Please direct all correspondence and book orders to:
National Society United States Daughters of 1812
1461-1463 Rhode Island Avenue NW
Washington, D.C. 20005
www.usdaughters1812.org

Library of Congress Control Number 76-135888

Published for the Society by
Gateway Press, Inc.
1001 N. Calvert Street
Baltimore, MD 21202-3897

www.gatewaypress.com

Printed in the United States of America

1812
ANCESTOR INDEX

VOLUME I
1892 - 1970

National Society
United States
Daughters of 1812

GATEWAY PRESS, INC.
Baltimore, MD   2005

Dedication

This 1812 ANCESTOR INDEX is dedicated to Mrs. Cecil Theodore Hays, Honorary President National. It was her idea, inspiration and progressive leadership which initiated this volume.

The National Society United States Daughters of Eighteen Hundred and Twelve will be in her debt not only for this work, but for her successful accomplishments as their President National during the years 1967-1970.

Disclaimer

This book is being reprinted as is.
There are errors.
Please, use this information merely as a guide.

National Society
United States Daughters of 1812

1892

1970

PURPOSES

The purposes of this society shall be to promote patriotism, to preserve and increase knowledge of the history of the American people, by the preservation of documents and relics, the marking of historic spots, the recording of family histories and traditions, the celebration of patriotic anniversaries, teaching and emphasizing the heroic deeds of the civil, military and naval life of those who moulded this Government between the close of the American Revolution and the close of the War of 1812, to urge Congress to compile and publish authentic records of men in civil, military and naval service from 1784 to 1815, inclusive, and to maintain at National Headquarters a museum and library of memorabilia of the 1784-1815 period, and to assist in the care and maintenance of our "Real Daughters" in every way that will add to their comfort and happiness.

CONSTITUTION
ARTICLE II

NATIONAL HEADQUARTERS of the
NATIONAL SOCIETY UNITED STATES DAUGHTERS OF 1812
1461 Rhode Island Ave., N.W., Washington, D. C. 20005

The National Headquarters was purchased in 1928 and serves as a Library and Museum of the Federal Period. The Society was founded January 8, 1892 for Patriotic and Educational Purposes by Mrs. Flora Adams Darling. It was incorporated in February 1901 by an Act of Congress.

The Flag Pole was part of the mast from the American frigate The Constitution, "Old Ironsides".

NATIONAL SOCIETY
UNITED STATES DAUGHTERS OF 1812

•

Founder and President General
Mrs. Flora Adams Darling

•

HONORARY PRESIDENTS NATIONAL

1892 - 1897
Mrs. Flora Adams Darling

1897 - 1915
Mrs. William Gerry Slade

1915 - 1919
Mrs. Robert Hall Wiles

1919 - 1923
Mrs. Clarence F. R. Jenne

1923 - 1927
Mrs. Samuel Preston Davis

1927 - 1931
Mrs. Samuel Z. Shope

1931 - 1934
Mrs. Robert James Johnston

1934 - 1937
Mrs. John Francis Weinmann

1937 - 1940
Mrs. Arthur J. O'Neil

1940 - 1943
Mrs. Percy Young Schelly

1943 - 1946
Mrs. Lloyd DeWitt Smith

1946 - 1949
Mrs. Lucius Willingham McConnell

1949 - 1952
Mrs. Frederick Brewster Ingram

1952 - 1955
Mrs. Frederic Gilbert Bauer

1955 - 1958
Mrs. Herbert Tylee Windsor

1958 - 1961
Mrs. Uel Stephens

1961 - 1964
Mrs. Charles William Crankshaw

1964 - 1967
Mrs. Frank Campbell Love

1967 - 1970
Mrs. Cecil Theodore Hays

NATIONAL OFFICERS 1967-1970

President National—Mrs. Cecil T. Hays, Atlanta, Georgia
First Vice-President National—Mrs. Ira J. Dietrich, Tulsa, Oklahoma
Second Vice-President National—Mrs. Robert Bachman, Washington, D.C.
Third Vice-President National—Miss Virginia F. Kuhn, Charleston, W.Va.
Fourth Vice-President National—Mrs. Loretta G. Thomas, Houston, Tex.
Chaplain National—Mrs. Enos H. Horst, Chambersburg, Pennsylvania
Recording Secretary National—Mrs. Earl L. Whitaker, Omaha, Neb.
Corresponding Secretary National—Mrs. Buton D. Basham, Atlanta, Ga.
Treasurer National—Mrs. Charles E. Dougan, McConnelsville, Ohio
Registrar National—Mrs. Michael J. Galvin, Washington, D.C.
Historian National—Mrs. George W. Davis, New Orleans, Louisiana
Librarian National—Mrs. James W. Reid, Detroit, Michigan
Curator National—Mrs. John O. McNelly, Annapolis, Maryland
Sergeant at Arms—Mrs. Miles B. Hopkins, Darlington, Maryland
Parliamentarian National—Mrs. Ralph Cox, Connellsville, Pennsylvania

NATIONAL OFFICERS 1970-1973

President National—Mrs. Ira J. Dietrich, Tulsa, Oklahoma
First Vice-President National—Mrs. Hugh W. Glover, Midland, Michigan
Second Vice-President National—Mrs. Miles Baldwin Hopkins, Darlington, Maryland
Third Vice-President National—Mrs. Harry M. Ives, Silver Lake, Kansas
Fourth Vice-President National—Mrs. Luther L. Tarbell, West Hartford, Connecticut
Chaplain National—Mrs. Gerald J. Laubenthal, Birmingham, Alabama
Recording Secretary National—Mrs. Garold C. Jenison, Phoenix, Arizona
Corresponding Secretary National—Mrs. Enos H. Horst, Chambersburg, Pennsylvania
Treasurer National—Mrs. Earl L. Whitaker, Omaha, Nebraska
Registrar National—Mrs. Michael J. Galvin, Washington, D.C.
Historian National—Mrs. Henry P. Boggs, DeLand, Florida
Librarian National—Mrs. Isaac D. Shank, Upper Montclair, New Jersey
Curator National—Miss Grace E. Lester, Fayetteville, New York
Sergeant at Arms—Mrs. Albert Charles Bauer, Beltsville, Maryland
Parliamentarian National—Mrs. Louis W. Patterson, Tulsa, Oklahoma

FOREWORD

The 1812 ANCESTOR INDEX of The National Society United States Daughters of 1812 is the second part of a publication approved April 1968 at the 76th Associate Council of the Society held in Washington, D.C.

The publication was proposed by Mrs. Cecil Theodore Hays, President National (1967-1970), as the project for her Administration. The publication was to consist of two parts: first, the National Membership Roster, listing the active members as of December 1, 1968, with the name of the 1812 Ancestor; and secondly, an Index of the 1812 Ancestors. Mrs. Michael J. Galvin was to serve as Chairman of the project with professional help furnished on approval of the Executive Committee.

Mrs. Cecil Theodore Hays, now Honorary President National, was the compiler of the membership lists submitted by the States for the National Membership Roster. The Roster, as planned but without the Index of Ancestors, was published and ready for distribution at the 77th Associate Council in April 1969. The publication of the Index of the 1812 Ancestors had become a separate project as the copy for the Index was not completed until July 1970, and the proofs completed January 1971.

Mrs. Michael J. Galvin, elected to the office of Registrar National for 1967-1970 and again for the term 1970-1973, has been the compiler and supervised all phases of the work, personally performing most of the tedious tasks of sorting information from the records of the Society from 1892 to June 1970. The work is monumental.

The National Membership Roster, published in 1969, is indispensible for use with the 1812 ANCESTOR INDEX.

Mrs. Ira J. Dietrich
President National
National Society
United States Daughters of 1812

Tulsa, Oklahoma
January 1971

TABLE OF CONTENTS

PREFACE

The 1812 ANCESTOR INDEX lists approximately 20,000 established ancestors, who had military or other service during the period from the close of the American Revolution, 1784, until the close of the War of 1812 in 1815. The ancestors, men and women, are listed with the names of their spouse, and the name of the child with his or her spouse that the descendant came through. This gives two generations for almost every ancestor, from the time of the organization of the Society in 1892 until June 15, 1970.

We sincerely hope that the 1812 ANCESTOR INDEX will be of help to prospective members of our Society, as well as to genealogists and historians.

Unfortunately, the earlier applications were much smaller and did not require as much data as we do today. When a Volume number is given after an ancestor it means future applicants must prove lineage to the ancestor.

We sincerely hope you find your copy of the 1812 ANCESTOR INDEX a valuable asset.

The Supplemental list following the end of the INDEX includes ancestors who have been established since the first list was sent to the printer.

ELEANOR STEVENS GALVIN
Registrar National, NSUSD of 1812

A

Aaron, Thomas b. Ga. d. Ark. 1864 m. Susanna V. Smith   Pvt. U.S. Inf.
son John m. Mary Butcher

Aball, John b.— d.— m.— Vol. 9   Sgt. Va. Mil.

Abbey, Amos b. Vt. 1773 d. N.Y. 1824 m. Nancy Chaffee   Pvt. N.Y. Inf.
daughter Olive Abbey m. Orrin Harte Fisher

Abbott, Lyman, Sr. b. Vt. 1787 d. N.Y. 1872   Maj. N.Y. Mil.
m. Anna Davis — son Lyman Jr. m. Clarissa Frances Derby

Abbott, Paul b. Conn. 1783 d. N.Y. 1831 m. Patty Eells   Capt. N.Y. Mil.
son James H. m. Elizabeth Louise Andrews

Abbott, William b. N.J. 1783 d. N.J. after 1814   Pvt. N.J. Mil.
m. Mary Patterson — son Isaac m. Elizabeth Fisher

Abbott, William b. N.H. 1748 d. N.H. 1793   Patriot N.H. 1787
m. Phebe Ballard — son Isaac m. Chloe Bayles

Abbott, William b. Conn. 1755 d. N.Y. 1832   Capt. N.Y. Mil.
m. Esther Green — son Paul m. Patty Eells

Abel, Daniel b. Ohio 1777 d. Ind. 1869 m. Sally Root   Capt. Ohio Mil.
son Homer m. Electa Hadsell

Abell, Simon b. Conn. 1767 d. Vt. 1851 m. Rachel Farnsworth   Musician
son Eliphalet m. Belinda Poole   Conn. 1812-13 Mil.

Abercrombie, Charles b. Va. 1742 d. Ga. 1819   Patriot Ga. 1798
m. Dicey Edwina Booth — son Leonard m. Sarah Comer

Abert, John James b. Md. 1788 d. D.C. 1863   Maj. Md. Mil.
m. Ellen Matlack Stretch — son Charles m. Constantia Bache

Abington, William b. Va. 1776 d. Mo. 1840   Pvt. Va. Mil.
m. (1) Miss Hardeman — son Hardeman m. Margaret Blaine

Abney, Joel b. S.C. 1772 d. S.C. 1816 m. Elizabeth   Cornet S.C.
son Mark m. Permelia Williams

Abraham (Abrams), Anthony b. N.Y. 1794 d. Wisc. 1869   Pvt. N.Y. Mil.
m. Cynthia Brownell — daughter Mary Ann m. James Merry

Abshire, Benjamin b. La. 1788 d. Tex. after 1854   Pvt. La. Mil.
m. Hannah Weed — daughter Lavinia m. James C. Moor

Abshire (Abshier), James b. Va. 1777 d. Ind. 1806   Pvt. Ohio Mil.
m. Elizabeth Overholtz — son Isaac m. Sarah Ballard

Acheson, Robert b. Pa. 1779 d. Pa. 1848   Pvt. Pa. Mil.
m. Martha Ramsey —son James R. m. Julia Ann McKnight

Acker, Joseph b. S.C. 1774 d. Tex. 1855   Pvt. Tenn. Mil.
m. Ruth Alexander — son Columbus m. Martha Mills

Ackerman, Joseph, III b. N.H. 1776 d. N.H. 1823   Lt. N.H. Mil.
m. Mary Day — son Joseph D. m. Mary Ann Plaisted

Ackerman, Tunis, Jr. b.— d. aft. 1793 N.Y. m.   Ens. N.Y. Riflemen
son Tunis, III m. Ann Crandall

Adair, John b. Pa. 1773 d. Pa. 1862 m. Esther Wilson   Pvt. Pa. Mil.
son James A. m. Isabel Eaty

Adair, John b. S.C. 1759 d. Ky. 1840   Gen. Ky. Mil.
   m. Catherine Palmer — daughter Ann P. m. John L. Bridges
   son Wm. Henry m. Elizabeth Cromwell
   daughter Isabella M. m. Benjamin F. Pleasants
   daughter Mary m. Mark Hardin

Adair, Walter b. Ga. 1783 d. Ga. 1836 m. Rachel Thompson   Pvt. Ga. Mil.
   son George W. m. Mary Martin
   son John T. m. Penelope Mayfield

Adair, William b.— d.— m. Margaret Vol. 18   Cpl. N.C. Mil.
   daughter Mary m. Peter Balton

Adam, James b.— d.— m.—   Justice Inf. Ct.
                                        Ga. 1810-15

Adams, Aaron b. Conn. 1782 d. Mo. 1868 m.— Vol. 5   Pvt. Conn. Mil.

Adams, Amos b. N.H. 1783 d. N.H. 1860   Pvt. N.H. Mil.
   m. Elizabeth McKinley — son George m. Ann Elizabeth Lee

Adams, Amos b.— d.— m.— Vol. 9   Pvt. N.Y. Mil.

Adams, Andrew b.— d.— m.— Vol. 1   Pvt. Conn. Mil.

Adams, Asa b. Mass. 1794 d. N.Y. 1868   Pvt. N.Y. Mil.
   m. Eliza Maria Merrill — son Asa M. m. Martha Ann Bradley

Adams, Baxter b. Mass. 1779 d. N.Y. 1870   Pvt. N.Y. Mil.
   m. Abigail Keith — son George Q. m. Charlotte Nickles

Adams, Chester b.— d.— m.— Vol. 3   Col. Mass. Mil.

Adams, Daniel b. N.J. 1773 d. N.J. 1863 m. Elizabeth Bartlett   Pvt. N.J. Mil.
   daughter Abigail Ann m. Charles Franklin Eastlack
   daughter Hannah G. unmarried   REAL DAUGHTER

Adams, David b. Va. 1780 d. Mo. 1862 m. Margaret Dickson   Lt. Ky. Mil.
   daughter Amanda C.I. m. Charles Holbert Allison
   son David m. Elizabeth Woods

Adams, David b. Conn. 1756 d. N.Y. 1833   Patriot N.Y. 1809
   m. Abigail Carver — daughter Martha Polly m. Timothy Chase

Adams, David b. 1789 d. Ohio 1862 m. Ellza Turner   Q.M. Ohio Mil.
   daughter Henrietta m. Benjamin Thompson

Adams, David b. Tenn. 1797 d. Tenn. 1853   Pvt. Tenn. Mil.
   m. Sarah Craft — daughter Josephine m. Milton Lee Clendenen
   Real Daughter

Adams, David Augustus b. Conn. 1784 d. Ohio 1855   Lt. Ohio Mil.
   m. Anna Tylee — daughter Sybil Maria m. Jesse Reeves

Adams, George b. N.J. d.— m. Sarah   Pvt. N.J. Mil.
   daughter Margaret m. James Theodore Tomlinson

Adams, George b. S.C. 1792 d. Tex. ca. 1850   Pvt. S.C. Mil.
   m. Lucinda Levice Jones — son Lemuel m. Caroline Norred

Adams, George, Jr. b. Del. 1786 d. Pa. 1862   Pvt. Pa. Mil.
   m. Sarah Fager — daughter Sarah C. m. Hugh Franklin McReynolds

Adams, Harden Stewart b.— d.— m.— Vol. 9   Pvt. Tenn. Vol.

Adams, Ignatius b. Pa. 1766 d. Pa. 1866   Pvt. Pa. Riflemen
   m. Honoria Burgoon — daughter Veronica m. Maurice O'Reilly

Adams, Isaac b. Mass. (Me.) 1794 d. Me. 1872   Pvt. Mass. Mil.
  m. Sarah Smith — daughter Catherine A. m. Silas Lowell Adams
REAL DAUGHTER

Adams, Israel b. Mass. 1780 d. N.H. 1865   Capt. N.H. Mil.
  m. Rhoda Harthorn — daughter Augusta m. Richard M. Smith

Adams, James b. Md. 1802 d. Ky. 1881   Drummer Md. Mil.
  m. Ann Pamelia Hill — daughter Margaret m. John Barnard Wathen
REAL DAUGHTER

Adams, James b. N.H. 1770 d. N.H. 1810   Capt. N.H. Mil.
  m. Abigail Hayward — daughter Polly m. Samuel Farwell

Adams, James b. N.Y. 1796 d. Ohio 1890   Pvt. Pa. Mil.
  m. Harriet Bailey — son Douglas W. m. Lydia
  son James C. L. m. Darlispka Eddy

Adams, Jeduthan b. Vt. 1793 d. Mich. 1853   Pvt. Vt. Mil.
  m. Lorinda Bradford — daughter Hannah m. Charles Henderson

Adams, John b. Mass. (Me.) 1783 d. Me.   Pvt. Me. Mil.
  m. Hannah Ridley — son John, Jr. m. Henrietta Hatch

Adams, John (of Medway) b.— d.— m.   Lt. Mass. Mil.
  Vol. 3

Adams, John b. Pa. 1769 d. Tenn. 1829   Pvt. Tenn. Mil.
  m. Margaret Kelsey — daughter Mary Agnes m. Edward Finnan

Adams, John b. Va. 1788 d. Tenn. aft. 1850 m. Margaret   Sgt. Tenn.
  son Benjamin m. Nancy Reynolds

Adams, John, Jr. b. Mass. 1777 d. Mass. 1834   Lt. Mass. Mil.
  m. Susan Davis — daughter Susan m. Elisha Fuller

Adams, John D. b. Pa. ca 1791 d. Ky. aft. 1871   Pvt. Ky. Regt.
  m. Rachel Fornier — son Thomas m. Pertamia Bailey

Adams, John Wilson b.— d.— m.—   Pvt. Del. Mil.
  Vol. 3

Adams, Joseph b. Mass. 1740 d. Mass. 1815   Patriot Mass. 1808
  m. Eleanor Carnes (Carney) — daughter Jane m. Peleg Bartlett

Adams, Joseph b. Va. 1749 d. N.C. 1837   Pvt. N.C. Mil.
  m. Winifred Rowland — son John m. Nancy White

Adams, Lemuel b. Va. 1797 d. Tex. 1892   Pvt. Tenn.
  m. Elizabeth Brewer — son Samuel m. Martha Murphy

Adams, Levi b. Mass. 1761 d. Vt. 1832   Pvt. Mass. Mil.
  m. Dolly Houghton — daughter Orinda m. Clark Lyman

Adams, Lyman b. Conn. 1779 d. Ill. 1851   Lt. Md. Mil.
  m. Matilda Glover — daughter Ann m. Adolph Berger

Adams, Mark b. Conn. 1788 d. N.Y. 1862   Pvt. N.Y. Mil.
  m. Mercy Brown — daughter Mary m. Abraham Caulkins

Adams, Martin b.— d.— m.—   Pvt. Ind. Mil.
  Vol. 8

Adams, Martin b. Ky. 1793 d. Ind. 1889   Pvt. Rangers U.S. Vol.
  m. Jane H. Davis
  daughter Clarinda Jane m. Thomas Duggan Fouts

Adams, Moses b. Mass. 1781 d. Mass. 1850   Adj. Mass. Mil.
  m. Ruth Perry — daughter Miranda W. m. Abel H. Perry

Adams, Nathan b. Conn. 1778 d. Mich. 1848   Adj. N.Y. Mil.
  m. Sally Cook — son Alvinza m. Betsy Cagwin

Adams, Nathan b.— d.— m.—   Pvt. N.Y. Mil.
  Vol. 7

Adams, Nathan b. Vt. 1794 d. Vt. 1857   Pvt. Vt. Mil.
  m. Caroline Hildreth — daughter Julia m. Edward J. Parker

Adams, Nathaniel F. b.— d.— m.—   Capt. N.H. Inf.
  Vol. 4

Adams, Nipper (Napier) b. 1755/60 d. Ga. 1830/40   Patriot Ga. 1810
  m. Mary Farmer — son Joshua, Sr. m. Martha Ursula Johnston

Adams, Peter b. Va. 1786 d. Va. 1854   Ens. Va. Mil.
  m. Harriet Byron Smith — son Fenton T. m. Anna E. Smith

Adams, Robert b. Pa. 1769 d. Ohio 1843   Cpl. Ohio Mil.
  m. Sarah Douglas — son Albert m. Nancy Coffey
  son Robert, Jr. m. Martha Clark

Adams, Robert b. S.C. 1798 d. S.C. 1852   Sgt. S.C. Mil.
  m. Charlotte Belton Pickens
  son James P. m. Margaret C. Johnstone

Adams, Samuel b. Mass. 1722 d. Mass. 1803   Patriot
  m. Elizabeth Checkley   Gov. of Mass. 1794-97
  daughter Hannah m. Thomas Wells

Adams, Samuel b.— d.— m.—   Surgeon Mass. Mil.
  Vol. 8

Adams, Samuel b. N.H. 1778 d. Vt. 1814   Capt. N.H. Mil.
  m. Elizabeth L. Prentice — son John m. Ruth Wade Dodge

Adams, Samuel b.— d.— m.— Vol. 16   Musician N.Y. Mil.

Adams, Samuel Griffin b. Va. 1776 d. Va. 1821   Adj. Va. Mil.
  m. Katherine Elizabeth Innes — son James I. m. Henrietta C. Bickley

Adams, Thomas b.— d.— m.—   Lt. Mass. Mil.
  Vol. 6

Adams, Thomas b. Mass. 1771 d. Ohio 1830   Pvt. Ohio Mil.
  m. Edith Oliver — son Thomas F. m. Rebecca Dickinson

Adams, William b. Va. 1784 d. Ky. 1844   Pvt. Ky. Vol.
  m. Rebecca Lawrence — son Willis m. Helen Hyatt

Adams, William b. 1791 d. Ohio 1848   Pvt. Ohio Mil.
  m. Mattie Stone — daughter Jane m. Thomas P. Day

Adams, William Ellis b. N.C. 1785 d. Ga. 1873   Capt. Ga. Mil.
  m. Mary (Rosser) Harris — son David R. m. Eliza H. Hudson

Adams, Zenas b. N.H. 1787 d. N.H. 1853   Pvt. N.H. Vol.
  m. Lydia Baker — daughter Elizabeth M. m. John Towne

Addams, Eli b. Md. 1785 d. Ohio 1870 m. Elizabeth Beeks   Pvt. Ohio Mil.
  son Christopher B. m. Sarah Gannaway

Addis, Isaac b. Pa. 1750 d. Pa. 1805 m. Jane Hegeman   Capt. Pa. Mil.
  son Joseph m. Susanna Lefferts

Adler, Christian F. b. Pa. 1787 d. Pa. 1867   Musician Pa. Cav.
  m. Mary Newman
  son Daniel N. m. Lydia Blue
  daughter Mary m. George W. Pierce

Adreon, Christian b. Md. 1776 d. Md. 1854   Capt. Md. Mil.
  m. Hannah Cornwell (Carsdwell)
  son William m. Susan Forsythe

Agan, Benjamin Leeland b. N.Y. 1795 d. N.Y. 1846   Cpl. N.Y. Mil.
  m. Eve Coonradt
  daughter Lucretia E. m. Gilbert Pierce   REAL DAUGHTER

Agey, (Achey-Egge), Jacob b. Pa. 1782 d. Pa. 1869   Capt. Pa. Mil.
  m. Sarah Bush
  daughter Anna Rebecca m. Dr. Reuel Stewart

Aiken, Alexander b. Ire. 1790 d. Pa. 1843   Cpl. Pa. Mil.
  m. Mary Carpenter
  daughter Jane m. William Bolton Lear

Ainsworth, Danforth b. Mass. 1791 d. Vt. 1860   Pvt. Vt. Mil.
  m. Lucy Lawson
  son Willard m. Annie Standish Charles

Airs, Thomas b. S.C. 1795 d. S.C. 1830 m. Sarah Ann Dorrell Pvt. S.C. Mil.
  daughter Lavinia Thursa m. John D. Murphy

Akers, Charles Raines b.— d.— m.— Vol. 15   Cpl. N.J. Mil.

Akers, William b. Va. 1740 d. Va. 1834   Patriot Va. 1789 & 1799
  m. Polly Blackburn
  son John m. Sallie Brown

Akin, Benjamin b. N.Y. 1762 d. N.Y. 1831   Patriot N.Y. 1800-02
  m. Martha Palmer — daughter Sarah m. Moses Hanzer

Akin, John H. b.— d.— m.— Vol. 7   Sgt. N.C. Mil.

Albee, Samuel b. Me. 1794 d. Me. 1868   Pvt. Mass. Mil.
  m. Jane Robinson (Fales)
  son Parker B. m. Rhoda Grover Andrews

Albin, Samuel b. Ohio 1787 d. Ohio 1841   Pvt. Ohio Mil.
  m. Mary McColby Adams — son Gabriel m. Lydia Glick

Albright, Jacob b. Pa. 1791 d. Pa. 1856 m. Ann   Pvt. Pa. Mil.
  daughter Emily Theresa m. T. Clarkson Whitson REAL DAUGHTER

Albritton, Thomas b. 1776 d. 1865   Pvt. Ga. Mil.
  m. Rhoda Strickland Parker
  daughter Jane m. Capt. James Jones, Jr.

Alburtis, (Albertis) John b. Va. 1778 d. Va. 1827   Pvt. Va. Mil.
  m. Nancy Van Meter — son Samuel m. Susan Mary Showers

Alcorn, William b. Pa. 1780 d. Pa. 1817 m.—   Pvt. Pa. Mil.
  son William M. m. Electa Howland

Alden, Briggs b. N.Y. 1796 d. Ia. 1891 m. Maria King   Pvt. N.Y. Mil.
  daughter Harriet M. m. David Montague Aspenwall

Alden, Isaac b. 1755 d. 1822 m. Irene Smith   prisoner British 1811-20
  son Philip Alden m. Margaret Riemer

Alden, Jonathan b. Mass. 1785 d. Ohio 1862   Pvt. Mass. Mil.
  m. (1) Lucy Bryant — daughter Mehitabel m. Moses True

Alder, Jonathan b. Pa. 1773 d. Ohio 1849 m. Mary Blont   Capt. Ohio Mil.
son Henry m. Elizabeth Millikin

Alder, Latimer E. b. Va. 1783 d. Kan. 1874   Pvt. Va. Mil.
m. Catherine Silcott — daughter Charlotte S. m. Samuel Price

Aldredge (Aldrease), Nathan b. N.C. or Ga. 1789   Pvt. Ga. Mil.
d. Ala. 1865 m. Alizannah Hanson
daughter Margaret Jane m. Lewis Gardner Davis

Aldrich, Timothy b.— d.— m.— Vol. 16   Lt. N.Y. Mil.

Aldridge, Samuel b. ca., 1777 d. Ohio after 1842   Pvt. Ohio 1813
m. Mary Ann Taylor—daughter Anna m. William Rumbaugh

Alexander, Ambrose b.— d.— m.— Vol. 4   Pvt.

Alexander, Andrew b. (W.) Va. 1773 d. (W.) Va. 1850   Pvt. Va. Mil.
m. Phoebe Bracken — daughter Mary D. m. Hugh McClaugherty
daughter Rebecca B. m. Samuel Kean

Alexander, Andrew Miller b. Md. 1788 d. La. k/a 1814   Pvt. Tenn. Mil.
m. Nancy Doran — son John D. m. Mary Rowena Baird

Alexander, David b.— d.— m.— Vol. 8   Pvt. Ky. Mil.

Alexander, George b. 1743 d. 1814   Patriot N.C. 1784-1786
m. Margaret Harris — daughter Narcissa m. Ransom Grey

Alexander, Hugh b. Pa. 1785 c. Pa. 1868   Pvt. Pa. Mil.
m. Elizabeth Brown — daughter Fanney m. George Jackson

Alexander, Jacob b. Pa. 1792 d. Pa. 1843   Pvt. N.Y. Mil.
m. Laura Belknap — son Squire m. Henrietta E. Sherman—Vol. 1
Jane E. (Dobie) Kellogg—Vol. 28

Alexander, James b. Pa. 1792 d. Ohio 1849 m. Sarah Crites   Pvt. Pa. Mil.
son John m. Margaret Martz

Alexander, James b. Pa. 1791 d. Pa. 1852   Pvt. Pa. Mil.
m. Margaret Holliday — daughter Margaret m. Alexander McKee

Alexander, James b. Pa. 1774 d. Pa. 1826   Ens. Pa. Mil.
m. Jane Sanderson — daughter Jane m. Charles Fausold

Alexander, John b. Pa. 1780 d. Ind. 1855   Pvt. Ohio Mil.
m. Elizabeth Stewart — son Joseph Samuel m. Matilda Jones

Alexander, John b. N.C. 1773 d. Ohio 1861   Pvt. Pa. Mil.
m. Mary Galloway — daughter Sarah m. Samuel Matthews

Alexander, John b. S.C. 1777 d. Ohio 1848   Patriot Mem. of Cong.
m. Isabelle Adair — daughter Isabella A. m. William T. Beall

Alexander, John Sr. b. Tenn. c. 1780 d. Tenn. 1831   Pvt. East Tenn.
m. Martha Ferguson son John m. Delilah Woods   Mil. 1814

Alexander, Milton King b. Ga. 1796 d. Ill. 1856   Sgt. Tenn. Mil.
m. Mary Shields — daughter Lucy m. Bruce Lamon Real Daughter

Alexander, Oliver b. Ire. 1732 d. Tenn. ca. 1812   Juror Tenn. 1807
m. Margaret Paul — son Ebenezer m. Elizabeth Rogers

Alexander, Robert M. b. S.C. 1790 d. S.C. 1836   Pvt. S.C. Vol.
m. Mary Brown Seaborn
daughter Matilda C. m. Mark Moore Johnson

Alexander, Silas b. N.C. 1796 d. Tenn. 1869   Pvt. West Tenn. Mil.
m. Mary Kennedy — son Linnaeus m. Adelia Daniel
son Thomas C. m. Ann Jane Long (Mabry)

Alexander, Thomas b. Va. 1774 d. Ohio 1845   Pvt. Va. Mil.
m. Sarah Huddleston — son Joel m. Roxalana Morris

Alexander, William b. Conn. 1787 d. Conn. 1867   Sgt. Conn. Mil.
m. Susan Day — son Luther D. m. Amelia Fay Young

Alexander, William b. Va. 1777 d. Ga. 1852 m. P__   Pvt. Ga. Mil.
daughter Elizabeth m. Mitchell N. Rice — Joseph Martin

Alexander, William b. Va. 1780 d. N.Y.C. 1821   Pvt. U.S. Inf.
m. Christina Fribbs — son James m. Mary Ann Wright

Alison, Robert b. Md. 1749 d. Tenn. 1826   Pvt. Tenn. Mil.
m. Martha McKinley — daughter Elizabeth A. m. William Deery

Alee, Isaac Reed b. Del. 1788 d. Mo. 1872   Cpl. Ohio Mil.
m. Sarah Parkhurst — son Jacob m. Catherine Wilson
daughter Sarah m. Philander Smith **REAL DAUGHTER**

Allemong, Henry b. N.C. 1790 d. N.C. 1822 m. Leah Shinn Pvt. N.C. Mil.
daughter Frances m. Mathew Plunkett

Allen, Archibald b. Va. 1795 d. Mo. 1877   Cpl. Va. Mil.
m. Nancy Hamilton — daughter Martha J. m. Henry T. Hunter

Allen, Barnabas W. b. Ky. 1791 d. Mo. after 1855   Pvt. Ky. Mil.
m. Amelia Lafernait   **1812**
son William Henderson m. Belle M. Burnett (Arabell)

Allen, Beverly b. S.C. 1766 d. Ky. 1817   Pvt. Ky. Rifle Reg.
m. Anna Hayes Singletary
daughter Sally A. m. James MacGruder Beall

Allen, Clark b. Conn. 1769 d. N.Y. 1851   Maj. Gen. N.Y. Mil.
m. Martha Thompson — son Elisha m. Jane Dixon

Allen, David b. Va. 1754 d. Va. 1818? m. Aphia Lewis Pvt. Va. Mil.
son David B. m. Martha Norfleet

Allen, Enos b. Conn. 1774 d. N.Y. 1858   Lt. N.Y. Mil.
m. Mrs. Ann Elizabeth Murray French
daughter Laura m. Richard Dunham

Allen, Hiram b. 1792 d. Ala. 1868 m. Polly   Pvt. Ga. Mil.
son William F. m. Sarah Jacoway

Allen, Isaiah b. Va. 1786 d. Mo. 1869 m. Rachel Brown Pvt. Mo. Mil.
son Joel m. Jemima Gardner

Allen, Jacob b. (Me.) 1784 d. Me. 1868   Pvt. (Me.) Mass. Mil.
daughter Margaret A. m. Rotheus M. Cole **REAL DAUGHTER**
daughter Mary J. m. Solon Royal

Allen, James b. Va. 1783 d. Ky. 1859 m. Durscilla Fawcett Col. Ky. Mil.
son John P. m. George Ann Baylor

Allen, James b. N.J. 1790 d. Ohio 1865   Pvt. Ohio Mil.
m. Elizabeth Van Gorder
daughter Artie (Artir) m. Amos Thornton

Allen, James b. Va. 1775 d. Va. aft. 1814   Lt. Col. Va. Mil.
m. Elizabeth Tate — son William m. Caroline Poage

Allen, James Sherman b. N.Y. 1773 d. Ind. 1838   Pvt. N.Y. Mil.
    m. Anna Mosher — daughter Harriett M. m. Erastus V. Adkins
    daughter Mehitabel Ann m. William Freedes Hadley

Allen, Jeremiah b. Mass. 1751 d. Mass. 1837   2nd Lt. Mass. Art.
    m. Abigail Rogers
    son Amenius (Americus) m. Rachael Weigert

Allen, Joel b. Mass. 1788 d. Vt. 1868 m. Lura Clapp   Pvt. Vt. Mil.
    son Reuben C. m. Sarah Ann Dewey

Allen, John b.— d.— m.— Vol. 17   Lt. Ind. Mil.

Allen, John b. N.Y. 1793 d. N.Y. 1876 m. Melissa Dewey   Pvt. N.Y. Mil.
    daughter Emma L. m. William S. Jones

Allen, John b. 1791 d. Ill. 1850 m. Martha Barrow   Pvt. Ohio Mil.
    daughter Martha Ann m. Wilson L. Meisenheimer

Allen, John b. Pa. 1788 d. Pa. 1854   Seaman U.S. Navy Pa.
    m. Alice Ann Schultz — son Henry R. m. Mary E. Thorn

Allen, John b.— d.— m.— Vol. 12   Comm. Man-of-War
    Vol. 12   Pa.

Allen, John b. Ky. 1789 d. Tenn. 1849 m. Peggy Huff   Lt. Tenn. Mil.
    daughter Katherine m. William McSween

Allen, John b. Va. 1788 d. Va. 1837 m. Sarah Bartlett   Sgt. Va. Mil.
    daughter Clarissa m. Lemuel Swiger

Allen, John b. Va. 1771 d. Ky. 1813 m. Jane Logan   Col. Ky. rifleman
    daughter Eliza m. Pierce Butler
    daughter Anna Maria m. (1) Crittenden (2) David R. Murray

Allen, Joseph b. Va. 1756 d. Ga. 1833 m. Agnes Patterson   Lt. Ga. Mil.
    daughter Elizabeth m. James Head

Allen, Joseph b. Va. 1774 d. Ky. 1862   Capt. Ky. Mil.
    m. Margaret Crawford — son Horace m. Eliza Ann LaRue
    son Alfred m. Mary Ellen Jennings

Allen, Joseph b. R.I. 1756 d. R.I. 1830   Capt. & Maj. R.I. Mil.
    m. Sallie Tillinghast — son John m. Honor Howard

Allen, Joseph b. Tenn. 1778 d. Tenn. 1858   Pvt. Tenn. Mil.
    m. Amanda Lowell — daughter Amanda m. William Wadley

Allen, Leonard b. Vt. 1795 d. N.Y. 1883   Pvt. N.Y. Mil.
    m. Eunice Knowlton — son Lebbeus m. Merve Warren

Allen, Levi b. Tenn. 1793 d. Ky. 1861 m. Elizabeth   Pvt. Tenn. Mil.
    son Eli B. m. (1) Mary Rebecca Ragland

Allen, Nathaniel b. Mass. (Me.) 1793 d. Ill. 1878   Pvt. U.S. Army 1814
    m. Mary Tinkham — son Nathaniel C. m. Emaline Johnson

Allen, Perez b. Mass. 1764 d. N.H. 1843   Maj. Mass. Mil.
    m. Mehitabel Richards — daughter Julia m. Ezra Cole

Allen, Reuben b. Va. d. Tenn. 1825 m. Mary Jones   Pvt. Tenn. Mil.
    son James R. m. Ann Nichols

Allen, Samuel b. 1789 d. 1873 m. Eliza Batsell   Pvt. Ky. Mil.
    daughter Keziah m. Abraham Harding, Sr.

Allen, Samuel b.— d.— m. Sarah Scattergood   Pvt. Pa. Mil.
    Vol. 5

Allen, Samuel b. Mass. 1767 d. Vt. 1832   Capt. & Pvt. Vt. Mil.
m. Catherine Campbell — son Solomon m. (2) Susan Westcott

Allen, Stephen b.— d.— m.—   Patriot N.Y.
Vol. 15

Allen, Thomas b. (Me.) Mass. 1783 d. Me. 1857   Pvt. Musician
m. Lydia Beals — son Alden m. Martha Ham Stevens   Mass. Mil.

Allen, Thomas b. N.J. 1781 d. N.J. 1855   Pvt. N.J. Mil.
m. Irene Lovelace (Loveless)
son Isaac m. Elizabeth A. Van Mater

Allen, Thomas b. N.C. 1787 d. Tenn. 1848 m. Betsy Ecklin   Cpl. N.C. Mil.
son Thomas, Jr. m. Roxanna Rogers

Allen, Thomas b. S.C. 1788 d. Ky. 1869   Pvt. Tenn. Mil.
m. (2) Ethelinda Harris (Faris)
daughter Rebecca Adelle unmarried   REAL DAUGHTER

Allen, William b.—d.—m.— Vol. 75   Capt. Ky. Mil.

Allen, William b. Tenn. 1790 d. Ark. 1846   Capt. La. Vol.
m. Mary Morgan son Abijah m. Celia Sutton Mebane

Allen, William b. Conn. 1777 d. Mich. 1867 m. Esther Goff Pvt. N.Y. Mil.
daughter Hannah A. m. Peter Van Tifflin
son Isaac P. m. Miranda Wallace Layton

Allerton, Archibald Montgomery b. Conn. 1790   Pvt. N.Y. Cav.
d. N.Y. 1863 m. Rebecca Chamberlain
son David m. Rachel Ward Hurd

Alley, Ephraim b.— d.— m.— Vol. 9   Pvt. Mass. Mil.

Alley, Jacob b. (Me.) Mass. d. (Me.) Mass.   Pvt. Mass. (Me.) Mil.
m. Alice Willis — daughter Margaret m. P. M. Cole

Alley, Peter b. 1782/3 d. 1858 m. —   Pvt. Ind. Mil.
son William m. Mary Jones

Allin, Thomas b. R.I. 1742 d. R.I. 1800   Brig. Gen. R.I. Mil.
m. Any Bicknell — son Ira m. Abigail Shores

Allison, Hugh b. N.C. 1771 d. Mo. 1846   Pvt. Ky. Mil.
m. Rebecca Sanders Hart — daughter Lucinda m. James Pearce
son Thomas W. m. Rosanna Snyder

Allison, John b. Pa. 1792 d. Ohio 1868 m. Elizabeth Stewart Pvt. Pa. Mil.
son James m. Keziah Vaughn

Allison, Robert b. Pa. 1755 d. Ohio 1812   Sol. Ind. Wars
m. Elizabeth Phillips — daughter Mary m. Nehemiah Davis

Allison, Robert b. Tenn. 1795 d. Tenn. 1861   Pvt. Tenn. Mil.
m. Mary McConnell Chester
daughter Apphia unmarried   REAL DAUGHTER
son George W. m. Malvina Smythe Mathews

Allison, Samuel Carroll b.— d.— m.— Vol. 16   Sgt. Ky. Mil.

Allison, Thomas Alexander b. N.C. 1794 d. N.C. 1854 Pvt. N.C. Mil.
m. Lettice — son Richard M. m. Elizabeth Carmichael Hampton

Allison, Uriah b. N.C. 1782 d. Tenn. 1829   Lt. Tenn. Mil.
m. Nancy Clark Cox — daughter Catherine Jane m. John W. Wester

Allison, William b. Ire. 1777 d. Pa. 1825 m. Julia Brandon Maj. Pa. Mil.
son Charles W. B. m. Sophronia Susanna Lee

Allyn, Israel b. Conn. 1790 d. Ohio 1873 m. Lucy Gallup   Sgt. Conn. Inf.
   son Abel G. m. Adaline Capron — son Austin m. Huldah Voris
   son George m. Alta Angeline Hall
   daughter Lydia m. Alvin Coe Voris

Allyn, Matthew b. Conn. 1794 d. Ohio 1862   Patriot Col. Conn.
   m. Clara Merrill   Mil. Mem. Conn. Legis.
   daughter Mary m. Henry Saxton

Almand, Thomas b. 1779 d. Ga. 1846   Pvt. Ga. Mil.
   m. Nancy David — son Alexander S. m. Christina Buffington

Almy, Langworthy b.— d.— m.— Vol. 3   Ens. R.I. Mil.

Alpuente, Francisco Boneventura de   Capt. La. Mil.
   b. La. 1791 d. La. 1841 m. Caterina Millon
   son Perez F. m. Charlotte Hepburn

Alston, Lemuel James b. S.C. 1760 d. Ala. 1836   Patriot S.C.
   m. Elizabeth Williams — son William W. m. Mary Haygood Burges

Alston, Willis b. 1750 d. N.C. aft. 1799   Congressman N.C.
   m. Elizabeth Wright   1797-9
   daughter Virginia m. Littleberry Orgain Willcox

Alter, Jacob b. Pa. 1789 d. Pa. 1865 m. Elizabeth Alter   Pvt. Pa. Vol.
   daughter Henrietta J. m. James Graham Finley

Alter, John, Sr. b. Pa. 1779 d. Ohio 1850   Pvt. Ohio Cav.
   m. Elizabeth Miller — son John, Jr. m. Eliza Dumm

Alverson, Elijah b.— d.— m.—   Pvt. S.C. Mil.
   son Elijah m. Fanny Vol. 70

Alvord, Daniel, Sr. b. Mass. 1758 d. N.Y. 1847   Patriot N.Y.
   m. Susanna Judd — son Daniel, Jr. m. Pamelia Sackett

Alvord, Daniel, Jr. b.— d.— m. Pamelia Sackett   Pvt. N.Y. Mil.
   Vol. 15

Alward, Nathaniel b. N.J. 1794 d. N.Y. 1848   Pvt. N.Y. Mil.
   m. Margaret S. Varnarsdale — daughter Mary m. William J. Taylor

Ambrose, Robert b. N.H. 1732-3 d. N.H. 1816   Patriot Mem. Legis.
   m. Mary Ethredge   1789 N.H.
   daughter Hannah m. John Church

Ames, Joseph b. Va. 1773 d. Va.   Capt. Va. Mil.
   m. Matilda (Tinney) Snead — son Levin S. m. Ann Priscilla Hornsby

Ames, Josiah b. Me. (Mass.) d. Me.   Cpl. Mass. (Me.) Mil.
   m. Sarah Stowers — daughter Jane m. Peter D. Perkins

Ames, William b. Vt. or N.Y. 1787 d. Mich. 1849   Musician N.Y. Mil.
   m. Amy F. Ferris — son Reuben C. m. Julia Ruth Pardee

Amis, Lincoln, b. N.C. 1776 d. Tenn. 1868   Sgt. Ky. Mil.
   m. Ann Nicholson — daughter Lucy H. m. John Reams Davis

Amis, Thomas b. N.C. 1744 d. Tenn. aft. 1793   Patriot Mem. Legis. 1788
   m. Alice Gale — son Dr. Lincoln m. Ann Nicholson   N.C.
   daughter Alice m. John Gordon

Amiss, Phillip Newport b. Va. 1779 d. Va. 1838   Col. Va. Mil.
   m. Polly Basey (Bayse) — daughter Edna m. Benjamin Pendleton

Ammen, David b.— d.— m.— Vol. 17   Pvt. Ohio Mil.

Ammidon, Calvin b. Mass. 1768 d. Mass. 1825   Patriot Mass.
m. Deborah Davis — daughter Deborah m. Chester Dresser

Amos, George b. (W) Va. 1794 d. (W) Va. 1853   Pvt. Va. Mil.
m. (Idna) Hawkins — son Edgar W. m. Dorcas Clayton
daughter Elizabeth m. William Beall

Amos, Robert, Sr. b. Md. 1741 d. Md. 1818   Pvt. Md. Mil.
m. Martha McComas — son Robert, Jr. m. Elizabeth

Amos, Robert, Jr. b. Md. 1771 d. Md. 1826 m. Elizabeth   Pvt. Md. Inf.
daughter Ann m. Thomas Mason Miller

Amos, William b. 1790 d. Md. 1878 m. Ruth   Pvt. Md. Mil.
daughter Mary Susan m. Thomas Edward Sanders

Amrine, Abraham b. Pa. 1761 d. Ohio 1849   Patriot Pa. & Ohio
m. Mary Woolford — daughter Susanna m. Joseph Worley

Amsden, Thomas Gates b. N.Y. 1797 d. Ohio 1876   Pvt. N.Y. Mil.
m. Lydia Chapman — daughter Sarah m. Joseph Peter Shoemaker

Anderson, Alexander O. b.— d.— m.— Vol. 12   Pvt. Tenn. Mil.

Anderson, Cornelius W. b. Ky. 1791 d. Ind. 1841   Pvt. Ky. Vol.
m. Permelia Leathers — daughter Permelia m. John M. Brown
REAL DAUGHTER

Anderson, Crawford b. S.C. 1793 d. Ky. aft. 1870   Pvt. Ky.
m. Jincy Cunningham — daughter Virginia m. Oliver H. Perry

Anderson, David b. Pa. 1771 d. Ohio 1843   Pvt. Ohio Mil. 1812
m. Esther Hollinshead — daughter Jane Duer m. Isaac Miover

Anderson, David Overton b. 1776 d. Tenn. 1839   Pvt. Tenn. Mil.
m. Sara Drake — son James P. m. Nancy Corn

Anderson, Eli b. Va. 1785 d. Va. 1814 m.—   Pvt. Va. Mil.
son John P. m. Ellen A. Truslon

Anderson, Ezekiel b. Pa. ca 1772 d. Ohio 1813   Pvt. Ohio
m. Margaret — daughter Jane m. George Feasel

Anderson, Francis b.— d.— m.— Vol. 15   Pvt. Md. Mil.

Anderson, Howell b. 1778 d. 1858 m. Elizabeth Denson   Pvt. S.C. Mil.
son Geo. Jeff m. Mary Pauline Killingsworth

Anderson, Isaac, Jr. b. Pa. 1796 d. Pa. 1865   Pvt. Pa. Mil.
m. Elizabeth Hayes Smith
son Benjamin S. m. Julia Rodman Schofield

Anderson, Isaac, Sr. b. Pa. 1760 d. Pa. 1838   Patriot Pa. 1803-7
m. Mary Lane — son Edward m. Catherine Highley
son Isaac, Jr. m. Elizabeth H. Smith
son Joseph E. m. Rebecca Workizer

Anderson, Jacob b. Ky. d. Ky. 1815 m. Lucinda   Sgt. U.S. Army
daughter Lucinda m. Robert Gammon

Anderson, James b. S.C. 1790 d. Tenn. 1858   Pvt. Tenn. Mil.
m. Sarah Hughes (1) — son Robert D. m. Sara Adelne Womack

Anderson, James b.-d. Ill. 1835 m. Mary   Pvt. Ill. Vol.
son Martin m. Lucy Ward

11

Anderson, James b. Va. 1765 d. Ill. 1851   Capt. Ky. Mil.
   m. Nancy (Ann) Rice Harris
   daughter Maria Caroline m. Austin Adams

Anderson, James Callaway b. Va. 1792 d. Mo. 1864   Ens. Va. Mil.
   m. Jane Robinson Moorman
   daughter Mary T. m. Asa Nathaniel Overall

Anderson, John b. Va. 1778 d. Ala. 1814   Lt. Col. Tenn. Mil.
   m. Elizabeth McNair
   daughter Louise m. Allen Kirklin(land)
   son Josiah M. m. Nancy Lamb

Anderson, John b. Va. 1750 d. Va. 1817   Col. N.C. (Tenn.)
   m. Rebecca Maxwell — daughter Jane m. John Henninger

Anderson, John William b. Md. 1800 d. D. C. 1861   Pvt. Md. Mil.
   m. Elizabeth Spellman
   daughter Clara Louise m. Edward Joseph Dowling
   REAL DAUGHTER

Anderson, John b. Va. 1750 d. Va. 1817   Col. N.C. (Tenn.)
   m. Martha B. Box son Harvey m. Mary Wellborn

Anderson, Joseph B. b.—d.—m.— Vol. 12   Sgt. Maj. Va. Mil.

Anderson, Oliver b. Ky. 1794 d. Ky. 1873 m. Mary Campbell Pvt. Ky. Mil.
   son John C. m. Anna Margaret Mason

Anderson, Samuel b. S. C. 1780 d. Ohio 1830   Pvt. Ohio Mil.
   m. Elizabeth Edminston — son William H. m. Mary Heiser

Anderson, Thomas F. b. S. C. 1779 d. Ga. 1875   Capt. S. C. Mil.
   m. Martha Box — son Harvey m. Mary Wellborn
   son James m. Martha Arrowood
   son Thomas, Jr. m. Jane Ballew

Anderson, Timothy b. Miss. 1797 d. Miss. 1850   Pvt. Tenn. Mil.
   m. Tinney Jane Dikes
   daughter Jane Elizabeth m. William Warren Wiles

Anderson, Vincent b. Va. 1775 d. Tex. 1840   Pvt. Ky. Mil. Vols.
   m. (1) Margaret Terry — son Crawford m. Jincy Cunningham

Anderson, William b. Va. 1760 d. Va. 1806 m. Sarah Early Patriot Va.
   son James C. m. Jane Robinson Moorman

Anderson, William b. ca 1760 d. bef. 1822 m. Frances   Pvt. S.C.
   daughter Elizabeth m. Anderson Killingsworth

Anderson, William b. Del. 1764 d. Va. 1839   Col. Va. Mil.
   m. Anne Thomas — son Francis T. m. Mary Ann Alexandria

Anderson, William b. Md. 1789 d. Ohio 1868   Pvt. Ohio Mil.
   m. Sarah Warnock — son James m. Mary Ann Wilson

Anderson, William b. Ire. 1781 d. Ohio 1828   Pvt. Ohio Mil.
   m. Melila Thompson
   son Benjamin m. Nancy Love

Andreas, Peter b. Pa. 1751 d. 1835 m. Thankful Washburn Capt. Pa. Mil.
   son John George m. Katherine Miller
   son Peter, Jr. m. Nancy Ann Miller

Andreas, Peter b. Pa. 1782 d. Ohio 1864   Pvt. Ohio Mil.
   m. Nancy Ann Miller — son John m. Sarah Sherretts

Andrews, Abraham b.- d.- m.-   Pvt. U.S. Inf.
   Vol. 14

Andrews, Artheur, III b. Pa. 1781 d. Pa. 1868   1st Sgt. Pa. Mil.
    m. Jane (1) — daughter Anna Amanda m. John Thomas Wentz

Andrews, Baker b. Va. 1790 d. Ill. 1832   Sgt. Va. Mil.
    m. Mary Peter Pegram
    son Nathaniel James m. Elizabeth Walker

Andrews, Charles b. 1793 d. N. Y. 1867 m. Anne Hummell   Pvt. N.Y. Mil.
    son John Wesley m. Henrietta

Andrews, Jacob Treworthy b. Mass. (Me.) 1791 d. Ohio 1840 Cpl. Vt. Mil.
    son William C. m. Catherine S. Hayward

Andrews, John b. Pa. 1794 d. Pa. 1823   Ens. Pa. Mil.
    m. Jane Patterson — son Robert C. m. Rhoda C. Kingsbury

Andrews, Tapley b. 1778 d. Tenn. m.-   Lt. Tenn. Mil.
    Vol. 31

Andrus, George b. N.Y. 1789 d. N.Y. 1846   paymaster N.Y. Mil.
    m. Angelina Betts
    daughter Almire m. Ellihu Allen Pierpont

Andrus (Andrews), James b. Ohio 1795 d. Ill. 1846   Pvt. Ohio Mil.
    m. Ourena Roberts — son Archibald R. m. Annetta Williams

Andruss, Isaac b. N.J. 1774 d. N.J. 1850   Maj. N.J. Mil.
    m. Mary Cook Halsted
    son Caleb H. m. Emma Sutherland Goble
    son Isaac, Jr. m. Lydia Austin

Angus, Daniel Page b.— d.— m.— Vol. 17   Capt. U.S. Navy 1812

Annelly, Gifford b. N.Y. 1794 d. N.J. 1854   Pvt. N.J. Mil.
    m. Rachel Morrison
    daughter Elizabeth m. Charles Warwick

Annin, John C. b. N.J. 1787 d. Mich. 1875 m. Mary Lane   Sgt. N.Y. Mil.
    daughter Maria H. m. Egbert C. Goodrich

Ansart, Felix b. Mass. 1783 d. Conn. 1874   Lt. U.S. Inf.
    m. Mary E. S. Prescott
    son Felix, Jr. m. H. Rowena Loomis

Antes, John Henry b. Pa. 1736 d. Pa. 1820   Col. Pa. Mil.
    m. Anna Maria Paul — daughter Elizabeth m. Phillip Barnhart

Anthony, John b. R.I. 1731 d. R.I. 1814 m. Rachel Bullock Ens. R.I. Mil.
    daughter Rachel m. Jesse Hopkins

Anthony, Joseph, Jr. b. Va. 1750 d. Ga. aft. 1810   Patriot Ga.
    m. Elizabeth Clark — son Anselm m. Sarah Menzies

Anthony, Lewis C. b. N.C. 1785 d. Mo. 1861   Pvt. Tenn. Mil.
    m. Nancy Kirby — son Thomas J. m. Cassandra Sutton

Anthony, Nicholas b.—d.—m.—   Pvt. N.Y. Mil.
    Vol. 5

Anthony, William b. Va. 1793 d. Mo. 1865   Lt. Tenn. Mil.
    m. Jane Branch Marshall
    son Richard m. Pocohantas Farmer

Anthony, William Banks b. Va. d. K/a New Orleans   Pvt. Tenn. Mil.
    m. Susan McLain — daughter Amanda m. Loddin Brodie

Apperson, John b. Va. 1794 d. Ill. 1877 m. Sidney Hanson   Pvt. Va. Mil.
    son William W. m. Barbara Ann Rhoades

Applegate, John b. 1758 d. N.J. 1863 m. Ann Eliza Cottrell Pvt. N.J. Mil.
    daughter Ella m. John G. Emmons   REAL DAUGHTER

Applegate, Thomas b. N.J. 1792 d. N.J. 1868   Teamster N.J.
    m. Hannah Thompson — daughter Althea m. Thomas Phillips

Applegate, Tunis b. 1771 d. Ky. 1846 m. Eleanor McGrew   Pvt. Ky. Mil.
    daughter Christina m. John Wheeler

Appleton, Thomas b. Mass. 1740 d. Mass. 1830   Pvt. Mass. Mil.
    m. Lydia Dane — son Daniel m. Polly Allen

Applewhite, James b. N.C. 1792 d. Miss. 1872   Pvt. Miss. Mil.
    m. Mary Regan — son Ralph m. (1) Josephine Brandt

Applewhite, Thomas b. Miss. 1790 d. Tex. 1861   Corp. Miss. Mil.
    m. Rachel Mixon — daughter Susan m. Harrison Presnall
    m. Elizabeth Oglesby — son James m. Fannie Grayson

Appley, Chester b. Conn. 1779 d. Conn. 1843   Pvt. Conn. Mil.
    m. Sarah Fitch — son Elhanon W. m. Hannah Starr

Appold, George b. Md. 1793 d. Md. 1853   Corp. Md. Mil.
    m. Elizabeth Boget — son George J. m. Mackall McKenzie
    m. Catherine Reese — daughter Catherine R. m. Oliver F. Lantz

Arbogast, Henry b. (W.) Va. 1770 d. W. Va.   Pvt. Va. Mil.
    m. Sophia Wade — daughter Margaret m. John Gall

Arbogast, Michael b. Germany 1734 d. (W.) Va. 1812   Patriot (W.) Va.
    m. Mary Elizabeth? — son Adam m. Margaret Hull

Arbuckle, Thomas b. Va. 1780 d. 1838 m. Jane Davis   Pvt. Ky. Mil.
    son Matthew m. Mary E. Trolinger

Arbuckle, William b. Va. 1752 d. (W.) Va. 1836   Capt. Ft. Randolph, Va.
    m. Catherine M. McPogue
    daughter Mary D. m. John Griffith Nelson

Archer, Allen b.— d.— m.—   Ens. Va. Mil.
    Vol. 17

Archer, Richard Henry b. Va. 1789 d. Tex. 1868   Pvt. Cpl. Va.
    m. Judith Ann Proudfit   Riflemen
    daughter Virginia m. John Hall Wise

Arey, James b. Mass. (Me.) 1795 d. Me. 1877   Pvt. Mass. (Me.)
    m. Nancy Merrille   Mil.
    daughter Jane C. m. William A. Brown

Argabrite, Martin b. Va. 1788 d. (W.) Va. 1869   Pvt. Va. Mil.
    m. Catherine Burdett — daughter Diana m. Wm. Hardman

Armantrout, Philip b. Va. 1797 d. Ill. 1869   Pvt. Va. Mil.
    son Jesse m. Louisa Davis
    daughter Margaret m. Robert Waggoner

Armistead, Francis b. Va. 1790 d. Mo.   Pvt. Va. Mil.
    m. Martha Grinnell — daughter Eliza S. m. Francis Merritt Hendrix

Armistead, George b. Va. 1780 d. Md. 1818   Lt. Col. U.S. Eng.
    m. Louisa Hughes
    daughter Georgianna F. L. m. William Stuert Appleton

Armistead, John Baylor b. Va. 1765 d. Va. 1845   Capt. Va. Mil.
   m. Anne B. Carter — son Robert L. m. Mary Carter

Armour, Hamilton b. Ire. 1750 d. Pa. 1838   Pvt. Pa. Mil.
   m. Jane Craig — daughter Mary Jane m. Samuel McCarty

Arms, Luman b. Mass. 1796 d. N.Y. 1884   Pvt. N.Y. Mil.
   m. Elizabeth Pierce — daughter Gertrude E. m. Charles M. Heath
   REAL DAUGHTER

Arms, Ralph b.— d.— m.— Vol. 4   **Pvt. Mass. Mil.**

Armstrong, Bela, Jr. b. Conn. 1790 d. Mich. 1827   Pvt. N.Y. Mil.
   m. Mary Palmer — son Sullivan m. Mary C. Sheldon

Armstrong, Darius b. Conn. 1795 d. Ohio 1857   Pvt. Conn. Mil.
   m. Mary Hazen — daughter Charlotte A. m. Mosier Ames

Armstrong, James b. Pa. 1748 d. Pa. 1828   Patriot Pa.
   m. Mary Stevenson — son John W. m. Catherine Shell

Armstrong, James A. b. Ire. ca. 1762 d. Pa. aft. 1850   Pvt. Pa. Rgt.
   m. Margaret Martin — son Hugh m. Jame McCoy
   son Martin m. Margaret Jamison

Armstrong, James W. b. prob. S.C. 1780/90   Asst. WM. Ga. Mil.
   d. Ala. 1835 m. Dorothy Tucker
   son James Francis m. Frances McDade

Armstrong, Job b. R.I. 1784 d. R.I. 1854   Ens. R.I. Inf.
   m. Adah Aldrich — son Job, Jr. m. Harriot C. Reynolds

Armstrong, John b.— d.— m.— Vol. 13   Sgt. Ohio Mil.

Armstrong, John b. Ga. 1768 d. Ill. 1851   Pvt. Tenn. Mil.
   m. Polly Dudley — son Robert m. Mahala M. Phillips

Armstrong, John b. ca. 1733/4 d. Tenn. 1829   **Pvt. Tenn. Mil.**
   m. Susannah Harrelson — son Alexander m. Nancy Ann Wells

Armstrong, John b.— d.— m.— Vol. 4   Capt. of Forts 1786

Armstrong, John b. Pa. 1793 d. Ohio 1865   Sgt. Ohio Mil.
   m. Isabella McVaig — daughter Margaret K. m. Hiram Garretson

Armstrong, John b. Pa. 1758 d. N.Y. 1843   **Brig. Gen. 1812**
   m. Alida Livingston   Sec. of War 1813/14
   daughter Margaret m. William B. Astor   Senator N.Y. 1800-04
                                    Min. to France 1804-10

Armstrong, John b. Ga. 1768 d. Ill. 1851   Pvt. Tenn. Mil.
   m. Mary Ann Dudley — son Robert m. Emilie Jane Sawrey

Armstrong, Peter b. Sweden 1777 d. Md. 1837   Pvt. U.S. Inf.
   m. Bathsheba Wood — daughter Mary Ann m. William Addison
   daughter Rachel Jane m. James W. Harvey

Armstrong, Richard b. Pa. 1794 d. Ohio 1845   Sgt. Ohio Mil.
   m. Electa Rumsey — son Elliott B. m. Mary Emma

Armstrong, Solomon b.— d.— m.— Vol. 9   Pvt. Md. Mil.

Armstrong, Thomas b. Ire. d. Md. 1824 m. Ellen Curran   Pvt. Md. Mil.
   daughter Eliza m. John T. Grindall

Armstrong, William b. Ky. 1795 d. Ill. 1879   Pvt. Ill. Mil.
   m. Susan H. Oden — son Joshua L (A.) m. Mary Ann Smith

Arnall, Richard b. Va. 1794 d. Va. 1880   Pvt. Va. Mil.
   m. Catherine Butler — daughter Jane m. Henry C. Ashby
   REAL DAUGHTER

Arnett, Andrew b. Va. ca 1760 d. Va. 1824   Capt. Va. Mil.
   m. Elizabeth Leggett — son Thomas m. Zarilda Price
   son Solomon m. Mary Cordray

Arnold, Benjamin Franklin b. N.Y. 1783 d. Ia. 1852   Pvt. Md. Mil.
   m. Euphema Bontte — son Benjamin F. m. Amanda Richardson

Arnold, James b. N.Y. 1785 d. Mich. 1865   Pvt. N.Y. Mil.
   m. Mary Slingerland — daughter Hannah Eliza m. Jonathan Ball

Arnold, John b. Va. 1782 d. Va. 1865   Lt. Va. Mil.
   m. Jane Humphries — son John Humphries m. Mary Peed

Arnold, John b. Md. 1783 d. Md. 1857   Pvt. Md. Mil. 1812
   m. Rebecca Ann Redmond — son Elijah m. Matilda Hammond

Arnold, Jonathan b. R.I. 1741 d. Vt. 1793   Patriot Vt. 1790
   m. Alice Crawford — daughter Freelove m. Noah Davis

Arnold, Michael b. N.C. d. Ill. 1862   Corp. East Tenn. Mtg.
   m. Fanny Funk   Gunmen — Roane Co.
   son William Mitchell m. Dorcas Hankins

Arnold, Peleg b.— d.— m.— Vol. 10   Capt. N.Y. Mil.

Arnold, Price b. Ky. 1771 d. Mo. 1830   Pvt. Mo. Mil.
   m. Elizabeth Pipes — daughter Mary m. Porter Jackman

Arnold, Samuel b. Mass. 1791 d. Mich. 1839   Mass. Navy 1814
   m. Mary Jackson — son Oscar m. Maria Deveny

Arnold, Solomon b. Ga. 1795 d. Ala. 1871   Pvt. Ga. Mil.
   m. Jennette C. Rush — daughter Martha R. m. Jesse Cary Cobb

Arnold, Stephen, Jr. b. Conn. 1781 d. Pa. 1861   Sgt. Pa. Mil.
   m. Martha Williams — son Rheuben D. m. Leah Santee

Arnold, Thomas Dickens b. Va. 1798 d. Tenn. 1878   Pvt. Va. Mil.
   m. Loretta Rose — daughter Martha W. m. John Coleman Marshall
   son Reuben m. Isabella Rogers Hape

Arnold, Wiatt b. Ky. 1792 d. Ky. 1847 m. Sally Rice   Pvt. Ky. Mil.
   daughter Louisa m. Abraham Newton Dale

Arnott, Andrew b. Pa. 1790 d. Ohio 1853   Pvt. Pa. Riflemen
   m. Jane Douglas — son John m. Louisa McMullen

Arrington, Joseph b.— d.— m.— Vol. 13   Pvt. N.C. Mil.

Arrison, Jeptha b. Eng. 1736 d. N.J. 1828   Corp. Pa. Mil.
   m. (2) - Bernhart — daughter Rosette m. Hugh Shotwell

Art, Bailey b.— d.— m.—   Pvt. Del. Vol.
   Vol. 15

Art, William b.— d.— m.—   Pvt. Ohio Mil.
   Vol. 6

Arthur, Ambrose b. 1776 d. Ky. 1859   Pvt. Ky. Mil.
   m. Jane Gilbert Fletcher — son Edward F. m. Susan Emma Routt

Arthur, Bradford b. 1772 d. N.Y. 1855 m. Rumah Ely Lt. N.Y. Mil.
 son Warren m. Almira Hough

Arthur, Joseph b. Pa. 1779 d. Ohio aft. 1829 Cpl. Ohio Mil.
 m. Mary McLaughlin Glasgow — son Joseph G. m. Nancy Ann Albin

Arthur, Lewis b. 1794 d. Ga. 1882 Pvt. Ga. Mil.
 m. Nancy Hartsfield — daughter Sallie m. Jabes Pleatus Hadaway

Arthur, Reuben b. S.C. 1774 d. S.C. 1833 Patriot S.C. 1808
 m. Mary Hannah Camber
 daughter Elizabeth D. m. James B. Diggs

Artman, Andrew b.— d.— m.— Pvt. Pa. Mil.
 Vol. 16

Artus, James b.— d.— m.— Sgt. Ky.
 Vol. 12

Asbury, William b. Va. ca 1785 d. Va. 1840 Ens. Va. Mil.
 m. Elizabeth Chafine
 son John Bertram m. Mary Adeline Garrett

Ash, Alexander Fleming b. S.C. 1785 d. Ga. 1848 2nd. Sgt. Ga.
 m. Elizabeth McCracken — son William m. Cynthia Turk

Ash, William b. Pa. 1771 d. Pa. 1850 m. Ann Fisher 2nd Sgt. Pa. Inf.
 daughter Elizabeth m. Nathan Rambo

Ashbrook, William b.— d.— m.— Pvt. Va. Mil.
 Vol. 12

Ashby, Turner b. Va. 1789 d. Va. 1834 Lt. Va. Mil.
 m. Dorothea Farrer Green
 daughter Mary m. George Vowles Moncure

Ashley, Samuel, Sr. b. Mass. 1720 d. N.H. 1792 Patriot N.H. 1791
 m. Eunice Doolittle — daughter Eunice m. Rev. Augustine Hibbard

Ashmead, Samuel b. Pa. 1710 d. Pa. 1794 Patriot Mem. Gen.
 m. Esther Morgan Assem. 1787 Pa.
 son Samuel, Jr. m. Ruth Robinson

Ashton, Burdett b. Va. 1709 d. Va. aft. 1800 Patriot Mem. Va.
 m. Anne Washington Legis. 1788
 daughter Sarah m. Nicholas Fitzhugh Deleg. 1799-1800

Ashton, James b. Ire. 1728-9 d. N.Y. 1802 Pvt. Ohio Mil.
 m. Elizabeth — daughter Rebekah m. George Barker

Ashton, Richard Watts b. Va. 1799 d. 1853 Pvt. Va. Mil.
 m. Mary Devereaux — son John D. m. Sara Janet Roberts

Askew, Josiah b. Tenn. 1792 d. Ill. 1845 Capt. Tenn. Mil.
 m. Hannah Bates — daughter Martha Jane m. William James Allen

Askey, (Asky, Ashy) Robert b. Pa. 1770 d. Pa. 1850 Capt. Pa. Mil.
 m. Mary (Polly) Evans — son Ellis m. Ann Woodle (Woodhul)

Aston, James b. Va. d. Va. 1840 m. Elizabeth Harris Pvt. Va. Mil.
 son James, Jr. m. Sophia Levinia Richeson (Richardson)

Atherton, Elisha b. Pa. 1765 d. Pa. 1818 m. Eunice Carver Ens. Pa. Mil.
 son James m. Nancy Raub

Atchley, Isaac b. Tenn. 1787 d. Tenn. 1854 Cpl. Tenn. Mil.
 m. Elizabeth Emma Smith — son Robert S. m. Louisa Clark

Atkins, James, Sr. b. Va. 1797 d. Tenn. 1826   Pvt. Tenn. Inf.
   m. Margaret Patterson — son James, Jr. m. Virginia Eliza Carr

Atkins, Joseph b. Mass. 1766 d. Mass. 1851   Patriot Mass. 1810-13
   m. Ruth Nickerson — daughter Martha m. Ebenezer Higgins

Atkins, Nathaniel, Jr. b.— d.— m.—   Pvt. Me. (Mass. Mil.)
   Vol. 12

Atkinson, George D. b.— d.— m.—   Capt. Md. Mil.
   Vol. 7

Atkinson, Henry b. N.J. 1789 d. N.J. 1875   Pvt. U.S. Dragoons
   m. Mary Abrams (Abrahams) — son James C. m. Sarah Powell

Atkinson, Jonathan b.— d.— m.—   Cpl. Mass. Mil.
   Vol. 7

Atkinson, Thomas Walton b. Va. 1777 d. Tenn. 1862   Ord. Sgt. Ky. Mil.
   m. Lizzie Hunley — daughter Frances J. m. Thomas Jefferson French

Atkinson, William b.— d. N.C. 1841 m. Susie Jessup   Pvt. N.C. Mil.
   daughter Etty Ann m. John Brown

Atlee, William Pitt b. Pa. 1772 d. Pa. 1815   Lt. Col. Pa. Mil.
   m. Sarah Light — daughter Elizabeth Amelia m. Alexander Varian

Atlie, William Augustus b.— d.— m.—   Patriot Pa. 1793
   Vol. 8

Attix, Aquilla b. Md. 1791 d. Md. m. Rebecca Chance   Pvt. Md. Mil.
   son James D. m. Sophrona Bowker

Atwood, Samuel b. Mass. 1735 d. Mass. 1796   Patriot Mass. 1785
   m. Bathsheba (Crosby?)
   daughter Bathsheba m. David Mays Chipman

Atwater, Samuel b. Conn. 1757 d. Conn. 1848   Patriot 1812
   m. Patience Peck — daughter Abigail Ann m. Levi Bradley

Atwood, Zaccheus b.— d.— m.— Vol. 16   Lt. N.Y. Mil.

Audrain, Peter F. b. France 1760 d. Mich. ca 1820   Patriot Mich. 1797
   m. Margaret Moore — daughter Caroline Maria m. Col. Starke

Augur, Daniel Page b.— d.— m.— Vol. 16   1st Mate Conn. Navy

Auld, Edward b. Md. 1789 d. Va. 1861   Sgt. Md. Mil.
   m. Elizabeth Dawson
   son Edward, Jr. m. Harriett Elizabeth Watkins

Auld, Hugh b. Md. 1767 d. Md. 1820   Lt. Col. Md. Mil.
   m. Zippora Wilson — son Hugh, Jr. m. Sophia Keithley

Auman, Henry b. Pa. 1789 d. Pa. 1874   Cpl. Pa. Mil.
   m. Catharine Buyman — son James m. Kate S. Boas
   son William m. Emma Eliza Posengarten

Aungst, George b. Pa. 1784 d. Ohio 1841   Pvt. Ohio Mil.
   m. Elizabeth Zimmerman — son Samuel m. Catherine Spayde

Austin, Gustavus b. Conn. 1764 d. Conn. 1855   Ens. Qm. Conn. Mil.
   m. Lydia Kent — son Thomas J. m. Charlotte Louise Hayden

Austin, James b. Va. 1791 d. Ky. 1879 m. Elizabeth Deel   Sgt. Ky. Mil.
   daughter Eliza Ann m. Owen Gathright
   daughter Martha A. M. m. Albert Ford

Austin, Jonah, Jr. b. Mass. 1753 d. Me. 1833   Pvt. Mass. Mil.
m. Sarah Foster — daughter Hannah m. Richard Lamb

Austin, Moses b. N.Y. 1782 d. N.Y. 1858   Pvt. N.Y. Mil.
m. Ruth Colburn — son Jonah m. Catherine Barclay

Austin, Peter b. Va. 1791 d. Va. 1835   Sgt. Cor. Va. Mil.
m. Sarah Leftwich — son William L. m. Ruth M. Bowdry
daughter Lucy Jane m. David Ball

Austin, Robert R. b.— d.— m.—   Pvt. N.Y. Mil.
Vol. 12

Austin, Silas b. N.Y. 1780 d. N.Y. 1841   Capt. N.Y. Mil.
m. Elizabeth Tompkins — son Joab m. Sarah Ann Young

Austin, William S. b. R.I. 1796 d. N.Y. 1857   Pvt. N.Y. Mil.
m. Lucy Barnes—daughter Mercy m. Peter Keck REAL DAUGHTER

Austin, William Wilson b. Va. 1787 d. Mo. 1843   Pvt. U.S. Inf.
m. Locke Thompson
daughter Elizabeth Reid m. John William Waddell
son William W., Jr. m. Jane Gordon

Autery (Autrey), Robert b. N.C. 1788 d. Ala. 1876   Pvt. U.S. Army
m. Elizabeth Till — son Urias m. Mary Jane Jordan

Avant, Ransome Davis b. Va. 1765 d. Ga. 1849   Capt. Ga. Mil.
m. Martha Smith — son Joseph m. Barbara Harrell

Avent, John b. Va. d. Va. 1821 m.—   Ens. Va. Mil.
daughter Elizabeth m. William Woodroof

Averill, Calvin Ketchum b.— d.— m.—   Aide N.Y. Mil.
Vol. 12

Averill, Daniel b. Conn. 1793 d. lost at sea 1836   Sailor & Pvt.
m. (1) Abigail Foote   Conn. Mil.
son Samuel m. Myrta Ann Fowler

Averill, Henry Ketchum b. N.Y. 1798 d. N.Y. 1881   Pvt. N.Y. Vol.
m. Elizabeth Platt — daughter Mary Eliazbeth m. Perrie E. Burch

Averill, Stephen b. Conn. 1730 d. Conn. 1810   Patriot Conn. 1785
m. Sarah Hendie — son Frederick m. Lucretia Waldo

Averill, Stephen Nobel b.— d.— m.—   Sgt. N.Y. Cav.
Vol. 16

Avery, Charles b. Conn. d. Conn. 1825 m. Lucy Griffin   Ens. Conn. Mil.
son Gordon m. Maria Gardner

Avery, David b. Conn. 1762 d. Conn. 1823   Ens. Conn. Mil.
m. Hannah Prentice Avery — son Alfred m. Elizabeth L. Pease

Avery, Ebenezer Punderson b. Conn. 1765 d. N.Y. 1840   Capt. N.Y. Mil.
m. Lovina Barnes — son Samuel m. Lucinda Jones

Avery, Elisha b. Conn. 1785 d. N.Y. 1815   Pvt. U.S. Inf.
m. Penelope Westcott
daughter Susan Caroline m. John Tillinghast

Avery, Henry b. Tenn. 1793 d. Mo. 1845   Pvt. Tenn. Mil.
m. Elizabeth Greene
son William L. m. Sophrona Caroline Williams

Avery, Isaac b. Conn. 1772 d. Ind. 1858 m. Sarah Brooks   Capt. N.Y. Mil.
daughter Charlotte Ann m. Daniel Ordway Gillette

Avery, Jasper b. N.Y. 1794 d. N.Y. 1865　　　　Sgt. N.Y. Mil.
　m. Sarah Sidmore — daughter Phebe M. m. William Barnard
　daughter Susan m. Adam Munk

Avery, Jesse b.— d.— m.—　　　　　　　　　　Pvt. N.Y. Mil.
　Vol. 14

Avery, John (Parke) b. Conn. 1788 d. Conn. 1820　　Sgt. Conn. Mil.
　m. Lucy Avery — daughter Betsey A. m. Nehemiah Dodge Perry

Avery, Parker, Jr. b.— d.— m.—　　　　　　　Patriot Conn. 1814
　Vol. 3

Avery, Samuel b. Vt. 1791 d. Mass. 1867　　　　Sgt. Mass. Mil.
　m. Mary Ann Wood Candler
　daughter Helen S. m. George R. Stetson

Avis, John, Sr. b. Va. 1776 d. Va. (W.) 1857　　　Pvt. Va. Mil.
　m. Elizabeth Haines — son John, Jr. m. Mary O'Neill

Axline (Exline), John b. Va. 1739 d. Va. 1833　　Patriot Va. 1812
　m. Christine Martin — son Henry m. Elizabeth Crooks

Ayars (Ayres), Shepherd b. N.J. 1789 d. Pa. 1857　　Lt. Pa. Mil.
　m. Mary Murray — daughter Sarah P. m. John Stanford Mullin

Aycock, Richard, Jr. b. Ga. 1780 d. Ga. 1859　　Sgt. Ga. Mil.
　m. Nancy Bradford — daughter Almeda m. James Hodge, Jr.

Aycrigg, Benjamin b. N.J. 1773 d. Canada 1818　　Lt. Capt. Maj.
　m. Susan Bancker — son John m. Jane Gardner　　N.Y. Mil.

Aye, Henry b. Md. 1794 d. Ohio 1869 m. Mary James　　Cpl. Ohio Mil.
　son Nathan, Jr. m. Lucretia Babcock

Aye, Jacob b. Md. 1793 d. Ohio 1871 m. Rebecca Hyde　　Pvt. Ohio Mil.
　son William S. m. Sarah Jane Mitchell

Ayer, Jonathan Shepherd b.— d.— m.—　　　　Pvt. Mass. Mil.
　Vol. 9

Ayer, Lewis Malone Sr. b. S.C. 1769 d. S.C. 1863　　Mem. Hou. Rep. 1806-8
　m. Sarah Kirkland — son Zacheus m. Mary　　Spkr. Hou. 1811 S.C.

Ayers, David b. N.J. 1793 d. Tex. 1881 m. Ann　　　Pvt. N.Y.
　son Frank m. Hattie Watson

Ayers, Frazee b.— d.— m.—　　　　　　　　Paymaster N.J. Mil.
　Vol. 14

Ayers, John b.— d.— m.—　　　　　　　　　Pvt. Mass. Mil.
　Vol. 16

Ayers, Moses b. N.C. d. Tenn. 1856 m. Mary　　　Pvt. Tenn. Mil.
　daughter Julia m. Frank Holland

Ayers, Nathan b.— d.— m.—　　　　　　　　Sgt. Va. Inf.
　Vol. 8

Ayers, David b. N.J. 1793 d. Tex. 1881　　　　　Pvt. N.Y. Mil.
　m. Ann Mosehall Smith
　daughter Eliza Perkins m. Robert Alexander

Ayers, William b. N.H. 1798 d. Mass. 1860　　　Pvt. N.H. Mil.
　m. Ann Baxter — daughter Martha m. Thomas Ayers

Aylor, Anthony b. N.C. 1792 d. Tenn. 1882　　　Pvt. Ga. Mil. 1814-15
　m. Mary Sharpe — daughter Martha L. m. Joseph Bradshaw

Ayres, Isaac b.— d.— m.—   Pvt. N.J. Mil.
   Vol. 15

Ayres, John b. N.J. 1799 d. N.J. 1859 m. Sarah   Cpl. N.J.
   son Robert m. Sarah Rice

Ayres, Mathias b. Va. 1781 d. Mo. 1851   Lt. Va. Mil.
   m. Nancy Gilliam Howell
   daughter Ann Elizabeth m. Fayette Henry Gillian
   son Samuel M. m. Priscilla Frances Priest

Ayres, William b. N.J. 1780 d. N.Y. 1842   Lt. N.Y. Mil.
   m. Abigail Freeman — daughter Angeline m. Nicholas Shoemaker

Ayres, William b. Pa. 1794 d. Ohio 1866   Pvt. U.S. Art.
   m. Elizabeth Simonton — son Samuel D. m. Ann Amelia Myers

B

Babb, John b. Germany 1727 d. Pa. 1811   Pvt. Pa. Mil. 1785
   m. Anna Maria Riel — daughter Catharine m. George Messinger

Babb, Joseph b. S.C. 1790 d. S.C. 1818   Pvt. S.C. Vol.
   m. Martha Hodges — son Joseph m. Mary Shaw

Babbitt, Samuel Gregory b. Mass. 1790 d. N.Y. 1878   Sgt. N.Y. Mil.
   m. Elizabeth Salisbury — daughter Verlona m. Schuyler Thompson

Babcock, Asa b. Conn. 1787 d. N.Y. 1869 m. Lydia   Cpl. N.Y. Mil.
   son George m. Hazel Green

Babcock, Asa b. Conn. 1786 d. N.Y. 1860   Capt. N.Y. Mil.
   m. Elizabeth Stanton Noyes
   son Edward H. m. Cynthia Catherine Lynde

Babcock, Asaph b. N.Y. 1793 d. Mich. 1873/5   Pvt. N.Y. Mil.
   m. (1) Samaira Fleming — daughter Louisa m. Henry Rice

Babcock, Barnes b. N.Y. 1794 d. Wisc. 1869   Pvt. N.Y. Mil.
   m. Asenath Grover — daughter Olive M. m. William G. Ritch

Babcock, Ezra b. Mass. 1794 d. N.Y. 1830   Sgt. N.Y. Inf.
   m. Elizabeth Blair — daughter Mary Ann m. George Swortfiguer

Babcock, Gideon b. R.I. 1744 d. N.Y. 1799   Lt. Maj. N.Y.
   m. Mary Christopher Chesebrough
   daughter Asa m. Elizabeth Stanton Noyes

Babcock, Joseph b. N.Y. 1790 d. N.Y. 1866   Drummer N.Y. Mil.
   m. Phoebe Burdick — daughter Phoebe C. m. Henry La Paugh

Babcock, Joshua b.— d.— m.—   Ens. N.Y. Mil.
   Vol. 14

Babcock, Nathan b. R.I. 1763 d. N.Y. 1843   Pvt. Conn. Mil.
   m. Ruth Hubbell — son Josiah H. m. Lorinda Chapin

Babcock, Phineas b.— d.— m.—   Lt. Col. N.Y. Mil.
   Vol. 10

Babcock, Stephen b.— d.— m.—   Pvt. Conn. Mil.
   Vol. 8

Babcock, William b. Mass. 1783 d. Mich. 1871   Lt. N.Y. Mil.
   m. Julia Reed — son Julius C. m. Maria Robinson

Babin, Simon b.— d.— m.—   Lt. La. Mil.
   Vol. 11

Bach, Warren N. b.— d.— m.—   Cpl. Conn. Mil.
   Vol. 7

Bachlott, John, Jr. b. Va. 1794 d. Ga. 1873   Patriot Ga.
   m. Hannah McGillis Howell
   daughter Martha Teasdal m. Archibald Johnson

Backenstose, Henry b. Pa. 1765 d. Pa. 1828   Pvt. Pa. Mil.
   m. Catherine Riedel — son John m. Susanna Ream

Bacon, Abel b. N.J. 1784 d. N.J. 1826   Capt. N.J. Mil.
   m. Mary Smith Harting — son Abel, Jr. m. Mary S.

Bacon, Abner b. Mass. 1758 d. N.Y. 1832   Capt. N.Y. Mil.
   m. Dotia Kirby — son David m. Susan Smith

Bacon, Ira b. Mass. 1796 d. Ia. 1857 m. Mary Baum   Pvt. Ohio
   daughter Mary m. James Noel

Bacon, Lyman b. Conn. 1792 d. Conn. 1850   Pvt. Conn.
   m. Phebe Morgan
   daughter Sarah Elizabeth m. Andrew Haskell Mills

Bacon, Septimus b. Conn. 1794 d. Pa. 1861   Pvt. Conn. Mil.
   m. Margaret LeBar — daughter Bethiah m. Alfred H. Boston
   daughter Marietta m. Julius Eilenberger
   daughter Susan L. m. John Miller Horton

Bacon, Williamson b. 1790 d. Mo. 1867 m. Susan Watson   Pvt. Mo. Mil.
   daughter Elizabeth m. George Bates

Badeau, Dr. Elias Cornelius b. N.Y. 1790 d. N.Y.   Surgeon's mate
   m. Anna Lockwood   N.Y. Mil.
   son Richard M. m. Mary Lewis Cromwell

Badollet, John b. Switz. 1758 d. Ind. 1837   Capt. Pa. Mil.
   m. Margaret Hanna — daughter Sarah m. John Caldwell

Badger, Bela b. Conn. 1791 d. Pa. 1852   Capt. Pa.
   m. Catharine Penelope Worrell
   daughter Catharine L. m. James Hankinson Hart

Badlam, Stephen, IV b. Mass. 1751 d. Mass. 1815   Gen. Mass. Mil.
   m. Mary Adams — son Stephen, V m. Nancy Clark

Bagby, John b. Va. 1793 d. Mo. 1870 m. Mildred Ward   Pvt. Ky. Mil.
   son John W. m. Elizabeth Terrill
   son Robert J. m. Permelia Troyman

Baggett, Micajah b. N.C. 1791 d. Ga. m. Catherine   Pvt. N.C. Mil.
   son Henry J. m. Susan Ann Ellis

Bagley, Daniel b.— d.— m.—   Pvt. U.S. Inf.
   Vol. 16

Bailes (Bales), David b. Va. 1762 d. Ohio 1849 m.—   Pvt. Va. Mil.
   son Moses m. (1) Mary Fish

Bailey, Caleb, Jr. b. R.I. 1765 d. R.I. 1840 m.—   Capt. R.I. Inf.
   Vol. 9

Bailey, DeVoue b. N.Y. 1751 d. N.Y. 1823   Patriot N.Y. 1808
   m. Elizabeth Smith — son William m. Mary M. Wixon

Bailey, Edmund b. Va. d. Va. 1847 m. Rebecca Clanton   Pvt. Va. Mil.
   son Josiah C. m. Sarah Howell

Bailey, Eliphalet b.— d.— m.—   Pvt. N.H. Mil.
Vol. 14

Bailey, Ephraim b.— d.— m.—   Cpl. N.Y. Mil.
Vol. 12

Bailey, Frederick b.— d.— m.—   Capt. Pa. Mil.
Vol. 14

Bailey, George Washington b.— d.— m.—   Pvt. U.S. Eng.
Vol. 15

Bailey, Hudson b. (Me.) Mass. 1786 d. Me.   Pvt. Mass. Mil.
m. Sarah Yeaton — daughter Elizabeth H. m. Asa T. Webster

Bailey, Jacob b. Vt. d. Vt. m.—   Gen. Vt.
daughter Adeline m. Moses Rogers Vol. 2

Bailey, John b. S.C. abt. 1790 d. La. 1872   Pvt. Ga. Mil.
m. Clarissa Joiner — daughter Brunette B. m. Pierre Hypolite Bahm

Bailey, John b. Mass. 1783 d. Mass. 1844   Capt. Mass. Mil.
m. Abigail Cross — son Joseph m. Sarah Ann Brachall

Bailey, John b. Vt. 1765 d. Vt. 1839   Capt. U.S. Army
m. Hannah Ladd — son Jeffrey A. m. Melissa Stevens

Bailey, Joseph b. Mass. (Me.) 1787 d. Me. 1843   Maj. Mass. Mil.
m. (2) Lydia Fitch — son Bradley m. Harriet Relief Wilbur

Bailey, Lansing b. N.Y. 1787 d. N.Y. 1866   Pvt. N.Y. Mil. 1814
m. Zada Parmelee — son Davis O. m. Rhoba Williams
m. 2d Sylvia Pratt daughter Harriet Jane m. Clark Hall

Bailey, Lewis J. b. N.H. 1796 d. Mass. 1874   Cpl. Mass. Mil. 1814
m. Sarah Fenno — daughter Nancy m. Samuel N. Fuller

Bailey, Nathan b. N.Y.C. 1786 d. N.Y. 1852   Capt. N.Y. Mil.
m. Catherine S. Gillespy — son Abraham C. m. Sarah V. Prescott

Bailey, Nathaniel b. Conn. 1768 d. Conn. 1817 m.—   Pvt. Conn. Mil.
daughter Clarissa m. William W. Richmond

Bailey, Robert b. Va. d. Va. m.—   Pvt. Va. Mil.
son Robert, Jr. m. Sallie Jackson Vol. 2

Bailey, Robert S. b. Va. 1787 d. Va. 1844   Qm. Va. Mil.
m. Roberta Ann Cox — daughter Julia m. George B. P. Bowis

Bailey, Thomas b. Va. d. Ky. m. Nancy Gentry   Pvt. Ky. Vol.
daughter Nancy m. John Holston

Bailey, Thomas b. Va. 1773 d. Ala. 1850's   Capt. Tenn. Mil.
m. Zilpha Lee — daughter Mary m. William Carroll Lee

Bailey, Thomas b. Mass. (Me.) 1787 d. Mass. (Me.) 1813   Privateer Mass.
m. Ellin Jansen — daughter Jane m. Charles C. Bishop   (Me.)

Bailey, William b. Va. 1798 d. D.C. 1887   Cabin Boy on Gun
m. (2) Lucinda Johnson   Boat Va. Navy
daughter Frances m. Edward P. Anderson

Bain, Bastian b. N.Y. 1795 d. N.Y. 1836   Lt. N.Y. Mil.
m. Moyca Huyck — daughter Julia A. m. Robert Wild

Bainer (Baynard), Henry b.—d. aft. 1815   Pvt. Md. Mil.
 daughter Mary m. Thomas Scott

Bair, John b. Pa. 1774 d. Pa. 1856 m. Catharine Grove Capt. Pa. Mil.
 daughter Lydia m. Joseph Bittinger

Baird, Barnes b.— d. N.Y. ca 1870 m. Eliza Barker Pvt. N.Y. Mil.
 daughter Julia m. Sylvanus Wolcott

Baird, Charles b. Mass. 1794 d. N.Y. 1857   Pvt. U.S. Vol.
 m. Sarah Barlow — daughter Julia m. Amos Bean

Baird, Isaac W. b. N.Y. 1797 d. N.Y. 1855   Pvt. N.Y. Mil.
 m. Elizabeth Becker — daughter Similda L. m. Frank D. Pease

Baird, James b. Pa. 1795 d. Mo. 1857 m.—   Pvt. Ohio Mil.
 son James m. Jane Stevenson

Baird, Robinson b. Pa. 1792 d. Ohio 1870   Pvt. Ohio Mil.
 m. Elizabeth Williamson
 daughter Nancy Newton m. Maj. James McIntire

Baird, Thomas b. Pa. 1778 d. Pa. 1864 m. Martha McGee Pvt. Pa. Mil.
 daughter Elizabeth m. John Coulter

Baird, Thomas James b.— d.— m.—   3rd Lt. N.Y. Art.
 Vol. 8

Baker, Abner b. Va. 1775 d. Ky. 1861   Pvt. Ky. Mil.
 m. Elizabeth Buford
 son Caleb H., Sr. m. Mrs. Elizabeth Martin Hudson
 daughter Frances Ann m. Wade Hampton Walker

Baker, Ashley Charles b. Spain 1796 d. N.Y. 1884 Pvt. N.Y. Mil.
 m. Eliza Jane Casterline — son John m. Anna Becker

Baker, Benjamin b.— d. N.Y. 1813 m. Bethia Crosby Pvt. N.Y. Mil.
 son Benjamin, Jr. m. Miriam Urania Hickox

Baker, Benoni b. Mass. 1773 d. Mass. 1844   Sgt. Mass. Mil.
 m. Hannah Eldridge — son Nehemiah m. Julia Anna Clary

Baker, Brown b. Nova Scotia 1772 d. Me. 1842 Maj. Mass. Mil.
 m. Hannah Robinson — daughter Belinda m. Benjamin Goodrich

Baker, Conrad b. Pa. 1768 d. Pa. ca 1830-5   Pvt. Pa. Mil.
 m. Susan Fraley — daughter Susan C. m. Thomas T. Webster
 daughter Louisa m. Samuel Cornell

Baker, Daniel b. N.J. 1753 d. N.J. 1814   Cpl. N.J. Art.
 m. Margaret Osborn — son Hedges (Hodges) m. Charlotte Crane

Baker, Daniel b. Conn. 1763 d. Ohio 1836   Pvt. Ohio Mil.
 m. Jerusha Parsons — son Daniel M. m. Lydia Gaylord

Baker, David b.— d.— m.—   Pvt. N.Y. Mil.
 Vol. 16

Baker, Elijah II b. N.Y. 1775 d. Ohio 1864   Pvt. N.Y. Mil.
 m. Lovina White — son Sanford G. m. Cynthia Almeda Webster

Baker, Guy Carleton b. Vt. 1787 d. Canada 1872 Pvt. N.Y. Mil.
 m. Marie Christine Strohn — son Guy Charles m. Catherine Garrison
 daughter Jane U. m. William Henry Bolte

Baker, Henry b.— d.— m.—   Pvt. U.S. Inf.
 Vol. 7

Baker, Henry b. Ohio 1788 d. Ohio 1855   Pvt. Ohio Mil.
    m. Mary Binkley — daughter Sophia m. William Binkley

Baker, Jacob S. b. N.Y. 1791 d. N.Y. 1859   Ens. Lt. N.Y. Mil.
    m. Elizabeth Garniss — son Garnis E. m. Sarah B. Dupignac

Baker, James b. Va. 1760 (Eng. 1761) d. Ky. 1833   Pvt. Ky. Vol.
    m. Sarah Davis — son Dixon R. m. Catherine Gannet (?)
    son John G. m. Catherine Blevins

Baker, Jesse b. N.C. d. Ky. m. Elizabeth Quicksall   Pvt. Ky. Mil.
    daughter Rebecca m. William Price Gathright Vol. 2

Baker, John b. Pa. 1786 d. Pa. 1865 m. Mary Neal   Pvt. Pa. Mil.
    daughter Catherine m. Francis Maurice Breene

Baker, John b. Va. 1750 d. Ky. 1834   Capt. Ky. Mil.
    m. Elizabeth Baker (cousin)
    daughter Elizabeth B. m. William Cheek

Baker, John b. Conn. 1773 d. N.Y. 1816   Capt. N.Y. Mil.
    m. Eleanor Banker — son Zebulon m. Elizabeth Albee

Baker, (Becker), (John) Mathias b. Pa. 1761 d. Pa. 1833   Patriot Pa.
    m. Esther Holder   1809
    son John (Becker) m. Elizabeth Austine

Baker, John b. S.C. 1722 d. Ga. 1792 m. Sarah   Col. Ga. Mil.
    daughter Sarah m. Michael Randolph

Baker, John Kelsey b. Mass. 1775 d. Mass. 1843   Pvt. Vt. Mil.
    m. Betsey Ross — son Robert Ross m. Harriet Ratcliffe

Baker, Peter b. Ger. 1781 d. Tenn. 1842   Pvt. Md. Mil.
    m. Elizabeth Wolf — son Peter, Jr. m. Rebecca Ann Wiley

Baker, Samuel b. N.Y. 1764 d. N.Y. 1852   Capt. N.Y. Mil.
    m. Esther Gustin
    daughter Welthia Ann m. Zeno Socrates Sellick

Baker, Samuel b. Mass. 1769 d. N.Y. 1867   Pvt. Mass. Mil.
    m. Betsey Tiffany — son Charles m. Almira Hunt

Baker, Samuel, Jr. b. Conn. 1775 d. Ill. 1852   Cpl. Ohio Mil.
    m. Margaret Kelly — son James m. Christiana Stansbury Roberts

Baker, Samuel b.— d.— m.—   2nd Sgt. Qm. Pa. Mil.
    Vol. 13

Baker, Thomas b.— d.— m.—   Pvt. Vt. Art.
    Vol. 15

Baker, Thomas b.— d.— m.—   Pvt. N.H. Mil.
    Vol. 16

Baker, William b. S.C. 1776 d. S.C. 1831   Pvt. S.C. Mil.
    m. Annie Phillips
    daughter Elizabeth Susan m. Alexander Owens

Balch, Amos P. b. Ky. d. Ill. 1846 m. Mary Sawyer   Sgt. Ky. Mil.
    daughter Charlotte M. m. Henry E. Sapp REAL DAUGHTER

Baldridge, Alexander Holmes b. Va. 1795 d. Ohio 1874   Sgt. Ohio Mil.
    m. Rosanna Monroe — daughter Dora m. Robert A. Stephenson
    REAL DAUGHTER
    daughter Laura B. m. Frank P. Torrence REAL DAUGHTER
    daughter Margaret Ann m. John Shaw

Baldwin, Augustus b. Conn. 1784 d. Mass. 1836   Sgt. Mass. Mil.
    m. Betsy Goodrich — son Joseph A. m. Mary Porter

Baldwin, David Nutler b.— d.— m.—   Pvt. N.Y. Mil.
    Vol. 12

Baldwin, Eli b.— d.— m.—   Pvt. Conn. Mil.
    Vol. 10

Baldwin, Hezekiah b. Conn. 1756 d. Conn. 1831   Patriot Conn.
    m. Elizabeth Hine — son Raymond m. Martha Platt

Baldwin, Jabez b. Mass. 1763 d. N.Y. 1844   Pvt. N.Y. Mil.
    m. Hannah Tucker — son Zebulon m. Betsey Clark

Baldwin, John b. Md. 1756 d. Ohio 1848 m.—   Cpl. Ohio Mil.
    daughter Mary m. Joseph Wade

Baldwin, John J. b. N.J. 1771 d. N.Y. 1846   Pvt. N.J. Mil.
    m. Lydia Dodd — daughter Sarah D. m. Anthony Denton Ball

Baldwin, Joseph b. Va. 1787 d. Pa. 1873   Capt. U.S. Inf.
    m. Isabel Cairnes — daughter Polly Ann m. G. A. Newton

Baldwin, Levi b.— d.— m.—   Pvt. Conn. Mil.
    Vol. 11

Baldwin, Raymond b. Conn. 1792 d. Conn. 1835   Capt. Conn. Mil.
    m. Martha Platt — son Theodore R. m. Delia Baldwin (?)

Baldwin, Robert b. N.J. 1774 d. N.J. Aft. 1814   Ens. N.J. Mil.
    m. Mary Gould — son Johnson G. m. Jane Broadwell

Baldwin, Stephen b. N.J. 1780 d. N.J. 1835   Capt. N.J. Mil.
    m. Hannah Morehouse — daughter Lydia m. Samuel Minor Bailey

Baldwin, Sylvester b. N.Y. 1784 d. Wisc. 1872   Cpl. N.Y. Mil.
    m. Phoebe Sherman — son Norman B. m. Emma Miles

Baldwin, William b. Ohio 1790 d. Ohio 1860   Pvt. Ohio Mil.
    m. Mary Martin — son Peter W. m. Susanna Ellis

Bales (Bailes), David b. Va. 1762 d. Ohio 1819 m.—   Pvt. Va. Mil.
    son Moses m. Mary Pish

Ball, Adonijah b. Mass. 1778 d. Ill. 1847   Sgt. U.S. Inf.
    m. Anna Gaston son Reuben m. Polly Dix Buell

Ball, Cyrus b. N.J. 1783 d. N.J. 1814/15 m. Sarah Cook   Pvt. N.J. Mil.
    son William C. m. Margaret Ann Ten Broeck

Ball, James b. Md. 1793 d. Md. 1858 m. Ann   Pvt. 27th Regt. Md.
    daughter Mary m. Thomas Fitzpatrick

Ball, James b. Mass. 1797 d. Mass. 1877   Pvt. Mass. Mil.
    m. Maria Tuttle
    daughter Mary Ann R. m. George William Brookings
    REAL DAUGHTER

Ball, James b. Va. 1775 d. (W)Va. 1855   Ens. (W)Va. Mil.
    m. Lucy Harden — daughter Lucy m. Thomas Gory Hogg

Ball, Dr. James Kendall b.— d.— m.—   Surgeon Va. Mil.
    Vol. 3

Ball, John Smith b. Va. 1773 d. Mo. 1849   Lt. Col. Mo. Mil.
    m. Nancy Opie
    daughter Nancy Opie m. Frederick Bates

Ball, Jonathan Dayton b. N.J. 1787 d. N.J. 1862   Pvt. Pa. Mil.
m. Mary Phillips — son William m. Elizabeth Dreppard

Ball, Joseph b. N.Y. 1769 d. N.Y. 1792 m. Cornelia Greene   Lt. N.Y. Mil.
daughter Cornelia G. m. Nathaniel Lester Lewis

Ball Joseph b. Va. abt. 1788 d. Mo. aft. 1838   Ens. Va. Mil.
m. Martha Kendell Lee — son David m. Lucy Jane Austin

Ball, William Lee b. Va. 1781 d. D.C. 1824   paymaster Va. Mil.
m. Mary Peirce — son Atherall m. Floride Calhoun Simonds

Ballard, James b. Va. 1778 d. Ky. 1858   Pvt. Ky.
m. Fanny Dabney Jarman — son Pleasant P. m. Mary Francis

Ballard, David Lovejoy b. N.H. 1785 d. Me. 185-   Pvt. N.H. Mil.
m. Submit Tarbox — son Benjamin W. m. Mary Ann Hall

Ballard, Thomas b. Va. 1751 d. S.C. 1843   Lt. Col. S.C. Mil.
m. Elizabeth Graham — daughter Mary m. William Russell
son Thomas P. m. Margaret Trusdel

Balliet, Stephen b. Pa. 1753 d. Pa. 1821   Patriot Pa.
m. Magdalena Burkhatter — son Stephen m. Susana Ihrie

Ballinger, James F. b.— d.—m.—   Ens. Ky. Mil.
Vol. 11

Ballou, Ebenezer b.—d.—m.—   Pvt. N.Y.
Vol. 2

Ballou, Ziba b. R.I. 1765 d. R.I. 1829 m. Molly Mason   Ens. R.I. Mil.
son Henry G. m. Sarah Little Fales

Balmer, Christian b. Pa. 1783 d. Pa. 1843 m. Margaret   Pvt. Pa. Mil.
son Christian, Jr. m. Elizabeth

Baltzell, George b. Md. 1777 d. Ky. 1837   Lt. 1st Regt. Ky. Inf.
m. Hannah Nelson — son George F. m. Rebecca Hill Long

Baltzy, John b. Pa. 1759 d. Ohio 1814   Patriot Pa. & Ohio
m. Lucinda Clapper (Clappero)
daughter Sarah m. Jacob Hoopingarner

Bancroft, John b. 1786 d. Pa. 1862 m. Deborah Kent   Ens. N.J. Mil.
daughter Hetty M. m. Michael R. Tallman

Bandy, Richard b. Va. 1771 d. Ark. m. Kizziah Pierce   Sgt. Tenn. Mil.
daughter Harriet E. m. Jacob Swift
daughter Jane Karon m. William Stone

Bane, Nathan b. Mass. or Va. 1750/6 d. Pa. 1825   Capt. Pa. Mil.
m. Charity Nelson — son Joseph m. Rhoda Peck

Bangs, Reuben b. Mass. 1760 d. Mass. 1822   Pvt. Mass. Mil.
m. Lucy Thayer — son Abel T. m. Judith Abbott

Banks, James b. Pa. 1765 d. Tenn. 1828   Maj. Gen. Pa. Mil.
m. Katherine Nelson — son David m. Miriam Lewis Hawkins
daughter Martha m. Hugh Wilson

Bankson, Andrew b. Tenn. 1787 d. Wisc. 1853   2nd Lt. Ill. Mil.
m. Elizabeth Moore — daughter Orinda m. Samuel G. Smith

Bankston, John b. Pa. 1758 d. La. 1823 m. Henrietta Coates Pvt. La. Mil.
son Spencer m. Louisa Watson — son Simeon C. m. Sarah Brewer
son Peter m. Tabitha Robertson

Bannan (Bennet), Benjamin b. Va. 1770 d. Pa. 1861   Pvt. Pa. Mil.
m. Sarah Dunn — son John m. Sarah Ann Ridgway

Bannan, John b. Pa. 1796 d. Pa. 1868   Pvt. Pa. Mil.
m. Sarah Ann Ridgway — son Francis B. m. Mary Repplier

Banning, Benjamin b. Conn. 1780 d. Ohio 1827   Pvt. Conn. Mil.
m. Mary Munger — daughter Amy Jane m. William E. G. Caldwell

Bannon, Michael b. Pa. 1789 d. Ind. 1871 m. Nancy Clark   Pvt. Ohio Mil.
daughter Elizabeth m. Harvey Fitzpatrick

Banta, Abraham b. Ky. 1789   Pvt. Ky. Mil.
d. k/a battle of the Thames 1813 m. Mary Demaree
daughter Nancy m. Andrew Carnine

Banta, David b. Pa. 1771 d. Ind. 1844 m. Mary DeMotte   Pvt. Ky. Mil.
son Isaac m. Eliza Barker

Banta, Hendrick b. N.J. 1717 d. Ky. 1805   Pioneer service
m. (2) Altie Demerest   against Ky. Indians
son Cornelius m. Mary Magdalena Shuck

Banta, Henry b. Ky. 1786 d. Ind. 1872 m. Jennie Fulton   Cpl. Ky.
son John Fulton m. Fidelia Ann Fugary

Banta, Henry b. Ky. 1787 d. Ind. 1833   2nd Cpl. Ky. Vol.
m. Mary Mitchell — son Abraham m. Rachel Van Osdoll
daughter Rachael m. Peter Banta

Banta, Henry b.— d.— m.—   Capt. N.J. Art.
Vol. 6

Banta, John Thomas b. N.J. 1768 d. N.Y.C. 1846   Patriot N.J. 1812-13
m. Cornelia Bogart
daughter Tynie(?) (Tryntie) m. Peter M. Bogart
(Pieter Mathews Bogert)

Banta, Peter (Petrus) b. N.J. 1773 d. N.Y. 1829   Pvt. N.Y. Art.
m. Dorothea Van Orden — daughter Ann m. James Ward

Banton, Joah (Jacob) b. Tenn. d. Tenn. m.—   Capt. Tenn. Mil.
daughter Elizabeth Ann m. Samuel Bolliver Giles

Bantz, William b.— d.— m.   Surgeon's Mate
Vol. 16   Md. Mil.

Barbee, Joshua b. Va. 1761 d. Ky. 1839   Lt. Col. Ky. Mil.
m. Elizabeth Hobson—daughter Sarah m. James Speed Hopkins

Barbee, William b. Va. 1759 d. k/a Ohio 1813   Pvt. Ohio Mil.
m. Mary Smith — daughter Sarah m. William Tullis

Barber, Charles b. N.Y. 1790 d. Pa. 1871   Fifer U.S. Rifleman
m. Sylvia Capron (1)—daughter Eliza A. m. Joseph A. Langworthy

Barber, Erastus b. N.Y. 1779 d. Ill. 186-   Pvt. N.Y. Mil.
m. Joanna Steele — son Austin J. m. Mary Eliza Stillman

Barber, Nathaniel b. 1759 d. Ohio 1826 m. Ann Watson   Sgt. Ohio Mil.
daughter Sarah m. Thomas Gatch

Barber, Noyes b. Conn. 1781 d. Conn. 1844   Capt. Conn. Mil.
m. Catherine Burdick — daughter Betsy Ann m. Belton Allyn Copp

Barber, Sheffield b. R.I. 1777 d. R.I. 1862   Capt. R.I. Mil.
m. Mary Palmer — daughter Comfort m. George Reynolds Sprague

Barbour, James b. Va. 1775 d. Va. 1842   Patriot Gov. of Va.
m. Lucy Johnson — son Benjamin J. m. Caroline Watson   1812

Barclay, Andrew b. Pa. 1790 d. Pa. 1859 m. Sarah Stark   Pvt. Pa. Mil.
daughter Catherine m. David J. Skinner

Barclay, George Washington b.— d.— m.—   Pvt. Md. Mil.
Vol. 6

Bard, David b. Pa. 1744 d. Pa. 1815 m. Elizabeth Diemor   Patriot Pa.
son Richard m. Elizabeth B. Dunlap   Memb. Congress 1795-1815

Bard, John, Sr. b. Conn. 1772 d. Pa. 1852   Pvt. Pa. Mil.
m. Alice Whipple — son John, Jr. m. Almeda Wilson

Bard, John, Jr. b. Conn. 1794 d. Conn. or Pa.   Pvt. Pa. Mil.
m. Almeda Wilson — son Cyrus m. Clarissa Kingsley

Bard, Richard b. Ire. 1736 d. Pa. m. Catharine Poe   Patriot Pa.
son Thomas m. Jane Cochran McFarland

Bard, Thomas b. Pa. 1769 d. Pa. 1845   Capt. Tenn. Mil.
m. Jane C. McFarland — son John m. Mary Poe Evans

Bare, David b.— d.— m.—   Pvt. Pa. Mil.
Vol. 12

Bare (Barre), John b. Md. 1791 d. Ohio 1871   Pvt. Md. Mil.
m. Mary Ann Shafer
daughter Rachel Marie m. Joseph Browning Wragg
REAL DAUGHTER

Barekman (Barkman), Abraham b. 1774 d. 1850   Ind. Mil.
m. Elizabeth Antis — son Wm. S. m. Diadema Morgan

Barfield, James b. N.C. 1780 d. Tenn. 1843   Pvt. Tenn. Mil. 1812/14
m. Frances Pendleton Gaines
son Frederick m. Mary Ann Benton Edney
son Henry P. m. Lucinda Pitts

Barger, Jacob b.— d. N.Y. m. Catherine   Pvt. N.Y. Mil.
daughter Sarah Anne m. Barney Lenning

Barker, Daniel b. Conn. 1786 d. Conn. 1864   Pvt. Conn.
m. Amy Pardee — daughter Mabel m. Leman Matthews

Barker, John, Jr. b.— d.— m.—   Pvt. Vt. Mil.
Vol. 16

Barker, Jonathan b. 1762 d. Canada 1814   Pvt. Vt.
m. Abiah Parker — son Messer m. Eliza Ann Bodley

Barker, Josiah b. Mass. 1763 d. Mass. 1847   Patriot Mass. 1786-1811
m. Penelope Hatch — son Josiah H. m. Mary C. Shattuck

Barker, Stephen b.— d.— m.—   Pvt. N.Y. Vol.
Vol. 17

Barker, William b. S.C. ca. 1762 d. S.C. 1841   Pvt. S.C. Mil.
m. Ann Williams — son Owen W. m. (2) Elizabeth Lyons

Barker, William b. Va. 1782 d. Tex. 1849   Lt. & Capt. Ind. Terr. Mil.
m. Abiah Hopkins — daughter Eliza m. Isaac William Banta

Barker, William Allen b. Va. 1796 d. Va. 1837   Pvt. Conn. Mil.
m. Sarah Hobbs
daughter Susan Frances m. George Peter Fiederling

Barkley, James b. Ky. 1796 d. Ky. 1855 m. Rebecca Hart   Pvt. Ky. Vol.
  son Benjamin F. m. Malinda Elizabeth Duncan

Barkley (Berkley), John B. b. Va. 1788 d. Ill. 1872   Pvt. Ohio Mil.
  m. Margaret DeVoss — daughter Elizabeth m. Cyrus Rine

Barkley, Joseph b. Md. 1784 d. Md. 1857   Sgt.-Maj. Md. Mil.
  m. Sallie D. Heath — daughter Angelina m. Stephen Dow Mills (2d)

Barkman, John (Barrackman) b. 1785 d. 1855   Pvt. Ind. Mil.
  m. Jane Hannah — son Thomas D. m. Rachael Jane Kirk

Barksdale, Jeffrey b. Va. 1762 d. Ga. 1836   Capt. Ga. Mil.
  m. Phoebe Stinson — son William m. Nancy Long

Barlow, Arnold b. Mass. 1779 d. Pa. 1825 m. Ann Brittin   Seaman Pa.
  son Thomas m. Elizabeth Bennet

Barlow, Elisha b. Mass. 1750 d. N.Y. 1828   Patriot N.Y.
  m. Sarah Barlow (cousin) — son Thomas m. Mary Clark

Barlow, Micah (Michael) b. Conn. 1756 d. Conn. 1840   Sgt. Conn. Mil.
  m. Elizabeth Holcomb — son Reuben m. Dorcas Converse

Barlow, Thomas b. Mass. 1772 d. N.Y. 1840   Capt. N.Y. Mil.
  m. Mary Clark — daughter Antis K. m. Platt B. Walker

Barnaby, Ambrose b. Mass. 1745 d. Mass. 1802 m.—   Patriot Mass. 1787
  son Stephen m. Lucy Hathaway

Barnard, John b. N.H. 1793 d. N.Y. aft. 1850   Pvt. N.Y. Mil.
  m. Abigail Hackett — daughter Rhoda m. Lorenzo Baird

Barndollar, Peter b. Pa. 1788 d. Pa. 1858   Pvt. Pa. Mil.
  m. Anna Martin — daughter Catherine m. Samuel Williams
  son Jacob m. Elizabeth Williams

Barnes, Amos b. Conn. 1786 d. Pa. 1855 m. Mary Belcher   Pvt. Pa. Mil.
  daughter Harriet D. m. Frederick B. Hamilton

Barnes, David Leonard b. Mass. 1760 d. R.I. 1812   Patriot R.I. 1812
  m. Joanna Russell — son George L. m. Eliza Greene Aborn

Barnes, Elijah b. Mass. 1766 d. N. Y. 1815   Lt. Col. N.Y. Mil.
  m. Salla Bogue — daughter Lucy m. David Hall

Barnes, James b. N.Y. 1796 d. N.Y. 1864   Pvt. N.Y. Mil.
  m. Amenda Noble —son Delos N. m. Caroline M. Wilson

Barnes, Jerimiah, Sr. b. N.Y. 1756 d. N.Y. 1840   Sgt. N.Y. Mil.
  m. Phoebe Amagansett — son Jonathan m. Mary

Barnes, Lovewell b. Mass. 1764 d. Mass. 1831   Lt. Col. Mass. Mil.
  m. Rebecca Eager — daughter Hepsibah m. John Bigelow

Barnes, Merritt Woodruff b. Conn. 1788 d. Conn. 1882   Cpl. Conn. Mil.
  m. Polly Foote — daughter Harriet m. Jonathan Sheldon Alling
  daughter Mary Jane m. Isaac P. Treat

Barnes, Miller b.— d.— m.—   Pvt. N.H. Mil.
  Vol. 10

Barnes, Samuel Clarke b. Conn. 1796 d. Ind. 1874   Pvt. N.Y. Mil.
  m. Miranda Nichols — son Samuel K. m. Eliza Jane Johnson

Barnes, William b. Pa. 1788 d. Ohio 1868 m. Sarah   Pvt. Pa. Mil.
  son Otho m. Susan

Barnett, James b. Pa. 1784 d. Ky. 1850 m. Sarah   Pvt. Ky. Mil.
daughter Sarah m. John Adamson

Barnett, James b. Va. 1749 d. Ky. 1835   Col. Ky. Mil.
m. Sarah Snodgrass — daughter Susannah m. Johnathan Evens

Barnett, Joel b. Va. 1762 d. Miss. 1851   Patriot Ga.
m. Mildred Meriwether — daughter Rebecca m. Michael Johnson

Barnett, Rezin b. Va. 1775 d. Va. 1821   Ord. Sgt. Va. Mil.
m. Elizabeth East — son Philip m. Mary Crigger

Barnett, Schuyler b. Va. 1782 d. Ky. 1856   Pvt. Ky. Mil.
m. Mary Durham Slade
daughter Margaret E. W. m. Napoleon B. Lewis

Barnett, Thomas b. Pa. 1761 d. Pa. 1836 m. Jane Finney   Pvt. Pa. Mil.
daughter Jane m. Henry H. Lutz

Barney, William b.— d.— m.—   Capt. U.S. Inf.
Vol. 14

Barney, Joshua b. Md. 1759 d. Pa. 1818   Commodore U.S. Marines
m. Anne Bedford — son John m. Elizabeth N. Hindman

Barnitz, George Sr. b. 1770 d. 1844   Apptd. Judge Pa. 1813-34
m. Catherine Spangler   York Co.
son George A. Barnitz, Jr. m. Marie Catherine Doudel

Barnum, Daniel b. Conn. 1772/5 d. Conn. 1852   Pvt. Conn. Mil.
m. Thankful Gorham — daughter Thankful m. Ira Knapp

Barnum, Eli b. Conn. 1770 d. Conn. 1848   Pvt. Conn. Mil.
m. Jerusha Clark — daughter Maria L. m. Ezra A. Clark

Barnum, Thomas b. Conn. 1749 d. N.Y. 1837   Lt. N.Y. Mil. 1808
m. Achsah Benedict — daughter Achsah m. Hezekiah Weston

Barnwell, John b. S.C. 1748 d. S.C. 1800   Maj. Gen. S.C. Mil.
m. Anne Hutson   State Senator 1784
son John Gibbes m. Sarah Bull

Barr, Francis b. Va. 1780 d. Ohio 1844   Pvt. Va. Mil. 1814
m. Nancy Wellington — daughter Mary m. James A. Gaines

Barr, James, Jr. b. Pa. 1782 d. Pa. 1835   Capt. Pa. Mil.
m. Polly R. Kelley — son Matthew R. m. Laura Wright

Barr, James b. Pa. 1753 d. Va. 1838 m. Rachel Ross   Fife Maj. Va. Mil.
daughter Hannah B. m. Christian Crum

Barr, Thomas b. Pa. 1772 d. Ohio 1861 m.—   Pvt. Ohio Mil.
son Thomas, Jr. m. Hannah Meyer

Barr, William b. Va. 1795 d. Ohio 1873   Pvt. Va. Mil.
m. Elizabeth Yoe — son William F. m. Georgiana Sprague

Barranger, John Francis, Sr. b. France 1777 d. Md. 1866   Pvt. Md. 1814
m. Alice (Else) White — son Lewis L. m. Barbara E. Dames

Barre, Daniel b. N.Y. 1773 d. N.Y. 1832   Adj. Maj. Brig. Comm.
m. Jane DeNyse   N.Y. Mil.
daughter Ann m. Jaques Van Brunt

Barrett, Chester b. Vt. 1794 d. Ky. 1867   Pvt. N.Y. Mil.
m. Mercy Harris — daughter Jane Elizabeth m. Thomas Lane
REAL DAUGHTER

Barrett, Daniel b. Mass. ca. 1760 d. Mass. aft. 1815   Patriot Mass. 1815
    m. Rebekah Bosworth   Town Clerk 1783-97
    son Marcus L. m. Nancy Peebles

Barrett, Eleazer b.— d. N.H. 1863 m. Alice Emerson   Pvt. N.H. Mil.
    daughter Clara D. m. Nathan Kendall Russ

Barrett, James b. Va. 1783 d. Va. 1840   Sgt. (W)Va. Mil.
    m. Sarah Hatfield — son Andrew m. Matilda Wells

Barrett, Phillip b. Pa. 1783 d. Pa. 1858   Pvt. Pa. Inf.
    m. Elizabeth Kuhler — son William m. Eleanor Williams

Barrett, Samuel Cecil b. Md. 1795 d. Md. 1825   Pvt. Md. Mil.
    m. Elizabeth Jarboe — son Samuel C., Jr. m. Elizabeth Ross

Barrett, Silas b.— d.— m.—   Pvt. N.Y. Mil.
    Vol. 11

Barrett, Willis b. Va. 1787 d. Ohio 1857   Pvt. U.S. Inf.
    m. Elizabeth Huff — son Isaac E. m. Druscilla Abrams
    son George Washington m. Lavinia J. Ramsey

Barringer, John Paul b. Ger. 1721 d. N.C. 1807   Patriot N.C. 1792-3
    m. Ann Elizabeth Iseman (Eisman)
    son John m. Christiana Burlinger

Barrow, John b. N.C. 1785 d. Ill. 1859 m. Mary Steele   Ens. Ky. Mil.
    daughter Jemima m. Thomas C. Burke

Barrows, Jacob b. Pa. 1797/8 d. Ohio aft. 1855   Pvt. Ohio Rifleman
    m. Anna Paulk — son Bradley P. m. Mary E. Stephens (Stephenson)

Barry, William b. Mass. 1776 d. Mass. 1855   Ens. Mass.
    m. Esther Stetson — son Henry m. Edith Adams

Bartholomew, Hayden b.— d.— m.—   Ens. Ky.
    Vol. 15

Bartholomew, Isaac b. Conn. 1761 d. N.Y. 1841   Capt. N.Y. Mil.
    m. Mrs. Lydia Deming Crampton
    daughter Minerva m. David Holbrook

Bartholomew, Isaac b. N.Y. 1776 d. N.Y. 1852   Frontiersman N.Y.
    m. Sally Lewis — daughter Harriet m. Ezra Brakeman

Bartholomew, John or Jonathan b. Pa. 1785 d. Ohio 1859   Pvt. Ohio Mil.
    m. Elizabeth Schleback — son Peter m. Emeline Welter

Bartholomew, Joseph b. N.J. 1766 d. Ill. 1840   Aid-de-Camp Ind. 1811
    m. Christiana Pickenpaugh (Pickenpaw)
    daughter Amelia m. Robert Hopkins
    daughter Catherine m. Thomas McNaught
    daughter Sarah m. Hugh Espey

Bartholomew, William b. Conn. 1788 d. Ohio 1868   Lt. Ohio Mil.
    m. Mary Boyd — son Lorenzo m. Malvina Booth

Bartlett, Aden b. Scot. 1794 d. Vt. 1863   Drum. N.H. Vol.
    m. Nancy Clough — son Sylander m. Julia Sawyer

Bartlett, Ballard b. Mass. (Me.) 1782 d. Me. 1854   Pvt. Mass. (Me.) Mil.
    m. Anne Allen Rogers — son Jeremiah m. Almira Pinkham

Bartlett, David, Jr. b. Mass. (Me.) 1781 d. Me. 1844   Pvt. Mass. Mil.
    m. Elizabeth Wilbur — daughter Harriett m. Ahira Sinclair
    daughter Eliza m. John H. Maddock

Bartlett, Ebenezer b. Mass. 1786 d. Mass. 1841   Pvt. U.S. Inf.
m. Martha Manley — son George W. m. Harriet Newal Foster

Bartlett, Hooker b. Vt. 1780 d. Wisc. 1864   Pvt. Vt. Mil.
m. Hannah Baldwin — son Albert M. m. Dorothy Higgins

Bartlett, Horace b. N.Y. 1795 d. Pa. 1888   Pvt. N.H. Mil.
m. Sally Woodworth — daughter Cynthia m. Edwin Huntley

Bartlett, Joshua b. N.C. 1768 d. Tenn. 1828   Pvt. Tenn. Mil.
m. Winney Williams or Herrin — son Nathan m. Narcissa Suttle

Bartlett, Josiah b.— d.— m.—   Patriot N.H. 1784-94
Vol. 14

Bartlett, Josiah b. N.H. 1787 d. 1863 m. Hannah Tine   2nd Lt. U.S. Inf.
son Alfred m. Mary M. Furber

Bartlett, Sanford H. b. Va. 1779 d. Va. 1816   3rd. Lt. Va. Mil.
m. Ann Maulsby — son Burgess D. m. Armenia Timms

Bartlett, William b. Va. 1763 d. Ky. 1820 m. (2) Phoebe   Ens. Ky. Mil.
son Ebenezer m. Rebecca Standiford

Bartley, George b.— d.— m.—   Pvt. N.Y. Mil.
Vol. 3

Barton, Benjamin b.— d.— m.—   Qm. N.Y.
Vol. 6

Barton, David b. Md. 1744 d. Tenn. 1815 m. Hannah Hill   Pvt. Tenn. Mil.
son Isaac m. Jane Barton (?)

Barton, Eleazar b. N.J. 1791 d. Ill. 1865   Pvt. N.J. Mil.
m. Rachael Bostede Read
daughter Rachel Amanda m. Rev. Edward C. Pratt

Barton, Hugh b. Va. d. Ala. 1853   Capt. Tenn. Mil.
m. Mary Shirley — son Roger m. Eudora Barry

Barton, Roberts b. Pa. 1788 d. Pa. 1859 m. Jane   4th. Sgt. Pa. Mil.
daughter Rachel m. John S. Harah

Barton, Seth, Jr. b. Md. 1795 d. La. 1850   Matross Va. Mil.
m. Mary L. Green — daughter Mary Louisa m. Addison L. Durrett

Barton, William b. Pa. 1794 d. Pa. 1855 m. Rachel Supple   Pvt. Pa. Mil.
daughter Caroline A.B.D. m. John Barry Farrell

Barwick, William b. 1787 d. Ga. 1881 m. Martha Outler   Pvt. Ga. Mil.
daughter Caroline m. Bennet Kea REAL DAUGHTER

Basford, Joseph b. N.H. 1787 d. Me. 1864   Pvt. Mass. Mil.
m. Lucy Alden — son Henry m. Eleanor Levensburg
daughter Louisa M. m. Gordon Lincoln Boynton

Bartram, Guerdon b.— d.— m.—   Maj. Conn. Mil.
Vol. 17

Baskett, William b. Va. 1741 d. Va. 1815   Patriot Va.
m. Mary Pace — son James m. Mildred Shepherd (2nd. cousin)

Baskin, John Craig b. Va. 1776 d. Va. 1833   Capt. Va. Mil.
m. Elizabeth Baskin (cousin)
daughter Peggy C. m. James C. Hamilton

Bass, Joel b. Conn. 1774 d. Vt. 1871 m. Polly Martin   Sgt. Vt. Mil.
son Joel M. m. Katherine W. Burnham

Bass, Nathaniel R. b. Va. 1775 d. Ky. 1849   Pvt. Va. Mil.
  m. Ruhama Price — son Andrew J. m. Nancy Conner

Bass, Obadiah (Boss, Barce Bearce) b. Mass. 1777   Musician U.S. Inf.
  d. Mass. 1849 m. Delia C. Goodwin
  son Albert G. m. Sarah Smith

Bassett, John b. Mass. 1793 d. Mich. 1874   Pvt. N.Y. Mil.
  m. Cynthia Benjamin — daughter Helen Emily m. John Stuart Craig

Bassett, Nathan b. Mass. 1785 d. N.Y. 1849   Pvt. N.Y. Mil.
  m. Rhoda Merry — daughter Rhoda L. m. William B. Manville

Basye, Henry b. Va. 1777 d. Mo. 1857 m. Elizabeth James   Pvt. Va. Mil.
  daughter Sarah J. m. Joseph Blosser

Batchelder, Joseph b.— d.— m.—   Pvt. Vt. Mil.
  Vol. 15

Batdorf, John b. Pa. 1780 d. Pa. 1857 m. Elizabeth Clup?   Pvt. Pa. Mil.
  son Peter m. Elizabeth Christ

Bate, Humphrey b. N.C. 1779 d. Tenn. 1856   Pvt. Tenn. Cav.
  m. Elizabeth Brimager — son James Henry m. Amanda Wetherall

Bateman, Enoch b. Tenn. d. Tenn. 1847   Pvt. Tenn. Mil.
  m. Melinda Stevens — son Robert m. Catherine Stevens

Bateman, Isaiah b. 1783 d. N.Y. 1860   Pvt. N.Y. Mil.
  m. Lucy Carpenter — son Melvin m. Henrietta Williamson
Bates, Edward — Vol. 10   Ensign Va. Mil.

Bates, Elihu m. Nancy Pierce — Vol. 7   Pvt. Vt. Mil.
  Pensioner

Bates, Frederick b. Va. 1777 d. Mo. 1825   Patriot Actg. Gov. Mo. Terr.
  m. Nancy Opie Ball
  daughter Emily Caroline m. Robert Alfred Walton

Bates, Gershom — Vol. 5   Pvt. U.S. Army

Bates, John b. Va. 1776 d. Ga. 1851   Lieut. S.C. Mil.
  m. Barbary Granger — daughter Lauritte m. Burrel Hulsey

Bates, Obadiah b. Mass. 1769 d. Mass. 1831   Pvt. Mass. Mil.
  m. Hannah Beal — son Elijah m. Sarah Fletcher

Battle, Elisha b. Va. 1723/4 d. N.C. 1799   Patriot Memb. Gen. Assy. 1788
  m. Elizabeth Summer — son William m. Charity Horn   N.C.

Bauman, Hans Dieter b. Pa. 1773 d. Pa. 1853   Major Pa. Mil.
  m. Margaretha Newhard — son Peter m. Polly Romig
  daughter Sarah m. Daniel Keiper

Baxley, George b. Md. 1771 d. Md. 1848   Pvt. Md. Mil.
  m. Mary Merryman — daughter Maria m. Augustus F. Seavers
  son Jackson m. Gertrude Minifee

Baxter, Andrew b. N.C. 1750 d. Ga. 1814   Lieut. Ga. Mil.
  m. Elizabeth Harris — daughter Mary L. m. William Green Springer

Baxter, Green Berry b. Va. 1778 d. Mo. 1857   Ensign Mo. Terr. Mil.
  m. Elizabeth Jones — daughter Mourning m. Conway

Bay, Robert b. Ohio 1777 d. Ohio 1855   Colonel Ohio Mil.
  m. Phoebe Lindley — son Thomas M. m. Rachel Buskirk

Bayard, James Ashton b. Pa. 1767 d. Del. 1815   Patriot Comm.
m. Anne Basset   at Ghent, Belgium
son James A. Jr., m. Ann Francis

Bayard, Stephen Adams b. Md. 1744   Patriot Judge Elections Pa.
d. Pa. 1815 m. Elizabeth Mackay
son George A. m. Ann Baders — daughter Susan B. m. James Ekin

Bayles, James b. N.Y. 1787 d. N.Y. 1863 m. Leah—   Capt. N.Y. Mil.
son Edward J. m. Maria Horton

Bayles, John B. — Vol. 11   Capt. Md. Mil.

Bayles, Reese b. Tenn. 1787 d. Tenn. 1814   Pvt. East Tenn. Vols. Mil.
m. Margaret Young — son John m. Adeline Gourley

Bayless, John b. Tenn. 1790 d. Tenn. 1841   Capt. East Tenn. Vols.
m. Susan Newton
daughter Sarah Margaret m. John Newton Corbett

Bayless. John b. Va. 1773 d. Tenn. 1858   Capt. East Tenn. Vols.
m. Elizabeth Jones daughter Rachel m. Robert Kirkpatrick

Bayless, Samuel b. Tenn. 1783 d. Ark. aft. 1851   Lt. E. Tenn. Regt. 1814-15
m. Sarah Ann Platte — daughter Sarah Rosite m. A. P. H. Jordan

Baylies, Nicholas b. Mass. 1768 d. Vt. 1847   Patriot—Supreme Court
m. Mary Ripley   Judge Vt.
son Nicholas m. Harriet Helen Cahoon

Baylor, Richard b. Va. 1750 d. Va. 1822   Patriot Justice
m. Anne Tilden Garnett Richards   Cty. Ct. Va. 1801
son Robert William m. Mary Catherine Moore

Bayman, Thomas b. Ohio 1795 d. Ohio 1867 m.—   Pvt. Ohio Mil.
son Charles H. m. Elmyra Berry

Bayne, Daniel b. Va. 1795 d. Va. 1848   Pvt. Va. Mil.
m. Elizabeth Ann Fuqua
daughter Sarah Frances m. William M. Eads

Bayne, Samuel b. Md. 1761 d. Ill.   Pvt. Ohio Mil.
m. Eleanor West — son James G. m. Catherine McCoy

Bays, Beverly b. Va. 1779 d. Ind. 1847   Sgt. Va. Mil.
m. Nancy Bays (cousin) — son Hubbard m. 2nd Edith James

Beach, Nathan b. N.Y. 1763 d. Pa. 1847   Capt. 1793 Maj. 1795 Pa.
m. Susan Thomas — daughter Desire m. Mason Crary

Beach, Rice Edwards b. Conn. 1770 — Vol. 9   Pvt. Conn. Mil.

Beach, Samuel Sevren b. prob. N.J. 1786   Lt. N.J. Mil. 1812
d. N.J. 1872 m. Jane Hoff
son Charles Hoff m. Ann Jackson

Beach, Warren N. — Vol. 7   Corp. Conn. Mil.

Beach, William b. N.Y. 1793 d. N.Y. 1877   Sgt. N.Y. Mil.
m. Sally Remington — daughter Mary C. m. Smith Sherman Wheeler

Beackley, Christian b. Pa. 1754 d. Pa. 1801   Pvt. Pa. Mil.
m. Mary Stroud — son Edward m. Catharine Welsh

Beackley, Edward b. Pa. 1785 d. Pa. 1834   4th Sgt. Pa. Mil.
m. Catherine Welsh — son John W. m. Ann Howey Miller

Beale, Thomas b. Pa. 1735 d. Pa. 1803   Patriot Memb. Conv. Pa. 1790
   m. Sarah Todhunter — son William m. Mary Henderson

Beale, William b. Pa. 1762 d. Pa. 1820   Lt. Col. Pa. Mil.
   m. Mary Henderson — son Joshua m. Hannah Coder

Beall, George S. b. Md. 1782 d. Ohio 1853   Sgt. Va. Flying Camp Mil.
   m. Susannah Hammond — son Henry m. Susan Priestly

Beall, John b. Md. 1781 d. 1831 m. Charlotte Jones   Pvt. Md. Mil.
   son William Rufus m. Martha Elizabeth McAtee

Beall, Reason — Vol. 6   Brig. General U.S. Army

Beall, Robert b. Va. 1767 d. Ga. 1832   Capt. Ga. Mil.
   m. Elizabeth Marshall — daughter Ann F. m. Edward Billups Young
   daughter Mary m. Henry Lockhart

Beall, Thaddeus II b. N.C. 1780 d. Ala. 1867   Justice Inf. Ct.
   m. Mary W. Jones   Columbia Co. Ga.
   son Augustus Romaldus m. Mary Ann Alford   1807/11

Beall, William b. Ga. 1795 d. Ga. 1851   Capt. Ga. Mil.
   m. Nancy Chandler — daughter Martha m. James L. Stephens

Beals, Isaac b. Mass. 1783 d. Mass. 1859   Fife Major Mass. Mil.
   m. Submit Monk — daughter Mary C. m. Barnard Clapp

Beam, Elijah b. Pa. 1791 d. Pa. 1869 m. Nancy Snee   Pvt. Pa. Mil.
   daughter Sarah m. Henry Huffman

Bean, Henry — Vol. 1   Pvt. N.H. Mil.

Bean, Phineas b. N.H. 1750 d. N.H. 1825   Patriot 1795-1825 N.H.
   m. Judith Snow — son John m. Nancy Hill   Civil Offices

Bean, William b.— d. Miss. 1815 m. Nancy Blevins   Pvt. Tenn. Mil.
   son Mumford m. Elizabeth Olive

Beard, David b. Conn. 1767 d. Conn. 1825   Surgeon Conn. Mil.
   m. Betsy Field — son John F. m. Lois Ann Wildman

Beard, John — Vol. 3   3rd Sgt. Md. Mil.

Beard, John b. Md. 1779 d. Ill. 1847 m. Mary Russell   Pvt. Ohio Mil.
   daughter Elizabeth m. James McKeen
   daughter Mary m. Salmon Lusk
   daughter Julia Ann m. Prier Wright

Beard, John b. Pa. 1733 d. W. Va. 1803   Patriot 1786-1795 Va.
   m. Jennet Wallace   Civil Offices
   son Samuel m. Margaret Walkup

Beard, Samuel b. Va. 1771 d. W. Va. 1850   Major Va. Mil.
   m. Margaret Walkup — son John m. Nancy McClintic

Beard, Thomas b. Va. 1776 d. W. Va. 1853 m. Mary Skyles   Col. Va. Mil.
   daughter Evelyn m. Benjamin Renick

Bearden, Roland b.— d. Ga. 1849 m. Elizabeth Herdage   Pvt. Ga. Mil.
   son John K. m. Mary Ann Waters

Beardsley, Lemuel b. Conn. 1777 d. Conn. 1837   Pvt. Conn. Mil.
   m. Polly Ann Hawley — daughter Ann Jeannette m. George Lyon

Beasley, Benjamin b. Va. 1773 d. Ohio 1851   Pvt. Tenn. Mtd. Mil.
   m. Ann Allentharp — son Harvey m. Eliza Killen

Beasley, Cornelius b. Va. 1780 d. Mo. 1871   Pvt. Va. Mil.
m. Martha Carr
daughter Jane Virginia m. William Sanford Hicks
daughter Julia B. m. Harrison Masters

Beasley, James b. Ga. c 1790 d. Tenn. 1848   Pvt. Ga. Mil.
m. Eliza E. (Henderson) Simmons
daughter Louisa R. m. Mark Hardin Taliaferro

Beaston, John b. N.J. 1787 d. at sea 1828   Pvt. N.J. Mil.
m. Submitter Edwards — daughter Susan m. John S. Somers

Beatty, David — Vol. 17   Pvt. Va. Mil.

Beatty, Francis b. Pa. 1789 d. Pa. 1872   Ensign Pa. Mil.
m. Isabel Williamson — daughter Sarah Ann m. John W. Stinson

Beatty, George — Vol. 5   Sgt. Pa. Mil.

Beatty, Hamilton b. Pa. 1785 d. Pa. 1871   Pvt. Pa. Mil.
m. Sarah A. Anderson — daughter Martha m. Joseph Baldridge
daughter Sarah Ann m. Samuel Adams

Beatty, James b. Md. 1770 d. Md. 1851   Agent Navy Dept.
m. Elizabeth Raymer
son James Jr. m. Mrs. Eliza Grant Bankston Wilmans

Beatty, James b. Va. 1793 d. Ohio 1890   Pvt. Ohio Mil.
son Newton m. Margaret Hidy

Beatty, James b. Pa. 1776 d. Pa. 1833   Pvt. Pa. Mil.
m. Margaret Pennell — son Caleb m. Phoebe Pyle

Beatty, William b. Ga. 1784 d. Ga. 1826   Patriot 1812 Ga.
m. Polly Drew — son William I. m. Nancy Bembry   Coroner

Beatty, William b. Pa. 1760 d. Va. 1830   Pvt. Pa. Mil.
m. Penny Bird — daughter Eliza m. James A. G. Ely

Beatty, William b. Pa. 1793 d. Ohio 1876   Pvt. Pa. Mil.
m. Mary Fulton — son David R. m. Clarissa Florence Shearer

Beaufait, Louis b. Ind. Terr. 1760 d. Mich. Terr. 1814   Col. Mich. Terr.
m. Catherine Peltier — son Francois m. Mary Weber   Mil.

Beaulieu, Jean b.—d.—m. 1794 Marie Poirer   Capt. Ill. Lt. Inf.
son Michel m. Elizabeth Ramey   Early Vol.

Beaver, Michael b. Va. 1775 d. Ind. 1844   Pvt. Ohio Mil.
m. Marguerite Zumwalt — son Henry m. Mary Hiestand

Beazley, James b. Va. d. Va. m. Elizabeth Mills   Pvt. Va. Mil.
daughter Mary Elizabeth m. George James Stephens

Beazley, Thomas b. Va. 1793 d. Mo. 1879   Corp. Va. Mil.
m. Elizabeth Woolfolk — daughter Mary Catherine m. Adrian Tandy

Bebout, Peter b. N.J. 1781 d. Pa. 1860 m. Isabelle Cooper   Pvt. Ohio Mil.
daughter Susan m. William Nemons Bebout

Bechtel, Christian b. Pa. 1752 d. Pa. 1814   Lieut. Pa. Mil.
m. Maria Catharine Bollman   Berks Co.
son John m. Magdalena Addams

Becker, David Harmon b. N.Y. 1786 d. N.Y. 1860   Pvt. N.Y. Mil. 1800
m. Maria Loucks — son David H. m. Hanna Lucks

Becker, Peter b. Pa. 1753 d. Pa. 1833 m. Catherine Carper   Pvt. Pa. Mil.
daughter Susan m. Mathias Sheets

Beckhorn, Job b. N.J. 1787 d. N. J. 1850   Pvt. Essex Co. N.J. Mil.
m. Sarah Crane — daughter Mary m. Thomas Crane

Beckley, David b. Conn. 1772 d. N.Y. 1850 m. Polly Reed   Pvt. N.Y. Mil.
daughter Ordelia m. Abiel Lathrop Jr.
son Ward m. Eliza Trumble

Beckwith, Abiah b. N.Y. 1784   Ensign 27th Regt. N.Y. Inf.
d. N.Y. 1874 m. Lorena Chadwick
son John W. m. Sophronia Dorr

Beckwith, Barnes b. Va. 1776 d. W. Va. 1855   Pvt. Va. Mil.
m. Elizabeth Peyton — daughter Mary P. m. Derich Hupp

Beckwith, Ezra b. Conn. 1789 d. Conn. 1871   Sgt. Conn. Mil.
m. Esther Smith — son Ezra S. m. Charlotte L. Bishop

Beckwith, Nathan b. N.Y. 1778 d. N.Y. 1865   2nd Lieut. Dutchess Co.
m. Mariette Pratt Pelton   N.Y Mil.
daughter Eliza Ann m. George Ogden Sr. REAL DAUGHTER

Beckwith, William Whitney b. Conn. 1793 d. Ohio 1861   Pvt. N.Y. Mil.
m. Ann Herrick — son Ephraim C. m. Frances Knight Forrest

Becnel (Becknell), Pierre Aime b. La. 1793 d. La. 1863   Pvt. La. Mil.
m. Emilie Haydel — son Octave m. Rose Aime Borne

Bedell, Daniel b. N.Y. 1765 d. N.Y. 1835   Colonel N.Y. Mil.
m. Mary Treadwell — son Benjamin W. m. Elizabeth J. Rolph

Bedinger, George Michael b. Pa. 1756 d. Ky. 1843   Major U.S. Inf. in St.
m. Nancy Keane   Clair's Exp. 1791 Repr.
daughter Sarah K. m. John Bedford   Ky. Leg. and Congress 1803/7

Beebe, Asa Jr. b. Conn. 1764 d. N.Y. 1851   Patriot Repr. 1796-1816
m. Sara Day   Vt. Leg. Bennington Co.
daughter Clarissa m. Isaac Foster Mack Sr.

Beebe, Peter b. Conn. 1792 d. Ohio 1849   Corp. Ohio Mil.
m. Betsey Vaughn — daughter Rexa Villa m. James Rice

Beecher, Enoch b. Conn. 1762 d. Conn. 1823   Patriot Civil Offices Conn.
m. Abigail Thomas — son Amos m. Charlotte Baldwin   1784-1808

Beecher, Hopestill b. 1777 d. Pa. 1823   Patriot - Co. Comm. Pa.
m. Abigail Rathbone — daughter Sarah m. Samuel K. Phillips

Beekman, Christopher b. N.J. 1730 d. N.J. 1829   Patriot Somerset Co.
m. Martha Veghte — son Garrett m. Margaret Quick   N.J. 1790

Beelar, Benjamin A. b. Tenn. 1794 d. Tenn. 1877   Pvt. Tenn. Mil.
m. Lucy Acree — daughter Susan F. m. Joseph de Cueto
REAL DAUGHTER

Beeler, George H. b. Va. 1796 d. Tex. 1861 m. Sarah   Pvt. Dist. Col. Mil.
daughter Seriah m. A. D. Rice

Beer, Enoch b. Pa. 1744 d. Pa. 1806   Patriot—Judge Ct. 1789
m. Mary Gloria Dieter   Northampton Co. Pa.
daughter Susannah m. Adam Marsh

Beers, James b. Vt. 1795 d. Vt. or N.Y. 1877   Pvt. U.S. Inf.
m. Hannah Butterfield — daughter Sarah Sabrina m. Zebulon Barton

Beers, John   Sgt. Conn. Mil.
    Vol. 3

Beers, Philo b. Conn. 1793 d. Ill. 1858   Pvt. Conn. Mil.
    m. Martha Stillman — daughter Caroline M. m. Andrew J. Kane

Beers, Timothy Phelps b. Conn. 1789 d. Conn. 1858   Surgeon Conn. Mil.
    m. Caroline Mills — daughter Abby P. m. Isaac Peck

Beeson, Henry Hodges b. Pa. 1788 d. Pa. 1869   Pvt. Pa. Mil.
    m. Anne Downer
    daughter Drucilla Ann m. Flavius Bowles Titlow

Beeson, William b. Va. 1772 d. Ohio 1840 m. Eva Vedder   Pvt. N.Y. Vols.
    son Harmon V. m. Rachel Lord Rupp

Beggs, Charles b. Va. 1775 d. Ill. 1869   Capt. Indiana
    m. Dorothy Tumbo — daughter Sarah m. John Epler   Terr. Mil.

Belcher, Joseph b. Mass. 1751 d. Mass. 1816   Pvt. Mass. Mil.
    m. Rachel Shute — son Joseph, Jr. m. Nancy Burrill

Belcher, Joseph, Jr. b. Mass. 1782 d. Mass. 1850   Pvt. Mass. Mil.
    m. Nancy Burrill — son Joseph III m. Serena Coates

Belcher, William b. Conn. 1772 d. Mass. 1851   Commander
    m. Sally Wilson   8th Conn. Regt.
    daughter Susan m. Charles Steele Thomson

Belden, Amos b. Conn. 1779 d. Mass. 1864   Pvt. Mass. Mil.
    m. Anna Day — son Joshua m. Charity M. Smith

Belding, Ludivicus b. Mass. 1791 d. Ark. 1833   Clerk and Steward
    m. Lydia Bassett   on "Regulator" Mass.
    daughter Maria m. William H. Gaines

Belfield, Thomas Meriwether b. Va. 1796 d. Va. 1873   Pvt. Va. Mil.
    m. Fanny Fairfax Sanford
    son Leroy D. m. Mary Elizabeth Spilman

Belknap, John Joshua b. N.H. 1790 d. Mich. 1884   Corp. N.H. Mil.
    m. Elvira Cantfield — daughter Sarah m. Arthur Callaghan

Bell, Benjamin b. N.C. 1790 d. N.C. 1839   Ensign, N.C. Mil.
    m. Lydia Tucker — son Samuel m. Sarah A. Hartsfield

Bell, David b. N.Y. 1770 d. N.Y. 1847   Capt. N.Y. Mil.
    m. Abigail Allen — son John A. m. Anne Hubbard Woodworth

Bell, Hugh b. Ireland 1791 d. Md. 1856   Pvt. Md. Mil.
    m. Ann Chambers — son Henry C. m. Betsy O. Stewart

Bell, Ignatious b. England 1755 d. Ky. 1824   Pvt. Northwestern
    m. Delilah — daughter Melinda m. John Doyle   Indian War

Bell, James b. Ga. 1789 d. Ga. 1848 m. Susan Bibb   Pvt. Ga. Mil.
    daughter Marianna E. m. Spencer Whitfield Taylor

Bell, John b. Va. 1770 d. Pa. 1855   Soldier Whiskey Rebellion
    m. Elizabeth Welsh   1794 - 1st Constable
    son James m. Hannah Jordan   of Indiana Co. 1806

Bell, John b. Ireland bef. 1774 d. Pa. 1815   Pvt. 16th Pa. Regt.
    m. Elizabeth Consor — son John m. Margaret Fullerton

Bell, John M. b. Ga. 1788 d. Ark. 1863 m.—   Pvt. Ky. Vol. Mil.
    daughter Eliza m. Samuel Carson

Bell, Jonathan b. N.C. 1782 d. Ala. 1842   Memb. Ga. Leg. 1814
   m. Judith Crump — son Joseph m. Martha Jones

Bell, Joseph b. Ireland 1765 d. Mo. 1846   Corp. Ky. Volunteers
   m. Helen Thompson — daughter Helen m. Levi Leithley

Bell, Joseph b. Ohio 1786 d. Ohio 1862 m. Sarah Young   Pvt. Ohio
   son John M. m. Eliza Jane Backenstow   Detached Mil.

Bell, Micajah S. b. Va. ca 1780 d. Va. by 1819   Corp. Va. Mil.
   m. Frances Mangum — son Josiah m. Nancy Brook

Bell, Pulaski Bott b. Va. ? d. Va. ?   2d Sgt. Va. Mil.
   m. Sarah Lacy Nailling — daughter Jackie m. Egbert E. Tansil

Bell, Richard b. Md. 1774 d. Md. 1850 m. Catherine Leaf   Sgt. Md. Mil.
   daughter Catherine m. William E. Hooper
   daughter Sarah Isabella m. Thomas S. Clark

Bell, Richard H. b. N.Y.C. 1794 d. N.J. 1846   Pvt. N.J. Mil.
   m. Lydia Waite — daughter Rachel m. Newel Yale

Bell, Thaddeus b. Conn. 1754 d. Conn. 1851   Memb. Conn. Leg.
   m. Elizabeth Howe — daughter Hannah m. Robert Scofield   1805-16

Bell, Thomas b. Va. 1754 d. N.C. 1830   Juryman Chatham
   m. Mary Lassiter — son Jonathan m. Judith Crump   N.C. 1781-1802

Bell, William b. Pa. 1778 d. Mo. 1876   Pvt. Ky. Mil.
   m. Malinda Grimes — son William A. m. Caroline Page Harvey

Bell, William b.— d.— m. Nancy Shipboy   Pvt. N.Y. Mil.
   Vol. 4

Bell, William b. Pa. 1783 d. Pa. 1841   Pvt. York Co. Pa. Inf.
   m. Anna Maria Polley — daughter Jane m. Thomas Bradley

Bell, William b. 1786 d. Ohio 1870 m. Jane Atwood   Pvt. Va. Mil.
   daughter Mary D. m. Lesley Lyon REAL DAUGHTER

Bellinger, Frederick   Pvt. N.Y. Mil.
   Vol. 14

Bellinger, John Henry b. N.Y. 1791 d. Ore. 1878   Pvt. N.Y. Mil.
   m. Mary Catherine Crane — son Edward H. m. Eliza Howard

Bellinger, Peter b. N.Y. 1760 d. N.Y. 1851   Pvt. N.Y. Mil.
   m. Alida Wagner — daughter Nancy m. Robert McChesney

Bellinger, William b. S.C. 1758 d. S.C. m. Harriet S. Field   Senator
   son Eustace m. Mary Kershaw   S.C. 1806

Bellows, John b. Mass. 1742 d. N.H. 1812   Legislator N.H.
   m. Rebecca Hulbard — son Josiah m. Lydia Preston

Belton, Francis S. b. Md. 1790 d. N.Y. 1861   2d. Lt., Major, Asst.
   m. Harriet Kirby — son Winfield S. m. Rebecca Todd   Adj. General

Belts, James Ellis b. Conn. 1794 d. N.Y.C. ? Vol. 1
   m. Maria Fordham
   daughter Mary Adelia m. Nathaniel W. Seat REAL DAUGHTER

Benagh, James b. Ireland 1783 d. Va. 1861 2 wives   Major Va. Mil.
   wife Sarah Perry — son Samuel m. Elizabeth Robertson
   wife Elizabeth M. Richardson — son George W. m. Mary W. Collier

Bender, George b. Mass. 1786 d. D.C. 1865   Capt. U.S. Army
   m. Mary Briscoe — daughter Anna Lucinda m. Robert Tansill

Benedict, Elisha Hubbell b. Ohio 1795 d. Kans. 1885   Pvt. Ohio Mtd. Mil.
m. Maria L. Simpson
daughter Sarah Ann m. Dr. James Allen McGinnis

Benedict, Isbow   Capt. Privateer Va. Navy
Vol. 17

Benedict, James b. N.Y. 1785 d. N.Y. 1863   Lieut. N.Y. Artillery
m. Isabel Fergerson — daughter Phebe A. m. William Penney

Benedict, Matthew b. Conn. 1770 d. N.Y. 1846 m. ?   Pvt. N.Y. Mil.
Vol. 12

Benedict, Stephen b. Conn. 1783/4 d. N.Y. ca 1840   Pvt. N.Y. Mil.
m. Polly Sherman — daughter Emmeline m. Martin Barnard

Benham, Richard b. Ohio 1791 d. Ohio 1870 2 wives   Pvt. & Corp.
wife Mariah Nutt — daughter Eliza m. John Van Arsdale   Ohio Mil.
wife Abigail Underwood — son George H. m. Millie Pence

Benjamin, Delsey b. N.Y. 1779 d. N.Y. 1857   Pvt. N.Y. Mil.
m. Anna Higbee — son James H. m. Minerva D. Chapman

Benjamin, Jesse   Ensign N.Y. Mil.
Vol. 11

Bennett, Aaron b. R.I. 1750 d. N.J. 1834   Gunner
m. Margaret ? — son Moses m. Patience Imlay   N.J. Artillery

Bennett, Amos b. N.Y. 1770 d. N.Y. 1840   Capt. N.Y. Mil.
m. Jeanette Stirling — son William m. Elma Strong

Bennett, Anthony b. Pa. 1777 d. Pa. 1859   Maj. Pa. Mil.
m. Nancy Espey — son Espey m. Esther Logan
son Thomas S. m. Sarah Ann Rounds

Bennett, Caleb Prew b. Pa. 1758 d. Del. 1836   Maj. Del. Artillery
m. Catherine Britton — daughter Eliza m. Charles Palmer Lisle

Bennett, Cornelius b. Mass. 1766 d. R.I. 1840   Sailing Master
m. Silvina Barlow   N.S.S. Adams
son Cornelius Jr. m. Emily Daboll   Mass. 1812/15

Bennett, George Washington b. N.Y. 1791 d. Ill. 1867   Sgt. N.Y. Mil.
m. Nabby Gunn — daughter Maria m. Thomas Hance

Bennett, Jacob b. N.Y. 1750 d. N.Y. 1821/4   Pvt. N.Y. Mil.
m. Barbara Brower — son Jacob m. Caroline Valentine

Bennett, Jacob b. N.Y. 1800 d. Mo. 1891   Pvt. N.Y. Mil.
m. Caroline Valentine — son Cornelius m. Anna Ross

Bennett, John b. Del. 1775 d. Ohio 1864   Corp. Ohio Mil.
m. Sarah Downs
son William m. Mary Maddux and Rhoda Van Buskirk

Bennett, John Sr. b. Va. 1760 d. Ohio 1814   Cpl. Ohio Mil.
m. 2nd Anna Stockham — daughter Hannah m. Samuel McDowell

Bennett, Joseph b. N.Y. 1794 d. Ky. 1868   Pvt. Ohio Mil.
m. Elizabeth Mills — daughter Lovina m. Henry Lantz

Bennett, Joseph   Drummer Vt. Mil.
Vol. 8

Bennett, Justus J. b. N.Y. 1788 d. Mich. 1878 m. Betsy ?   Sgt. N.Y. Mil.
son Timothy R. m. Susannah Stone

Bennett, Lewis b. Va. 1778 d. Ohio 1863 m. Jane McLain   Capt., Major
    daughter Jane m. Frederick Williams   (W) Va. Mil.

Bennett, Mitchel b. Va. 1784 d. Ala. 1859   Pvt. Ga. Mil.
    m. Martha Didama Turner — son James W. m. Ann Newton

Bennett, Oliver b. Conn. 1793 d. Conn. 1841   Pvt. Conn. Mil.
    m. Fanny Hempstead — daughter Miranda m. Rhodes Burrows

Bennett, Peter b. Md. 1793 d. Iowa 1859   Pvt. Ohio Mil.
    m. Mary Pinkerton — son James m. Nancy Peirsol

Bennett, Richard b. N.Y. 1783 d. N.Y. 1856   Pvt. N.Y. Mil.
    m. Marian Rood — daughter Eliza Ann m. John Turner

Bennett, Rufus S. b. Conn. 1761 d. Pa. 1842   Pvt. Pa. Mil.
    m. Martha ? — son Rufus Hiram m. Henrietta Leader   1784/7

Bennett, Solomon   Capt. N.Y. Mil.
    Vol. 13

Bennett, Thomas b. N.Y. 1769 d. N.Y. 1861   Pvt. N.Y. Mil.
    m. Charity Hedges — son David J. m. Dorothea Morse

Bennett, Dr. Walter b. Ireland 1745 d. Ky. 1812   High Sheriff
    m. Jemima Wyatt   Halifax Co.
    son Walter Jr. m. Fannie Reynolds   Va. 1801

Bennett, William b. Md. 1787 d. Ohio 1874   Pvt. U.S. Infantry
    m. Margaret Slusser — daughter Sarah m. James Foraker

Bensley, David b. R.I. 1755 d. N.Y. 1847   Capt. N.Y. Mil.
    m. Elizabeth Rushton — son William m. Mary Bunnell

Benson, Daniel b. N.Y. 1764 d. Ohio 1848   Major N.Y. Mil.
    m. Electa Haskins — son Elias m. Lydia Sprague

Benson, Elias b. N.Y. 1797 d. Mich. 1874   Pvt. N.Y. Mil.
    m. Lydia Sprague — son Oscar P. m. Mary Alma Short

Bent, David b. Mass. 1730 d. Mass. 1798   Surveyor of Highways
    m. Lucy Moore   & Tax Collector
    son Thaddeus m. Abigail Howard   Mass. 1787/8

Bentley, Daniel b. Conn. 1789 d. Conn. 1876   Sgt. Conn. Mil.
    m. Esther Wheeler — son Edwin D. m. Augusta Lindsley

Bentley, James b. England 1785 d. Mich. 1864   Sgt. Mich.
    m. Amanda Barker — son James Jr. m. Mary Bartlett   Volunteers

Bentley, Thomas   Pvt. N.Y. Infantry
    Vol. 17

Benton, David b. Conn. 1768 d. N.Y. 1803   Paymaster
    m. Nancy Pitts — son Ebenezer m. Lavinia Freeman   N.Y. Mil.

Benton, Noah Lester b. Vt. 1794 d. Ill. 1839   Pvt. Vt. Mil.
    m. Priscilla Marshall Hall
    daughter Ruby Ann m. Addison Gardner Bragg

Bentrages, John b. Germany 1792 d. Ohio 1874   Pvt. Ohio Mil.
    m. Mary Rainsberger — son Isaac W. m. Mary Cairns

Berger, Daniel b. Pa. 1786 d. Pa. 1842   Pvt. Pa. Mil.
    m. Catherine Weaver — son David m. Mary Jane McIlhaney

Berger, Samuel   Pvt. Ohio Mil.
    Vol. 15

Berkeley, Thomas N. b. Va. 1790 d. Ill. 1871   Lieut. Fairfax Co.
  m. Nancy McCullough   Va. Mil.
  son James H. m. Elizabeth Ann Davidson

Berkey, John Jr. b. Germany 1745 d. Pa. 1815   Pvt. Pa. Mil.
  m. Sarah Schmidt — son John m. Susanna Whips   1785/90

Berlin, Israel b. Pa. 1793 d. Pa. 1881   Pvt. Pa. Mil.
  m. Christine Minium — daughter Mary m. George Watson

Berlin, Philip b. Germany 1793 d. Va. 1870   Pvt. Va. Cavalry
  m. (2) Sarah Jane ?
  daughter Mary J. m. John W. Metz REAL DAUGHTER

Bernard, Elysee Leon b. France 1785 d. La. 1859   Pvt. La. Cavalry Mil.
  m. Edesie Tricon — daughter Eugenie m. James Henry Suydam

Bernard, Stephen b. N.C. 1771 d. N.C. aft. 1813   Captain U.S. Navy
  m. Mosley Davis — daughter Hepsebah m. Calvin T. Davis

Berrien, John b. N.J. 1759/60 d. Ga. 1815   Treas. State Ga. 1796/1800
  wife Wilhelmina S. E. Moore — daughter Julia m. John Whitehead
  wife Margaret McPherson — son John P. m. Eliza Cecil Hunter

Berrien, John McPherson — Vol. 8   Pvt. Ga. Light Dragoons
  daughter Louisa m. Ephraim Seabrook REAL DAUGHTER

Berry, Elisha C. b. Md. 1790 d. Ohio 1846   Patriot — gave aid to cause
  m. Nancy A.? — son Thomas H. m. Luxima Hughes

Berry, John b. Va. 1793 d. Va. 1874   Pvt. Va. Troops
  m. Catherine Shryock
  daughter Sarah Elizabeth m. Henderson M. Folsom

Berry, John Nalley b. Md. c 1774 d. Md. 1842   Pvt. 43rd Regt. Md. Mil.
  m. Mildred Robey
  daughter Jane E. m. James Henry Montgomery

Berry, Nathaniel b. Mass. 1793 d. Me. 1876   Corporal Mass. Mil.
  m. Betsy Woodbury — son Harris B. m. Lucy A. Gragg

Berry, Watson — Vol. 3   Lieut. Mass. Mil.

Berry, William Sr. b. Va. 1755 d. Ind. 1819   Pvt. Ind. Mil.
  m. Clara Feagin — daughter Mary m. Berry Cantwell

Berryhill, John b. Va. 1792 d. Ohio 1870   Pvt. Va. Mil.
  m. Rachel James — daughter Angeline m. William W. Foster

Berryhill, Samuel b. Pa. 1759 d. Pa. 1816   Capt. Dauphin Co. Pa. Mil.
  m. Mary Brunson
  daughter Margaret C. m. George Phillip Wiestling

Bertholf, Jacobus b. N.Y. 1776 d. N.Y. 1844   Capt. Orange Co. N.Y. Mil.
  m. Mary Wisner — son Henry W. m. Ann Eliza Cooper

Berwick, Joseph b. La. 1784 d. La. 1853   Sergeant La. Mil.
  m. Eleanor Comstock — son David m. Louisa Garrett

Best, Jacob b. Ga. 1779 d. Ga. 1864   Pvt. Ga. Detached Mil.
  m. Elizabeth Newton — daughter Louisa m. George W. Hodges

Best, John b. Ireland 1786 d. Pa. 1856   Pvt. Pa. Mil.
  m. Hannah MacCombs — son Thompson m. Selina Brackin

Bethea, Tristram b. S.C. 1776 d. Ala. 1851   Capt. S.C. Mil.
  m. Mrs. Anna Pearce — daughter Mary m. Robert Hamer

Betzer, Jacob b. Pa. 1782 d. Ohio 1871   Pvt. Ohio Mil.
   m. Rosanna Barbara Metzger
   son William m. Mary Ann Creachbaum

Biays, James b. 1760 d. Md. 1822   Lt. Col. Md. Cav. Mil.
   m. Sarah Jackson — daughter Fannie m. Henry Hammond

Bibb, James b. Va. 1754 d. Ky. 1846 m. Nancy Fleming   Sgt. Ky. Mil.
   son Fleming m. Kitty Ellis

Bibb, Peyton b. Va. 1784 d. Ala. 1841 m. Martha Cobb   Capt. Ga. Mil.
   daughter Frances m. Walter C. Jackson

Bibb, Thomas b. Va. 1793 d. Ala. 1871   Pvt. U.S. Mounted Rangers
   m. Elizabeth Fielder
   daughter Amanda m. Milton McCarty — REAL DAUGHTER
   daughter Lucy m. E. S. Johnson — REAL DAUGHTER
   daughter Myra unm. — REAL DAUGHTER
   son Thomas H. m. Carolyn Hobbs

Bibb, William — Vol. 14   State Senator Ga.

Bickel, Anthony b. Va. 1790 d. Ohio 1860   Pvt. Va. Mil.
   m. Diana Chapell — son Aaron m. Savannah Porter

Bickerstaff, Robert b. Ga. 1781 d. Ga. 1838   Ensign Ga. Mil.
   m. Nancy Robertson — daughter Harriett m. Creed Taylor Wise

Bickle, James b. Va. 1790 d. Ind. 1844 m.?   Pvt. Va. Mil.
   daughter Adeline E. m. Thomas Kane — REAL DAUGHTER

Bickley, John b. Va. 1790 d. Va. 1864   Ensign Va. Regt.
   m. Elizabeth Brown
   daughter Nancy G. m. James H. Dickinson

Biddle, Absolum b. Va. 1740 d. Ga. 1810   Judge Inferior Ct. 1786
   m. Ruth Jackson — daughter Martha m. Warren Stone

Biddle, James Dundas II b. Pa. 1760 d. Pa. 1821   Sgt. Berks Co. Pa. Mil.
   m. Frances — son John M. m. Lydia Collins

Biddlecome, Orin — Vol. 10   Pvt. N.Y. Mil.

Bidwell, Charles b. Conn. 1787 d. Tenn. 1848   2nd Lieut. Tenn. Mil.
   m. Martha Binkley — daughter Julia Ann m. Pierce Crutcher

Bieber, John b. Pa. 1748 d. Pa. 1846 m. Elizabeth Schaeffer   Pvt. Pa. Mil.
   son Dewalt m. Elizabeth Sassaman

Bieber, Michael b. Europe 1740 d. Pa. 1832   Pvt. Northampton
   m. Anna Marie Fenstermacher   Co. Pa. Mil. 1784
   daughter Anna Margaret m. Jacob Dreisbach

Bienvenue, Alexandre de Vince b. La. 1784 d. La. 1855   Pvt. La. Mil.
   m. Charlotte Uranie de la Barre
   son Charles N. m. Estelle Dupre
   daughter Virginie Charlotte m. Charles Fagot de la Garciniere

Bienvenue, Pierre Terville De Vince b. La. 1797   Pvt. La. Mil. 1815
   d. La. aft. 1822 m. Genevieve S. Kerlegan
   son Charles G. m. Hersalie de la Houssaye

Bienvenu, Henrietta DeGrondel b. 1762   Nursed wounded Soldiers
   d. La. 1833 m. Alexandre Devince Bienvenu
   son Francois m. Genevieve Fontenette

Bierly, Daniel b. Pa. 1760 d. Pa. Pvt. Schuykill Co. Pa. Mil.
m. (1) Elizabeth Settele
son John L. m. Susannah Biessel

Biery, Peter b. Pa. 1795 d. Pa. 1870 m. Mary Keck Pvt. Pa. Infantry
daughter Eliza m. Samuel Lightcapp

Bigelow, Asa — Vol. 5 Pvt. Vt. Volunteers

Bigelow, Nathan b. ? d. N.Y. 1859 m. Clarinda F. Barker Pvt. N.Y. Mil.
son Daniel F. m. Charlotte M. Barnes

Bigelow, Timothy II — Vol. 7 Pvt. N.Y. Mil.

Bigelow, Timothy b. Mass. 1767 Mass Legislator 1792-1815
d. Mass. 1821 m. Lucy Prescott
son Rev. Andrew m. Amelia S. Stanwood

Bigelow, William b. Mass. 1751 Judge Windham Co. Vt. to 1814
d. Vt. 1814 m. Damaris Hapgood — son Levi m. Hannah Goodrich

Bigger, Samuel b. Ireland 1735 d. Ohio 1820 Pvt. Lancaster Co. Pa. Mil.
m. Abigail Wilson — son Matthew m. Margaret Findley

Biggs, Benjamin b. N.J. 1752 d. W. Va. 1823 General Va. Mil.
m. Priscilla I. — son Benjamin F. m. Lydia Ann Carney

Biggs, John b. Scot. 1752 d. Tenn. 1838 Pvt. West Tenn. Mil.
m. Isabella Wilson — son William m. Margaret Temple

Biggs, William b. N.C. 1788 d. Mo. 1846 Pvt. Ky. Mil.
m. Elizabeth McCune — daughter Nancy m. William A. Hutcherson

Bilby, John — Vol. 15 Ensign N.Y. Lt. Inf.

Billings, Jarvis b. N.Y. 1796 d. Minn. 1884 Pvt. N.Y. Mil.
m. Almira Partridge — son Henry O. m. Amanda M. Waring

Billings, Sanford b. Conn. 1736 d. Conn. 1806 Capt. Conn. Mil.
m. Lucy Geer — son Gilbert m. Lucy Swan

Billmeyer, Martin b. Pa. 1782 d. Pa. 1855 Pvt. Pa. Mil.
m. Margaret Himmelreich — daughter Catharine m. Isaac Blue

Bills, Hartwell b. Mass. 1792 d. Wisc. 1882 Pvt. Mass. Mil.
m. Sarah Lucy Legg — son Jason m. Susan Cork

Bills, William — Vol. 17 Pvt. N.Y. Volunteers

Billups, Samuel b. Va. 1795 d. Va. 1869 Soldier 1812 Va.
m. Sarah W. Chandler son Joseph Sampson m. Nancy C. McClure

Binder, John Jacob b. Ger. 1736 d. Pa. 1804 Capt. Pa. Mil.
m. Marie Magdalena Weisbach — son William m. Mary Rice

Binder, William Weisbach b. Pa. 1768 Pa. State Repr. Phila.
d. Pa. 1842 m. Mary Rice and Delaware Cos. 1794
son William m. Louise E. Stam

Bingham, Abel b. N.H. 1786 d. Mich. 1865 Lieut. N.Y. Mil.
m. Hannah Brown — daughter Sophia m. John Buchanan

Bingham, John — Vol. 12 Pvt. Conn. Mil.

Bingham, Thomas — Vol. 6 Pvt. U.S. Artillery

Binn, John b. Ky. 1798 d. Ky. 1859 m. Hester Ann Griffith Pvt. Ky. Mil.
daughter Nannie H. m. Dr. W. H. Tucker

Binns, Thomas N. b.—d.—m. Frances Pearson   QM. Va. Mil.
son William m. Mary Salter

Bird, Abraham b. Va. d. Va. aft. 1787   Memb. Va. Leg. 1786-7
m. —Zeigler — son Abraham m. Catherine Fry

Bird, Amos b. Va. 1737 d. Mo. m. Sarah —   Judge Greene Co. Tenn.
son John m. Mary Gillespie

Bird, Philemon b. Va. 1743 d. Ga. 1810 m. Mary Lee   Capt. Va. Inf. 1796
daughter Mary m. William Ogletree

Bird, William b. Va. 1795 d. D.C. 1855   Pvt. Accomac Co. Va. Mil.
m. Hester Mears — son John H. m. Georgiana Polkinhorn

Birdsell, Daniel b. N.Y. 1795 d. N.Y. 1850   Pvt. N.Y. Mil.
m. Lucy Babcock — daughter Lucy m. Jacob Bonesteel

Birge, John b. N.Y. d. N.Y. m. Nancy Little   Drummer N.Y. Mil.
daughter Celestine m. Nathan Pendleton Wilcox

Bisbee(y), Benjamin b. Vt. 1791 d. N.Y. 1880   Pvt. N.Y. Mil. 1812/13
m. Nancy Ladd — daughter Frances A. m. Oliver Cromwell Smith

Bisbee, John Fuller, b. Mass. 1777 d. N. Y. 1865   Sgt. N.Y. Mil.
m. Chloe C. Burrell — son Hiram m. Caroline Blood

Bisbing, Henry b. Pa. 1792 d. Pa. 1866   Pvt. Pa. Vol. Rifleman
m. Ann Singlewood — daughter Ann m. Isaac M. Bonsall

Biscoe, James b. Md. 1776 d. Md. 1853 m. Anne Farnandis   Pvt. Md. Mil.
daughter Jane A. m. John H. Norris

Bishop, Benjamin b. N.Y. 1764 d. Conn. 1850   Pvt. N.Y. Mil.
m. Lucy Hyde — daughter Emeline m. Ichabod Brackett

Bishop, David b. Conn. d. Ohio m. Anne Hinman   Pvt. Ohio Mil.
daughter Eliza m. Uriah J. Singletary

Bishop, Elijah — Vol. 7   Major N.Y. Mil.

Bishop, Frederick b. Conn. 1792 d. Mass. 1855   Pvt. Conn. Mil.
m. Olive Bassett — daughter Nancy m. Birney Buddington
son William F. m. Sarah A. Crittenden

Bishop, Henry Neely b. S.C. 1792 d. Tex. 1869   Ensign S.C. Mil.
m. Hannah Long — son John N. m. Louvincy Harris

Bishop, Jonathan b. Conn. 1754 d. Conn. 1840   Pvt. N.Y. Volunteers
m. Anna Allen — son Giles m. Phoebe Waite

Bishop, Levi b. Conn. 1794 d. N.Y. 1882   Corp. Conn. Mil.
m. Sally Miner — daughter Sophia m. Dr. Asa J. White

Bishop, Levin b. Md. 1789 d. Mo. 1880   Pvt. Bourbon Co. Ky. Mil.
m. Judith Boothe — son David m. Maria Ann Evans

Bishop, Lucius — Vol. 7   Pvt. Vt. Mil.
daughter Thetis m. Elbert Harrison Putnam
REAL DAUGHTER

Bishop, Peter b. N.Y. 1779/80 d. N.Y. 1850/5   Ensign 1805 Lt. 1807 N.Y.
m. Mary Wood — son Asa m. Elizabeth Berner

Bishop, Thomas Fitch b. Conn. 1763   Selectman Farmington
d. Conn. 1851 m. Lucy Foote   Conn. 1811-14
son Jacob m. Diana Frisbie

Bishop, William b. Va. 1794 d. Ill. 1855   Pvt. Ohio Mil.
m. Margaret Lake — daughter Sarah m. Hiram M. Ayers

Bispham, Benjamin b. N.J. 1790 d. N.J. 1844   Pvt. N.J. Mil.
m. Ann Ivens — daughter Elizabeth m. Urias Shinn

Bissell, Daniel Russell b. Conn. 1766 d. Mo. 1833   Brig. Gen. Conn. Mil.
m. Deborah Sebor — daughter Mary m. Risdon H. Price

Bissell, Ezekiel III b. Conn. 1781 d. N.Y. 1853   Ensign N.Y. Mil.
m. Annie Hurlbut — son Ralph m. Mary C. Packard

Bissell, John b. Conn. 1761 d. Conn. 1831   Capt. Conn. Mil. 1809
m. Hannah Kilbourn — son Herman m. Caroline Pierce

Bissell, Lewis Russell b. Conn. 1770 d. La. 1832   Major U.S. Army 1790-2
m. Fannie Wilson — son Lewis R. m. Electa West

Bittenbender, Jacob b. Pa. 1753 d. Pa. 1844   Justice of Peace
m. Dorothy—   Luzerne Co. Pa. 1800
daughter Catherine m. Martin Herter

Bittick, John R. b.— d. Tenn. 1837   Pvt. Tenn. Mil.
m. Cynthia Rakestraw — son Green m. Gallie Brownlow

Bivin, John b. Ky. 1798 d. Ky. 1857/9   Pvt. Ky. Mil.
m. Hester Ann Griffith — daughter Nannie m. Dr. William S. Tucker
REAL DAUGHTER

Bixby, Appleton b. Mass. 1786 d. Ohio —   Pvt. Ohio Mil.
m. Margaret Rowland — daughter Harriet m. Richard W. Reynolds

Bixby, Ephraim b. Vt. 1778 d. Mich. 1869   Pvt. N.Y. State Mil.
m. Phoebe Adams — daughter Susannah m. Samuel Hunt

Bixby, Samuel b. 1789 d. Mo. 1880 m. Judith   Pvt. Ky. Mil.
daughter Margaret m. Peter Booth

Bixby, Samuel b. Mass. 1739 d. N.Y. 1820   Memb. Civic Comm.
m. Hannah Powers   N.Y. 1785 & 91
son Samuel m. Lois Moss

Bixby, Samuel — Vol. 8   Pvt. Vt. Mil.

Black, Andrew b. Ireland 1772 d. Ohio 1861   Ensign Ohio Mil.
m. Jane Livingston — son Samuel m. Sara Davis

Black, James b. Ohio 1772 d. Mo. 1872   Lieut. Ohio Mil.
m. Rebecca Pottinger — son James m. Julia Wells
son William m. Julia Wells?

Black, James b. Ire. d. Ohio 1850   Pvt. Pa. Mil.
m. Catherine McDowell (McDonald)
daughter Miriam m. Jesse Overlander

Black, James b. Pa. 1777 d. Va. 1860   Minister to soldiers
m. Nancy McMurran — son Joseph E. m. Mary S. Trigg

Black, James b. Va. 1774 d. W. Va. 1859   Pvt. Va. Mil.
m. Elizabeth Rice — son Samuel m. Amanda Jane McCutchen

Black, James Augustus b. S.C. 1793 d. D.C. 1888   Lieut U.S. Infantry
m. Sarah E. Logan — daughter Mary P. m. John Logan Black

Black, Joseph b. S.C. 1763 d. S.C. 1843   S.C. Senator
m. Mary Burnette — son Samuel R. m. Martha Ann Kirkland

Black, Robert b.— d. Pa. 1815 m. Hannah Jones   Pvt. Union Co. Pa. Mil.
daughter Mary m. Daniel Heller

Black, Samuel b. Ire. 1776 d. Ohio 1867   Pvt. Md. Artillery
m. Betsey Cross — daughter Winefield m. Robert H. Winram

Black, Samuel b. Va. 1782 d. Ohio 1830   Pvt. Va. Mil.
m. Louisa Ferguson — son Samuel m. Sarah Alexander

Black, Thomas b. Va. 1745/6 d. Va. 1814   Capt. Pittsylvania Co.
m. — Skipworth   Va. Mil.
son Thomas m. Elizabeth Dews

Black, William b. Pa. 1784 d. Ohio 1866   Pvt. Franklin Co.
m. Elizabeth Burget   Ohio Mil.
son Edward R. m. Susan Shoemaker
daughter Martha m. Joseph Hassenflug

Black, William b. Pa. 1770 d. Pa. 1853   Pvt. Cumberland Co. Pa. Mil.
m. Catherine — daughter Jane m. William Okeson

Blackburn, Anthony b. 1780 d. 1866   Raised Company in 1812
m. Hester McGrew   Comm. Captain
son Abiram m. Elizabeth McGrew

Blackburn, Ephraim b. Pa. 1774 d. Pa. 1801   Capt. Chester Co. Pa. Mil.
m. Prudence Rich — daughter Prudence m. James Carter

Blackburn, John b. Va. 1747 d. Tenn. 1818   Justice Jeff. Co. Tenn. 1793
m. Janet Matthews — son Andrew m. Catherine McGirk

Blackburn, John Maxwell b. Pa. c 1772 d. Ohio 1836   Pvt. Ohio Mil.
m. Sarah — son Henry L. m. Margaret Madden
son John H. m. Eliza Stier

Blackburn, John Porter b. N.C. 1786 d. Tex. 1855   Pvt. Tenn. Mil.
m. Nancy Churchill
daughter Frances O. m. William Roscoe Chalk
son John D. G. m. Mary Ann Chambers
son Merryweather m. Julia A. Lyell

Blackburn, Thomas b. Ky. 1780 d. Ky. 1867   Lieut. Ky. Mtd. Mil.
m. Willina Burbridge — son Robert m. Hannah Marsh
daughter Betty m. Charles Horace Benton

Blackford, Thomas Thornberg — Vol. 4   Pvt. Md. Art. Mil.

Blackledge, William b. N.C. d. N.C. 1828   Congressman 1803-13
m. Alice Wharton — daughter Louisa m. George Whitfield

Blackman, Elijah b. Mass. prob. 1741 d. Mass. 1822   Capt. & Major Mass.
m. Elizabeth Hall — daughter Polly m. Abner Pease   Mil.

Blackman, James Butler b. Conn. 1784 d. Conn. 1806   Pvt. Conn. Mil.
m. Fanny Beckwith — daughter Emily C. m. John M. Speidel

Blackman, William b. N.Y. 1785/90 d. Ohio 1856   Capt. N.Y. Mil.
m. Miss Curtis — son Jerome L. m. Belinad Darden

Blackmer, Ephraim b. N.Y. 1795 d. N.Y. 1872   Sgt. N.Y. Mil.
m. Tirza Moreley
daughter Thankful m. William Henry Harmon

Blackmer, William D. b. Tenn. 1796 d. Tenn. 1878   Pvt. Tenn. Mil.
m. Jane Davis
daughter Jerusha Ann m. Watkins Hopkins Dodson

Blackshear, David b. N.C. 1764 d. Ga. 1837   Brig. Gen. Ga. Mil.
  m. Frances Hamilton
  son Elijah F. m. Mary Ann LaFayette Hamilton
  son Everard H. m. Isabella M. C. Hamilton
  son James H. m. Caroline L.

Blackwell, Grant b. Va. c 1782 d. Ky. 1847   Pvt. Ky. Mtd. Vol. Mil.
  m. Lucy Latham — son Thomas C. m. Virginia Taylor

Blackwell, Jesse b. Va. 1780 d. Mo. 1832   Capt. Mo. Terr. Mil.
  m. Mrs. Catherine W. Reyburn
  son William Henry m. Mary A. Holmes

Blackwell, John b. Va. 1778 d. Va. 1835   Pvt. Va. Mil.
  m. Mary Edmondson
  daughter Elizabeth m. Robert Blackwell Jones

Blackwell, Thomas — Vol. 13   Pvt. Va. Mil.

Blagdon, Joshua — Vol. 4   Corp. Mass. Mil.

Blain, Thomas b. N.Y. 1765 d. N.Y. 1839   Pvt. Orange Co. N.Y. Mil.
  m. Esther Scott — daughter Jane m. Philo Stone

Blair, Hugh b. Ire. 1792 d. Pa. 1824   Pvt. Pa. Mil.
  m. Anna Maria Gilbert — daughter Abigail Anne m. Henry Snyder

Blair, Jeremiah b. Mass. 1795 d. N.Y. 1878   Pvt. N.Y. Mil.
  m. Susan J. Clarke — son Arvin H. m. Ella A. Ensign

Blair, John — Vol. 17   Pvt. Va. Mil.

Blair, Thomas b. Pa. 1755 d. Pa. 1814   Lieut. Westmoreland Co.
  m. Eleanor Evans   Pa. Mil.
  son Thomas m. Susan Dunica

Blair, Thomas b. N.C. 1773 d. Tenn. 1846   Pvt. 4th Regt. West. Tenn.
  m. Eleanor Doak   Mil. 1812
  daughter Amanda Jane m. Joseph Poindexter

Blair, Thomas b. N. or S.C. 1780   Pvt. East Tenn. Mtd. Mil.
  d. Tenn. 1866 m. Hannah Stone
  son Samuel J. m. Nancy Walker

Blaisdell, Ebenezer b. N.H. 1778 d. N.H. 1813   Pvt. U.S. Inf.
  m. Nancy Noyes — son James W. m. Mercy Wentworth

Blaisdell, Enoch b. N.H. 1779/80   Lieut. Ind. Mtd. Rangers
  d. Ind. 1847/8 m. Susanna Ferris
  son Sherwood M. m. Reliance Chase

Blaisdell, Walter Robie b. Mass. (Me.) 1776   Lt. Col. Mass. Mil.
  d. Me. 1831 m. Sarah Tyler
  son John T. m. Mary Gove Herrick

Blake, John Jr. b. Mass 1753 d. Me. 1842   Capt. U.S. Army
  m. Mary Dupree — son Charles m. Mary Winchester

Blake, Joseph b. Md. 1760 d. Md. 1843   Capt. Calvert Co. Md.
  m. Elizabeth Benson   Home Guards
  son Joseph m. Lucy C. Groverman

Blake, Lewis b. Va. 1796 d. Ind. 1881 m. Polly Edgar   Pvt. Va. Mil.
  daughter Polly L. m. Johnston Ross Talman

Blake, Simeon b. Mass. 1771 d. Ohio 1833   Pvt. Ohio Mil.
  m. Lavinia Peck — daughter Sybil m. Josephus Noyes

Blake, Thatcher b. Mass. 1774 d. Me. 1838   Driver Mass. Art. Mil.
m. Sarah Evans — daughter Elizabeth m. Ephraim Sumner

Blakemore, Thomas b. Va. 1770 d. Ala. 1835   Pvt. Ga. Mil.
m. Elizabeth Hudson — son Joseph m. Nancy Saxon

Blakeslee, Caleb lived Rowe, Mass. — Vol. 6   Civil Offices 1795/1809

Blakeslee, Manning b. Conn. d. Conn. 1832/3   Pvt. Conn. Mil.
m. Sally Wilmot — son Sherman m. Nancy M. Mix

Blakeslee, Matthew Gilbert b. Conn. 1781 d. Mass 1831   Pvt. Conn. Mil.
m. Rhoda Dorman — son Charles W. m. Martha Waters (Blair)

Blanchard, Augustus b. N.H. 1746 d. N.H. 1809   Town Clerk, Selectman
m. Bridget Lovewell   Repr. Gen. Ct. N.H.
daughter Priscilla m. John Crosby

Blanchard, Nathan b. Mass. (Me.) 1784 d. Me. 1868   Pvt. Mass. Mil.
m. Eliza Mitchell — daughter Alemena C. m. John Wesley Hanson

Blanchard, William b. N.Y. 1772 d. N.Y. 1854   Capt. N.Y. Mil.
m. Hannah Whitmarsh — son Asabel m. Elizabeth Brown

Blanchard, William b. Vt. 1796 d. Ill. 1883   Pvt. & Capt. Cortland Co.
m. Betsey Donohue   N.Y. Mil.
daughter Emily Ann m. William Parker
daughter Mary Elizabeth m. Thomas J. Fauber

Bland, Charles b. Va. 1765 d. Ky. 1842 m. Phillis Pope Pvt. Ky. Mil. 1812
son Alemander m. Margaret Bourne

Blanding, Ebenezer b. Mass. 1754   Civil Offices Royalston, Mass.
d. N.Y. 1844 m. Nancy Wheeler   & Richmond, N.H. 1800/9
son Otis m. Abigail Barrus

Blanding, Lamech b. Mass. 1759 d. Ill. 1839   Selectman Vt. 1794
m. Lydia Lambert — daughter Betsey m. Abiah Fuller

Blankenship, John b. Ky. 1792 d. Mo. 1851 m.—   Pvt. Ky. Vol.
daughter Lucy Ann m. Thomas S. Williams

Blankenship, Levi b. Va. 1789 d. Va. 1860   Pvt. Va. Art.
m. Permelia — son William Henry m. Margaret Ann Barnett

Blayney, Charles b. Ire. 1789/90 d. Va. 1860   Corp. Va. Mil.
m. Nancy Faris — son James m. Margaret Atkinson

Blecker, John — Vol. 6   Pvt. Pa. Mil.

Blevens, Daniel b. Ky. 1794 d. Mo. 1875   Pvt. Mo. Terr. Mil.
m. Lucy Roberts — son Daniel M. m. Margaret C. Sandys

Blevins, Armistead b. Va. 1775 d. Tenn. aft. 1814   Pvt. Tenn. Vol.
m. Keturah Carter
son Hugh A. m. Mrs. Sarah Willis Coopender

Blevins, Dennis Van O. b. N.Y. 1796 d. N.Y. 1879   Pvt. N.Y. Mil.
m. Betsy — daughter Catharine m. Aaron Cornish

Blevins, Hugh Armstrong b. prob. Tenn. 1796   Sgt. West Tenn. Mil.
d. Ark. 1859 — m. Mrs. Sarah Willis Coopender
daughter Mary Willis m. Polk Bishop — REAL DAUGHTER

Blish, Daniel b. N.Y.? 1782 d. 1820 m. Beulah Wilcox   Capt. N.Y. Mil.
son Daniel m. Mary Houghton Bruce

Blish, Zenas b. Mass. 1793 d. Ohio 1870   Pvt. Phila. Co. Pa. Mil.
  m. Vashti Ingersol — daughter Lydia m. Horace Steele

Bliss, Francis b. Mass. 1793 d. Minn. 1882   Pvt. Conn. Mil.
  m. Nancy J. Harington
  daughter Esther unm. — REAL DAUGHTER

Bliss, Frederick b. Mass. 1764 d. Vt. 1841   Town Ofcr. Calais, Me. 1795
  m. Hannah Patience Cole
  daughter Lucy m. Welcome Cole

Bliss, Ichabod b. Mass. 1768 d. Mass. 1835   Town Treas. Brimfield
  m. Mehitabel Sebbins   Mass. 1812/13
  son Thomas m. Sarah King

Bliss, John b. Mass. 1727 d. Mass. 1809   Civil Offices Mass.
  m. Abiel Colton — daughter Lucy m. Edward Morris

Bliss, Reuben b. Mass. 1726 d. Mass. 1808   Selectman Springfield
  m. Elizabeth Hitchock   Mass. 1784/95
  son Calvin m. Lucy Hale

Blocker, Jesse b. S.C. 1750 d. S.C. 1831 m. Eliza Malone   Pvt. S.C. Mil.
  son William J. m. Mary Douglass Butler

Blocker, John — Vol. 16   Corp. U.S. Inf.

Blodgett, Elijah b. Mass. 1751 d. N.Y. 1839   Town Clerk Oneida Co.
  m. Mary Branch — son Eliphaz m. Mary Cutler   N.Y. 1788/90

Blodgett, Samuel b. Conn. 1751 d. Vt. 1838   Constable 1804, Selectman
  m. Mary Palmer   Cornwall, Vt. 1787/1800
  daughter Rhoda m. Abraham Williamson

Blood, Francis b. Mass. 1735 d. N.H. 1814   Col. 1789; Gen. 1795 N.H.
  m. Elizabeth Spaulding — daughter Elizabeth m. Elias Boyton

Blood, Joseph — Vol. 14   Pvt. Vt. Mil.

Blood, Sewall — Vol. 16   Sgt. N.Y. Mil.

Bloodgood, Aaron b. N.J. 1738 d. N.J. 1813   Councilman N.J. 1789/92
  m. Abigail Carman — son William m. Doziah Freeman

Bloodgood, William b. N.J. 1770 d. N.J. 1842   Constable 1787 Perth
  m. Doziah Freeman   Amboy, N.J.
  son Aaron m. Jane Harned

Bloodworth, Thomas b. N.C. 1755 d. Ga. 1836   Justice of Peace
  m. Tamsa Proctor   Hanover Co. N.C. 1784
  son Hiram B. m. Mary Abbott Croley

Bloomer, Daniel b. N.Y.? d. Ohio 1855 m.—   Pvt. N.Y. Mil.
  son Abraham m. Margaret Stoutenburg

Blossom, Reuben b. Mass. 1786 d. N.Y. 1857   Col. N.Y. Mil.
  m. Lydia Ingram — daughter Mary m. Gavin Thomson

Blouin, Charleville b. 1791? d. 1882 N.C. or La.?   Pvt. La. Mil.
  m. Rosalie Part — son Leon m. Elizabeth Potter

Blount, Francis b. Va. 1776 d. Va. 1856   Ensign Va. Mil.
  m. Elizabeth Doswell Harris
  daughter Maria m. William Phillips

Blount, Reading b. N.C. 1757 d. N.C. 1807   Maj. Gen. N.C. Mil. 1800
  m. Lucy Harvey — son Wiley m. Delia Blakemore

Blowers, Moses Sr. b. N.Y. 1774 d. N.Y. 1862 m.— Pvt. N.Y. Mil.
son Moses m. Emily Lucinda Stewart

Blue, Ezekiel b. N.J. 1745 d. N.J. 1811 Assessor Somerset Co. N.J.
m. Martha Voorhees 1799/1807
daughter Mary m. Peter Van Vleet

Blue, Isaac Samuel b. Pa. 1785 d. N.Y. 1813 Capt. Pa. Mil.
m. —Gray — son Isaac m. Catherine Billmeyer

Blue, John b. N.C. 1776 d. N.C. 1831 m. Effie Gilchrist Capt. N.C. Mil.
daughter Jeannette m. William Buchanan Sr.

Blue, Michael b. ?1784 d. Ohio 1875 m. Nancy Chaney Pvt. Ohio Mil.
daughter Rebecca m. James De Weese

Blystone, Henry b.— d.— m. Julia Eckefurner — Vol. 27 Pvt. Pa. Mil.
daughter Harriet m. Mahlon Reeves

Blythe, David b. S.C. 1790 d. S.C. 1871 m. Evelyn McClure Sgt. S.C. Mil.
daughter Lillian M. m. William Mayfield

Board, James b. Va. 1731 Patriot Bedford Co. Va. 1796
d. Ky. bef. 1823 m.—
daughter Nancy m. Nathaniel Shrewsbury

Board, John b. Va. 1754 d. Va. 1821 Capt. Bedford Co. Va. Mil.
m. Jane Harwood 1795
daughter Mary m. William Horsley

Boardman, James b. Conn. 1785 d. N.Y. 1842 Lieut. U.S. Army Conn.
m. Lydia Tyler Foote
daughter Martha F. m. William Ackermon

Boatner, John Wesley b. S.C. 1793 d. Miss. 1864 Pvt. S.C. Mil.
m. Rachel Agner — son John m. Ellen Barnett

Boatwright, Benjamin b. Va. 1769 d. Va. 1816 Pvt. Va. Mil.
m. Elizabeth Blackburn — son William m. Sally Gates

Boatwright, Leonard b. Va. 1793 d. Va. 1856 Pvt. Cumberland Co.
m. Susannah Stokes Rogers Va. Mil.
son James A. m. Mary Louise Sanderson
son William m. Mary Anderson

Boaz, David R. b. Va. 1790 d. Ky. 1862 Pvt. 42nd Regt. Va.
m. Susan Stubblefield — daughter Susan m. Joseph Godwin
son Peter m. Louisa Ryan

Bobart, Charles C. b. Md. 1790 d. Md. 1869 Corp. Md. Mil.
m. Charlotte Swift — son Charles C. m. Georgia Schley

Bobbitt, Isham b. N.C. 1754 d. Ill. 1836 Pvt. Ky. Mil.
m. Elizabeth — daughter Nancy m. John Crisman

Bobbitt, John b. Va. 1759 d. Va. 1829 Pvt. Amherst Co. Va. Mil.
m. Amelia Hill — son Tillman m. Mary Hill

Bocee, John b. N.Y. 1788 d. Ill. 1868 Pvt. Chautaqua Co.
m. Phoebe Bardner N.Y. Mil.
daughter Mary m. Nathan Elliot Roberts

Boddie, George b. N.C. 1769 d. N.C. 1842 Repr. & Sen. N.C. Leg.
m. Susanna Parham Hill Nash Co. 1800-15
daughter Rebecca m. James Peters

Boddie, William b. N.C. 1749 d. N.C. 1817   Tax Collector N.C. 1784
m. Martha Jones — daughter Mary m. Col. John Sanders

Boden, John b. Pa. 1783 d. Pa. 1849   Brig. Gen. Pa. Vol.
m. 1st Jane Clark — son John C. m. Jane Clark

Bodley, Thomas b. Md. 1792 d. Ill. 1879   Pvt. N.Y. Mil.
m. Pauline Conger — son Oliver m. Susan Uhler

Boehm, Anthony b. Pa. 1770 d. Pa. 1848   Lieut. Pa. Mil.
m. Catharine Geissinger — daughter Mary m. James Mohr

Bogan, Benjamin Lewis b. Va. 1795   Pvt. D.C. Alexandria Co. Mil.
d. Va. 1870 m. Sarah W. Ott
daughter Susan S. m. George Henry Varnell

Bogardus, Ephraim A. b. N.Y. 1795 d. N.Y. 1866   Pvt. N.Y. Mil.
m. Hannah Rea — son Charles m. Mary Helen Briggs

Bogardus, Lewis b. N.Y. 1738 d. N.Y. 1808   Sgt. N.Y. State Mil.
m. Anna Mills — daughter Eleanor m. Pasco Noxon

Bogart, Joseph Outen b. N.Y. 1768 d. N.Y.C. 1837   Major N.Y. Mil.
m. Jane Fink — daughter Josephine O. m. Daniel A. Webster

Boggess, Giles Sanford b. Tenn. 1797 d. Tex. 1881   Pvt. Tenn. Mil.
m. Sarah Bryant — son Bennett m. Texas Rogers

Boggs, Alexander Lowry b. Md. 1792 d. Md. 1856   Pvt. Md. Mil.
m. Susan Greer — son John Greer m. Rosetta Graham

Boggs, Ezekiel b. Va. 1787 d. Ohio 1870   Corp. Ohio Mil.
m. Elizabeth Brown — daughter Alice m. Moses Clark Carrick

Boggs, John b. Ohio 1775 d. Ohio 1861   Capt. Pickaway Co. Ohio Mil.
m. Sarah McMeechin — son Moses m. Margaret Scott Cook

Boggs, William b. Scotland d. Va. m.—   Pvt. Va. Mil.
son Robert m. Abigail Carr

Bogle, Andrew b. Scot 1753 d. Tenn. 1813   Justice Peace Tenn. 1795
m. Elizabeth Campbell — son Joseph m. Mary Glass

Bohon, George b. Scot. c. 1770 d. Ky. 1817   Pvt. Ky. Mil.
m. Ann Woods — son Joseph m. Elizabeth Magruder

Bohon, William b. Ky. 1787 d.— 1866 m. Nancy   Lieut. Ky. Mil.
son Thomas B. m. Susanna I. Stotts

Boise, Chester b. Mass. 1788 d. Ohio 1856   Sgt. U. S. Inf.
m. Roxy Ann Todd — son William P. m. Lydia Loring Savercool

Boley, John b. Pa. 1779 d. Pa. 1860 m. Mary Downer   Pvt. Pa. Mil.
daughter Sarah Ann m. Jacob Lashells

Bolling, Christopher b.— d. La. 1815 in service   Pvt. 2nd Div. La. Mil.
m. Catherine Higgins — daughter Bridget H. m. Robert Ferguson

Bolling, William Luther b. Va. 1782 d. Ill. 1840   Pvt. Ky. Mil.
m. Elizabeth Waters — son Wesley B. m. Nancy Drake

Bolling, William b. Va. 1777 d. Va. 1845   Capt. Va. State Mil.
m. Mary Randolph — daughter Ann M. m. Joseph Kendall Weisiger

Bolliger, George Frederick b. N.C. 1770 d. Mo. 1842   Capt. Mo. Terr. Mil.
m. Elizabeth Hunsucker   1800—Member
daughter Sarah m. (1) ____ Frizel   Mo. Terr. Assembly 1812
(2) Ralph Daugherty

Bolmer, Isaac b. N.J. 1781 d. Ill. 1869   Lieut. N.J. Mil.
    m. Lena Brown — daughter Charlotte S. m. Otto Van Tuyl

Bolton, James b. Mass. (Me.) 1768 d. Me ?   Corp. Mass. Mil.
    m. Elizabeth Pettengill — daughter Thankful m. Henry Coon

Bond, Henry b. Va. 1772 d. Ohio 1854   Pvt. Ohio Mil.
    m. Elizabeth Wall — daughter Amy m. Eneas Fountain

Bond, John Pearson b. S.C. 1768 d. S.C. 1822   Representative S.C.
    m. Abigail Fairchild   Leg. 1806-8
    daughter Hepzibah m. John Bates

Bond, Joseph b. Va. 1787 d. Ga. 1840 m. Mary Lewis   Pvt. Ga. Mil.
    son Lewis A. m. Mary Bacon

Bond, Major Lewis b. N.J.— d. N.J.— m.—   Ensign U.S. Inf.
    daughter Sarah S. m. Thomas J. Paxton

Bond, Thomas Talbott b. Md. 1792 d. Md. 1875   **Pvt. Md. Mil. 1814**
    m. Mary Ann Bond (cousin)
    son Beverly m. Elizabeth R. Lumsdon

Bonebrake, Peter b. Pa. 1755 d. Pa. 1821   Pvt. Pa. Mil.
    m. Catherine Cook — daughter Magdalena m. Peter Small

Bones, Thomas b. Ireland 1758 d. N.Y. 1830   **Pvt. Pa.**
    m. Susannah Rowland — son James m. Eliza Knight

Bonnell, Matthew b. N.J. 1785 d. Ind. 1863   Pvt. Ohio Mil.
    m. Ruth Florea — daughter Mary Ann m. William Crips

Bonnell, Paul b. N.J. 1762 d. Ohio 1820   Pvt. U.S. Inf.
    m. Mary Pierson (Parsons) — daughter Rachel m. Aaron Jewell

Bonner, Jesse A. b. Va. 1774 d. ? 1847   Surgeon's Mate Va. Mil.
    m. Elizabeth Herter — son Moses H. m. Ann Robertson

Bonner, John Young, b. N.C. 1795 d. N.C. 1877   Pvt. N.C. Troops
    m. 2nd Clarissa G. I. Trippe
    son Bryan T. m. Clarissa Sparrow Trippe

Bonner, William b. S.C. 1783 d. Tex. 1877   Ensign S.C. Troops
    m. Ann Lee Joel — daughter Mary m. Joseph McGrary
    daughter Sue m. Andrew Samuel Bonner

Bonnett, John b. Va. c. 1785 d. Va. 1816 m. Eve   Capt. 6th Reg. Va. Mil.
    son Lewis m. Mahala

Bonnett, Lewis b. Va. 1778 d. Ohio 1863   Major Va. Mil.
    m. Jane McLain — daughter Jane m. Frederick Williams

Bonney, Benjamin b. Mass. 1739 d. Mass. 1803   Col. Hampshire Co. Mil.
    m. Hannah Day   1787/9
    daughter Hannah Day m. Isaac Nobel Dayton

Bonney, Gethro — Vol. 7   Capt. N.Y. Mil.

Bonney, John — Vol. 3   Pvt. Mass. Mil.

Bonney, Ruffus L. b. Mass. 1800 d. N.Y. 1885   Pvt. U.S. Inf.
    m. Arvilla Smith
    daughter Arvilla m. William H. Scott — REAL DAUGHTER
    daughter Lucinda M. m. Edwin R. Green — REAL DAUGHTER

Boog, John b. Scot. 1775 d. Ga. 1825   1st Lieut. Ga. Mil. 1812
    m. Mrs. Isabella Kelly King Turner
    daughter Mordina Jane m. Henry Hamilton Floyd

Booker, Edward b. Pa. 1740 d. Va. 1836   Pvt. Cumberland Co. Va. Mil.
m. Patsy Taylor
daughter Amanda Elizabeth m. James Armistead Taylor

Booker, William Marshall b. Va. 1786 d. Va. —   Pvt. Va. Mil.
m. Sally G. Blankinship
son William M. Jr., m. Mary Archer Warriner

Boomer, Benjamin b. Mass. 1763 d. N.Y. m. Mary Collins   Pvt. N.Y. Mil.
daughter Esther m. Ezra Mason

Boone, Bryant b. 1789 d. 1837 m. Martha R. Phipps   Pvt. Tenn. Mil.
son William Felton m. Agnes Walker Alloway

Boone, Daniel b. Pa. 1734 d. Mo. 1820   Indian Fighter Ky.
m. Rebecca Bryan   Lt. Col. Kanawha Co. Va.
daughter Lavinia m. Joseph Scholl   Mil. 1789
son Jesse m. Chloe Van Bibber
daughter Susannah m. William Hays

Boone, Jesse Bryan b. Ky. 1775 d. Mo. 1820   Justice Greenup Co.
m. Chloe Van Bibber   Ky. 1804-11
daughter Minerva m. Wynkoop Warner

Boone, Nathan — Vol. 17   Pvt., Capt., Maj.
daughter Mary m. R. L. Hosman—REAL DAUGHTER   Tenn. Mil.

Boone, Samuel Sr. b. Pa. 1728 d. Ky. 1807/11   Surveyor Ky. 1785/1807
m. Sarah Day — son Squire m. Anna Grubbs

Boone, Squire b. Pa. ? d. Ind. 1815   Memb. Ky. Leg Jefferson Co.
m. Jane Van Cleve   1788
son Enoch M. m. Eliza Lucy Goldman

Boone, William — Vol. 9   Pvt. N.Y. Mil.

Booth, Abel — Vol. 8   Pvt. Conn. Mil.

Booth, David — Vol. 10   Pvt. Va. Mil.

Booth, Elisha Jr. b. Conn. 1789 d. Ohio 1868   Pvt. Vermont Mil.
m. Nancy Kinsley — son Elisha m. Kate Preston
daughter Malvina B. m. Lorenzo Bartholomew

Booth, Rodam H. b. Va. 1775 d. Va. 1850   Pvt. Northumberland
m. Elizabeth Christian   Co. Va. Mil.
son Cyrus m. Priscilla Routt

Booth, William b. Va. 1783 d. Ill. 1854   Capt. Randolph Co.
m. Deborah Hart   (W.) Va. Mil.
son Elijah m. Sarah Beckley
son James H. m. Susannah Elizabeth Bexroad
son John m. Elizabeth Radcliffe
daughter Malinda m. John Wilson

Boothe, Charles b. Va. 1780 d. Ala. 1845   Quarter Master Va. Vol.
m. Lucy Ann Abernathy
son George W. m. Martha Caroline Gaston

Borden, Benjamin b. Md. 1780/2 d. Md. 1821   Pvt. Md. Mil.
m. Jane Prather — daughter Louise B. m. Samuel Rice

Bordner, Jacob b. Pa. 1754 d. Pa. 1837   Lieut. Berks Co. Pa. Mil.
m. Anna Marie Brosz — daughter Juliana m. John Weber

Boren, James b. 1781 d. 1864 m. Jane Blair   Pvt. West Tenn. Mil.
daughter Martha Jane m. Gabriel L. Long

Borne, Antoine b. La. 1783 d. La. 1816　　　　Fusilier La. Mil.
　m. Rosalie Rodriguez son Antoine m. Arthemise Fanchaux

Borie, Simon b. France 1784 d. Pa. 1872 m. Ann Kean　　Pvt. Pa. Mil.
　son Joseph Albert m. Rebecca Segurland

Boring, Greenberry b. Tenn. 1784 d. Tenn. 1874　　Pvt. Tenn. Mil.
　m. Mary Ruble — son John m. Laura

Boroughs, Charles b. Va. 1795 d. Ind. 1876　　　Pvt. Ohio Mil.
　m. Jane Haris — Jonathan m. Ellen C. Swain

Bosler, John b. Pa. 1765 d. Pa. 1824 m. Catharine Gish　　Pvt. Pa. Vol.
　son John Jr. m. Anna Webbert

Boss, Daniel C. b. Eng. c. 1785 d. Pa. 1828　　　Pvt. Pa. Mil.
　son Daniel m. Anna Hague

Boucher, Charles b. Quebec 1776 d. Mich. 1864　　Oath of Alleiance 1812
　m. Julie La Vallee — son Michael m. Margaret La Saga

Boucher (de Monbreun), Jacques Timothe　　Commandant of Kaskaskia
　b. 1747 ? d. 1826 ?　　　　　　　　　　　　　　　Ill.
　m. Marguerite Theresa Archange Gibault 1783
　daughter Theresa Archange m. Alexis Doza Sr.

Boudeman, Isaac, b. Pa. 1765 d. Pa. 1841　　Lieut. Northumberland
　m. Jane McBride　　　　　　　　　　　　　　　Co. Pa. Mil.
　son George m. Margaret Crossley

Boughton, Claudius Victor b. Mass. 1784　　Sgt. or Lieut. N.Y. Mil.
　d. N.Y. 1831 m. Elizabeth Boardman and Clarissa Boeber Hotchkiss
　daughter Esther Maria m. James Wood Emerson (thru Clarissa)
　daughter Delia Ann m. Cromwell Lloyd (thru Elizabeth)

Bostick, Absalom b. Va. c. 1740　　Member House of Commons
　d. N.C. 1803 m. Bethenia Perkins　　　　N.C. 1788/9
　son Manhoah m. Jane Scales

Bostick, Littleberry b. Ga. 1751 d. Ga. 1823　　Memb. Richmond Co.
　m. Rebecca Beall　　　　　　　　　　　　Ga. Assy. 1800/2
　son Littleberry Jr. m. Mary Ann Martha Walker

Bostick, Littleberry Jr. b. Ga. 1776　　　Justice of Peace Ga.
　d. Ga. 1855 m. Mary Ann Martha Walker
　daughter Elizabeth W. m. Campbell Raiford

Bostick, Manoah b. N.C. 1780 d. Ill. 1840　　Major Cabell Co.
　m. 2. Frances Taliaferro Harvie　　　　　Va. Mil.
　daughter Martha Ann m. William Wilkins Andrews
　1st wife Jane Scales
　daughter Mary Frances m. David Buckner
　son Peter Lewis m. Mary Virginia Gary

Boston, John b. Va. 1774 d. Pa. 1862　　　Sgt. Pa. Mil.
　m. Elizabeth Albert — son John Jr. m. Maria Morrison

Bosworth, Amos — Vol. 10　　　　　　　　Lieut. N.Y. Mil.

Boszor, Henry b. c. 1784 d. Mich. 1862　　Svc. in Mich. Mil.
　m. Polly Boosinger
　daughter Elizabeth m. Joseph G. Chapman

Botkin, Charles b. Ohio 1792 d. Ohio 1869　　　Pvt. Ohio Mil.
　m. Dorcas Tuttle — son Zebedee T. m. Cynthia Ann Smith

Bottum, Bishop — Vol. 7　　　　　　　　Pvt. Vt. Cav. Inf.

Boughton, Jared b. N.Y. 1766 d. N.Y. 1852   Pvt. N.Y. Mil.
  m. Olive Stone — son Charles S. m. Caroline Lettice Markham

Boughton, Jared b. N.Y. 1780 d. N.Y. 1821   Pvt. N.Y. Mil.
  m. Abigail Marvin — son Egbert m. Mary Marvin

Boughton, Jared b. 1781 d. 1858   Pvt. 1st Reg. N.Y. Mil.
  m. Mary Webb of Conn.
  son Ralph Leonard m. Anna Jane Gibson

Bouldin, John b. Md. 1760 d. Md. 1830   Capt. Md. Cav.
  m. Mary Askew — son Alexander J. m. Susan Hutton

Boullemet, Roland b. France 1771 d. La. 1848   Corp. La. Mil.
  m. Elizabeth Le Camp
  son Stephen m. Elizabeth Watkins

Bourne, Michael b.— d. at sea 1818 m. Charlotte Mars   Pvt. Pa. Mil.
  son Stephen m. Marian Jordan

Bourne, Walker b. Va. 1790 d. Ky. 1873   Pvt. Ky. Mil.
  m. Willey Belfield or Jameson
  daughter Kitty m. Mattias Gossett
  daughter Pamela m. Henry Lane Stone
  daughter Sarah m. Alfred Ratliff

Bourne, William IV b. Va. 1743 d. Va. 1836   Patriot — gave aid in
  m. Rosmond Jones   Grayson Co. Va.—civil offices
  daughter Patience m. Jonathan Thomas

Boush, Nathaniel Sr. b. Va. 1778   Pvt. Southampton Co. Va. Mil.
  d. Va. 1831 m. Polly Coleman
  son Nathaniel m. Jane Chatham

Boutrager, John b. Ger. 1792 d. Ohio 1874   Pvt. Ohio Mil.
  m. Mary Rainsberger — son Isaac W. m. Mary Cairns

Bowden, William b. Va. 1783 d. Va. 1823   Soldier Va. Inf.
  m. Mildred Davis — son Lemuel J. m. Martha Shackelford

Bowdry, Samuel Perin b. Ky. 1795 d. Mo. 1869   Pvt. Ky. Mil.
  m. Sallie McDaniel
  daughter Ruth m. William Leftwich (Austin)
  son Bennett W. m. Eliza Victor Bailey (mothers's name Sallie Kirtley)

Bowe, Erastus b. Vt. 1784 d. Ohio 1864   Sgt. Ohio Mil.
  m. Eleanor Swinnerton
  son Erastus Guilford m. Mary E. Hart

Bowell, Bazel b. Pa. 1786 d. Pa. 1874   Pvt. Fayette Co. Pa. Mil.
  m. Elizabeth Kyle — daughter Malinda m. James Shoaf

Bowell, Thomas b. Wales 1754 d. 1815 m. Ann ?   Pvt. Pa. Mil. 1812-13
  daughter Mary m. Robert Brownfield, Jr.

Bowen, Ezra b. N.H. 1783 d. Vt. 1841   Lieut. Vt. Mil.
  m. Lois Aldrich Haris — son Nathan A. m. Roxinda Barett

Bowen, Haile Jr. b. R.I. 1794 d. R.I. 1876   Pvt. R.I. Mil.
  m. Elizabeth Johonnot
  son Charles William m. Mary Richardson

Bowen, Oswald b. Md. 1789 d. Md. 1835   Pvt. Cecil Co. Md. Mil.
  m. Sarah Ricketts — son John R. m. Elizabeth Temanns
  son William m. Sarah Ann Garrett

Bowen, Owen Jones b. Pa. 1762 d. Ga. 1826   Capt. Franklin Co. Pa.
m. Nancy Jones   Horse Troops 1793/4
son Thomas J. m. Nancy Yarbrough

Bowen, Samuel A. b. Tenn. 1790 d. Mo. 1852   Lieut. Ky. Mil.
m. Amanda Stone — daughter Amanda S. m. Archibald M. Matson

Bower, Christopher b. Pa. 1759 d. Pa. 1826   Pvt. Pa. Mil.
m. Catherine E. — daughter Justina m. Jacob Hummel

Bower, Gustavus M. b. Va. 1790 d. Mo. 1864   Surgeon's Mate Ky. Mil.
m. Martha Crockett — daughter Isabella M. m. W. Y. Slack

Bower, William b. Pa. 1794 d. Pa. 1843   Pvt. Pa. Mil.
m. Catherine Moore — daughter Elizabeth m. Henry Benner
son William D. m. Emily Robinson

Bowers, John b. Pa. 1789 d. Pa. 1841   Ensign Pa. Mil.
m. Mary Huntzman — son Thomas m. Rebecca Marple

Bowers, Valentine b. Tenn. 1788 d. Tenn. 1867   Pvt. Tenn. Mil.
m. Abigail L. Buck — daughter Eliza G. m. Abraham Nave

Bowie, John Fraser b. Md. 1781 d. Miss. 1823   Major Miss. Terr. Vols.
m. Phoebe Cochrane
daughter Elizabeth Anne m. Thomas M. Dawson

Bowie, Thomas b. Md. 1767 d. D.C. 1823   Colonel Md. Mil.
m. Margaret Belt — son John m. Anna Margaretta Gantt

Bowker, Charles b. N.H. 1787 d. Mass. 1872   Pvt. Mass. Mil.
m. Martha Whitten — son Franklin m. Elizabeth J. M. Stoddard

Bowker, Isaiah b. 1766 d. Ohio 1845   Pvt. Ohio Mil.
m. Hannah Whitten Cresher
daughter Mary m. James W. Leach

Bowles, Lyddal Bacon b. Va. 1783 d. Va. 1835   Pvt. Va. Mil.
m. Sarah Waller Price — daughter May m. Henry Ramey

Bowles, Thomas b. Md. 1765 d. N.Y. 1832   Pvt. Md. Mil. 1794
m. Sarah Price — daughter Eleanor m. William Begole

Bowles, Thomas C. b. Md. 1796 d. Iowa 1857   Pvt. Md. Mil.
m. Jane Rogers — son David D. m. Nancy J. Bowles ?

Bowly, Daniel b. Md. 1745 d. Md. 1807   Senator Md. Leg. 1791/2
m. Ann Stewart
daughter Rebecca M. m. Peter Octavius Wirgman

Bowman, Abraham b. Va. 1775 d. Ill. 1855   Justice of Peace Ohio
m. Mary Varner — son Abraham Jr. m. Agnes Turley

Bowman, Abraham b. Pa. 1782 d. Pa. 1850   Pvt. Pa. Mil.
m. Frances Rugh — daughter Susan m. David Baker

Bowman, Andrew b. Pa. 1783 d. Pa. 1859   QM. Pa. Mil.
m. Mary Sarah Hale — son Edward H. m. Elizabeth Ann Byles

Bowman, Horace — Vol. 9   Corp. N.Y. Mil.

Bowman, Isaac Hite b. Va. 1757 d. Va. 1826   Patriot Civil Svc. 1792 Va.
m. Chary Chinn
daughter Elizabeth m. Joseph Murdock Fauntleroy

Bowman, Peter b. Pa. 1783 d. Pa. 1861   Lieut. Somerset Co. Pa. Mil.
m. Mary Horner — son William m. Sarah Woy

Bowman, Samuel b. N.Y. 1790 d. Pa. 1857   Pvt. Mercer Blues Pa. Mil.
m. Sarah Alexander — son Samuel Jr. m. Catherine M. Fleming

Bowne, Peter b. N.J. 1772 d. N.J. 1835   Pvt. N.J. Mil.
m. Ann Thompson — son Spafford m. Ann Denice

Bowser, John b. Pa. 1740 d. Pa. 1813 m. Mary ?   Pvt. Pa. Mil. 1786/9
son Samuel m. Anna Catherine Snider

Bowser, Noah b. Pa. 1750 d. Pa. 1830   Pvt. York Co. Pa. Mil.
m. Eunice Ditto — son John S. m. Elizabeth Baker

Bowsher, Anthony b. Pa. 1792 d. Ohio 1861   Pvt. Ohio Mil.
m. Sarah Reeder — daughter Mariam m. Henry C. Blacker

Boxley, George b. Va. d. Ind. 1865 m. Hannah Jenkins   Ensign Va. Mil.
daughter Virginia m. Zimra Hussey

Boyce, Isaac b. N.Y. 1764 d. N.Y.C. 1791   Pvt. N.Y. Mil.
m. Elizabeth Covert son John m. (1) Martha Rogers

Boyce, Joseph b. Vt. 1790 d. Vt. 1870   Pvt. Vt. Dragoon
m. Malinda Child — son Amos E. m. Roxanna A. Britton Comstock

Boyd, Alexander — Vol. 14   3rd. Sgt. Md. Mil.

Boyd, David b. Pa. 1743 d. Pa. 1831   Expert Rifleman
m. Elizabeth Henderson   Allegheny Co. Pa.
daughter Nancy m. Thomas Gilson

Boyd, George Washington b. Va. 1796 d. Ohio 1837   Pvt. Ohio Mil.
m. Nancy Baird
daughter Sarah Ann m. William S. Rodgers

Boyd, James b. Pa. 1787 d. Ky. 1839   Pvt. Ky. Mil.
m. Margaret Gibson
son Charles W. m. Jane McCurdy

Boyd, John — Vol. 15   Seaman Md. Navy

Boyd, John b. 1777 ? d. Tenn. 1837   Pvt. Tenn. Mil. 1814/15
m. Elizabeth Leath — daughter Mary m. Alfred Cross

Boyd, Joseph b. Va. 1797 d. Tenn. 1874   Pvt. Tenn. Mil. Pens.
m. Margaret Lilburn—daughter Sarah Jane m. Benjamin Alvin Pettitt
son Thomas G. m. Louisa Rebecca Thomas

Boyd, Richard — Vol. 14   Pvt. Ga. Mil.

Boyd, Thomas b. Md. 1781 d. N.Y. 1828   Pvt. N.Y. Art. Vols.
m. Polly Farnham Johnson
son John A. m. Sally Maria Sergeant

Boyd, Thomas Duckett b. Md. 1767 d. Va. 1820   Pvt. Va. Vols.
m. Mary Magruder — son Thomas J. m. Minerva Ann French

Boyd, William b. Ire. 1776 d. Del. 1844   Sgt. Del. Trps.
m. Margaret Gamble — daughter Sophia m. John Power

Boyden, Daniel b. Mass. 1778 d. Mass. 1828   Musician Mass. Regt.
m. Hannah Crawford — daughter Charlotte m. Frederick W. Burt

Boyer, Christopher b. Pa. 1737 d. Pa. 1817   Pvt. Pa. Mil.
m. Catherine Reifsnyder — son Jacob m. Susannah Schaffer

Boyer, Henry b. Pa. 1778 d. Pa. 1857   Pvt. Lebanon Co. Pa. Rangers
m. Sarah Krebe — daughter Catherine K. m. John Rhoads

Boyer, John b. Md. 1782 d. Ind. 1835   Sgt. Ind. Mil.
    m. Mary Rowe — daughter Sarah m. Harding Hancock, Sr.

Boyer, John George b. Pa. 1780 d. Ohio 1855   Corp. Ohio Mil.
    m. Gertrude Schaeffer — daughter Christina m. John Barnhart

Boyer, Samuel b. Pa. 1797 d. Pa. 1842   Pvt. Schylkill Co., Pa. Mil.
    m. Elizabeth Reed — son Zaccur P. m. Catherine C. Williams

Boyer, Valentine Jr. b. Pa. 1760 d. Pa. 1850   Lieut. Berks Co. Pa. Mil.
    m. Elizabeth Kuehn — son Samuel K. m. Elizabeth Reed

Boykin, Solomon b. N.C. 1792 d. N.C. 1844   Pvt. N.C. Brig.
    m. Mary Wright — son Louis M. m. Lizzie Corbett

Boykin, Thomas b. N.C. 1788 d. N.C. 1859   Capt. Sampson Co. N.C. Mil.
    m. Elizabeth Fennell — daughter Louisa m. Carr Hargrove
    son Robinson T. m. Cynthia Ann Hobbs

Boyle, Alexander b. 1771 (?) d. 1841   Pvt. Ky. Mtd. Mil.
    m. Mary Carpenter — daughter Mary m. Henry Teles Terrell

Boyle, Richard b. (?) 1787 d. Ohio 1859 m. Sarah Locke   Pvt. Ohio Mil.
    son David m. Althea Couch

Boyle, Thomas b. Mass. 1776 d. at sea 1825   Capt. Privateer Svc. Mass.
    m. Mary Gross — daughter Amanda C. m. Dr. John H. Owings

Boyles, Henry b. Pa. 1786 d. Ill. 1846   Pvt. Pa. Mil.
    m. Sarah Butler Hiller — daughter Nancy m. John William Read

Boyles, Thomas b. Pa. 1774 d. Ohio 1866 m. Ann Bonar   Pvt. Ohio Mil.
    daughter Margaret m. James Connor

Boynton, James G.   Vol. 6   Pvt. U.S. Inf.

Boynton, Jonathan   Vol. 16   Pvt. N.Y. Mil.

Boynton, Nathaniel b. N.H. 1785 d. Me. 1868   Pvt. Me. Terr. Mil.
    m. Besey Clark — son Gorham L. m. Louisa M. Basford

Boys, James b. N.Y. 1795 d. N.Y. 1817   Pvt. N.Y. Mil.
    m. Susan Tichenor
    son James K. m. Catherine Tenbrook Minier

Boys, Nathan b. (?) bef. 1770 d. Pa. 1803   Peace Commr. Phila. 1793/7
    m. Mary Reynolds — son John m. Anna St. Clair

Bozeman, Howell   Vol. 16   Pvt. La. Mil.

Brabham, John b. S.C. 1776 d. S.C. 1836 m. Martha Moye   Pvt. S.C. Mil.
    son Hampton m. Harriet E. Kirkland

Bracken, Charles b. Ky. 1788 d. Ky. 1831   Corp. Ky. Mil.
    m. Elizabeth Crowdus
    son Charles F. m. Nancy Ellen Nield

Bracken, John Oliver b. Ire. 1791 d. Tex. 1848   Pvt. Ky. Mtd. Vol. Mil.
    m. Anne Grymes Richards
    son Edward R. m. Sarah A. Watkins

Brackenridge, Robert b. Pa. 1783 d. Ind. 1859   Capt. Ohio Rifle Mil.
    m. Hannah Cully Northup — son Joseph m. Eliza J. Walpole

Braddock, John b. Pa. 1744 d. Pa. 1818   Pvt. Washington Co. Pa. Mil.
    m. Sarah — son Moses m. Sarah Langdon

Braden, James b. Pa. c. 1770 d. Pa. 1824   Major Pa. Mil. 1811
m. Eleanor — daughter Penelope m. Edward Hannah

Bradford, Charles b. Mass. 1788 d. La. 1828 m__   Corp. Mass. Art. Inf.
son Joseph R. m. Sarah Jane Tappan Wordman

Bradford, Daniel Morgan b. Va. 1793 d. Ala. 1869   Pvt. Tenn. Vol. Mil.
m. Mary Brook Lamkin
daughter Ellen D. m. John Marshall Fariss — REAL DAUGHTER
son Henry C. m. Anna Watkins

Bradford, David b. Md. 1765 d. Ohio 1834   Patriot—Civil offices Ohio
m. Barbara Grimes — daughter Sophia m. James Ramsey Balbridge

Bradford, George G. b. Pa. 1787 d. Pa. 1840   Sgt. Pa. Mil.
m. Margaret McCandless
son John m. Margaret Rebecca Andrew

Bradford, Rev. Henry b. 1761 d. 1838 Pvt. 5th Brig. 3rd. Reg. N.C. Mil.
m. Sarah Crowell — son John m. Mary Belbeck

Bradford, Henry b. Va. 1758 d. Tenn. 1815   Brig. Major Tenn. Mil.
m. Mrs. Elizabeth Payne Blakemore
son Priestley m. Elizabeth Jouette

Bradford, James M. b. Va. 1795 d. Ill. 1852   Pvt. Ky. Mil.
m. Aseneth Talbott — son William T. m. Grizella Ann Parkinson

Bradford, John b. (?) 1790 d. Minn. 1852   Lieut. Md. Mil.
m. Mary Armistead — son John m. Anna Swanson

Bradford, Simon b. Ky. 1797 d. Tenn. 1865   Pvt. Ky. Mil.
m. Isabel Anderson
daughter Ida m. A. B. Vauaro — REAL DAUGHTER

Bradford, William b. Conn. 1779 d. Mich. 1837   Pvt. N.Y. Mil.
m. Concurrence Bonfoey — son David m. Lydia Hall

Bradford, William b. Va. 1760 d. Ala. 1831   Pvt. Va. Mil.
m. Mary Ellen Steele — daughter Catherine m. John Waddell

Bradley, Anson b. Conn. 1783 d. Conn. 1850   Lt. Col. Conn. Mil.
m. Grace Benham — son William H. m. Caroline Holmes

Bradley, Ariel b. Conn. 1792 d. Ohio 1859 Sgt. Trumbull Co. Ohio Mil.
m. Laura Barstow — daughter Reumah m. Buell Pelton

Bradley, Elam b. Conn. 1774 d. Conn. 1857   Representative Conn.
m. Lowly Dickerman — daughter Julia m. Leonard Todd

Bradley, James Terry b. Ky. 1786 d. Mo. 1850   Pvt. Ohio Mil.
m. Sally Bruan Grimes — son George William m. Elizabeth Davis

Bradley, Jesse b. Conn. 1736 d. Mass. 1812 Del. to Ratify Const. Conn.
m. Mamre Ives   1788
son Daniel m. Patience Cooper

Bradley, Philip Burr b. Conn. 1738 d. Conn. Judge Fairfield Co. Conn.
m. Ruth Smith   1782/1806
daughter Ruth m. Nathan Dauchy Jr.

Bradley, Phineas Sherman   Vol. 9   Pvt. Conn. Mil.

Bradley, Samuel Jr.   Vol. 3   Midshipman, Mass.

Bradley, Thomas b. Ky. 1785 d. Ky. 1823 m. Fanny Bush   Pvt. Ky. Mil.
son Thomas M. m. Cynthia Swan

Bradley, William b. Dela. 1785 d. Dela. 1841   Pvt. Sussex Co. Del. Mil.
m. Hester Nicholson — son William H. m. Phillis Ralph

Bradley, William b. S.C. 1785 d. S.C. aft. 1855   Pvt. S.C. Mil.
m. Elizabeth Cave — son John W. m. Julia Wilson

Bradshaw, James b. Va. (?) d. Va. 1849   Pvt. Nottaway Co. Va. Mil.
m. Nancy A. Hudson — son Richard E. m. Sara Bagley Waugh

Bradshaw, John b. d. Ky. m. Catherine Huffman   Pvt. Ky. Mil.
daughter Mary Ann m. Robert J. Holmes

Bradshaw, Richard b. N.C. 1788 d. Tenn. 1872   Pvt. Tenn. Mil.
m. Lydia Prigmore — son Richard H. m. Jane P. Rawlings

Bradshaw, William b. Va. 1790 d. Ind. 1860   Pvt. Va. Mil.
m. Margaret Coyner   Nottaway Co.
daughter Elizabeth m. John Reynolds
daughter Mary m. John Russell Hussey — REAL DAUGHTER

Bradstreet, Daniel Moore   Vol. 16   Pvt. N.H. Mil.

Bradstreet, Thomas b. Vt. 1795 d. Ill. 1877   Pvt. N.H. Mil.
m. Clarissa Todd
daughter Martha Jane m. George Thomas Patrick
REAL DAUGHTER

Bradt. Cornelius b. N.Y. 1765 d. N.Y. 1826   Pvt. N.Y. Mil.
m. Annatje Pieterse — son Peter m. Anna Marie Stevens

Brady, Hugh b. Pa. 1796 d. Ill. 1874 m. Polly Reed   Pvt. Pa. Mil.
son Hugh m. Mary M. Gunn

Brady, John b. N.Y. 1780 d. N.Y. 1858 m. Lydia Parks   Seaman N.Y.
daughter Hannah M. m. Wing Kelley Walbridge

Braham, Samuel b. Ire. 1790 d. Pa. 1874   Pvt. Pa. Mil.
m. M. A. Patton
daughter Asenath M. m. Samuel E. McCleary — REAL DAUGHTER

Brainard, Ansel Jr. b. Conn. 1765 d. Ohio 1855   Musician Conn. Mil.
m. 1st Mary Warren — son Alvah m. LaFlavia Salina Harris

Brainard, Edward b. Mass. d. Vt. m. Vol. 1   Pvt. Vt. Mil.
son David m. Nancy Sawyer

Brainard, Othinel b. 1793 d. 1872 m. Asenath Ross   Pvt. N.Y. Mil.
son Whitney Joshua m. Jane Harriet Cady

Brainerd, Asahel b. Conn. 1740 d. N.Y. 1822   Capt. Conn. Mil.
m. Experience Ackley
son Benjamin m. Mrs. Mary E. Slocum Kitman

Brainerd, Chauncey b. Conn. 1795 d. N.Y. 1861   Pvt. Conn. Mil.
m. Narcissa Post — son Wilbur F. m. Catherine M. Holmes

Brainerd, David Sr. b. Conn. 1748 d. Ohio 1828   Capt. Conn. Mil. 1791
m. Hannah Willard — son David m. Martha Clark

Brainerd, Ezra   Vol. 9   Lt. Col. Conn. Mil.

Brainerd, Silas b. Conn. 1757 d. Conn. 1847   Pvt. Conn. Mil.
m. Lucinda — son Erastus m. Mary Wells Stancliff

Bramham, Nimrod b. Va. 1769 d. Va. 1845   Lieut. Va. Mil.
m. Margaret Marshall — daughter Sarah Wyatt m. William A. Bible

Branch, John Jr. b. N.C. 1782 d. N.C. 1863   Civil Service 1813/15
m. Eliza Fort — daughter Margaret m. Daniel Smith Donelson

Branch, Nicholas b. 1780 d. Tenn. aft. 1817   Pvt. Tenn. Mil.
m. Elizabeth Hurst — son James W. m. Nancy Mathews

Brand, Stephen b. 1793 d. N.Y. 1873 m. Phebe Moore   Pvt. N.Y. Mil.
son Graton M. m. Adelaide Mary Tyler

Brandenburg, Mathias b. Va. 1790 d. Ohio 1822 Vol. 2   Pvt. Lt. Art.
m. Esther — son Absalom m. Hettie Frankes

Brandenburg, Solomon b. Germany 1760 d. Ind. 1851   Pvt. Ky. Det. Mil.
m. Susan Wiseman
daughter Martha Ellen m. William Jasper Conrad

Brandon, Alexander b. Pa. 1748 d. W. Va. 1813   Col. W. Va. Mil. 1812
m. Elizabeth Robinette — son James R. m. Anna Lucretia Hole

Brandon, George b. N.C. 1770 d. Tenn. 1844   Capt. West Tenn. Vol. Mil.
m. Sidney McGuire — daughter Nancy m. John Pruitt Dunn

Brannan, Benjamin b. Pa. 1739 d. Pa. 1825   Brig. Gen. Pa. Mil. 1793
m. Eunice Estey   Judge Dela. Co. Pa. Ct. 1794
daughter Abigail m. John McKinley

Brannan, Thomas b. Md. 1787 d. Md. 1834   Sgt. Md. Mil.
m. Rebeckah Maddox
son James M. m. Eliza Jane Alexander

Brant, Jacob b. N.J. 1784 d. N.J. 1821   Matross N.J. Art.
m. Mary Donnelly Bedell — daughter Sarah Ellen m. Henry Gorham

Brantley, Benjamin b. N.C. 1791 d. Ark. 1867   Pvt. N.C. Mil.
m. Susanna F. Blodgett
daughter Maryanna m. Charles B. Davidson

Brantley, Green D. b. N.C. 1795/6 d. Ala. 1849   Pvt. Ga. Mil.
m. Elizabeth Holifield
daughter Kate m. William B. Augustus — REAL DAUGHTER

Brashear, Otho b. Ky. 1793 d. Ky. 1875 m. Mary Wills   Pvt. Ky. Mil.
son Thomas m. Lydia Ash

Brashears, Merida b. S.C. 1793 d. Mo. 1883   Pvt. S.C. Mil.
m. Elizabeth McGuire — son Solomon m. Ann Lyons

Brashears, Otho b. and d. ____ m. Ruth Brown   Pvt. Pa. Mil.
son Levi m. Aggie Watts Turner

Bratton, George b. 1786 d. 1853   Pvt. Ky. Det. Mil.
m. Elizabeth Ann Thompson
daughter Sarah Rebecca m. Wilmouth A. White

Bratton, William b. Va. 1778 d. Ind. 1841   Pvt. Ky. Mil. 1812/15—
m. Mary H. Maxwell   member Lewis & Clark Exp. 1804/6
son George m. Cynthia Ann Moore
daughter Grizella Ann m. Stephen Fields

Braun, Adam b. Pa. 1742 d. Pa. 1828   Pvt. Lancaster Co. Pa. Mil.
m. Catherine — son William m. Elizabeth Balmer

Brawner, Henry b. Md. 1791 d. Md. 1838   Lieut. Md. Mil.
m. Maria Campbell Gates — son James C. m. Caroline Ould

Bray, John H. b. Ohio 1779 d. Ohio 1875   Pvt. Ohio Mil.
m. Hannah Shelton — son Edward m. Lucy Jane Gilmore

Brayton, Jeremiah b. 1793 d. Wisc. 1869   Fifer N.Y. Mil.
m. Maria Manville
daughter Louise M. m. George Sawin — REAL DAUGHTER

Brazeale, John b. Tenn. d. Tenn. 1843   Sgt. East Tenn. Vol.
  m. Elizabeth Margrave
daughter Elizabeth m. Robert Mosby Eastland

Brazie, Cornelius b. N.Y. 1783 d. N.Y. 1861   Pvt. N.Y. Mil.
  m. Lucretia Snook — son Cornelius E. m. Emeline G. Dyer

Bready, David b. Md. 1796 d. Md. 1869   Pvt. Frederick Co. Md. Mil.
  m. Anne Elizabeth Kelly
son David F. m. Martha A. C. Yowell & Octavia H. Cashell
son Samuel K. m. Anne Rabbitt

Breckenridge, Alexander b. Va. 1743 d. Ky. bef. 1813   Civil Officer 1784
  m. Magdalene Gamble; Mary Chadd   Washington Co. Va.
  son George m. Elizabeth Cowan

Breckenridge, Robert b. c. 1743 d. 1812/14   Lt. Ky. Mil. 1795
  m. Mary Doak — daughter Mary m. Walter Caldwell

Breidinger, Peter b. Pa. 1756 d. Pa. 1806   Pvt. Northampton Co. Pa. Mil.
  m. Anna Maria Glass — daughter Elizabeth m. Valentine J. Uhler

Brent, Hugh b. Va. 1739 d. Ky. c. 1813   Civil Officer Ky.
  m. Elizabeth Baxter — daughter Mary m. Hugh McIlvain

Brent, John b. S.C. 1779 d. Miss. 1884   Pvt. Miss. Inf.
  m. Magdalen Turnipseed
son John A. m. Rebecca Kaigler

Brent, John b. Va. 1755 d. Miss. aft. 1820 m.—   Sgt. Miss. Terr. Mil.
son Preston m. Elizabeth Briley

Brent, Robert b. Md. 1759 d. Md. 1819   Paymaster U.S.A. 1808
  m. Dorothy Leigh — son William L. m. Maria Fenwick

Brent, Thomas b. S.C. 1792/8 d. Miss. c. 1870   Pvt. Miss. Terr. Mil.
  m. Sarah Briley — daughter Angeline m. Robert Glover Alexander

Brett, Ezra b. Mass. 1779 d. Me. 1854   QM. Mass. Mil.
  m. Alice Robinson — son George W. m. Susan Stevens Whariff

Brewer, Abraham b. N.Y. 1763 d. N.J. 1826   Pvt. N.J. Mil.
  m. Phebe Maybee — daughter Rachel m. David Lawrence Breeme

Brewer, Daniel b. 1791 d. Md. 1855 m. Mary Mish   Capt. Md. Mil.
daughter Mary Elizabeth m. John Rufus Smith

Brewer, James Drury b. Ky. 1797 d. Mo. 1856   Pvt. Ky. Mil.
  m. Aloysia Manning — daughter Aloysia m. Timon Rufus Manning

Brewer, John Jr. b. Va. 1762 d. Va. 1814   2nd. Lieut. Va. Mil.
  m. Ann Cooper (?) — daughter Mary m. Henry Riddick

Brewer, Samuel   Vol. 14   Major Mass. Mil.

Brewer, Samuel b. N.Y. 1789 d. N.Y. 1885   Pvt. N.Y. Mil.
  m. Elizabeth Hess — son Michael m. Eliza Maria Sharp

Brewer, William b. N.C. 1790 d. Ill. 1874   Pvt. Tenn. Mil.
  m. Jane McKnight — son Thomas m. Mary Hutton

Brewer, Willis Hamlin b. Ga. 1790 d. Miss. 1869   Pvt. Ga. Troops
  m. Mary Walpole — son Samuel B. m. Rebecca Attaway

Brewster, Ephraim b. Vt. 1782 d. N.Y. 1880   Orderly Sgt. N.Y. Mil.
  m. 1st Adah Harmon — daughter Adah Almira m. Jonathan Peabody

Brewster, Jonathan Jr. b. Conn. 1781 d. N.Y. 1842   1st Lieut. Vt. Mil.
  m. Polly Everts — daughter Harriet m. James Risley Dickinson

Brewster, Joshua b. Mass. 1761 d. Mass. 1832   Capt. Mass. Navy
m. Ruth Chandler — daughter Hannah m. Hosea Delano

Brewster, Joshua b. Mass. 1763 d. Mass. 1861   Pvt. Mass. Mil.
m. Elizabeth Ellis — daughter Adaline F. m. John W. Perry

Brewster, Levi b. 1799 d. 1873 m. Lydia Case Waterman   Pvt. 1812
son Richard m. Sarah Emeline Knowles

Brewster, Samuel b. N.Y. 1740 d. N.Y. 1824   State Senator N.Y. 1805/8
m. Freelove Williams — daughter Harriet m. James Caldwell

Brewster, Sanford b. Conn. 1788 d. Ohio 1857   Pvt. Conn. Mil.
m. Lucy Avery Swan — daughter Lucy Ann m. Josiah Lacy Botsford

Brewster, Stephen   Vol. 12   Pvt. N.Y. Mil.

Brewster, Timothy b. Conn. 1759   Selectman Pawlet Vt. 1812/13
d. N.Y. 1848 m. Temperance Andrus
son Ephraim m. Adah Harmon

Brewster, Wadsworth b. Conn. 1737 d. Conn. 1812   Selectman 1792 Conn.
m. Jerusha Newcomb — son Jasper m. Theodosia Lyman
daughter Lydia m. Daniel Lyman

Brewster, William b. Vt. 1794 d. en route to Cal. 1848   Pvt. N.Y. Mil.
m. Sarah Todd Maltby — daughter Charlotte F. m. John R. Bowler

Brian, Hardy b. S.C. 1759 d. La. 1815   Pvt. Fla. War 1810
m. Jemima Morgan — son Francis m. 2nd Salomie Causey
son Solomon M. m. Ann Maynard Chase Sands

Brian, James Jr. b. 1794 d. 1878   Pvt. S.C. Mil. 1814/15
m. Susan Collins — daughter Mary Adeline m. Daniel Franklin Hall

Brian, Solomon Morgan b. S.C. 1792 d. La. 1864   Lieut. La. Mil.
m. Ann Maynard Chase Sands
son William S. m. Mary Frances Ligan

Brice, James b. Md. 1751 d. Ohio 1832   Repr. Pa. Leg. 1794 Commr. 1797;
m. Hester Johnson   Tax Coll. Pa. 1798/1804
son Barnet m. Mary Miller

Brice, James b. S.C. 1768 d. S.C. 1845 m. Jane Wilson   Sgt. S.C. Mil.
son Robert m. Margaret Simonton

Bricker, Henry b. Pa. 1790 d. Ohio 1855   Pvt. Pa. Mil.
m. Rachel Kneesel — son William R. m. Esther Elizabeth Taylor

Bricker, Peter b. Pa. 1764 d. Pa. 1837 m. Eva Holstine   Pvt. Pa. Mil.
son David m. Lucinda Peterson

Brickey, William b. Va. 1780 d. Tenn. 1856   Pvt. East Tenn. Mil.
m. Eleanor Dobkins — son John m. Nancy Ann King

Bridge, Jesse b. N.Y. 1787 d. N.Y. 1863   QM. Sgt. U.S. Inf.
m. Margaret Love — daughter Juliett m. William Albert Farrington

Bridges, John L. b. Va. d. Ky. 1859   Pvt. Va. Troops
m. Anna Palmer Adair — daughter Isabelle m. Robert L. Scruggs

Bridgfort, David b. Va. 1793 d. Tenn. 1841   Corp. Nottaway Co. Va. Mil.
m. Mariah Dandridge Hobbs — son Thomas O. m. Carolyn Jane Gray

Briest, William b. N.J. 1786 d. N.J. 1856   Pvt. N.J. Mil.
m. Margaret Crossley — daughter Mary Ann m. Joseph Thomas

Brigance, Charles Newton b. Tenn. 1790 d. Tenn. 1855   Pvt. Tenn. Mil.
m. Frances Dyer — son Harvey m. Mary Jane Hester

Briggs, Allen b. Vt. 1788 d. Mich. 1868   Sgt. N.Y. Mil.
    m. Amanda Seymour — son Mansel M. m. Mary Ann Shepard

Briggs, Asa B.   Vol. 22 m. Jane Winslow   Pvt. Vt. Mil.
    son Flavius J. m. Sophronia Wilson

Briggs, George b. Mass. 1758 d. Mass. 1823   Ensign Mass. Mil.
    m. Elizabeth Goff — son George m. Cynthia Jones

Briggs, John Perkins b. Mass. (Me.) 1791   Capt. & Surgeon U.S.A.
    d. Me. 1838 m. Dorthea Fifield Boynton
    daughter Hannah B. m. David Parker Strout

Briggs, William Gilkey b. Ky. 1794 d. Mo. 1866   Corp. Ky. Vol. Mil.
    m. Rhoda Wright — daughter Louise O. m. Hiram Brooks

Brigham, Elijah b. Mass. 1751 d. D.C. 1816   Member U.S. Congress 1810/16
    m. Sarah Ward—daughter Catherine Martha m. George Henry Lowe

Brigham, Joel b. Mass. 1785 d. Ohio 1840   Lieut. N.Y. Mil.
    m. Polly Ann Durkee — son Joel m. Betsy Lyon

Brigham, Thomas b. Conn. 1742 d. Conn. 1800   Lieut. Conn. Mil.
    m. Susanna Eels — son Alexander m. Sarah Whitten

Bright, John b. Ky. 1787 d. Ky. 1848   Capt. Ky. Mil.
    m. Elizabeth Morrison — daughter Mary m. Thomas M. Lillard

Bright, Thomas b. 1779 (?) d. Ohio 1846   Pvt. Ohio Mil.
    m. Clarissa Ferris — daughter Margaret m. Stephen S. Mapes

Brightman, Daniel b. R.I. 1771 d. Ohio 1851   Pvt. Mass. Mil.
    m. Elizabeth Brownell — son Alvan m. Pamelia Clapp Douglas

Brightman, George Claver b. R.I. 1791 d. Tex. 1857   Pvt. Ind. Terr. Mil.
    m. Nancy Moore daughter Emaline C. m. Charles Arden Russell
    son Lyman m. Harriet C. Howard

Brill, Henry   Vol. 17   Pvt. Ohio Mil.

Brimm, Richard b. Va. (?) d. Va. aft. 1823 m. Patsy Dram Pvt. Va. Mil.
    son Joseph m. Sally

Brindley, Asa Riggs b. Ga. 1795 d. Ala. 1883   Pvt. Ga. Riflemen
    m. Mary Bowen — daughter Hester m. Wiley Lafayette Casey

Brindley, James b. Va. 1765 d. W. Va. 1838   Constable Va. 1796
    m. Rebecca Hughes — daughter Mary m. Richard Morrison

Briner, Samuel b. Pa. 1784 d. Pa. 1861   Pvt. Pa. Mil.
    m. Elizabeth Koch — daughter Esther m. Daniel Jackson Werner

Brinker, Abraham b. Pa. 1774 d. Pa. 1850   Capt. 2nd Inf. Pa. Mil.
    m. Louisa Moser — daughter Amy Matilda m. William Richey

Brisbane, Adam Fowler b. S.C. 1754 d. S.C. 1797   Memb. Constitutional
    m. Mary Camber   Conv. S.C.
    daughter Mary Hannah C. m. Reuben Arthur

Briscoe, Alexander b. Md. 1786 d. Pa. 1820   Pvt. Md. Art.
    m. Mary Wilson — daughter Sarah Ann m. Dixon Stansbury Miles

Briscoe, Andrew Logan b. Va. 1776 d. Mo. 1858   Lieut. Ky. Mil.
    m. Anne Kavanaugh — daughter Sallie m. Samuel Cole

Briscoe, Parmenas b. Va. 1784   Gen. Miss. Terr. Mil.
    d. at sea 1851 bur. Pac. Ocean m. Mary Montgomery
    son James M. m. Susan Mason
    son Robert P. m. Adaline Mayes

Briscoe, Thomas b. Va. 1791 d. W. Va. 1868   Ensign Va. Mil.
m. Juliet Wood Hite
daughter Frances Amelia m. William B. Gallaher Sr.
daughter Juliet B. m. Norman Miller

Bristol, Anson b. Vt. 1778 d. Mich. 1855 m. Deborah (?)   Pvt. N.Y. Mil.
daughter Hannah m. Hiram Hall

Bristow, Archibald b. Va. 1774 d. Ky. 1848   Pvt. Ky. Mtd. Riflemen
m. Philadelphia Bourne — son James H. m. Frances Coolidge

Britain, Calvin b. Mass. or N.Y. 1770/1   Lt. Col. N.Y. Mil.
d. Mich. 1840 m. Mary — daughter Mary B. m. James Warren
daughter Sarah m. Oliver Stevens

Britt, Anderson Smith b. Va. 1789 d. Ark. 1847   Pvt. Tenn. Mil.
m. Mary Wilks — son John Henry m. Sue Ann Hunt

Britt, Bolling b. Va. 1795 d. Ill. 1857/8 m. Mary Gautier   Pvt. Va. Mil.
son William N. m. Bessie Belson

Britt, William S. b. Va. 1785 d. Va.   Sgt. U.S. Vol.
m. Mary Cowan Wallace — daughter Mary m. William Obed Britt

Brittain, Joseph b. N.C. 1756 d. Tenn. 1823   Lieut. Tenn. Mil.
m. Dorothy Horner
daughter Amelia Louise m. John Fleming Ferguson

Brittain, Zeboeth b. N.J. 1746 d. Pa. 1790   Pvt. Northampton Co. Pa. Mil.
m. Elizabeth Mars — son John m. Margaret Albertson

Britten, Nathanial   Vol. 16   Pvt. U.S. Inf.

Brittingham, Purnell b. Md. 1779 d. Ohio —   Pvt. Ohio Mil.
m. Mary Neill — son James N. m. Susannah Adams

Britton, Joseph b. Pa. 1756 d. Pa. 1830 m. Mary Frain   Pvt. Pa. Mil.
daughter Mary m. William Carvell

Britton, Nathaniel b. N.J. — d. N.Y. 1815 m. Sarah Horn   Pvt. U.S. Inf.
daughter Mary m. Samuel Cooley

Broadwater, Charles b. 1778 d. 1859   Pvt. Md. 50th Regt.
m. Mary M. Beaver — son William C. m. Jane Warnick
son Ashford m. Rachel Malvina Loyler

Broadwater, Charles b. Va. 1781 d. Va. 1840 m. Mary Ripes   Pvt. Mil.
son Jefferson m. Mary Beckner

Broadwell, James b. Ohio 1797 d. Ill. 1878 m. Betsy Pratt   Pvt. U.S. Inf.
daughter Cynthia m. Alexander B. Irwin

Broadwell, Lewis b. Conn. 1791 d. Conn. 1844   Pvt. Conn. Mil.
m. Betsey Folliott — son John S. m. Catherine Morrow

Brobeck, Jacob b. 1780 d. 1845 m. Catherine Cooper   Pvt. Va. Mil.
son Henry m. July Ann Mooney

Brock, Hayden b. S.C. 1791 d. S.C. 1862   Sgt. U.S. Inf.
m. Mary A. Braswell — son James H. m. Susan Blackmon

Brockman, Moses b. Va. 1775 d. Ind. 1849   Patrolman Boone Co. Ky.
m. Eleanor — daughter Susannah m. Elijah Rogers

Brockway, Tiffany b. N.Y. 1774 d. N.Y. 1866   Lt. Col. N.Y. Mil.
m. Lucy Alvord — son Tiffany m. Cornelia Babcock

Brodhead, Charles W. b. N.Y. 1742　　Memb. N.Y. Assembly Ulster Co.
d. N.Y. 1799 m. Sarah Hardenberg
son Wessel m. Annetje Hardenbergh

Brodnax, Edward Brookings b. Va. 1785 d. Ga. 1862　　　Pvt. Ga. Mil.
m. Frances V. Brooking — daughter Marie Ann m. Joseph Mann
son Samuel m. Marguerite Acock

Brodnax, Robert b. Ga. 1784 d. Ala. 1874　　　　　Lieut. Ga. Vol.
m. Olive Whitaker — daughter Rebecca V. m. James M. Winston

Brodnax, Robert b. Va. 1787 d. N.C. —　　　　　　Pvt. Mil.
son Edward m. Alice Henderson Jones

Brokaw, John b. N.J. 1741 d. N.J. m. Cornelia　Pvt. Somerset Co. N.J. Mil.
daughter Cornelia m. Tunis Covert

Bromley, Dewey b. Conn. 1787 d. Conn. 1874　　　Corp. Conn. Mil.
m. Lucretia Caswell — son Gurdon J. m. Asenath Lewis

Bronaugh, William b. Va. 1775 d. Mo. 1859　Pvt. Kanawah Valley W. Va.
m. Mary Catherine Peyton
son Christopher m. Ann Elizabeth Waters

Bronston, Thomas Springer b. 1791 Pa. d. Ky. 1869　　Corp. Ky. Mtd. Vol.
m. Lucy A. W. Clark
daughter May Ann m. William Smith Collins
daughter Samira M. m. Dr. James Edward Baker
son Jacob m. Carrie Evans

Brooke, Benjamin b. Pa. 1793 d. Ohio 1874　　　　Pvt. Ohio Mil.
m. Martha Taylor — daughter Elizabeth B. m. John Higgins

Brooke, Francis Taliaferro b. Va. 1763 d. Va. 1851　　Lt. Col. Va. Cav.
m. Mary Randolph Spotswood
son Robert S. m. Margaret Lyle Smith

Brooke, William b. Pa. 1788 d. Pa. 1866　　　　　Lieut. Pa. Mil.
m. Eliabzeth Geiger — son Franklin G. m. Sarah D. Irwin

Brooking, Edwin or Edward　　　Vol. 11　　　　Sgt. Va. Mil.

Brooking, William b. Va. 1764 d. Va. 1840　　　　　Pvt. Va. Mil.
m. Elizabeth Barret — daughter Elizabeth m. John Mann

Brooks, Alfred Sayre b. Conn. 1794 d. N.Y. 1863　　　Pvt. N.Y. Mil.
m. Fannie Cone — son Horatio D. m. Amanda P. Dewey

Brooks, Bartemus b. Vt. 1786 d. Wisc. 1875　　　　Pvt. N.Y. Mil.
m. Elizabeth O. Smith
daughter Electa E. unm. — REAL DAUGHTER

Brooks, Daniel b. N. J. 1751 d. N.Y. 1816 m. Pattie　Corp. N.Y. Mil.
son Zebulon m. Amanda Paull

Brooks, James b. Md. 1782 d. Md. 1832 m. Judith Seward　Corp. Md. Mil.
son George W. m. Elizabeth McCarter

Brooks, James Allen b. Pa. — d. Ky. 1833　　　　　Lieut. Ky. Mil.
m. Elizabeth Garrard
daughter Eliza Jane m. John Regis Alexander

Brooks, John b. Ga. 1786 d. Ga. 1875 m. Nancy Nunn　　Ensign Ga. Mil.
son Terrell J. m. Nancy Matthews

Brooks, John　　　Vol. 17　　　　　　Pvt. Ky. Vol. Mil.

Brooks, John b.— 1769 d. Md. 1869   Capt. U.S. Inf.
m. Mary Conway — son William C. m. Sarah Maria Roberts

Brooks, John b. — d. N.C. — m. Isabella Graves Kerr   Pvt. S.C. Mil.
son John K. m. Isabella Malone

Brooks, John b. Pa. 1778 d. Pa. 1845   Pvt. Pa. Mil.
m. Catherine Greenawait
daughter Julia P. m. Boyle Irwin McClure

Brooks, Moses b. Va. 1760 d. Tenn. 1830   Pvt. Knox Co. Tenn. Mil.
m. Mrs. Agnes Gamble Fowler
daughter Jane m. Robert Clark McRee
son Joseph A. m. M. Almeda McMillan

Brooks, William b. Pa. 1788 d. Pa. 1866   Lieut. Pa. Mil.
m. Elizabeth Geiger — son Franklin G. m. Sarah D. Irwin

Brooks, William S. b. Mass. 1781 d. Vt. 1865   Lieut. U.S. Navy
m. Eleanor Forman — son Francis W. m. Matilda C. Smith

Brookshire, Nathaniel b. Tenn. 1793 d. Texas 1853   Pvt. West Tenn. Mil.
m. Mary Ann Hooks — son Arolaus K. m. Argiva Wheaton
son James S. m. Henrietta Streppe

Brosius, Jacob b. Pa. 1744 d. Md. 1822 m. Katherine—   Pvt. Pa. Mil.
son Jacob m. Maria Eve Meyer

Bross, Henry b. N.J. 1764 d. N.J. 1827 m. Nancy Hall   Pvt. N.J. Det. Mil.
son Henry Hall m. Elizabeth Keeler

Bross, Henry Hall b. N.J. 1796 d. NYC 1843   Pvt. Musician 1814 Inf.
m. Elizabeth Keeler — son Robert S. m. Susan Thomas

Brough, John b. Pa. 1787 d. Va. 1873   Pvt. Botetourt Co. Va. Mil.
m. Catherine Peters — son Daniel m. Elizabeth Rader

Broughton, Nicholson b. Mass. 1790 d. Mass. 1873   Mass.
m. Mrs. Nancy Harris Hooper   Sailing Master Privateer
daughter Ellen I. m. Henry E. Waiter

Broughton, William b. Conn. 1785 d. N.Y. 1838   Ensign N.Y. Mil.
m. Sally Blakely — daughter Vallonia m. Isaac Wycoff Quick

Broughton, Zephron b. Vt. 1791 d. Pa. 1856   Sgt. N.Y. Vols.
m. Elizabeth Warriner — son Jonah R. m. Temperance Udell Sturgis

Brouse, Michael Jr. b. Pa. 1775 d. Ohio 1859   Sgt. Ohio Mil.
m. Susannah Wilt — daughter Julia Ann m. Samuel Engle

Broutin, Francois Andre Narcisse b. 1759 d. La. 1818   Capt. 7th Inf. La.
m. Francisca Rochon
daughter Irene Francois m. Louis J. B. de Bellevue

Broward, Francis b. France 1755 d. Fla. 1817   Patriot — took Oath
m. Rebecca   Loyalty 1813

Broward, John b. S.C. 1795 d. Fla. 1865 m. Margaret Tucker   Patriot 1815
son John m. Margaret Tucker
son Montgomery m. Elizabeth Broward (cousin)

Brower, Abraham b. N.Y. 1763 d. N.J. 1826   Pvt. N.J. Mil.
m. Phoebe Maybee — daughter Rachel m. David Lawrence Broome

Brower, Nazareth b. N.Y. 1756   Capt. Dutchess Co. N.Y. Mil.
d. N.Y. 1817 m. Jane —
daughter Elizabeth m. John D. Smith

Brower, Thomas L.　　Vol. 13　　　　　　　　　Corp. N.Y. Art.

Brown, Aaron b. Conn. 1781 d. Conn. 1870　　　　Pvt. Conn. Mil.
　m. Mary Wilcox — son Theophilus M. m. Mary Louise Geer

Brown, Aaron b. Mass. 1773 d. Mass. 1844 m.—　　Pvt. Mass. Mil.
　son James m. Ruth Eames Swan

Brown, Abel b. Vt. 1792 d. Vt. 1845　　　　　　　Pvt. Vt. Mil.
　m. Priscilla Hodgkins
　daughter Jane m. Sullivan Demary

Brown, Abraham b. Va. 1793 d. Pa. 1851　　　Fayette Co. Pa. Brig.
　m. Mary Brownfield　　　　　　　　　　　　　Lieut. 1812
　son Isaac m. 2nd Mary Jane Grier

Brown, Amos b. Mass. 1784 d. Vt. 1863　Selectman Northfield Vt. 1814
　m. Sarah Norris — daughter Jane m. Charles Wesley Smith

Brown, Andrew Anderson b. Va. 1779 d. Va. 1850　　Pvt. Va. Mil.
　m. Mary R. Duncan — son John Fleming m. Ann Eliza Reynolds

Brown, Benjamin b. Mass. 1720　　　　　Repr. Gen. Ct. 1783/5 Mass.
　d. Mass. 1802 m. Sarah Reed
　daughter Sarah m. Nathaniel —

Brown, Beriah b. R.I. 1715 d. R.I. 1792　　　High Sheriff R.I. 1784/92
　m. Elizabeth — daughter Sarah m. Benjamin Wait

Brown, Bezaleel b. Va. 1754 d. Va. 1829　Sheriff Albemarle Co. Va. 1805
　m. Mary Thompson — daughter Elizabeth m. Jesse Garth

Brown, Charles b. N.H. 1787 d. N.H. 1855　　　　Pvt. N.H. Mil.
　m. Lydia Woods — son Eldredge m. Emily de la Vergue

Brown, Clement　　Vol. 13　　　　　　　　　Capt. Ohio Mil.

Brown, Daniel b. N.Y. 1786 d. N.Y. 1867 m. Sally Winch　Pvt. Mass. Mil.
　daughter Amorite m. Ashel Champney — REAL DAUGHTER

Brown, David b. Ga. 1774 d. Ga. 1828　　　　　　Corp. Ga. Mil.
　m. Elizabeth Wells — son David M. m. Winifred Tarver

Brown, David b. R.I. 1757 d. Mass. 1849　　　　Pvt. Mass. Mil.
　m. Chloe Carpenter
　daughter Mary m. Nathaniel Dana Jr.

Brown, David b. N.Y. 1794 d. N.Y. 1881 m. Rosetta Moore　Pvt. N.Y. Mil.
　son Chauncey W. m. Susan Lobar

Brown, David b. Pa. 1778 d. Ohio 1868　　　　　Pvt. Ohio Mil.
　m. 1st Margaret McTeear — daughter Martha m. Gabriel Barr

Brown, Ebenezer b. Va. 1770 d. N.Y. 1833　　　　Capt. N.Y. Mil.
　m. Hannah Darling — son Pliney J. m. Elizabeth Mitchel

Brown, Elijah b. Va. 1778 d. Ala. 1845　　　　　　Pvt. Va. Mil.
　m. Nancy Edmundson
　daughter Rebecca m. Joab Bagley

Brown, Elisha b. R.I. 1796 d. N.Y. 1842　　　　　Pvt. N.Y. Mil.
　m. Anna Calkins — son Anson m. Harriet Marilla Negus
　son Henry P. m. Mary Esther Adams

Brown, Ephraim b. Mass. 1765　　Selectman Cumberland Co. Me. 1802
　d. Me. 1840 m. Huldah Richardson
　son Joseph m. Elizabeth Hunt

Brown, Ephraim b. Mass. 1776   Ensign Ontario Co. N.Y. Mil.
d. N.Y. 1851 m. Hannah Huddleston
son Ephraim E. m. Jerusha Weston
son Timothy m. Sophia Hopping

Brown, Eppes b. Ga. 1766 d. Ga. 1827   Brig. Gen. Ga. 1810
m. Elizabeth Shackleford
son Alfred E. W. m. Virginia Brooking

Brown, Felix b. Va. 1778 d. Mo. 1855 m. Agnes Boaz   Pvt. Va. Cav. Mil.
daughter Elizabeth A. m. Richmond Pearson

Brown, George b. Ky. 1799 d. Mo. 1876 m. Mary Cole   Pvt. U.S. Inf.
son Andrew J. m. Catherine Kreiter

Brown, George b. Pa. 1773 d. Ohio 1828 m. Alice Hardesty   Pvt. Ohio Mil.
daughter Alice m. James Taggart
son William m. Mary M. Young

Brown, Henry b. N.C. 1793 d. Tenn. 1845   Sgt. Tenn. Mil.
m. Nancy Ellington Marshall
daughter Nancy T. m. Iley Nunn Selph

Brown, Isaac b. Vt. c. 1775 d.— m.—   Pvt. Vt. Mil.
son William m. Susan Cheeseman

Brown, Jacob   Vol. 9   Brig. Gen. N.Y. Vols.

Brown, Jacob b. Pa. 1783 d. Ill. 1863 m. Letitia —   Pvt. Ohio Mil.
son Isaac m. Virginia Hutchinson

Brown, Jacob b. Tenn. 1789 d. Tenn. 1860   Pvt. Tenn. Vol. Mil.
m. Sara Million — daughter Nancy H. m. Bright Johnson

Brown, Jacob b. Va. — d. Tenn. 1814   Pvt. Tenn. Mil.
m. Christeney Rainey
son Isaac m. Margaret P. Williams

Brown, Jacob Sr. b. S.C. 1736   2d Major Wash. Co. N.C. Mil. 1784
d. Tenn. 1785 m. Ruth Gordon
son Jacob m. Elizabeth Bird

Brown, Jacob Jr. b. S.C. 1761 d. Tenn. 1838   Magistrate & Senator
m. Elizabeth Bird   Tenn. Leg. 1815
daughter Mary m. John Hunter

Brown, Jacob Roberts b. Va. 1742 d. S.C. 1805   Judge Newberry Co. S.C.
m. Christine Nealy   Memb. S.C. Leg.
daughter Caroline M. m. Dr. Anthony F. Golding

Brown, Jacob Stymets b. N.Y. 1786 d. N.Y.C. 1841   Lieut. N.Y. Mil.
m. Eunice Thompson — son Jacob S. m. Mary Cornelia Davis

Brown, James b. N.C. 1796 d. Tex. 1863   Pvt. Tenn. Mil.
m. 3rd Mary McDaniel
daughter Mary Louise m. James Rives — REAL DAUGHTER

Brown, James III b. Mass. 1750 d. Ohio 1816   Capt. Ohio Mil.
m. Isabel Oliver — son Hiram James Luke m. Rosanna Perry

Brown, James S. b. Va. 1796 d. Mo. 1855 m. Mary Varner   Pvt. Va. Mil.
daughter Elizabeth m. Francis K. Tucker

Brown, James Scott   Vol. 17   Sgt. Va. Mil.

Brown, Jeremiah b. Mass. 1780 d. N.Y. 1863   Capt. N.Y. Mil.
m. Abigail Davis — daughter Diantha C. m. John Eglinton Maxwell

Brown, Jesse b. Mass. 1775 d. Mass. 1832   Musician Mass. Mil.
    m. Dolly Faulkner — daughter Clarissa m. John Carter

Brown, John   no data   Constable, Sudbury, Mass.

Brown, John   Vol. 16   Pvt. N.H. Mil.

Brown, John b. S.C. 1795 d. Ill. 1871   Pvt. Ohio Mil.
    m. Elizabeth Porter — son Alexander P. m. Nancy Travis

Brown, John b. Pa. 1742 d. Pa. 1826   Pvt. Lancaster Co. Pa. Mil. 1795
    m. Catherine —
    son Martin m. Maria Diffendorffer

Brown, John b. N.C. 1779 d. Tenn. 1846   Col. & Brig. Gen. E. Tenn. Mil.
    m. Nancy Clark Cox
    daughter Eliza Jane m. William Porter Martin—REAL DAUGHTER
    daughter Rachel m. John H. Greer — John Coleman
    son Robert A. m. Mary Jane Roddye — this son thru wife
       Mary Moore Allison

Brown, John b. Vt. 1793 d. N.Y. 1878 m. Michal Sykes   Pvt. Vt. Mil.
    daughter Julia m. David W. Hawley

Brown, John b. Va. 1788 d. Mo. 1861   Pvt. Bath Co. Va. Mil.
    m. Mrs. Julia Brown Carthrae
    daughter Kate m. H. A. Baldwin — REAL DAUGHTER

Brown, John Doggett b. Va. 1789 d. Va. 1867   Ensign Va. Mil.
    m. Catherine Semple — daughter Sarah m. William Keating

Brown, John M. b. N.Y. 1746 d. N.Y. 1839   Judge Schoharie Co. N.Y. 1795
    m. Gitty Hager — daughter Elizabeth m. John Taft

Brown, John Riggs b. Md. 1775 d. Md. 1814   2nd Lieut. Md. Mil.
    m. Sarah Griffith Gassaway
    son Samuel m. Elizabeth Jenkins

Brown, John Wesley b. Va. 1788 d. Tenn. 1849   Pvt. E. Tenn. Mil.
    m. Margaret Kencheloe—son George K. m. Mary Mahoney

Brown, Jonas   Vol. 14   Lieut. Marines on Saratoga

Brown, Jonathan b. Conn. 1753 d. N.Y. 1836   Repr. Albany Co., N.Y. Leg.
    m. Lucy Douglas   1791/1801
    daughter Olive m. Thomas Rattoone

Brown, Joseph b. Tenn. 1780/90 d. Mo. 1848   Pvt. Tenn. Mil.
    m. Mary Leland Webster — son Joseph m. Louisa Collins

Brown, Joseph b. N.C. 1772 d. Tenn. 1868   Capt. Tenn. Mil.
    m. Sarah Thomas — son David F. m. Jane Frances Polk McNeal

Brown, Joshua b. Mass. (Me.) 1787 d. Canada 1860/5   Pvt. Mass. Mil.
    m. Marcia Boughner — daughter Mary Jane m. Joshua Harvey
    daughter Sarah Anne m. Asa Jarvis Foote

Brown, Joshua b. Ohio 1788 d. Ohio 1883 m. Actious Hall   Pvt. Ohio Mil.
    daughter Charlotte m. Peter Lockwood

Brown, Joshua b. Tenn. 1792 d. Tenn. 1841   Pvt. Tenn. Mil.
    m. Frances Blakely — son James L. m. Martha Jane Hall

Brown, Josiah b. Mass. 1744 d. Mass. 1826   Lieut. Mass. Mil. 1781/7
    m. Ann How — son Jesse m. Dolly Faulkner

Brown, Lewis Smith b. Va. 1795 d. Mo. 1856   Corp. Va. Mil.
    m. 3rd Ann M. Tolle
    daughter Lucy Maria unm. — REAL DAUGHTER

Brown, Luke b. Mass. 1795 d. Me. 1890   Pvt. Mass. Mil.
m. Polly Gilman — son George O. m. Caroline H. Fox

Brown, Mackey b. Ga. 1797 d. Ga. 1874 m. Sally Rice   Pvt. Tenn. Mil.
daughter Edna Eliza m. Berryman Hicks Turner

Brown, Marvin b. Conn. 1795 d. N.Y. 1886   Pvt. U.S. Inf.
m. Sally Wright
daughter Didama m. Allen James M. Stevenson

Brown, Micah b. Conn. 1776 d. Vt. 1863   Capt. Vt. Mil.
m. Phoebe Merriam — son Cyril James m. Ann Deborah Day

Brown, Moses b. Mass. 1742 d. at sea 1804   Commander U.S. Navy
m. Sarah Coffin — son William m. Katherine Jones

Brown, Nathaniel b. Mass. 1771 d. Mass. 1849   Selectman Waltham Mass.
m. Sarah Stearns   1812/13
daughter Anna m. Jesse Edson Farnsworth

Brown, Nathaniel b. Vt. 1784 d. Ill. 1843   Ensign Vt. Mil.
m. Dolly Benedict — son Samuel H. m. Fidelia Munsell

Brown, Noah   Vol. 16.   Ship Builder N.Y.

Brown, Park b. Conn. 1759 d. Conn. 1840   Memb. Conn. Leg. 1812
m. Mary Curtis
daughter Sarah Maria m. Samuel Hinman Brown

Brown, Peter b. Va. 1782 d. Va. 1818 m. Sarah Franklin   Pvt. Va. Mil.
daughter Donna Elvira m. John Roland Smith

Brown, Robert b. 1786 d. 1858 prob. Conn.   Pvt. Conn. 30th Reg.
m. Ann Maria Noyes—daughter Emma Louise m. George Clark Wells

Brown, Robert Tarver   Vol. 12   Capt. Mo. Terr. Mil.

Brown, Solomon b. N.C. 1794 d. Mo. 1834   Pvt. Surry Co. N.C. Mil.
m. Lydia Adams — daughter Rachel m. David Nelson Terry

Brown, Tarlton b. S.C. 1757 d. S.C. 1845   Col. S.C. Mil.
m. Amelia Matthews — daughter Almedia m. Preston Harley

Brown, Theron b. N.Y. 1793 d. N.Y. 1859   Pvt. Buffalo Co. N.Y. Mil.
m. 1st Clarissa Harmon
son Volney P. m. Sarah Rebecca Avery
m. 2nd Ann Marie Hammond
son Charles m. Martha Elizabeth Hubbard

Brown, Thomas b. Tenn. — d. Tenn. 1849   Capt. Tenn. Mil Hawkins Co.
m. Sarah Sizemore — son Iredell C. m. Mary Willis

Brown, William b. Md. 1796 d. Md. 1838   2nd Lieut. Md. Mil.
m. Anne Waters Perry
daughter Susannah Delilah m. Edward Augustus Cockney

Brown, William   Vol. 7   Surgeon's Mate Mich. Mil.

Brown, William b. N.Y. 1794 d. N.Y. 1873   Pvt. N.Y. Mil.
m. Angeline Campbell
daughter Lydia A. m. Evan Griffith — REAL DAUGHTER

Brown, William b. Va. 1759 d. Va. 1838   Col. Va. Mil.
m. Elizabeth Beverly — son John B. m. Mary Ransay

Brown, William b. N.J. 1794 d. N.J. 1861   Pvt. 3d Regt. N.J. Mil. 1814
m. Jemima Newbury — daughter Sarah m. James L. Brand

Browne, Samuel J. b. Eng. 1788 d. Ohio 1872   Bearer of dispatches
m. Esther Attee — son George S. J. m. Emma Carpenter

Brownell, Benjamin Jr. b. Mass. 1760 d. Mass. 1830   Pvt. Mass. Mil.
m. Abigail Milk — son Jireh m. Sarah Kirby

Brownfield, John b. Va. 1792 d. Mo. 1851   Pvt. Augusta Co. Va. Mil.
m. 1st. Susannah Fauber — son Thomas m. Elizabeth Grove
m. 2nd Catherine Shover
son Abraham m. Surilda Margaret Gourley

Browning, Charles b. 1777 d. 1843 prob. Va.   Pvt. 35th Va. Mil. Reg.
m. Miss Roadcap — son John Wesley m. Matilda Wagner

Browning, James b. Va. 1745 d. Ky. 1812   Ensign 17th Ky. Reg.
m. Susannah Hickman — daughter Mary m. Taliferro Browning

Browning, Jeffrey Hazard b. R.I. 1762 d. R.I. 1820   Ensign R.I. Mil.
m. Martha Potter — son John W. m. Bathsheba Knowles

Browning, William Winston b. Va. 1794 d. Va. —   Pvt. Va. Mil.
m. Sarah Farrow
daughter Sarah Louise m. Dr. William James Knox

Brownlaw, Joseph A. b. Va. c. 1790 d. Tenn. 1816   3rd Lieut. Tenn. Mil.
m. Catherine Ganaway — daughter Nancy m. John S. Martin

Brownley, Robert b. Va. — d. Va. —   2nd Sgt. Va. Mil.
m. Elizabeth Williams — son William m. Bolina Thursa Moss

Brownson, Hector b. Conn. 1789 d. N.Y. 1875   Sgt.-Maj. U. S. Inf.
m. Lucy Gallup
daughter Mary E. m. William R. C. Clark — REAL DAUGHTER

Broyles, Cain b. S.C. 1788 d. Tenn. 1864   Major Ga. Mil.
m. Lucinda Nash — son Aaron R. m. Martha Helen Brown

Broyles, Cornelius b. — 1790 d. Tenn. 1862   Pvt. East Tenn. Mil.
m. Mary Farley — son O. G. m. Susan W. —

Brubaker, John b. Pa. 1779 d. Pa. 1852   Lieut. Berlin Pa. Rifle Mil.
m. Sarah Faust — daughter Henrietta m. Allen B. Rose

Bruen, Daniel Benjamin b. N.J. 1769   Matross Essex Co. N.J. Mil.
d. N.J. 1849 m. Aureantia Harris
son Isaac H. m. Mary Ann Pierson

Brundage, Moses b. Pa. — d. Pa. 1872 m. —   Pvt. U.S. Art.
son Chester B. m. Marie Josephine Mitchell

Bruner, Elias b. Md. 1756 d. Md. 1826   Pvt. Md. Mil.
m. Mary Elizabeth Zimmerman
son Daniel m. Mary Kemp

Brunk, Joseph b. Md. 1777 d. Ohio 1858 m. Polly South   Pvt. Ohio Mil.
son Joseph m. Mary Jane Dunton

Brunner, Casper, b. Pa. 1776 d. Pa. 1832   Pvt. Lancaster Co. Pa. Mil.
m. Ann Marie Schaffner — son Peter m. Sarah Gibbs

Brunson, Alfred b. Conn. 1793 d. Wisc. 1882   Quar. Sgt. U.S. Inf.
m. Caroline S. Birge
daughter Ella Caroline unm. — REAL DAUGHTER
daughter Elizabeth m. Eugene L. Hitchock — REAL DAUGHTER

Brusstar, Samuel Sr. b. N.J. 1738 d. Pa. 1824   Ensign Pa. Mil.
m. Rebecca Tabor — son Samuel m. Catharine Sutter

Brusstar, Samuel Jr. b. N.J. 1765 d. Pa. 1798   in Whiskey Reb. 1794
   m. Catharine Sutter — son Peter m. Sarah Hinchman Baspham

Bruton, Simon b. N.C. — d. N.C. 1823 m. Tierce —   Lt. Col. N.C. Mil.
   daughter Eleanor m. Robert G. Pridgeon

Brutzman, Abel b. Pa. 1790 d. Pa. 1848 m. Elizabeth Shaffer Pvt. Pa. Mil.
   son John A. m. Elizabeth Sigman

Bryan, Edward b. N.C. 1764 d. Ga. 1825   Memb. N.C. Assembly
   m. Penelope Blackshear — son Elijah m. Elizabeth —   1789

Bryan, Frederick b. Va. 1796 d. Ohio 1856   Capt. Williamburg
   m. Martha Wills Lee — daughter Mary Elizabeth   Va. Mil.
   m. William Gilliam

Bryan, James Cambell b. N.C. 1776 d. N.C. 1832   Pvt. Ga. Mil. Memb.
   m. Anne Averette —   House of Commons N.C. 1807/13
   son James A. m. Catharine Holloway

Bryan, John Thomas b. N.C. 1770 d. N.C. 1845   Memb. Hse. Commons
   m. Rachel Whitfield — daughter Nancy   Jones Co. N.C. 1800
   m. Henry Roberts

Bryan, Kedar b. N.C. 1748 d. N.C. 1807   Memb. Hse. Commons N.C.
   m. Mary Whitfield   1797/8
   daughter Rachel m. Gibson Sloan

Bryan, Lewis b. N.C. 1782 d. N.C. 1850 m. Mary Dudley   Pvt. N.C. Mil.
   daughter Ann Maria m. William Woodbridge Stiles
   son John Lewis m. Mary Ann Fitchett
   son Lewis A. m. Belle Hilliard

Bryan, Luke b. Ky. 1784 d. Ind. 1857   3d Sgt. Ky. Mil.
   m. Mary Saunders — son John S. m. Harriett Hartman

Bryan, Nathan b. N.C. 1748/50 d. Pa. 1798   Congressman N.C. 1795/8
   m. Winifred —
   daughter Winifred m. Bryan Whitfield
   son John Thomas m. Rachel Whitfield

Bryan, Needham b. N.C. 1725 d. N.C. 1800   Memb. Prov. Cong. 1794
   m. Nancy Smith — daughter Winifred m. Nathan Needham

Bryan, Peter b. Va. 1755 d. Tenn. 1810   Indian Fighter and
   m. Betty Hubbard   Memb. Tenn. Conv. 1796
   son Thomas m. Nancy Cate

Bryan, Thomas b. Ga. 1793 d. Ga. 1878   Pvt. Ga. Mil.
   m. Mary Dooley
   son James T. m. Elizabeth H. Blackwell
   son William M. m. Jane E. Mabry

Bryan, William b. N.C. 1780 d. N.C. 1819   Pvt. Pitt Co. N.C. Mil.
   m. Mary Manning
   son Littleberry m. Ann Moring Teel

Bryant, Amos b. 1789 ? d. ? m. Polly Woodward   Pvt. 1st Me. Brig.
   son Moses W. m. Elvecy Andrews

Bryant, David b. Vt. 1791 d. Pa. 1875   Pvt. Pa. Troops
   m. Abigail Hillard
   son Elias Mather m. Lydia Maria Wheaton

Bryant, Joseph b. S.C. 1795 d. Ark. 1873   Pvt. Tenn. Mil.
   m. Margaret Hart — daughter Elizabeth m. Jeremiah Shannon

Bryant, Joseph b. Va. 1788 d. Ohio 1831 m. Nancy Carter   Pvt. Va. Mil.
daughter Nancy m. Philip Wait

Bryant, Reuben b. Mass. 1769 d. Mass. 1846   Pvt. Mass. Mil.
m. Julia Danforth
son George Fay B. m. Jane Miller Baker

Bryant, Walter b. N.H. 1710 d. N.H. 1807   Surveyor, Town
m. Elizabeth Folsom   Moderator 1789
daughter Elizabeth m. Edward Hall Burgin

Bryant, Zebulon b. Mass. 1782 d. Me. 1881   Pvt. Mass. Mil.
m. Desire Richmond — daughter Zilpha m. William Pratt Jr.

Buchanan, John b. Pa. 1759 d. Tenn. 1832   Sgt. Major Tenn. Mil.
m. Sarah Ridley — daughter Elizabeth m. Thomas Hardeman Everett

Buchanan, John b. Va. 1772 d. Tenn. 1820   Pvt. Tenn. Mil.
m. Margaret Edmondson — son Joseph m. Martha Edmiston

Buchanan, Robert b. N.J. 1780 d. Ky. 1872   Pvt. Va. Mil.
m. Sarah T. Watkins — daughter Emeline m. Mortimer Givens

Buchanan, Samuel b. N.C. 1780 d. S.C. 1860   Sgt. S.C. Mil.
m. Mary Morrow — daughter Jane Emeline m. Conrad Wakefield

Buchanan, Samuel b. Pa. 1791 d. Mich. 1854   Sgt. N.Y. Mil.
m. Elizabeth Steward — son John Claudius m. Sophia Bingham

Buchanan, Thomas b. Ky. 1794 d. Ill. 1876   Pvt. Ky. Mil.
m. Elizabeth Anderson — son William T. m. Talitha Crane

Buchanan, Thomas b. N.Y. 1791 d. Conn. 1867 m.   Sgt. N.Y. Art. Mil.
son Millford D. m. Mary S. Wheeler

Bucher, John Jacob   Vol. 5   Pvt. Pa. Mil.

Buck, Benjamin b. Md. 1779 d. Md. 1848   Lieut. Md. Art.
m. Catharine Reese — son John M. m. Eleanor E. Coe
daughter Josephine M. m. David C. Landis
daughter Margaret Ann m. Robert B. Porter

Buck, Benjamin b. Md. 1795 d. Md. 1841   Cornet Baltimore Cav. Md. Mil.
m. Jane Herbert — son Hezekiah B. m. Emily C. Hoover

Buck, Horace b. Mass. 1791 d. N.Y. 1863   Fifer, N.Y. Mil.
m. Betsey Burgess — daughter Marietta m. Nathan Smith Joslin

Buck, Isaiah b. Va. 1797 d. W.Va. 1892   Corp. Ohio Mil.
m. Catharine Waugh — son James H. m. Sarah B. Frost
by wife Mary Catherine Culp
daughter Elizabeth Mary m. Spriggs REAL DAUGHTER

Buck, Jasper b. N.C. 1792 d. Ill. 1841 m. Sophia Corbett   Pvt. N.C. Mil.
son John H. m. Cynthia Ann Wagle

Buck, Lemuel b. Vt. 1791 d. N.Y. 1858 m. Masa Parsons   Pvt. Vt. Mil.
son Harmon A. m. Julia Webber

Buck, Thomas b. Va. 1756 d. Va. 1842   Pvt. Va. Cav. Mil.
m. Anne Richardson — daughter Letitia A. m. John M. Blakeman

Buck, Zebediah b. Mass. 1770 d. Me. 1846   Pvt. Mass. (Me.) Mil.
m. Sarah Marshall — daughter Emily m. Samuel Brackett Furber

Buckey, John b. Md. d. Md. 1829 m. Susan Hauser   Pvt. Md. Mil.
daughter Mary m. William Hoover Wentzell

Buckey, Peter b. Md. 1770 d. W.Va. aft. 1800   Constable 1800 Randolph
m. Christina Marteney — son George m. Elizabeth Hart   Co. Va.
daughter Mary m. Archibald Earle

Buckingham, John   Vol. 10   Pvt. Conn. Mil.

Buckingham, Jonas b. 1769 d. N.Y. 1815   Pvt. N.Y. Mil.
m. Deborah Homan — son John m. Abigail Howell

Buckles, Henry b. Va. m.—   Vol. 25   Corp. Ohio Mil.
son Joseph m. Elizabeth Arnel

Buckley, John b. Va. 1783 d. Kansas 1875 m.   Pvt. Ky. Vols.
son Jacob C. m. Mary E. Seeders

Buckley, Joshua Jr.   Vol. 16   Major Ky. Mtd. Vols.

Bucklin, David b. R.I. 1777 d. Ind. 1845   Pvt. R.I. State Troops
m. Amy Miller — daughter Cornelia m. John Gilbert

Buckminster, Lawson   Vol. 3   Lieut. R.I. Mil.

Buckner, Aylett b. Va. 1745 d. Ky. aft. 1815   Sgt. U.S. Riflemen
m. Judith Presley Thornton — daughter Kate T.
m. John Young Taylor

Buckner, Ezra b. Tenn. 1797 d. Tenn. 1861   Pvt. Tenn. Vol. Mil.
m. Elizabeth Duncan — daughter Emily Ann
m. John Anderson Smith

Buckwalter, John b. prob. Pa. 1735 d. Pa. 1808 Pvt. Lancaster Co. Pa. Mil.
m. Catherine — son Henry m. Madalena Kauffman

Budd, Gilbert b. N.Y. 1758 d. N.Y. 1825   Lt. Col. N.Y. Mil.
m. Frances Jerow — daughter Mary m. Angevine Thorne

Budd, William b. N.J. 1773 d. Pa. 1849   Pvt. Mercer Co. Pa. Mil.
m. Druscilla Hulse — son Joseph L. m. Teressa Rankin

Buell, Truman b. Conn. 1786 d. Conn. 1867   Sgt. Conn. Mil.
m. Nancy Hinman — son Albert m. Nancy Noyes

Buffam, Jedediah b. R.I. 1737 d. N.H. 1808   Treasurer Richmond N.H.
son George m. Deliverance Winslow

Buffington, Joseph b. Pa. 1737 d. S.C. 1798   Coroner S.C. 1785
m. Mary Aston Few — daughter Mary m. Thomas Gordon

Buford, James b. Va. 1746 d. Tenn. aft. 1820   Justice Peace Tenn. 1800
m. Priscilla Ragsdale — son James m. Mary Giddens

Buford, Paschal b. Va. 1791 d. Va. 1875   Pvt. Va. Mil.
m. Frances Ann Otey — son James H. m. Lucy Elvira Hanson

Buford, William b. S.C. c 1760 d. Ala. 1817 Lt. Col. Miss. Terr. Mil. 1811
m. Martha — daughter Mary m. Jesse A. Cooper

Bugbee, Nehemiah b. Mass. 1777 d. Mass. 1848   Pvt. Mass. Arty.
m. Hannah Bardwell — daughter Catherine m. Obed Newton

Bugbee, William II b. Mass. 1770 d. Mass. 1843   Pvt. Mass. Mil.
m. Rebecca Champney — son John B. m. Hannah

Bulkeley, Joseph b. Conn. 1742 d. Conn. 1821 Repr. Conn. Assy. 1787/1814
m. Mary Williams — son Henry m. Martha Tucker
daughter Mary m. Joseph Butler

Bull, Daniel b. N.Y. 1762 d. N.Y. 1849   Pvt. Montgomery Co. N.Y. Mil.
m. Catharine Miller — daughter Hannah m. Alexander Thompson

Bull, Elijah b. Pa. 1769 d. Pa. 1847   Pvt. Pa. Det. Inf.
m. Margaret Steel — daughter Sarah m. Charles Rettew

Bull, James b. Conn. 1772 d. 1831 m. Margaret Pond   Pvt. Va. Mil.
    son Jabez B. m. Mary Ford

Bull, Walter   Vol. 5   Pvt. Ohio Mil.

Bull, William b. Conn. 1781 d. N.Y. 1868   Pvt. N.Y. Mil.
    m. Mary Foster — daughter Laura m. William Warren
    daughter Sarah m. William P. Warren

Bull, William b. Va. 1779 d. Ill. 1852   Pvt. Va. Inf. Mil.
    m. Esther Fowler Goodwin — daughter Eleanor C.
    m. William M. Arnold
    son Milton m. Nancy Newlon

Bullard, Benjamin   Vol. 9   Surgeon N.Y. Mil.

Bullard, James b. Eng. 1750 d. N.C. 1832   Justice of Peace 1810
    m. Sarah Pittman — son Robert   Randolph Co. N.C.
    m. Katherine McLean

Bullis, John b. Vt. 1783 d. N.Y. 1861 m. Sally Parish   Pvt. N.Y. Mil.
    son Levi m. Abbie R. Dibble

Bullock, William b. Ire. 1792 d. Ind. 1871   Pvt. Pa. Mil.
    m. Margaret Smith — son William m. Matilda Hamilton

Bullock, William T. b. Md. 1760 d. Ind. 1844 Patriot—manned fort during
    m. Sarah Ord — daughter Catherine m. John Brenton   War 1812

Bunbury, William b. Va. 1789 d. Va. 1848   Pvt. Va. Mil.
    m. Katherine Chesley — daughter Sarah Louisa
    m. Phillip S. Lanham

Bunce, William Sheafe b. N.Y. 1795 d. N.Y. 1859   Pvt. N.Y. Mil.
    m. Mary Freeman — son William C. m. Mary Carpenter

Bundy, Nathan b.— d. 1832 m. Adah Melinda Nicholson   Pvt. Tenn. Mil.
    son H. S. m. Caroline Paine

Bunker, Alexander b. N.Y. 1782 d. N.Y. 1813   Pvt. N.Y. Mil.
    m. Elizabeth Lake — son Marvel G. m. Susan Ann Reeves

Bunker, William Mitchell b. Mass. 1797 d. Ky. 1870   Corp. Ky. Mil.
    m. Lydia Coleman — son Jethro m. Julia Ann Sabine

Bunnel, Isaac b. Conn. 1738 d. Pa. aft. 1812   Patriot—furn. supplies Pa.
    m. Eleanor Barcalow — daughter Mary   Mil. 1812
    m. William Bensley

Bunner, Joseph Jr. b. Va. 1798 d. W.Va. 1844   Pvt. Va. Mil.
    m. Christina Hamilton — son Archibald H. m. Eliza Jane Davidson

Buntin, John b. Ky. 1775 d. Ind. 1857   Pvt. Ind. Terr. Mil.
    m. Elizabeth Hawkins — son James m. Hulda Bowen

Bunting, John b. Md. 1782 d. Md. 1847   Pvt. 51st Md. Regt.
    m. Mary Somerville — son Rev. James m. Eleanore Shenwell

Burbank, Nahum b. Mass. 1781 d. N.Y. 1864 m. Eunice Cates Pvt. Vt. Mil.
    daughter Rosamond m. Eleazer Robbins

Burbank, Stephen b. 1799 d. Vt. 1882   Pvt. Mass. Mil.
    m. Mehitabel Rowell — daughter Delia Ann m. William N. Stevens

Burch, Asa b. N.Y. 1775 d. N.Y. 1854 m. Abigail Rose   Capt. N.Y. Mil.
    son Varnum m. Amanda Chapin

Burch, Benjamin b. Va. 1765 d. Ill. 1831 m. Ann Williams   Pvt. Ky. Mil.
    daughter Ella Ann m. William Wright
    daughter Jane D. m. Thomas Wright
    son Walter m. Ann Chastain

Burch, Hiram b. Conn. 1796 d. Ohio   Pvt. & River Pilot
  m. Nancy Whiting — daughter Mary W. m. Rufus Putnam Ijams

Burch, John b. Ga. 1770 d. Tenn. 1829   Pvt. Ky. Mil.
  m. Elizabeth Hampton — daughter Sarah m. William Jack

Burch, Wyatt b. N.Y. 1792 d. N.Y. 1864   Pvt. N.Y. Mil.
  m. Lucinda Brooks — daughter Sabrina Mardula
  m. William Jones Avery

Burckhartt, Christopher Frederick b. Md. 1756 d. Mo. 1827
  m. Elizabeth Hobbs   Fort Builder Frontier Defense Mo. 1811/12
  son George F. m. Ruth Dorsey

Burdett, Humphrey H. b. S.C. 1780 d. Ala. aft. 1858   Pvt. S.C. Mil. 1815
  m. Isobella — daughter Sarah Ann m. John Duke Taylor

Burdick, Benjamin b. Conn. 1776 d. Conn. 1855 m. Meribah Sgt. Conn. Mil.
  son Benjamin F. m. Mrs. Rosina Mitchell Sprague

Burdick, Maxson b. R.I. 1794 d. Vt. 1875   Pvt. Vt. Mil.
  m. Rebecca O'Brien — son Oscar F. m. Sarah Luce Frisbie

Burdick, Samuel b. R.I. 1788 d. R.I. 1854   Lieut. R.I. Mil.
  m. Sarah Sheffield — son Anderson m. Martha Howard

Burford, David b. N.C. 1791 d. Tenn. 1864 Lieut., Brigade Major U.S. Inf.
  m. Elizabeth Watkins Alexander — son Robert A. m. Mary E. Lowe

Burford, John b. N.C. 1758 d. Ala. 1835   Patriot Ala.
  m. "Granny" Kitchen — son John Jr. m. Emily H. Johnson Garrison
  daughter Mary Nancy m. George Starnes

Burford, John Jr. b. 1787 d. Ala. 1852   Pvt. Tenn. Vol. Mil.
  m. 2d Mrs. Emily Hopson Johnson Garrison — daughter Florence M.
  m. William Ellis Murphy

Burger, Michael b. Pa. 1763 d. Mo. 1869   Corp. East Tenn. Mil.
  m. Margaret Parrott — son Abraham m. Sarah Lawson

Burger, Samuel b. Pa. 1790 d. Ohio 1862 m. Mary Levan   Pvt. Va. Mil.
  daughter Catherine m. Joseph Rinehart REAL DAUGHTER
  son Tobias m. Lydia Deitz

Burgess, Gideon b. R.I. 1774 d. N.Y. 1856   Ensign R.I. Mil.
  m. Sallie French — son William m. Lois Bemis Harding

Burgess, Michael b. Md. 1754 d. Md. m. Sarah Warfield   Capt. Md. Mil.
  son Thomas m. Honor Dorsey

Burgess, William B. b. La. 1784 d. La. 1864   Pvt. La. Mil.
  m. Elizabeth Richardson — son Louis A. m. Caroline Maes

Burgin, Edward Hall b. N.H. 1741 d. N.H. 1813   Justice Peace 1794
  m. Elizabeth Bryant — daughter Nancy Y.   Allentown, N.H.
  m. John Sargent Sr.

Burk, John b. Pa. 1794 d. Pa. 1873   Pvt. Chester Co. Pa. Mil.
  m. Ann Hampton — daughter Hannah m. John Quidland

Burk, Thomas b. Va. 1795 d. Ind. 1852 m. Sarah Givens   Pvt. Va. Mil.
  daughter Martha Jane m. Thomas Woods

Burk, William M. b. Pa. 1771 d. Ill. 1856   Capt. Scioto Co. Ohio Mil.
  m. Elizabeth McCormick — son Oliver H. P. m. Elizabeth Thompson

Burke, Ora M. b. Vt. 1795 d. Vt. 1855/6   Drummer U.S. Infantry
  m. Mary Ann Howard — daughter Ann Mahala
  m. Jonathan G. Eddy REAL DAUGHTER

Burkhalter, Peter Sr. b. Swit. 1731 d. Pa. 1805 Repr. Pa. Assembly 1784/8
   m. Eva C. Deshler — daughter Catherine m. George Seitz
   daughter Magdalena m. Stephen Balliet

Burkhalter, Peter Jr. b. Pa. 1769 d. Pa. 1825 Capt. Northampton Co. Pa.
   m. Elizabeth — son Jacob m. Elizabeth Reed   Mil.

Burkhart, John b. Md. 1787 d. Oreg. 1856   Pvt. Tenn. Vol. Mil.
   m. Rebecca Baltzell — son Oriolanus m. Lavena Goff

Burkitt, Thomas b. N.Y. 1763 d. Ohio 1836   Seaman U.S. Navy
   m. Polly Wheller — daughter Rebecca m. Thomas Newton Moore

Burks, James Lyon   Vol. 10   Orderly Sgt. Tenn. Mil.

Burks, Rowland P. b. Va. 1792 d. Mo. 1875   Corp. Va. Mil.
   m. Sarah Ann Ware — daughter Emma Louise m. Andrew J. Marsh
   REAL DAUGHTER

Burleson, Isaac b. 1795 d. Tenn. 1865 m. Julian Barner   Pvt. Tenn. Mil.
   daughter Kate Augusta m. Edwin Wells Talley REAL DAUGHTER

Burleson, James Sr. b. N.C. 1775 d. Texas 1836   Capt. Tenn. Mil.
   m. Elizabeth Shipman — son James Jr. m. Ann Elizabeth Earpe
   daughter Sarah m. Robert T. Thrasher

Burleson, John b. N.Y. 1797 d. N.Y. m. Sarah Bugbey   Pvt. N.Y. Mil.
   son John H. m. Anna McIntyre

Burley, Jacob b. Pa. 1771 d. Pa. 1854   Sheriff Green Co. Pa. 1802/5
   m. Mary Hughes — daughter Cassandra m. Reason Howard
   daughter Sarah m. William J. Howard

Burley, Josiah b. N.H. 1763 d. N.H. c 1819 m.   Pvt. N.H. Mil.
   son Winthrop M. m. Sarah Bean Giles

Burley, Winthrop b. N.H. 1795 d. N.H. 1860   Pvt. N.H. Mil.
   m. Sarah Bean Giles — daughter Ellen m. Satchel C. Dore

Burlingham, Nathan   Vol. 5   Capt. Mass. Mil.

Burlinghame, Richardson b. Vt. 1771 d. N.Y. 1840 Ensign Tioga Co. N.Y.
   m. Lydia Fitch — son Victor Monroe m. Lydia Thayer   Mil.

Burnam, Andrews b. Mass. 1786 d. Wisc. 1872   Pvt. N.Y. Mil.
   m. Phebe Roberts — daughter Huldah E. m. Martin Grider

Burnam, Hickerson b. Tenn. 1791 d. Texas aft. 1856 Pvt. 2nd Tenn. Vol.
   m. Sarah Kern — daughter Ann Zora   Regt.
   m. David William Crews

Burnell, Joseph b. Mass. 1725 d. Mass. 1807 Capt. Shay's Rebellion Mass.
   m. Hannah Tucker — son John m. Mary Bannister

Burnet, Isaac Gouverneur b. N.J. 1784 d. Ohio 1856   Civil Officer Ohio
   m. Keturah Winn Gordon — daughter Gertrude   1808/12
   m. Rev. Charles Pierson Jennings

Burnet, William b. Pa. 1776 d. W.Va. 1815   Drummer Pa. Mil.
   m. Mary Douglass — daughter Hannah T. m. Sylvanus G. Moler

Burnett, Stephen Grover b. N.J. 1794 d. Ind. 1862   Pvt. U.S. Arty.
   m. Hannah Creel — daughter Rosetta m. Robert Briggs

Burney, Arthur b. Ga. 1773 d. Fla. 1842   Tax Receiver Ga. 1807
   m. Sarah C. Blount — son Greene m. Sarah Ball

Burney, William b. N.C. 1760 d. N.C. aft. 1806 Road Overseer N.C. 1789
   m. Mary Mebane — daughter m. David Thomas

Burnham, Benjamin b. Mass. (Me.) 1782 d. Me. 1878 Sgt. Mass. (Me.)
   m. Naomi Royal — son George W. m. Olivia Jellerson Libby Mil.

Burnham, Charles Chester b. Conn. 1789 d. Pa. 1873   Pvt. Va. & Pa. Mils.
m. Sophia Kreitzer — daughter Loretta m. Leo Standwood
REAL DAUGHTER
m. Susannah Starne — daughter Sarah m. James H. Walker

Burnham, James b. Vt. 1782 d. Vt. 1815 m. Jemima Grow   Pvt. Vt. Mil.
daughter Harriet m. Luban Putnam

Burnham, James b. Vt. 1790 d. Ill. 1843   Pvt. Vt. Mil.
m. Fannie Hibbard — son Luther m. Charlotte Joslyn

Burnham, Jesse b. Ky. 1792 d. Texas 1883   Pvt. Tenn. Mtd. Mil.
m. Temperance Baker — daughter Amanda
m. 2d John Thompson Holman

Burnham, Jonas b. Mass. (Me.) 1796/7 d. Me. 1889   Midshipman U.S.
m. Mrs. Mary L. Wells Hart — daughter Marie S.   Frigate
m. David Holqin REAL DAUGHTER

Burnham, Joshua P. b. Vt. 1788 d. Vt. 1831   3d Lieut. U.S. Inf.
m. Roxana Martin — son Daniel M. m. Rosina A. Ramsdell

Burnley, Henry b. Va. 1756 d. Ga. 1835   Justice Peace Warren Co. Ga.
m. Lucy Barksdale Davenport — daughter Hannah   1794/6
m. James Crowder

Burns, Benjamin b. N. C. 1780 d. Ala. bef. 1860 Pvt. N.C. Mil. Rutherford
m. Susannah Smith — daughter Harriet S.   Co.
m. Nathaniel Hughes Dobbins

Burns, John b. N.H. 1755 d. N.Y. 1852   Pvt. Mass. Mil.
m. Sarah Smith McMasters — son David m. Susanna Knight

Burns, William Howard b. Va. 1766 d. W.Va. 1811   Postmaster Md. 1802
m. Philadelphia Burbridge — son James m. Nancy Ingman

Burnside, James   Vol. 17   Pvt. Ky. Mil.

Burnside, Thomas   Vol. 11   Chairman War Comms. Pa.

Burr, Aaron b. Conn. 1784 d. Vt. 1864 m. Rebecca Cook   Capt. Vt. Mil.
daughter Mary P. m. John Preston Olds

Burr, Isaac Jr. b. Conn. 1790 d. Ill. 1871   Pvt. Jefferson Co. N.Y. Mil.
m. Lydia Fuller — son Hiram F. m. Mary Hower

Burrill, Joseph b. Mass. 1761/2 d. Mass. 1818   Pvt. Mass. Mil.
m. Sarah Belsher — daughter Nancy m. Joseph Belcher Jr.

Burris, George b. Va. 1790 d. Mo. 1872 m. Lydia Ewing   Pvt. Ohio Mil.
son George m. Elizabeth Henry

Burritt, Charles b. Conn. 1786 d. N.Y. 1866   Ensign N.Y. Mil.
m. Orpha Tucker — daughter Harriett m. David G. McClure

Burrough, Isaac b. N.J. 1784 d. N.J. 1823   Patriot, Haddon N.J.
m. Mary Evaul — son Thomas m. Elizabeth Steelman

Burroughs, Benjamin b. Vt. 1786 d. N.Y. 1865   Pvt. N.Y. Mil.
m. Eunice Morgan — son Benjamin m. Meranda Rose

Burroughs, John   Vol. 15   Pvt. Ohio Mil.
daughter Maragaret J. m. James R. Routh REAL DAUGHTER

Burroughs, John b. Del. 1787 d. Md. 1867   Pvt. Del. Mil.
m. Mary Robinson — daughter Mary Ann m. Alexander Jackson

Burroughs, John b. 1793 d. 1862 Served as Substitute in Capt. Short's Co.
m. Martha Chambers — daughter Lucinda   Ohio Mil.
m. Cornelius Murray

Burroughs, Peter b. Va. 1796 d. Tenn. 1840　　　　Pvt. Va. Mil.
　m. Elizabeth Atkinson — son Thomas F. m. Nancy Smallman

Burrows, Daniel Jr. b. Conn. 1794 d. Conn. 1851　　　Pvt. Conn. Mil.
　m. Mary Hempstead — son Rhodes m. Miranda Bennett

Burt, Daniel b. N.Y. 1776 d. Ohio 1846 m. Sally Foght　Pvt. N.Y. Mil.
　son Washington m. Georgianna Fisk

Burt, James　　Vol. 9　　　　　　　　　　　　　Pvt. N.Y. Arty.

Burt, John Jr. b. S.C. 1779 d. Miss. 1844　　　Pvt. Miss. Terr. Mil.
　m. Magdalin Turnipseed — son John A. m. Rebecca Kaigler

Burton, Isaac b. Del. 1782 d. Del. 1823 m. Hetty Lamb　2nd Sgt. Del. Mil.
　daughter Anna m. Thomas L. Waples

Burton, May Jr. b. Va. 1752 d. Va. 1829 m. Sarah Head　Sheriff 1811 Pa.
　daughter Lucy m. James Collins

Burton, Simon b. N.H. 1795 d. Mo. 1880　　　Pvt. U.S. Riflemen
　m. Abigail Clark Baldwin — daughter Mindwell
　m. Joseph A. Langworthy

Burton, Thomas　　Vol. 13　　　　　　　Pvt. East Tenn. Mil.

Burwell, Lewis b. Va. 1779 d. Va. 1847 m. Sallie Green　Pvt. Va. Mil.
　son Abram m. Elizabeth Peterson

Burwell, Nathan b. Conn. 1768 d. N.Y. 1852 Capt. Herkimer Co. N.Y. Mil.
　m. Nancy Smith — daughter Elizabeth m. Peter Newman Jr.

Burwell, Nicholas b. Va. 1794 d. Ohio 1879　　　Pvt. Va. Mil.
　m. Sallie Fenton — son Samuel m. Margaret

Bush, Abraham b. Va. 1780 d. Ohio 1851　　　　Pvt. Ohio Mil.
　m. Phoebe Peterson — son Abraham m. Catherine

Bush, Adam b. N.Y. 1790 d. N.Y. 1865 m. Mary Stansel 2nd Sgt. N.Y. Mil.
　daughter Eliza m. Isaac Thomas
　daughter Juliann m. James Thornton
　daughter Mary Jane m. Enos McLaughlin

Bush, Isaac b.— d. Miss. 1827 m. Hetty Bruce　　Pvt. Miss. Terr. Mil.
　m. Charlotte Castillo — son William m. Elizabeth Bryant
　m. 2d Mrs. Zilpha Bryant
　son David m. 2d Clarissa Ann Ashley

Bush, Isaac d. Miss. 1827 m. Hetty Bruce　　　Pvt. Miss. Terr. Mil.
　daughter Harriet E. m. Daniel Slack

Bush, John b. Pa. 1747 d. Pa. 1823 m. Catherine Leimbach　Capt. Pa. Mil.
　daughter Sarah m. Jacob Agee

Bush, John b. Pa. 1773 d. Pa. 1844 m. Esther McHose　Pvt. Pa. Mil.
　son John m. Elizabeth Lynn

Bush, John b. Va. 1767 d. Ky. 1847 m. Sally Craig　Pvt. Ohio-Va. Mil.
　son John C. m. Mary Wright Gaines

Bush, Jonathon b. Va. 1780 d. Ky. c 1857　　　Pvt. Ky. Vol. Mil.
　m. Mary Stevens Rawlings — son James S. m. Mary Jane Adams

Bush, Nelson b. Ky. 1789 d. Ky. 1874 m. Nancy Neil　Pvt. Ky. Mil.
　daughter Mary Jane m. William Webber

Bush, Philip b. Va. 1737 d. Ky. 1819 m. Frances Vivion　Capt. Ky. Mil.
　daughter Margaret m. Tandy Quisenberry

Bush, Pleasant b. Ky. 1791 d. Ky. 1853　　　　Ensign Ky. Mil.
　m. Jane Bush (maiden name) — daughter Emmerine
　m. Isaac Conkwright

Bush, Richard b. N.Y. 1782 d. N.Y. 1846 m. Charity Bedle Pvt. N.Y. Mil.
daughter Elizabeth m. William T. Anderson

Bush, Roland b. Mass. 1793 d. Wisc. 1886 Corp N.Y. Mil.
m. Harriet Phelps — son Alfred Henry m. Cordelia De Voe

Bush, Roswell b. Eng. 1796 d. N.Y. 1873 m. Pvt. N.H. Mil.
son Roswell m. Ann Canfield

Bush, Thomas b. N.C. 1793 d. Ill. 1881 Pvt. Tenn. Mil.
m. Sarah W. Swift — son Carrol J. m. Clarissa Massy

Bush, William b. S.C. 1786 d. Ga. 1839 m. Joicy King Pvt. Ga. Mil.
daughter Melissa m. Dr. William R. Wellborn
son William m. Harriet Jones

Bush, William b. Va. 1758 d. Ky. 1843 Pvt. Va. Mil.
m. Elizabeth Shearer Collester — son William m. Malinda Finch

Bush, William Martin b. N.C. c 1759 d. N.C. 1799 Sheriff Jones Co. N.C.
m. Penelope Lane — son Nathan B. m. Mary R. Harrison 1787/9

Bushong, George b. Va. 1793 d. Tenn. 1852 Pvt. East Tenn. Mil.
m. Sarah Pyle — son William m. 2d Elizabeth Peebler

Bushnell, Doud b. Conn. 1762 d. Vt. 1845 m. Lucy Joyce Pvt. Vt. Mil.
son Daniel m. 2d Mary Brown

Busick, James b. Md. d. Md. 1850 Ensign Md. Mil.
m. Elizabeth Webster — daughter Elizabeth m. Levin Richardson

Bussey, Henry Green b. Md. 1784 d. Md. 1820 Capt. Md. Mil.
m. Elizabeth S. Harris — son Bennett Francis m. Mary Anne Black

Bussey, Hezekiah b. Md. 1748 d. Ga. 1796 m. Amy Justice Peace Ga. 1790
son Benjamin m. Mary Burgamy

Butler, Bailey b. Va. 1779 d. Tenn. 1842 Capt. West Tenn. Mil.
m. Mary Stafford — daughter Mariann m. John Bayless Anderson

Butler, Benjamin II b. Pa. 1738 d. Pa. 1830 Corp. Bucks Co. Pa. Mil.
m. Sarah Davis — son Simon m. Charity Lomison

Butler, David b. Conn. 1760 d. Ohio 1815 m. Olive Henry Pvt. Conn. Mil.
son Charles m. Dorcas Pratt

Butler, David b. Vt. 1788 d. N.Y. 1863 m. Polly Kinsley Pvt. N.Y. Inf.
son Ormond m. Lamira Holmes

Butler, Ezekiel Vol. 11 Pvt. N.Y. Mil.

Butler, Edward b. Mass. 1780 d. Me. 1849 2nd Lieut. Mass. (Me.) Mil.
m. Mehitabel Norton — son Edward m. Sally Hersey

Butler, George b. Conn. 1750 d. Mass. 1837 Pvt. Mass. Mil.
m. Chloe Bidwell — son James B. m. Lydia Plank

Butler, George Pollard b. Va. 1780 d. Miss. 1865 Pvt. Ga. Det. Mil.
m. Polly Faulkner Heard — son Decatur N.
m. Martha Ann Wilkinson

Butler, Henry b. Mass. 1754 d. N.H. 1813 Major Gen. N.H. Mil.
m. Isabelle Fiske — daughter Sally C. m. John Haley

Butler, Henry Todd b. Tenn. 1794 d. Tenn. 1876 Pvt. Tenn. Mil.
m. Musidora McNairy — son John D. m. Dionitia Anne Marks

Butler, Ignatious b. Eng. 1755 d. Ky. 1824 Pvt. Northwestern Indian War
m. Delilah — daughter Melinda m. John Doyle

Butler, James b. Md. d. Md. 1860 m. Anne Jones Pvt. Md. Mil.
daughter Emily m. Peter Smith

Butler, John Vol. 17 Lieut. Pa. Mil.

Butler, John b. Va. 1791 d. Ind. 1864 m. Hannah Smith   Pvt. Ky. Mil.
son William F. m. Melissa Paris

Butler, Joseph b. Pa. 1779 d. Pa. 1862 m. Esther Greene   Pvt. Pa. Mil.
son Joseph G. m. Temperance Orwig

Butler, Joseph D. b. Va. 1792 d. Ind. 1880   Pvt. Mason Co. Ky. Mil.
m. Eleanor B. Hayden — son Joseph C. m. **Malinda Purcell**

Butler, Ormond b. Vt. 1775 d. Mo. 1860 m. Abigail Rudd   Pvt. N.Y. Mil.
daughter Susan m. John H. Button

Butler, Peter b. Ky. 1789 d. Oregon 1856   Pvt. Ky. Det. Mil.
m. Rachel Murphy — daughter Elizabeth Ann m. Edward Ground

Butler, Richard P.   Vol. 16   Adj. Gen. & Inspector Ky. Mil.

Butler, Samuel   Vol. 12   Fifer, Mass. Mil.

Butler, Seth b. Mass. 1782 d. Mass. 1864 m. Mary   Lieut. Mass. Mil.
son John Calvin m. Margaret Putnam

Butler, Thomas   Vol. 16   Corp. Marine Corps U.S.S. Frigate
Constitution Mass.

Butler, Thomas b. Ire. 1782 d. Ill. 1857 m. Hannah Farr   Sgt. Pa. Mil.
son Thomas M. m. Adelaide A. Pronty

Butler, Thomas Langford b. Ky. 1789 d. Ky. 1880   Lieut. 28th U.S. Inf.
m. Sarah Hawkins — daughter Mary Ellen   Regt.
m. Philip Turpin

Butler, William b. Pa. 1772 d. Pa. 1831   Pvt. Indiana Co. Pa. Mil.
m. Elizabeth McMurtry — son William D. m. Mary Jane Morton

Butler, William Edward b. Pa. 1789 d. Tenn. 1884   Surgeon Tenn. Vols.
m. Patsy Thompson Hays — son William Ormond
m. Martha Ann Hale

Butt, Henry b. Va. 1764 d. Ohio 1820   Pvt. Ohio Ind. Battalion
m. Margaret Crim — daughter Salome m. James Davis

Butt, Lemuel Boush b. Va. 1792 d. Va. bef. 1829   Ensign Va. Mil.
m. Abigail Porter Godfrey — daughter Virginia Frances
m. Benjamin Henry Capps

Butt, William Moses b. Va. 1781 d. Va. 1848   Capt. Va. Mil.
m. Priscilla Banks — son Moses E. m. Jerusha Ready and
Henrietta Allen

Buttles, Avery b. Conn. 1791 d. Ohio 1864   Drum Major Ohio Mil.
m. Harriet Kilbourne Carl — son Levi m. Jennie E. Wright

Buttolph, David b. Vt. 1791 d. Vt. 1869 m. Almira Little   Pvt. Vt. Mil.
son William W. m. Mary Ann Manney

Button, Jesse L. b. N.Y. bef. 1800 d. N.Y. 1840   Pvt. N.Y. Mil.
m. Abbey E. Thurber — son Darius m Sarah Van Veghten

Button, Simeon b Conn. 1757 d. N.Y. 1836 Lieut. Rensselaer Co. N.Y. Mil.
m. Ruth Eddy — son Jesse L. m. Abby E. Thurber

Buttrick, Cyrus b. Mass. 1786 d. Mass. 1859   Corp. Mass. Mil.
m. Susannah Wooley Bentley — daughter Susan C.
m. John W. Bartlett

Butts, Christian b. Pa. 1790 d. N.Y. 1888 m. Elizabeth   Pvt. Pa. Mil.
son Simon m. Sarah E. Way

Butts, Daniel b. Conn. 1782 d. N.Y. 1859   Capt. Oneida Co. N.Y. Mil.
m. Annis Bradford — daughter Esther C. m. Samuel J. M. Mersereau

Butts, Daniel b. Va. 1777 d. Va. 1850   Capt. Va. Mil.
  m. Ariadne E. Smith — daughter Marie E. m. Robert Dunlop

Butts, Daniel Claiborne   Vol. 17   Capt. Va. Inf.

Butts, Iah   Vol. 15   Pvt. N.Y. Mil.

Butts, Job b. R.I. 1796 d. N.Y. 1877 m. Helen Livermore   Pvt. N.Y. Mil.
  daughter Chloe m. Alexander Bailey REAL DAUGHTER

Butts, Noah b. R.I. 1770 d. Mass. 1817   Pvt. R.I. Arty. Mil.
  m. Lydia Daggett — son John W. m. Mehitabel Wentworth

Butts, Thomas b. N.Y. 1789 d. N.Y. 1867   Pvt. N.Y. Mil.
  m. Amanda Waters — daughter Lizzie M. m. Dickinson C. Griffith
  son Thomas m. Amanda Waters

Buxton, Daniel b. Vt. 1790/1800 d. Ohio 1835 m. Eliza   Pvt. Vt. Mil.
  son Darius V. m. Sarah S. Bradbury

Buxton, George Washington b. Md. 1779 d. Md. 1853 Ensign Montgomery
  m. Mary Ann Trail — son George W.   Co. Md. Mil.
  m. Honor Stevens

Buzzell, Jotham b. Mass. (Me.) 1793 d. Me.   Sgt. U.S. Inf.
  m. Mary Walker — daughter Sarah m. Milbury Jacobs

Byerly, Andrew b. Pa. 1763 d. Pa. 1851 m. Christina Fruit   Capt. Pa. Mil.
  daughter Margaret m. Solomon Waggoner

Byerly, Daniel b. Pa. 1760 d. Pa.   Pvt. Berks Co. Pa. Mil.
  m. 1st Elizabeth Settle — son John L. m. Susannah Biessel

Byerly, John b. Pa. 1787 d. Pa. 1871 m. Irma E. Harmon   Pvt. Pa. Mil.
  daughter Rachel m. George Schall

Byers, Jacob b. Pa. 1798 d. Pa. 1876 m. Mary M. Shakely   Pvt. Pa. Mil.
  son Albert m. Margaret Henlen

Byers, James b. Pa. c 1760 d. Ohio 1828 m.   Pvt. Pa. Frontier Mil.
  son Moses W. m. Mary Ann Brandenburg

Byers, Joseph Alexander b. S.C. 1790 d. Ala. 1873   3rd Lieut. S.C. Mil.
  m. Rebecca Bowman — son Edward m. Lorena McBrayer

Byers, Michael b. Md. 1792 d. Md. 1876   Pvt. Md. Mil.
  m. Margaret R. Duttera Fredericks — son Joshua m. Martha Wilson

Byington, Amos Fox b. S.C. 1793 d. Ga. 1874   Pvt. Ga. Mil.
  m. Nancy Freeney — son James L. m. Jane Caroline McLendon

Bynum, Wade Hampton Turner   Vol. 17   Pvt. Miss. Terr. Mil.

Byrd, John b. Pa. 1776 d. Pa. 1856   Pvt. Phila. Co. Pa. Mil.
  m. Esther Ely — son Charles m. Molly Geller

Byrd, Joseph b. Va. 1795 d. Tenn. 1858 m. Anne Pride   Corp. Tenn. Mil.
  son John H. m. Mary Ann Ballard

Byrd, Richard b. 1790 d. Mo. m. Sarah Birch   Pvt. Tenn. Gunmen
  daughter Mary Ann m. Benjamin Allen O'Bannon

C

Cabiniss, Elijah b. Ga. 1796 d. Ark. 1870 m. Annie Bussey   Pvt. Ga. Mil.
  daughter Harriet m. Asahel L. Carlock

Cabell, Benjamin William Davidson b. Va. 1793 d. Va.   Ensign Va. Mil.
  m. Sallie Epes Doswell   1812
  son George C. m. Mary Harrison Baird
  son John Roy m. Martha Wilson
  son William L. m. Harriette Amanda Rector

Cabell, Joseph b. Va. d. Va. m. Mary Hopkins   Col. Va. Mil.
daughter Ann m. Robert Carter Harrison   Vol. 2

Cabell, Joseph b. Va. 1780 d. Ky. 1836   Capt. 16th Green Co. Ky. Regt.
m. Rachel Mann — son Samuel m. Catherine M. Allen   1803

Cabell, Landon   Vol. 3   Patriot Va.

Cabell, Nicholas b. Va. 1750 d. Va. 1803   Patriot, Va. Assembly 1785-1803
m. Hannah Carrington
daughter Mary Anne m. Benjamin Carrington

Cabell, William H. b. Va. 1772 d. Va. 1853   Governor, Judge, Va.
m. Agnes S. B. Gamble — son E. Carrington m. Anna M. Wilcox

Cable, Jacob b. Tenn. 1782 d. Tenn. 1833 m. ? Vol. 30   Pvt. Tenn. Mil.

Cable, James b. N.Y. 1780 d. Ohio 1822 m. Lucy Read Pvt. N.Y. State Art.
daughter Lucy R. m. William Barnett

Cade, John b. N.C. 1736/42 d. N.C. aft. 1793   Patriot—Mem. N.C.
m. Elizabeth Hobson Adair   Convention
daughter Agnes m. Andrew Fulmore

Cadman, George b. R.I. 1760 d. N.Y. 1839 m. Desiah Beebe   Pvt. N.Y. Mil.
daughter Rebecca m. Elijah Sprague

Cadmus, Abraham H. b. N.J. 1789 d. N.J. 1864   Corp. N.J. Mil.
m. Mariah Brown — son Moses m. Sophia Jane Weakley

Cadmus, Andrew b. N.J. 1794 d. Ill. 1886   2nd Corp. N.Y. Mil.
m. Elizabeth Kinney Cole — son Richard m. Fidelia Bailey

Cadot, Claudius b. Ohio 1793 d. Ohio 1875 m. Nancy Ball   Pvt. Ohio Mil.
daughter Eliza Jane m. Peter Feurt Boynton

Cadwell, Timothy b. Conn. 1747 d. Conn. or Mass.   Pvt. Mass. Mil.
m. Rhoda Kellogg — son Austin m. Anna Holcomb

Cady, Calvin b. N.H. 1774 d. Vt. 1819 m. Hepzibeth Bruce Pvt. N.Y. Mil.
daughter Roxanne m. Paschal Hatch

Cady, David b. Conn. 1703 d. Conn. 1788   Patriot Conn. 1785
m. Hannah Whitmore — son Joseph m. Zerviah Hosmer

Cady, George Washington b. Conn. 1776 d. N.Y. 1854 Pvt. Conn. Mil.
m. Sally Gates — son Silas m. Susanna Coffin

Cady, Isaac b. Vt. 1765 d. Vt. 1851 m. Eunice Houghton   Pvt. Vt. Mil.
son Jacob m. Betsy E. Coolidge
daughter Wealthy m. Reuben Jenney

Cady, Joseph b. Conn. 1727 d. Conn. 1794   Patriot, Selectman Conn.
m. Zerviah Hosmer — son Manesseh m. Elizabeth Hutchins

Cady, Manasseh b. Conn. 1758 d. Vt. 1833   Patriot Vt.
m. Elizabeth Hutchins — daughter Lucy m. David Huggins

Cage, William b. Va. 1746 d. Tenn. 1811   Memb. N.C. Assy. from
m. Elizabeth Douglass   Sullivan Co. 1784/5
daughter Priscilla m. William Hale

Cahill, Nicholas   Vol. 4   Col. Va. Mil.

Cahoon, Joel Butler   Vol. 12   Pvt. Ohio Mil.

Cahoon, William b. R.I. 1774 d. Vt. 1833   Major General Vt. Mil.
m. Nancy Shaw — daughter Harriet Helen m. Nicholas Baylies

Cain, Michael b. Ireland 1750 d. Ky. 1848   Pvt. Ky. Mil.
m. Elizabeth Warmores — son John m. Olive Dinsmore

Cain, Nathan b. ? d. Ky. m. Mary   Pvt. Ky. Mil.
son Albert m. Eliza

Cain, Thomas b. Va. ?d. Ky. 1849 m. Oney Meador Pvt. Va. Mil.
son William H. m. Mary Walker

Calder, John b. S.C. 1761 d. Ga. 1845   Pvt. Ga. Mil.
m. Phoebe Horton or Houghton
daughter Mary m. Allen Beverly Powell

Caldwell, Adam b. Ireland 1763 d. Tenn. 1819 Pvt. Tenn. Mil.
m. Phoebe Gallion — son John m. Lucinda Whey

Caldwell, Alexander b. Ireland 1780 d. Ohio 1844 Pvt. Ohio Mil.
m. Jane Boyd — son Alexander m. Charlotte Morris

Caldwell, Crawford b. Ireland 1789 d. Ohio 1872 Pvt. Ohio Mil.
m. Sarah McClure — son Alan m. Elinor Jane Winegar

Caldwell, David b. Pa. 1725 d. N.C. 1824   Patriot - N.C.
m. Rachel Craighead — son Alexander m. Sallie Davidson —
son Samuel m. Elizabeth Lindsey

Caldwell, Hugh b. Va. 1786 d. Tenn. 1853 Pvt. E. Tenn. Mtd. Gunmen
m. Malinda Lucretia Gault — son Hugh m. Polly Bayless

Caldwell, John b. Md. 1779 d. D.C. 1865   Pvt. Ky. Vol. Mil.
m. Hannah Hinds — daughter Ann S. m. William N. Caldwell

Caldwell, John K. b. Ky. 1789 d. Mo. 1830   Pvt. Ky. Vol.
m. Sally Utterback — son Walter K. m. Lucinda Crow

Caldwell, Perrine b. Va. 1764 d. Tenn. 1854   Pvt. Ky. Mil.
m. Elizabeth Worsham — son George m. Sarah Elizabeth Easley

Caldwell, Samuel b. Va. 1770 d. Ky. 1835 m. Anna General, Ky.
son William P. m. M. Jane Jackson

Caldwell, Samuel Walker b. Ky. 1787 d. Ky. 1862 Pvt. Ky. Mil.
m. Betsey — daughter Susan M. m. William M. Northcraft

Caldwell, Thomas Alfred b. Tenn. 1798 d. Calif. 1852 Corp. W. Tenn. Mil.
m. Elizabeth Hughes — daughter Virginia E. m. William Wells

Calhoun, Angus b. Scotland 1782 d. Tex. aft. 1825 Capt. Ga. Mil.
m. Winifred Ryals
son Thomas B. m. Catherine Johanna McAllister

Calhoun, George b. Pa. 1754 d. Ky. 1835 Patriot - Surveyor Ky.
m. Susan C. Cotton   1800-8
son Samuel m. Nancy Ann Knight

Calhoun, John b. N.Y. 1790 d. N.Y. 1875   Corp. N.Y. Mil.
m. Hannah Jeffries — daughter Catherine m. James R. Parks

Calhoun, William Sr. b. Ireland c. 1750 d. Pa. c 1800 Pvt. Pa. Rangers
m. Mary — son William Jr. m. Elizabeth H. Moon

Calhoun, William Jr. b. Pa. 1786 d. Pa. 1836   Capt. Pa. Mil.
m. Elizabeth Hutchinson — son John m. Nancy Stevenson

Calkins, Abraham   Vol. 10   Corp. N.Y. Mil.

Calkins, David b. N.Y. 1787 d. Iowa 1863 m. Patience Drew Pvt. N.Y. Mil.
son Jonathan m. Amanda Rider

Call, Moses b. N.H. 1755 d. N.H. 1842 m. Sarah Boynton Pvt. Mass. Mil.
son Nathan m. Susanna Webster

Call, Nathan b. N.H. 1793 d. N.H. 1859   Pvt. Mass. Mil.
m. Susanna Webster — daughter Mary Elizabeth m. Noah Little

Callaway, Charles b. Va. 1785 d. Mo. 1834   Pvt. Ky. Mil.
     m. Elizabeth Eubank — son Stephen m. Ann Eliza Edwards

Callaway, Hatton W. b. N.C. 1791 d. Ga. 1863   Pvt. N.C. Mil.
     m. Martha Hughes — daughter Amy Mary m. Louis Curbow

Callaway, James b. Mo. 1783 d. Mo. 1815   Capt. Mo. Terr. Mil.
     m. Nancy Howell — son William B. m. Malinda Silvey

Callaway, Jesse b. Ga. 1796 d. Ga. 1875   Sgt. Ga. Mil.
     m. Mary Catherine Kirby
     son Luke Henry m. Angie Harris

Callmus, Levi   Vol. 14   Pvt. Md. Artillery

Calmes, Marquis b. Va. 1775 d. Ky. 1834   Brig. Gen. Ky. Vols.
     m. Priscilla Hale — daughter Sarah m. Simeon Bohannon

Calvert, Ralls b. Va. 1767 d. Va. 1815   Patriot - Va. 1811
     m. Mary Wade Strother
     son Jeremiah S. m. Priscilla Smithers

Calvert, William b. 1781/3 d. Mo.? m. Elizabeth Fine   Lieut. Tenn. Mil.
     daughter Mary Ann m. Thomas J. Plemmons

Cameron, George b. 178- d. ? m. Martha Casteel   Pvt. Pa. Mil.
     daughter Nancy Jane m. Jacob Newton Billingsley

Cameron, James b. N.Y. 1794 d. N.Y. 1858 m. Dinah Coman   Pvt. N.Y. Mil.
     son Charles m. Laura Case

Cameron, William liv. Northumberland Co. Pa.   Vol. 5   Pvt. Pa. Mil.

Camp, Abner b. Va. 1770 d. Ga. aft. 1850   Pvt. N.C. Mil.
     m. Elizabeth Ragsdale — son Edmund m. Mary Reynolds

Camp, Elisha b. N.Y. 1786 d. N.Y. 1856 m. Sophia Hale   Capt. N.Y. Mil.
     son George H. m. Mary Alice Smith

Camp, Ephraim   Vol. 21   Pvt. N.J. Mil.

Camp, Hardin   Vol. 11   Pvt. U. S. Rangers

Camp, Joseph b. S.C. 1777 d. Ga. 1854 m. Martha   Pvt. Ga. Mil.
     daughter Elizabeth m. James Brock REAL DAUGHTER

Camp, Samuel b. Conn. 1753 d. Ga. 1827   Patriot - Surveyor Gen. Ga.
     m. Mary Banks — daughter Mary m. Sims Kelly

Campbell, Alexander b. (Me.) Mass. 1790 d. Me. 1863 Sgt. Me. Dist. Mass.
     m. Nancy McFadin — son Robert m. Catherine Rogers

Campbell, Beasley b. Miss. or La. 1795 d. La. 1887   Pvt. La. Mil.
     m. Mary Franklin — daughter Minerva m. Ezekiel Young

Campbell, Benjamin b. Pa. ? d. Pa. aft. 1811   Lt. Pa. Mil.
     m. Sarah Tietsworth — daughter Mary m. Joseph McClow

Campbell, Charles   Vol. 1   Lt. Ky. Mil.

Campbell, Charles b. N.Y. ? d. N.Y. 1814   Pvt. N.Y. Inf.
     m. Hanah Swart(z) — daughter Elena m. William Schell —
     daughter Maria m. John Jacob Haines

Campbell, Charles b. ? 1777 d. Pa. 1791   Vol. 17   Lieut. Pa. Mil.

Campbell, Daniel b. N.H. 1762 d. N.H. 1829   Pvt. N.H. Mil.
     m. Ann Houston — daughter Susannah m. Thomas H. Dickey

Campbell, David b. Va. 1750 d. Tenn. 1812   Judge Tenn. 1796
     m. Elizabeth Outlaw — son Thomas J. m. Sarah Bearden

Campbell, David b. Va. 1793 d. Va. 1853   2d Lieut. Va. Mil.
m. Ann Ryburn — son Joseph L. F. m. Josephine Bondurant

Campbell, Dougal b. Va. 1776 d. W. Va. 1844   Major Va. Mil.
m. Sarah Wallace Lyle
daughter Isabella M. m. Hiram McKoun

Campbell, Farguard b. Scotland 1721 d. N.C. 1810   Patriot - Senator
m. Isabella McAllister   N.C. Gen. Assembly 1791/3
daughter Isabella m. John Smith

Campbell, Hamilton Crockett   Vol. 12   Pvt. West Tenn. Vols.

Campbell, Isaac b. Va. 1766 d. Tenn. 1832   Pvt. Tenn. Mil.
m. Susannah Smith — son Smith m. Nancy Allen

Campbell, Jacob b. Pa. 1789 d. Pa. 1871   Capt. Pa. Mil.
m. Eliza Allen — daughter Lavina m. John Blythe

Campbell, James   Vol. 1   Capt. Md. Mil.

Campbell, James b. 1783 d. N.C. aft. 1830   Major N.C. Det. Mil.
m. Sarah Miller Vaughan — daughter Harriet m. Samuel A. Ford

Campbell, James b. Ky. 1793 d. Mo. 1872   Pvt. Tenn. Mil.
m. Eliza Ann Jennings
son Granville K. m. Louisa Jane Walker

Campbell, James b. Va. 1788 d. Mo. 1872   Swordmaster Va. Mil.
m. Lucinda Spiller Gwatkin
daughter Catherine m. William Luckett

Campbell, James Austin b. Va. 1787 d. La. 1830   Capt. Va. Inf.
m. Mary Massie Vaughan — son Gilbert R. m. Elizabeth Spurlock

Campbell, John b. Va. 1768 d. Va. 1843   Major Ky. Frontier Mil. 1790/4
m. Dorcas Tate — son Spotswood M. m. Nancy Faught Pratt

Campbell, John Livingston b. ? 1779 d. ? 1859   Pvt. Ohio Mil. &
m. Eliza McCulloch Haghey   Ky. Mil.
daughter Elizabeth m. Thomas Henry Taylor

Campbell, Matthew b. Pa. 1758 d. Ohio 1819   Pvt. Ky. Mtd. Vols.
m. Mary Shelby   & Sgt. Ky. Mil.
daughter Levisa Jane m. James Power

Campbell, Moses b. Ky. 1788 d. ? m. Tabitha   Pvt. Pa. Mil.
son Edmund m. Elizabeth Ann

Campbell, Peter b. Scotland 1795 d. N.Y. 1886   Pvt. N.Y. Mil.
m. Elsie Clarke
daughter Lovina m. John Park REAL DAUGHTER

Campbell, Richard b. N.J. 1855 d.— m. Mary Lee   Pvt. N.J. Mil.
son Richard Jr. m. Sarah Webb   (Sussex Co.)

Campbell, Robert b. Pa. 1770 d. Ohio 1813   Pvt. Pa. Light Dragoons
m. Elizabeth Boone — daughter Jane m. Nathaniel Cooper Weede

Campbell, Robert Jr. b. S.C. 1789 d. England 1862   Capt. U.S. Rifles S.C.
m. Carolina Morland
daughter Agnes (unm.) REAL DAUGHTER

Campbell, Samuel b. Scotland 1790 d. N.Y. 1859   Pvt. N.Y. Mil.
m. Maria Mulford — daughter Helen C. m. Martin W. Palmer

Campbell, Samuel   Vol. 19   Pvt. Tenn. Mil.

Campbell, Samuel b. Va. d. Ill. 1867   Pvt. - Drummer Va. Mil.
   m. Julia F. Grimes — daughter Elizabeth m. Lewis Dyer
REAL DAUGHTER

Campbell, Whitaker b. prob. Va. 1727 d. Va. 1814 m. ?   2nd Lieut. Va. Mil.
   daughter Mary m. Benoni Carlton Sr.   (Middlesex Co.)

Campbell, William b. Ky. 1793 d. Calif. 1885   Pvt. Ky. Mtd. Mil.
   m. Sarah McNary — daughter Ann Laurette m. Ira Joseph Lovell

Campbell, William b. Va. 1769 d. Ohio 1819   Pvt. Ohio Mil.
   m. Mary Stricklett — daughter Sarah Ann m. Daniel Kirkendall

Campbell, William b. Va. 1791 d. Ohio 1852   Pvt. U. S. Rangers
   m. Jane O'Neal — daughter Margaret m. Camden Cutright
   daughter Elizabeth m. Arthur Burt

Campbell, Wyatt b. Va. d. Va. m ?   Pvt. Va. Mil.
   son Cabe C. m. Martha Jane Davis

Camper, Peter b. Va. 1793 d. W. Va. 1878   Pvt. Va. Mil. (Bortetourt Co.)
   m. Ellender P. Obenschein
   daughter Mary E. m. Alexander McPherson

Campfield, Jabez b. N.J. 1738 d. N.J. 1821   Patriot — Justice 1794/6
   m. Sara Ward   Morris Co., N.J.
   son William m. Hannah Tuthill

Canan, John b. Ireland 1746 d. Pa. 1831 m. Margery Dean   Patriot Va.
   son Moses m. Mary Henderson

Canary, Christian b. Va. 1790 d. Ky. ?   Pvt. Ky. Mil.
   m. Nancy Jane South — son MacHenry m. Emily Hunley

Candler, John Jr.   Vol. 17   Master Mate USS Constitution, U.S.N.

Canfield, Enos b. N.Y. 1767 d. N.Y. 1825   Capt. N.Y. Mil.
   m. Polly Robertson — son Amos m. Eleanor Knapp

Canfield, Gold b. N.Y. 1770 d. N.Y. 1814   Pvt. N.Y. Mil.
   m. Nancy Keeler Hayes — daughter Mary Ann m. James Robertson

Canfield, John b. Conn. 1740 d. Conn. 1786   Patriot — Conn. Senator
   m. Dorcas Buel — son John M. m. Fanny Harvey   1786

Canfield, Joseph b. c. 1755 ? d. N.J. ? m. Phebe Baldwin   Pvt. N.J. Mil.
   daughter Hannah m. James Peck

Canfield, Lewis L. b. N.Y. 1796 d. N.Y. 1878   Pvt. N.Y. Mil.
   m. Mehitabel Cox
   daughter Rhoda Ann m. Samuel A. Patterson

Canfield, Samuel   Vol. 8   Patriot — Judge & Member Conn.
                              Leg. — in Shay's Rebellion

Cannon, John b. 1740 prob. Va. d. Pa. 1798 m. Polly   Justice Peace 1790
   son Joshua m. ?   Repr. Wash. Co. Pa. to Assy.

Cannon, Robert b. Pa. 1780 d. Ill. 1854   Pvt. Ky. Mil.
   m. Elizabeth Cheatham — son Obediah C. m. Sarah Ann Noel

Cannon, Thomas b. Tenn. 1791 d. Tex. 1870   Pvt. Tenn. Mil.
   m. Elizabeth Brown — daughter Nancy G. m. James Henry Williams

Canoles, William Stansbury b. Md. 1785 d. Md. 1865   Pvt. Md. Mil.
   m. Ann Fuller — daughter Susan Mariah m. John G. Brendel

Cantrelle, Michel b. La. 1750 d. La. 1814   Judge 1805/12 La.
  m. Magdalene Celeste Andry
  son Joseph m. Louise Dejean
  daughter Rose C. m. Jean Baptiste Armant

Cantwell, Berry b. Va. 1781 d. Ind. 1843   Pvt. Ind. Mil.
  m. Mary (Polly) Berry — daughter Catherine m. Thomas Garrett

Capps, Solomon b. Va. 1780 died Va. 1820/30   Pvt. Va. Mil.
  m. Mrs. Sarah Walker Braithwaite
  son Benjamin Henry m. Virginia Frances Butt

Cardwell, James b. 1776 d. N.Y. ? m —— Thompson 2nd Lieut. N.Y. Cav.
  daughter Anne m. Bernard Savage

Cardwell, John b. Va. 1786 d. Ky. 1879   Pvt. Ky. Mil.
  m. Margaret Arnold — daughter Mary Elizabeth m. William Priestly

Carey, Daniel b. Mass. 1762 d. Mass. (Me.) 1791   Lieut. Mass. Mil.
  m. Phebe Doty — daughter Hannah m. Abner Shaw

Carey, Isaac b. Pa. 1794 d. Ohio 1866   Pvt. Ohio Mil.
  m. Catharine Eylar — son Joshua m. Mary E. Rudolph

Carey, Samuel b. N.Y. c 1780 d. N.Y. 1866 m ?   Pvt. & Teamster
  daughter Polly m. Elias Blount   N.Y. Mil.

Carey, Samuel b. Pa. 1752 d. Ohio 1823   Justice Peace Ross Co. Ohio
  m. Rachel Doane (McPherson?)
  son John m. Margaret Green

Carey, Samuel b. N.Y. 1758 d. Pa. 1842   Ensign Pa. Mil.
  m. Mrs. Rosanna Cary Slocum
  daughter Laura m. Marton Downing

Carey, Zenas b. Mass. 1792 d. N.Y. 1873 m. Olive Brown   Pvt. N.Y. Mil.
  daughter A. Rosaltha (unm.) REAL DAUGHTER

Carhart, William b. Ohio 1795 d. Iowa 1884   Pvt. Ohio Mil.
  m. Josephine E. Simmons
  daughter Mary m. Alphonso A. Rice

Carleton, John b. N.H. 1787 d. N.H. 1869 m. Fanny Lewis Pvt. N.H. Mil.
  son William D. m. Clarissa Wells

Carlock, Abraham b. Va. 1765 d. Ill. 1843   Pvt. West Tenn. Mil.
  m. Abigail Osborne — son Abraham W. m. Mary A. Goodpasture

Carlock, Isaac   Vol. 16   Pvt. Tenn. Mil.
  son Andrew

Carlton, Harris b. Va. 1793 d. Va. 1865 m. Jane Lumpkin   Sgt. Va. Mil.
  daughter John Ella m. Edward Campbell

Carlton, James b. Va. 1790 d. Mo. 1854   Ensign Va. Mil.
  m. Philena Askins — daughter Irene m. Thomas Gillespie
  REAL DAUGHTER

Carlton, Peter b. Conn. 1786/7 d. Ohio 1861   Pvt. Ohio Mil.
  m. Clarissa Ladd — son Caleb D. m. Julia Hine

Carlton, Robert b. Va. 1786 d. Va. 1814 m. Sarah   Pvt. Va. Mil.
  daughter Lydia Ann m. Archer A. Farmer
  son Thomas R. m. Nancy Hart

Carman, John b. N.Y. 1797 d. N.Y. 1852   Pvt. N.J. Mil.
  m. Mary Bloomfield — son Jarvis m. Emeline Seamon

Carmichael, Calvin b. N.Y. 1796 d. N.Y. 1849   Pvt. & Fifer N.Y. Mil.
    m. Nancy Ellicotte — daughter Emma unm. REAL DAUGHTER
    daughter Lorena unm. REAL DAUGHTER
    m. Lamira R. Seybolt
    daughter Adeline L. m. William T. Bicknell Sr.

Carmichael, John b. Pa. 1780 d. Pa. 1865   Pvt. Pa. Mil.
    m. Margaret Morrison — son Hugh m. Lucy A. E. Buckner
    m. Charlotte Wible — son Aaron m. Margaret Henderson

Carmon, Joshua b. N.C. 1789 d. N.C. 1875   Staff Major N.C. Mil.
    m. Mrs. Ann McIver Tyson — son Samuel m. Eliza Wells

Carmouche, Pierre b. France c. 1740 d. La. 1822   Member 1st Grand
    m. Genevieve Rousseau   Jury St. James La. 1805
    daughter Narcisse m. Francoise Paugue Bock

Carnal, James b. Va. 1780 d. Va. 1862   Pvt. Carolina Co. Va. Mil.
    m. Ann Fletcher — son Archibald m. Elizabeth Oder

Carnes, James b. Va. ? d. Ohio 1836 m. Mary Satterday   Pvt. Va. Mil.
    son Alfred H. m. Sarah Ann Crothers

Carnes, John b. ? d. Pa. 1819 m. Jane   Pvt. Pa. Mil.
    daughter Jane m. Thomas Copeland   Westmoreland Co.

Carney, John b. c. 1787 d. La. 1820/32   Pvt. La. Vol.
    m. Mary Elizabeth Como — son John P. m. Mary A. Smith

Carney, Solomon b. prob. N.Y. 1796 d. N.Y. 1854   Pvt. N.Y. Mil. 1812/13
    m. Mary Belcher — daughter Mary m. Eli Miller

Carney, Thomas b. Va. 1768 d. W. Va. 1846   Pvt. Harrison Co. W. Va.
    m. Mary Parsons — daughter Hannah m. Levi Casto   Mil.

Carothers, James b. ? 1792 d. Tenn. 1865   Pvt. Tenn. Mil.
    m. Pamelia Sellers Noble
    daughter Elizabeth N. m. George Logan Neely

Carothers, Samuel M. b. N.C. 1789 d. Miss. 1845   Pvt. West Tenn. Mil.
    m. Naomi Brown — son Samuel B. m. Mary Terrell Howlette

Carpenter, Alanson   Vol. 9   Sgt. Vt. Mil.
    daughter Jennie A. m. George Restle — REAL DAUGHTER
    daughter Lulu B. m. J. W. Melchior — REAL DAUGHTER
    daughter Mae D. unm. — REAL DAUGHTER

Carpenter, Amos b. Vt. 1790 d. N.Y. 1871   Pvt. N.Y. Mil.
    m. 2d Delaney Farnsworth
    daughter Alice m. George Hecox — REAL DAUGHTER
    daughter Mary Orpha m. John C. Shaffert — REAL DAUGHTER

Carpenter, Benjamin b. Mass. 1726 d. Vt. 1804   Patriot Memb. Gov.'s
    m. Annie — daughter Rhoda m. Samuel Nichols   Council Mass. 1788
    son Joseph m. Eunice

Carpenter, Benjamin   Vol. 9   Patriot - Civil - Vt.

Carpenter, Chester b. Vt. 1787 d. Vt. 1872   Orderly Sgt. Vt. Mil.
    m. Hannah Kendell — son Charles m. Betsy Hinman

Carpenter, Comfort b. Vt. 1775 d. Vt. 1853 m. Betsy Foster   Pvt. Vt. Mil.
    daughter Polly m. Thomas Trask

Carpenter, Daniel b. Vt. 1796 d. Colo. 1884   Pvt. N.Y. Mil.
    m. Sally Northway — son William B. m. Emeline Grove

Carpenter, David b. N.C. 1798 d. N.C. 1890   Pvt. N.C. Mil.
m. Catherine May — son Jacob m. Elizabeth Burton

Carpenter, Elijah Jr. b. Conn. 1789 d. Conn.   Pvt. Conn. Mil.
m. Phebe Wilson — daughter Laura m. Edwin S. Stanley

Carpenter, George b. Pa. 1791 d. Ohio 1859   Pvt. Ohio Mil.
m. Rebecca L. Clough — daughter Catherine C. m. Azor Bunyan

Carpenter, Harvey b. 1788 d. N.Y. 1837   Paymaster N.Y. Mil.
m. Sally Clark — son William C. m. Adaline Dalrymple

Carpenter, Jacob b. Pa. 1767 d. Pa. 1803   Patriot Treas. Pa. 1801-3
m. Catherine Martin — daughter Catherine m. David Miller

Carpenter, James b. R.I. ? d. 1859 prob. N.Y.   Pvt. N.Y. Mil.
m. Hannah Tourtellot — son W. Timothy m. Sarah Ann Joslyn

Carpenter, James b. Conn. 1741 d. Vt. 1813   Patriot Member
m. Irene Ladd — daughter Lucy m. Ralph Turner   Vt. Leg. 1785

Carpenter, John b. N.J. ? d. N.J. 1831 m. Anna Van Cleve   Pvt. N.J. Mil.
daughter Eliza m. Peter Beekman

Carpenter, John b. 1783 d. Ohio aft. 1871   Pvt. Ohio Mil.
m. Mary Yoho — daughter Ella m. John Richardson

Carpenter, Joseph b. Mass. 1783 d. N.Y. 1855   Corp. Mass. Vol. Mil.
m. Hannah Olmsted — daughter Julia m. John Daly Platt

Carpenter, Jotham b. Mass. 1750 d. R.I. aft 1798   Patriot - Justice Peace
m. Hannah Gulley   R.I. 1777/98
son Jotham Jr. m. Sarah Dexter

Carpenter, Marshall   Vol. 14   Pvt. Vt. Mil.

Carpenter, Moses b. N.Y. 1751/2 d. N.Y. 1829   Patriot - Cty. Treas. N.Y.
m. Elizabeth Bunyon — daughter Elizabeth m. James Wisner

Carpenter, Nathaniel   Vol. 9   Pvt. Vt. Mil.

Carpenter, Parker   Vol. 13   Lieut. Conn. Mil.

Carpenter, Silas b. N.Y. 1781 d. N.Y. 1855   Pvt. N.Y. Mil.
m. Phoebe Ann Penny
daughter Phoebe Ann m. William Burtis Skidmore

Carpenter, Solomon b. Conn. 1732 d. Conn. 1836   Patriot Conn.
m. Elizabeth Walker — son Frederick W. m. Clarissa Symonds Bull

Carpenter, Stephen b. N.Y. 1795 d. Mich. 1866   Corp. N.Y. Mil.
m. Hannah Scovil — son Benjamin m. Malvina Nixon

Carr, Caleb b. N.Y. 1778 d. N.Y. 1840 m. Lucinda Harris   Col. N.Y. Mil.
son Caleb Lawrence m. Frances C. Baker

Carr, Charles Vol. 17   Pvt. N.Y. Mil.

Carr, Dabney b. Va. 1793 d. Mo. 1872   Pvt. Va. Cav. Mil.
m. Mary M. Appleberry
daughter Pocahontas m. David James Milroy

Carr, Elias b. N.C. 1775 d. N.C. 1822   Corp. N.C. Mil.
m. Cecelia Johnston — son James J. m. Elizabeth J. Hilliard

Carr, Jesse b. Va. 1771 d. Va. 1846 m. Frankie Seward   Sgt. Va. Mil.
daughter Frances E. m. James Dunlevy

Carr, John b. S.C. 1773 d. Tenn. 1858 m. Sally Gage   2d Lieut. Tenn. Vols.
daughter Sarah m. Samuel Wallace

Carr, Jonathan b. ? d. Ind. 1845 m. Martha   Pvt. Ind. Terr. Mtd. Vols.
son John m. Sarah Comer

Carr, Thomas Dabney b. Ga. 1790 d. Ga. 1830   Capt. Ga. Mil.
m. Anne Bell Watkins — daughter Susan F. m. James Corbin Avery

Carr, Thomas S.   Vol. 10   Pvt. Va. Cav. Mil.

Carr, Timothy b. N.H. 1784 d. Ill. 1850   Patriot Vt. 1814
m. Elvira Sally Drew—son Merrill P. m. Phebe Ann Huffman

Carrell, James b. Pa. 1776 d. Pa. 1863 m. Ellen Carnahan   Sgt. Pa. Mil.
son William m. Sarah Laughlin

Carrell, John b. Pa. 1784 d. Ohio 1858 m. Mary E. Wirt   Ensign Ohio Mil.
son Thomas m. Emily Bacon

Carrico, Joseph b. Md. 1792 d. W. Va. 1869   Pvt. Va. Mil.
m. Sebath Holbert — son Albert C. m. Appolonia Miller

Carrie, Joseph b. France 1773 d. Ga. 1835   Patriot Ga. 1809/14
m. Mary Eubanks — son Gaspard T. m. Angeline Blodgett

Carriger, Christian b. Pa. 1779 d. Calif. 1846   Patriot — Tenn. Leg.
m. Levicy Ward   1812/15
daughter Elizabeth m. James White Nelson
daughter Mary Lincoln m. James F. Cass

Carriger, Godfrey Jr. b. Pa. 1769 d. Tenn. 1827   Lt. Tenn. Mil.
m. Elizabeth Lovelace Crawley
daughter Elizabeth m. Reuben Brooks
son Jackson D. m. Edna George Dugger
daughter Margaret R. m. David Bishop

Carrington, Daniel b. Mass. 1785 d. Vt. 1840   Pvt. Vt. Mil.
son Charles V. m. Mary M. Brennan

Carrington, Leverett b. Conn. 1797 d. Conn. 1885   Pvt. Conn. Mil.
m. Polly L. Perkins — daughter Mary L. m. James Lawrence

Carroll, James b. N. C. 1770 d. Tenn. aft. 1830   Pvt. Tenn. Vols.
m. Sarah Bruce — daughter Elizabeth m. John Gunn

Carroll, John b. Miss. Terr. 1795 d. La. 1873   Pvt. La. Mil.
m. 1st Susannah — daughter Louisa m. Thomas Lyles

Carroll, John Bond Vol. 8   Pvt. Md. Mil.

Carroll, Samuel b. S.C. c. 1788 d. Tenn. 1840   Pvt. Tenn. Inf.
m. Hulda Davy—daughter Mary m. A. M. Van Dyke

Carroll, William b. Pa. 1788 d. Tenn. 1844   Major General
m. Cecilia Bradford   Tenn. Mil.
son William Henry m. Eliza Jane Breathitt

Carson, Charles Smith   Early Vol.   Pvt. Pa. Mil.

Carson, John b. N.C. d. Va. 1815 m. Rachel Cox   Pvt. N.C. Mil.
son Elisha m. Susanna Marsh

Carson, John b. Pa. 1789 d. Ind. 1875 m. Sarah Gamble   Pvt. Ohio Mil.
son Joseph G. m. Sarah Ann McConnell

Carson, Samuel b. Pa. 1788 d. Ohio 1867 m. Elizabeth   Pvt. Ohio Mil.
daughter Hannah m. Alanson Cory

Carson, Simon C. b. Va. 1769 d. Va. 1856   Lieut. Va. Mil.
  m. Martha Williams
  son Jared W. m. M. Harriet McKay

Cart, George b. Va. 1783 d. Ind. 1849   Corp. Va. Mil.
  m. Margaret Paxton — son Andrew m. Mary Slife

Carter, Alexander b. Va. 1784 d. Miss. 1844   Pvt. N.C. Mil.
  m. Mary Davis — son James m. Hannah M. Weir

Carter, Asa b. Mass. 1798 d. Mass. 1853   Pvt. N.Y. Vol. Silver
  m. 2d Ellinor Carleton   Gray Mil.
  daughter Huldah m. Seth William Merrill

Carter, Benjamin b. Conn. 1764 d. N.Y. 1833   Pvt. N.Y. Mil.
  m. Phoebe Austin — son Benjamin E. m. Vilette White

Carter, Clement b. Del. 1783 d. Md. 1862 m. Eliza Tittle   Pvt. Md. Mil.
  son Edward F. m. Mary Ann Ross Heckrotte

Carter, Curtis b. Va. 1778 d. Va. 1850   Pvt. Va. Mil.
  m. Letitia La Tellier
  son Jesse W. m. Margaret B. Campbell
  daughter Virginia L. m. Joseph Jackson White

Carter, Elijah b. Mass. 1742 d. Mass. 1813   Patriot, Civil Ofr.
  m. Jane Goodrich — son Elisha m. Lucy Eaton   Fitchburg, Mass.

Carter, Isaac b. N.C. d. Miss. 1834 m.—   Pvt. Miss. Terr. Mil.
  son Henry m. Nancy Tate

Carter, Jabez, Jr. b. N.Y. 1792 d. N.Y. 1868   Pvt. N.Y. Mil.
  m. Hannah Kenyon — son George W. m. Sarah Waters

Carter, Jesse   Vol. 7   Pvt. West Tenn. Mil.

Carter, John   Vol. 6   Pvt. Del. Mil.

Carter, John b. N.H. 1759 d. N.H. 1847   Lt. Col. N.H. Vols.
  m. Lucy Cavis Wells — son Hiram m. Sally Mayhew
  son Nathaniel m. 1st Elizabeth Robertson

Carter, John b. Va. 1783 d. Ala. 1850 m. Elizabeth Day   Pvt. Va. Mil.
  son John R. m. Jemima

Carter, Joshua b. Md. 1766 d. Del. 1816 m. Ann Liston   Lt. Col. Del. Mil.
  son James T. m. Sarah Ann Daphin

Carter, Landon b. Va. 1760 d. Tenn. 1800   Patriot - Memb.
  m. Elizabeth Maclin   Tenn. Conv. 1796
  son Alfred M. m. Evalina B. Perry

Carter, Rawley Williamson b. Va. 1788 d. Va. 1847   Sgt. Va. Mil.
  m. Anna J. Robertson — son George A. m. Bettie Anne Womack

Carter, Richard b. Md. 1759 d. W. Va. 1835 m. Mary Beall   Pvt. Va.
  son Samuel H. B. m. Amanda Bishop   Cav. Mil.

Carter, Richard B. b. Va. 1793 d. Ohio 1842   Sgt. Va. Mil.
  m. Esther Rogers — daughter Emily B. m. Aschel Clark Cochran

Carter, Robert b. S.C. 1781 d. Ga. 1844 m. Sarah McDaniel   Pvt. S.C. Mil.
  son Ezekiel M. m. Elizabeth McElroy

Carter, Samuel b. Conn. 1770 d. N.Y. 1855   Capt. R.I. Mil.
  m. Nancy Reynolds — son Benjamin P. m. Phebe Davis
  daughter Elizabeth m. James F. Clark

Carter, Thomas b. Mass. (Me.) 1789 d. Me. 1871   Pvt. Mass. (Me.) Mil.
    m. Mehitabel D. Moulton
    son Benjamin F. m. Dorcas Ann Snow

Carter, William b. Va. bet. 1760/70 d. Ky. 1848   Pvt. Ky. Mil.
    m. Unity Bates — son Braxton m. Mary Ewing

Carter, William b. S.C. 1781 d. Miss. 1844   Lieut. Miss.
    m. Hannah Cole   Terr. Mil.
    daughter Mahala m. Jacob Leonard Amacker

Carter, William b. 1786 d. 1816 m. Mary Gibbon   Lieut. U.S. Navy
    son John F. m. Louisa Rhodes

Carter, Zeboam b. 1772 d. Iowa 1853   Lt. Col. N.Y. Mil.
    m. Olivia Hanchett — daughter Deborah S. m. George Jackson, Jr.

Cartmell, Martin b. Va. 1797 d. Tenn. 1864   Pvt. Tenn. Mil.
    m. Jemima Sharp — son R. H. m. Mary J. Baldwin

Cartwright, Peter b. Va. 1785 d. Ill. 1872   Chaplain Ky. Mil.
    m. Frances Gaines — son Valentine m. Cythelia Scott

Carver, Isaac b. Pa. 1792 d. Pa. 1843 m. Lydia Brace   Corp. Pa. Mil.
    daughter Ann m. Joseph Harding

Carver, James b. N.C. 1796 d. Mo. 1847   Pvt., Capt., Maj.
    m. Sarah Gimblin — son James m. Sarah   N.C. Mil.
    son John m. Rebecca Jenkins
    daughter Margaret C. m. James F. Bostick

Carver, John b. Mass. 1774 d. Mass. 1829   Pvt. Mass. Mil.
    m. Huldah Pratt — son John m. Lucy Hammond

Carver, John C. b. Va. 1788 d. Ky. 1873   Pvt. Va. Mil. 1814/15
    m. Nancy Carver (cousin) — son James m. Jane Thomas

Cary, Benjamin b. N.Y. 1763 d. Pa. 1830   Ensign Pa. Mil. 1793
    m. Mercy Abbott — daughter Martha m. Peter Mensch

Cary, John B. b. N.J. 1790 d. N.J. 1872   Capt. N.J. Mil.
    m. Hannah Hammond — son Stephen S. m. Anna E. Whittemore

Cary, Nathan Hulse b. N.Y. 1793 d. N.Y. 1863   Pvt. N.Y. Det. Mil.
    m. Fanny Sylvia (Depew) Dilly
    son Alexander D. m. Florilla Stedge

Cary, Nathaniel b. Va. 1792 d. Mo. 1852   Seaman U.S. Sea
    m. Sophia Cary (cousin)   Fencibles Va.
    daughter Cynthia m. James Trotter

Case, Benajah Sr. b. Conn. 1738 d. Conn. 1790   Patriot - Grand
    m. Lydia Woodruff   Juror Conn.
    son Benajah m. Anna Moses

Case, Israel P. b. Conn. 1781 d. Ohio 1832   Capt. Ohio Mil.
    m. Laurinda Morrison — daughter Mila m. Alvin Case

Case, John b. Mass. 1789 d. Ind. 1864 m. Rhoda Sisson   Pvt. Mass. Mil.
    son George S. m. Julia Chase

Case, Lester b. Conn. 1789 d. Ohio 1866   Pvt. Ohio Mil.
    m. Matilda Bancroft
    daughter Lucretia m. John Nelson Ferris

Case, Noah O.   Vol. 8   Pvt. N.Y. Mil.

Case, Ozias   Vol. 16   Pvt. Conn. Mil.

Case, Philetus b. Conn. 1782 d. Conn. 1857   Pvt. Conn. Mil.
   m. Lucinda Reed — daughter Mercy Lavinia m. Oliver Beach

Case, Reuben b. N.Y. 1796 d. Wisc. 1877   Pvt. N.Y. Mil.
   m. Meribeth Griswold
   daughter Elizabeth m. James Vanderlyn

Case, Stephen b. N.Y. 1771 d. Mich. 1872   Pvt. N.Y. Mil.
   m. Betsy Norwood — daughter Elida Ann m. Robert Brown

Case, William b. Conn. 1776 d. N.Y. 1853   Patriot - Justice Peace
   m. Cynthia   N.Y. 1809 & 3rd Sgt.
   son Charles C. m. Esther A. Green   N.Y. Mil.

Casey, Wanton b. R.I. 1760 d. R.I. 1842   Lieut. Ohio Mil.
   m. Elizabeth Goodall — son Silas m. Abby Perry Pearce

Casey, William b. Va. 1754 d. Ky. 1820   Patriot - Memb. Ky. Leg.
   m. Jane Montgomery — daughter Anne m. John Montgomery

Cash, Isaac b. Pa. 1761 d. Pa. 1813 m. Sally Gore   Ensign Pa. Mil.
   son Isaac m. Sarah Hepburn

Cashon, Samuel b. Va. 1780 d. Va. 1883   Pvt. Va. Mil.
   m. Elizabeth Wilkinson — daughter Harriet m. William B. Roberts

Casler, John H.   Vol. 8   Pvt. N.Y. Mil.

Cason, George b. Va. 1792 d. Mo. 1877   Pvt. Va. Mil.
   m. Mariah E. Partlow
   daughter Mary Jane m. Bennett C. Brown

Cass, Jonathan b. N.H. 1773 d. N.H. 1847   Sgt. N.H. Mil.
   m. Abigail Dow — son Gilman D. m. Fanny Tilton

Cass, Moses b. N.C. 1778 d. N.C. 1854 m. Lucy Jones   Lieut. N.C. Mil.
   son William m. Ruth Cox — son James m. Mary Lincoln

Cassard, Gilbert   Vol. 5   Pvt. Md. Mil.

Cassell, John b. Md. 1785 d. Ky. 1815   Pvt. Ky. Mil. Det.
   m. Hester Farra — son Samuel F. m. Sally Boone Bryan

Cassidy, Edward b. Ireland bef. 1780 d. Pa. 1831   Pvt. U.S. Army
   m. Eleanor McShane — daughter Mary m. Jefferson Douglass
   daughter Nancy m. Hamilton Griffin

Cassidy, William b. Pa. 1784 d. Pa. 1865 m. Sarah Hoffman   Pvt. Pa. Mil.
   daughter Mary Ann m. Abraham Lamer

Cassidy, William b. Ireland 1761 d. Miss. 1847   Pvt. S.C. Mil.
   m. Hannah Dees — son Allen m. Harriet James

Cassin, John b. Pa. 1760 d. S.C. 1822 m.—   Commodore Charleston
   daughter Eliza m. Joseph Tarbell   S.C. Naval Station
   son Stephen m. Margaret Abernathy

Cassin, Stephen b. Pa. 1783 d. D.C. 1857   Commodore U.S.N. at
   m. Margaret Abernathy   Battle of Lake
   son Joseph R. m. Anne Elizabeth Williams   Champlain 1814

Castellan, Stephen Henry b. Spain c. 1794 d. Ga. 1886   Pvt. Ga. Mil.
   m. Mary Sanders — daughter Martha m. William H. Lewis

Castle, Daniel b. Conn. 1782 d. Ohio 1862   Sgt. Ohio Mil.
     m. Mrs. Mary Watrous Willard
     daughter Nancy P. m. Henry Lawton Morrison

Castle, Jonathan b. Vt. 1788 d. Ohio 1834   2d Lieut. Vt. Mil.
     m. Frances P. O'Brien
     daughter Julia Laura m. John Lynde Green

Castleman, Asa b. Ga. 1780 d. Ga. c. 1828   Rifleman Ga. Mil.
     m. Margaret Davis — daughter Annie m. Jabel Faulkner

Casto, Jonathan b. Va. 1794 d. W. Va. 1851   Pvt. Va. Mil.
     m. Magdalene Wetherholt — son Benjamin m. Mary Craig

Caswell, Gilbert b. N.Y. 1755 d. N.Y. 1812   Patriot - Justice Peace
     m. Hannah Foster   N.Y. 1791/1812
     daughter Elizabeth m. Willard Jackson

Cate, Isaac b. Vt. 1795 d. Vt. 1857   Corp. U.S. Inf. - Vt.
     m. Clarissa Knight — son George W. m. Levara S. Brown

Cather, Robert b. Md. 1771 d. Ill. 1849   Pvt. Indian Wars; Sheriff
     m. Sarah Hyde   1799; Sgt. Pa.
     daughter Rebecca H. m. Charles Chase   Mil. 1812/14

Cather, Thomas b. Va. 1751 d. S.C. 1803   Patriot - S.C.
     m. Rachel Miles   Legislator 1786
     son Thomas M. m. Sarah McPherson Postell

Cathey, Alexander b. N.C. 1783 d. Ala. 1866   Pvt. Tenn. Mil. Vols.
     m. Mary Locke — daughter Ann m. Alfred Avery

Caton, Michael b. Ireland 1798 d. D.C. 1885   Pvt. D.C. Mil.
     m. Sarah King — son Thomas m. Ariana Dole

Caulk, Richard b. Md. 1768 d. Mo. 1821 m. Sarah Long   Col. Mo. Mil.
     daughter Sarah Elizabeth m. Alton Long

Causten, James H. b. Md. 1788 d. Md. 1874   Pvt. Md. Vols. in
     m. Eliza Myer   defense D.C.
     daughter Alice E. m. Benjamin F. Fisher

Cauthen, William B. b. S.C. 1790 d. S.C. 1884   Pvt. S.C. Mil.
     m. Nancy Ingram — son John M. m. Matilda Bruce

Cauthorn, Godfrey b. Va. 1784 d. Va. 1849   Pvt. Va. Mil.
     m. Harriett Bryon Starke — son Richard S. m. Elizabeth G. Brown

Cave, William b. Va. 1749 d. Ky. 1839 m. Rachel   Patriot - Justice Peace
     daughter Nellie Ellen m. Joseph Hon Jr.   Va. 1784/87

Cavender, John b. Del. 1790 d. Del. 1837 m. — Jones   Pvt. U.S. Light Art.
     son James m. Ann Willis

Cavet, John b. 1770 d. Pa. 1847   Pvt. Pa. Mil.
     m. Jane Anne (McKean) Hughey
     daughter Margaret m. John Hughey

Caywood, William b. N.J. 1783 d. N.Y. 1853   Pvt. N.Y. Mil.
     m. Mahalath Walker — daughter Ann Lovena m. Jacob Ennis

Cease, Jacob b.— d. Mexico 1848   Capt. Pa. Mil.
     m. Catherine Elizabeth Cole — daughter Sarah m. Daniel Shure

Chace, Russell b. R.I. 1777 d. N.Y. 1862   Capt. N.Y.
     m. Esther Rice — son Supply m. Amanda Winegar   State Troops

Chadbourne, Nahum b. Mass. (Me.) 1784 d. Me. 1857   Quartermaster
 m. Desire Watson — son George m. Harriet Boyington   Mass. Mil.
Chadwick, David   Vol. 17   Capt. Vt. Mil.

Chadwick, Elihu b. N.J. 1759 d. Pa. 1837   Capt. N.J. Mil. 1785
 m. 2d Rebecca Jeffrey   Patriot - Justice Peace
 daughter Sarah m. William Lewis, Jr.

Chaffey, John b. R.I. 1762/4 d. Vt. 1858   Pvt. Conn. Mil.
 m. Patty Tubbs — daughter Julia Ann m. Willis Grant

Chalk, John b. Md. 1777 d. Md. 1829   Pvt. Md. Mil. 1814
 m. Cassandra Kindell — daughter Ruth m. Israel Gosnell   wounded

Chalmers, Peter b. Mass. (Me.) 1779 d. N.Y. 1870 Corp. Mass. (Me.) Mil.
 m. Margaret — son Edwin R. m. Elizabeth —

Chamberlain, Daniel Jr. b. Mass. 1782 d. Mass. 1860   Pvt. Mass. Mil.
 m. Jerusha Burnap — son Dexter H. m. Sarah Moulton N. Wallace

Chamberlain, Enoch b. Mass. 1778 d. Mass. 1841   Pvt. Mass. Mil.
 m. Lucy Holbrook — son William m. Rachel Davis

Chamberlain, Henry   Vol. 15   Pvt. Vt. Mil.

Chamberlain, Isaac b. Vt. 1782 d. Ohio 1863   Sgt. Vt. Mil.
 m. Polly Harriman — daughter Sarah m. James B. Sprague

Chamberlain, John b. Pa. 1776 d. Pa. 1854   Pvt. Pa. Vols.
 m. Elizabeth Zeller — son Willam m. Mary Ann Joyce

Chamberlain, Joseph b. Vt. d. Vt. 1839   Pvt. Vt. Mil.
 m. Electra Sayers — son Mark A. m. Mary E. Bartholomew

Chamberlain, Joshua b. N.H. 1770 d. Me. 1857   Colonel Mass. Mil.
 m. Anna Gould — son Ebenezer M. m. Phoebe Ann Hascall

Chamberlain, William b. N.Y. 1771 d. N.Y. 1850   Patriot - Judge 1808/17
 m. Lucy Park — son Park m. 2d Mary Rebecca White   N.Y. Court

Chambers, Alexander b. Ky. 1792 d. Mo. 1862   Pvt. Ky. Mil.
 m. Sarah Boring — daughter Frances m. John S. Clayton
REAL DAUGHTER
 daughter Harriett m. Dr. Thomas Booth

Chambers, Benjamin b. Pa. 1749 d. Md. 1816   Brig. Gen. Md. Mil.
 m. Elizabeth Forman — son Ezekiel F. m. Sara G. Bowen

Chambers, Enoch b. N.C. 1776 d. Ind. 1850   Pvt. Ind. Terr. Mil.
 m. Margaret Brown — daughter Martha m. John Burroughs

Chambers, Ezekiel F. b. Md. 1788 d. Md. 1867   Capt. Md. Mil.
 m. Sara G. Bowen — daughter Elizabeth A. m. Rev. Clement F. Jones

Chambers, James b. Ky. 1793 d. Ill. 1877   2nd Sgt. Ky. Vols.
 m. Nancy Bucy — son James R. m. Elizabeth Dickey

Chambers, John   Vol. 11   Pvt. Mo. Terr. Mil.

Chambers, John b. N.J. 1780 d. Ky. 1852   Aide-de-Camp
 m. Hannah Taylor   Gen. Harrison
 daughter Jane m. John Samuel Forman

Chambers, Thomas   Vol. 11   Pvt. Mo. Terr. Mil.

Chambers, William   Vol. 10   Pvt. Ky. Mil.

Chambers, William   Vol. 8   Sgt. Md. Mil.

Chambers, William b. Va. d. Va. 1809   Capt. Va. Lt. Inf. 1793
    m. Ann Heatherly — son Mustoe m. Mary Lewis

Champion, Littleberry b. S.C. 1774 d. Ga. c 1823   Pvt. Ga. Mil.
    m. Hannah — son Jason m. Frances Sheffield

Champlin, Christopher b. Conn. 1787 d. Ill. 1858   Sgt. Conn. Mil.
    m. Betsey Sterling Lee
    daughter Cordelia m. Joel West Armstrong
    daughter Mary C. m. Cyrus Bentley Lewis

Chandler, Isaac Hollingsworth b. Pa. 1794 d. Ohio 1856   Pvt. Pa. Mil.
    m. Alice Armstrong — daughter Mary m. William R. Douglas

Chandler, James b. Ga. 1780 d. Ga. 1815 m. Rebecca—   Pvt. Ga. Mil.
    son Mordecai m. Elizabeth Banks

Chandler, Samuel b. Vt. 1795 d. Iowa 1893   Pvt. N.Y. State Mil.
    m. Eliza Kenyon — daughter Martha A. m. William Andrew White

Chandler, Simeon b. Mass. 1766 d. Ill. 1846   2d Lieut. Mass. Mil.
    m. Elizabeth Bigelow — son Simeon m. Almira Bradford

Chandler, Wadsworth b. Mass. 1769 d. Mass. 1842   3rd Sgt. Mass. Mil.
    m. Mercy — son Wadsworth m. Selina

Chandler, William b. Mass. 1761 d. Mass. c. 1840   Pvt. Mass. Mil.
    m. Louisa Shumway — daughter Lucy m. Ruel Gilbert

Chaney, James Walter b. Md. d. Ky. 1866   Pvt. U.S. Volunteers
    m. Lucinda Janey Dulaney
    daughter Annie Eliza m. Warren Milander James Gordon
    REAL DAUGHTER

Chapin, Ashbel b. Mass. 1765 d. Mass. 1840   Capt. Mass. Troops
    m. Eleanor Van Horn — son Titus m. Emily McKinstry

Chapin, Caleb b. Mass. 1736 d. Mass. 1815   Capt. Shay's Rebellion Mass.
    m. Rebecca Bascom — son Consider m. Esther Wallace

Chapin, Charles Jr. b. Mass. 1772 d. N.Y. 1854   Pvt. N.Y. Mil.
    m. Clarissa Day — daughter Roxy m. Anthony Barney

Chapin, Nathaniel   Vol. 16   Pvt. N.H. Mil.

Chapline, Moses W. b. Va. 1789 d. W. Va. 1840   General Va. Mil.
    m. Elizabeth Miller Fox
    daughter Josephine m. Thomas B. Pheby

Chapman, Avery b. Conn. 1781 d. N.Y.—   Musician Conn. Mil.
    m. Welthian Thomas — daughter Eunice T. m. William Crumb

Chapman, Benjamin b. Va. 1779 d. N.C. 1846   Capt. N.C. Mil.
    m. Isabella Gee — daughter Isabella m. Arthur Lewis

Chapman, George Henry b. Conn. 1789 d. Conn. 1877   Capt. Conn. Mil.
    m. Lucie Tully — daughter Harriet m. Dr. Amos Chesebrough

Chapman, Henry P. b. N.Y. 1793 d. N.Y. 1875   Pvt. N.Y. Mil.
    m. Nancy Middlebrook — daughter Martha m. George E. Knox

Chapman, John b. Va. 1740 d. Va. 1815   Lieut. Va. Mil. 1790
    m. Sallie Abbott — son George m. Patience Clay

Chapman, Peter   Early paper   Corp. N.Y. Mil.

Chapman, Phineas b. Conn. 1773 d. Vt. 1842   Pvt. Vt. Vols.
    m. Hannah Eldridge — daughter Sarah m. Horace Doud

Chapman, Richard b. N.C. 1782 d. Ill. 1870   Pvt. Va. Mil.
  m. Celia Davenport
  daughter Miriam Ann m. Ambrose Mitchell

Chapman, Simeon b. Conn. 1785 d. Ohio 1861   Pvt. Ohio Mil.
  m. Phoebe J. Beardsley — son Asahel A. m. Mary E. Newcomer
  son Phinehas B. m. Celia Valentine

Chapman, William b. Tenn. 1782 d. Ky. 1862   Pvt. Tenn. Mil.
  m. Anne E. Chamberlain
  daughter Lucy B. m. Isaac M. Cox   REAL DAUGHTER

Chappell, John b. S.C. 1794 d. S.C. 1853   Pvt. S.C. Mil.
  m. Grace Goodwyn — daughter Rebecca m. Jacob Bookman

Chappell, Oliver b. Conn. 1779 d. N.Y. 1854   Ensign N.Y. Mil.
  m. Rachel Ensworth — son Homer P. m. Mary Doane Wright

Chappell, William L. b. England 1792 d. Mo. 1855 m.—   Pvt. Md. Mil.
  daughter Mary J. m. Joshua H. Alexander   REAL DAUGHTER

Charlock, Henry A. b. N.Y. 1796 d. N.Y. 1876   Pvt. N.Y. Mil.
  m. Charlotte Ablin Nichols
  son Abraham m. Margaret Scofield

Charnal, James   Vol. 6   Pvt. S.C. Mil.

Charter, Nathaniel   Vol. 14   Sgt. Va. Mil.

Chase, Henry b. R.I. 1775 d. R.I. 1850   Capt. Conn. 1802/4
  m. Anna Brownell — son Henry Chase m. Harriet King

Chase, Jacob b. Mass. 1790 d. Mass. 1856   Sgt. Mass. Mil.
  m. Elizabeth Sprague
  daughter Sophronia m. John B. Hawthorne

Chase, Manning   Vol. 8   Adjutant N.Y. Mil.

Chase, Moses b. Mass. 1727 d. N.H. 1799   Patriot - Presidential
  m. Hannah Brown — son Moody m. Rebecca Chapman   Elector N.H.

Chase, Nathaniel b. Mass. 1748 d. N.Y. 1826   Pvt. N.Y. Mil.
  m. Rachel Pierce
  son Reuben m. Mrs. Hannah Merrifield Esty

Chase, Samuel b. Md. 1741 d. Md. 1811   Vol. 17   Patriot - Judge
                     General Court Md. 1811

Chase, Samuel Sr. b. Mass. 1707 d. N.H. 1800   Patriot - Justice
  m. Mary Dudley — son Samuel m. Silence Stowe   Peace 1784

Chase, Silas William Cooper b. Vt. 1773 d. Vt. 1818   Sgt. Vt. Mil.
  m. Mary Somonds — son Autumnus m. Mary A. Peterson

Chatfield, Joel b. Conn. 1756 d. Conn. 1836   Pvt. Conn. Mil.
  m. Ruth Stoddard — son Joel R. m. Mary Tomlinson

Chatfield, Sherman b. Conn. 1789 d. Ill. 1833   Pvt. N.Y. Mil.
  m. Deborah Wood — son Alonzo m. Mary Graves
  daughter Eliza Ann m. Pierre LePitre

Chauncey, Isaac   Vol. 14   Commander Naval Forces

Chauncey, John b. Md.— d.— Mo. m. Cordelia—   Lieut. U.S. Army
  daughter Mary E. m. Squire Boon Green

Chazal, Jean Pierre b. West Indies 1779 d. France 1826   Commander
   m. Elizabeth C. A. de la Lande   Privateer Saucy Jack
   son Pierre August m. Ellen Austin

Cheatham, John B. Jr. b.— d. Tenn.—   Capt. Tenn. Cav. Mil.
   m. Lavinia O. Dawson — daughter Medora m. William Ryder

Cheatham, Obediah Pride b. Va. 1796 d. Ga. 1850   Pvt. Ga. Mil.
   m. Charity Bryan
   son Rufus S. m. Annie Elizabeth Loyless

Cheek, Henry b. c. 1790— d. Miss. aft. 1834   Pvt. La. Mil.
   m. Margaret Allison Hill
   daughter Margaret N. m. Robert Miller IV

Cheek, Henry Hoskins   Vol. 8   Lieut. Miss. Mil.

Chesebrough, Elihu   Vol. 10   Pvt. Conn. Mil.

Chellis, John b. Vt. 1793 d. N.Y. 1876 m. Sally Bullard   Pvt. Vt. Mil.
   daughter Caroline m. Dr. Samuel Fitch REAL DAUGHTER
   daughter Sarah unm.   REAL DAUGHTER

Chenault, James b. Va. 1775 d. Ark. 1830 m.—   Pvt. Va. Mil.
   daughter Margaret m. Isaiah Vanzant

Cheney, Ephraim   Vol. 16   Pvt. Vt. Mil.

Cheney, Luke b. Md. 1793 d. Md. 1825   Ensign Md. Mil.
   m. Matilda Shawen — daughter Amanda m. John H. Strider

Chenowith, Absalom b. Va. 1767 d. Ky. 1842   Pvt. Ky. Mil.
   m. Lydia Ann Ross — daughter Angelina m. Emanuel Stucky

Chenowith, Arthur b. Va. 1755 d. Ohio 1821   Corp. Ohio Mil.
   m. Elizabeth Williams — son Absalom m. Mary Brown

Chenowith, John b. Md. 1755 d. Va. 1831   Capt. W. Va. 1794
   m. Mary Pugh   other civil offices
   daughter Mary m. John W. Stalnaker
   son Robert m. Edith Skidmore

Cherry, Benjamin b. Tenn. 1795 d. Tenn. 1876   Lieut. East Tenn. Mil.
   m. Emily E. Nugent
   daughter Jennie Minerva m. Hugh L. Crownover REAL DAUGHTER
   daughter Josephine m. Jack Clark   REAL DAUGHTER

Cherry, James b. Pa. 1789 d. Ohio 1863   Corp. Pa. Vol. Mil.
   m. 2d Hannah Ross Dean
   daughter Anna H. L. unm.   REAL DAUGHTER

Cherry, Roderick b. N.C. 1790 d. N.C. 1840   Memb. Hse. Commons
   m. Jennie Cherry (cousin)   N.C. 1815-17
   son Marcus C. S. m. Arcena Best

Cherry, Samuel b. Ire. 1756 d. N.Y. 1856   Capt. N.Y. Mil.
   m. Ann Wallace — son Samuel m. Abigail Delano

Cherry, Thomas Perrin b. Pa. 1759 d. Ohio 1829   Pvt. Pa. Mil.
   m. Elizabeth Hurst — son Nathaniel m. Katherine Martin

Cherry, William b. N.J. 1793 d. Ohio 1859   Corp. N.J. Mil.
   m. Hannah Foote — daughter Adeline m. Homer J. Austin

Cheshire, Tennison b. Md. 1791 d. N.C. 1854   Pvt. N.C. Mil.
m. Barbara Mock — daughter Emily Melissa m. Robert Blackwell
daughter Nancy C. m. Major Wilson Gowan
daughter Mary M. m. William Wyche Wilson
daughter Samantha C. m. John W. Wilson

Chesley, Jonathan b. 1784 d. 1863 m. Phebe West   at Plattsburg,
daughter Phebe m. John Liddiard   N.Y. 1814

Chesley, Robert b. Md. c. 1782 d. Va. c. 1825   Pvt. Va. Mil.
m. Elizabeth Bunbury
son William S. m. Mary Ann Forneyhough

Chesley, Simeon Jr. b. Conn. 1767 d. Ohio 1843   Pvt. Conn. Mil.
m. Anna Higby — daughter Mary Frances m. Tillotson King

Chew, John Hamilton   Vol. 17   Capt. Md. Mil.

Chick, James b. Mass. 1783 d. Me. 1855   Pvt. Mass. Mil.
m. Susan West
daughter Sarah Elizabeth m. Edward H. Knight REAL DAUGHTER
son James M. m. Mary Jane Warren

Chickering, Hartshorn b. Mass. 1780 d. Mass. 1825   Pvt. Mass. Mil.
m. Mary Smith — son James m. Nancy Bailey

Chickering, Thomas Balch   Vol. 17   2d Lieut. U.S. Art.

Child, John Throop b. R.I. 1790 d. R.I. 1866   Memb. Council
m. Mary Ann Mason   War 1812/13 R.I.
daughter Molly Turner m. Frank B. Lawton REAL DAUGHTER

Childress, Robert   Vol. 8   Pvt. East Tenn. Mil.

Childs, Andrew b. Pa. 1789 d. Pa. 1864   Ensign Pa. Mil.
m. Margaret Arnwine — son Andrew Jr. m. Margaret M. Price

Childs, Jonathan   Vol. 8   Sgt. Vt. Mil.

Chiles, David b. Ky. 1767 d. Ky. 1834   Brig. Gen. Ky. Mil.
m. Frances Craig — son Lewis C. m. Elizabeth B. Craig

Chiles, John Henry b. Va.— d. Mo. 1838   Major East Tenn.
m. Sarah Ballenger — son Joel F. m. Azubah Skinner   Mtd. Vol.

Chinn, Chichester b. Va. 1771 d. Ky. 1814   Memb. Ky. House
m. Susanna Withers   Repr. 1799
daughter Margaret m. Robert McCausland   Senate 1910/14

Chinn, George G.   Vol. 13   4th Corp. Ky. Vols.

Chinn, Richard Henry   Vol. 11   Pvt. Ky. Mil.

Chipman, Lemuel   Vol. 17   Pvt. N.Y. Mil.

Chipman, Timothy Fuller b. Mass. 1761 d. Vt. 1830   Major Gen. Vt. Mil.
m. Polly Smith — daughter Huldah m. Ephraim Holland

Chisam, John b. S.C. 1780 d. Tenn. 1855   Pvt. Tenn. Mtd. Spies
m. Mary Harris — son William m. Mary Lodema Cotton

Chisum, James b. Tenn. 1774 d. Tenn.—   Pvt. Tenn. Mtd. Mil.
m. Elizabeth — daughter Mary m. John Johnson

Chittenden, Thomas b. Conn. 1730 d. Vt. 1797   1st Gov. Vt. 1778/97
m. Elizabeth Meiggs — son Truman m. Lucy Jones

Chotard, Henry b. St. Domingo 1787 d. Miss. 1870   Asst. Adj. Gen.
    m. Fanny (Francis) Minor   Miss. Terr. Mil.
    daughter Amenaide m. Edward Knight Chaplain

Chrisman, George b. N.C. 1765 d. Ky. 1850   Corp. Ky. Mil.
    m. Elizabeth Hagler — son Peter m. Mary Williams

Christ, George   Vol. 16   Corp. Pa. Mil.

Christ, Henry b. Germany 1718 d. Pa. 1789   Civil Officer 1789
    m. Elizabeth — daughter Elizabeth m. Peter Batolf

Christian, Daniel b. Pa. 1800 d. Pa. 1878 m. Mary Ebert   Pvt. Pa. Mil.
    daughter Lowden m. Rev. Thomas Watson

Christian, Gideon b. Va. c. 1785 d. Va.   Pvt. Va. Cav. Mil.
    m. Miss Apperson — son William E. m. Anne E. Taylor

Christian, Thomas b. Pa. 1787 d. Mich. 1856   Pvt. Pa. Mil.
    m. Hannah Shipley Cole
    son Edmund P. m. Mary Hawley Foster

Christian, Turner b. Va. 1759 d. Va. 1830 m. Susan Walker   Pvt. Va. Mil.
    son Robert W. m. Elizabeth Jones

Christian, William   Vol. 11   Corp. Va. Mil.

Christie, Israel b. Va. 1793 d. Mo. 1873   Pvt. Ky. Mil.
    m. Elizabeth Cook — daughter Sara m. James Anderson Wade

Christie, Robert   Vol. 14   Fifer Pa. Mil.

Christopher, William b. Del. 1775 d. Del. 1831   Corp. Del. Mil.
    m. Sarah Howell — daughter Mary R. m. John Collins Morris

Christy, Daniel b. N.Y. 1791 d. Ohio 1874   Adj. N.Y. Mil.
    m. Alma Green — daughter Sara E. m. Frederick Walter

Chubb, Milo   Vol. 15   Pvt. N.Y. Mil.

Church, Elijah b. Conn. 1792 d. Wisc. 1877   Pvt. N.Y. Mil.
    m. Violet Holcomb — son Cyrus m. Mary Boorman

Church, Gideon b. Conn. 1761 d. Pa. 1793   Pvt. Pa. Mil.
    m. Abigail Harris — son William m. Lucinda Carver

Church, Jeremiah C. b. R.I. 1787 d. Conn. 1860   Pvt. Conn. Mil.
    m. Susan Burdick — daughter Emeline m. Israel Rodolphus Hicks

Church, Malachi b. Mass. 1732 d. Vt. 1790   Courier Mass. Mil.
    m. Elizabeth Miller — son Malachi Jr. m. Lucy Blakeslie

Church, Nathan b. R.I. 1782/92 d. N.Y. 1868   Pvt. N.Y. Mil.
    m. Samantha More — son Zara m. Caroline Knapp

Church, Philip b. Vt. 1790 d. N.Y. 1870   Corp. N.Y. Det. Mil.
    m. Tryphena Titus — son Philip T. m. Mary Walton

Church, William b. Ky. 1782 d. Ky. 1823   Capt. Ky. Mil.
    m. Kate Oliver — son John m. Polly Steele

Church, William b. Mass. (Me.) 1775 d. Ohio 1817   Pvt. Mass. Mil.
    m. Elizabeth Daniels — son Joseph m. Elizabeth Buxton

Churchill, Benjamin b. Conn. 1791 d. Ill. 1893   Pvt. N.Y. Mil.
    m. Catherine Strader — son Levi H. m. Marion E. Williamson

Churchill, Caleb b. Mass. 1757 d. Vt. 1856   Selectman 1804/10 Vt.
m. Sarah Hawley   Surveyor 1811
daughter Betsey m. Anson Manley

Churchill, Darius b. Vt. 1793 d. N.Y. 1862   Pvt. N.Y. Mil.
m. 1st Tryphenia Adeline Newton
son Samuel m. Jemima Devel Jackson

Churchill, Jesse Jr. b. Conn. 1757 d. N.Y. 1828   Chaplain N.Y. Mil.
m. Hannah Boardman — son William B. m. Almira Humes

Churchill, Stephen W. b. N.Y. 1791 d. 1879   Pvt. N.Y. Mil.
m. Margaret Dates — son Zaccheus N. m. Sarah Beardsley

Churchill, William Boardman b. Vt. 1794 d. Ill. 1856   Corp. N.Y. Mil.
m. Almira Humes
daughter Caroline E. m. John Augustine Bingham
son Jesse m. Ann Sherman

Cilley, Joseph b. N.H. 1734 d. N.Y. 1799   State Senator N.H.
m. Sarah Longfellow   Maj. Gen. N.H. Mil.
son Jonathan m. Dorcas Butler

Cilley, Joseph b. N.H. 1791 d. N.H. 1888   Capt. N.H. Mil.
m. Elizabeth Williams — son Joseph N. m. Mary B.
daughter Victoria E. m. Thomas B. Bartlett

Clabaugh, William I. b. Md. 1781/2 d. Tenn. 1863   Pvt. Tenn. Mil.
m. Lavinia King
son William II m. Elizabeth Jean Henley

Clack, John b. Tenn. 1795 d. Ala. 1869   Pvt. East Tenn. Mil.
m. Prudence Rowden
son William S. m. Amanda Melvina Manning

Clack, Raleigh b. Va. 1772 d. Tenn. 1842   Pvt. East Tenn. Mil.
m. Martha Kerr
son William M. m. Isabella Gist Wilson
son John m. Prudence Rowden thru different wife Mary Reynolds

Clack, Spencer b. Va. 1783 d. Tenn. 1854   Pvt. Tenn. Mil.
m. Lucy Williams Jones
son Thomas J. m. Mary Emeline Hadley

Clack, Spencer b. Va. 1746 d. Tenn. 1832   Lawmaker Tenn.
m. Mary Beavers — son Raleigh m. Mary Randles   1796-1832

Claflin, Cornelius b. N.Y. 1788 d. Mich. 1857   Pvt. N.Y. Mil.
m. Phoebe Fuller — son Cornelius m. Sarah E. Kincaid

Claggett, Samuel b. Va. — d. Va. 1846 m. 2d Julia Sanford   Pvt. Va. Mil.
daughter Frances m. William Francis

Claiborne, Charles A. b. Va. 1792 d. Ohio 1864   Pvt. Va. Mil.
m. Mahala Pettus — son William L. m. Lydia Hulitt

Clapp, David b. Mass. 1744 d. Mass. 182-   Repr. Mass. Leg. 1794/99/1800
m. — No further data   Vol. 6   Capt. Mass. Mil.

Clapp, Thaddeus b. Mass. 1770 d. Mass. 1860   Civil Officer Del. Co. Conv.
m. —Achsah Parsons   1812 Mass.
son Luther m. Lucy Parsons Pomeroy

Clapsaddle, George b. N.Y. 1767 d. N.Y. 1832-40   Lieut. N.Y. Mil.
m. Anna Deigert — son John m. Louisa Cain (Waterman)

Clapsaddle, William b. N.Y. 1762 d. N.Y. 1827   Lt. Col. Herkimer Co.
m. (Miriah) Elizabeth Haner (Hayer)   N.Y. Mil.
daughter Nancy m. Ichabod Tanner
son Peter m. Mary Steele

Clardy, William b. Va. 1787 d. Va. 1853 m. Annie Ferell   Pvt. Va. Mil.
daughter Paulina m. Robert Henry Bradner

Clark, Abraham b. Conn. 1782 d. Conn. 1847   Ensign Conn. Mil.
m. Lurana Champion — son Erastus m. Emily Crandall

Clark, Abraham b. Md. 1794 d. Md. 1839   Ensign, Lieut. Q.M. U.S. Inf.
m. Maria Clark — son John M. m. Ann M. Boswell

Clark, Amasa b. Conn. 1764 d. Conn. 1847   Sgt. Conn. Mil.
m. Elenor Fuller — son Thomas m. Peggy Hazen

Clark, Andrew b. Pa. 1774 d. Pa. 1851 m. Anna Simpson   Sgt. Pa. Mil.
son John S. m. Sabra Perlina Hill

Clark Baley Erles b. Md. 1768 d. Md. 1816   Lieut Md. Cav.
m. Elizabeth Van Horn — daughter Maria m. Abraham Clark

Clark, Caleb b. Vt. 1791 d. N.Y. 1868 m. Clarissa Tripp   Pvt. N.Y. Mil.
daughter Marrietta E. m. Seth B. Tibbets
son William m. Statira Joslin

Clark, Calvin b. Md. 1790 d. Pa. 1840 m. Tacy Coughlin   Sgt. U.S. Inf.
daughter Rebecca Ann m. Edward T. Wills

Clark, Charles II b. N.Y. 1762 d. N.J. 1821   Actg. Gov. N.J. 1812/15
m. Anna Youmans — son Charles III m. Mary Eleanor Carswell
daughter Elizabeth m. Jonas Smith
son Samuel J. m. Rachel Clark

Clark, Christopher b. Va. 1767/8 d. Va. 1828   Memb. Congress 1804
m. Elizabeth Hook
daughter Susan Jane m. Dr. Thomas Evans

Clark, Daniel b. — 1794 d. Tenn. 1881   Pvt. Tenn. Mil.
m. Catherine Henry
daughter Martha Jane m. Arch or Henry Porter

Clark, Eleazer b. Mass. 1764 d. Mass. 1832   Capt. Mass. Vol. Mil.
m. Sarah Clark (rel.)   Shay's Reb.
son Eleazer m. Anna Lippincott

Clark, George b. Pa. 1772 d. Ohio 1825 m. Hannah Vaughn   2d Lieut.
son George Jr. m. Jane Nairn   Ohio Mil.

Clark, George Washington b. Va. 1797 d. Nebr. 1892   Pvt. Va. Mil.
m. Jane R. Shelton — daughter Narcissa m. Thomas Huston

Clark, Henry James b. Va. 1794 d. Ill. 1874   Musician Va. Mil.
m. Mary Lewis Mansfield
son Henry S. m. Frances Elizabeth Cassidy
daughter Mary C. m. U. S. Hodge

Clark, Hermon Munson b. Conn. 1789 d. Ohio 1865   Surgeon N.Y. Mil.
m. Laura Daviess — son Theodore F. m. Lencie Tuller

Clark, Isaac b.— d.— m. Hannah Crittendon   Col. U.S. Inf.
daughter Modena m. Gideon Dyer Cobb

Clark, James b. Ire. (N.J.) 1762 d. Mo. 1852   Qm. Ohio Mil.
m. Ann Griffith — son Bazabel W. m. Elizabeth Myers
daughter Sarah m. George Pfouts

Clark, James b. Pa. 1742 d. Pa. 1824   Major Ind. Wars
  m. Barbara Sanderson   Pa. 1786
  son William m. Sarah Woodward

Clark, James b.— 1787 d. Pa. 1871 m. Anna Means   Pvt. Pa. Mil.
  daughter Catherine m. John McNees

Clark, Jesse b. Va. 1778 d. Ohio 1861 m. Jane Grant   Pvt. Ohio Mil.
  daughter Sarah Y. m. John Moore

Clark, John b. N.Y. 1776 d. N.Y. 1856 m. Rhoda —   Pvt. N.Y. Mil.
  son Laomi m. 1st Lydia Powers

Clark, John b. N.C. 1776 d. Ala. 1832 m. Nancy Williamson   Major Gen.
  daughter Elizabeth m. John McGrew   Ga. Mil. 1812

Clark, John b. N.C. 1780 d. Ga. 1870 m. Susan Parke   Pvt. S.C. Mil.
  daughter Nancy Amelia m. Thomas W. Sims

Clark, John b. Md. 1777 d. Iowa 1862 m. Sarah   Pvt. Ohio Mil. 1812/13
  son John m. Lucy A. Knauss

Clark, John   Vol. 14   Major Pa. Mil.

Clark, John   Vol. 15   Pvt. S.C. Mil.

Clark, John L. b. R.I. 1772, d. N.Y. 1856 m. Eliff Calkins   Qm. N.Y. Mil.
  daughter Fanny m. Smith C. Bateman

Clark, Jonathan b. Mass. (Me.) 1777 d. Me. 1857   Sgt. Mass. (Me.) Mil.
  m. Sarah Young — son Socrates m. Harriet Todd

Clark, Joseph   Vol. 4   Pvt. — Me.?

Clark, Joseph b. Va. 1776 d. at Dudley's Defeat 1813   Pvt. Ky. Mil.
  m. Jane Frame — son William Joseph m. Matilda Park

Clark, Julius Deming   Vol. 3   Pvt. Vt. Riflemen

Clark, Moses A.   Vol. 17   Pvt. Vt. Mil.

Clark, Nathaniel b. Mass. (Mc.) 1786 d. Me. 1850   Pvt. Mass. Mil.
  m. Mary Gilpatrick Adams Small
  daughter Martha m. Samuel Stephens Felt

Clark, Newton b. Conn. 1788 d. N.Y. 1879   Corp. N.Y. Mil.
  m. Elizabeth Cone — daughter Clarissa Ann m. Rutson Rea

Clark, Oliver   Vol. 15   Pvt. Conn. Mil.

Clark, Oliver b. Mass. 1756 d. Mass. 1824   Pvt. Mass. Mil.
  m. Phebe Parsons — son Julius m. Hannah Pelton

Clark, Oramel b. Conn. 1792 d. Ill. 1863 m. Judith Wroe   Corp. Mass. Mil.
  daughter Carline I. m. John M. Amos

Clark, Rufus b. Conn. 1763 d. Pa. 1846   Pvt. Conn. Mil.
  m. Phebe Blanchard — daughter Almeda m. William Goodwin

Clark, Samuel   Vol. 9   Pvt. N.H. Mil.

Clark, Samuel b. Pa. 1770 d. Pa. 1860 m. Mary Custer   Civil Officer Pa.
  daughter Sarah m. John Gillespie

Clark, Samuel H. b. N.H. 1791 d. N.J. 1882   Adjutant
  m. Alice Barker Wilson   Mass. Mil.
  daughter Alice m. Benjamin Boynton Rollins
  daughter Ruth M. m. Walter Hardy   REAL DAUGHTER

Clark, Timothy b. 1794 d. 1863 m. Caroline Thayer   Pvt. N.Y. Mil.
son Francis Eugene m. Lavine C. J. Scott

Clark, Thomas   Vol. 15   Mem. Conn. Leg. 1797/1802

Clark, Thomas b. Mass. 1745 d. Vt. 1836   Selectmen 1786/96 —
m. Catherine Ward   Repr. Gen. Ct. 1789/90 Vt.
son Thomas m. Martha Bond Tenney

Clark, Vachel b. Ky. d. Mo. m. — Adams   Pvt. Ky. Mtd. Vols.
daughter Permelia Ann m. Joseph Perry Russell

Clark, Waters b. Conn. — d. La. 1814 m. Eunice Benjamin   Maj. U.S. Inf.
son Sheldon S. m. Mary Emeline Casson

Clark, William b. Ky. 1790 d. Ky. 1870 m. Betsey Darnaby   Pvt. Ky. Mil.
daughter Anne Elizabeth m. Thomas Corbin Wood

Clark, William b. Pa. 1784 d. Ohio 1824/5   Col. Ohio Mil.
m. Kitturah Brown
son Edward B. m. Elizabeth Thompson
son Milton Lee m. Jane Isabel Woodside

Clark, William b. Va. 1798 d. Va. 1898 m. Eliz. Winston   Adj.
daughter Missouri m. Richard L. Ricks   Va. Mil.

Clark, William Jr. b. Va. 1789 d. Ala. 1833 m. Susan Adams   Lieut.
daughter Isabelle Martha m. Joseph C. Bradley   Va. Mil.

Clark, William Weston b. 1781 d. 1835   Pvt. 5th Det. Pa. Mil.
m. Margaret Young — daughter Nancy m. William Dorrance

Clarke, Benjamin Jr. b. N.J. 1766 d. N.J. 1820   Capt. N.J. Mil.
m. Mary Howell — son Charles m. Gertrude Anderson Perrine

Clarke, Elijah b. N.C. 1736 d. Ga. 1809   Indian Fighter
m. Hannah Arrington   Ga.
daughter Fanny m. Edwin Munger

Clarke, Gideon b. R.I. 1738 d. R.I. 1817   Just. Peace 1793/7 R.I.
m. Eunice Browning — son Silas m. Ruhamah Cross

Clarke, Joseph b. Va. 1793 d. Ky. 1875 m. Harriet Julian   Pvt. Ky. Mil.
daughter Mary Ann m. James L. Sneed

Clarke, Robert b. Md. 1782/5 d. Wash., D.C. 1833   Pvt. Md. Mil.
m. Jane McDaniel — daughter Frances L. m. John Ober

Clarke, Samuel b. Mass. 1791 d. Mass.— m. Alice Nelson   Pvt. Mass. Mil.
daughter Ruth M. m. Walter Hardy

Clarke, William b. R.I. 1778 d. N.Y. 1843   Pvt. N.Y. Mil.
m. Sally Hamilton — son Joseph m. Julia A. Eddy

Clarkson, Aquilla b. Va. 1786 d. Ill. 1865   Pvt. East Tenn. Mil.
m. Frances Young — son Franklin S. m. Eliza Kelley

Clarkson, Charles Smith b. Va. 1792/3 d. Mo. 1872   Maj. and Asst. Dist.
m. Charlotte A. R. Dunlop   Paymaster U.S. Army Ohio
son James D. m. Elvira Scott

Clarkson, John b. Va. bef. 1790 d. Va. 1836   Sgt. Va. Mil.
m. Mary Gatewood — son John H. m. Sarah Ann Wright

Clarkson. Richard P. b. N.H. 1782 d. Ind. 1849   Lieut. Mass. Mil.
m. Mary Simpson
son Tisdale D. m. Hannah W. Ferguson

Clarridge, Edmund b. Md. 1789 d. Ohio 1868   Pvt. Ohio Mil.
  m. Eleanor McCafferty
  daughter Elizabeth m. Isaac McClimans

Clary, Ethan Allen b. Mass. 1777 d. Mass. 1849   Lieut U.S. Inf.
  m. Electa Smith — daughter Caroline m. Samuel Saxton

Clay, Green b. Va. 1757 d. Ky. 1828 m. Sallie Lewis   General
  son Cassius M. m. Mary Jane Warfield   Ky. Vol. Mil.
  daughter Eliza m. John Speed Smith
  daughter Paulina m. William Rodes

Clay, Henry b. Va. 1779 d. Ky. 1863 m. Margaret Helm   2nd Lieut.
  son Francis P. m. Susan Ryon Wornall   Ky. Mtd. Riflemen
  son Samuel m. Nancy Tucker Wornall

Clay, John Ingram b. Va. 1790 d. Mo. 1873   Pvt. Ky. Mil.
  m. Martha Alice Eldridge
  son Samuel P. m. Emily Kell

Clay, Woodson b. Va. 1797 d. Tenn. 1824   Pvt. West Tenn. Vol. Mil.
  m. Orpha Kennedy
  daughter Ann m. Albert Green

Claybrooks, Edward b. Va. 1776 d. Ky. 1854   Pvt. Va. Mil.
  m. Dicie Bayley — son James B. m. Susan Keith

Clayton, Beverly William b. Va. 1789 d. Ark 1873   Pvt. Ky. Mtd. Mil.
  m. Sally Ryan — son Beverly W. m. Mary C. Kerr

Clayton, John b. Pa. 1792 d. Pa. 1871   Fifer Ind. Blues Pa. Mil.
  m. Sarah Ann Clark
  son John M. m. Sarah Ann Zebley

Clayton, John b. Va. 1790 d. Tenn. 1864   Pvt. West Tenn. Mil.
  m. Mrs. Ellen Mayfield Bridges
  daughter Mary Jane m. Isaac Newton (Hulme)
  daughter Nancy m. James Love Johnston

Claytor, Coleman b. Va. 1796 d. Ill. 1871   Pvt. Va. Mil.
  m. Phoebe Ann Buchanan
  son John A. m. Hester Ann Jones

Cleaver, David b. N.J. 1770 d. Ky. 1829   Lieut. Col. Ky. Mil.
  m. Letitia Griffey — son Stephen D. m. Lucy Ann Murray

Cleek, John b. 1777 — d. 1848 — m. Jane Owin   Pvt. 2nd Reg. Pa. Mil.
  son John II m. Sarah Kimes Givens

Clegg, John Polk b N.C. 1792 d. Ark. 1854 m. Martha Boone   Pvt.
  son Benjamin F. m. Nancy Bassett   N.C. Mil.
  daughter Nancy m. Elias D. Culpepper

Cleghorn, James b. N.C. bef. 1775 d. Ga. 1831   Officer Ga. Mil.
  m. Nancy Jones — son Almomach m. Rosa B. Cash

Cleghorn, James b. Va. 1787 d. Va. 1875 m. Rachel James   Pvt. Va. Mil.
  daughter Hannah m. James Bell Walker

Clem, Michael b. Va. 1777 d. W.Va. 1858   Pvt. Va. Mil.
  m. Mary Elizabeth Walter
  daughter Rebecca m. Washington Marteney

Clemens, Alexander b. Mass. (Me.) 1793 d. Ohio 1886   Pvt. N.Y. Mil.
  m. Angeline Hollister — son Phineas H. m. Alice Douglas

Clemens, Edward b. Md. 1787 d. Ind. 1849 m. Mary Morris   Sgt. Md. Mil.
    son James J. m. Elizabeth Kerr

Clement, Adam b. Va. 1739 d. Va. 1813   Sheriff Va. 1791
    m. Agnes Johnson   Capt. Mil. 1787
    daughter Susanna m. Temple Perkins

Clement, Jeremiah   Vol. (early)   Sgt. Dist. Me. Mil.

Clement, John b. N.J. 1769 d. N.J. 1855   Adj. & Major N.J. Mil.
    m. Hannah Chew — son Aaron m. Mary Ann Albertson

Clements, John b. Va. 1764 d. Md. 1870 m. Eliza Wingate   Pvt. Md. Mil.
    daughter Martha m. John T. Hope

Clements, Peter b. N.Y. 1785 d. N.Y. 1842   Pvt. N.Y. Det. Mil.
    m. Lydia McBride — son Isaac m. Nancy Bigelow Thomas

Clements, Robert b. Va. 1783 d. Mo. 1879   Pvt. Va. Mil.
    m. Elizabeth Thomas
    daughter Elizabeth m. Pierce Lamb Dye

Clements, Thomas b. Va. 1792 d. Ind. 1861   Pvt. 15th Regt.
    m. Winifred (Richardson)   Ky. Mil. 1814/15
    son Thomas m. Catherine Marshall McIntosh

Clemm, William b. Md. 1779 d. Md. 1826 m. Harriet Poe   Pvt. Md. Mil.
    daughter Josephine E. m. Neilson Poe

Clemons, Alexander   Vol. 17   Pvt. N.Y. Mil.

Clemons, Hine b. c 1770 d. N.Y. 1855 m. Elizabeth —   Pvt. N.Y. Mil.
    daughter Rachel Elizabeth m. Mark H. Kidder

Clemons, Samuel Peet   Vol. 15   Pvt. Conn. Mil.

Clemson, Elihu B. b. Pa.— d.— 1845 m. Maria Oliver   Lt. Col. U.S. Inf.
    daughter Mary C. m. Joseph Olden

Clemson, James III b. Pa. 1727 d. Pa. 1792   Justice of Peace Pa.
    m. Margaret Heard
    son John m. Mary Elizabeth Haines

Clendenin, Alexander b. Va. c. 1754 d. Va. ? 1829   Ensign 1791 (W.)Va.
    m. Catherine Spencer — son Andrew m. Rebecca Edwards

Clendenin, William b. Va. 1753 d. (W.) Va. 1828   Major Indian War
    m. Margaret Handley   1788/9
    daughter Sophia m. John Miller

Cleuverius, Benjamin b. Va. 1778 d. Va. 1843   Major Va. Mil.
    m. Dorothy Gibson
    daughter Harriet Elizabeth m. Francis Thornton

Cleveland, Augustus b. Conn. 1778 d. N.Y. 1826   Capt. N.Y. Mil.
    m. Sally Cushman — son Moses m. Tryphena Bates

Cleveland, Erastus b. Conn. 1771 d. N.Y. 1858   Lt. Col. N.Y. Mil.
    m. Rebecca Berry — daughter Jeannette m. Hamilton Putnam

Cleveland, George Columbus b. Ga. 1790 d. Ga. 1883   Pvt. Ga. Mil.
    m. Nancy Cleveland (cousin)
    daughter Melvina E. m. Fred Eastman Vining

Cleveland, Harvey   Vol. 15   Sgt. N.Y. Mil.

Cleveland, Henry Wilson b. Va. 1798 d. Ky. 1874   **Pvt. Ky. Mil.**
  m. Elizabeth Bare
  son James A. m. Sarah Ellen Raywood or Raymond
  son Oliver A. m. Americus F. Casey

Cleveland, John b. Va. 1730 d. S.C. 1825   **Capt. Ga. Mil. 1791**
  m. Mary McCann   **Legislator 1789**
  son Benjamin m. Margaret Holland
  son William m. Nancy Harrison

Cleveland, John b. Conn. 1779 d. Ohio 1861   **Pvt. N.Y. Mil.**
  m. Silvia Phillips — son John P. m. Sarah Hatch

Cleveland, Joseph b. Mass. 1738 d. (Me.) Mass. 1816   **Sgt. Mass.**
  m. Dorothy Cragain   **(Me.) Mil.**
  son Timothy m. Jane McFadden

Cleveland, Moses b. Vt. 1799 d. Wisc. 1894   **Pvt. N.Y. Mil.**
  m. Tryphena Bates — son Charles m. Sophia King

Cleveland, Robert b. Va. 1744 d. N.C. 1812/18   **Presidential Elector**
  m. Aley Mathis   **N.C. 1809**
  son Eli m. Mary Ragon

Cleveland, Timothy b. Mass. (Me.) 1770 d. Me. 1853   **Pvt. Me. Mil.**
  m. Jane McFadden — daughter Sarah m. McKenney Hilton

Clever, Charles   Vol. 12   **Pvt. Vt. Mil.**

Clever (Klever, Kleber), Martin b. Pa. 1760 d. Pa. 1825   **Pvt.**
  m. Catharine —   **Pa. Mil.**
  daughter Catharine m. Jacob Lehman

Clew, James Beach   Early Vol.   **Capt. Pa. Mil.**

Clifton, Daniel b. Del. 1765 d. Del. 1827   **Pvt. Del. Troops**
  m. Catherine Hargis
  daughter Catherine m. Thomas Albert Maguire

Cline, Andrew b. Pa. 1791 d. Ind. 1862   **Pvt. Ohio 1813-14**
  m. Hannah Kistler — son William Kline m. Angeline Hamilton

Cline, James b. Va. bef. 1794 d. Ohio 1836   **Pvt. 5th Reg.**
  m. Christena Hershberger   **Va. Mtd. Riflemen**
  daughter Amanda m. Levi Tarr

Cline, Philip b. Va. 1781 d. Ohio 1865 m. Mary Turner   **Pvt. Ohio Mil.**
  son George W. m. Catherine Feagins

Clingman, George Washington b. Pa. 1779 d. Ill. 1856   **Lieut. Ohio Mil.**
  m. Mary Ann Bright
  son John B. m. Sarah Parker Turner

Clizbe, Daniel or Darius b. N.J. 1786 d. N.Y. 1869   **Pvt. N.Y. Mil.**
  m. Mary Jones — son Samuel J. m. Marie A. Chamberlain

Clizbe, Jonathan b. N.J. 1779 d. N.Y. 1850   **Lieut. N.Y. Light Inf.**
  m. Hannah Glass — son Ira m. Mary Mahoney

Clopper, Andrew b. N.Y.C. 1771 d. Md. m. Ann Torrence   **4th Sgt. Md.**
  daughter Rachel m. Henry Basil Waring   **Fencibles**

Clopton, John b. Va. 1756 d. Va. 1816 **Memb. Congress 1795, 99, 01-16 Va.**
  m. Sarah Bacon — son John B. m. Maria G. Foster

Clopton, John B. b. Va. 1789 d. Va. 1860 **Sgt. Maj. Va. Mil. New Kent Co.**
  m. Maria Foster — son Francis B. m. Mary Boyd

Close, Stephen b. Conn. 1769 d. N.Y. 1817 Memb. Assembly N.Y. 1810/12
m. Joanna Baxter — son Samuel m. Susan Dwinell

Clough, Aaron b. Conn. 1763 d. Ohio 1823   Lieut. Ohio Mil.
m. Sarah Delano — daughter Julia m. Daniel Oakes

Clough, John b. Mass. (Me.) 1787 d. Wisc. 1855   Pvt. Mass. Vol. Mil.
m. Sybil Howard — daughter Harriet m. Benjamin Webster

Clough, John b. Mass. 1777 d. N.Y. 1826   Sgt. N.Y. Art.
m. Mary Throop Chapman
son Simeon D. m. Marie Louise Hyatt

Clough, William b. Mass. 1797 d. Kans. 1866   Ensign Mass. Mil.
m. Mary Ann Elliott
son William m. Mrs. Mary Ann Scott Embry

Clover, Lewis Peter b. N.J. 1790 d. N.Y. 1879   Prisoner at
m. Bridget Murphy   Dartmoor, Eng.
son William Charles m. Mary Earle

Clover, Peter b. Pa. 1791 d. Ohio 1846   Pvt. Ohio Mil.
m. Elizabeth Wridner
son Elkanah m. Susan Gardner

Clower, John b. Ga. 1780 d. La. 1837   Pvt. 13th Reg.
m. Polly Pleasants   Miss. Mil.
daughter Matilda m. Thomas M. Donahoo

Cloyd, James Barr b. Pa. 1779 d. Tenn. 1861   Pvt. Tenn. Mil.
m. Mary Patton — daughter Jenny B. m. Enos Campbell

Cloyd, Joshua b. Va. 1784 d. Ohio 1862   Corp. Ohio Mil.
m. Edith Southerland
daughter Sarah Amanda
m. Martin L. McWhinney — REAL DAUGHTER
daughter Malinda m. Alfred B. Brown — REAL DAUGHTER

Cluley, John Jr.   Vol. 9   Pvt. Pa. Art. Mil.

Cluley, John Francis Jr.   Early Vol.   Memb. Hse. Deleg.
                                       Va. 1784/6 Justice

Clute, Peter b. N.Y. 1765 d. N.Y. 1835   Pvt. N.Y. Mil.
m. Engeline Van Slyck — daughter Catharine m. Johannes Teller

Clyborne (Claiborne), Charles A. b. Va. 1792   Pvt. Amelia Co.
d. Va. 1864 m. Mahala Pettus   Va. Mil.
son William L. m. Lydia Hulitt

Clymer, Daniel Cunningham b. Pa. 1748   Repr. Berks Co., Pa.
d. Pa. 1810 m. Mary Weidner   1783/91
son Edward T. m. Mary Catherine Hiester

Coates (Coats), Benjamin b. Mass. 1785   Pvt. Mass. Mil.
d. Mass. after 1833 m. Mary Kimball   (Night Guards)
daughter Serena m. Joseph Belcher

Coates, William b. Pa. — d. Pa. —   Pvt. Pa. Mil.
m. Miss Catesby   Vol. 1
daughter Susan Juliet m. George Franklin Klingle

Cobb, John b. Pa. 1788 d. Pa. 1866 m. Mary Swingle   Pvt. Pa. Mil.
daughter Amy m. William A. Allen

Cobb, Jonathan b. Mass. 1770 d. Mass. 1845   Pvt. Mass. Mil.
m. Sibel Miller
son William H. m. Candide Josephine Casanovas

Cobb, Matthias   Vol. 7   Matross, N.J. Inf.

Cobb, Thomas b. N.J. 1760 d. N.J. 1845   Sgt. N.J. Mil.
m. Clara Rosina de Tabera
son Delphin B. m. Anna McLeod

Coble, Eli b. Ohio 1790 d. Ind. 1864 m. Mary Smith   Pvt. Ohio Mil.
son Nicholas S. m. Martha Pence

Cochram, William b. — d. S.C. — m. Mary —   Pvt. S.C. Mil.
daughter Jane m. Reuben McElroy

Cochran, Andrew   Vol. 6   Pvt. Ohio Mil.

Cochran, Barnabas b. N.J. 1774 d. Ohio 1846   Pvt. Ohio Mil.
m. Charlotte Stites
daughter Charlotte m. Francis Smith
daughter Sylvitha m. Thomas Greenwell Cockerill

Cochran, David b. c 1790 ? d. S.C. 1828   Corp. 2d Regt. S.C. Troops
m. Mary Laird — daughter Margaret m. William D. Weathersbee

Cochran, James b. N.H. 1748 d. N.H. 1822   Selectman, Dept. Sheriff;
m. Elizabeth McKeen Nesmith   Coroner 1794-1822 N.H.
son James m. Jane Moore

Cochran, John b. Mass. (Me.) 1749 d. Maine 1839   Pvt. Mass. (Me.) Mil.
m. Mary Adams — daughter Mary m. Parker Jewett

Cochran, John b. Pa. 1781 d. Ohio 1864   Quartermaster Sgt. Ohio Mil.
m. Tamar Howard
daughter Elizabeth m. William Shelton
son John m. Margaret Starrett
daughter Sarah Jane m. Joseph Stewart

Cochran, John b. Va. 1794 d. Va. 1884   Pvt. Augusta Co.
m. Margaret Lynn Lewis   Va. Mil.
daughter Mary P. L. m. John Montgomery — REAL DAUGHTER

Cochran, Nathaniel b. Pa. 1757 d. (W.) Va. 1808   Capt. Harrison Co.
m. Elizabeth Ford   Va. Mil.
son James m. Amanda Brumage
son John m. Sarah B. Morgan

Cochran, Robert b. Vt. 1746 d. N.Y. 1812   Capt. Vt. Mil. 1792
m. Mary Miller — daughter Jeannette m. Asahel Haskins

Cochran, Samuel   Vol. 10   Pvt. Ohio Mil.

Cochran, Samuel b. Pa. 1763 d. Pa. 1829   Brigade Inspector
m. Rebecca —   Pa. Mil.
son James m. Jane Mackateney

Cochran, William b. Ire. 1792 d. Ala. 1858   Pvt. N.Y. Mil.
m. Martha Dickey or m. Matilda Swan Johnston
son Thomas m. Nancy Ann Manning

Cocke, Harrison Henry   Vol. 15, 16, 13   Commodore U.S. Navy

Cocke, John Hartwell b. Va. 1780 d. Va. 1866   Brig. Gen. Va. 1814
m. Ann Blaus — son Philip m. Sally E. C. Bowdin

Cocke, Walter Travis   Vol. 15   Capt. U.S. Inf.

Cockrell, James b. Mo. 1785 d. Mo. 1843   Pvt. Mo. Terr. Mil.
m. Nancy Maria Stovall — daughter Mary m. James H. Longacre

Cockrill, John II b. N.C. 1757 d. N.C. 1837   Patriot 1789 N.C.
m. Mrs. Ann Robertson Johnston
son John III m. Elizabeth B. H. Underwood

Cockrill, Thomas b. Ire. 1768 d. Md. 1815   Lieut. Md. Mil.
m. Rebecca Ward Veazey (2)
son James J. m. Mary Evelyn Ford

Codding, Abiather b. Vt. 1775 d. Vt. 1861   Pvt. Vt. Det. Mil.
m. Mariana (Meriam) Marble
son James or Jonas m. Rachel Tillotson

Codman, Frederick b. Mass. (Me.) 1793 d. Md. 1854   Pvt. Mass. (Me.)
m. Margaret Green   Mil.
daughter Elizabeth m. James Edward Ford

Coe, Joel b. Conn. 1758 d. N.Y. 1846   Ensign N.Y. State Mil.
m. Huldah Robinson Horton
daughter Huldah m. Walter Bennet

Coe, Joseph b. Pa. 1796 d. Iowa 1855 m. Sarah Winans   Pvt. Ohio Mil.
daughter Esther m. Edwin Keech Morse

Coen, Edward b. Md. 1794 d. W.Va. 1881   Pvt. Md. Mil.
m. Grace Murray — son Charles M. m. Elizabeth P. Robb

Coenhoven, Christian   Vol. 6   2nd Lieut. N.Y. Mil.

Coffee, John b. Va. 1772 d. Ala. 1833 m. Mary Donelson   Brig. Gen.
son Andrew J. m. Elizabeth Atwood Hutchinson   Ga. Mil.

Coffee, John b. Va. 1782 d. Ga. 1836   Gen. Ga. Mil. Creek War
m. Ann Penelope Bryan   1813/14
son John B. m. Marcella Griffin
son Peter H. m. Susan Ann Rogers

Coffeen, William b. Vt. 1775 d. Wis. 1864   Adj. N.Y. Mil.
m. Bathsheba Lynde — daughter Rosalinda m. Benjamin S. Budd

Coffey, Jesse b. 1784 ? d. 1850 prob. Ky.   Capt. 1st Co. Ky. Mil.
m. Elizabeth Riffe — daughter Hannah m. John S. Coulter Jr.

Coffey, John b. Pa. 1772 d. Ohio 1853 m. Ruth Mitchell   Capt. Ohio Mil.
daughter Isabella m. Watson Douglass

Coffin, Moses   Vol. 15   Pvt. Vt. Mil.

Coffin, Tristram b. Mass. 1733 d. Mass. 1803   Pvt. Mass. Art. 1785
m. Anne Davis
daughter Eunice m. Nathan Emery Coffin

Coggeshall, William b. R.I. 1752 d. R.I. 1823   Mem. Gen. Assy.
m. Molly Finney   R.I. 1804/6
son Josiah m. Mary Pierce Finney

Cogswell, William   Vol. 9   Judge, Pittsford, N.Y.

Cohorn, John C. Jr.   Vol. 8   Capt. Va. Mil.

Cokefair, Zebulon b. N.J. 1798 d. N.J. 1859   Pvt. N.J. Det. Mil.
m. Catherine Carl
son Ephraim m. Eliza Terhune

Colbert (Colvert, Calvert), William b. Va. 1792 d. Va. 1841   Pvt. Va. Mil.
m. Mary Guy — daughter Virginia m. Thomas Cunningham

Colburn, Andrew   Vol. 12   Pvt. N.Y. Mil.

Colburn, Isaac Jr. b. Mass. 1766 d. Mass. 1845   Selectman, Auditor,
m. 1st Elizabeth Dexter   Assessor Dedham, Mass. 1802/14
daughter Lucy m. Cortus Harmon Lincoln

Colburn, William b. Mass. 1793 d. Ill. 1869   Pvt. Mass. Mil.
m. Achsah Phelps — son Daniel W. m. Lucinda Huffmaster

Colby, Enoch   Vol. 3   Pvt. N.H. Vols.

Colby, Enoch Eastman   Vol. 9   Ensign N.Y. Mil.

Colby, Ephraim   Vol 13, 14   Drummer Vt. Mil.

Colcord, Ivory b. Mass. (Me.) 1799 d. Ill. 1865   Fifer Mass. (Me.)
m. Elzina Smith   Mil. 1812
son William H. m. Fianna V. Linerode

Cole, Abram b. N.Y. 1793 d. N.Y. 1878   Sgt. N.Y. Mil.
m. Polly Benjamin — son Noah H. m. Olive Ann Lusk

Cole, Ezekiel b. Pa. 1756 d. Pa. 1829 m. Elizabeth Hess   Sgt. Pa. Mil.
son William m. Elizabeth Laubach

Cole, Gershom b. Mass. (Me.) 1782 d. Me. 1859   Pvt. U.S. Inf.
m. Polly Besse — son George W. m. Miranda Cooper

Cole, Hannah Allison b. Va. 1764 d. Mo. 1843 Defender Frontier Mo. 1814
m. William Temple Cole — son Samuel m. Sarah Briscoe
son William m. Nancy Wood

Cole, Hezekiah b. R.I. 1765 d. N.Y. 1814   2nd Major R.I. Troops
m. Bethani Arnold — son Arnold m. Ruth Hopkins

Cole, Ira b. N.Y. 1791 d. N.Y. 1871 m. Sarah Kingsley   Pvt. N.Y. Mil.
daughter Diana m. Asa Lyman Hazelton REAL DAUGHTER

Cole, John b. N.H. 1754 d. 1814/15 m. Keziah Dore   Pvt. N.H. Mil.
daughter Mary m. George Hill

Cole, Joseph b. prob. Md. 1752 d. Md. 1821   Pvt. Baltimore Mil. 1794
m. Sophia Osborn — son Ernestus m. Mary Kemp

Cole, Levi b. N.H. 1790 d. Iowa 1868 m. Lygusta Allen   Pvt. N.H. Mil.
daughter Caroline m. George Batchelder

Cole, Seth Martin b. Vt. 1795 d. Ind. 1872   Pvt. N.Y. Vols.
m. Fanny Warren — daughter Eliza Jane m. William Patten

Cole, Thomas b. S.C. 1790 d. Ala. 1865 m. Elizabeth Horn, Ensign Ga. Mil.
daughter Caroline m. Lewis Hutchison Jr.
daughter Sarah m. Mason Creed Kinney

Cole, William b. 1785 d. 1843 m. Cassandra Smallwood   Pvt. Md. Mil.
son James S. m. Charlotte Quick

Cole, William b. N.Y. 1777 d. N.Y. 1847   Lieut. N.Y. Mil.
m. Elizabeth Root — son William Jr. m. Laura Bunce

Cole, William Carter b. Va. 1793 d. N.C. 1841   Corp. Va. Mil.
m. Elizabeth Murphy — son James Reid m. Mary Parish King

Cole, Armistead b. Va. 1782 d. Va. aft. 1867   Pvt. Va. Mil.
m. Elizabeth Quarles — son Alfred G. A. m. Rebecca W. Worsham
daughter Evelyn m. Roger Boisseu REAL DAUGHTER

Coleman, Benjamin b. N.C. 1746 d. N.C. 1813   Memb. Gen. Assy. N.C.
m. Elizabeth Goodman — daughter Nancy m. Mickleberry Ferrell

Coleman, Daniel   Vol. 6   Capt. Pa. Mil.

Coleman, Daniel   Vol. 17   Lt. Col. Va. Mil.

Coleman, Elijah b. Mass. 1782 d. Ohio 1856   Surgeon Ohio Mil.
    m. Amey Wilkins — daughter Molly C. m. Robert Boyd
    REAL DAUGHTER

Coleman, Henry Embry b. Va. 1768 d. Va. 1837   Lt. Col. Va. Mil.
    m. Anne Gordon — son Thomas G. m. Nancy Ann Sims Clark

Coleman, Isaac b. Va. 1796/7 d. Ind. 1867   Sgt. Ohio Mil.
    m. Rachel H. Thompson Crumsy (2) — daughter Martha
    m. Emil H. Schintz REAL DAUGHTER

Coleman, John b. Pa. 1776 d. Pa. 1865   Pvt. Pa. Mil.
    m. Martha Eaton or Katon — daughter Nancy m. John Neal

Coleman, Robert L. b. Va. 1786 d. Va. 1854   Capt. Va. Mil.
    m. Matilda Minor — daughter Mary Orrell m. George Fleming

Coleman, Samuel b. Mass. 1768 d. N.Y. 1857   Capt. N.Y. Mil.
    m. Abigale Dole — son Charles D. m. Marinda Miner

Coleman, Samuel McCullock b. (W.) Va. 1794 d. Ind. 1865 Lieut. Ohio Mil.
    m. Mary W. Brooks — daughter Sarah A. m. Robert Harlow Hanna

Coleman, Thomas b. Va. 1770 d. Tenn. 1826   Sgt. West Tenn. Mil.
    m. Clarissa White — daughter Eliza P. m. Robert Crosby

Coleman, Zur b. Mass. 1789 d. Mich. 1852   Sgt. U.S. Light Art.
    m. Sally Nearpass — son Eli M. m. Jane Mensch (Mench)

Coles, Edward b. Va. 1786 d. Pa. 1868   Secy. to Pres. Madison 1812/15
    m. Sally Logan Roberts — son Edward Jr. m. Bessie M. Campbell

Coles, Isaac b. Va. 1747 d. Va. 1813   Memb. Va. Leg. 1789
    m. Katherine Thompson — son Robert T. m. Eliza Fearn Patton

Colestock, Jonas b. Pa. 1765 d. Pa. 1850   Lieut. Pa. Mil.
    m. Margaret Seese — son Joseph m. Isabella Speer

Coley, William Buckner b. Va. 1799 d. Ill. 1875   Capt. Va. Mil.
    m. Elizabeth McClain — son Thomas

Colfax, Robert   Vol. 10   Lieut. Conn. Mil.

Colgin, Edward Broadnax b. Va. 1789 d. Ala. 1860   Pvt. Va. Mil.
    m. Caroline Binns — son George James m. Caroline Eveline Taylor

Colladay, Charles b. Pa. 1764 d. Pa.   5th Sgt. Pa. Mil. Vols.
    m. Ann McLane — daughter Frances m. John Buddy Bergman

Collier, Charles Miles b. Va. d. Va. 1827   Capt. Va. Mil.
    m. Ann Armstead Marshall — son Charles Miles Jr.
    m. Sarah Ann Cowles

Collier, Daniel b. Md. 1764 d. Ohio 1835   Col. Ohio Mil.
    m. Elizabeth Prather — daughter Katherine m. James Jackson

Collier, Franklin b. Ky. 1790 d. Ky. 1832   Repr. Ky. Leg. from Nicholas
    m. Mary M. Basye — daughter Elizabeth   Co. 1805/10
    m. Robert Binns Ellis

Collier, James   Vol. 75   Pvt. Vt. Mil.

Collier, James b. Va. 1793 d. Iowa 1859 m. 2d Mary M.   Pvt. Va. Art. Mil.
    daughter Clementine m. William Bowman Ross REAL DAUGHTER

Collier, John b. Va. c 1770 d. Ky. 1819/20 m. Hannah   Major Va. Mil.
    son Franklin m. Mary M. Basye

Collier, William b. Ky. 1792 d. Mo. 1870 m. Susan Higby   Pvt. Ky. Vols.
    son Luther m. Frances C. Brauner

Collin, David   Vol. 6   Sgt. N.Y. Mil.

Collins, Barbee b. Va. 1778 d. Tenn. 1843   Capt. West Tenn. Mil.
m. Mary Woods — daughter Ann m. Joseph Nuckles

Collins, Daniel b. (Scot., Ire.) 1764 d. Pa. 1845   Pvt. Pa. Mil.
m. Ruth Craton (1) — son John m. Susannah Prall

Collins, Dillard b. Va. 1760 d. Ky. 1812   Memb. Ky. Leg. 1797/1801
son Dillard Jr. m. Sarah Montague

Collins, Elijah b. Md. 1786 d. Ohio 1865   Pvt. Ohio Mil.
m. Hannah Fenton — son Samuel F. m. Elizabeth Stout

Collins, Hugh b. S.C. 1773 d. Ill. 1845   Pvt. Ill. Terr. Mil.
m. Elizabeth Lane — daughter Mary Ann m. George Girtman

Collins, Isaac b. Md. 1789 d. Md. 1870   Pvt. Md. Mil.
m. 1st Frances Hardman Snyder — daughter Frances W.
m. Dr. Robert Kennedy

Collins, John   Vol. 4   Ensign Ind. Mil.

Collins, John b. R.I. 1717 d. R.I. 1795 m.   Vol. 10   Gov. R.I. 1789
no further data

Collins, John Wharton   Vol. 17   Pvt. La. Mil.

Collins, Lemuel Jr. b. Mass. (Me.) 1781 d. Me. 1851 Pvt. Mass. (Me.) Mil.
m. Sally Greenleaf — daughter Mahala m. John Williamson

Collins, Moses S. b. c 1787 d. c 1840 m.   Capt. Miss. Mil.
son Benjamin m. Lucinda Duncan

Collins, Nathaniel b. 1771 d. 1821 m. Roxada Evans   Ensign 1796
son Albert Gallatin m. Lucy Emeline Fairchild

Collins, Nathaniel Madison b. Ky. 1787 d. Miss. 1860   Pvt. Tenn. Mil.
m. Susan Burroughs (1) — son Andrew J. m. Malinda Breakfield

Collins, Reuben   Vol. 8   Corp S.C. Mil.

Collins, Thaddeus b. Mass. 1762 d. N.Y. 1828   Pvt. N.Y. Mil.
m. Esther Foster — son Moses F. m. Mary Wade

Collins, William b.— d. Ark. m. Viena Kukendall   Pvt. Ind. Terr. Mil.
son Alexander W. m. Nancy Jones

Collinsworth, Edmond   Vol. 10   Pvt. West Tenn. Mil.

Colman, Samuel b. Mass. 1768 d. N.Y. 1857   Capt. N.Y. Mil.
m. Abigail Dole — son Anson m. Catherina Kimball
son Charles m. Marinda Miner
son Hamilton m. Nancy Sprague

Colson, James b. Ga. 1782 d. Ga. m. Frances Johnston   Lieut. Ga. Mil.
daughter Nancy m. Augustus Thompson Burton

Colson, Jonah   Vol. 5   Selectman Weymouth Mass.

Colton, Herman b. Mass. 1786 d. N.Y. 1878   Pvt. N.Y. Mil.
m. Lucina Warriner — son Chauncey m. Angeline Read

Colvard, John Stokley b. 1771 d. Ga. m. Sarah Gibson   Pvt. Ga. Mil.
son Joseph Arthur m. Frances M. Brown

Colver, (Culver) John b. Conn. 1799 d. Conn. 1881   Drummer Conn. Mil.
m. Susan Geer — son John Jr. m. Helen Rathbun

Colville, Robert Jamison b. Va. 1791 d. Ohio 1833   Constable Va.
m. Hanna A. Watson — son David H. m. Mary Elizabeth Pritchard

Colvin, George b. Pa. 1765 d. Ohio 1855 m. Phoebe   Pvt. Ohio Mil.
  daughter Eleanor m. Amos McLouth

Colvin, George b. Va. 1797 d. Ohio 1881   Pvt. Va. Mil.
  m. Melevey Broyles — daughter Susan Jane m. John Oxley

Colwell, John b. Pa. 1768 d. Pa. 1831   Lieut. Pa. Mil. 1796
  m. Nancy Smith — daughter Jane m. George M. Phillips

Combs, Fielding b. Ky. 1791(96) d. Mo. 1879   Pvt. Ky. Vol. Mil. Det.
  m. Mary (Polly) Foreman — daughter Sarah Anne
  m. Aden Atterberry
  son William Leslie m. Nancy H. Byers Smith

Combs, Leslie b. Ky. 1793 d. Ky. 1881   Cadet or Capt. Ky. Mil.
  m. Margaret Trotter — daughter Georgie m. William A. Warner

Combs, William b. Va. 1786 d. Ky. 1866   Lieut. Ky. Mil.
  m. Elizabeth Blanton — daughter Margaret m. Albert Bridgeford

Comings, (Cummings) Alexander b. Ire. 1750 d. Pa. 1842 Civil Officer Pa.
  m. 2d Jane Livingston — son James m. Christena McMillan

Comins, Free b. Mass. 1790 d. Mass. m. Abigail Dresser Capt. Mass. Mil.
  daughter Augusta m. Fisk Bacon

Compton, Henry b. Ky. 1784 d. Tenn. 1873 m. Sarah C.   Capt. Tenn. Mil.
  son Philip N. m. Lucy Trimmer

Compton, Stephen b. N.J. c 1765 d. N.Y. 1851   Sgt. N.Y. Mil.
  m. Anna Van Sickle — daughter Catherine m. Jacob Linderman

Comstock, Adam b. R.I. 1739 d. N.Y. 1819 Judge, State Leg., Pres. Elector
  m. Margaret McGregor — son John m. Mary Williams   1793/1808

Comstock, Arnon b. Mass. 1779 d. N.Y. 1850   Lieut. N.Y. Mil. 1811
  m. Irene Morris — daughter Mary m. Addison Brill
  REAL DAUGHTER

Comstock, Ezekiel b. Mass. 1795 d. N.Y. 1889 m. Mary G. Pvt. N.Y. Mil.
  son Rufus m. Martha Havens

Comstock, Peter b. Mass. 1796 d. N.Y. 1874   Pvt. N.Y. Mil.
  m. 1st Lucy Campbell Jackson — daughter Demmis Dewey
  m. Charles White Kellogg
  m. 2d Eliza Brewster — daughter Katherine Brewster unm.
  REAL DAUGHTER

Comstock, Samuel b. Conn. 1790 d. N.Y. 1870   Ensign Conn. Mil.
  m. Elizabeth Turner — son Samuel Francis m. Mary Mason Turner

Conant, Airs b. Eng. d. Ill. 1848 m. Mary Pepper   Pvt. 1st Reg. Ga. Mil.
  son John B. m. Mary E. Atkins

Conant, Ezra b. Mass. 1723 d. N.H. 1804   Clerk Warwick Mass. 1789/92
  m. Millicent Newell — son Amos m. Elizabeth Erskine

Conant, George Jr. b. Mass. 1762 d. Mass. 1831   Assemblyman Mass.
  m. Hannah Walden — daughter Sarah M. m. Ephraim L. Williams

Conant, Nathan (Nathaniel) b. Mass. 1743 d. Mass. 1820   Selectman
  m. Esther Emery — son Levi   Townsend Mass.
  m. Eunice Saunderson

Conaway, (Conway) Michael b. Md. 1780 d. Ohio 1853   Pvt. Ohio Mil.
  m. Martha Hoagland — daughter Elizabeth m. George McKinney
Condit, Moses b. N.J. 1760 d. N.J. 1838 m. Hannah Smith Pvt. N.J. Vols.
  son William m. Maria Stryker

Condit, Nathaniel Ogden b. N.J. 1789 d. N.J. 1862 N.J. Mil. Quartermaster
m. Mary Ann Bedford — son Melvin S. m. Eliza Ann Provost

Condit, Stephen b. N.J. 1771 d. N.J. 1849   Sgt. N.J. Mil.
m. Elizabeth Harrison — daughter Charlotte m. Isaac Bond

Coney, Luke b. Mass. 1792 d. N.Y. 1855 m. Mary Emens   Pvt. N.Y. Mil.
daughter Margaret m. Charles Clark

Conkey, Adam b. N.Y. 1793 d. N.Y. 1884 m. Elizabeth Lee Capt. N.Y. Mil.
daughter Adelia M. m. Thomas Wilson REAL DAUGHTER

Conklin, David Preston Jr.   Vol. 14   Pvt. U.S. Inf.

Conklin, Jonathan Titus b. N.Y. 1782 d. N.Y. 1860   Pvt. N.Y. Mil.
m. Mary Elizabeth Sammis — son John F. m. Elizabeth Martin

Conlin, John b. Ire. d. Pa. after 1878 m. A. Quakeress   Capt. Pa. Mil.
son James T. m. Mercy Coats

Conn, Oliver b. N.Y. 1796 d. Wisc. 1883   Pvt. N.Y. Mil.
m. Harriette Burdick — daughter Lucy m. Samuel H. Conn (rel.)

Connell, Giless b. S.C. 1774 d. Tenn. 1827   Pvt. Tenn. Mtd. Inf.
m. Jane Tinsley — son John T. m. Mary B. Fort

Connelly, Bernard   Vol. 16   Corp Md. Mil.

Conner, Cornelius b. Va. 1759 d. Pa. 1832   Capt. Pa. Mil.
m. Elizabeth Carroll — daughter Margaret m. Matthew Borland

Conner, Edmund   Vol. 14   Pvt. Vt. Mil.

Conner, Wilson b. S.C. 1768 d. Ga. 1844   Capt. Ga. Vol. Riflemen
m. Mary Cook — son James G. m. Penelope Ryals
son Thomas B. m. Sara Wall

Conner, Samuel b. Va. 1783 d. Ind. 1863   Capt. Ind. Terr. Mil.
m. Nancy Hyde — son Albert m. Eliza Anna Connor ?
m. Elizabeth Claycomb
son Terrence m. Nancy Tate
m. Sarah Claycomb
son Frederick m. Mary Hyde

Conrad, Joseph b. Pa. 1759 d. Pa. 1822   Pvt. Pa. Mil.
m. Anna Maria Seitzinger — son Jacob m. Rebecca Fisher

Conrey, John b. N.J. 1760 d. Ill. 1834   Corp. & Sgt. Ohio Vols.
m. Sarah Calvin — son Abram m. Elizabeth Taylor

Constant, Jacob b. Va. 1787 d. Ky. 1813   Pvt. Ky. Mtd. Vol. Mil.
m. Elizabeth Judy — son Rezin N. m. Mrs. Mary Lindsay Herbert

Constantine, Bernard   Vol. 9   Pvt. Rep. Blues Ga. Mil.

Contee, John b. Md. 1794 d. Md. 1839   Lieut. U.S. Marine Corps
m. Ann Snowden — son Charles m. Elizabeth Childs

Convers, David   Vol. 17   Drummer N.Y. Mil.

Converse, Israel   Vol. 7   Repr. to Cong. from Vt.

Conway, George b. Va. 1789 d. Ala. 1827   Ensign Ala. Mil.
m. Sarah Newbold Howard — daughter Eliza F. m. Drury Thompson

Conway, Joseph b. Va. 1763 d. Mo. 1830   Pvt. Mo. Terr. Inf.
m. Elizabeth Caldwell — son Samuel m. Mourning Baxter

Conwell, James b. Del. 1786 d. Ind. 1849   Ensign Del. Mil.
m. Winifred Harris King — daughter Caroline
m. William Pitt Murray

Conwell, Stephen b. 1786 d. 1841   Pvt. Ohio Mil. 1812/13
    m. Martha Mills — daughter Eliza m. Samuel F. Bunnell

Conwell, Thomas b. Tenn. d. Tenn.   Vol. 26   Pvt. Tenn. Mil.
    m. Elizabeth Robertson — daughter Nancy
    m. Plummer Willis Shafner REAL DAUGHTER

Conwell, Yates Stokeley b. Pa. 1783 d. Pa. 1865   Ensign Pa. Mil.
    m. Anna Craft — son John B. m. Elizabeth Fulton

Cook, Ezekiel b. N.Y. 1784 d. N.Y. m. Amy Smith   Major N.Y. Mil.
    daughter Sophrona m. Lorenzo D. Hathaway

Cook, Francis   Vol. 5   Pvt. Mass. (Me.) Mil.

Cook, Horace b. N.Y. 1789 d. N.Y. 1877 m. Helen Beaman   Pvt. N.Y. Mil.
    daughter Cynthia A. m. Henry J. Davis

Cook, John b. Pa. 1770 d. Pa. 1829   Pvt. Pa. & Ohio Mil.
    m. Elizabeth Evans — son Miles m. Mary Fisher

Cook, John b. Scot. 1787 d. Ga. 1823 m.   Pvt. S.C. Mil.
    son John Jr. m. Sarah B. Hall

Cook, Joseph   Vol. 17   Postmaster Pittsgrove N.J., Justice of Peace N.J.
                                                           1808-13

Cook, Marvin b. 1799 d. Ohio c 1875 m. Clarissa   Pvt. N.Y. Mil.
    son Orange H. m. Eva Felber

Cook, Peter Gordon   Vol. 12   Pvt. N.Y. Mil.

Cook, Philip b. S.C. 1775 (Ga. 1785) d. Ga. 1841   Major U.S. Inf.
    m. Ann Wooten — daughter Martha P. m. Isaac Winship
    son Philip m. Sarah Lumpkin

Cook, Prentice B. b. Conn. 1793 d. Mass. 1853   Pvt. Conn. Mil.
    m. Elizabeth Osborn — daughter Mary Elizabeth m. Lewis Parks

Cook, Samuel b. Va. 1784 d. Va. 1834 m. Sarah Turner   Sgt. Va. Mil.
    son Samuel S. m. Mildred Dawson

Cooke, Andrew B. b. N.Y. 1789 d. N.Y. 1838 m.   Surgeon U.S. Navy 1812
    daughter Elizabeth P. m. R. D. Stearns REAL DAUGHTER

Cooke, Benjamin b R.I. 1768 d. R.I. 1846   Lieut. R.I. Mil.
    m. Abigail Church — son Russel m. Mary Vinal Otis

Cooke, George Mason b. Va. 1792 d. Va. 1866   Ensign & Adj. Va. Mil.
    m. Anne Jane Carter — daughter Rosa M. m. James Goss Bramham
    REAL DAUGHTER

Cooke, John b. Va. d. Ky. 1817   Clerk for Claims State Md.
    m. Catherine Burton Nourse — daughter Maria B. m. Thomas Winn

Cooke, John b. Mass. 1737 d. N.H. 1810   Selectman N.H. 1785
    m. Mary Godfrey — son Godfrey m. Abigail Hubbard

Cooke, Joseph b. Conn. 1735 d. Conn. 1821   Selectman & Leg. Conn.
    m. Lucretia Post — son Nathan m. Abigail Beckwith   1784/94

Cooke, Richard Fielding b. Va. 1787 d. Tenn. 1870/7 2nd Lieut. Tenn. Mil.
    m. Margaret Cox — daughter Adaline m. Hickman Dowell
    son Boliver H. m. Alice Galena Kessell

Cooke, Samuel b. Mass. 1755 d. Vt. 1834   Memb. 2nd Vt. Leg. 1809/14;
    m. Mehitabel Marsh   Memb. Constitutional Conv. 1814
    daughter Emma m. Alva Spaulding

Cool, Keyes P. b. 1795 d.— m. Julia   Vol. 2   Pvt. Vt. Mil.
    daughter Sarah A. m. Henry Spencer

Colidge, Luther b. Vt. 1781 d. Vt. 1856   Surveyor, Vt. 1814
    m. Betsey Jenny — daughter Amanda m. Harmon McWain

Coombs, Asa b. Me. 1796 d. Wash. 1888   Pvt. Mass. Mil.
    m. Lucretia Mann — son Thomas P. m. Abbie T. Sheldon

Coombs, Edward P. b. Pa. 1791 d. Wisc. 1849   Pvt. Pa. Mil.
    m. Nancy Hickman — daughter Carrie m. George H. Greer
    REAL DAUGHTER
    daughter Rachel P. m. Joseph Chambers

Cooms, Charles Rensselaer b. Conn. 1794 d. Conn. 1877   Musician Conn.
    m. Hannah Sargent Chaffee — daughter Mary S.   Mil.
    m. Jabez Lucien Bowen

Cooms, John   Vol. 4   Pvt. U.S. Inf.

Coon, Oliver b. N.Y. 1796 d. Wisc. 1883   Pvt. N.Y. Mil.
    m. Harriette Burdick — daughter Lucy m. Samuel H. Coon (rel.)

Coonrod, John Sr. b. Va. or Pa. 1771(69) d. Ohio 1831   Sgt. Ohio Mil.
    m. Sarah Davis — son John Jr. m. Sarah Tuttle

Coonrod, Peter (later Conrad) b. Va. 1793 d. W.Va. 1868   Pvt. Va. Mil.
    m. Phoebe Hartley — son John m. Hannah H. Parsons   1814-15

Cooper, Ira b. Conn. 1795 d. N.Y. 1860 m. Diantha Doane   Corp. N.Y. Mil.
    daughter Caroline E. m. Bestow Dexter REAL DAUGHTER

Cooper, Isaac b. (W.) Va. 1792 d. W.Va. 1870   Lieut. Col. Va. Mil.
    m. Sarah P. Chalfant — daughter Mary A. m. George Kiger

Cooper, James b Ire. c 1775 d. Ohio aft. 1825   Pvt. Ohio Mil.
    m. Jane Robinson — son John m. Barbara Moore

Cooper, John b. Mass. 1765 d. Me. 1845   Brig. Gen. Mass. Mil.
    m. Elizabeth Savage — son William m. Eliza Balch Dutton

Cooper, Joseph b. Va. 1787 d. S.C. 1842   Pvt. S.C. Mil.
    m. Sarah Franklin — daughter Virginia A. m. Robert F. Babb

Cooper, Sarshel b. Va. 1763 d. Mo. 1815   Capt. 3 Mo. Frontier Forts
    m. Ruth Hancock — son Joseph m. 2d Frances Marshall

Cooper, Thomas b. Va. 1733 d. Ga. 1799   Memb. Va. Const. Conv. 1788
    m. Sarah Anthony — daughter Elizabeth m. Thomas Stovall

Cooper, Thomas b. Va. 1788 d. Ohio 1851   Pvt. Ohio Mil.
    m. Hannah Stewart — son John m. Helen Oliver

Cooper, William b. Ire. 1783 d. Pa. 1875   Pvt. 76th Reg. Pa. Mil. 1812
    m. Mary — son James m. Mary DeVaul Spence

Copeland, Hezekiah Balch b. Tenn. 1789 d. Va. 1872   Sgt. Va. Mil.
    m. Mary Anne Kincaid — daughter Cornelia
    m. George Ross McIntosh REAL DAUGHTER
    daughter Julia Ann m. William Nathaniel Woodruff
    REAL DAUGHTER

Copeland, Josiah b. N.C. 1729 d. N.C. 1791   Memb. N.C. Assembly from
    m. Sarah — daughter Tamar m. Benjamin Gordon   Chowan Co.

Copeland, Nathaniel b. Mass. (Me.) 1794 d. Me. (Mass.) 1850   Pvt. Mass.
    m. Eunice Philbrick — son William Henry   (Me.) Mil.
    m. Lucinda Lowe

Copeland, Thomas b. Pa. 1776 d. Pa. aft. 1837   Pvt. Pa. Mil.
    m. Jane Carnes (Kerns, Kearnes) — daughter Mary Jane
    m. Miller Stephen Speakman

Copenhaver, George   Vol. 13   Pvt. Va. Det. Mil.

Copenhaver, Henry b. Va. 1791 d. Va. 1869   Pvt. Va. Mil.
  m. Barbara Phillipi — son James Henry m. Sarah Snodgrass

Copley, Joseph Jr. b. N.Y. 1781 d. Ill. 1863   2d Lieut. N.Y. Mil.
  m. Mary Hickok — son Isaac m. Elizabeth Rood

Copp, Daniel Dennison b. Ga. 1799 d. Ga. 1859   Pvt. Ga. Troops
  m. Eunice Waldo — daughter Mary E. m. Aaron Wilbur

Copp, David b. N.H. 1738 d. N.H. 1817   Memb. N.H. Leg. 1790/2
  m. Margaret Palmer — son Amasa m. Charlotte K. Atkinson

Copp, George Washington b. N.H. 1776 d. N.H. 1822/3 Pvt. U.S. Army
  m. Mary Abrams — daughter Nancy W. m. Aaron P. Goodwin

Copp, Squire Joshua b. N.H. 1741 d. Vt. 1804   Justice of Peace; Judge
  m. Sarah Poore — son George W. m. Mary Abrams   Inf. Ct. N.H.

Corbett, James b. Tenn. d. Tenn.   2d Lieut. East Tenn. Mil.
  m. Polly Gresham — son Michael M. m. Nancy Gilbreath

Corbin, James b. Va. 1790 d. Ky. 1867 m. Elizabeth Hurst   Pvt. Va. Mil.
  daughter Amanda Eliz. m. William Andrew Gosnell

Corbin, William b. Md. 1750 d. Pa. 1817   Patriot Huntington Co. Pa.
  m. Elizabeth — son William Jr.   on military list 1788
  m. Mary Hagey

Corbly, Stephen b. Ohio 1792 d. Ohio 1830   Sgt. 1st. Ohio Reg. Mil. 1813
  m. Margaret Riggs — son Stephen D. m. Julia Ann Gerard

Cordery, Absalom   Vol. 16   Pvt. N.J. Mil.

Corell, William b. N.Y. 1785 d. N.Y. 1843   Capt. N.Y. Mil.
  m. Diantha Covell (cousin) — daughter Diantha m. Martin Smith

Corey, Parley b. N.H. 1776 d. N.Y. 1853 m. Polly Babbitt   Pvt. N.Y. Mil.
  son Albert m. Sarah Oakes

Corey, Timothy Jr.   Vol. 7   Capt. Mass. Mil.

Corgan, Patrick b. Ire. 1775 d. Ill. c 1850   Pvt. Tenn. Mil.
  m. Rhoda Newsom — son Charles m. Mary Messamore
  son William m. Mary Parmelee

Corless, Ephraim   Vol. 15   Lieut. Vt. Mil.

Cornelius, Daniel   Vol. 12   Sgt. U.S. Rangers

Cornelius, James b. Va. 1786 d. N.C. aft. 1814   Pvt. Va. Mil.
  m. Lucy Forkner — son Joseph m. Maria Hauser

Cornell, Ashabel Sr. b. Conn. 1754 d. N.Y. 1835   Capt. N.Y. Mil.
  m. Susanna Gaylord — daughter Hannah m. Samuel Lefferts

Cornell, Lewis b. N.Y. 1755 d. N.Y. 1836   Ch. Flushing Town Mtg. 1798
  m. Jane — son William H. m. Elizabeth Doughty Justice Peace N.Y.

Cornell, Richard b. N.Y. d. N.Y. 1839 m. Mary Hogeman   Pvt. N.Y. Mil.
  daughter Ella E. m. Benjamin Franklin (Flushing)

Corning, Peter b. Mass. 1796 d. Mass. 1880   Pvt. Mass. Mil.
  m. Mollie Pierce — daughter Hannah m. Hooper A. Appleton

Cornwall, Daniel b. N.Y. 1781 d. N.Y. 1849 m.   Pvt. N.Y. Mil.
  son Elias m. Amy J. Randall

Cornwall, John b. Conn. 1738 d. N.Y. 1812   Repr. Leg. from Cornwall
  m. Abigail Maltbee — daughter Lydia m. Noah Rogers   1787/8

Corr, Jesse b. Va. d. Va. 1846 m. Frankie Seward   Sgt. Va. Mil.
  daughter Frances Elizabeth m. James Dunlevy

Corry, Ebenezer M.   Vol. 4   Pvt. Mass. (Me.) Mil.

Corser, William b. N.H. 1758 d. N.Y. 1812   Pvt. U.S. Inf.
   m. Abigail Gordon — son William Jr. m.

Corwin, Daniel Jr. b. N.Y. 1779 d. N.Y. 1871   Corp. N.Y. Mil.
   m. Mary Reynolds — daughter Charity Ann m. Silas Gilbert Corwin

Corwin, David   Vol. 4   Pvt. N.Y. Mil.
   daughter Sarah m. Evans REAL DAUGHTER

Corwin, Silas B. b. N.Y. 1786 d. 1865 m. Sarah Little   Pvt. N.Y. Mil.
   son Parmanas m. Caroline Roe

Cory, James b. Ky. 1794 d. Ohio 1846   Corp. Ross Co. Ohio Mil. 1812
   m. Rebecca Sperry — daughter Mary m. Jonathan Jones
   daughter Serena m. Anthony Ross
   son Hiram S. m. Mary A. Rine

Cory, Nathaniel b. Va. 1771 d. Mo. 1844   Seaman Sea Fencibles
   m. Sophia — daughter Cynthia m. James Trotter

Cosby, Winkfield   Vol. 13   Pvt. U.S. Inf.

Cosgrove, Christopher b. Conn. 1777 d. N.Y. 1842   Lieut. N.Y. Mil.
   m. Rebecca Allison — daughter Mary m. Luther Abbott

Cosgrove, Joseph b. N.J. 1742 d. Md. 1833 m. Mary North   Pvt. N.J. Mil.
   son Christopher m. Rebecca Allison

Cosnahan, Joseph b. S.C. 1788 d. Miss. 1874   Pvt. Ga. Mil.
   m. Elizabeth Hamilton — daughter Henrietta
   m. Jacob Franklin Polatty

Cotten, Richard Carney b. N.C. 1792 d. N.C. aft. 1862   Capt. N.C. Mil.
   m. Peggy — son Richard C. m. Charlotte Adelaide Mann

Cotterman, Michael b. Pa. 1782 d. Ohio 1877   Pvt. Ohio Mil.
   m. Eva Shubert — son Michael Jr. m. Mary Hopson

Cotton, James Jr. b. N.J. 1787 d. W.Va. 1837   Pvt. Pa. Mil.
   m. Jemima Chaffin — daughter Achsah m. John Fordney

Cotton, John b. Tenn. 1790 d. Tex. 1853   Pvt. Miss. Vol. Co.
   m. Jane Belina Kelley — daughter Mary Ann   Dragoons 1814
   m. James C. Smith

Cotton, Samuel b. N.H. 1780 d. N.H. 1852 m. Sally Fernald, Pvt. N.H. Mil.
   son Joseph P. m. Jerusha Tucker

Cotton, Samuel b. Eng. 1774 d. N.Y. 1839   2d Lieut. N.Y. Cav.
   m. Lucy Gilbert — daughter Elizabeth Ann m. Enos Smith Halbert

Cottrell, William b. Va. 1785 d. Va. 1838 m. Susan Halsey Corp. Va. Mil.
   son Peter m. Rosa Cosby

Couenhaven, Christian   Vol. 15   2d Lieut. N.Y. Mil.

Coulter, Alexander b. Md. 1760 d. Md. 1828   Pvt. Md. Mil. 1794
   m. Esther McCaskey — daughter Hannah m. Benjamin Hood

Coulter, Alexander H. b. N.C. 1776 b. Ga. 1854   Ensign Tenn. Vol. Mil.
   m. Margaret McReynolds — son William M.
   m. Minerva Lawrence Sutton

Coulter, Charles b. Ire. 1785 d. Pa. 1874   Pvt. Pa. Mil.
   m. Betsy Cornelius — son John m. Jane Clark

Coulter, John b. prob. Va. 1775 d. Mo. 1813 Pvt. 1803/6 in Lewis & Clark
   m. Sally — son Hiram m. Margaret Davis   Expedition

Coulter, Thomas   Vol. 17   Pvt. Ky. Mil.

Coulter, Thomas b. N.C. 1790(95) d. Tenn. 1876(74) 2nd Lieut. Tenn. Mil.
m. Rebecca Parks — son James P. m. Mary Ann McDonald
son Thomas J. m. Joanna Gamble

Councill, James N. b— d.— m. Mary Ann (Marian)   Sgt. Va. Mil.
son Benjamin m. 1st Charlotte

Counselman, Jacob b. Md. 1782 d. Md. 1831 Lieut. & Paymaster Md. Mil.
m. Elizabeth Flinn — son Jacob Jr. m. Mary Wigart

Countryman, John N. b. N.Y. 1788 d. N.Y. 1868   Pvt. N.Y. Mil.
m. Ann Eygabrode — daughter Eliza m. John Wallace

Courtney, James b. Pa. 1793 d. Pa. 1874   Seaman on Sloops President &
m. Polly Davies — son Andrew J.   Saratoga, U.S. Navy
m. Phebe Angelina Hayes
daughter Jane L. m. Burnham Miller Sherwood

Courtney, Robert b. Ire. 1771 d. Ky. 1837   Pvt. Ky. Mtd. Vols.
m. Jane Stuart Wishard — daughter Elizabeth m. Frazier Peters

Courtney, Robert Sr.   Vol. 12   Capt. Va. Mil.

Courtney, Robert Jr.   Vol. 12   2d Lieut. Va. Mil.

Courtright, John D. b. Pa. 1779 d. Ohio 1863(52)   Capt. Ohio Mil.
m. Elizabeth Grubb — son Jesse Drake m. Sarah Stout

Courvoisier, John Francis William b. Switz. 1751   Civil Officer Ga.
d. Ga. 1811 m. Mary Fox — son John F. W. Jr.
m. Amelia Rebecca Rudolph

Couse, James b. N.Y. 1794 d. 1864 m. Lydia Wetmore   Pvt. N.Y. Mil.
son Ambrose W. m. Caroline Condit

Covell, James b. N.Y. 1777 d. Pa. 1865 m. Rebecca Pierce Lieut. N.Y. Mil.
son Calvin T. m. Elizabeth Coleman

Covell, Jonathan b. Conn. 1758 d. N.Y. 1830   Pvt. Pa. Mil.
m. Rhoda Kimberly — daughter Rhoda Sophia m. Ebenezer Martin

Covert, Tunis Jr. b. N.J. 1777 d. N.Y. 1849   Lieut. N.Y. Mil.
m. Cornelia Brokon — son Abraham B. m. Mary Van Nuys

Covington, John b 1791 d. Tenn. 1873   Pvt. East Tenn. Mil.
m. Catherine Stickley — daughter Mary Ann m. John Kelly

Covington, Thomas D.   Vol. 12   Pvt. Va. Mil.

Covington, William b. N.C. 1742 d. Tenn. 1817   Pvt. Tenn. Cav.
m. Catherine Roberts — daughter Elizabeth m. Henry Pate

Cowan, John b. S.C. d. Tenn. 1836/7   Capt. Mtd. Vols. Franklin Co.
m. Elizabeth — son William M. m. Elizabeth   1814/15

Cowan, Jedediah H. b. Mass. 1778 d. Me. 1840   Sgt. Mass. (Me.) Mil.
m. Jane — daughter Joannah m. Isaac Winn

Cowan, John b. N.C. 1757 d. N.C. 1827   Juror Rowan Co. N.C. 1784
m. Jane Cowan — daughter Jane m. John B. Burke

Cowan, John b. S.C. d. Tenn. 1836/7 Capt. Mtd. Vols. Franklin Co. 1814-5
m. Elizabeth — son William M. m. Elizabeth
son Nathaniel S. m. Josephine B. Kelly

Cowan, John b. Va. 1784 d. Va. 1869 m. Mary Pickering   Sgt. Va. Mil.
son Jacob m. Delia Allebough

Cowan, John   Vol. 16   Pvt. U.S. Mtd. Rangers

Cowan, William M. b. N.C. 1740 d. N.C. 1806 Juror Rowan Co. N.C. 1784
m. 1st Ann Jinkins — daughter Jane m. John Cowan

Cowan, William b. Va. 1783 d. 1817　　　　　　　　Ensign Va. Inf.
m. Bathsheba McBride — daughter Harriett A. m. Strother Moore

Cowart, John b. France d. Ga. 1821 m. Michel Williams　　Capt. Ga. Mil.
daughter Mary m. Joseph Jackson

Cowdry, Ezra　　Vol. 17　　　　　　　　　　　Pvt. Mass. Mil.

Cowen, Matthew b. N.C. 1777 d. Tenn. aft. 1855　　　Capt. Tenn. Mil.
m. Catherine Trousdale — daughter Delia m. Chester Calhoun Sadler
daughter Elizabeth M. m. John Trousdale, Jr.

Cowgill, Elisha b. Va. 1771 d. Ind. 1855　　　　　　Pvt. Ky. Mil.
m. Ann Stanton Tarvin — daughter Martha m. Henry Clay Smith

Cowles, Benjamin b. Mass. 1769 d. N.Y. 1854　Judge Ct. Common Pleas.,
son Zina H. m. Elizabeth Leavens　　　　　Memb. N.Y. Assembly

Cox, Ancil b. Va. 1791 d. Ill. 1873 m. Lucy H. Palmer　Pvt. Ky. Mtd. Inf.
son Albert W. m. Emily Antle

Cox, Aris b. Va. 1773 d. Ga. 1867 m. Ruth Box　　　Pvt. Ga. Mil.
son Matthew m. Rebecca White

Cox, Caleb　　Vol. 14　　　　　　　　　　　Capt. La. Mil.

Cox, Caleb b. Md. 1796 d. Tenn. 1879　　　　　　Pvt. Tenn. Mil.
m. Nancy Ann Carriger — daughter Ruth Emaline m. William Cass

Cox, Carey b. N.C. 1778 d. Ga. 1871 m. Martha Rountree　Ensign Ga. Mil.
son Orren D. m. Emily T. Moore
son Willis m. Elizabeth Moore

Cox, Coleman b. Tenn. 1793 d. Tenn. 1847　　　Pvt. East Tenn. Vols.
m. Roxana Foster — son Isaac M. m. Luck Rodman

Cox, Henry b. Va. 1778 d. Va. 1817 m. Mary Traylor　　Ensign Va. Mil.
son James H. m. Martha Reid Law

Cox, Henry b. Va. 1774 d. Ala. 1821 m. Judith Eldridge　Ensign Va. Mil.
daughter Judith E. m. John Wyatt Harris

Cox, (Coxs) Ichabod b. prob. Ga. 1769 d. Ga. 1861 Justice Peace 1799-1812
m. Mary Rowan — daughter Mary　　　　　　　Jones Co. Ga.
m. William Rushing

Cox, James b. Va. 1769 d. Ky. 1846　　　　　Major Ky. Vol. Mil.
m. Mary Cox (cousin) — son David H. m. Catherine Forman

Cox, John　　Vol. 13　　　　　　　　　　　Pvt. Pa. Mil.

Cox, John b. Pa. 1781 d. Pa. 1854 m. Martha Pedan　　Lieut. Pa. Mil.
daughter Mary Louise m. Charles Maclay

Cox, Joseph b. N.J. 1778 d. Ohio 1830　　　Pvt. Pa. Light Dragoons
m. 2d Lydia Ellsworth — son Elijah m. Jemima Blaylock

Cox, Josiah b. 1796 m. Elizabeth Willson　　　　Pvt. N.C. Det. Mil.
son William W. m. Margaret Ann Bryan

Cox, Larkin b. Md. 1789 d. Tenn.　　　　　　Pvt. West Tenn. Mil.
m. Jane Hardenbrook — son John m. Elizabeth

Cox, Moses b. Md. 1781 d. (W.) Va. 1861　　Capt. Monongalia W.Va. Mil.
m. Jane Musgrave — son Ulysses D. m. Emily Jane Lowe

Cox, Robert　　Vol. 11　　　　　　　　　　Pvt. S.C. Mil.

Cox, Thomas b. N.Y. 1792 d. N.Y. 1848 m. Sally Bump　Pvt. N.Y. Mil.
son James W. m. Hannah Gilbert

Cox, William b. Md. d. Tenn. m. Mary Ruth Boring   Pvt. East Tenn. Mil.
son Caleb m. Nancy Ann Carriger

Cox, William Sitgreaves b. Pa. 1780 d. Minn. 1874   Pvt. Pa. Mil.
m. Elizabeth (Jane Eliza) Banks — daughter Charlotte S.
m. Daniel N. Pope
son Eugene St. Julien m. Mariah H. Mayhew

Coyner, Jacob b. Pa. 1774 d. Ohio 1826 m. Mary Byers   Ensign Va. Mil.
daughter Fanny m. John Clark

Coyner, Robert b. Va. 1794(99) d. Ohio 1874   Pvt. (Corp.) Va. Mil.
m. Margaret Gwinn — son David Silas m. Matilda Heizer

Crabbe, Plunkett   Vol. 6   Pvt. Pa. Mil.

Crabbs, Henry b. Ger. 1734 d. Pa. 1812/15   Ensign Pa. Mil.
m. Sarah Keller — son Henry Jr. m. Anna George

Cracraft, Charles b. Md. 1746/8 d. Pa. 1824   Ensign Pa. Mil.
m. Ellen Atkinson — son William m. Sarah Saxe

Craft, James Steele   Vol. 4   Sgt. Pa. Mil.

Craft, William b. N.Y. 1791 d. Pa. 1871 m. Anna Keator   Sgt. N.Y. Mil.
son Lewis m. Jane Harris

Cragin, John b. Mass. 1769 d. N.H. 1853 m. Ruth Heald   Capt. N.H. Mil.
son Abner B. m. Martha Shepherd

Craig, David b. Ky. 1789 d. Mo. 1883 m. Sarah Whiteside   Pvt. Ky. Mil.
son Francis M. m. Sarah M. Fullington

Craig, James b. Va. 1762 d. Va. 1834 m. Ann Montgomery   Pvt. Va. Mil.
daughter Celinda m. William E. Kyle Sr.

Craig, John b. Va. 1782 d. Va. 1876 m. Nancy Cain   Pvt. Va. Mil.
son John Jr. m. Jane Morgain

Craig, Robert b. Va. 1787   Vol. 9   Pvt. Ky. Mil.

Craig, Samuel b. N.J. 1796 d. N.J. 1879   Pvt. N.J. Mil.
m. Catherine Danzenbaker — daughter Margaret
m. Ebenezer Wright

Craig, Thomas b. Pa. 1742 d. Pa. 1832   Brig. Gen. Pa. Mil.
m. Mary Jane Hamilton — daughter Mary Jane m. Hamilton Armour

Craig, William b. Ire. d. Pa. 1838 m. Jane Smilie   Capt. Pa. Mil.
son John S. m. Jane Springer

Craigg, James Henry b. Va. 1795 d. Va. 1884   Pvt. Va. Mil.
m. Mary McManaway — son James S. m. Lucinda St. Clair

Crain, Isaac   Vol. 10   Pvt. Tenn. Mil.

Crain, Nathaniel b. Va. 1792 d. Ky. 1889   Pvt. Ky. Mil.
m. Mrs. Cynthia Keller Sharp — daughter Cinderella
m. Cyrus Edwards
daughter Sammie A. m. William Henry Edmunds

Cram, Jonathan b. Vt. 1779 d. Vt. 1869 m. Lydia Smith   Pvt. Vt. Mil.
son Joel m. Sophronia Adams

Cram, William b. N.H. 1788 d. Me. 1843 m. Lucinda White, Pvt. Mass. Mil.
daughter Lucinda W. m. Moses Wadsworth Farr

Cramer, (Cramner) Richard b. N.J. 1791 d. Ind. 1883   Pvt. N.J. Mil.
m. Mary Bowker — son Job m. Mary Lancaster

Crandall, Asa b. R.I. 1778 d. N.Y. 1846   Pvt. N.Y. Mil.
m. Mrs. Susan Babcock Kingsley — son Jerome B. m. Julina Rice

Crandall, Beman   Vol. 12   Corp. U.S. Inf.

Crandall, Robert b. R.I. 1769 d. R.I. aft. 1810   Justice Peace R.I.
m. Margaret — daughter Hannah m. Joseph Belcher

Crandall, Simeon   Vol. 12   Pvt. N.Y. Mil.

Crandell, William b. N.Y. 1796 d. N.Y. 1881   Pvt. N.Y. Mil.
m. Ruth Underhill — daughter Mary unm. REAL DAUGHTER

Crane, Belden b. Conn. 1770 d. Ohio 1856   Town Treas. Shersville Ohio
m. Asenath Bigelow — son Frederick m. Sarah Weber Hanks

Crane, Elias B. b. N.J. 1789 d. N.J. 1869   Corp. N.J. Det. Mil.
m. Esther Maxwell — daughter Mary Ann m. Nathan Meeker Winans
son Smith Emon m. Phoebe Beach

Crane, Elihu b. Conn. 1791 d. Pa. 1876 m. Nancy Crane   Sgt. Pa. Mil.
daughter Wealthy m. Jason Jared Tichnor

Crane, Henry b.— d.— m. Anna Chilton Thomas   Vol. 2   Capt. Ohio Mil.
daughter Virginia m. Atlas Lacock Stout

Crane, John b. Mass. 1730 d. Mass. 1800   Repr. Mass. Leg. 1788
m. Rachel Terry — daughter Rachel m. Reuben Tisdale

Crane, John b. N.J. 1755 d. N.J. 1837 m. Phebe Ross   Corp. N.J. Det. Mil.
son Elias m. Esther Maxwell

Crane, John Caleb b. N.J. 1757 d. N.J. 1812   Capt. N.J. Mil., Pa.
m. Sarah Myer — son Henry m. Sarah Day   Insurrection
son Simeon H. m. Amanda Taylor

Crane, John b. N.J. d. k/a Fallen Timbers, Ohio Vol. 2, Colonel Ohio Mil.
son Henry m. Anna Chilton Thomas

Crane, Josiah   Vol. 11   Pvt. N.J. Mil.

Crane, Levi L. b. Mass. 1793 d. Mass. 1864   Pvt. Mass. Mil.
m. Maria Gushee — daughter Emily E. m. John Fraser
REAL DAUGHTER

Crank, George b. Va. 1784 d. Va. 1865 m. Margaret Gaines Pvt. Va. Mil.
daughter Mary Catherine m. William Henry Wayland

Cranson, Asa b. Mass. 1760 d. N.Y. 1841 m. Zillah Fuller, Capt. Mass. Mil.
daughter Huldah m. Samuel Goodwin

Cranson, Elisha b. Mass. 1720/1 d. Mass. 1804 Repr. Mass. Gen. Ct. 1784-7
m. Abigail Baldwin — son Asa m. Zillah Fuller

Cratty, Robert b. Pa. 1784 d. Ohio 1887   Ensign Pa. Mil.
m. Ellen Porter — daughter Mary m. Christian Gast

Cravens, Jeremiah b. Ky. 1790 d. Ky. 1849   Ensign Ky. Mil.
m. Harriet Earle — daughter Elizabeth m. John Graham Gooch

Crawford, Caleb b. N.Y. 1771 d. Ind. 1829   Cornet N.Y. Mil.
m. Phoebe Elizabeth Kniffin — daughter Emeline
m. Henry Fairbanks

Crawford, Charles b. Va. 1738 d. Ga. 1813   Del. Const. Conv. Ga. 1784-9
m. Jane Maxwell — daughter Mary Ann m. Peter Crawford (cousin)

Crawford, Daniel b. Va. 1778 d. Ohio 1846   Pvt. Ohio Mil.
m. 2d Margaret Robinson — son Daniel Jr. m. Mary McBeth

Crawford, James b. Va. 1759 d. Ind. 1836   Memb. Const. Conv. Ky. 1792
m. Rebecca Anderson — daughter Elizabeth m. Beverly Vawter

Crawford, John b. Pa. 1748 d. Pa. 1812   Lieut. Pa. Mil. 1786
     m. Isabelle Parker — son Ebenezer m. Janet Grant

Crawford, John   Vol. 6   Pvt. Vt. Det. Mil.

Crawford, John b. Ireland d. Va. or La. 1864   Pvt. Va. Mil.
     m. Margaret Holmes — daughter Mary Ann m. Elihu Whitley Beggs

Crawford, Samuel b. Va. 1752 d. Ky. 1821 m.   Pvt. Ky. Vol. Mil.
     daughter Eleanor m. James Jennings

Crawford, Thomas b. N.C. 1784 d. Ala. 1844   Capt. Creek Campaign 1814
     m. Mary Davidson — son Dr. James W. m. Sarah Huey

Crawford, Thomas b. Ky. 1793 d. Ky. 1885   Pvt. Ky. Mil.
     m. Mrs. Sarah Schooling (Sherrill) — daughter Sarah Frances
     m. Harvey Nelson Mitchell REAL DAUGHTER

Crawford, William b. Md. d. N.Y.C. 1839   Pvt. Md. Mil.
     m. Elizabeth Cook — daughter Frances A. m. George D. Chenoweth

Crawford, William b. Ireland 1769 d. Pa. 1846   Pvt. Pa. Mil.
     m. Nancy Morrow — son Matthew m. Mary Slater

Creamer, (Cramer) George Washington   Vol. 17   Pvt. Pa. Mil.

Creamer, Joshua b. Md. 1788 d. Md. 1853   Pvt. Md. Mil.
     m. Margaret Smith — son Thomas m. Jane L. Brown

Crebs, Henry b. Va. d. Va. m. Elizabeth White   Pvt. Va. Mil.
     son David H. m. Jennie Cook

Creech, Richard b. N.C. 1730 d. S.C. 1808   Leg. & Sen. S.C. 1806/8
     m. (2) Mrs. Mary Williams — son William m. Susan Kirkland

Creed, Wilson b. 1793 d. 1830   Ensign and QM Sgt. 1813/15
     m. Lucinda Stubblefield — son William S. m. Nancy S. Wright

Creekmore, Robert Warren b. Va. 1792 d. Miss. 1869   Sgt. N.C. Mil.
     m. Nancy McGowen — daughter Nancy m. John Clark Martin
     son Hiram C. m. Ann Eliza Wier

Creese, John b. Pa. 1755 d. Pa. 1833   Lieut. Pa. Vol. Mil.
     m. Elizabeth D. — son Samuel m. Margaret Young

Creigh, John Sr. b. Ireland 1741 d. Pa. 1813   Lieut. Cumberland Co. Pa.
     m. Jane Huston — son Dr. John m. Eleanor Dunbar   Mil.

Creigh, John b. Pa. 1773 d. Pa. 1848 m. Eleanor Dunbar   Capt. Pa. Mil.
     son John D. m. Caroline Ramsey Williamson

Creighton, John   Vol. 17   Pvt. Va. Mil.

Crenshaw, Charles b. Va. 1749 d. S.C. 1814   Pvt. Va. Mil.
     m. Eunice White — son Anderson m. Mary Chiles

Crenshaw, Freeman b. Va. 1776 d. Ala. 1853   Pvt. Tenn. Mil.
     m. Elizabeth Terrell Martin — daughter Martha D. m. N. C. Malone

Crenshaw, Robert Jr. b. S.C. 1775 d. S.C. 1816   Legislator S.C.
     m. Dorothy Abell — son Ephraim A. m. Margaret Ewart Adams

Cresap, James Daniel b. Md. 1770 d. Md. 1836   Member Md. Leg. 1812/15
     m. Abigail — daughter Mary m. John T. Singleton

Cressey, Joseph   Vol. 10   Pvt. Mass. (Me.) Mil.

Cretors, Ezekiel b. Pa. 1776 d. Ohio 1862   Pvt. Ohio Mil.
     m. Mary Susanna Foglesong — son Jacob m. Anna Perrott

Creuzet, Charles b. France 1793 d. Ohio 1880 Seaman & Vol. for defense
     m. Genevieve Pistor — daughter Emily   of Baltimore
     m. Charles Henking

Crigler, Lewis b. Va. 1796 d. Mo. 1860 m. Pamelia DePew   Corp. Va. Mil.
daughter Elizabeth m. Joseph Page

Crim, Adam   Vol. 14   Pvt. N.Y. Mil.

Crippen, James b. Ohio 1782 d. Ohio 1856   Lieut. Ohio Mil.
m. Polly Beebe — son James R. m. Paulina

Cripps, Christian b.— d. Ky. 1788 m. —   Indian Fighter Ky.
daughter Margaret m. Gov. Charles Anderson

Crispin, George   Vol. 9   Sgt. N.J. Mil.

Cristman, George Frederick b. N.Y. 1790 d. N.Y. 1871   Pvt. N.Y. Mil.
m. Mary Bell — son William m. Charlotte Ward

Criswell, James   Vol. 6   Lieut. Pa. Mil.

Criswell, John b. Pa. 1788 d. Iowa 1873 m. Rebecca Kilgore, Pvt. Md. Mil.
daughter Keziah m. Reuben Alexander

Crittenden, Joel   Vol. 5   Corp. D.C. Mil.

Crittenden, Josel   Vol. 12   Corp. Ky. Mil.

Crittenden, John Jordan b. Ky. 1787 d. Ky. 1863   Major Ky. Mil., Memb.
m. Sarah O. Lee (1)   State Leg. from Logan Co. 1811-17
daughter Sarah Lee m. Edward Howe Watson

Crittenden, William b. Conn. 1754 d. Mass. 1842   Pvt. Conn. Mil.
m. Mary Brayman — daughter Lucy m. Eli Hale

Crittenden, William Gatewood b. Va. 1787 d. Va. 1830   Pvt. Va. Mil.
m. Mary Thomas — son John L. m. Susan J. Eustace

Crittenton, Harvey b. Mass. 1794 d. N.Y. 1884   Pvt. 55th Reg. N.Y. Mil.
m. Phoebe Matteson — son Levi m. Charlotte Farman
daughter Phoebe A. m. James A. Cole REAL DAUGHTER

Crittenton, Jason b. Conn. 1761 d. N.Y. 1813   Corp. N.Y. Mil.
m. Keziah Cushman Brown — son Stephen m. Charlotte Dunham

Crocker, Calvin   Vol. 6   Pvt. Mass. Mil.

Crocker, Gurdon b. Conn. 1786 d. Conn. 1872   Pvt. Conn. Mil.
m. Sarah Caulkins — son Albert G. m. Abigail C. Haynes

Crocker, James   Vol. 9   Pvt. Mass. (Me.) Mil.

Crocker, Thomas b. N.H. 1788 d. Me. 1872   Ensign Mass. (Me.) Mil.
m. Clarissa Stovall — daughter Mary Elizabeth
m. Jesse Phillip Daniel

Crockett, Andrew b. Va. 1745 d. Tenn. 1821   Major Va. Mil.
m. Sally Elliott — son Samuel m. Joanna Sayers

Crockett, Anthony b. Va. 1756 d. Ky. 1838   Major Ky. Mil. 1812
m. Mary Robertson — daughter Mary   Memb. Ky. Leg. 1790
m. William B. Hawkins

Crockett, David b. Tenn. 1786 d. Texas 1836   Sgt. Tenn. Mtd. Gunmen
m. (2) Elizabeth Patton   Scout, Indian Fighter
daughter Matilda (Wid Tyson) m. James Wilson
m. Elizabeth Finley
son John W. m. Martha Hamilton

Crockett, John Daniel b. 1777 d. Ind. 1866   Pvt. 2nd Regt. Ind. 1813
m. Mary Covert — son Thomas D. m. Sarah Sales Smith

Crockett, Robert b. 1769 d. 1835   Pvt. 37th Va. Reg.
m. Letitia Saunders — son Stephen Saunders m. Mary S.

Crofford, (Crawford) James Thomas b. 1796 d. Tenn. 1863, Pvt. Tenn. Mil.
m. Jane Brown Porter — daughter Louisa M. m. Robert Fain Looney

Crofoot, David b. Conn. 1787 d. N.Y. 1861 m. Eliza   2d Lieut. N.Y. Mil.
son Osmond D. m. Maria Samson

Crofoot, Isaac b. Conn. 1784 d. Wisc. 1868 m. Sallie   Corp. N.Y. Mil.
son Lewis m. Lovina Wilcox

Cromwell, James b. N.Y.C. 1789 d. N.Y. 1870   Pvt. N.J. Reg. U.S.A.
m. Catherine Kemp — son Gilbert m. Sarah Bradley   1812/15
son John m. Mary Eliza Parsons

Croninger, John b. Pa. 1775 d. Pa. 1852   Corp. U.S. Inf.
m. Margaretta R. Culp — daughter Catherine A. V. m. Jacob H. Lutz

Cronise, Henry   Vol. 12   Pvt. Md. Mil.

Cronk, Hiram   Vol. 6   Pvt. (N.Y.)

Crook, Charles Jr. b. Md. 1794 d. Md. 1882   Pvt. Md. Mil.
m. Angelique Laedrich — daughter Angelique
m. Charles McCullough Smith REAL DAUGHTER

Crooker, Gamaliel   Vol. 13   Ensign Mass. (Me.) Mil.

Crooke, John b. Md. 1766 d. Ky. 1849   Pvt. Ky. Mtd. Vols.
m. Ann D. Reeves — daughter Rebecca m. John Thurman

Crooke, Ozias b. Md. 1745 d. Ky. aft. 1810, Constable Madison Co. Ky. 1805
m. Rebecca Stephens (Stevens) — son John m. Ann D. Reeves

Crooks, Alexander b. 1777 d. Ohio 1856 m. Margaret   Pvt. Ohio Mil.
daughter Nancy m. Wilson Brown

Crooks, William b. Mass. 1766 d. Ohio 1855   Major Ohio Mil.
m. Jemima Dickinson — daughter Sally Merina m. Josiah Westland

Crosby, Jedediah b. Mass. 1776 d. N.Y. 1830   Lieut. Col. N.Y. Mil.
m. Mabel Austin — daughter Polly C. m. Joseph Latham

Crosby, Josiah b. Mass. 1730 d. N.H. 1793   Patriot—gave aid N.H.
m. Sarah Fitch — son John m. Priscilla Blanchard

Crosby, Thomas Baker b. Mass. 1793 d. Ill. 1872   Pvt. N.Y. Mil.
m. (1) Lucina Crego — son Hiram Lester m. Ruth Parmalee

Croshaw, William b. N.J. 1780 d. N.Y. 1813   Pvt. U.S. Inf. 1812
m. Martha Budd — daughter Rebecca m. Charles Bodine

Crosier, Jason b. Mass. 1773 d. Ohio 1865   Pvt. Mass. Mil.
m. Almira Newton — daughter Maria m. Luke DeVoe

Cross, George b. N.Y. 1789 d. N.Y. 1861   Corp. N.Y. Art. Vols.
m. Mary Elizabeth Nellis — daughter Catherine m. Ithiel Corbett

Cross, George W. b.—d. S.C. 1816 m. Charlotte Teazevant Capt. S.C. Lt. Inf.
daughter Sarah S. m. Daniel Russell

Cross, John   Vol. 13   Pvt. Va. Mil.

Cross, Joseph b. Mass. 1776 d.— m. Anne M. Lowe   Capt. Mass. Mil.
daughter Catherine Anne m. Robert P. Farris

Cross, Richard b. Va. 1750 d. Tenn. 1802 m. Ann Maclin   Pvt. Va. Mil.
son Maclin m. Mary Hall

Cross, Solomon Jr. b. Vt. 1786 d. Ohio 1831   Pvt. N.Y. Det. Mil.
m. Mariah Wilcox — daughter Lucinda m. John Lansing Pray

Crossin, George b. Ohio 1797 d. Ohio 1848   Pvt. Ohio Mil.
m. Charlotte Morrison — daughter Susannah m. Zebulon Dickinson

Crossley, Thomas b. Pa. 1710 d. Pa. 1791   Pvt. Pa. Mil.
  m. Caroline Chapman — son Jesse m. Elizabeth Fullmer

Crouse, Daniel b. Va. 1790 d. Va. 1818 m. Catherine Cline   Pvt. Va. Mil.
  daughter Mary Ann m. B. F. Moomaw

Crow, Charles Donnally Lewis b. Va. 1790 d. Tex. 1870, Pvt. Ky. Mtd. Vols.
  m. Nancy Kirk — son Benjamin F. m. Elizabeth Jane Lee

Crow, John b. 1769 d. in service 1813   Pvt. 23rd Regt. U.S. Inf.
  m. Mary Hawk — son Edmund m. Hannah Fuller

Crow, Levi b. S.C. aft. 1775 d. Miss. 1847   Pvt. Miss. Mil.
  m. Svbil Hammett 2d Susanna Hart — daughter Martha Ann
  m. Henry H. Bell

Crow, Walter   Vol. 4   Pvt. Ky. Mil.

Crowell, Aaron b. N.J. c 1750 d. N.J. 1814   Surveyor Highways N.J.
  m. Abigail Brown — son Job m. Caroline Beach

Crowell, Henry b.— d. Ala. 1840 m. Sarah Catherine Cantey   Capt. Ga.
  daughter Martha m. Edward Ward Wright   Mil.

Crowell, Job b. N.J. 1779 d. N.J. 1854   Overseer Orange Co. N.J. 1812
  m. Caroline Beach — son Aaron B. m. Catherine J. Schoner

Crowell, Samuel b. N.J. 1766 d. Pa. 1834 m. Mary Walker Lieut. Pa. Mil.
  son Samuel III m. Mary Jane Link

Crozier, William   Vol. 16   Pvt. Md. Mil.

Crum, Cornelius   Vol. 16   Lieut. Pa. Mil.

Crumb, Arnold Jr. b. Conn. 1795 d. Conn. 1873   Musician Conn. Mil.
  m. Lucinda Lamphere — daughter Augusta J.
  m. James Alden Peabody REAL DAUGHTER
  daughter Isophine I. m. Rollin Mathewson Harris
  REAL DAUGHTER

Crump, Benjamin   Vol. 11   Pvt. Va. Mil.

Crump, Gilbert b. Pa. 1782 d. Ky. 1860 m. Letitia Dixon   Pvt. Va. Mil.
  son Thomas m. Wilmuth Ann Dixon

Crump, Joseph b. Va. d. N.C. 1796   Juryman Chatham Co. N.C. 1794
  m. Martha Johnson — daughter Judith m. Jonathan Bell

Crump, Joshua b. Va. 1784 d. Va. 1851   Sgt. Va. Mil.
  m. Sarah Kimbrough — daughter Mary T. m. William Christian

Crutcher, James b. Va. 1755 d. Ky. 1823 m. Ann Poore Major Ky. Mil.
  son Norval m. Sarah Pollock

Crutcher, James b. Ky. 1795 d. Ky. 1874   Vol. 6   Pvt. Ky. Mil.

Cubberly, William b. N.J. 1759 d. Ohio 1842   Pvt. Ohio Mil.
  m. Mary Sinclair — daughter Eliza m. Henry Richmond

Culbertson, James b. Ga. 1788 d. Ga. 1863   Pvt. Ga. Mil.
  m. Sarah Wilkinson — son John P. m. Romelia Bird

Culbertson, John b. Pa. 1779 d. Pa. 1830   Lieut. (Brig. Gen.) Pa. State
  m. Margaret Greer — son Thomas G.   Mil. 1811
  m. Sarah Ann Steele

Culbertson, Robert b. Pa. 1764 d. Pa. 1851   Vol. 6   Pvt. Pa. Mil.

Culbertson, Robert b. Pa. c 1781 d. Ohio 1815   Pvt. Ohio Mil.
  m. Mary Peoples — daughter Jane m. Thomas Forsythe Jones

Culp, Frederick b. Va. 1768 d. Ala. 1864   Drummer Va. Mil.
  m. Mary Flanagan — daughter Catherine m. Thaddeus Chewning

Culpepper, Mariner b. Ga. 1793 d. Ga. 1838   Ensign Ga. Mil.
   m. (2d) Jane Greer McCeary — son James M. m. Nancy Kemp

Culver, George b. N.Y. 1772 d. N.Y. m. Ruth   Capt. N.Y. Mil.
   daughter Phoebe m. Luman Harrison

Culver, Jeremiah b. Vt. 1796 d. Vt. 1876 m. Cynthia Foster   Pvt. Vt. Mil.
   son George W. m. Harriet Royce

Culver, John b. Conn. 1799 d. Conn. 1881   Drummer Conn. Mil.
   m. Susan Greer — son John Jr. m. Helen Rathbun

Culver, Moses   Vol. 9   Pvt. Conn. Mil.

Culver, Timothy   Vol. 9   Capt. Ohio Mil.

Cumby, William b. Va. 1795 d. Ill. 1857 m. Mrs. Anna Bell   Pvt. Va. Mil.
   son Vincent C. m. Laura Watt

Cummings, David   Vol. 14   Capt. U.S. Inf.

Cummins, Charles b. Pa. 1744 d. Pa. 1821   Furnished supplies during
   m. Elizabeth — daughter Agnes Nancy   Whiskey Rebellion
   m. Patrick Hayes

Cummins, Francis b. S.C. 1751 d. Ga. 1832   Memb. Constit. Conv. N.C.
   m. Sarah Thompson — daughter Elizabeth
   m. Archibald Laurinda McKinley

Cummins, (Cummings) George Jr. b. 1764/5   Pvt. West Tenn. Mil.
   d. Tenn. 1830/9 m. Mary McQuiston — daughter Sally
   m. Rev. John Bond
   daughter Elizabeth m. William R. Phipps
   daughter Harriet m. George A. Huddleston
   son William m. Jennie Ensley

Cummins, (Cummings) Guy Carlton b. N.Y. 1789 d. Ill. 1862   Pvt. N.Y.
   m. Eleanore Wheeler — daughter Jane   Mil.
   m. William Duff REAL DAUGHTER
   daughter Waity m. Daniel Duff

Cummins, Joseph b. Ire. d. Tenn. m. Nancy Browning   Pvt. Va. Mil.
   daughter Mary Ann m. Benjamin Wilkinson

Cummings, Levi b. N.Y. 1784 d. Ill. 1856   Vol. 8   Pvt. U.S. Inf.

Cummins, (Cummings) Samuel b. N.C. 1751/2 d. N.C. 1798/9 Memb. Gen.
   m. Mary Sheels — son David m. Elizabeth Fielder   Assem. N.C. 1812

Cummins, (Cummings) Seth b. 1785 d. N.Y. 1857   Pvt. N.Y. Mil.
   m. Lucinda Haley — daughter Lorinda m. Stephen Landon

Cummins, William   Vol. 15   Pvt. Pa. Mil.

Cunningham, Hugh b. Pa. 1768 d. Pa. 1859   Corp. Pa. Mil.
   m. Christine Caster (Castner) — son Syrus m. Jane McElroy
   son John R. m. Anna Emily Neal
   son William C. m. Hannah Gladden

Cunningham, James b.—d.—m.—   Messenger for Va. Assem. from
   daughter May m. Sylvester Ward   Randolph Co. 1789

Cunningham, Jesse b. N.C. 1772 d. N.C. 1827   Pvt. N.C. Det. Mil.
   m. Polly Moore — son William m. Mrs. Edith Gibbons Edwards

Cunningham, John b S.C. 1750 d. Ga. 1829   Col. Ga. Mil. 1786
   m. Ann Davis — son John Jr. m. Mary Carleton

Cunningham, John b. N.C. 1774 d. Ala. 1859   Wagon Master Tenn.
  m. Hannah Lewis — son Lewis   Vol. Mil.
  m. Charlotte Temple Campbell

Cunningham, John W.   Early Vol.   Brig. Gen. Pa. Mil.

Cunningham, Robert b.—d. Tenn. m. Mary Simmerson   Pvt. Tenn. Vols.
  son John M. m. Elizabeth Hicks Marion La Fontaine

Cunnington, William b. Eng. 1738 d. S.C. 1804 Lieut. Col. S.C. Mil. 1788
  m. Elizabeth Sophia — daughter Eliza Sophia m. Louis Senf Tharin

Curfman, Adam b. Md. 1789 d. after 1814 m.   Pvt. Md. Mil. 1814
  son Christian m. Rebecca Carman

Curman, Christian (Christopher) b. Md. 1789 d. W.Va. 1882 Pvt. Md.
  m. Rebecca Carman — son Samuel Henry   Mil. 1814
  m. Mary Ann Cain

Curlee, Cullen b. N.C. 1786 d. Tenn. 1853   Musician Tenn.
  m. Eleanor McFerrin — daughter Elizabeth m. Benjamin Stanley

Currie, Ezekiel b. N.C. 1792 d. N.C. 1855   Pvt. 43d Inf. N.C. Mil.
  m. Lydia Mangum — son John Henry m. Samanthia Ann Smith

Currier, Sylvanus b. N.H. d. N.H. m. Anna Hardy   Pvt. N.H. Vol.
  son Alfred m. Deborah Ball Powers

Curry, James b. Va. 1794 d. (W.) Va. 1855   Pvt. Pendleton Co., Va. Mil.
  m. Sally Curry (maiden name) — daughter Mary J.
  m. Nimrod C. Brake
  son William H. m. Mary E. Wilson

Curry, John b. Ky. 1780 d. Ill. 1833   Fife Major Ky. Mil.
  m. Charity Smith — daughter Letitia m. William Perry Gilliland

Curry, John b. N.C. 1789 d. Ala. 1879 m. Jane Weaver Pvt. Ala. Mil.
  daughter Georgia m. Oliver Wiley

Curtis, Abijah Birdsey   Vol. 15   Major Conn. Mil.

Curtis, Abner b. Mass. 1782 d. Me. 1864 m. Lydia Turner Pvt. Me. Mil.
  daughter Joanna m. Martin Bates

Curtis, David b. Mass. 1790 d. N.Y. 1838 m. Mercy Willey Pvt. Vt. Inf.
  daughter Wealthy m. Charles Caldwell

Curtis, Edmund b. Va. 1757 d. Va. 1857   Sgt. Va. Mil.
  m. Mrs. Martha Moreland Chisman — daughter Anne C.
  m. Seaton Elliott

Curtis, Ezra S. b. N.Y. 1790 d. Ohio 1864   Pvt. drummer Ohio Mil.
  m. Irene Sprague — daughter Mary R. m. Thomas O. Sager

Curtis, Frederick b. 1760 d. Mass. 1830 m. Persis Brown Pvt. Mass. Mil.
  daughter Dorcas m. Daniel Goodell

Curtis, John b. Mass. 1793 d. Me. 1875   Pvt. Mass. (Me.) Mil.
  m. Pheobia Jepson (Juftson) — daughter Abigail P.
  m. John Q. A. Atwood

Curtiss, Abijah b. Mass. 1773 d. Mass. 1834   Major Mass. Mil.
  m. Betsy Stevenson — son Charles A. m. Sabrina Robinson

Curtiss, John b. Conn. 1739 d. Conn. 1801   Memb. Conn. Conv. to
  m. Mary Lewis — daughter Lavina   Ratify U.S. Const.
  m. Selah Deming

Curtiss, Thaddeus b. Mass. 1764 d. Ohio 1834   Pvt. Ohio Mil.
    m. 2d Ester Bates — daughter Olive A. m. Ira Gardner

Cushing, Daniel Lewis b. Mass. 1764 d. Ohio 1815 m.—   Capt. U.S. Art.
    daughter Hannah L. m. John M. Gallagher

Cushing, Thomas b. Mass. 1725 d. Mass. 1788   Vol. 10   Lt. Gov. Mass.

Cushman, Artemas b. Mass. 1781 d. Vt. 1863   Pvt. Vt. Mil.
    m. Phebe Spear — son Earl S. m. Mary Elizabeth Lambe

Cushman, Caleb b. Mass. 1779 d. Me. 1859   Pvt. Mass. (Me.) Mil.
    m. Mary (Polly) Buck — daughter Zilpha m. Amory Hamilton

Cushman, Consider b. Mass. (N.Y.) 1755(65) d. N.Y. 1818(15) Capt. N.Y.
    m. Phebe Townsend — daughter Sophia   Mil. 1788/93
    m. Lewis Boyd

Cushman, George b. Mass. 1799 d. Mass. 1875   Pvt. Mass. Mil.
    m. Louisa Hayward — son Elbridge m. Elizabeth B. Shantleff

Cushman, Peter Newcomb b. Conn. 1780 d. Wisc. 1848   Corp. N.Y. Mil.
    m. Sarah Kellogg — daughter Cynthia Maria
    m. Danford Newton Barney

Cushwa, David b. Md. 1777 d. Md. 1849   Capt. Wash. Co. Md. Mil.
    m. Catherine Resley — daughter Catherine m. Henry McLaughline

Custer, Jonathan b. Pa. 1768 d. Pa. 1823   Pvt. Berks Co. Pa. Mil.
    m. Rosannah Ludwig — son David L. m. Catherine Kline

Cathbertson, David b. N.C. 1768 d. N.C. 1835   Memb. House Commons
    m. Janet Monteith — son Josiah   Anson Col. N.C. 1810/13
    m. Mary Hasty

Cutler, Abner b. 1792 d. 1878 m. Mary M. Weston   Pvt. Buffalo, N.Y.
    daughter Mary Martha m. Henry Hinklin

Cutler, Asa b. Vt. 1776 d. N.Y. 1834/5   Pvt. N.Y. Mil. Det.
    m. Sally Wadley — son Asa m. 2d Caroline Mattice

Cutler, David b. Mass. 1730 d. N.Y. 1806/7   Memb. Alarm List Mass.
    m. Dorcas Reed — daughter Lydia m. Israel Meade

Cutler, Ebenezer b. Mass. 1790 d. Vt. 1867   Pvt. U.S. Vols. from N.Y.
    m. Zipha — son Frederick L. m. Mary

Cutler, Ephraim b. Mass. 1767 d. Ohio 1853   Capt. Ohio Mil.
    m. Leah Atwood — son Charles m. Maria Walker

Cutler, Jarvis b. Mass. 1768 d. Ind. 1844   Major N.W. Terr. Mil.
    m. Philadelphia Cargill — daughter Elizabeth A.
    m. Rev. John Burnett

Cutter, Amos   Vol. 3   Pvt. N.Y. Mil.

Cutter, Joseph b. N.J. 1789 d. N.J. 1848 m.   Cornet N.J. Cav.
    daughter Harriet P. m. Matthias van Deveer

Cutter, Joseph b. N.J. 1787 d. N.J. 1869 m. Lydia Gravett   Pvt. N.J. Mil.
    daughter Elizabeth M. m. John Benham

Cuyler, John Bleeker b. N.Y. 1790 d. N.Y. 1839   Pvt. N.Y. Mil.
    m. Phebe Hoffnagle — son Elbert A. m. Ruth Jane Titus

Cypert, Jesse b. Tenn. 1781 d. Tenn. 1856   Pvt. West Tenn. Mil.
    m. Jemima Worthen — daughter Elizabeth m. John Merrow
    daughter Felicia Ann m. Littleberry L. Mack
    daughter Sarah Wade m. Joseph M. Copeland
    son Thomas P. m. Temperance Brown

Cyrus, William b. N.C. 1794 d. W.Va. 1867   Pvt. (W.) Va. Mil.
   m. Leah Toney — daughter Caroline C. m. David Hanson Johnson
REAL DAUGHTER

D

Dade, Robert Townshend   Vol. 17   Capt. Md. Inf.

Daffan, William b. Va. c. 1777 d. Va. 1855 m. Ann Davis   Pvt. Va. Mil.
   son James A. m. Anna Maria Shelkett

Dail, Daniel b. Md. 1791 d. Md. 1863 m. Elizabeth Block   Pvt. Md. Mil.
   daughter Mary C. m. Lemuel G. Taylor

Daily, Russell b. Conn. 1786 d. Mich. 1858   Seaman U.S. Frigate
   m. Mary Furness — daughter Mary Ann   United States 1811
   m. Julius Hoyt Spalding

Dalby, Richard Henderson b. Va. 1788 d N.C. 1831   Pvt. N.C. Mil.
   m. Fannie Mitchell — daughter Sophia m. John D. Bullock

Dale, Adam b. Md. 1768 d. Ala. 1851 m. Mary Hall   Capt. Smith Co.
   son Edward W. m. Anne Lewis Moore   Tenn. Mil.
   daughter Margaret H. m. John Philips
   daughter Sarah Hill m. Nathan Vaught
   daughter Sophia W. m. Dr. Robert Turner

Dale, Elijah Pearson b. Ky. 1795 d. Mo. 1865   Pvt. Ky. Mil.
   m. Frances V. Shelton — son Robert R. m. Olive Canzada Cox

Dale, George C.   Vol. 12   Pvt. Ky. Mil.

Dale, Samuel b. 1773 d. Pa. 1842 m. Eliza Gundecker   Col. Pa. Mil.
   son Samuel F. m. Eliza McClelland

Dale, Thomas Jr. b. Md. 1778 d. Tenn.   Pvt. Tenn. Mtd. Gunmen
   m. Elizabeth Hammond — son William J. m. Mary Elizabeth O'Reilly
   m. Rachel Irons — son William m. Martha Goodpasture

Dallas, Alexander James   Vol. 8   Commodore U.S. Navy

Dally, John b. Conn. 1786 d. N.Y. 1823 m. —   Cornet N.Y. Mil.
   son Joseph George m. Mary Elizabeth Vance

Dalrymple, David b. Mass. 1762 d. Pa. 1840   Pvt. Pa. Mil.
   m. Polly Richardson — son Corning m. Polly Goodenough

Dana, Austin b. Mass. 1795 d. Vt. 1870   Pvt. Vt. Mil.
   m. Susan Trowbridge Gale — daughter Sarah Ann
   m. Horatio Sanford

Dana, Francis b. N.Y. 1797 d. N.Y. 1872 m. Harriett Mosher   Pvt. N.Y.
   son John H. m. Maria Wiborn   Mil.

Dana, Henry b. Mass. 1768 d. Vt. 1851   Pvt. Whitefield Vt. 1805
   m. Martha Pike — son Harvey m. Sally Foster

Dana, Nathaniel b. Mass. 1740 d. R.I. 1822   Ensign R.I. Mil.
   m. Elizabeth Peyton — son Nathaniel m. Mary Brown   1788 & 93

Daneker, John Jacob b. Md. 1798 d. Md. bef. 1870   Pvt. Md. Mil.
   m. Ann Jarvis — son John F. m. Mary Carter

Danforth, David b. Vt. 1797 d. Vt. 1835 m. Sophronia Beach   Pvt. Vt. Mil.
   son Allen m. Edna Gilman

Danforth, Luther b. Vt. 1781 d. N.Y. 1807   Pvt. N.Y. Mil.
   m. Henrietta Ellsworth — daughter Harriett
   m. Cornelius Van Horn Stafford

Danforth, Thomas Paine   Vol. 8   Capt. N.Y. Mil.

Daniel, Allen b. Va. 1738 d. Ga. 1814 m. Mary Allen   Pvt.
    daughter Elizabeth m. Aaron Johnson   Gentlemen at Arms Ga. Mil.

Daniel, Charles b. Va. 1736/7 d. Ky. 1826   Memb. Quar. Sessions
    m. Sarah Tate — son Enos m. Mary Nelson   Campbell Co. N.Y.

Daniel, James b. Ga. 1794 d. Ga. 1859   Pvt. Ga. Mil.
    m. (2d) Delilah Wilson — daughter Martha J. m. John L. Smith
    REAL DAUGHTER

Daniel, James b. 1796 d. Tenn. 1872 m. Elizabeth   Pvt. Tenn. Mil.
    son Jesse m. Phoebe Ann

Daniel, John b. Va. 1756 d. Va. 1809 m. Martha Terrell   Capt. Va. Mil.
    son John T. m. Harriet Washington Fitzhugh

Daniel, John Moncure b. Va. 1769 d. Va. 1813   Surgeon U.S. Army
    m. Margaret Eleanor Stone — daughter Margaret E.
    m. Walker Peyton Conway

Daniel, Moses b. S.C. 1765 d. Ga. 1853 m. Charlotte Kinsley, Capt. Ga. Mil.
    daughter Charlotte D. m. Norman McDuffie

Daniell, George W. b. N.C. 1782 d. Ga. 1845 m. Mary Gonto   Pvt. Ga. Mil.
    daughter Nancy m. John Graham

Daniell, William b. N.C. 1743 d. Ga. 1840   Capt. Ga. Mil. 1800
    m. Mary Melton — son Robert m. Naomi Burnett

Daniells, John   Vol. 16   Lieut. N.Y. Mil.

Daniels, James b. N.C. 1762 d. Va. 1841   Pvt. N.C. Mil.
    m. Nancy Ann Venable — son Nathaniel C. m. Ann Harriet Bullock

Daniels, John Zadoc b. N.C. 1775 d. N.C. 1850   Pvt. N.C. Mil.
    m. Elizabeth Lewis — son Dudley m. Emeline Curtis

Daniels, Nathaniel b. Mass. 1791 d. Mass. 1835   Pvt. Mass. Mil.
    m. Ann (Nancy) Hay — son Edward m. Ione Flora Gove

Daniels, William b. Va. 1772 d. Va. 1872   Justice Peace 1803
    m. 1st Catherine Stalnaker — son Madison   Constable 1805
    m. Eleanor Skidmore

D'Antignac, Louis Jean Baptist Chamberon   Justice Peace 1804
    b. France 1749 d. Ga. 1827 m. Hannah DuBose   Richmond Co. Ga.
    son William M. m. Mary Ann Campbell Hariss

Darby, Benjamin b. S.C. 1777 d. S.C. m. Susan Eliz. Burns   Pvt. Ga. Mil.
    daughter Mary m. Eli Henderson

Darby, Philip b. Md. 1775 d. prob. Tenn. or Miss.   Capt. West Tenn. Mil.
    m. Nancy Davis — son Henry m. Martha Williams

Darcy, John b. N.J. 1760 d. N.J. 1822 m. Phebe Johns   Brig. Gen. N.J. Mil.
    son John S. m. Eliza Grey

Darden, Washington b. Va. 1781 d. Miss. 1830   Capt. Miss. Mil.
    m. Ann Sharkey — son Stephen m. Katherine Mays

Darke, William b. Pa. 1736 d. Va. 1801   Brig. Gen. U.S. Troops Va.
    m. Sarah Delayea — daughter Mary m. Thomas Rutherford

Darley, John b. Eng. 1765 d. Pa. 1853   Lieut. Marines U.S. Navy
    m. Eleanor Wesley — son Alford G. m. Mary Browne

Darling, John b. Vt. 1786 d. N.Y. 1867 m. Hannah Pennock Sgt. N.Y. Mil.
daughter Betsey m. Jerome Hill
daughter Lucinda m. Byrom Helms

Darling, Joseph   Vol. 17   Pvt. Mass. Mil.

Darnell, Jeremiah b. Va. 1789 d. Ohio 1866   Pvt. Va. Mil.
m. Narcissa Coppedge — daughter Ann M. m. David W. Ritchey

Darrington, John   Vol. 9   Lt. Col. U.S. Army

Darrow, George b. — d. Ohio 1861 m. Olive Gaylord Major Ohio Mil.
daughter Eliza m. (3rd) Orren McNeill

Darrow, James b. N.Y. 1777 d. N.Y. 1816   Vol. 1   Lieut. N.Y. Art.

Darrow, James b. 1789 d. Ohio 1875   Fife Major Ohio Mil.
m. Elizabeth Rose — daughter Harriet Melissa m. Jonas Butterfield

Darrow, Zadock W. b. Conn. 1792 d. Ind. 1852   Pvt. Conn. Mil.
m. Nancy Smith — son Hezekiah S. m. Janette Van Benschoten

Darst, Isaac b. Mo. 1789 d. Mo. 1852 m. Phebe   Pvt. Mtd. Mil. Mo. Terr.
daughter Tevelda m. Stuart A. Hall

Dasher, John Martin b. N.C. 1738 d. Ga. 1812   Commissioner 1796
m. 1st Susannah Schaffer—son Solomon m. Maria Wylly   Effingham
m. 2d Elizabeth   Co. Ga.

Dashiell, George b. Md. 1770 d. N.Y. 1852   Pioneer Clergyman Del. 1793
m. Esther Handy — son Alfred H. m. Ann Ridgely   Md. 1797

Dashiell, Henry b. Md. 1769 d. Md. 1830   Capt. Md. Marine Art.
m. Mary Leeke — son Nicholas L. m. Louisa Turpin Wright

Dashiell, Matthias b. Md. 1778 d. Md. 1835   Maj. Md. Mil.
m. Rebecca Emmet Whitelock — son Cadmus
m. Harriet or Henrietta Waters Walters
daughter Virginia R. E. m. George Washington Dashiell (rel.)

Daubenspeck, George b. Pa. 1776 d. Pa. 1857   Pvt. Northampton Co.
m. Ann Margaret Meals — son Lewis   Pa. Mil.
m. Mrs. Ruth Christie Coulter

Dauchy, Nathan Sr. b. Conn. 1746/7 d. Conn. 1824   Civil Officer 1787/1815
m. Mary Smith — son Nathan m. Ruth Bradley

Daughdrill, John b. S.C. 1782 d. Miss. 1850   Pvt. Miss. Mil.
m. Winnie Harrell — son James H. m. Elizabeth J. Rawls

Daughterty, Daniel   Vol. 16   Pvt. Pa. Mil.
Daulton, Moses b. Va. 1760 d. Ky. 1819   Capt. Silver Grays
m. Mary Fristoe — daughter Margaret m. James G. Arnold

D'Aunoy, Fevre Etienne b. La. 1778 d. La. 1855   Pvt. La. Mil.
m. Rosema Barabino — daughter Rosema m. Joseph Hernandez

Davenport, Benjamin b. Va. 1783 d. W.Va. 1830   Lieut., Adj. Va. Mil.
m. Elizabeth — daughter Margaret S. m. Ambrose W. Cramer

Davenport, John b. Va. 1777 d. Ga. 1858 m. Nancy Davis   Pvt. Ga. Mil.
daughter Anne E. m. Edwin D. Coleman

Davenport, John b. Mass. 1760 d. Ind. 1838   Pvt. N.Y. Mil.
m. Eunice Hawk — son Lewis m. Sarah Horner

Davenport, Richard b. Va. 1775   Col. 17th Reg. U.S. Inf. 1812/15
d. Miss. 1818 m. Elizabeth Tadlock   in Ky. Mil. 1799/1809
son Charles F. m. Catharine McPherrin
son Patrick H. m. Eliza Ann Bohannon

Davenport, William Sr.   Vol. 11   Pvt. Mass. Mil.

David, Benjamin b. Pa. 1776 d. Pa. 1817 m. Jerusha Brown Pvt. U.S. Inf.
daughter Sarah m. George Christman

David, Charles Stansbury b. Md. 1795 d. Md. 1856 m.   Pvt. Md. Mil.
daughter Achsah G. m. Sewell B. Scott

David, Isaac Jr. b. Va. 1754 d. Va. 1828   Memb. Va. Hse. Delegates fr.
m. Elizabeth Kirtley — son Robert   Orange Co.
m. Augustina Shumate

David, Jacob White b. Va. 1790 d. Ga. 1871   Pioneer Minister Ga.
m. Betsy Margaret Almond — son William J.
m. Elizabeth Dean Taylor

Davidson, Asa b. Tenn. 1790 d. Tenn.   Corp. East Tenn. Mil.
m. Martha West — daughter Mary N. m. Joel Terrell

Davidson, David b. Va. 1790 d. Va. 1859   Pvt. Campbell Co. Va. Mil.
m. Caroline Laye — daughter Mary Jane unmarried
REAL DAUGHTER

Davidson, James b. Va. 1777 d. Ky. 1861   Col. Ky. Mil.
m. Harriet C. Ballinger — daughter Mary W. m. Charles G. Reeves

Davidson, James b. Va. 1795 d. Va. 1861   Pvt. & Courier Va. Mil.
m. Mary Harrison Butts — daughter Nora Fontaine Maury
unmarried   REAL DAUGHTER

Davidson, Lewis b. Pa. 1773 d. Ohio 1832 Matross Georgetown D.C. Art.
m. Mary — son Thomas L. m. Rebecca Walker

Davidson, Samuel b. Va. 1766 d. Ill. 1845   Maj. Lincoln Co. Ky. Mil.
m. Sarah Logan — daughter Anne M. m. Israel Jennings Jr.
daughter Mariah m. Charles Jennings

Davidson, Samuel W. b. N.C. 1781/2 d. N.C. 1858   Rep. N.C.
m. Martha McRee — daughter Rachel A.   Assembly 1811
m. John Burgin

Davidson, Thomas Sr. b. Ohio 1791 d. Ohio 1870   Pvt. Highland Co.
m. Sarah Collins — son Thomas m. Amanda Malcolm   Ohio Mil·

Davie, William Richardson b. Eng. 1756   Brig. Gen. N.C. 1798 - Gov. N.C.
d. S.C. 1820 m. Sarah Jones   Ambassador France 1799
daughter Mary H. m. Uriah Blanchard

Davies, William Washington b. Ga. 1792 d. N.C. 1862   Lieut. U.S. Inf.
m. Charlotte M. Howard — daughter Martha E. W.
m. Robert Hamilton Bigger

Davis, Abisha b. Md. 1754 d. Md. 1815   Lieut. Worcester Co.
m. Mary Brevard — daughter Elizabeth m. Peter Whaley   Md. Mil.

Davis, Abner b. Pa. 1782 d. Pa. 1863   Pvt. Lancaster Co. Pa. Mil.
m. Barbara Hess — son Abner m. Abigail Andrews
daughter Ann m. Jacob Keech

Davis, Abraham b. 1782 d. Pa. 1863 m. Ruth Mead   Lieut. Pa. Mil.
daughter Susan m. Nathan Whitney

Davis, Benjamin b. Va. 1784 d. Ala. 1863 m. Martha Taylor   Lieut. Ga. Mil.
daughter Louisiana C. m. John Harvin Barlow

Davis, Benjamin b.—d.— m. Jerush Brown — see Benjamin David

Davis, Charles Stansbury b.—d.— m. Priscilla Galloway
see Charles S. David — also Surgeon's Mate

Davis, Daniel b. Mass. 1713 d. Mass. (1799 Me.)   Memb. Mass.
   m. Mehitabel Lathrop — daughter Mary   Prov. Congress 1774-1799
   m. George Lewis

Davis, Daniel b. Mass. 1793 d. Me. 1860   Pvt. Mass. (Me.) Mil.
   m. Hannah Grant — son Samuel S. m. Evelyn Hooker

Davis, Daniel b. N.H. 1766 d. N.H. 1842 m. Mary Brown   Pvt. N.H. Mil.
   son Enoch m. Armittai Bartlett
Davis, David   Vol. 13   Capt. Mass. Mil.

Davis, David Sr. b. Italy 1764 d. Ill. 1827   Pvt. U.S. Inf. - N.Y. & Ill.
   m. Jane Smith — son David Jr. m. Blanche Keating
   daughter Rebecca   REAL DAUGHTER

Davis, Ebenezer b. Mass. 1790 d. Me. 1861   Pvt. Mass. Troops
   m. Philippi Wilson — daughter Lucy Ann m. Henry Collom

Davis, Elijah b. Pa. 1760 d. Md. 1829   Memb. Md. Senate 1811
   m. Mary Gouldsmith Garretson — son Septimus
   m. Frances Ann Griffith

Davis, Ezra b. N.H. d. N.H. m. Mary Garland   Musician U.S. Inf.
   son Jesse B. m. Jane P. Voorhees

Davis, Frederick b. Mass. 1791 d. N.Y. 1865   Pvt. N.Y. Mil.
   m. Lucia Holmes — daughter Harriet E. m. Artemas Adams

Davis, George b. N.J. 1774 d. N.J. 1824   Musician N.J. Troops
   m Mary Brokaw — son Isaac m. Mary Scott

Davis, George b. Va. c. 1765 d. Mo. 1838   Pvt. Ohio Mil.
   m. 2d Elizabeth Botkin — son Charles m. Sally Kennedy

Davis, Greeley   Vol. 13   Pvt. N.Y. Mil.

Davis, Henry b. Ga. 1787 d. Ga. 1851 m. Rachel Bellah   Pvt. Ga. Mil.
   daughter Martha Ann m. Joseph Reagan

Davis, Henry   Vol. 19   Pvt. Ohio Mil.

Davis, Henry B. b. N.Y. d. Ohio 1842   Pvt. N.Y. Mil
   m. Sally G. Spaulding — son William A. m. Sarah Ann Williams

Davis, Ichabod b. 1776 d. Mich. 1849 m. Mary Frisbie   Capt. N.Y. Mil.
   daughter Mary H. m. Oliver Wentworth

Davis, Isaac m. Elizabeth Kirtley — see Issac David

Davis, James b. Va. 1779 d. Ky. 1835   Pvt. Ky. Mtd. Mil.
   m. Eilzabeth Shepherd — daughter Mahalie m. Pleasant Foster

Davis, James b. 1775 d. Ohio 1813 m. Mary Hickman   Capt. Ohio Terr. Mil.
   daughter Lydia m. Isaac Phillips, Jr.

Davis, James b. Va. 1785 d. Va. 1823   Capt. Norfolk Co. Va. Mil
   m. Sarah Wilkins — son James A. m. Sarah C. Carmichael

Davis, Jehiel b. 1787 d. Mich. 1872 m. Phebe T.   Pvt. N.Y. Mil.
   daughter Angeline M. m. Albert Davis

Davis, Jeremiah b. N.H. 1796 d. N.Y. 1856   Pvt. N.H. Mil.
   m. Elizabeth Dickerson Miles — daughter Ellen
   m. Chester Hayden Freeman

Davis, John b. Ire. 1757 d. N.J. 1828 m. Mary Bartholomew   Pvt. N.J. Art.
   son Thomas m. Ann Bartholomew

Davis, John b. 1760 d. prob. N.C. 1840   Justice Wayne Co. N.C. 1803
   m. Charity — daughter Mary Davis m. Alexander Carter

Davis, John   Vol. 5, 7, 8, 9,   Pvt. Pa. Mil.

Davis, Jonathan b. Md. or Va. 1765/70 d. Ga. 1819   Lieut. Col. Ga. Mil.
m. Mary Eliz. Waller — daughter Elmyra E.
m. David Brady Mitchell Moore

Davis, Joshua b. Vt. 1777 d. Vt. 1850 m. Mary Polls   Pvt. Conn. Mil.
son Tuial ? B. m. Fanny Cutler

Davis, Josiah b. Conn. 1779 d. Vt. 1870 m. Sarah Averill Pvt. Conn. Mil
daughter Louisa P. m. Joseph MacNeill

Davis, Nathaniel b. Va. 1784 d. Miss. 1857   Pvt. Ky. Vol. Mil.
m. Martha Bowe — son Hugh m. Sarah Rachael Jones

Davis, Nathaniel b. Vt. 1787 d. N.Y. 1845 m. Sophonia Reed Pvt. Vt. Mil
son Richard M. m. Rowena Wells

Davis, Paschal b. Va. 1793 d. Ohio 1862 m. Nancy L. Toone Pvt. Va. Mil.
daughter Elizabeth m. Washington Davis

Davis, Reuben (Samuel) b. Va. 1792 d. W.Va. 1868 Ensign Hamshire Co.
m. Eleanor Dean — son David D. m. Susan Vance Wilson   Va. Mil.

Davis, Richard b. Va. 1746/7 d. Ky. 1812   Col. Ky. Frontier 1806
m. Nancy Chiles — son Thomas C. m. Elizabeth Dabney

Davis, Robert b. N.Y. 1777 d. N.Y. 1876   Lieut. N.Y. Det. Mil.
m. Leah Van Horne — son Philip m. Olive Harrington

Davis, Samuel b. Md. 1795 d. Md. 1876 m. Eliza Sturgis   Pvt. Md. Mil.
daughter Elizabeth m. George Ward Airey   REAL DAUGHTER

Davis, Samuel b. Vt. 1786 d. Ohio 1868   Pvt. Ontario Co. N.Y. Mil.
m. Laura Louisa Spicer — son Justus Barker m. Susanna Murlin

Davis, Samuel Boyer b. Del. 1766 d. Del. 1854   Lieut. Col. U.S. Inf.
m. (1) Rosa Eliz. de Botsfontaine — son Horatio
m. Naomi du Bourg de Ste Colombe
son Samuel B. Jr. m. Anne Catherine Warner

Davis, Shannon b. Pa. 1791 d. N.Y. 1854 m. Elizabeth Adams   Sgt. Pa. Mil.
daughter Mary Ann m. John B. Shank

Davis, Stephen b. N.Y. 1771 d. N.Y. 1834 m. Zilpha Spencer Patriot N.Y.
son John L. m. Elizabeth Worden

Davis, Stephen b. Va. 1789 d. Va. 1856/9   Pvt. Dinwiddie Co. Va. Mil.
m. Susan E. Elder — daughter Edna m. John McClure Goodwin

Davis, Thomas b. Md. 1782 d. N.Y. 1857   Capt. N.Y. Mil. 1811
m. Sarah Shekell — daughter Sarah A. m. Joel H. Prescott
son Samuel m. Hannah W. Case

Davis, Thomas b. N.C. 1764/5 d. N.C. 1822   Brig. Gen. N.C. Mil.
m. Mary Owen — daughter Maria O. m. James Alves

Davis, Thomas Chiles b. Va. 1799 d. Mich. 1813   Surgeon Ky. Mil.
m. Elizabeth Dabney — son Thomas C.
m. Rebecca Fifield Rutherford Grace

Davis, William b. Del. 1770 d. Del. 1824   Sgt. Del. Mil.
m. Elizabeth Harrington — daughter Ann C.
m. Thomas Robinson Finsthwait

Davis, William   Vol. 11   Ensign N.Y. Mil.

Davis, William b. Md. 1784 d. Ohio 1871 m. Livinia Parker   Pvt. Ohio Mil.
daughter Maria m. Joshua Daugherty

Davis, William b. S.C. c. 1748 d. S.C. 1801   Repr. S.C. 1786
  m. Mrs. Rebecca Hardin Weakley — daughter Martha m. Henry Rice

Davis, William b. Va. 1786 d. Ga. 1869   4th Sgt. Tenn. Mil.
  m. Elizabeth Brickey — daughter Winifred B.
  m. John Scott Henderson

Davis, William b. Del. 1782 d. Ohio 1854   Pvt. Monongalia Co.
  m. Sarah Pride — son Jehu m. Susan Honley   W.Va. Mil.

Davis, William   Vol. 14   Sgt. Tenn. Mil.

Davis, William T. b. Va. 1790 d. Va. 1854   Pvt. Va. Mil.
  m. Sarah Boston — son George W. m. Mary Rose Powell

Davison, Edward b. Va. 1750 d. Ohio 1827   Pvt. Ky. Mil.
  m. Elizabeth Ikes or Eikes — son John m. Elnora Van Wagoner

Davison, Ezra b. Nova Scotia 1765 d. N.Y. 1834   Juryman N.Y. 1807
  m. Diadamia Smith — son Daniel P. M. m. Malinda Maxon

Davison, Isaac b. W.Va. 1790 d. Ohio 1851 m. Sarah Curl   Pvt. Ohio Mil.
  daughter Margaret m. David V. Pringle

Davy, William b. Eng. 1773 d. Md. 1850   Pvt. Md. Mil.
  m. Anna Hammond Foulds — daughter Margaret
  m. James Hyland Cox

Dawson, Bernard b. Va. 1789 d. Ill. 1853 m. Elizabeth Lowe   Pvt. Va. Mil.
  son Edward L. m. Olive L. Yeamans

Dawson, George b. Eng. 1760 d. Ga. 1824   Pvt. Ga. Mil.
  m. Mrs. Kate Marston Skidmore — daughter Martha
  m. David Corsby

Dawson, James b. Ire. 1747 d. Pa. 1834   Signed Oath Allegiance 1793
  m. Catherine Morrow — daughter Catharine   Pa. Mil. 1794
  m. James McBurney

Dawson, John Wells b. Ky. 1792 d. Ia. 1865   Corp. Ohio Mil. or
  m. Ann Cheney — daughter Clarinda   Wagon Master Ohio
  m. Alexander R. Miller
  daughter Nancy Jane m. William Henry Harrison

Dawson, Mackall b. Md. 1770 d. Pa. 1830 m. Rachel Porter   Pvt. Pa. Mil.
  son Thomas m. (2d) Eliza Eggleson

Dawson, Nicholas b. Md. 1750 d. Md. 1806   Magistrate Frederick Co.
  m. Elizabeth Bayne (2) — son Samuel   Md. 1785
  m. Sarah Ann Bayne

Dawson, Nicholas b. Md. 1772 d. Ohio 1856   Pvt. Pa. Mil.
  m. Rachel Moore — son William m. Ann Irwin

Dawson, Samuel b. Md. 1787 d. Va. 1845 m. Sarah Bayne   Capt. Md. Mil.
  daughter Elizabeth m. Richard Ayres

Day, Hezekiah b. Mass. 1768 d. Vt. aft. 1822   Opponent of Shay's
  m. Elizabeth Wickham — son Chester m. Esther Patrill   Rebellion

Day, Horatio b. Md. 1793 d. Va. 1834 m. Elizabeth Sullivan   Pvt. D.C. Mil.
  daughter Honoria m. Theodore P. Stallings

Day, John III b. Tenn. 1795 d. Tenn. 1853   Corp. East Tenn. Mil.
  m. Frances Holdeway — daughter Elizabeth
  m. William Claiborne McCoy
  son Jesse m. Alice Cantwell

Day, Joseph   Vol. 7   Capt. Conn. Mil.

Day, Morgan b. Va. 1781/1791 d. Mo. 1861 m. Lucinda P. Corp. Ky. Mil.
   daughter Sarah Amanda m. Isaac D. Herndon
   son William H. m. Martha Montgomery

Day, Samuel b. Mass. 1743 d. N.Y.   Ensign Ontario Co. N.Y. Mil.
   m. Lois Merrick — son Loring m. Sarah Parker

Day, Samuel b. N.Y. 1764 d. N.Y. 1857 m. Sarah Parker   Pvt. N.Y. Mil.
   daughter Martha m. Ira Phillips

Day, Sylvester b. Vt. 1778 d. Pa. 1851 m. Avis Bliss   Surgeon U.S. Inf.
   son Hannibal m. (1) Maria Houghton

Day, William b. Mass. 1780 d. Minn. 1862   Pvt. Mass. Mil.
   m. Lucy Augusta Thompson — son Leonard m. Lois Averill

Day, William b. N.J. 1759 d. 1815   Capt. 4th Reg. Pa. 1794
   m. Damaris Foster — son William Jr. m. Nancy Bonnel

Dayton, Elias b. N.J. 1737 d. Pa. 1807   Major Gen. N.J. Mil. 1793
   m. Catherine Elizabeth Chandler — daughter Jane T. C.
   m. William Berrian

Dayton, Jehiel b. N.Y. 1772 d. N.Y. 1840   Capt. N.Y. Mil.
   m. Mary Parkhurst — son Gaius m. Pleades Kingsley

Dayton, John G. b. Conn. 1787 d. N.Y. 1863   Ensign Conn. Mil.
   m. Hannah Beardsley — daughter Asenath A. m. Charles M. Platt
   son Russell m. Dally Titus

Deake, Jabez b. N.Y. 1788 d. N.Y. 1846 m. Sophia Bowen Pvt. N.Y. Mil.
   son Jabez m. Elizabeth Church

Deal, George b. Va. 1779 d. Ohio 1851   Ens. Ohio Mil.
   m. Catherine Hott — son George, Jr. m. Esther Ann Johnson

Deal, Peter   Vol. 10   Lt. Pa. Mil.

Deal, William b. N.C. 1774 d. N.C. 1824 m. Mary Herman Pvt. N.C. Mil.
   son William Jr. m. Catherine Smyre

DeAlpuente, Francisco Bonaventura b. La. 1783 d. La. 1841 Capt. La. Mil.
   m. Charlotte Mathilda Antoinette Hepburn — daughter Marie
   m. J. W. Bailey
   m. Dona Catharina Mellon — son Francois R. m. Zoe le Breton des
   Chappelles

Dean, Abraham b. Pa. 1763 d. Ohio 1806   Lt. Ohio 1783-90
   m. Sarah Stewart —daughter Margery m. Adam B. Wilson

Dean, Burkett b. Va. 1775 d. Ga. aft. 1814   Ens. Ga. Mil.
   m. Sarah Carleton — daughter Elizabeth Ann
   m. James Morrison Broadfield

Dean, Ezra   Vol. 13   2nd Lt. Ohio Mil.; Ens. U.S. Inf.

Dean, Isaac b. Va. 1789 d. W.Va. 1870 m. Anna Conway   Pvt. Va. Mil.
   daughter Belle m. George Schaefer   REAL DAUGHTER
   daughter Louvenia   REAL DAUGHTER
   son Rufus C. m. Anna Bell Linn

Dean, Jacob b. Md. 1747 d. Pa. 1829/31   Pat. Pa. 1792-1803
   m. Nancy Lovell — son Zecheriah m. Allie Thompson

Dean, James   Vol. 11   Capt. U.S. Inf.

Dean, James Savage b. N.Y. 1790 d. Mo. 1839   Lt. U.S. Inf.
   m. Harriet Marie Christy — daughter Cornelia Van m. J. G. Tilford

Dean, John b. Conn. 1795 d. Conn. 1876 m. Sarah A. Tillman   **Pvt. U.S. Inf.**
  daughter Virginia T. m. George R. Prowell

Dean, Peter L.   Vol. 6   **Pvt. N.J. Mil.**

Dean, Peter L. b. N.J. 1791 d. Ohio 1883   **Rif. N.J. Mil.**
  m. Elizabeth Meeker — daughter Phebe m. Aaron Clark

Dean, Samuel F. b. Pa. 1760 d. Pa. 1856   **Capt. Pa. Mil.**
  m. Martha Camp   **Sheriff**
  son Edward m. Mary Ann Crawford
  son John m. Sarah Jane Crawford
  son Thomas m. Jane Wright

Dean, Thomas   Vol. 3   **Maj. Mass. Mil.**

Dean, Thomas b. Ky. 1765 d. Ky. 1834 m. Sarah   **Pa. House of**
  daughter Sarah Jane m. Edward Maxwell Dean   **Rep. 1809**

Dean, Zecheriah b. Md. 1772 d. Pa. 1862   **Pat. Pa. 1813-14**
  m. Allie Thompson — son Abner m. (1) Susannah Remley

Dear, George b. Conn. 1791 d. N.Y. 1854 m. Eunice   **Pvt. U.S. Inf.**
  daughter Catharine m. William Winch

Dearing, William Lynch Smith b. Va. 1796 d. Tenn. 1876   **Pvt. Va. Mil.**
  m. Mary Terry Harrison — daughter Virginia
  m. Hugh Lawson White Hill

Dearth, George A. b. Eng. 1762 d. Pa. 1846   **Capt. Pa. Mil.**
  m. Elizabeth Mills — daughter Mary m. Thomas Nelan

Deason, Absalom b. Tenn. 1781 d. Ala. 1845   **Pvt. Tenn. Mil.**
  m. Miss Yerby — son Absalom, Jr. m. Katherine Ray

Deason, Joseph b. S.C. d. Ga. 1845 m. Jelico Cates   **Pvt. Ga. Mil.**
  son John m. (3) Mary Jane Howell

Deatherage, George b. Va. 1791 d. Va. 1834   **4th Sgt. Va. Mil.**
  m. Catherine Waters — son John L. m. Ann Eliza Fant

de Berry, Lemuel b. Va. 1757 d. N.C. 1817   **Pvt. Va. Mil.**
  m. Delphia Ellis — son William E. m. Eliza Ellen Morrison

DeBlanc, Joseph Carlos b. La. 1776 d. La. 1856   **Capt. La. Mil.**
  m. Madalena LaCour — son Louis Eloi m. Julie Hebert

DeBlois, James b. Mass. 1784 d. Mass. 1862   **Sgt. Mass. Mil.**
  m. Sally Duncklee — son Albert m. Emma Bruce

Dech, Andrew b. Pa. 1790 d. Pa. 1854   **Pvt. Pa. Mil.**
  m. Catherine Heller — son Solomon m. Matilda Magdalina Driesbach

de Chalmette, Ignace de Lino b. La. 1755 d. La. 1815   **Pvt. La. Mil.**
  m. Victoire de Vaguine
  daughter Heloise m. Pierre de Verges de St. Sauvour
  daughter Victoire m. Antoine G. Cruzat

Decker, Andrew Dingman b. N.J. 1791 d. N.J. 1847   **Pvt. N.J. Mil.**
  m. Elizabeth Overpeck — son Moses V. m. Sarah Ann Spangenberg

Decker, Luke b. Pa. 1760 d. Ind. 1825   **Lt. Col. Ind. Mil.**
  m. Sarah Kuykendall — son John m. (1) Mrs. Diana D. Riley

de Coursey, William Jr.   Vol. 4   **Pvt. Ga. Mil.**

Deem, Phillip b. Pa. 1783 d. W.Va. 1865   **Pvt. W.Va. Mil.**
  m. Rachel Kidwiler — son James J. m. Elizabeth Bradley

Deffenbaugh, Daniel b. Pa. 1785 d. Pa. 1867   **Pvt. Pa. Mil.**
  m. Barbara Riffle — son Eli m. Sarah Dusenberry

Deffenbaugh, Daniel K. b. Ohio 1798 d. Ohio 1885   Drummer Ohio Mil.
 m. Nancy Ann Armstrong — daughter Angeline
 m. William Cephas Stahl   REAL DAUGHTER
 son James m. Lydia Stump

De Freest, John, Jr. b. N.Y. 1780 d. N.Y. 1844   Maj. N.Y. Mil.
 m. Elizabeth Ann Knickerbocker — daughter Elizabeth Ann
 m. Francis Nicoll Sill

Defriez, Henry I   Vol. 3   Sailing Master of the "Brutus" 1812

DeGarmo, Martin b. N.Y. 1788 d. N.Y. 1869   Courier N.Y. Mil.
 m. Esther Willse — daughter Catherine m. John Tefft

DeGroot, James b. N.Y. 1777 d. N.Y. 1847 m. Susan Perkins   Sgt. Pa. Mil.
 daughter Sarah m. John Green

DeGroot, William b. N.Y. 1751 d. N.Y. 1840   Pvt. N.Y. Mil.
 m. Anne La Tourette — son William, Jr. m. Jane Bishop

DeHart, Cornelius b. N. J. 1776 d. N.Y. 1859   Pvt. N.J. Mil.
 m. Prudence Cheeseman — son James m. Ann DeWitt

de Haven, Moses b. Pa. 1765 d. Pa. 1812   Maj. Pa. Mil. 1794
 m. Margaret Bisbing — son Samuel m. Elizabeth Sharp

de Hoa, Manuel b. Spain d. La. 1821 m. Rosalie Jourdan   Pvt. La. Mil.
 son Pierre m. Emilie Elizabeth de la Ronde

DeJarnett, James b. Va. 1777 d. Ky. 1859 m. Elizabeth Sims   Maj. Ky. Mil.
 son Christopher m. Hannah Tribble
 son Josiah m. Mahala Boyce

de Kernion, Charles La Bedeyere Huchet b. La. 1796   Pvt. La. Mil.
 d. La. 1846 m. Euphemie Aimee Lambert
 son Louis D. m. Blanche DuPuy

de la Houssaye, Louis Alexandre le Pelletier b. La. d. La.   Pvt. La. Drag
 m. Charlotte Pellerin — son Louis Jr. m. Elizabeth M. de Blanc

de la Houssaye, Louis Alexandre le Pelletier b. St. Martin   Pvt. La. Drag
 d. La. m. Elisabeth Marcelite de Blanc
 son Louis A le P, Jr. m. Helene Sidomie Perret

de Lamater, Isaac, Jr. b. N.Y. 1791 d. Mich. 1878   2nd Lt. N.Y. Mil.
 m. Diadema Barnes — daughter Maria K. m. Hiram Tuthill

Delano, Jesse b. Mass. 1780 d. N.J. 1867   Pvt. N.Y. Mil.
 m. Rachel Beach Sickles — son Jesse, Jr. m. Marie Nuttman

DeLano (De Lannoy), Thomas, Jr. b. N.Y. 1760   Capt. U.S. Inf.
 d. N.Y. 1835 m. Olive Griswold — son Ira B. m. Polly Rogers

Delany, Henry Field b. Va. 1795 d. Ky. 1831   Capt. Ky. Mil.
 m. Rhoda Prince — son William S. m. Gabriella Rebecca Shropshire

Delany, William b. Ire. 1776 d. Md. 1856 m. Ellen McClane   Pvt. Md. Mil.
 daughter Mary C. m. Patrick Flannagan

de la Ronde, Pierre Denis, II b. La. 1762 d. La. 1824   Col. La. Mil.
 m. Elizabeth Eulalie Guerbois — daughter Adelaide A.
 m. Pierre A. Ducros
 daughter Emilie E. m. Pierre de Hoa Cacho
 daughter Felicie m. Pierre Jorda

de la Shumate, Louis b. Va. 1770 d. Va. 1861   Pvt. Va. Mil.
 m. Mary Chadwell — daughter Augusta Ann m. Robert Davis

de Laughter, George b. S.C. 1760 d. S.C. 1830 m. Charlotte   Juror S.C.
 son Solomon m. Susanna Trailer

de Lemos, Fernando Gayoso b. Miss. 1797 d. La. 1837   Lt. La. Mil.
  m. Lodoiska Perez — daughter Felicite G. m. Charles Tennent

De Lesdernier, Lewis Frederick b. Me. 1785 d. Me. 1816   Cpl. Mass. Mil.
  m. Anna Aymar — son Lewis F. m. Eliza Stetson
  daughter Phebe m. George H. Robbins

Delo, George b. Pa. 1773 d. Pa. 1848   Pvt. Pa. Mil.
  m. Eva Catherine Kuhns — daughter Elizabeth m. George Keiser

De Lyon, Isaac   Vol. 3   Sgt. Ga. Mil.

Demarest, David Peter b. N.J. 1738 d. N.Y. 1820   Ens. Pa. Mil.
  m. Hester Brower — son David D. m. Hannah Van Saun

Demary, Silas b. N.H. 1766 d. Vt. 1838 m. Sally Rand   Lt. Vt. Mil.
  son Sullivan J. m. Jane Howard Brown

Demeritt, Richard, Jr. b. Vt. 1799 d. Calif. 1850   Capt. Supply Vessel
  m. Martha Ricker   on Lake Champlain
  son Albert m. Elizabeth F. Lanpher

Deming, Timothy b. Conn. 1788 d. Conn. 1879   Pvt. Conn. Mil.
  m. Eliza Wing — daughter Antoinette m. Franklin Comstock

Demond, Abel b. Mass 1799 d. Mass. 1864   Pvt. Mass. Mil.
  d. N.Y. 1864 m. Catherine Brooks—son Joseph m. Permelia Sampson

DeMond, Cornelius b. N.Y. 1788 d. N.Y. 1869   Pvt. N.Y. Mil.
  m. Mary Yaples — son John Y. m. Priscilla Hiltc

de Mongreun (Monbreun), Jacques Timothe   Commandant Ill. 1786
  Boucher (Archange Gibault) b. Canada 1747 d. Tenn. 1836
  m. Marguerite (Theresa) — daughter Madame Therese A.
  m. (2) Alexis Doza

DeMoss, John b. Ky. 1789 d. Ind. 1852 m. Sarah Irwin   Sgt. Ohio Mil.
  son James m. Elizabeth Dodson

DeMoss, William b. Tenn. 1794 d. Mo. 1848   5th Cpl. Tenn. Cavalry
  m. Abiah Charter — daughter Hannah m. Samuel Bryan

Demott, Isaac   Vol. 12   Pvt. Pa. Mil.

Denbo (D'Enbeau), Joseph b. Pa. 1779 d. Ind. 1851   Lt. Ind. Mil.
  m. Jane Lowry Martin and Nancy Woodfield
  son Francis M. m. Margaret Bell
  son Jacob m. Mariah Grant

Denby, William b. Va. 1791 d. Va. 1861 m. Mary Deshon   Pvt. Va. Mil.
  son Andrew J. m. Hariett Virginia Phillips
  son William m. Mary DeShon

Deneen, Samuel (Hackett) b. N.J. 1766 d. Mich. 1849   Pvt. Ohio Mil.
  m. Phoebe Nixon — son William L. m. Verlinda Beall Moore

de Neuveille, Louis Charles de Blanc b. La. 1753   Commissioner La. 1803
  d. La. 1825 m. Elizabeth Pomponne d'Erneville
  son Maximillien m. Aspasie Castillo

Denice, Garret b. N.J. 1772 d. N.J. 1813 m. Elizabeth Davis   Pvt. N.J. Mil.
  daughter Ann m. Spafford Bowne

Denig, George   Vol. 3   Surgeon's Mate Pa. Mil.

Denison, Henry b. Conn. 1782 d. Va. 1822   Chaplain Navy 1810
  m. Eliza Ann Read — daughter Eliza Ann   Purser 1812
  m. Isaac Newton Brown

Denison. Isaac b. Conn. 1790 d. Conn. 1855　　　　Pvt. Conn. Mil.
　m. Livinia Fish — daughter Eliza T. m. Dudley W. Stewart

Denison, Jonathan b. Conn. 1780 d. Conn. 1828　　　Pvt. Conn. Mil.
　m. Catherine Brown — daughter Betsey Permelia m. Galusha Owen

Denison, Samuel b. Ohio 1783 d. Ohio 1869　　　Capt. Ohio Mil.
　m. Elizabeth Steward — son John m. Susannah Fite

Dennard, Bird b. Ga. 1780 d. Ga. 1835 m. Rhoda Marshall　Pvt. Ga. Mil.
　son James E. m. Elizabeth Fuller

Dennard, Isaac b. S.C. 1776 d. Ga. 1854 m. Mary Harris　Pvt. Ga. Mil.
　daughter Harriet m. James Parrott

Dennard, Jacob b. S.C. 1750 d. Ga. 1810 m. Harriet　　Lt. Ga. Mil.
　son Isaac m. Mary Harriss

Denning, William b. N.Y. 1740 d. N.Y. 1819　N.Y. Rep. & U.S. Senator
　m. Sarah Harvyhurst — daughter Luctetia Ann m. Nathan Shaber

Dennis, Eben Jacob b. N.Y. 1796 d. Ohio 1886　　　Sgt. N.Y. Mil.
　m. Amanda Caldwell — son Lloyd B. m. Celestina Yale

Dennis, Purnell J. b. Md. 1790 d. Ohio 1866　　　Pvt. Ohio Mil.
　m. Sarah Baggs — daughter Sarah Ann m. Elbert Chittum

Dennis, Richard b. N.J. 1771 d. Ky. 1845 m. Susan Salter Smith　Col. Inf.
　daughter Adelaide M. m. Dr. Frederick Speck
　daughter Rebecca m. Rev. Theopholis Wylie

Dennis, Schooley b. N.Y. 1784 d. Mich. 1860 m. Anna Mabee　Sgt. N.J. Mil.
　daughter Susan m. William Marrs

Denniston, Ezekiel b. N.Y. 1774 d. N.Y. 1859　　　Lt. N.Y. Mil.
　m. Margaret Pulver — son Charles m. Maria Thomas

Denniston, John b. N.J. 1795 d. N.J. 1874　　　Pvt. N.J. Mil.
　m. Rachel Vanderbeck — daughter Eliza m. Benjamin F. Freeman

Denny, Henry b. Pa. 1785 d. Ohio 1835　　　Pvt. Pa. Mil.
　m. Elizabeth Keener Morgan — daughter Amanda m. John Yager

Denny, James b. Pa. 1767 d. Pa. 1815 m. Isabella Barr　Col. Ohio Mil.
　daughter Janet S. (2) m. Ralph Osborn

Denny, John b. Ky. 1795 d. Wash. 1875 m. Sally Wilson　Sgt. Ky. Mil.
　son Arthur A. m. Mary Ann Boren (Boven, Baln)

Denny, Joseph Cyrus b. Ohio 1794 d. Ill. 1871　　　Pvt. Ohio Mil.
　m. Phoebe Ross — son Elvira m. Emily (?) Stout

Denny Robert b. Pa. 1753 d. Ind. 1826 m. Rachel Thomas　Sgt. Mass.
　son Samuel m. Dorothy Goffe　　　　　　　　M&D Rifleman

Dent, George b. Md. 1752 d. Md. 1812　　Md. Mem. Legis. Speaker,
　m. Susannah Marbury Cromwell　　Pres. of Senate, U.S. Rep.
　son Frederick F. m. Ellen Bray Wrenshall　　　1785-1801

Dent, Richard b. Md. 1778 d. Ala. 1846 m. Nancy Thomas　Pvt. Ga. Mil.
　son William S. m. Mary Witherspoon

Dent, William S. b. Ga. 1759 d. Ga. 1813 m. Virlinder　　Justice of
　son William Jr. m. Fannie Graham　　　　　　　Peace Ga.

DePue (DePew), Benjamin b. N.Y. 1729 d. Pa. 1811 m.　Justice Pa.
　daughter Sarah m. Michael Seely

Depuy, Ephraim b. N.Y. 1785 d. N.Y. m. Rachel Alleger　Lt. N.Y. Mil.
　son Ephraim, Jr. m. Isabelle/Fitz Randolph

DeRevere, John   Vol. 5   Cpl. N.Y. Mil.

Derr, Martin b. Pa. 1781 d. Pa. 1858 m. Sarah Clawges   Ord. Sgt. U.S.
    son Henry H. m. Sallie Britton   Light Drag
    son John C. m. Rebecca Adamas (Streeton)

Deer, Michael   Early Vol.   Pvt. Pa. Mil.

Derrick, Biby (Bibie) Lake b. Vt. 1796 d. N.Y. 1865   Bugler N.Y. Mil.
    m. Statira Felton — daughter Helen D.   REAL DAUGHTER
    m. James Monroe Merritt

de Ridder, Simon b. N.Y. 1765 d. N.Y. 1832   Brig. Gen. N.Y. Mil.
    m. Maria Van Schaick — son Abram G. L.   1807-17
    m. Mary S. Schermerhorn

de Saussure, Henry William b. S.C. 1763 d. S.C. 1837   Directed U.S.
    m. Eliza Ford — son Henry A. m. Susan Boone   Mint 1794
    son William Ford m. Sarah Jones Davie

Desferges, Louis b. France 1775 d. La. 1852 m. Isabel Dupre   Carbineer
    son Louis m. Marie Blanchet

Desha, Joseph Holmes b. Pa. 1768 d. Ky. 1842   Maj. Gen. Ky. State
    m. Peggy Bledsoe   Rep. 1802, State
    son Lucius m. Eliza Jean Moore   Senator 1802-7

Deslondes, Rosalie Picou b. La. d. La. 1845   Converted her home into a
    m. George Deslondes — daughter Rosalie   Hospital La.
    m. Bartholemy Jourdan

Desnoyers, Peter Jean b. France 1772 d. Mich. 1846   Lt. Mich. Mil.
    m. Marie Louise Gobaille — daughter Victoire m. Henry S. Cole

De Vane, Benjamin b. N.C. 1796 d. Fla. 1879   Cpl. N.C. Mil.
    m. Mary Rodgers — son Benjamin F. m. Nancy J. Blanton

DeVault, Abraham b. Va. 1791 d. W.Va. 1863 m. Mary Steele   Pvt. Va. Mil.
    son Edward S. m. Helen H. Haun

de Villere, Jacques Phillippe b. 1761 d. 1838   Maj. Gen. La. Mil.
    m. Jeanne Henrietta Fazende — daughter Marie Adele
    m. Hugnes de la Vergue

de Villere, Rene Gabriell Roy b. La. 1785 d. La.   Maj. La. Mil.
    m. Marie Magdelaine Eulalie de Farmele
    son Francis Pierre m. Malvina Crluzat

Devin, Clayton b. Va. 1793 d. Mo. 1868   Pvt. Pittsylvania
    m. Margaret West — daughter Massa Louisa   Co. Va.
    m. Abner Benton Hughes

De Vol, Gilbert b. R.I. 1736 d. Ohio 1821 m.   Pat. assoc. Justice
    daughter Mary m. Andrew McCluer   of Superior Ct. R.I.

Dew, John b. N.C. 1764 d. N.C. 1811 m. Sarah Thomas   Pat. Civil Offices
    daughter Mary m. John Barnes   N.C.

de Weese, Lewis b. Del. 1769 d. Ohio 1840   Grand Juror Township
    m. Mary McKelvey   Trustee Clerk Ohio
    son James m. Rebecca Blue   1809-12

Dewey, Chauncey   Vol. 8   Sgt. N.Y. Mil.

Dewey, Daniel   Vol. 3   Pvt. Conn. Mil.

Dewey, Truman Chittenden b. Vt. 1794 d. Ind. 1875   Pvt. N.Y. Mil.
    m. Wealthy Farman — daughter Joanna m. Andrew Talcott Norton

DeWitt, Charles b. N.Y. 1727 d. N.Y. 1787   Pat. mem. 3 Provincial
    m. Blandina DuBois   Congress N.Y. 1785
    son Garrett m. Catherine Ten Eyck

Dexter, David b. N.H. 1785 d. Me. 1872   Pvt. Mass. (Me.) Mil.
    m. Margaret Boyd McCurdy — son Joshua L. m. Sarah Jane Smith

Dexter, Jabez b. N.H. 1790/1 d. Wisc. 1871 m. Acenath   Pvt. Vt. Inf.
    daughter Nancy m. Israel Cross

Dexter, John b. R.I. 1783 d. Wisc. 1862   Qtr. Mtr. N.Y. Mil.
    m. Sophia Winsor — son John J. m. Sarah Lovejoy

Dey, William b. N.J. 1758 d. Va. 1816 m. Agnes Bates   Pvt. N.J. Mil.
    son William B. m. Susan Spratley

de Young, Isaac b. Holland 1794 d. Pa. 1868   Music N.Y. Art.
    m. Elizabeth Morange — daughter Bluma m. Jacob Gans (Gaus)

DeZeng, Frederick Augustus b. Ger. 1757 d. N.Y. 1838   Maj. N.Y. Mil.
    m. Mary Lawrence — daughter Maria A. m. William Sears Stow

Dibble, Noah b. N.Y. 1788 d. N.Y. 1864 m. Abagail Crippen   Sgt. N.Y. Mil.
    son Ichabod m. Candance Denison

Dibble, Tompkins (Thompkins) b. N.Y. d. N.Y. 1813   Pvt. U.S. Inf.
    m. Honer Lewis — son Bartlett L. m. Clela Reed

Dibert, John b. Pa. 1747 d. Pa. 1807 m. Eve Ickes   Ens. Pa. Mil. 1786
    son David m. Elizabeth Fickes

Dibrell, Charles Lee b. Va. 1757 d. Tenn. 1840   Capt. Ky. Troops
    m. Martha Burton — daughter Lee Anne
    m. George Washington Gibbs

Dibrell, Edwin b. Va. 1794 d. Va. 1872   Pvt. Va. Mil.
    m. Martha Shrewsbury — son James A. m. (2) Jane Emily Pryor

Dickason, John H. b. Va. 1779 d. Tenn. c. 1856 m. Shelton   Lt. Tenn. Vol.
    son John S. m. Mary Louise Dickerson

Dicken, James Turner b. N.C. 1790 d. Miss. 1864   4th Sgt. Ga. Mil.
    m. Lucy Barksdale Burnley — daughter Mary Jane
    m. Joseph Harman

Dickenshied, Charles Frederick b. Pa. 1792 d. Pa. 1881   Surgeon's Mate
    m. Catherine Eberhard—son John C. m. Amanda Steinman   Pa. Mil.

Dickerson, William Terry b. (W.)Va. 1778 d. La. 1815   Pvt. U.S. Inf.
    m. Nancy Royall — son Achilles A. m. Nancy McWhorter Jones
    son Washington R. m. Mary Jane Danial Stone

Dickey, George b. Ky. 1792 d. Ohio 1889   Pvt. Ohio Mil.
    m. Salome Weidner — daughter Katherine J.   REAL DAUGHTER
    m. John Frederick Eichler

Dickey, James b. N.H. 1775 d. 1860 m. Mary Clark   Pvt. N.H. Mil.
    daughter Annis m. Chandler Chase   & Waiter

Dickey, Patrick b. Ire. 1768 d. Ohio 1816   Capt. Ohio Mil.
    m. Margaret McClelland — daughter Catherine m. Daniel Bowdle

Dickins, Robert b. Eng. 1741 d. N.C. 1804 m. Mary Brown   Justice of
    son Samuel B. m. Jane Vaughan   Peace 1787 mem. of House
                                                     of Commons N.C. 1789

Dickins, Samuel b. N.C. 1781 d. Tenn. 1840   Mem. of N.C. Gen. Assem.
    m. Jane Vaughan — son Thomas m. Martha Bolling Eppes   1813-15

Dickinson, Daniel b. 1794 d. 1862 m. Sarah Maria Becker   Qtr. Mst. &
son Daniel S. m. Libbie Palmer Hoskins   Staff Officer N.Y.

Dickinson, David b. N.J. 1791 d. N.J. 1822   Pvt. N.J. Mil.
m. Mary C. Griffith — daughter Hannah m. Jarvis Shriner

Dickinson, Isaac b. Va. d. Ky. 1842 m. Nancy Robinson   Lt. Va. Mil.
son William M. m. Margaret E. Couls

Dickinson, James C. b. 1781 d. 1844 m. Mary Sandidge   Pvt. Va. Mil.
son Roscoe Cole m. Emily Harris

Dickinson, John b. Mass. 1744 d. N.Y. 1816 m. Lois Biglow   Pvt. N.Y. Mil.
son John C. m. Sophia Fitch

Dickinson, Ralph b. Va. 1788 d. Va. 1870   Cpl. Va. Mil.
m. Ann F. Quisenberry — son John Q. m. Mary S. McCluer

Dickson, Benjamin b. Pa. 1767 d. S.C. 1840 m. Mary Anderson   Patriot S.C.
son William m. Mary Anderson

Dickson, David b. S.C. 1750 d. Ga. 1830 m. Martha Cureton   Pat. Ga.
son Michael m. Rebecca Aubrey
son William m. Harriet Catchings

Dickson, David, Jr.   Vol. 11   Surgeon Miss. Mil.

Dickson, Isaac b. Md. 1767 d. 1840 m. Susannah Larsh   Brig. Gen. Md. Mil.
son Isaac N. m. Mary Jane Sears

Dickson, John b. Pa. 1786 d. Ill. 1860   Pat. Ind. 1810-11
m. Elizabeth Ann Lambert — daughter Rebecca m. William Durham

Dickson, Joseph b. d. Ind. 1812 m.   Vol. 32   Killed by Indians   Ind.
daughter Elizabeth m. Malcolm McFadden

Dickson, Marshall b. Conn. or N.Y. 1760 d. Pa. 1834   Pvt. Pa. Mil.
m. Phoebe Oakley — daughter Elizabeth m. Oliver Stark

Dickson, Thomas b. 1780 d. Tenn.   Pvt. E. Tenn. Mil.
m. Elizabeth McMahon — son Milton M. m. Maria Jane Graham

Dickson, William b. N.Y. 1783 d. Ill. 1869   Capt. N.Y. Mil.
m. Elizabeth Barron — son James m. Ruth Ann Kelly

Diehl, John b. Pa. 1796 d. Pa. 1867 m. Julian Snyder   Pvt. Pa. Mil.
daughter Sarah Ann m. Jacob S. Hollinger

Diehl, Simon Jacob b. Europe 1738 d. Pa. 1819   Pvt. Pa. Mil.
m. Anna Elizabeth Wagner — daughter Anna Margaret
m. John Werheiser

Diffenderfer, Jacob B. b. Pa. 1787 d. Pa. 1861   Pvt. U.S. Art.
m. Sarah McElroy — daughter Sarah M. m. David M. Witmer

Diffenderfer, Samuel b. Pa. 1791 d. Ohio 1853 m. Mary Higo   Sgt. Pa. Mil.
daughter Carolina Matilda m. Matthew Littleton

Diefendorf, George b. N.Y. 1765 d. N.Y. 1823/4   Capt. N.Y. Mil.
m. Catherine Fox — daughter Catherine m. Cornelius Van Camp

Diggs, Beverly b. Va. 1784 d. Md. 1862 m. Maria Ross   Lt. Comm.
son Charles Francis m. Camilla Maria Hall   Ft. McHenry 1814

Diggs, James Barnes b. Va. 1793 d. La. 1855   Pvt. La. Mil.
m. Elizabeth A. Dale Arthur — daughter Elizabeth A.
m. John Edwards   REAL DAUGHTER

Dike, Thomas b. Conn. 1744 d. Conn. 1813   Selectman Justice of Peace
m. Dorothy Davidson — daughter Lucy   Conn. 1785
m. Noah Shumway

Dilks, Joseph   Early Vol.   Sgt. N.J. Mil.

Dill, Matthew b. Ire. 1726 d. Pa. 1812 m. Jane Bracken   Pa. 1789-90
    son Thomas m. Mary Boyd   Del. to Const. Assem.

Dill, Vincent Lemuel b. N.Y. 1795 d. N.Y. 1868   Pvt. N.Y. Art.
    m. Margaret Hurley — daughter Margaret W.
    m. William Cook Disbrow

Dillahunty, John b. Md. 1747 d. Tenn. 1816   N.C., Tenn. 1760-90
    m. Hannah Neal — son Thomas   Land Commissioner
    m. Sarah Becton   Preacher

Dillard, James S. b. Va. 1755 d. Va. 1832 m. Jane Stark   Capt. Va. Mil.
    son Joseph S. m. Polly Bradford

Dille, Lewis Brooks b. 1783 d. 1854 m. Bathsheba Leveridge   Lieut.
    son Aurora m. Catherine Cornwell McCarty   Ohio Mil.

Dille, (Dilly) Lewis b. Pa. 1786 d. Pa. 1863 m. Jane Elliott Pvt. Pa. Mil.
    son David W. m. Emaline Corbin

Dillenbach, Martinus I. b. N.Y. 1786 d. N.Y. 1859   Lt. N.Y. Mil.
    m. Elizabeth Everson — daughter Catherine m. James Wagner

Dilley, Abraham b. N.J. 1785 d. Ohio 1875   Pvt. Ohio Mil.
    m. Jane Wilson McClurg — daughter Sarah
    m. Manson Lewis Gooderl

Dillman, Frederick William b. Pa. 1788 d. Ind. 1836   4th Cpl. Ky. Mil.
    m. Mary Bowman — son Jacob A. m. Mary Elizabeth

Dillman, Peter b. Pa. 1781 d. Pa. 1858 m. Susanna Krause Capt. Pa. Mil.
    son Daniel K. m. Catherine Dunkelberger

Dillon, John b. Va. 1790 d. Ind. 1875 m. Sarah Bonnell   Cpl. Ohio Mil.
    daughter Rebecca E. m. Aaron Sutton

Dillon, William b. Pa. 1792 d. Mich. 1876   Cpl. N.Y. Mil.
    m. Eliza Stone Whitman — daughter Janett m. Abraham Millage
    REAL DAUGHTER — son Marvin m. Estella Harmon

Dilly, Abraham   Vol. 14   Pvt. Ohio Mil.

Dingman, Daniel W. b. N.J. 1775 d. Pa. 1862   Lt. Pa. Mil.
    m. Mary Westbrook — son Andrew m. Caroline Eliza Sayre

Dinsmore, Adam b. Pa. 1790 d. Pa. 1832   Pvt. Pa. Mil.
    m. Margot Findly — daughter Diantha m. Robert J. McCartney

Dipert (Dibert), John b. Pa. 1747 d. Pa. 1807 m. Ene Ickes Pvt. Pa. Mil.
    son David m. Elizabeth Fickes

Disbrow, John b. N.J. 1784 d. N.J. 1841   Pvt. N.J. Mil.
    m. Elizabeth Applegate — son John, Jr. m. Jane Price

Disbrow, Samuel Warne b. N.J. 1778 d. N.Y. 1873   Capt. N.Y. Mil.
    m. Sarah Cook — son William C. m. Margaret Wessells Dill

Disler, Jacob b. 1780 d. Ohio 1846 m. Catherine Fry   Pvt. Pa. Mil.
    daughter Lydia m. John Warner

Disler, Jacob   Vol. 9   Pvt. Pa. Mil.

Dismukes, James b. Ga. 1784 d. Ga. m. Gilliam Cooper   Pvt. Ga. Mil.
    daughter Frances P. m. Dr. Isaac Rhodes Waller

Dismukes, William b. N.C. abt. 1785 d. N.C. aft. 1833   Maj. Field Officer
    m. Elizabeth Ward Pegues   N.C. 1807 Justice of
    son James W. m. Mary Agnes White   Peace N.C. 1807

Disney, Jarett b. Md. d. Md. 1845 m. Ann Jeffers   Pvt. Md. Mil.
daughter Mary Ann m. Thomas Cockey Bamber

Ditman, John b. 1795 d. Md. 1846 m. Rachel Johnson   Pvt. Md.
son Thomas m. Maria Hopkins

Dively, Michael b. Pa. 1787 d. Pa. 1840   Sgt. Pa. Mil.
m. Julianna Schwartz — daughter Caroline E. m. William Smith

Dix, Timothy b. N.H. 1770 d. Canada 1813   Lt. Col. U.S. Inf.
m. Lucy Dix Hartwell — son Roger S. m. Mary B. Beanes
m. Rachel Burbank
son Timothy m. Lucy Hartwell

Dixon, Adam b. Va. 1785 d. Tenn. 1870 m. Hannah L. Erwin   Capt. Va.
son Thomas J. m. Katherine C. Kinnard

Dixon, John b. ca 1795 d. 1877 m. Elizabeth Boyd   Pvt. Tenn. Mil.
son Columbus F. m. Sarah Ann Springer

Dixon, (Dickson) John b. Va. 1790 d. S.C. 1820-30   Pvt. S.C. Mil.
m. Elizabeth Lee — son John Lee m. Nancy Maria Cheves

Dixon, Luther   Vol. 15   Col. Vt. Mil.

Dixon, Payne   Vol. 10   Pvt. Ky. Mil.

Dixon, Thomas b. Scot. 1752 d. Vt. 1823 m. Lydia Griffith   Capt. Vt. Mil.
daughter Lydia m. Calvin Fletcher

Dixon, Thomas Jr. b. Va. 1793 d. Ohio 1879   Pvt. Va. Mil.
m. Margaret Krantz — son John K.   Fife, Maj.
m. Armilda Brakefield

Dixon, William George b. S.C. 1783 d. Miss.? m.   Pvt. Miss. Mil.
son Thomas m. Sarah Ann Simms

Doak, David b. Va. 1779 d. Ohio 1864 m. Nancy Ann Best   Pvt. Va. Mil.
son David F. m. Isabella Sigler

Doak, Rev. Samuel b. Va. 1740 d. Tenn. 1830   Pat. Tenn. 1795
m. Esther Houston Montgomery — son John Whitfield
m. Jane H. Alexander

Doane, Isaiah b. Mass. 1753 d. Mass. 1805   in Shay's Rebellion 1787-1794
m. Hannah Bartlett — daughter Hannah m. Seth Wells

Doane, Simeon b. Vt. 1786 d. N.Y. 1866 m. Joanna Wood   Pvt. Vt. Mil.
daughter Minerva M. m. Robert D. Gillespie

Doane, Timothy   Vol. 12   Pvt. Ohio Mil.

Dobbin, John b. Eng. 1773 d. Tenn. 1859 m. Nancy Herring   Lt. Tenn. Mil.
son William A. m. Ellis Jane Lockridge

Dobbins, William b. Nova Scotia 1790 d. Me. 1881   Pvt. Mass. Mil.
m. Miriam Beal — son Daniel W. m. Julia Eliza Comstock

Dobbs, David b. Va. ca 1790 d. Ga. 1872   Lt. Ga. Mil.
m. Elizabeth McMullan — son David J. m. Martha Josephine Prothro

Dobson, John b. Va. 1795 d. Va. 1828 m. Susan Stokes   Pvt. Va. Mil.
son William m. Margaret M. Hayes

Dobyns, Thomas b. Va. 1770 d. Ky. 1829   Pvt. Ky. Mtd. Mil.
m. Frances Key — son Thomas J. m. Martha Caroline Sharpe

Dockham, Jonathan   Vol. 1   Pvt. N.H. Mil.

Dockstader, Nicholas b. N.Y. 1750 d. N.Y. 1812   Lt. N.Y. Mil.
  m. Catherine Van Der Werken — daughter Catherine
  m. Adam Vrooman Snyder
  son Nicholas m. Sarah Yates

Dodd, Amos b. N.J. 1781 d. N.J. 1851 m. Mary Canfield   Sgt. N.J. Mil.
  daughter Harriet N. m. James McCracken

Dodd, John b. N.C. 1760 d. Miss. 1825 m. Elizabeth Wright Lt. Miss. Mil.
  daughter Elizabeth m. John Springs Roach

Doddridge, John b. Md. 1745 d. Pa. 1791 m. Mary Wells   Pat. Pa. 1786-91
  daughter Ruth m. Joseph Huff

Dodds, John b. Del. 1781 d. Ill. 1856 m. Harriet Thompson   Pvt. Va. Mil.
  son Alexander m. Joan Caudle

Dodds, John Craig b. S.C. 1783 d. Ky. 1860 m.   Capt. Ky. Mil.
  daughter Pernicia m. William D. Cook

Dodge, Abraham   Vol. 3   Capt. Mass. Mil.

Dodge, Ananiah b. Mass. 1770 d. Mass. 1846   Lt. Mass. Mil.
  m. Elizabeth Janes — daughter Susan m. Cornelius Mellny

Dodge, David b. Mass. 1783 d. Mass. 1858 m. Huldah   Capt. Mass. Cavalry
  daughter Elizabeth S. m. Robert Schouler

Dodge, Henry Samuel b. N.Y. 1783 d. N.Y. 1826   Col. N.Y. Mil.
  m. Jane Dey Varick — son John V. m. Augusta Alice DuPuy

Dodge, Josiah   Vol. 10   Pvt. U.S. Inf.

Dodge, William b. Vt. 1778 d. Ill. 1854 m. Matilda Lyon   Pvt. Vt. Mil.
  son Jabez S. m. Almeda Jane Powers

Dodson, Elias b. Va. 1786 d. Tenn. 1847   Pvt. Tenn. Mil.
  m. Maria Marshall — son Marshall m. Emily Brown

Dodson, William b. Md. 1786 d. Md. 1833   Capt. Md. Mil.
  m. Amelia Brown — son Robert A.   Sailing Master U.S. Navy
  m. Hester A. Keithley

Doe, David b. Mass. (Me.) 1776 d. Me. m. Anna Taylor   Pvt. Mass. (Me.)
  daughter Ann m. Calvin Ballard Snow   Mil.

Doe, John b. N.H. 1749 d. Mass. 1819 m. Abigail Giddings   Pat. 1785-95
  daughter Martha m. David Marston   Mass. (Me.)

Doer (Durr), Conrad b. Holland 1793 d. Lost at Sea   Pvt. D.C. Mil.
  m. Elizabeth Reynolds — daughter Mary Elizabeth
  m. Walter Lindsay

Doggett, Armstead b. Va. 1792 d. Ohio 1847   Pvt. Va. Mil.
  m. Mary Allison — son Cary A. m. Mary Ellen Huffman

Doll (Dull), Christian b. Pa. 1794 d. Pa. 1875   Pvt. Pa. Mil.
  m. Mary Rosenberger — daughter Elizabeth m. Samuel Diehl

Dolliver, William Henry b. 1798 d. 1844   Mst. Mariner
  m. Adeline Sayward — daughter Sarah Elizabeth
  m. Ignatius Gilbert (1) Hiram Holmes (2)

Dolph, Charles b. Conn. 1783 d. Conn. 1815   Pvt. Conn. Mil.
  m. Rosanna Carltin — son William m. Rhoda Watrous

Dolph, Moses b. Conn. 1756 d. Pa. 1826 m. Anna McArthur   Ens. Pa. Mil.
  son Alexander m. Susan London

Dolson (Dalson), Tunis b. N.Y. 1783 d. N.Y. 1859   2nd Lt. N.Y. Cavalry
  m. Pruella Kniffen — son William m. Rachel DuBois

Donaldson, H. W. Richard b. Mich. 1793 d. Mich. 1868   Soldier Mich.
   m. Maria Palmer — —daughter Julia m. Constantine G. Young

Donaldson, James Ewing b. N.J. 1792 d. Ohio 1842   Pvt. Ohio Mil.
   m. Synthia Dodge — son David M. m. Sarah Elizabeth Lattimer

Donaldson, John   Vol. 8   Capt. Pa. Vol.

Donaldson, Robert b. 1791 d. Va. 1869/70   Pvt. Va. Mil.
   m. Elizabeth Burch — daughter Elizabeth Jane m. Francis A. Jones

Donally, William b. Va. 1792 d. Tenn. 1842 m. Sarah McQueen Pvt. N.C.
   son William m. Alice Moore

Donelson, John b. Va. 1718 d. Ky. 1785   Lt. Col. N.C., Tenn. Mil. 1780
   m. Rachel Stockley — son John m. Mary Purnell
   son Severn m. Elizabeth Rucher
   son William m. Charity Dickinson

Donelson, John b. Va. 1756 d. Tenn. 1830 m. Mary Purnell   Pvt. Tenn. Vol.
   son Stokely m. Phila Ann Lawrence

Donnally, Andrew b. Va. d. Va. 1825 m. Jeanne McCreary   Va. Assembly
   daughter Mary m. Ruben Slaughter   1790, Justice 1791, Sheriff 1814

Donnell, James b. Pa. 1769 d. Ky. 1850 m. Hannah   Pvt. Pa. Mil.
   son Samuel m. Sophia Meek

Donnell, John b. Ire. d. Md. 1827 m. Ann Tasher Smith   Pvt. Md. Mil.
   daughter Ann T. m. Edward D. Kemp

Donnelly, Thomas b. N.Y. 1764 d. N.Y. 1835   Ens. N.Y. Inf.
   m. Ruth Pettinger — daughter Marie m. Samuel Knower

Donnelly, William b. Va. 1792 d. Tenn. 1842   Pvt. N.C. Mil.
   m. Sarah McQueen — son Richard A. m. Matilda Sullivan
   son William K. m. Alice Moore
   son John M. m. Amanda Wagner

Dooley, Esom B. b. N.C. 1793 d. Miss. 1871 m. Patsey Pvt. E. Tenn. Mil.
   son Isaac M. m. Susan

Dooley, Job b. 1786 d. 1854 m. Lucy Searcy   Pvt. Ky. Mil.
   son Underwood D. m. Martha Dooley (Cousin)

Doolittle, Ormus b. Conn. 1789 d. N.Y. 1872   Pvt. N.Y. Mil.
   m. Lydia Rood — daughter Caroline m. Abel Webster

Doom, Benjamin b. Ky. 1782 d. Ky. 1854   Capt. Ky. Mil.
   m. Cassandra Phillips — son James M. m. Sallie Ewing Norse

Doran, Alexander b. Pa. 1760 d. Tenn. 1814   2nd Lt. Tenn. Mil.
   m. Elizabeth Lowry — daughter Elizabeth m. Caleb Smith
   daughter Rebecca m. Richard Donnelly
   daughter Janette m. John Ward
   daughter Nancy m. Ezekiel Smith
   m. Sarah Reed
   son Joseph m. Lucy G. Fry (Foy)

Dority, Benjamin b. 1793 d. 1865 m. Nancy Foster   Pvt. U.S. Inf. 1815
   son Charles m. Olive Bates

Dorman, Charles P. b. Va. d. Va. 1849   Adj. Va. Mil.
   m. Amanda E. McCue — son William B. m. Margaret C.

Dorman, David b. Va. 1790 d. Ohio ca 1849   Pvt. Va. Vol.
   m. Catherine Bickel — son Solomon m. Margaret Youmans

Dorman, Joel b. Conn. 1786 d. Ohio 1870 m. Nancy Hart Pvt. Conn. Mil.
daughter Millicent m. William Myron Cobb

Dorr, Ebenezer Vol. 17 Capt. in Dartmoor Prison

Dorrance, Benjamin b. Conn. 1767 d. Pa. 1834 Pat. Lt. Pa. Mil.
m. Nancy Ann Buckingham — son Charles m. Susan E. Ford

Dorrance, George b. Conn. 1786 d. N.Y. 1841 Lt. Mass. Mil.
m. Ann Olney Warner — son Albert A. m. Juliette Salome Gregor
daughter Mary m. Silas Fish

Dorrance, Joseph b. Vt. 1777 d. Vt. 1849 Pvt. Vt. Mil. 1810
m. Esther Martin — son George Town Clerk Selectman
m. Hannah Putnam Walcott

Dorsey, Clement b. Md. 1778 d. Md. 1848 Pat. Md. 1812
m. (1) Priscilla Hebb — daughter Ann Eliza
m. Richard Brooks Dorsey

Dorsey, Edward Worthington b. Md. 1793 d. Mo. 1858 4th Sgt. Md. Mil.
m. Eleanor Elizabeth Brown — daughter Anna B. m.—
REAL DAUGHTER

Dorsey, John b. Md. 1785 d. Va. 1821 Pvt. Va. Mil.
m. Elizabeth Dorsey (cousin) — son William M.
m. Margaret Arnold Hudson

Dorsey, John b. Md. 1773 d. Md. 1841 m. Sarah Hammond Pvt. Md. Mil.
daughter Mary m. Samuel P. Bailey

Dorsey, Walter b. Md. 1771 d. Md. 1823 Chief Justice Md. 1799
m. Hopewell Hebb — son John R. m. Mary Catherine Johnson

Dory, George b. Pa. 1790 d. Pa. 1887 Pvt. Pa. Mil.
m. Harriet McElvania — daughter Charlotte m. Matthias Plank

Doudle, Jacob b. Pa. 1760 d. Pa. 1837 Pvt. Pa. Mil.
m. Catherine Dinckel (Dinkel) — daughter Sarah Ann
m. Adama Klinefelter

Douds, Robert b. Ger. d. Pa. 1843 m. Rachel Willison Pvt. Pa. Mil.
son Joseph W. m. Margaret Beggs

Dougherty, John b. S.C. 1788 d. Ga. 1870 m. Nancy Gantt Pvt. Ga. Mil.
son Eli G. m. Mary Elizabeth Fletcher

Doughty, Charles J. b. N.Y. 1770 d. Mich. 1855 Lt. N.Y. Mil.
m. Mary Williams — son Cortlandt W. m. Almira Pierce

Doughty, Daniel b. Va. ca 1772 d. Ind. 1835 Pvt. U.S. Inf.
m. Ann McCauley — son Joseph m. Catherine

Doughty, Enoch b. N.J. 1792 d. N.J. 1871 Pvt. N.J. Mil.
m. Charlotte Clark — daughter Abigail m. David Somers Blackman

Douglas, David, Sr. b. Va. 1777 d. Ohio 1854 Sgt. Ohio Mil.
m. Sarah Matthews — son David H. Jr. m. Dorothy Koakum

Douglas, James b. Mass. 1778 d. N.Y. 1851 Lt. N.Y. Cavalry
m. Catharine Billings — daughter Abby m. Dr. Alfred Gray

Douglas, Levi b. (W.)Va. 1784 d. (W.)Va. 1871 Cpl. Va. Mil.
m. Nancy Haley — son William m. Mary Nutter

Douglas, Samuel b. Conn. 1781 d. Conn. aft. 1814 Music Conn. Mil.
m. Sarah Strickland — daughter Nancy Ann
m. Gurdon Crocker Beckwith

Douglass, George b. Miss. 1790/1 d. Miss. 1852 Pvt. Ga. Mil.
m. Susannah Carlisle — daughter Martha A. m. James M. Stanfill

Douglass, James b. Ire. 1754 d. S.C. 1825 m. Jane   Capt. S.C. Mil.
daughter Agness (Nancy) m. John McCardell
son Robert m. Ruth Perry

Douglass, Watson b. Pa. 1782 d. Ohio 1833   Capt. Ohio Mil.
m. Isabella Coffey — son Addison C. m. Mary E. Robertson

Dousman, John   Vol. 8   Qtr. Mst. Mich. Mil.

Douthit, John b. N.C. 1777 d. Ind. 1854   Pvt. N.C. Rangers
m. Mary (Nancy) Ellen White — son Ira m. Sarah Ellis

Dove, Benjamin b. Eng. 1768 d. N.Y. 1824   Pvt. N.Y. Mil.
m. Margaret Howell — daughter Mary Ann m. Samuel Wright

Dover, John b. Va. 1789 d. Mo. 1859 m. Jemima Stevens   Sgt. Va. Mil.
daughter Amanda m. Alexander Zeigler

Dow, Henry, Jr. b. Conn. 1794 d. Ind. 1873   Pvt. Conn. Mil.
m. Mercy Kinne — daughter Sarah M. m. William Burnes

Dow (Dowe, Doe), John b. Vt. 1791 d. Ill. 1846   3rd Lt. Vt. Mil.
m. Cordelia Hull — daughter Phoebe H. m. John W. Councill

Dowd, William Moore b. N.C. 1792 d. Ark. 1868   Capt. N.C. Mil.
m. Ann Henrietta Gillespie (Smith) — son William F.
m. Anne Williamson Brown

Dowden, Zachariah   Vol. 17   Pvt. Md. Mil.

Dowdell, John A. b. Va. 1795 d. Ill. 1865   Sailor Va.
m. Elizabeth English — son James m. Mary Stevens

Dowdle, Allen b. S.C. 1795 d. Ark. 1858   Pvt. S.C. Mil.
m. Martha Mintre Cavenah — daughter Amanda
m. Thomas Allen Watkins
son Robert A. m. Rebecca Aylett Taylor
daughter Mary N. m. Daniel Harehan

Dowdle, Peter   Vol. 17   Pvt. Pa. Mil.

Dowling, Jabez b. S.C. 1770 d. Ga. 1848   Justice of Peace S.C. 1801
m. Rebecca Walker — son Jabez L. m. Honor Davis

Down, Benjamin Clark b. Pa. 1793 d. Pa. 1863 m.   Ens. N.J. Mil.
Vol. 17

Downing, John b. Va. 1789 d. Kan. 1859 m. Mary Boiles   Pvt. Ohio Mil.
son George m. Lavina Van Buskirk

Downing, Michael b. Ire. 1769 d. Ind. 1852   Pvt. Ind. Mil.
m. Mary Ann Wells — son John m. Pernina Mundaul (Mundeene)

Downing, Samuel Sr. b. Va. d. Va. 1839 m. Mary Edwards   Maj. Va. Mil.
son Samuel Jr. m. Catherine Ellen Payne

Downes, Hawkins b. Md. d. Md. 1831   Pvt. Md. Mil.
m. Sarah Hall Vandeford — daughter Anne m. Ezekiel Wootters

Dowman, Joseph Ball b. Va. 1787 d. Va. 1857 m. Priscilla   Capt. Va. Mil.
daughter Jane Elizabeth m. Henry Fithugh

Downs, James b. Va. 1777 d. Ohio 1848 m. Ann Snodgrass   Pvt. Ohio Mil.
son James Jr. m. Susannah Crough Immell

Downs, John b. Md. 1788 d. Del. 1849 m. Rebecca Morton   Sgt. Del. Mil.
son John m. Susannah Cubbage
daughter Mary E. m. Thomas H. A. Purnell

Downs, Jehu   Vol. 6   Pvt. U.S. Rangers

Downs, Moses b. Conn. 1734 d. Conn. 1822 m. Ann Hinman Conn. 1788
    son Nathan m. Susanna Little   Key-Keeper

Downs, Nathan b. Conn. 1761 d. Conn. 1819   1788, 1799 Constable,
    m. Susanna Tuttle — son Henry   Surveyor, Selectman
    m. Sarah Ann Botsford

Doxey, John Sanford   Vol. 10   Qtr. Mst. Sgt. Tenn. Vol.

Doyle, Charles Carroll   Vol. 10   Pvt.

Doyle, Elisha b. Pa. 1790 d. Neb. 1872 m. Sarah Ann Fister Pvt. Pa. Mil.
    son Thomas G. m. Charlotte Catherine Postlewaite

Dozier, W. Allen S. b. Va. 1785 d. Va. 1839   Capt. Va. Mil.
    m. Nancy Shackleford — son Stephen B. m. Evelina Elliott

Draffen, William b. Va. 1793 d. Ky. 1873 m. Nancy Marr Pvt. Va. Mil.
    daughter Mary Elizabeth m. John Uriah Houser

Drake, Abraham Stout b. N.J. 1781 d. Ky. 1831   Capt. Ky. Mil.
    m. Hannah Prall — daughter Eliza m. Gabraiel Stout Slaughter

Drake, Adam b. N.J. 1784-99 d. Mich. 1874   Pvt. N.J. Mil.
    m. Lydia Marie Foote — daughter Ada Bell m. Jacob H. Bastedo
    REAL DAUGHTER
    daughter Amanda C. m. William E. Jordan   REAL DAUGHTER
    daughter Augusta m. Stephen Scott   REAL DAUGHTER
    daughter Florence m. William Mathews   REAL DAUGHTER
    daughter Sarah Louise m. Ernest Theodore Winters
    REAL DAUGHTER

Drake, Ephraim b. ca Va. 1760 d. Tenn. 1816   Justice of Peace Ky. 1798
    m. Ann Buchanan — daughter Sarah m. David O. Anderson

Drake, Jonathan b. N.H. 1758 d. N.H. 1848 m. Sarah Ward, Pvt. N.H. Mil.
    daughter Sarah m. Amos Seavey

Drake, Philip b. N.Y. 1789 d. N.Y. 1822 m. Phoebe Maxim, Pvt. N.Y. Mil.
    daughter Eliza m. David Lawton

Drake, Warren b. Mass. (Me.) 1784 d. Me. 1820   Sgt. Mass. (Me.) Mil.
    m. Melinda Lothrop — son Daniel m. Mary Rollins

Drake, Zephaniah b. N.J. 1792 d. Ohio 1837 m. Mary Dennis, Pvt. N.J. Mil.
    son Manning m. Henrietta Roberts

Draper, William b. N.C. 1785 d. N.C. 1834   Pvt. N.C. Mil.
    m. Talitha Parker — son James B. m. Mary A. S. Parker

Drapier, Gideon b. 1782 d. Ind. 1860 m. Polly   Lt. Col. N.Y. Mil.
    son Ariel Euclid m. Martha Marie Spencer

Dreisbach, Jacob b. Pa. 1759 d. Pa. 1817   Lt. Pa. Mil
    m. Anna Margaret Bieber — son Jacob Jr. m. Magdalena Bliem
    daughter Mary M. m. Jacob Boyer

Dreisbach, Peter b. Pa. 1757 d. Pa. 1810   Pvt. Pa. Mil.
    m. Susanna Beisel — son Simon m. Elizabeth Lerch

Dreisbach, Simon Jr. b. Bavaria 1730 d. Pa. 1806   Pa. 1784 Mem. Council
    m. Dorothea Dies — son Jacob m. Anna Margaret Bieber of Censors
    son Peter m. Susanna Beisel

Drennan, William b. S.C. 1768 d. Ill. 1847 m. Mary Thomas Pvt. S.C. Mil.
    son John L. m. Nancy J. Dodds

Drennen, Samuel b. Pa. 1786 d. Md.   Pvt. Md. Mil.
  m. Mrs. Deborah Thompson McBride — son William G.
  m. Nancy Wardwell

Drenning (Drennen, Drinnen), William b. Pa. 1796   Pvt. Pa. Mil.
  d. Pa. 1877 m. Mary Boyd — son Richard W. m. Sophie Wicks

Dresback, Benjamin b. Pa. 1789 d. Ohio 1857   Pvt. Ohio Mil.
  m. Mary Pontius — daughter Susan m. William Roberts

Dresser, Mark b. Mass. (Me.) 1795 d. Me. 1841   Pvt. Mass. (Me.) Mil.
  m. Mary Lord — daughter Mehitabel L. m. John Patten Perkins

Dresser, Thomas b. Mass. 1790 d. Me. 1878   Pvt. Mass. Mil.
  m. Caroline Curtis — son Joseph m. Lucy Hurd

Drewry, Henry T.   Vol. 17   Pvt. Va. Mil.

Drinkwater, Perez   Vol. 4   Lt. on Privateer Lucy

Dritt, Jacob b. Pa. d. Pa. 1818 m. Baird   Brig. Gen. Pa. Mil.
  daughter Elizabeth m. Joseph Shewalter

Dromgoole, Edward Sr. b. Ire. 1752 d. Va. 1835   Magis. Va. 1790-1812
  m. Rebecca Walton — son Thomas

Drown, Benjamin, b. (W.)Va. 1794 d. (W.)Va. 1855   Corp. Va. Mil.
  m. Joanna Davis — son Benjamin m. Sarah Elizabeth Riggs
  son Rufus P. m. Sarah Chadwick

Drummond, Benjamin b. Va. 1792 d. Ohio m. Mary   Sgt. Ohio Mil.
  son James m. Hepziah Staley

Drury, Elijah b. N.Y. 1792 d. Pa. 1880 m. Abigail Cheney Pvt. N.Y. Mil.
  daughter Polly G. m. John Wesley Pettis

Drury, Samuel b. Md. 1759 d. Md. 1843 m. Ann Ijams   Pvt. Md. Mil.
  son Henry C. m. Mary Ann Owens
  daughter Ruth m. Benjamin Welch

Drury, Samuel Jr. b. Md. 1792 d. D.C. 1867   Mattross D.C. Mil.
  m. Mary Nolan — son William P. m. Mary Elizabeth Lenman

Dryden, Joshua   Vol. 10   Maj. Md. Mil.

Dryden, Joshua b. Md. 1792 d. Md. 1879   Cpl. Md. Art.
  m. Anne Maria Roberts — son Joshua J. R. m. Cordelia E. Owings

Dubbs, Jacob b. Pa. 1790 d. Pa. 1858 m. Catherine   Drummer Pa. Mil.
  daughter Mary m. John Bowermaster

DuBois, Isaac b. N.Y. 1774 d. N.Y. 1830   Capt. N.Y. Inf.
  m. (1) Catherina Tewilliger — daughter Elizabeth m. Solomon Deyo

DuBois, Joel b. N.Y. 1762 d. N.Y. 1844   Capt. N.Y. Mil.
  m. Annatze (Nancy) — son Isaac J. m. Catherine Hunter

DuBose, Elias b. S.C. 1737 d. S.C. 1789 m. Lydia Cassels   Rep. S.C. 1785
  son Jesse m. Rebecca Wilds   Justice 1785 S.C. Commissioner of
                                                            Navigation

Ducatel, Germain b. Fra. 1775 d. La. 1849   Surgeon La. Troops
  m. Clemerce de la Muloniere — daughter A. Josephine Clementine
  m. LeGardeur de Tilly
  daughter Amedee m. Aline Bertus
  daughter Odalie m. Louis Henri (Bilie) Pilie

Duck, Samuel b. 1792 d. Ohio 1844   Pvt. Ohio Mil.
  m. Catherine Longabaugh — daughter Anna Jane m. Jacob Horner

Duckworth, John b. Va. 1781 d. Ind. 1840/43   Pvt. Ky. Mil.
     m. Nancy Clifton — son Isaac m. Serena Beard

Duddeth, John   Vol. 36   Pvt. Va. Mil.
     daughter Mary m. Elijah Stone

Dudley, John b. Va. 1757 d. Ga. 1820   Capt. Ga. Mil.
     m. Elizabeth Jones — son William m. Elizabeth Ewing

Dudley, Samuel b. N.H. 1720 d. Me. 1797   Defender Me. 1785-97
     m. Mary Ladd — son Eliphalet m. Mary Gilman

Dudley, Trueworthy b. 1757 d. Lake Champlain 1814   Pvt. in Rev. & 1812
     m. Sarah Stevens — son Wm. m. (1) Harriet Ann Hardy

Duduit, Gillaume b. Fra. 1769 d. Ohio 1835   Ind. Spy Ohio Mil.
     m. Agnes Dessot — son Frederick m. Helen Hannah Gilruth

Duff, John   Vol. 9   Pvt. Pa. Mil.

Duffel, Henry Leonard b. S.C. 1791 d. La. 1859(67)   2nd Lt. U.S. Art.
     m. Mary L. West — son Edward J. m. Mary Ellen Seay
     daughter Jennie S.   REAL DAUGHTER

Duffield, William b. Pa. 1773 d. Pa. 1848   Pvt. Pa. Mil.
     m. Mary Johnston — son Charner m. Mahalia Cunningham

Dufphey, William L. b. Ire. d. N.C. m.   Capt. U.S. Inf.
     son Richard m. Prudence

Dugan, John b. N.J. 1791 d. Pa. 1851   4th Cpl. Pa. Mil.
     m. Lydia (Holmes) (Nolnier) — son Ashley m. Margaret M. Shively

Dugger, Jarrot (Jarred) b. Va. d. Ill. 1850   Pvt. (W.)Va., Tenn. Mil.
     m. Sarah M. Neale — son Jefferson F. m. Alice Hayes
     m. Mary McAdams
     son John m. Sarah Neale

Dugger, John b. N.C. 1780 d. Tenn. 1867   Ens. E. Tenn. Mil.
     m. Mary Engle — son Samuel m. Hannah Potter

Dugger, Julius (C.) b. Va. 1760 (Scot. 1750)   Pvt. E. Tenn. Mil. 1814
     d. Tenn. 1838 m. Mary Hall   Pvt. Ky. Mil. 1812-13
     daughter Elizabeth m. Elisha Rainbolt
     son John m. Mary Engle
     daughter Nancy D. m. James Jordan George
     daughter Mary m. Michael Pierce

Dugger, Julius A. b. Tenn. 1764 d. Tenn. 1862   Pvt. Tenn. Mil.
     m. Elizabeth Robinson — daughter Lydia m. John Blevins

DuHamel, James (2) b. 1795 d. Md. 1869 m. Martha Seth   Pvt. Md. Mil.
     daughter Arminta Maria m. James Francis Moulton

Duke, Andrew b. N.C. 1730 d. Ga. 1798   mem. Gen. Assem. N.C. 1789
     m. Keziah Anderson — daughter Rebecca m. James Reid

Duke, Francis   Vol. 7   Pvt. Va. Mil.

Dulaney, Samuel   Vol. 3   Pvt. Md. Mil.

Dulin, Smith b. Va. 1792 d. Iowa 1879 m. Frances   Pvt. Va. Mil.
     daughter Elizabeth m. Emanuel Renner

DuMont, Henry b. N.Y. 1791 d. N.Y. aft. 1823   Pvt. N.Y. Mil.
     m. Sarah Houtaling — daughter Letitia Maria m. John Lewis Fisher

Dunbar, Butler b. Conn. 1791 d. Iowa 1868   Music Conn. Mil.
     m. Lucina Painter — son Edward Lucian m. Julia Warner

Dunbar, George Towers, Sr. b. Md. 1774 d. Md. 1843   Pvt. Md. Mil.
    m. Frances Worthington McCannon — son George T. Jr.
    m. Caroline Eliza Robinson

Dunbar, Isaac b. Miss. 1788 d. Miss. 1849   Cor. 2nd Lt. Miss. Terr. Caval
    m. Elizabeth Marshall Wilkinson — daughter Anna Maria
    m. Thomas Affleck

Dunbar, Samuel b. Scot. 1779 d. Pa. 1857   Pvt. Pa. Mil.
    m. Mary Ann McQuiston — son Samuel, Jr. m. Martha Oliver

Dunbar, William b. Ire. 1752 d. S.C. 1798   Legis. S.C. 1783-87
    m. Elizabeth Robinson — son George R. m. Mary S. Fickling

Duncan, Alexander b. Scot. 1780 d. Ohio 1861   Pvt. Ohio Mil.
    m. Susan Robb — son Samuel R. m. Sarah Elizabeth Miller

Duncan, Arnold b. Pa. 1776 d. Ga. 1851   Lt. Pa. Mil.
    m. Martha Petterson — son Daniel m. Rachel Harrington

Duncan, Charles b. Va. 1779 d. Va. 1839   Sgt. Va. Mil.
    m. Mary Ann Woods — daughter Ann E. m. Henry Modena

Duncan, Charles b. Va. 1770 d. Va. 1856   Sgt. Va. Mil.
    m. Elizabeth Herndon — daughter Elizabeth
    m. James William Shackleford

Duncan, John   Vol. 14   Pvt. Ohio Mil.

Duncan, James b. Pa. 1747 d. S.C. 1843   Pvt. S.C. Mil.
    m. Elizabeth Fincher — daughter Charlotte m. Byrd Murphy

Duncan, John b. Pa. 1774 d. Pa. 1855 m. Susan Leech   Pvt. Ohio Mil.
    daughter Mary V. m. S. F. DeFord

Duncan, Jonathan b. Pa. 1791 d. Iowa 1876 m. (2) Agnes L., Pvt. Pa. Mil.
    daughter Ida Belle m. James William King

Duncan, Joseph b.—d.— m. Elizabeth Caldwell   Vol. 2   Ens. U.S. Inf.
    daughter Julia m. Edward Payson Kirby   REAL DAUGHTER

Duncan, Joseph b. Ky. 1780 d. Ky. 1809   Cpl. Ky. Mtd. Mil.
    m. Nancy Bowls — son Joseph m. Amanda Clardy

Duncan, Robert b. Pa. 1777 d. Ohio 1843 m. Mary Mann   Sgt. Ohio Mil.
    daughter Nancy m. Martin Morrison McClure

Duncan, Titus b. Ky. 1795 d. Ohio 1855 m. Jamima King   Pvt. Ohio Mil.
    son William m. (1) Mary Hurley
    son Lewis C. m. Frances Westenhaver

Duncan, Wesley Leland b. Va. 1791 d. Va. 1886   Sgt. Va. Mil.
    m. Sallie Woodford Camden (cousin) — son Daniel Lewis
    m. Ida Sharon (McCorkell)

Dunckel, Nicholas F. b. N.Y. 1793 d. Mich. 1879   Sgt. N.Y. Troops
    m. Catherine Countryman — daughter Matilda m. Cornelius Dietz

Dunckel, Peter b. 1742 d. 1827   Pvt. N.Y. Mil. 1786-7
    m. Anna Elizabeth Wolf — daughter Catherine Dinkel
    m. Jacob Doudel

Duncklee, John   Vol. 10   Pvt. N.H. Mil.

Dungan, David Davis b. Pa. 1787 d. Pa. 1880   Sgt. Maj. Pa. Mil.
    m. Isabella McFerren — son Warren S. m. Abby Kingman Procter

Dunham, Calvin b. Conn. 1754 d. N.Y. 1840   Pvt. Mass. Mil.
    m. Ruth Noble — son Alpheus m. Amarillis Oviatt

Dunham, Josephus b. Conn. 1773 d. Ohio   Pvt. Ohio Mil.
    m. Betsy Huntington — daughter Samantha m. Daniel McAlmont

Dunham, Obadiah b. Conn. 1730 d. Vt. 1831   Justice of Peace Vt.
  m. Lucy Gillette — daughter Lydia m. John Downer

Dunham, Othniel b. Vt. 1786 d. Vt. 1868   Lt. Vt. Mil.
  m. Charlotte Peak — son Samuel C. m. Hannah Meserve

Dunham, Peleg K. b. R.I. d. R.I. 1822 m.   Midshipman R.I. Navy
  daughter Phoebe m. George Grieves

Dunkin, Peter b. Pa. 1792 d Ind. 1863 m. Polly Martin   Pvt. Ohio Mil.
  son Benjamin m. Jane Rhine

Dunlap, Alexander   Vol. 10   Pvt. Conn. Mil.

Dunlap, John b. Pa. 1794 d. N.Y. 1835 m. Nancy Brown   Pvt. Pa. Mil.
  daughter Mary Evalina m. John Dodd

Dunlap, William b. Va. 1771 d. Va. 1827 m. Ann Greer   Pvt. Va. Mil.
  daughter Esther Ann m. Charles Hector Triplett

Dunlap, Wililam I.   Vol. 11   Sgt. N.Y. Mil.

Dunman, Joseph b. d. Va. m. Elizabeth I. Kilpatrick   Pvt. Va. Mil.
  son Pleasant W. m. Mary Jane Jenkins

Dunn, Alexander b. Pa. 1770 d. Pa. 1823   Justice of Peace Pa. 1809
  m. Mary McFadden — son James m. Maria Thompson

Dunn, David, Sr. b. N.C. 1786 d. Miss. 1863   Pvt. Miss. Terr. Mil.
  m. Lavinia Gladsburn — son Evander G. m. Sarah Ella Stonestreet

Dunn, George F.   Vol. 12   Pvt. Ohio Mil.

Dunn, Henry b. Miss. 1770 d. Miss. 1854   Capt. Miss. Terr. Mil.
  m. Elizabeth Scott — son Valeria Henry m. Mary Ann Bostwick

Dunn, James b. Pa. 1800 d. Pa. 1874 m. Maria Thompson   Pvt. Pa. Mil.
  son Socrates A. m. Sarah Richardson

Dunn, John   Vol. 5   Pvt. Ohio Mil.

Dunn, John b. Va. 1782 d. Va. 1848   Pvt. Va. Mil.
  m. Elizabeth Wood Johnson—son Elijah J. m. Susan Ann Sandridge

Dunn, Robert   Vol. 13   Ens. Pa. Mil.

Dunn, Thomas b. Va. 1787 d. Va. 1874   Sgt. Va.
  m. Temperance Pierpont — daughter Martha m. Michael Sheets

Dunnegan, John   Vol. 16   Pvt. Tenn. Mtd. Mil.

Dunning, Jonathan b. N.J. 1770 d. N.J. 1836   Pvt. U.S. Inf. N.J.
  m. Rachel Crane — daughter Rachel m. Lawrence Low

Dunsmore, Phineas b. Mass. 1771 d. Ohio 1823   Capt. N.H. Cavalry
  m. Polly Page — son Heil m. Susannah Mellor

Dunsmore (also Dunsmoor), Samuel b. N.H. 1790 d. Vt. 1863, Pvt. Vt. Mil.
  m. Anne Powers — daughter Sarah Ann m. Duan Snow
  son William m. Fanny Maria Ainsworth

Dunton, James, Sr. b. Mass. (Me.) 1783 d. Me. 1875   Pvt. Mass. Mil.
  m. Polly Patterson — son James Jr. m. Dorothy A. Weeks

Dunwell (also Dundwell), Henry b. Conn. 1791 d. N.Y. 1861, Pvt. N.Y. Inf.
  m. Mary Deitz — daughter Polly m. John B. Chamberlain

Dunwoody, Patrick McClain b. 1789 d. Tenn. 1854   Lt. Tenn. Mil.
  m. Esther Bare — D. H. m. L. J.

du Pont, Eleuthere Irenee b. Fran. 1771 d. Pa. 1834 m.   Capt. Del. Vol.
  son Alexis Irenee m. Joanna Maria Smith

Durfee, Thomas b. R.I. 1759 d. R.I. 1829   Mem. Gen. Assy. R.I. 1787-97
m. Mary Lowden — daughter Elizabeth m. Samuel Warren

Durfee, Thomas b. Mass. 1721 d. Mass. 1796   Senator 1780-87
m. Patience Borden — son Charles   Del. to Conv. 1788
m. Welthe Hathaway

Dupree, David Daniel b. Va. 1784 d. Ga. 1857   Capt. Ga. Mil.
m. Elizabeth — daughter Elinor H. m. Luke Stevens
son George G. m. Sara Jane Brown

Dupree, Jacob (Dippery) b. Pa. 1789/90 d. Pa. 1866   Pvt. Pa. Mil.
m. Maria Gross (Kross) — son Jeremiah m. Lydia Klapp

Dupuy, Samuel b. Ky. 1779 d. abt. 1840   Sheriff Ky.
m. Mary Ann Fawcett — daughter Amanda m. Aaron Goza

Durant, Ruben   Vol. 17   Pvt. U.S. Inf.

Durden, Burch b. Ga. 1787 d. Ala. 1875 m. Polly Trammell   Pvt. Ga. Mil.
daughter Elizabeth S. m. Henry Loggins

Durden, Joshua b. Ga. 1775 d. Ala. 1825 m. Gilley Baker   Ga. 1812-14
daughter Martha Emily m. John Merritt   Sword Maker

Durham, John b. N.C. 1760 d. Ohio 1852 m. Mary   Music Va. Mil.
son Ralph m. Elizabeth Elliot

Durham, Thomas b. N.C. c 1760 d. Tenn. 1823   Juror Tenn. 1809
m. Rebecca Allen — son Thomas, Jr. m. Elizabeth Chiles Johnson

Duryea, George b. N.Y. 1777 d. N.Y. 1846 m. Anny Hubbs   Pvt. N.Y. Mil.
daughter Patience E. m. Eliphalet Wicks Smith

Duryee, William b. N.J. 1784 d. Mich. 1872   Pvt. N.Y. Mil.
m. Sarah Groot — son Isaac G. m. Lydia Augur Budington

Dutch, Holly M. b. Mass. 1793 d. Me. 1866   Cpl. U.S. Inf.
m. Elizabeth Greenlaw — son Darius P. m. Lydia Storer

Dutch, William   Vol. 15   Lt. N.Y. Mil.

Dutton, John b. Md. 1797 d. Md. 1877 m. Sara Parks   Pvt. Md. Mil.
son John R. m. Annie Le Tournau
daughter Mary Hosanna m. Cornelius Lowry Willis
daughter Sarah Matilda m. James Lloyd Baylies

DuVal, Alexander de la Planche b. 1793 d. 1851   Pvt. Tenn. Mil. Inf.
m. Margaret Gwin — daughter Matilda K. m. John H. Baskette

DuVal, John Pope b. Va. 1791 d. Fla. 1855   Brig. Gen. Va. Troops
m. Ann Fouche Tebbs — son Harvie S. m. Olivia Harrison

Duvall, Henry b. Md. 1778 d. Md. 1819   Adj. Md. Mil.
m. Elizabeth Boone — son Grafton B. m. Elizabeth Duvall (cousin)

Duval, William Pope b. Va. 1785/4 d. D.C. 1854   Capt. Ky. Mil.
m. Nancy Haynes   Mem. Cong. Ky. 1813-15
daughter Laura H. m. Arthur Maury Randolph
daughter Mary m. Matthew Hopkins
son Thomas Howard m. Laura Peyton

Dwinal, Jacob Jr. b. Mass. 1793 d. Mass. 1851   Pvt. Mass. Mil.
m. Sarah Cushwan — son Charles H. m. Rosalia Houghton

Dye, George b. Pa. 1786 d. Ind. 1847 m. Sarah Calvert   Pvt. Ohio Mil.
son Samuel H. m. Melissa B. Hague

Dye, John Hixson b. Va. 1785 d. Va. 1826   Ens. Va. Mil.
m. Ann Hixson Johnson — daughter Emily m. James H. Simpson
son Henry Clay m. Diana Mathis

Dyer, Clement Clinton b. Tenn. 1799 d. Tex. 1864   Pvt. Tenn. Mil.
   m. Sarah Stafford — son James F. m. Sarah Catharine Barnett

Dyer, David Dalton b. Va. 1791 d. Mo. 1844   Pvt. Va. Mil.
   m. Nancy Reynolds Salmon — daughter Sarah Ann
   m. Albert Gallatin Mason

Dyer, Joel Sr. b. 1754 d. Tenn. 1825 m. (1st wife)   2nd Maj. Tenn. Mil.
   daughter Sophia W. m. William Randolph Hess

Dyer, William Bootes b. Md. d. D.C. m. Anne March   Capt. Md. Mil.
   daughter Sarah Rebecca m. Robert Wheeler Bates

Dygert, John B. b. N.Y. 1792 d. N.Y. 1854   Cpl. N.Y. Mil.
   m. Elizabeth Devendorf — daughter Elizabeth m. Frederick Myers

Dygert, Rudolph b. N.Y. 1768 d. N.Y. aft. 1825   Maj. N.Y. Mil.
   m. Elizabeth Ehle — son John R. m. Maria Wock

Dyre (Dyer), Joseph b Pa. 1754 d. Pa. 1835   Pvt. Pa. Mil.
   m. Mrs. Christian Thomas Frankford — daughter Catherine C.
   m. John G. Teese

Dysinger, George Sr. b. Pa. 1786 d. N.Y. 1847   Pvt. Pa. Mil.
   m. Elizabeth Hollenbeck — son George Jr. m. Anna Mary Miller

E

Eads, William Lovern b. (W.)Va. 1783 d. W.Va. 1871   Pvt. U.S. Inf.
   m. Elizabeth Douglas — son James D. m. Minerva Foster

Eager, Uriah Jr. b. Mass. 1740 d. Mass. 1813   Selectman Marlboro
   m. Triphosa Bush — son Moses m. Sarah Stratton

Eagle (Eakle), John (Baker) b. Va. 1778 d. Va. c 1840   Pvt. Va. Mil.
   m. Elizabeth Barger (1) — daughter Annie
   m. Martin Coiner (Coyner)

Earhart (Earheart), Jacob b. Pa. 1773 d. Ohio aft. 1812   Pvt. Ohio Mil.
   m. Elizabeth — son Joseph B. m. Elizabeth Bean

Earl, Danford b. Vt.? 1771 d. N.Y. 1851   Pvt. N.Y. Regt.
   m. Phebe Andrews — son Wheaton m. Alsena Andrus

Earl, John b. N.Y. 1792 d. Ohio 1883 m. Mary Perry   Pvt. N.Y. Mil.
   son Lucurgus m. Corinthia Bassett

Earl, Samuel G. b. Va. 1760 d. S.C. 1833   Capt. S.C. Inf.
   m. Harriett Harrison — daughter Nancy m. John McClanahan

Earle, Archibald b. Va. 1788 d. W.Va. 1842   Major Va. Mil.
   m. Mary Buckey — daughter Maria m. George Ward

Earle, Baylis b. Va. 1734 d. S.C. 1825 m. Mary Prince   Ct. Judge
   son Aspasio m. Mary Montague   Spartansburg, S.C. 1791

Earle, Elias b. Va. 1762 d. S.C. 1823   Congressman Greenville
   m. Frances Robinson   Dist. S.C. 1805/20
   daughter Elizabeth R. m. George W. Earle
   son Robinson m. Eliza Williams Thompson
   daughter Sarah m. James Harrison

Earle, Izaias b. 1753 d. Va. 1826 m. Sarah Brownley   Maj. Va. Mil.
   son Archibald m. Mary Buckey

Earle, James b. Mass. 1765 d. N.Y. 1857   Seaman, Sea Fensibles N.Y.
   m. Elizabeth Soule — daughter Prudence m. Samuel Welch

Earle, John b. Va. 1766 d. en rte. fr. Miss. to S.C. 1820   Trumpeter
  m. Nancy Holland — son Ezias m. Isabella Herndon   Ky. Mil.

Earle, John Baylis b. Va. 1766 d. S.C. 1836   Adj. Insp. Gen. S.C.
  m. Sarah Taylor — son Baylis B. m. Eliza Ann Harrison

Earll, Richard b. N.Y. 1773 d. N.Y. 1831   Pvt. N.Y. Det. Mil.
  m. Mercy Willetts — daughter Mary W. m. William Weaver

Earll, Robert b. Nova Scotia 1759   Brig. Gen. 1804/8 N.Y. Mil.
  d. N.Y. 1833 m. Elizabeth Hodges   Memb. Assembly N.Y. 1811
  son Hiram m. Cynthia Root
  daughter Phoebe m. Benoni Danks
  son Robert Jr. m. Phoebe

Early, Joel b. Va. 1760 d. Ga. 1806   Just. Peace Wilkes Co. Ga. 1792/5
  m. Lucy Smith — daughter Mary (Polly) m. George Watkins

Early, Joseph b. Va. 1770 d. Ind. 1842   Pvt. Ky. Mtd. Mil.
  m. Catherine Drennan — daughter Mary m. Willis Bell

Early, Peter b. Va. 1773 d. Ga. 1817   Memb. Congress, Supreme Ct.
  m. Anne Adams Smith — daughter Lucy   & Gov. Ga.
  m. Richard Jones

Early, William b. 1776 d. Ky. 1813   Ensign Ky. Vols.
  m. Hannah Laughlin — son Dr. James H.
  m. Rebecca Cummins Sammons

Earnest, Henry b. Ky. 1790 d. Ky. 1833 m. Fannie Harris   Pvt. Ky. Vols.
  son Robert H. m. Leann Elizabeth Cockrill

Easley, John S. b. Va. 1792 d. W.Va. 1869   Pvt. Va. Mil.
  m. Agnes C. White — daughter Harriet m. Henley French

East, Thomas b.— d. La. k/a 1815 m. Mary Day   Pvt. La. Mil.
  son John m. Frances Collins

Easterling, William b. N.C. 1757 d. S.C. 1839   Judge Marlboro Co. S.C.
  m. Elizabeth Covington Sands — son John   1807/39
  m. Nancy Ann Covington

Eastin, Thomas   Vol. 12   Pvt. Ky. Mil.
  daughter Frances m. William B. Wait REAL DAUGHTER

Eastlack, Samuel b. N.J. 1740 d. N.J. 1798   Pvt. N.J. Mil.
  m. Mary Turner — son Amos m. Rachel Cawman

Eastland, Thomas b. Va. 1775 d. Tenn. 1860   QM. Gen. Ky. Mil.
  m. Nancy Mosby — son Robert Mosby m. Elizabeth Brazeale

Eastman, Azariah b. Vt. 1795 d. N.Y. 1865   Pvt. N.Y. Mil.
  m. Percie Parsons — son Chauncey m. Amitta Philena Nims

Eastman, Cyprian b. Conn. 1749 d. Vt. 1798   Capt. Vt. Inf.
  m. Rosanna Nelson — son Luther m. Lydia Eastman

Eastman, Irad b. Conn. 1789 d. N.Y. 1864   Pvt. N.Y. Mil.
  m. Azudah Skinner — daughter Lydia L. m. Jefferson Brown

Easton, Giles b. Md. 1762 d. Md. 1842   Pvt. Md. Mil.
  m. Rebecca Grumes — son Giles Jr. m. Sarah Shook

Easton, Nathaniel Peck   Vol. 16   Pvt. N.Y. Mil.

Eastwick, Thomas b. Pa. 1775 d. N.Y. 1816   Pvt. U.S. Inf.
  m. Margaret McCalla — son Andrew M. m. Lydia Ann James

Eaton, Ebenezer b. N.H. d. N.Y. 1838 m. Deborah Vose   Sgt. N.H. Vols.
  daughter Matilda m. William Gilmore

Eaton, Eli   Vol. 17   Pvt. Conn. Mil.
  daughter Maria Antoinette m. Benjamin Taylor REAL DAUGHTER

Eaton, Jacob b. N.H. 1788 d. Vt. 1833 m. Tamar Lovley   Pvt. Vt. Mil.
  son Ralph H. m. Eliza Knapp Dickerman

Eaton, Johnston b. Pa. 1776 d. Pa. 1847 m. Eliza Cannon   Capt. Pa. Mil.
  daughter Martha C. m. Samuel C. Sturgeon

Eaton, Parley b. N.Y. 1794 d. N.Y. 1872 m. Phila Barnes   Pvt. N.Y. Mil.
  daughter Roxana m. Newell Hine
  son Volney m. Alida Herkimer

Eaton, Roswell b. N.Y. 1796 d. N.Y. 1863   Pvt. N.Y. Mil.
  m. Margaret Reals — daughter Cathren E. m. Isaac Sadler

Eavenson, Eli b. Pa. 1760 d. Ga. 1829 m. Rachel Seal   Pvt. Pa. Mil.
  son George m. Polly Hilly

Eberhard, Barnes b. Pa. 1783 d. Pa. 1882 m. Susan Henry   Pvt. Pa. Mil.
  son Gabriel m. Catherine Yeater

Eberly, (also Everly) David b. Pa. 1781 d. Pa. 1860   Lieut. Pa. Mil.
  m. Catharine Frankenberger — daughter Rebecca
  m. Christian D. Hertzler

Ebersole, (also Eversole) Jacob b. Hol. 1765 d. Ohio 1848 Corp. Ohio Mil.
  m. Catherine Albaugh — son John m. Hannah Hartzel

Elbert, Peter b. 1774 d. Pa. 1846 m. Mary Landy   Pvt. Pa. Vols.
  son James L. m. Barbara Richards

Eby, Christian b. Pa. 1734 d. Pa. 1807 m. Veronica Hershey Pvt. Pa. Mil.
  son Sem m. Anna Frantz

Echols, Benjamin b. Ga. 1785 d. Ga. 1870 m. Elizabeth Ellis Pvt. Ga. Mil.
  daughter Julia Ann m. James Madison Veach

Eckenrode, John b. Pa. 1767 d. Pa. 1849 m. Anna Mary   Pvt. Pa. Mil.
  son George m. Mary Kelly

Eckles, Joseph b. Pa. 1797 d. Pa. 1857   Pvt. Pa. Mil.
  m. Susan Kelly Lytle (2) — son John T. m. Arabella Louise Powell

Eckles, Robert B. b. 1794 d. Ga. 1861   Pvt. Ga. Mil.
  m. Eliza Griffin Paxson — daughter Susan Laura
  m. Terrell C. Hawthorn

Eckles, Thomas b. Pa. 1766 d. Pa. 1842   Capt. Pa. Mil.
  m. Martha Haggerty — son Joseph m. Mrs. Susan Kelly Lytle
  daughter Susanna m. John Van Gorder

Eddens, John   Vol. 10   Pvt. N.C. Mil.
  daughter Sarah Ellen m. Larkin Davis   REAL DAUGHTER

Eddy, Allen W. b. Vt. 1793 d. Mich. 1878   Pvt. N.Y. Mil.
  m. Clorinda Castle — daughter Anna m. Clement Kemp

Eddy, Gilbert   Vol. 14   Brig. Gen. N.Y. Mil.

Eddy, Henry b. Vt. 1798 d. Ill. 1849 m. Mary Jane Marshall Pvt. N.Y. Mil.
  daughter Elizabeth K. m. Charles Carroll

Eddy, John b. Mass. 1780 d. R.I. 1866   Ensign R.I. Mil.
  m. Martha Jenckes Tefft — daughter Amanda M. m. Robert Goodwin

Eddy, Jonathan b. Vt. 1782 d. Vt. aft. 1820   Moderator, Selectman
  m. Temperance Lewis — daughter Polly   1798/1800
  m. Edward Wade

Eddy, Tisdale, b. N.Y. 1762 d. N.Y. 1828   Major N.Y. Mil.
m. Elizabeth Button — son Devotion C. m. Isabella Campbell

Edens, Austin b. Va. 1770 d. Ala.   Pvt. East Tenn. Mil.
m. Mary Amanda White — daughter Tempe m. Joseph Abele

Edgar, Henry Russell b. Va. 1779 d. Mo. 1890 ?   Sgt. Ky. Mil.
m. Jane McCurdy Martin — daughter Sarah Martin m. Henry Wood
REAL DAUGHTER

Edgar, Matthias B. b. N.Y. 1789 d. N.Y. 1865   Capt. N.Y. Mil.
m. Catherine Hatfield — son William m. Mary Babcock

Edgar, Robert b. Va. 1770 d. Ohio 1838   Scout Ohio Mil.
m. Margaret Gillespie — daughter Jane Ellen m. Augustus George

Edge, Isaac b. N.J. d. N.J. 1859 m. Frances Ogden   Drummer N.J. Mil.
son Isaac Jr. m. Margaret Ward Doyle

Edgerly, Samuel Jr. b. N.H. 1765 d. N.H. 1854   Pvt. N.H. Mil.
m. Lydia Shepherd (Johnson) — daughter Lydia m. Ira Aasker

Edgerton, Simeon b. Conn. 1732 d. Vt. 1809   Selectman Vt. 1781/91
m. Abiah Hough — son Jacob m. Esther Reed

Edgington, Isaac b. 1746 d. Ohio 1846   Pvt. Ohio Mil.
m. (3d) Sarah Brown — daughter Jane m. William Pellitt

Edic, Jacob Jr.   Vol. 15   Pvt. N.Y. Mil.

Edington, William C. b. Va. 1783 d. Ohio 1864   Pvt. Va. Mil.
m. Polly (Mary) Hart — daughter Elizabeth A.
m. Wiliam F. Forsaker

Edloe, William b. Va. 1786 d. Va. 1846   2nd Lieut. Va. Mil.
m. Elizabeth Lowry Allen — daughter Elizabeth E.
m. John Royster Armistead

Edminster, John (Jonathan) b. Mass. 1769 d. Mass. 1840   Pvt. Mass. Mil.
son James m. Lydia Knight

Edmiston, (also Edmundson) John b. Va. 1763   Capt. Ky. Mil.
d. River Raisin k/a 1813, m. Margaret Montgomery
daughter Margaret m. Chandler Prewitt

Edmiston, John b. Va. 1788 d. Ohio 1853   Corp. Ohio Mil.
m. Malinda Teeter — son John F. m. Susan Jane Pricer
daughter Mary m. William Brown

Edmiston, William b. Tenn. 1792 d. Tenn. 1874   Lieut. Tenn. Mil.
m. Priscilla Reid — son William Jr. m. Sarah E. Murray

Edmiston, William b. Va. 1795 d. Ill. 1885   Pvt. Tenn. Mil.
m. Sarah Askins — son James A. m. Martha Little

Edmonson, Robert Spilsbee b. Va. 1780 d. Miss. 1863   Pvt. Va. Mil.
m. Nancy Singleton — son John C. m. Mary Smith (Coleman)

Edmunds, William b. Ga. 1775 d. Ga. 1840   Lieut. Ga. Mil.
m. Catherine Cole — son Roscoe m. Nancy Bagby

Edmunds, William b. 1776 d. Tenn. 1863   Pvt. Mtd. Gunmen Tenn.
m. Mary Ann Penn — daughter Martha Ann m. Haiden Trigg Curd

Edmundson, Joseph b. Pa. 1746/56 d. Pa. 1822 m. Sarah   Capt. Pa. Mil.
son Caleb m. Rebecca Phillips   1794

Edson, Nathaniel b.— d. Mass. m.—   Vol. 22   Capt. Mass. Mil.
daughter Lucy m. George Burrell Stone

Edwards, Benjamin b. Va. 1752 d. Ky. 1826   Memb. Cong. 1795 Md.
  m. Margaret Beall   Mem. of Const. Conv. Md. 1788
  daughter Elizabeth m. John Gray

Edwards, Brice b. Va. 1776 d. Mo. 1850   Maj. Va. Mil.
  m. Martha Barksdale — son John A. B. m. Elizabeth James

Edwards, Caleb b. Mass. (Me.) 1795 d. Me. 1885   Pvt. Mass. (Me.) Mil.
  m. Hannah Welch — daughter Cordelia M. m. Ansel Fields Brooks

Edwards, Daniel, Sr. b. La. 1787 d. La. 1877   Pvt. La. State Troops
  m. Mary Cooper — son Nicholas S.   Mem. Leg. Council 1810-15 La.
  m. Adaline Bankston

Edwards, David L. b. N.C. 1778 d. Tenn. 1817   Pvt. Tenn. Mil.
  m. Eva Lazene — son Amos m. Elizabeth Wilburn

Edwards, Edward b. Va. 1763 d. Tenn. 1863   Pvt. Va. Mil.
  m. Mary Howlett — son Edward C. m. Nicey Stover Ross

Edwards, Evan b.— d. S.C. 1796 m.—   Memb. S.C. Leg. 1785
  son Charles m. Catherine Lee

Edwards, James b. Va. 1792 d. Ga. 1852   Pvt. Ga. Mil. 1813
  m. Patsy Hamilton — daughter Sarah m. Sherod Lindsey

Edwards, James b. Va. 1789 d. Ohio 1835   Sgt. Ohio Mil.
  m. Elizabeth Carr — daughter Sarah Jane m. James Robinson

Edwards, James Lewis   Vol. 11   Lieut. U.S.M.C.

Edwards, John b. Wales 1776 d. Ohio 1815   Pvt. Pa. Mil.
  m. Mary MacGregor — son David m. Rebecca Lamborn

Edwards, John Crawford b. Va. 1765 d.— m. Patience Byrd Pvt. S.C. Mil.
  son Henry C. B. m. Mahala Acrean Merritt

Edwards, Richards b. R.I. 1770 d. R.I. 1843 m. Mary Howard   QM. R.I. Mil.
  daughter Hannah m. Rev. John G. Dorrance (1)

Edwards, Richard b. Va. 1767 d. Va. 1861   Corp. Va. Mil.
  m. Sally Williams — daughter Julia Ann m. Joseph Woodson

Edwards, Sanford b. S.C. 1784 d. Ohio 1874   Pvt. West Tenn. Mil.
  m. Mary Thetford — son William H. m. Lucinda Dockings

Edwards, Timothy b. Mass. 1738 d. Mass. 1813   Prob. Judge Mass.
  m. Rhoda Ogden — daughter Mary m. Mason Whiting

Eells, Nathaniel b. Conn. 1757 d. N.Y. 1851   Capt. N.Y. Mil.
  m. Martha Hamlin — daughter Patty m.

Effner, Valentine b. N.Y. 1776 d. N.Y. 1865   Major N.Y. Mil.
  m. Elizabeth Martin — daughter Catherine m. Charles Whiting

Egdell, Henry   Vol. 13   Pvt. Md. Mil.

Eggleston, Edward b. Va. 1761 d. Va. 1812   Pvt. U.S. Dragoons, Va.
  m. Judith Booker — son Joseph C. m. Mary Jane Craig

Eggleston, Rowland b. 1796 d. Conn. 1876   Pvt. Conn. Mil.
  m. Betsey Collins — son William F. m. Narcissa Graham

Eheart, (also Ahartz) Michael L. b. Va. d. Va.   Pvt. Va. Mil.
  m. Elizabeth Harrison Cannady — son Andrew J.
  m. Pamelia Harrison

Ehler, Thomas b. Pa. 1796 d. Ind. 1876   Pvt. Pa. Mil. 1st Regt.
  m. Catherina Fasnacht   1st Brig. Lebanon Co. 1814/15
  daughter Rosana m. William O'Brien

Eichelberger, George S.   Vol. 4   Corp. Md. Mil.

Eichelberger, Leonard b. Pa. 1750 d. Pa. 1811 Constable, Judge of Ct. of
 m. Elizabeth Smyser — son John   Appeals Pa. 1785
 m. Katharine Coover

Elam, Jesse b. Ga. 1782 d. Texas 1854 m. Rosa Evans   Pvt. U.S. Inf.
 son Isaac m. Margaret Lanham

Elam, Joel b. Va. d. Va. m.   Pvt. Va. Mil.
 daughter Elizabeth m. James T. Gray

Elbert, Henry Dalton b. Md. 1768 d. Ky.   Lieut. Md. Mil.
 m. Rebecca Starkey — son John L. m. Frederica Jacoby

Elder, Jesse b.— d. Ky. 1858 m. Mary Jane Davis   Pvt. Ky. Mil.
 daughter Mary Jane m. Silas Marion Jasper

Elderkin, Jedidiah b. Conn. 1718 d. Conn. 1793   Justice Conn. 1789-91
 m. Anne Wood — daughter Judith m. Jabez Huntington

Eldred, Rufus b. Conn. 1773 d. N.Y. 1838   Lieut. N.Y. Mil.
 m. Hannah Smith — daughter Adaline m. Francis Xavier Boschert

Eldredge, Aaron b. N.J. 1771 d. N.J. 1819   Lieut. N.J. Mil.
 m. Harriet Langdon — son Jeremiah m. Harriet Tomlin

Eldredge, Anthony H. b. Pa. 1794 d. Ill. 1888   Pvt. D.C. Guards 1812/13
 m. Susannah Vance — son William V. m. Mary Fuller

Eldridge, Peter b. Ga. or N.C. 1784 (1797) d. Texas 1884   Pvt. Ga. Mil.
 m. Sarah M. — son John D. m. Mary Kerr
 daughter Sarah Amanda m. John Lightfoot Gulley
 REAL DAUGHTER
 daughter Tennie m. James Kilborne Harris   REAL DAUGHTER

Eldridge, Peyton Randolph b. Pa. 1769 d. Ky. 1849 Pvt. Matross Va. Mil.
 m. Mary Guinn — daughter Martha Alice m. John Ingram Clay

Elkin, Robert b. Ky. 1794 d. Ky. 1874 m. Polly Salter Corp. Ky. Mtd. Mil.
 son Thomas A. m. Katie Claire Simpson

Elkins, James, Sr. b. Va. 1755 d. Ky. 1836   Drummer Va. Mil.
 son James Jr. m. Lucinda Osborne

Ellerbe, Thomas b. S.C. 1749 d. S.C. 1808   Org. Chatham Lt. Horse Trp.
 m. Obedience Gillespie — son Thomas   1789 S.C.
 m. Leslie Margaret Prince
 son William m. Elizabeth Crawford

Elliott, Asa b. N.Y. 1785 d. Mich. 1852   Pvt. N.Y. Art. Mil.
 m. Elizabeth Williams — son Charles E. m. Lucy M. Barber
 son Jesse m. Henrietta Delamar

Elliott, Benjamin b. Pa. 1791 d. Pa. 1858   Pvt. Pa. Mil.
 m. Jane Smith — daughter Sarah m. James A. Stephenson

Elliott, Burgess b. Va. 1768 d. Ohio 1846   Pvt. Ohio Mil.
 m. Sarah Acklin (Ackley) — daughter Elvira m. John C. Washburn

Elliott, David b. Pa. 1783 d. Ohio 1823   Capt. Ohio Mil.
 m. Elizabeth Swart — son David W. m. Mary Elizabeth Hull

Elliott, George b. Gibralter 1783 d. Md. 1854   Pvt. Md. Mil.
 m. Hannah Rush — daughter Emma m. Lewis Waggner

Elliott, George b. Pa. 1792 d. Pa. 1853 m. Elizabeth   Pvt. Pa. Mil.
 son William m. Elizabeth Hazen

Elliott, Henry b. Md. 1774 d. Md. 1844   Pvt. Md. Mil.
 m. Nancy Conway — daughter Adaline m. John Thompson

Elliott, James b. Pa. 1791 d. Kansas 1865   Pvt. Pa. Rangers 1811
  m. Nancy Agnes Shields — daughter Ruth Jane
  m. Richard Emery Derrick

Elliott, Jesse Duncan b. Md. 1784 d. Pa. 1845   Capt. U.S. Navy
  m. Frances C. Vaughan — daughter Fannie m. Jacob R. Spangler
  son Washington L. m. Harriett Eloise Jones

Elliott, John b. Md. d. Md. 1829   Capt. Md. Mil.
  m. Elizabeth Hambleton — son William H. m. Catharine Hentz

Elliott, John b. Pa. 1791 d. Pa. 1876   Capt. Pa. Mil.
  m. Marietta Keeler — daughter Melissa m. John Franklin Dodge

Elliott, Samuel b. N.H. 1775 d. N.H. 1826   Pvt. N.H. Mil.
  m. Anna Pulsifer — son Edmund m. Sarah Smith

Elliott, Samuel b. Md. 1745 d. Ky. 1825   Pvt. Va. Mil. 1805
  m. Mary Oldham — son Robert m. Polly Kirkpatrick

Elliott, Thomas b. N.C. or Va. 1758/68 d. Tenn. 1863, Pvt. East Tenn. Mil.
  m. Elizabeth Bullner — daughter Barbara m. William Frazier
  son David m. Rachel Stout

Elliott, William Jr. b. S.C. 1761 d. S.C. 1808   Legislator S.C.
  m. Phoebe — son Stephen m. Anne Hutson Habersham

Ellis, Ethelrid b. S.C. 1771 d. N.C. 1849 m.   Pvt. S.C. Mil.
  daughter Sarah m. Issaac Faulkner

Ellis, Henry b. Va. 1782 d. Ill. 1857   Pvt. Ohio Mil.
  m. Charity Harper — daughter Maria Louisa m. Allen Hegler

Ellis, James b.— d. Ky. 1832 m. Elizabeth Overfield   Lieut. Ky. Mtd. Vols.
  daughter Elizabeth m. Reason Downing

Ellis, Jeremiah b. Pa. 1779 d. Ohio 1857   Pvt. Ohio Mil.
  m. Ann Underwood — son Washington m. Aris Parker

Ellis, Jesse b. Pa. 1782 d. Ohio 1878 m. Sabina Brooks   Musician Ohio Mil.
  daughter Cinderilla m. Armstrong Howland

Ellis, John b. Ky. 1777 d. Ill. c 1845 m. Anna Cook   Corp. Ky. Mil.
  daughter Nancy m. Benjamin Barr

Ellis, John   Vol. 10   Maj. Gen. Mass. Mil.

Ellis, John b. Mass. 1742 d. Mass. 1827   Selectman Ashfield 1784
  m. Molly Dimmick — daughter Hannah m. Apollas Williams

Ellis, Judah   Vol. 12   Pvt. N.Y. Mil.

Ellis, Levi D. b. S.C. 1791 d. Ill. 1857   Patriot—made gun stocks
  m. Cynthia Bradford — son Jacob W. m. Sarah Kreider

Ellis, Samuel b. Va. 1791 d. Ky. 1879   Ensign Tenn. Mil.
  m. Elizabeth Gaines — son John m. Mary A. Lester
  son Robert m. Amanda Jane Lewis

Ellis, Walter b. Va. 1790 d. Mo. 1877   Pvt. Ky. Mil.
  m. Cynthia Ann Wells — daughter Columbia m. Thomas H. Branham

Ellison, John b. Ire. 1779 d. Ohio 1829 m. Anna Barr   Pvt. Ohio Mil.
  daughter Mary K. m. William Ellison

Elliston, Jacob Percy b. Va. d. Ky. m. Elizabeth Heiter   Lt. Col. Ky.
  son Robert m. Sally Mountjoy   Vol. Mil.

Ellwood, Isaac   Vol. 5   Pvt. N.Y. Mil.

Ellwood, John b. Del. 1788 d. Ind. 1855　　　　Sgt., Corp. Del. Mil.
m. Ann Ellsbury — son Levi C. m. Elenor Kirkman

Elmore, John b. Mass. 1766 d. N.Y. 1840　　　　Ensign N.Y. Mil. 1803
m. Elizabeth Hay — daughter Euretta m. Dr. Edward Kane

Elmore, John Archer b. Va. 1762 d. Ala. 1834　　　Brig. Gen. Ala. Mil.
m. (2d) Nancy Martin — son Physil R. m. Susan Nesbitt

Elson, John Harris b. Va. (Md.) 1771 d. Ohio 1822　　　Capt. Ohio Mil.
m. Margaret Wiggins — daughter Charity m. Robert Wilson
son Richard m. Fredericka S. Boegel and Anna Brandon

Elston, Isaiah b. N.J. 1788 d. Ind. 1831　　Pvt. Ind. Terr. U.S. Rangers
m. Sarah Rutherford — son Joseph m. Elizabeth Stephenson

Ellsworth, Moses b. Conn. 1767 d. Ohio 1833　　　　Pvt. Ohio Mil.
m. Mary M. Bumgardner — daughter Ann m. Jeremiah Botkin

Ellsworth, William C. b. Conn. 1769 d. Vt. 1850　　　　Pvt. Vt. Mil.
m. Jane Beckett — son Alba m. Eliza Ellen Barnes

Elting, Robert b. Vt. or N.Y. 1785 d. N.Y. 1841　　Lt. Col. N.Y. Mil.
m. Hannah Gale — daughter Jane Elisabeth m. Louis Walsh

Elwood, Richard P. b. N.Y. 1750 d. N.Y. 1825　　　Corp. N.Y. Mil.
m. Catherine Bell — daughter Susannah m. John Wilson

Ely, Isaac b. Va. 1775 d. Mo. 1857 m. Mary Judy　　　Pvt. Ky. Mil.
son Benjamin m. Martha Bonaparte Layne

Ely, Merrick b. Mass. 1793 d. Ohio 1838　　　　Pvt. Ohio Mil.
m. Lovisa Farnum — daughter Lucinda m. Luke Dewey Johnson

Emberson, John b. Va. 1798 d. Texas 1850　　Pvt. Tenn. Mil. 1812
m. Matilda Carter — daughter Eliza m William M. Williams

Embich, Jacob b. Pa. 1754 d. Pa. 1819　　　　Lieut. Pa. Mil.
m. Maria Catherine Gatz — daughter Sara m. John Peter Shindel

Embrey, Daniel b. Va. 1790 d. Va. aft. 1868　　Pvt. Va. Mil. 1814
m. Winifred — son Edward E. m. Missouri Ann Jackson

Embrey, Robert b. Va. 1773 d. Va. 1857 m. Sarah Glass　　Sgt. Va. Mil.
son Stanton G. m. Mary Delia Miller

Emerson, Asa b. Mass. 1780 d. Ohio 1855 m. Sally　　Musician Mass. Mil.
daughter Miriam m. John Anson Ackley

Emerson, Daniel　　Vol. 7　　Mem. Gov's. Council, State Leg. N.H.

Emerson, Ezekiel b. R.I. 1767 d. Ohio 1856　　　Lt. Col. R.I. Mil.
m. Patience Burlingame — son George m. Phebe Sherman
daughter Nancy m. Dutee Sherman

Emerson, James b. 1787 d. Mo. 1863 m. Nancy Tuggle　Pvt. Ky. Vol. Mil.
son Simpson m. Catherine Owen

Emerson, Nathaniel　　Vol. 15　　　　　Pvt. N.Y. Mil.

Emery, Henry b. Pa. 1789 d. Pa. 1872 m. Sarah Horn　Ensign Pa. Mil.
son Jacob m. Rebekah Martin

Emery, John b. Mass. 1788 d. Ohio 1862　　　　Pvt. Ohio Mil.
m. Susan Bartlett — son Dr. John m. Elizabeth Wheeler

Emery, John b. Mass. d. Ohio m. Elizabeth Wheeler　　Pvt. Ohio Mil.
son Samuel m. Henrietta Reese

Emery, Robert b. Mass. 1764 d. Me. 1825   Pvt. Me. Mil.
   m. Temperance Mathews — son George Arnold m. Mary Libby

Emison, Thomas b. Pa. 1776 d. Ind. 1836   Lieut. Ind. Mil.
   m. Jennet Holmes — son James M. m. Emmeline Scott

Empie, Philip b. N.Y. 1797 d. N.Y. 1848 m. Eliza Burdick   Fifer N.Y. Mil.
   daughter Marie m. James B. Hill

Engle, George Sr. b. Pa. 1750 d. Ky. 1826   Memb. Ct. Pleas. 1796
   m. Elizabeth Sturm — son Peter m. Mildred Chick   Tenn.

Engle, James b. Pa. 1757 d. Pa. 1827 Vol. 6   Speaker Pa. Hse. Repr. 1809

English, Green b. Ga. 1795 d. Ga. 1877   Pvt. Ga. Mil.
   m. Mary Carr Morgan — daughter Eliza m. Jonathan Proctor Milner

English, James b. N.J. 1757 d. N.J. 1816   Pvt. N.J. Det. Mil.
   m. Hannah Perrine — son John m. Mary Perrine

English, John b. Va. 1793 d. Texas 1868   Capt. Tenn. Mil.
   m. Elizabeth Choate — son James D. m. Ella Beavers

English, Joshua m. Sarah Adamson   2nd Lieut. S.C. Mil.
   son Joseph m. Harriet Fitzpatrick

English, Levin Nelson b. Md. 1792 d. Oregon 1876   Pvt. Ky. Mtd. Mil.
   m. (2d) Mary Tate Daley —daughter Elizabeth
   'm. James Dority Riggs   REAL DAUGHTER
   daughter Mahala m. Reuben Riggs   REAL DAUGHTER
   daughter Nancy m. Thomas M. Elliott   REAL DAUGHTER

Ennis, Sylvanus b. N.Y. d. N.Y. 1831 m. Mary Dobbs   Pvt. U.S. Arty.
   son Sylvanus S. m. Caroline Brown

Enochs, Enoch b. Va. 1750 d. Ohio 1835   Pvt. Va. Mil., Capt. Pa. Mil.
   m. Rebecca Morris — daughter Elizabeth   Frontier Svc. Ind. Wars
   m. Isaac Morris

Ensor, John B. b. Md. 1791 d. Md. 1880   Pvt. Md. Mil.
   m. Delilah Chilyoat —son John C. m. Ruth Cott Duncan

Ensor, Thomas b. Tenn. 1790 d. Tenn. 1875   Pvt. Tenn. Mil.
   m. Hannah Jobe — son David J. m. Mrs. Mary May Bailey

Ensor, William b. Md. 1760 d. Md. 1834   Pvt. Md. Mil.
   m. Rachel Ann Canoles — son John Edward m. Eliza Ann Hopkins

Enyeart, David b. Pa. 1787 d. Pa. 1857   Sgt. Pa. Riflemen
   m. Margaret Housholder — son Isaac m. Margaret Isenberg

Enyeart, (Enyard) William b. Holland d. Pa. 1828   Pvt. Pa. Mil.
   m. Catherine Schell — son David m. Margaret Housholder

Epler, George b. Pa. 1791 d. Pa. 1874 m. Eva Barlet   Pvt. U.S. Inf.
   son George Jr. m. Josephine C. Read

Epperson, John b. Va. 1783 d. Ga. 1862 m. Emilie Bell   Pvt. Ga. Vols.
   daughter Nancy m. James Jordan

Eppes, Daniel b. Va. 1776 d. Va. 1836 m. Sarah G. Jones   Major Va. Mil.
   son John m. Louisa Emiline McCain

Erb, John b. Pa. 1793 d. Ind. 1872 m. Nancy Myers   Teamster Pa. 1814
   son William m. Norrie A.

Erisman, Abraham b. Pa. 1771 d. Pa. 1829   Pvt. Pa. Mil.
   m. Catherine Muller (Miller) — son Abraham Jr.
   m. Catharine Meroni

Erskine, Martin b. 1790 d. N.J. 1874 m. Mary Alexandria   **Pvt. Va. Mil.**
daughter Ann M. m. William Edward Jones

Ervin, Charles b. Pa. 1784 d. Ind. 1848 or 1835   **Sgt. Ohio Mil.**
m. Sarah Bennett — daughter Rebecca L. m. Jonathon Moom
daughter Mary m. Peter L. Runyon Sr.

Erwin, Alexander b. Pa. 1750 d. N.C. 1830   **Memb. Leg. N.C.**
m. Sarah Ann Robinson — daughter Catherine m. John Erwin
(prob. cousin)

Erwin, Charles b. Pa. 1791 died at sea 1828   Commander Privateer Pa.
m. Eliza Spooner — daughter Sarah C. m. Jacob Ellis

Erwin, David b. N.J. 1758 d. N.Y. 1831   Built Block House at
m. Catherine Munson — son Cornelius M.   Ft. Covington N.Y.
m. Lucinda Fairman

Erwin, Francis b. S.C. 1766/7 d. S.C. 1839   **Pvt. N.C. Mil.**
m. Mrs. Mary Moore — son William L. m. Anne B. Williamson

Erwin, Robert b. Pa. d. Ohio 1854 m. Jane Frazer   **Pvt. Ohio Mil.**
son Robert Jr. m. Rebecca Law

Erwin, Samuel b. Pa. 1770 d. N.Y. 1836   **Capt. U.S. Inf.**
m. Rachel Hickman — son Arthur H. m. Frances Mary McKean

Eskridge, Hector J. b. Va. 1772 d.—m.—   **Pvt. Va. Mil.**
son Thomas O. m. Mary Peyton Matson

Espy, James S. b. Pa. 1788 d. Pa. 1872 m. Mary Huling   **Pvt. Pa. Mil.**
daughter Anna m. Hugh H. Stockton

Esselstyn, John Broadhead, b. N.Y. 1774 d. N.Y. 1857   **Major N.Y. Mil.**
m. Clarissa Stanley — daughter Maria S. m. Abram Nelson Brooks

Essig, Jacob b. Ohio 1791 d. Ohio 1874   **Corp. Ohio Mil.**
m. Elizabeth Weaver — son William H. m. Ann Eliza Cowell

Estes, James b.— d. Ga. 1842 m. Elizabeth Phillips   **Pvt. Ga. Mil.**
daughter Sara m. Robert L. Hays

Estes, Joel b. Va. 1780 d. Va. 1833   **Capt. Va. Mil.**
m. Sarah Langhorne Bates — son Moreau P. m. Mary Quarles Noel

Estes, William b. Va. 1792 d. Miss. 1871   **Sgt. QM. Va. Mil.**
m. Susan Shelton — daughter Ann Maria m. James C. Hiller

Estes, William Forston b. Va. 1790 d. Ky. 1862   **Pvt. Ky. Mtd. Mil.**
m. Margaret Miller — son William L. m. Elvira Colbert

Etzler, John b. Md. 1790 d. Ill. 1860   **Ensign Va. Mil.**
m. Mary Magdalene Peters — daughter Elizabeth
m. Abraham McNeill

Eubank, Jonathan b. 1784 d. Ky.? 1862   Ky. Mil. at Battle of New
m. Stacey Reeder — son Carson T. m. Mary Hunt   Orleans 1815

Eubank, Joseph b. Va. 1797 d. Ky. 1842   **Pvt. Va. Mil.**
m. Nancy M. Smith — son John m. (3rd) Fetna Isabel Jackson

Eubank, Robert b. N.C. 1780 d. Miss. 1860   **Pvt. Tenn. Mil.**
m. Margaret Conley — daughter Malinda E. m. Calvary Williams

Eubank, William   Vol. 11   **Pvt. Va. Mil.**

Evans, Daniel b. Pa. 1776 d. Ohio 1840 m. Mary Roland   **Pvt. Ohio Mil.**
daughter Esther J. m. William S. Town

Evans, David b. Pa. 1794 d. Pa. 1855   Corp. Pa. Mil.
    m. (1st) Elizabeth Lunn — daughter Mary m. Charles S. James

Evans, Dudley b. (W.)Va. 1766 d. (W.)Va. 1844   Lt. Col. Va. Mil.
    m. Ammarah Williams — daughter Margaret m. Jacob Miller

Evans, Edward   Vol. 3   Pvt. N.H. Mil.

Evans, James b. Pa. 1773 d. Pa. 1842 m. Charlotte Brooke   Pvt. Pa. Mil.
    daughter Anna m. John Barlow
    son Thomas B. m. Rebecca Robinson

Evans, Jeremiah b. Pa. d. Pa. m. Rachel McMullen   Pvt. Pa. Mil.
    daughter May Poe m. John Bard

Evans, John b. (W.)Va. 1792 d. Texas 1852   Pvt. Ky. Vol. Mil.
    m. Nancy Plummer — son Louis H. m. Mary Lewellon

Evans, John b. S.C. 1760 d. St. Tamany   Pvt. La. Mil.
    m. Mary Ann Graham — daughter Mary Ann m. Antonio Rousseaux

Evans, John b. Va. 1737 d. Va. 1834 m. Ann Martin   Clerk of Ct. 1809
    daughter Margaret   Va. Del. to Const. Convention 1788
    m. Dudley Evans Dent

Evans, John b. Md. 1768 d. W.Va. 1849   Patriot W.Va.
    m. Gilly C. Strother — daughter Louise S. m. John Henry Hoffman

Evans, John Jr. b. S.C. 1786 d. S.C. 1863   Pvt. S.C. Mil.
    m. Mary Parham — daughter Rhoda m. James Carlisle Posey

Evans, John R. b.—d.—m.—   Capt. Md. Mil.
    daughter Ann Marshall m. William Brown

Evans, Joseph Porter b. Mass. 1786 d. Mass. 1823   Sgt. Mass. Mil.
    m. Phoebe Howland — son David m. Catharine Glass

Evans, Lemuel b. Del. 1776 d. Ill. 1848   Pvt. Del. Mil.
    m. Jerusha Veasey (1) — son Samuel B. m. Nancy Hougham

Evans, Leroy b. Va. 1793 d. Va. 1863   Pvt. Va. Mil.
    m. Mary Frances Mills — son Robert K.
    m. Sarah Catherine Patterson

Evans, Pierce b. Ky. 1793 d. Ohio 1862   Sgt. Ohio Mil.
    m. Mary Ann Brauscher — daughter Mary Ann
    m. John C. Arrowsmith

Evans, Samuel b. Md. 1725 d. Md. aft. 1800   Patriot 1788
    m. Anne Marshall — son John R. m. Elizabeth Marshall

Evans, Samuel b. Md. d. Ohio 1853   Ensign Ohio Mtd. Mil.
    m. Mary Foreman — son Foreman m. Anna Ferris (2)

Evans, Solomon b. Md. 1760 d. Md. 1852 m. Lovey   Patriot Md.
    son Denwood m. Hannah

Evans, William b.— d. Ga. 1815 m. Betsey   Justice Ga. 1798
    daughter Elizabeth m. Thomas Hibeler

Evans, William b. 1789 d. 1852 m. Rachel Stokes   Pvt. Ohio Mil.
    son Moses Evans m. Elizabeth Antrim

Evans, William Bradley b. Md. or Pa. 1794 d. Ohio 1873   Pvt. Va. Mil.
    m. Elizabeth Heister — son Cornelius S. m. Catherine Ellis

Evarts, Gilbert b.—d.— m. Rebecca Chapin   Vol. 24   Town Officer Conn.
    son Timothy m. Hannah Bigelow

Evarts, John b.—d.— m. Summit Stone   Vol. 24   State Officer Conn.

Evarts, Timothy b. Conn. 1708 d. Conn. 1786   Town Repr. Conn.
    m. Submit Stone — son Gilbert m. Rebecca Chapin

Eveleth (also Eveleigh, Evelyn), Nathaniel b. Mass. 1736   Capt. Mass. Mil.
    d. Maine 1824 m. Sarah Chandler Mason — son Nathaniel
    m. Judith Ruth Parsons

Eveleth, Nathaniel Mason Jr. b. Mass. (Me.) 1764   Lt. Mass. Mil.
    d. Maine 1849 m. Judith Ruth Parsons — daughter Judith
    m. Zebulon Rowe Jr.

Everett, John b. Va. 1788 d. Va. 1871   Capt. Va. Mil.
    m. Sarah Woodson (Dedman) — son Talton W. m. Elizabeth Moore

Everett, Thomas b. Md. 1742 d. N.C. 1837   Pvt. N.C. Mil.
    m. Elizabeth Covington — son Lawrence m. Mary Thomas

Everhard, Barnes b. Pa. 1783 d. Pa. 1883 m. Susan   Pvt. Pa. Mil.
    son Gabriel m. Catherine

Everhart, John   Vol. 12   Pvt. Pa. Mil.

Everitt, John Sr. b. Ga. 1754 d. Ga. 1828   Justice Peace 1795/6
    m. Sarah Fagan — son John Jr. m. Mary Jones

Eversole, Abraham b. Md. 1791 d. Ind. 1883   Pvt. Va. Mil.
    m. Elizabeth Allemong — son Benjamin m. Mary Dorman

Eversole, Jacob b. Pa. 1765 d. Ohio 1848   Corp. Ohio Mil.
    m. Catherine Albaugh — son John m. Hannah Hetzel
    daughter Mary Ann m. Jacob Sponhourer

Everton, Thomas Jr. b. N.C. 1782 d. Ind. 1844   Pvt. Ky. Mil.
    m. Mehitabel Luce — daughter Ellen m. Harrison Fox

Everts, Aranthus b. 1782 d. 1867 m. Margaret Matthews   Lt. Col.
    son Robert E. m. Julia Ann Sloan   N.Y. Inf.

Everts, Luther b. Conn. 1771 d. Vt. 1846   2nd Pvt. N.Y. Mil.
    m. Deborah Newcomb — son Luther m. Matilda Brintnell

Everts, Martin b. Conn. 1765 d. Vt. 1842   Pvt. N.Y. Mil.
    m. Electa Noble Foote   daughter Eliza L. m. Gardner C. Cady

Ewell, James b. Va. 1746 d. Va. 1809   Col. Va. Mil.
    m. Mary Ewell (cousin) — son James B. m. Sophia Douglass

Ewell, Jesse b. Va. 1743 d. Va. 1805   Memb. House Del. 1789/90 Va.
    m. Charlotte Ewell — son Jesse m. Mildred Beale
    daughter Margaret m. Finley Adams   REAL DAUGHTER

Ewing, Alexander   Vol. 8   Pvt. Pa. Mil.

Ewing, Alexander b. Pa. 1763 d. Ind. 1822   Col. Ohio Mil.
    m. Charlotte Griffith — son Samuel H. m. Hannah Race

Ewing, Alexander b. Pa. 1750 d. Pa. 1825   Lieut. Pa. Mil.
    m. Jane Wilson — son James m. Prudence Manifold
    daughter Mary m. John McMillan

Ewing, Charles b. Md. 1793 d. Ohio 1849   Pvt. Md. & Va. Mil.
    m. Theresa Ireland — daughter Mary m. Thomas J. Cline

Ewing, Finis b. Va. 1773 d. Mo. 1841   Chaplain Tenn. Mil.
    m. Margaret Davison — daughter Margaret m. Ewing Sloan
    daughter Winifred m. Henry Rubey

Ewing, James b. 1784/9 d. 1876   Pvt. — packhorse driver
    m. Elizabeth Sutton — son Marquis m. Eliza J. Fouracre

Ewing, John b. S.C. 1763 d. Ind. 1828   Justice Peace Ind.
    m. Margaret Adair — daughter Isabel Ann m. John Skinner

Ewing, Robert m. Mary Ann Beymer   Vol. 33   Pvt. Ohio Mil.
    daughter Elizabeth m. William Chapplear

Ewing, Robert b. Va. 1760 d. Ky. 1832   Brig. Gen. Ky. Brigade—1812
    m. Jane McLean   Mem. of Ky. Leg. —1788-1814
    daughter Elizabeth D. m. Thomas J. Townsend
    daughter Mary B. m. Philip McDonald (Mary)
    son Ephraim m. Jane P. McIntyre

Ewing, Robert Allen b. Tenn. 1792 d. Mo. 1857   Corp. Ky. Mtd. Vols.
    m. Jane Ramsey — son Gilson T. m. Eliza Carolyn Jackson

Ewing, Thomas b. Pa. 1791 d. Ind. 1860   Ensign Ohio Mil.
    m. Elizabeth Levi — daughter Charlotte E. m. G. W. Mac Flynn

Ezell, Michael b. Va. 1764 d. N.C. 1809   Lieut. Va. 1795
    m. Priscilla Rives — daughter Elizabeth m. John Roper Wilson

F

Fagan, Robert Lanier   Vol. 6   Sgt. Tenn. Mil.

Fager, John   Vol. 5   Pvt. Pa. Mil.

Fahnestock, Henry b. Md. 1778 d. Md.   Pvt. Md. Vol.
    m. Catherine Latshow — son Benjamin L. m. Elizabeth Houpt

Failing, Daniel b. N.Y. 1792 d. N.Y. m. Susan Roof   Lt. N.Y. Mil.
    son Daniel m. Lydia Perrine

Failing, John b. N.Y. 1777 d. N.Y. 1850   Capt. N.Y. Mil.
    m. Maria Timmerman — son Henry m. Margaret Sailor

Failing John A. b. N.Y. 1792 d. N.Y. 1874 m. Jane Jordan   Pvt. N.Y. Mil.
    son John Wesley m. Eliza

Failing, Warner b. N.Y. 1786 d. N.Y. 1865   Pvt. N.Y. Mil.
    m. Elizabeth Stansel — daughter Ellen M. m. Joseph Webb Reade

Fairbank, Chester   Vol. 6   Sgt. U.S. Inf.

Fairbanks, Benjamin b. Mass. 1746 d. Me. 1828   Me. 1784-1800 Civil
    m. Keturah Luce — daughter Abigail m. Rufus Allen   Officer

Fairbanks, Calvin b. Mass. 1780 d. Vt. 1836   Capt. Vt. Mil.
    m. Jenny Ayers — son Calvin, Jr. m. Lydia Chamberlain

Fairbanks, Jason   Vol. 15   Lt. N.Y. Mil.

Fairchild, Lewis b. N.J. 1781 d. Lost on Sloop "Wasp"   Purser on
    m. Mary Amelia — son Lewis J. B. m. Anna Mathews   "Wasp" N.J.

Fales, Nathaniel b. R.I. 1720 d. R.I. 1801 m. Sarah Little   Rep. R.I. 1784
    son William m. Mary Smith

Fales, Stephen Smith b. R.I. 1783 d. R.I. 1839   Clerk in Supreme Ct.
    m. Phebe Wardwell — son Charles J. E.   R.I. 1814
    m. Susan James Usher

Fall, Henry Jr. b. Conn. 1791 d. Limerick 1831   Pvt. N.Y. Mil.
    m. Amy Bailey — daughter Lorina m. Henry Woodworth

Falls, William b. N.C. 1784 d. N.C. 1870 m. Sarah Dickson   Pvt. N.C. Mil.
    son Thomas D. m. Rachel Wells

Fancher, Thaddeus b. Conn. 1777 d. Ohio 1854   Sgt. N.Y. Mil.
   m. Sally Mead — son William m. Mary Vanscoy

Fancher William b. Pa. 1793 d. Ohio 1878   Pvt. Ohio Mil.
   m. Evaline Brown — daughter Mary Selina m. Joseph Bigelow Powell
   REAL DAUGHTER

Fannin, Francis   Vol. 14   Pvt. Md. Mil.

Fannin, Laughlin b. Va. c 1750 d. Ga. 1806 m. Winifred   Del. to Ga. 1795
   daughter Susannah m. Nathan Arendall   Const. Conven.

Fanning, Charles b. Conn. 1749 d. Conn. 1837   Rep. to Conn. Leg. 1792-
   m. Anne Brewster — daughter Sophia m. Charles C. Barstow   1814

Fant, George Buckner b. Va. 1790 d. Mo. 1843   Pvt. Va. Rgt.
   m. Ann Strother Ficklin — daughter Ann Eliza
   m. John Landy Deatherage

Fargo, Thomas (Turner) b. Conn. 1769 d. Conn. 1861   Pvt. Mass. Mil.
   m. Ann Comestock — daughter Armenia m. John Harris

Faris, William Jr. b. Va. 1772 d. (W.)Va. 1848   Lt. & QM. Ohio Mil.
   m. Susannah Curtis — duaghter Nancy m. Charles Blayney

Farmer, James b. Mass. 1780 d. Me 1823   Capt. Mass. Mil.
   m. Elizabeth Webb Sears — son William B.
   m. Emeline Janette Powe

Farmer, James R. b. Md. 1789 d. Ohio 1857   Pvt. Md. Mil.
   m. Margaret Robins — daughter Sarah Jane   REAL DAUGHTER
   m. (1) Alexander Nugent (2) Philip Uhrich

Farmer, John b. N.C. 1792 d. Ill. 1871 m. Mary Phillips   Pvt. N.C. Mil.
   son Nathan C. m. Mathilda Carr

Farmer, Joseph b. N.C. 1795 d. N.C. 1846 m. Mary Barnes   Pvt. N.C. Mil.
   daughter Susan m. Benjamin Lancaster

Farmer, Millis b. Va. d. La. m. Susannah McGowan   Sgt. La. Mil.
   daughter Elizabeth m. Solomon Feazel

Farmer, Samuel b. Tenn. 1784 d. Tenn. 1866   Pvt. Tenn. Mil.
   m. Sarah Childers — daughter Malinda m. Thomas Martin

Farnsworth, Alden b. N.H. 1785 d. Vt. 1849 m. Abigail   Sgt. U.S. Inf.
   daughter Hulda M. m. William Kingsley Dow

Farnum Jonathan   Vol. 5   Matross N.Y. Art.

Farr, Aaron b. N.H. 1775 d. N.Y. 1852 m. Polly Wilcox   Pvt. N.Y. Mil.
   daughter Lucy m. Jeremiah Wright

Farr (Pharr) Henry b. N.C. 1768 d. N.C.   Pvt. N.C. Mil.
   m. Margaret Bain — son Walter Smiley m. Jane Howie

Farr, Stephen b. N.Y. 1780 d. N.Y. 1872 m. Heiress Towne   Pvt. N.Y. Mil.
   daughter Alma m. Emory Steele

Farrand, Daniel b. N.J. 1764 d. N.J. 1829   Maj. N.J. Mil.
   m. Phoebe Plume — daughter Electa m. James Quinby

Farrar, Jesse Carter   Vol. 14   Pvt. Va. Mil.

Farrar, Joseph b. 1780 d. N.Y. 1852 m. Sarah Henry   Ens. U.S. Inf.
   son Solon m. Almira Jane Richardson

Farrar, Josiah b. Mass. 1780 d. N.Y. 1814   Ens. & Capt. N.Y. Mil.
   m. Elizabeth Briggs — daughter Sally Ann
   m. Woodbridge Cottle George

Farrar, Perrin b. Va. 1799 d. Ark. 1823   Pvt. Va. Mil.
    m. Rebecca Sampson — son John P. m. Sallie E. Jones

Farrens (Ferren, Farence), John b. Pa. 1791   Pvt. Pa. Lt. Inf.
    d. Ore. 1862 m. Nancy Hixon — son John Francis
    m. Eliza Ann Finley

Farrington, March b. Mass. 1762 d. N.Y. 1817   Drummer N.Y. Mil.
    m. Pauline Fitch — daughter Betsy Ann m. Henry More, Jr.

Farrior, John Jr. b. N.C. 1786 d. N.C. 1850   Pvt. N.C. Mil.
    m. Sarah Sandlin — daughter Mary Jane   Surveyor 1809
    m. Jesse Brown Southerland

Farrow, William b. Va. 1771 d. Ky. 1841   Maj. Ky. Mil.
    m. Elizabeth Shores — daughter Jane S. m. John Hillis

Fauble, John   Vol. 5   Cpl. Md. Mil.

Farwell, Absalom b. N.J. 1782 d. Me. 1854   Pvt. Mass. Mil.
    m. Lydia Washburn Prince — son Horatio R. m. Helen Amelia Ellis

Farwell, Jacob b. Mass. 1792 d. Mass. 1886   Sgt. Mass. Mil.
    m. Frances Pamelia Stratton — daughter Eliza Jane
    REAL DAUGHTER
    m. William A. Butts

Fassett, Benjamin b. Mass. 1757 d. Vt. 1816   2nd Lt. Vt. Mil.
    m. Mrs. Hetty Schenk Alvah — daughter Mary D. m. Gordon Hayes

Faulkner, Francis Sr. b. Mass. 1728 d. Mass. 1805   Mass. 1760-1797
    m. Rebecca Keyes   Town Clerk, Board of Action Chairman,
    son Francis Jr. m. Ann Robbins   Justice Mass.

Faulkner, Henry b. Va. 1773 d. Ky. 1850   Pvt. Ky. Mil.
    m. Frances Howell — son Jonas m. Nancy Bowen

Faulkner, James   Vol. 15   Maj. Va. Mil.

Faulkner, John b. Va. abt. 1755 d. Ky. aft. 1812   State Senator 1812
    daughter Susanna m. John Pennybaker

Faulkner, William b. Ire. 1755 d. Ohio 1834 m. Mary   War of 1812 Pa.
    son Anthony W. m. Lucy Higdon   or Ohio

Fauntleroy, Muse Sr. b. Va. 1757 d. Pa. 1839/40   Lt. Pa. Mil.
    m. Mary Jones — son Muse Jr. m. Susan Graham

Faurot, Isaac b. N.Y. 1790 d. N.Y. 1879 m. Sally Jaques Sgt. N.Y. Mil.
    son Abram m. Emily Frances Brooks

Fausold (Fassold), Jacob b. Ger. 1765 d. Pa. 1814   Pvt. Pa. Mil.
    m. Catherine Barbara Schriber — son Charles m. Jane Alexander

Fausold, Valentine b. Ger. 1765 d. Pa. 1824   Pvt. Pa. Mil.
    m. (2) Catherine B. Schriver (Schriber)
    son Charles m. Jane Alexander
    son George m. Mary Krieger
    son Henry m. Catharine Weiser
    daughter Sarah Ann m. George Zimmerman
    daughter Susanna X m. Abraham Wolf

Faust, John (Foust) b. Pa. 1785 d. Pa. 1861 m. Dorothy Cable Pvt. Pa. Inf.
    son Jacob m. Eliza Clark

Fay, Benjamin Jr. b. Mass. 1774 d. Mass. 1834   Selectman Mass.
    m. Beulah Stow — son William   1786-1792
    m. Elizabeth Crane Lankton

Fay, Lyman C. b. 1795 d. N. Y. 1839 m. Sarah Smith   Pvt. N.Y. Troops
daughter Mary Annis m. George Edward Hinman

Fayssoux, Peter b.—d.—   Midshipman U.S. Navy
m. Rebecca Irvine   Vol. 18

Feagin, Henry   Vol. 16   Pvt. Ky. Vol.

Feagin Henry b. Ky. d. Ind. m. Frances Colbert   Pvt. Ky. Mil.
daughter Joanna m. Nathan L. Jones

Feagles, Jacob Hallock b. N.Y. 1792 d. N.Y. 1862   Pvt. N.Y. Mil.
m. Susan Winans Roe — son Nathaniel R. m. Elizabeth Ryerson

Fearn, Robert b. Va. 1795 d. Ala. 1856   Pvt. Va. Mil., Tenn. Mil. 1812
m. Eliza Maria Henderson — son Robert Jr. m. Elizabeth Lee Coles

Fearn, Dr. Thomas b. Va. 1789 d. Ala. 1863   Surgeon (W.)Tenn. Vol.
m. Sallie Bledsoe Shelby—daughter Maria E.   REAL DAUGHTER
m. William Willis Garth
daughter Catherine E. m. Matthew Weaver Steele
daughter Lucie Lee m. George Miller   REAL DAUGHTER

Feaster, Andrew Jr. b. S.C. 1793 d. Fla. 1869   Cpl. S.C. Mil.
m. Mary De Saussure Norris — son Elbert H.
m. Caroline Matilda Teague

Feather, Isaac b. Pa. 1753 d. Pa. 1836 m. Mary Bickel   Lt. Pa. Mil.
son Solomon m. Christine Louise Greisemer

Featherston, Charles Henry b. Va. 1790 d. Va. 1868   Pvt. Va. Mtd. Mil.
m. Elizabeth Thornton — son Everard m. Marianne Goodwin

Featherstun, Burrell b. Va. 1784 d. Miss. 1874   Pvt. Va. Mil.
m. Rebecca Adams — son William m. Margarette Presgrove

Fee, George J. b. Pa. 1795 d. Iowa 1880 m. Mary Porter   Pvt. Pa. Mil.
daughter Sarah Ellen m. Isaac Harrington Brown

Fee, John b. Md. 1753 d. Mo. 1858 m. Elizabeth Meek   Lt. U.S. Art.
son Daniel m. Elizabeth Walker

Feeck, Jacob Jr. b. N.Y. 1772 d.—m.—   Pvt. N.Y. Mil.
daughter Margaret m. Peyton L. Farrell

Feelemyer, Francis b. Ger. d. Md. 1851 m. Julia A. Casey   Sgt. Md. Mil.
daughter Laura Virginia m. (1) Alfred J. Browne

Fegan, Daniel b. 1793 d. 1864 m. Magdalena Killinger   Pvt. Pa. Mil.
son Daniel Jr. m. Sarah Magd. Dutter

Feight, John (Fight), b. Pa. 1793 d. Pa. 1877   Pvt. Pa. Mil.
m. Sarah Lowery — daughter Maria m. Phillip Fisher

Felder, Daniel b. S.C. 1781 d. S.C. 1841 m. Rachel Young   Capt. S.C. Inf.
daughter Martha A. m. Henry Hitt Meredith

Felder, John b. S.C. 1793 d. Miss. 1875   Pvt. Miss. Terr. Mil.
m. Elizabeth Sandell — son Wyatt W. m. Sarah Curtis

Felker, Charles b. N.H. 1794 d. N.H. 1887 m. Polly Swain   Pvt. N.H. Mil.
son Hiram m. Betsey Dame Canney

Fell, Isaac b. Eng. 1758 d. Ga. 1818   Pvt. Ga. Guards 1789
m. Elizabeth Shick — son Frederick S.   Mem. of City Council 1812
m. Harriet Hoskins Nesler

Fellows, Abiel b. Conn. 1762 d. Mich. 1833   Col. Pa. Troops
m. Catherine Mann — son Elebias A. m. Sarah Smith

Fellows, Jonathan b. N.H. 1764 d. N.H. 1842   Pvt. N.H. Mil.
m. Eleanor Weeks — son Joseph m. Mary Ann Marks

177

Fellows, Moses b. N.H. 1755 d. N.H. 1846   N.H. Selectman
    m. Sarah Stevens — son Reuben m. Sarah Emery

Felps, Joseph b. Ga. 1796 d. La. 1839 m. Louisa Taylor   Cpl. La. Mil.
    daughter Laura m. George W. Munday

Felt, Jehiel b. Conn. 1769 d. N.Y. 1842   Capt. N.Y. Troops
    m. Mehitabel Davis — son Jehiel R. m. Sarah Jane Moore

Felton, Cornelius Conway   Vol. 6   Pvt. Mass. Mil.

Felton James b. Mass. 1738 d. Mass. 1804   Mem. of Gen. Ct.
    m. Sarah Houlton — daughter Susannah   Mass. 1801
    m. Samuel Kellogg Jr.

Felton, Skelton b. Mass. 1784 d. N.Y. 1851   Lt. Mass. Mil.
    m. Lucinda Adams — daughter Lucinda m. Charles H. Miller

Fenley, William b. Va. 1784 d. Ky. 1863 m. Mary Lewis   Pvt. Va. Mil.
    son William H. m. Elizabeth M. Ford

Fenn, Eli b. Ga. 1784 d. Texas 1840   Pvt. Ga. Vol.
    m. Sarah Fitzgerald — son John R. m. Rebecca Matilda Williams

Fenwick, Philip b. Md. 1789 d. D.C. 1863   Pvt. D.C. Mil.
    m. Mary Ann Stewart   Vol. 6

Fergus, Samuel b. Pa. 1763 d. Pa. 1853 m. Mary Paxton   Pat. Pa.
    daughter Margaret m. Thomas Maxwell

Ferguson, Andrew b. Pa. 1766 d. Pa. 1855   Ens. Pa. Mil.
    m. Hester Graham — daughter Eleanor G. m. Thomas Brown

Ferguson, Andrew b.— d. Va. 1880 m. Margaret Kelley   Cpl. Va. Mil.
    son Andrew C. m. (3) Mallissa Routh

Ferguson, Charles Wesley b. Va. 1792 d. W.Va. 1878   Pvt. Va. Mil.
    m. Lucinda Hoffman — daughter Kate m. George W. Johnson

Ferguson, Fergus b. 1798 d. 1836 m. Elizabeth B. Gooch   Pvt. Va. Mil.
    daughter Lucy Frances m. Thos. L. Disharoon

Ferguson, James   Vol. 3   Capt.

Ferguson, James b. S.C. 1782 d. Miss. 1847   Pvt. S.C. Mil.
    m. Rebecca Guthrie — son James E. m. Fanny Phillips Fitzpatrick

Ferguson, John b. N.Y. 1753/5 d. Vt. 1815   1st Rep. Vt. 1798-1809
    m. Chloe Case — daughter Hannah m. Jiet Delano Swift

Ferguson, John b. Mass. 1782 d. N.Y. 1872   Sgt. N.Y. Mil.
    m. Clara Wilson — daughter Lydia M.
    m. Albert Russell Ralph   REAL DAUGHTER

Ferguson, John b. Mass. 1740 d. Mass. 1792   Rep. Gen. Ct. 1789 Mass.
    m. Dorothy Hamilton — daughter Mary m. John Collester

Ferguson, Robert b. Ire. or Md. 1787 d. La. 1857   Pvt. La. Mil.
    m. Mary Bolling — daughter Mary Jane m. James Walker Draughon

Ferguson, William b. S.C. 1793 d. S.C. 1874 m. Mary   Pvt. S.C. Mil.
    daughter Elizabeth A. m. John Waters

Ferneyhough, Milton b. Va. 1785 d. Mo. 1852   Pvt. Va. Inf.
    m. Martha Edwards — daughter Sarah Ann H.
    m. James Thaddeus Webb

Ferree, Jeremiah b. Pa. 1782 d. Pa. 1856 m. Sarah Orr   Capt. Pa. Mil.
    daughter Mary m. William Orr
    daughter Sarah m. John Sharp Anderson

Ferree, Joel b. Pa. 1771 d. Ohio 1813   Lt. Col. Pa. Mil.
  m. Christianna Kuykendall — daughter Rebecca m. Andrew Bedell

Ferrell, Lewis Wells b. Va. 1796 d. W.Va. 1875   Pvt. Va. Mil.
  m. Martha C. Loving — son Garland T. m. Celina Webster Sexton
  m. Mary Wells — daughter Mary Etta m. William McClain

Ferris, Charles b. N.Y. 1790 d. Pa. 1877   Pvt. N.Y. Inf.
  m. Elizabeth Robbins — daughter Lydia A. m. William B. Haworth

Ferris, George b. Conn. 1791 d. Conn. 1874   Pvt. Conn. Mil.
  daughter Mary m. William Henry Peck

Ferris, Isaac Jr. b. Conn. 1768 d. Ohio 1844   Pvt. Ohio Mil. 1793
  m. Elsie Thornhill — son Isaac C. m. (1) Elizabeth Parmeter

Ferris, Jesse Owen b. N.Y. 1800 d. N.Y. 1891   Pvt. N.Y. Mil.
  m. Jane S. Edgerly — daughter Marian
  m. Henry Taylor, Jr.   REAL DAUGHTER

Ferris, Jonathan b. N.Y. 1779 d. N.Y. 1838   Capt. N.Y. Mil.
  m. Jane Ourer — son Jesse O. m. Jane S. Edgerly

Ferris, Peter b. N.Y. 1724 d. Vt. 1816 m. 2nd wife   Mem. of Vt. State
  son Squire m. Deidamia Callender   Assem. 1786

Fessenden, John b. Mass. 1729 d. Mass. 1793   State Senator 1787-1791
  m. Elizabeth Wyman — son Thomas m. Olive Dixon

Fessenden, John   Vol. 11   Pvt. Mass. (Me.) Mil.

Fessenden, William   Vol. 3   Pvt. Mass. Mil.

Fettyplace, William b. Mass. 1780 d. Mass. 1867   Owner Privateers
  m. Mehitable Story — daughter Mary L. F. O.   Mass.
  m. Lewis Endicott

Fickes, Isaac b. Pa. 1746 d. Pa. 1827 m. Rachel   Pvt. Pa. Mil.
  daughter Elizabeth m. David Dilbert

Fickett, Isaac   Vol. 8   Seaman Mass. Navy

Ficklin, Charles b. Va. d. Va. 1816 m. Mary Strother   Pvt. Va. Mil.
  daughter Harriett Drucilla m. Charles Morehead Johnson

Field, Aaron b. Mass. 1722 d. Mass. 1800   Selectman Mass. 1784
  m. Eunice Frary — daughter Chloe m. Samuel Shattuck

Field, Cephas b. Mass. 1785 d. Mich. 1861   Music N.Y. Art.
  m. Elizabeth Taylor — daughter Nancy m. William Pullen

Field, Harvey b. Conn. 1790 d. Vt. 1878 m. Persis Church Pvt. Vt. Mil.
  daughter Emily m. S. Newel Marsh

Field, John b. Va. 1763 d. Mo. 1833 m. Sarah Wood   Capt. Va. Mil.
  son James W. m. Elizabeth Yancy

Field, Joseph b. Va. 1791 d. Va. 1815 m. Elmira Wood   Cpl. Va. Mil.
  son Joseph Jr. m. Susan Frances Brown

Field, Peter, Jr. b. Conn. 1783 d. N.Y. 1847/8   Pvt. N.Y. Mil.
  m. Ann Aiken — daughter Mary
  m. Dr. Abram Thomas Van Gaasbeek

Field, Pliny Ashly b. Vt. 1783 d. N.Y. 1817   Pat. Vt. or N.Y.
  m. Olivia Babcock — daughter Caroline A. m. George Hedge

Field, William b. Vt. 1791 d. Mich. 1872   Pvt. Vt. Mil.
  m. Orpha Haskell — son William Lysander m. Mary Ann Scott

Fielder, Obediah Martin Benge b. Ga. 1789 d. Ga. 1857   Capt. Ga. Mil.
   m. Elizabeth Thornbury Heard — son Herbert
   m. Mary Telulah Blance(?)
   son James M. m. Roxanna Williamson

Fields, Miles   Vol. 15   4th Cpl. Ga. Mil.

Fields, William b. Ire. 1746 d. Ky. 1830 m. Mrs. Wright   Pvt. Ky. Mil.
   son Daniel m. Elizabeth Childs
   son Samuel m. Elizabeth Childs

Fields, William b. Va. ca 1791 d. Va. m. Mary Martin   Pvt. Va. Regt.
   daughter Mary m. John B. Fickle

Fiero, Christian (John Christian) b. N.Y. 1758   Mem. Town Meeting
   d. N.Y. 1826 m. Maretje Meier (Myer)   N.Y.
   daughter Ann m. James Halladay

Fiester, Jacob b. Pa. 1782 d. Pa. 1818 m. Mary Robb   Ens. Pa. Mil.
   son Benjamin m. Mary Sones
   daughter Susannah m. Isaac Shipman

Fife, William Jr. b. Pa. 1793 d. Pa. 1844 m. Mary Thomas   Pvt. Pa. Mil.
   daughter Nancy Jane m. Joseph Garretson

Fifield, Samuel b. N.H. 1772 d. N.H. m. Abigail   Pvt. N.H.
   daughter Betsey m. John Beedy

Figgatt, Spencer b. Va. 1772 d. Va. 1865   Pvt. Va. Mil.
   m. Mary Katherine Dodd — son Rutherford H.
   m. Sarah Jane Bridgland

Fikes, Michael b. N.Y. 1785 d. N.Y. 1859   Pvt. N.Y. Mil.
   m. Mary Fetterly — son George m. Jane Scouten

Fillebrown, Samuel Sprague   Vol. 9   Pvt. U.S. Inf.

Finch, Isaac   Vol. 4   Maj. Vt. Mil.

Finch, John W. b. N.C. 1793/5 d. Tenn. abt. 1830   Pvt. N.C. Mil.
   m. Judith Hockaday — son James M. m. Melissa Montgomery

Finch, Jonathan b. 1759 d. 1831 m. Jemina Ferris   Chaplain N.Y. Mil.
   son Joshua m. Betsy Clement

Finck, Andrew Acker b. N.Y. 1784 d. N.Y. 1872   Lt. N.Y. Mil.
   m. Delia Getman — son Edward m. Susan J. Mumford

Finck, Christian II b. N.Y. 1759 d. N.Y. 1841   Capt. N.Y. Troops 1800
   m. Elizabeth Suite — son Christian III m. Phoebe Clinton Rockwell

Finck, John Jr. b. Pa. 1789 d. Ohio 1842 m.   Drummer Ohio Mil.
   daughter Cecilia m. Edward T. Droege

Findlay, John b. Pa. 1766 d. Pa. 1838   Lt. Col. Pa. Mil.
   m. Nancy Brownson — daughter Mary B.
   m. Judge George Paul Torrence
   son William I. m. Sarah Hamilton

Findley, David b. Ire. 1762 d. Ohio 1849   Pvt. Pa. Mii.
   m. Jane Mitchell — son Abel m. Mary Irwin

Findley, Kenneth b. Scot. 1769 d. S.C. 1828   Pvt. & Spy S.C. Mil.
   m. Sarah Moffitt — son Kenneth A. m. Mary Coker

Fink, Johnston b. Pa. 1785 d. Ohio c 1850   Pvt. Ohio Mil.
   m. Susan Myers — son Henry m. Elizabeth Goldsborough

Finley, John b. Pa. 1748 d. Ky. 1837 m. Hannah Duncan   Maj. 1793
   daughter Betsy Ann m. Joseph Belt Faris

Finley (Findley), Joseph b. Md. 1766 d. Pa. 1860   Ens. Pa. Mil.
m. Frances Moore — daughter Jane M. m. John Power Woods

Finn, James b. N.Y. 1792 d. N.Y. 1857 m. Polly Lindsay   Pvt. N.Y. Mil.
daughter Frances M. m. John Clapp

Finnell, Charles Wesley b. Va. 1792 d. W.Va. 1878   Pvt. Va. Mil.
m. Lucinda Hoffman — daughter Ann Rebecca m. Henry S. Hayes
son Charles W. Jr. m. Lucy Evans
daughter Kate m. George W. Johnson   REAL DAUGHTER
daughter Margaret m. Jesse J. Fitch   REAL DAUGHTER

Finnell, Collin b. Ga. 1792 d. Ala. 1848   Pvt. Ga. Mil.
m. Nancy Ferguson Brown — son Adoniram Judson
m. Narcissa Durrett
daughter Julia Ann J. m. William Richard Hall   REAL DAUGHTER

Finnell, Jonathan b. Va. 1771 d. Ky. 1842 m. Rhoda Green   Sgt. Ky. Vol.
son Azariah m. Celia Jane Pullen

Finnell, Robert b. Va. 1777 d. Va. 1858 m. Martha Thorne   Pvt. Va. Mil.
daughter Sarah Margaret m. George Weaver

Finney, John   Vol. 17   Capt. Va. Mil.

Finney, Levi b. Vt. 1787 d. Vt. 1846 m. Orphal P. Clark   Col. Vt. Mil.
daughter Caroline F. m. William H. Barker

Fish, Samuel b. Vt. 1791 d. N.Y. 1859   Pvt. N.Y. Mil.
m. Betsey Londrey — daughter Sarah
m. William Hemstreet   REAL DAUGHTER

Fish, Uriah b. Conn. 1780 d. N.Y. 1863   Pvt. N.Y. Mil.
m. Lovina Carpenter — son Samuel m. Sally Crosby

Fishbourne, William b. Pa. 1760 d. S.C. 1819   Maj. Gen. S.C.
m. Mary Snipes — son Robert m. Harriet Chalmers

Fisher, Adams Jr. b. Ky. 1782 d. Mo. 1860   Pvt. Ky. Mtd. Vol.
m. Nancy Edwards Waller — son George W. m. Mary Ellen Crow

Fisher, George b. Pa. 1766 d. Pa. 1853   Capt. Pa. Mil.
m. Anne Shippen Jones — son Edward H. m. Hannah Sevelle Medicus

Fisher, George b. Md. 1782 d. Pa. 1848   Maj. Pa. Mil.
m. Christianna Hovis — son Benjamin m. Elizabeth Hildebrand

Fisher, George Frederick b. N.C. 1755 d. Ala. 1837   Col. Miss. Terr. 1813
m. Catherine Sosserman — daughter Mary m. Robert Haden

Fisher, Henry b. N.Y. 1756 d. N.Y. 1820 m. Sarah Babcock   Lt. N.Y. Mil.
daughter Elizabeth m. Robert Clark Maxwell

Fisher, Henry b. N.J. 1773 d. N.J. 1826 m. Mary Brokaw   Pvt. N.J. Mil.
daughter Ellen m. Sylvanus Ayres

Fisher, John b. Pa. 1762 d. Pa. 1815 m. Mary Alleman   Pvt. Pa. Mil.
daughter Elizabeth m. John Anderson

Fisher, John b. N.J. 1795 d. N.J. 1870 m.   Pvt. N.J. Mil.
son Louis m. Ann Moore

Fisher, John Boleyn b. Pa. 1768 d. Ky. 1870   Capt. Va. Mil.
m. Mary Leftredge Brown — son Robert H. m. Margaret Cessna
son Louis m. Louisa Davis

Fisher, Samuel b.—d.— m. Mary Ann Rouke   Sgt. La. Mil.
daughter Henrietta R. m. Jos. Lawrence

Fisher, Thomas b. Del. 1763 d. Del. 1835   Brig. Gen. Del. Mil.
    m. Elizabeth Evans — son Henry P. m. Mary Hazzard Young

Fisher, Thomas b. Pa. 1784 d. Wisc. 1852 m. Mary McGuire   Maj. Pa. Mil.
    son James m. Margaret Gordon

Fisk, Abraham   Vol. 14   Maj. Ky. Vol.

Fisk, Abraham J. b. N.Y. 1784 d. Ky. 1830   Capt. N.Y. Inf.
    m. (1) Sarah Peters — son Robert W. m. Mary Orpha Ransom

Fisk, Enoch b. Vt. 1796 d. Vt. 1884 m. Susan Muzzey   Pvt. Vt. Mil.
    son Seymour N. m. Betsey Noyes

Fisk, James b. Mass. 1763 d. Vt. 1844 m. Priscilla West   Mem. of U.S.
    son James Nathaniel m. Simona Smith   Cong. Vt. 1805-15

Fisk, Jonathan b. Mass. 1790 d. Ind. 1853   Ens. Mass. Mil.
    m. Susannah Williams — daughter Georgiana m. Washington Burt

Fisk, Samuel b. N.Y. 1794 d. Ohio 1879 m. Margaret Jack   Pvt. N.Y. Mil.
    daughter Bessie m. William A. Crittenden   REAL DAUGHTER

Fisk, William Robey b. N.H. 1779 d. N.Y. 1867   Pvt. U.S. Inf.
    m. Hannah Martin — daughter Sarah Frances m. Ebenezer Bush

Fiske, David   Vol. 3   Pvt. Mass. Mil.

Fiske, Ebenezer b. Mass. 1776 d. Mass. 1810   Mass. 1795-1802
    m. Dolly Gould — daughter Clynda   Hogreave & Surveyor
    m. Harvey Fuller

Fislar, (Fisler) John b. N.J. 1762 d. Ind. 1833   Pvt. Ind. War 1790
    m. Sarah Plascutt — daughter Elizabeth m. Joseph Brown

Fitch, Ephraim b. Conn. 1736 d. N.Y. 1823   Del. to Gen. Ct. Mass. 1788
    m. Lydia Root — daughter Lydia   Cons. Conv. 1779-1780
    m. Richetson Burlingame

Fitch, Frederick   Vol. 12   Surgeon N.Y. Mil.

Fitch, Gideon   Vol. 17   Pvt. Md. Mil.

Fitch, John b. Mass. 1758 d. N.Y. 1824   Lt. N.Y. Mil.
    m. Hannah Hollenbeck — daughter Lydia m. Richetson Burlingame

Fitts, Christopher b. N.J. 1791 d. N.J. 1828   Pvt. N.J. Mil.
    m. Mary Petty — son Jacob m. Eliza Dusenbery

Fitzgerald, Thomas b. N.Y. 1796 d. Mich. 1855   Cpl. N.Y. Mil.
    m. Mary Baldwin — son Jerome B. m. Isabel Sweet

Fitzgerald, William b. Va. 1749 d. Va. 1818   Capt. Va. Mil.
    m. Sarah Eppes — daughter Elizabeth m. Littlebury Jones

Fitzhugh, George b.— d. Va. 1819 m. Elizabeth   Sailing Mst. Navy
    daughter Eliza Virginia m. John Crawley

Fitzhugh, George b. Va. 1751 d. Va. 1810   Pat. Justice Va. 1788
    m. Humphrey Frances Toy Tabb — daughter Frances T.
    m. John Bolling Stith Fitzhugh

Fitzhugh, Philip b. Va. 1790 d. Va. 1836 m. Mary Aylett   Cpl. Va. Mil.
    son Thaddeus m. Laura Charlotte Sharpe

Fitzpatrick, Joseph b. Ga. 1788 d. Ga. 1830   Sgt. Ga. Mil.
    m. Nancy Hunter — daughter Julia Ann m. John Johns Fariss

Fitzsimmons, Caleb   Vol. 8   Pvt. Pa. Mil.

Flack, John b. N.Y. 1789 d. Ill. 1876   Pvt. N.Y. Mil.
m. Elizabeth Nelson — daughter Martha J. m. Harvey Downey

Fleming, Daniel b. Pa. 1761 d. Pa. 1819   Pvt. Pa. Lt. Drag.
m. Susanna Johnson — son Samuel m. Catherine Larimer

Flagg, John b. Mass. 1778 d. Mass. 1861 m. Sarah Ward Pvt. Mass. Art.
daughter Rhoda m. Darius Rice

Flanagan, Ambros b. Va. 1780 d. Ala. 1864   Lt. Va. Mil.
m. Diama Lodiase — son John Daniel
m. Maria Chewing (Mary Jane Robinson) ?

Flander, Jacob Clock b. N.Y. 1791 d. N.Y. 1876   Cpl. N.Y. Mil.
m. Angeline Lasher — son Walter m. Amanda Hase

Flannagan, William b. Va. 1781 d. Va. 1873   Pvt. Va. Mil.
m. Sarah Curd Johnson — son Benjamin m. Ann Timberlake

Flansbrugh, Jacob b. N.Y. 1788 d. N.Y. 1815   Pvt. N.Y. Mil.
m. Celia McKidney — daughter Ann Maria m. William Lunn Reston

Fleck, George b. Ger. 1748 d. Pa. 1836 m. Mollie Weeks Clerk of Ct. Pa.
daughter Catherine m. Daniel Crissman

Fleming, Daniel b. Pa. 1761 d. Pa. 1819   Pvt. U.S. Inf.
m. Susanna Johnston — son Mathew m. Eliza Caldwell
son Samuel m. Catharine Larimer

Fleming David L. b. N.J. 1781 d. N.Y. 1862   Capt. N.Y. Art.
m. Elizabeth Lanning — son Robert L. m. Laura Ilett

Fleming, James b Pa. 1797 d. Pa. 1878 m. Rebecca Lowry Pvt. Pa. Mil.

son Robert L. m. Martha E. Fleming(?)

Fleming, John b. Pa. 1780 d. Mich. 1863   Capt. N.Y. Mil.
m. Susanna Horton — daughter Mary Ann m. Silas J. Moore
m. Elizabeth Moore
son William m. Elizabeth Sullivant

Fleming, John b. N.J. 1789 d. N.J. 1850 m. Catharine Raub Pvt. N.J. Mil.
son David m. Mary Ann

Flesher, Isaac b. Va. 1796 d. Va. 1841   Pvt. Va. Mil.
m. Elizabeth Bonnett — son Andrew J. m. Sarah M. Weaver

Fletcher, James b. Va. 1758 d. Va. 1825 or 45   Pvt. Va. Mil.
m. Edy Bywaters and Mary Patterson
son James P. m. Philadelphia Menefee

Fletcher, John b. N.J. 1789 d. N.J. 1858 m. Hannah Wallace Pvt. N.J.
daughter Elizabeth W. m. John Cawman Eastlack

Fletcher, John Gould b. N.C. 1760 d. Ark. 1803   N.C. & Tenn. Indian
m. Mary Elizabeth Lewis — son Henry L. m. Mary Lindsay Fighter

Fletcher, Samuel b. Mass. 1745 d. Vt. 1814   Brig. Gen. N.Y. Troops
m. Mehitabel Hazeltine — daughter Valinda m. Foster Young

Fletcher, Thomas b. Va. 1749 d. Va. 1820   Sheriff Va. 1814
m. Elishea Drummond — son Thomas Jr. m. Elizabeth Wallop

Fletcher, Thomas b. 1780 d. aft. 1825   Mem. of Legis. 1803-06 Ky. Maj.
m. Nancy McIlhenney — daughter Margaret   Ky. Mil. 1813
m. William Temple Washington

Fletcher, William b. Mass. 1765 d. Mass. 1830   Pvt. Music Mass. Mil.
m. Lois Wood — son David W. m. Sarah Estabrook

Fletcher, William b. Mass. 1745 d. Mass. (Me.) 1819   Pvt. Mass. Mil.
    m. Sarah Parritt — daughter Sarah m. Amos Heald

Flickinger, John b. Pa. 1758 d. Pa. 1833   Pvt. Pa. Mil.
    m. Nancy Hanschy — daughter Mary m. Henry Stouffer

Fling, James b. Va. 1786 d. Ind. 1867 m. Rebecca Fluhart Pvt. Va. Mil.
    son George m. Margaret A. Thorp

Fling, Richard b.—d.—m.—   Vol. 17   Pvt. Va., Pvt. Lt. Drag.
    daughter Angeline Allene m. Charles M. Heller REAL DAUGHTER

Flint, Porter b. Mass. 1763 d. Ohio m. Lucy Farewell   Pvt. Vt. Mil.
    son Jacobe m. Eliza Aplin

Florence, William b. Va. 1774 d. Ohio 1870   Mem. of Legis.
    m. Fanny Robinson — son Robinson m. Elizabeth Williams

Flory, John (Johannes) b. Pa. 1761 d. Pa. 1827   Pvt. Pa. Mil.
    m. Elizabeth Illick — son Peter m. Mary Zeisloff

Flournoy, Thomas b. Va. 1775 d. Ga. 1857   Brig. Gen. Ga. Mil. 1812-14
    m. Sophia Davies — daughter Emily Agnes
    m. Joseph Stockton Canfield
    daughter Sarah Ann m. Charles Dixon Williams
    daughter Martha m. Dr. John Carter

Flower, Horace   Vol. 15   Capt. Ohio Mil.

Flower, Zephon b. N.Y. 1787 d. Ohio 1860   Sgt. N.Y. Mil.
    m. Margaret Glazier — son Hiram D. m. Mary Cheney Perry

Flowers, George b. Pa. 1786 d. Pa. 1839 m.   Pvt. Pa. Mil.
    daughter Mary Ann m. Joseph Blair

Flowers, William Wallace b. S.C. 1788 d. S.C. 1859   Pvt. S.C. Mil.
    m. Jeannette Colding — daughter Jeannette m. James Young Calhoun

Floyd, John b. S.C. 1769 d. Ga. 1839   Gen. Ga. Mil.
    m. Isabella Maria Hazzard   Leg. & Congressman
    son Henry H. m. Mordina Jane Boog
    daughter Mary H. m. Everett Hamilton

Floyd, John b. Va. 1789 d. Ill. 1848 m. Elizabeth Johnson Sgt. Ky. Vol.
    daughter Nancy H. m. William Harlan

Fluskey, John b. N.Y. d. N.Y.   Vol. 1   Maj. N.Y. Mil.
    m. Charity Horning (Haring) — son Lu (?) m. Emma R. Lincoln

Fly (Flye), John b. Mass. 1778 d. Me. 1819   Cpl. Mass. Mil.
    m. Lydia Hamilton Dodge — daughter Julia Ann
    m. George W. Philbrick

Foard, Joseph   Vol. 13   2nd Lt. Md. Mil.

Foard, Levi George b. Md. 1779 d. Md. m. Ann Bayard Capt. Md. Mil.
    son Richard J. m. Susan Jefferson

Foble (Fowble), William b. Ger. d. Md. 1816   Pvt. Md. Mil.
    m. Helen Marsilius — son John m. Mary Elizabeth Disney

Fogel, John b. Pa. 1774 d. Pa. 1838   Brig. Inspector Pa. Mil.
    m. Catherine Stettler — son Solomon m. Anna Stahler

Fogelsanger, David b. Fra. 1763 d. 1834   Pvt. Pa. Mil. 1784
    m. Gertraut Minich — son David Jr. m. Lydia Diehl

Foley, Moses b. Va. c. 1750 d. Ky. aft. 1823 m. Rachel Justice Ky.
    son Thomas m. Leanna Rector   1800-1820

Follett, Benjamin b. Pa. 1774 d. Ohio 1831   Lt. Vt. Mil.
   m. Mercy Noble — son Benjamin Jr. m. Emily Cultbertson

Follett, Martin Dewey b. N.Y. 1765 d. Vt. 1831   Capt. Vt. Mil.
   m. Persis Fassett — son Martin D. Jr. m. Lurania Winchell

Folse, Louis b. La. 1776 d. La. aft. 1820   2nd Lt. La. Mil.
   m. Rosa Roussel — son Pierre Honore m. Constance Boyer

Folsom, Benjamin b. 1788 d. Me. 1875 m. Charlotte   Sgt. Mass. Mil.
   daughter Josephine m. Allan McLean

Folsom, Isaac b. N.H. 1792 d. Ark. 1865   Sgt. N.H. Mil.
   m. Lucia Davis Morton — daughter Harriet
   m. Patrick Henry Childress

Folsom, Joseph b. N.H. 1775 d. Me. 1827   Pvt. Mass. (Me.) Mil.
   m. Deborah Sinnott — son Richard O. m. Isabella Patterson

Folsom, Nathaniel   Vol. 3   Pres. of Con. N.H.

Folts, Jacob C. b. N.Y. 1775 d. N.Y. 1831   Lt. N.Y. Mil.
   m. Elizabeth Steele — son Benjamin m. Jane Harwood
   daughter Dorothy m. John Edick
   son James m. Mary Piper

Folts, Melchert M. b. 1789 d. 1851 m. Catherine Herter   Pvt. N.Y. Mil.
   son Adam W. m. Helen Maria Alvord

Folts, Warner b. N.Y. 1777 d. N.Y. 1837   Pvt. N.Y. Mil.
   m. Elizabeth Getman — son Daniel m. Mary Getman

Fonda, Henry b. N.Y. 1766 d. N.Y. 1828 m. Hester Mabie   Maj. N.Y. Mil.
   son Henry Jr. m. Ann Veeder

Fontaine, Aaron b. Va. 1753 d. Va. 1823   Capt. Va. Mil.
   m. Barbara Terrell — son James m. Deborah Hobbs

Fontaine, Henry b. Md. d. Md. m. Mrs. Betsy Eyzey Bennett Lt. Md. Art.
   daughter Elizabeth M. m. Theodore G. Dashiell

Foos, Joseph b. Pa. 1767 d. Ohio 1832   Brig. Gen. Ohio Mil.
   m. Margaret Phifer — daughter Clara m. Thomas Rood Norton

Foose, Conrad b. Pa. 1745 d. Pa. 1820   Pvt. Pa. Mil.
   m. (2) Catherine Ruek? — son Jacob m. Mary Taylor

Foote, Avery b. N.Y. 1791 d. N.Y. 1867   Pvt. Music NY. Mil.
   m. Joanne Osgood — son Warren m. Rhoda Reed

Foote, Calvin b. Conn. 1785 d. Pa. 1879 m. Polly Burton   Pvt. Pa. Mil.
   son Lester B. m. Susan G. Scott

Foote, Clark b. Vt. 1791 d. Md. 1883 m. Harriott Bordman Cpl. Vt. Mil.
   daughter Harriott m. Louis L. Leggett

Foote, Justus b. Conn. 1781 d. Vt. 1829   Capt. Vt. Mil.
   m. Harriet Sylvester Graham — son Charles K. m. Sarah Lyon

Forbes, Colin Van Gelder b. N.Y. 1776 d. N.Y. 1865   Lt. N.Y. Mil.
   m. Eliza Bullock — daughter Amanda L.
   m. George Washington Gerard

Forbes, Jotham b. Mass. 1776 d. Ohio 1838   Surgeon Maj.
   m. Nancy Olmstead — daughter Frances m. Angus McKinley

Forbes, Silas b. N.C. 1782 d. N.C. m. Brittania Jones   Pvt. N.C. Mil.
   son John J. m. Elizabeth Bell

Forbes, William b. 1777 d. Ind. 1833 m. Rebecca Robinson   Pvt. Ohio Mil.
daughter Rebecca m. Jared Brush Mershon

Forbes, William G. b. N.Y. 1751 d. N.Y. 1840   Lt. N.Y. Mil.
m. Catherine Maria Van Gelder — son Colin V. m. Eliza Bullock

Forbis, (Forbes) James b. Va. 1755 d. Ky. 1839   Capt. Ky. Vol. Mil.
m. Sally Hubbard — daughter Martha m. Charles P. Taylor

Forbush (Furbush), David b. Mass. 1779 d. N.H. 1865   Lt. N.H. Mil.
m. Susannah Proctor — daughter Mary R. m. Richard Hayes

Force, Peter b. Pa. 1795 d. Pa. 1868 m. Elizabeth   Powder Boy Perry's
son John S. m. Elizabeth Hammer   Flag Ship Pa. 1814

Ford, Adam b. Mass. 1784 d. N.Y. 1830?   Pvt. N.Y. Mil. 1812, 1814
m. Susanna Heisey — son John C. m. Sarah Ann Coomes

Ford, Angustus Freeman b. 1783 d. 1857 m. Elizabeth Helt   Ohio Mil.
daughter Susannah m. Elijah B. James

Ford, Benjamin b. Eng. 1794 d. N.Y. 1854 m. Abby Pope   Pvt. N.Y. Mil.
daughter Jane m. Charles Edwin Platt

Ford, Charles Fleming b. d. Va. m. Patsy Butler   Capt. Va. Mil.
daughter Elizabeth K. m. John Swetman

Ford, Daniel Alden b. Mass. 1791 d. Mass. 1868   Sgt. Mass. Art.
m. Abigail Farrar — daughter Mary Catherine m. Jacob Bates

Ford, George W. b. Md. 1795 d. Md. 1887   Pvt. Md. Mil.
m. Elizabeth Ann Dorsey — son James D. m. Mary Hall

Ford, Ira b. Mass. 1787 d. Mass. 1841 m. Anna Sherman   Pvt. Mass. Mil.
son William S. m. Zilah Jeanette Myers

Ford, James b. S.C. 1775 d. Ky. 1833 m. Susan Miles   Capt. Ill. Terr. Mil.
daughter Cassandra m. Charles Henry Webb

Ford, James b. Va. 1778 d. Ky. 1856 m. Annie Newton   Pvt. Ky. Mil.
daughter Pauline S. m. William Parrott Stone
son Thomas R. m. Emeline Smith

Ford, John b. N.Y. 1784 d. N.Y. 1846 m. Clarissa Coe   Capt. N.Y. Mil.
daughter Ellen m. Samuel F. Kinney

Ford, Lemuel b. Va. 1788 d. Ind. 1850   Sgt. Ky. Mil.
m. Hannah McDowell — daughter Elizabeth m. Jesse Perdue

Ford, Mahlon b. N.J. 1756 d. Ohio 1820   Capt. U.S. Art.
m. Sophia B. Spencer — son George W. m. Isabelle Carothers

Ford, Warren b. Conn. 1787 d. Vt. 1866 m. Sally French   Pvt. Vt. Mil.
daughter Philinda m. Sidney Hervey Weston

Ford, William b. Va. 1788 d. Va. 1834   Capt. U.S. Inf. Va.
m. (2) Elizabeth Allen Hore — son Nathaniel W.
m. Margaret Ursula Waller

Ford, William W. b. S.C. 1785 d. Ky. 1841   Sgt. Maj. Ky. Mil.
m. Elizabeth Metcalf — daughter Elizabeth M.
m. William Hendricks Fenley

Fordham, Abraham Jr. b. N.Y. 1755 d. N.Y. 1810   Lt. N.Y. Mil.
m. Mehitabel Howell — son Merritt m. Mary Ann Harris

Foreman, Charles b. Pa. c. 1790 d. (W.)Va. 1834   Pvt. Pa. Mil.
m. Ann Parks — son Robert P. m. Roseanna Schaal

Forman, Elijah b. N.C. 1787 d. Ala. 1848   Pvt. Tenn. Mil.
   m. Catherine Strickland — daughter Sarah Ann m. Abraham Blevins

Foreman, John   Vol. 5   Pvt. Tenn. Mil.

Forman, John b. Pa. 1773 d. Pa. 1845 m. Catharine Eck   Pvt. Pa. Mil.
   son David m. Leah Seavers

Forman, John b. Pa. d. Ohio 1848 m. Willey Lewis   Pvt. Tenn.
   daughter Elizabeth m. Peter De Haven

Forman, William b. Va. 1773 d. Ala. 1850   Pvt. S.C. Mil.
   m. Elizabeth Owens — daughter Mary E. m. Robert George

Forman, William b. Va. d. Va. m.   Vol. 24   Pvt. Va. Mil.
   son Reuben m.

Forney, Adam b. Pa. 1780 d. Ohio 1861 m. Sarah May   Cpl. Ohio Mil.
   son David m. Eliza Jane Copelen

Forney, Daniel Morgan b. N.C. 1784 d. Ala. 1847   Maj. N.C. Art.
   m. Harriet Brevard — daughter Anna m. Samuel D. J. Moore

Forney, Peter b. N.C. 1756 d. N.C. 1834   Mem. House of Commons,
   m. Nancy Abernathy   State Senate Rep. in U.S.
   son Jacob m. Sabina Swope Hoke   N.C. 1794-1815
   daughter Mary m. Christian Reinhardt

Forrest, Archibald b. Md. 1780 d. Ohio 1857 m. Mary Hall   Pvt. Ohio Mil.
   son Joseph H. m. Vancaline Vance

Forrest, James b. Md. 1786 d. Md. 1845   Pvt. Md. Mil.
   m. Susannah Fenwick — daughter Maria T. m. Mathias Beal

Forest, John b. Va. 1783 d. Va. 1857 m. Harriet Morgan   Pvt. Va. Mil.
   daughter Delaney Haddison m. James White
   m. Mrs. Elizabeth Knight Miller
   daughter Susan Frances m. Alexander Marchant

Forrey (Furry, Furree), John Sr. b. Pa. 1734 d. Pa. 1787   Pvt. Pa. Mil.
   son Lawrence m. Miss Zingmaster   1787

Forester, John b. Pa. 1777 d. Pa. 1863 m. Mary Elder   Col. Pa. Mil.
   son Rheodore m. Amanda Bryan

Forster, John b.—d.—m.—   Brig. Gen. Pa. Vol.
   daughter Ellen Foster Bent   REAL DAUGHTER

Forsythe, Benjamin b. N.C. 1772 d. N.C. 1814   Capt. U.S. Rifles
   m. Bethina Hardin Ladd — daughter Elizabeth B.
   m. Samual Smalling

Forsythe, James Jr. b. Pa. 1756 d. Pa. 1850   Pvt., Sgt. Pa. Mil.
   m. Susannah Kuykendall — son Joseph m. Sarah Jane Covert
   son Benjamin m. Margaret Carroll

Fort, Robert Diggs b. N.C. 1795 d. Tenn. 1886   Pvt. Tenn. Mil.
   m. Elizabeth Ann Joyner — daughter Frances
   m. William Wallace Ware

Fort, Tomlinson b. Ga. 1787 d. Ga. 1859   Pvt. Fla. Vol.
   son John P. m. Tallulah Ellis

Fortier, Michel, Jr. b. La. 1750 d. La. 1819   Lt. Col. La.
   m. Rosa Aimee (Marie Rose Durel) — daughter Alcee
   m. Marie Lanauze
   son Louis Edmond m. Felicite M. La Branche

Fossett, John b. Md. 1786 d. Md. 1870 m. Arabella German   Sgt. Md. Mil.
daughter Zania m. William Hamilton

Foster, Abijah (Elijah) b. N.H. 1768 d. N.Y. 1814   Lt. Col. N.Y. Mil.
m. Fanny Rogers — son Daniel R. m. Electa Rich

Foster, Daniel b. Mass. 1776 d. Me. m. Phelena Pettingill   Pvt. Mass. Mil.
son Daniel Jr. m. Rebecca Eaton

Foster, Edward Jr. b. Mass. 1769 d. N.Y.   Maj. Mass. Mil.
m. Vise Shurtleff — son Otis m. Polly Nott

Foster, Ephraim H.   Vol. 10   Pvt. Tenn. Art.

Foster, Isaac Preston b. N.J. 1792 d. N.J. 1872   Sgt. N.J. Mil.
m. Rosena Diament — son Charles C. m. Eunice Sockwell

Foster, James b. N.Y. 1797 d. Iowa 1868 m. (1) Polly Hix   Pvt. N.Y. Mil.
daughter Julia m. James Butler

Foster, John b. Pa. 1788 d. Pa. 1860 m. Jane Fetz   Pvt. Pa. Mil.
daughter Rachel m. John Hankins

Foster, John II b. Border Md. & Va. 1771 d. Ohio 1832   Soldier Ohio
m. Mary Prather — daughter Nancy m. William Morgan

Foster, Jonas b. N.Y. 1792 d. Ohio 1883   Fife-Maj. N.Y. Mil.
m. Lavina Pierce — son Lemuel T. m. Susanna B. Alexander

Foster, Joseph Farnum b. N.H. 1784 d. N.H. 1844   Ens. N.H. Mil.
m. Mary Jewett — son Orin m. Harriet Mallard

Foster, Peter b. Va. 1780 d. N.C. 1840   Lt. N.C. Mil.
m. Elizabeth Keeble — daughter Mary Ann
m. Edward Taylor Fowlkes

Foster, Peyton b. Ky. 1791 d. Mo. 1872 m. Polly Daniel   Pvt. Ky. Mil.
daughter Jeanette m. Edmund Greenwood

Foster, Philip Hoyt b. 1790 d. Me. 1854 m. Patty Stanwood   Pvt. Me.
son Philip m. Carrie Woodworth

Foster, Ransom b. Va. 1783 d. Ga. 1856 m. Nancy   Sgt. Va. Art.
son Ira R. m. Mildred Creighton Crooks

Foster, Richard b. N.H. 1762 d. N.H. 1833   Pvt. N.H. Mil.
m. Sarah Greeley — daughter Susan m. Chellis Currier

Foster, Robert D. b. Va. 1795 d. Va. 1869   Pvt. Va. Mil.
m. Elizabeth Mitchel — daughter Amanda m. Joseph Moody

Foster, Stephen b. R.I. 1784 d. Ohio 1862   Capt. N.Y. Mil.
m. Mary Germond — son John H. m. Nancy M. Boardman

Foster, Thomas b. Ohio 1789 d. Ohio 1875 m. Sarah Raper   Lt. Ohio Mil.
son Joseph R. m. Susan Ricker

Foster, William Barclay b. Va. 1779 d. Pa. 1855   Dep. Comm. of Purchas.
m. Eliza Clayland Tomlinson — son Morrison   Pa.
m. Rebecca Shields Snowden
son Stephen C. m. Jane Denny McDowell

Fouke, Jacob   Vol. 11   Pvt. Va. Mil.

Foulk, Willis   Vol. 8   Capt. U.S. Inf.

Foulkrod, Philip b. Pa. d. Pa. m. Frances   Pvt. Pa. Mil.
daughter Barbara m. William Stoker

Foulks, Christopher b. Pa. 1771 d. Mo. 1845   Capt.
m. Margaret Crundy — daughter Elizabeth m. Joseph Liggett

Fowler, Alvin   Vol. 8   Pvt. N.Y. Mil.

Fowler, Archibald   Vol. 5   Pvt. Pa. Mil.

Fowler, Asa   Vol. 17   Pvt. Va. Mil.

Fowler, Charles M. b. Va. 1785 d. Ky. 1833   Sgt. Ky. Mil.
m. Lydia Heaton — son William m. Hannah Whitley Ashcraft

Fowler, Christopher b. Va. 1782 d. Va. 1816   Cpl. Va. Mil.
m. Constance Christian Oglesby — daughter Sallie S.
m. Edmund W. Harris

Fowler, Frederick William b. Conn. 1789 d. Ohio 1868   Pvt. Ohio Mil.
m. Mary Inman — daughter Sarah Elizabeth
m. William Usher Montgomery

Fowler, Israel b. N.Y. 1771 d. N.Y. 1852   Capt. N.Y. Home Guard
m. Ruth Reynolds — son Platt m. Emily Dean

Fowler, John   Vol. 3   Music Mass. Mil.

Fowler, Pexcel b. N.Y. 1772 d. West Indies 1830   Maj. N.Y. Navy
m. Anne Magdalene Aymar — daughter Hannah m. Daniel Talmage

Fowler, Samuel b. Ga. 1790 d. Ala. 1860 m. Eunice Pope   Pvt. Ga. Mil.
son Jefferson J. m. Georgia Hurst

Fowler, Trueworthy   Vol. 8   Pvt. N.H. Mil.

Fowles, Albert b. Mass. 1797 d. Mass. 1827   Cpl. U.S. Inf.
m. Harriet Dike — son Charles D. m. Susan Jackson

Fox, Angustus Carlton   Vol. 9   Lt. N.Y. Mil.

Fox, Charles   Vol. 14   Cpl. Md. Mil.

Fox, Daniel Christopher b. N.Y. 1777 d. N.Y. 1847   Adj. N.Y. Mil.
m. Elizabeth Lampman — daughter Ann m. James C. Adams

Fox, Daniel C. b. N.Y. 1783 d. N.Y. 1865   Adj. N.Y. Mil.
m. Margaret Hess — daughter Laney m. Jacob Winne

Fox, Edward b. Va. 1797 d. Va. 1837   Pvt. Va. Mil.
m. Emily P. Campbell — son Edward C. m. John Ella Carlton

Fox, George   Vol. 14   Pvt. Pa. Mil.

Fox, James b. Tenn. d. Mo. m.   Vol. 23   Pvt. W. Tenn. Mil.
son Elijah m. Sarah Ann Akard

Fox, John b. Ind. 1795 d. Ind. 1885 m. Katherine Miller   Pvt. Ind. Mil.
son John W. m. Anna J. Compton

Fox, Joseph b. Pa. c. 1795 d. Ill. 1879 m. Lois Jordan   Pvt. Pa. Mil.
daughter Beulah m. Jacob Casper Cain

Fox, Josiah b. Eng. 1763 d. Ohio 1847 m. Ann Miller   U.S. Navy
daughter Elizabeth M. m. Moses W. Chapline   Shipbuilder

Fox, Leonard b. Conn. 1792 d. Conn. 1866   Pvt. Conn. Mil.
m. Hannah Nicholson — daughter Eliza Ann m. Leonard Pitkin

Fox, Lewis b. Ger. d. Ohio 1855 m. Mary Weaber   Pvt. N.Y. Mil.
son Jacob L. m. Mary Shull

Fox, Nathaniel b. Va. 1763 d. Va. 1820   U.S. Inspector of Tobacco Va.
m. Mary Carver King — daughter Mary B. m. Bowler F. Cocke

Fox, O'Hara D. T. b. N.Y. 1793 d. N.Y. 1848   Sgt. N.Y. Mil.
m. Ellen Scott — son O'Hara D.T. Jr. m. Maggie Hardman

Fox, Stephen b. Conn. 1760 d. Ind. 1842 m. Mary Bates   Pvt. Ohio Mil.
son John m. Katharine Miller

Fox, William Jr. b. S.C. 1793 d. S.C. 1862   Pvt. S.C. Mil.
   m. Rebecca Huffman — daughter Caroline C.
   m. Archibald Campbell Williams

Foxworthy, William b. Va. 1753 d. Ky. 1837   Pvt. Va. Mil.
   m. Clarissa Calvert — daughter Charlotte m. John Fleming

Frailey, Jacob b. Pa. 1786 d. Pa. 1860   Cpl. Pa. Mil.
   m. Mary Ann Troyer — son Henry m. Frances Stoner

Frailey, Leonard   Vol. 6   Maj. Md. Mil.

Frambes, Job b. N.J. 1788 d. N.J. 1884 m. Hannah Irelan   3rd Lt. N.J. Mil.
   son Lewis S. m. Charlotte Irelan
   son Richard I. m. Mary Tilton

Frame, James b. Pa. ca. 1790 d. Ill. 1845 m. Mary Thompson   Pvt. Ohio
   daughter Mary m. George Rounsavell

Frame, John b. Va. 1778 d. Tenn. m. Sarah Wallace   Pvt. Ky. Mil.
   son Prior P. m. Susanna Young

Francis, Lewis b. Ky. 1790 d. Ky. 1855 m. Ede Kennedy   Pvt. Ky. Mil.
   son Joe m. Edna Kennedy
   daughter Susan m. John B. Francis

Francisco, James Anderson b. Va. 1786 d. Ala. 1839   Pvt. Va. Mil.
   m. Judith Woodson Michaux — son Robert L. m. Keziah Black

Frank, Nathaniel b. Conn. 1776 d. N.Y. 1824 m.   Maj. N.Y. Mil.
   son Eliza A. m. Lovader Lucas

Frankeberger, Jesse b. 1791 d. 1870   3rd Sgt. Ohio Mil.
   m. Rosannah Rinehart — daughter Jane m. Allen Hendryx

Franklin, Andrew   Vol. 13   Pvt. Ohio Mil.

Franklin, Anthony b. Va. 1778 d. Ohio 1859   Maj. Ohio Mil.
   m. Mary Nelson — daughter Maria m. John Spargur

Franklin, Benjamin b. Mass. 1706 d. Pa. 1790   Mem. U.S. Const. Pa.
   m. Deborah Read — daughter Sarah m. William Rache

Franklin, Eber b. Vt. 1791 d. N.Y. 1875   Pvt. N.Y. Mil.
   m. Martha Kimble — son George W. m. Diana P. Russell

Franks, Henry   Vol. 14   Pvt. Pa. Mil.

Fray, Isaac b. Pa. 1792 d. Ohio 1846 m. Mary   Pvt. Ky. Mil.
   son Samuel m. Sarah Tomblin

Frazee, Ephraim b. Ky. 1792 d. Ky. 1824   Pvt. Ky. Mil.
   m. Susan M. Doniphan — son Ephraim S. m. Frances E. Austin

Frazee, William b. N.J. 1763 d.— m. M. Bogardus   Pvt. N.J. Mil.
   daughter Rebecca m. L. W. Lowree

Frazer, James   Vol. 6, 10   Surgeons Mate Tenn. Vol.

Frazer, Jeremiah b. Va. 1776 d. Ky. 1852   Pvt. Ky. Mil. 1813
   m. Martha Walter — son James m. Catherine Turner Leavel

Frazer, Josiah   Vol. 11   Sgt. Md. Mil.

Frazier, James b. Mass. d. Mass. m. Eliza Hammond   Pvt. Mass. Mil.
   daughter Mary D. m. Francis B. Macker

Frazier, Jacob b.— d. Ohio 1843 m. Rebecca Morris   Ens. Ohio Mil.
   daughter Louisa m. Samuel Kesler

Frazier, James   Vol. 3   Pvt. Mass. (Me.) Mil.

Frazier, James E. b. Va. 1776 d. Ohio 1846 m. Sarah Evans   Pvt. Va. Mil.
daughter Phoebe m. Jacob Hoover

Frazior, Ebenezer b. Tenn. 1795 d. Tex. 1864   Cpl. Tenn. Vol.
m. Julia Franklin Titus — son Robert E. m. Mary Ann Olivia Stone

Frear, William b. Pa. 1792 d. Pa. 1874   Pvt. Pa. Mil.
m. Hannah Wheelock — son James m. Sarah Osterhout

Frederick, Lewis b. Va. 1755 d. Ind. 1826-1830   Pvt. Battle of Tippecanoe
m. Elizabeth — son Michael C. m. Mary Linda

Freeby, George b. Eur. 1778 d. Pa. 1854   Cpl. Pa. Mil.
m. Catharine Eckhardt — daughter Catharine m. Samuel Buell (Bull)

Freedley, Jacob   Vol. 14   Pvt. Pa. Mil.

Freeland, Egbert b. 1784 d. 1868 m. Sarah Goldsmith   Pvt. Md. Vol.
daughter Helen Augusta m. James Madison Scott

Freeland, (Freeman) John b. Ky. d. Ky. 1836 m.   Pvt. Ky. Mil.
son George W. m. Mary Robinson

Freeman, Ermund b. Conn. 1764 d. Vt. 1854   Capt., Maj. N.H. Mil.
m. Zilpha Poole — son Otis m. Mary Kimball

Freeman, George b. Mass. (Me.) 1772   Pvt. Mass. (Me.) Mil. 1790
d. Me. 1844 m. Tamson Richardson
daughter Judith S. m. Israel Atherton

Freeman, Israel b. N.J. 1791 d.— m. Anne Vorhees   Pvt. N.J. Mil.
son Edgar m. Mary Swan Tunison

Freeman, Jedediah b. N.J. 1773 d. Pa. 1861   Pvt. Pa. Mil.
m. Jeanette Jaques — son William m. Lucinda Spalding

Freeman, John b. Ga. 1793 d. Tex. 1864 m. Susannah Baker   Pvt. Ga. Mil.
son Robert F. m. Nancy Garner Willingham

Freeman, John b. N.J. 1786 d. N.Y. 1869 m. Lydia Briggs   Pvt. N.Y. Mil.
daughter Maryette m. Stephen J. Raymond

Freeman, John b. Va. c. 1756 d. Ga. 1806   Capt. Ga. Mil.
m. Catherine Carlton — daughter Rebecca m. Shaler Hillyer

Freeman, Joshua b. N.C. 1750 d. Tenn. 1831   Pvt. E. Tenn. Vol.
m. Lucinda (Lucy) King — daughter Temperence m. Reuben Grant

Freeman, Nathaniel   Vol. 8   Gen. Mass.

Freeman, Nathaniel b. Mass. (Me.) 1792 d. Me. 1869   Pvt. Mass.(Me.) Mil.
m. Eliza B. Hutchinson — daughter Mary C.
m. William Freeman (Relative)

Freeman, Samuel b. Mass. 1773 d. N.Y. 1819   Pvt. Inf. N.Y.
m. Mary Johnson — son Samuel Jr. m. Sarah A. V. White

Freeman, Timothy b. Mass. 1747 d. Me. 1823   Rep. Gen'l. Ct. Me.
m. Zurinah Nickerson Harroich   1804-1809
daughter Susannah m. Thomas Deane

Freeman, William b. Pa. 1796 d. Pa. 1872   Pvt. Pa. Mil.
m. Lucinda Spalding — son John S. m. Rebecca C. Culbertson

Freer (Frear), Jonas E. b. N.Y. 1790 d. Mich. 1854   Matross N.Y. Art.
m. Sarah Cooley — son Alva m. Phoebe Ann Streeter

French, Abel   Vol. 4   Pvt. N.Y. Mil.

French, Chauncey b. Mass. 1795 d. Ohio 1868   Pvt. Mass. Mil.
m. Cynthia Fowler — son Nelson m. Martha Bailey

French, David   Vol. 11   Pvt. Conn. Mil.

French, Ebenezer b. Mass. (Me.) 1789 d. Me. 1865   Sgt. Mass. (Me.) Mil.
   m. Sibyl Dutton — daughter Mary A. m. Moses Fellows Jr.

French, Elkanah b. N.Y. 1796 d. N.Y. 1882   Pvt. N.Y. Mil.
   m. Maggie Cronwell — daughter Agnes
   m. George Franklin Sibley   REAL DAUGHTER

French, Hains   Vol. 14   Maj. U.S. Army

French, Joel b. N.Y. 1780 d. N.Y. 1868   Pvt. N.Y. Mil.
   m. Sally Safford — daughter Thankful S. m. Lucius Whitney

French, John 2nd b. Conn. 1783 d. Conn. 1848   Capt. Conn. Mil.
   m. Elizabeth Rogers — daughter Ann S. m. Charles Henry Smith

French, Joseph b. N.J. 1767 d. Pa. aft. 1799   Pvt. Pa. Mil.
   m. Anna Robertson — son Daniel m. Amy Tingle

French, Leonard b. Mass. 1793 d. Wisc. 1856   Pvt. Mass. Art.
   m. Mary Wallace — daughter Bethia M.
   m. James Bennett   REAL DAUGHTER

French, Micah b. Vt. 1792 d. Ia. 1889 m. Azubah Purdy   Pvt. N.Y. Vol.
   son Micah Jr. m. Rebecca Hague

French, Nathaniel b. Mass. 1760 d. Vt. 1834   Pvt. Mass. Mil.
   m. Susannah Brown — daughter Lucinda m. Hezekiah Maynard

French, Noah b. N.J. 1754 d. N.Y. 1846 m. Mary Rolfe   Capt. N.J. Mil.
   son Henry m. Hannah Miller

French, Robert b. D.C. 1788 d. D.C. 1835   Surgeon's Mate U.S. Army
   m. Helen Dickson Gautier — son Robert S.
   m. Sarah Ann (Dobb) Evans

French, William b. 1787 d. Ohio 1836   Pvt. Ohio Mil.
   m. Elizabeth Davison — son George m. Elizabeth Atmur
   son Samuel D. m. Margaret Roberts

French, William b. Va. 1789 d. Va. 1822 m. Martha Taylor   Lt. Va. Mil.
   daughter Martha T. m. Layton James Hansberger

Freshour, Abraham b. Va. 1787 d. Ohio 1824   Pvt. Ohio Mil.
   m. Elizabeth House — son Abraham J. m. Juliana White Bryant

Frey, Peter b. 1792 d. Tenn. 1856   Pvt. W. Tenn. Mil.
   m. Evelina Hutchinson — daughter Zerilda m. Alex Robertson

Friend, Joseph Sr. b. Md. 1747 d. Pa. 1806   Mil. Substitute
   m. Rachel Rose — son John m. Elizabeth Fuffner
   son Jonas m. Mary Ann Rissler

Frier, Henderson b. N.C. 1775 d. Ga. 1835   Pvt. Ga. Mil.
   m. Delilah Williams — son Jarvis J. m. Nancy Williams

Frisbie, Frederick (W.) b. N.Y. 1789 d. N.Y. 1869   Cpl. Conn. Mil.
   m. (3) Polly Ludington — daughter Catherine E.
   m. Russell Granis Smith

Frist, John b. Del. 1789 d. Ohio 1847 m.   Pvt. Del. Mil.
   son John m. Susannah Stidham

Fristoe, Amos b. 1792 d. 1872 m. Susan Waller Withers   Sgt. Va. Mil.
   daughter Mary Jane m. Aaron Jenkins

Fristoe, Richard Marshall b. Tenn. 1789 d. Mo. 1845   Lt. E. Tenn. Gunmen
   m. Mary P. Sullivan — daughter Beersheba m. Henry Younger
   daughter Frances m. Dr. Lydal W. Twyman
   daughter Laura Matilda m. Reuten Harris

Fristoe, Thomas L. b. Va. c. 1775 d. Bef. 1817   Capt. Va. Mil.
   m. Lydia Wells — son Amos m. Susan Waller Withers

Fristoe, Thomas b. Tenn. 1796 d. Mo. 1872   Ens. Tenn. Mil.
   m. Nancy Johnson — daughter Susan m. Jordan Bentley

Fritz, Christian William b. Pa. 1744 d. Pa. 1797   Draftee Pa. Mil.
   m. Eva Margaret Dorwortan — son Valentine   1783-1790
   m. Susan Palm

Fritz, Martin Luther Jr. b. Pa. 1794 d. La. 1850   Pvt. Ind. Mil.
   m. Sara Johanna Huffman — daughter Catharine
   m. John Zebulon Vaughn

Froman, Paul b. Pa. 1776/8 d. Ind. 1866   Pvt. Ind. Regt.
   m. Keziah Pickett — daughter Mary m. Solomon Walden

Fross, Rufus   Vol. 14   Pvt. N.Y. Mil.

Frost, John b. N.C. 1770 d. Ala. aft. 1820   Capt. N.C. Mil.
   m. Rebecca Boone — son Ebenezer m. Elizabeth Gaither

Frost, John b. 1775 d. 1836 m. Rhoda Miles   Capt. Tenn. Mil.
   son Samuel Miles m. Harriet Hunter (Head)

Frost, Phineas b. Mass. 1792/4 d. Minn. 1869   Pvt. Mass. (Me.) Mil.
   m. Abagail Bean — son James C. m. Mary Airity and Sarah Sloan

Fry, (Frey) George b. Pa. 1781 d. Pa. 1850   Pvt. Pa. Mil.
   m. Anna Maria Sleeger — son George, Jr. m. Mary Spangler

Fry, Henry b. Va. 1738 d. Va. 1823   Del. to Va. Assy. Va. 1785
   m. Susanna (Sukey) Walker — son Wesley m. Susannah (Sukey)

Fry, Jacob   Vol. 15   Cpl. N.Y. Mil.

Fry, John III b. Pa. 1781 d. Pa. 1814 m. Sophia Cope   Pvt. Pa. Mil.
   son John IV m. (2) Mary Gibbs

Fry, Joseph b. Va. 1788 d. Va. 1866 m. Katherine Keckley   Pvt. Ohio Mil.
   son Eli J. m. Leah Finley

Fry, Michael b. Eng. 1758 d. Pa. 1856 m. Nancy Howard?   Pvt. Pa. Mil.
   daughter Catherine m. John Long m. (1) Katherine O. Kelly(?)

Fryback, John b. Pa. 1788 d. Ohio 1875   Sgt. Ohio Mil.
   m. Lititia Emerson — son James m. Mary W. Sharp

Frye, Abraham b. Pa. 1750 d. Pa. 1800 m. Agnes Ann   Pat. 1794
   daughter Christina m. John Snapp
   daughter Rebecca m. Joseph Foreman

Frye, Samuel b. Pa. 1778 d. Pa. 1833   Pvt. Pa. Mil.
   m. Elizabeth Van Voorhis — son Solomon m. Charlotte Scott

Fryer, John b. Pa. 1793 d. Pa. 1875 m. Sarah Mace   Pvt. Pa. Mil.
   daughter Sarah Ellen m. John K. Kerbaugh

Frysinger, George b. Pa. 1781 d. Pa. 1870   Mem. Assy., Capt. Pa.
   m. Elizabeth Ritter — son William m. Henrietta Stine   1813, 1814

Fugate, Levi b. Va. 1795 d. Ky. 1874 m. Haney   Pvt. Tenn. Mil.
   son Martin m. Elizabeth Smith

Fulk, John b. Va. 1776 d. Ohio 1858 m.   Pvt. Ohio Mil.
   Vol. 8

Fulkerson, John   Vol. 13   Lt. Va. Mil.

Fuller, A. Theodore Foster b. R.I. 1792 d. Ohio 1857   Capt. Ohio Mil.
   m. Mary Swain — daughter Harriet Augusta m. James A. Haskell

Fuller, Calvin P. b. Mass. 1782 d. N.Y. 1868   Sgt. Mass. Mil.
m. Mary Perry — son Daniel P. m. Nancy Crawford

Fuller, James b. Conn. 1788 d. Conn. 1894   Pvt. Conn. Mil.
m. Pamela Warner — daughter Dorianne m. S. W. Skinner

Fuller, John b. N.H. d. Me. m. Rachel Auld   Sgt. (Mass.) (Me.) Mil.
son Jason m. Jane McClintock

Fuller, John   Vol. 11   Pvt. Conn. Mil.

Fuller, John B. b. N.Y. 1783 d. N.Y. 1848   Pvt. N.Y. Mil.
m. Margaret Allison — son Nelson m. Pamelia Tupper

Fuller, John Smith b. Mass. 1789 d. N.H. 1865   Pvt. Mass. Mil.
m. Ann Guppy Hanson — son Edward N. m. Augusta E. Morrison

Fuller, Levi b. N.Y. 1782 d. Mich. 1865 m. Daraxa McLouth   Lt. N.Y. Mil.
son Thomas m. Emaline Richards

Fuller, Luther b. Conn. 1766 d. N.H. 1841   Pvt. N.H. Regt.
m. (2) Lydia Hutchins — son Peter C. m. Rebecca Blodgett

Fuller, Moses b. N.Y. 1783 d. N.Y. 1869 m. Sarah Neely   Pvt. N.Y. Mil.
daughter Elizabeth m. William Cupid

Fuller, Moses b. N.Y. 1784 d. Ill. 1878   Cpl. Ohio Mil.
m. Elizabeth Prillaman — daughter Clarissa m. Samuel Abner

Fuller, Perley b. 1782 d. 1856 m. Rebecca Rogers   Pvt. N.Y. Mil. 1813
son Richard m. Camilla Isham

Fullerton, James b. Scot. 1788 d. N.Y. 1872   Pvt. N.Y. Mil.
m. Susannah Barr — son Daniel m. Hannah Meech

Fulmer (Follmer), Jacob b. Pa. 1738 d. Pa. 1804   Pat. Rep. Pa. 1794
m. Anna Catherine Walters — son John m. Mary Haupt

Fulmer, Jacob C. b. N.Y. 1784 d. N.Y. 1848   Pvt. N.Y. Mil.
m. Mary Rasbach — daughter Nancy m. John Helmer

Fulton, Hugh b. Vt. 1759 d. Ky. 1816   Maj. Ky. Justice 1797
m. Jane Rogers — daughter Martha S. m. Joseph How

Fulton, James b. Scot. 1751 d. Pa. 1833   Mem. Pa. Assy. 1802-4
m. Margaret Miller — son James J.   Pres. Elector 1815
m. Ann Ramsey

Fulton, James b. 1763 d.— m. Agnes Thompson   Pvt. Pa. Mil.
son James m. Jane Hayes

Fulton, Mahlon b. Va. 1790 d. Ohio 1852 m. Jane S. Jett   Ens. Va. Mil.
daughter Sara Ara m. William Parker Collins   1814

Fulton, Philip b. Md. 1777 d. Ohio 1841 m. Sarah Hanna   Sgt. Ohio Mil.
son Philip S. m. Rebecca Belle Adair

Fulton, Robert b. Pa. 1765 d. N.Y. 1815   Mat. Aid U.S. Navy
m. Harriet Livingston — daughter Cornelia m. Edward Chas. Crary

Fulton, William Savin   Vol. 17   Cpl. Md. Mil.

Fults (Fulk), Peter b. Va. 1788 d. Ohio 1863   Pvt. Ohio Mil.
m. Frances Rankin (2) — son Jacob m. Catherine M. Glaze
son John m. Anna Any Bush

Funk, Abraham b. Va. 1770 d. Ohio 1848 m. Catherine   Pvt. Pa. Mil.
daughter Mary m. Isaac Hammell

Funk, Jacob b. Va. c. 1790 d. Ohio aft. 1854 m. Peggy   Pvt. Ohio Mil.
daughter Winnie m. David H. Dennis

Funk, Nimrod b. Va. 1794 d. Ill. 1879 m. Evey Leib   Pvt. Tenn. Mil.
daughter Rosa Jane m. John Newland Gray

Funk, Samuel b. Va. 1768 d. Ill. 1836 m. Elizabeth Cordell   Pvt. Pa. Mil.
son Jacob m. Milly Hassler
daughter Martha Jane m. Greenville Tankersley and John C. Gibbs
son Nimrod m. Evey Leib

Funston, John b. Pa. 1750 d. Pa. 1844 m. Mary Aten Pvt. Pa. Mil. 1784
son Jessie m. Sarah Templeton

Funston, Thomas b. Pa. 1789 d. Ohio 1859   Pvt. Ohio Mil.
m. Nancy Hubbard — daughter Nancy Elizabeth
m. James Marshall White

Fuqua, Nathan b.—d. Miss. 1852 m. Milly Carter   Capt. Tenn. Mil.
daughter Nancy m. William Henry Riggan

Fuqua, Peyton b. Va. 1783 d. Va. 1827   Pvt. Ens. Va. Mil.
m. Mary McGee — daughter Elizabeth m. Daniel Bayne

Fuqua, Samuel   Vol. 17   Pvt. Va. Mil.

Fuqua, William Sternin b. Eng. 1776 d. La. 1830   Maj. La. Mil.
m. Betsy Baker — daughter Sophy M. m. Nathaniel D. Fuqua

Furber, Richard b. N.H. 1753 d. N.H. 1848   Brig. Gen. N.H. Mil.
m. Mary Wingate Powers — son Pierce P. m. Mehitabel Winckley

Furlong, Thomas W. b. Mass. (Me.) 1793 d. Me. 1861   Pvt. Mass. Mil.
m. Elizabeth Jordan — son Benjamin m. Eliza Wylie Worthly

Furlong, William b. Mass. 1767 d. Md. 1814   Pvt. Md. Mil.
m. Sarah Johnson — son John m. Mary Ann Pawley

Furman, Jonathan b. N.Y. 1786 d. N.Y. 1863   Pvt. N.Y. Mil.
m. Dorothey Keeler — son Joseph m. Sarah Ann Morrell

Furney (Furneyhough), Milton   Vol. 10   Pvt. Va. Mil.

Furr, Paul b. N.C. 1786 d. Ga. 1867 m. Sarah Griffith   Pvt. Ga. Mil.
son Leonard W. m. Parthenia Lane

Furry, John, Sr. b. Pa. 1734 d. Pa. 1787 m.—   Pvt. Pa. Mil.
son Lawrence m. (1) Miss Zingmaster

G

Gabbert, David b. Tenn. 1793 d. Iowa 1855   Pvt. Ky. Mil.
m. Katherine Giles — son Henry m. Eliza Jane McGarvey

Gable, Harmon b. S.C. 1793 d. S.C. 1884 m. Mary Rampey Pvt. S.C. Mil.
son William m. Margaret E. Walker

Gable, John b. Pa. 1795 d. Pa. 1878   Pvt. Conn. Mil.
m. Margaret B. Fleming — daughter Anna E. m. David Hastings

Gage, Moses b. N.H. 1795 d. N.H. 1854 m. Polly Smith Pvt. N.H. Mil.
son Isaac m. Lydia L. Burrington

Gager, David b. Conn. 1784 d. Conn. 1853   Sgt. Conn. Arty.
m. Polina Bingham — son Rufus m. Matilda Dimon

Gaillard, Peter b. S.C. 1757 d. S.C. 1833   Capt. S.C. Mil.
m. Elizabeth Porcher — son Thomas m. Marianne Palmer

Gaillard, Peter b. 1782 d. S.C. 1815   Recognized Patriot 1813,
m. Elizabeth Gourdin   Mem. of House Rep. S.C.
son Alfred S. m. Addie Du Bose

Gaines, Bernard b. Va. 1769 d. Ky. 1839   Capt. U.S. Inf. Va.
    m. Sarah Force Cooke — son Gustavus C.
    m. Catherine Mary Cromwell, also Ann Gibson

Gaines, George Strother b. N.C. 1784 d. Miss. aft. 1813   Col. Ala. Mil.
    m. Ann — son George W. m. Eliza Earle

Gaines, James b. Va. 1742 d. Tenn. aft. 1830   Rec. Pat. N.C. Legislature
    m. Elizabeth Strothers   Pres. Elec. 4 Presidents Tenn.
    daughter Anna m. Richard Waggener
    daughter Elizabeth m. Samuel Moore

Gaines, James Taylor b. N.C. d. Tenn. 1821   Pvt. Tenn. Mil. Asst.
    m. Frances Gale Rogers — daughter Mary E.   Qr. Master
    m. James McKinney

Gaines, John Long b. Va. 1777 d. Va. 1827   Pvt. Va. Mil.
    m. Joanna Saunders — son Robert S. m. Rebecca Myers

Gaines, John P. b. Va. 1795 d. Oregon 1858   Pvt. Ky. Vol.
    m. Margaret Burnside Wands — daughter Catharine F.
    m. Homer Greene   REAL DAUGHTER

Gaither, Basil b. Md. 1721 d. N.C. 1802   Rec. Pat. N.C. Legis. 1788-1802
    m. Margaret Watkins — daughter Ellen m. Isaac Jones

Gaither, Frederick b. Md. 1768 d. Md. 1843   Capt. Md. Mil.
    m. Jane Gartrell — daughter Rebecca m. Nicholas Dorsey Warfield

Gaither, John b. Md. 1781 d. Md. 1860 m.   Sgt. Md. Mil.
    son John, Jr. m.

Galbraith, James b. Pa. 1743 d. Pa. 1802   Rec. Pat Surveyor Hyways
    m. Martha McClelland — son Samuel   Overseer of Poor 1787
    m. Ann Morrison

Galbraith, John b. Pa. 1739 d. Pa. 1802 m. Mary McColly   Capt. Pa. Mil.
    daughter Elizabeth m. Patrick Hays
    daughter Nancy m. Robert Stockton

Galbraith, Samuel b. Pa. 1767 d. Ohio 1841   Capt. Pa. Mil.
    m. Ann Morrison — daughter Elizabeth m. Matthew Steen

Galbreath, Benjamin b. Ky. d. Mo. 1868   Lt. Ky. Mil.
    m. Elizabeth Sanderson — daughter Maria Louise
    m. James Dickson Burns

Galbreath, Thomas b. Tenn. 1784 d. Ill. 1847   Pvt. East Tenn. Mil.
    m. Margaret White — daughter Eveline m. Sanford Harned

Gale, Peter Jr. b. Mass. 1780 d. Vt. 1851   Pvt. Vt. Mil.
    m. Hannah Tottingham — daughter Matilda m. James Henry

Gale, Summers   Vol. 6   Major Vt. Mil.

Gallaher, John Savage b. Va. 1796 d. D.C. 1877   Pvt. Va. Mil.
    m. Catherine Shannon — daughter Mary Helen
    m. George Edward Senseney

Gallaher, Philip b. Pa. 1793 d. Wisc. 1875   Pvt. Pa. Mil.
    m. Elizabeth Clark — son Joseph W. m. Elizabeth Dougherty

Gallaher (Gallagher), Thomas b.— d. Pa. 1821 m. Ann   Adj. Pa. Mil.
    daughter Martha m. William Johnson (Johnston)

Gallup, Erastus b. Conn. 1795 d. Conn. 1876   Pvt. Conn. Mil.
    m. Judith Rauthman — daughter Celia m. Joseph Gallup

Gallup, John Adam b. Conn. 1795 d. Ill. 1875   Pvt. Conn. Mil.
    m. Polly Barber — son Ralph W. m. Rebecca Reeder

Gallup, Russel b. Conn. 1791 d. Conn. 1869   Sgt. Conn. Mil.
    m. Hannah Morgan — daughter Sarah m. William M. Gray

Galpin, George b. Conn. 1781 d. Conn. 1870   Pvt. U.S. Inf. Conn.
    m. Content Hinman — son Joseph A. m. Caroline Goddard

Galt, Alexander b. Va. 1793 d. Va. aft. 1851   Act. Ass't. Apothecary Gen.
    m. Mary Silvester Jeffery — son William m. Mary Williams Ware

Gamble, James b. N.C. 1793 d. Tenn. 1875   Pvt. Tenn. Mil.
    m. Susan Beeler — daughter Sarah V.
    m. Capt. Charles William Coker   REAL DAUGHTER

Gamble, John Sr. b. Ire. 1760 d. Ga. 1817   Lt. Ga. Mil.
    m. Margaret Lawson — son James m. Mary

Gamble, Robert   Vol. 7   Pvt.

Gambrill, John b. Md. d. Md. m. Abigail Green   Pvt. Md. Mil.
    daughter Elizabeth m. Richard Watts Hook

Games, Gideon b. Md. 1792 d. Mo. 1846   Pvt. Ky. Mounted Mil.
    m. Abigail Toner — son Craig m. Patsy Craig

Gann, John Sr. b. 1775 d. Pa. 1842   Pvt. Pa. Mil.
    m. Catherine Christ — son John Jr. m. Adalene Cruse

Gano, John Stites   Vol. 5   Major Gen. Ohio Mil.

Gano, Richard M. b. N.Y.C. 1776 d. Ky.   Gen. Ky. Mil.
    m. Elizabeth Ewing — son John A. m. Mary Catherine Conn

Ganong, Jeremiah b N.Y. 1766 d. Ohio 1839   Pvt. N.Y. Mil.
    m. Elizabeth Townsend — son Jeremiah m. Rebecca Cole

Gansevoort, Leonard Jr. b. N.Y. 1754 d. N.Y. 1834   Rec. Pat., Del. to
    m. Maria Van Rensselaer   Congress, State Sen., Probate Judge
    daughter Elizabeth R. m. Theodorus Ross

Gant, Thomas b. Va. 1795 d. Ky. 1858 m. Marie Mott   Pvt. Ky. Mil.
    son James m. Mary Ann Steers

Garber, Michael III b. Pa. 1769 d. Va. 1845   Capt. Va. Mil.
    m. Margaret Smith — daughter Elizabeth M.
    m. William Adam Menzies

Garbutt, William b. Eng. 1786 d. N.Y. 1867   Lt. N.Y. Mil.
    m. Elizabeth Dow — son William D. m. Marion McVean

Gard (Le Garde), Gershom b. N.J. 1736 d. Ohio 1807, Capt. Ohio Mil. 1800
    m. Phoebe Huntington — daughter Jemima m. Peter Keen

Gard (Guard), William b. Pa. 1777 d. Ind. aft. 1834   2nd Sgt. Ohio Mil.
    m. Sarah Campbell — daughter Eliza W. m. James Henry

Gardiner, Benjamin b. R.I. 1750 d. R.I. 1819   Rec. Pat., Justice of
    m. Mary Howland — son John H.   Peace R.I.
    m. Hannah Dyer Allen

Gardiner, Jacob   Vol. 6   Musician N.Y. Mil.

Gardiner, James   Vol. 4   Pvt. Pa. Mil.

Gardiner, Lawrence Dempster b. Scot. 1794 d. N.Y. 1867   Pvt. N.Y. Mil.
    m. Sarah Anne Groot—daughter Sara L. (single) REAL DAUGHTER

Gardiner, Nathaniel   Vol. 4   Pvt. N.Y. Arty.

Gardinier, John S. b. N.Y. 1765 d. N.Y. 1817   Capt. N.Y. Mil.
   m. Jane Van Epps — son Charles m. Lucy Smith also Jane Starin

Gardner, Charles b. Conn. 1795 d. Conn. m.   Pvt. Conn. Mil.
   daughter Mary C. m. Alfred Hart

Gardner, Cullen Bryant b. N.C. 1788 d. Tenn. 1865   Qtr. Master Sgt.
   m. Sallie L. Franklin — daughter Mary Jane   Tenn. Mil.
   m. David Grant Herring   REAL DAUGHTER

Gardner, David b. Mass. 1786 d. at Sea—War 1812   Pvt. Mass. Mil.
   m. Polly Paine — daughter Olive m. Robert Clemons

Gardner, David Miller b. N.J. 1788 d. N.Y. 1867   Pvt. N.Y. Mil.
   m. Lucy Scott — daughter Minerva C. m. Elijah Cooley Odell

Gardner, Francis b. Va. 1787 d. Va. 1844 m. Ann Bell   Pvt. Va. Mil.
   daughter Sarah H. m. Henry Sterrett

Gardner, John b. Mass. 1764 d. Mass. 1829   Rec. Pat., Mass. Shipbuilder
   m. Hannah Sampson — son David m. Polly Paine

Gardner, John b. N.Y. 1791 d. Wisc. 1879   Pvt. N.Y. Mil.
   m. Elizabeth Smith — daughter Frances m. Jonathan Niles Fellows

Gardner, Julius b. N.Y. or Mass. 1793 d. Ohio 1854   Pvt. N.Y. Mil.
   m. Ruth Odell — son Daniel O. m. Amy A. Spring

Gardner, Nathaniel b. Conn. 1750 d. N.Y. 1829   Ens. N.Y. Mil.
   m. Sarah Jenkins — daughter Lydia m. Stephen Walker

Gardner, Samuel Knapp b. Mass. 1781 d. Mass. 1850   Pvt. Mass. Navy
   m. Mary Marsh — daughter Mary m. Nathan Bryant, Jr.

Gardner, William b. N.C. 1781 d. Miss. 1840   Pvt. Miss. Detached Mil.
   m. Mary Neal — son William, Jr. m. Eugenia Moore

Gares (Garis), John b. Pa. 1750 d. Pa. 1832   Pvt. Pa. Mil.
   m. Elizabeth Stout — son Abraham m. Sarah Smith

Garfield, Nathaniel Jr. b. Mass. 1793 d. N.Y. 1853   Pvt.—Drummer
   m. Charlotte Harwood — daughter Julia   N.Y. Mil.
   m. Amasa Harwood Martin

Garland, Christopher b. Va. 1752 d. Va. 1812   Rec. Pat., Mem. Va.
   m. Sarah Burton — daughter Mildred   House of Del. 1799
   m. Allen Howard Kidd

Garland, James   Vol. 9   Capt. Va. Mil.

Garland, James b. Va. 1722 d. Va. 1812   Magistrate 1783, Sheriff 1791
   m. Mary Rice — daughter Mary m. Col. James Woods
   son Nathaniel m. Jane Rodes

Garlin, John C. b. N.H.   Vol. 7   Pvt. U.S. Inf.

Garlington, James b. Ga. (Miss.) 1786 m. Sarah Jones   Pvt. Miss. Mil.
   son Moses D. m. Ann Moore

Garlock, Jacob b. N.Y. 1761 d. N.Y. 1848   Pvt. N.Y. Mil.
   m. Catharine Young — daughter Nancy m. Isaac Young

Garner, Samuel b. S.C. 1788 d. Ark. 1846 m. Rachel Pugh   Pvt. Tenn. Mil.
   daughter Elvira m. Chauncey Garner
   son William S. m. Mary Peppers

Garnett, Reuben   Vol. 12   Capt. Va. Mil.

Garnsey, Moses b. N.H. 1781 d. N.Y. 1851 m. Polly Grout   Pvt. N.H. Mil.
   daughter Rhoda m. Walter Woodward

Garrard, James b. Va. 1749 d. Ky. 1822   Col. Va. Mil.
   m. Elizabeth Montjoy — son William M. m. Matilda Ann Coburn

Garrard, James b. Va. 1773 d. Ky. 1838 m. Nancy Lewis Lt. Col. Ky. Mil.
   son Thomas L. m. America G. Coleman

Garrard (Gerrard, Jarod, Gerard), William b. N.Y. 1778   Lt. N.Y. Mil.
   d. N.Y. 1839 m. Mary Gertrude Johnston — son George W.
   m. Amanda Lent Forbes

Garrett, Francis E. b. Tenn. 1786 d. Ill. 1840   Pvt. Tenn. Mil.
   m. Elinor Blair — son Alfred m. Jane Hulett Graves

Garrett, James b. Va. 1775 d. Tenn. 1852 m. Martha   Pvt. Tenn. Mil.
   daughter Martha m. Littleton Vaughan

Garrett, Joab b. S.C. 1764 d. Ind. 1837   Pvt. Ind. Riflemen
   m. Rachel Harmon — son Thomas m. Catherine Cantwell

Garrett, John b. Md. 1794 d. Md. 1861 m. Eliza Drummond Pvt. Md. Mil.
   son John m. Anne E. Bean

Garrett, Joseph b. Va. 1784 d. Mo. 1855 m. Mary Rieger   Capt. Va. Mil.
   daughter Mary B. m. James Dawson

Garretson, John Connor b. N.Y. 1785 d. N.Y. 1875   Pvt. N.Y. Mil.
   m. Eliza Ann Lake — daughter M.E.D. m. Albert M. Holbrook

Garrison, Nehemiah b. Va. 1776 d. Ga. 1862   Capt. Ga. Mil.
   m. Sallie Evans — daughter Elizabeth m. John Evans

Garrison, William   Vol. 13   Capt. N.J. Mil.

Garrigues De Flaugeac, Antoine Paul Louis   Brig. General
   b. 1780 d. 1845 m. Marie Louise Fontenot   La. Mil. 4th Brig.
   daughter Marie Louise Irma m. Louis Felix Lestrapes

Garth, Jesse Winston b. Va. 1788 d. Ala. 1867   Lt. Col. Va. Mil.
   m. Unity Spotswood Dandridge — daughter Sarah D.
   m. Charles F. M. Dancy
   son William W. m. Maria Eliza Fearn

Garth, Thomas b. Eng. 1740 d. Va. 1812, Magistrate 1791, Sheriff 1807 Va.
   m. Judith Bowcock or Long — son Jesse m. Elizabeth Garth

Garwood, Jesse b. Pa. 1792 d. Ohio 1865 m. Sidney Gregg Sgt. Pa. Mil.
   son Bani m. Ruth

Gary (Geary), Thomas b. S.C. 1761 d. Ala. 1818   Pvt. S.C. Mil.
   m. Rebecca Jones — daughter Sara m. Charles Davenport

Gaskill, David   Vol. 5   Pvt. Ohio Mil.

Gaskill, Jonathan b. N.H. 1739 d. N.H. 1790   Rep. Gen. Court N.H.
   m. Hannah Estes — daughter Hannah m. Caleb Buffum

Gaskill, Silas b. R.I. 1743 d. N.Y. 1818 m. Sarah Jillson Rec. Pat., N.Y.
   son Wilder m. Lucy   elected Poormaster 1791

Gaskill, Wilder b. N.H. 1772 d. N.Y. 1822 m. Lucy   Rec. Pat., N.Y.
   son Stephen G. m. Sarah Lewis   Postmaster 1800

Gaskins, Spencer b. Va. d. Va. 1825 m. Mary   Pvt. Va. Mil.
   son Enrico m. Sarah Ann Hall

Gatch, Philip b. Md. 1751 d. Ohio 1835   Assoc. Judge Ohio 1803
   m. Elizabeth Smith — daughter Ruth m. Michael Swing

Gates, Ardel b. Vt. 1792 d. Maine m. Aurelia Hall   Pvt. N.Y. Mil.
   son William W. m. Fannie Stark

Gates, Charles Jr. b. S.C. 1788 d. S.C. 1871 m. Rose Reid   Pvt. S.C. Mil.
son Charles F. m. Susan E Ragsdale

Gates, Ezra b Conn. 1749 d. N.Y. 1841 m. Mercy   Ens. N.Y. Mil.
son Elijah m. Polly Walker

Gates, Jacob b. Pa. 1795 d. Pa. 1878 m. Mary Bowers   Pvt. U.S. Arty.
son Martin m. Anna Beamer

Gates, James R. b. Va. 1789 d. Va. 1871 m. Judith Forsee   Corp. Va. Mil.
son William B. m. Bettie Curtis Belcher

Gates, Lemuel b. Mass. 1758 d. Pa. 1806   Capt. U.S. Arty. & Engineers
m. Lydia (Bliss) Whitmore — daughter Lydia   1800/5
m. Joseph Denny Learned

Gates, Pearly (Perly, Purly) b. Conn. 1767 d. N.Y. 1813   Capt. N.Y. Mil.
m. Orpha Scott — daughter Sabra m. Enock Fobes

Gates, Robert   Vol. 8   Capt. Conn. Mil.

Gates, Silvanus b. Mass. 1748 d. Pa. 1836   Corp. Mass. Mil.
m. Elizabeth Graham — daughter Alpheus W. m. Orillo Bigelow

Gates, Timothy Minck, Jr. b. (Me.) Mass. 1777 d. Ill. 1844 Pvt. Ohio Mil.
m. Margaret Hughes — daughter Mary M. m. Seth Baker II

Gates, William b. Va. d. Texas 1829   Pvt. Ky. Mt. Mil.
m. Catherine Calloway — daughter Jane m. (2) Dr. Duke A. Perry

Gatewood, John b. Va. 1785 d. Ohio 1868   Pvt. Va. Mil.
m. Margaret Bryson — daughter Elizabeth m. John Choguill

Gatlin, John William b. N.C. 1780 d. Miss. 1820   Pvt. Miss. Vol.
m. Amanda Reeves — son William m. Angeline Allen

Gaugler, William b. Pa. 1793 d. Pa. 1870   Pvt. Pa. Vol.
m. Margaret Eyer — son Simon Peter m. Lorinda Jane Eastep

Gaumer, John Adam b. Pa. 1752 d. Pa. 1841 m. Regina   Pvt. Pa. Mil.
son John Adam Jr. m. Christine Wescol

Gautier, Samuel John Sinclair Fargis b. N.Y. 1785   2nd Lt. N.Y. Arty. Mil.
d. N.Y. 1845 m. Elizabeth Fawpell — daughter Mary Louise
m. Amedee Constance
daughter Eliza m. Cornelius L. Sidell

Gautier, Thomas Nicholas b. France d. N.C. 1848   Lt. U.S. Navy
m. Eliza Ann Brown — daughter Lucy J. m. John Kirkpatrick

Gaverick, John b. Pa. 1799 d. Pa. 1875   Pvt. Pa. Mil.
m. Regina Backenstone — daughter Elizabeth m. John Poorman

Gay, Apollos b. Conn. 1788 d. Conn. 1864 m. Lucy Pease Pvt. Conn. Mil.
son William P. m. (1) Harriet Louisa Clark

Gayoso, (de Lemos) Fernando b. Miss. 1797 d. La. 1837   Lt. La. Mil.
m. Victoria Lodoiski Perez — son Fernando Jr.
m. Zilphia Sunedricker

Gear, Hezekiah H. b. Conn. 1791 d. Ill. 1877   Sgt. Mass. Mil.
m. Charlotte Clark — daughter Charlotte m. George W. Girdon
daughter Clarissa m. James C. H. Hobbs   REAL DAUGHTER

Gearhart, John b. Pa. 1754 d. Pa. 1840 m. Catherine Gray Pvt. Pa. Mil.
son Isaac Elias m. Mary Magdalene Ream

Geary, James b. Pa. 1795 d. Ohio 1865   Pvt. Pa. Mil.
m. Margaret Provines — son Alexander m. Belinda Hillyer

Geary, Thomas b. S.C. 1761 d. Ala. 1818 m. Rebecca Jones   Pvt. S.C. Mil.
    daughter Sarah (Gary) m. Joseph W. Davenport also   1791
    Charles Davenport

Gebhart, Emanuel (also Gephart) b. Pa. 1788   Pvt. Ohio Mil.
    d. Ohio 1868 m. Elizabeth La Rose — son Noah L.
    m. Martha Cotterman

Geiger, Henry b. Pa. 1789 d. Ohio 1862   Pvt. Pa. Mil.
    m. Julia Ann Rhubush — son Levi m. Rosalinda Gleason

Geller, John b. Pa. 1789 d. Ohio 1880 m. Sarah Bainter   Pvt. Pa. Mil.
    son John H. m. Louisa Crawford
    son Milton m. Louisa Crawford

Gemmill, David b. Pa. 1780 d. Md. 1840 m. Margaret Wiley   Pvt. Md. Mil.
    son James m. Susanna Grim

Gendron, Jean Baptiste, Jr. b. Ill. 1770 d. Ill.1805/10   Militiaman Ill. 1790
    m. Marie Louise Boutillet — son Luke m. Marie Odeille Tullier

Gentry, David b. Ky. 1787 d. Mo. m. Susannah Maupin   Pvt. Ky. Mil.
    daughter Elizabeth m. Michie Maupin

Gentry, Reuben Estes b. Va. 1785 d. Mo. 1839   Pvt. Mo. Mil.
    m. Elizabeth White — son Joel W. m. Jael Woods Hocker
    son Richard m. Alzira Miller
    son William m. Ann Redd Major

Genung, Aaron b. N.J. 1787 d. N.Y. 1879 m. Rebecca Snyder   Pvt. N.Y.
    son Luther G. m. Phebe Banfield

George, Daniel b. N.H. 1785 d. N.H. 1844 m. Mary Bean   Lt. U.S. Inf.
    son Charles m. Margaret Warren

George, Isaac b. N.Y. 1788 d. N.Y. 1831   Pvt. N.Y. Mil.
    m. Debora Ann Hayes — son Isaac O. m. Harriet Lamira Storre

George, William b. Md. 1790/1 d.— m. Ann Price   Pvt. Md. Mil.
    son Washington C. m. Sarah Currell

George, William b. Va. 1790 d. W.Va. 1871   Pvt. Va. Mil.
    m. Nancy Easthern (Eastham) — daughter Kate m. H. S. Williams
    daughter Margaret Anne m. Rev. John Calvin Rece

George, William b. 1789-90 d. Ill. 1872 m. Nancy Hazlett   Sgt. Ohio Mil.
    daughter Mary m. James M. Ward

George, Woodbridge Cottle b. N.H. 1790 d. Mich. 1827   Sgt. U.S. Inf.
    m. Sally Ann Farrar — daughter Mary Caroline
    m. William Miller Cary

German (Germain), Obadiah b. N.Y. 1766/7   Brig. Gen. N.Y. Mil.
    d. N.Y. 1842 m. Ann Lewis — son Sutherland m. Mary Wiswell

Gernand, Christian b. Pa. 1746 d. Pa. 1824   Pvt. Pa. Mil.
    m. Magdelena Yost — son George m. Barbara Hain

Gerrish, Andrew b. Maine (Mass.) 1783 d. Me. 1834   Pvt. Mass. Mil.
    m. Rosannah Coombs — daughter Charlotte m. John S. Merchant

Gess (Gest), John b. Ky. 1774 d. Ky. 1849 m. Anne Winn   Pvt. Ky. Mil.
    son John W. m. Mary Ann Spurr

Getchell, Dennis b. Mass. (Me.) 1724   Rec. Pat., member General Court
    d. Mass. (Me.) 1792 m. Nancy or Margaret   Me. 1786
    daughter Lydia m. Joseph Boswell

Getman, Daniel b. N.Y. 1791 d. N.Y. 1881/2   Sgt. N.Y. Mil.
    m. Delilah Timmerman — daughter Anna m. Jeremiah Wait

Getman, Frederick Jr.   Vol. 6   Capt. N.Y. Mil.

Getzendanner, Jacob (of Adam) b. Md. 1760 d. Md. 1836   Capt. Md. Mil.
    m. Elizabeth Moyer — son Thomas G. m. Catherine Baer

Gibbens, Daniel Lewis b. Mass. 1786 d. Mass. 1853   Lt. Mass. Mil.
    m. Mary R. Howe — son Edwin Augustus
    m. Mary Elizabeth Chandler
    daughter Elizabeth m. William V. Taylor

Gibbons, William   Vol. 16   Pvt. Pa.

Gibbony, John b. 1790? d. aft. 1830 m. Miss Jones   Paymaster 47th Reg.
    daughter Mary Ann m. John Jefferson Dunn   Md.

Gibbs, David b. Conn. 1788 d. Ohio 1840   Pvt. U.S. Army
    m. Elizabeth Lockwood — daughter Sarah Louisa
    m. (2) William A. Mowry   REAL DAUGHTER

Gibbs, George W. b. N.C. 1785 d. Tenn. 1870   Capt. Tenn. Inf.
    m. Lee Dibrell — son Quesney m. Sarah Dorsey

Gibbs, Jonas b. Mass. 1762 d. Ohio 1834 m. Rachel Daniel   Pvt. Ohio Mil.
    son Jason m. Elizabeth Coonrod

Gibbs, Reuben Marshall b. Conn 1794 d. Conn. 1871   Sgt. U.S. Inf.
    m. Katherine Cole — daughter Sarah Eliza m. Turney Hall

Gibbs, Robert (Foster) b. Ky. 1794 d. Mo. 1868   Pvt. Ky. Mil.
    m. Fanny Pemberton — son John P. m. Mary Ann Rothwell

Gible (Givler), Henry b. Pa. 1765 d. Pa. 1835   Pvt. Pa. Mil.
    m. Rebecca Line — son David m. Mary Jane Eckman

Gibony, Andrew   Vol. 11   Corp. Mo. Mil.

Gibson, Abel b. Mass. 1784 d. "out west" 1828   Sgt. Vt. Mil.
    m. Achsah Puffer — son John A.
    m. Mrs. Mary Samantha Davis Hooper

Gibson, Alexander b. N.Y. 1790 d. N.Y. 1871   Pvt. N.Y. Vol.
    m. Caroline Stuart — daughter Eliza Ann May m. James N. New
    REAL DAUGHTER

Gibson, Charles b. Pa. 1750 d. Pa. 1803 m. Esther Graham   Pvt. Pa. Inf.
    son Charles Jr. m. Agnes Simpson

Gibson, Charles b. Pa. 1772 d. Pa. 1814   Pvt. Pa. Mil.
    m. Agnes (Nancy) Simpson — son Joseph Dean m. Ann Dunwoody

Gibson, David b. Va. 1795 d. W.Va. 1870   Sgt. Major Va. Mil.
    m. Ann Markee Van Meter — daughter Elizabeth I.
    m. John Park Wilson

Gibson, Jacob b. Pa. 1775 d. Pa. 1843 m. Jane Brush   Pvt. Pa. Mil.
    daughter Jane E. m. William Armstrong

Gibson, James b. Pa. 1775 d. Pa. 1854/5   Lt. Qrmaster Pa. Mil.
    m. Rebecca Knox — son John L. m. Martha Kirk Porter

Gibson, James b. Pa. 1776 d. (W.)Va. 1847   Capt. Va. Mil.
    m. Susan Gregg — son James D. m. Elizabeth Daniel Hurst
    son John T. m. Frances Williams Davenport
    son J. Gregg m. Susan Watters

Gibson, James   Vol. 8   Pvt. Md. Mil.

Gibson, John   Vol. 14   Pvt. Pa. Mil.

Gibson, John b. N.C. 1790 d. Ga. m. Sarah Messer   Pvt. N.C. Mil.
son Samuel W. m. Nancy Conley

Gibson, John b. Pa. 1784/6 d. Ill. 1872 m. Elizabeth Yates   Pvt. Pa. Mil.
daughter Maria m. James Marshall Trenary

Gibson, Robert   Vol. 13   Pvt. Ohio Mil.

Gibson, Samuel b. 1734 d. 1820   Selectman N.H. 1814, Supt. School Comm.
m. Elizabeth Stewart — daughter Margaret m. John Patten

Gibson, Thomas b. Ky. or Va. 1788 d. Ky. 1877   Sgt. Ky. Mil.
m. Elizabeth Cowan — daughter Elizabeth C.
m. Samuel Fulton Cowan

Gibson, William F. b. N.J. 1793 d. Va. 1858   Pvt. Va. Mil.
m. Nancy Longest — daughter Martha G. m. William Wyatt

Giddens, James b. Va. 1784 d. Tenn. 1818   Capt. Tenn. Mil.
m. Priscilla Buford — daughter Amanda S. m. Joseph H. Fry
son James M. m. Caroline Allen Thomason

Giddings, Joshua R.   Vol. 12   Pvt. Ohio Mil.

Giffin, David Doane b. Mass. 1766 d. N.Y. 1840   Capt. N.Y. Mil.
m. Jerusha Thompson — son Nathan F. m. Mary Galloway
son William C. m. Mary Dawson

Giffin, David   Vol. 14   Capt. N.Y. Mil.

Gifford, James   Vol. 16   Fifer N.J. Mil.

Gifford, James M. b. N.J. 1786 d. N.J. 1860   Pvt. N.J. Mil.
m. Christianna Sooy — daughter Hannah P. m. Joseph Scull
son Daniel E. m. Emily Frazier

Gifford, John   Vol. 14   2nd Lt. N.Y. Mil.

Gifford, Stephen b. N.Y. 1793 d. N.Y. 1866   Capt. N.Y. Mil.
m. Abigail Covell — daughter Sarah A. m. Sylvester Zeluff

Gifford, Stephen b. Conn. 1780 d. N.Y. 1865   Capt. N.Y. Mil.
m. Hannah Warner — daughter Delia m. Chester C. Blodgett
daughter Martha A. m. Roswell Woodruff Sherman

Gifford, Thomas Bethuel b. Pa. 1781 d. Pa. 1815   Pa. Navy, Mate on
m. Elizabeth Cline — son Samuel   Ship "Paoli"
m. Eliza Van de Bogart

Gilbert, Butler b. Conn. 1747 d. N.Y. 1827   Town Supervisor 1796
m. Abigail Woodhouse — son William m. Martha Greene

Gilbert, Peter b. Mass. 1796 d. N.Y. 1870 m. Eliza Skelton   Seaman N.Y.
daughter Louisa m. George Washburn   **REAL DAUGHTER**

Gilbert, Sylvester b. Conn. 1755 d. Conn. 1846   Rec. Pat., Mem. Conn.
m. Patience Barber — daughter Sophia   Legis. 1780-1812
m. Stuart Beebe

Gilbert, William   Vol. 12   Pvt. Tenn. Mil.

Gilbreath (Galbreath), Benjamin b. Va. 1787 d. Mo. 1868   Lt. Ky. Mil.
m. Elizabeth Sanderson — daughter Maria m. James Dickson Burns

Gilbreath, James b. Va. 1780 d. Ill. 1820   Pvt. Ill. Mil.
m. Isabella Findley — son John Randolph m. Caroline Amanda Hill

Gilchrist, John b. S.C. 1758 d. S.C. 1829   Pvt. S.C. State Troops
m. Mary Holmes — daughter Jane (Jincy) m. Lewis Glanton

Gildersleeve, Philip b. N.Y. 1757   Master Carpenter, Shipbuilder, Conn.
d. Conn. 1822 m. Temperance Gibbs   for Gov't. 1798
daughter Cynthia m. Edward Lewis

Giles, Harvey   Vol. 8   Pvt. Ky. Mil.

Gill, Nicholas b. Md. 1776 d. Ohio 1844 m. Mary Ambrose   Pvt. Md.
son Edward William m. Mary Catherine Waddell

Gill, Thomas b. Pa. d. Pa. 1849 m. Rachel McCord   Pvt. Pa. Mil.
son Robert m. Margaret Woods

Gillespie, David Lewis b. Va. 1783 d. Va. 1856   Pvt. Va. Mil.
m. Nancy King — son David W. Jr. m. Sarah Virginia Kelly

Gillespie, Henry b. Va. 1784 d. Ohio 1862   Pvt. Va. Mil.
m. Elizabeth Moody — son Benjamin m. Elizabeth May

Gillespie, Robert b. Ohio 1778 d. Ohio 1854   Pvt. Ohio Mil.
m. Mary Robinson — son Robert D. m. Carolin Bolser

Gillespie, Robert b. Ire. 1785 d. N.Y. 1850   Adjutant N.Y. Mil.
m. Martha Johnson — son Robert Jr. m. Henrietta Payne

Gillespie, William Cage b. Tenn. 1794 d. Miss. 1868   Pvt. Tenn. Vol.
m. Margory Bell — son George m. Alexena Lampkin

Gillet, Johiel b. N.Y. 1786 d. Mich. 1867 m. Martha Lakore   Pvt. N.Y. Mil.
son Paul W. m. Caroline H. Rogers

Gillett, Griswold b. 1780 d. Wisc. 1863   Sgt. Ohio Mil.
m. Clarissa Tracy — son Seth Augustus m. Melinda Pease

Gillett, Plumley   Vol. 9   Pvt. N.Y. Mil.

Gillette, Zaccheus Phelps b. Conn. 1776 d. Wisc. 1865   Sgt. U.S. Inf.
m. Clarissa Humphrey — son Charles L. m. Eliza Ann Hanna

Gillham, Samuel b. N.C. or S.C. 1778 d. Ill. 1826   Sgt. & Lt. Ill. Mil.
m. Anna Patterson — daughter Louisa m. Samuel Parker Gillham
(cousin)

Gilliam, Hartwell b. Vt. 1793 d. Ohio 1883   Pvt. Va. Mil.
m. (2) Sarah Townsend Routt — daughter Susan
m. Thomas Chestnutt   REAL DAUGHTER

Gilliam, Robert b. Va. 1740 d. Va. 1820   Rec. Pat., Trustee Va.
m. Lucy Shelton — son John m. Hannah Sampson

Gilliam, Samuel b. Va. 1774 d. Va. 1815 m. Susan Bolling Pvt. Va. Mil.
son John W. m. Mary C. Goodwyn
daughter Maria m. Thomas Claiborne Willson

Gilliland, Eli (Elijah) b. Tenn. 1784 d. Texas 1867   Pvt. Tenn. Vol.
m. Kesiah Haynie — son Haynie m. Sarah Jane McClellan

Gilliland, Samuel b. N.Y. 1776 d. at sea 1815   Asst. Surgeon U.S. Navy
m. Margaret Bleeker — daughter Mary M. m. William P. Magee

Gillis, Dougal P. b. Scot. 1795 d. Tenn. 1876   Pvt. Ala. Mil.
m. Sarah McFaddin — daughter Anna Belle m. John H. Sinclair

Gillis, Enos b. N.Y. 1788 d. Pa. 1854 m. Lucretia Hart   Pvt. N.Y. Mil.
daughter Jane m. Joseph S. Hyde

Gilmer, Campbell b. Ky. 1792 d. Iowa 1865   Sgt. Ky. Mil.
m. Martha Morrison — daughter Henrietta m. James Smith Welpton

Gilmer, George b. Va. 1743 d. Va. 1796   Magis., Sheriff, Del. House,
m. Luck Walker — daughter Susan   1784 Va.
m. Zachariah Shackleford

Gilmore, Arunah b. Vt. 1792 d. N.Y. 1855   Pvt. N.Y. Mil.
   m. Judith Whitcomb — daughter Sarah Eliza
   m. Rev. Judson C. Barber

Gilmore, George Washington b. Ga. 1794 d. Texas 1873   Pvt. Tenn. Mil.
   m. Nancy Newton — son Stephen Heard m. Frances Caroline Brown

Gilmore, James b. Va. 1750/5 d. Ky. 1822   Rec. Pat., Justice of Peace Ky.
   m. Martha McElwee — daughter Ann m. David Lee Woodstock

Gilmore, Rufus b. Mass. 1787 d. Me. 1872   Adjutant, Mass. (Me.) Mil.
   m. Julietta Metcalf Fairbanks — daughter Julietta M.
   m. George Peaslee Brown

Gilmore, Wm. b. 1760 d. 1836 m. Martha Lackey   Pvt. Va. Mil. (7th)
   daughter Agnes Nancy m. Jonathan Paxton   Corp. 39th Reg.

Gilruth, James b. Va. 1793 d. Iowa 1873   Qrtmster Sgt. Ohio Mil.
   m. Hannah Korms — daughter Hannah Helen m. Frederic Dudint

Gilson, Thomas b. Pa. 1765 d. Pa. 1813 m. Nancy Boyd   Pvt. Pa. Mil.
   daughter Nancy m. James Whitaker, III

Gist, Cornelius Howard b. Md. 1770 d. Va. 1830   Rec. Pat., Sheriff Md.
   m. Clara Reinecker — son Joseph m. Elizabeth Colver (Culver)

Gist, Rezin Hammond b. Md. 1787 d. Ky. 1834   Lt. U.S. Inf.
   m. Rachel Dawson — daughter Anna R. m. David Howell

Gist, Thomas b. Md. 1789 d. Md. aft. 1814   Pvt. Md. Mil.
   m. Edith Wheeler — son Thomas W. m. Harriet Ann Smith

Given, James b. Va. 1781 d. Va. or Iowa 1835   Pvt. Va. Mil.
   m. Elizabeth Graham — son John H. m. Cynthia A. Given
   daughter Nancy m. William Berry

Givens, John   Vol. 8   Pvt. Ky. Vol.

Givens, William b. Va. 1780 d. Ky. 1837   Pvt. Ky. Mil.
   m. Elizabeth Prather — son Mortimer m. Emiline Buchanan

Givens, William b. Ky. 1782 d. Ohio 1863   Sgt. Ohio Mil.
   m. Rachel Stockham — son Allen F. m. Mary Smith
   son William Jr. m. Elizabeth Elliott

Glascock, Scarlet   Vol. 13   Pvt. Mo. Mil.

Glascock, Thomas b. Va. 1796 d. Ky. 1872   Pvt. Ky. Mil.
   m. Elizabeth Asbury — son Albert R. m. Anne Elizabeth Parks

Glasgow, Hugh b. Pa. 1769 d. Pa. 1818   Mem. U.S. Congress
   m. Elizabeth Ramsay — son John   Pa. (1813-1817)
   m. Lydia Cooper Morgan

Glass, Henry b. Va. 1783 d. N.C. 1861 m.   Ensign Va. Mil.
   daughter Patience m. Joseph Jennings

Glass, James b. Ga. d. Ga. 1861 m. Sarah Arline   1st Lt. Ga. Mil.
   son Samuel B. m. Elizabeth P. Jordan

Glass, Thomas b. Va. 1792 d. Va. 1862   Lt. Va. Mil.
   m. (1) Catherine Wood — son William W.
   m. Nannie Rebecca Campbell

Glass, Willis b. Va. 1780 d. Va. 1835 m. Nancy Dupuy   Patriot
   son John Stephen m. Mary Terry

Glaze, Thomas   Vol. 15   Pvt. Ga. Mil.

Glazebrook, James Richard   Vol. 17   Pvt. Va. Mil.

Glazebrook, John   Vol. 13   Pvt. Va. Mil.

Glazebrook, Julius Caesar b. Va. 1752 d. Ind. 1837   Pvt. Va. Mil.
    m. Mary — son James R. m. Catherine Snead

Glazier, John   Vol. 5   Pvt. Pa. Inf.

Gleason, Elon b. Conn. 1786 d. Conn. 1873   Sgt. Conn. Mil.
    m. Sarah Belden — daughter Henrietta m. David M. Rogers

Gleason, Joel b. 1782 d. Wisc. 1864 m.   Ens. Lt. N.Y.
    daughter Annette m. Michael Jackson

Gleason, Salem b. N.Y. 1789 d. Kan. 1865   Pvt. La. Inf.
    m. Polly Houghton — daughter Nancy Marie
    m. Capt. W. Orvis Hubell

Gleeton, Thomas b. S.C. d. S.C. m. Kizin Bolen   Pvt. S.C. Mil.
    son Absalom m. Nancy Bonnett

Glenn, Thomas b. 1781 d. Ill. 1864   Pvt. Ill. Mil.
    m. (1) Malinda Milligan — daughter Nancy F.
    m. Robert A. Glenn (cousin)

Glenn, William   Vol. 6   Pvt. Pa. Mil.

Glidden, Arnold b. Mass. (Me.) 1754 d. Me. 1841   Pvt. Mass. Mil.
    m. Hannah Davis — daughter Hannah m. Samuel Sewell Cram

Glidden, John b. (Me.) Mass. 1790 d. Me. 1864   Capt. Mass. (Me.) Mil.
    m. Mary Jordan Lorett — son Sam G. m. Martha A. H. Fisher

Glines, Benjamin b. N.H. 1764 d. 1813 in battle N.Y.   Pvt. N.H.
    m. Love Leavitt — son David m. Matilda Rowe

Glisson, Daniel b. N.C. 1759 d. N.C. 1830   Rec. Pat., 1794 State Legis. N.C.
    m. Elizabeth Herring — daughter Sarah m. George F. Kornegay

Glover, Chesley b Va. 1761 d. Ky. 1829   Pvt. Ky. Vol.
    m. Mary Guerrant — daughter Ann m. William Smart

Glover, Nathan b. Ohio 1786 d. Ohio m. Mary Jones   Sgt. Ohio Mil.
    son John M. m. Isabelle Hannah Miller

Glover, Philip b. Md. 1795 d. Ore. 1872 m. Sarah Koontz   Pvt. Md. Mil.
    son Charles P. m. Clarissa Palmer

Glover, Samuel   Vol. 15   Pvt. Md. Mil.

Goddard, Calvin b. Mass. 1768 d. Conn. 1842   Rec. Pat., Mem. Conn.
    m. Alice C. Hart — son George C.   Legis., Mem. Congress
    m. Catherine Staples

Goddard, Edward b. Md. d. D.C. 1833   Vol. 6   Pvt. D.C. Mil.

Goddard, Hezekiah b. Mass. 1771 d. Conn. 1851   Qtrmster Gen. Conn. Mil.
    m. Phoebe Halsey — daughter Paulina m. John Mason

Goddard, James   Vol. 16   Pvt. Va. Mil.

Goddard, James Thomas b. Va. 1793 d. Ill. 1877   Pvt. Va. Mil.
    m. Maria Davis McHaney — son James T. Jr. m. Winifred Spiller

Goddin, John Jr. b. Va. 1780 d. Va. 1865   Sgt. Va. Mil.
    m. Rozanna Ford — son Adolphus m. Martha Isabella Syme

Godfrey, Andrew b. N.J. 1791 d. N.Y. 1867   Capt. N.J. Mil.
    m. Sarah Stephenson — daughter Mary m. David Budd Hallinger

Godfrey, Benjamin b. S.C. 1789 d. S.C. 1852 m. Rachel Hart   Sgt. S.C. Mil.
    son James W. m. Eleanor Crodes

Godfrey, John b. Mass. 1754 d. Mass. 1827/9   Vol. 8   Pvt. Mass. Mil.

Godfrey, Richard   Vol. 5   Pvt. N.Y. Mil.

Godfrey, Richard b. N.Y. 1776 d. N.Y. 1817   Capt. N.Y. Mil.
     m. Elizabeth Brownell — daughter Mary m. Ira Camp

Godfrey, Robert b. Va. 1788 d. Ky. 1859 m. Eleanor Payne   Pvt. Ky. Inf.
     daughter Sarah Ellen m. James Monroe Hammond

Godwin, Robert b. Va. 1794 d. W.Va. 1874 m. Mary Barb   Pvt. Va. Mil.
     daughter Nancy Ann m. Abraham Loar   REAL DAUGHTER

Goff, Elisha b. Ky. 1795 d. Ky. 1831 m. Nancy Hedges   Pvt. Ky. Mil.
     son John H. m. Martha Chandler Prewitt

Goff, Hezekiah b. Conn. 1753/4 d. Vt. 1848   Pvt. Vt. Mil. 1813
     m. Annah Ward — daughter Clarissa m. Bradford Powell

Goff, Hiram b. Va. 1779 d. Va. 1840 m. Margaret Rush   Major W.Va. Mil.
     son John R. m. Eunice Johnson

Goff, Salathiel b. Germany 1748 d. Va. 1791   Rec. Pat., Va. Justice of Peace
     m. Elizabeth Gray — daughter Nancy Ann m. Benjamin Riddel

Goiare (Gior, Guyer), Joseph b. Detroit 1775 d. Mich. 1879   Pvt. Mich. Mil.
     m. Mary Burg — son Oliver m. Elizabeth Ragan
     son Eli m. Jane Phillips

Gold, Daniel b. Va. 1768 d. N.C. 1851 m. Miss Griffin   Mem. House of
     son Milton m. Martha Fourtune   Commons, Justice of Peace N.C.

Golden, Daniel b. N.Y. 1774 d. N.Y. m. Mary Perkins   Sgt. N.Y. Mil.
     son Ezra m. Harriet Day

Goldsborough, Robert b. Va. 1795 d. Ohio 1840   Pvt. Va. Mil.
     m. Catharine Corbin — daughter Elizabeth m. Henry Fink

Goldsbury, William b. Mass. 1762 d. Vt. 1815   Pvt. Vt. Mil.
     m. Bathsheba Walker — son Joel m. Charlotte Collyer

Goldsmith, Nathaniel b. N.H. 1780 d. Mass. 1845   Boatswain on
     m. Nancy Taylor — daughter Elizabeth S.   "Rattlesnake"
     m. William Henry Clough   P.O.W. 1814

Goldthwaite, Sylvester b. N.Y. 1789 d. N.Y. 1875   N.Y. Mil. Drummer
     m. Elizabeth Peck — daughter Benoni m. Lamar Clark

Gollahon, Robert b. N.C. 1780 d. Va. 1843 m. Ann Tilson   Pvt. Va. Mil.
     daughter Mary m. Joseph Park Bonham

Good, Jacob b. Pa. 1791 d. Pa. 1881   Pvt. Pa. Mil.
     m. Elizabeth Cortright — son Charles m. C. Adelaide

Goodale, Isaac b. Mass. 1732 d. Mass. 1808 m. Huldah Burt   Rec. Patriot
     son Isaac Jr. m. Jemima Warner

Goodall, Nathaniel b. Vt. 1796 d. Wisc. 1883   Pvt. N.Y. Mil.
     m. Fanny Kent — son Louis K. m. Eva Pamela Jencks

Goode, Philip b. Va. 1745 d. Va. 1821 m. Ann Jones   Pvt. Va. Mil.
     son Thomas m. Elise Royal Jones

Goode, Richard b. Va. or N.C. 1762 or 1780 d. Ky. 1846 m.   Pvt. Ky. Mil.
     son Robert H. m. Mattie Ann Stafford

Goode, William b. Va. 1778 d. Mo. 1844 m. Polly Cabell   Rec. Pat., Mem.
     daughter Elizabeth R. m. Matthias Smith Link   Ky. Legis. 1815

Goodell, Roswell   Vol. 10   Corp. Conn. Mil.

Goodenough, David b. N.Y. 1735 d. N.Y. 1814   Pvt. N.Y. Mil.
   m. Abigail Rice — daughter Polly m. Corning Dalrymple

Goodhue, James b. Mass. 1789 d. Ind. 1852   Ens. U.S. Inf.
   m. Rebecca Bosworth — daughter Mary Martha m. Alexander Dixon

Goodhue, Richard Shatswell b. Mass. 1794   Pvt. Mass. (Me.) Mil.
   d. Me. 1856 m. Sarah W. Quincy — son Daniel m. Eleanor Heseltine

Goodman, John b. Pa. 1762 d. Ohio 1830   Capt. Pa. Mil.
   m. Charlotte Shuck — son David m. Elizabeth Cullum

Goodman, John b. Pa. 1763 d. Pa. 1856   Rec. Pat., Mem. Pa. Legis. 1813
   m. Katherine Hyneman — daughter Charlotte m. John Whiteman

Goodman, John Davidson   Vol. 15   Seaman Md. Navy

Goodman, Moses   Vol. 6   Capt. Conn. Mil.

Goodner, James b. Tenn. 1792 d. Tenn. 1883   Corp. Tenn. Mil.
   m. Martha Fite — son Thomas C. m. Jennie (Goodner?)

Goodnight, John b. 1788 d. 1845 m. Margaret   Pvt. N.C. 7th Reg.
   son Abraham Goodnight m. Lydie Brian

Goodnight, John b. Ky. 1794 d. Ill. 1879 m. Agnes Jones   Pvt. Ky. Mil.
   son Thomas m. Susan Pittman

Goodnight, John b. Va. 1765 d. Ky. 1841 m. Ruth Davis   Pvt. Ky. Mil.
   son Michael m. Comfort McCormick

Goodnight, Michael b. Ky. 1789 d. Mo. 1861   Pvt. Ky. Inf.
   m. Comfort McCormack — daughter Nancy m. Milton Durrell

Goodnough, Calvin b. 1761 d. Vt. 1835 m. Betsy Parker   Pvt. Vt. Mil.
   son Jesse m. Almira Robinson

Goodnough, Jesse b. Vt. 1790 d. Vt. 1884   Pvt. Vt. Mil.
   m. Almira Robinson — son Frank Aurelian m. Mary Myers

Goodrich, John b. Vt. 1791 d. Pa. 1844 m. Leva Hopkins   Pvt. N.Y. Mil.
   son William B. m. Maria Clarissa McNitt

Goodrich, John Martin b. Vt. 1778 d. Vt. 1867   Pvt. N.Y. Mil.
   m. Amy Haskell — son Christopher m. Mary Ellen White

Goodrich, Samuel Griswold b. 1793 d. Conn. 1860   Pvt. Conn. Mil.
   m. Mary Booth — daughter Emily m. Nathaniel Smith
   REAL DAUGHTER

Goodsell, John   Vol. 15   Pvt. Conn. Mil.

Goodspeed, Luther   Vol. 9   Pvt. Mass. Mil.

Goodwin, Benjamin b. (Mass.) Me. 1784 d. Me. 1858   Capt. Mass. Mil.
   m. Sally Lilly — daughter Nancy J. m. Alfred Lee
   REAL DAUGHTER

Goodwin, Hiram b. 1792 d. N.H. 1877 m. Draxy Gowell   Pvt. Mass. Mil.
   son George W. m. Susan Hood

Goodwin, Jacob Sr. b. N.H. 1770 d. Pa 1847   Pvt Pa. Mil.
   m. Mary Kinnan — son Isaac m. Sally Ann Cook

Goodwin, John Chapman b. Va. 1779 d. Va. 1845   Pvt. Va. Mil.
   m. Anna Rhodes Thompson — son James Robert m. Elizabeth Boxley

Goodwin, Nathaniel   Vol. 3   Major Gen. Mass. Mil.

Goodwin, Robert Morris   Vol. 17   Ens. Lt. Md. Mil.

Goodwin, Robert b.—d.— m. Jane Tulluck   Pvt. Va. Mil.
daughter Mary m. Joseph Graves

Goodwin, Simeon b. N.H. 1789 d. Ohio 1855   Orderly Sgt. Vt. Mil.
m. Phebe Chandler — son Hill C. m. Ruth L. Swing

Goodwin, William b. Va. 1782 d. Va. 1861 m. Nancy Carter   Pvt. Va.
daughter Susan m. James Cranford

Goodwyn, Joseph   Vol. 15   Col. U.S. Army

Goodwyn, William b. S.C. d. S.C. prior to 1804   Rec. Pat., Justice of
m. Grace Weston — daughter Grace   Quorum S.C. 1800
m. John S. Chappell

Goodyear, John b. Pa. 1784 d. Pa. 1864   Corp. Pa. Mil.
m. Ann Burkholder — son John Jr. m. Caroline Flennard

Gookin, John Wingate b. N.H. 1788 d. Me. 1856   Capt. U.S. Arty.
m. Elizabeth Dearborn Smith — son Seth S. m. Phebe Ann Dole

Gordon, Elias b. Pa. 1782 d. N.Y. 1863 m. Sarah Kinne   Pvt. N.Y. Mil.
daughter Sophia Ann m. Luther Smith

Gordon, Ephraim b. N.H. 1782 d. N.H. 1829 m. Anne Rowe Pvt. N.H. Mil.
son Simon m. Maria Robinson

Gordon, George b. Pa. 1764 d. Ohio 1842   Dragoon Ky., Dis. of Va.,
m. Sarah Winn Moss — daughter Keturah W.   Coroner O.
m. Isaac Gouverneur Burnett

Gordon, John b. Va. 1763 d. Tenn. 1819 m. Dolly Cross Capt. Tenn. Mil.
daughter Louisa P. m. Felix Kirk Zollicoffer

Gordon, Robert b. Pa. 1796 d. Ohio 1872   Sgt. Pa. Mil.
m. Susanna B. Winslow — son Thomas W.
m. Minerva Elvira Scoville

Gordon, Samuel b. Md. 1751 d. Ky. 1840   Pvt. Ky. Mil.
m. Elizabeth Brannen — son Christopher m. Karenhappock Harrison

Gordon, Thomas b. Scot. 1759 d. Ohio 1818   Pvt. Ohio Mil.
m. Ezeabelle (Isabel) — son Robert m. Susanna Bacon Winslow

Gordon, Thomas   Vol. 16   Pvt. Tenn. Vol.

Gordon, Thomas Kennedy b. Ky. 1792 d. Tenn. 1880   Capt. Tenn. Mil.
m. Elizabeth Lane — daughter Helen m. Mr. Walker
REAL DAUGHTER
daughter Lydia A. N. D. m. Dr. Thomas Cathy White
REAL DAUGHTER

Gordon, William b. N.H. 1753 d. N.H. 1818   Capt. N.H. Mil.
m. Hannah Ladd — daughter Clarissa m. Nathaniel Davis

Gordon, William Fitzhugh b. Va. 1787 d. Va. 1857   Pvt. Va. Mil.
m. (2) Elizabeth Lindsay — daughter Hannah E.
m. William J. Robertson

Gore, Joshua b. Va. 1784 d. Va. 1866   Corp. Va. Mil.
m. Elizabeth Roundtree — daughter Frances m. John Thomas Grant

Gore, Obediah b. Conn. 1744 d. Pa. 1821 Mem. Pa. Assembly, Just. of
m. Anna Avery — daughter Welthy Ann   Peace Pa.
m. John Spalding

Gorham, John   Vol. 11   Pvt. Mass. Mil.

Gorham, John   Vol. 14   Sgt. N.Y. Mil.

Gorham, Nathaniel b. Mass. 1738 d. Mass. 1796 Rec. Pat., Mem. & signer
m. Rebecca Call — daughter Rebecca   of Constitution 1785/7
m. Warham Parks

Gorham, Shubel b. Mass. 1781 d. N.Y. 1857   Pvt. N.Y. Mil.
    m. Mary Carpenter — daughter Lydia m. Henry P. Sanger

Gorin, John b. Va. 1763 d. Ky. 1837   Major Ky. Mil.
    m. Elizabeth Franklin — son John Jr. m. Eliza Wilson
    daughter Sarah H. m. Dr. George Rogers

Gorrell, Ralph b. N.C. 1735 d. N.C. 1816   Rec. Pat., Mem. Gen. Assem.
    m. Mary Kerr — son Robert m. Rebecca Doak   N.C. 1784

Gorton, Joseph b. N.Y. 1786 d. Ohio 1820   Capt. Ohio Mil.
    m. Rachel Goetchins — daughter Nancy m. Fletcher Sells

Gorton, Joseph b. Conn. 1773 d. N.Y. 1851   Rec. Pat., Tax Receiver N.Y.
    m. Charlot Schriver — son Ethan m. Mary Sague

Gorton, William b. R.I. 1750 d. Conn. 1826   Pvt. Conn. Mil.
    m. Wealthian Tellinghast — daughter Phebe m. Charles Campbell

Goss, Benjamin Sr. b. Va. 1742 d. Ga. 1813   Pvt. Ga. Cavalry of Horse
    m. Elizabeth Hamilton — son Benjamin Jr. m. Susannah Davis

Gossard (Gossett), John b. Pa. 1778 d. Ohio 1837   Pvt. Ohio Mil.
    m. Elizabeth Valentine — son James m. Elizabeth C. Messmore

Gossett, John b. Ky. 1791 d. Ohio 1853 m. Polly Eyler   Corp. Ohio Mil.
    daughter Rachael m. Amos Chaney Jr.

Gossett, Joseph b. Va. 1794 d. Ind. 1860   Sgt. Ohio Mil.
    m. Rebecca Warnock — son Jacob m. Rebecca

Gotham, John   Vol. 14   Corp. N.Y. Mil.

Gould, Abram Scott b. Vt. 1778 d. N.Y. 1868   Pvt. N.Y. Mil.
    m. Mary Nixon — daughter Agnes M. m. Charles Wheeler
    REAL DAUGHTER

Gould, Daniel b. N.Y. 1796 d N.Y. 1890   Pvt. N.Y. Mil.
    m. Fanny Demmon — daughter Clarissa A. m. Hezekiah Barnes
    REAL DAUGHTER

Gould, Ebenezer b. Conn. 1755 d. N.Y. 1809   Capt. N.Y. Mil.
    m. Rhoda Robbins — son Daniel m. Corlenthy Woodcock

Gould, Isaac b. Mass. ca. 1745 d. Mass. aft. 1819   Pat., Surveyor of
    daughter Dolly m. Ebenezer Fisk   Lumber, Tithing

Gould, Jacob b. Mass. c. 1755 d. Mass. 1857   Pvt. Mass. Mil.
    m. Lydia Thayer — daughter Joanna T. m. Shepard Simonds

Gould, Peter Warren b. Vt. 1789 d. N.H. 1873   Pvt. Mass. (Me.) Mil.
    m. Cynthia Flint — daughter Susan E. m. Leonidas Pierce

Gould, Simeon b. (Me.) Mass. c. 1785 d. Me. 1834   Pvt. Mass. Mil.
    m. Abigail Stewart — son Ingraham m. Anna Tucker Leaming

Gould (Gold), Thomas b. N.C. 1794 d. Ala. 1874   Corp. Tenn. Mil.
    m. Nancy Holland — son David m. Nancy Ann Foster

Gove, Elijah b. N.H. 1751 d. N.H. 1816 m. Sarah Mills   Rec. Pat.,
    son Squires m. Dolly Atwood   Constable N.H. 1784

Gove, Enos Sanborn b. N.H. 1786 d. Vt. 1802   Pvt. Vt. Mil.
    m. Mercy Eastman — son Hiram E. m. Mary Elizabeth Dennison

Gove, Jonathan b. Mass. 1746 d. N.H. 1818   Rec. Pat., Physician
    m. Mary Hubbard — son George B. R.   N.H. Senate
    m. Hannah Woodbury

Gove, Samuel   Vol. 2

Gover, Samuel b. Md. 1786 d. Md. 1861 m. Mary C. Wilson   Pvt. Md. Mil.
daughter Sarah Jane m. William Ward

Gowdy, Samuel b. Pa. 1790 d. Ky. 1878 m. Nancy Burnett   Pvt. Ky. Mil.
son Alfred F. m. Sarah Lois Hotchkiss

Gowdy, Samuel b. Conn. 1737 d. Conn. 1811   Rec. Pat.—Town
m. Abiah Pease — son Samuel Jr. m. Alice Gleason   Official Conn.

Gowen, Levi b. (Me.) Mass. 1790 d. Me. 1851   Pvt. Mass. Mil.
m. Deborah Hawkes — son William m. Mary A. Pride

Grable, Joseph b. Md. 1745/50 d. Ky. 1805   Capt. Ky. Mil.
m. (2) Druscilla Brown — son Samuel m. Rebecca Baker Bridwell

Grable, Joseph b. Md. 1745 d. Ky.1804/5 m. Lydia Forman   Capt. Ky. Mil.
daughter Mandania m. Philip Weller

Gradeless, William b. Md. 1789 d. Ind. 1855   Pvt. Ohio Mil.
m. Rebecca Waugh — daughter Elizabeth m. Samuel Nickey

Grafton, David b. Mass. (Me.) 1782/3 d. Texas 1822   Capt. Mass. Mil.
m. Jane West — son David Jr. m. Olivia Joy

Graham, Edward b. S.C. 1790 d. Iowa 1875 m. Molly Milton   Pvt. U.S. Inf.
daughter Susan m. Amos Sawyer

Graham, Henry   Vol. 9   Lt. N.Y. Cavalry

Graham, James b. Va. 1784 d. Texas 1867   Pvt. Miss. Mil.
m. Elizabeth Ann Floyd — daughter Prudence Ann
m. Sharp Runnels Whitley

Graham, John b. Va. 1765 d. Ky. 1835 m. Rebecca Mitten   Pvt. Ky. Mil.
daughter Elizabeth m. Thomas P. Johns
daughter Sophia m. William Henry Layne

Graham, John Kennedy b. Pa. 1783 d. Ind. 1841   Pvt. Ind. Mil.
m. Elizabeth Veach — son Ferdinand m. Abbie Ayers Day
m. Mary Ann Huff — daughter Caroline m. James Belton

Graham, Joseph b. Pa. 1789 d. N.C. 1836   Brig. Gen. N.C. Vol.
m. Isabella Davidson — son George F. m. Martha Ann Eppes Harris

Graham, Joseph   Vol. 11   Sgt. Md. Mil.

Graham, Thomas b. Va. 1786 d. Va. 1869   Capt. Va. Mil.
m. Amand Elizabeth Koontz — son Franklin P. m. Dorcas A. Cobb
daughter Mary Diana m. Stephen B. Bradshaw

Graham, Zachariah Goodwin b. S.C. 1793 d. S.C. 1880   Pvt. Miss.
m. Eliza Mason — daughter Mamie E.

Grammer, John b. Va. 1754 d. Va. 1836   Rec. Pat., 1st Postmaster,
m. Elizabeth Timberlake — daughter Sallie   1st Ct. Clerk
m. Peter Franklin Rieves

Granger, Elihu b. Conn. 1771 d. N.Y. 1842   Major N.Y. Mil.
m. Apema Granger (cousin) — son Gaius m. Sallie Emery

Granger, Lyman b. N.Y. d. Mich. 1868 m. Achsah Wells   Pvt. N.Y. Mil.
daughter Prudence W. m. Pierce G. Wright

Grant, Isaac b. Va. 1778 d. Va. 1858 m. Mary Patterson   Pvt. Va. Mil.
son John T. m. Frances Gore

Grant, Isaac b. (Me.) Mass. 1787 d. Me. 1866   Pvt. Mass. (Me.) Mil.
m. Lydia Knight — daughter Cordelia Anna m. Samuel Jarvis Noble

Grant, James b. N.Y. 1770 d. N.Y. 1837   Rec. Pat., Mem. N.Y. Assem.
   m. Christina McPherson — son James Jr.   1814-15
   m Theodosia Delavan

Grant, William III b. Va. 1761 d. Ky. 1814   Pvt. Ky. Mil.
   m. Susannah Moseby — daughter Mary m. John Whiting Moore

Grant, Zebulon b. Conn. 1776 d. N.Y.C. 1835   Pvt. N.Y. Mil.
   m. Anna Moore — daughter Catharine Eliza m. Isaac Plumb

Granwiss, Simeon Jr.   Vol. 17   Pvt. Conn. Mil.

Graves, Abraham   Vol. 15   Ens. N.Y. Mil.

Graves, Azariah b. 10-29-1768 d. 3-1-1850   Lt. Col. N.C. Mil. 1806
   m. Elizabeth Williams   Brig. Gen. 1810
   daughter Rebecca Williams Graves m. Dr. Henry Lee Graves

Graves, Eliphalet W. b. N.Y. 1791 d. Kan. 1873   Pvt. N.Y. Mil.
   m. Hannah Carpenter — daughter Huldah m. John Barr Everhart

Graves, Elisha   Vol. 15   Corp. N.Y. Mil.

Graves, Ira   Vol. 15   Pvt. N.Y. Mil.
   daughter Jennie m. George Austin   REAL DAUGHTER

Graves, Jacob b. Va. 1779 d. Va. 1854   Capt. Va. Mil.
   m. (1) Fannie White — daughter (2) Elizabeth W.
   m. Paschal Graves

Graves, John b. Va. 1720 d. N.C. 1790 m. Isabella Lea   Rec. Pat., Mem.
   daughter Mary m. John Kerr   State Assem. 1788

Graves, Joseph b. Conn. 1787 d. N.Y. 1875 m. Anna   Lt. N.Y. Vol.
   daughter Delia Josephine m. Erasmus Darwin Allen

Graves, Joshua   Vol. 14   Pvt. U.S. Inf.

Graves, Josiah b. 1773 d. Ohio 1838 m. Hannah Cooley   Lt. Ohio
   son Volorus m. Louisa Warren

Graves, William A. b. Va. 1790 d. Va. 1839   Brigade Qrtrmster Va.
   m. Agnes Brown Branham — daughter Sarah Anne
   m. Joseph C. Deming

Gray, Alexander McFarland b. Va. 1788 d. Va. 1859   Pvt. Tenn. Mil.
   m. Harriet Mason — daughter Lucy A.
   m. Stephen Jett Nickels   REAL DAUGHTER
   daughter Margaret C. m. Jonathan C. Wood   REAL DAUGHTER
   daughter Mary m. Travis H. Flanary   REAL DAUGHTER

Gray, Gabriel b. Scot. 1762 d. Va. 1844   2nd Lt. Va. Mil
   m. Rebecca Wilson — son Thomas W. m. Sallie Wither Lucas

Gray, George b. Ire. 1775 d. Ill. 1840   Pvt. Miss. Mil.
   m. Margaret McKinney — son John N. m. Rosa Jane Funk

Gray, Henry b. N.H. 1786 d. N.H. 1876 m. Dorothy Otis   Pvt. N.H. Mil.
   son Solomon F. m. Lovinia Perkins

Gray, Isaac b. Pa. 1792 d. Ohio 1846 m. Mary   Pvt. Ky. Mil.
   son Samuel m. Sarah Tomblin

Gray, Isaac b. Pa. 1774 d. Ky. 1841 m. Nancy Anderson   Capt. Ky. Mil.
   daughter Mary Elizabeth m. Green V. Caldwell
   son William m. Elizabeth Newman

Gray, James b. Conn. 1759 d. Pa. 1847   Pvt. Pa. Mil.
   m. (1) Parthenia White — son Silas m. Omira Wilson

Gray, James   Vol. 11   Pvt. Mass. Mil.

Gray, John b. Va. 1791 d. Tenn. 1868 m. Rachel Harland   Lt. Va. Mil.
daughter Elizabeth m. J. C. Hammer

Gray, John Putnam b. Va. 1776 d. Va. 1869   Capt. Va. Mil.
m. Anna Rebekah Campbell — son Marquise D. m. Anne R. E. Jordan

Gray, Richard b. Md. d. Md. 1831 m. Elizabeth Burton   Pvt. Md. Mil.
daughter Louisa m. Henry D. Hoffman

Gray, Silas b. N.Y. 1792 d. Iowa 1846 m. Omira Wilson   Pvt. N.Y. Mil.
son Argalna W. m. Emeline Dent
son Hosea W. m. Ann McQuarry Smith

Gray, Thomas b. S.C. d. S.C. m. Elizabeth   Pvt. Ga. Mil.
son Stephen Alfred m. Mary Winifred Grace

Gray, William b. 1750 d. 1825   Lt. Gov. 1810/11, Mem. Mass.
m. Elizabeth Chipman — son Wm. Rufus   Senate 1807/8
m. Mary Clay

Grayson, Peter Wagener b. Va. 1770 d. Ala. 1816   Col. Va. Mil.
m. Kitty Callaway Thorpe — son Edward B. m. Juliette Mix

Greathouse, William b. Ky. d. Mo. 1876   Pvt. Ky. Mil.
m. Sarah Beale Van Swearinger — daughter Mary E.
m. Henry Watson   REAL DAUGHTER

Greeley, Joseph   Vol. 9   Rep. N.H. Gen. Ct.

Greeley, Joseph b. N.H. 1756 d. N.H. 1840 m. Sarah   Rep. N.H. Governor
son Seneca m. Priscilla Fields

Greeley, Samuel b. N.H. 1747 d. N.H. 1824   Rec. Pat., Mem. N.H. Legis.
m. Mary Leavitt — son Gilman m. Betsey V. Thompson

Green, Alpheus Wortley b. 1790 d. Md.   Pvt. Md. Mil.
m. Margaret Rhemm — daughter Mary m. Alpheus W. Greene

Green (E), Benjamin b. N.Y. 1783 d. N.Y. 1866   Pvt. N.Y. Vol.
m. Lydia Gardner — son David C. m. Lovina Sweet

Green, David b. Pa. 1795 d. Pa. 1875 m. Phoebe Darrow   Pvt. Pa. Mil.
daughter Aurilla m. Orlin Chanberlain

Green, Forest b. Ga. d.— m. Elizabeth Clower   Pvt. Ga. Mil.
son Daniel M. m. Nancy Henson

Green, Grief b. Va. 1770 d. Va. 1844 m. Rebecca Mayo   Lt. Col. Va. Mil.
daughter Martha T. m. James Lanier

Green, John b. Pa. 1784 d. Pa. 1852 m. Hannah   Pvt. Pa. Mil.
son John C. m. Catharine Reider

Green, John b. S. C. 1790 d. Ala. 1882 m. Nancy Jones   Corp. Ga.
son Christopher m. Maryan Watson

Green, John   Vol. 6   Purser U.S. Navy

Green, John   Vol. 15   Purser Va. Navy Ship "Hornet"

Green, John Sims b. Pa. 1794 d. Pa. 1876   Pvt. Pa. State Fencibles
m. Elizabeth Henly — son Walter K. m. Marion Wolcott

Green, Joseph Lodd   Vol. 14   Corp. N.Y. Mil.

Green, Joseph Strother   Vol. 6   Pvt. Ky. Mil.

Green, Joshua b. N.Y. 1782 d. Minn. 1869   Pvt. N.Y. Mil.
m. (2) Jane Atkins — daughter Affa Maye m. Ernest Woodworth
REAL DAUGHTER

Green, Richard b. Va. 1755 d. Va. 1823 m. Sarah   Pvt. Va. Mil.
son George m. Miss Lipscomb

Green, Thomas b. Pa. 1785 d. Pa. 1831 Qrtmster Pa. Mil., builder of ships
m. Nancy Eckels — daughter Debora m. Lorenzo Dow Childs
REAL DAUGHTER
son O.H.P. Green, Sr. m. Eliza Ann Mitchell

Green, Samuel b. Conn. 1768 d. Conn. 1859   Capt. Conn. Mil.
m. Mary Starr — son Charles m. Sophia Haskell Tudor

Green, William b. Va. 1745 d. S.C. 1815   Deputy Surveyor S.C.
m. Phereby — son Absolom m. Miss Stallings
son Reuben m. Elizabeth Bates

Green, William   Vol. 17   Pvt. Va. Mil.

Green, William b. 1769 d. Pa. 1840 m. Elizabeth Shomo Major Pa. Mil.
daughter Ester m. Phillip Haffa

Green, William H.   Vol. 15   Pvt. Ga. Mil.

Greenawalt, John   Vol. 6   Pvt. Pa. Mil.

Greene, Allen J. b. Va. 1782 d. Texas 1845   Pvt. Va. Mil.
m. Nancy Porter Hunt — daughter Elizabeth B.
m. William Etheridge

Greene, Elisha Barton b. N.H. 1786 d. Ohio 1845(?) Sgt. U.S. Inf.
m. Lydia McLaughlin — daughter Mandane
m. Judge Benjamin Johnston

Greene, Jesse b. Tenn. 1791 d. Mo. 1847 m. Mary Todd Pvt. Tenn. Mil.
daughter Isabella L. (single) REAL DAUGHTER
daughter Mary E. m. Mr. Crenshaw REAL DAUGHTER

Greene, Nathaniel b. R.I. 1787 d. R.I. 1831   Ens. R.I. Mil.
m. Martha Fones Northup — daughter Mary D.
m. Thomas W. Clarke

Greene, Samuel b. Conn. 1784 d. Conn. 1860   Lt. Conn. Mil.
m. Betsey Holmes — son Samuel Jr. m. Mary Ann Crandall

Greenleaf, Christopher   Vol. 14   Physician N.Y. Mil.

Greenlee, David b. Va. 1781 d. Va. 1850   Pvt. Va. Mil.
m. Hannah J. Grigsby — son Dr. R. B. m. Amanda Boone Gifford

Greenlee, Elisha   Vol. 16   Pvt. Miss. Mil.

Greenman, Benjamin b. N.Y. 1757 d. N.Y. 1841   Pvt. N.Y. Mil.
m. Lydia Brown — son Russell m. Lydia Minor

Greenwood, Daniel b. Mass. 1704 d. Mass. 1812 Rec. Pat., Selectman
m. Sarah Adams — daughter Zeviah m. Peter Woodbury Mass. 1787

Greer, Aaron b. S.C. 1779 d. La. 1853 m. Susannah   Pvt. Miss. Mil.
son Wesley m. Mary Keele

Greer, Andrew Sr. b.— d. 1806 m. Mary Vance Rec. Pat., Comm.
son John m. Rebecca Bowney   Tenn. 1796

Greer, John b. Va. 1762 or 1774 d. Tenn. 1835   Pvt. Tenn. Mil.
m. Rebecca Bowney — son Thomas m. Mary Artic Johnson

Greer, Robert   Vol. 9   3rd Lt. Ga. Mil.

Gregg, George b. Va. 1776 d. Va. 1866   Pvt. Va. Mil.
   m. Elizabeth Wilson — daughter Nancy m. Anthony Conard

Gregg, John b. Va. 1760-70 d. Tenn. 1847   Civil Officer, Just. of Peace,
   m. Hannah Piercy — daughter Anna   Mem. Gen. Assbly.
   m. Jacob Kelly

Gregg, John b. Va. 1786 d. Ind. 1857   Pvt. Ky. Mil.
   m. Frances Spillman (Spellman) — daughter Lucy O.
   m. James Williamson Cooper
   daughter Sarah m. Samuel Cones

Gregg, John Polk b. N.C. 1792 d. Ark. 1854   Pvt. N.C. Mil.
   m. Martha Boone — daughter Nancy C. m. Elias D. Culpepper

Gregg, Leslie   Vol. 10   Corp. Vt. Mil.

Gregg, Samuel   Vol. 7   Pvt. Pa. Mil.

Gregg, William Taylor b. N.H. 1792 d. N.Y. 1865   Pvt. N.Y. Mil.
   m. Esther Mallory — son Albert B. m. Susan Salome White

Gregory, Israel b. Maine (Mass.) 1780 d. Maine 1887   Pvt. Mass. Mil.
   daughter Amelia m. Thomas Rivers

Gregory, Johiel Jr. b. N.Y. 1782 d. Ohio 1823   Capt. Ohio Mil.
   m. Sally Van Dolah — son John, III m. (2) Mary Ann Henline

Gregory, Luther   Vol. 4   Pvt. U.S. Inf.

Gregory, Umbleton S. b. Va. 1798 d. Texas 1864   Pvt. Va. Mil.
   m. Mary Hewitt also Amanda Malvina Crooks
   daughter Virginia E. m. Seaman Oscar Eidman Jr. — 1st wife
   daughter Phynetta m. James W. Mahon — 2nd wife
   daughter Malzena m. Andrew C. Zumwalt — 2nd wife

Gregory, William   Vol. 15   Pvt. Va. Mil.

Greisimer, Isaac C. b. Pa. 1785 d. Pa. 1823   Lt. Pa. Mil.
   m. Hanna Mineker — daughter Christine L. m. Solomon Feather

Grenell, Benjamin Persons b. N.Y. 1790 d. N.Y. 1864   Pvt. N.Y. Mil.
   m. Kezia Freeman — son Ezra Orosco m. Abby Wardwell

Gresham, Elijah b. Va. 1781 d. Va. 1859/60   Pvt. Va. Mil.
   m. Maria Goode — son Edwin James m. Josephine P. Lumpkin also
   Fannie Williams

Gresham, Samuel b. Va. 1740 d. Va. c. 1820   Pvt. Va. Mil.
   m. Mary Faulkner — son John m. Martha Lumpkin

Gress, Jacob b. Pa. 1793 d. Pa. 1883 m. Mary Lauffer   Pvt. Pa. Mil.
   son Henry m. Susan Rugh Seanor

Grier, James b. Ire. 1770 d. N.C. c. 1840   Pvt. N.C. Mil.
   m. Jane Bingham — son John B. m. Sarah Boyd

Griffin, John b. Ky. 1773 d. Ky. 1854 m. Mary James   Pvt. Ky. Mil.
   son James N. m. Sarah M. Vardaman

Griffin, Jones b. Tenn. 1784 d. Ala. 1836 m. Mary Lee.   Capt. Tenn. Mil.
   son John A. m. Malinda Burgess

Griffin, LeRoy   Vol. 13   Pvt. Ky. Vol.

Griffin, Samuel Jr. b. Conn. 1775 d. Pa. 1821   Capt. Pa. Mil.
   m. Anna Blake — daughter Clarissa m. Joseph Stanton

Griffin, Solomon b. Va. 1777 d. Ky. 1869 m. Mary Bull   Pvt. Ky. Mil.
   son Tamer m. Pouncy Anderson

Griffin, William b. N.Y. 1781 d. N.Y. 1847   Lt. N.Y. Mil.
  m. Alida Maybie — daughter Clarissa m. Isaac Newton Pardy
  son James M. m. Jane Brizee

Griffis, John   Vol. 13 & 16   Sgt. Tenn. Vol.

Griffith, Henry Jr. b. Md. 1794 d. Md. 1866   Pvt. Md. Mil.
  m. Ruth Plummer (See Howard) — son William H.
  m. Laura V. Duvall

Griffith, Hezekiah b. Me. 1792 d. Me. 1878   Sgt. Me. Mil.
  m. Lyndia Fuller — daughter Flora L. m. Jess W. Tirrell

Griffith, Howard b. Md. 1794 d. Md. 1866   Pvt. Md. Mil.
  m. Ruth Plummer (See Henry) — daughter Sarah
  m. Cyrus Sumner Maynard

Griffith, Isaac b. Pa. 1764 d. Ohio 1834 m. Ann   Major Pa. Mil.
  daughter Margaret m. William Stage

Griffith, John b. Mass. (Me.) 1787 d. Me. 1848   Pvt. Mass. Mil.
  m. Nancy Wormell — son William A. m. Mary C. Reynolds

Griffith, Moses b. Va. 1770 d. Va. 1842 m. Nancy Costin   Pvt. Va. Mil.
  son John m. Ann

Griffith, Samuel b. Mass. 1766 d. Mo. 1815 m. Sarah   Capt. U.S. Vol.
  daughter Mary m. Wilson Lee Overall

Griffith, Thomas b. Md. aft. 1776 d. Md. 1838   Capt. Md. Mil.
  m. Harriet W. Simpson — son Thomas D. m. Charlotte M. Inglehart

Griffith, William b. Wales 1775 d. W.Va. m. Anne Wells   Pvt. Va. Mil.
  daughter Rachel m. Thomas Chapman

Griggs, John b. N.J. 1790 d. Mo. 1876 m. Susan Williams Pvt. Ky. Mil.
  son Seth m. Massa Warner

Griggs, Solomon   Vol. 16   Pvt. Ohio Mil.

Grim, (M), Jacob b. Pa. 1754 d. Pa. 1833   Lt. Col. Pa. Mil.
  m. Catherine Hottenstein — son David m. Catherine Knabb

Grimes, Charles b. Va. 1770 d. Ky. 1837 m. Jane Winn Capt. 8th Reg.
  daughter Maria m. George E. Monroe   Ky. 1804

Grimes, George b. Pa. 1792 d. Ohio 1858 m. Isabel Smith Ens. Ohio Inf.
  son Robert R. m. Caroline Frances Green

Grimes, George b. Va. 1790 d. Ind. 1869   Pvt. Va. Mil.
  m. Elizabeth Donahoe — son William m. Evelyn Balch
  son George Jr. m. Eliza Ann Anderson also Clarissa Kennedy

Grimes, John b. Md. 1794 d. Ohio 1871   Pvt. Ohio Mil.
  m. (3) Nancy Weaver — daughter Belle m. William D. Cryder

Grinnell, William b. Md. 1778 d. N.Y. 1864   Sgt. Md. Mil.
  m. Diademia Brown — son William H. m. Caroline Pomeroy

Grisham, Austin b. N.C. 1771 d. Ill. 1853   Pvt. Tenn. Mil.
  m. Fanny Powers — son James m. Martha R. Garrison

Griswold, Ashbel b. Conn. 1733 d. Conn. aft. 1813   Sgt. Conn. Mil.
  m. Elizabeth Woodruff — daughter May m. Ebenezer Cadwell

Griswold, Chester b. Conn. 1782 d. Md. 1868 m. Rhoda Capt. N.Y. Vol.
  son Benjamin B. m. Catherine F. Onderdonk

Griswold, Hezekiah b. Conn. 1773 d. N.Y. 1836   Pvt. Conn. Mil.
  m. Mary Denslow Thrall — daughter Mary m. Alanson Watkins

Griswold, Jabez, Jr. b. Conn. 1764 d. N.Y. 1827   Pvt. N.Y. Mil.
   m. (1) Ann Spencer — son Norman F. m. Deborah Richmond

Griswold, Julius b. Conn. 1784 d. Conn. 1863   Pvt. Conn. Mil.
   daughter Charlotte Ann m. (1) Philo Howe Cummings

Griswold, Sylvester   Vol. 16   Fifer, N.Y. Mil.

Griswold, Wareham, Jr. b. Conn. 1791 d. Conn.   Lt. Conn. Mil.
   m. Sylvia Clark — daughter Delia C. m. Nathan Frankon

Groce, Jared Ellison b. Eng. 1740   Delegate Ga. Convention 1798
   d. Ga. 1803 m. Sarah Sheppard — son Jared E. Jr.
   m. Mary Ann Waller

Gros, Laurence   Vol. 17   Rec. Pat., Mem. N.Y. Legis. 1806-1807

Gross, George   Pvt. Pa. Mil.

Grout, Elijah b. Mass. 1732   Selectman 1794, Just. of Peace 1800
   d. N.H. 1807 m. Mary Willard — son Amasa m. Lucinda Heywood

Grout, Josiah b. N.H. 1772 d. Vt. 1853 m. Sarah White   Major Vt. Mil.
   daughter Catherine m. Orris L. Ballard

Grove, Francis b. 7-14-1781 d. 3-9-1844   Pvt. 5th Div. 41st Reg. York Co.
   m. Janet Cross — son Thomas Cross m. Sarah Croskey

Grove, Jacob b. Pa. 1780 d. Pa. 1866 m. Margaret Parke   Pvt. Pa. Mil.
   son William m. Hannah Withrow

Grove, John b. Pa. 1793 d. Pa. 1859   Pvt. Pa. Mil.
   m. Catherine Elizabeth Arnold — son John A. m. Mary Boadenhamer
   son Samuel m. Maria Strombaugh

Grove, Thomas b. abt. 1750 d. 1802   Oath of Allegience to Pa. June
   m. Margaret Sinard — son Francis   1789. Voted Oct. 1789
   m. Jannet Cross

Groves, Allen b. N.C. 1780-90 d. Tenn. 1850 m. Mary Uzzell   Pvt. Tenn.
   son James m. Jane Covington

Groves, David b. Vt. 1771 d. Ohio 1855   Sgt. Ohio Vol.
   m. Elizabeth Stipp — daughter Mary m. Absolem Neff

Groves, Peter b. Ohio 1792 d. Ohio 1847   Pvt. Ohio Mil.
   m. Sarah Swickard — daughter Martha Jane
   m. John Samuel Andrews   REAL DAUGHTER

Grow, Edward b. Mass. (Me.) 1722   Col. Mass. (Me.) Mil.
   d. Mass. (Me.) 1785 m. Olive Farnham — daughter Hannah
   m. Josiah Chase

Grubb, Elijah b. Va. 1789 d. Va. 1845   Pvt. Va. Mil.
   m. Mary Ann Saunders — daughter Mary Ann m. Robert McKendree

Gruber, Jacob b. Pa. 1794 d. W.Va. 1881   Pvt. Va. Mil.
   m. Martha Baughman — son Josiah m. Susannah Couchman

Grundy, George   Vol. 5   Pvt. Va. Mil.

Guild, Lewis b. Mass. 1795 d. Mass. 1882   Drummer Mass. Mil.
   m. Greta Smith — daughter Elvira m. Obed Wilson Paine

Guild, Nathaniel b. Mass. 1791 d. Mass. 1868   Pvt. Mass. Mil.
   m. Harriet Perry — son Lavoise N. m. Hannah Tuft

Guilde, Henry   Vol. 14   Sgt. N.Y. Mil.

Guile, Samuel b. Conn. 1781 d. Pa. 1847   Pvt. Conn. Mil.
   m. Hannah Coleman — son Silas B. m. Catherine Chase

Guillanden, Emil b. France 1790 d.— m. Rosina Duncan   Pvt. U.S. Arty.
daughter Catherine m. Henry Hannington

Guinn, Andrew b. Va. 1752 d. Ala. 1832 m. Mary Dudley   Pvt. Ky. Mil.
son Richard m. Mary Clay

Guinn, William G. b. N.C. 1795 d. Tenn. aft. 1871   Pvt. Tenn.
m. Lydia Price — daughter Elizabeth m. John L. Barbour

Guion, Elijah b. N.Y. 1770 d. N.Y. 1844   Capt. N.Y. Mil.
m. Elizabeth Marshall — son John M. m. Elizabeth Ives Wheaton

Guion, Isaac b. N. Y. 1755 d. Miss. 1823 m. Sarah Lewis   Major N.Y. Mil.
son John Isaac m. Cornelia Hall

Gulick, Joachim b. N.J. 1764 d. N.Y. 1840   Pvt. N.J. Mil., Capt. of
m. Jane Wycoff (Wyckoff) — son Abraham   Teamsters
m. Rebecca Vedder
son William m. Ann Maria Parkes

Gulick, William Gano b. N.J. 1786 d. Ohio 1832   Lt. Ind.
m. Sarah Adams — son Martin m. Eleanor Welch

Gullette, Robert b. Del. d. 1843 m. Sarah Morris   Pvt. Delaware Troops
daughter Mary E. m. Mark D. Strout

Gunckel, Michael b. Pa. 1787 d. Ohio 1857   Capt. Ohio Mil.
m. Barbara Shuey — son George W. m. Julia Ann Ayres

Gunn, John b. N.C. 1780 d. Tenn. 1817   Pvt. Tenn. Mil.
m. Elizabeth Carroll (2) Wm. Hubbard — son John C.
m. Caroline Williamson
son William C. m. Elizabeth Susan Moreland

Gunn, Reuben b. Va. 1782 d. N.C. or S.C. 1822   Pvt. U.S. Arty.
m. Miss Henderson — son Charles m. Venetta Page

Gurley, Davis b. N.C. 1792 d. Texas 1861   Pvt. Tenn. Mil.
m. Patience Bland Smith — son Davis R. m. Louisa Wells Earle

Gurley, William b. Ire. 1757 d. Ohio 1848   Rec. Pat., Defender Ohio
m. Susannah Beatty — son William D.   Frontier
m. Nancy Jane Stevenson

Gustin, Alpheus Jr. b. N.Y. abt. 1755 d. Vt. 1814   Postmaster Va.
m. Margaret Strange — son Aburdy m. Eleanor Chew   1802-1814

Guth (Good), Henry b. Pa. 1796 d. Pa. 1865   Pvt. Pa. Mil.
m. (2) Catharine Hoffman — son Amos S. m. Catherine Nyce

Guthridge, John b. Va. 1776 d. Ohio 1829   Wagon Master Ohio Mil.
m. Margaret Parkinson — son Harrison P. m. Emily Williamson

Guthrie, Henry Pigg b. Pa. 1793 d. Ohio 1869   Pvt. Va. Mil.
m. Mary Catherine Stedman — daughter Sarah Frances
m. Daniel L. Pratt

Guthrie, John b. Pa. 1749 d. Pa. 1832 m. Sarah Davis   Capt. Pa. Mil.
son John Jr. m. Elizabeth Fielding

Guy, Joseph b. N.C. 1767 d. Ala. 1830   Rec. Pat., State Senator N.C. 1811
m. Esther Sharpe — son Martin W.   Just. of Peace 1810
m. Hester Ann Hardy

Guy, Robert   Vol. 17   Sgt. Va. Mil.

Guyer, Benjamin b. Pa. 1782 d. Pa. 1850 m. Sarah Holden   Pvt. Pa. Mil.
son Benjamin F. m. Mary Ann Zebley

Guyor, Joseph b. Mich. 1783 d. Mich. 1887   Pvt. Mich. Mil.
   also (Gior, Goiare, Gaillard)
   m. Mary Margaret Bourg or (Mary Burke Monroe)
   son Eli m. Jane Story Phillips
   daughter Emily m. Anthony Roberts, Sr.

Gwinn, Andrew b. (W.) Va. 1788 d. (W.) Va. 1863   Lt. Va. Mil.
   m. Mary Newsome — daughter Eliza (3rd wf.) m. Wilson Lively

Gwinn, James b. Md. 1774 d. Md. 1835 m. Catherine Megill   Pvt. U.S. Inf.
   daughter Anne m. William Benjamin Irwin

H

Haas, Charles b. Pa. 1784 d. Pa. 1862 m. Mary Sweeney   Sgt. Pa. Mil.
   daughter Hannah Rebecca m. John Ketcham Babcock

Haas (Hause, Haus), John b. Va. 1756 d. Ohio 1827   Sgt. Va. Mil.
   m. Elizabeth Wilkins — daughter Sarah m. Joseph F. Parrett

Hackett, Trueworthy b. Vt. 1789 d. Vt. 1858 m. Ada Rich   Pvt. Va. Mil.
   daughter Mary m. Charles Allen

Hackett, William b. N.C. 1776 d. Ga. aft. 1829 Rec. Pat., Justice of Peace
   m. Mary Covington — son Albert T.   Ga. 1813-1817
   m. Sarah Jane Payne

Hackley, Lott b. Ky. 1779 d. Mo. 1847 m. Elizabeth Perry   Pvt. Ky. Mil.
   son Francis H. m. Ann Eliza White

Hackstaff, William G. b. N.Y. 1795 d. Conn. 1869   Pvt. N.Y. Mil.
   m. Anna Garr — daughter Clara m. Robert Adams
   also Charles S. MacDonough   REAL DAUGHTER

Hackworth, Joseph b. Va. 1789 d. Ky. 1844   Pvt. Ky. Mil.
   m. Catherine Saunders — daughter Amanda m. George Smith Wright
   son James M. m. Linda Smith

Haddaway, Daniel Lambden b. Md. 1788 d. Md. 1848   Pvt. Md. Mil.
   m. Clementine Hughes — daughter Matilda m. Caleb T. Holden

Haden, William b. Va. 1770 d. N.C. 1845 m. Mary Hamm   Pvt. U.S. Inf.
   daughter Vienna Louise m. Madison Rowzee

Hadley, Smith b. 1765 d. Ohio 1850 m. Sarah   Corp. & Sgt. Ohio Mil.
   son Savannah m. Martha Riddle

Hadley, Stephen b. N.J. 1786 d. Mich. 1860   Corp. N.Y. Mil.
   m. Elizabeth Owens — daughter Elsie m. Peter Evans

Hagaman, Abraham b. N.Y. 1790 d. N.Y. 1860   Sgt. N.Y. Mil.
   m. Martha Carpenter — son Abraham m. Eunice Wilcox

Hagaman, John J. b. N.Y. 1792 d. N.Y. m. Sarah Frye   Pvt. N.Y. Mil.
   daughter Abby F. m. Benjamin Franklin Hall

Hager, Nathan b Mass. 1744/5 d. Mass. 1802   Patriot, Civil Officer
   m. Anna Bigelow — son Isaac m. Eunice Stedman   1788-1800

Hageman, Simon b. Ohio or N.J. 1795 d. Ind. 1872   Pvt. Ohio Mil.
   m. Elizabeth Shuff — son Thomas J. m. Louisa Polin

Hagen (Higgins), Samuel b. Mass. (Me.) 1792   Corp. Mass. (Me.)
   d. Mass. (Me.) 1877 m. Hannah Skillings — son Milton
   m. Esther E. Libby

Hager, Lucas   Vol. 12   Pvt. N.H. Mil.

Haggard, John, II b. Ky. 1794 d. Ky. 1858   Pvt. Ky. Mil.
    m. Mourning Quisenberry — son Clinton S. m. Nannie Kate Lunsford

Hagler, Abraham b. (W.)Va. 1790 d. Ohio 1865   Rec. Pat., Just. of Peace
    m. Dolly Stookey (2) — son Allen   Ohio 1813
    m. Maria Louisa Ellis

Hagler, Benjamin Jones b. N.C. 1791 d. Ill. 1865   Pvt. Tenn. Mil.
    m. Elizabeth Graham — son James G.   Musician N.C. Mil.
    m. (2) Clarissa Falls
    son John G. m. Elizabeth Stevenson
    daughter Susan E. m. A. D. Reed   REAL DAUGHTER

Hagler (Hagley), Isaac b. Va. 1793 d. Ohio   Pvt. Ohio Mil.
    m. Susan Stookey — daughter Matilda Jane m. Daniel McLean

Hagler, Phillip b. Pa. d. N.C. 1845 m. Mary Long   Pvt. N.C. Mil.
    daughter Margaret H. m. Drury Morgan

Hagler, William b. N.C. aft. 1782 d. N.C. 1856   Pvt. N.C.
    m. Elizabeth Mullens — son John m. Edith Triplett

Haight, Daniel b. Vt. 1791 d. Vt. 1842   Pvt. Vt. Mil.
    m. Mariah or Harriet Hatch — son William T.
    m. Harty Caroline Eddy

Haigler, John b. Va. 1791 d. Kan. 1875   Pvt. (W.) Va. Mil.
    m. Phoebe Morl Skidmore — son Elijah M. m. Letitia Hays

Hail, Stephen also Hale b. Va. 1783 d. Va. 1854   Sgt. Va. Mil.
    m. Frances Boume — daughter Rosamond B. m. Clarke S. Nuckolls

Hain (Hehn), William b. Pa. 1786 d. Pa. 1861   Capt. Pa. Mil.
    m. Anna Hain (same name) — daughter Elenora
    m. Emanuel Sharman

Haines, Levi b. Va. 1779 d. Ohio 1824 m. Nancy Rush   Pvt. N.Y. Mil.
    daughter Nancy H. m. William Brewer   REAL DAUGHTER

Haines, Moses   Vol. 6   Sgt. N.Y. Mil.

Hair, David b. S.C. 1791 d. S.C. 1843 m. Levicy Reed   Pvt. S.C. State
    daughter Ella Rebecca m. Samuel Hutchins Still   Troops

Hair, James b. Md. 1777 d. Pa. 1826   Rec. Pat., Just. of Peace Pa. 1811
    m. Rebecca McKown — daughter Mary m. Isaac Van Voorhis

Hair, John b. S.C. 1794 d. S.C. 1868 m. Mary Jowers   Pvt. S.C. Mil.
    son James W. m. Nancy A. Barr

Hair, John b S.C. abt. 1785 d. S.C. aft. 1849 m. Mary   Pvt. S.C. Mil.
    son Joseph m. Mary T. Veitch

Hair, John Henry b. S.C. 1788 d. S.C. 1854 m. Mary Burt?   Pvt. S.C. Mil.
    son Darling J. m. Rebecca Walker

Hairston, George b. Va. 1750 d. Va. 1827   Lt. Col. Va. Mil.
    m. Elizabeth Perkins — son George m. Louisa Hardyman

Haislip, John b. N.C. 1787 d. Tenn. 1876 m. Sarah Wade   Pvt. Tenn. Mil.
    son Calvin W. H. m. Martha Robinson Drake

Hakes, Jesse   Vol. 14   Pvt. U.S. Inf.

Halbert, James, Jr. b. Va. 1785 d. Ill. 1858   Pvt. Va. Mil.
    m. Nancy Rennolds — daughter Mary L. m. Rezin Harlan Constant
    daughter Sarah m. James S. Taylor

Halcomb, Hiram b. N.C. 1789 d. Ky. 1869 m. Isabella West   Pvt. Tenn.
    son Amos m. Isabella Catherine Sivley   Rangers

Hale, Daniel   Vol. 16   Lt. N.Y. Mil.

Hale, Daniel b. Mass. 1758 d. Mass. 1830   Rec. Pat., Mem. Mass. Legis.
m. Cynthia Buffington — son Jonathan m. Rosana West   1806

Hale, Joseph b. Tenn. 1789 d. Tenn. 1873   Capt. Tenn. Mil.
m. Rebecca C. Landrum — son Young L. m. Lucy Jane

Hale, Joshua b. abt. 1767 d. Ohio 1813 m. Mary   Pvt. U.S. 24th Inf.
son Nicholas m. Rhoda Crouch

Hale, Levi b. Vt. 1790 d. N.Y. 1862 m. Anner Durkee   Corp. Vt. Mil.
son Colwell D. m. Ann Jeanette Clift
daughter Louisa m. Harry Buel Collins

Hale, Lewis b. Va. 1750 d. Va. m. Mary Burwell   Capt. Va. Riflemen Mil.
son Francis m. Elizabeth Buroughs

Hale, Samuel b. 1771 d.— m. Rebecca Carlton   Pvt. Mass. Mil.
daughter Mary H. m. Moses Harrison Palmer

Hale, Stephen, Sr. b. Va. 1783 d. Va. 1854 m. Frances Bourn   Sgt. Va. Mil.
daughter Sophia P. m. Dr. W. M. Mitchell

Hale, William   Vol 16   Pvt. Pa. Mil.

Hale, William B. b. 1790 d. 1880   Pvt. 7th Reg. Va. Mil.
m. Sarah Wade — son David m. America A. Easter

Haley, John b. (Me.) Mass. 1780 d. (Me.) Mass. 1817 Seaman U.S. Frigate
m. Margaret Lee — son Nathan G. m. Mehitabel Barnes Lee

Haley, Simeon b. Conn. 1781 d. Conn. 1859   Capt. Conn. Mil.
m. Priscilla Avery Burrus — daughter Catharine m. Albert Haley

Haling, William b. Conn. 1793 d. Conn. 1871   Pvt. Conn. Mil.
m. Abigail Hall — daughter Sarah Ann m. Thomas G. Lucas

Hall, Abraham Bashara b. N.J. 1786 d. N.Y. 1872   Sgt. N.Y. Mil.
m. Sarah Haight — daughter Harriet N. m. Truman P. Handy

Hall, Alpheus b. Conn. 1757 d. Vt. 1841   Rep. State Legis. Vt. 1809-1816
m. Mercy Blinn — son Lorenzo m. Marcia Phelps

Hall, Asahel b. Conn. 1792 d. N.Y. 1877   Surgeon's Mate Conn. Mil.
m. Catherine R. Vanderburgh — son George V. m. Mary H. Gleason

Hall, Bainbridge b. Va. 1784 d. Ind. 1855 m. Polly Nicolas   Pvt. Ky. Mil.
son Yelverton P. m. Martha Ellen Stillwell

Hall, Benedict William b. Md. 1790 d. N.C. 1843   3rd Lt. Md. Mil.
m. Mary Calhoun — daughter Elizabeth B. m. Horatio L. Whitridge

Hall, Clark b. Va. 1793 d. Ohio 1877   Pvt. Va. Mil.
m. Mary Jane Johnston (Smithfield?) — son Joseph
m. Rachel E. McGrew

Hall, Daniel, Jr.   Vol. 10   Major N.Y. Mil. 1802-7

Hall, George b. Conn. 1770 d. N.Y. 1840   Rec. Pat., Postmaster Super. &
m. Theodocia Keeler — son Daniel K. m. Sarah Olin   Surrogate

Hall, Grafton   Vol. 17   Pvt. Md. Mil.

Hall, Henry b. R.I. 1765 d. Vt. 1841 m. Sally Gray   Lt. Vt. Mil.
son Hiram Henry m. Lucy Everts

Hall, Henry G. b. Conn. 1789 d. Mich. 1872 m. Ruth Stark   Pvt. Conn. Mil.
son James A. m. Mary A. Sherman

Hall, Jacob   Vol. 11   Pvt. Pa. Mil.

Hall, James   Vol. 8   Pvt. Pa. Mil.

Hall, Joel b. Ky. 1786 d. Ill. 1881 m. Mary Clarke   Pvt. & Pack Horse
    son Randolph m. Almeda Lianda Woods   Driver Ky. Mil.

Hall, John b. Va. 1773 d. Va. 1852 m. Patsy   Pvt. Va. Mil.
    son William m. Lucy

Hall, John   Vol. 11   Capt. Md. Mil.

Hall, Johnson b. Conn. 1794 d. N.Y. 1870 m. Polly Andrews   Sgt. N.Y. Mil.
    son Johnson L. m. Marcelia Wood

Hall, Jonathan b. Va. 1774 d. Tenn. 1848   Rec. Pat., Civil Officer Tenn.
    m. Johanna Barton — son William K.   1806
    m. Martha Winn McConnell

Hall, Levi b. (Me.) Mass. 1787 d. Me. 1851   Lt. Mass. Mil.
    m. Jane Emery — daughter Hannah H. m. Rev. Almon Libby

Hall, Martin b. Vt. 1793 d. Pa. 1887 m. Emily Lamb   Corp. Vt. Mil.
    daughter Samantha m. Alpheus Woods Gates, Jr.

Hall, Robert b. Ire 1777 d. N.Y. 1841 m. Nancy Gilmore   Lt. N.Y. Mil.
    son George m. Alzuma Sanders

Hall, Robert M. b.— d. Ky. m. Sallie Gilkey   Pvt. Ky. Mil.
    daughter Maria m. Dr. John H. Reynolds

Hall, Roland b. N.Y. 1783 d. N.Y. 1837 m. Lydia Harris   Capt. N.Y. Mil.
    son Augustus m. Clarissa Mills
    son Rozell H. m. Jeannette C. Smith

Hall, Roland   Vol. 14   Capt. N.Y. Mil.

Hall, Samuel b. Mass. 1778 d. Pa. 1854   Lt. N.J. Inf.
    m. Polly Daroxa Basset — daughter Polly D. m. Valentine B. Tiffany

Hall, Samuel b. Mass. 1780 d. Iowa 1856 m. Hannah Chapin   Lt. N.Y. Mil.
    son Cyrus m. Mary Ann E. Davis

Hall, Silas Hill b. Jamaica d. Mo. m. Keturah Dillarde   Pvt. Va. Mil.
    daughter Keturah m. Harrison Harris

Hall, Street   Vol. 30   Del. to Conven. Conn. 1788

Hall, Thomas   Vol. 15   Pvt. Vt. Mil.

Hall, William b. Va. 1756 d. Ky. 1811 m. Urcilla Woodward   Capt. Ky. Mil.
    son Bazil m. Sallie Hammond
    son Green m. Mary Barnes

Hall, William b. Conn. 1800 d. Ohio 1869   Pvt. Conn. Mil.
    m. Margaret Kinney — son Thomas F. S. m. Katherine Rigdon

Hall, William b. N.C. 1775 d. Tenn. 1856   Brig. Gen. Tenn. Mil.
    m. Mary Brandon Alexander — daughter Martha Anne
    m. La Fayette Sharp
    son William H. m. Sarah Winceanna McDaniel

Hall, William b. N.C. 1785 d. Ga. aft. 1852   Pvt. Ga. Mil.
    m. Sara Hicklin — daughter Charlotte M.
    m. Rufus Augustus Roberson

Hall, William b. Vt. 1790 d. Mich. 1861 m. Polly Curtis   Lt. Ohio
    daughter Susan m. Daniel B. Fenton

Hall, William b. Ky. 1793 d. Ky. 1859 m. Malinda Stone   Pvt. Ky. Mil
son John m. Eliza Jane Thompson

Halladay, Daniel E. b. Conn. 1735/6 d. N.Y. 1818 m. Anna Higley   Pat.
son Nathan Halladay m. Susannah Adams

Hallam, Giles Russell b. Conn. 1776 d. Conn. 1863   Commander Conn. &
m. Lucy Williams — son Isaac W.   Paymaster
m. Nancy Courtney Hallam

Hallenbeck, Isaac b. N.Y. 1767 d. N.Y. 1855   Corp. N.Y. Mil.
m. Magdalena Slingerland — son Garret m. Martha Trotter

Haller, (Heller, Hollar) Peter b. 1762 (Swit. Pa. or   Pvt. Pa. Mil.
Germany) d. Pa. 1851 m. Katherine Swigert — son Peter Jr.
m. Nancy Waggoner

Halliburton, Martin b. 1776 d. Mo. 1860   Orderly Sgt. Tenn. Mil.
m. Frances Turner — daughter Frances m. William Harrison Nichols

Hallock, Benjamin b. N.Y. 1787 d. N.Y. 1863   Ens. N.Y. Mil.
m. Fannie Gilbert — son John Elijah m. Loretta Gould

Hallowell, Joseph   Vol. 5   Sgt. Del. Mil.

Halsey, Abraham b. N.Y. 1790 d. N.Y. 1857   Pvt. N.Y. Mil.
m. Anne Wright Gosman — son James M. m. Jane Pearl Lord

Halsey, Frederick b. N.Y. 1761 d. N.Y. 1838   Chaplain N.Y. Mil.
m. Letitia Platt — daughter Caroline m. James Bailey

Halstead, Jonathan b. N.J. 1769 d. Ga. 1814   Rec. Pat., U.S. Agent
m. Isabella Neil — son Daniel N. m. Harriett Tyler   (Factor) Ga.

Ham, John   Vol. 6   Musician Mass. (Me.) Mil.

Hamblen (Hamlin), Gershom b. Mass. (Me.) 1779   Rec. Pat., Collector
d. N.Y. 1805 m. Lydia Freeman   & Petition Signer
daughter Eliza m. Julius Tuttle

Hamblen, Ichabod b. Mass. (Me.) 1791 d. Me. 1871   Pvt. Mass. Mil.
m. Lydia Webb Fickett — son Samuel m. Maria F. Flint

Hamill, John   Vol. 10 and 11   Pvt. Pa. Mil.

Hamilton, Adam C. b. c. 1780 d. Tenn. aft. 1831   Pvt. Tenn. Mil.
m. Sarah Elizabeth Atterbury — son Oliver P. m. Helen Kirkpatrick

Hamilton, Andrew b. S.C. 1794 d. Texas 1859 or 1867   Capt. S.C. Mil.
m. Deliliah Smith — daughter Emeline m. James Brown
son Young H. m. Mary Smith

Hamilton, David b. Tenn. 1794 d. Tenn. 1879   Pvt. Tenn. Mil.
m. Cibella Griffin — daughter Parmelia m. Michael Keenan

Hamilton, Erastus b. Mass. 1790 d. N.Y. 1857   Surgeon Mate N.Y. Mil.
m. Harriet Miller — son Edward J. m. Isabella Reed

Hamilton, James b. Va. 1783 d. W.Va. 1854   Pvt. 2nd Va. Mil.
m. Clarissa Fleming — daughter Christiana m. Marshall Jackson

Hamilton, James b. Ire. 1746/7 d. Ga. 1817   Rec. Pat., Many Civil Offices
m. Ann Fox Napier — daughter Ann Elizabeth
m. Samuel Watkins Goode

Hamilton, John b. Pa. 1770 d. Pa. 1856   Capt. Major Pa. Mil.
m. Sara Courtney — son Matthew m. Ruth Steele

Hamilton, John Craig b. Va. 1777 d. Mo. 1857   Lt. Va. Mil.
m. Sarah Craig — son John M. m. Sarah Susan Moore

Hamilton, Joseph DeVance b. Md. 1795 d. La. 1861   Pvt. La. Mil.
m. Margaret Webb — son William Ignacious
m. Mary Elizabeth Brown

Hamilton, Joseph P. b. Tenn. 1795/6 d. Ark. 1884   Pvt. Tenn. Mil.
m. Julia Ann Hardin — son John V. m. Harriet Plant

Hamilton, Paul b. S.C. 1762 d. S.C. 1816 Rec. Pat., Controller, Secy. of
m. Mary Wilkinson — daughter Margaret   Navy, Governor S.C.
m. Gov. Benjamin Whitemarsh

Hamilton, Robert b. Tenn. 1796 d. Texas 1876   Pvt. Tenn. Mil.
m. Elizabeth Bethea — son Thomas S. m. Elizabeth Ballard

Hamilton, Robert b. Pa. 1768 d. Ky. 1817 m. Mary Edward Pvt. Ky. Mil.
daughter Spicy G. m. John Thomson

Hamilton, Rufus b. Mass. 1757 d. Mass. 1817   Rec. Pat., Rep. Legis.
m. Polly Kingsbury — son Isaac m. Mahala

Hamilton, William   Vol. 17   Major Ga. Mil.

Hamilton, William b. Va. 1789 d. Va. 1870 Major & Brigade Inspector
m. Mary Bryan — daughter Mary m. John L. Hodges   Ga. Mil.

Hamilton, William B.   Vol. 9   Sgt. Ohio Mil.

Hamilton, William Sutherland b. N.C. 1789 d. Pa. 1872 Lt. Col. 3rd Rifle.
m. Eliza Caroline Stewart — son Jones Stewart   War 1812
m. Fannie Buck

Hamler, Alexander b. Pa. 1790 d. Ohio 1875   Pvt. Pa. Mil.
m. Mary Brenner — son Samuel George m. Harriet Howe

Hamlett, James b. N.C. 1795 d. Tenn. 1887   Pvt. Tenn. Mil.
m. Jane Cullen Atkins — daughter Margaret Ann
m. David Halliburton   REAL DAUGHTER
daughter Mary Jane m. Wesley W. Morrison

Hamlin, Salmon b. Conn. 1763 d. N.Y. 1821   Capt. Mass. Mil.
m. Margaret Vanderburg — daughter Pauline m. Mark Dewey

Hamm, Daniel b. Pa. 1759 d. Pa. 1832 m. Elizabeth Winter Pvt. Pa. Mil.
son John William m. Esther Lefevre

Hammer, Jonathan b. Ger. 1771 d. Tenn. 1851   Pvt. Tenn. Mil.
m. Agnes (Kup or Keep?) — son William m. Mariah Temple

Hammersley, William b. Va. 1789 d. Va. 1860   Pvt. Va. Mil.
m. Malinda Hays — daughter Sarah Elizabeth m. David Williamson

Hammon, John Loren   Vol. 12   Pvt. N.Y. Mil.

Hammond, James b. N.Y. 1786 d. N.Y. 1875   Pvt. N.Y. Mil.
m. Mary Corrigan — son Edmund J. m. Rachel Knapp

Hammond, Job b. Va. 1754 d. Ky. 1844   Sgt. Ky. Mil.
m. Nancy Anne Stone — son Davis S. m. Anne Eliza Long

Hammond, John D. b. N.Y. 1780 d. N.Y. 1840   Ens. N.Y. Mil.
m. Hellanah Settle — son John W. m. Mary Viola Watkins

Hammond, Josiah b. Conn. 1760 d. Conn. 1844   Pvt. Conn. Mil.
m. Abigail Durkee — son Josiah, Jr. m. Elizabeth Moseley

Hammond, Phillip b. Md. 1753 d. Ala. 1832   Indian Scout Ky.
m. Christina Cook — daughter Sallie m. Bazil Hall

Hammond, Rawleigh b. 1756 d. S.C. 1838 m. Mary Y. Pvt. Ga. Mil.
son Samuel m. Nancy Twitly

Hammond, Samuel b. Va. 1757 d. S.C. 1842   Rec. Pat., U.S. Congress
m. Eliza Amelia O'Keefe   Col. Commandant
daughter Margaret Ellen m. Samuel Kingman

Hammond, Theodore b. Conn. 1789 d. Ill. 1856   Pvt. Ohio Mil.
m. Mary Fisk (2) — son Theodore m. Julia Reynolds

Hammond, Thomas b. N.C. 1777 d. Ga. 1864 m. Ann Allen   Pvt. Ga. Mil.
son Thomas S. m. Eliza Anne Merritt

Hammond, Urial b. Conn. 1781 d. Conn. 1868 m. Sally Holt   Lt. Conn. Mil.
son Alfred m. Cynthia Storer

Hammons (Hammonds), Leroy b. Va. d. Tenn. 1843   Lt. Col. Tenn. Mil.
m. Mary Hampton — daughter Elizabeth m. Charles L. Sullivan

Hampton, Thomas b. Ky. 1786 d. Ky. 1843   Pvt. Ky. Mil.
m. Emily Pemberton Jones — daughter Mary Belle
m. Albert Williams Smith

Hampton, William b. Va. 1781 d. N.C. 1831 Patriot N.C. Mem. Committee
m. Nancy Bryan — daughter Philadelphia A.   of Safety
m. George Williams Brown

Hancock, Joel b. 1788 d. 1863   **Pvt. Ky.**
m. Jane Lintner — daughter Harriet Hancock m. Ezra Clark

Hancock, William b. Va. 1749 d. Ky. 1857 m. Ann Hill   Pvt. Ky. Mil.
daughter Winefred m. William Henry Harrison

Hancock, Zebina b. N.Y. 1788 d. N.Y. 1833   Pvt. N.Y. Mil.
m. Laura Preston — son Andrew H. m. Louisa Young

Hancox (Hancock), Peleg b. Conn. 1787 d. Conn. 1855   Sgt. Conn. Mil.
m. Betsey Burdick — son Joseph N. m. Emeline Pendleton

Hand, Aaron b. N.J. 1779/80 d. N.J. 1852   Pvt. N.J. Mil.
m. Rebecca Mulford — daughter Rebecca Ann m. James Wiley

Hand, Charles b. Va. 1792 d. Ill. 1852   Pvt. Va. Mil.
m. Elizabeth Hendricks — son Charles D. m. Julia Ann Pavey

Hand, Jonathan, Jr. b. N.J. 1780 d. N.J. 1834   Capt. N.J. Mil.
m. Mrs. Sarah (Moore) Wilson — daughter Esther m. Elijah Husted

Hand, Thomas b. N.J. 1794 d. Pa. 1868   Pvt. Ohio Mil.
m. Rebecca Whitaker — daughter Mary N. m. William G. Reynolds

Hand, William b. N.J. 1764 d. N.J. 1814 m. Sarah Shaw   Pvt. N.J. Mil.
son William, Jr. m. Nancy Terry

Handley, James Sr. b. N.C. bef. 1750 d. bef. 1823   Del. N.C. Conventions
m. Molly Cato? — daughter Keziah m. Batt Lee

Handley, John Sr. b. Va. 1746 d. (W.) Va. 1811   Major Va. Mil.
m. Mary Harrison — son Archibald m. Susan Kincaid
son Samuel m. Sarah Walker Harmon

Handley, John   Vol. 17   Pvt. Va. Mil.

Handy, William   Vol. 3   Capt. Schooner "Resolution" Mass.

Hanford, Alford b. Conn. 1790 d. Conn. 1828   Pvt. Conn. Mil.
m. Elizabeth Fitch — daughter Angeline A.
m. Ignatius Theophilus Chutkowski

Hanks, Amos b. 1780 d. 1859   Corp. 50th Reg. N.Y. Mil.
m. Polly Fisk — son Fisk Hands m. Mary Louisa Rubbelee Hicks

Hanks, Chichester b. Ky. 1781 d. Ky.   Pvt. Ky. Light Inf.
    m. Elizabeth Allin (Penney) — daughter Susan Mary
    m. William F. Bond

Hanks, Fielding b. N.C. 1784 d. Ky. 1861 m. Lydia Harper   Corp. Ky. Vol.
    daughter Ann m. James Cox

Hanley, Peter b. Pa. 1771 d. Pa. 1854 m. Owensline   Capt. Pa. Mil.
    daughter Sarah J. m. Charles H. Richards

Hanna, Thomas b. Ire. 1760 d. Ohio 1839 m. Jane Cowden   Pvt. Pa. Mil.
    son Thomas, Jr. m. Jemima Patterson

Hannah, George b. Va. abt. 1782 d. Va. 1870   Capt. Va. Mil.
    m. Lucy Morton — son George C. m. Anne Eliza Spraggins

Hanes, Peter b. 1777 d. Ky. 1861 m. Nancy Bibb   Sgt. Tenn. Vol.
    son William M. m. Gabrilla Wright

Hannah, Edward b. Pa. 1792 d. Pa. 1876   Sgt. Pa. Mil.
    m. Penelope Breadin — daughter Margaret m. Elijah Corbin

Hannah, William C. b. Va. 1796 d. Va. 1837   Pvt. Va. Cavalry
    m. Jane Clack Thornton — daughter Ann Elizabeth
    m. Robert Nicolson

Hannum, John b. Pa. 1740 d. Pa. 1799   Patriot, held many offices Pa.
    m. Alice Parks — son Richard M. m. Charlotte Rustin

Hansberger, Adam b. Va. 1751 d. Va. 1815   Major Va. Mil.
    m. Catherine Nall — daughter Catherine m. Jacob Hansberger

Hansberger (Hansbarger), Henry b. Va. 1794   Pvt. Va. Riflemen
    d. Va. 1867 m. Miss Bear — son Layton J. m. Martha Taylor French

Hansbrough, Joel b. Va. 1779 d. Ky. 1844 m. Lucy Gooch   Lt. Ky. Mil.
    son Thomas m. Mary Thomas Stone

Hansbrough, Morias b. Ky. 1792 d. Ky. or Ind. 1880/1   Corp. Ky. Mil.
    m. Catherine Smith — daughter Martha m. Thomas B. Smith
    son Morias, Jr. m. Amelia Hubbard

Hansell, John Walker b. Va. 1782 d. Ala. 1866   Capt. U.S. Inf.
    m. Orpha Hite Wood — daughter Josephine (single)
    REAL DAUGHTER
    son John H. m. Martha Elizabeth Jackson

Hanson, John b. Md. 1715 d. Md. 1789   Rec. Pat., Mem. of Congress 1784
    m. Jane Contee — son John F. m. Rose Anna Evans

Harbaugh, Daniel   Vol. 5   Capt. Ohio Mil.

Harbaugh, William b. Pa. 1779 d. Ohio 1833   Pvt. Ohio Mil., Qrtmstr.
    m. Sarah Springer — daughter Rachel   Gen., 1st Postmaster
    m. Warwick Martin

Harbin, Joshua b. Md. d. bet. 1790 & 1792   Served in Knox Co. N.W. Terr.
    m. Elizabeth — daughter Cassandra m. Michael Thorn   Mil.

Harbison, Aaron b. 1793 d. 1860 m. Nanc Dyer   Pvt. Tenn. Mil.
    son Pryor L. m. Mary A. C. Claiborne

Harbison, Francis b. Pa. 1758 d. Pa. 1823   Pvt. Pa. Mil.
    m. Katherine Hart — daughter Jane m. James Ewing

Harcall, William b. N.Y. 1789 d. Wis. 1863   Pvt. N.Y. Mil.
    daughter Martha m. Jenodor Ten Eyck   REAL DAUGHTER

Harcourt, Daniel b. Md. 1798 d. N.D. 1889 m. Jane McCaw   Pvt. Ky. Mil.
    daughter Betsey m. Felix Conner

Harcum, Lee Peyton b. Va. 1777 d. Md. aft. 1835   Ens. Va. Mil.
m. Betty Polk — son Henry L. m. Elizabeth Ann Allen

Hardcastle, Thomas b. Md. 1737 d. Md. 1808   Judge of Orphan's
m. Henrietta Downs — son Aaron m. Miss Starkey   Ct. Md.

Hardee, John   Vol. 5   Major Ga. Mil.

Hardeman, Thomas b. ca. 1750 d. Tenn. 1833   Lt. Tenn. Vol.
m. Mary Perkins — son Blackstone m. Ann Bunch

Harden (Harding), Freeman b. Mass. 1783 d. Me. aft. 1873   Pvt. Mass. Mil.
m. Thankful Stetson — son Jared m. Cynthia Roundy

Hardenburgh, Abraham J. b. N.Y. 1777 d. N.Y. 1845   Lt. Col. N.Y. Mil.
m. Margaret Du Bois — son Josiah m. Cornelia Dubois

Hardesty, Abraham (Abram) b Md. 1789 d. Ohio 1865   Pvt. Ohio Mil.
m. Elizabeth Marshall — son John m. Sarah Ann Correll

Hardesty, Isaac   Vol. 7   Sgt. Va. Mil.

Hardie, Robert b. Pa. 1798 d. Md. 1881   Midshipman Navy
m. Emily Jane McClure — daughter Ella H. (single)
REAL DAUGHTER
daughter Emily A. (single)   REAL DAUGHTER

Hardin, David b. Va. ca. 1765 d. Miss. 1844 m. Sarah Gist   Capt. Ky.
daughter Eliza m. Edmond Willis

Hardin, James b. Ga. 1794 d. Ga. 1854 m. Julia Staples   Pvt. Ga. Mil.
son Thomas Stephen m. Mary J. Coarts

Hardin, John b. Va. 1753 d. Ohio 1792   Qtrmstr. Ky. 1789
m. Jane Davis — daughter Elizabeth m. Ebenezer Hancock

Hardin, Joseph b. Va. 1734 d. Tenn. 1818   Rec. Pat., Legis. Tenn. 1794
m. Jane Gibson — son Joseph, Jr. m. Zany Dillahunty also
Sarah Drake
son Gibson, Sr. m. Sarah Gallaher

Hardin, Mark b. Va. 1750 d. Ga. 1817   Rec. Pat., Lt. Ga. Mil. Magistrate
m. Frances Newsom — daughter Martha m. Jacob Garrard   1794

Hardin, Mark, Jr. b. Ky. 1773 d. N.C. m. Frances Hill   Major Ga. Mil.
son Pleasant m. Tabitha Gentry

Hardin, Mark b. Va. 1738 d. Ga. 1817   Rec. Pat., Just. of Peace
m. Mary Hunter — son James m. Mary Freeman

Hardin, Martin b. Va. 1785 d. Ky. 1857 m. Rosannah Fisher   Pvt. Ky. Mil.
daughter Laetitia m. Jesse Vandaman

Harding, Abraham b. Conn. 1744 d. Pa.   2nd Major N.Y. Mil.
m. Huldah Tryon — son Amos m. Phoebe Tripp

Harding, Dexter b. N. Y. 1796 d. Ark. 1862   Pvt. Drummer N.Y. Mil.
m. Jane Allen — son Henry Allen m. Mary Ann Harper

Hardy, Humphrey b. N.C. c. 1743 d. N.C. 1809   Rec. Pat., Just. of Peace
m. Mrs. Morning Smith — son Jonathan   N.C. 1785-1795
m. Susanna Sheppard

Hardy, Jonathan b.— d. Ala. 1816 m. Susanna Sheppard   Pvt. Miss. Mil.
daughter Hester Ann m. Martin Winston Guy

Hare, Daniel b. Pa. 1789 d. Ohio 1866 m. Sarah Ross   Sgt. Ohio Mil.
son Marquis de L. m. Mary Alice Alexander

Hare, Jacob b. Pa. 1790 d. Ind. aft. 1835   Pvt. Ohio Mil.
m. Betsey Freshour — son Doone or Deluney m. Rebecca Burk

Hare, Jacob b. N.C. 1790 d. Ark. 1857 m. **Emma** Wheeler   **Pvt. N.C. Mil.**
    son Thomas m. Bettie Tuberville

Harford, Samuel b. Conn. 1762 d. N.Y. 1808 m. Ann   **Lt. Conn. Mil.**
    daughter Lucretia m. **Jesse Camp**

Harford, Thomas b. N.Y. 1798 d. Ohio 1870   **Pvt. N.Y. Mil.**
    m. Eliza Ann St. John — daughter Orpha Jeanette
    m. Joseph Trimble Barr

Harkness, James b. S.C. 1780 d. Ga. 1851   **Lt. Ga. Mil.**
    m. Rosannah Baskin — daughter Anne B. m. Robert B. Price

Harl, Baldwin b. Va. 1790 d. Mo. 1893 m. **Mary** Gates   **Pvt. Ky. Mil.**
    son John P. m. Mary Mannen

Harlan, Bonham b. Pa. d. Ill. 1845 m. Jane Baxter   **Pvt. Tenn. Mil.**
    son William m. Nancy H.

Harlan, James b. Va. 1755 d. Ky. 1816 m. Sarah Caldwell   **Lt. Ky. Vol.**
    son Jehu m. Clarissa Black

Harle, Baldwin II b. 1767 d. aft. 1823   **Major Cav. 1796**
    m. Rosanna Huffman — son Baldwin Harle III
    m. Mary Hightower Lea

Harley, James b. S.C. 1777 d. S.C. 1845 m. Jane Ann Creech, **Pvt. S.C. Mil.**
    son James M. m. Susan Frances Harley (cousin)

Harlow, Amaziah b. Mass. 1788 d. Mass. 1862   **Sgt. Mass. Mil.**
    m. Mrs. Ruth Rogers Bartlett Drew — daughter Martha D.
    m. John Boutell also George H. Devens   **REAL DAUGHTER**

Harlow, Levi b. Mass. 1745 d. Vt. 1833 m. Silence Cobb   **Patriot Vt.**
    son Barnum m. Susannah Reed

Harlow, William b. N.Y. 1779 d. Ohio 1818   **Pvt. N.Y. Mil.**
    m. Mary Conklin — daughter Martha Ann m. Pardin Sheldon

Harman, Elias b. N.C. 1780 d. Va. 1856 m. Polly Davis   **Ens. Va. Mil.**
    son James W. m. Nora Jeanette Patton

Harmon, Andrew b. Pa. 1768 d. Pa. 1838   **Pvt. Pa. Mil.**
    m. Irma Catherine Sandles — daughter Irma E. m. John Byerly

Harmon, Benjamin b. (Me.) Mass. 1795 d. Me. 1841   **Pvt. Mass. Mil.**
    m. Priscilla Hanscom — son Walter B. m. Martha J. Cary

Harmon, Henry b. Va. 1777 d. Va. 1854   **Pvt. Va. Mil.**
    m. Elizabeth Persinger — —son Eli F. m. Margaret Brumfield
    daughter Sarah m. Wm. B. Triplett

Harmon, Henry b. Isle of Man. 1726 d. Va. 1822   **Pvt. Va. Mil.**
    m. Nancy Wilburn — daughter Rhoda N. m. William Neel

Harmon, John b. Conn. 1789 d. Ohio 1871   **Corp. Ohio Mil.**
    m. Philinda Chapman — son Robert O. m. Mary Fitzgerald

Harmon, Thomas b. (Me.) Mass. 1762 or 1780 d. Me. 1834, **Pvt. Mass. Mil.**
    m. Lydia Elden (Elders) — son Flanders m. Jane Norton

Harn, John b. Md. 1789 d. Md. 1852 m. Charlotte Hay   **Pvt. Md. Mil.**
    daughter Ellen Dorcas (Miss)   **REAL DAUGHTER**

Harne, Baltzer b. Pa. 1754 d. Pa. 1826   **Pvt. Pa. Mil.**
    m. Catherine Kreber — son David m. Susanna Wolf

Harness, Solomon b. Va. 1762 d. Va. 1839   **Pvt. Va. Cavalry 1814**
    m. Catherine Stump — daughter Frances Ann m. Barnett Hoe Foley

Harper, James   Vol. 11   Lt. Va. Mil.

Harper, Travis (Francis) b. N.C. 1737 d. N.C. 1790 Patriot, Just. of Peace
m. Elizabeth Bright — son Francis m. Theresa Hopton   N.C. 1787

Harper, William b. S.C. 1784 d. S.C. 1831 m. Catherine Huey   Pvt. S.C.
daughter Mary m. Matthew Biggart Kirk

Harpold, Solomon b. Va. 1796 d. W.Va. 1888   Pvt. Va. Mil.
m. Melinda Shinn — daughter Elizabeth m. Solomon Wallace Stone
daughter Mazilla m. James M. Kessel
son Solomon W. m. Samantha Jane Sayre

Harrell, Asa b. N.C. 1794 d. Tenn. 1870   Pvt. Tenn. Mil.
m. Elizabeth Granade — son Jesse Lee m. Rhoda Ann Robinson

Harrell, Asa b. N.C. 1779 d. Ga. 1851   Pvt. Ga. Mil.
m. Elizabeth Keen — son John A. m. Jeanette Hendley
son Willis m. Sophia Henley

Harrell, Francis b. N.C. 1781 d. N.C. 1830 m. Betsy Owens Pvt. N.C. Mil.
son John A. m. Emma Lanie Lee

Harrell, James b. N.C. 1792 d. N.C. 1858   Pvt. Va. Mil.
m. Frances Waddy Wise — son Joseph H. m. Emily Taylor Uzzell

Harrell, Levi b. N.C. 1777 d. Ga. 1865 m. Elizabeth Holt   Pvt. Ga. Mil.
son William m. Sophia Hendley

Harrell, Samuel b. N.C. 1740 d. N.C. 1811 Rec., Pat., Clerk of Court N.C.
m. Sally Bond also Mary Freeman — son Abner m. Jennie Yates
son Willis W. m. Louise Granburg

Harrell, William   Vol. 4   Pvt. Ga. Mil.

Harrington, Cyril b. Vt. 1782/3 d. N.Y. 1855   Pvt. 76th N.Y. Regt.
m. Rachel Madison — daughter Almira m. Adney Carley

Harrington, James   Vol. 16   Drummer, N.Y. Mil.

Harrington, Stephen b. Conn. 1777 d. Ohio 1812   Capt. Ohio Mil.
m. Sarah Holcomb — son Henry m. Hannah Reeder Dungan

Harrington, William D.   Vol. 8   Capt. Del. Mil.

Harris, Abner Nelson b. Va. 1795 d. Va. 1859   Pvt. Va. Mil.
m. Lucy Overton — daughter Clara M. m. Henry Daniel Gardner

Harris, Allen b. N.C. 1787 d. N.C. 1827   Pvt. N.C. Mil.
m. Lennie or Tennie Wood — son John Crump m. Melinda Popham

Harris, Asa   Vol. 17   Capt. or Major N.Y.

Harris, Benton   Vol. 5   Major Del. Troops

Harris, Ephraim b. N.J. 1732 d. N.J. 1794   Pat., Judge N.J. Ct. Mem. &
m. Jane Pierson — son Pierson   Speaker of Assembly 1778-1793
m. Judith Nixon

Harris, Henry Harrison b. N.C. 1791 d. Ala. 1863   Pvt. Ga. Mil.
m. Lucinda Pittman — son Noah Marion m. Catherine Cooksey

Harris, James b. N.C. 1777 d. Tenn. 1863   Capt. Tenn. Mil.
m. Ann (Nancy) Thomson — daughter Ann W. m. Hartwell Freeman

Harris, James b. Va. 1750 d. Va. 1794   Rec. Pat., Surveyor & other
m. Mary Cheagle — daughter Judith m. George Winston   Civil Off.

Harris, James b. N.C. 1792 d. Ind. 1854 m. Naomi Lowis   Pvt. Ind. Mil.
son Milton R. m. Matilda Bradbury

Harris, Jeptha Vining b. Ga. 1782 d. Ga. 1856   Brig. Gen. Ga. Mil.
    m. Sarah (Sally) Hunt — son James Walton m. Martha Watkins

Harris, John b. Ire. 1724 d. Pa. 1794   Rec Pat., Mem. Gen. Assbly.
    m. Jane Harris (cousin) — daughter Jean m. James Patterson

Harris, John b. Md. 1775 d. Md. 1834   Pvt. Md. Sea Fencibles (Rejected)
    m. Ruth Gunstall — daughter Ann Delia m. Thomas Miles Moore

Harris, John L.   Vol. 14   Pvt. N.Y. Mil.

Harris, Joshua b. Va. 1795 d. Ohio 1859   Pvt. Ohio Mil.
    m. Jane Badger — son William B. m. Dinah Byers

Harris, Micajah b. Ga. 1792 d. Ga. 1847 m. Mary Butler   Pvt. Ga. Mil.
    daughter Pernaty m. John G. Hammonds

Harris, Nathaniel Snell b. Mass. 1791 d. Me. 1859   Pvt. Mass. Mil.
    m. Eliza Adams — son Everett m. Ella R. Freeman Lothrop

Harris, Nelson b. Ga. 1764 d. Ga. 1815 m. Sara   Pvt. Ga. Mil.
    son Alston G. m. Ann Gray

Harris, Richard   Vol. 17   Pvt. Ky. Mil.

Harris, Robert b. Va. 1772 d. Va. m. Rebecca Rice   Pvt. Va. Mil.
    son Robert W. m. Mary M. Perkins

Harris, Samuel Woods b. Va. 1793 d. Mo. 1852   Pvt. Va. Cavalry
    son Edwin E. m. Margaret Ann Cox

Harris, Tyree b. Va. 1765 d. Ky. 1840 m. Rachel Brown   Pvt. Va. Mil.
    son Overton D. m. Lettie Pierce

Harris, William b. S.C. abt. 1778 d. S.C. 1820 m. Martha   Pvt. S.C.
    son George m. Elizabeth Cartledge

Harris, William Overton b. Va. c. 1785 d. Va. 1861   Corp. Va. Light Inf.
    m. Mary Ann Tyler — daughter Mary E. H.
    m. Joseph Shelton Meredith

Harris, William W. b. N.C. 1788 d. S.C. 1875   Major 12th Regt. Tenn.
    m. Elizabeth Golightly — son David G. m. Emily Lyles

Harrison, Batteal b. Va. 1780 d. Ohio 1857   Capt. Ohio Mil.
    m. Elizabeth Scott — son Benjamin m. Martha Reeves
    son Scott m. Frances Young

Harrison, Daniel b. Va. 1763 d. Tenn. 1817 m. Anne Smith   Pvt. Va. Mil.
    son Daniel, Jr. m. Elizabeth Weaver

Harrison, Edmond b. Va. 1769 d. Ind. 1844 m. Mary Stinson   Corp. Va. Mil.
    daughter Desdemona m. Jonathan McCarty

Harrison, Isham b. S.C. 1788 d. Miss. 1861   Pvt. S.C. Mil.
    m. Harriet Kelley — daughter Eliza Ann m. Baylis Wood Earle

Harrison, Jabez   Vol. 15   N.J. Mil.

Harrison, John   Vol. 17   Major Va. Mil.

Harrison, John Dawson b. Va. 1788 d. Va. 1853   Pvt. Va. Mil.
    m. Elizabeth Corlin — daughter Mary H. m. Isaac Kell

Harrison, Micajah b. Va. 1788 d. Ky. 1850 m. Polly Payne   Pvt. Ky. Mil.
    son Jilson P. Sr. m. Sidney Ann Norton

Harrison, Reuben b. S.C. 1760 d. S.C. 1835   Pvt. S.C. Inf. & Tenn. Mil.
    m. Sara Burgess — son Willoughby m. Elizabeth Rives

Harrison, Reuben Jr. b. Va. 1780-4 d. Mo. 1844   Major Ky. Mounted Mil.
m. Elizabeth T. Hill — daughter Susan M. m. John S. Franklin

Harrison, Robert b. Va. 1780 d. Va. 1826   Capt. Va. Mil.
m. Charlotte Thomas Pretlow — son Benjamin P.
m. Martha Louisa Williams
son Dr. Robert m. Susan Epps Williams
son William H. m. Agnes Heath

Harrison, Thomas   Vol. 12   Pvt. Va. Mil.

Harrison, William b. 1760/3 d. Ohio m. Mary Bunting   Pvt. Ohio Mil.
son John m. Jane Miller

Harrison, William H. b. N.J. 1792 d. Pa. 1874   Pvt. N.J. Mil.
m. Rebecca Lippincot — —son Edward m. Susan (L'or)

Harrison, William Henry b. Va. 1773 d. D.C. 1841   Major Gen. U.S. Army
m. Anna Symmes — son John S.   Ohio, Pres. of U.S.
m. Elizabeth Irwin

Harriss, Daniel b. Mass. 1775 d. N.Y. 1813   Pvt. Mass. Mil.
son Daniel m. Mary Windsor

Harrod (Herrod), Samuel b. Ky. 1776 d. Ohio 1857   Capt. Ohio Mil.
m. Mary Paullin — daughter Polly m. Jacob Carr

Harrouff, Andrew b. Holland 1786 d. Pa. c. 1870   Sgt. Pa. Mil.
m. (1) Magdelena Kuhns — son John m. Katherine Dimeler

Harry, John b. Md. 1782 d. Md. 1866   Pvt. Md. 43rd Regt.
m. Harriet Beall Williams — daughter Harriet B.
m. John Wm. Chesley

Harry, John b. Md. c. 1791 d. Ill. 1852 m. Mary Ashbury   Pvt. Md. Vol.
son George I. m. Elizabeth P. McGary

Harsh, John Henry, Sr. b. Pa. 1734 d. Pa. 1819   Pvt. Pa. Mil.
m. Maria Margaritha Scholl — son John H. Jr. m. Magdalena

Harshman, Christian b. Germany 1744 d. Md. 1816   Rec. Pat., Pres.
m. Catherine Grossnickle — daughter Christina   Elector, Md.
m. George Warner (Werner)

Harshman, Henry b. Va. 1797 d. Ind. 1843   Pvt. Ohio Mil.
m. Mary Magdalene Fogle — son Moses m. Elizabeth Leah Everding

Hart, James b. Mass. 1770 d. N.J. 1814 m. Martha Rice   Pvt. Mass. Mil.
daughter Mary m. Levi Cheney

Hart, Josiah b. Va. 1764 d. Ky. 1845 m. Judith Tanner   Pat.
son Thomas m. Lucy Ashley

Hart, John b. Pa. 1786 d. Ohio 1865 m. Susan Dunbar   Pvt. Pa. Mil.
daughter Rebecca m. Abraham Rhodenbaugh

Hart, Robert b. Ga. 1776? d. Ga. 1839   Sgt. Ga. Mil.
m. Sarah Patterson — son Jesse m. Talitha Waller

Hart, Robert b. Va. 1776 d. Ga. 1839 m. Elizabeth Bowen   Sgt. Ga. Mil.
daughter Mazie m. Herndon Patterson

Hart, Rufus b. Conn. d. Ohio 1840 m. Esther Cotter   Lt. N.Y. Mil.
daughter Lucinda m. Edward Sumner

Hart, Thomas   Vol. 12   Corp. U.S. Dragoons

Hart, William b. Conn. 1786 d. N.Y. 1834 m. Delia Willis   Lt. N.Y. Mil.
son John Jay m. Mary E. Gidley (adopted Matthews)

Hart, William b. Mass. (Me.) 1774 d. Me. 1837   Pvt. Mass. (Me.) Mil.
m. Martha Wall — daughter Lucy m. Jeremiah Grover

Hart, William b. Va. 1784 d. Ark. 1873 m. Nancy Peoples   Pvt. Ga. Mil.
son William L. m. Elizabeth Carter

Hartley, Michael b. S.C. 1785 d. Ga. 1832   Pvt. N.C. Mil.
m. Polly Harris Heuler — son Frederick m. Massilva Lovelace

Hartley, Michael b. S.C. 1785 d. Ga. 1882   Pvt. N.C. Mil.
m. Mary Harris or Harrison — son James D. m. Parmelia Jackson

Hartman, Frederick b. Pa. 1794 d. (W.) Va. 1859   Pvt. Pa. or Va. Mil.
m. Nancy Jenkins — son Elliott m. Martha Ellen Pixler
son George F. C. m. Amanda Whisler

Hartman, George b. Pa. 1793 d. Pa. 1878 m. Edith Weaver   Capt. Pa. Mil.
son Dr. William D. m. Mary J. Kable

Hartman, Jacob b. N.Y. 1777 d. N.Y. 1859 m. Hannah Cox   Pvt. N.Y. Mil.
son Jacob, Jr. m. Eunice Jane Wherry

Hartman, Peter b. Pa. 1784 d. Pa. 1849   Pvt. Pa. Mil.
m. Margaret Metzler — son Peter m. Margaret Fetters

Hartsell, I. A. b. Tenn. 1777 d. Tenn 1858   Pvt Tenn. Vol.
m. Mary Norton — son Paul Anthony m. Margaret Jane Reagan

Hartshorn, Ryal b. Conn. 1789 d. N.Y. 1857 m. Jane Kingsley   Sgt. Conn.
daughter Hannah m. Marcus Schenck

Hartsook, Peter b. Md. 1792 d. Iowa 1864 m. Ann Wooten   Pvt. Va. Mil.
son William m. Catherine Smoot

Hartsough, Henry b. N.Y. 1772 d. N.Y. 1826   Lt. N.Y. Mil.
m. Sarah Van Ness — daughter Johannah m. John Scribner

Hartzell, George b. Pa. 1733 d. Pa. 1795   Capt. Pa. Mil.
m. Catherine Nyce — son George Jr.
m. Catherine Krohen (Cron-Kron)

Hartzell, George, Jr. b. Pa. 1770 d. Pa. 1850   Lt. Pa. Mil.
m. Catherine Krohen (Cron-Kron) (1) — daughter Nancy
m. James Harkins

Hartzog, Daniel b. S.C. 1774 d. S.C. 1826 m. Susannah Zorn   Pvt. S.C.
daughter Elizabeth m. Nelson Bodiford

Hartzog, Frederick b.—d.— m. Rany Bowell   Sgt. Pa. Arty.
daughter Elizabeth m. John Chick

Harvey, Ambrose   Vol. 10   Pvt. Conn. Mil.

Harvey, Henry b. Md. d. Md. aft. 1814   Pvt. Md. Mil.
m. Sarah McDaniel — son George W. m. Nancy Sly

Harvey, Jacob b. France 1789 d. Md. 1835 m.—   Pvt. Md. Mil.
daughter Maria m. Phillip A. Moltz

Harvey, James b. Md. 1792 d. Ill. 1859   Pvt. Ohio Mil.
m. Mary Ann Billingsley — daughter Hannah m. William M. John

Harvey, Lewis b. Va. 1785 d. Va. 1842   Pvt. Va.
m. Frances Thacker Burwell — son Matthew m. Martha Hannah

Harvey, Lewis b. Va. 1786 d. Va. 1856   Pvt. Va. Mil.
m. Frances Thacker Burwell — daughter Sarah M.
m. Dr. William Richards

Harvey, Rufus b. Mass. 1758 d. Vt. 1807   Rec. Pat., Just. of Peace Vt.
m. Sarah Jones — son Charles R. m. Olive Willard   1794-1807

Harvey, Samuel b. Conn. 1769 d. Conn. 1826   Pvt. Conn. Mil.
m. Sarah Cone — son James m. Amanda Dunham

Harvin, John b. S.C. 1790 d. S.C. 1869 m. Nonie Nowell   Pvt. S.C. Mil.
daughter Frances Lucy m. Thomas Weeks

Harwood, Nathan   Vol. 14   Pvt. Vt. Rifleman

Hasbrouck, Solomon Peters b. N.Y. 1784 d. N.Y. 1841   Ens. N.Y. Mil.
m. Magdalene Lefevre — daughter Ann m. Ebenezer Kilby

Hasbrouck, Stephen   Vol. 4   Lt. Col. N.Y. Mil.

Hasbrough, Morias b. Ky. 1794 d. Ky. 1881   3rd Corp. Ky. Vol.
m. Catherine Ball Smith — daughter Mary m. Moses Irwin

Hascall, William   Vol. 13   Pvt.

Haselton, Urial b. Vt. 1788 d. Vt. 1853 m. Amy Eddy   Lt. Vt. Mil.
son Chester E. m. Charlotte Augusta Allbee

Hash, Philip b. Va. 1790 d. Mo. 1849 m. Sarah Nance   Pvt. Ky. Mil.
son John m. Mildred Elkins

Haskell, Henry   Vol. 14   Pvt. N.Y. Mil.

Haskell, James   Vol. 10   Corp. Mass. Mil.

Haskell, James b. Mass. 1774 d. Mass. 1811   Corp. Mass. Mil.
m. Sarah Pollard — son Nahum m. Lucy Perrin Denison

Haskell, Nathaniel   Vol. 9   Lt. Col. N.Y. Mil.

Haskell, Samuel, Jr. b. Mass. 1749 d. Me. 1825   Pvt. N.Y. Mil.
m. Ruth Safford — daughter Mercy m. John Herring

Haskell, Stephen b. Mass. 1763 d. Mass. 1847   Pvt. Conn. Mil.
m. Rachel Larned — son Amasa m. Amanda Paull

Haskew, William Sr. b. Va. 1775 d. Tenn. 1827   Pvt. 1st Regt. Tenn.
m. Catherine Breedlove — son William Jr.   Inf. 1813
m. Telitha Courley

Haskins, Samuel b. Mass. 1789 d. N.Y. 1866   Pvt. N.Y. Mil.
m. Christiana Jones — son Isaac J. m. Amanda Bennett

Haslet, Robert b. Pa. 1777 d. Pa. 1841   Corp. Pa. Mil.
m. Elizabeth Bilger — daughter Elizabeth m. Samuel Kepner

Haslett, Thomas b. N.Y. 1781 d. N.Y. 1848   Ens. N.Y. Mil.
m. Eunice Curtis or Antis — daughter Anne E. m. Abram Post
daughter Caroline m. Thomas McClumpha

Hastings, George W. b. prob. Mass. 1785 d. Canada   Pvt. N.Y. Mil.
daughter Emily m. John Robbins

Hastings, James   Vol. 6   Pvt. Mass. Mil.

Hastings, Levi b. N.H. 1776 d. N.H. m. Edith Farr   Pvt. N.H. Mil.
son Thaddeus m. Adaline

Hastings, Matthew b. Mass. (Me.) 1796   Pvt. Mass. (Me.) Mil.
d. Maine 1878 m. Ann C. Cutter — daughter Jenie C.
m. Joseph Tyler   REAL DAUGHTER

Hastings, Thomas b. Mass. 1776 d. N.Y. 1856   Pvt. N.Y. Mil.
m. Huldah Carey — daughter Huldah m. Seth Perry Fargo

Haston, David b. Tenn. 1777 d. Tenn. 1860   Juror 1811, Overseer of
m. Margaret — son Isaac m. Elizabeth Sparkman   Roads 1812 Tenn.

Hatch, Edmund b. N.C. 1721 d. N.C. Rec. Pat., Mem. of Senate N.C.
m. Lucy Richards — daughter Lucy 1798-1799
m. Needham Whitfield

Hatch, Robert b. Mass. 1758 d. S.C. 1814 Ship Pilot, U.S. Schooner
m. Mary Roulain — daughter Ann Susannah "Alligator"
m. Thomas Sweeny

Hatch, Silvanus b. Mass. 1789 d. Mass. 1855 Capt. Mass. Coast Guard
m. Tirzah — daughter Clarissa m. Gustavus Howland

Hatch, Sylvanus b. Mass. 1788 d. Texas 1885 Pvt. La. Mil.
m. Pamelia Louise (Nicholson) Brown — son Davis W.
m. Sarah Bodfish Hatch (cousin)

Hatch, Timothy b. Conn. 1757 d. Conn. 1838 Pvt. Mass. Mil.
m. Lucretia Rockwell — son Timothy L. m. Sarah Walker Shepard

Hatcher, John b. Va. 1756 d. Va. 1837 Major Va. Mil. 1794
m. Nancy Gentry — son John, Jr. m. Mary Flippen

Hatfield, Nathan b. 1770 d. Ill. 1843 Ens. Ohio Mil.
m. Deborah Betts — daughter Sarah m. Stephen Hahn

Hathaway, Lynde b. Mass. 1782 d. Mass. 1822 Capt. Mass. Mil.
m. Nancy (Mary) Evans — daughter Laura E.
m. Richard Briggs Palmer

Hathaway, Paul b. Mass. 1788 d. Ill. 1883 Pvt. N.Y. Mil.
m. Melissa Landon

Hathaway, Zephaniah b. Mass. 1767 d. Ohio 1860 Rec. Pat., Surveyor of
m. Silence Alden — daughter Sally Hwys. Juror. Vt.
m. George Comstock, Jr.

Hatheway, Samuel b. Conn. 1760 d. Conn. 1813 Pvt. Conn.
m. Lorinda Morris — son Amos m. Mary Thrall

Hathorn (Hathorne), Seth b. Mass. 1782 d. Mass. 1865 Pvt. Mass. Mil.
m. Rebecca Thwing — son Seth, Jr. m. Amy Hathorn
son Warner m. Priscilla Eaton

Hattan, John b. Md. 1784 d. Ohio 1841 Pvt. Md. Mil.
m. Sarah Frances Collins — son William M. m. Maria Heinman

Hatton, James Hamilton b. Pa. 1782 d. Pa. 1817 Vol. 7 Sgt. Pa. Mil.

Hauck (Houck), William b. Pa. 1781 d. Md. 1856 Capt. Md. Cavalry
m. Catherine Frank — daughter Julia m. Melchior Allgire

Haught, Peter b. 1780 d. Va. 1848 m. Elizabeth Jenkins Pvt. Va. Mil.
son Evan m. (1) Mary Santee

Haughton, Charles b. N.C. ca. 1730 d. N.C. 1805 Major N.C. Mil.
m. Tamer Benbury — son John m. Mary Ryan Hooker

Haupt, Henry b. Pa. 1763 d. Pa. 1841 m. (1) Mary Pvt. U.S. Inf.
son John m. Rebecca Brandt

Hauptman, Daniel b. Md. 1791 d. D.C. 1873 Pvt. Md. Mil.
m. Ann Margaret Michael — son George W. m. Elizabeth M. Brady

Hauser, Daniel b. N.C. 1794 d. N.C. m. Susanna Holder Pvt. N.C. Mil.
son Lisanius C. m. Elias C. Rominger

Hausman, Jacob Moser b Pa. 1788 d. Pa. 1863 Pvt. Pa. Mil.
m. Mary Dorothy Reinhard — son Jacob R. m. Lucetta Steltz

Haven, Jesse b. N.J. 1781 d. Iowa 1862   Pvt. Ill. or Ohio Mil.
m. Rebecca or Margaret Hinthorn(?) — daughter Dorcas
m. Benjamin Wheeler
son Hiram m. Sarah Ann Trimmer
son Jesse D. m. Martha Maria Curtis

Havens, Silas b. Conn. 1794 d. Conn. 1857   Pvt. Conn. Mil.
m. Maryetta Griffin — son Herman E. m. Jessie Freeman Beebe

Havens, Van Rensselaer b. N.Y. 1773 d. N.Y. 1854   Rec. Pat., Notable
m. Catherine Cebra Webb — daughter Catherine E.   Aid N.Y.
(single)   REAL DAUGHTER
daughter Frances Maria m. Rev. Samuel Burr S. Bissell

Hawes, Samuel II b. Va. 1727 d. Va.   Rec. Pat., Va. Legis. 1785
m. Ann Walker — son Richard m. Katherine Walker

Hawk, Benjamin b. Pa. d. Pa. 1841/2 m. Rachel   Pvt. Pa. Mil.
son Benjamin W. m. Maria L. Scaife

Hawk, Philip b. Va. 1792 d. Ohio   Pvt. N.Y. or Ohio Mil.
m. Mary Balentine — son John B. m. Penelope Dragoo

Hawkes, Ezra b. Mass. d.— m. Sally Tolman   Pvt. Mass. Mil.
son Ezra, Jr. m. Mary Ann Berry

Hawkes, Ira b. Mass. 1766 d. Vt. m. Cynthia Mitchell   Pvt. Vt. Mil.
son Abner m. Ruth Van Duzen

Hawkins, Benjamin b. R.I. 1759 d. R.I. 1836   Lt. R.I. Light Inf. 1787-1791
m. Elizabeth Arnold — son Oliver H. P. m. Alzada Irons

Hawkins, Benjamin b. N.C. 1734 or 54 d. Ga. 1816   Col. Rec. Pat., Senator
m. Sarah Chambers — daughter Mary   N.C. 1795
m. Ezekiel Hawkins
son Robert m. Ann Featherstone

Hawkins, Benjamin Worthington b. Ky. 1793   Pvt. Ky. or Ohio Mil.
d. Ind. 1857 m. Ruth Thompson — daughter Hadassah Maria
m. Martin Joseph Maher also Thomas Hamilton Bradford

Hawkins, Byrd b. Ohio 1800 d. Ohio 1854   Pvt. Ohio Mil.
m. (1) Diana Heath — daughter Elizabeth m. J. Parker

Hawkins, Elijah b. Ky. 1790 d. Mo. 1841   Sgt. Ky. Mil.
m. Sophia Bradford — daughter Eleanor B. m. Rev. Younger R. Pitts

Hawkins, Nathaniel b. 1791 d.— m. Abigail Glover   Ens. N.Y. Mil.
daughter Delia m. David Bayles

Hawkins, Willis Alston b. N.C. 1794 d. Ga. 1883   Pvt. Ga. Mil.
m. Elizabeth Boone — son Sion B. m. Julia Kelsey

Hawley, Abel b. Vt. 1776 d. N.Y. 1862 m. Elinor Morgan   Sgt. N.Y. Vol.
son Thomas m. Elvira Knapp

Hawley, Abel b. Conn. 1763 d. Conn. 1855   Capt. Conn. Mil.
m. Hepsa Blackman — son Abel W. m. Anna Deitz

Hawley, Gideon   Vol. 14   Lt. U.S. Inf.

Hawley, Gideon b. Conn. 1763 d. Vt. 1813   Lt. Vt. Mil.
m. Lavinia Darrah — son Gideon, Jr. m. Elizabeth Caldwell

Hawley, James b. Conn. 1787 d. Vt. 1836   Rec. Pat., Notable Civil
m. (2) Martha Stevens — daughter Sophia   Services, Vt.
m. Tertius Leach

Hawley, John b. Conn. 1750/1 d. Pa. 1811   Rec. Pat., Judge of Election
    m. Mary Newton — son John, Jr.   Conn. 1808
    m. Merab Andrews Hitchcock

Hawley, Peter b. Pa. 1771 d. Pa. 1854   Capt. Pa. Mil.
    m. Phoebe Crenshire — daughter Sarah J. m. Charles H. Richards

Hawley, Pierce b. Vt. 1789 d. Ark. 1858   Sgt. Vt. Mil.
    m. Sarah Schrader (Schroeder) — son Gideon
    m. Mary Cordelia Holcomb
    daughter Priscilla m. John Young

Hawley, Samuel   Vol. 13   Capt. N.Y. Mil.

Hawn, Adam b. N.Y. 1796 d. Wis. 1876 m. Eliza Lewis   Pvt. N.Y. Mil.
    son Jerome P. m. Elmira Gillett

Hay, Andrew P. b. Ky. 1790 d. Ind. 1849   Surgeon's Mate Ky.
    m. Sarah Stites Fannie Bainbridge Gano — daughter Julia B.
    (2) m. Edward A. Cobb REAL DAUGHTER
    daughter Sarah Frances (1) m. Edward A. Cobb

Hay, Daniel   Vol. 15   Lt. Ky. Mounted Vol.

Haydel, George b. La. 1794 d. La. 1852   2nd Lt. 5th Regt. La. Mil. 1814-15
    m. Natalie Haydel (cousin) — daughter Angele Haydel
    m. Paul E. Briant

Hayden, Bartholomew b. Va. d. Ky. 1848   Ens. Ky. Vol.
    m. Julia Gleason — daughter Julia m. Gen. Joshua Burton

Hayden, James b. (Me.) Mass. 1797 d. Ill. 1872   Pvt. U.S. Inf.
    m. Judith Sawyer — daughter Julia A. m. Josiah Deyo

Hayden, John b. N.J. 1749 d. Pa. 1836 m. Charity Gard   Capt. Pa. Mil.
    son Jacob, Sr. m. Sophia Shacklett

Haydon, Benjamin b. Va. 1760 d. Ky. 1845   Pvt. Ky. Mounted Vol.
    m. Hannah McPike — daughter Elizabeth m. Benjamin F. Elston

Haydon, James b. Va. 1763/6 d. Ky. 1840   Pvt. Ranger & Indian Spy
    m. Susannah Gore — son Fountain T. m. Elizabeth Duvall Ky. Mil.

Hayes, Dennis   Vol. 8   Pvt. Mass. (Me.) Mil.

Hayes, Ebenezer b. Mass. 1783 d. Ohio 1848   Corp. Ohio Mil.
    m. Pauline Ford — son Roswell m. Minerva Allen

Hayes, Hanson b. N.H. 1792 d. N.H. 1851   Lt. N.H. Troops
    m. Sophia Swazey (wid. John T. Hanson) — daughter Mary D.
    m. Brackett Merrill
    son John H. m. Henrietta Dwight Stone

Hayes, Jeremiah   Vol. 8   Lt. N.Y. Mil.

Hayes, Jeremiah b. N.Y. 1780 d. N.Y. aft. 1817   Lt. N.Y. Mil.
    m. Lydia Chamberlain (1) — son Reuben M. Elsa Fuller

Hayes, Joel b. Conn. 1728 d. Conn. 1800   Rep. Gen. Assbly.
    m. Rebecca Post — son Joel m. Mary Bliss   Conn. 1786-1792

Hayes, Lester b. Conn. 1790 d. Ohio 1828   Pvt. Ohio Mil.
    m. Mathilda Bushnell — daughter Stella m. John J. Jacobi

Hayes, Samuel D. b. N.H. 1796 d. N.H. 1884   Musician N.H. Mil.
    m. Comfort Chesley — son Charles W. m. Ellen Weeks

Hayes, Sylvester b. Vt. 1792 d. Ohio aft. 1844   Sgt. N.Y. Mil.
    m. Fanny Bassett — daughter Achsah O. m. Christopher Avery

Haymond, William Jr. b. Md. 1771 d. Va. (W.Va.) 1848   Pvt. Va. Mil.
m. Cynthia Carroll — son Augustus m. Rebecca Madera

Haynes (Haines), George b. Va. 1736 d. Tenn. 1834   Sgt. Tenn. Mil.
m. Margaret McInturff — daughter Mary Magdelene
m. George Swingle

Haynes, John b. Ga. 1794 d. Texas 1870   Pvt. Ga. Mil.
m. Elizabeth Traylor — son Dunstan m. Mary Horn

Haynes, Robert b. N.C. 1790 d. Tenn. 1844   Pvt. Tenn.
m. Elizabeth Patton — son William m. Susan Coucn

Haynie, Lawrence (Lally) b. Va. 1794 d. Mo. 1841   Pvt. Va. Mil.
m. Margaret Sarah Damron — daughter Margaret Judith
m. Joseph Franklin Handley

Haynie, (Haney) William b. Va. 1780 d. Ill. 1870   Pvt. Va. Mil.
m. Elizabeth Bayless Frost — son Isham m. Elizabeth Cooper
daughter Martha J. m. Dr. Thomas Williams

Hays (Hayes), Corkins b. N.Y. 1791 d. Ohio 1887   Pvt. N.Y. Troops
m. Amy Dake — son Benjamin C. m. Hannah Frost

Hays (Hayes), Patrick b. Pa. d. Pa. 1823   Capt. Pa. Mil.
m. Nancy Cummins — daughter Jane Louise m. Jacob Levergood

Hays, William b. Ky. 1792 d. Ohio 1872 m. Jane Lynn   Corp. Ohio Mil.
daughter Letitia m. Elijah Morl Haigler

Hayslip, John b. Va. 1781 d. Ohio 1840   Lt. Ohio Mil.
m. Letitia Campbell — son Joseph W.
m. Lemyra Elizabeth Montgomery

Hayward, Ira b. Mass. 1782 d. Mass. aft. 1831   Pvt. Mass. Mil.
m. Olive McLaughlin — son Ira A. m. Sarah Caroline Tripp

Hazard, Sylvester Robinson b. R.I. 1791 d. R.I. 1875   Sgt. R.I. Mil.
m. Gulielma Babcock — daughter Abby R.
m. William Attmore Whaley

Hazel, John b. S.C. c. 1785 d. S.C. 1849/1850 m. Mary   Pvt. S.C. Mil.
son Dr. Joseph m. Mary T Veitch

Hazeltine, Ballard b. N.H. 1769 d. N.Y. 1836   Capt. N.H. Mil
m. Sally Noyes — son Peter m. Sarah Rieves

Hazelton, John b. Pa. 1758 d. Ohio 1834   Lt. Pa. Inf.
m. Barbara Slaughter — daughter Betsy m. Samuel Skinner

Hazelton, Roswell b. 1790 d. Ohio 1874   Corp. Ohio Vol.
m. Wealthy Fenton — daughter Wealthy m. John Hutchinson

Hazen, William Blackwell b. Pa. d.— m. Nancy Lamour   Sgt. Pa. Mil.
daughter Celia Jane m. Joseph Ritner Shepard

Hazlett, Samuel b. 1790 d. Ind. 1882 m. Nancy Miller   Pvt. Ind. Mil.
son James Z. m. Isabella Jones

Hazzard, George b. Del. 1789 d. Del. 1830   Commissary Del. Mil.
m. Ann Hazzard (nee) — son George W. m. Mary Eleanor Elder

Hazzard, Simpson   Vol. 5   Pvt. Del. Mil.

Headington, Nicholas b. Md. 1789 d. Ind. 1856   Pvt. Md. Mil.
m. Ruth Phillips — daughter Katherine m. David Braddock

Headley, Samuel b. N.J. 1774 d. Pa. 1838   Capt. & Surgeon N.Y. Mil.
m. Ann Farichilds — daughter Harriet m. Jess C. Horton

Headrick, John B. b. Tenn. 1799 d. Mo. 1890   Pvt. U.S. Riflemen Mil.
m. Maria Blair Worth — son Peter m. Angela Meyers

Heald, Israel b .Mass. (Me.) 1793 d. Me. 1882 Pvt. Mass. (Me.) U.S. Inf.
m. Jane Standish — daughter Mary G. m. Ambrose Buck
daughter Nancy W m. William Jackman

Heald, Nathan b. N.H. 1775 d. Mo. 1832   Major U.S. Army
m. Rebecca Wells — son Darius m. Martha Hunter

Heald, William b. Mass. 1788 d. Md. 1861   Pvt. U.S. Inf.
m. Belinda Eleanor Simmons — daughter Alice H.
m. Michael D. Groverman   REAL DAUGHTER

Heap, George b. Pa. 1771 d. Ill. 1855   Pvt. Ohio Light Dragoons 1812-15
m. Elizabeth Saunders — daughter Margaret m. George Hill

Heaps, John b. Md. 1788 d. Md. 1876 m. Martha Alexander   Capt. Md. Mil.
daughter Sarah Ann m. John James Fulton

Heard, Joel b. Ala. 1788 d. Texas 1869   Pvt. Miss. Mil.
m. Nancy Gilmore — son Humphrey m. Ellen Foster

Heard, John, Jr.   Vol. 3   Pvt. Mass. Mil.

Heard, Oliver b. Mass. (Me.) 1794 d. Maine   Pvt. Mass. (Me.) Mil.
m. Lucy Worcester Smith — daughter Abigail m. Moses Shaw

Heard, Stephen b. Va. 1720 d. Ga. 1815   Rec. Pat., Governor of Ga. 1784
m. Mary Faulkner — daughter Ann? m. Sherwood Wilkinson

Heath, Daniel b. Conn. 1761 d. Ind. 1841   Pvt. N.Y. Mil.
m. Azuba Reynolds — daughter Phylinda m. Francis B. McBeth

Heath, Ephraim b. Va. 1790 d. Texas 1866   Sgt. Va. Mil.
m. Sally Titmash — son John O. m. Martha Ann Jones

Heath, Henry, Sr. b. Mass. 1786 d. N.Y. 1875   Sgt. N.Y. Mil.
m. Mary Casler — son Asahel H. m. Mary Geraldine Mannering

Heath, Josiah Wilson b. Md. 1771 d. Md. 1819   Capt. Md. Mil.
m. Mary Harris — daughter Parthenia M. m. James Culton

Heath, Samuel b. c. 1750 d. Md. 1829 m. Margaret Turpin   Lt. Md. Mil.
daughter Sally D. m. Joseph Barkley

Heatherly, Benjamin b. Va. 1769 d. Mo. 1850   Pvt. Ohio Mil.
m. Rebecca Crook — son James m. Sarah Maupin

Heavenhill (Havenhill), Oliver b. Ger. 1739 d. Ky.   Pvt. Ky. Mil. 1791
son George m. Sarah Clark

Hebard, Diah b. Vt. 1783 d. Vt. 1831   Pvt. Vt. Mil.
m. Sarah Averill — son George D. A. m. Margaret E. D. Marven

Heck, Godfrey b. Md. 1777 d. Ind. 1858   Pvt. Ky. Mil.
m. Elizabeth Kimmer — son Nicholas m. Sarah Stiles

Heckathorn, John b. Va. 1781 d. Ohio 1853   Corp. Ohio Mil.
m. Dorothy Shambaugh — daughter Barbara m. Ethan Terry

Heckert, Peter   Vol. 9   Pvt. Pa. Mil.

Hedden, Luther b. N.Y. 1787 d. N.Y. 1868 m. Sally Townley   Pvt. N.Y. Mil.
son Richard T. m. Emily Brown

Hedden, Thomas b. Pa. 1764 d. N.Y. 1813   Pvt. N.Y. Arty.
son Jedediah m. Mary Bender

Hedges, David b. N.Y. 1744 d. N.Y. 1817   N.Y. State Assembly 1786-9,
m. Charity Howell — daughter Abigail m. Hiram Sanford   1804-7

Hedges, John   Vol. 13   **Ens. Va. Mil.**

Hedges, Joseph   Vol. 13   **Lt. Va. Mil.**

Hedges, Joseph b. Md. 1764 d. Ky. m. Sarah Biggs   Sgt. Ohio Mil.
son Jonas m. Anne Shortridge

Hedges, Silas b. Va. 1736 d. Va. (W.Va.) 1811   Rec. Pat., Recruiting
m. Margaret Hoagland — daughter Margaret   Officer Va.
m. Jacob Fouts

Hedges, Silas, Jr. b. Va. 1777 d. Ohio m. Mary Cox   Pvt. W.Va. Mil.
daughter Nancy m. Absolom Fouts

Hedrick, Henry b. Va. 1793 d. W.Va. 1890   Pvt. W.Va. Mil.
m. Nancy Livesey — daughter Mary m. Charles McClung

Heermance, Martin b. N.Y. 1765 d. N.Y. 1824   Brig. Gen. N.Y. Mil.
m. Sarah Kierstede — daughter Cornelia m. Archibald Smith

Heffner (Hafner, Heavner), John b. N.C. 1793 d. N.C. 1873 Pvt. N.C. Mil.
m. Susannah Rudisill — son Solomon m. Sadie Reinhardt

Heilman, Daniel b. Pa. 1795 d. Pa. 1820 m. Gertrude Diehl   Pvt. U.S. Army
son Daniel D. m. Elizabeth Hauck

Heilman (Hehlman), John Adam b. Pa. 1774 d. Pa. 1833   Pvt. Pa. Mil.
m. Eva Margaret Abney — daughter Catherine m. Peter Myers

Heintz, b. Md. 1799 d. Pa. m. Catherine McCord   Pvt. Pa. Mil.
son Silas m. Elizabeth Shenkle

Heiskell, Peter b. Va. 1760 d. Va. 1840   Capt. Va. Mil.
m. Susanna Wetzel — daughter Caroline m. John Boys Breckenridge

Heizer (Hiser), Samuel b. Va. 1781 d. Ohio 1832   Pvt. Va. Mil.
m. Mary Ware — daughter Mary Jane m. William H. Anderson
daughter Matilda m. David Silas Coyner

Heldenbrand, Michael b. Pa. 1766 d. Ohio 1850   Pvt. Pa. Mil.
m. Elizabeth Schlenger (Slanker) — son Adam m. Ann King

Heller, Joseph b. Pa. 1756 d. Pa. 1838 m. Margaret Butz   Pvt. Pa. Mil.
daughter Catharine m. Andrew Dech

Hellums, John b. 1782 d. aft. 1878   Capt. Griffith's Co. Miss. Mil.
m. Margaret Prewitt — son Jacob Hellums m. Cyntha White

Helm, Peter b. Pa. 1784 d. Pa. 1853 m. Carolina Phillips   Pvt. Pa. Mil.
son Peter, Jr. m. Lucy Heichold (Hirchold)

Helman, Michael b. 1791 d. 1861 m. Mary Manon   Pvt. Pa. Mil.
son Lawrence C. m. Susannah Wilkenson

Helmershausen, Charles   Vol. 16   Sgt. Mass. Mil.

Helms, Cadwalader Morris b. Pa. 1791 d. Pa.   Pvt. Pa. Mil.
m. Elizabeth M. — son Isaac m. Phoebe Mower Robinson

Helton, Peter b. N.C. 1750 d. Ind. 1856 m. Lavenia   Pvt. S.C. Mil.
son Arthur, Sr. m. Margaret Munsey

Hemingway, Enos b. Conn. 1755 d. Conn. 1845   Rec. Pat., Mem. of Conn.
m. Sarah Hemingway (cousin) — son Willet   Gen. Assembly
m. Sarah Rowe

Hemingway, James b. N.Y. 1788 d. Mich. 1881   Pvt. N.Y. Mil.
m. Phebe Hart — daughter Hannah m. Thomas Babcock

Henderson, Bennett b. Va. 1750 d. Va. 1793   Patriot, Magis. Va. 1783-1791
m. Elizabeth Lewis — daughter Nancy C. m. Matthew Nelson

Henderson, James, Jr. b. N.C. 1775 d. La. 1814   Lt. Col. Tenn. Vol.
  m. Margaret Dickson — daughter Margaret B. m. Daniel McKisick

Henderson, John b. Va. 1775 d. Va. 1875   Pvt. Va. Mil.
  m. Sallie Quisenberry — daughter Elizabeth M. m. Joseph Dent

Henderson, John b. Pa. 1780 d. Pa. 1847 m. Anna Jackson Pvt. U.S. Inf.
  son Joseph m. Nancy Wilson

Henderson, John   Vol. 6   Pvt. N.J. Mil.

Henderson, Jonas (Josiah) b. Va. 1784 d. Va. 1875   Ens. Va. Mil.
  m. Elizabeth Thomas — daughter Eleanor m. George Pearis Pepper

Henderson, Joseph   Vol. 12   Lt. Ky. Vol.

Henderson, Peter H. b. Md. 1790 d. Md. 1835   Pvt. Md. Mil.
  m. Mary Booth — son Benjamin F.
  m. Ann Elizabeth (Harris) Williams

Henderson, Samuel b. 1740 d. 1819   Overseer of Roads N.C. 1808
  m. Priscilla Miles — daughter Sarah m. George Halcomb

Henderson, Samuel b. S.C. 1776 d. Ga. 1828   Rec. Pat., Just. of Peace,
  m. Isabella — son John Milton m. Rutha Sharp   Senator

Henderson, Thomas b. N.C. 1751 d. N.C. 1821   Pat., Mem. N.C. Assembly
  m. Jane Martin — daughter Mary   House Commons & Senate
  m. John Lacy

Henderson, Thomas or William b. Pa. 1752   Pvt. 17th Regt. Pa. Mil.
  d. Pa. 1846 m. Mary Patterson — daughter Matilda
  m. Samuel McCourtney

Henderson, William   Vol. 9   Pvt. Ky. Vol.

Henderson, William H. b. Va. 1764 d. Ala. 1841   Pvt. Md. Mil.
  m. Mary Hale — son John H. m. Minerva Banard

Henderson, William Steel b. N.C. 1778 d. Tenn. 1860   Pvt. Tenn. Mil.
  m. Elizabeth Baldridge — son William F. m. Nancy Kerr

Hendree, George   Vol. 9   Pvt. Va. Mil.

Hendricks, Abraham b. 1749 d. Pa. 1819   Pat., Pa. Legis.
  m. Anne Jamison — son Thomas m. Elizabeth Trimble

Hendricks, Andrew b. Pa. 1785 d. Pa. 1868   Sgt. Pa. Mil.
  m. Catherine Martin — son John m. Judith Keifer

Hendricks, James b. Pa. 1784 d. Pa. 1829   Pvt. U.S. Inf.
  m. Martha E. Burns — son Adam m. Rachel Bowler Stephens

Hendricks, Thomas b. Pa. 1773 d. Pa. or Ind. 1835   Capt. Pa. Mil.
  m. Elizabeth Trimble — daughter Mary m. Silas Stewart

Henderickson, Daniel b. N.J. 1787 d. N.J. 1858   Capt. N.J. Mil.
  m. Catherine Bedle — daughter Eliza m. Samuel Applegate

Hendrickson, John b. N.Y. 1797 d. Ill. 1877 m. Polly Curtis, Pvt. N.Y. Mil.
  son Norman G. m. Emily Townsend

Hendrix, Solomon b. Tenn. 1790 d. Tenn. 1864   Capt. Tenn. Mil.
  m. Susanna Hart — son Harrison m. Aditha Taylor

Hendry, Dr. John Anderson b. N.J. 1786 d. N.Y. 1834 Surgeon N.J. Mil.
  m. Abigail Chambers — son Charles F. m. Ann Frances Kelly

Hening (Henning), William Waller b. Va. 1767/8   Adjut. Gen. Va.
     d. Va. 1828 m. Agatha Banks — daughter Anna Matilda
     m. James Cabiness
     daughter Eliza L. (Mrs. Spottswood) m. John F. Schermerhorn

Heningway, Enos b. Conn. 1755 d. Conn. 1845   Rec. Pat., Mem. Conn.
     m. Sarah Hemingway (cousin) — son Willet   Assembly 1797-1809
     m. Sarah Rowe

Henion, Cornelius b. N.J. 1793 d. Mich. 1862   Pvt. N.J. Mil.
     m. Rebecca Markel — son Henry M. m. Minerva Huntington

Henley, David b. Mass. 1749 d. Wash. D.C. 1829 Rec. Pat., Commissary of
     m. Sarah Heselrigge — son Arthur H.   war supplies Tenn.
     m. Anne Evelina Moore

Hennon, Joseph b. Pa. 1761 d. Pa. 1841   Rec. Pat., Founder of Presby.
     m. Margaret Morrow — daughter Mary   Church, Pa. 1800
     m. William James McConahy, Sr.

Hennon, Thomas b. Tenn. 1781 d. S.C. 1868   S.C. Mariner, Schooners
     m. Mary Naves   Sparrow, Saratoga & Lawrence
     daughter Martha m. Stephen Smith

Henry, David b. Pa. 1776 d. Ohio 1834   Sgt. Ohio Riflemen
     m. Sarah Robinson — son John H. m. Isabel Wallace (Zimmerman)

Henry, Elijah b. Va. d.— m. Lorana Alexander   Pvt. Ky. Vol.
     son Joseph m. Jemima Jane Raeburn

Henry, Gawen   Vol. 8   Capt. Pa. Mil.

Henry, James b. Mass. d. La. m. Margaret Ann   Vol. 2   Pvt. La. Mil.
     daughter Margaret Ann m. Charles McMillan

Henry (Hendry), James b. N.C. 1750 d. N.C. 1816   Rec. Pat., Mem. Gen.
     m. Mary Murphy — daughter Catherine   Assembly N.C.
     m. Charles Stevens

Henry, James b. Ohio d. Ohio 1840 m. Priscilla Wagner   Pvt. Ohio Mil.
     daughter Harriet E. m. Henry Andrew

Henry, James Jr. b. Conn. 1765 d. Ohio 1840   Ens. Conn. Mil.
     m. Hannahritta Waterman — son Warren m. Mary Ellen Gerls

Henry, Jeremiah b. Pa. d. Pa. 1819 m. Elizabeth Caine   Pvt. Pa. Mil.
     son Jeremiah L. m. Jane Fitz Randolph

Henry, John W. b. abt. 1791 d. 1824   Pvt. Ky. Mil.
     m. Nancy Barnett — son James Henry m. Nancy Bordman

Henry, Joseph b. Pa. 1796 d. Pa. 1892 m. Maria   Pvt. Pa. Mil.
     son John A. m. Caroline E. Frantz

Henry, Robert b. Pa. 1772 d. Pa. 1844 m. Anne Burns   Pvt. Pa. Mil.
     daughter Anne m. Moses Hart

Henry, Robert Jenkins b. Md. 1781 d. Md. 1843   Brig. Gen. Md. Mil.
     m. Mary Dennis Handy — son Samuel H. m. Frances Ann Elliott

Henry, Samuel b. Va. 1762 d. Tenn. 1824 m. Mary   Lt. Tenn. Mil. 1792
     son William W. m. Margaret Montgomery   Civil Serv. 1795

Henry, Thomas b. Ire. 1781 d. Pa. 1849 m. Sarah James   Capt. Pa. Mil.
     son Evan James m. Lucy Maxwell Rigg

Henry, William b. Va. 1761 d. Ky. 1824   Major Gen. Ky. Mil. 1812
     m. Elizabeth Julia Flournoy — son Gustavus A. m. Marion McClure
     son Patrick m. Bettie Claiborne West
     son William m. Cornelia Vanasour Gano

Henry, William b. Pa. 1757 d. Pa. 1821   Patriot, made muskets for Army
m. Sabina Schropp — son William, Jr. m. Maria Rittenhouse

Hensel, David b. Va. 1793 d. Mo. 1843   Corp. Va. Mil.
m. Nancy Callender Miller — daughter Hester Ann m. Blair Hogan

Hensel, William b. Pa. 1755 d. Pa. 1842   Pvt. Pa. Mil.
m. Maria Eve East — son John W. m. Elizabeth Myers

Henshaw, Hiram b. Va. 1771 d. Va. 1845 m. Mary McConnell, Pvt. Va. Mil.
daughter Martha Jane m. Zephaniah Silver

Henshaw, Nicholas b. Va. 1763 d. Pa. 1821   Ens. 8th Co. 4th Bn. Pa. Mil.
m. Margaret McConnell — daughter Mary m. Thomas Clark   1791

Henshaw (Hancher), Thomas b. Va. 1783 d. Ohio 1862   Pvt. Md. or Va. Mil.
m. Eleanor Brown — son Joseph m. Rebecca Tanquary

Henshy (Henshie), Henry b. Pa. 1761 d. Ohio 1825   Pvt. Pa. Mil.
m. Barbara — son Henry, Jr. m. Mary Brouse

Henton, Benjamin b. Pa. 1761 d. Va. 1807   Rec. Pat., Bondsman for
m. Sarah Hopkins — son David   Sheriff Va.
m. Elizabeth Moyers (Myers)

Henton, David b. Va. 1786 d. Mo. 1870   Pvt. Va. Mil.
m. Elizabeth Myers (Moyers) — daughter Rebecca C.
m. John Elias Corder

Henton, (Hinton), John C. b. Va. 1778 d. Mo. 1853   Pvt. Va. Mil.
m. Katherine Keith — son Alexander K. m. Mary McHenry
son Walter B. m. Rebecca Demaries Cooley

Henton (Hinton), Silas b. Va. 1792 d. Va. 1852   Sgt. Va. Mil.
m. Susan H. Gwinn — son D. Benjamin m. Lizzie Wilson

Hentz, Jacob b. Pa. 1795 d. Pa. 1871 m. Susan Rhodes   Pvt. Pa. Riflemen
daughter Catharine m. William Hambleton Elliott

Hepburn, Roderick b. Scot. 1780 d. N.Y. 1873   Pvt. Mass. Mil.
m. Mary Miller Burlingame — daughter Mary A. m. John O. Keeler
REAL DAUGHTER

Hepburn, William b. Ire. 1753 d. Pa. 1821   Brig. Gen. Pa. Mil.
m. Elizabeth Huston — son John m. Caroline Wheeler

Herbach, Yost b. Pa. 1741 d. Md. 1831 m. Eva Bahn   Rec. Pat., Mem.
son Jacob m. Maria Laucks   Legis. Pa. 1799

Herbert, Charles   Vol. 16   Pvt. Md. Mil.

Herbert (Harbert), Thomas b. N.J. 1783 d. Ohio 1833   Sgt. Ohio Mil.
m. Elizabeth Curran — son Samuel m. Emma Varina Schibli

Herbst, Peter b. Pa. 1767 d. Pa. 1847   Pvt. Pa. Mil.
son John m. Permilla Ann Elliott

Hereford, John Wesley b. Va. 1790 d. Va. 1832   Pvt. Va. Cavalry
m. Juliet Harrison — daughter Mary A. B. m. Daniel DaShiell

Herndon, Fleetwood b. Va. 1792 d. Mo. 1871   Lt. La. Vol.
m. Martha Bradley — daughter Harriet V. m. David Guitar
REAL DAUGHTER
son John m. Eliza C.

Herndon, James b. Va. 1791 d. Mo. 1857   3rd Sgt. Va. Arty.
m. Ann Perkins — son Archelaus M. m. Maria Ann Dickinson
son Grief P. m. Elizabeth Gay Baird
son Isaac O. m. Amanda Day
daughter Martha H. m. Lewis Bell Ely

Herndon, James, Sr. b. Va. c. 1732 d. Ky. 1815   Rec. Pat., Constable
  m. Isabella Thompson — daughter Frances   Overseer N.C. 1784-98
  m. Amos West

Herod, Peter b. 1787 d. 1880   Trumpeter and Pvt. 2nd Reg.
  m. Rebecca Key — son Benjamin Franklin   Mounted
  m. Judith Haynie

Herrick, Daniel   Vol. 3   Brig. Gen. Ohio Mil.

Herring, Jacob   Vol. 7   Ens. Md. Mil.

Herrington, John b. N.Y. 1794 d. N.Y. 1852   Pvt. N.Y. Mil.
  m. Maria Schermerhorn — daughter Elizabeth H.
  m. Joseph Mason Holmes

Hersey, Nathaniel b. Mass. 1744 d. Mass. (Me.) 1817   Pvt. Mass. Mil.
  m. Lucy White — daughter Sally m. Freeman Butler

Heskett, Benjamin b. 1775 d. Ohio 1857 or 1859   Pvt. Ohio Mil.
  m. Pharaby Crouse — daughter Rachel Jean
  m. George W. Gallagher   REAL DAUGHTER

Hess, George H. b. N.Y. 1773 d. N.Y. 1840   Pvt. N.Y. Mil.
  m. Mary Elizabeth Yerdon — son George m. Catherine Wormuth

Hess, William b. Pa. 1767 d. Miss. 1815   Prin. Forage Master
  m. Margaret Davies — son William R.   Tenn. Mil. 1813
  m. Sophia Western Dyer

Hesser, John b. Pa. 1761 d. Pa. 1825   Musician Pa. Mil.
  m. Elizabeth Fry — son William m. Catherine Paul

Hester, Chisholm b. Va. 1782 d. Ark. 1863   Pvt. Va. Mil.
  m. Mary Sumner — daughter Mary Ann m. James A. Cason

Hester, John Dippolt   Vol. 8   Pvt. N.J. Mil.

Hester, Matthew C. b. Va. 1785 d. Ga. 1857   Pvt. Ga. Mil.
  m. Cynthia Phillips — son Albert G.
  m. Mrs. Susan Elizabeth Hester Allen

Hester, Thomas b. Va. 1782 d. Mo. 1841-2   Pvt. Va. Mil.
  m. Mary Egleston Baynham — daughter Martha
  m. Benjamin Harrison Moore
  daughter Virginia T. m. Robert Dulin

Hetrick, Christian b. Pa. 1765 d. Pa. 1827   Brig. Gen. Pa. Mil.
  m. Catharine — son John W. m. Wilhelmina Wolfrom

Hevener, George b. Va. 1784 d. W.Va. 1872 m. Eva Propst   Pvt. Va.
  son John m. Sarah McMullen

Hewes, Shubael b. Mass. 1732 d. Mass. 1813 Rec. Pat., Civil Officer, Mass.
  m. Martha Frye — daughter Hannah m. William Cooper Hunneman

Hewins, Ebenezer b. Mass. 1764 d. Maine 1824   Rec. Pat., Collector &
  m. Zilpha Cummings — son John   Committeeman Mass.
  m. Rozana Rockwood

Hewitt, Hazael b. 1793 d. Tenn. 1859/60   Sgt. Tenn. Vol.
  m. Caroline S. Newsome — daughter Mary Anne
  m. Ashbury Travis Pegues

Hewitt, Jeptha b. Vt. 1780 d. N.Y. 1851   Pvt. & Fifer N.Y. Mil.
   m. Lurancy Button — son Renssalaer S. m. Sarah Everest

Hewitt, Moses b. N.Y. 1786 d. N.Y. 1830 m. Jane Stedman   Pvt. N.Y. Mil.
   daughter Ruth m. Elisha King   REAL DAUGHTER

Hiatt, Elijah b. Va. 1771 d. Ky. 1853 m. Patsy Allen   Pvt. Ky. Vol.
   daughter Almira m. Josiah Burnside

Hiatt, Jesse b. N.C. 1782 d. Iowa 1857 m. Mary Proctor   Pvt. Ill.
   son Reuben m. Nancy (1)

Hibbard, Jonathan I.   Vol. 8   Pvt. U.S. Inf.

Hibbard, Lovell b. Conn. 1774 d. Vt. 1848   Lt. Col. Conn. Mil.
   m. Lois Whitney — daughter Susan S. m. Isaac Bradshaw Emerson

Hibbard, Orlin b. Vt. 1783 d. Vt. 1868 m. Chloe Kingman   Pvt. Vt. Mil.
   son Elisha m. Rebecca Ransom Clark

Hibben, James b. Pa. 1795 d. Ohio 1871   Sgt. Pa. Mil.
   m. Ann Watson Allison — daughter Mary Jane m. A. S. Ballard

Hibben, Thomas b. Pa. 1760 d. Pa. 1833 m. Mary Entrekin   Capt. Pa. Mil.
   son James m. Ann Watson Allison
   son John m. Phoebe Millhouse

Hibschman, Henry   Vol. 16   Lt. Pa. Mil.

Hibshman, Henry b. Pa. 1774 d. Pa. 1859   Lt. Pa. Mil.
   m. Hannah Sweitzer — daughter Mary Ann m. Henry Keller
   son Lewis R. m. Hannah Shay

Hibsham, Jacob b. Pa. 1772 d. Pa. 1852   Brig. Gen. Pa. Vol.
   m. Elizabeth Atkinson — son John m. Magdalena Shirk

Hick, William S. b. Nova Scotia 1784 d. N.J. 1820   Capt. N.Y. Mil.
   m. Mary Weeden — daughter Hannah Dean m. Francis Asbury Day

Hickernell, Frederick b. Pa. 1772 d. Pa. 1845   Pvt. Pa. Mil.
   m. Margaret Gehr — daughter Lucy Ann m. William Armstrong

Hickerson, David b.— d. 1834 m. Nancy Tallaferro   8th Reg. 3rd Co.
   daughter Sarah m. Isaac Lusk   N.C. Mil.

Hickey, William b. Va. 1797 d. Ohio 1890   Pvt. Va. Mil.
   m. Harriett Moore — daughter Elizabeth m. Henry A. Metz
   REAL DAUGHTER

Hicklin, James b. Tenn. 1796 d. Mo. 1875   Pvt. Ga. Mil.
   m. Nancy Paterson Beason — daughter Mary
   m. Augustus O. Persinger   REAL DAUGHTER
   son William m. Elizabeth Gill

Hickman, David b. Va. 1747 d. Ky. 182?   Sgt. Va. Mil.
   m. Clara McClanahan — son Thomas m. Sarah Moss Prewitt

Hickman, David McClanahan b. Ky. 1788 d. Mo. 1851   Pvt. Ky. Mil.
   m. Cornelia Ann Bryan — daughter Sarah Ann
   m. Dr. Archibald Young

Hickman, Jacob b. Va. 1776 d. Pa. m. Elsie Way   Pvt. Va. Mil.
   son Jacob S. m. Catherine Litman
   daughter Nancy m. Edward Pindell Coombs
   son William W. m. Mary McCune

Hickman, Joseph b. S.C. 1787 d. Ala. 1861   Pvt. S.C. Mil.
   m. Martha A. Pullen — daughter Mary C.
   m. James Augustus Burgin

Hickman, Nathaniel b. Del. 1792 d. Ohio 1864   Pvt. Del. Mil.
m. Phoebe Prettyman — son Daniel m. Jane Blauvelt

Hickman, Thomas b. Ky. 1782 d. Ky. 1849 m. Sarah Prewitt Pvt. Ky. Mil.
daughter Clara m. Dr. Jones H. Flourney

Hickok, Andrew b. N.Y. 1781 d. N.Y. 1865   Pvt. Drummer & Musician
m. Betsey Philips — son Andrew Jr.   N.Y. Mil.
m. Mary Jane Sherborn

Hickok, Stephen D.   Vol. 17   Pvt. N.Y. Mil.

Hickox, Eri b. Conn. 1790 d. Ohio 1864 m. Alma Hoadley Pvt. Ohio Mil.
daughter Alma Hoadley m. Dr. David G. Wilder REAL DAUGHTER
daughter Miriam Unrania m. Benjamin Baker

Hickox, Harvey b. N.Y. 1785 d. N.Y. m. Lydia West   Corp. N.Y. Mil.
daughter Iris W. m. Giles Arnold

Hicks, Edward   Vol. 7   Pvt. S.C. Mil.

Hicks, George b. (Mass.) Me. 1779 d. Me. 1879   Musician Mass. Mil.
m. Hannah Allen — daughter Abigail m. Dennis Doughty

Hicks, John H. b. Ga. 1778 d. La. 1815 m. Elizabeth   Pvt. Ga. Mil.
son Stephen G. m. Eliza Rice Maxey

Hicks, Thomas b. Va. 1725 d. N.C. 1797 Rec. Pat., Mem. House Commons
m. Elizabeth Williams — son Thomas Jr.   N.C. 1778-1797
m. Mary Faison

Hicks, Thomas b. Va. 1796 d. Va. 1870 m. Lucy Alsop   Pvt. Va. Mil.
son Thomas m. Ann Bradford

Hicks, William b. N.Y. 1792 d. Mich. 1877 m. Nabby Younglove   Pvt. Mich.
daughter Helen m. Philo Dunsmore

Hicks, Willis b. Md. 1792 d. Ohio 1867   Sgt. Ohio Mil.
m. Frances White — son Ebenezer N. m. Jane Robinson
daughter Minerva m. William T. Rittenhouse
daughter Rachel m. William Junk

Hicks, Wyatt   Vol. 15   Pvt. Ga. Mil.

Hicky, Philip b. 1778 d. La. 1859 m. Anna Mather   Col. La. Mil.
daughter Caroline S. m. Morris Barker Morgan

Hide (Hyde), John b. Va. 1794 d. Va. 1826 m. Sarah   Pvt. Va. Mil.
daughter Ellen m. Andrew Warwick Cameron

Hider, Michael b. N.C. 1743 d. N.C. 1790 m. Elizabeth Wood Pvt. N.C. Mil.
son John m. Rosannah English

Higginbotham, Joseph Cabell b. Va. 1782 d. Va. 1842   Col. Va. Mil.
m. Lucy Neville Wills — son Joseph C. Jr. m. Angeline E. Plunkett

Higginbotham, Samuel b. Va. d. Ga.   Rec. Pat., Justice Inferior Court Ga.
m. Jane Satterwhite — son John S. m. Annie Staunton

Higgins, Richard b. Va. 1770 d. Ky. 1843 m. Sally Allen   Pvt. Ky. Mil.
son Joel m. Anne Louise Gibson

Higgins, Robert b. Pa. 1744 d. Ohio 1825   Rec. Pat., Builder of Ky. Fort
m. Sarah Wright — son Gideon m. Sidney Ann A. Steenberger

Higgins, Solomon   Vol. 8   Pvt. N.Y. Mil.

Higgins, William, II b. Va. 1742 d. Tenn. 1805   Defender of Higgins
  m. Dinah Tribble — daughter Mary   Block House Ky. 1786
  m. James Hardage Lane

High, Jacob b. Md. 1793 d. Ind. 1873 m. Sarah Nichols   Pvt. Md. Mil.
  daughter Katherine m. Chauncey King

High, Joseph b. N.J. 1794 d. Ind. 1874 m. Mary Dare   Pvt. N.J. Mil.
  son Benoni-Benjamin m. Sarah M. Sparks

Hildenbrand (Hildebrand), Michael b. Pa. 1766 d. Pa. 1850   Pvt. Pa. Mil.
  m. Elizabeth Schlenger (Slankee) — son Adam m. Ann King

Hiler, Eleazer b. N.J. 1790 d. Mich. 1873   Corp. N.J. Mil.
  m. Harriett Sturdevant — daughter Martha Phedora
  m. Hanson H. Rogers

Hill, Aaron b. N.Y. 1789 d. Iowa 1870 m. Pamelia Winston   Pvt. N.Y. Mil.
  son Ebenezer m. Hannah Mariah Barber

Hill, Amos b. Mass. 1787 d. Ill. 1869 m. Lucinda Cutler   Lt. Mass. Mil.
  son William m. Sarah Francis Scott

Hill, Andrew Uriah b. N.Y. 1774 d. N.Y. 1847   Pvt. N.Y. Mil.
  m. Catherine North — son John m. Sarah Hollister

Hill, Benjamin b. S.C. 1793 d. S.C. 1844 m. Lucy Whitten   Pvt. S.C. Mil.
  son Jacob W. m. Martha Louise Whitten

Hill, Caleb b. Conn. 1770 d. Vt. 1814 m. Cynthia Strong   Capt. Vt. Mil.
  daughter Barbara m. Ezra Pike
  son Calvin m. Mercy Pike
  son Harry m. Ann Tompkins Ladue
  son Ira m. Minerva Augusta Thomas
  daughter Rhoda m. Jesse Ashley Clark

Hill, Calvin b. N.Y. 1795 d. Vt. 1831 m. Mary Pilse   Corp. Vt. Mil.
  son Henry C. m. Cornelia L. Scott

Hill, Daniel H. b. N.J. 1750 d. Tenn. 1848   Pvt. Tenn. Vol.
  m. Ellenor (Eleanor) Noodings(?) — son Massey m. Lucinda Harle

Hill, Daniel b. Conn. 1797 d. Pa. 1872   Vol. 8 & 10   Pvt. U.S. Inf.

Hill, David b. N.Y. 1770 d. N.Y. 1817 m. Amelia Stanbury   Pvt. N.Y. Inf.
  daughter Amelia m. Eber Deane

Hill, Ebenezer b. N.Y. 1778 d. N.Y. 1862   Corp. N.Y. Mil.
  m. Elizabeth Hurlburt — son William W. m. Sarah Townsend

Hill, Ebenezer b. Mass. 1771 d. N.Y. 1835   Pvt. N.Y. Mil.
  m. Sarah Ambley (Ambler) — daughter Sally m. Ephraim Warner

Hill, Frederick b. Pa. 1773 or 1778 d. Pa. 1823   Capt. Pa. Mil.
  m. Catharine Conner — son Jacob m. Anna Achenback

Hill, George b. Tenn. 1793 d. Ark. 1849 m. Nancy Harpole   Pvt. Ky. Mil.
  son James m. Ida Smith

Hill, Ira Jr. b. Vt. 1787 d. Ohio 1866   Capt. Ohio Mil.
  m. Welthea Little — son Hervey D. m. Angeline M. Dye

Hill, Jacob   Vol. 9   Sgt. Miss. Mil.

Hill, Jacob b. Tenn. 1796 d. Tenn. 1878 m. Jane Lemons   Sgt. Tenn. Mil.
  daughter Sarah Prudence m. David Lacy

Hill, Jacob Killingsworth b. S.C. 1795 d. Miss. 1856 Sgt. S.C. or Miss. Mil.
  m. Rebecca G. Sims — daughter Sarah Ann m. Hamden McKey

Hill, James b. Mass. 1773 d. Mass. 1852   Qrtmstr. Mass. Mil.
m. Ann Adams — daughter Eliza m. Elijah Allen

Hill, James b. Pa. 1777 d. Pa. 1862   Ens. Pa. Mil.
m. Ann Hill (daughter of George Hill — daughter Margaret
m. Richard Morton

Hill, James b. Conn. 1760 d. Ky. 1816 m. Betsey Chittenden   Pvt. Ohio Mil.
son Thomas C. m. Lovina Tupper

Hill, James b. N.H. 1783 d. N.H. 1829   Pvt. Home Guard N.H.
m. Sally M. Griard — son Alfred
m. Marie Louise Francoise Adroise Brigitaire Brasdefer

Hill, Jehu b. Del. 1768 d. Del. 1817 m. Arcadia Stockley   Capt. Del. Mil.
son Cord H. m. Sarah Paynter

Hill, Joab b. 1775 d. 1847 m. Elizabeth Lane   Col. & Capt. La.
son Claiborne m. Polly Gates

Hill, John b. N.Y. 1786 d. Iowa 1869 m. Sarah Ann Haight   Pvt. N.Y. Mil.
daughter Esther Ann m. James Morgan

Hill, John Langdon b. Mass. (Me.) 1797 d. Me. 1847   Rec. Pat., Army
m. (1) Silence Alexander Cushing — son George L.   Mass. (Me.)
m. Anna Cummings Larrabee

Hill, Joseph b. Ire. 1748 d. Pa. 1828   Just. of Peace, Pa. 1795
m. Elizabeth Ackley — son James Hill m. Nancy Ann Hill

Hill, Joseph b. Pa. 1774 d. Ind. 1862 m. Keziah Bartley   Ens. Pa. Vol.
son Johnathan m. Nancy Hurt Foree

Hill, Joseph Briggs b. N.Y. 1786 d. Va. 1833   Ens. Mass. Mil.
m. Harriet Hempstead — son Edw. Norris Hill m. Harriet Nelson
daughter Frances Ellen m. Enoch Russell Hinckley

Hill, Mark Langdon b. Me. 1772 d. Me. 1842 Rec. Pat., Judge & Legis. Me.
m. Mary McCobb — daughter Cordelia m. Sumner P. Heald

Hill, Nathaniel J.   Vol. 17   Pvt. N.Y. Mil.

Hill, Philip Gray   Vol. 12   Pvt. Conn. Mil.

Hill, Rees b. Va. 1776 d. Va. 1852   Col. Commander Pa. Mil.
m. Nancy Heaton — daughter Mary m. Thomas Hughes Roseberry

Hill, Robert b. Va. 1766 d. Va. 1862 m. Elizabeth Franklin   Lt. Va. Mil.
daughter Arethusa H. m. Thomas Baldwin Purcell

Hill, Samuel   Vol. 9   Corp. Va. Mil.

Hill, Samuel b. Va. 1792 d. Tenn. 1865 m. Lovey Murden   Pvt. Va. Mil.
daughter Sarah m. James S. Carruthers

Hill, Samuel b. N.H. 1776 d. N.Y. 1848 m. Sally Bartlett   Lt. N.Y. Mil.
son Asahel m. Lorenda Lawrence

Hill, William K. b. N.C. 1794 d. Tenn. 1841   Pvt. Tenn. Mil.
m. Rebecca K. Harris — son John Orlando m. Joanna Weaver

Hilliard, Minor b. Conn. 1764 d. Vt. 1845 m. Abigail Hill   Pvt. Vt. Mil.
daughter Dimmis m. Israel Palmer

Hilliard, (Hilgirt, Hilyard, Hillyard), Peter b. Pa. 1754 Mem. Pa. Legis.
d. Pa. 1834 m. Elizabeth Hauk (Hauck)   1814-1815
daughter Catherine m. Christian Memch

Hilliard, William b. 1784 d. 1872   Pvt. under Capt. Lord &
m. Elizabeth Lewis — son Henry L. m. Malvina   Col. Dalfsen

Hillyer, Justin b. Mass. 1773 d. Ohio 1846   Pvt. & Fifer Ohio Mil.
    m. Adah Munson — daughter Ada m. Jonathan Clapp

Hillyer, Lawrence b. N.Y. 1734 d. N.Y. 1809   Rec. Pat., Material Aid N.Y.
    m. Ann Lakerman — daughter Emma m. Peter Cortelyou

Hillyer, Shaler b. Conn. 1776 d. Ga. 1820   Capt. Ga. Mil.
    m. Rebecca Freeman — son Junius m. Jane S. Early Watkins

Hilton, Edgar b. Mass. (Me.) 1782 d. Me. 1849   Sgt. Mass. (Me.) Mil.
    m. Betzey Hilton (cousin) — daughter Rachel m. Oliver Waugh

Hilton, John b. Mass. (Me.) 1756 d. Me. 1835   Pvt. Mass. Mil.
    m. Rachel Gray — daughter Hepzibah
    m. Joshua Hilton (prob. relative)

Hilton, John   Vol. 8   Pvt. N.Y. Mil.

Hilton, Joshua b. Mass. (Me.) 1790 d. Me. 1876   Pvt. Mass. Vol.
    m. Sarah Heald — son McKenney m. Sarah Cleveland

Hilyer, Simon b. N.J. 1762 d. N.J. 1822 m. Elner Vactor   Pvt. N.J. Mil.
    daughter Mary m. Martin M. Nevius

Hinckley, Amasa b. Conn. 1772 d. N.Y. 1858   Ens. N.Y. Mil.
    m. Lucretia McDonald — son Charles G. m. Pamelia Comstock

Hinckley, Gilbert b. Conn. 1778 d. Ohio 1843   Capt. N.Y. Mil.
    m. Betsy Turner — son Harry G. m. Charlotte Baldwin

Hinckley, Philip b. Mass. 1747 d. Mass. 1843 m. Mary Covil   Mariner
    son Philip Jr. m. Edith Baker

Hindes, James Bateman b. Md. 1775 d. Md. 1847   Pvt. Md. Mil.
    m. Mary Ann Johnson — daughter Caroline M.(single)
    REAL DAUGHTER
    son Samuel B. m. Margaret I. Delphey

Hinds, Simon b. N.C. 1769 d. Tenn. 1840   Capt. Tenn. Mil.
    m. Elizabeth Stone — son John m. Rhoda Webb

Hinds, Thomas b. Mass. 1780 d. N.Y. 1846 m. Phebe Bent   Pvt. N.Y. Mil.
    son William W. m. Minerva Burroughs

Hines, John b. 1771 d. 1853   Major 61st Reg. 20th Brig. Ky. Mil.
    m. Sarah Davis — daughter Eliza J. C. m. Phillip Loving

Hinkle, Christopher b. Pa. 1790 d. Ohio 1860 m. Mary Jane   Pvt. Ohio Mil.
    daughter Sarah m. Robert Griffin

Hinkle, Daniel b. Va. 1786 d. Ill. 1847 m. Ruth Lee   Pvt. Ohio Mil.
    daughter Elizabeth m. Isaac Preston

Hinman, Edward W. b. Conn. 1773 d. Ohio 1843   2nd Major N.Y. Mil.
    m. Lucy Mather — daughter Eunice m. Thomas Hough

Hinman, Joel b. Conn. 1748 d. Conn. 1813   Rec. Pat., Mem. State Legis.
    m. Marie Sevill(?) — daughter Caroline A.   Conn.
    m. Henry Wheaton Goodwin

Hinman, Russell   Vol. 15   Pvt. N.Y. Mil.

Hinsdale, Horace Seymour b. N.Y. 1792 d. N.Y. 1858   Pvt. N.Y. Mil.
    m. Sarah Ogden — son Henry B. m. Mary Ann Hatch

Hinton, William b. Eng. 1749 d. Pa. 1839 m. Martha   Capt. Pa. Mil.
    daughter Elizabeth m. William Ross

Hipkins, John   Vol. 10   Pvt. Va. Mil.

Hipple, Henry b. Pa. 1780 d. Pa. 1864 m. Jane Garrett   Pvt. Pa. Mil.
    son Jesse M. m. Sarah Upright

Hiscock, Jesse b. Mass. (Me.) 1794 d. Me. 1842   Pvt. Mass. Mil.
  m. Jennie Sewell Wheeler — son James M. m. Leonora Parker Wilton

Hitch, Mardy E. b. Mass. 1775 d. Mass. 1858   Pvt. Mass. Mil.
  m. Betsy Delano — son Obed F. m. Mary Gage Buswell

Hitch, John b. Md. 1773 d. S.C. 1849 m. Katherine Hanna   Civil Service
  daughter Katherine m. Clark Stewart

Hitchner, John George b. Ger. 1759 d. N.J. 1829   Pvt. U.S. Inf.
  m. Miss Miller — son John m. Sarah Johnson

Hite, Isaac b. Va. 1758 d. Va. 1836   Corp. Va. Mil.
  m. Eleanor Conway Madison — daughter Eleanor
  m. Dr. Cornelius C. Baldwin
  daughter Elenor H. m. Davison E. Baldwin

Hite, Isaac b. Va. 1753 d. Ky. 1795   Rec. Pat., Surveyor Ky. 1785
  m. Harriet Smith — son Jacob m. Elizabeth W. Sneed

Hite, James b. Va. 1776 d. Va. 1832 m. Juliet Wood Baker   Major Va. Mil.
  daughter Juliet W. m. Thomas Briscoe

Hite, Joseph b. Va. 1780 d. Ind. 1862 m. Frances Berry   Pvt. Ohio Mil.
  son Jonas m. Levinna Huffman

Hoadley, Calvin b. Conn. 1769 d. Ohio 1846?   Capt. Ohio Mil.
  m. Miriam Terrell — daughter Alma m. Eri Hickox

Hoagland, John b. N.Y. 1759 d. N.Y. 1831   Lt. Col. N.Y. Mil.
  m. Phebe Baird — daughter Margaret m. John Hendrick

Hoar, Allen b. R.I. 1768 d. R.I. 1837   2nd Major R.I. Mil.
  son Joseph S. m. Lucy Ann Burr

Hobart, Baxter b. Mass. 1790 d. N.Y. 1879   Ens. N.Y. Mil.
  m. (1) Eliza Potter — son Melin W. m. Eunice Louisa Pierce

Hobart, Nehemiah b. Mass. or N.H. 1773 d. N.Y. 1852   Pvt. N.Y. Mil.
  m. Rachel Shattuck and Lydia Randall — daughter Lucetta
  m. Zaccheus Newcomb Weston
  son Daniel m. Kezia Wesson

Hobbs, (William) Hubbard b. Va. 1746 d. Va. 1817   Pvt. Va. Mil.
  m. Martha Meredith — daughter Elizabeth m. James C. Fennell

Hobbs, James b. Eng. d. Va. m. Sarah Elizabeth Dollard   Pvt. Va. Mil.
  daughter Sarah E. m. William A. Barker

Hobbs, Joseph Jr. b. Md. d. Ky. 1809   Rec. Pat., Mem. Ky. House of Rep.
  m. Ann Maynard — daughter Sarah m. Greenberry Dorsey   1792

Hobbs, Joshua b. Md. 1740 d. Ky. aft. 1806   Civil Service 1792
  m. (1) Selman — son Eli m. Elizabeth Hamilton

Hobbs, Samuel b. Md. 1768 d. Md. aft. 1820   Corp. Md. Mil.
  m. Mary Eccles Ridgely — son John R. m. Charlotte Riley

Hobby, Thomas b. Conn. 1770 d. N.Y. 1866   3rd Corp. Conn. Mil.
  m. Mary Ferris — son Uriah m. Anne Sophia Wilcox

Hobensack, George b. Pa. 1791 d. Pa. 1830   Pvt. U.S. Inf. Pa.
  m. Hannah Carver — daughter Ann C.
  m. Isaacher Morris Rhoads, Jr.

Hobson, Matthew b. Va. 1782 d. Ala. 1851   Corp. Va. Mil.
  m. Elizabeth Mary Ann Mounger — daughter Eliza Ann
  m. William Giles Jones
  daughter Imogen m. William David Lee

Hocker, William b. Md. 1773 d. Mo. 1849   Pvt. Ky. Mounted Mil.
    m. Sarah Lawrence — son William Jr. m. Margaret Jane Turner

Hodge, Andrew b. Va. 1770 d. Ohio 1858 m. Isabella Mateer   Pvt. Ohio Mil.
    daughter Jane M. m. Jeremiah Yeazel

Hodges, George Washington b. S.C. 1792 d. S.C. 1876   Sgt. S.C. Mil.
    m. Rebecca Douglas — daughter Ann m. Joseph Stokes

Hodges, John b. Vt. 1787 d. Pa. 1879 m. Theodosia Alford   Pvt. Vt. Mil.
    son James M. m. Lucinda M. Nichols

Hodges, William b. Va. 1789 d. Ohio 1861   Pvt. Md. Mil.
    m. Elizabeth Groves — son Michael m. Louisa Johnson

Hodnett, John   Vol. 8 & 9   Ensign

Hoerner, John b. Pa. 1783 d. Pa. 1874   Major Pa. Mil.
    m. Magdalena Ebersole — son John Jr. m. Mary Rauch

Hoeye, John b. Ire. 1789 d. Iowa 1872 m. Mary Moore   Pvt. Ohio Mil.
    son Gordon R. m. Amanda Bobo

Hoffman, Daniel b. Pa. 1784 d. Pa. 1830   Vol. 5   Pvt. Pa. Mil.

Hoffman, John b. Pa. 1793 d. Pa. 1875 m. Barbara Bowman   Corp. Pa. Mil.
    son John Jr. m. Ann Mary Enterline

Hoffman, Samuel   Vol. 12   Pvt. N.J. Mil.

Hoffman, William b. Nova Scotia 1782 d. Texas 1845   Lt. U.S. Army
    m. Catherine Driscoll — daughter Amelia Frances
    m. Edmund B. Alexander

Hoffman, William b.— d. Pa. 1823 m. Susanna   Pvt. Pa. Vol.
    son Philip W. m. Barbara Stellwagon

Hogan, James b. S.C. 1790 d. Ga. 1854   Pvt. S.C. Mil.
    m. Elizabeth Gibson — son Thomas m. Emily Jane Jordan

Hogan, Reuben b.— d. Fla. m.—   Rec. Pat. 1812-1813 Fla. Rebellion
    son Luis Zacarias m. Maria Suarez Taylor

Hogan, William b. 1792 d. 1853 m. Sarah Clifton   Pvt. S.C. Mil.
    daughter Elizabeth Susan m. Samuel Andrew Weaver

Hogeboom, Stephen b. N.Y. 1744 d. N.Y. 1814   Rec. Pat., Mem. N.Y.
    m. Hilletja Waller (?) — daughter Nancy   Assembly & State Ser.
    m. Benjamin Moore

Hogeland, Isaac   Vol. 14   Pvt. Pa. Mil.

Hogg, James b. Pa. 1785 d. Ohio 1865   Pvt. Pa. Riflemen
    m. Elizabeth McCaughey — daughter Sarah m. Thomas McGlenn

Hogg, John b. S.C. 1794 d. S.C. or Miss. 1866   Pvt. S.C. Mil.
    m. Rachel Simms — son John Jr. m. Jane Miller

Hogle, Jeremiah b N.Y. 1773 d. N.Y. 1843   Lt. N.Y. Mil.
    m. Catherine Lucas — daughter Catherine m. Sebra Mosher

Hoisington, Abishai b. Vt. 1769 d. Ohio 1859   Teamster Vt. Mil., Civic
    m. Lucinda Hastings — son John M. m. Josephine Park   Offices

Hoitt, Joshua b. Mass. 1750 d. N.H. 1835   Patriot, Selectman N.H.
    m. Betsey Gerrish — son Daniel m. Rhoda Rawlings   1792-1800

Holbrook, Benajah b. Mass. 1772 d. Mich. 1855   Lt. N.Y. Mil.
    m. Judith Badger — son Milton m. Sarah Bronson

Holbrook, Benjamin b. Eng. 1778 d. Pa. 1859   Pvt. Pa. Marine Arty.
  m. Jane Campbell — son Benjamin F. Jr.
  m. Prudence Sophia Godshall

Holbrook, Henry b. Ire. 1791 d. Ill. 1842   Pvt. N.H. Mil.
  m. Abigail White — son Henry H. m. Caroline Ross

Holbrook, James   Vol. 14   Ens. Mass. Mil.

Holbrook, Nehemiah b. Mass. 1745 d. Mass.   Lt. Mass. Mil.
  m. Elizabeth Hobart — son Nehemiah, Jr. m. Sarah Wild

Holbrooks, Jesse b. Va. 1764 d. Ga. 1844   Sgt. Ga. Mil.
  m. Susannah Meanley — daughter Sarah m. John Arendall

Holcomb, Amos b. Conn. 1732 d. Vt. m. Mary Dibble   Pvt. Vt. Mil.
  son Jesse m. Phebe Loop

Holcomb, Benjamin   Vol. 14   Sgt. N.Y. Mil.

Holcomb, Diadorus b. Conn. 1780 d. N.Y. 1859   Surgeon & Paymaster
  m. Sybil Spaulding Wright — daughter Minerva   N.Y. 1809
  m. William J. Cutting

Holcomb, Hezekiah, Sr. b. Conn. 1726 d. Conn. 1794   Rec. Pat. Mem. Conn.
  m. Susanna Alderman — son Abel m. Elizabeth Pinney   Assembly

Holcombe, Benjamin   Vol. 7   Rec. Pat., Just. of Peace, Judge N.J.

Holcombe, Diodorus b. Conn. 1780 d. N.Y. 1859/60   Surgeon N.Y. Mil.
  m. Sylvia Loveland — daughter Almira S. m. George Warren Cole

Holcombe, Jesse b. Vt. 1770 d. Vt. 1846   Pvt. Vt. Mil.
  m. Mehitabel Winchell — son Jesse, Jr. m. Phebe Loop

Holcombe, (James) Philemon b. Va. 1720 d. Va. 1804 Rec. Pat., Va. Court
  m. Ann Walthall — daughter Elizabeth m. John Bibb Jr.   Officer

Holden, Daniel b. Me. 1771 d. Ohio 1854   Major Me. Arty.
  m. Hannah Greene — son William m. Malinda Shinkle

Holden, Jabez b. Mass. 1735 d. Mass. 1787   Rec. Pat. Mass.
  m. Rachel Farnsworth — son Samuel m. Jane Farnsworth

Holden, James b. Mass. 1750 d. Mass. 1827   Rec. Pat., Surveyor Mass.
  m. Hannah Bacon — daughter Abigail m. Amherst Morse   1784

Holden, John b. 1765 d. Ohio 1842 m. Jane Reilly   Pvt. Ohio Mil.
  daughter Jane m. Thomas Hunt

Holden, Lyman   Vol. 4   Pvt. Vt. Mil.

Holden, William b. Mass. 1795 d. Ill. 1862 Pvt. Drummer Mass. Riflemen
  m. (2) Catherine G. Childs — daughter Elizabeth B.
  m. Kendall P. Morse
  daughter Emma T. m. John B. Reid

Holden, John   Vol. 6   Col. Ky. Mil.

Holderby, Robert b. Va. 1788 d. (W.) Va. 1852   Pvt. Va. Mil.
  m. Susan Ann Chapman — son George W. m. Adelaide C. Hite
  daughter Susan m. Thomas J. Jenkins   REAL DAUGHTER

Holdridge, John b. N.Y. 1794 d. Ill. 1879 m. Rachel Biggers Pvt. N.Y. Mil.
  daughter Alice m. James Sherman

Holdridge, William b. N.Y. 1790 d. N.Y. m.—   Qtrmster. N.Y. Mil.
  son Darius

Hole, John b. Va. 1785 d. Ohio 1868   Rec. Pat., **Wagoner Va.**
   m. Catherine Hanna — son Lemuel m. Unity C. Stanley

Holeman, Alexander b. Pa. 1790 d. Pa. 1874   Pvt. Pa. Mil.
   m. Clarissa Sexton — son Ashbel m. Nancy Shelmadine

Holland, James   Vol. 12   Rec. Pat., **State Senator N.C.**

Holland, James b. Tenn. 1790 d. Ala. 1858 m. **Myra Davis**   Sgt. **Tenn. Mil.**
   son Newton m. Huldah Wilson

Holland, Stephen b. Va. 1785 d. Pa. 1840   Pvt. Pa. Mil.
   m. Polly McConehey — son Charles T. m. **Docia Craghead**

Hollen, Andrew B. b. Ind. 1793 d. Ind. 1835   Pvt. Ind. Mil.
   m. Nancy Brown Richards — son James H.
   m. Elizabeth Anne Graham

Hollenback, Martin b. Va. d. Va. 1849 m. Eleanor Hampton   Pvt. Va. Mil.
   daughter Sarah Ann m. Manoah Nathan Cardwell

Hollenbeck, William A. b. N.Y. 1784 d. N.Y. 1871   Pvt. N.Y. Mil.
   daughter Clarissa m. John A. Vincent

Holley, Daniel b. Conn. 1785 d. Conn. 1852   Paymaster 16th Reg. Conn.
   m. (2) Maria Jones — son Samuel C. m. Mary Ann Beard   Mil.

Holliday, Joseph   Vol. 16   Sgt. Ky. Mil.

Holliday, William b. Pa. 1750 d. Ind. 1819   Rec. Pat., Mem. House
   m. Jane Andrew — daughter Sarah   Commons N.C. 1813
   m. Aaron Maris

Hollingsworth, John W. b. Md. 1784 d. Pa. 1843   Pvt. Pa. Mil.
   m. Margaret Fullweiner — daughter Mary m. Cornelius Sutton

Hollister, Charles b. N.Y. 1785 d. N.Y. 1865   Lt. N.Y. Mil.
   m. Plemna Lewis — daughter Flora Ann m. Henry Boomer
   REAL DAUGHTER

Hollister, Silas b. Mass. 1778 d. N.Y. 1851 m. Rachel   Pvt. N.Y. Mil.
   son Alonzo F. m. Harriett M.

Holloway, Edward b. S.C. 1778 d. Ga. 1850   1st, 2nd Lt. U.S. Inf.
   m. Nancy — daughter Virginia m. William Traylor

Holloway, John b. Va. 1764 d. Ill. 1844   Adjutant Ky. Mil.
   m. Millie Burch — daughter Elizabeth m. Hugh Lunby

Holloway, Samuel b. Ky. 1795 d. Ky. 1882   Pvt. Ky. Mil.
   m. Jane Spencer — son William m. Mary Goodman

Hollman, Joseph   Vol. 8   Pvt. Md. Mil.

Holman, John b. Ky. 1787 d. Oregon 1864   Pvt. Ky. Mil.
   m. Betsy L. Duval — daughter Mary Ann
   m. James Lyburn Clinkenbeard
   son James D. m. Rachel Hixon Summers

Holman, Samuel   Vol. 4   Fifer Pa. Mil.
   daughter Ann E. m. Samuel Alleman   REAL DAUGHTER

Holmes, Benjamin b. Vt. 1790 d. N.Y. 1859   Corp. Vt. Reg.
   m. Eunice Hawley — daughter Chloe m. Jason W. Stearns

Holmes, Ethan b. 1771 d. N.Y. 1813   Capt. N.Y. Mil.
   m. Rebecca Wheeler — son William W. m. Julia Priscilla Vibbert

Holmes, Gabriel Jr. b. N.C. 1769 d. Wash., D.C. 1829   Rec. Pat., N.C.
m. Mary Hunter — daughter Jane   Assembly as Senator
m. John D. Beatty

Holmes, Halsey b. Conn. 1792 d. Conn. 1827   Sgt. Conn. Mil.
m. Jerusha Foster — son Frederick O. m. Isabella Anderson

Holmes, James Lewis b. Va. 1785 d. Texas 1836   Capt. Ky. Mil.
m. Nancy or Ann Griffith — son George N. m. Sarah Layton Jones
son James M. m. Elizabeth Ewens

Holmes, Jeremiah b. Conn. 1782 d. Conn. 1872 m. Anne   Capt. U.S. Navy
son Isaac D. m. Ellen Kemp

Holmes, John   Vol. 5   Capt. Pa. Mil.

Holmes, John Stout b. N.J. 1762 d. N.J. 1821   Cornet, N.J. or Pa. Mil.
m. Sarah Hendrickson — son Daniel m. Rhoda Van Meter
daughter Mary m. Albert Van Brunt

Holmes, Joseph b. Va. 1771 d. Ohio 1868   Capt. Ohio Mil.
m. Sarah McNabb — son Asa S. m. Mary McCoy

Holmes, Josiah b. S.C. 1787 d. Ga. 1865   Sgt. Mass. Mil.
m. Amelia Williams — son William C. m. Martha Elizabeth Holmes

Holmes, Samuel b. Pa. 1784 d. Ky. 1876   Pvt. Ohio Mil.
m. Mary Ann Hosick (Sarah) — son Samuel H. m. Lucindy Mitchell

Holmes, Samuel b. Pa. 1785 d. Ky. 1884 m. Sarah   Pvt. Ohio Mil.
daughter Terza B. m. James McLaughlin

Holsberry, John b. aft. 1780 d. 1862 m. Margaret Poling Ens. Va. Mil.
son Martin m. Abigail Stalnaker
daughter Rachael m. Andrew Stalnaker

Holsopple, Henry b. Pa. 1778 d. Ohio 1812   Soldier in Army
m. Susanna LeFevre — son Isaac m. Christena Hoffman

Holt, Erastus b. Conn. 1778 d. Vt. 1875   Rec. Pat., Mem. of Vt. Const.
m. Sally Parmenter — son Paul m. Almira Dean   Conven.

Holt, George b. Va. 1777 d. Va. 1836 m. Margaret   Pvt. Va. Artily.
son George Jr. m. Elizabeth Anne Savage

Holt, Stephen b. N.H. 1779 d. N.H. 1846 m. Mary Knox Pvt. Mass. Mil.
son Albert m. Mary White Ames

Holt, William b. N.C. 1785 d. Mo. 1866   Capt. N.C. Troops
m. Bettie Rainey — son Benjamin R. m. Sarah Elizabeth King

Holton, Jeremiah   Vol. 13   Lt. Mass. (Me.) Artil.

Holton, John A. b. Md. 1786 d. Ky. 1869   Pvt. Ky. Mil.
m. Frances E. Fenwick — son Llewellyn m. Frances P.

Holton, Richard b. N.J. 1770 d. Ohio 1842-50   Pvt. Ohio Mil.
m. Margaret Sparks — son William H. H. m. Amanda Combs

Holtzman, Samuel b. Md. 1788 d. (W.) Va. 1849   Pvt. D.C. Mil.
m. Sarah Theresa Sweeney — son William F. m. Jeannette Brookin

Hood, David b. Pa. 1794 d. N.Y. 1873   Pvt. N.Y. Mil.
m. Elizabeth Burrough — son Silas M. m. Mrs. Mary F. Pratt

Hood, Frederick b. Pa. 1779 d. Pa. 1865   Pvt. Pa. Mil.
m. Margaret Higgins — daughter Catharine H.
m. George England Lockwood

Hood, Gerhard b. Pa. 1756 d. Pa. 1814 m. Mary Wentz   Pvt. Pa. Mil.
son Frederick m. Margaret Higgins

Hooe, John b. Va. 1729 d. Va. aft. 1790   Rec. Pat., Justice Va. 1790
m. Anne Fowke — son Bernard m. Mary Symmes Chickester

Hook, Conrad   Vol. 3   Capt. Md. Mil.

Hook, Solomon b. Md. 1781 d. Md. 1840 m. Eliza Watts   Sgt. Md. Mil.
son Richard W. m. Elizabeth Gambrill

Hook, Thomas b. Md. 1790 d. Md. 1869   Lt. Md. Mil.
m. Sarah Worthington — daughter Martha m. William J. Phillips

Hook, Thomas b. (W.) Va. 1783 d. Mo. 1861   Lt. Va. Mil.
m. Elenor McVicker — son Adison m. Mary Catherine Carlyle

Hooke, Robert b. Va. 1776 d. Va. 1852   Capt. Va. Mil.
m. Elizabeth Walker — daughter Elizabeth J.
m. Robert Kenney Wilson
daughter Jinnette Mary Lucy Margaret m. Charles Ashby Van Lear

Hooker, Joshua Freeman b. N.C. 1795 d. Ark. 1866   Pvt. Tenn. Mil.
m. Frances Ridley Winn — daughter B. m. R. Kinman

Hooper, Enoch b. S.C. c. 1775 d. Miss. 1815   Capt. Ky. Mil.
m. Letitia Birding — daughter Elizabeth m. Mathias Cook

Hooper, James b. Md. 1804 d. Md. 1898   Seaman Md. Navy
m. Ann Elizabeth Brannan — daughter Avarilla m. Edward J. Codd
daughter Julia A. m. James A. Boyle
daughter Maria m. Thomas Kemp

Hooper, John   Vol. 15   Pvt. U.S. Inf.

Hooper, William b. Eng. 1788 d. Md. 1863   Pvt. Md. Mil.
son William E. m. Catherine Bell

Hooven (Hoven), Benjamin b. Pa. 1783 d. Pa. 1815   Pvt. U.S. Inf.
m. Janet Elsron — son James E. m. Emeline Henry

Hoover, Jacob b. Pa. 1790 d. Ohio 1852 m. Ann Marie Huber   Pvt. U.S. Inf.
daughter Lou. Henrietta m. Levi Heidelbaugh

Hoover, Peter b. N.Y. 1787 d. N.Y. 1879   Corp. N.Y. Mil.
m. Gertrude Siebert — son Eli m. Catherine Walrath

Hoover, Peter b. N.Y. 1787 d. N.Y. 1879   Corp. N.Y. Mil.
m. Magdelena Bloodough — daughter Betsy C. m. Philip Helmer

Hopkins, Caleb Sr. b. Mass. 1769 d. Mass. 1831   Pvt. Mass. Mil.
m. Priscilla Atwood — son Caleb, Jr. m. Elizabeth Augusta Dennis

Hopkins, Caleb b. Vt. 1770 d. N.Y. 1818 m. Dorothy Baybee   Col. N.Y.
son Marvin m. Jane Phelps

Hopkins, Cyrus b. N.Y. 1782 d. N.Y. 1863   Qtrmstr. N.Y. Mil.
m. Charlotte Bissell — son Cyrus B. m. Fanny Lankin

Hopkins, David b. R.I. 1748/9 d. N.Y. 1813   Rec. Pat., Senator N.Y.
m. Hannah Parrish — daughter Hannah m. Aaron Hayden
son Henry m. Mary E. Casey

Hopkins, David b. Mass. 1753 d. Md. 1824   Major U.S. Army
m. Isabella Ford — son William L. m. Susanna Rebecca Warfield

Hopkins, Elisha b. Mass. (Me.) 1788 d. Me. 1870   Pvt. Mass. (Me.) Mil.
m. Miriam Sprague — daughter Mary Jane Merritt
m. Andrew Chauncy Munsey

Hopkins, James b. N.J. 1763 d. N.J. 1826   Rec. Pat., Mem. of
    m. Rebecca Clement — daughter Elizabeth L.   Governor's Council
    m. Thomas Redman

Hopkins, John b. Ire. ca. 1732 d. Va. bef. 1791   Del. Va. 1784-8
    m. Jean Gordon — daughter Sarah m. Benjamin Benton

Hopkins, John b. S.C. 1765 d. S.C. 1831   Rec. Pat., Mem. of Rep. &
    m. Amy Goodwyn — son William m. Emma Goodwyn   Senate S.C.

Hopkins, Hiram b. 1798 d. 1879   Pvt. Vt. Mil.
    m. Mary Reynolds — daughter Mary Etta Hopkins
    m. Wm. Clark Gay

Hopkins, Joseph b. Vt. c. 1770 d. Ohio 1812/13   Pvt. Ohio Mil.
    son Harris m. Christina Cherry

Hopkins, Mark b. Mass. 1779 d. Mich. 1828   Capt. N.Y. Mil.
    m. Anastatia L. Kellogg — son Samuel F. m. Mary Ann Keeney

Hopkins, Russel b. Conn. 1797 d. Conn. 1878   Pvt. Conn. Mil.
    m. Hannah Paddock — daughter Maria Josephine m. Billings Neff

Hopkins, Samuel b. Va. 1750 d. Ky. 1819   Major Gen. Ky. Mil.
    m. Betty Bugg — daughter Elizabeth B. m. Philip Barbour

Hopkins, Solomon b. N.Y. 1787 d. N.Y. 1875   Pvt. N.Y. Mil.
    m. Lavisa Everett — daughter Susan
    m. William Stoutenburgh De Groff

Hopkins, Timothy S.   Vol. 9   Major Gen. N.Y. Mil.

Hopper, Daniel Cox b. Md. 1777 d. Md. 1849   Lt. Md. Mil.
    m. Maria Thomas — daughter Mary Louise
    m. Charles Washington Ridgely

Hopper, John b. Va. 1751 d. Ind. 1852 m. Anna Wilson   Pvt. Ky. Mil.
    daughter Elizabeth m. John Turpin

Hoppin (Hepping), Curtis b. Conn. 1785 d. N.Y. 1868   Ens. N.Y. Mil.
    son Bushrod E. m. Henrietta L. Parmenter
    son Franklin B. m. Sarah McConnell

Hopson, Simeon Jr. b. 1786 d. 1855   Drummer N.Y. Mil.
    m. Ruth Cowing — son Wm. A. Hopson m. Jane (Hannah?) Scofield

Hord, Elias b. Va. 1773 d. Ky. 1821 m. Ann Triplett   Pvt. Ky. Mil.
    son Francis T. m. Elizabeth S. Moss
    son Lewis m. Elvira Stillwell
    son Thornton m. Nancy Bolling

Hord (Hoard), James b. Va. d. Va. 1822 m. Agatha Sinclair Pvt. Va. Mil.
    son Dr. Ambose m. Elizabeth B. James

Horine, Benjamin b. 1780 d. 1852   Ens. Mo. Mil.
    m. Catherine Shook — daughter Elizabeth m. Wm. Henry Hulsey

Horn, Abraham b. Pa. 1756 d. Pa. 1826   Lt. Col. Pa. Mil.
    m. Susannah Hay — daughter Marie m. Jacob Shipe
    son Joseph m. Catherine Barthold
    son Melchor m. Isabella Trail

Horn, John b. Tenn. 1795 d. Ind. 1853   Pvt. Ky. Mil.
    m. Margaret Bottom (1) — daughter Jeanette m. Lewis Wayland

Hornbeck, Benjamin b. Va. 1754 d. (W.) Va. 1827 Rec. Pat., Just. of Peace
    m. Lydia Currence — son Joseph   Va. 1806-1815
    m. Nancy Light (?)

Hornbeck, Samuel b. Ky. 1789 d. Ohio 1862   Pvt. Ohio Mil.
    m. Mary Hutson — son Samuel, Jr. m. Sarah Correll

Hornblower, Josiah b. N.J. 1767 d. N.J. 1848   Surgeon, N.J. Mil.
    m. Annetje Merselis — son William m. Sarah Romeyn

Horner, James Yard   Vol. 8   Pvt. Va. Mil.

Horner, John Jr. b. 1793 d. 1878   Pvt. 36th Reg.
    m. Sarah Sparks — son John Valentine m. Elizabeth D. Patterson

Horner, Major b. Va. 1789 d. Mo. 1867   Sgt. Va. Mil.
    m. Keturah Morgan — son James S. m. Louisa Jane Kingsbury

Horner, William Edmonds b. Va. 1793/5 d. Pa. 1853   Surgeon's Mate
    m. Elizabeth Welsh — daughter Agnes   Va. Mil.
    m. Adolph Buschbeck   REAL DAUGHTER
    daughter Emily V. m. William Horner (relative)

Horney, Daniel b. Md. or N.C. 1786 d. Ohio 1865   3rd Sgt. Ohio Mil.
    m. Margaret Calloway — son Jefferson E. m. Margaret Griffith

Horrell, John b. Pa. 1781 d. Pa. 1859   Col. Pa. Mil.
    m. Margaret Trimmel (Trimble) — son Irwin m. Harriet Ressman

Horsford, Samuel b. Conn. 1762 d. Conn. 1808   Lt. Conn. Mil.
    m. Anna Densmore — daughter Lucretia m. Jesse Camp

Horsley, William b. Va. 1776 d. Va. aft. 1811   Rec. Pat., Grand Juror
    m. Mary Board — son Burrell m. Nancy Shrewsbury   Va. 1800

Horton, Craven b. Va. 1760 d. Va. 1835   Lt. Va. Mil.
    m. Mary Lawrence (?) — son William Henry m. Ann Clarkson

Horton, Daniel b. N.Y. 1788 d. N.Y. 1868   Ens. N.Y. Mil.
    m. Haddassah Seevers — daughter Maria F.
    m. Jerome Bonaparte Peterson

Horton, Horace b. Conn. 1793 d. Ill. 1883   Pvt. Conn. Mil.
    m. Clarissa Stevens — son Hobart m. Octavia Udell

Horton, Isaac b. Va. 1790 d. Tenn. 1856   Pvt. Va. Mil.
    m. Rhoda Richardson — daughter Margaret m. Guy Smith Hail Ellis

Horton, James b. N.Y. 1773 d. N.Y. 1834   Pvt. N.Y. Mil.
    m. Martha White — son George m. Sabra Mills

Horton, Jo W. b. N.C. 1792 d. Tenn. 1846   Pvt. Tenn. Mil.
    m. Sophia Weston Davis — son John D. m. Maria Graham Cannon

Horton, John b. Va. 1777 d. Va. aft. 1850   Pvt. Va. Mil.
    m. Jane Sargent — son Henderson m. Arminda Jane Mitchell

Horton, Joseph W. b. N.C. 1792 d. Tenn. 1846   Pvt. Pa. Mil.
    daughter Elizabeth m. Alexander Fall, Sr.

Horton, Jotham b. Mass. 1787 d. Mass. 1864   Rec. Pat., Ironworker 1797
    son Jotham, II m. Robey Warren

Horton, Samuel b. N.Y. 1792 d. N.Y. 1851   Pvt. N.Y. Mil.
    m. Mary Galloway — daughter Cynthia E. m. Abram Norris

Horton, Thomas b. Vt. 1795 d. Ohio 1886   Pvt. & Drummer N.Y. Mil.
    m. Mary Carter — son Orson m. Eliza Ann Croan

Horton, William   Vol. 6 & 14   Rec. Pat., N.Y. Legis.

Horton, William b. S.C. 1758 d. Tenn. aft. 1798 m.—   Rec. Pat.,Civil Officer
    son Claiborne m. Margaret Ingram   Tenn.

Hosack, David b. Pa. 1790 d. Pa. 1844 m. Rebecca Paxton Pvt. Pa. Mil.
son John J. m. Martha Barnes

Hosford, Aaron b. Mass. 1787 d. N.Y. 1879 m. Sarah Pvt. N.Y. Mil.
son Almer m. Elizabeth Ann

Hoshall, Jesse b. Prussia or Holland 1758 Lt. Md. Mil.
d. Md. 1830 or 1840 m. Mary Hurst —son Bennett
m. Elizabeth Williams

Hoskins, John b. Md. 1782 d. Ohio 1861 Pvt. Ohio Mil.
m. Elizabeth Davis — daughter Susan m. George Gordy

Hoskins, William b. Va. 1791 d. Miss. 1873 Pvt. Va. Mil.
m. Mildred Miller Hall — son Napolean m. Frances Walton

Hosley, Eli b. Vt. d. Pa. 1868 m. Angeline Arms Pvt. Vt. Cavalry
daughter Sybil m. David Doing

Hosmer, Jonathan, Jr. b. Mass. 1734 d. Mass. 1822 Sgt. Mass. Mil.
m. Submit Hunt — son Simeon m. Sarah Whitcomb

Hosmer, Sherman b. Conn. 1785 d. N.Y. 1877 Corp. N.Y. Mil.
m. Fanny Slack — daughter Hannah m. Holland Wilder

Hoss, Isaac b. Tenn. 1784/6 d. Tenn. 1829 Pvt. U.S. Inf.
m. Hannah Bayless — son Henry m. Anna Maria Sevier
daughter Mary m. John Smith

Hott, Peter b. Va. 1780 d. Ohio 1856 Pack Horseman
m. Margaret Wright — son George m. Jane Dean

Hottel, Joseph II b. Va. 1795 d. Va. 1878 Pvt. Va. Mil.
m. Catherine Snarr — son Elias m. Julia A. McInturff

Houck, William b. Md. 1781 d. Pa. 1851 Pvt. Pa. or Md. Mil.
m. Catherine Frank — son Jacob F. m. Eve Ebaugh
daughter Julia m. Melchior Allgire

Houeye, John b. France 1782 d. La. 1861 Corp. La. Mil.
m. Martha Wheat — daughter Martha m. Joseph Killian

Hough, David b. Conn. 1753 d. N.H. 1828 Rec. Pat., Mem. of Congress
m. Abigail Huntington — daughter Lucinda m. Jacob Ela

Hough, Samuel L. Vol. 3 Lt. Conn. Mil.

Hough, Thomas b. Pa. 1761 d. Pa. m. Hannah Tompkins Major Pa. Mil.
son Jonathan T. m. Helen Neff

Houghtaling, Henry b. N.Y. 1789 d. N.Y. 1861 Pvt. N.Y. Mil.
m. Maria Van Denbergh — daughter Ann Eliza m. Amos Hotaling

Houghtaling, William b. N.Y. 1798 d. N.Y. 1833 Sgt. N.Y. Mil.
m. Nancy Able — son Richard m. Mary Jane Mahaney

Houghton, Rufus Vol. 6 Pvt. U.S. Inf.

Houpt, John b. Pa. 1789 d. Pa. 1831 m. Rebecca Brandt Pvt. Pa. Mil.
son Isaiah Brant m. Elizabeth Neidig

House, Abraham b. N.Y. 1773 d. N.Y. 1851 m. Maria Smyth Pvt. N.Y. Mil.
daughter Katherine m. Daniel I. Diefendorf

House, John b. 1787 d. 1865 Pvt. Md. Mil.
daughter Emily m. George Enoch Bingey

House, Joseph b. N.Y. 1745 d. N.Y. 1823 Major N.Y. Mil.
m. Elizabeth Youngs — son Abraham m. Maria Smith

Houston, James b. Va. 1757 d. Tenn. 1844   Rec. Pat., Mem. Constitution
 m. Polly Gillespy — daughter Esther Jane   Convention
 m. Samuel Cowan
 daughter Phoebe m. Robert Tedford

Houston, James Fisher b. Ire. 1785 d. Md. 1842   Capt. Md. Mil.
 m. Agnes Butler — daughter Elizabeth C. m. Robert Gwynn

Houston, John b. Del. 1780 d. Del. 1828   Qtrmstr. Del. Mil.
 m. Elizabeth Wiltbank — daughter Elizabeth W. m. Henry Dunning

Houston (Huston), John b. Pa. 1743 d. Pa. 1809   Capt. Pa. Mil.
 m. Susanna Wright — daughter Martha m. Joseph Mifflin

Houston, Robert b. 1790 d. Tenn. 1840   Sgt. Tenn. Mil.
 m. Margaret Cunningham — son Robert A. m. Savannah Kinnebrew

Houston, Sam b. Va. 1793 d. Texas 1863   Tenn. Mil.
 m. Margaret Moffett Lea — daughter Margaret
 m. Weston L. Williams
 daughter Nancy Elizabeth m. Joseph Clay Stiles Morrow
 daughter Nettie m. Wm. S. L. Bringhurst   REAL DAUGHTER

Hover, Jacob A. b. N.Y. 1792 d. N.Y. 1880   Pvt. N.Y. Mil.
 m. Anna Ostrander — daughter Mary J. m. Albert de Myer

Hovey, Benjamin b. Mass. 1758 d. Ohio Terr. 1804   Lt. Mass. Mil.
 m. Lydia Haven — daughter Alphena m. James Glover

Hovey, Josiah b. Conn. 1747 d. N.Y. 1820   Ens. N.Y. Mil.
 son Elithalet m. Sallie Rowley Knapp

Hovey, Simeon b. Conn. 1781 d. Conn. 1869   Pvt. Conn. Mil.
 son William B. m. Charlotte Eliza Turner

Howard, Daniel b. R.I. 1752 d. R.I. 1827   Rec. Pat., Just. of Peace, Clerk
 m. Dorothy Clarke — son Clarke m. Amey Cranston   & Judge

Howard, Ichabod b. Mass. 1754 d. Mass. 1841 Rec. Pat., Civil Office Mass.
 m. Molly Keith — son Henry m. Mary Emily Ware

Howard, James b. N.C. 1735 d. N.C. 1790 Rec. Pat., Justice of Court N.C.
 m. Cassandra Brice — daughter Cassandra B.
 m. (2) Jaspe Rogers Ashworth Jr.

Howard, James b. N.H. 1774 d. N.Y. 1855   Capt. N.C. Mil.
 m. Patience Balch — son Seth m. Lany Bonch

Howard, Jeremiah b. Mass. 1756 d. N.H. 1837   Rec. Pat., Clerk of Court,
 m. Sally Humphreys — son Jeremiah, Jr.   N.H. 1812
 m. Lucy Johnson

Howard, John b. N.C. 1725/30 d. N.C. 1785   Lt. N.C. Mil.
 m. Mary Ashburn — daughter Amelia
 m. Joseph Howard, Sr. (cousin)

Howard, John Williams   Vol. 17   Pvt. N.Y. Mil.

Howard, John William b. Vt. 1791 d. Wisconsin 1862   Officer N.Y. Mil.
 m. Mary Bonn — son John W. m. Eliza Celinda Cone

Howard, Joshua b. Conn. 1771 d. Conn. 1859   Pvt. Conn. Mil.
 m. Mary Elderkin — daughter Martha m. Anderson Burdick

Howard, Joshua   Vol. 5 & 14   2nd Lt. Mass. Mil.

Howard, Samuel b. Conn. 1752 d. Conn. 1816   Pvt. Conn. Mil.
 m. Rachel Talcott — son Walter m. Ruth Kenney

Howard, Thomas b. Pa. 1758 d. Ohio 1825   Pvt. Pa. Mil.
m. Elizabeth Armstrong — son Robert A. m. Priscilla Nelson

Howard, William b. 1779 d. Ohio 1861 m. Mary Rose   Pvt. Ohio Mil.
son Albert C. m. Susannah Teegarden

Howard, William Sanders b. S.C. 1793 d. Ga. 1885   Sgt. S.C. Mil.
m. Anna Thorne — son George W. m. Sarah Margaret Robinson
son William S. Jr. m. Georgia V. Walker

Howard, Zephaniah b. Conn. 1788 d. N.Y. 1847   Pvt. Conn. Mil.
m. Olive Smith — daughter Sabrina m. Joseph Cottrell Hanchett

Howe, Benjamin b. Vt. 1788 d. Vt. 1849 m. Sabra Washburn Pvt. Vt. Mil.
son Isaac m. Sarah Ide

Howe, Daniel b. Md. 1764 d. Pa. 1843 m. Hannah Day   Pvt. Pa. Mil.
son William m. Elizabeth

Howe, Daniel b. Va. 1758 d. Va. 1838   Lt. Va. Mil. 1786-93, Sheriff 1796
m. Nancy Haven — son William H. m. Mary Margaret Fisher

Howe, James b. Va. 1789 d. Ill. 1867   Pvt. Ohio Mil.
m. Catherine Tethero (Tudero) — daughter Rebecca Jane
m. Robert Barkley Stephenson

Howe, Joseph b. Conn. 1777 d. N.Y. 1862 m. Amy Reed   Capt. N.Y. Mil.
son Ira B. m. Charity Helmer

Howe, Mark b. Mass. 1736 d. N.H. 1818   Major, Surgeon N.H. 1785
m. Mary Payson Rowley — son Eliphalet P. m. Abigail Robinson

Howe, Peter b. Mass. 1756 d. Ohio 1842   Rec. Pat., Just. of Peace Ohio
m. Orinda Fuller — son Sylvanus m. Abigail Durfee

Howe, Samuel b. Conn. 1769 d. N.Y. 1854   Sgt. N.Y. Mil.
m. Polly Caroline Fitch — son James W. m. Emma Davis

Howe, Thomas Yardley b. Pa. 1777 d. N.Y. 1855   2nd Lt. U.S. Inf.
m. Elizabeth Woodruff — daughter Mary Y. m. Ezekiel Gilbert Gear

Howe, William   Vol. 17   Pvt. Conn. Mil.

Howell, David b. Ky. 1797 d. Ky. 1874 m. Anna K. Gist   Pvt. Ky. Mil.
daughter Henrietta m. Jere E. Rogers

Howell, David b. N.J. 1773 d. N.J. 1844 m. Sally Burnett Pvt. N.J. Mil.
daughter Tace m. Elam Williams Bonnell

Howell, Elisha b. Del. 1784 d. Ohio 1872   Pvt. Del. Mil.
m. Louisa Hickman — daughter Charlotte m. James German
daughter Nancy R. m. Adam Miller

Howell, Francis   Vol. 11   Pvt. Mo. Mil.

Howell, Jacob   Vol. 17   Pvt. N.J. Mil.

Howell, John b. Va. 1784 d. Ohio 1844   Capt. Ohio Mil.
m. Eleanor Mercer — son Ingabee m. Grammer Jones

Howell, Richard b. Del. 1754 d. N.J. 1803   Rec. Pat., Governor of N.J.
m. Keziah Burr — son William B. m. Margaret Graham Kemp

Howell, William Burr b. N.J. 1749 d. Ala. 1863   Lt. N.J. Inf.
m. Margaret Kempe — daughter Varina B. m. Jefferson Davis

Howes, Samuel, II. b. Va. 1727 d. Va.   Rec. Pat., Va. Legis. 1785
m. Anne Walker — son Richard m. Katherine Walker

Howland, Abraham   Vol. 3   Pvt. Mass. Mil.

Howland, Humphrey b. Mass. 1750 d. N.Y. 1862   Rec. Pat., N.Y. Legis.
   m Sarah T. Field — daughter Mary S.   1812
   m. John Jacobs Thomas

Howland, Ichabod b. Mass. 1782 d. Ohio 1852   Sgt. Ohio Mil.
   m. Mary Alice Beam — son Armstrong m. Cinderella Ellis

Howland, John b. Mass. 1758 d. Ohio 1841 m. Jane Beam   Pvt. Ohio Mil.
   son Stephen m. Mary Black

Howland, Richard   Vol. 16   Corp. N.Y. Mil.

Howland, Richmond   Vol. 16   Corp. N.Y. Mil.

Howland, Solomon M. b. N.C. 1790 d. N.C. 1853   Pvt. N.C. Mil.
   m. Mrs. Mehitabel Masters Mayo — daughter Sarah J.
   m. David Morris

   Howland, William   Vol. 15   Pvt., Ship's Carpenter

Hoxsie, Stephen b. R.I. 1713 d. R.I. 1793   Rec. Pat., Just. of Peace R.I.
   m. Elizabeth Kenyon — daughter Elizabeth K.   1791
   m. Thomas Woodmansee Rogers

Hoy, John Bush b. Ky. 1793 d. Ky. 1867   Pvt. Ky. Vol.
   m. Sarah P. Martin — daughter Lavinia S.
   m. Daniel Boisseau Price

Hoy, Patrick b. Ire. 1783 d. S.C. 1860   Rec. Pat., Munitions Maker S.C.
   m. Elizabeth Coan — son John m. Nancy Rogers

Hoyer, Jacob b. Pa. 1793 d. Pa. 1834 m. Lucetta Brus   Pvt. Pa. Mil.
   son George m. Justina Margaret Hippey

Hoyman (Heiman, Homan, Hohman), Henry b. Pa. 1785 d. Pa. aft. 1850
   m. Elizabeth Uhl   Pa. Mil., Pvt. & Drum Major
   son Henry, Jr. m. (2) Mrs. Catherine Hay Shaffer

Hoyt, Aaron b. Conn. 1778 d. N.Y. 1847 m. Sophia Brooks   Pvt. N.Y. Mil.
   son Aaron m. Sarah M. B. Jordan

Hoyt, David Cole b. N.Y. 1788 d. N.Y. 1841 m. Betsy Frost   Pvt. N.Y. Mil.
   son David L. m. Mary Brooks
   daughter Lucy m. Halsey Hadley

Hoyt, Ebenezer b. Conn. 1779 d. Conn. 1819   Pvt. Conn. Mil.
   m. Polly Stebbins — son Ebenezer B. m. Mary Jane Reynolds

Hoyt, Henry Jr. b. Conn. 1780 d. Ga. 1823 m. Sarah Brower   Lt. U.S. Inf.
   daughter Clarissa B. m. Lewis Bradley Ayres

Hoyt, Ira b. Conn. 1785 d. Conn. m. Laura Gregory   Pvt. Conn. Mil.
   son Starr m. Phoebe Finch

Hoyt, Jacob b. Conn. 1762 d. Conn. 1832 m. (2)   Rec. Pat., Juror Conn.
   daughter Sarah m. Azer Tuttle   1804

Hoyt, John b. N.Y. 1783 d. Ohio 1875 m. Lydia Plympton   Pvt. U.S. Inf.
   daughter Alma G. m. Walter S. Barnes

Hoyt, Noah b. Conn. 1753 d. N.Y. 1827 m. Mary Seeley   Pvt. N.Y. Mil.
   son Joseph L. m. Mary Jane Norman

Hubball, Ebenezer b. Eng. 1785 d. Md. 1849   Pvt. Md. Mil.
   m. Sarah Broome — son Ebenezer, Jr. m. Jane Talbott

Hubbard, David Elizur b. Conn. 1778 d. Conn. 1830   Rec. Pat., Judge &
   m. Pamela Hollister — daughter Caroline   Rep. of Conn. Legis.
   m. Eleazur W. Hollister

Hubbard, Isaac b. Conn. 1791 d. N.Y. 1868　　　　　Pvt. N.Y. Mil.
　　m. Samantha Gurnsey — son William M. m. Susan Evans

Hubbard, John b. Conn. 1751 d. Conn. 1837　　　　Deputy 1791 Conn.
　　m. Martha Bradley (2) — son William m. Abigail Heaton

Hubbard, Joseph b. Va. 1760 d. Ga. 1830 m. Cynthia Bennet　　Capt. Ga. Mil.
　　daughter Elizabeth m. Jacob Wise

Hubbard, Noadiah b. Conn. 1765 d. N.Y. 1859　　　　Major N.Y. Mil.
　　m. Eunice Ward — son Ward m. Clarissa Fish

Hubbard, Salmon　　Vol. 16　　　　　　　　　Pvt. N.Y. Mil.

Hubbard, Sela　　Vol. 9　　　　　　　　　　Pvt. N.Y. Mil.

Hubbard, Stephen b. Conn. 1798 d. Wisc. 1868　　　Pvt. Conn. Mil.
　　m. Esther Scofield — daughter Elizabeth m. Ebenezer Hadley

Hubbard, William b. Conn. 1787 d. Ohio 1863　　　　Capt. N.Y. Mil.
　　m. Katharine Hurlburt — daughter Catherine m. O. H. Fitch

Hubbel, Vernon b. Conn. 1788 d. Mich. 1870　　　　Pvt. N.Y. Mil.
　　m. Lucy Deake (Dake) — daughter Betsey Maria m. James B. Cass

Hubbell, Ephraim　　Vol. 9　　　　　　　　Pvt. U.S. Inf.

Hubbell, William D. b. N.Y. 1798 d. Mo. 1883　　　Pvt. N.Y. Mil.
　　m. Elizabeth E. Price — son John Price m. Anna Maria Morton

Huber, Tobias b. Pa. 1789 d. Pa. 1873　　　　　　Pvt. Pa. Mil.
　　m. Charlotte Elder — son Joseph De B. m. Virginia Johnson

Hubert, David b. Miss. 1782 d. Miss. 1830　　　　Pvt. Miss. Mil.
　　m. Philadelphia Runnels — son Benjamin m. Anna Maria Simpson

Hubley, Adam b. Pa. 1759 d. Pa. 1798 Memb. Pa. Assembly fr. Lancaster
　　m. Lydia Field　　　　　　　Co. 1783/7 State Sen. 1790/1

Huddleston, John　　Vol. 11　　　　　　　　Pvt. Tenn. Mil.

Huddlestun, George b. Va. 1778 d. Ky. 1851　　　　Pvt. Va. Mil.
　　m. Susannah Slack — son Barnett G. m. Susan Minter

Hudgins, Houlder I. b. 1738 d. 1815　　　　　Vet. Rev. War Va.,
　　m. 2nd Mary Gwyn — son John L. Hudgins　Defense Comm. 1812
　　m. 2nd Mary Anderson

Hudgins, John b. Va. 1793 d. Va. 1827　　　Master Mate U.S. Navy
　　m. Harriet Miller — son Robert M. m. Helen Skinner

Hudgins, William b. Va. 1786/9 d. Mo. 1874　　　　Pvt. Va. Mil.
　　m. Nancy Blake — son William B. m. Mary Frances Wirt

Hudnall, John (Smith) b. Va. 1763/7 d. Va. 1844/5　　Pvt. Va. Mil.
　　m. Martha Newman — daughter Cena m. William Henry Hardy
　　daughter Elizabeth m. William Edgar

Hudson, George b. Pa. 1744/5 d. Pa. 1820　　　　Pvt. Pa. Mil.
　　m. Isabella Abernathy — son John m. Eleanor Moreland
　　son William m. Melinda Doyle

Hudson, Hiram (Hyrum) b. 1798 d. 1867　　　　Pvt. Va. Mil.
　　m. Nancy E. Vanhook — daughter Ellen S. m. Henry W. Long

Hudson, John b. S.C. 1772 d. Ga. 1838 m. Elizabeth Morgan　Lt. Ga. Mil.
　　son John N. m. Amanda Melvina Stewart

Hudson, Joshua b. N.C. 1770 d. Ga. 1855　　Justice of Peace Ga. 1805
　　m. Elizabeth — daughter Martha m. Henry B. Gober

Hudson, Larkin Rutherford b. Va. 1792 d. Va. 1850   Pvt. Va. Mil.
   m. Mary Wingfield — daughter Mary Frances
   m. Thomas Jefferson Johnson

Hudson, Lemuel b. N.Y. 1789 d. N.Y. 1868   Surgeon's Mate N.Y. Mil.
   m. Mary Treadwell Woodruff — daughter Julia m. Lot Davis

Hudson, Richard b. N.Y. d. N.Y. 1828   Ens. Lt. N.Y. Mil.
   m. Rachel Akerly (Ackerly) — daughter Phebe Rachel
   m. Thomas Terry

Hudson, Robert b. Va. 1780 d. Va. m. Elizabeth Jones   Pvt. Va. Mil.
   daughter Margaret A. m. William Dorsey

Hudson, Shadrach b. 1780 d. Ohio 1842   Pvt. Ohio Mil. 1791-1813
   m. Lydia Winans — daughter Abigail m. Isaac Carey

Hudspeth, William b. N.C. 1778 d. Mo. 1867   Major Ky. Mil.
   m. Tabitha Beall — son George W. m. Elizabeth C. Jesse
   son Thomas J. m. Cynthia Hambright

Hueston (Hewson), Matthew b. Pa. 1771 d. Ohio 1847   Capt. Ohio Mil.
   m. Catherine Davis — daughter Mary Jane m. Robert Harper

Huett, John b. Pa. 1763 d. Pa. 1825 m. Susanna Bechtel   Pvt. Pa. Mil.
   daughter Christina m. John Hiester

Huffaker, George b. 1757 d. Tenn.   Corp. Tenn. Mil.
   son Henry m. Polly French

Huffman, George b. N.C. 1780 d. N.C. 1848   Capt. N.C. Mil.
   m. Susannah Houck — son Langdon m. Amy Miller

Huffman, George Peter b. Pa. 1775 d. Ind. aft. 1860   Pvt. Ky. Mil.
   m. Cynthia Jones — son Edmund m. Louise Ann Rightsell

Huffman (Hoffman), Johannes Peter b. N.J. 1766   Pvt. N.J. Mil.
   d. N.J. 1841 m. Mary Willett — daughter Anne
   m. Noah Sharp Cramer

Huffman, Joseph b. Pa. 1782 d. Pa. 1839 m. Susannah Horn   Pvt. Pa. Mil.
   daughter Anne m. John Dague, II

Huffman, Michael John b. Va. 1783 d. Ill. 1872   Pvt. Va. Mil.
   m. Susannah E. Summers — daughter Phebe Ann m. Merrill P. Carr

Huffmaster, Joseph b. Va. 1782 d. Tenn. 1874   Pvt. Tenn. Mil.
   m. Elizabeth Waitzell (Weitzel) — son James W.
   m. Sarah Herrington
   daughter Lucinda m. Levi Campbell

Hufman, Peter b. Va. 1776 d. Mo. 1854 m. Susannah Senate   Pvt. Mo. Mil.
   daughter Margrate S. m. Squire Green

Hugg, Enoch b. Del. 1794 d. Del. 1833   4th Sgt. Del. Mil.
   m. Margaret Walker — daughter Rebecca Jane
   m. William Henry Chandler

Huggins, David, Jr. b. N.H. 1788 d. Vt. 1868 m. Lucy Cady   Pvt. Vt. Mil.
   daughter Harriette G. m. Cyrus Fisher

Hughes, Anthony b. Va. 1765 d. Va. 1860 m. Nancy Palmore   Ens. Va. Mil.
   son Josiah m. Sallie Ellyson

Hughes, Charles b. Ky. 1793 d. Mo. 1857   Pvt. Ky. Mil.
   m. Elizabeth Lawless — daughter Nancy m. Noah Kingsbury

Hughes, Edward Edwin b. Pa. 1792 d. Ill. 1873   Corp. Pa. Riflemen
   m. Mary Hice/Heiss/Hiess — daughter Susannah
   m. (1) James K. Wakefield

Hughes, Felix b. Pa. 1774 d. Pa. 1828 m. Mary Donnelly   Pvt. Pa. Mil.
    son Francis m. Elizabeth Hempstead

Hughes, Hugh b. Pa. 1755 d. Pa. 1816   Rec. Pat., Just. of Peace Pa. 1793
    m. Mary Hutton — son James, Sr. m. Hannah Swetland

Hughes, James b. Va. 1785 d. Tenn. 1841   Pvt. Tenn. Vol.
    m. Mary W. Edmiston — son Franklin m. Elizabeth Bernice Tinnon

Hughes, John b. Va. ca. 1790 d. Tenn. 1845   Pvt. Tenn. Mil.
    m. Cathrine Bryant (Briant) — son George W.
    m. Lucinda Hamm Vincent

Hughes, John b. Va. 1776 d. Tenn. 1860   Vol. 19   Rec. Pat., Va.
    daughter Rachel Jane m. Samuel Henderson

Hughes, John, Jr. b. Va. 1763 d. Ky. 1842   Major Ky. Mil.
    m. Anne Meriwether — son James N. m. Louisa Adaline Russell

Hughes, Jonathan b. Va. 1790 d. Ohio 1830   Pvt. Ohio Vol.
    m. Elizabeth McKnight — daughter Charlotte m. Jeremiah Porter

Hughes, Leaven b. 1796 d. Ind. 1874 m. Barbara McNay   Pvt. Ky. Mil.
    son William P. m. Edey Ann Lewman

Hughes, Reuben b. Va. 1766 d. Va. 1851 m. Elizabeth Estes Pvt. Va. Mil.
    daughter Lucy m. James French

Hughes, Thomas b. Va. 1749 d. Pa. 1823 m. Elizabeth Swan Pvt. Pa. Mil.
    daughter Martha m. Barnet Neel   Justice, 1792
    daughter Nancy m. James Curl
    daughter Sarah m. Mathias Roseberry

Hughes, Thomas b. Va. 1750 d. Ky. 1826 m. Lucy Tandy   Major Ky. Mil.
    son Elliott M. m. Jane McConnell

Hughes, Thomas b. Pa. 1789 d. (W.) Va. 1849   Pvt. Pa. Mil.
    m. Mary Odenbaugh — son Alfred m. Mary Kirby Adrain

Hughes, William b. Pa. 1781 d. Pa. 1840   Pvt. Pa. Mil.
    m. Elizabeth Barnett — daughter Rachel m. William Kelley

Hughes, William b. Va. d. S.C. m.—   Pvt. S.C. Mil.
    daughter Elizabeth m. Jeremiah Stokes

Hughes, William b. Va. 1735 d. Va. 1813   Patriot, Sheriff 1797 Va.
    m. Mary Ball — daughter Hannah m. Edward Thomas

Hughey, John b. S.C. 1793 d. Florida 1881   Pvt. Ga. Mil.
    m. Hannah Morris Pearson — daughter Mary M.
    m. Alexander Calvin Martin

Hughey, Robert b. Va. 1796 d. Tenn. 1830 m. Mary Lain Sgt. Tenn. Mil.
    son Beverly D. m. Talitha Estes

Hulbert, John b. Conn. 1735 d. Mass. 1815   Rept. Mass. Gen. Ct. 1788
    m. Mercy Hamlin — son Peyton Randolph m. Sarah Youngs

Hulin, Peter   Vol. 16   Pvt. N.Y. Mil.

Hulings, David Watts b. Pa. 1794 d. Md. 1858   2nd Corp. Pa. Mil.
    m. Maria Holmes Patton — daughter Elizabeth W.
    m. Chauney Andrus Reynolds

Hull, Benjamin b. Va. 1782 d. (W.) Va. 1862   Pvt. Va. Mil.
    m. Sayy Cundiff — daughter Catherine N.
    m. Abraham Pennybacker Byrd

Hull, Daniel, Jr. b. Conn. 1766 d. N.Y. 1842   Major N.Y., 1802 Mem. State
    m. Phebe Green — daughter Sally m. Eliphalet Jones   Legis.

Hull, Eli b. Conn. 1764 d. N.Y. 1828 m. Sally Beckwith Pvt. N.Y. Mil.
son Josiah m. Anna Graves

Hull, John b. N.J. 1780 d. Ill. 1833 m. Rebecca Bennett Pvt. Ohio Mil.
son Benjamin m. Lucinda Allen
son Samuel m. Lucy Tully

Hull, Henry b. Va. 1760 d. (W.) Va. 1836 Pvt. Va. Mil.
m. Elizabeth Hawkins — son John m. Sophie Derieux

Hull, William b. Conn. 1753 d. Mass. 1825 m. Sarah Fuller Pvt. Mass. Mil.
daughter Julia K. m. Joseph Wheeler

Hull, William b. Conn. 1753 d. La. 1825 Vol. 7 General U.S. Army

Huls, Henry b. Pa. 1764 d. Pa. 1851 m. Priscilla Hoagland Major Pa. Mil.
daughter Sicky m. James McCully

Hulse, John b. N.J. d. N.J. 1815 m. Eliza Pvt. N.J. Mil.
son Ralph m. Margaret Stillwell

Hultz, George Vol. 13 Pvt. Ohio Mil.

Humber, Robert Christian b. Va. 1783 d. Ga. 1842 Pvt. Ga.
m. Mrs. Mary Ellis Waller Davis — son Robert C. Jr.
m. Sarah E. R. Ingram

Humbert, Abraham b. N.Y. 1783 d. Pa. 1841 Pvt. N.Y. Mil.
m. Hannah James — daughter Rebecca m. Robert Hustead

Hume, Moses b. Mass. 1787 d. Mich. 1864 m. Sarah Stewart Sgt. N.Y. Mil.
son Stephen T. m. Permelia Stewart

Humes, Hamilton b. Pa. 1784 d. Pa. 1859 Pvt. Pa. Vol.
m. Ann Elmira Bailey — daughter Rachel m. Samuel Humes

Hummel, Frederick b. Pa. 1758 d. Pa. 1802 Major Pa. Mil.
m. Rachel Pickard — son Jacob m. Justina Bower

Hummel, Jacob b. Pa. 1791 d. Pa. 1847 m. Justina Bower Capt. Pa. Mil.
daughter Justina m. Benjamin F. Feaster

Hummel, Valentine Vol. 12 Pvt. Pa. Mil.

Hummell, Frederick Vol. 6 Pvt. Pa. Mil.

Humphrey, Allen b. Conn. 1773/7 d. Ohio 1825 Lt. Ohio Mil.
m. Polly Bodwell — son Elijah H. m. Emily Eliza Shayes

Humphrey, Jacob b. Pa. 1751 d. Pa. 1826 Rec. Pat., Mem. of Pa. Legis.
m. Jane Charlesworth — daughter Nancy m. Jacob Johns

Humphrey, John G. Vol. 16 Pvt. Va. Mil.

Humphrey, Josiah H. b. N.Y. 1784 d. N.Y. 1836 Capt. N.Y. Troops
m. Esther Doball — son Josiah W. m. Louise Smith

Humphrey, Thomas b. Pa. 1774 d. Pa. 1822 Major Gen. Pa. Mil.
m. Euphemia Hart — daughter Eliza H. m. Samuel Wentz

Humphrey, William C. b. N.Y. 1780 d. N.Y. 1858 Sgt. N.Y. Mil.
m. Mary C. Coddington — daughter Jane m. Seth Harris

Humphreys, David b Pa. 1775 d. Va. 1850 Sgt. Va. Regt.
m. Catherine Keyes — son George m. Janet L. Henderson

Humphreys, Decius b. Conn. 1789 d. Iowa 1873 Lt. Conn. Mil.
m. Laura Adams — daughter Hannah m. Samuel Wiss Brown

Humphreys, George Vol. 8 Rec. Pat., Civil Offices Conn.

Humphreys, Moses   Vol. 9   Pvt. Tenn. Mil.

Humphreys, Richard b. Va. 1793 d. Tenn. 1879   Corp. Va. Mil.
m. Matilda Hartman — son James C. m. Dicey A. Bacon

Humphreys, Uriah b. Ky. 1796 d. Mo. 1843   Pvt. Ind. Mil.
m. Rachel Gordon — son Elisha E. m. Mary Ann Dobbins

Hungate, John b. Va. 1774 d. Ky. 1813 m. Molley Coffman Pvt. Ky. Mil.
daughter Salley m. James Ray

Hungerford, Henry   Vol. 12   Capt. Va. Mil.

Hungerford, John Washington b. Va. 1787 d. Va. 1850 Asst. Aid-de-Camp
m. Eleanor Ann — daughter (2) Eleanor Ann   Va. Mil.
m. Frederick Dodge Wheelwright

Hungerford, Timothy   Vol. 15   Farrier N.Y. Mil.

Hunt, Daniel b. R.I. 1769 d. R.I. aft. 1813   Major R.I. Mil.
m. Susanna Northrup — daughter Ruth Ann m. Aurin Miller

Hunt, David b. Tenn. 1778 d. Tenn. 1841   Pvt. Tenn. Mil.
m. Elizabeth Larkin — son David L. m. Martitia Shelton

Hunt, Eustace   Vol. 13   Ens. Va. Mil.

Hunt, Horatio b. Md. 1790 d. Ohio 1875 m. Matilda Roby Pvt. Md. Mil.
son John L. m. Susan C. Gregory

Hunt, James b. N.J. 1758 d. N.Y. 1837   Rec. Pat., Mem. of N.Y. Legis.
m. Mary Cochrane — daughter Ann m. Henry A Halsey   1799

Hunt, James b. Va. 1791 d. Neb. 1875 m. Mary Jordan Pvt. Ohio Mil.
daughter Margaret m. Robert Anderson Jones

Hunt, James Jr. b. N.C. 1762 d. Ga. 1832   Pvt. Ga. Mil. 1798
m. Jemima Carter — son Richard C. m. Mary Davis Harris

Hunt, Job b. Md. 1785 d. Md. 1825 m. Mary Ann Boyd   Pvt. N.J. Mil.
son Samuel m. Martha McCleary Beall

Hunt, Josiah (Jonah) b. Vt. 1792 d. Mass. 1864   Pvt. Mass. Mil.
m. Experience Colton — son Henry C. m. Caroline S. St. Clair

Hunt, Stephen b. N.Y. 1770 d. N.Y. 1831   Lt. N.Y. Mil.
m. Jane Delamater — son James m. Sarah Nicholas Burr
son Peter Underhill Fowler m. Jane Hunt

Hunt, Thomas b. Mass. 1754 d. Ill. 1808   Vol. 8   Col. U.S. Inf.

Hunter, Charles W. b. N.C. 1787/90 d. N.C. aft. 1815   Major N.C. Mil.
son Major H. m. Elizabeth Lynch

Hunter, Emanuel b. S.C. 1787 d. Ill. 1874 m. Judith Lee Pvt. Tenn. Mil.
son Allen m. Elizabeth Lee

Hunter, George Washington b. Va. 1776 d. Va. 1856   Capt. Va. Mil.
m. Angeline Moore — son George W. Jr. m. Mary Angeline Conrad

Hunter, Jacob b. N.C. 1766 d. Tenn. 1836 m. Anne Clarke Pvt. Tenn. Mil.
son John m. Mary Brown

Hunter, John b. Ireland 1750/2 d. S.C. 1803 m. Sarah   Judge S.C.
daughter Rachel m. John Garlington

Hunter, John b. Conn. 1784 d. N.Y. 1850   Rec. Pat., Just. of Peace N.Y.
m. Susanna — daughter Eliza m. Chauncy Seymour

Hunter, John b. Pa. 1751 d. Ohio 1829 m. Margaret Watt   Pvt. Ohio Mil.
  daughter Margaret m. George Robinson Sr.

Hunter, John, Jr. b. N.C. 1792 d. Tenn. 1850   Capt. Tenn. Mil.
  m. Mary Brown — son Thomas E. R. — m. Louisa Jane Brooks

Hunter, John, Sr. b. N.C. d. Tenn. 1823   Rec. Pat., Mem. of Tenn. Legis.
  m. Barbary Bowman — son Jacob m. Anne Clark

Hunter, Jonathan b. Va. 1771 d. Va. 1819   Pvt. Va. Mil.
  m. Frances James — son Josiah W. m. Cornelia Anne Whitehurst

Hunter, Joseph   Vol. 10   Major Mo. Vol.

Hunter, Richard Arell b. Va. 1785 d. Md. 1816   Corp. U.S. Inf.
  m. Mary Ann Goldsmith — son William F. m. Mary Kincaid

Hunter, Robert b. Pa. 1782 d. Pa. 1860   Pvt. Pa. Mil.
  daughter Elizabeth m. John Ross

Hunter, Robert b. Pa. c. 1780 d. Ohio 1837   Pvt. Ohio Mil.
  m. Elizabeth Murray — daughter Isabel m. John Lemon

Hunter, Samuel b. N.C. 1777 d. Texas 1846   Lt. Col. N.C. Mil.
  m. Rebecca Bruce — daughter Rebecca J. m. Blackstone Hardeman

Hunter, William   Vol. 8   Capt. Pa. Mil.
  daughter Jane m. John J. Baldwin   REAL DAUGHTER

Huntington, Andrew b. Md. or Conn. 1745 d. Conn. 1824   Rec. Pat., Judge
  m. Hannah Phelps and/or Lucy Coit   Probate Court Conn.
  son Charles P. m. Maria Perit
  son Joseph m. Eunice Carew

Huntington, Chandler b. Conn. 1778 d. Ind. 1845   Corp. N.Y. Mil.
  m. Anna Wallace — son Spencer W. m. Sarah Taffe

Huntington, Miller   Vol. 13   Pvt. N.Y. Vol.

Huntley, Seth T. b. Conn. 1779 d. Iowa 1856   Pvt. Musician Conn. Mil.
  son Charles m. Polly Davison

Huntt, Henry b. Md. 1782 d. Wash. D.C. 1838   Surgeon U.S. Navy
  daughter Minnie m. Robert Ransom, Jr.

Hurd, Asa b. N.Y. 1790 d. N.Y. 1877 m. Louisa Stowell   Pvt. N.Y. Mil.
  daughter Emily Hurd m. Benj. Bidlack

Hurd, Benjamin b. Mass. (Me.) 1777 d. Mass. (Me.) 1858   Corp. Mass.
  m. Joanne Chadbourn — son Isaiah m. Mary Smith   Mil.

Hurd, Ebenezer b. Conn. 1774 d. N.Y. 1865 m.—   Pvt. N.Y. Mil.
  son Benjamin m. Almira E. Sheldon

Hurd, Isaac b. Vt. 1793 d. Pa. 1891 m. Eliza Tyler Darling   Pvt. Vt. Mil.
  daughter Martha M. m. John Long

Hurd, Isaac b. N.J. 1794 d. N.J. 1881   Pvt. N.J. Mil.
  m. Jane Armstrong Pitney — daughter Mary Elizabeth
  m. James Reynolds   REAL DAUGHTER

Hurd, Zera b. Conn. 1789 d. Ill. 1866 m. Abigail Gilbert   Pvt. Conn. Mil.
  daughter Anne J. m. Patterson Jenkins

Hurford, John b. Pa. 1760 d. Ohio 1846 m. Sarah Hayes   Pvt. Pa. Mil.
  daughter Rachel m. Jacob Jehu Pickering

Hurlburt, Jehiel b. Conn. d. Ohio 1813   Pvt. Ohio Mil.
  m. Sibyl Martindale — daughter Juliet m. William Tylee

Hurlbut, Samuel   Vol. 5   Rec. Pat., Civil Officer Conn.

Hurley, James b. Pa. 1777 d. Pa. 1866 m. Catherine Stump   Pvt. Pa. Mil.
son George m. Leah Miller

Hurley, Zachariah b.—d.— m. Mary Manning   Pvt. Ohio Mil.
son William m. Mary Boots

Hurst, Henry b. (W.) Va. 1777 d. Ind. 1854   Major, Aide-de-camp U.S.
m. Nancy Stanhope — son William H.   Army
m. Anne Isabella Bodley

Hurstler, George   Vol. 9   Pvt. Ohio Mil.

Hurt, John B. b. Va. 1773 d. Va. 1822   Pvt. & Drummer Va. Mil.
m. Anne Newman — son Thomas m. Anne Elizabeth Burke

Husband, Isaac b. Pa. 1771 d. Pa. 1858 m. Anne King   Cornet Pa. Mil.
son Philip m. Magdalene Fredeline

Hussey, Albert Manchester b. Mass. 1778 d. Mass. 1839   Mem. of Relief
m. Elizabeth Starbuck — son James Albert   Comm. Mass.
m. Ellen Landrigan

Hussey, George   Vol. 4   Patriot

Husted, William b. N.Y. 1795 d. Mo. 1877 m. Sivilla Ann   Pvt. N.Y. Mil.
daughter Annie m. William L. Weller   REAL DAUGHTER

Huston, John b. Eng. 1782 d. Ohio 1830 m. Mary Haggerty   Sgt. Ohio Mil.
son John, Jr. m. Aurilla J. Vandergrift

Huston, John, Jr. b. Pa. 1795 d. Pa. 1869   Pvt. Pa. Mil.
m. Eliza Weakley — son John W. m. Sarah Line

Huston, Samuel b. Ire. 1760 d. Pa. 1820   Brigade Inspector Pa. Mil.
m. Nancy Agnes Lecky — son James m. Katherine Davis

Huston, William b. Va. 1776 d. Ohio c. 1850   Capt. Ohio Mil.
m. Nancy Boyd — son Samuel J. m. Elizabeth Leonard

Huston, William Jr. b. Pa. 1765 d. Island in Gulf of Mexico 1822   Capt.
m. Susanna Boyd — daughter Elizabeth m. Silas W. Cole   Ohio Mil.

Hutchins, John b. Del. 1793 d. Del. 1873   Pvt. Md. Mil.
m. Charlotte Knolls (Voshill) — son Nathan m. Elizabeth Shaw
daughter Sarah m. Clement White

Hutchins, Jonathan, Jr. b. Mass. (Me.) 1793   Pvt. Mass (Me.) Mil.
d. Maine 1878 m. Naomi Bradbury — son Jonathan m. Sarah Ellery

Hutchins, Richard b. Md. 1741 d. Md. 1826   3rd Corp. Md. Mil.
m. Zana Standiford — son William m. Mary Rampley

Hutchinson (Hutcherson), Joseph b. Va. 1746 d. Ky. 1818   Rec. Pat., Clerk
m. (?) Marshall — son Thomas m. Catherine Phillips   of Court Ky.

Hutchinson, Joseph b. Sweden 1790 d. N.Y. 1876   Sgt. N.Y. Mil.
m. Polly Sexton — daughter Sophronia m. Anson Doty

Hutchinson, Lewis b. Va. 1760 d. Va. 1832   Pvt. Va. Mil.
m. Keziah Hutchinson (cousin) — son William m. Jemima Padgett

Hutchinson, Robert b. Scot. 1790 d. Mass. 1861   Pvt. Mass. Mil.
m. Elizabeth Ellis — daughter Adeline F. m. John W. Perry

Hutchinson, Zenas b. Conn. 1770 d. N.Y. 1854   Surgeon N.Y. Mil.
m. Fannie Tyler Smith — daughter Harriet m. Edward Barber Smith

Hutson, John b. Del. 1781 d. Ohio 1826   Teamster Ohio, Pack Horse Service
m. Elizabeth Clymer — son James m. Elizabeth Stults

Hutt, John b. Va. 1763 d. Ohio 1835   Pvt. Va. Artil., 1813
 daughter Kate Spencer m. John James Robinson

Hutton, James Hamilton Vol. 7   Sgt. Pa. Mil.

Hyde, Comfort Starr b. Conn. 1784 d. Conn. 1868 Capt. Conn. Cavalry
 m. Abigail Hough — son John m. Emily Augur

Hyde, Henry b. Vt. 1774 d. N.Y. 1818   Rec. Pat., Town Officer N.Y.
 m. Caroline Noyes — daughter Therina m. George Tibbetts

Hyder, Michael b. Va. or N.C. 1743 d. Tenn. or N.C. 1790 Pvt. N.C. Mil.
 m. Elizabeth Woods — son Jacob m. Hannah Rockwell   1784
 son John m Rosanna English
 son Michael Jr. m. Martha Locherd

Hyer, William b. N.Y. 1775 d. N.Y. 1851/2 Pvt. & Matross N.Y. Vol.
 m. Jane — son George W. m. Catherine Gaffit

Hyland, Henry Miles b. Md. 1796 d. Md. 1851 Pvt. Kent County Mil.
 m. Marcia Maria Grant — daughter Anna Austusta
 m. Howard McEwen

Hyland, Stephen b. Md. 1793 d. Md. 1855   Pvt. Md. Mil.
 m. Mary Jane Maulden — daughter Eleanora m. John Hahn Delks

Hyneman, John M. b. Pa. 1771 d. Pa. 1816   Adjutant Gen. Pa. Mil.
 m. Catherine Katzeninmoyer — daughter Clara Jane
 m. James Beidler

Hynes, Andrew Vol. 6   Capt. Tenn. Mil.

Hyser, Jeremiah b. N.Y. abt. 1800 d. N.Y. 1880   Pvt. N.Y. Mil.
 m. Hannah Miller — daughter Margaret Eliza
 m. Lewis Preston Traver

I

Ice, Jacob Sr. b. Pa. 1777 d. Ohio 1850   Pvt. Ohio Mil.
 m. Susanna Butler — son Minor m. Hannah Rebecca Shelt

Ice, Jesse b. (W.) Va. 1786 d. Ind. 1863 m. Sarah Hickman Capt. Va. Mil.
 son Ezekiel T. m. Rebecca Bohn

Iddings, Joseph b. Pa. 1785 d. Pa. 1845   Pvt. Pa. Inf.
 m. Hannah Hoopes (Hooper) — daughter Levinah m. James Davis
 daughter Phoebe Ann m. John Cannon Reed

Iden, Jonathan b. Va. 1785 d. W.Va. 1875   Pvt. Va. Mil.
 m. Catherine Jolly — daughter Emily Amanda m. Zed Smith I

Iders, James b.—d.—m.   Pvt. Va. Mil.
 daughter Margaret m. Henry Stanley REAL DAUGHTER

Igou, Joshua Sr. b. Pa. 1760 d. Pa. 1833 Pat. Pa. 1808-14, Co. Supervisor
 m. Mary Roller — son John Jr.   and Overseer of Poor
 m. Matilda Meredith

Ijams, John b. Md. 1789 d. Md. 1879 m. Catherine Barnes Ens. Md. Mil.
 son William Henry m. Isabel King

Iles, (Oiles, Isles, Oler) Henry b. New England 1749 Pvt. Va. Mil. 1788-9
 d. Ohio 1814 m. Maria Margaretta Stein (Stine)
 son Adam m. Jane Cloton
 son John m. Elizabeth Sanders

Imboden, Benjamin b. Va. 1791 d. Ark. 1858 m. Mary Hunter Pvt. Va. Mil.
 daughter Susan C. m. Green Russell Jones

Ingalls, Darius b. N.Y. 1793 d. N.Y. 1867   Sgt. N.Y. Mil.
 m. Achsah Cobb — daughter Isabella A. m. James Martin Stagg

Ingalls, Israel b. N.H. or Mass. (Me.) 1793   Pvt. N.H. Mil.
  d. Ohio or Ill. 1835 m. Mary Lord — daughter Elizabeth
  m. Joseph Bradley Varnum Butler

Ingalls, Marvin (Marion) b. Conn. 1787 d. Conn. 1847   Pvt. Conn. Mil.
  m. Amelia Spaulding — daughter Olive m. Pulaski P. Carter

Ingalsby, John   Vol. 12   Pvt. N.Y. Mil.

Ingerson, John b.— d. aft. 1829   Tax Collect. Pat., 1798-1815
  m. Eleanor Holmes — daughter Dorothy m. Moses Woodward

Ingham, Samuel Delucenna b. Pa. 1779 d. N.J. 1860 Pat., mem. of Cong.
  m. Deborah Kay Hall — daughter Eliza R.   Pa. 1813
  m. Rev. Georgia Hale, D. D.

Inghram (Ingram), William Sr. b. Md. 1750 d. Pa. 1809   Capt. Pa.
  m. Agnes Fee — son William Jr. m. Sarah Adams

Inghram, William Jr., b. Pa. 1794 d. Pa. 1843   Pvt. Pa. Mil.
  m. Sarah Adams — daughter Eliza m. John T. Hook

Ingram, David b. Ga. 1780 d. Ga. 1831   Pvt. Ga. Mil.
  m. Margaret Ross (Rofs) — daughter Eleanor
  m. Francis Marion Clark

Ingram, John b. N.C. 1772 d. N.C. 1835 m. Charity Bell Pvt. N.C. Mil.
  daughter Isa Bell m. John Lawrence

Inman, Shadrach (Shadrack) b. Tenn. 1793   Sgt. E. Tenn. Mil.
  d. Tenn. 1852 m. Sarah Keys Henderson — daughter Elizabeth K.
  m. William McDermott Bradford

Innes, Robert b. Ky. 1773 d. Ky. 1865   Lt. Col. Va. Mil.
  m. Hannah Egleston — son Robert m. Catherine Coun

Ioor (Joor), John b. S.C. (1783) 1780 d. S.C. 1836   Col. Miss. Mil.
  m. Emily Richardson — daughter Caroline B.
  m. Edward Waring Ioor (cousin)
  son John C. m. Alise Sophia Jones

Ireland, Clement b. N.J. 1762 d. N.J. 1835   Pvt. N.J. Mil.
  m. Deborah Conover — daughter Keturah m. Daniel Samson

Ireland, Elijah b. N.J. 1780 d. N.J. 1823 m. Rachel Somers Pvt. N.J. Mil.
  daughter Leah m. Joseph Davis

Ireland, Japhet b. N.J. 1776 d. N.J. 1859   Pat., Postmaster N.J. 1814
  m. Mary Somers — daughter Hannah m. Job Frambes

Ireland, Thomas b. N.J. 1782 d. N.J. 1829   Pvt. N.J. Mil.
  m. Mary Williams — son Thomas Jr. m. Sarah Ann Scull

Ireland, William b. Pa. 1772 d. N.Y. 1840 m. Mary   Capt. N.Y. Mil.
  son George m. Alice Connor

Ireson, James H. b.— d. Miss. 1826 m. Hannah Swayze Sgt. Miss. Mil.
  son Lansford O. m. Lydia Jane Lassley

Irish, Perry   Vol. 3   Pvt. N.Y. Mil.

Ironmonger, James b. Va. 1777 d. Va. 1859   Pvt. Va. Mil.
  m. Mrs. Mary Custis Chandler Wise — daughter Euphemie
  m. William Hopkins

Irvine, Abram b. N.C. 1770 d. S.C. 1824 m. Sarah Graham Col. N.C. Mil.
  daughter Charlotte L. m. Gilbert Sarratt

Irvine, Christopher   Vol. 16   Col. Va. Mil.

Irvine, Isaiah Tucker b. Va. 1783 d. Ga. 1856   Capt. Ga. Mil.
     m. Isabella Henderson — daughter Louise T. m. Lewis Lanier Davis

Irvine, William b. Ire. 1741 d. Pa. 1804   Brig. Gen. U.S. Inf., Pat., mem.
     m. Anne Callender — son Callender   of Cong. Pa., Pres. Elector
     m. Patience Elliot
     daughter Rebecca m. Dr. Peter Fayssoux
     son William Jr. m. Mary Carson

Irving, John Pinkney b. Eng. 1786 d. Miss. 1871 m.—   Sgt. Md. Mil.
     son Joe A. m. Mary Elizabeth Simpson

Irwin, Abner b. Va. 1781 d. Md. 1841   Pvt. Md. Mil.
     m. Elizabeth Benjamin (Berryman) — son William B. m. Ann Gwinn

Irwin, Eliphalet b. Pa. 1773 d. Pa. 1830   Pvt. Pa. Mil.
     m. Margaret Marshall — son John M. m. Catherine Rees

Irwin, James b. Pa. 1779 d. Pa. 1873 m. Sarah   Pvt. Pa. Mil.
     daughter Rachel m. Martin Irwin (cousin)

Irwin, John b. Pa. 1788 d. Pa. 1879 m. Sarah La Fever   Pvt. Pa. Mil.
     daughter Harriet m. Hezekiah D. Gamble

Irwin, John b. 1788 d. Ky. 1884 m. Jemima Stockton   Pvt. Ky. Vol.
     daughter Emily m. Demuel Hardin

Irwin, John Lawson b. N.C. 1755 d. Ga. 1822   Brig. Gen. Ga. Mil.
     m. Rebekah Sessions — son Alexander m. Margaret Moore

Irwin, John Lawson b. Ga. 1793 d. Miss. 1841   Lt. Miss. Mil.
     m. Elizabeth Mitchell — daughter Elizabeth B. m. Henry Felix Cook

Irwin, Mary Pattison (Mrs.) b. Ire. 1754 d. Pa. 1826   Pat. 1812
     m. John Pattison — son John Jr. m. Hannah Taylor

Irwin, Robert b. 1740 d. N.C. 1800   Pat., Legis. N.C. 1797-1800
     m. Mary Alexander — son William m. Lydia Birdsong

Irwin, Robert b. Ire. 1774 d. Wisc. 1851   Lt. Adj. Pa.
     m. Catherine Singer — son Alexander J. m. Frances Pamelia Smith

Irwin, William b. (W.) Va. 1773 d. (W.) Va. 1826   Capt. Va. Mil.
     m. Elizabeth Snodgrass — daughter Sarah m. John Moore

Irwin, (Irvine) William McNeill b. Pa. 1779 d. Pa. 1854   Col. U.S. Inf.
     m. Rachel Patton Tipton — daughter Jane m. Levi Bailey Croy

Iseminger, George Jr. b. Md. 1792 d. Ill. 1867   Pvt. Md. Mil.
     m. Mary Elizabeth Myer — daughter Elizabeth
     m. Charles Farmer Brooking   REAL DAUGHTER

Ish, John b. Pa. 1786 d. Ark. aft. 1850   Sgt. Tenn. Mil.
     m. Cynthia (Edmiston) — daughter Sarah J. m. Frank Parke (Fish)

Isham, Jirah b. Conn. 1760 d. Vt. 1837   Brig. Gen. Conn. Mil.
     m. Lois Kellogg — son Samuel K. m. Sarah Hull

Isherwood, Pilgrim b. Pa. 1787 d. Pa. 1871   Pvt. Pa. Mil.
     m. Rebecca Alfred — daughter Lovina m. James R. Durham

Ives, Ambrose b. Conn. 1736 d. Mass. m. Deborah   Ens. N.Y. Mil.
     son Timothy m. Sallie Hill   1783-1821

Ives, Timothy b. Mass. 1767 d. Pa. aft. 1834   Pat. Pa. 1814, Co.
     m. Sarah Hill — daughter Mary m. Uriah Leete   Commissioner

Ivy (Ivey), Sampson b. Va. 1761 d. Ga. 1814 or later   Lt. Ga. 1799-1814
     m. Milly — daughter Jency (Jane) m. Harris McKinney

Ivy, Thomas b. Ga. 1784 d. Miss. 1836 m. Margaret Gibson   Sgt. Ga. Mil.
son Byrd m. (2) Caroline Jemima Cockrell

J

Jack, Patrick b. Pa. ca. 1745 d. Pa. 1817   Cpl. Pa. Mil. 1794
m. Margaret Bryant — son James m. Mary Alcorn

Jack, William b. N.C. d. Mo. m. Esther Harris   Lt. E. Tenn. Vol.
daughter Bethenia m. William B. Almond

Jackman, Benjamin b. N.H. 1743 d. N.H. 1836   2nd Lt., Reg. Qtrmstr.
m. Jane Woodman — son Joshua m. Dorothy Sweat

Jackson, Anson b. N.Y. 1793 d. Mich. 1876 m. Almira Gibbs   Pvt. N.Y. Mil.
son George W. m. Margaret McLouth

Jackson, Elzaphan (Elzy) b. S.C. 1795 d. Miss. 1874   Pvt. La. Mil.
m. Martha E. Causey — daughter Bertha B.
m. Sherrod Richard Quin   REAL DAUGHTER
daughter Elsie m. Hillery A. Quin   REAL DAUGHTER

Jackson, George b. Ire. 1780 d. N.Y. 1854   Capt. N.Y. Mil.
m. Margrette Baxter — son George Jr. m. Deborah Sheldon Carter

Jackson, George Washington b. Va. 1771 d. W.Va. 1876   Capt. U.S. Inf.
m. Hetta Taylor — son Alfred Henry m. Mary Blair Paxton
son James T. m. Phoebe Ann Wilson

Jackson, George Washington   Vol. 17   Lt. Va. Mil.

Jackson, Henry b. Eng. 1778 d. Ga. 1840   Pat., France 1813, Sec. Am.
m. Mrs. Martha Jaquelin Rootes Cobb — son Henry R.   Legation
m. Cornelia A. Davenport

Jackson, James b. Ire. 1782 d. Ala. 1840 m. Sarah Moore   Pat. Ala.
son James Jr. m. Elizabeth Perkins
son William M. m. McKieman(?)

Jackson, James b. Ire. d. Md. 1851   Pvt. Md. Mil.
m. Bethiah Rennie Moore — daughter Sarah m. Alexander Parks

Jackson, James b. Ire. 1782 d. Ala. 1840 m. Mary Steele   Pat. 1814
son James Jr. m. Sarah Moore

Jackson, James b. N.Y. 1782 d. N.Y. 1864   Pvt. N.Y. Mil.
m. Margaret Wands — daughter Sarah Eleanor m. Martin Fay

Jackson, James b. 1777 d. Ill. 1830 m. Rachel   Pvt. Ohio Mil.
son James M. Jr. m. Minerva Wolfskill

Jackson, John b. Pa. 1780 d. Ill. 1865   Cpl. Pa. Mil.
m. Asenath Moore — son John m. Adelaide Stuall
daughter Lucinda m. Bazell Foster Tipton

Jackson, John Jr. b. 1774 d. aft. 1804   Adj. N.Y. Mil.
son Benjamin m. (2) Clarissa McCormick

Jackson, Joseph   Vol. 13   Adj. N.Y. Mil.

Jackson, Levi b. Conn. 1779 d. Pa. c. 1847   Pvt. Conn. Mil.
m. Hannah Mechum — daughter Rachel P. m. Abram K. Noss

Jackson, Mark b. Ga. d. Tenn. m.—   Cpl. Ga. Mil.
son Harbard m. Martha Gill

Jackson, Robert b. 1760 d. N.Y. 1829 m. Elbertje Hogeboom   Capt. N.Y.
son Isaac m. Esther DeForest

Jackson, Samuel b. Eng. 1755 d. N.Y. 1845   2nd Maj. N.Y. Mil.
m. Lovysa Hyer — son Samuel C. m. Delia Sheldon

Jackson, Samuel b. Pa. 1757 d. Pa. 1834 m. Margaret Cree   Pvt. Pa. Mil.
daughter Jane C. m. Levi Hart

Jackson, Solomon Redman b. 1789 d. Del. 1863   Ens. Va. Mil.
m. Ann Cleveland — daughter Mary m. James M. Kiger

Jackson, Williams F. b. Ga. 1790 d. Ala. 1855   Capt. Ga. Mil.
m. Harriett Crawford — son Winfield S. m. Ethelia Jane Cobb

Jacobs, Bennett b. Ky. 1783 d. Ia. 1861 m. Nancy Watts   Pvt. Ky. Mil.
son Austin m. Hannah Hamilton Walker

Jacobs, Joseph b. N.H. 1777 d. Vt. 1817 m. Sarah Drew   Pvt. Vt. Mil.
daughter Louisa m. Robert Scott Bell

Jacobs, Joshua   Vol. 3   Capt. U.S. Inf.

Jacobs, Justin b. Mass. 1788 d. Wisc. 1878   Pvt. Mass. Mil.
m. Polly Sargeant — daughter Emily m. Madison Gillingham

Jacobs, Presley b. Va. 1774 d. Va. 1852 m. Elizabeth Chew Sgt. Va. Mil.
daughter Emily m. John Nicholas Webb

Jacoby, Peter b. 1766 d. Pa. 1814 m. Mary Lomison   Ens. Pa. Mil.
son George m. Sarah Ann Eylenberger
daughter Susannah m. Solomon Welch

Jacoby, Ralph b. Va. 1768 d. Ohio 1822 m. Christiana Brice 3rd Lt. Ky. Inf.
daughter Christiana m. Thomas Benson Whitledge

James, Ashbury   Vol. 11   Pvt. N.C. Mil.

James, Enoch   Vol. 12   Pvt. Mass. Mil.

James, John b. N.Y. 1789 d. N.Y. m. Mary Dan Hickerson Pvt. N.Y. Mil.
daughter Elizabeth W. m. John Frederick Kellers

James, John Jr. b. Mass. 1766 d. Mass. 1826   Pvt. Mass. Mil.
m. Patience Clapp — daughter Eliza m. John Taylor

James, Thomas b. N.C. 1797 d. Tenn. 1870 m. Judith   Pvt. Ky. Mil.
daughter Frances m. Col. W. A. Hoskins

James, William b. N.C. 1795 d. Tenn. 1872   Pvt. U.S. Army
m. Sarah Elizabeth Williams(?) — daughter Roberta W.
m. Robert Allen Williams

Jameson, Archibald b. Scot. 1772 d. Pa. 1847   Pvt. Pa. Mil.
m. Jane Lowry — daughter Nancy m. Matthew Stuart

Jameson, David b. 1752 d. 1839 m. Mary Mennis   Justice 40 Yrs. Va.
son Geo. Wash. Jameson m. Susan Ann Day

Jameson, Thomas III b. Ky. 1783 d. Ky. 1819   Pvt. Ky. Mil.
m. Sarah Smith — son Willey B. m. Walker Bourne

Jamison, Harrison b. 1793 d. 1861 m. Ellender Barnes Pvt. Mo. Mil.
son James Barnes m. Mary Jane Wear

Jamison, Henry Downs b. Ga. 1795 d. Tenn. 1857   Pvt. W. Tenn. Mil.
m. Elizabeth Batey — daughter Julianna m. Isaac Ledbetter

Jamison, Hugh b. Pa. 1784 d. Pa. 1873 m. Jane Stuart   Lt. Pa. Mil.
son John M. m. Angeline Thomas

Jamison, Jacob b. Ky. 1786 d. Ohio 1865   Pvt. Ohio Mil.
m. Isabell Hopkins — daughter Margaret m. John Stuckey

Jamison, Jacob Lockhart b. Ky. 1786 d. 1865   Pvt. Ohio Mil.
  m. Druscilla Harrison — son Jacob L. m. Martha Ann Brown

Jamison, James b. Ire. 1742 d. Pa. 1828   Pat. Pa. 1795-6, Constable
  m. Sarah Ireland — daughter Rebecca m. Abraham Walker

Jamison, John   Vol. 17   Pvt. Pa. Mil.

Jamison, John b. Va. 1783 d. Va. 1866 m. Catherine Boone   Pvt. Va. Mil.
  son Henry m. Sallie Showalter

Jamison, John b. Va. 1780 d. La. 1819 m. Mary Anson   Major La. Mil.
  daughter Harriet M. m. John Durst

Jamison, John Harvey   Vol. 11   Pvt. Va. Mil.

Jamison, John W.   Vol. 15   Pvt. Pa. Mil.

Jamison, Joseph b. Pa. 1768 d. Md. 1847   Maj. Md. Art.
  m. Catherine Wallace — daughter Catherine E.
  m. Henry Clay Ridgely
  m. Ann Jackson
  daughter Jane m. James Ridgely

Janupin (Janurin), George Jr. b. N.H. 1794 d. N.H. 1882 Pvt. N.H. Art.
  m. Sarah Dodge — daughter Dorothy Anne m. William Waldo Curtis

Jaqua, Richard b. N.Y. 1787 d. Ohio 1878   Pvt. N.Y. Mil.
  m. Elizabeth Wiltsee — son Uriah D. m. Abigail Conley

Jaquith, Amasa b. Mass. 1793 d. Ohio 1871 m. Lydia King Pvt. N.Y. Mil.
  son Tillison m. Mrs. Lucinda (Devinney) Manley

Jared, John b. Va. 1787 d. Ill. 1844 m. Elizabeth Bandy   Pvt. Va. Mil.
  daughter Miriam Louesa m. Caleb Bair

Jared (Jarrod), William b. Va. 1758 d. Tenn. 1827   2nd Lt. Tenn. Mil.
  m. Elizabeth Raulston — son Moses m. Malinda Bryne

Jarrett, Asbury b. Md. 1796 d. Md. 1884   Pvt. Md. Mil.
  m. Eliza Sophronia Lefevre — son Asbury B.
  m. Elizabeth Wallace Galloway

Jarrett, David b. 1792 d. 1867 m. Elvira Elizab. Hulme   Pvt. Va. Mil.
  daughter Pauline Jarrett m. Anderson Rochelle Moores

Jarrett, Nicholas   Vol. 14   Pvt. Va. Mil.

Jarrett, Young b. Va. d. (W.) Va. aft. 1830 m. Nancy Hill Pvt. Va. Mil.
  son Lemuel m. Martha Jane Malone

Jarvis, Joseph Russell b. Mass. 1795 d. Ill. 1869 Midshipman N.Y. Navy
  m. Josephine   REAL DAUGHTER   Vol. 7

Jarvis, William   Vol. 4   Pvt. N.Y. Mil.

Jasper, Thomas b. Ky. 1774 d. Ky. 1838 m. Betsy Denham Pvt. Ky. Mil.
  son Oliver P. m. Sireny (Serena) Chesney

Jayne, Benaiah b. Pa. 1790 d. Pa. 1854 m. Mary Whitaker Pvt. N.Y. Mil.
  son Benaiah G. m. Florence E. M. Palmer

Jayne, Morris b. N.Y. 1763 d. N.Y. 1842 m. Mary Biggs   Capt. N.Y. Mil.
  son Isaac m. Sarah Brewster   (Cavalry)

Jaynes, Thomas R. b. Va. 1789 d. Va. 1858   Lt. Va. Mil.
  m. Ann Bell Satchell — daughter Mary S.
  m. George Parker Scarburgh

Jefferson, James b. Va. 1793 d. W.Va. 1874   Pvt. Va. Mil.
  m. Zervia Freeland — son James Jr. m. Malinda Mundell

Jefferson, Samuel Allan b. Va. 1776 d. Va. 1855　　　Sgt. Va. Mil.
　　m. Elizabeth Ann Jefferson (cousin) son James H.
　　m. Kittie Grace Jefferson (2nd cousin)
　　son John G. m. Margaret A. Townes

Jeffery, Jehoiada　　　Vol. 11　　　　　　　　　　Pvt. Mo. Mil.

Jeffords, Amasa b. Mass. 1768 d. N.Y. 1834　　　Capt. Mass. Mil.
　　m. Susannah Cleveland — son Allen C. m. Ann Eliza Robinson

Jeffries, James b. Pa. 1791 d. Pa. 1863 m. Mary Echard　　2nd Lt. Pa. Mil.
　　son E. Harper m. Mary B.
　　daughter Mary F. m. James Ogborn

Jeffries, John b. Pa. 1759 d. Pa. 1832 m. Anne Wilson　　2nd Lt. Pa. Mil.
　　son Thomas m. Amelia Landis

Jelks, William b. N.C. d. Ga. 1827 m. Mary Wallace　　　Pvt. Ga. Mil.
　　son James O. m. Mary Polhill

Jenckes, David b. R.I. 1739 d. R.I. 1828　　　Smithfield Grenad R.I.
　　daughter Lydia m. Oliver Harris

Jenings, James b. Va. 1771 d. Ky. 1828　　　Pat. Judge Ky. 1799
　　m. Eleanor Crawford — son Jefferson m. Susan Peachey Nicolson

Jenkins, Andrew b. N.J. 1779 d. N.J. 1849 m. Lydia Wiltsee　Pvt. N.J. Mil.
　　daughter Lydia Ann m. Hampton Williams

Jenkins, Benedict b. Md. 1789 d. Md. 1837　　Prize Mst. Navy Schooner Md.
　　m. Adeline Murphy — son John T. m. Hulda Amelia Spencer

Jenkins, Benjamin b. Pa. 1794 d. Pa. 1835　　Vol. 7　　Pvt. Pa. Mil.

Jenkins, Eleazer b. Pa. 1751 d. Pa. 1824 m. Rebecca Dunlap　　Capt. Pa. Mil.
　　daughter Sarah m. James Weir

Jenkins, Hiram b. 1780 d. 1857 m. Deborah Allison or Ellison　　Pvt.
　　son Aaron m. Mary Jane Fristoe

Jenkins, John b. S.C. 1794 d. S.C. 1854　　　Pvt. S.C. Mil.
　　m. Elizabeth Grimball Clark — son John Jr. m. Marcelline Murray

Jenkins, John b. Conn. 1751 d. Pa. 1827 m. Bethia Harris　　Lt. Col.
　　son James m. Elizabeth Breese　　　　　　　　Pa. Mil. 1790

Jenkins, John J. b. Md. 1789 d. Md. 1845 m. Mary Ann　　Sgt. Md. Mil.
　　daughter Mary J. m. George C. P. Davis

Jenkins, Joseph b. S.C. 1761 d. S.C. 1828　　Pat. S.C. Senate 1811-13
　　m. Elizabeth Evans — son John m. Elizabeth Grimball Clark

Jenkins, Philip b. Pa. 1789 d. Ark. 1871 m. Mary Shaver　　Pvt. Ky. Mil.
　　daughter Sarah B. m. William B. Kellenbarger

Jenkins, Robert b. Mass. 1772 d. N.Y. 1819　　　Maj. N.Y. Art.
　　m. Christain Dayton — daughter Caroline M.
　　m. Samuel Pomeroy White

Jenkins, Thomas b. R.I. 1776 d. N.Y. 1861 m. Sarah Gardnier　　Pat. N.Y.
　　daughter Catharine m. Richard T. Hartshorne

Jenkins, William　　　Vol. 5　　　　　　　　　Pvt. Md. Troops

Jenkins, William Smythe b. Va. 1782 d. Ky. 1847　　　Cpl. Va. Mil.
　　m. Nancy Carter — son Joseph C. m. Elizabeth Berkshire

Jenks, Boomer King b. Vt. 1789 d. N.Y. 1865　　　Pvt. N.Y. Mil.
　　m. Clarissa Herrick — daughter Charlotte m. George Brown
　　son Henry V. m. Jane Elizabeth Fox

Jenks, Boomer b. R.I. 1761 d. Vt. 1847   Pat. 1798-1805, Trustee, Juror,
  m. Anna King — son Boomer K. m. Clarissa Herrick   Surveyor

Jenks, Ira   Vol. 15   Pvt. N.Y. Mil.

Jenney, Ebenzer b. Mass. 1773 d. Vt. 1866   Capt. Vt. Mil.
  m. Chloe Parker — son Hiram M. m. Margaret McDonald

Jennings, Burr b. Conn. c. 1768 d. Conn. 1845   Cpl. Pa. Mil.
  m. Mercy Morehouse — daughter Matilda m. Eli Couch

Jennings, James b. Va. d. Va. 1838 m. Mary Hawkins   Pvt. Va. Mil.
  daughter Martha m. Lewis Wilmer Wrenn

Jennings, Robert b. 1794 d. 1861 m. Luvincy Hill   Pvt. S.C.
  daughter Mary I. m. John H. Rochelle

Jennings, Samuel b. Mass. 1762 d. Me. 1842   Pvt. Mass. Mil.
  son Perez S. m. Joanna Lane

Jennings, William b. Va. 1771 d. Ky. 1831   Brig. Gen. Ky. Mil.
  m. Nancy Ballinger — daughter Eliza A. m. Samuel Lush

Jennison, Daniel b. Mass. 1757 d. Mass. 1839   Capt. Mass. Mil.
  m. Mollie Putnam — son Joseph m. Hannah Ryan

Jerman, Hezekiah b. Va. 1785 d. Va. m. Mary Robey   Pvt. Va. Mil.
  daughter Mary Ann m. Matthew Mayhugh

Jernigan, Hardy b. S.C. 1766 d. Ga. 1836   Pvt. Ga. Mil.
  m. Frances Colbert — daughter Martha Matilda m. Richard Burch

Jesup, Thomas Sidney   Vol. 7   Maj. Gen. U.S. Inf.

Jeter, John b. Va. 1774 d. Va. 1823 m. Jane   Capt. Va. Mil.
  son John T. m. (2) Ann

Jett, Daniel b. Va. 1762 d. Ga. 1830 m. Sarah Smith   Capt. Ga. Mil.
  daughter Nancy m. Samuel Skidmore

Jett, James b. Va. 1784 d. Va. 1841   Lt. Va. Mil., Justice of Peace
  m. Mary Livingston — son John m. Irene Wolfe

Jett, Stephen Jr. b. N.C. 1780 d. Ky. 1839   Pvt. Ky. Vol.
  m. Rachel Milor — daughter Susannah m. Claiborne Crawford

Jetton, Isaac b. Tenn. 1793 d. Tenn. 1843   Pvt. Tenn. Mil.
  m. Henrietta Elam — daughter Jane m. Charles Bluford Walker

Jewel, Ebenezer b. Conn. 1789 d. Mich. m. Anna Jones   Pvt. N.Y. Mil.
  son Edward m. Jane K. Dunham

Jewell, William Gilbert b. 1779 d. Ohio 1862   Pvt. Ohio Mil.
  m. Jane Keener — son William m. Sarah Jane George

Jewett, Aaron b. N.H. 1781 d. 1852 m. Nancy Smith   Pvt. N.H. Mil.
  daughter Eliza Jane m. Hezekiah Smith

Jewett, Nathan b. N.H. 1781 d. N.Y. m. Mille Gragg   Pvt. N.Y. Mil.
  son George W. m. Helen Cornell

Jewett, Thomas b. Conn. 1736 d. Vt. 1812 m. Eunice Slafter   Pat. Vt.
  son Thomas F. m. Elsie Green

Jipson, Ruben b. Vt. 1788 d. N.Y. 1813 m. Betsy Boss   Pvt. N.Y. Mil.
  daughter Catherine m. Rilus Eastman

Jobe, Daniel b. N.C. 1760 d. 1864 m. — Pryor   Pvt. Ky. Vol.
  son John m. Sarah Farmer
  son Joseph m. Elizabeth Phillips

Jobe, John b. Miss. 1801 d. Miss. 1890   Pvt. Tenn. Mil.
    m. (1) Sarah Farmer — son Joseph m. Elizabeth Phillips

John, Abel b. N.C. 1786 d. N.C. 1825 m. Isabella Reid   Pvt. Ky. Vol.
    son Joseph R. m. Rosanna Jane Smith

Johns, Robert b. Va. 1784 d. Ala. 1862 m. Frances Clarke   Pvt. S.C. Mil.
    daughter Frances m. John Waters Youngblood
    daughter Nancy Norman m. John Cogburn

Johns, Stephen Stewart b. Md. 1777 d. Md. 1844   Maj. Md. Mil.
    m. Nancy Franklin — son Kensy m. Betty Stuart

Johnson, Anson b. Conn. 1790 d. Ohio 1865   Pvt. Ohio Mil.
    m. Maria Oviatt — son Almon A. m. Catherine E. Robinson

Johnson, Baker b. Md. 1787 d. Fla. 1838   Capt. Md. Cavalry
    daughter Mary Catherine m. John Robert Dorsey

Johnson, Charles   Vol. 13   Pvt.
    daughter May Bishop Johnson m. Mr. Hall (Horatio)
    REAL DAUGHTER

Johnson, Chauncey b. Vt. 1799 d. Tex. m.—   Pvt. Conn. Mil.
    daughter Caroline m. Louis Eilers

Johnson, Daniel b. Conn. 1775 d. N.Y. 1869   Pvt. Conn. Mil.
    m. Lucretia Prout — son Seth m. Lovina Adams

Johnson, Daniel b. N.C. 1789 d. Tenn. 1871   Pvt. Tenn. Mil.
    m. (2) Polly Gray Young — daughter Angelina
    m. Benjamin Chapman

Johnson, David b. Vt. 1796 d. Wisc. 1877 m. Keziah Dodson   Pvt. N.Y. Mil.
    daughter Jane m. John Adams

Johnson, David   Vol. 11   Lt. Ohio Mil.

Johnson, David   Vol. 18   1813
    daughter Margaret E. m.—   REAL DAUGHTER

Johnson, David b. Va. 1782 d. S.C. 1855   Pat. Governor S.C. 1812
    m. Barbara A. Herndon — son David Jr. m. Frances Wallace

Johnson, Ebenezer   Vol. 8   Surgeon's Mate N.Y. Mil.

Johnson, Elias   Vol. 16   Pvt. Del. Mil.

Johnson, Enos   Vol. 11, 12, 13   Capt. Conn. Mil.

Johnson, Ezekiel   Vol. 14   Pvt. N.Y. Cavalry

Johnson, George   Vol. 17   Pvt. Va. Mil.

Johnson, George   Vol. 9   3rd Lt. Md. Mil.

Johnson, Gideon b. S.C. 1787 d. La. 1854   Sergt. S.C. Mil.
    m. Nancy Sweat — daughter Mary m. Henry Clay Avery

Johnson, Greef b. 1788 d. 1862 m. Mary Hellums   Capt. Miss. Mil.
    daughter Malinda m. Zachariah T. Tankersley
    son William Davis m. Lizzie (Betty) Martin

Johnson, Hardy b. Tenn. 1777 d. Ala. 1846   Pvt. Tenn. Mil.
    m. Betsy Libran — son Stephen m. Martha Brown

Johnson, Henry b. Ky. 1794 d. Miss. 1862   Pvt. Ky. Mil.
    m. Betsey J. Flournoy — daughter Emily m. Frank Tilford

Johnson, Jacob b. Md. 1792 d. Ind. 1881   Pvt. Md. Mil.
    m. Magdalane Vertinbecker — daughter Martha m. Joseph Heth

Johnson, James   Vol. 11   Lt. Col. Ky. Vol.

Johnson, James b. S.C. 1777 d. S.C. 1850   Capt. S.C. Mil.
   son James Jr. m. Sylvania Bruckhalter

Johnson, (Johnston), James b. Pa. 1773 d. Pa. 1860   Pvt. Pa. Mil.
   m. Mary Johnson (cousin) — son Samuel m. Anna Hudler

Johnson, James b. Va. 1774 d. Ohio 1845   Pvt. Ohio Mil.
   m. Mildred Boling Pate — son Boling m. Andeline Pavey

Johnson, James b. Va. 1774 d. D.C. 1826   Lt. Col. Ky. Vol.
   m. Nancy Payne — daughter Nancy m. Edmund Pendleton Pope
   son Milton C. m. Mary Botts

Johnson, Joel b. N.J. 1783 d. N.J. 1834 m. Mary Bird   Pvt. N.J. Mil.
   daughter Eliza m. John Cunningham

Johnson, John b. Pa. 1794 d. Pa. 1862   Sgt. Pa. Mil.
   m. Rebecca Baker — son Francis m. Margaret Kelly

Johnson, John b. Pa. 1775 d. Ohio 1857   Pvt. Ohio Mil.
   m. Rebecca Baker — son Joseph m. Mary Cosner

Johnson, John (Joseph) b. Pa. 1791 d. Ohio 1850   Capt. Ohio Mil.
   m. Mary Ann — son James B. m. Jane Pullin

Johnson, John b. N.J. 1760 d. N.J. 1824   Pvt. N.J. Mil.
   m. Sarah McDonald — son Joseph m. Mary M. Wyckoff

Johnson, John Clarke b. Ga. 1794 d. Ga. 1856   Pvt. Ga. Mil.
   m. Behetheland Berryman Lingo — son Henry R.
   m. Mary Elizabeth Hunt
   son William L. m. Ann Elizabeth Kunze

Johnson, John T. b. Ky. 1788 d. Mo. 1856   Aid to Gen. Harrison
   m. Sophia Lewis — daughter Mary Sophia m. Jon. R. Viley (John)

Johnson, Joseph b. N.Y. 1785 d. W.Va. 1877   Capt. Va. Mil.
   daughter Elizabeth m. John Sidney Horner

Johnson, Joseph b. N.J. 1792 d. N.J. 1830   Pvt. N.J. Mil.
   m. Mary Magdalen Wyckoff — son Joseph Jr. m. Theodosia Scholfield

Johnson, Joshua b. Conn. 1757 d. Ill. 1849   Chaplain N.Y. Mil.
   m. Fannie Fancher — daughter Mary Emily m. Lovett Partridge

Johnson, Oliver   Vol. 12   Sgt. Conn. Mil.

Johnson, Philo S. b. N.Y. 1786 d. N.Y. 1872   Pvt. N.Y. Mil.
   m. Anna Maria Nash — daughter Alice Sophia m. John C. Ioor
   daughter Anna Maria m. Hamilton Peck   REAL DAUGHTER

Johnson, Moses b. Mass. 1777 d. N.Y. 1829   Pvt. Mass. Mil.
   m. Eunice Sanborn — daughter Helena Abigail C. m. John Kane

Johnson, Richard Sr. b. 1763 d. 1825   House of Rep. S.C. 1810-1812
   m. Mrs. Sarah Beckett Stanyarme — son Dr. Wm. S.
   m. Sarah Green

Johnson, Richard b. N.Y. 1794 d. Ind. 1875   Sgt. Ky. Mil.
   m. Keziah Vanosdol — son Joseph m. Margaret Parker

Johnson, Robert b. Va. 1745 d. Ky. 1815   Justice Va. 1786, Senator 1792,
   m. Jemima Suggett — daughter Betsy   Maj. Ky. Mil. 1813
   m. John Payne
   son Joel m. Verlinda Offert
   daughter Sally m. William Ward

Johnson, (Johnston), Robert b. N.C. (Va.) 1787   Lt. Tenn. Mil.
   d. Tenn. 1856 m. Mary McLaren — son Josephus S.
   m. Amanda Herrin

Johnson, Samuel b. Tenn. 1798 d. Md. 1871   Pvt. U.S. Army 1814
   m. Josephine Gonzales — son Joseph Taylor m. Ann S. Harvey

Johnson, Samuel b. Pa. 1744 d. Ky. 1827 m. Fannie   Pvt. Ky. Vol.
   son John Jack m. Lucy Huston

Johnson, Samuel b. Vt. 1789 d. Vt. 1850   Pvt. Vt. Mil.
   m. Elizabeth Hoveyol — son William F. m. Rosana Pennock

Johnson, Seth   Vol. 15   Pvt. U.S. Inf.

Johnson, Stephen b. Conn. 1786 d. N.Y. 1860   Lt. N.Y. Mil.
   m. Mercy Pierce — son Stephen Jr. m. Althea Pierce

Johnson, Thomas   Vol. 5   Pvt. N.Y. Mil.

Johnson, Thomas Simpson Sr. b. Vt. 1779 d. Ia. 1867   Pvt. Ind. Mil.
   m. Elizabeth Tharp — son Thomas S. Jr. m. Elizabeth Wright

Johnson, Waite b. N.Y. 1790 d. Pa. 1868 m. Lydia Stevens   Pvt. N.Y. Mil.
   daughter Nancy m. William Carl

Johnson, William b. Va. 1750/60 d. Ga. 1821   Pat., Sheriff, Justice, N.C.
   m. Nancy Hill — daughter Nancy H.
   m. Lodowick Meriwether Hill (2nd cousin)
   daughter Martha P. m. (2) William O. Martin

Johnson, William b. (Va.) Del. 1781 d. Ohio 1833   Cpl. Ohio Mil.
   m. Jane B. Dowden — son Isaac McC m. Casander Dick
   daughter Jane Eliza m. John Mitchener

Johnson, William b. N.C. 1794 d. N.C. 1883   Pvt. N.C. Mil.
   m. Temperance Kiser — son Tip m. Eliza Jackson

Johnson, William b. Va. 1792 d. Ohio 1885   Pvt. Va. Mil.
   m. Catherine Lang — daughter Sarah Helen m. S. G. Johnston

Johnston, Benjamin b. Va. d. Mo.   Ens. Mo. Terr. Mil.
   m. Miss Thompson — son W. m. Ruth Dixon

Johnston, Benjamin Albright b. Va. 1795 d. Mo. 1880   Pvt. Va. Mil.
   m. Mary Crabtree — son Lysander m. Lois Ellen Ross
   daughter Salina Docia m. John Jackson Beagles

Johnston, Bryant b. Ky. 1782 d. Ky. m. Ellen Reaugh   Pvt. Ky. Mil.
   daughter Eurithe Q. m. John Ramsey

Johnston, Daniel b. Ire. 1748 d. N.J. 1822   Pvt. Pa. Mil.
   m. Mary Haille — son Joseph m. Margaret Beatty

Johnston, David b. Va. 1768 d. W.Va. 1846   Pvt. Va. Mil.
   m. Mrs. Sallie Chapman Miller — son Oscar F. m. Elizabeth French

Johnston, David b. Pa. 1785 d. Pa. 1857   Pvt. Pa. Mil.
   m. Susanna Riale — son Robert m. Wilhelmina McHenry

Johnston, Jacob Sr. b. Eng. 1740 d. Ind. 1818   Pvt. Ky. Mil.
   m. Feriby Warren — son Jacob Jr. m. Feriby Warren Long

Johnston, John b. 1767 d. 1818 m. Isabel Craig   Lt. N.C. Mil.
   son John Jr. m. Charity Tate

Johnston, John   Vol. 15   Pvt. Conn. Mil.

Johnston, Matthew b. N.C. 1790 d. N.C. 1857   Pvt. N.C. Mil.
   m. Elizabeth Register — daughter Mary m. James Finley Bland
   REAL DAUGHTER

Johnston, Nathan b. 1794 d. 1869   Capt. S.C. 1812
   m. Elizabeth McCoy (McKoy) — son Nathan Henry
   m. Louisa Catherine Johnson

Johnston, Richard b. Ohio 1792 d. Ohio 1875   Seaman Ohio
   m. Elziabeth Blackburn Davidson (Davison) — son Finley B.
   m. Roxanna Hardesty

Johnston, Rudolph   Vol. 17   Pvt. Va. Mil.

Johnston, Thomas   Vol. 5   Pvt. N.Y. Mil.

Johnston, Washington b. Va. 1795 d. Mo. 1879   Pvt. Ky. Mil.
   m. Mary E. Hardin — son Wesley P. m. Sarah A. Snider

Johnston (Johnson), William b. Canada 1782   Pvt. N.Y. Frontier
   d. N.Y. 1870 m. Ann Randolph — daughter Maria m. Alonzo Reed

Joiner, Asahel (Asel) b. Vt. 1773 d. N.Y. 1876   Pvt. N.Y. Mil.
   m. Lavinia Darby — daughter Lucy m. Peter Conklin

Joiner, Nathan b. S.C. abt. 1777 d. La. c. 1835/40   Pvt. La. Mil.
   m. Milindy Fruney — daughter Clarissa Lucindy m. John Bailey

Jolliff, William b. Pa. 1761 d. W.Va. 1827   Pvt. Va. Mil.
   m. Catherine Collins — daughter Elizabeth m. Benjamin Hayhurst

Jolly, Samuel b. Md. 1794 d. Ohio 1864   Pvt. Ohio Mil.
   m. Susanna Creekbaum — son Samuel F. m. Harriett Ann Glasscoe

Jones, Aaron b. Va. 1781 d. Ohio 1853 m. Sarah Bunn   Sgt. Ohio Mil.
   son Abel m. Catherine Dresbach

Jones, Abraham b. Va. 1752 d. Ga. 1811   Ga. Aud. 1794, Jus. Inf. Ct.
   m. Sarah Bugg   1799-1802, State Senate 1792
   daughter (2) Martha B. m. Dr. Thomas Moore

Jones, Adam b. 1765 d. Ga. 1830 Ga. Justice of Peace 1810-15, of Inf. Ct.
   m. Serisy — son John m. Ann

Jones, Allen   Vol. 16   Senator N.C. 1784-87

Jones, August   Vol. 16   Sgt. Mo. Mil.
   daughter Pauline m. James D. Russell   REAL DAUGHTER

Jones, Augustus b. Kaskaskia d. Tex. 1887   Sgt. N.W. Terr.
   m. Mary Barger — daughter Fannie   REAL DAUGHTER

Jones, Benjamin b. Va. 1750 d. N.C. 1821   Legis. N.C. 1791-4
   m. Elizabeth Foster — daughter Lucy m. Moses Cass

Jones, Branch b. Va. 1775 d. Ark. 1851   Capt. E. Tenn. Mil.
   m. Mary Van Pelt — son Daniel F. m. Mariah Louise Hotchkiss

Jones Bridger b. Va. 1753 d. Ga. 1819   Justice of Inf. Ct. Ga. 1808-19
   m. Rachel Barry — daughter Rachel m. John Wise

Jones, Cadwallader b. Va. 1788 d. N.C. 1861   Capt. Va. Mil.
   m. Rebecca Edwards Long — daughter Alice C. m. Allen C. Jones

Jones, Cyrus b. (Me.) Mass. 1791 d. Me. 1846   Pvt. Mass. Mil.
   m. Rebecca Tyler — daughter Lucy A. m. Peter Weare Brown
   son Wesley m. Sophia P.

Jones, Daniel b. N.C. 1790 d. Tenn. 1876 m. Mary   Pvt. Tenn. Cavalry
   daughter Mary m. John Weigart

Jones, David b. Del. 1736 d. Pa. 1820   Chaplain Pa. Mil.
   m. Ann Stillwell — daughter Eleanor m. John Garrett

Jones, Edward b. Va. 1754 d. D.C. 1829   Chief Clerk U.S. Treasury Dept.
m. Louise Maus — son John A. m. Ann Maria Major

Jones, Erastus Lyman b. N.Y. 1790 d. Wisc. 1854   Pvt. N.Y. Mil.
m. Abigail Ingersoll — son John N. m. Elizabeth Green Clark

Jones, Fielding b. Va. 1756 d. Ky. m. Sarah Hardin   Pvt. Ky. Mil.
son Peter m. Matilda C. Sibley

Jones, Gardiner b. N.Y. 1760 d. N.Y. 1825   Pvt. N.Y. Mil.
m. Elizabeth Morris — daughter Elizabeth m. Stephen Lewis

Jones, Hampton b. Va. c. 1773 d. Ky. c. 1829   Lt. Ky. Mil.
m. Matilda Crowder — daughter Jane m. (2) Leander F. Danforth

Jones, Henry b. S.C. 1795 d. Miss. 1833   Pvt. Miss. Mil.
m. Mary Spurlock — daughter Elizabeth Ann
m. Andrew Jackson Robinson
son William m. Katherine Burris

Jones, Henry P. b. Ga. 1788 d. Ga. 1853   **Lt. Ga. Mil.**
m. Sarah Vickers — son James V. m. Mary Elizabeth Hurt
daughter Penelope E. m. John Troupe Shewmake

Jones, Hugh Andrew b. Md. 1791 d. Md. 1864   Pvt. Md. Mil.
m. Rebecca Ann Kidd — son John F. m. Helen Creswell

Jones, Humphrey b. 1770 d. 1853   War of Wabash Indians Ky. 1791
m. Susannah Gentry — son James m. Lucretia Smith

Jones, Isaac b. Conn. 1748 d. Conn. 1813 m. (1) Mary Pond   Pat., Conn.
daughter Hannah m. Nehemiah Woodruff

Jones, James   Vol. 16   Sgt. Ky. Vol.

Jones, James b. Va. 1774 d. Ky. 1849 m. Mary Buster   Pvt. Ky. Mil.
daughter Eliza m. Micajah Phillips
daughter Hannah m. Jonathan B. S. Frisbie

Jones, John b. Ire. 1780 d. Tenn. 1868   Capt. Tenn. Mil.
m. Charlotte Blaine — daughter Rebecca
m. William Carroll Sullivan
daughter Susanna m. William S. Woolford

Jones, John Jr. b. Va. 1764 d. Va. 1840   Mem. Va. Assy., Capt. Va. Mil.
m. Lucy Binns Cargill — son John m. Mary Ann Walker

Jones, John Sr. b. Va. 1735 d. Va. 1793   Mem. of Va. Senate 1784-90
m. Elizabeth Binns — son John Jr.   Co. Clerk Va. 1790-93
m. Lucy Binns Cargill

Jones, John b. Md. 1755 d. Md. 1848   Lt. Col. Md. Mil.
m. Cassandra Chew — daughter Mary Ann m. George Fisher

Jones, John b. Pa. 1781 d. Pa. 1858 m. Catharine Clover   Pvt. Pa. Mil.
son John Jr. m. Lucinda Fulton

Jones, John b. Tenn. 1789 d. Tenn. 1869 m. Annis Manes   Pvt. Tenn. Mil.
son James F. m. Nancy Peck

Jones, John Blair b. N.J. 1779 d. Pa. 1849   **Pvt. Pa. Mil.**
m. Elizabeth Phillips — son John P. m. Susan Jane Long

Jones, John Leftridge b. Va. 1797 d. Ind. 1883   Pvt. Va. Mil.
m. Ann Lewis — daughter Minerva m. William M. Davis
REAL DAUGHTER
son William W. m. Urania Hicks

Jones, Joseph b. S.C. 1779 d. Ga. 1849   **Capt. Ga. Mil.**
m. Sarah Anderson — son John m. Jane Adaline Dunwoody

Jones, Joseph b. Ga. 1780 d. Ga. 1846   Capt. Ga. Mil.
  m. Elizabeth Screven Lee Hart — son James N.
  m. Sarah Jane Norman

Jones, Joshua b. W.Va. 1760 d. W.Va. 1813   Pvt. Va. Mil.
  m. Jane McMullain — son Henry m. Mary Lough
  daughter Prudence m. Arnold James Eddy

Jones, Lewis b. Conn. 1771 d. Pa. 1848   Ens. Pa. Mil.
  m. Sarah Benedict — son Benjamin m. Caroline Arista Harvey

Jones, Mahlon b. Md. 1793 d. N.C. 1868   Pvt. Md. Mil.
  m. Sarah E. Hancock — daughter Anna Celeste
  m. Moses G. Hamburger   REAL DAUGHTER

Jones, Mathew b. Pa. c. 1788 d. Ohio 1847/8   Pvt. Ohio Mil.
  m. Sarah Thoroughman — son Samuel m. Sophia Huyskell

Jones, Matthew b. S.C. 1774 d. Ill. 1855   Pvt. Tenn. Mil.
  m. Rachel Gallagly — daughter Lucinda R. m. John M. Haggard

Jones, Nathaniel b.—d.—m.—   Legis. N.C.
  daughter Mary Jane Daniel Stone Dickerson   REAL DAUGHTER
  m. Washington Riborn

Jones, Nathaniel b. N.C. 1745 d. N.C. 1815   Judge N.C.
  m. Amelia Millicent Blanckord — daughter Sarah E. m. John Lane

Jones, Obediah b. S.C. 1762/3 d. Ala. 1825   Fed. Judge Miss. 1805
  m. Jane Elizabeth Cowden — son Thomas M. m. Joanna G. Lindley

Jones, Otis George b. Vt. 1796 d. Vt. 1873   Pvt. Vt. Mil.
  m. Fanny Buckmaster — son Dana George m. Ellen Bucklin
  daughter Patty Agnes m. Wranslow Holton

Jones, Peter b. Va. 1751 d. Va. 1815   Maj. Va. Mil.
  m. Sally Glenn Bacon — daughter Julia m. Dr. Henry May

Jones, Pleasant b. Va. 1782 d. Ill. 1847 m. Sarah   Pvt. Va. Mil.
  son James m. Eliza Dressor
  daughter Mary Minerva m. James McCracken

Jones, Randall b. Ga. 1786 d. Tex. 1873   Capt. Miss. Terr. Mil.
  m. Mary Andrus — daughter Sallie C. m. Joseph Bruckmiller

Jones, Richard   Vol. 5   Pvt. N.Y. Mil.

Jones, Richard b. Va. 1794 d. Va. 1852   Ens. Va. Mil.
  m. Elizabeth Campbell Epes — daughter Sallie F.
  m. Dr. Reps Connalley

Jones, Richard   Vol. 10, 11   Pvt. N.Y. Mil.

Jones, Richard Stith   Vol. 7   Col. Va. Mil.

Jones, Richard b. Va. 1793 d. Ala. 1883   Sgt. Maj. Ga. Mil.
  m. Lucy Early — daughter Daniella m. Joseph Wheeler

Jones, Roger   Vol. 6   2nd Lt. U.S. Marines
  daughter Virginia Bird   REAL DAUGHTER

Jones, Roger b. Va. 1763 d. Va. 1836   Pvt. Va. Mil.
  m. Rebecca Boone — daughter Nancy m. Joseph Barker

Jones, Samuel b. 1755 d. 1831   Capt. Tenn. Mil. 1808
  m. Elizabeth Goodloe — son Edward D.
  m. (Anne E., Katherine Willis)

Jones, Spottswood   Vol. 11   Pvt. Va. Mil.

Jones, Tarpley b. Ky. 1794 d. Ohio 1852   Pvt. Ohio Mil.
    m. Phoebe Calvin — son Samuel M. m. Elizabeth Gray

Jones, Taylor E. b. Mass. 1790 d. Ohio 1870   Cpl. N.Y. Mil.
    m. Hannah Esty — son William E. m. Augusta Bump

Jones, Thomas b. Ga. 1794 d. Miss. 1869   Pvt. Miss. Mil.
    m. Elizabeth Stovall — son Thomas H. m. Nettie Carney

Jones, Thomas Anderson b. Md. 1797 d. W. Va. 1883   Pvt. Md. Vol.
    m. Catherine Luella Smith — son William P.
    m. Frances Christine Kerr

Jones, Thornton   Vol. 7   2nd Lt. W. Tenn. Mil.

Jones, William   Vol. 4   Capt. Ga. Mil.

Jones, William b. N.J. 1789 d. Mo. 1874   Pvt. Ohio Mil.
    m. Jane Corken — son Fletcher m. Mary Ann Ring

Jones, William   Vol. 8   Pvt. Pa. Mil.

Jones, William b. Va. 1782 d. Mo. 1879   Pvt. Va. Mil.
    m. Catherine Hudnall — daughter Mattie   REAL DAUGHTER
    daughter Sallie m. Isaac Waters   REAL DAUGHTER

Jones, William Dibrell b. Va. d. Va. 1874   Pvt. Va. Mil.
    m. Judith Baker Le Grand—son Louis D. L.
    m. Louisa Thomas Flippen

Jones, Willis b. N.C. 1784 d. Tenn. 1834   Cpl. Tenn. Mil.
    m. Elizabeth Gee — daughter Rachel A. m. Madison Monroe Russell
    son Wiley m. Sarah Jane Dodson

Jones, Willis H. b. N.C. 1797 d. Tex. 1861   Pvt. N.C. Mil.
    m. Mary Holmes Taylor — daughter Mary Anna
    m. John Edward Sterne

Joor, John B. b. S.C. 1780 d. Miss. 1830   Capt. Miss. Mil., Indian War and
    m. Emily Richardson   Gen. Battle New Orleans
    daughter Caroline B. m. 3rd Edward Waring Joor

Jordan, Archibald Steele b. Pa. 1774 d. Pa. 1859   Inspector Pa.
    m. Rebecca Turner — son James P. m. Rachel Alexander

Jordan, Benjamin b. Va. 1772 d. Tenn.   Pvt. W. Tenn. Vol.
    m. Elizabeth Johnston — son Benjamin F. m. Elvira Byler

Jordan, Dillon   Vol. 8   Pvt. N.C. Mil.

Jordan, Edward b. Va. 1745 d. Va. 1820 m. Susanna   Maj. La. Mil.
    son Miles m. Harriet Pettus

Jordan, Hezekiah b. Va. 1789-90 d. Va. 1833 m. Polly Hoffman   Pvt. Va.
    daughter Elizabeth m. Wm Shoemaker

Jordan, Ichabod b. Mass. (Me.) 1770 d. Me. 1865   Capt. Mass. (Me.)
    m. Mary Coffin — son Enoch C. m. Mary Cleeves

Jordan, Jacob b. Ger. 1760 d. Ohio 1849 m. Mary Ann Sivers   Pvt. Pa. Mil.
    son David m. Elizabeth Dowler

Jordan, John b. Va. 1777 d. Va. 1854 m. Lucy Winn   2nd Lt. Va. Mil.
    son Samuel m. Hannah Davis

Jordan, Jubal b. Va. 1792 d. Va. 1858   Cpl. Va. Cavalry
    m. Prescilla Williamson — daughter Ann E. R. m. Marquis D. Gray

Jordan, Merritt   Vol. 8   4th Cpl. Va. Mil.
    daughter Pauline Jordan m. Rogers   REAL DAUGHTER

Jordan, Notley b. N.C. 1795 d. Va. 1879   Pvt. Va. Mil.
m. Nannie Anderson Woodall (2) — daughter Bettie J.
m. James Richard Elliott   **REAL DAUGHTER**

Jordan, Robert b. Pa. 1748 d. Pa. 1835   Pvt. Pa. Mil.
m. Catherine Redding — daughter Nancy m. Enoch Crissman

Jordan, Samuel b. S.C. 1793 d. S.C. 1876   Pvt. S.C. Mil.
m. Mary Ansley — daughter Emma Lucretia
m. James Warren Wideman

Jordan, Thomas b. N.C. d. Ga. 1840 m. Catherine Daniel   Lt. Ga. Mil.
son Elisha W. m. Penny Ann Watkins

Jordan, Tristam b. (Me.) Mass. 1731 d. Me. 1821   Senator Mass. 1787
m. Hannah Goodwin — daughter Elizabeth m. William Vaughan
son William m. Sallie Raymond B. Keating

Jordan, Warren b. N.C. 1784 d. Tenn. 1843   Mem. Legis. Ga. 1812
m. Juliette Anna Daniell — daughter Sarah Geraldine
m. John Raymond Worrill

Jordan, William b. (Me.) 1767 d. Me. 1820   Pvt. Mass. (Me.) Mil.
m. Anna Leach — son Dominicus m. Kezia Dingley

Jordan, William b. Md. 1794 d. Md. 1853 m. Helen Ogg   Pvt. Md. Mil.
son James W. m. Delila Ann Shilling
son Ellias m. Mary Welsh

Jordan, Dillon b. Ire. 1773 d. N.C. 1837   Vol. 6   Pvt. N.C. Mil.

Jorey, John b. Md. 1780 d. Md. 1865 m. Eliza Buckingham   Pvt. Md. Mil.
daughter Adeline m. Charles Edward Kemp

Joseph, Daniel b. d. Ohio 1847 m. Annis Jackson   Pvt. Va. Mil.
son Harvey J. m. Mary Ross

Joy, Francis b. Mass. d. Mass. m. Susan Ramsdell   Pvt. U.S. Art.
son Francis H. m. Sarah Goodwin

Joy, Edward b. Md. 1776 d. Md. 1864 m. Elizabeth Wheeler   **Pvt. Md. Mil.**
son Edward Jr. m. Rachel Ann Willington

Joyce, Daniel Benedict b. N.Y. d.— m. Mary Place   Fife Maj. U.S. Inf.
daughter Anne Almira m. Sherman Horace Sterling

Joyce, John b. Ire. 1755 d. Ga. 1827 m. (2) Martha   Capt. Ga. Mil.
son Garten m. Hester J. Hardin

Joyce, Thomas Boyce b. Pa. 1788 d. Pa. 1849   Sgt. Pa. Mil.
m. Sarah Ann Higgins — daughter Mary Ann
m. William Chamberlain
daughter Jane m. Samuel Lair Mintzer

Joyner, Absalom Belton b. S.C. 1794 d. S.C. 1873   Pvt. S.C. Mil.
m. Martha Jane Sturgeon — daughter Gabrielle
m. Julius Peter Larsevick   **REAL DAUGHTER**
daughter Janie m. Washington Sherman Hodge
m. Annie Carroll
son Nicholas C. m. Cassandra Darrell

Joynes, William b. Va. 1780 d. Va. 1856 m. Hester Rogers   Cpl. Va. Mil.
son Edward D. m. Ann Catherine Scott

Judd, Jesse b. Conn. 1785 d. N.Y. 1859   Pvt. N.Y. Mil.
m. Anna (Alvira) Dayton — son Alonzo B. m. Julia White
daughter Lovisa A. m. Simon P. Smith   **REAL DAUGHTER**

Judy, John b. Ky. 1791 d. Ill. 1874 m. (1) Lydia Hull   Pvt. Ohio Mil.
    son Amaziah m. Hopy Ann Nicholson

June, Ezra b. Conn. 1784 d. Conn. 1866 m. Sarah Hoyt   Pvt. Conn. Mil.
    daughter Rachel m. George Hubbard

Jungkurth, Christopher (Jungwith, Christian)   Pvt. Pa. Blues
    b. Pa. 1799 d. Pa. 1874 m. Ann Fisher — daughter Rebecca
    m. Sylvester Crout Markle

Justice, James b. Pa. 1794 d. Ohio 1873 m. Eliza Moore   Pvt. Ohio Mil.
    daughter Statia Eliza m. John Wesley Failing (relative)

Justice, William b. N.C. 1765 d. Tenn. 1830   Pvt. N.C. Mil.
    m. Nancy Brantley — daughter Elizabeth m. Green Utley

K

Kaigler, David b. S.C. 1788 d. Ga. 1858   Cpl. Tenn. Mil.
    m. Anna Barbara Craps
    daughter Annie E. B. m. Benjamin G. Christie

Kaler, Matthias b. Ger. 1751 d. Pa. 1825 m. Katherine Sands   Capt. Pa. Mil.
    son John m. Elizabeth Umsted
    daughter Katherine m. John Cox

Kalfus, Henry Frederick b. Ger. 1756 d. Ky. 1833   Pvt. Ky. Mil.
    m. Anna Fisher — son James F. m. Sarah Ann Etley

Kalfus, Jacob Watts   Vol. 7   Pvt. Ky. Mil.

Karr, Thomas b. Pa. 1793 d. Ill. 1878   Pvt. Ohio Mil.
    m. Mrs. Elizabeth Edwards Kitchell
    son Thomas J. m. Elizabeth Low

Karshner (Kershner), Jacob b. Pa. 1775 d. Ohio 1863   Pvt. Ohio Mil.
    m. Mary Magdelene Dunkleberger — son John m. Phoebe Swinehart

Kasey, John b. Va. c. 1780 d. Va. 1860 m. Jane Saunders   Ens. Va. Mil.
    daughter Julena Jane m. Jesse Morgan

Kaster (Castor), Philip b. 1777 d. 1865 m. Elizabeth Fox   Pvt. Pa. Mil.
    son John Elick m. Susannah Lobaugh

Kauffman (Kaufman), Jacob b. Pa. 1794 d. Pa. 1849   Pvt. Pa. Mil.
    m. Catherine Martin — daughter Maria m. Joseph Bomburger

Kavanuagh, Charles, Sr. b. Va. 1726 d. Ky. 1796   Del. to 1st Cons.
    m. Ann Coleman — son William m. Hannah Woods   Conv. 1792

Kaylor, George   Vol. 3   Pvt. Md. Mil.

Kean, Andrew b. Ire. 1775 d. Va. 1837   Surgeon Va. Mil.
    m. Martha Winston Callis
    daughter Leonora L. m. Duarte Horace Monteiro de Barros

Kearney, James   Vol. 7   Pvt. N.J. Mil.

Kearney, John A. b. Ire. 1790 d. Mex. 1847   Surgeon U.S. Navy
    m. Mary M. Forrest
    daughter Kate m. James L. M. Henry REAL DAUGHTER

Kearney, Stephen Watts b. N.J. 1794 d. Mo. 1848   Capt. U.S. Inf.
    m. Mary Radford — son Charles m. Annie Stewart
    daughter Ellen m. Western Bascome REAL DAUGHTER

Kearsley, Jonathan   Vol. 1   1st Lt. U.S. Mil.

Keefer, Daniel b. Pa. 1795 d. Ind. 1872   Pvt. U.S. Cavalry
  m. Charlotte Englebright — son William B. m. Sarah A Mower

Keeler, Daniel b. Conn. 1750 d. N.Y. m. Abigail Isaacs   Justice N.Y. 1794
  daughter Theodocia m. George Hall

Keeler, Edward b. 1761 d. N.J. 1826 m. Elizabeth Gray   Pvt. N.J. Mil.
  daughter Deborah m. Joseph Furman
  daughter Elizabeth m. Henry Hall Bross

Keeler, Elijah   Vol. 7   Pvt. Conn. Mil.

Keeler, Henry Jr. b. Pa. 1757 d. Pa. 1826 m. Hannah Lemlar   Ens. Pa. Mil.
  daughter Elizabeth m. Phillip Berrett

Keely, Henry b. Pa. 1791 d. Pa. 1833 m. Mary McCoy   Sgt. Pa. Mil.
  daughter Phoebe m. Edward Nixon

Keen, Timothy Thomas b. Conn. 1779 d. Md. 1847   Sgt. Md. Mil
  m. Harriet Bayless — son Nathaniel B. m. Susan Eleanor Davis

Keene, Jarius b. Mass. 1766 d. Me. 1844   Capt. Mass. (Me.) Inf.
  m. Lucy Knight — son William m. Anna Barbour Lombard

Keeney, Ithiel b. Conn. 1755 d. Conn. 1837   Town Treasurer
  m. Letitia Lockwood Bunce   Conn. 1789-1812
  son Lockwood m. Ann Maria Shipman

Keeney, Leonard b. Conn. 1790 d. Conn. 1866   Pvt. Conn. Mil.
  m. Mary Hollister — son Charles H. m. Emily Augusta Munnson

Keeney, Michael b. Va. d. Tenn. m. Mary Leech   Pvt. E. Tenn. Mil.
  son Calvin L. m. Mary E. Boatwright

Keeney, Seth b. Pa. 1798 d. Pa. 1849 m. Mary Wall   Pvt. Pa. Mil.
  son Ephraim m. Elizabeth Neigh

Keeney, Thomas b. Conn. 1751 d. Pa. 1840   Defender of Frontier
  m. Mercy Lamb — son Elijah m. Cynthis Forbes

Keep, Martin b. Mass. 1774 d. N.Y. 1845   Lt. Col. N.Y. Mil.
  m. Hepsibeth Hotchkiss — daughter Emily m. Richard M. Graham

Keesecker, Conrad b. Va. d. Va. 1813 m. Frances Parker   Rifleman Va. Mil.
  son Andrew m. Clara Roberg

Kefer (Keifer) Henry b. Ger. 1771 d. Pa. 1841 m. Ann   Pvt. Pa. Mil.
  son Washington m. Elizabeth Moss

Keffer, Anthony b. Pa. 1790 d. Pa. 1856 m. Sarah Shillingford   Pvt. Pa. Mil.
  daughter Eliza Ann m. Hugh Duffy

Kehoe, John b. Pa. 1783 d. Pa. 1861 m. Rebecca Robinson   Lt. Pa. Mil.
  daughter Nancy m. James Nicholls

Keifer, Joseph b. Md. 1784 d. Ohio 1850 m. Mary Smith   Pvt. Ohio Mil.
  son Joseph W. m. Eliza Stout
  daughter Sarah m. Richard Youngman

Keilholtz, William b. Md. 1777 d. Md. 1815 m. Magdalena   Cpl. Md. Mil.
  son William m. Lydia

Keiper, Daniel b. Pa. 1794 d. Pa. 1870 m. Sarah Bowman   Pvt. Pa. Inf.
  daughter Clara M. m. William H. Deshler REAL DAUGHTER

Keirstead, John A. b. N.J. 1769 d. N.J. 1857   Capt. N.J. Mil.
  m. Polly Williams—daughter Margaret m. John Van Ness

Keister, Phillip b. Pa. 1780 d. Pa. 1863 m. Margaret Shaffer   Pvt. Pa. Mil.
  son Paul m. Mary Neiman

Keith, Benjamin Franklin b. Ky. 1792 d. Ky. 1878   Cpl. Ky. Mil.
  m. Ruanny Walters — son Enos m. Mary Berry

Keithly, William b. 1793 d. 1883 m. Charlotte Castilo   Ky. Ranger
  daughter Ruth Christine m. Jos. Warren Savage

Keller, Casper b. Pa. 1796 d. Pa. 1837 m. Elizabeth Brant   Capt. Pa. Mil.
  son Henry m. Rachel Trent

Keller, Daniel b. Va. 1790 d. Md. 1870 m. Margaret Taylor   Pvt. Va. Mil.
  son Daniel m. Mary Jane Thistle

Keller, Edward b. Conn. 1761 d. N.J. 1826 m. Elizabeth Gray   Pvt.N.J. Mil.
  daughter Elizabeth m. Henry (Hall) Bross

Keller, Jacob b. Pa. 1761 d. Pa. 1830 m. Christina Hoover   Pvt. Pa. Mil.
  son John m. Elizabeth Hershberger

Keller, John b. Pa. 1785 d. Ohio 1859 m. Elizabeth Mitzell   Pvt. Ohio
  daughter Catherine m. Henry Bowlus Jr.

Kelley, George b. Va. 1782 d. Ind. 1868 m. Elizabeth Harrell   Pvt. Ohio Mil.
  son James m. Hannah Goodlander

Kelley, James b. Conn. 1721 d. Conn. 1813   Pvt. Conn. Mil.
  m. Rebecca Sherman — daughter Hannah m. Oliver Lewis Sr.

Kelley, John b. W.Va. 1796 d. W.Va. 1866 m. Mary Yoke   Cpl. (W.)Va. Mil.
  son James L. B. m. Annie Mary Beohm

Kelley (Kelly), Joshua Jr. b. Md. 1790 d. Ind. 1863   Pvt. Ky. Mil.
  m. Rebecca Eliot — son William B. m. Margaret Ann Greene

Kelley, William b. Va. 1777 d. Va. 1854 m. Mary Lawson   Pvt. Va.
  son John m. Tacy Davis

Kelley, William Bowdoin b. N.H. 1769 d. N.H. 1825   Col. N.H. Mil.
  m. Polly Smith — son Benjamin F. m. Isabel G. Goshorn

Kellogg, Benjamin b. Mass. 1761 d. N.Y. 1850   Sgt. N.Y. Mil.
  son Jeremiah m. Eunice Dodge

Kellogg, Eleazer b. Conn. 1749 d. N.Y. 1818 m. Esther Filler   Sgt. U.S. Inf.
  son Whiting m. Marinda Burr

Kellogg, Elisha b. N.Y. 1772 d. N.Y. 1857 m. Persis Dunham   Lt. N.Y. Mil.
  son Aaron m. Charlotte Webber

Kellogg, Rev. Ezra Benedict b. 1795 d. 1878   Sgt. Ohio
  m. Anna Thompson — daughter Eleanore m. Dr. Wyllys Hull

Kellogg, Israel b. Conn. 1792 d. Conn. 1868   Pvt. Conn. Mil.
  m. Jerusha Pease — son Julius A. m. Abbie Jane Kellogg

Kellogg, Jonathan b. Conn. 1767 d. Pa. 1869   Justice 1808 Pa.
  m. Elizabeth Smith — son William m. Sarah Vosburg

Kellum, Edward b. Tenn. 1787 d. Tex. 1863   Pvt. W. Tenn. Mil.
  m. Karenhapoc Tabor
  daughter Emily Caroline m. John Baird Puckett

Kelly, Daniel b. Ire. 1737 d. N.Y. 1834 m. Mary   Pvt. N.Y. Vol.
  daughter Mary m. Aaron Norcross Sr.

Kelly, James b. Ohio (Pa.) 1776 d. Ohio 1837   Pvt. Ohio Mil.
  m. Elizabeth Lane (Lain) — daughter Polly m. Aaron Cole
  daughter Rachel m. Lowman Pratt

Kelly, Jonathan b. N.J. 1769 d. Pa. 1849 m. Agnes Taylor   Pvt. Pa. Mil.
son Amiziah m. Rebecca McBride

Kelly, Joseph b. Va. 1767 d. Ky. 1858 (53) (51)   Capt. Ky. Mil.
m. Elizabeth Mallory — daughter Mary m. Joel P. Thomasson
daughter Sarah m. Thomas Ecton

Kelly, Joseph b. Va. d. Ky. 1822 m. Jane Buster   Pvt. Ky. Vol. Mil.
son Joseph N. m. Elizabeth McMillan

Kelly, Joseph b. Ky. 1785 d. Ohio 1849 m. Mary Detrow   Lt. Ky. Vol.
son Jacob m. Felinda Farewell

Kelly, Moses b. S.C. 1775 d. Ala. 1837 m. Margaret   Capt. S.C. Dragoons
son Isham H. m. Elizabeth Ruth Herbert

Kelly, Samuel b. Va. 1776 d. Ky. 1834 m. Nancy Kennedy   Pat. Ky. 1809-
son Clinton m. Moriah M. Crain

Kelly, Sims b. N.C. 1784 d. Ala. 1860 m. Mary Camp   Pvt. Tenn.
son Albert G. m. Permelia Miller (Emily Jane Marshall)
son Samuel C. m. Annie Elizabeth Pace
son William C. m. Mary Ann Hollingsworth

Kelly, Thomas Davis b. Md. 1786 d. Ga. 1850   Lt. U.S. Inf.
m. Phoebe Caroline Bryan
daughter Mary Eugenia m. John Henry Bitting REAL DAUGHTER

Kelly, William Durham b. N.C. 1783 d. Miss. after 1860   Pvt. Tenn. Vol.
m. Mrs. Miriam (Lloyd) O'Rear — son Willis A. m. Ruth Duncan

Kelly, William b. 1783 d. 1850 m. Ruth Prigmore   Pvt. Tenn. Mil.
son John m. Nancy Hendrick (Hendrix)

Kelly, William Somes b. N.H. 1761 d. N.H. 1832   Selectman N.H. 1804
daughter Prudence B. m. Ezekiel Foster

Kelse, George b. Pa. 1793 d. Pa. 1867 m. Mary Shedron   Pvt. Pa. Mil.
daughter Martha m. William H. Good
daughter Mary m. William Eccleson

Kelsey, J. Havens b. N.Y. 1784 d. N.Y. 1805   Capt. N.Y. Inf.
m. Deborah Scudder — son John Budd m. Sarah

Kelso, John Russell II b. Md. 1791 d. Md. 1880   Cpl. Md. Mil.
m. Martha Balderston
daughter Mary Esther m. Alexander Maitland Carter

Kelton, Robert b. N.C. 1776 d. Tenn. 1826   Pvt. W. Tenn. Mil.
m. Rachel Jetton — son William P. m. Lucinda White

Keltz, George Jr. b. Pa. 1758 d. Pa. 1857 m. Sarah Shannon   Lt. Pa. Mil.
daughter Rebecca m. Mahlon Norris

Kemmerer, John Philip b. Pa. 1759 d. Ohio 1827   Pvt. Pa. Mil.
m. Rose Ann Hyle (Heil) — son Joseph m. Salome Bowser

Kemp, Gilbert b. Md. 1785 d. Mo. m. Rebecca Curfman   Capt. Md. Mil.
son Stephen m. Ann Knauff

Kemp, Joseph b. Md. 1781 d. Md. 1835   Capt. Md. Mil.
m. (2) Alice Ridgeway — son William m. Henrietta Lambdin

Kemp, Thomas b. Md. 1779 d. Md. 1824 m. Sophia Horstman   Pvt. Md. Mil.
daughter Sophia m. William Haddaway Dawson

Kemper, John b. Va. 1768 d. Va. 1856 m. Martha Fisher   Maj. Va. Mil.
daughter Isabella N. m. Francis Morgan Stone

Kendall, Alexander b. Va. 1785 d. Ohio 1821   Pvt. Va. Mil.
 m. Elizabeth Addison — son Welford m. Jennette B. Turpen

Kendall, Francis b. Pa. 1767 d. Pa. 1851 m. Jane Gibson Capt. Pa. Mil.
 son Francis m. James E. Merryfield

Kendall, Joshua Vol. 4   Selectman Vt. 1802

Kendall, William b. Ky. 1784 d. Ohio 1840 m. Edith Stokes Pvt. Ohio Mil.
 son William Jr. m. Elizabeth Brown

Kendig (Kendrick), John b. Pa. 1745 d. Pa. 1823   Pvt. Pa. Mil.
 m. Elizabeth Eshleman — daughter Veronica m. Martin Brenneman

Kendrick, James O'Burke b. Va. 1786 d. Mo. 1840   Maj. Ky. Mil.
 m. Harriet Belt — daughter Cordelia m. Michael Finnin

Kendrick, Samuel b. Va. 1795 d. Va. 1860   Pvt. Va. Mil.
 m. Clarinda Spengler
 daughter Eleanor Frances m. David English Armstrong

Kenison, David b. Me. 1736 d. Ill. 1852 m. 4 times   Pvt. Ill.
 son Isaac m. Lucy — son Joab m. Annie Holmes

Kennan, George b. Mass. 1752 d. Vt. 1830   Justice Selectman
 m. Abigail Sherman — son Thomas m. Sally Lathrop Vt. 1794-1804

Kennedy, Andrew b. Va. 1780 d. Ill. 1844   Pvt. Ky. Mil.
 m. Margaret Woolery — daughter Sarah M. m. Richard Bandy

Kennedy, Daniel b. N.C. 1744 d. Tenn. 1802   Civil Officer
 m. Margaret Hughes   N.C.-Tenn.
 daughter Margaret Ann m. John Ewing McClure

Kennedy, Evander Vol. 6   Pvt. Tenn. Mil.
 daughter Elizabeth G.

Kennedy, (Cannady), James b. Va. 1794 d. Tenn. 1838 Pvt. E. Tenn. Mil.
 m. Jane Holt Cox
 daughter Elizabeth m. Frederick William Vanuxem
 son William m. Melissa Gareett

Kennedy, John b. Pa. 1781 d. Ohio 1851   Pvt. U.S. Lt. Dragoons
 m. Margaret Wolfe — son Moses m. Nancy F. Kendrick

Kennedy, John III Vol. 9   Pvt. Vt. Mil.

Kennedy, John Vol. 17   Pvt. Pa. Dragoons

Kennedy, Martin b. Fra. 1768 d. Del. 1851 m. Mary Mains Pvt. Del. Mil.
 daughter Cecilia m. Patrick H. Flynn

Kennedy, Samuel Barnet Vol. 5   Sgt. Vt. Mil.

Kennedy, Thomas b. Pa. 1785 d. Pa. 1859 m. Catherine Flick Pvt. Pa. Mil.
 son James m. Catherine De Groff

Kennedy, William b. (Me.) Mass. 1774 d. Me. 1838 Cpl. U.S. Vol.
 m. Jane Hodge — son James m. Phoebe Alley

Kennedy, William Doak b. Pa. 1791 d. Pa. 1861/2   Pvt. Pa. Mil.
 m. Anne Maria Sherbourne — son Joseph S. m. Elizabeth M. Peltz
 son William S. m. Rebecca Bates

Kennon, John b. Va. 1784 d. Ga. 1831   Pvt. Va. Mil.
 m. Rachel Bobo Corly (widow)
 daughter Jenniford m. Frances Fretwell

Kennon, Richard Vol. 11   Lt. La. Mil.

Kent, Ephraim b. N.J. 1765 d. N.J. 1821   Pat. N.J. 1814
   m. Rachel (Edmunds) Foster
   daughter Deborah m. John Bancroft III

Kent, William Samuel   Vol. 12   Pvt. Mo. Mil.

Kentner, Amos, b. Conn. 1790 d. N.Y. 1858   Pvt. N.Y. Mil.
   m. Lucinda Clark
   daughter Susan M. m. Dohn Kilham (Heman)   REAL DAUGHTER

Kenyon (Kinyon) Asa b. N.Y. 1780 d. N.Y. 1836   Pvt. N.Y. Mil.
   m. Catherine Paddock — son Yates m. Mary House

Kepler, Jacob b. Md. 1793 d. Pa. 1877   Pvt. Pa. Mil.
   m. Ann Margaret Peiffer — son Samuel W. m. Martha C. Strouss

Kepner, Jacob b. Ohio 1784 d. Ill. 1864   Cpl. Ohio Mil.
   m. Catherine (Violet) Sidener — son Jacob Jr. m. Violet Maxfield

Kepner, John b. Pa. 1791 d. Pa. 1827 m. Mary Heefner (2)   Pvt. Pa. Mil.
   son Levi C. m. Sarah Ann Stover (Davis)

Kerby, Francis Marion b. S.C. 1794 d. Tenn. 1880   Pvt. W. Tenn. Mil.
   m. Barbara Brown (1) — son James V. m. Fannie Murphy
   daughter Medoria m. Wm. W. Ferguson

Kern, Joseph Sr. b. Pa. 1788 d. Ohio 1883   Pvt. Ohio Mil.
   m. Barbara Markley — son Joseph Jr. m. Sarah M. McKee

Kernion, Charles La Bedoyere Huchet de b. La. 1796   Pvt. La. Mil.
   d. La. 1846 m. Euphemie Aimee Lambert
   son Dangeville Redoyere la m. Blanche Dupuy

Kerr, Archibald b. Ire. 1777 d. Pa. 1843 m. Nancy Nichol   1st Sgt. Pa. Mil.
   daughter Mary Ann m. Ephraim Chidester

Kerr, David b. Pa. 1791 d. Ohio 1864 m. Rachel Sweek   Lt. Pa. Mil.
   son David Jr. m. Rozanna Premer

Kerr, George b. Scot. 1762 d. Pa. 1836 m. Eleanor Wilson   Capt. Pa. Mil.
   son John A. m. Eliza Jane Hutchinson

Kerr, James b. Pa. 1788 d. Ohio 1869 m. Mary McClellan   Lt. Ohio Mil.
   son William m. Mary Elizabeth West

Kerr, Joseph b. Scot. 1760 d. Va. (W.) 1843   Pvt. Pa. Mil.
   m. Jane Chambers — son John S. m. Nancy Leab

Kerr, Nathaniel Preston b. Pa. 1780 d. Ohio 1813   Pvt. Ohio Mil.
   m. Mary Gallagher — son Nathaniel P. Jr. m. (2) Ann Eliza Boggs

Kerr, Samuel b. Pa. 1792 d. Ohio 1882 m. Annie Smith   Pvt. Pa. Mil.
   daughter Sarah m. James McLaughlin

Kerr, William III b. Pa. 1794 d. Pa. 1862   1st Sgt. Pa. Mil.
   m. Margaret Irvin McClellan — son Irvin m. Elizabeth Jane Bunny

Kerr, William b. Pa. 1758 d. Pa. 1832 m. Margaret Young   Sgt. Pa. Mil.
   daughter Elizabeth m. Joseph Lowry

Kerrick, Edwin b. Va. 1792 d. 1867 m. Harriett P. Drummond   Pvt. Va. Mil.
   son John W. m. Sarah E. Deatherage

Keslar (Kester) George b. Md. 1787 d. Ind. 1857   Pvt. Ohio Mil.
   m. Catherine Horn — son John m. Margaret Ann Chisholm

Kessler, John Sr. b. Pa. 1761 d. Pa. 1840   Pvt. Pa. Mil.
   m. Abigail Anderson — son John Jr. m. Catherine Voight

Ketcham, David b. N.Y. 1773 d. N.Y. 1869   Lt. N.Y. Mil.
   m. Abigail Nostrand — daughter Hannah m. Jesse Oakley

Ketteyman, Andrew   Vol. 5   Pvt. Pa. Mil.

Key, Barzilla G.   Vol. 8   Pvt. S.C. Mil.

Key, Tandy Watts b. Va. 1786 d. Ga. 1840   Capt. Ga. Mil.
   m. Nancy J. Beatty — daughter Harriet E. m. Maxwell Rufus Berry

Key, Francis Scott b. Md. 1779 d. Md. 1843   Lt. D.C.
   m. Mary Tayloe Lloyd
   daughter Maria Lloyd m. Henry Maynadier Steele

Kibby, Thomas b. N.Y. 1784 d. N.Y. m. Electia Rexford   Pvt. N.Y. Mil.
   daughter Ruby Ann m. Hobart Read Tuttle

Kibby, Walter b. Conn. 1795 d. N.Y. 1868 m. Lydia Barber   Pvt. N.Y. Mil.
   son Delos L. m. Addie L. Reynolds

Kidd, Burgess b. Va. ca. 1772 d. Va. 1815 m. Sarah Daniels   Pvt. Va.
   daughter Nancy m. Nathan Davis

Kidd, John b. Ire. 1782 d. Pa. 1874 m. Anna McNealy   Pvt. Pa. Mil.
   son James M. m. Mary Caughey

Kidd, William Jr. b. Va. 1787 d. Ill. 1876 m. Susan Logan   Sgt. Va. Mil.
   son Willis N. m. Nancy Parks

Kidwell, Jonas b. Md. 1779 d. Md. 1824 m. Anne   Pvt. Md. Mil.
   daughter Anne m. George Cashell Wheatley

Kieffer, Dewald b. Ger. 1735 d. Pa. 1830   Capt. Pa. Vol. Mil. 1793
   m. Hannah Fox — son Abraham m. Catharine Beaver

Kierstede, John Aaron b. N.J. 1769 d. N.J. 1847   Capt. N.J. Mil.
   m. Polly Williams — son Aaron m. Sara Pier

Kies, (Keyes) Joseph b. Scot. 1753 d. N.Y. 1834   Pvt. N.Y. Mil.
   m. Mary Nichols — son John m. Betsy Locke

Kiggins, Thomas b. Va. 1791 d. Mo. 1870   Pvt. Ky. Vol. Mil.
   m. Elizabeth England — son John m. Mrs. Elizabeth Lyon Beck

Kight, Cornelius b. Md. 1792 d. Md. 1856 m. Mary Dawson   Pvt. Md. Mil.
   daughter Mary Ellen m. William Meakins Owens

Kight, John   Vol. 3   Cpl. Mass. Mil.

Kilbourne, John b. Vt. 1765 d. N.Y. 1847   Town Clerk Selectman
   m. Anne Ashley   Justice of Peace
   son Dr. Henry m. (2) Mrs. Lucy Maples Dyke   Vt. 1785-1815

Kilby, Allen b. 1772 d. 1854 m. Theda Darris   Pvt. N.Y. Mil.
   son Eben O. Kilby m. Caroline M. Osgood

Kile, (Kilde), George S. b.— d.— D.C. after 1823   Seaman U.S. Navy
   m. Deborah Jennings — daughter Margaret m. James Fort

Kilgore, William b. Va. 1770 d. Nr. Lake Erie 1814   Capt. Ohio Mil.
   m. Margaret Cochran — daughter Mary m. Joseph Lindley Robinson

Kilham, Heman b. Mass. 1786 d. N.Y. 1847 m. Maria Doben   Sgt. N.Y. Mil.
   son Doben H. m. Susan Minerva Kilham

Killam, Charles b. Pa. 1788 d. N.Y. 1859 m. Sarah Bingham   Pvt. N.Y. Mil.
   son Powell m. Margaret Ferguson

Killgore, Mathew b. Eng. c. 1740 d. Ohio 1823 m. Mary   Tax Collect 1787
   son Thomas m. Hetty Sanders   Judge 1785 Pa.

Killian, Jacob b. Pa. 1761 d. Pa. 1828 m. Susanna Beck   **Pvt. Pa. Mil.**
   son Abraham m. Sarah Brown

Killingsworth, Anderson b. 1789 d. 1866 m. Elizabeth Anderson   **Sgt. S.C.**
   daughter Pauline m. George Anderson

Killmore, George   Vol. 15   **Pvt. N.Y. Mil.**

Kimball, Charles   Vol. 4   **Pvt. Mass. (Me.) Mil.**

Kimball, Daniel b. Mass. (Me.) 1794 d. Me. 1878   **Cpl. Mass. (Me.) Mil.**
   m. Ruby Curtis — son Augustus H. m. Sophia Hunter Streeter

Kimball, Erastus b. Mass. 1788 d. N.Y. 1874   **Pvt. N.Y. Mil.**
   m. Elizabeth Reals — son Harrison m. Caroline Sayles

Kimball, Jeremiah b. Mass. 1788 d. N.Y. 1854   **Sgt. N.H. Mil.**
   m. Roxana King
   daughter Mary Jane m. Moses Howard Cross REAL DAUGHTER

Kimball, Oliver Jr. b. N.H. 1745 d. N.H. 1821   **Selectman N.H. 1793**
   m. Mary Allen — daughter Mary K. m. Benjamin Coates

Kimberlin, John b. Va. 1751 d. Ind. after 1834 m. Ruth Jones   **Pat. Ind., Ky.**
   daughter Elizabeth m. Barnet B. Whitlatch

Kimberly, Hazard b. Conn. 1775 d. N.Y. 1827   **Capt. N.Y. Mil.**
   m. Eliza Robbins — son John R. m. Aurelia Aldrich

Kimberly, Nathaniel   Vol. 3, 7, 9   **Pvt. Md. Mil.**

Kimberly, Nathaniel b. Conn. (Md.) 1775   **Pvt. Md. Wash. Blues**
   d. Md. 1836 m. Ann Tuttle (Tittle)
   daughter Amelia S. K. m. Dr. J. F. C. Hadel
   son Jeremiah McK. m. Olevia Stansbury

Kimble, Elijah Sr. b. Eng. 1782 (Md. 1779) d. Ohio 1852   **Pvt. Ohio Mil.**
   m. Mary Ann Bradford — son Elijah Jr. m. Clarinda Bradford

Kimbrough, Duke b. N.C. 1762 d. Tenn. 1849   **Tenn. 1799-1849**
   m. Eunice Carlock   **Preacher**
   son Bradley m. Martha Wilcox Whitaker

Kimmel, Jacob b. Pa. 1757 d. Pa. 1824 m. Mary Hoffman   **Pvt. Pa. Mil.**
   son Solomon m. Mary Catherine Good

Kincaid, George William b.— Md. d. Pa. 1830   **Pvt. Pa. Mil.**
   m. Jane Linthicum — daughter Ella m. George Hoover

Kincaid, John H. b. Ohio 1779 d. Ohio 1824   **Col. Ohio Mil.**
   m. Sarah Hannah — daughter Elizabeth m. John B. McClanahan
   son John H. m. Barbara Lawrence

Kincaid, Mathew b. Pa. 1793 d. Ohio 1871   **Cpl. Pa. Mil.**
   m. Rebekah Curtis — son Paul R. m. Lo Ruhamah Dunn

Kincaid, William T. b. Pa. 1786 d. Ill. 1876 m. Elizabeth Mace   **Pvt. Ky. Vol.**
   son John M. m. Temperance Rattan

Kincheloe, Stephen b. Va. d. Ky. m. (2) Elizabeth Tyler   **Sgt. Ky. Vol.**
   son William H. m. Margaret Lynn (1)

Kinchen, Uriah b. Ga. 1780 d. Ga. 1836   **Cpl., Lt. Ga. Mil.**
   m. Sarah Elizabeth Smith — son George T. m. Clarissa Ann Hester

Kindred, Edward b. Va. 1785 d. Ill. 1872 m. Rachel Webb   **Lt. Tenn. Mil.**
   daughter Martha Jane m. William Lewis Moss

King, Abraham b. Ga. 1797 d. S.C. 1855 m. Anis Taylor   Pvt. S.C. Mil.
daughter Rachel m. George Washington Lewis

King, Adam b. D.C. 1765 d. D.C. m. Grace Doyle   Maj. D.C. Mil.
daughter Mary E. m. Richard T. Queen

King, Asa b.— d. N.J. 1833 m. Abigail Shoneberger   Pvt. N.J. Mil.
daughter Ann m. William Wood Carman

King, Christian b. Ger. 1784 d. Ohio 1852   Pvt. Ohio Mil.
m. Margaret Basore (Bashore) — son Michael m. Franey Auspach

King, Dan b. Conn. 1791 d. R.I. 1864 m. Cynthia Pride   Pvt. Conn. Mil.
son Charles P. m. Ellen Bethia Thompson

King, Darius b. Pa. 1796 d. N.Y. 1886 m. Caroline Poulder   Pvt. N.Y. Mil.
Vol. 28

King, Elijah b. Va. c. 1771 d. Ky. 1843   Sheriff, Ky. 1813-14
m. Elizabeth Smith   Co. Justice, Ky. 1808-10
daughter Sarah m. John Eakins

King, James b. Va. or Md. 1777 d. W. Va. 1864   Lt. Va. Mil.
m. (2) Emma Short — daughter Margaret m. Henry Chidester

King, James b. N.J. 1771 d. N.J. 1838 m. Sarah Ann Curran   Cpl. N.J. Mil.
son Elias B. m. Mary Arnot

King, James b. Eng. 1752 d. Tenn. 1825   Treaty Commissioner
m. Sarah Goodson   Tenn. 1805
son James Jr. m. Mourning M. Watkins

King, James Moore b. N.C. 1792 d. Tenn.   Cpl. Tenn. Mil.
m. Martha Batey—son Charles H. m. Ann Wood

King, John b. Vt. 1790 d. Ill. 1850   Pvt. Vt. Lt. Dragoons
m. Anna Sturdevant
daughter Myranda m. Washington Reed Wallace

King, John b. Mass. 1787 d. Pa. 1842 m. Betsey Kilson   Capt. Pa. Mil.
son Rufus P. m. Mary Sebrina James

King, John b. Va. 1798 d. Ohio 1873 m. Jane Finley   Pvt. Va. Mil.
daughter Mary m. Michael Bulger

King, John Christian b. Ger. 1754 d. Ohio 1823   Pat. Va. 1786-1792
m. Ann Bane — son Peter m. Mary Magdalene Whitmer

King, John Edwards b. Va. 1757 d. Ky. 1828   Brig. Gen. Ky. Mil.
m. Sarah Clifton — son Alfred m. Nancy Haggard
son Milton m. Susan Wiles
son William m. Emily Wakefield

King, Nathan b. N.Y. 1787 d. Ia. 1867 m. Rebecca Conant   Pvt. N.Y. Mil.
son Noah L. m. Mary Lown

King, Peter b. Ger. 1782 d. Ohio 1858   Cpl. Ohio Mil.
m. Mary Magdalene Whitmer—daughter Rebecca m. Isaac Zartman

King, Robert b. N.J. 1785 d. N.J. 1869 m. Jane Griffith   Pvt. Pa. Art.
son Griffith m. Elizabeth Vanderhoof

King, Thomas b. Va. 1760 d. Ky. bef. 1838   Capt. Ky.
m. Elizabeth Cotton; Anna — daughter Sarah m. Elijah Dodson

King, Thomas Sr. b. Pa. 1754 d. Tenn. 1847 m. Susan Sharp   Pvt. N.C. Mil.
son William m. Martha Crouch

King, Thomas Frothingham b. Mass. 1785 d. N.Y. 1871   Pvt. N.Y. Mil.
m. Submit Jaynes—son Seymour m. Anice E. Lebo

King, William b. Va. 1770 d. Ohio 1836 m. Sarah Green Pvt. Ohio Mil.
 daughter Jemima m. Titus Dungan

King, William b. Ire. 1771 d. D.C. 1854 Sgt. D.C. Mil.
 m. Christina Gozler Fowler —son James m. Charlotte Meyers Libbey

King, William b. Tenn. 1796 d. Tenn. 1868 Pvt. Tenn. Mil.
 m. Martha Crouch — son Louallen m. Amanda Weessner

King, William b. Nova Scotia 1786 d. N.Y. 1829 1st. Lt. Mass. Mil.
 m. Eliza Ingersol — son Frederic H. m. Catherine Marie Pierce

King, William b. Va. c. 1780 d. Tenn. 1869 Indian Fighter N.C.-Tenn
 m. Elizabeth Willson — daughter Catherine m. William Tarwater

King, William Jr. b. 1761 d. Vt. 1840 m.— Pvt. Mass. Mil.
 daughter Celinda m. Lewis Underwood

Kingan, William b. Ire. 1786 d. Pa. 1863 m. Christena Sarver Pvt. Pa. Mil.
 daughter Armada m. John A. Hutchman REAL DAUGHTER

Kingman, John b. Conn. 1770 d. N.Y. 1859 m. Mariam Isbell Col. N.Y. Mil.
 son Charles m. Nancy Root

Kingsbury, Andrew b. Conn. 1759 Comptroller of Public Accts.
 d. Conn. 1837 m. Mary Osborn Conn. 1791
 daughter Harriet m. Russell Talcott

Kingsbury, Emmons b. Mass. 1779 d. Me. 1862 Capt. Mass. (Me.) Mil.
 m. Hannah Ryder — son Otis m. Sarah Hathorn (Hawthorne)

Kingsley, Charles b. Mass. 1795 d. N.Y. 1863 Cpl. N.Y. Mil.
 m. Parmelia Boutelle — son Ashbel S. m. Harriett C. Pardee

Kinnard, Jacob b. Pa. 1793 d. Pa. 1866 m. Mary Carter Pvt. Pa .Mil.
 daughter Anne m. John G. Water

Kinnear, William Vol. 7 Pvt. U.S. Inf.

Kinney, Joseph Vol. 10 Pat. Civil Offices

Kinney, William b. Scot 1782 d. Fla. 1815 Pvt. Tenn. Mil.
 m. Eliza Mothershed — daughter Eliza M. m. Benjamin Rogers White

Kinsey, John Vol. 7 Lt. Pa. Mil.

Kinsler, Herman b. S.C. d. S.C. 1828 m.— Pat. Mem. of Ct. S.C. 1789
 son John m.—

Kinsley, Benjamin Aaron Vol. 14 Pvt. Vt. Mil.

Kinsley, Ben Alva b. Vt. 1796 d. Vt. 1870 Pvt. N.Y. Mil.
 m. Catharine Montague — son Guy m. Lucinda Ellsworth
 son Alonzo m. Alsie Emmarett Brown

Kinsley, Daniel b. Mass. 1764 d. Vt. 1828 m. Lucy Montague Pvt. N.Y. Mil.
 son Ben Alva m. Catharine Montague

Kinzie, John Vol. 17 1812 U.S. Indian Agt.

Kip, Henry b. N.J. 1770 d. N.J. 1840 Surgeon N.J. Mil.
 m. Catherine Garrison — son Peter m. Clarissa Merselis

Kip, Samuel b. N.Y. 1771 d. N.Y. 1833 m. Elizabeth Howell Ens. N.Y. Mil.
 son Samuel Jr. m. Nancy H. Fowler

Kirby, Clinton b. N.C. 1791 (ca.) d. Ala. 1876 Pvt. Tenn. Inf.
 m. (1) Mariah P. Trice—son Thomas m. Mary Boyd

Kirgan, Arthur b. Ky. 1795 d. Tex. 1866 m. Sarah Bland   Pvt. Ky. Mil.
daughter Martha m. W. H. Smith REAL DAUGHTER

Kirk, George b. S.C. 1790 d. S.C. 1873 m. Ellen Mayfield   Pvt. S.C. Mil.
daughter Mary Eleanor m. Felix G. Whitlock

Kirkendall, Daniel David b. Pa. 1792 d. Ohio 1853   Pvt. Ohio Mil.
m. Sarah Ann Campbell — daughter Mary m. Thomas Craig

Kirker, Thomas b. Ire. 1760 d. Ohio 1837 m. Sarah   Governor of Ohio
Smith — son George S. m. Mary M. Cunningham   Civil Offices
daughter Rebecca A. m. Dr. D. M. McConoughy   Ohio 1807-8
son William m. Esther Williamson

Kirkham, Thomas b. Ga. 1786 d. Miss 1832   Lt. Miss. Mil.
m. Elizabeth Prewett — daughter Anne T. m. Joseph Warder

Kirkpatrick, Amos b. Ky. 1779 d. Tenn. 1861   Sgt. W. Tenn. Mil.
m. Sarah Green Ellis — son Ellis m. Anne Fowler

Kirkpatrick, Andrew b. N.J. 1775 d. Ohio 1859   Sgt. Ohio Mil.
m. Elizabeth Baldwin — son John (Kirk) m. Susan Bingham

Kirkpatrick, James b. S.C. 1770/77 d. Ala. 1847   Pvt. Pa. Regt.
m. Sarah Pettijohn — son Robert H. m. Mary Elizabeth Norman

Kirkpatrick, James b. Va. 1791 d. Ohio 1829   Pvt. Ohio Mil.
m. Mary Kincaid — son Thomas M. m. Hattie Foster

Kirkpatrick, John b. Pa. 1774 d. Ohio 1865   Pvt. Ohio Mil.
m. Agnes Johnston — son John m. Nancy Ogden

Kirkpatrick, Joseph b. 1786 d. Tenn. 1852   Capt. Tenn. Mil.
m. Charity Hodge — daughter Jane E. m. George Smith Williamson

Kirkpatrick, James b. Va. 1791 d. Ohio 1829   Pvt. Ohio Mil.
m. Mary Kincaid — daughter Sarah m. Thomas Kirkpatrick Ewart

Kirkwood, Joseph b. Del. 1784 d. Ohio 1856   Lt. Ohio Mil.
m. Margaret Gillespie
daughter Catharine S. m. Dr. James McCune McConahey

Kirtley, Jeremiah b. Va. 1783 d. Ky. 1844 m. Sally Johnson   Adj. Ky. Inf.
daughter Almedia m. William Watts

Kiser, Daniel (Kaiser) b. 1790 d. 1860 m. Lucy Turley   Sgt. Va. Mil.
daughter Nancy m. Martin Austin Gauldin

Kiser, Daniel b. Va. 1782 d. Va. m. Mary   Pvt. D.C. Mil.
daughter Mary A. m. Samuel Koiner

Kiser, John b. Pa. 1790 d. Pa. 1868 m. Eleanor Howell   Pvt. Pa. Mil.
daughter Mary Ann m. Richmond Barge, Jr.

Kiser, Philip b. 1773 d. Ohio 1817 m. Elizabeth Kite   Capt. Ohio Mil.
daughter Anna m. Daniel Snyder

Kitchell, Aaron   Vol. 15   N.J. Civil Officer

Kitchen, Joseph b. N.J. 1763 d. W. Va. 1835   Pvt. Va. Mil. 1813/14
m. (2) Catherine Ghulic
daughter Alena (Alley) m. Kezekiah Thatcher

Kithcart, Joseph b. Pa. 1770 d. Ohio 1814   Ohio Surveyor 1808
m. Elizabeth Cunningham — son Cunningham m. Jane Dunlap

Kittle, John   Vol. 13   Pvt. Va. Mil.

Klase, Valentine Sr. b. Pa. d. Pa. 1812   Lt. Pa. Mil.
  m. Mary Eva Smitten — son Abraham m. Elizabeth Smith

Kleckner, Anthony b. Pa. 1793 d. Pa. 1860 m. Sarah   Pvt. Pa. Mil.
  son Robert m. Catherine Brungard

Kline, George b. Pa. 1791 d. Pa. 1844 m. Margaret Demars   Pvt. Pa. Mil.
  son James m. Mary D. Mumford

Kline, Harman b. 1760 d. Pa. 1823 m. Diana Robbins   Capt. Mil.
  son Morris m. Elizabeth Lee

Kline, Jacob   Vol. 12   Cpl. Ohio Mil.

Kline, Morris b. Pa. 1785 d. Mich. 1871 m. Elizabeth Lee   Pvt. Pa. Mil.
  son Eli m. Anna Maria Bender

Kline, (Cline), Philip b. Pa. 1792 d. Pa. 1869   Pvt. Pa. Mil.
  m. Elizabeth Rewalt
  daughter Elspy Rebecca m. Andrew Jackson Polk

Klinefelter, Adam b. Pa. 1796 d. Pa. 1871   Pvt. 1814 Pa. Mil.
  m. Sarah Ann Doudel — daughter Elizabeth Ann m. Philip King

Klinefelter, Michael b. Ger. 1736 d. Pa. 1807   Capt. Pa. Mil. 1799
  m. Anna Maria Elizabeth (2)   Sheriff, Pa. 1807
  son Adam m. Sarah Ann Doudel

Kling, John George b. N.Y. 1780 d. N.Y. 1867   Capt. N.Y. Mil.
  m. Lane Dailey — son George m. Diana Shafer

Klippinger (Clippinger), Anthony b. Pa. 1753 d. Pa. 1806   Pvt. Pa. Mil.
  m. Anna Margretta Heckman — son John H. m. Elizabeth Kuntz

Klippinger (Clippinger), Frederick b. Pa. 1749 d. Pa. 1802   Pvt. Pa. Mil.
  m. Maria Barbara Best — daughter Catherine m. George Cressler

Klock, George J.   Vol. 14   Pvt. N.Y. Mil.

Klock, Peter b. N.Y. 1778 d. N.Y. 1873 m. Nancy Stawing   Capt. N.Y. Mil.
  daughter Catharine m. Leonard Hodgkins

Knaggs, Whitmore b. Ohio 1762 d. Mich 1827   Scout for Gen. Wayne
  m. Josette Labadie — son George B. m. Laura Bosley

Knap, Edward b. 1763 d. Ohio 1821 m. Esther   Corp. Mass. Mil.
  daughter Sythenia m. Francis Carner

Knapp, Auren b. Conn. 1795 d. Ore. 1876   Pvt. Mass. Mil.
  m. (1) Sarah Maria Burrell — son Richard B. m. Minnie A.

Knapp, Caleb b. W. Va. 1787 d. W. Va. 1830   Juror etc. Va. 1792-1813
  m. Elizabeth — son Moses m. Elizabeth Anderson

Knapp, Henry b. Vt. 1787 d. Vt. 1859 m. Lucy Keyes   Pvt. Vt. Mil.
  daughter Sophia m. Samuel Udall Richmond REAL DAUGHTER

Knapp, James b. N.Y. 1796 d. N.Y. 1853 m. Jane Elwood   Sgt. N.Y. Mil.
  son Edward m. Jennie C. Graham

Knapp, John H.   Vol. 7   Sgt. N.Y. Mil.

Knapp, John H. b. Conn. 1787 d. Conn. 1878   Capt. Conn. Mil.
  m. Esther Turney — son Rufus m. Caroline Trubee

Knapp, John Holly b. 1791 d. Ia. 1837 m. Harriet Seeley   Sgt. N.Y. Mil.
  daughter Almeda Ann m. Joseph S. Douglas

Knapp, Jonathan (John) b. Conn. 1756 d. N.Y. 1817   Sgt. N.Y. Mil.
m. Abigail Palmer — son Lyman m. Adeline Maxwell

Knapp, Robert b. N.Y. 1793 d. N.Y. 1859 m. Sarah Phillips   Pvt. N.Y. Mil.
daughter Rachel m. Edmund Jordan Hammond

Knauss (Knouse), George Frederick b. Pa. 1748 d. Pa. 1817   Pvt. Pa. Mil.
m (2) Maria M. Saeger — son Solomon m. Maria Magdalena Keck

Knauss (Knouse), Solomon b. Pa. 1781 d. Pa. 1853   Pvt. Pa. Mil.
m. Magdelena Keck — son Jesse m. Sarah Heinly

Knerr, Andrew b. Pa. 1758 d. Pa. 1840   Pvt. Pa. Cavalry
m. Catherine Elizabeth Schall — daughter Catherine m. Paul Kramlich

Knickerbocker, Andrus b. N.Y. 1792 d. N.Y. 1873   Pvt. N.Y. Mil.
m. Margaret H. — daughter Lanny m. William Heal

Knight, Ephraim b. Mass. (Me.) 1776 d. Me. 1851   Pvt. Mass. (Me.) Mil.
m.— — son Ephraim Jr. m. Betsey

Knight, George b. Va. 1784 d. Miss. 1869   Pvt. La. Mil.
m. Charity Hamilton — son Mark m. Martha Shepherd

Knight, Giles b. Pa. 1719 d. Pa. 1799 m. Elizabeth James   Mem. of Leg.
son Israel m. Sarah Tyson   Pa. 1791

Knight, Jacob b. R.I. 1784 d. R.I. 1856   2nd Maj. R.I. Mil.
m. Freelove Fiske — son Dexter m. Cynthia Louise Hart

Knight, James b. N.C. about 1782 d. N.C. 1847 m.—   Ens. N.C. Mil.
daughter Druscilla m. Simons Bythel Staton

Knight, John b. Ky. d. Ky. 1873 m. Nancy Dowden   Capt. Ky. Mil.
daughter Elzina m. Stephen Lee

Knight, John b. Ire. d. N.Y. 1815 m. Seclinda House   Pvt. N.Y.
daughter Mary Ann m. David Ross

Knight, Jonathan   Vol. 4   Capt. Vt. Mil.

Knight, Nathaniel b. Mass. (Me.) 1775 d. Me. 1832   Sgt. Mass. (Me.) Mil.
m. Hannah Mugford — son George W. m. Hannah Jackson Davis

Knight, Richard b. Pa. 1793 d. Pa. 1869   Pvt. Pa. Mil.
m. Elizabeth Ewing — son Luther m. Virginia Gardner

Knight, Richard b. N.Y. 1767 d. Pa. 1849 m. Sarah Berry   Pvt. Pa. Mil.
daughter Anne m. B. Franklin Gregory REAL DAUGHTER

Knight, Samuel b. Mass. 1730 d. Vt. 1804   Chief Judge of Supreme Ct. 1791
m. Mary — son John m. Sally Allen   Delegate to Convention 1793

Knight, Solomon b. Mass. (Me.) 1794 d. Me. 1850   Pvt. Mass. (Me.) Mil.
m. Polly Pratt — daughter Eliza J. m. Daniel G. Whitney

Knight, Wade H. b. N.C. 1798 d. Tenn.   Pvt. Tenn. Mil.
m. Elizabeth Knight — son George W. m. Margaret Brown

Knisely, David b. Va. 1768 d. Ohio 1860 m. Mary Rhodes   Pvt. Ohio Mil.
son Joseph m. Isabella Watts

Knoop, John b. Pa. 1767 d. Ohio 1842 m. Barbara Holstein   Pvt. Ohio Mil.
daughter Nancy m. Isaac Sill Sheets

Knowles, William b. Del. 1785 d. Del. 1857   Pvt. Del. Mil.
m. Nelly Collins (1)
daughter Hester Eleanor m. Rev. Fletcher E. Marine

Knowlton, Isaac b. N.Y. 1797 d. N.Y. 1883   Pvt. N.Y. Mil.
m. Rachel Whitbeck — daughter Almira Pamelia m. Archibald Jennings

Knowlton, Samuel b. Mass. (Me.) 1783 d. Ohio 1857   Pvt. Mass.(Me.) Mil.
m. Olive Butler — son Samuel Jr. m. Julia Hadley

Knox, John   Vol. 16   Pvt. W. Tenn. Mil.

Knox, John M.   Vol. 11   Pvt. Ky. Mil.

Knox, Samuel b. Ire. 1756 d. Md. 1832 m. Grace Gilmour   Md. Preacher
daughter Martha m. William Swan

Knox, William b. Vt. 1780 d. N.Y. 1839 m. Rhoda Gould   Capt. N.Y. Mil.
daughter Mary Ann m. John N. Cole

Knox, William   Vol. 16   Lt. N.Y. Mil.

Koch, Henry b. Pa. about 1787 d. Pa. 1824   Pvt. Pa. Mil.
m. Catherine Gerhart — daughter Susannah m. Robert Payne

Koenig, Mathias b. Ger. 1734 d. Pa. 1810   Cpl. Pa. Mil.
m. Eva Christina Hartzell — son George David m. Margaret Ringle

Koger, Joseph b. S.C. 1779 d. Miss. 1866 m. Mary Murray   Capt. S.C. Mil.
daughter Martha Matilda m. Joshua Thomas Heard

Koger, Joseph Jr. b. S.C. 1779 d. Miss. 1866 (73)   Capt. S.C. Troops
m. Abigail Sleigh Milhous (Mrs.?)
daughter Elizabeth m. Isaac Murray

Kohl (Cole), Jacob b. Pa. 1752 d. Pa. 1827   Sgt. Pa. Mil.
m. Elizabeth Buck — son Jacob B. m. Mary Ann Messenkop

Kolb, John William b. Md. 1776 d. Md. 1835   Lt. Md. Mil.
m. Eve (Maria Ann) Miller — son William m. Catherine Crum

Kolb, Peter b. S.C. 1762 d. Ga. 1835   Mem. House of Rep.
m. Theny Gates — son Martin m. Susan Butt   1813-14

Kollock, Shepard b. Del. 1750 d. N.J. 1839   Judge N.J. 1804
m. Susannah Arnett
daughter Susan Davis m. John Witherspoon (Rev.)

Koons, (Kuntz) Peter b. Pa. 1759 d. Pa. 1847   Pvt. Pa. Mil.
m. Margaret Snyder — daughter Lydia m. John D. Howard
daughter Polly m. Nicholas Border

Koontz, John b. 1760 d.—m. Jane Crum   Vol. 1   Col. Va. Mil.
son Jacob m. Maria Gilbert Graham

Kormany, Martin b. Pa. 1794 d. Va. 1857   Pvt. Va. Mil.
m. Elizabeth Weaver — son David m. Rachel Scherrer

Kornegay, Harget b. N.C. 1794 d. N.C. 1875   Pvt. N.C. Mil.
m. Susan Simmons — son Simmons m. Eliza Loftin

Krake, Henry b. N.Y. 1787 d. N.Y. 1879   Pvt. N.Y. Mil.
m. Elizabeth Baxter — son John A. m. Sarah Elizabeth Turner
daughter Sallie m. Cornelius Bart

Kreamer, Daniel Sr. b.— d.— m. Miss Kern   Vol. 27   Pvt. Pa. Mil.
son Daniel Jr. m. Miss Neese

Krepps, John b. 1764 d. Pa. 1845 m. Mary Gillespie   Pvt. Pa. Mil.
son Samuel J. m. Elizabeth Brooke

Krom, Jacobus G. b. N.Y. 1772 d. N.Y. 1854 m.—   Pvt. N.Y. Mil.
son John m. Margaret

Kresge, Conrod b. Swit. c. 1740 d. Pa. 1805   **Pvt. Pa. Mil.**
  m. Anna Margaret Kohl — son Conrad Jr. m. Elizabeth Marie Kunkle

Krum, Mathew b. N.Y. 1779 d. N.Y. 1863   **Matross N.Y. Mil.**
  m. Margaret Van Denmark — son Abram P. m. Catherine Mott

Kuder, Solomon b. Pa. 1790 d. Ohio 1873 m. Catherine Row   **Pvt. Ohio Mil.**
  daughter Caroline m. Edward Ketcham
  daughter Catherine m. Edwin Tuller
  daughter Margaret Ann m. John Lewis McColley
  daughter Victoria V. m. Edward Barney Beverstock

Kuntz, Henry b. Pa. 1794 d. Ohio 1877 m. Catharine Kromisk   **Pvt. Pa. Mil.**
  son Henry Jr. m. Mary Ruth Zimmerman (2)

Kuntze, Lewis b. Fra. 1783 d. Ga. 1837 m. Gertrude Wingate   **Sgt. Ga. Mil.**
  daughter Ann m. William Lingo Johnson

Kurtz, Abraham b.— d. Pa. 1799 m. Barbara Blanck   **Pvt. Pa. Mil. 1787**
  son John m. Magdalina Gockley

Kurtz, John   Vol. 17   **Lt. D.C. Mil.**

Kyle, Joshua Sr. b. Pa. 1766 d. Ohio 1842 m. Mary Stewart   **Ens. Pa. Mil.**
  daughter Anna m. Cornelius Tomson   **Pvt. Ohio Mil.**

Kyle, Samuel b. Pa. 1777 d. Ohio 1857 m. Rachel Jackson   **Sgt. Ohio Mil.**
  son Roland C. m. Anna Jackson Dunlap   **Asso. Judge Ohio**
  son Thomas B. m. Margaret J.   **Surveyor of Ohio 1810**

L

LaBranche, Alexandre b. 1751 d.—   **Col. La. Mil. 1814-15**
  m. Marie Jeanne Piseros   **La. Leg. 1812**
  daughter Marie Feliete m. Louis Edmond Fortier

Lacey, (Lacy), James b. Tenn. (N.C.) 1771 d. Tenn. 1847   **Pvt. Tenn. Mil.**
  m. Nancy Edens — son John m. Nancy Hyder

Lachman, Christian   Vol. 11   **Pvt. Pa. Mil.**

Lacock, Abner b. Va. 1770 d. Pa. 1837   **Brig. Gen. Pa. Mil. 1802**
  m. Hannah Eddy — son Atlas E. m. Louisa Lyon   **Pa. Senator 1813**
  son Atlas E. m. Louisa Lyon
  daughter Bethsheba m. Ephrion Pentland

Lacy, Charles Christian b. Va. 1775 d. Va. 1832   **Lt. Va. Mil.**
  m. Frances Washington Terrill
  daughter Mary Elizabeth m. Dr. William Cox

Lacy, William Sterling b. 1791 d. Ark. 1880   **Maj. Tenn. Mil.**
  m. (2) Julia Eldredge
  daughter Fannie m. Daniel B. Lester REAL DAUGHTER
  son Watson E. m. Sallie Holcombe

LaFargue, Francois b. West Indies 1783(82) d. La. 1863   **Pvt. La. Vol.**
  m. Rosalie Jacques Nicholas
  daughter Marie Melanie m. Edouard Lafonta

La Faucherie, John b. ca. 1750 d. after 1837 m.—   **Teamster N.J. Inf.**
  son F. Rostain LaFaucherie m. Louisa Pitcher

Lafferanderie, Lucien b. Fra. 1792 d. La. 1850   **Pvt. La. Mil.**
  m. Marianna Dolille Dupart
  daughter Jean Marie m. Olympe Quingard

Laidler, John b. British Isles. 1783 d. Ga. 1856   **Pvt. Ga. Mil.**
  m. Elizabeth Watkins—son John Jr. m. (1) Catherine Elizabeth Fudge

Lake, Daniel William b. N.Y. 1780 d. N.Y. 1835   Pvt. N.Y. Mil.
    m. Mary Gifford — son Arthur G. m. Anna G. Delaney

Lake, Edward D. b. Conn. 1776 d. N.Y. 1831   Ens. N.Y. Inf.
    m. Lois Dennison — son Dennison m. Harriet Arnold

Lake, George Bixby Sr. b. Mass. 1750 d. Vt. 1816   Capt. Vt. Mil.
    m. Sarah Lovejoy — son George B. Jr. m. Mary Ritter

Lakey, (Locke, Lockey), Francis b. N.C. 1768 d. N.C. 1812   Pvt. N.C. Mil.
    m. Mary — son Abraham B. m. Nancy Phillips

Lakin, John G. b. N.H. 1795 d. N.Y. 1870   Cpl. U.S. Mil.
    m. Catherine Evans — daughter Jane m. Daniel Candee
    son Lafayette m. Hannah E. Corwin

Lamb, Chester Sr. b. Mass. 1777 d. N.Y. 1820   Cpl. Mass. Mil.
    m. Hannah Bates — son Chester Jr. m. Mary Crooks

Lamb, David b. Mass. 1758 d. Mass. 1815 m. Judith Fitts   Cpl. Mass. Mil.
    daughter Eleanor m. Martin Twichell

Lamb, David b. S.C. 1792 d. Tenn. 1842   Pvt. Tenn. Vol.
    m. Hester Landaum — daughter Mary Jane m. Andrew Shinall

Lamb, Isaac b. N.C. 1765 d. N.C. 1825 m. (1) Mary Norman   Sheriff N.C.
    daughter Nancy D. m. Josiah Earle

Lamb, John b. Ky. 1790 d. Ky. 1878 m. Lucy Porter   Pvt. Ky. Mil.
    daughter Kerrilla m. Emery Whitaker

Lamb, Nahum b. Mass. 1759 d. Mass. 1842   Pvt. & Co. Clerk
    m. Lydia Daggett — son Jason m. Nancy Cruver   Clerk of Mass. 1792

Lamb, Peter b. Va. 1781 d. Ohio 1867 m. Mary Walters   Capt. Ohio Mil.
    daughter Louisa Jane m. David Eversole

Lamb, Solomon b. N.Y. 1780 d. Ind. 1848   Pvt. Ind. Terr. Mil.
    m. Elizabeth H. Shepherd — daughter Helen m. James Thomas Morgan

Lambden, (Lamdin), James Morsell b. Md. 1790 d. Md. 1869, Cpl. Md. Mil.
    m. Emily Banning — daughter Emily m. John Mauldin

Lambert, Isaac b. Mass 1771 d. Me. 1861   Pvt. Mass. (Me.) Mil.
    m. Mary Strout — daughter Jane S. m. Nelson Dingley Jr.

Lambert, Lewis b. N.Y. 1773 d. N.Y. 1862 m. Mary Caskey   Pvt. N.Y. Mil.
    daughter Jane m. Solomon Dunning

Lambden, James Morsele   Vol. 5   Pvt. Md. Mil.

Lambkins, Samuel L. b. N.C. 1777 d. Ky. 1820   Pvt. N.C. Mil.
    m. Rachel Moores — daughter Sarah H. m. Martin D. Noland

Lamoreux, Thomas b. N.Y. 1748 d. Pa. 1829   Pvt. Pa. Mil. 1790
    m. Keturah Tuttle — son James m. Sarah Hunter
    daughter Martha m. Samuel Pringle
    daughter Temperance m. Matthias Van Loon
    son Joshua m. Martha Ives

Lamoreux, William b. N.Y. 1796 d. Wisc. 1880   Pvt. N.Y. Mil.
    m. Harriett Barnard — daughter Ormenta F. m. William F. Schley

LaMotte, John b. Md. 1796 d. Md. 1884 m. Rachel Hoover   Pvt. Md. Mil.
    son William Oliver m. Catherine Althouse

Lampkin, John b. Va. 1739 d. Va. 1830   Capt. Va. Troops
   m. Mrs. Mary Story Lee — daughter Mary m. William Freeman

Lampkin, Lewis, b. N.C. 1786 d. Ga. 1840 m. Andelica Ryan   Pvt. Ga. Mil.
   son Edward m. Mary Liza P. Wright

Lanaux, Charles Julien b. La. 1792 d. Cuba 1826   Pvt. La. Vol.
   m. Aglee Roussell
   daughter Caroline m. Jules Delery

Lanaux, Phillippe b. 1752 d. 1816   Capt. Maj. La. Vol.
   m. Angelique Bozonnier — son Charles Julian m. Aimee Aglae Roussel

Lancaster, Joseph Bradford b. Ky. d. Fla. c. 1840   Capt. Ky. Vol.
   m. Anna Blair — son William m. Josephine Morgan

Lancaster, Washington b. Ga. 1784 d. Ga. 1869   Sgt. Ga. Mil.
   m. Nancy Wilson — son William W. m. Pheriby Wilson

Lance, William b. Ger. d. N.J. m. Margaret Apgar   Pvt. N.J. Mil.
   son William Jr. m. Sarah Taylor

Lance, William b. N.J. d. N.J. m. Sarah Tayor   Vol. 26   Pvt. N.J. Mil.
   daughter Hariet T. m. Andrew Cregar

Land, Nathaniel D. b. Va. 1783 d. Va. 1845   Sgt. Va. Lt. Inf.
   m. Mary Rochelle — son Henry C. m. Mary R. Marabel

Land, Peter b. Va. 1763 d. Va. 1845 m. Elizabeth Keeling   Capt. Va. Mil.
   son Edward C. m. Elizabeth Smith Foreman
   daughter Lovy m. Thomas Keeling

Landers, Joseph Jr. b. Mass. 1722 d. Conn. 1801   Mem. of Conn. Legis.
   m. Sarah — son Seth m. Susan Stone

Landiss, Isaac b. N.C. 1788 d. Ill. 1867 m. Esther King   1st Sgt. Tenn. Mil.
   daughter Catherine m. William Speaks, Jr.

Landis, John b. Pa. 1755 d. Pa. 1837 m.—   Pvt. Pa. Mil. 1794-7
   son John Jr. m. Anna Bachman

Landis, Joseph b. Pa. 1795 d. Ohio 1865   Pvt. Pa. Mil.
   m. Hetty Diffenderfer — daughter Susanna m. John Sapp

Landrum, Thomas b. 1759 d. 1833 m. Nancy Bell   Lt. Col. Ga. Mil.
   daughter Mary (Polly) m. William Norton

Landry, Pierre Joseph b. 1770 d. 1843   Capt. La. Mil.
   m. Larguerite Rosalie Capdeville
   son Benjamin Achille m. Pauline Breaux Amore

Lane, Dutton b. Md. 1778 d. Wisc. 1816 or 1827   Lt. Ohio Mil.
   m. Martha Prichard — son Richard m. Grace Sunderland

Lane, Isaac b. Md. 1760 d. Tenn. 1851 m. Sarah Russell   Capt. Tenn. Mil.
   daughter Mary m. Elijah Hurst   1796-1801 Civil Services

Lane, James b. Pa. 1789 d. Ill. 1852 m. Janette Wishart   Lt. Pa. Mil.
   son Robert P. m. Mary Brice

Lane, James Hardage b. Va. 1764 d. Ky. 1849   Lt. Ky. Mil.
   m. Mary Higgins — daughter Sally m. Samuel Stone

Lane, Job b. Conn. 1787 d. Vt. 1859   Pvt., Teamster Conn. Mil.
   m. Sarah Terrill — son Henry m. Mary Parker Peck

Lane, Joel b. N.C. c. 1746 d. N.C. 1795   Senator N.C. 1782-92
   m. (2) Mary Hinton — son John m. Sarah E. Jones

Lane, Roswell b. 1798 d. N.Y. 1870 m. Jerusha Rhoades   Pvt. N.Y. Mil.
daughter Sarah m. Brooks Bowman Hazelton

Lane, Samuel b. N.J. 1776 d. N.J. 1849 m. Catherine King   Pvt. N.J. Mil.
son Peter D. m. Almyrah Thompson

Lane, Samuel b. Pa. 1745 d. Pa. 1814   Pvt. Pa. Mil. 1784
m. Phoebe Coates — daughter Priscilla m. James Irwin

Lane, Thomas   Vol. 12   Pvt. Ga. Mil.

Lane, Thomas b. Va. 1764 d. Ga. 1829 m. Nancy Healy   Pvt. Ga. Mil.
son John A. m. Ann (Nancy) Pettyway Mayfield

Lane, Tidence b. 1789-8 d. Tenn. (Miss.) 1851   Col. Qtr. Mst. W. Tenn. Mil.
m. Abigail Hewes Thomas — daughter Elizabeth m. Robert A. Clark
son James T. m. Quintinia Moss

Lane, William Tidence   Vol. 12   Pvt. E. Tenn. Mil.

LaNeuville, Adolph b. Fra. 1758 d. Fra. 1835   Adj. Inspect. Gen. La.
m. Marie Louise de Seville — son Adolphe Jr. m. Albina T. Y. Alvarez

Lang, George b. N.H. 1791 d. N.H. 1882 m. Susan Davis   Music N.H. Mil.
son Benjamin F. m. Hannah Elizabeth Harvey

Lang, John (Jack) b. West Indies 1793 d. Mass. 1838   Seaman U. S. Navy
m. Phebe B. Lamos — daughter Mary Elizabeth m. Joel Eaton Foster

Lang, Samuel b. N.H. 1761 d. (Me.) Mass. 1803   3rd. Sgt. (Me.) Mass. Mil.
m. Irana Damon — son John D. m. Ann Elmira Stackpole

Langford, Jarius b. Ga. 1778 d. Ark. 1859 m. Mary Christie   Pvt. Ga. Mil.
son William C. m. Martha
m. Rebecca Bishop — daughter Narcissa m. Archibald Johnston

Lanier, Alexander Chalmers b. N.C. 1779 d. Ind. 1820   Maj. Ohio Mil.
m. Druscilla Doughty — son James F. D. m. Elizabeth Gardner

Lanier, James b. Va. 1724-6 d. N.C. c. 1786   Mem. of Comm. of Safety
m. Mary Cooke — son Sampson m. Elizabeth Massey   1785 N.C.

Lanier, Lewis b. Va. 1756 d. Ga. 1839   Maj. Ga. Mil.
m. Esther Butts Thorne — son Isaac m. Sarah Hurst

Lank, Elzey   Vol. 13   Pvt. Del. Mil.

Lanning, Elijah   Vol. 16   Fifer N.J. Mil.

Lansdale, John Wesley b. Md. 1791 d. Md. 1836   Capt. Md. Mil.
m. Miranda Stevenson — son Francis Asbury m. Harriett Ann Morrow

Lansdown, George   Vol. 9   Ens. Va. Mil.

Lantz, Andrew b. Pa. 1773 d. Pa. 1859   Pvt. Pa. Mil. 1798
m. Mary Sanover — son Andrew Jr. m. Mary Bailey

Lantz, Jonas b. Va. 1787 d. Va. 1853 m. Eleanor Arbogast   Pvt. Va. Mil.
daughter Phoebe m. Amos Wimer

Lapretre, Jean Baptiste b. La. 1800 d. Va. 1871   Pvt. La.
m. Sophie Andry — daughter Amanda m. Juan Manuel Oriel

Lapsley, John b. Va. 1783 d. Mo. 1859 m. Mary Wear McKee   Lt. Ky. Mil.
daughter Miriam M. m. Warner Wallace

Lapsley, William b. Ky. 1793 d. Mo. 1843 m. Sarah R. Alcorn   Pvt. Ky. Mil.
daughter Mary Ann m. William Bishop REAL DAUGHTER

Larimer, Isaac   Vol. 12   Ens. Ohio Mil.

Larimore, Robert b. Va. 1796 d. Ohio 1856 m. Mary Smith   Cpl. Va. Mil.
   son Robert Jr. m. Amelia Stoddard

Larison, Theodorus b. N.J. 1773 d. Pa. 1857   Pvt. N.Y. Vol.
   m. Elizabeth Updyke — son John m. Mary Huntley

Larkin, Elam b. Vt. 1792 d. N.Y. 1866 m. Lucy Robinson   Drum N.Y. Mil.
   son Lorenzo D. m. Julia Griffith (2)

Larkin, John b. Vt. 1786 d. N.Y. 1865 m. Sarah Wood   Lt. N.Y. Mil.
   son Elam L. m. Martha Norton
   son Eleazer J. m. Helen Stetson

Larman, Francis b. Fra 1780 d. Va. 1865 m. Lucy Hibdon   Pvt. N.Y. Mil.
   daughter Rosetta m. Issac T. Graham

Larned, Charles b. Mass. 1793 d. Mich. 1834   Gen. Ky. Mil.
   m. Sylvia Easton Coll
   daughter Jane H. m. Alpheus Starkey Williams

LaRonde, Pierre Denis de b. La. 1762 d. La. 1824   Senator & Mem. of
   daughter Emilie E. m. Pierce de Hoa   La. Constit. Conv. 1812

Larrabee, Adam b. Conn. 1787 d. Conn. 1869   Capt. U.S. Inf.
   m. Hannah Lester
   daughter Emeline H. m. George Perkins REAL DAUGHTER

Larrabee, Daniel b. (Me.) Mass. 1782 d. Me. 1862 or 1864   Lt. Mass. Mil.
   m. Mary Quimby — daughter Betsey S. m. William Dearing
   daughter Mary Ellen m. Joseph Newcomb

Larrabee, Samuel   Vol. 9   Ens. Mass. (Me.) Mil.

Lassell, William C.   Vol. 13   Pvt. Md. Mil.

Latham, Charles b. Va. 1766 d. Ala. 1855 m. Susan Graves   Pvt. Tenn. Mil.
   son William m. Mary Katharine Braziel

Latham, Henry Bradford b. N.Y. 1770 d. N.Y.   Shipmst. N.Y. 1808-16
   m. Delia Harnet — daughter Sarah m. William Crum

Latham, James b. N.C. 1770 d. N.C. 1834 m. Rebecca   Justice N.C. 1796
   son James Jr. m. Penny

Latham, Joseph b. Conn. 1789 d. N.Y. 1867   Ens. Qtr. Mst. N.Y. Mil.
   m. Polly Crosby — daughter Helen m. John Hazzard
   son Rev. Joseph m. Lydia Nelson

Lathrop, Daniel b. Conn. 1789 d. Pa. 1842 m. Miss Perkins   Col. Pa. Mil.
   daughter Jane m. William McKune

Lathrop, John Hatch b. N.Y. 1789 d. N.Y. 1856   Capt. N.Y. Mil.
   m. Susan Froman — daughter Caroline A. m. Philo Remington

Lathrop, Oliver   Vol. 8   Surgeon N.Y. Cav.

Latil (Latillel), Joseph Timecourt b. 1796 d. 1857   Pvt. La. Mil.
   m. Mercelite Clermont
   daughter Josephine Timecourt m. Louis Henry Tabary

Laton, John b. Va. 1777 d. N.C. 1852 m. Catherine Dry   Pvt. N.C. Mil.
   son Franklin A. m. Martha Ann Solomon

LaTourrette, Peter b. N.Y. 1766 d. N.Y. 1854 m. Mary   Maj. N.J. Mil.
   daughter Elizabeth m. Peter Vlerebome

Latshaw, Peter b. Ger. 1744 d. Pa. 1840   **Pvt. Pa. Mil.**
   m. Mary Susannah Close — son John m. Catherine Haines

Lauderdale, James b. Va. ca. 1739 d. Tenn. aft. 1820   **Lt. Va. 1793**
   m. Miss Mills — son John m. Amelia Wood

Laufman, Jacob Craven b. Pa. 1793 d. Ill. 1877   **Vol. Penn. 1814**
   m. Margaret Keefer — son Keefer m. Harriet Shively

Laughlin, John   Vol. 5   **Pvt. Pa. Mil.**

Laughlin, (Laflin) John b. Vt. 1785 d. N.Y. 1846   **Pvt. Vt. Mil.**
   m. Deborah Bishop — daughter Aurilla m. Nahum Wilson

Laughlin, Mathew b. Pa. 1784 d. Ohio 1857   **Pvt. Ohio Mil.**
   m. Nancy Spillars — daughter Martha m. William Sly

Laurence, William b. N.Y. 1797 d. N.Y. 1854   **Sgt. N.Y. Mil.**
   m. Eva Phillips — son John m. Cornelia Francis Porter

Lauterman, Peter b. Ky. 1795 d. Ill. 1866   **Pvt. Ky. Mil.**
   m. Eliza Sellar Purvines
   daughter Sarah Sophia m. Mathew D. Irwin

Lavake, William b. Mass. 1794 d. Mass. 1872   **Pvt. Mass. Art.**
   m. Lucinda Tower — daughter Mary Ann m. (2) George F. Chapin

Lavenburg, Frederick b. Ger. 1758 d. Pa. 1845   **Pvt. Pa. Mil.**
   m. Catherine Minnig — son John m. Rebecca Kerbe

Law, John Archibald b. Conn. 1789 d. R.I. 1879   **Pvt. Conn. Mil.**
   m. Asha Carnal Aldrich — son William A. m. Mary Henry

Law, Samuel b. N.H. 1782 d. Mass. 1859 m. Mercy Adams   **Lt. Mass. Mil.**
   daughter Susan m. William Taylor

Lawler, Isaac b. 1793 d. aft. 1874 m. Patsy Crunk   **Pvt. Miss. Mil. 1812-13**
   son Abner Jackson m. Lorinda Coplin Lister

Lawrence, Benjamin b.— d.— m. Euphamy Borden Vol. 24   **Pvt. N.J. Mil.**
   son Joseph m. Mary E. Newell

Lawrence, Edward b. Me. 1778 d. Me. 1844   **Pvt. Me. 1799**
   m. Abigail Wells — son Daniel m. Sophia Eliz. Duel

Lawrence, James   Vol. 7   3rd. Lt. U.S. Inf.

Lawrence, John b. Mass. (Me.) 1750 d. Me. 1837, Lt. Col. Mass. (Me.) Mil.
   m. Mary Moore — son Samuel m. Susannah Allen

Lawrence, Joseph b. (Me.) Mass. 1765 d. Me.   **Pvt. Mass. Mil.**
   m. Rhoda Russell — daughter Sophronia m. John Pratt (?)

Lawrence, Joseph b. N.Y. 1790 d. Tex. 1853   **Pvt. N.Y. Mil.**
   m. Henrietta Fisher — son Solomon F. m. Julia Alice Rhea

Lawrence, Joseph (William) b. N.Y. 1770 d. Mich. 1847   **Lt. Col. N.Y. Mil.**
   m. Sybil Heath — daughter Irene Azubah m. Samuel Beach
   son James N. m. Mary B. Goodman

Lawrence, Joseph Wheelock b. Mass. 1786 d. Wisc. 1869   **Pvt. Vt. Mil.**
   m. Elizabeth Sherman — son George W. m. Isabelle Sipek

Lawrence, Nathaniel b. N.Y. 1761 d. N.Y. 1797   **Att'y. Gen. 1792-5**
   m. Elizabeth Berrien — daughter Margaret m. Philip Lindsley

Lawrence, Peter P.   Vol. 10   **Pvt. N.C. Mil.**

Lawrence, Robert b. Va. 1793 d. Va. 1866 m. Elizabeth Allen   Pvt. Va. Mil.
daughter Sarah m. Edward Godwin

Lawrence, Samuel b. Mass. (Me.) 1781 d. Vt.   Sgt. Maj. Mass. Mil.
m. Susannah Allen — daughter Lorenda m. Asahel Hill

Lawrence, William   Vol. 13, 9

Lawrence, Zachriah b. Mass. (Me.) 1786 d. Ia. 1868, Lt. Mass. (Me.) Mil.
m. Harriett Holbrook — son Perry m. Matilda Hunter

Lawrence, Zalmon Bigelow b. 1790 d. 1819   Pvt. Mass. Mil.
m. Letitia A. Averill — daughter Letitia m. Henry Green Bread

Laws, James b. Mass. 1772 d. Mass. 1860   Pvt. Mass. Mil.
m. Thankful Metcalf — son Hosea m. Fanny Jane Ames

Lawson, Epaphroditus b. Va. ca. 1781 d. Va. 1829   Pvt. Va.
m. Nancy Longworth — daughter Nancy m. William B. Rupard

Lawson, Isaac b. Va. 1788 d. Ill. 1864 m. Nancy Anderson   Sgt. Va. Mil.
son John A. m. Ellen Daughtery

Lawson, Robert b. Eng. d. Md. m. Mary MacAllister Vol. 2   Capt. Md. Mil.
son Robert Jr. m. Mary Quin

Lawson, Robert b. Ire. d. Md. m. Margaret Quinn Vol. 1   Capt. Tenn. Mil.
daughter Margaret m. Herbert Stella REAL DAUGHTER

Lawson, Roger b. Va. 1730 d. Ga. 1803   Register of Probate 1784-1790 Ga.
m. Hannah Thompson   Navigation Commissioner
son Andrew T. m. Mary Moore Barry

Lawson, Thomas b.— d. Ill. 1848 m.—   Vol. 2   Maj. Ky. Mil.
daughter Martha m. James C. Cochran

Lawton, George b. R.I. 1770 d. R.I. 1835   R.I. Justice 1803-4
m. Patience Turner —son Moses T. m. Elizabeth Tillinghast Harris

Lawton, Joseph James b. 1777 d. 1858/9   House Rep. S.C. 1804
m. Phoebe Jane Mosse
son Benjamin Wm. m. Josephine Barksdale Polhill

Lawton, William   Vol. 4   Surgeon's Mate Mass. Mil.

Laylin, John b. Pa. 1791 d. Ohio 1877 m. Olive Clark   Pvt. Ohio Mil.
daughter Mary Ette m. William Roberts

Layport, George b. Fra. c. 1735 d. Ohio 1814   Indian Fighter Ohio
m. Nancy Agnes Havelin—daughter Nancy m. William (Bill) Wilson

Layton, John b. N.J. 1734 d. N.J. 1814 m. Sarah   Pvt. N.J. Vol.
Somers Neill—son Peter m. Margaret Heath

Layton, Louder b. Del. 1770 d. Del. 1849   Pvt. Del. Lt. Inf.
m. Sarah Sipple—daughter Nancy m. Rhodes Franklin Hemmons

Layton, Thomas b. N.Y. 1795 d. N.Y. 1879   Pvt. N.Y. Mil.
m. Mariah Palmer — daughter Mary J. m. William Long

Lea, Major   Vol. 11   Pvt. Miss. Mil.

Lea, Zachariah b. 1776 d. 1845   Capt. Miss. Mil. 1812-1813
m. Sabrina Clay & Jane McKnight
son Alfres Mead m. Elizabeth Garner

Leach, Daniel b. Conn. 1777 d. N.Y. 1831 m. Eve Corbett   Ens. N.Y. Mil.
daughter Mary m. Ira Wood

Leach, James b. N.H. 1780 d. N.Y. 1814 m. Sally Batchelder   Pvt. Vt. Mil.
daughter Emily m. Charles Francis Smith

Leadbetter, Gardner   Vol. 17   Pvt. Va. Mil.

Leake, Thomas A. b. S.C. 1797 d. Tex. 1865   Pvt. S.C. Mil.
m. Charlotte Dillard — son Moses H. m. Harriett Ann Lowry

Leakin, Shepperd, Church b. Md. 1790 d. Md. 1867   Capt. U.S. Army
m. Margaret Dobbin — son George A. m. Anna Maria Clarke Miller

Leaming, Daniel Mack   Vol. 14   Cpl. N.Y. Mil.

Lear, Thomas b. Va. 1769 d. Mo. 1830 m. Mary Fagen   Pvt. Ky. Mil.
son William B. m. Nancy A. White

Leary, Peter   Vol. 3   Lt. Md. Mil.

Leatherman, Michael b. Md. 1761 d. Pa. 1811   Pvt. Md. Mil.
m. Catherine Palmer — daughter Sarah m. Robert Guthrie

Leatherwood, Zachariah b. Md. d. Ohio m. Catherine   Pvt. Md. Mil.
daughter Eliza m. Philip Jacob Zink

Leaulieu, Jean b. Ill. d. m. Marie Poirer   Capt. Ill. Terr. Mil.
son Michael m. Elizabeth Ramey

Leaverton, John Foster b. Eng. 1755 d. Ohio 1838 m.—   Pvt. Ohio Mil.
son Solomon m. Lettie Ann Thompson

Leavenworth, Henry   Vol. 12   Vol. Vt. Mil.

Leavenworth, Henry b. Conn. 1783 d. 1834   Brig. Gen. U.S. Army
m. Elizabeth Eunice Morrison — son Jesse H. m. Elvira Caroline Clark

Leckey, John b. Pa. 1763 d. Pa. 1821 m. Elizabeth   Pvt. Ohio Mil.
son Alexander m. Sarah Anderson

LeCount, John H. b. N.Y. 1794 d. Wisc. 1878 m. Esther Day   Pvt. N.Y. Mil.
daughter Celia m. Wilson B. Kinyon

Ledbetter, Gardner b. Va. 1786 d. Va. 1864/5 m. Nancy Jones   Pvt. Va. Mil.
daughter Martha C. J. m. John J. Slaughter

Ledbetter, Henry b. Va. 1771 d. N.C. 1857   Pvt. U.S. Inf.
m. (2) Mrs. Anna Prichard Dunn
daughter Mary W. m. Thomas Jefferson Smith

Lee, Amherest (Amherst) b. Vt. 1789 d. Ind. 1841   Pvt. Vt. Mil. 1814
m. Cynthia Taft — son Thomas m. Mary Ann Rush

Lee, Asa   Vol. 17   Pvt. Conn. Mil.

Lee, Braxton b. Va. 1766 d. Tenn. 1839   Juror Va. 1791-1810 Tenn. Judge
m. Elizabeth Hatcher — daughter Judith m. Manuel Hunter

Lee, Charles   Vol. 17   Sheriff Va. 1784

Lee, Daniel   Vol. 6   Pvt. N.Y. Mil.

Lee, David b. Conn. 1784 d. N.Y. 1862 m. Mary Whitcomb   Pvt. N.Y. Mil.
daughter Mary m. Rev. Henry Hawkins

Lee, George b. Conn. 1767 d. N.Y. m. Elizabeth Bennett   Capt. N.Y. Mil.
son George D. m. Pamela Ruland

Lee, Henry b. Va. 1756 d. Ga. 1818 m. Matilda Lee   Maj. Gen., Gov.
daughter Lucy G. m. Bernard Moore Carter   Va. 1794-98

Lee, Isaac b. N.C. ca. 1776 d. Ala. 1856   Pvt. Tenn. Mil.
m. Elizabeth Pruitt (Prewett)
daughter Diana Amelia m. Swan Hardin Skelton
daughter Malvina m. Ezekiel Abner Powell

Lee, James Sr. b. Va. 1778 d. Va. 1851 m. Mary Mahorney   Pvt. Va. Mil.
son James Jr. m. Elizabeth Staples

Lee, Jeptha Byram, b. N.Y. 1794 d. N.Y. 1884   Pvt. N.Y. Mil.
m. Catherine Cortright — son Philip m. Nancy Jane Cunion

Lee, John (C.) b. Va. 1793 d. Va. 1874   Pvt. Va. Cavalry
m. Catherine Newell — daughter Rebecca m. Adam Crisman

Lee, Jonathan b. N.Y. 1752 d. N.Y. 1812 m. (1) Elizabeth   Lt. Col. N.Y. Mil.
son Elias m. Patty Watkins

Lee, Joshua b. Va. 1779 d. Va. 1844   Pvt. Va. Mil. 1814
m. Elizabeth Simpson
daughter Maragret m. William Simpson Patton

Lee, Levi b. Va. 1791 d. Tex. 1864 m. Mary Marcus   Sgt. W. Tenn. Mil.
daughter Catherine m. Joshiah Taylor

Lee, Major b. Miss. 1771 d. Tenn. 1822   Pvt. Miss.-Tenn. Mil.
m. Lavinia Jarnigan — son Pryor m. Minerva Heard

Lee, Needham Sr. b. N.C. 1770 d. Ala. 1820   Lt. Tenn. Mil.
m. Susan Bailey—daughter Elizabeth m. William Action
son Needham Jr. m. Nancy Wharton
son William C. m. Mary Bailey

Lee, Richard Evers b. Va. 1748 d. Va. 1814 m. Letty Kelly   Va. Mayor 1807
son William Ludwell m. Sarah McKenney

Lee, Richard Henry b. Va. 1790 d. Va. 1883   Cpl. Va. Mil.
m. Rebecca Andrews — daughter Frances T. m. William E. Andrews

Lee, Richard Henry b. Va. 1756 d. Ga. 1818   Maj. Gen. U.S. Army
m. Matilda Lee — daughter Lucy m. Barnard Moore Carter

Lee, Roswell b. N.Y. 1777 d. Mass. 1833 m. Phebe Potter   Lt. Col. Inf.
son Henry W. m. Lydia Morton

Lee, Stephen Collander b. Pa. 1793 d. Ill. 1880 m. Honora(h)   Sgt. Pa. Mil.
son Darius B. m. Mary J.

Lee, Stephen D. b. S.C. 1750 d. S.C. 1807   Commissioner S.C. 1796
m. Dorothea Smiser Alison — son Paul S. H. m. Jane Elizabeth Martin

Lee, Whitaker, b. Va. 1778 d. Va. 1835 m. Anne Kirby   Sgt. Va. Mil.
son Robert G. H. m. Margaret Burnham

Lee, William Carroll b. Tenn. 1796 d. Ala. 1884   Pvt. Tenn. Mil.
m. Mary Bailey — daughter Teresa m. William Orr

Lee, William Dallam b. Md. 1785 d. Md. 1828   Capt. Md. Mil.
m. Ann Wilson — daughter Frances Ann m. William G. Wilson

Leeds, Joshua b. Conn. 1775 d. Conn. 1822   Ens. Conn. Mil.
m. Peace Partridge—daughter Mary m. Elihu Hakes Jr.

Leeper, Robert b. Pa. 1777 d. Pa. 1862   Capt. Pa. Mil.
m. Nancy Agnes Harper—daughter Agnes m. Jonathan Duncan

Leer, Jacob Jr. b. Pa. 1769 d. Pa. or Ohio 1827   Pvt. Pa. Mil.
m. Mary Frances Stutsman—son Abraham m. Mary Esther Miller

Leeright, Minor b. Va. 1780 d. Ind. 1840   **Ens. Ky. Mil. 1797**
   m. Elizabeth Simmons—son John S. m. Albier Kimmel

Leeson, Richard Largent b. Ohio 1786 d. Ind. 1854   **Capt. Ohio Mil.**
   m. Jane Dooley — son Moses D. m. Elizabeth Mundell

Leet, Samuel M. b. Conn. 1794 d. Ill. 1882 m. Anna Atwood   **Pvt. Conn. Mil.**
   son John M. m. Sarah Tucker

Leete, Daniel Brown   Vol. 15   **Customs Officer Conn.**

Lefevre, John b. Pa. 1776 d. Pa. m. Elizabeth Kephart   **Lt. Pa. Mil.**
   son Daniel m. Elizabeth Swinehart

LeFevre, Lawrence b. Pa. 1764 d. Pa. 1830 m. Veronica Alter   **Pvt. Pa. Mil.**
   son John m. Rebecca Rhine

Leflour, Louis b. Fra. d. Ark. 1835   **Pvt. Miss.-Tenn. Mil.**
   m. Rebecca Cravat — son Benjamin m. Polly Ann Juyan
   son Forbis m. Anne Mary Maurer

Leftwich, Augustine Jr. b. Va. d. Va. m. Mary Turner   **Pvt. Va. Mil.**
   son Peyton m. Mildred Fuqua

Leftwich, Jabez b. Va. 1766 d. Ala. 1855   **Maj. Gen. Va. Mil.**
   m. Delilah Stovall — daughter Pamelia m. Andrew Drake

Leftwich, Jesse b. Va. ca. 1770 d. Va. 1845 m. Eudosia Trigg   **Capt. Va.**
   son John m. Sarah Lane

Leftwich, Littleberry b. Va. 1751 d. Va. 1823   **Maj. Va. Mil.**
   m. Frances Hopkins — daughter Sally m. Michajah Stone

Leftwich, Thomas b. Va. 1740 d. Va. 1816   **Col. Va. Mil.**
   m. (3) Jane Stratton   **Sheriff Va. 1794**
   daughter Catherine G. m. James C. Brown

Leftwich, Thomas b. Va. 1740 d. Va. 1816   **Col. Va. Mil.**
   m. (2) Bethunia Ellis — daughter Susannah m. David Thurman

Legg, Samuel b. Va. 1782 d. Tenn. 1866 m. Jane Hafely   **Lt. Tenn. Mil.**
   son Cornelius A. m. Sarah R. Harris

Legier, de la Tour, Louis Joseph Rene b. Fra. 1751, Official Dr. La. Prison
   d. La. 1827 m. Marie Jeanne Compain
   son Dr. L. J. R. m. Jeanne Louise Fourmy

Lehman, John b. Pa. 1743 d. Pa. 1824 m. Anna Baer   **Pvt. Pa. Mil.**
   son John m. Elizabeth Baer

Leigh, John b. Va. 1797 d. Ala. 1826 m. Susan Ann Brantley   **Sgt. Va. Mil.**
   son John D. m. Miriam Dean Rabun

Leigh, Paschal Greenhill b. Va. 1769 d. Va. 1856   **Capt. Va. Mil.**
   m. Elizabeth A. Scott — daughter Anne m Simeon Buford Fleshman

Leinbach, Christian b. Pa. 1791 d. Pa. 1866   **Pvt. Pa. Mil.**
   m. Susanna Althouse — son Elias m. Caroline Hoch

Leinbach, Daniel b. Pa. 1746 d. Pa. 1817   **Capt. Pa. Mil.**
   m. Mary Magdelena Hartman   **Mem. of Pa. Assembly 1790**
   son Jacob m. Mrs. Catherine Schill Epler
   son Thomas H. m. Elizabeth Reise Seibert

Leitheiser, Hartman b. Pa. 1760 d. Pa. 1829   **Capt. Pa. Mil.**
   m. Elizabeth Sauerbier
   daughter Ann Catherine m. Johan Christian Lockman

Lemming, John b. Ohio 1780 d. Ohio 1866   **Pvt. Ohio Mil.**
  m. Phebe Applegate — daughter Susan m. Abram Smyser

Lemmon, James b. Md. 1765 d. Tex. 1858 m. Sarah Carr   **Pvt. Ky. Mil.**
  son John m. Elizabeth Johnson

Lemon, Isaac b. Pa. c. 1760 d. Pa. 1842 m.—   **Pvt. Ohio Mil.**
  son John Jr. m. Isabel Hunter

Lemon, Samuel b. Pa. 1740 d. Pa. 1815 m. Margaret   **Pvt. Pa. Mil. 1794**
  son Issac m.—

Lenard, Robert   Vol. 14   **Pvt. Tenn. Vol.**

Lenoir, William b. Va. 1751 d. N.C. 1839   **Senate N.C. 1787-95**
  m. Ann Ballard — daughter Mary m. Charles Gordon

Lent, James b. Pa. 1782 d. Pa. 1881 m. Chloe Parks   **Pvt. Pa. Mil.**
  daughter Catherine m. Simeon Rockwell

Lent, Joseph b. Pa. 1786 d. Pa. 1863 m. Mary Ann Johnson   **Pvt. Pa. Mil.**
  daughter Anna m. Jesse Smith

Lentner, Jacob b. Pa. 1776 d. Ohio 1849 m. Lydia Russel   **Adj. Del. Troops**
  daughter Hester m. William Rowell

Lentz, John b. Pa. 1793 d. Pa. 1875 m. (3) Elizabeth High   **Sgt. Pa. Mil.**
  son Franklin Pierce m. Clara A. Olewine
  m. Julia Winter Barnett — daughter Julia m. William Morris

Leonard, Asa b. Mass. 1759 d. N.Y. 1836   **Commissioner of Schools**
  m. Olive Churchill   **1808 N.Y.**
  son Levi m. Isabella Avery   **Fence Viewer 1813**

Leonard, John b. N.J. 1765 d. N.Y. 1831 m. Mary Pitney   **Lt. N.Y. Mil.**
  daughter Martha m. John Waldron

Leonard, John b. N.J. 1790 d. Ky. 1837 m. Harriet McQuiddy   **Pvt. Ky. Mil.**
  son James Francis m. Ruth Marion Browne

Leonard, John b. Pa. 1768 d. Pa. 1847   **Capt. Pa. Mil.**
  m. Margaret Kline — daughter Clara E. m. Daniel Vondersmith

Leonard, Jonathan b. Conn. (Mass.) 1777 d. N.Y. 1868   **Capt. N.Y. Mil.**
  m. Persis Henshaw — son Herman m. Jane Goodrich

Leonard, Thomas b. Md. 1781 d. Texas 1870   **Juror Tenn. 1810-15**
  m. Lara Lauderdale — daughter Matilda Caroline m. Gordy C. Clifton

Leonard, William b. Conn. 1752 d. R.I. 1828   **Qtr. Mst. R.I. Mil. 1799-1800**
  m. Mrs. Angell — daughter Elizabeth m. Ephraim Brown

Lepretre, Jean Baptiste b. La. 1790 d. La. 1871   **Pvt. La. Vol. 1815**
  m. Sophia Andre — daughter Alice m. Jules Aldige

Lerch, Peter Sr. b. Pa. 1764 d. Pa. 1813   **Pvt. Pa. Mil.**
  m. Anna Margaret Riegel — daughter Elizabeth m. Simon Dreisbach

Lescure, Edward P. b. Pa. 1797 d. Pa. 1883   **Seaman Pa. Navy**
  m. Sarah Ferguson — daughter Annie m. Martin H. Stutzbach

Leslie, George   Vol. 13   **Pvt. Pa. Mil.**

Lester, Ezekiel b. d. Ga. m. Celia Cock   **Justice Ga. 1797-1799**
  daughter Cynthia m. Thomas Low

Lester, James Lord b. Conn. 1785 d. Conn. 1870   **Qtr. Mstr. Conn. Mil.**
  m. Nancy Wheeler Griswold — son Andrew m. Mary Harris

Letcher, Stephen Giles b. Va. 1742 d. Ky. 1823   Pvt. Ky. Vol.
    m. Elizabeth Perkins — daughter Elizabeth m. David McKee

Letherbury, Peregrin b. Del. 1775 d. Del. 1851   Pvt. Del. Mil.
    m. Amelia Wright — son John W. L. m. Ann McCall

Letton, (Litton) Caleb b. Md. 1768 d. Ky. 1850   Pvt. Ky. Mil.
    m. Mary Wilcoxen
    daughter Millicent C. A. m. Michael Strother Kern

Leverich, Edward b. N.Y. 1763 d. N.Y. 1833   Capt. N.Y. Mil. 1814
    m. Patience Moore—daughter Anna L. m. James Milnor Peck

Levy, Lewis b. Eng. 1777 d. Pa. 1861   Cornet Ga. Lt. Dragoons
    m. Ann Patterson — son Lewis m. Phoebe Fite

Lewis, Alanson Freeman   Vol. 7   Pvt. Conn. Vol.

Lewis, Amos Jr. b. Mass. 1794 d. N.J. 1875   Pvt. Mass. Mil.
    m. Ana H. McIntyre — daughter Adelaide m. John Steelman

Lewis, Amos Sr.   Vol. 10   Constable Mass.

Lewis, Andrew b. Va. 1779 d. Va. 1825 m. Maria Walton, Surgeon Va. Mil.
    daughter Lucy m. George Washington Shanks

Lewis, Andrew Jr. b. Va. 1759 d. Va. 1844   Capt. Va. Mil.
    m. Elizabeth Strother Madison
    daughter Agatha S. m. Elijah McClanahan

Lewis, Asa Jr. b. N.Y. 1795 d. Mich. 1859   Pvt. U.S. Inf.
    m. Anna Bentley — son Cyrus B. m. Mary Christophene Champlin

Lewis, Asa Sr. b. R.I. 1762 d. N.Y. 1843   Pat. N.Y. 1792-1800
    m. Bridget Rix — son Asa Jr. m. Anna Bentley

Lewis, Augustine, b. Va. 1784 d. Ga. 1859 m. Louisa Booking   Pvt. U.S. Inf.
    son Francis B. m. Elizabeth Brodnax

Lewis, Bissel   Vol. 9   Capt. Va. Mil.

Lewis, Brittain b. Miss. 1796 d. Miss. 1851   Pvt. Miss. Mil.
    m. Nancy McCaskill — son Albert G. m. Barkley Lemon
    daughter Margaret m. Jesse M. Fuller

Lewis, Daniel b. N.C. ca. 1760 d. Ala. 1833   Sgt. Ga. Mil.
    m Sarah Sinkfield — daughter Harriet m. Lawson Keener

Lewis, Fielding   Vol. 15   Pvt. Ga. Mil.

Lewis, Horatio Gates b. Conn. ca. 1780 d. Mass. 1847   Maj. Conn. Mil.
    m. Betty Bailey — daughter Ann Eliza m. Asa Miner

Lewis, Jabez York b. N.Y. 1790 d. Mass. 1884   Drummer N.Y. Mil.
    m. Lydia Ann Foster — son Charles B. m. Eunice Wyeth
    m. Sarah (Day) Draper — daughter Lauretta m. DeEsting Harris

Lewis, James b. Va. 1756 d. Tenn. 1849 m. Lucy Thomas   Pvt. Tenn. Mil.
    daughter Mary Elizabeth m. (1) Dyer Moore

Lewis, James b. Va. 1784 d. Ga. m. Sarah Darby   Lt. Va. Inf.
    son Hamilton W. m. (2) Elizabeth Wiley Hart

Lewis, John b. N.Y. 1780 d. N.Y. 1867 m. Olive Whipple   Pvt. N.Y. Mil.
    son John Jr. m. Mary Simmons

Lewis, John   Vol. 11   Pvt. U.S. Vol.

Lewis, John b. N.C. 1733 d. Ga. 1818   Ga. Legis. 1815
    m. Nancy Lavinia Ward — son Jesse m. Mary Clifton

Lewis, Joseph Francis b. Eng. ca. 1750 d. Ky. aft. 1799   Maj. Ky. 1792
  m. Sarah Whitley — daughter Mary m. Joel Owsley

Lewis, Joseph   Vol. 12   Pvt. Ohio Mil.

Lewis, Joseph b. Pa. 1778 d. Pa. 1836   Pvt. Pa. Mil.
  m. Frances Montgomery
  daughter Elizabeth Ann m. Edward Pennington

Lewis, Joshua b. Va. 1772 d. La. 1833   Lt. La., La. Justice
  m. America Lawson — son Alfred J. m. Mrs. Elise M. Power
  son John Hamden m. Anna L. Von Ettendalh (2) Henriette Baham

Lewis, Lewis b. Va. 1790 d. W. Va. 1873 m. Polly Seckman   Pvt. Va. Mil.
  son Benjamin F. m. Mary Anderson

Lewis, Martin b. Conn. 1761 d. Mich. 1854   Capt. N.Y. Mil.
  m. Abigail Thayer — daughter Eveline Helen m. William Wheeler

Lewis, Nathaniel b. Conn. 1747 d. Conn. 1839, Conn. Town Officer 1802-5-9
  m. Sarah Gridley — daughter Sylvia m. Isaac Upson

Lewis, Philip Jr. b. 1778 d. Ohio 1851 m. Nancy Umble   Ohio Legis. 1804
  daughter Delilah K. m. Asher W. Tinder   Paymaster Ohio Mil.

Lewis, Reuben b. 1772 d. Ky. 1836   Pvt. Ky. (Mich. Mil.) ? ?
  m. Miss Worthington — son Silas m. Lydia Butts Chilson

Lewis, Richard b. Va. 1764 d. S.C. 1831   Mem. Constit. Conv. S.C. 1789
  m. Sarah — daughter Nancy Elvira m. Joseph Van Shanklin

Lewis, Russell   Vol. 9, 10, 11   Pvt. Conn. Mil.

Lewis, Samuel b. N. C. 1780 d. Ky. 1828 m. Elizabeth   Pvt. N.C. Mil.
  son Eddin m. Winifred Easley

Lewis, Samuel b. Va. 1785 d. Tex. 1838 m. Sarah Lemasters Pvt. Ind. Mil.
  daughter Julia m. Lewis Donaho

Lewis, Silas b. N.Y. 1797 d. Mich. 1853   Pvt. Ohio-Tenn. Cavalry
  m. Lydia Butts Chilson — son Samuel B. m. Mary Elizabeth Viles

Lewis, Thomas b. Ire. 1718 d. Va. 1790   Mem. of Con. 1788 Va.
  m. Jane Strother—son William B. m. Margaret Hite
  daughter Elizabeth m. Thos. Meriwether Gilmer

Lewis, Thomas b. Va. 1749 d. Ky. 1809 m. Elizabeth Payne Capt. U.S. Inf.
  daughter Elizabeth m. James A. Brown

Lewis, Warner b. Va. 1786 d. Va. 1873   Pvt. Va. Mil.
  m. Ann Susannah Latane — son Thomas W. m. Ann Ursula Latane

Lewis, William b. Conn. 1727 d. Vt. 1806 m. Naomi   Vt. Civil Officer
  son Joseph m. Experience Burr

Lewis, William b. Md. 1755 d. Md. 1827   Capt. Md. Mil.
  m. Mary Fockler (Fackler) — daughter Elizabeth m. George Shryock

Lewis, William   Vol. 16   Lt. Col. Ky. Mil.

Lewis, William b. N.Y. 1783 d. Ind. aft. 1860   Sgt. N.Y. Mil.
  m. Sarah (Miller) Butler — son John M. m. Mary Jane Coryell

Lewis, William Terrell b. Va. 1718 d. Tenn. 1802   Mem. House of
  m. Sarah Martin   Commons N.C. 1785-8
  daughter Elizabeth m. John Fielder

Lewis, Zebulon b. R.I. 1734 d. N.Y.   Capt. N.Y. Mil. 1791-98
  m. Mary York — son Jabez Y. m. Lydia Ann Foster

Libby, Daniel   Vol. 5   Capt. U.S. Inf.

Libby, Josiah b. (Me.) Mass. 1794 d. Me. 1846   Pvt. Mass. Mil.
  m. Mary Palmer — daughter Abby m. George Shackford

Lide, (Lloyd) Robert b. Va. 1734 d. S.C. 1802   Justice S.C. 1791
  m. Sarah Kolb — daughter Mary m. Robert Hodges

Ligget, Henry b. Va. 1795 d. Tenn. 1861   Sgt. Tenn. Mil.
  m. Elizabeth Center
  daughter Sarah Elizabeth m. Richard L. Caldwell

Liggett, Alexander b. Va. 1791 d. Ohio 1859   Cpl. Ohio Mil.
  m. Ruhama Moore — son William W. m. Elizabeth J. Crawford

Light, Henry b. Pa. 1760 d. Pa. 1830 m. Magdalena Funk   Pvt. Pa. Mil.
  son Henry (Fuller) m. Barbara Wenger

Lightfoot, Thomas E. b. Va. 1770 d. Ala. 1830   Pvt. Tenn. Mil.
  m. Sarah Allen — daughter Narcissa W. m. John Miller

Lighthall, William b. N.Y. 1756 d. N.Y. 1822   Pvt. N.Y. Mil.
  m. Sarah Marselis — son Ahasueras m. Margaret Peeke

Lighthizer, Henry b. Ger. 1783 d. Ohio 1866 m. Sarah Fonce   Pvt. Md. Mil.
  son Henry Jr. m. Elizabeth George

Lightner, Henry   Vol. 17   Ens. Pa. Mil.

Lightner. Jacob b. Pa. 1788 d. Ind. 1847 m. Sarah Harris   Pvt. Pa. Mil.
  daughter Juliana m. Alphonsus N. DeLauney

Lightner, William b. Pa. 1774 d. Pa. 1825   Pvt. Pa. Mil.
  m. Esther Brenneman — daughter Leah m. James Johnstin

Ligon, (Liggin) David Gaddy b. Va. 1791 d. Ala. 1871   Pvt. Ga. Mil.
  m. Mary Parker Nelson — son Noel N. m. Rebecca Dorsett

Ligon, William Blackman b. Va. 1788 d. Miss. aft. 1850   Ens. U.S. Inf.
  m. Eliza Lawn — daughter Elizabeth m. Lemuel J. Quin

Lile, John M. b. Ga. 1795 d. Mo. 1870 m. Margaret Witt   Pvt. Ky. Mil.
  son William Henry m. Elizabeth Parks

Lillard, Abraham b. Va. 1791 d. Tenn. 1873   Pvt. Tenn. Mil.
  m. Jane Harrison — daughter Minerva m. Joseph E. Taylor

Lillard, David b. Va. 1782 d. Ky. 1861 m. Mary Spencer   Lt. Ky. Mil.
  daughter Artimissia m. Thomas J. Turley, Sr.

Lillie, Henry b. Scot. 1794 d. Conn. 1880 m. Frances Smith   Pvt. Conn. Mil.
  daughter Cornelia L. m. Robert L. McChristie
  son Henry B. m. Harriett E. Brewer
  daughter Lydia A. m. Henry W. Mason

Liliord, Christopher b. Ky. 1795 d. Ky. 1855   Pvt. Ky. Mil.
  m. Miss Minerva Lillard
  daughter Alma T. m. John I. Felix REAL DAUGHTER

Lilly, Isaac   Vol. 16   Pvt. Mass. (Me.)) Mil.

Lincecum, Gideon b. Ga. 1793 d. Tex. 1873 m. Sallie Bryant   Pvt. Ga. Mil.
    daughter Cassandra m. George John Durham   Tax Collector Ga.
    son Dr. L. G. m. Kate Lauderdale

Lincoln, Amasa b. Mass. 1787 d. Vt. 1857 m.—   Vol. 5   Pvt. Vt. Mil.

Lincoln, Caleb b. Mass. 1789 d. Ohio 1850   Pvt. U.S. Inf.
    m. Elizabeth Lincoln — son Caleb m. Polly Hance
    daughter Elizabeth L. m. Charles S. Vorwerk

Lincoln, George b. Ky. 1792 d. Mo. 1848   Pvt. Ky. Mil.
    m. Julia Ann Gatewood — daughter Fannie m. Isaac Newton Hockaday
    son John K. m. Elmira Malone
    daughter Julia m. John McMichael
    m. Fannie Morton — son George m. Julianna

Lincoln, Luther b. Conn. 1787 d. N.Y. 1862   Pvt. Vt. Mil.
    m. Samantha Sanford — son John m. Harriett Sawtelle

Lindenmuth, John Michael b. Ger. 1790 d. Pa. 1830   Pa. Justice of Peace
    m (2) Anna Katharina Geschwindin   1784-90
    daughter Catherine m. Christian Hartzog
    son Martin m. Catherine

Linder, Jacob b. Va. 1775 d. Ill. aft. 1821 m. Dicy Woods   Pvt. Ill. 1810
    son Isham m. Sarah Vaughn

Lindsay, John b. 1789 d. Tex. 1853 m. Martha   2nd. Tenn. Mil.
    son Noah m. Frances Walker

Lindsey, Andrew b. Pa. 1789 d. Pa. 1834 m. Jane Davison   Maj. Pa. Mil.
    son John m. Martha Small

Lindsey, Henry   Vol. 10   Ens. Ky. Vol.

Lindsay, Rufus Herrick b. Vt. 1798 d. N.Y. 1866 m.—   Pvt. Vt. Mil.
    daughter Harriette m. George T. Griswold REAL DAUGHTER

Lindsay, Benjamin b. N.Y. 1794 d. Ohio 1857   Pvt. N.Y. Mil.
    m. Abigail Moor — daughter Roxanna m. Jacob Eckert, Jr.

Lindsay, John b. N.C. 1769 d. N.C. 1828   Gen. Assem. N.C.
    m. Elibabeth Wilson — son Andrew m. Sarah Moch

Lindsey, John H. b. Scot 1790 d. Ohio 1855 m. Mary Keel   Capt. Ohio Mil.
    son William J. m. Lucinda Eliza Gardner

Lindsey, Jonathan Woodby b. R.I. 1778 d. R.I. 1854   Lt. R.I. Mil.
    m. Hannah Easterbrooks — daughter Abby m. Hiram Luther
    daughter Martha m. Henry Hight Dimond
    daughter Mary m. Mayberry Luther Lincoln

Lindsay, Nathaniel b. Mass. 1771 d. Mass. 1842   Capt. Mass. Navy
    m. Sarah Barker — daughter Mary Rebecca m. John Blacklee Payne

Lindsey, Parham b. Va. 1788 d. Ga. 1863 m. Polly Wise   4th Sgt. Ga. Mil.
    son Sherod m. Sarah Edwards

Lindsey, Philip b. Va. 1792 d. Va. 1875 m. Sallie Gilmore   Pvt. Va. Mil.
    son John B. m. Mary Catherine Smaltz
    m. Maria Lindsey (cousin)
    daughter Mary E. m. Joseph T. Davenport

Lindsley, Abraham Bradley b. N.J. 1786 d. D.C. 1851   Lt. U.S. Inf.
    Vol. 10, 13

Line, (Lyne) Abraham b. Pa. 1758 d. Pa. 1820   Pvt. Pa. Mil.
    m. Christina Eby — son Henry m. Frances Douer

Line, George b. Pa. 1724 d. Pa. 1798 m. Salome Carpenter   Ens. Pa. Mil.
son David m. Anna Bear

Lininger, John b. Ger. 1783 d. Pa. 1850 m. Polly Reisinger   Pvt. Pa. Mil.
daughter Lydia m. John Schever

Linkenhoger (Lenkinogan), George b. Va. 1775 d. Va. 1853   Pvt. Va. Mil.
m. Elizabeth Stone — daughter Lucy Ann m. Madison Monroe Switzer

Linscott, Andrew D. b. (Me.) Mass. 1785 d. Me. 1838   Pvt. Mass. Mil.
m. Polly Chaney — son Josiah m. Mary Small

Linsley, Joel b. Conn. 1756 d. Vt. 1819   Town Clerk, Rep. of Legis.
m. Lavina Gilbert   Selectman Vt.
son Horace m. Abigail Matthews

Linthicum, Abner b. Md. 1763 d. Md. 1848 m. Rachel Jacobs   Capt. Md. Mil.
son Hezekiah m. Matilda Phillips
son William m. Elizabeth Sweetzer

Linthicum, Samuel   Vol. 9   Pvt. Md. Mil.

Lippincott, Samuel b. N.J. 1762 d. Ohio 1836   Pvt. Pa. Mil.
m. Elizabeth Morgan — daughter Jane m. William Scott

Lippencott, Samuel b. N.J. d. N.J. m. Rosannah English   Cpl. N.J. Mil.
daughter Rebecca M. John Shinn

Lipscomb, John   Vol. 9   Ens. Va. Mil. 1802-4

Lipscomb, William b. Va. 1731 d. S.C. 1810   Justice 1805 S.C.
m. Elizabeth Smith — son William Jr. m. Elizabeth Hall

List, (Leist) David b. Pa. 1777 d. Ohio 1840
m. Catherine Spade — son John D. m. Catherine Valentine

Lister, Josiah Dunlap b. N.C. 1792 d. Tex. 1858   Capt. Miss.-Tenn. Mil.
m. Sarah Johnston — son Albert D. m. Ophelia Richardson

Lister, William b. Va. 1772 d. Ohio 1876 m. Mary Hurt   Pvt. Ohio Mil.
daughter Mary Alice m. Matthew W. Cannon

Liswell, Thomas b. Conn. 1758 d. Conn. 1814   Pvt. U.S. Army
m. Hannah Crosby — daughter Lovisa m. John Sykes

Litchfield, Ensign b. Mass. 1778 d. N.Y. 1840   Pvt. Mass. Mil.
m. Mary Hayden — son Levi m. Nancy French

Litchfield, Israel Clark b. N.Y. 1791 d. Ohio 1873   Pvt. N.Y. Mil.
m. Chloe Keith — daughter Susan m. Thomas R. Brown

Litman, John b. Del. 1778 d. Pa. 1854 m. Elizabeth Morris   Pvt. Pa. Mil.
daughter Clarinda m. John Lyons

Little, David b. Mass. 1760 d. Mass. 1825   Capt. Mass. Mil.
m. Abigail Noyes   Rep. Mass. 1810-12
daughter Elizabeth m. Samuel Brookings

Little, George b. Mass. 1754 d. Mass. 1809   Commander of Protector
m. Rachel Rogers   Mass. Navy
son Edward m. Edy Rogers
daughter Rachel W. m. Joseph Healey

Little, Gray b. N.C. 1765 d. N.C. 1824   Maj. N.C. Mil. 1805-10
m. Sylvia Peninah Ann Thigpen
daughter Lydia m. Elijah L. Manning

Little, James b. Va. 1779 d. Ga. 1815   3rd Lt. Ga. Mil.
m. Nancy Ann McDonald — son James M. m. Louise Anne Headen

Little, Joseph b. Scot. 1732 d. Vt. 1817 m.—   Pvt. Vt. Mil.
    son Rufus m. Eunice Brown

Little, Stephen b. N.H. 1774 d. Me. 1852 m. Rebecca Dodge   Pvt. Me. Art.
    daughter Harriet m. Nathan Sawyer

Little, Thomas   Vol. 6   Capt.

Littlepage, James Beverly b. Va. 1798 d. Va.   Pvt. Va. Mil.
    m. Susan Shanklin Van Ansdale
    son Charles P. m. Jeanne Anaise Perret

Littlefield, James Pennell b. Mass. or Vt. 1792 d. Mich 1856   Pvt. N.Y. Mil.
    m. Anne Saunders — son Benjamin F. m. Anne Elizabeth Phelps

Littleton, Mathew b. Md. 1785 d. Ohio 1848   Lt. Ohio Mil.
    m. Sophia Harper — son Matthew Jr. m. Caroline Matilda Diffenderfer

Litzenberg, (er), George b. Pa. 1792 d. Pa. 1866   Cpl. Pa. Mil.
    m. Tacy Malin — son Charles A. m. Mary Ann Shillingford

Livaudias, Francois Enoul de b. La. 1782 d. La. 1813   Mem. Const. Conv.
    m. Anna Williams   La. 1812
    son Francis B. m. Estelle Mortimer

Livermore, Abner b. Mass. 1774 d. Mich. 1861   Sgt. N.Y. Mil.
    m. Melinda Bassett — daughter Melinda B. m. Mowry Thatcher

Livermore, Charles b. Vt. 1784 d. Vt. 1833   Lt. Adj. Vt. Mil.
    m. Sibyl Eggleston — son Lemuel m. Rebecca Ray

Livermore, Daniel b. N.Y. 1801 d. N.Y. 1889   Pvt. N.Y. Mil.
    m. Elmina Lamberton — son Daniel Jr. m. Ella Brigham

Livermore, Levi b. Conn. 1796 d. Conn. 1837   Pvt. N.Y. Inf.
    m. Anna Van Schaick
    daughter Lucy Maria m. Horace Orville Gilmore REAL DAUGHTER
    daughter Mary Elizabeth m. James Eben Gilmore REAL DAUGHTER
    son Solomon m. Aliva Whitney

Livers, Arnold b. Md. 1768 d. Md. 1837 m. Mary Brawner   Pvt. Md. Mil.
    daughter Caroline m. John F. Elder

Livingston, Adam b. N.Y. 1790 d. N.Y. 1826 m. Amy Spence Pvt. N.Y. Mil.
    daughter Rachel m. Milton B. Deland

Livingston, Peter b. Va. 1776 d. Va. 1815   Ind. Fighter Va. 1794
    m. Elizabeth — daughter Mary m. James Jett
    son William m. Annie Fleenor

Livingston, Peter b. Scot. 1788 d. N.C. 1862   Pvt. N.C. Mil.
    m. Isabella McGoogan — daughter Eliza m. John McInnis

Lloyd, Eli b. Pa. 1775 d. Ohio 1857 m. Elizabeth Campbell   Pvt. Pa. Mil.
    son Eli. Jr. m. Elizabeth Adeline King

Lloyd, James b. Md. 1742 d. Md. 1815   Judge Md. 1783-1815
    m. Sarah Martin — son Robert G. m. Mary Ruth

Lloyd, John b. Pa. 1791 d. Ill. 1866 m. Catherine Van Hise Pvt. Ohio Mil.
    daughter Sarah m. David Strawn

Lloyd, John b. Va. 1795 d. N.J. 1877 m. Jane Perry   Pvt. Md. Mil.
    daughter Jane m. Warren Vreeland

Lobdell, Jacob Jr. b. Mass. 1771 d. N.Y. 1847   Capt. N.Y. Mil.
    m. Hannah Boughton — daughter Clarisa m. Ebenezer Stone
    son George A. m. Almira Austin Preston

Lobingier, Christopher b. Pa. 1740 d. Pa. 1798   **Rep. Pa. 1791-3**
   m. Elizabeth Miller — daughter Mary m. George Kimmel

Locke, Francis b. N.C. 1791 d. N.C. 1853   **Cpl. Tenn. Mil.**
   m. Sarah Alexander
   daughter Mary E. m. Davidson Alexander Underwood

Lockett, Osborne b. Va. 1769 d. Va. 1836   **Ens. Va. Mil. 1811-14**
   m. Agnes Branch Scott — son Thomas Francis m. Sallie Waller Dixon

Lockett, Philip   Vol. 4   **Pvt. Va. Mil.**

Lockhart, John Hobson b. S.C. 1796 d. Ala. 1874   **Pvt. S.C. Mil.**
   m. Nancy Edwards — daughter Joyce P. m. Drury Martin

Lockhart, Josiah b. Va. 1782 d. Va. 1853   **Brig. Gen. Va. Mil.**
   m. Nancy Odell — daughter Emeline Grace m. Daniel Clinton Lovett
   daughter Rebecca Anne m. Robert Madison Campbell
   daughter Sallie D. m. John Addison
   son Thomas J. m. Rebecca Hollingsworth

Lockhart, Robert b. Ky. 1793 d. Ohio 1858   **Pvt. Ohio Mil.**
   m. Sarah Hemphill — son Robert E. m. Alice A. Stevenson

Lockheart, Hiram b. Pa. 1791 d. Pa. 1867   **Pvt. Pa. Mil.**
   m. Nancy McCullough
   daughter Mahala m. Martin V. Gould REAL DAUGHTER

Lockhart, Thomas b. Ky. 1796 d. Ind. 1867 m. Leah May   **Pvt. Tenn. Mil.**
   daughter Laura m. D. J. Hubbell REAL DAUGHTER

Lockhart, William b. Conn. 1775 d. Conn. 1817   **Pvt. Conn. Mil.**
   m. Sally Johnson — daughter Louisa Jane m. Josiah Boardman

Lockhart, William   Vol. 10   **Lt. Pa. Mil.**

Lockwood, Ebenezer b. Conn. 1736 d. N.Y. 1821   **Judge N.Y. 1791**
   m. Hannah Smith — son Horatio m. Bethia Close Lockood (2 cousin)

Lockwood, Richard b. Del. 1788 d. Del. 1875   **Pvt. Del. Art.**
   m. Mary Rothwell Wilson — daughter Lydia Ann m. Samuel Price

Lofland, Nehemiah   Vol. 15   **Lt. Del. Mil.**

Lofland, Smith b. Del. 1764 d. Ky. 1838 m. Jane Harrison   **Capt. Va. Mil.**
   son William S. m. Margaret Clarke

Lofland, Wm. Smith b. Va. 1793 d. Tex. 1873   **2nd Capt. Ky. Mil.**
   m. Margaret Clark — son Matthew Clark m. Mary Alice Nalley
   son Jasper B. m. Mary Blanton

Loftin, Joseph b. N.C. 1777 d. N.C. 1834 m. Mary Becton   **N.C. 1812-15**
   daughter Mary A. Eliza m. Simon S. Becton   Mem. of Assembly

Logan, Alexander b. 1782 d. Ky. 1845   **2nd Sgt. Ky. Mil.**
   m. Verlinda Claggett Offutt (1)
   son Alexander Henry m. Mary Ann Cowherd

Logan, Allen b. Ky. 1791 d. Ky. 1835 m. Martha Givens   **Pvt. Ky. Vol.**
   son Hugh m. Mary Ann Lee

Logan, Beatty (Baty) b. Va. 1788 d. Ky. 1872   **Pvt. Ky. Mil.**
   m. Martha Everhart — daughter Rosannah m. Joseph Lloyd Ray

Logan, Henry b. Pa. 1784 d. Pa. 1866 m. Martha O'Hail   Pvt. Pa. Inf.
   daughter Josephine F. m. Dr. William D. Bailey REAL DAUGHTER

Logan, Hugh b. Va. 1745 d. Ky. 1816   Gen. Ky. Mil. 1784-92
    m. Sarah Woods   Rep. Ky. 1794
    daughter Jennie m. George Carpenter   Senator 1800-1806

Logan, John b. Ire. 1752 d. Ohio m. Mary   Capt. Ohio Mil.
    son John Jr. m. Eleanor Latimer

Logan, John b. Va. 1744 d. Ky. 1807   Pat. Senator Ky. 1792-5
    m. Sarah Jane McClure — daughter Elizabeth m. Edwin Lanier Harris

Logan, Joseph b. Md. 1787 d. Md. 1850 m. Mary Powell   Pvt. Md. Mil.
    daughter Mary Ann m. John Cooke

Logan, Robert b. Ky. d. 1813 m. Betsy Tinsley   Lt. U.S. Army
    son William m. Lydia Hocker

Logan, Samuel b. Va. 1780 d. Mo. 1843 m. Nancy Orr   Pvt. E. Tenn. Mil.
    daughter Sarah m. Jesse Day

Logan, William b. Va. 1787 d. Va. 1858   Lt. Va. Mil.
    m. Elizabeth Crawford
    son James (John) H. m. Mary Gamble Crawford

Lomax, John Tayloe b. Va. 1781 d. Va. 1862   Officer Va. Mil.
    m. Charlotte Thornton — daughter Cornelia m. J. Alexander Kelly

Lonas, Adam b. N.Y. 1787 d. N.Y. 1865   Pvt. N.Y. Mil.
    m. Katherine Quackenbush — daughter Margaret m. Stephen Burdick

Long, Abraham b. Pa. 1743 d. Pa. 1794 m. Maria   Pvt. Pa. Mil.
    son David m. Catherine Hershey

Long, Benjamin b. S.C. c. 1740 d. S.C. 1816   Sheriff S.C.
    m. Priscilla Turner — daughter Mary m. Henry Coate

Long, Edward Jennings b. Mass. 1771 d. N.H. 1824   Maj. N.H. Mil.
    m. Dorothy Abigail Rogers
    son Nathaniel R. m. Caroline White Smith.

Long, Gabriel b. Va. 1781 d. Mo. 1822   Ens. Mo.-Tenn. Mil.
    m. Elizabeth Lewis — son Alton m. (1) Sarah Long Caulk

Long, Hugh b. Pa. 1796 d. Ohio 1884 m. Sally Hinkle   2nd Maj. Pa. Mil.
    daughter Martha A. m. L. H. De Lander

Long, John Jr. b. 1773 d. 1854 m. Nancy Kinkaid   Pvt. Ky. Mil.
    daughter Jane Kinkaid m. George W. Saunders

Long, John b. Ire. d. Tenn. 1825   Mem. Gen. Assembly Tenn. 1796
    m. Mrs. Jane Young (Henry) — son Joseph m. Mary Davis

Long, Joseph b. Ger. 1783 d. Pa. 1832 m. Margaret Kuntz   Ens. Pa. Mil.
    son George M. m. Sarah Jane Carr
    son William m Susan Miller

Long, Kennedy b. Ire. 1763 d. Md. 1821   Lt. Col. Md. Mil.
    m. Elizabeth Kennedy
    daughter Emelia Juliana m. Thomas Worthington

Long, Mathew b. Mass. 1757 d. N.Y. 1821 m. Betty Hawes   Pvt. U.S. Vol.
    daughter Polly m. Stephen Landers

Long, Nicholas b. N.C. d. N.C. 1819 m. Mary McKinney   Col. U.S. Inf.
    son John J. m. Frances

Long, Solomon b. N.C. 1782 d. Ky. 1833   4th Sgt. Ky. Vol.
    m. Hannah Travis — son Samuel m. Margaret Berry

Long, William b. Ire. 1740 d. Pa. 1793 m. Hannah Young   Capt. Pa. Mil.
  son Joseph m. Sarah Miller

Long, William Lindsay b. Va. 1789 d. Mo. 1849   Lt. Mo. Mil.
  m. Elizabeth Sappington — son John F. m. Fannie E. Piukin
  daughter A. Malvina m. Joseph Sale Berry
  daughter Mary m. Thos. E. Wright

Longacre, Daniel b. Pa. 1740 d. Pa. 1812   Pvt. Pa. Mil. 1785-90
  m. Elizabeth — son Henry m. Elizabeth Sell

Longley, Edmund b. Mass. (Me.) 1792 d. Me. 1862   Sgt. Mass. Art.
  m. Abigail Sawtelle — son Charles W. m. Elizabeth Ann Swift (1)

Longley, John b. N.Y. 1782 d. Ind. 1867   Chaplain Ohio Mil.
  m. Frances Hendrickson — son Edward R. m. Martha Ann Crane
  daughter Hariette m. John Wilson

Longley, Thomas   Vol. 6   Cpl. Ky. Mil.

Longshore, Euclydus (Euclides) b. S.C. 1792 d. S.C. 1861   Pvt. S.C. Mil.
  m. Gracie McConnell — daughter Mary m. John Edward Reagan
  daughter Permelia Eliza m. Timothy Letcher Pittman

Longshire, Isaiah b. Pa. 1791 d. Pa. 1836 m. Ann Folwell   2nd Lt. Pa. Mil.
  son Ashbel B. m. Maria J. Righter

Longwell, James b. Ire. 1754 d. Ohio c. 1820   Pvt. Ohio Mil.
  m. Nellie Slack — daughter Nancy m. Joseph Leonard

Loomis, Daniel b. Conn. 1761 d. N.Y. 1833   Lt. Col. N.Y. Mil.
  m. Mary Huston — son Daniel Jr. m. Paulina Day

Loomis, Ham b. Mass. 1758 d. Mass. 1827   Selectman Mass. 1803
  m. Elizabeth Allen — son Ham Jr. m. Anne Burrit

Loomis, Israel Jr. b. Conn. 1768 d. Mich. 1835 m. Mary Lee   Pvt. N.Y. Mil.
  son Daniel m. Caroline B. Seelye

Loomis, Noah b. Mass. 1724 d. Mass. 1808   Selectman Mass. 1803
  m. Rhoda Clark — son Ham Sr. m. Elizabeth Allen

Loper, John b. N.J. 1782 d. N.J. 1855 m. Sarah Mateer   Pvt. N.J. Mil.
  daughter Deborah m. Charles L. Clark

Loper, John b. Pa. 1785 d. 1812 m. Elizabeth Trepania   Pvt. Pa. Mil.
  daughter Mary m. Gideon Bright Sommers

Lord, Oliver b. Mass. (Me.) 1799 d. Me. 1890   Pvt. Me. (Mass.) Mil.
  m. Eliza Ingersoll — son George W. m. Caroline Gullison Small

Lord, Philip b. Mass. 1787 d. Vt. 1859 m. Mariam Twitchell   Pvt. Vt. Mil.
  son Alvin m. Sarah Bucklin

Lord, Thomas b. Mass. 1736 d. Mass. 1810 m. Leonard Smith   Pvt. Mass.
  son Gardiner m. Sally Smith

Lord, William b. Conn. 1785 d. Conn. 1820 m. Harriet Ely   Pvt. Conn. Mil.
  daughter Harriet m. James Walling

Lord, William Sr. b. 1750 d. Ga. 1828 m. Sarah   Legis. Ga.
  son Steven m. Elizabeth Ann Johns

Lord, William   Vol. 14   Pvt. N.Y.

Loring, David   Vol. 13   Pvt. N.Y. Mil.

Loring, Isaac b. Mass. 1775 d. Mass. 1850 m. Sarah Smith   Pvt. Mass. Mil.
  daughter Sarah m. John Salter Boden

Loring, Lunsford b. Va. 1778 d. Va. 1856 m. Margaret N.   Capt. Va. Mil.
son John H. m. Louise Seymore Williamson

Loring, Matthew   Vol. 3   Bombadier Mass. Navy

Lorton, Lewis R. b. N.Y. 1796 d. N.Y. 1849   Pvt. N.Y. Mil.
m. Sarah Westervelt — son Alfred H. m. Sarah Mulford

Lother, Robert b. Va. 1765 d. W. Va. 1832   Sgt. Va. Mil.
m. Catherine Cain — daughter Catherine m. Thomas Ireland

Lothrop, Daniel b. Eng. d. Maine m. Miss Lane   Vol. 2   Maj. Mass.
son John m. Polly Thayer

Lothrop, Peter   Vol. 3   Capt. Mass. Mil.

Lott, Johnnes b. 1763 d.—m. Nellie Suydam Vol.1   Pvt. N.Y. Mil.
daughter Phebe m. John Spader

Lott, Johannes b. N.Y. 1785 d. N.Y. 1858 m. Abigail Bergen   Pvt. N.Y. Mil.
son Hendrick m. (1) Caroline Way

Louchnore, (Lauchner) Joseph b. Pa. 1787 d. Pa. 1866   Pvt. Pa. Mil.
m. Marie Handerk — daughter Elizabeth m. William Boyer

Loud, John b. N.Y. 1778 d. N.Y. 1866 m. Rachel Ritemen   Pvt. N.Y. Mil.
son James S. m. Huldah Pursell

Loude, Ebenezer b. Mass. 1795 d. Mass. m. Sarah   Powder Boy on Frigate
daughter Ellen L. m. Mr. Tripp   Chesapeake

Loughead, James Brown   Vol. 7   Pvt. N.Y. Mil.

Loughry, John   Vol. 8   Capt. Pa. Mil.

Lourey, Alexander b. 1767 d. Tenn. 1846   Col. Tenn. Mil. 1814-15
m. Annie Gist — son James m. Jane Meek

Love, Eliza Matilda Lee b. Va. 1790 d. Mo. 1875   Pat. 1814
m. Richard Henely Love — daughter Flora Lee m. William Johnson

Love, Robert b. S.C. 1784 d. Miss. 1865   Sgt. Miss.-Tenn. Mil.
m. Sallie Catching — daughter Harriet Emily m. Hugh C. McLaurin

Love, Robert Elliott b. S.C. 1791 d. Miss. 1833   Sgt. Miss.-Terr. Vol.
m. Pameila Canty McCullough
son Mathew M. W. m. Mary Ellen Wall Ives

Love, Ward b. Ky. 1795 d. Tex. 1878 m. Jane Wilson   Pvt. Ky. Inf.
daughter Elinor Jane m. John W. Darlington

Lovejoy, Eleazer b. S.C. 1779 d. Ga. 1834   Pvt. S.C. Mil.
m. Mary Pennington — son Welcome C. m. Penelope C. Parker

Loveland, John b. Conn. 1785 d. Conn. 1857   Elector 1812
m. Nancy Dunham — son George H. m. Christina La Tour

Loveland, John b. Conn. 1740 d. Conn. 1809   Capt. Conn. 1805
m. Mrs. Esther Buck Seward — son Justus m. Mary Robbins (Robins)

Loveland, Solomon b. Conn. 1787 d. N.Y. 1866   Drummer N.Y. Mil.
m. Clorinda Chidester — son John C. m. Derilla Tracy Deming

Lovell, James b. Mass. 1788 d. 1836   Surgeon U.S. Army
m. Margaret Mansfield
son Joseph Jr. m. Louisa Quitman (Chadbourne)

Lovell, John b. Md. 1786 d. Md. 1861 m. Nancy Lockerd   Pvt. Md. Mil.
son Thomas m. Jane Ann Cushing

Lovelace, James, b. N.C. 1779 d. Ga. 1860 m. Mary Stapler   Sgt. Ga. Mil.
son Lucius B. m. Obedience Robinson

Loveridge, Amasa   Vol. 1   Pvt. Conn. Mil.

Lovett, Aaron b. Pa. 1796 d. N.Y. 1870 m. Hester Noble   Pvt. N.Y. Mil.
daughter Catherine m. James Lawrence Stewart

Lovett, James b. N.Y. 1796 d. N.Y. 1888   Pvt. N.Y. Mil.
m. Emmeline Tallman
daughter Isabel m. Earl Gardner REAL DAUGHTER

Low, Cornelius b. Va. 1730 d.— m. Catherine McKenny   Pvt. N.Y. Mil.
son William m. Julia Ann Mathews

Low, Jacob I. b. N.Y. 1788 d. N.Y. 1867   Pvt. N.Y. Mil.
m. (1) Elizabeth Bends — son David H. m. Marietta Osborn

Lowe, (Low) John b. Va. 1797 d. Ohio 1851   Pvt. Ohio Mil.
m. Hannah Ayles — daughter Miriam m. David Thornton Brown

Lowe, Joseph b. Md. 1795 d. Ia. 1879 m. Sarah McCauley   Sgt. Va. Mil.
son Ausborn Eugene m. Sarah Wyckoff

Lowe, William Gibson b. Md. 1771 d. Pa. 1827   Pvt. Del. Mil.
m. Sarah Graham — daughter Mary H. m. Marcellus Edward Keene

Lowell, John E. b. Mass. 1757 d. Mass. (Me.)   Sgt. Mass. (Me.) Mil.
m. Sarah or Hannah Rogers — daughter Sarah m. James B. Lowell

Lowman, Barnard b. Pa. ca. 1769 d. Va. 1847   Postmaster Va.
m. Margaret Bell — son William m. Sally Eagon

Lowman, William b. Pa. 1774 d. Va. 1839 m. Margaret Agner   Pvt. Va. Mil.
son David m. Rachel Tribbet

Lowrey, Thomas b. Ire. 1737 d. N.J. 1806   U.S. Marshall
m. Esther Fleming   N.J. 1791-1805
son William m. Martha Howe   Mem. of Leg.

Lowrey, William b. N.J. 1759 d. N.J. 1802   Sheriff N.J. 1780-91
m. Martha Howe — daughter Mary m. Thomas Alexander

Lowry, Jacob Jr.   Vol. 17   Pvt. Pa. Mil.

Lowry, Robert James b. S.C. 1783 d. Miss. 1825   Lt. Miss. Mil.
m. Eliza Wren — son James Francis m. Melissa Emma Clark

Lowther, Alexander b. Va. 1791 d. Va. 1864 m. Sarah Ireland   Pvt. Va. Mil.
son Jesse m. Hannah Leeson

Loy, Nicholas b. Pa. 1770 d. Pa. 1848 m. Catherine Kuhn   Pvt. Pa. Mil.
son Andrew m. Maria Wormley

Loyal, Jesse   Vol. 4   Pvt. Ga. Vol.

Lucas, Bennet b.— d.— m. Sarah Ann Wiesner Vol. 28   Pvt. D.C. Mil.
daughter Susanna m. Aloysius Dyer

Lucas, Edward b. W. V. 1790 d. W. Va. 1858   Lt. W. Va. Mil.
m. Mary Ellen Johnson — son James B. m. Ellen Brooks

Luce, David b. N.J. 1769 d. Ind. 1839 m. Elizabeth Carter   Pvt. Ky. Vol.
daughter Mehitabel m. Thomas Everton

Luce, Rowland b. Conn. 1776 d. Me. 1862   Pvt. Mass. (Me.) Mil.
m. (2) Eunice Mason — son Jesse m. Lydia Hurd

Luce, Thomas b. Mass. 1786 d. Me. 1884   **Pvt. Mass. (Me.) Mil.**
 m. Mehitabel Hodges — son Daniel m. Emily Ladd

Luckett, Benjamin b. Md. 1787 d. Ky. 1866   **Ens. Ky. Mil.**
 m. Maria Holton — daughter Mary Eliz. m. Basil Gaither Smith

Luckey, George b. N.Y. 1793 d. Ohio 1839   **Pvt. N.Y. Art.**
 m. Elizabeth Culver — daughter Priscilla m. James Brooke, Jr.

Ludlam, Anthony b. N.J. 1792 d. N.J. 1826   **Pvt. N.J. Mil.**
 m. Mrs. Mary Mayhew Fortiner
 daughter Martha m. John Peterson Jr.

Lufkin, Moses Vol. 3   Drum Mass. Mil.

Lukins, John b. Pa. 1720 d. Pa. 1789 m. Sarah   Surveyor General
 son Charles m. Margaret Sanderson   Pa. 1784

Lum, Joseph Cooke Vol. 11   Selectman, Mem. of Gen. Assembly
                     Conn.

Lum, Obadiah b. N.J. d. N.Y. 1830 m. Elizabeth Holmes **Pvt. N.J. Mil.**
 daughter Abigail Ann m. Abraham Sypher

Lumpkin, John b. Va. 1762 d. Ga. 1834 m. Lucy Hopson Ga. 1796-1813
 son George m. Sarah Pope   Mem. of Leg. 1796
 son Joseph H. m. Callender Grieve   Elector 1800

Lumbkin, Robert b. Va. 1770 d. Va. 1879 m. Sarah Hutchinson **Pvt. Va.**
 daughter Martha m. Benjamin Hilton

Lunceford, Jacob Judy b. Ill. 1793 d. Ill. 1862   **Pvt. Ill. Mil.**
 m. Maria Ann Russell
 daughter Mary Agnes m. Clement Lloyd Allen **REAL DAUGHTER**
 m. Temperance Waller — daughter Elizabeth m. Frank Horine

Lunday, Theophilus b. Va. d. Ga. after 1800   Pat. Ga. Leg. 1784
 m. Frances McLin — son Robert m. Mary Fox Courvoisier

Lundy, Ebenezer b.—d.—m. Hannah Bard Vol. 95
 daughter Elizabeth m. John Meldrum
 son James M. m. Margaret Chase

Lunsford, (Luntzford), Jacob Vol. 17   **Pvt. Ill. Terr. Mil.**

Lupher, Jacob b. Pa. 1792 d. Pa. 1874 m. Martha Hill **Pvt. Pa. Mil.**
 daughter Martha m. Samuel Allen Hawthorne

Lupton, William Boyer b. Md. 1780 d. Md. 1820   **Pvt. Md. Mil.**
 m. Martha La Rue — son Elisha F. m. Martha Jane Davidson

Luse, Daniel Vol. 17   Cpl. Pa. Mil.

Luse, Nathan b. N.J. 1747 d. N.J. 1813 m. Demaris **Col. N.J. Mil.**
 son Nathan B. m. Mary Perry

Lusk, James b. Pa. 1793 d. Pa. 1850 m. (2) Catherine Apgar **Pvt. Pa. Mil.**
 daughter Sarah m. Abraham Stockton

Lusk, Salmon b. Vt. 1788 d. Ind. 1869 m. Mary Beard **Lt. Vt.**
 daughter Lydia m. William Brown

Luther, Jeremiah b. Mass. 1787 d. Kansas 1849 Seaman U.S. Navy
 m. Deborah
 daughter Mary Ann m. Horace Freeman **REAL DAUGHTER**

Luttrell, Lewis b. Tenn. 1786 d. Tenn. 1855   Sgt. Maj. Tenn.
 daughter Malinda m. Alexander Reeder

Lutz, Jacob D. b. Ohio 1790 d. Ohio 1866 m. Polly Broucher   Sgt. Ohio Mil.
son Eli m. Catherine Fetherolf

Lutz, Jacob H. b. Pa. 1791 d. Ohio 1844   Sgt. Ohio Mil.
m. Elizabeth Wolfley — daughter Caroline m. George H. Fickhardt

Lutz, Samuel b. Pa. 1789 d. Ohio 1890   Pvt. Ohio Mil.
m. Elizabeth Fetherolf — daughter Harriet m. Robert Zurmehly
daughter Rachel m. Christopher Patrick

Lumsden, John b.— d. Ga. 1845 m. Melindia Sanford   Lt. Ga. Cavalry
son Thomas R. m. Virginis Pearce Leonard

Lusk, David b. Va. 1770 d. Ky. 1840   Lt. Va. Mil.
m. Rachel Huffman (Hoffman) — son Winston C. N. m. Ellenor Brown

Lyford, Burleigh (Biley) b. N.J. 1755 d. N.H. 1830   Pvt. N.H. Mil.
m. (2) Dorothy Blake — son Epaphras K. m. Sarah Rollins Fletcher

Lyke, Samuel   Vol. 13   Pvt. N.Y. Mil.

Lyle, Robert b. Pa. 1754 d. Pa. 1843 m. Mary Gilliland   Sgt. Pa. Mil.
son Robert Jr. m. Sarah Rea

Lyles, Aromanus b. S.C. 1743 d. S.C. 1820   Ens. S.C. Mil.
m. Rebecca Valentine — son Thomas m. Mary Collins Woodward

Lyman, Francis b. Conn. 1755 d. Ohio 1840   Indian Fighter Ohio
m. Abigail Coles — son Joseph m. Lavinda Woodworth

Lynch (Linch), James b. Ky. 1791 d. Ky. 1846   Pvt. Ky. Mil.
m. Elizabeth Burnet (Riddle)
daughter Patience E. m. Edward Durbin

Lynch, John Raymond b. N.Y. 1767 d. Pa. 1802-4   Surgeon's Mate N.Y.
m. Jean Clarke — son Francis C. m. Caroline Billand   Engineer

Lynch, Peyton b. Ire. d. La. 1832   Pvt. Va. Mil. 1813
m. Ann Eliza Montgomery   Farrier 1814
son George m. Rosa Elizabeth Bright

Lynch, Stephen b. Va. 1777 d. Miss. 1863 m. Polly   Pvt. Miss. Vol.
son William m. Eliza Mann

Lyne, William b. Va. 1740 d. Va. 1808   Mem. Const. Conv.
m. Lucy Foster—son Henry m. Lucy Martin   Va. 1788

Lyon, Aaron Woodruff b. N.J. 1797 d. Calif. 1888   Pvt. Pa. Mil.
m. Cara Jeannette Hutchins
daughter Marie L. m. James Orlando Colwell
daughter Sarah W. m. REAL DAUGHTER

Lyon, Burr, b. Conn. 1794 d. N.Y. 1867   Pvt. Conn. Mil.
m. Malinda Churchill — son John M. m. Julia G. Eells

Lyon, Daniel b. Conn. 1795 d. N.Y. 1842   Pvt. N.Y. Mil.
m. Polly Strickland — son Newton T. m. Caroline Smith

Lyon, Nathaniel b. Vt. 1770 d. N.Y. 1836 m. Hepsibah Rugg   Pvt. N.Y. Mil.
daughter Martha m. Eli Bates

Lyon, James b. Va. 1783 d. Ky. 1828 m. Patsy Neil   Pvt. Ky. Vol.
son James Jr. m. Louise Olive Gunn

Lyon, John   Vol. 17   Pvt. N.Y. Mil.

Lyon, Matthew b. Ire. 1750 d. Ark. 1822   Mem. Congress Vt. 1796-1800
m. Mary Hosford   Shipyard Ky. 1812
daughter Anne m. John Messenger

Lyon, Noah b. Pa. 1790 d. Pa. 1858 m. Elizabeth Pettit   Pvt. Pa. Mil.
    son Peter m. Elizabeth Kern

Lyon, Samuel b. N.Y. 1776 d. N.Y. 1851 m. Hannah Merritt   Pvt. N.Y. Mil.
    daughter Lavina m. Charles Stuart Booth

Lyons, Elias b. 1786 d. Wisc. 1847 m. Lucy Phillips   Pvt. N.Y. Mil.
    son Elisha m. Harriet Vosburg

Lytle, James   Vol. 11   Pvt. Md. Mil.

Lytle, John b. Pa. 1755 d. Pa. 1822 m. Rachel Kenney   Justice Pa. 1808
    son John Jr. m. Eleanor Henderson

Lytle, Samuel b. W.Va. d. Pa. m. Elizabeth Askins   Vol. 24   Pvt. Pa. Mil.
    daughter Katherine m.—

M

Maben, Thomas (N.) b. Ky. 1792 d. Ky. 1872   Pvt. Ky. Mil.
    m. Mary P. Sawyers   Todd Co.
    son William M. m. Hannah Sawyers

Mabry, Seth b. Va. 1752 d. Tenn. 1803   Pat. Justice Va. 1786-7
    m. Elizabeth Seawell — daughter Nancy E. m. William Seawell

MacCorkle, Alexander b. Va. 1773 d. Va. after 1820   Capt. Va. Mil.
    m. Mildred Welch — son Thomas m. Susan Alexander

MacCubbin, Moses b. Md. d. Md. m.—   Pvt. Md.
    daughter Mary Ann m. William McNeir

MacDaniel, Ezekiel Sr. b.—d.—m. Ann Moore   Lt. D.C. Mil. 1814
    daughter Mary Ann m. Gibson F. Hill, Sr.

MacDonough, Thomas   Vol. 7   Commodore U.S. Navy

McDonough, Thomas b. Del. 1747-8 d. Del. 1795   Justice Del. 1788-93
    m. Mary Vance — daughter Hannah m. James Pennington
    son James m. Lydia Laroux

Mace, Henry, b. 1771 d. Ill. 1867 m. Druscilla Andrews   Cornet Ill. Mil.
    daughter Christina m. James Berry Needles

Machen, John b. S.C. 1777 d. S.C. 1861 m. Dicy Holland   Sgt. S.C. Mil.
    daughter Mary W. m. Lawson Terry Arnold

MacIntyre, Malcolm   Vol. 15   Pat.

Mackay, Aeneas b. N.Y. 1796 d. Mo. 1850 m. Helen LaGate   Pat. N.Y.
    daughter Charlotte M. m. Benjamin Bogey

Mackenzie, Cosmo b. Md. 1770 d. Md. 1809   Ens. Md. Mil.
    m. Sarah (Taylor) Mackall — son Thomas m. Tacy Bruges Norbury

MacKenzie, James b. Scot. 1776 d. Ohio 1875   Capt. Ohio Mil.
    m. Eleanor Burrows — son Samuel B. m. Mary Campbell Frazer

MacKenzie, James b. Del. 1794 d. Wisc. 1871   Pvt. Pa. Mil.
    m. Lucintha Rountree — daughter Mary L. m. John H. Barnett

MacKenzie (McKinsey), Kenneth b. Pa. 1770 d. Pa. 1846   Pvt. Pa. Mil.
    m. Sarah Newberry — daughter Jane m. Samuel Rowland

MacKenzie, Thomas b. Md. 1794 d. Md. 1866   Pvt. Md. Mil.
    m. (1) Tacy Bruges Norbury
    daughter Sarah M. m. George Julius Appold

Mackerly, Michael b. N.J. 1770 d. Ohio 1853   Sgt. N.J. Mil.
  m. Martha McCurdy — daughter Emily m. Alfred Dickey
  son Louis m. Margaret Sloane
  daughter Mary m. James Douglass

Mackie, Thomas b. Scot. d. Pa. 1821 m. Joanna Cook   Pvt. Pa. Mil.
  daughter Eliza m. Francis Gurney Smith

MacKoy, John b. Ga. 1772 d. Ky. 1843 m. Levina Fuqua   Pvt. Ky. Mil.
  son Moses F. m. Hannah Lawson

MacKrill, Samuel   Vol. 13   Pvt. Ohio Mil.

Maclay, John b. Ire. 1707 d. Pa. 1804   Pat. Pa. Legis. 1790, 2, 4
  m. Janet McDonald — daughter Elizabeth m. Samuel Culbertson

Maclay, Samuel   Vol. 10   Senator Pa.

MacLay, William Plunket b. Pa. 1774 d. Pa. 1842   Pat. Mem. Assem.
  m. Jane Holmes   1807-8
  son David m. Elizabeth Richardson   Judge 1809 Senate 1812
         Congress 1814

MacMillian, John   Vol. 13   Maj. S.C. Vol.

MacMurphy, Daniel Jr. b. Ga. 1788 d. Ga. 1839   Sgt. Maj. Qtr. Mst. Ga. Mil.
  m. Mary Drummond Lamb
  daughter Susannah C. m. Augustus de Cotte

MacMurphy, George G. b. Va. 1782 d. S.C. 1814   Adj. S.C. Mil.
  m. Keziah Parish Martin — daughter Sarah m. John M. Adams

MacNeil, David Breckenridge b. Vt. 1787 d. Vt. 1863   Col. Vt. Mil.
  m. Hannah Havens — son Charles H. m. Abigail Douglass Bentley

Macomb, Alexander b. Mich. 1782 d. D.C. 1841, Brig. Gen. U.S. Army 1814
  m. Catherine Navarre — daughter Alexandrine M. m. Henry Stanton
  daughter Jane Octavia m. Morris S. Miller

Macon, Henry b. 1790 d. 1863 m. Elizabeth Ozier   Pvt. N.C. Mil.
  son John A. m. Elizabeth A. Morris

Macon, Nathaniel b. N.C. 1757 d. N.C. 1837   Pat. Rep. N.C. 1791-1815
  m. Hannah Plummer — daughter Elizabeth K. m. William John Martin

MacPherson, George   Vol. 7   Capt. N.Y. Mil.

Macrae, John Jr. b. Va. 1791 d. Va. 1850   Capt. Va. Mil.
  m. Euphan Washington — daughter Euphan W. m. William Henry Roy

Madam, Henry   Vol. 11   Pvt. N.Y. Mil.

Madara, William b. N.J. 1777 d. N.J. 1843 m. Abigail Turner   Lt. N.J. Inf.
  daughter Abigail m. Thomas Simpkins

Madden, William b. Pa. 1790 d. Pa. 1872   Pvt. Pa. Mil.
  m. Elizabeth Flickenger — son Charles m. Mary Shivley

Maddox, Sherwood, Jr.   Vol. 17   Pvt. Ky. Mil.

Madison, George   Vol. 17   Maj. Ky. Mil.

Magee, Daniel b. N.C. 1795 d. Tex. 1871 m. Sally Allen   Pvt. Miss. Mil.
  daughter Nancy Ann E. m. David Catching Dickson

Mager, William Vol. 4   Pvt.

Maggard, Adam b. W. Va. 1778 d. Va. 1832   Ens. (W.) Va. Mil.
  m. Sarah White—son David m. Pernicia Gary

Magill, Hugh b. Pa. ca. 1767 d. Ky. about 1814   Lt. Va. Mil.
     m. Margaret Dougherty — daughter Rebecca m. Washington Hocker

Magnon, Jaques   Vol. 11   Pat. La.

Magoon, John   Vol. 3   Pvt. Mass. (Me.) Mil.

Magruder, Samuel   Vol. 17   Pat. Justice Md. 1784-5

Magrue, Paul   Vol. 14   Pvt. Ohio Mil.

Mahan, Edward b. Va. 1772 d. Ala. 1855 m. Rachel Reagan   Pvt. Tenn. Mil.
     son Jesse W. m. Martha McCrimmon

Mahon, William Pope b. Va. 1796 d. Mo. 1865   Va. Mil.
     m. Permelia Goodman — son Thomas Jefferson m. Rebecca Baker

Major, John Sleet b. 1789 d. 1872   Pvt. Ky. Mil.
     m. Lucinda Smith Slaughter
     daughter Sarah Belle m. Wilson Hunter Smith

Major, Thomas Porter b. Va. 1782 d. Ky. 1850   Pvt. Ky. Vol.
     m. Margaret Alexander
     daughter Nancy S. m. Robert Madison Crenshaw

Malary, Henry b. Vt. 1781 d. Ill. 1853 m. Polly Bent   Ens. N.Y. Mil.
     daughter Mary m. Peter Martin Becker

Malcomson, Joseph b. Ire. d. Pa. after 1851 __Vol. 5   Pvt. Pa. Mil.

Maley (Mealey), John b. Va. 1778 d. Va. 1832 m. Sarah Rice   Pvt. Va. Mil.
     son Sidney m. Arena Deadwyler

Mallard, Abraham b. 1780 d. Mass. 1858 m. Sally Dana   Sgt. Mass. Mil.
     daughter Harriet m. Orin Foster

Mallet, Lewis Jr. b. Conn. 1734 d. Conn. 1804   Pat. Leg. Conn. 1789
     m. Mary Merwin — son Lewis III m. Anna Beach

Mallett, John Goldsmith Charles b. Conn. 1785 d. La. 1883   Sgt. Ohio Mil.
     m. Margaret — daughter Laura Ann m. Jesse Pease

Mallette, Abraham b. Ga. 1788 d. Ga. 1867   Pat. Sheriff Ga.
     m. Catherine Kennedy — daughter Margaret M. m. Robert Brazil Crum

Mallory, James b. Conn. 1772 d. N.Y. 1825   Lt. N.Y. Mil.
     m. Amelia Hunt — son Stirling m. Elsie Bentley Greenwich

Mallory, John F. b. Va. 1778 d. N.C. 1860 m. Polly Coleman   Pvt. Va. Mil.
     son John Thomas m. Sarah Boyd

Mallow, Henry b. Va. 1773 d. Ohio 1849 m. Sarah Popyay, Capt. Ohio 1812
     son William m. Sarah

Mallow, Michael b. Va. 1793 d. Tex. 1863   Pvt. Va. Mil.
     m. Charlotte Ghortner — son Lewis C. m. Dorcas C. Fitzhugh

Maloon, Simon b. Mass. (Me.) 1795 d. Me. 1873   Pvt. Mass. Mil.
     m. Sally Phoebe Drake
     daughter Jane Deborah m. John Henry Johnson

Malott, David b. Md. 1777 d. Ohio 1870 m. Rebecca (1)   Pvt. Ohio Mil.
     son Hiram m. (1) Matilda Smith

Malott, Hiram   Vol. 13   Pvt. Ky. Vol.

Maltby, Isaac   Vol. 15   Brig. Gen. Mass. Mil.

Manchester, George b. R.I. 1764 d. N.Y. 1856 m. Jael Kent   Capt. N.Y. Mil.
     son Stephen m. Meriba Chamberlin

Manchester, Thomas b. Vt. 1770 d. Vt. 1852   Pvt. Vt. Mil.
   m. Elizabeth Kelley — daughter Elizabeth m. George Sutherland

Mandeville, Nicholas b. N.J. 1765 d. N.J. 1820   Pat. Rep. N.J. Leg.
   m. Elizabeth VanNess — son Simon V. m. Catharine Crane   1813-15

Mandeville, Cornelius W. b. N.J. 1789 d. N.J. 1856   Capt. N.J. Mil.
   m. Maria Berry — daughter Sarah M. m. Josiah H. Zabriskie

Maner, John Seth b. S.C. 1785 d. S.C. 1862   Leg. S.C. 1808
   m. Kitty Morgandollar — son Samuel P. m. Mary Ann Lawton

Manley, Nathan b. Mass. 1750 d. N.Y. 1833   Pat. Vt. 1786
   m. Hannah Kent — daughter Hannah m. James Blinn Sr.

Manlove, Vincent b. Del. 1780 d. Ohio 1854 m. Martha Gans   Pvt. Del. Mil.
   son Vincent Jr. m. Mary Trease

Mann, Cain b. Va. 1792 d. Va. 1852   Pvt. Va. Mil.
   m. Priscilla Belcher or Mary Berkley
   son Cain Jr. m. Virginia Andrews or Mary M. Andrews

Mann, Daniel b. Mass. 1770 d. N.Y. 1814   Sgt. U.S. Art.
   m. Elizabeth Hamblin — daughter Catherine m. Azariah Edwards

Mann, David b. Mass. (Me.) 1794 d. Ind. 1867   Pvt. Music N.Y. Mil.
   m. Sarah Dunbar Smith
   daughter Rachel F. m. Howard B. Acuff REAL DAUGHTER

Mann, George b. 1780 d. Pa. 1873   Pvt. U.S. Rifleman
   m. Elizabeth Ream — daughter Sarah Elizabth m. George Barrow

Mann, Luke b. Ga. 1736 d. Ga. 1800 m. (1) Ann Butler   Ga. Senator 1789
   son Thomas m. (2) Harriet Sleigh   for Bryan Co.

Manning, Anthony   Vol. 15   Lt. Md. Mil.

Manning, Clarkson b. N.J. 1794 d. Ohio 1888 m. Phoebe Cory Pvt. N.J. Mil.
   daughter Elsy A. m. Squire Ayers

Manning, John Sr. b. S.C. 1782 d. S.C. 1844 m. Lititia Lee   Pvt. S.C.
   son Elisha m. Rebecca Edwards
   son John m. Eliz. Harvey
   son Melea m. Mary Kinney

Manring (Mannering), Jourdan Marchial b. Ohio 1790 d. Ohio 1864
   m. Sarah Knox   Lt. Ohio Mil. 1814-15
   son Andrew Jerrerson m. Sarah Ewing
   son Thira m. Ann Best Smith

Mansfield, William b. Va. 1790 d. Ky. 1849 m. Gracey Noel   Pvt. Va. Mil.
   son Richard m. Array

Manson, David Jr. b. Pa. 1789 d. Ohio 1823   Pvt. Ohio Mil.
   m. Sarah Cornwall — son Mahlon D. m. Caroline Mitchell

Manson, Joseph Pettigrew b. (Me.) Mass. 1793 d. Me. 1883   Pvt. Mass. Mil.
   m. Ursula Edgerly — son Nathaniel m. Hannah Weymouth

Mansur, James b. Vt. c. 1790 d. Wisc. 1860 m. Sarah   Pvt. Mass. Mil.
   daughter Mary m. Abner Reynolds

Mantle, Edmond   Vol. 15   Sgt. N.Y. Mil.

Manton, Anthony b. La. 1793 d. La. 1876 m. Ann Eliza McKee   Seaman La.
   daughter Eliza Ann m. John McCartney Taylor

Manuel, William b. 1788 d. Ky. 1823 m. Starling Cameron   Pat. Ky.
   son Philip m. Rebecca Wheeler

Manvill, Ira b. Conn. 1762 d. Pa. 1803 m. Mary Reynolds   Pat. Pa.
    son Ira G. m. Eliza Deremer

Manwell (Manuel), John b. Mass. (Me.) 1796 d. Me. 1883
    m. Mary Hammond   Pvt. Mass. (Me.) Mil.
    son John Jr. m. Huldah Jane Poland

Mapes, James   Vol. 16   Pvt. U.S. Rifleman

Mapes, Moses b. N.Y. 1789 d. Ohio 1861   Pvt. N.Y. Mil.
    m. Elizabeth Hawkins — son George W. m. Martha Danison

Mapes, Rufus b. N.Y. 1795 d. Ohio 1874 m. Abigail Allen   Pvt. N.Y. Mil.
    son Cassius C. m. Augusta A. Frissell

Maple, William b. N.J. 1779 d. Ill. 1848 m. Mary Fuller   Pvt. Ohio Mil.
    son William Jr. m. Sarah Cowgill

Maples, William C. b. Va. 1766 d. Ala. 1847   Sgt. Tenn Mil.
    m. Nancy Long — son James m. Edith Caroline Patterson

Marable, Edward b. Va. 1789 d. Va. 1860   Pvt. Va. Mil.
    m. Elizabeth Major
    daughter Martha W. m. Thomas Jefferson Morecock

Marable, William H. b. Va. 1795 d. Va. 1854   Pvt. Va. Mil.
    m. Elizabeth Hunt
    daughter Mary R. m. Henry Carter Land REAL DAUGHTER

Marable, William J.   Vol. 14   Pvt. Pa. Mil.

Marbury, Leonard b. La. 1750 d. La. 1795   Pat. Const. Conv. 1789 Ga.
    m. Ann Sommerville — daughter Eliza m. Samuel Dunbar

March, William b. Mass. 1792 d. Vt. 1824 m.—   Pvt. Vt. Mil.
    daughter Philadelphia m. Nehemiah Horton

Marcy, Nathaniel b. Conn. 1733 d. Conn. 1798   Pat. Conn. 1785-6
    m. Hannah Grosvenor — son Alfred m. Rebekah Perrin

Marham, Jabez b. Mass. 1743 d. Mass. 1831   Tax Coll. 1813
    m. Anna Shurtleff — son Jabez m. Ruth Chubbuck   Carver, Mass.

Maris, David   Vol. 4   Pvt. Pa. Mil.

Markham, Abijah   Vol. 12   Pat. U.S. Gov.

Markham, George b. Va. 1783 d. Va. 1850   Capt. Va. Mil.
    m. Fanny Garland—daughter Martha M. m. Solomon Carr

Markham, William b. Conn. 1762 d. N.Y. 1826   Pat. N.Y. 1812
    m. Phebe Dexter — son Wayne m. Anna Brown

Markland, Edward Jr. b. Md. 1796 d. Md. 1841   Pvt. Md. Mil.
    m. Frances Crates McJilton
    daughter Alice E. m. Sylvester E. Penning

Markle, Abraham b. Pa. 1762 d. Ohio 1841   Pvt. Ohio Mil.
    m. (1) Rachel Blackburn — son Abram m. Harriett Johnson

Markle, Gaspard   Vol. 9   Pat. W. Va.

Markle, George   Vol. 9   Pat. W. Va.

Markle, Joseph   Vol. 7   Capt. Pa. Mil.

Marks, Heston (Hastings) b. 1795 d. 1846 m. Sivility Powell   Pvt. Ga. Mil.
    son John Harvie Marks m. Matilda Thornton

Marpet, Joshua b. S.C. 1788 d. Ga. 1863 m. Sarah Longshore   Pvt. S.C. Mil.
    son Robert L. m. Sophonia Ann Peek

Marple, John Abraham b. Pa. 1770 d. W. Va.   Pvt. Pa. Mil.
    m. Barbary Weaver — son John William m. Ruth Reger

Marquis, Thomas b. Va. 1753 d. Ohio 1827 m. Jean Park   Lt. Pa. Mil.
    son William m. Sarah Marquis (cousin)

Marriner, Silas   Vol. 4   Seaman on Dash

Marriott, James Homewood b. Md. 1771 d. Md. 1835   Pvt. Md. Vol.
    m. Rachel Waters — son Alpheus W. m. Adalia Hammond

Marriott, John b. Fra. 1776 d. Md. 1845 m.—   Pvt. Md. Mil.
    daughter Le Sutte m. George C. Tucker

Marschalk, John b. N.Y. 1776 d. N.Y. 1860   Capt. N.Y. Mil.
    m. Sophia Stediford—son Gerard S. m. Clarissa Mary Dodge

Marsh, Charles b. Conn. 1775 d. N.Y. 1837   2nd Lt. U.S. Inf.
    m. Martha Howe — son Darius W. m. L. Cordelia Heaton

Marsh, Elias M. b. N.J. 1794 d. Ohio 1865 m. Sarah Clark   Pvt. N.J. Mil.
    son Robert S. m. Julia Weidman

Marsh, Henry b. Pa. 1786 d. Pa. 1857   Pvt. Pa. Mil.
    m. Magdalena Maisle — son Joseph m. Eliza Cecelia Von Steuben

Marsh, Joel b. Conn. 1791 d. Ohio 1867   Drummer N.Y.
    m. Nancy Cartwright — daughter Mary m. Robt. Bloomfield

Marsh, John   Vol. 6   Pvt. Pa. Mil.

Marsh (March), John b. Pa. 1750 d. Pa. 1821   Cpl. Pa. Mil.
    m. Susanna Catharine — daughter Maria Magdalena m. Henry Marsh

Marsh, Joshua b. Mass. 1765 d. Mass. 1855   Mem. of Mass. Train Band
    m. Mindwell Crosbee — son Joshua Jr. m. Mary Hawley

Marsh, Luman   Vol. 14   Sgt. N.Y. Mil.

Marsh, Thomas Hartshorne b. Mass. 1776 d. Me. 1870   Capt. Mass. Mil.
    m. Sarah Curtis Bronsdon — son Lucius B. m. Caroline Elizabeth Mann

Marshall, Alexander b. S.C. 1787 d. Ill. 1864   Pvt. S.C. Mil.
    m. Mary McMillan — daughter Jane T. m. Isaiah John Brooke
    son John m. Ann Richey

Marshall, Coleman   Vol. 17   Cpl. Va. Mil.

Marshall, Davis   Vol. 4   Ens. Vt. Mil.

Marshall, Elijah b. N.H. 1766 d. N.H. 1838 m. Mary Pierce   Pvt. N.H. Mil.
    daughter Elizabeth m. Benjamin Hayward

Marshall, Gilbert b. Tenn. 1789 d. Ark 1847   Pat. Ill. Surveyor
    m. Nancy Stinett — daughter Mary Jane m. Samuel Wright Williams

Marshall, James b. Va. 1735 d. N.C. 1818 m. Abbe Garrusib   Pat. N.C.
    daughter Lucy m. James Turner

Marshall, James b. Va. 1771 d. Tenn. 1836 m. Margaret Wilson Lt. Ky. Mil.
    son Gilbert m. Judith Adaline Drake

Marshall, Jesse b. Pa. 1784 d. Ohio 1866   Lt. Ohio Mil.
    m. Mary Gabrielle Serot Carteron — daughter Mary G. m. Vinton Price
    son Jesse Jr. m. Marie Avilgne Serot

Marshall, John b. Va. 1755 d. Pa. 1835   Chief Justice of Supreme
   m. Mary Willis Ambler   Ct. 1801
   son Thomas m. Margaret W. Lewis

Marshall, John b. Ky. 1784 d. Ohio 1867 m. Fanny Martin   Pvt. Ohio Mil.
   daughter Hetty m. George Kiler

Marshall, John b. Eng. 1773 d. Ga. 1833   Pvt. Ga. Mil.
   m. Elizabeth McGill — son Charles L. m. Mary Catherine Ross

Marshall, John b. R.I. 1764 d. N.Y.   Pat. Justice Peace
   m. Lydia Brown — son Thomas m. Effie Jones   N.Y. 1814

Marshall, Orra   Vol. 3   Pvt. Vt. Mil.

Marshall, Peletiah b. Mass. 1782 d. Me.   Pvt. U.S. Inf. Mass.
   m. Martha Skillings — son Hammond m. Mary Maddox

Marshall, Robert b. Md. 1790 d. Md. 1872   Pvt. Md. & D.C. Mil.
   m. Charlotte Brown — son George R. W. m. Sarah Anne Waring

Marshall, Robert b. Va. 1757-8 d. Ky. 1814   Pvt. Ky. Mil.
   m. Mary Ann Simpson — son Robert Jr. m. Elizabeth Evans

Marshall, Samuel b. Ire. 1772 d. Pa. 1846 m. Jane Moon   Pvt. Pa. Mil.
   son Samuel Jr. m. Margaret Smith

Marshall, Samuel b. Pa. 1750 d. Ohio 1816   Pvt. Ohio Mil.
   m. Nancy Haylesrigg (Hazelrigg)
   son Jesse m. Mrs. Mary G. S. Carteron

Marshall, Scott b. Pa. 1788 d. Pa. 1864 m. Jane McClure   Pvt. Pa. Mil.
   daughter Eliza m. Elliott Ferguson

Marshall, Thomas b. Va. 1730 d. Ky. 1802   Pat. Leg. Va. 1787
   m. Mary R. Keith — son Thomas Jr. m. Frances Maitland Kennan

Marshall, William   Vol. 10   Pvt. Ohio Mil.

Marshall, William   Vol. 15   Lt. Del. Mil.

Marshall, William b. Tenn. 1788 d. Ky. 1849   Pvt. Ky. Mil.
   m. Elizabeth Henry Williams
   daughter Elizabeth H. m. Samuel Davies Blackburn

Marshall, William b. Va. 1782 d. Ky. 1857   Pvt. Ohio Inf.
   m. Elizabeth Kercheval — daughter Laurentine K. m. John Carrigan

Marston, Nathaniel b. N.H. 1776 d. Me. 1848   Lt. Mass. Mil.
   m. Eleanor Watson — daughter Mary m. Arthur Neal

Marteney, William b. Md. 1770 d. W.Va. 1847   Del. to Gen. Asso. Va.
   m. Eunice Eastburn — daughter Martha Ellen m. John Phares
   son Washington m. Rebecca Clem

Matthias, Daniel b. Holland 1734 d. Pa. after 1802   Pvt. Pa. Mil. 1794
   m. Catherine Warner — son Michael m. Catherine Cope

Martin, Aaron Jr. b. Conn. 1772 d. Vt. 1861 m. Mary Martyn   Pvt. Vt. Mil.
   son Minot m. Nancy Densmore

Martin, Bethel b. N.Y. 1793 d. N.Y. 1841 m. Nancy Horton   Pvt. N.Y. Mil.
   son Timothy m. Victoria Patnode

Martin, Charles b. Va. 1715 d. W. Va. 1800   Pat. Del. to Assm. Va.
   m. Elizabeth Burrows — son Spencer m. Polly Snider

Martin, Charles b. Va. 1796 d. Ia. 1843   Pvt. Va. Mil.
   m. Elizabeth Morgan — son Charley m. Maria Louisa Glasscock

Martin, Elijah b. Ky. 1768 d. Ohio 1842 m. Rebecca Boggs   Capt. Ohio Mil.
son Alexander B. m. Prudence McNoun

Martin, Elijah b. Pa. 1751 d. Ga. 1819   Ens. Ga. Mil.
m. Mary Van Der Burg — son Levi m. Jemima Harris

Martin, George W. b. N.C. 1792 d. Miss. 1854   Pvt. Tenn. Mtd. Gunsman
m. Lucinda R. Donelson — daughter Elizabeth D. m. Jacob M. Hoffa

Martin, Hiram, b. S.C. 1790 d. S.C. 1844 m. Jane Bobo   Pvt. S.C. Mil.
son Jefferson m. Louise Dodd

Martin, Hudson b. Ky. 1794 d. Ky. 1838   2nd Sgt. Ky. Troops
m. Elizabeth Richard — daughter Judith m. Samuel C. Hughes

Martin, Hutson, b. Va. 1783 d. Wash. 1862   Pvt. Ohio Mil.
m. Martha Laycock — son William m. Ceraphina Wetherbee

Martin, James b. S.C. 1788 d. Ga. 1869 m. Esther Bogan   Pvt. Ga. Troops
son Charles m. Rachel Anna Leslie

Martin, James b. R.I. 1751 d. R.I. 1807 m.—   Pat. Mem. Gen. Ass. R.I.
daughter Amelia m. Ira Kent   1794/1804

Martin, James b. Pa. 1734 d. Pa. 1809   Pat. Assy. Judge Pa. 1785/91
son Abraham A. m. Martha R. Minie

Martin, Jesse b. Mass. 1778 d. N.Y. 1841   Pvt. N.Y. Mil.
m. Hannah Hicks (Hix) — son Jesse Jr. m. Sarah Ann Decker

Martin, John b. Pa. 1772 d. Pa. 1844 m. Alice Kendig   Capt. Pa. Mil.
daughter Mattie m. J. Henry Mehaffey

Martin, John b. Va. 1751 d. S.C. 1813 m. Elizabeth Terry   Lt. S.C. Mil.
daughter Sarah m. John Cheney

Martin, John b. S.C. 1794 d. Miss. 1864 m. Alsie Gill   Pvt. Miss. Mil.
son Albert J. m. Sarah Ann Given
son John Jr. m. Effie Ovier Weathesby

Martin, John b. Va. 1783 d. Ohio 1850 m. Mary   Capt. Pa. Mil.
daughter Gerncia m. Ludwig Weber

Martin, John B. b. Pa. 1794 d. Pa. 1854 m. Jane Ann Maxwell   Pvt. Pa. Mil.
daughter Rachel W. m. Jacob McDonald

Martin, John D. Sr. b. 1795 d. 1860 m. Sarah Dickens   Pvt. Tenn. Mil.
son John D. Jr. m. Mary Ruth Davidson

Martin, John L. b. Pa. 1783 d. Pa. m. Sarah Loots   Capt. Pa. Mil.
daughter Mary m. Nickolas Borden Wean

Martin, John Peter b. Ger. 1775 d. Md. 1856 m.—   Pvt. Md. Mil.
daughter Martha Ellen m. Cornelius Trump REAL DAUGHTER

Martin, Joseph b. Va. 1785 d. Va. 1856 m. Sally Hughes   Col. Tenn. Mil.
son Jesse m. Cecelia Reid

Martin, Joseph b. Va. 1740 d. Va. 1808   Brig. Gen. Va. Mil.
m. (1) Sarah Lucas — son Brice m. Malinda Perkins
m. (2) Susannah Graves — son Joseph Jr. m. Sallie Hughes

Martin, Joshua b. Ga. 1794 d. Ga. 1874 m. Sarah S. Shields   Pvt. Ga. Mil.
son John S. m. Harriet Hewell Lansford

Martin, Nathaniel b. N.J. 1762 d. N.J. 1854 m. Phila Potter   Pvt. N.J. Mil.
son Humprhey m. Isabella Teasdale

Martin, Reuben b. Conn. 1746 d. Vt. 1838 m. Sarah Williams   **Pvt. Vt. Mil.**
son Stoddard m. Abigail Squires

Martin, Richard Francis b. 1763 d. Miss. 1856 m. Ann   **Pvt. Miss. Mil.**
son Thomas F. m. Elizabeth Slater

Martin, Robert b. Md. 1754 d. Ga. 1832 m. Eleanor Jones   **Ens. Ga. Mil.**
daughter Eleanor m. Jesse Short

Martin, Robert B. b. Ky 1788 d. Mo. 1849 m. Polly Crutcher   **Pvt. Ky. Mil.**
daughter Nancy m. Samuel Bowling REAL DAUGHTER

Martin, Simeon b. Mass. 1775 d. Canada 1816   **Capt. Mass. Mil.**
m. Esther Mason — daughter Rhoby m. Isaac Dean

Martin, Thomas b. N.J. 1759 d. Pa. 1828   **Pvt. Pa. Mil.**
m. Mary Montgomery — son Lewis m. Sarah Foster Berryhill

Martin, Wait   Vol. 13   **2nd Lt. N.Y. Mil.**

Martin, Wait   Vol. 16   **Pvt. Vt. Mil.**

Martin, Walter b. Mass. 1764 d. N.Y. 1834   **Brig. Gen. N.Y. Mil.**
m. Sarah Turner — son John W. m. Lavinia Lee

Martin, William   Vol. 10   **Capt. N.Y. Mil.**

Martin, William b. Va. 1765 d. Tenn. 1846   **Lt. Col. Tenn. Vol.**
m. Frances Ferriss — son Wilson m. Mary Bridgewater
daughter Sallie m. Thomas T. Young

Martin, William b. N.H. 1786 d. Vt. 1879 m. Sabra Axtell   **Pvt. Vt. Mil.**
son Bowman B. m. Catherine Davis Pratt

Marvin, Benjamin b. Conn. 1762 d. N.Y. 1822 m. Mehitabel   **Pvt. N.Y. Mil.**
daughter Clarinda m. Joseph Mott

Marin, Thomas b. Conn. 1763 d. N.Y. 1835 m. Anna Norton   **Sgt. N.Y. Mil.**
son Henry m. Caroline K. Jones

Mase, Simeon   Vol. 8   **Ens. N.Y. Mil.**

Mask, Pleasant M. b. N.C. 1787 d. Tenn. 1847   **Capt. N.C. Mil.**
m. Winifred T. Pemberton
daughter Margaret Jane m. Dr. Charles Alfred Gantt

Mason, Christopher Jr.   Vol. 3   Pat. Mem. Gen. Ct. Mass. 1784

Mason, Hezekiah b.— d.— Ia. m. Sybil Eddy   Vol. 21   **Pvt. N.Y. Mil.**
son Hezekiah E. m. Ruth Gowan

Mason, James b. Va. 1790 d. Mo. 1873 m. Lucinda Jameson   **Pvt. Va. Mil.**
daughter Eliza m. C. S. W. Taylor

Mason, John b. Pa. 1793 d. Pa. 1878 m. Jane Shaw   **Pvt. Pa. Mil.**
son Joseph m. Eugenia Achsah Anderson

Mason, Joseph b. Tenn. 1790 d. Tenn. 1871   **Lt. Tenn. Mil.**
m. Edith McClure—son Allen J. m. (2) Martha Jane Fitzhugh

Mason, Noah Sr. b. Mass. 1782 d. Ill. 1834   **Pvt. U.S. Vol.**
m. Lucinda Stetson — son Noah Jr. m. Martha Nuckolls

Mason, Peter b. Ct. 1786 d. Ohio 1856 m. Sebra Day   **Pvt. Ct. Mil.**
Vol. 26

Mason, Robert b. Va. 1752 d. m.—   Vol. 31   **Pvt. Va. Mil.**
daughter Mary m. Silas Crispin

Mason, Thomas b. Tenn. 1792 d. Ill. 1847   Pvt. Tenn. Mil.
  m. Eleanor Thurston
  daughter Harriett M. m. James Anderson Thompson

Mason, William b. Ct. 1790 d. Minn. 1882 m. Lovina Lyon   Cpl. U.S. Inf.
  daughter Keziah m. Charles Eaton

Mason, William b. N.C. 1760 d. N.C. 1840 m. Nancy Acree   Pvt. N.C. Inf.
  son Turner m. Sarah Wilson

Massee, Needham b. N.C. 1779 d. Ga. 1859 m. Sarah Little   Capt. Ga. Mil.
  son Drewry W. m. Susan E.

Massey, Benjamin b. Md. 1790 d. Pa. 1864   Capt. Md. Mil.
  m. Elizabeth Ware — son Hiram m. Anna Dotterer

Massey, James   Vol. 16   Pvt. Tenn. Mil.

Massie, Charles b. Va. 1727 d. Va. 1817 m. Mary Davis   Pat. Va.
  son Thomas m. Lucy Davis

Massie, Josia b. Va. 1786 d. Va. 1852 m. Elizabeth Ball   Lt. Va. Mil.
  son Joseph C. m. Messiniah Elizabeth Sessums

Massie, Peter b. Va. 1789 d. Mo. 1837   3rd Lt. Mo. Mil.
  m. Charlotte Rodney—son William m. Fannie Keith

Mastin, John Gilbert b. Del. 1793 d. Ky. 1867 m. Jane Miller   Pvt. Ky. Vol.
  daughter Ann Mary m. Davis Edwards REAL DAUGHTER

Matheny, Charles R. b. Va. 1786 d. Ill. 1839 m. Jemima Ogle   Pvt. Ill. Mil.
  daughter Maria Carolina m. Stephen Strode Whitehurst

Mather, Demas b. Ct. 1767 d. Vt. 1833 m. Louise Marine   Capt. Ct. Mil.
  son George William m. Elvira Warren

Mather, John b. Pa. 1792 d. Pa. 1880 m. Mary Ann Lindsay   Sgt. Pa. Mil.
  son Thomas m. Hannah Ann Barr

Mather, Joseph b. Ct. 1750 d. Ct. 1833 m. Polly Burritt   Ens. N.Y. Mil.
  daughter Eunice m. Asahel Pannfield

Mather, Moses b. Ct. 1719 d. Ct. 1806 m. Elizabeth Whiting   Pat. Ct.
  son Noyes m. Catherine

Mather, Phineas b. Vt. 1751 d. Vt. 1838   Pat. Selectman Vt.
  m. Huldah Taylor   1792/6
  son Elihu m. Eunice Miller

Mather, Samuel b. Pa. 1784 d. Ohio 1864   4th Sgt. Ohio Mil.
  m. Lucy or Luvicy — daughter Mary m. John Peale

Mathews, Isaac b. Va. 1781 d. Ill. 1863   Pvt. Ohio Mil.
  m. (2) Susannah Sibert — daughter Ann REAL DAUGHTER

Mathews, Joseph b. Ohio 1792 d. Ka. 1871   Pvt. Ohio Mil.
  m. Hannah Bayless — daughter Amelia m. John Vandeman

Mathews, James A. b. Va. 1756/8 d. Ky. 1824   Pvt. Ky. Mil.
  m. Catherine Mizner — son George W. m. Margaret Jane Davis

Mathews, Sampson b. Va. 1767 d. Tenn. 1848   Lt. W. Tenn. Mil.
  m. Elizabeth Johnson — son Joseph R. m. Sallie B. Ryan

Mathews, Valentine b. Mass. (Me.) 1790 d. Me. 1869   Pvt. U.S. Inf.
  m. Nancy Moore — daughter Marcena G. m. Thomas Lord

Mathewson, William B. b. 1745 d. N.Y. 1835   Pvt. U.S. Inf.
    m. Tabitha Chaffee — daughter Prudence m. Shirland Rose

Mathias, Griffith b. Md. 1786/7 d. Md. 1851   Pvt. Md. Mil.
    m. Susannah Hufford — son Philip m. Eleanor Stimmel

Mathiot, Jacob b. Pa. 1790 d. Pa. 1873 m. Anna Wisler   Pvt. Pa.
    daughter Mary m. George W. Ralston

Mathis, Jesse b. N.C. 1794 d. Tenn. 1875   Gunner U.S. Vol. 1815
    m. Mary Murphy
    daughter Martha Ann m. Harris E. Owen REAL DAUGHTER

Matlack, James b. N.C. 1780 d. Mo. 1867 m. Martha Gunn   Cpl. N.C. Mil.
    daughter Mary m. Ashley G. Lea

Matlack, Josiah b. N.J. 1777 d. N.J. 1838 m. Sarah Ellis   Adj. N.J. Mil.
    son Samuel B. m. Mrs. Deborah Snyder

Matlack, Timothy b. N.J. 1736 d. Pa. 1829 m. Ellen Yarnall   Pat. Pa. 1793
    daughter Martha m. Rev. Robert Blackwell

Matson, John b. Abt. 1780 d. 1819   Pvt. Tenn. Mil.
    m. Sarah (Sally) Nichols
    son Wm. Hatcher m. Elizab. Emeline Limbaugh

Matson, Uriah b. Ire. 1745 d. Pa. 1817 m. Belle   Pvt. Pa. Mil.
    son John m. Mary Thompson

Matthews, Elijah Jr. Vol. 14   Pvt. N.J. Mil.

Mathews, Isaac Vol. 3   Lt. Mass. Mil.

Matteson, Abraham Jr. b. Vt. 1781 d. N.Y. 1831   Maj. N.Y. Troops
    m. Elizabeth Woodward — son Hiram m. Alvira Brooks

Matteson, Thomas b. R.I. 1764 d. N.Y. 1820   Pvt. N.Y. Vol.
    m. Eunice Le Valley — son Cyrus m. Catherine Maydole

Matthews, Absalom E. b. 1790 d. Ill. 1853 m. Esther Green   Pvt. Tenn. Mil.
    son Andrew J. m. Hulda Ann Swafford

Matthews, George b. 1766 d. Pa. 1869 m.—   Lt. Pa. Mil.
    son James B. m. Mary Thompson

Matthews, John b. Ct. 1778 d. Mo. m. Penelope Morris   Pvt. Ohio Mil.
    son George Q. m. Anne Cocoran

Matthews, Joseph Jr. b. N.C. 1775 d. Tex. 1855   Sgt. Miss. Mil.
    m. Penina Lucinda Crisp — daughter Nancy E. m. A. C. C. Bailey

Matthews, Orrin b. N.Y. 1789 d. N.Y. 1841 m. Hannah Burr   Sgt. N.Y. Mil.
    daughter Sally Maretta m. William G. Reeves

Matthews, William Vol. 9   Ens. Md. Mil.

Mattison, Ebenezer b. N.Y. 1790 d. N.Y. 1852   Sgt. N.Y. Mil.
    m. Roxana Greene — son Ephraim m. Elizabeth Sherman

Mattox, Elijah Jr. b. Ky. 1791/4 d. Ohio 1883   Pvt. Ohio Mil.
    m. Elizabeth Medaris — daughter Amelia m. Henry Bonnell

Mattox, John b. 1760 d. Ga. 1826 m. Sarah   Lt. Ga. Mil.
    son Elijah m. Lavinia Johnson

Mauger, Frederick b. Pa. 1788 d. Ohio 1869   Cpl. Pa. Mil.
    m. Hester Reisswide — son James m. E. Jane Ford

Maulding, Morton b.—d. Ky. m. Vol. 20   Pat. Legis. Ky.
    daughter Dicey m. Ragland Langston

Maupin, John b. 1783 d. 1814 m. Elizabeth Richardson   Capt. Mo.
    son Amos m. Rebecca Heatherly

Maupin, John D. b. Va. 1798 d. Ka. 1885 m. Mary J. Cobb   Pvt. Va. Mil.
    son Fleming C. m. Mary E. S. Brown

Maurer, John b. 1777 d. Pa. 1834 m. Susannah Strickler   Pvt. Pa. Mil.
    son Samuel m. Elizabeth Hoffman

Maurer, John Peter, b. Pa. 1757 d. Pa. 1847   Ens. Pa. Mil.
    m. Elizabeth Crawford (Craffort) — son Henry m. Elizabeth Leibley

Maury, James b. Va. 1746 d. Va. 1840   Pat. Amer. Consul to
    m. Margaret Rutson   Liverpool 1812/15
    son William m. Sarah Mytton Hughes

Mauzy, John A. b. 1789 d. Ia. 1842 m. Mary Gooding   Pvt. U.S. Inf.
    daughter Julia A. m. William Carr REAL DAUGHTER

Maxey, James b. Va. d. Ill. 1874/5 m. Maria Cook   2nd Lt. Ky. Mil.
    son John C. m. Farnetta Turner Lloyd

Maxey, James b. Va. 1760-70 d. Va. aft. 1840 m. Sally Agee   Pvt. Va.
    son Isaac m. Elizabeth Sowles   1814/15

Maxfield, Eliphalet b. N.H. d. Me. 1860 m. Judith Alley   Pvt. N.H.
    son James m. Elvira Foster

Maxson, Jesse b. N.Y. 1791 d. N.Y. m. Betsey Brown   Sgt. N.Y. Mil.
    daughter Angenette m. Isaac Kellogg REAL DAUGHTER

Maxwell, Bedwell b. Va. 1789 d. Va. 1845 m. Nancy Utter   Pvt. Va. Mil.
    son Amos m. Ruhama Morris

Maxwell, David Hervey b. Ky. 1786 d. Ind. 1854   Surgeon U.S. Rangers
    m. Mary Dunn — son James D. m. Louise J. Howe
    daughter Mary m. Mark Shryer REAL DAUGHTER

Maxwell, John b. N.J. 1755 d. N.J. 1828   Pvt. N.J. Lt. Dragoons
    m. Anna Hubbell — daughter Esther m. Elias Crane

Maxwell, Thomas Vol. 11   Pvt. Va .Mil.

May, George b. Pa. 1730 d. Pa. 1798 m.—   Ens. Pa. Mil.
    daughter Barbara m. Leonard Groninger

May, John b. Ga. 1775 d. Miss. 1851   Pvt. Miss. Mil.
    m. Mrs. Elizabeth Thomas Barnes (2)
    son James M. m. Retta Ann Coburn

May, John Spearman b. Va. 1790 d. Va. 1863   Sgt. Va. Mil.
    m. Margaret Poindexster — son John S. m. Frances Newcomb

May, Jonathan b. Mass. 1793 d. Ia. 1879 m. Abigail Higby   Pvt. N.Y. Mil.
    daughter Theresa E. m. Robert Hawley

May, Thomas b. 1787 d. 1845 m. Anne Elizabeth Byng   Pvt. D.C. Mil.
    son George Thomas m. Emma Holmes Hale

Mayberry, Henry b. Va. 1755 d. Tenn. 1832/   Ens. Tenn. Mil. 1796/1811
    m. Mary Carnes — daughter Hannah E. m. George Kinzor
    son Michael m. Margaret Williams

Mayer, Lewis Vol. 3   Pvt. Md .Mil.

Mayes, Sherrod b. Va. 1737 d. Tenn. 1834   Pat. Va. 1784
    m. Elizabeth Smith — son William m. Susannah (Mayes) Bridges

Mayfield, James b. Ky. 1784 d. Ind. 1855 m. Amelia Hinkle   Sgt. Ky. Mil.
    daughter Elizabeth M. m. Absalom Smith

Mayhall, John b. Ky. 1792 d. Ky. 1862   Pvt. Ky. Rifleman
    m. Bettie Ann Wiggs
    daughter Edna m. Reuben M. Brown REAL DAUGHTER

Mayhall, Timothy b. 1774 d. 1840 m. Hester Hutton   Pvt. Ky. Vol.
    daughter Sarah m. William Jackson

Mayhall, William b. Ky. 1778 d. Ky. 1860 m. Jane Ward   Pvt. Ky. Mil.
    son Samuel W. m. Louisiana Bartlett Alsop

Mayhew, Jonathan Vol. 9   Pvt N..Y. Mil.

Maynard, Amos b. Mass. 1771 d. N.Y. 1829 m. Amy Neal   Maj. N.Y. Mil.
    daughter Emma m. Warren Rinner

Mayo, David b. Mass. 1793 d. Ga. 1868   Pvt. Vt. Mil.
    m. Marie Julia Bruckner — daughter Julia B. m. John Mills Clarke

Mayo, Stephen b. Va. 1757 d. Va. 1847 m. Ann   Pvt. Va. Mil.
    son Jacob m. Eliza Gordon

Mays, Fleming Bingham b. Va. 1795 d. Va. 1847   Pvt. Va. Mil.
    m. (1) Mrs. Micah Thorp Vaughn
    son Jonathan F. B. m. Mrs. Mattie J. C. Shepherd

Mays, Sherrod b. Va. 1737 d. Tenn. 1825 m. Elizabeth Smith   Pat. Va.
    son Thomas D. m. Elizabeth Bridges

Mays, Thomas Washington b. S.C. 1784 d. Pa. 1873   Pvt. Pa. Mil.
    m. Henrietta Myers — daughter Mary m. Abraham Kearns

Mays, Samuel b. Va. 1765 d. S.C. 1816 m. Nancy Gregsby   Brig Gen. S.C.
    son Enoch m. Chotilde Linton

Mayse, William b. Ohio 1786 d. Ohio 1856   Qtr.Mst. Ohio Mil.
    m. Nancy Burgess — daughter Mary m. John Kirkpatrick

Mazuzan, Mark W. b. Ct. ca. 1771 d. Ct. 1854   Pvt. Vt. & Ct.
    m. Diana Fuller — son Erastmus m. Amy Mead

McAdams, John b. Ky. 1791 d. Ill. 1849 m. Eda Horn   Pvt. Ky. Mil.
    daughter Mary Tabitha m. Wesley White

McAdams, John Sr. b. Ire. 1737 d. Tenn. Aft. 1793 m. Ann   Pat. Tenn. 1784
    son John m. Martha Rogers

McAdams, Joseph b. Pa. 1757 d. Ill. 1840 m. Sarah Bradford   Pvt. Pa. 1786
    son Thomas B. m. Mary Hunt

McAdden, Thomas b. N.C. 1793 d. Tenn. 1825   Pvt. Tenn. Vol.
    m. Harriet Reditt — son Hugh m. Kate Walker

McAfee, Robert B. b. Ky. 1784 d. Ky. 1847   Capt. Ky. Mil.
    m. Mary Caldwell — daughter Nancy C. m. William Archer Hooe

McAllister, William b. Mass. 1797 d. Mich. 1879   Pvt. Mass. Mil.
    m. Elizabeth Gunn — daughter Nancy m. Dr. Joseph Eastman

McArthur, Arthur b. Va. 1789 d. Va. 1856 m. Elizabeth   Ens. Ohio Mil.
daughter Lucy m. William Webster Sturgeon

McArthur Duncan b. N.Y. 1772 d. Ohio 1839   Gen. Ohio Mil.
m. Nancy McArnold — son James m. Hannah Smith

McArthur, John b. Ohio 1770 d. Ohio 1838 m. Laney   Lt. Ohio Mil.
son Thomas m. Nancy Morton

McArtor (McCartor, McArthor),
Moses Taylor b. Pa. 1780 d. Ohio 1873 m. Sarah Wilson   Pvt. Va. Mil.
son Thomas W. m. Elizabeth Ann Exley

McAvoy, George b. N.J. 1796 d. Ohio 1837   Surgeon's Mate U.S. Inf.
m. Sarah Bowne — daughter Mary A. B. m. John Pearl Haggott

McBride, Barzilla b. N.C. 1790 d. N.C. 1858   Pvt. W. Tenn. Mil.
m. Rachel Wilson — son Hiram m. Mary Farthing

McBride, Isaac b. Pa. 1780 d. Ohio 1844 m. Miss Mead   Pvt. Ohio Mil.
son John m. Mahala Ann Robinson

McBride, James b. Va. 1787 d. Ill. 1851 m. Nancy Taylor   Pvt. E. Tenn. Inf.
son William m. Nancy Manley

McBride, William Vol. 16   Maj. Tenn. Mil.

McBroom, Robert b. Pa. 1795 d. Ohio 1881   Pvt. Ohio Mil.
m. Nancy Vinson, Cantwell
daughter Minerva Priscilla m. Jacob Iles

McBurney, James b. Scot. or Pa. 1747 d. Pa. 1816   Pat. Justice Pa.
m. Martha McGoffin — son James m. Catharine Dawson

McBurney, John Vol. 6   Pvt. Ohio Mil.

McCabe, John b. Va. 1796 d. Va. 1889   Pvt. Va. Mil.
m. Elizabeth Nelson Simpson
son Charles P. m. Margaret Ann Mitchell

McCague, Thomas Vol. 15   Pvt. Ohio Mil.

McCall, Andrew b. S.C. 1790 d. Tenn. 1841   Sgt. Mass. Art. Mil.
m. Janette Todd — son Joseph W. m. Victoria Adelaide Wilson

McCall, Charles b. Pa. 132 7d. Ga. 1816   Pat. Ga. Legis. 1798-1808
m. Celete Ann Williams — son Francis m. Sarah Pearce
daughter Nancy m. Stephen McCoy
son William m. Mary Pearce

McCall, Charles b. Va. 1732 d. Ga. 1816 m. Nancy Williams   Pat. Ga.
daughter Nancy m. Stephen McCoy

McCall, John Cooper b. N.Y. 1786 d. N.Y. 1861   Ens. Pa. Mil.
m. Mary Williams — daughter Eunice B. m. William Basto(w)

McCall, Notgomery b. Ky. 1786 d. Ia. 1855   Pvt. Ohio Mil.
m. Charlotte McCain — daughter Margaret m. Samuel J. Parks

McCall, Thomas b. N.C. 1764 d. Ga. 1840   Surveyor Gen. Ga. 1786-95
m. Elizabeth Mary Ann Smith — daughter Janet H. m. Ira E. Stanley
daughter Margaret S. m. Jeremiah Hansley

McCallister, Richard b. Scot. 1725 d. Pa. 1795 m. Mary Dill   Pat. Pa.
daughter Nancy m. Patrick Hayes

McCann, Francis b. Md. 1792 d. Ark. 1870 m. Sarah Crumez   Pvt. Pa. Mil.
daughter Sarah m. J. M. Giles

McCants, David b. 1781 d. 1864 m. Maria Young Livingston   1st Lt. La.
daughter Valeria Blanche m. James R. Freeman

McCarroll, John b. Va. 1789 d. Ky. 1862 m. Eliza Kelly   Sgt. Tenn. Mil.
son James Edwin m. Susan Lavinia Stephenson

McCartney, Andrew b.—d. Va. 1858 m. Susanna Trevey   Pvt. Va. Mil.
son James W. m. Nancy Frye
daughter Mary Jane m. Washington Kyle

McCartney, George b. Pa. 1764 d. Pa. ???? m. Rebecca   Pvt. Pa. Mil.
son John m. Rhoebe Massey

McCartney, James b. Scot. 1745 d. Pa. 1814 m. Taggart   Music. Pa. Mil.
son Robert m. Mary Mitchell

McCartney, John b. Pa. d. Pa. 1820 m. Hannah Elliott   Pvt. Pa. Mil.
daughter Caroline m. Charles Coolidge

McCartney, Robert b. Scot. 1763 d. Pa. 1841   Music Pa. Mil.
m. Mary Mitchell — son Samuel m. Mary Jane Armour

McCartney, Samuel b. Pa. 1790 d. Pa. 1871   Pvt. Pa. Inf.
m. Mary Jane Armour — son Robert m. Diantha Dinsmore

McCartney, Samuel b. Pa. 1753 d. Pa. 1817   Pvt. Pa. Mil.
m. Nancy Penelope Young — son Jacob m. Margaret Shearer

McCartney, Samuel b. Pa. ca. 1786 d. Pa. 1866 m. Mary   Pvt. Vt. Mil.
daughter Malinda m. Joshua Eckman

McCarty, Enoch b. Va. 1783 d. Ind. 1857 m. Elizabeth Logan, Ens. Ind. Mil.
son Enoch M. m. Amanda Bibb

McCarty, William b. Va. 1799 d. Va. 1845 m. Lucinda Beale   Cpl. Va. Mil.
daughter Olivia m. Albert F. Yerby

McCarty, William b. Pa. 1766 d. Pa. 1813 m. Mary Lloyd   Pat. Pa.
son Lloyd m. Jane McClintock

McCarty, William Downman b. Va. 1794 d. Va. 1845   Officer on
m. Frances Ravenscroft (Ball) Carter   "Constitution" 1812
daughter Lavinia m. Littleton Downman Mitchell

McCasland, James b. Pa. 1770 d. Pa. 1840 m. Martha Bell   Pvt. Pa. Mil.
daughter Harriett m. John C. Aughinbaugh

McCausland, Robert b. 1773 d. 1851 m. Margaret Scott Chinn   Gen. La. Mil.
daughter Jane m. Gabell Breckinridge Chinn
son Marcus m. Gertrude Phillips
son Robert Emmett m. Mary Louise Sweeny

McCaw, William Henry b. S.C. 1785 d. S.C. 1837   Surgeon S.C. Inf.
m. Frances Hunt Todd — son William H. Jr. m. Charlott McGee

McChesney, David b. N.J. 1795 d. Ky. 1839 m. Anna Webster   Matross Ky.
son John m. Sarah Payne

McChord, John b. Pa. 1786 d. Ia. 1885 m. Jane Sawyer   Pvt. Ohio Mil.
daughter Nancy Caroline m. James Huston

McClain, Charles b. Md. 1789 d. Md. 1862   Pvt. Md. Mil.
m. Julia Ann Eichelberger — daughter Mary m. David Hartsocke

McClain, John b. Va. 1776 d. Va. 1860 m. Mary Wheeler   Pvt. Va. Mil.
son Thomas A. m. Mary Jane Duncan

McClanahan, Alexander b. Ire. 734 d. Va. 1819   3rd Lt. Tenn. Mil.
m. (2) Elizabeth Clymer — son Philip m. Leathy Ritchie

McClanahan, Elijah b. 1779 d. Va. 1857   Lt. Col. Va. Mil. 1814/15
m. Agatha S. Lewis — daughter Elizabeth M. m. Pleasant M. Cox

McClanahan, William b. Va. 1740 d. Va. 1819/20   Lt. Col. Va. Mil.
m. Sarah Nelly — son Elijah m. Agatha S. Lewis

McClanahan, William b. Tenn. d. Tenn. 1832 m. Lydia   Pvt. Tenn. Mil.
son Thomas m. Frances Huddleston

McClaugherty, James b. Scot. 1780 d. Va. 1854   Sgt. Va. Mil.
m. Sallie Mullins — son Hugh m. Mary Davis Alexander

McCleary, John b. N.Y. 1765 d. Ill. 1837 m. Margaret   1st Lt. Pa. Mil.
Glenn — daughter Susan m. Peter Miller

McClellan, Hugh b. Ire. 1744 d. Mass. 1816   Col. Mass. Mil. 1787
m. Sarah Wilson — daughter Jane m Samuel Bolton

McClellan, Isaac B. b. Ire. 1775 d. N.C. 1840   Cpl. Adj. Tenn. Mil.
m. Margaret — son William W. m. Teressa

McClellan, John b. 1785 d. Ohio 1839 m. Lydia Spencer   Pvt. Ohio Mil.
son Ezra S. m. Catherine Ann Kinsell

McClellan, John b. N.C. 1765 d. Ark. 1842 m. Mary Wallace   Lt. Tenn. Mil.
son William m. Martha Roby

McClellan, Samuel b. Pa. 1787 d. Md. 1858   Sgt. Md.
m. Eva Maria Elizabeth Raborg-Hussars
daughter Eliza Amelia m. Franklin Hersh

McClellan, Samuel b. N.J. 1792 d. La. 1855   Pvt. U.S. Inf.
m. (3) Mildred Womack — son James W. m. Mary Amanda Chaffin

McClelland, Elias b. Pa. 1784 d. Pa. bef. 1820   Pvt. Pa. Mil.
m. Mary McKinney — son John J. m. Nancy McGlaughlin

McClelland, James b. Pa. 1774 d. Mo. 1833   Pvt. Pa. Mil.
m. Susan Ammons — daughter Elizabeth m. Warren Woodson

McClelland, John b. Ire. 1762 d. Pa. 1853 m. Mary Findley   Ens. Pa. Mil.
son Francis m. Margaret Brownlee

McClendon, Francis (Frank) b. Ga. 1790 d. La. 1884   Pvt. Ga. Mil.
m. Ann Watson — son Robert W. m. Sarah Bethia Newcomb

McClendon, Joseph b. Ga. 1751 d. Ga. 1837 m. Olive Blake   Pvt. Ga. Mil.
son Jonathan J. m. Sarah Jane Kirby

McCleskey, David Henderson b. 1783 d. 1879   Lt. Ga. Mil.
m. Martha Jarrett — son James Jarrett m. Anna Dunagan

McCleskey, James b. Pa. 1775/6 d. Ga. 1842   Capt. Ga. Mil.
m. Isabella Ray (Rhea) — son James R. m. Frances Mary Wood

McClintick, William Vol. 14   Pvt. Ky. Mil.

McClintock, Joseph b. Pa. 1781 d. La. 1817   Pay Mst. U.S. Army
m. Sarah McCullough — daughter Catharine m. William McElroy

McClintock, Robert b. Va. 1762 d. W. Va. 1845 m. Jane Mann   Pat. Va.
daughter Nancy m. John Beard

McClintock, William b. Va. 1790 d. Ohio 1860   Pvt. Ohio Mil.
    m. Margaret C. Buchanan — son James m. Anna Yontz (Yountz)

McCloud, Samuel b. Va. 1794 d. Ind. 1877   Pvt. Ohio Mil.
    m. Margaret Burley — daughter Sarah m. John William Gerard

McCluer, Robert b. Va. 1792 d. Mo. 1834   Surgeon Va. Mil.
    m. Sophia Campbell
    daughter Janetta (Jeannetta) m. Dr. J. B. Muschany

McClung, John b. W. Va. 1782 d. W. Va. 1815   Capt. Va. Mil.
    m. Anne Crawford — daughter Amanda m. Joel McPherson

McClure, Francis b. Ire. 1740 d. Pa. 1843   Pa. Legis. Judge 1809/11
    m. Margaret — son Andrew m. Margaret Abraham
    son Francis M. m. Rebecca Criswell

McClure, James b. Ky. 1791 d. Ill. 1865 m. Mary Givens   Pvt. Ind. Mil.
    son Samuel H. m. Missouri Meek

McClure, James Vol. 16   Lt. S.C. Mil.

McClure, John Vol. 14   1812

McClure, John b. Ire. d. Md. m. Jane Napier   Capt. Md. Mil.
    son John C. m. Mary Ann

McClurkin, John b S.C. 1790 d. Ia. 1865   Pvt. S.C. Mil.
    m. Margaret C. Wright — son Thomas m. Julia Ann

McCollum, Archibald b. Scot. 1785 d. Ind. 1837   Pvt. Ohio Mil. 1815
    m. Jamima R. Lane — daughter Nancy Ann m. Samuel F. Wiser

McCullough, James Brown b. N.C. 1788 d. Ind. 1868   Cpl. Ind. Mil.
    m. Margaret Maxwell
    daughter Margaret m. Sampson McMillen Houston

McComas, Elisha b. Va. 1770 d. Va. 1849   Col. U.S. Army Va.
    m. Annie French — son William m. Mildred Ward

McComas, Nicholas, D. b. 1790 d. 1878 m. Love Prudence Evans   Md. 1812
    daughter Sarah Augusta m. Francis Pond Timms

McComb, John b. Pa. 1789 d. Ohio 1849   Pvt. Ohio Mil.
    m. Mary Catherine Conrad — son Abraham m. Rebecca Shade

McComb, Joseph Vol. 6   Pvt. Ohio Mil.

McConathy, Jacob b. Del. or Pa. 1766 d. Ky. 1827   Capt. Ky. Mil.
    m. Elizabeth McCarty — son Asa m. Rebecca Berry

McConathy, James b. Va. 1792 d. Mo. 1866 m. Eliza Craig   Pvt. Ky. Mil.
    daughter Anne m. Alfred C. Wilson
    son Henry m. Betty Norwood

McConnel, Robert b. Pa. 1776 d. Ohio 1841   Brig. Gen. Ohio Mil.
    m. Mary Adams — daughter Rebecca m. Hon. James Moore

McConnell, Alexander Vol. 11   Pvt. Va. Mil.

McConnell, Alexander b. Pa. 1791 d. Ohio 1853   Pvt. Pa. Mil.
    m. Polly Adams
    daughter Virginia m. Addison A. Adair REAL DAUGHTER

McConnell, Alexander b. Pa. 1790 d. Pa. 1874 m. Ann Berry   Pvt. Pa. Mil.
    son William m. Anna McCherkan

McConnell, Archibald b. N.C. 1795 d. Tenn. 1847   Pvt. Tenn. Mil.
  m. Eliza Houston
  daughter Cynthis Artemesia m. Nathan N. London
  son William J. m. Pamela Jane Elliott

McConnell, Charles b. N.Y. 1776 d. N.Y. 1827   Pvt. N.Y. Mil.
  m. Sally Sammons — son Asa m. Elizabeth Jones

McConnell, John b. Ky. 1774 d. Ill. 1834   Pvt. Ky. Mil.
  m. Elizabeth Butts Clarkson
  daughter Rebecca E. S. m. Warren O. Parker REAL DAUGHTER

McConnell, John b. Tenn. 1779 d. Tenn. 1858   Pvt. Tenn. Guman
  m. Anna Townsend — son James m. Hester
  daughter Mary Ann m. Joshua Roberts
  daughter Sally m. Thomas J. Payne
  son William m. Sarah L. Bell

McCord, Russell Paul b. S.C. 1793 d. Fla. aft. 1873   Pvt. S.C. Mil.
  m. Elizabeth May Hall — daughter Sarah G. m. William Spann Knox

McCormack, Levi b. Va. 1789 d. Va. 1853 m. Jane Graham   Sgt. Va. Mil.
  son Harrison m. Mary DeHaven

McCormick, George b. Va. 1769 d. Ohio 1851   Pvt. U.S. Levies 1st Reg.
  m. Frances Malone Armstrong — daughter Fanny m. Isaac K. Young

McCormick, George b. Ire. 1757 d. Pa. 1802 m. Rachel Moore   Ens. Pa. Mil.
  son George B. m. Amelia James

McCormick, George b. Va. 1742 d. Ky. 1820 m. Mary Chaplin   Pvt. Va. Mil.
  daughter Comfort m. Michael Goodnight

McCormick, James b. Pa. 1757 d. Pa. 1850   Pvt. Va. Mil.
  m. Mary Margaret Taylor — daughter Araminta m. Henry B. Goucher
  son Noble m. Miss Brown
  son Samuel m. Elizabeth Gregg
  son William T. m. Susan Colestock

McCormick, James b. Pa. 1760 d. Pa. 1847   Pvt. Pa. Mil.
  m. Martha Cochran — daughter Clarissa m. Cyrus Hewitt
  daughter Rachel m. Thomas Shepherd

McCormick, John b. S.C. 1761 d. aft. 1814   Sgt. Ga. Mil.
  m. Sarah (Sally) Moore — daughter Fransinia m. Barnett Cody

McCormick, Moses b. Pa. 1792 d. Pa. 1839   Pvt. Pa. Mil.
  m. Elizabeth Buttermore — son George m. Lucinda Teele

McCormick. Walter b. Ky. 1793 d. Ill. 1865 m (1) Ellen Jane   Pvt. Ky. Mil.
  daughter Ann Mildred REAL DAUGHTER

McCown, John b. Pa. 1788 d. W. Va. 1850 m. Sarah Stone   Pvt. Va. Mil.
  son James m. Samantha Smith

McCoy, Alexander Vol. 12   Pvt. Pa. Mil.

McCoy, Daniel Vol. 11   Lt. U.S. Rangers

McCoy, Daniel b. Md. 1794 d. Ohio 1876   Pvt. Ohio Mil.
  m. Sarah Slaughter — daughter Lois m. Louis Igo

McCoy, James b. Ky. d. Ky. 1861 m. Elizabeth Stuckey   Pvt. Ohio Mil.
  son Abraham m. Margaret Hoppess
  daughter Elizab. June m. Abraham Post

McCoy, John b. Ky. 1789 d. Ill. 1851 m. Isabella Baird   Pvt. Ohio Mil.
   daughter Catherine m. James G. Bayne

McCoy, John b. Pa. 1771 d. Ohio 1844 m. Margaret Kerr   Pvt. Ohio Mil.
   son John M. m. Harriet Hughs
   son William K. m Margaret Affleck

McCoy. (Mackoy) John b. Ga. 1772 d. Ky. 1843   Pvt. Ky. Mil.
   m. Lavinia Fuqua — son Moses F. m. Hannah Lawson

McCoy, John b. Pa. 1793 d. Ill. 1854 m. Sabra Clark   Pvt. Vt. Mil.
   daughter Mary M. m. Dr. William Barrett

McCoy, William b. S.C. 1776-8 d. S.C. aft. 1843   Pvt. S.C. Vol.
   m. Elizabeth Floyd — son Owens G. m. Martha Mason Coker

McCracken, Adam b. Ire. 1775 d. Pa. 1859 m. Mary Gillespie   Cpl. Pa. Mil.
   son James m. Araminta Moore

McCracken, James b. N.C. 1778 d. Ill. 1829   Pvt. Ill. Vol.
   m. Nancy Houtchin — son James m. Mary Minerva Jones

McCrackin, Otho b. Md. 1790 d. Mo. 1878 m. (1) Jane Bell   Pvt. Ky. Mil.
   son Otho m. Mary McFarlane (McFarland)
   m. (2) Sarah Carter Wilson
   daughter Mary m. Willard F. Harris REAL DAUGHTER

McCracken, Thomas b. Md. 1778 d. Mo. 1859   Pvt. W. Tenn. Mil.
   m. Elizabeth Holmes — son James m. Anne Douglas
   son Joseph m. Mary Bodine

McCracken, Virgil b. Ky. 1779 killed at River Raisin   Capt. Ky. Mil.
   m. Martha Caldwell — daughter Mary Bird m. Thomas Jessee

McCrary, Benjamin b. N.C. 1785 d. Mo. 1878   Ens. Tenn. Mil.
   m. Polly Coleman — daughter Lucy m. William E. Hackley

McCrea James b. Pa. 1796 d. Pa. 1875   Pvt. Ens. Pa. Mil.
   m. Elizabeth Gordon — daughter Margaret A. m. Joseph Snivley

McCreedy, Gamaliel b. N.Y. 1781 d. N.Y. 1859   Pvt. N.Y. Mil.
   m. Celia Howe — son Lois E. m. Chauncey Howe

McCreless, George L. b. 1793 d. Ala. 1872   Pvt. S.C. Mil.
   m. Elizabeth Dorn — son John M. m. Hannah Moore

McCrory, Thomas b. Ire. 1776 d. Tenn. 1819   Col. Tenn. Mil.
   m. Rachel L. Leggett — son Charles S. m. Martha Douglas Caldwell

McCuistion, James b. N.C. 1758 d. Tenn. 1826   Pvt. N.C. Mil.
   m. Jean Nicholson — son Anthony m. Nancy Winsette

McCuiston, Thomas b. N.C. 1762 d. N.C. 1853   Capt. Tenn. Inf.
   m. Mary Nicholson — daughter Elizabeth m. James Lanier

McCulloch, Alexander b. Va. 1777 d. Tenn. 1846   Pvt. Tenn. Mil.
   m. Frances Lenoir — son Henry E. m. Jane Isabelle Ashby

McCullough, James b. Pa. 1791 d. Ohio 1873   Pvt. U.S. Inf.
   m. Mary Mackey — son Robert E. m. Jane Hoey

McCullough, James Brown b. N.C. 1788 d. Ind. 1868   Cpl. Ind. Mil.
   m. Margaret Maxwell — daughter Margaret m. Sampson M. Millan

McCune, James b. Pa. c. 1730 d. Pa. 1808   Pat. Justice Pa. 1784
   m. Elizabeth Rotherham — son Joseph m. Mary Shannon

McCune, John b. Pa. 1774 d. Pa. 1836 m. Catherine Bell   Pvt. Pa. Mil. 1793
son James m. Rosenna Graham

McCune, John b. Pa. 1764 d. Pa. 1814 m. Mary Boyles   Pvt. Pa. Mil.
daughter Sarah m. John Cone

McCune, John b. Pa. 1793 d. Pa. 1855 m. Sally Anne Duncan   Cpl. Pa. Mil.
daughter Jane Mary m. Rev. Samuel S. Wylie

McCune, Samuel b. Pa. 1766 d. Pa. 1813 m. Hannah Brady   Ens. Pa. Mil.
son William m. Mary Ann Hays

McCune, William b. Pa. 1777 d. Pa. 1828   Pvt. Pa. Vol. 1812/14
m. Nancy Agnes Shannon — daughter Sarah Ann m. John Bowman

McCurdy, Alexander b. Ire. 1744 d. Pa. 1839   Training Officer Pa. Mil.
m. Jane Henderson (Heridenon) — daughter Jane m. James Duncan

McCurry, John b. Scot. 1776 d. Ga. 1857 m. Sarah   Pvt. Ga. Regt.
daughter Nancy m. James E. Brown

McCutchen, Samuel b. Va. 1789 d. Ohio 1835   Pvt. Ohio Mil. 1812/13
m. Rosanna Bright — daughter Ann m. Benjamin Foster

McCutchen, William b. Va. 1760 d. Ga. 1827 m. Anne Shaw   Pvt. Ga. Mil.
son Benjamin R. m. Jane Bell

McClure, Alexander b. Ire. 1788 d. Pa. 1873   Pat. Material Aid
m. Sarah Trevor — daughter Sara Ann m. George Hogg

McClure, John b. Pa. 1792 d. Pa. 1872 m. Susan Hull   Maj. Pa. Mil.
daughter Martha m. Josiah McElwain

McClure, John Charles b. Ire. 1775 d. Md. 1825   Capt. Md. Rangers 1807
m. Mary Ann Thornburgh — daughter Emily Jane m. Robert Hardie

McClure, Matthew b. Ire. 1719 d. N.C. 1805 m.—   Pat. Justice N.C. 1789
daughter Jane m. (2) William Kerns

McClure, Samuel b. Pa. 1777 d. Ohio 1855   Soldier Prob. Va.
m. Sarah Baldwin
son James B. m. Hannah Leaverton

McClure, Thomas Vol. 9   Pvt. Ohio Mil.

McClure, William b. 1789 d. 1861 m. Lucretia Chapman   Pvt. Va. Mil.
son William Landon m. Louisa Booth

McClure, William b. Pa. 1759 d. Pa. 1823   Pvt. Pa. Mil.
m. Margaret McKeehan — son James M. m. Rachel Patterson

McDade, Charles b. Ga. 1790 d. Ala. 1839 m. Edna Fields   Pvt. Ga. Mil.
daughter Elizabeth m. Richard Jolley
daughter Frances m. James F. Armstrong

McDade, William b. S.C. 1778 d. Ala. 1835   Pvt. Ga. Art. 1814
m. Mary Germany — son James G. m. Nancey Miller

McDaniel, Redman b. prob. Md. c. 1766 d. Ky. aft. 1814   Pvt. 1814 Ky.
m.— daughter Rachel m. William Leathers   Det. Mil.

McDavid, John b. S.C. 1788 d. S.C. 1854 m. Susannah Davenport   Pvt. Va.
son Richmond m. Harriet L. Acker
daughter Susan Adeline m. William Hamilton Roberts

McDermot, James b. Pa. 1795 d. Pa. 1888 m. Jane Fleming   Pvt. Pa. Mil.
daughter Margaret Jane m. Franklin Nichol

McDill, James b. Ire. 1760 d. Ill. 1854   Lt. Ohio Mil.
   m. Margaret Chestnut — son Samuel m. Nancy Findley

McDonald, Alexander b. Va. 1763 d. Ky. 1843   Pvt. Va. Mil.
   m. Elizabeth Taylor — son Zachariah m. Sallie Yokum

McDonald, Daniel b. Ga. 1780 d. Ga. 1856   Cpl. Ga. Mil.
   m. Margaret Buchan — son James m. Serena Swain

McDonald, Ebenezer b. Scot. 1790 d. Ohio 1859   Pvt. Ohio Mil.
   m. Annie E. Kelly — daughter Mary A. m. David Hanger

McDonald, Edward b. Va. 1761 d. Va. 1855   Magistrate Va.
   m. (1) Mary Rowland — son James m. Kitty Jones

McDonald, Henry Brown Vol. 8   Pvt. Tenn. Mil.

McDonald, Hugh Vol. 17   Pvt. Va. Mil.

McDonald, James Vol. 9   Col. U.S. Inf.

McDonald, James b. Mass. (Me.) 1777 d. Me. 1856   Pvt. Mass. (Me.) Mil.
   m. Rachel Webb — son Thomas m. Hannah P. Proctor

McDonald, James b. N.J. 1785 d. Mich.   Pvt. U.S. Inf. N.Y.
   m. Helena Marsac — son Bosiel m. Teresa Henrietta Moran

McDonald, James b. N.C. 1776 d. Ala. 1848   Pvt. N.C. Mil.
   m. Joanna Cicati — daughter Katharine m. Samuel Carnochan

McDonald, William b. Ga. 1772 d. Ga. 1844   Pvt. Ga. Mil.
   m. Pheriba Farrow — son Daniel m. Matilda Powell

McDonald, William (Jackson) b. Scot. c. 1789 d. Ala. 1827   Cpl. Miss. Mil.
   m. Elizabeth Perkins — son William Jr. m. Cynthia Ann Madison

McDonough, Henry b. Md. 1754 d. Pa. 1822   Justice 1801
   m. Jane Hamilton — son David m. Levina Weir

McDonough, Thomas b. Del. 1747/8 d. Del. 1795   Pat. Assy. Justice 1793/5
   m. Mary Vance — daughter Lydia C. m. Zacharias Roberts

McDow, William Loftin b. 1794 d. 1870 m. Jane Ramsey   Sgt. S.C. Vol.
   son Arthur m. Sarah Arabella Edwards
   daughter Mary m. Andrew Neville

McDowell, Alexander Vol. 13   Pvt. Pa. Mil.

McDowell, Daniel b. Pa. 1763 d. N.Y. 1806 m. Ruth Drake   Capt. N.Y. Mil.
   daughter Phoebe m. Abraham Miller

McDowell, James b. Va. 1760 d. Ky. 1843   Maj. Ky. Mil.
   m. Mary Paxton Lyle — daughter Isabella m. John Poage Campbell

McDowell, John b. Pa. 1768 d. Pa. 1837 m. Sarah Gettys   Ens. Pa. Mil.
   son John 2nd. m. Elizabeth Henderson

McDowell, John Adair b. Ky. 1789 d. Ohio 1823   Asst. Adj. Gen. Ky. Mil.
   m. Lucy Todd Starling — daughter Ann m. John Winston Prince

McDowell, Joseph Jr. b. Va. 1756 d. N.C. 1801   Pat. Del. to Assem. N.C.
   m. Margaretta Moffett — daughter Sarah m. John Mathews

McDowell, Matthew b. Pa. 1790 d. Pa. 1853 m. Jane Jackson   Capt. Pa. Mil.
   son Matthew S. m. Rachel Frances Nash

McDowell, Robert b. 1752 d. 1838 m. Hannah Twining   Pvt. Pa. Mil.
   daughter Sarah m. William Worthington

McDowell, Samuel Jr. b. Ky. 1764 d. Ky. 1817   Capt. Ky. Mil.
  m. Anne Irvine — daughter Sarah m. Jeremiah A. Minter

McDowell, Samuel Sr. b. Va. 1735 d. Ky.   Pat. 1st Marshall Ky. 1787
  m. Mary McClung — daughter Mary m. William Starling
  son Samuel Jr. m. Anne Irvine

McDowell, Thomas b. Ky. 1790 d. Ky. 1873   Pvt. Ky. Mil.
  m. Lumilla Sholes — son Sigel m. Clara Belle McGrew

McDowell, Thomas b. Eng. 1760 d. Pa. m. Ruth MacIntyre   Pvt. Pa. Mil.
  son Joseph m. Rebekah Warren English

McDowell, William b. Ohio 1785 d. Ohio 1834   Pvt. Ohio Mil.
  m. Sarah Dever — son James m. Frances Wilson

McEachron, Peter b. N.Y. 1748 d. N.Y 1841   Capt. N.Y. Mil. 1803/15
  m. Maria Kilmer (Kilmore) — daughter Catherine m. Adam I. Dings

McElderry, Thomas b. Va. 1790 d. Ala. 1883   Scout, Lt. Tenn. Vol.
  m. Martha Ann Dozier Winn
  daughter Achsah Elizabeth REAL DAUGHTER
  son George T. m. Mary Irion
  m. Frances Turner Edmonds
  daughter Louisa A. m. Elbert Sevier Jennison REAL DAUGHTER

McElheny, Tobert b. Pa. 1775 d. Ohio 1825   4th. Sgt. Ohio Mil.
  m. Jane Karr — daughter Juliana K. m. William Barrett

McElrain, Samuel b. Va. 1794 d. Ill. 1848 m. Penelope Able   Pvt. Ky. Mil.
  son William A. m. Angelina A. Sowell

McElroy, James Erwin b. Pa. 1781 d. Ohio 1826   Capt. U.S. Inf.
  m. Isabella Malvina Glenn — daughter Sarah m. William Glendening

McElwain, Robert b. Pa. 1779 d. Ohio 1824 m. Jane Taylor   Capt. Ohio Mil.
  daughter Nancy m. Simon Stuckey
  son Thomas N. m. Sarah Ann Mouser

McElwee, William b. Tenn. 1798 d. Tenn. 1883   Pvt. Tenn. Mil.
  m. Lucinda Eblen — daughter Anne Eliza m. George Washington Nixon

McElwrath, Joseph b. N.C. d. Tenn. 1825 m. Elizabeth   Capt. Tenn. Mil.
  daughter Rebecca m. David Alexander

McEwen, Christopher E. b. Ky. 1790 d. Tenn. 1868   Capt. Tenn. Mil.
  m. Narcissa Newson
  daughter Mary H. m. Robert Anderson McLemore

McEwen, David b. N.C. 1756 d. Tenn. 1821   Lt. Tenn. Mil.
  m. Margaret Erwin — daughter Eleanor C. m. Henry Cannon Stevens
  son James m. Elizabeth Goff

McEwen, David Kerr b. Tenn. 1781 d. Tex. m. Lydia   2nd Lt. Tenn. Mil.
  Lane — daughter Elizabeth m. Azariah Jesse Hood

McEwen, James b. N.C. 1782 d. Tenn. 1821 m. Betsy Goff   Maj. Tenn. Mil.
  son Christopher m. Martha Carr
  daughter Emeline m. Zacheus German
  daughter Margaret Matilda m. William Alexander

McFadden, Thomas b. Mass. (Me.) 1740 d. Me. 1840   Pvt. Mass. (Me.) Mil.
  m. Hannah Savage — daughter Jane m. Timothy Cleveland

McFadin, Andrew Jr. b. 1786 d. Ind. 1847   Pvt. Ind. Mil.
  m. Rebecca Hogan — son Andrew H. m. Elizabeth Alice Stott

McFall, William b. Mo. 1794 d. Mo. 1873 m. Mary Ann   Pvt. Ky. Mil.
    son Jonathan m. Armilda

McFarlan, James Vol. 6   Pvt. N.Y. Mil.

McFarland, John b. Tenn. 1788 d. Ill. 1840   Pvt. Ohio Mil.
    m. Catherine — daughter Theresa m. William McAnulty

McFarland, John b. Scot. 1750 d. Tenn. 1824   Pvt. Tenn. Mil.
    m. Nancy Manees — son James m. Dicy Billero

McFarland, William b. Mass. 1756 d. Pa. 1823   Pat. Coroner, Justice Pa.
    m. Hannah Kelsey — daughter Rebecca m. John Carter

McFeely, Thomas b. Pa. 1780 d. Ind. 1859   Pvt. Ohio Mil.
    m. Elizabeth Rogers — son Isaac N. m. Sarah Milroy

McFerran (McFarron), John b. Md. 1798 d. W.Va. 1868   Sgt. Md. Mil.
    m. Elizabeth Wright Moore — daughter Jean m. Thomas Sweeney

McGannon, Zachariah Vol. 14   Pvt. Ky. Mil.

McGary, Hugh b. Va. 1770 d. Ind. 1842 m. Mary C.   Maj. In.d Mil.
    daughter Clarissa H. m. Thomas Jefferson Dobyns

McGavock, Jacob b. Va. 1790 d. Tenn. 1878   Pvt. Tenn. Art.
    m. Louise Caroline Grundy
    daughter Sarah m. Dr. John Berrien Lindsley
    daughter Anne Elizabeth m. Henry Dickinson
    son Felix G. m. Mary Manoah Bostick

McGee, David b. Scot. 1762 d. Ala. 1857 m. Mary Cook   Pvt. Ky. Vol.
    son Sampson m. Polly Finch

McGehee, William b. Ga. 1782 d. Miss. 1851 m. Jane   Lt. Miss. Mil.
    daughter Elizabeth K. m. Benjamin Wright Leggitt

McGeorge, Reuben Vol. 14   Pvt. Va. Mil.

McGill, George Vol. 8   Pvt .U.S. Inf.

McGill, Hugh b. Ire. 1777 d. N.Y. 1861 m. Clarissa Johnson   Pvt. U.S. Inf.
    daughter Sarah m. Thomas Sullivan

McGinnis, Edmund b. Va. c. 1770 d. Ind. or Mo. 1827   Justice W.Va.
    m. Sarah — son Allen A. m. Eliza Holderby

McGinnis, John b. Ire. 1780 d. in service 1814   Pvt. Tenn. Mil.
    m. Nancy Brown — daughter Mary m. James Perdee

McGinty, Robert b. Va. 1746 d. Ga. 1841   Pat. Judge Ga.
    m. Deborah Wright — son Geo. W. Sr. m. (3) Naomi Elvira Moore

McGowan, Daniel Vol. 11   Pvt. Md. Mil.

McGowan, Patrick b.—d. N.Y. 1818 m. Hannah   Pvt. N.Y. Dragoons
    daughter Julia Ann m. Cyrus Hewitt

McGown, Samuel William b. Ky. d. Ky. m. Nancy   Pvt. Ky. Mil.
    daughter Mary Elvira m. Felix Grundy Mattheny

McGraw, Isaiah b. 1760 d. Ky. 1850 m. Mary   Pvt. Ky. Mil.
    son James m. Mary Ellis

McGregor, Archibald b. Scot 1779 d. N.C. 1863   Pvt. N.C. Mil.
    m. Mary Jane McMillan — daughter Mary M. m. Malcolm Johnson

McGregor, John b. Tenn. 1794 d. Tenn. 1825   Sgt. Tenn. Mil.
    m. Milberry Donelson — son Andrew m. Eudora Anderson

McGrew, James b. Pa. 1779 d. W.Va. 1873 m. Isabella Clark   Col. Va. Mil.
son James C. m. Persus Hagens

McGrew, John b. Pa. 1766 d.—m. Vol. 1   Joined Gen. Harmar's Army
daughter Esther Jane m. Niebel REAL DAUGHTER

McGrew, Nathan b. Pa. 1746 d. Pa. 1828   Ens. Pa. Mil.
m. Martha Hendricks — son Samuel m. Deborah McGrew (cousin)

McGriff, Patrick b. Ire. c. 1750 d. Ga. 1810   Pat. Senator Ga. 1804-8
m. Mary Hall — son William m. Sarah Speight

McGuier, Daniel b. 1775 d. N.Y. 1827 m. Sarah Whitney   Pvt. N.Y. Mil.
daughter Lucy m. Thomas J. Eddy

McGuigan, James b.— d.— m. Ann Vol. 1   Pvt. Pa. Mil.
daughter Elizabeth m. William

McGuinnes, John b. Pa. 1777 d. Pa. 1852   Pvt. Pa. Mil.
m. Elizabeth Conley Horn — son William m. Catharine Marshall

McGuire, Richard b. Md. 1771 d. Pa. m. Eleanor Byrn   Capt. Md. Mil.
son Joseph m. Rosina Cupp

McHenry, James b. Pa. 1779 d. Pa. 1812   Maj. Pa. Mil.
m. Elizabeth Stutchel — daughter Mary m. Asa Crossman

McHenry, William b. Pa. 1785 d. Pa. 1815 m. Lydia Law   Pvt. Pa. Mil.
son Alexander m. Mary Jane Love

McIlhany (McElhenny),
William b. Pa. 1770 d. Pa. aft. 1800   Pvt. Pa. Mil. 1789
m. Rebecca Lee — son William Jr. m. Catherine Schultz

McElhenny, Robert b. Pa. 1761 d. Pa. 1822 m. Martha King   Capt. Pa. Mil.
son Victor K. m. Agnes Elizabeth W. Orr

McElroy, Samuel b. Va. 1781 d. Ark. 1853   Pvt. Mo. Mil.
m. Elizabeth McLain — son Hammet m. (1) Elizabeth Davis

McIlvain, John b. Pa. 1779 d.—m. Hannah Martin   Cpl. La. Mil.
daughter Georgiana Jane m. Francis Cook

McElvain, William b. Scot. 1794 d. Pa.   Capt. U.S. Inf.
m. Wilhemina Messing — daughter Cordelia m. Ephraim Stonesipher

McIntire, John b. Va. 1787 d. Ind. 1837 m. Mary Bumgarner   Pvt. Va. Mil.
daughter Mary m. Archibald Williamson

McIntire, Thomas Vol. 13   Pvt. Pa. Mil.

McIntire, William b. Va. 1750 d. Ky. 1792   Maj. Va. Mil.
m. Elizabeth Shepherd — daughter Eleanor m. Zadoc Springer

McIntosh, Hampden Vol. 11   Pvt. Ga. Art.

McInvaine (McElwain), Robert b. Pa. 1781 d. Pa. 1853   Pvt. Pa. Mil.
m. Jane Shannon — daughter Sarah Jane m. John Leonard Wiest

McIver, Evander Roderick b. S.C. 1791 d. Ala. 1837   Officer S.C. Mil.
m. Ann Elizabeth Cowan
daughter Margaret J. m. Benjamin F. Williamson

McKay, John b. Scot. 1770 d. Ala. 1859 m. Sarah Campbell   Pvt. Ala. Vol.
daughter Ann Catherine m. Elkanah L. Shuford

McKee, Andrew Vol. 5   Pvt. Pa. Mil.

McKee, Jabish b. N.Y. 1780 d. Ohio 1857   Pvt. N.Y. Mil.
son Eldridge m. Rebecca Morris

McKee, Joseph b. Pa. 1789 d. Ohio 1881   Sgt. Ohio Mil.
  m. Maragert Eakins — son Richard m. Elizabeth Poole

McKee, William b. Ire. 1735 d. Ky. 1816   Mem. Va. Conv. 1788
  m. Miriam McKee (cousin) — son David L. m. Elizabeth Letcher

McKeehan, Samuel b. Va. 1767 d. Pa. 1863   Surgeon's Mate Pa. Mil.
  m. Elizabeth Blair — daughter Elevyn m. John Shurr

McKenny, Abner b. Mass. (Me.) 1777 d. Me. 1860   Pat. (Me.) Mass.
  m. Mary Newcomb — son James m. Lucy Ann Fenderson

McKenny, Jonathan Vol. 17   Pvt. Mass. Mil.

McKenzie (McKensey), Eli. b. Md. 1793 d. Ohio 1874   Pvt. Ohio Mil.
  m. Mary Ann Kemper — son Joshua m. Martha J. Newman

McKenzie, John b. N.C. 1777 d. Mo. 1868 m. Agnes Gibson   Pvt. N.C. Mil.
  son James B. m. Mary
  daughter Mary m. John Clark
  daughter Sallie m. Sashley Lucas Wood

McKenzie, John b. Md. 1786 d. Ohio 1866 m. Elizabeth Hare   Pvt. Ohio Mil.
  daughter Julia Ann m. William Igou

McKenzie, William b. Ire. 1758 d. Ga. 1835   Pvt. Ga. Mil.
  m. Eleanor Campbell — daughter Mary Ann m. James Means

McKim, John Jr. b. Md. 1766 d. Md. 1842 m. Margaret Telfair   Pat. Md.
  son David T. m. Sarah Beatty

McKimey, Anthony Vol. 12   Pvt. Ohio Mil.

McKinney, Abraham Smith b. Pa. 1791 d. Ill. 1872   Pvt. Pa. Mil.
  m. Margaret Reynolds — daughter Anna m. Gen. David Perkins Grier

McKinney, James b. Pa. 1789 d. Ind. 1872   Pvt. Ohio Mil.
  m. Mary Flynn Irby — son Moses B. m. Nancy Ann Leabo

McKinney, John Sr. b. Va. 1757 d. Ky. 1837   Capt. Ky. Mil. 1794
  m. Hannah Evans — daughter Jane m. Ray Moss

McKinney, Samuel b. Pa. 1786 d. Pa. 1871   Pvt. Pa. Mil.
  m. Rachel McKinney (relative)
  daughter Margaret m. Joseph Chambers

McKinsey, Benjamin Jr. b.—d. N. Y. 1846   Pvt. Md. Mil.
  m. Elizabeth Purnell —son James m. Catherine Nickels

McKinsey, Nehemiah b. S.C. 1795 d. Ind. 1874   Pvt. Ohio Mil.
  m. Catherine Elliot — son Urban C. m. Indiana Shoemaker

McKinstry, John b. Pa. 1775 d. Ohio 1827   Pvt. Ohio Mil.
  m. Elizabeth Brooks — son Robert m. Eliza Bean

McKnight, William b. Pa. 1789 d. Pa. 1828   Capt. Pa. Mil.
  m. Susan Boyer — daughter Anna Maria m. Charles Artman

McLain (MacLean), Charles Jr. b. N.C. 1772 d. N.C. 1858   Pvt. U.S. Inf.
  m. Elizabeth Hughes — daughter Lucinda m. Richard Morris

McLaughlin, John b. Md. 1784 d. Ind. 1851   Fifer Md. Mil.
  m. Elizabeth Copp — son Charles H. m. Thomasine Hocking

McLean, Archibald b. Pa. 1712 d. Pa. 1788 m. Mary Leach Pat. Pa. 1785
  daughter Hester m. Jacob Scudder

McLean, Charles b. Conn. 1769 d. N.Y. 1813 m. Anna Babcock Lt. U.S. Inf.
  daughter Betsy m. William Yeomans

McLean, Ephraim b. Scot. 1730 d. Ky. 1823   Mem. House Repr. Ky. 1800
m. Elizabeth Davidson — son William m. Margaret Miller

McLean, Hugh b. N.C. 1772 d. N.C. 1852   Pvt. N.C. Mil.
m. Margaret Peabody — daughter Mary m. William Bolin

McLean (McLane), John b. N.C. c. 1772 d. N.J. aft. 1841   Capt. N.C. Mil.
m.— son Hiram m. Harriett Moore

McLellan, David b. Mass. (Me.) 1786 d. Me. 1860   Pvt. Mass. Mil.
m. Betsey Phinney — daughter Mary P. m. Royal Thaxter Twombly

McLellan, James b. Mass. (Me.) 1777 d. Me. 1854   Pat. Mass. 1812
m. Lydia Osgood — daughter Lydia m. Winslow Hawkes

McLellan, William b. Mass. (Me.) 1797 d. Ohio 1878   Qtr. Mast. Mass. Mil.
m. Margaret Rebekah Wright — daughter Ann Eliza m. John M. Deer

McLemore, John b. S.C. 1775 d. Ga. aft. 1850   3rd Lt. Ga. Mil.
m. Catherine or Crissey Clifton Patrick
son John H. m. (1) Sally Good Kirkland

McLendon (McClendon), Samuel Jr. b. Ga. 1787 d. La. 1849   Cpl. Ga. Mil.
m. Mary Cook — son James m. Louisa Annie C. Tait

McLeod, John Vol. 8   Pat. Legis. Pa. 1811-13

McLucas, James b.—d. Me. (Mass.) 1814   Mus. (Mass.) Me. Mil.
m. Elizabeth Chick — daughter Eunice m. Alexander Ham

McMachen, Samuel b. Md. 1788 d. Md. 1830   Pvt. Md. Mil.
m. Elizabeth Moelinger Smith — son John m. Mary Murray

McMahan, James b. Pa. 1768 d. N.Y. 1846   Capt. N.Y. Mil.
m. Mary McCord — daughter Sarah Ann m. Austin Smith

McMahan, John b. Ire. 1728 d. Tenn. 1800   Pat. Justice N.C.
m. Isabella Barnes — daughter Rosannah m. Samuel Fain

McMahan, John b. Ohio 1793 d. Ill. 1856 m. Rachel   Pvt. Ohio Mil.
daughter Hariet m. William A. Ewing

McMahon, Samuel Doak b. Tenn. 1789 d. Tex. 1851   3rd Lt. Tenn. Vol.
m. Phebe Young — daughter Margaret T. m. Acton Young

McMahon, William b. Va. 1780 d. Ala. 1846   Capt. Va. Mil.
m. Rebecca Patton — son Ahser W. m. Jane Barksdale Jackson
son John J. m. Hariet C. Shackleford

McMahon, William b. Va. 1749 d. Ohio 1794   Scout, Maj. Va. Mil. 1792
m. Ann Cox — son Joseph m. Ann Hurst and Rebecca Hunt

McManaway, James b. Va. 1796 d. Va. 1845   Pvt. Va. Mil.
m. Nancy Barton — son Charles H. m. Nancy Anne Wright

McMaster, James b. Pa. 1783 d. Pa. 1819 m. Charlotte Black   Pvt. Pa. Mil.
son Joseph m. Rebecca Strausbach

McMath, Samuel b. Pa. 1783 d. Mich. 1826   Capt. N.Y. Mil.
m. Mary Fleming — son Robert m. Betsey Caroline Huggins

McMeeken, Hanse b. Pa. 1791 d. Ia. 1862   Pvt. Pa. Mil.
m. Margaret Marshall — daughter Eleanor m. David F. Young

McMichael, John b. Ga. 1777 d.—m. Frances Lawrence   Pvt. Ga. Mil.
daughter Nancy Emily m. William M. Tomlinson

McMichael, John b. Pa. 1758 d. Pa. 1817 m. Mary Crawford　　Capt. Pa. Mil.
　　son Thomas m. Sarah Mason
　　son John Sr. m. Mary Level
　　son Robert m. Abigail Adsit

McMichie, William Vol. 8　　　　　　　　　　　　　　Adj. S.C. Regt.
　　daughter Maggie m. T. S. Calhoon REAL DAUGHTER

McMillan, John b. Pa. 1782 d. Pa. 1857　　　　　　　　Pvt. Pa. Mil.
　　m. Rebecca Arbuckle — daughter Elizabeth m. John Marquis

McMillan, John Vol. 15　　　　　　　　　　　Maj. S.C. Troops
　　daughter Margaret m. Finley Adams Burke REAL DAUGHTER

McMillan, John b. N.C. 1786 d. Miss. 1866 m. Charity Jones　Pvt. Miss. Mil.
　　daughter Lavicy J. m. Winston Wilkinson

McMillan, Malcolm b. 1778 d. 1829 m. Jo Anna Jacobs　　Sgt. Tenn. Mil.
　　son Robert m. Nettie Trimble

McMillan, Peter E. b. S.C. 1791/2 d. Ga. 1877　　　　　Soldier Ga.
　　m. Sarah Kerbow — daughter Celia m. James Sell

McMillin, David b. S.C. 1761 d. Tenn. 1827 m. Mary Mathis　Lt. Tenn. Vol.
　　son Robert m. Rachel Caldwell

McMillian, Hugh b. N.C. 1784 d. Tenn 1847　　　　　Sgt. Tenn. Mil.
　　m. Margaret McLeod — son John m. Elizabeth Williams

McMorris, Thomas b. Va. 1782 d. Ohio 1842 m. Celia Young　Pvt. Va. Mil.
　　son William S. m. Melissa Ann Durflinger

McMurphey, Daniel b. Ire. 1737 d. Ga. 1819　　　　Pat. Legis. Ga.
　　m. Susannah Crosley — daughter Jane m. William Anderson Cobb

McNabb, Absalom b. Tenn. 1779 d. Tenn. 1858　　　　Lt. Tenn. Mil.
　　m. Mary Lusk — son Robert L. m. Eliza Ann Boyd

McNabb, William b. Tenn. 1786 d. Tenn. 1860 m. Agnes M.　Pvt. Tenn. Mil.
　　son William S. m. Susan H.

McNair, John b. Ky. 1796 d. Wisc. 1852 m. Hannah McBride　Ens. U.S. Inf.
　　daughter Jennie m. William L. Blackman REAL DAUGHTER

McNary, David b. Pa. 1771 d. Pa. m. Janet Edgar　　　Pvt. Pa. Mil.
　　son Samuel m. Margaret Templeton

McNaught, Thomas Vol. 6　　　　　　　　　　　Pvt. Ind. Mil.

McNeil, Daniel b. N.H. 1764 d. Ill. 1839 m. Martha Parker　Sgt. N.H. Mil.
　　son Parker m. Jane McLaren

McNeill, David b. N.H. 1794 d. N.Y. 1861 m. Martha Parker　Pvt. N.Y. Mil.
　　son James m. Margaret

McNeir, William b. Md. 1798 d. Pa. 1861　　　　　　Pvt. Md. Mil.
　　m. Mary Maccubbin
　　son George A. R. m. Margaret Emma Henning

McNitt, Samuel b. Mass. 1772 d. N.Y. 1861　　　　Capt. N.Y. Mil.
　　m. Hannah Foster — daughter Elizabeth m. Elam Parsons

McNutt, William Black b. Tenn. 1783 d. Tenn. 1842　　Pvt. Tenn. Mil.
　　m. Margaret Gillespie — daughter Jane A. m. Warren Caldwell

McPike, Richard b. Md. 1791 d. Ohio 1871 m. Marie LaRue　Cpl. Ohio Mil.
　　son James m. Nancy Woolford

McPherson, Elijah (Daniel) b. Tenn. 1789 d. Ga. 1875　Pvt. Tenn. Rifleman
　　m. Sarah Small — son Henry L. m. Jerusha P. McCalman

McPherson, George Vol. 7 — Capt. N.Y. Mil.

McPherson, Henry Hendley Vol. 14 — 2nd Lt. Md. Mil.

McPherson, James b. Pa. 1760 d. Ohio 1837 — Guide Pa. & Ohio
m. Dorothy Tullis — daughter Martha m. Robert Miller

McPherson, John b. S.C. d. at sea 1806 — Pat. Legis. S.C.
m. Susannah Miles — daughter Ann m. James Creighton

McPherson, William b. N.Y. d. Ala. 1891 m. Susan S. Speer — Pvt. N.Y. Mil.
daughter Roxanna Margaret m. Janes Mallard

McQuaide, Andrew b. Pa. 1790 d. Pa. 1830 — Pvt. Pa. Mil.
m. Elizabeth Kirkwood — daughter Elizabeth m. Thomas Hughes

McQueen, Donald b. Md. 1787 d. N.C. 1867 — Pvt. 1813 Prisoner of War
m. Katherine McQueen — son Alexander m. Caroline Adams

McQueen, John (A. L.) b. 1787 d. Mo. aft. 1856 — Pvt. Ky. Mil.
m. Calrissa Byram — son William B. m. Jerusha Vaughan

McQueen, Joseph b. Ire. 1787 d. N.Y. 1862 — Sgt. N.Y. Mil.
m. Deborah Knight — son Joseph Jr. m. Betsey Loop

McQuiddy, James b. Va. 1788 d. Ky. 1859 — Pvt. Ky. Lt. Dragoons
m. Jane Perry — daughter Martha m. Ephraim Lillard

McRainey, Malcolm b. Scot. 1784 d. N.C. 1847 m. Effa Shaw — Pvt. N.C.
daughter Margaret m. John Brown

McSpadden, Samuel b. Va. 1756 d. Tenn. 1844 — Cpl. Tenn. Inf.
m. Sarah Keys — daughter Darcus m. John Henderson

McVean, John b. N.Y. 1798 d. Ohio 1850 — Pvt. N.Y. Mil.
m. Palemia Stark — daughter Etta m. Bryon Pope REAL DAUGHTER

McWhinney, Matthew b. Tenn. 1792 d. Ohio 1859 — Pvt. Tenn. Vol.
m. Temperance Kendrick
daughter Mary Jane m. Charles Beall Cooper

McWhinney, Thomas b. Ire. 1755 d. Ohio 1828 — Pvt. Tenn. Mil.
m. Eleanor Bell — son Matthew m. Temperance Kendrick
son William m. Elizabeth Kendrick

McWhinney, William b. Tenn. 1789 d. Tenn. 1824 — Cpl. Tenn. Gunman
m. Elizabeth Kendrick — son James m. Mary Bell

McWhorter, John b. Scot. 1739 d. N.Y. 1813 — Capt. N.Y. Mil.
m. Bethiah Hall — daughter Jennett m. Zera Tanner

McWilliams, John Cleveland b. Ky. 1787 d. Mo. 1858 — Sgt. Ky. Mil.
m. Nancy Hockaday — son John Q. A. m. Emma McCord

McWilliams, John T. b. Wales d. Pa. 1832 — Pvt. Pa. Mil.
m. Sarah A. Dickson — son John P. m. Amanda Jane Snyder
son Robert S. m. Amy Marple Corson

McWillie, Adam, b. Ire. 1766 d. S.C. 1827 — Lt. Col. S.C. Mil.
m. Ann McCullough
daughter Margaret D. m. Dr. William McCulloch

Meacham, Philip b. Conn. 1761 d. Mass. 1836 — Pvt. Mass. Mil.
m. Abigail Leland — son Parson P. m. Aseneth Smith

Mead, Brush (Bush) b. Conn. 1797 d. Ohio 1873 — Music Cpl. Conn. Mil.
m. Mary Hess — son Napoleon B. m. Carrie Carl

Mead, David b. N.Y. 1752 d. Pa. 1816   **Maj. Gen. Pa. Mil.**
   m. (1) Agnes Wilson — son William m. Mary Ann Bell

Mead, Ebenezer b. Conn. 1748 d. Conn. 1818   **Conn. Mil. 1801**
   m. Nancy — daughter Rheumah m. Timothy Dwight Walker

Mead, Henry Vol. 16   **Capt. Vt. Inf.**

Mead, John b. N.Y. 1756 d. Pa. 1819   **Pvt. Pa. Mil.**
   m. Catherine Foster — son John m. Sarah Huffman

Mead, Josiah b. Vt. 1775 d. Vt. 1853   **Sgt. Vt. Mil.**
   m. Eusebia Humphrey — son Hiram m. Mary Anna Young

Mead, Rufus b. Vt. 1764 d. Vt. 1824 m. Betty Rockwell   **Sgt. Vt. Mil.**
   daughter Amy m. Erastus Mazuzan Corwall

Mead, Samuel Vol. 9   **Sgt. Va. Mil.**

Mead, Shadrach F. Vol. 16   **Cpl. N.Y. Mil.**

Mead, Solomon b. Ct. 1769 d. N.Y. 1861 m. Hannah Knapp   **Capt. N.Y. Mil.**
   daughter Finnette m. Jacob Countryman

Mead, Zadoc (K.) b. N.Y. 1775 d. N.Y. 1833 m. Nancy Knapp   **Pvt. U.S. Vol.**
   daughter Nancy m. William Reynolds

Meade, David b. N.Y. 1752 d. Pa. 1816   **Maj. Gen. Pa. Mil.**
   m. Agnes Wilson — daughter Margaret m. William Moore

Meade, Stephen b. N.Y. 1793 d. Ind. 1879   **Pvt. N.Y. Mil.**
   m. Mary Pritchard — son Martin E. m. Mahala Yeager

Meaders, Barney b. Ga. 1783 d. Ga. 1861   **Pvt. Ga. Mil.**
   m. Jane Garrison — son Christopher m. Candace Garrison
   daughter Jane m. Osborne Phillips Quillian

Means, Isaac, Jr. b. Va. 1774 d. W.Va. 1875   **Maj. Va. Mil.**
   m. Catherine Smith — daughter Mary m. Nathan Hall

Mears, Jesse b. N.C. 1794 d. N.C. 1878 m. Sarah Bell   **Pvt. N.C. Mil.**
   daughter Delilah Anne m. George S. Thomas REAL DAUGHTER

Mears, John b. Mass. 1764 d. Me. 1854 m. Mary Parker   **Pvt. Mass. Mil.**
   son James m. Sarah Cross

Mears, William b. Va. d. Va. 1837 m. Bridgett Bull   **Pvt. Va. Mil.**
   son John B. m. Sarah Jane Ames

Meason, Thomas b. Pa. 1776 d. Wash. 1813 m.— Vol. 5   **Gen. Pa. Mil.**

Mebane, David b. N.C. 1760 d. N.C. 1844   **Mem. N.C. Gen. Assm.**
   m. Anne Allen   **1808-9-10**
   son Elbridge m. Susan Moore
   son Alexander m. Frances Mitchell

Mebane, John A. b. N.C. 1790 d. N.C. 1864   **Surgeon N.C. Mil.**
   m. Celia Sutton — daughter Celia m. Abijah Allen

Mecum, James b. Mass. 1793 d. Ill. 1877 m. Julia Dewey   **Corp. Mass.**
   son Charles Burt m. Frances Ellen Richards

Medbury, Abner b. R.I. 1774 d. N.Y. 1845   **Pat. Coroner N.Y. 1813-14**
   m. Rhoda Blackmar — son Hiram m. Nancy Sanders

Medders, John b. Md. 1773 d. Md. 1855   **Lt. Md. Mil.**
   m. Hannah Whittington — son George W. m. Araminta Spry

Medley, Ambrose Vol. 13   **Pvt. Va. Mil.**

Medley, James B. b. Va. d. Va. m. Mary Owen Bowman   Pvt. Va. Mil.
daughter America L. m. Henry Harding REAL DAUGHTER

Meehan, John Silva b. N.Y. 1790 d. D.C. 1863   Cpl. Pa. Mil.
m. Margaret J. Monington
daughter Susan M. m. Algernon Sidney Taylor

Meek, Jeremiah b. Md. 1776 d. Ind. 1839   Judge Ind. 1810
m. (2) Catherine Williams — son John m. Sarah Hunt

Meek, John Vol. 5   Pvt. Ohio Mil.

Meek, Samuel b. 1732 d. Pa. 1799 m. Charity   Pvt. Pa. Mil.
son William m. Margaret Thomas

Meeker, Forrest b. Ct. 1768 d. Del. 1840   Sgt. Ohio Mil.
m. Patience Hulburd — daughter Clarissa m. Esbon Husted

Meeker, Stephen B. Vol. 12   Pvt. N.J. Mil.

Meeks, John b. S.C. 1783 d. Tenn. 1877   Ens. Ga. Mil.
m. Elizabeth Henderson — son John H. m. Eleanor Atkins

Meeks, Joseph (K.) b.— d.—   Pvt. N.Y. Mil.
m. Sarah Clark Van Dyk — son John m. Elizabeth Bush

Meggison, Thomas H. b. N.C. 1790 d. Va.   Pvt. Va. Mil.
m. Elizabeth Davidson — daughter Gincy m. Rev. George Everett

Megrue, Paul b. Md. 1791 d. Ohio 1872 m. Nancy Newton   Pvt. Ohio Mil.
son William m. Mary Ann Osborn

Meigs, Daniel Bishop b. Ct. 1762/3 d. Vt. 1849   Pat. Vt. 1805-12
m. Huldah Brownson — son John m. Lucretia Fuller

Meigs, Henry b. Ct. 1782 d. N.Y. 1861 m. Julia Austin   Adj. N.Y. Mil.
son Theodore D. m. Julia E. Tooker

Meldrum, John b. N.J. 1742 d. N.J. 1815 m. Sarah   Pat. N.J. 1811
son John Jr. m. Elizabeth Lundy

Mellichamp, Saint Lo b. S.C. 1789 d. S.C. 1877   Lt. S.C. Mil.
m. Margaret Gedded Lorimore — son Saint Lo m. Amelia MacMillan

Melott, Theodore b. Fra. 1752 d. Ohio 1840 m. Millie   Pvt. Pa. Mil.
son Jacob m. Abigail Truex

Melsheimer, Henry Vol. 12   Sgt. Md. Mil.

Melton, Reubin b. N.C. 1757 d. N.C. 1831 m. Sally Jones   Pvt. N.C. Mil.
daughter Sally m. Isaiah Green

Melton, Samuel b. Va. 1789 d. S.C. 1861 m.—   Pvt. Va. Mil.
son Samuel Jr. m. Mary Helen Gore

Melvin, James b. Md. 1793 d. Neb. 1877 m. Sarah   Sgt. U.S. Inf.
son George m. Laura

Menary, James b. 1760 d. 1835 m.—   Brig. Gen. Ohio Mil.
daughter Jane m. James McCreary

Mench (Mensh), Alexander b. Pa. 1797 d. Pa. 1874   Sgt. Pa. Mil.
m. Susanna Rosensteel — son Isaac m. Lucinda Steiner

Mengle, Benjamin b. Pa. 1786 d. Pa. 1864 m. Sarah Weiser   Pvt. Pa. Mil.
daughter Sophia m. Peter Brehm

Mendoza, Jose Joaquin Fernandez Y. b. Cuba 1751 d. La. 1859   Pat. Spy La.
m. Henrietta Elana Juerre
daughter Therese F. m. Marquis Jean Francois de Cruzel

Mercer, Herman b. Ga. 1784 d. Ga. or Fla. 1853/63   Capt. Ga. Mil.
m. Elizabeth Andrews — daughter Mahala m. John Wesley Jordan

Mercer, Simeon Vol. 6   Pvt. Miss. Mil.

Meredith, Obed b. Va. 1769 d. Ohio 1814 m. Rebecca Draper   Pvt. Ohio Mil.
son Jesse m. Polly Beatty

Meriwether, David b. Va. 1755 d. Ga. 1822   Brig. Gen. Ga. Mil. 1797
m. Frances Wingfield — son John G. m. Mary Hays (Hayes)

Meriwether, John Garland b. Ala. c. 1784 d. Ala. 1836   Lt. Ga. Mil.
m. Mary Hays — daughter Frances Eliza m. William King Crenshaw

Merkel, Christopher b. N.Y. 1761 d. N.Y. 1840 m.—   Pvt. N.Y. Art.
daughter Ellen m. Joseph Perkins

Merrell, Eli. b. N.C. 1787 d. Tex. 1849   Pvt. N.C. Mil.
m. (1) Nancy McCrary — son Benjamin m. Margaret Fleming

Merriam, Sylvester b. N.Y. 1785 d. Ohio 1855   Sgt. N.Y. Dragoons
m. Cynthia Johnson — son Stephen J. m. Fidelity Humphrey

Merrick, Joseph b. Mass. 1739 d. N.Y. 1824   Ens. Mass. Mil.
m. Deborah Leonard — son Gad m. Sybil Harrison

Merrill, Asa Vol. 14   Pvt. N.H. Mil.

Merrill, Edward b. Mass. (Me.) 1791 d. Me. 1848   Pvt. Mass. Mil.
m. Elizabeth Googins — daughter Mary A. m. Bartlett Pillsbury

Merrill, James b. Mass. 1775 d. N.H. 1855   Pvt. N.H. Mil.
m. Elizabeth Heath — daughter Abigail S. m. John Snyder Jr.

Merrill, John Dow b. N.H. 1796 d. Mass. 1886   Fifer Mass. Mil.
m. Mary Barter — daughter Persis m. Isaac Holbrook

Merrill, Robert b. Mass. 1776 d. Ohio 1858   Capt. Mass. Mil.
m. Margery Somerby — son Robert Jr. m. Adaline Poinier

Merrill, Samuel b. N.H. 1793 d. Mass. 1856   3rd Lt. N.H. Mil.
m. Sarah Newell — son Samuel R. m. Mary Smith

Merrill, Stephen S. b. 1798 d. 1863 m. Elizabeth Marshall   Pvt. Mass.
daughter Diana Jane m. Henry W. Smith

Merriman, Joel b. Ct. 1799 d. Mich. 1886   Music Ct. Troops
m. Chloe Gaylord — son Chauncy G. m. Susanna Porter

Merriman, Thomas Vol. 9   Capt. Me. (Mass.) Mil.
daughter Sarah A. m. Samuel L. Johnson REAL DAUGHTER

Merritt, John Vol. 16   Pvt. Del. Mil.

Merwin, James b. Ct. 1777 d. N.Y. 1865 m. Esther Smith   Pvt .N.Y. Mil.
son Alanson m. Amanda Kimball

Meserole, Bernard Johnson Vol. 8   Aid to Gen. Johnson N.Y. Mil.

Meserve, William b. N.H. 1753 d. N.H. 1824   Commander of Privateer 1796
m. Deborah Bartlet — son Charles H. m. Mary Young

Mesick, Thomas I. b. N.Y. 1786 d. N.Y. 1868   Lt. N.Y. Mil.
m. Elizabeth Shinkle — daughter Elizabeth m. Charles W. Fox

Messenger, Campbell b. 1795 d. Ohio 1866   Pvt. Ohio Vol.
   m. Charlotte Wilcox — son Madison C. m. Mary Samantha Pratt

Messenkop, John Adam b. Pa. 1794 d. Pa. 1860   Pvt. Pa. Mil.
   m. Charlotte Bansman — son Hiester M. m. Sarah Gorman

Messinger, George b. Pa. 1755 d. Pa. 1825   Pvt. Pa. Mil.
   m. Catharine Babb — daughter Sarah m. Valentine Werkheiser

Messmore, John b. Swit. 1733 d. Pa. 1813 m. Susan Wise   Pvt. Pa. Mil.
   son Isaac m. Martha Dunlap

Metcalfe, John III b. Va. 1760 d. Ky. 1826   Pvt. Ky. Mil.
   m. Amelia Shackleford —son Thomas m. Margaret Alsop

Metcalfe, Thomas Vol. 11   Capt. Ky. Vol.

Metcalf, William b.— d. Miss. 1835 m. Esther Kuykendall Col. Tenn. Mil.
   daughter Elizabeth m. John R. Duke
   daughter Grace B. m. Robert St. Clair Rayburn

Metz, Jacob b. Ger. 1781 d. Ohio 1860   Drum Maj. Ohio Mil.
   m. Anna Marie — daughter Elizabeth M. m. David Sprinkle

Meyer, Henry Vol. 17   Pvt. Pa. Mil.

Meyers, Matthew Vol. 9   Lt. Commander N.Y. Inf.

Michael, Jacob b. Md. 1772 d. Md. 1855   Capt. Md. Mil.
   m. Mrs. Susanna Osborn Crane
   son William H. m. Henrietta Maria Denny

Michel, Laurent Camile b. Md. 1797 d. Pa. 1878   Pvt. Marine Corps
   m. Mary Elizabeth Smythe
   daughter Annie Elizabeth m. William Davidson Alexander

Mickey, Robert b. Pa. 1747 d. Pa. 1827 m. Ezemiah Kelly   Pvt. Pa. Mil.
   son James m. Lucetta Carothers

Mickley, Jacob Jr. b. Pa. 1794 d. Pa. 1888 m. Anna Kerine   Pvt. Inf. Pa.
   son Edwin m. Matilda E. Fogel
   daughter Rebecca m. Samuel Thomas

Mickley, Jacob b. Pa. 1766 d. Pa. 1857   Pvt. Pa. Mil. 1794
   m. Catherine Scrieber — son Jacob Jr. m. Anna Kerine
   daughter Anna m. Andrew Sheldon

Middleton, Alexander G. b. Ga. 1796 d. Ga. 1859   Pvt. Ga. Mil.
   m. Mary Townsend — daughter Marcella V. m. Allen B. Purdom

Middleton, William H. B. b. Ohio 1793 d. Ohio 1834   Pvt. Ohio Mil.
   m. Phoebe Brown — daughter Julia m. Jacob Tulleys

Miksch, John Frederick b. Pa. 1782 d. Ohio 1837   Pvt. U.S. Inf.
   m. Elizabeth Haber — son William m. Anna Enterline

Milam, James b. Va. 1792 d. Ky. 1865 m. Susan Noel   Pvt. Ky. Vol.
   son John T. m. Elizabeth Morgan

Milam, John b. Va. 1772 d. S.C. 1857 m. Sallie Fuller   Pvt. Ga. Mil.
   son Milton m. Martha Workman

Milburn, Jonathan b. Va. 1772/6 d. Tenn. 1811   Pvt. Ky. Vol.
   m. Nancy Ann — daughter Mary Ann m. George W. Carder

Milburn, Samuel b. Md. 1795 d. Md. 1875   Pvt. Md. Mil.
   m. Rebecca Hutchins — daughter Eleanora m. John Ivy Herrick

Mileham, William b. Pa. 1796 d. N.J. 1866   Pvt. Pa. Mil.
   m. Margaret McKinney
son William Jr. m. Levinah Hazen Wintamute

Miles, Abram b. Ga. 1788 d. Ala. 1873   Sgt. Dragoons Ga. Mil.
   m. Lucinda H. Simmons — daughter Louise G. m. D. H. Floyd

Miles, John Jr. b. Eng. 1777 d. N.J. 1852   Lt. N.J. Inf.
   m. Mary Brittingham — daughter Lydia m. David Middleton Carslake

Miles, Reuben b. Ct. 1782 d. N.Y. 1844 m. Sarah Hallock   Pvt. N.Y. Mil.
   daughter Sarah E. m. Addison Hulse

Milikin, Daniel Vol. 6   Qtr. Mst. Ohio Mil.

Millage (Middagh), George b. N.Y. 1774 d. N.Y. 1839   Pvt. N.Y. Mil.
   m. Margaret — son Charles m. Enylan Onderkerk

Millar, John b. Va. c. 1790 d. Tex. 1843   Pvt. Va. Mil.
   m. Elizabeth Payne — son Daniel m. Susan Lockett

Millar, William b. Va. 1778 d. Ohio 1863   Pvt. Ohio Mil.
   m. Mary Sudduth — son Adam m. Nancy Robinson Howell
   daughter Ann m. Isaac Decker Millar

Millard, William J. b. N.Y. 1796 d. Ind. 1877   Fifer N.Y. Mil.
   m. Betsey J. Ball — daughter Terressa A. m. John Danner

Millauden, Laurent b. Fra. 1786 d. La. 1868   Pvt. La. Mil.
   m. Marie Marthe Elmore Montreuil
   daughter Jeanne Henriette m. Charles Casimir Gardanne

Milleman, George b. Md. 1772 d. Md. 1850   Sgt. Md. Mil.
   m. Roseanna Coleman
   daughter Georgiana m. Charles Rutherfond Taylor

Miller, Abraham b. Ky. d. Ky. m.— Givens   Lt. Ky. Vol.
   daughter Deborah m. John Carpenter

Miller, Abraham b. N.Y. 1775 d. N.Y. 1853 m. Amey Evans   Pvt. N.Y. Mil.
   daughter Ruhamey m. Benjamin Van Nosdall

Miller, Abraham b. Pa. 1777 d. Pa. 1839 m. Susannah Ruch   Pvt. Pa. Mil.
   daughter Salome m. Joseph Biery

Miller, Abraham b. Holland 1735 d. N.Y. 1815   Pat. Judge N.Y. 1791
   m. Winchey McDowell —son Abraham Jr. m. Phoebe McDowell

Miller, Andrew b. Scot. 1773 d. Va. aft. 1855   Cpl. Va. Art. 1813/14
   m. Isabelle Yeman — son Thomas m. Margaret A. Neel

Miller, Andrew b. N.C. d. Mo. 1825 m. Jean Wilson   Pvt. N.C. Mil.
   son William m. Sarah Elizabeth Shults

Miller, Andrew b. Pa. 1756 d. Pa. 1842   Pat. Pa. 1795-8
   m. Anna Elizabeth Stoudt — daughter Hannah m. Andrew Swalm

Miller, Daniel Vol. 6   Pvt. Pa. Mil.

Miller, Daniel b. Va. d. 1825 m. Elizabeth Deshler   Pvt. Va. Mil.
   son John H. m. Jemima Davis Clark

Miller, Daniel b. N.Y. 1763 d. N.Y. 1839 m. Betsy Miller   Pat. N.Y. 1803
   son Daniel S. m. Ann Kip Bailey

Miller, Daniel b. Pa. 1791 d. Pa. 1859 m. Christina Frank   Pvt. Pa. Vol.
   daughter Elizabeth m. James Stover

Miller, David b. 1788 d. Wisc. 1863 m. Alvina Wolven   Pvt. N.Y. Mil.
daughter Huldah m. Peter Bell

Miller, Ezra b. N.Y. 1790 d. N.Y. 1856   Pvt. N.Y. Mil.
m. Zerirah Hulda Park — daughter Catherine E. m. Calvin Huson Jr.

Miller, Frederick b. Ger. 1758 d. La. 1815 m. Ann Custer   Pvt. Ky. Mil.
daughter Ann Margaret m. Abraham Miller
son Adam m. Susanna Settles

Miller, Frederick b. Pa. d. La. 1815 m. Elizabeth Sells   Pvt. Ky. Mil.
daughter Elizabeth m. George C. Baker

Miller, George b. Tenn. 1796 d. Tenn. 1877   Pvt. Mo. Mil.
m. Susan Massengil — daughter Alice m. Samuel Bishop

Miller, George b. Tenn. 1794 d. Ohio 1840   Cpl. Ohio Mil.
m. Elizabeth Morgan Ross
daughter Sarah Jane m. William H. Stoneman REAL DAUGHTER

Miller, Henry b. Pa. 1777 d. Canada 1813 m. Sarah Riley   Pvt. U.S. Inf.
son Henry Jr. m. Sarah Wood Scott

Miller, Henry b. Pa. 1751 d. Pa. 1824   Brig. Gen. Pa. Mil.
m. Sarah Ann Ursula Rose — son Henry Jr. m. Barbara Kremer
daughter Nancy m. David Finley

Miller, Jacob b. Pa. 1775 d Pa. 1861 m. Ann Maria Ott   Sgt. Va. Rifleman
son John D. m. Elizabeth Whitehall

Miller, James b. Ky. 1791 d. Mo. 1878   Pvt. Ky. Mil.
m. Nancy Walton Baker — son Joseph E. m. Velvia Ann Stanmire

Miller, James b. N.H. 1758 d. Pa. 1839   Pat. Me. (Mass.) 1793-5
m. Elizabeth Nesmith — daughter Elizabeth m. Casper Reel

Miller, Jeremiah b. N.Y. 1777 d. N.Y. 1839   Brig. Gen. N.Y. Inf.
m. Phebe Baker — daughter Rosalie m. Edward Mulford Baker

Miller, Jeremiah b. N.Y. 1741 d. N.Y. 1824   Maj. N.Y. Mil.
m. Sarah Van Allen Hogeboom — daughter Sarah H. m. John L. Groot

Miller, Jesse b. Mass. 1772 d. Mass. 1845   Pvt. Mass. Mil.
m. Levina Thurston
son Elkanah m. (2) Deborah Crowell (Richardson) Gleason

Miller (Millar), Jesse b. Pa. 1767 d. 1853 m. Elizabeth Weister   Pvt. Pa. Mil.
daughter Ann m. William Iddings

Miller, John b. Va. 1750 d. Ky. 1806   Pat. Memb. Ky. Legis. 1792-4
m. Jane Dulaney — son Thomas m. Anna Woods

Miller, John b. Va. 1793 d. Ind. 1875 m. Sarah F.   Pvt. Va. Mil.
daughter Alice May m. Finley Franklin

Miller, John b. N.J. 1769 d. N.J. 1834   Pvt. N.J. Mil.
m. Rachel Dissway Wilson — son Robert W. m. Deborah Flock

Miller, John b. Md. 1787 d. Md. 1882   Capt. & Col. Md. Regt.
m. Mary M. Knode — son William Mathias m. Henrietta Norrid

Miller, John b. Pa. 1743 d. Pa. 1810 m. Margaret Ganter   Sheriff, Pa.
daughter Anna m. Phillip Schaeffer

Miller, John b. N.C. 1763 d. N.C. 1854   Commissioner N.C. 1786
m. Christina Bolick — son Ephraim m. Amy Isenhower

Miller, John b. Pa. 1777 d. Pa. 1858 m. Magdalena Schantz   Sgt. Pa. Mil.
son John Jr. m. Hannah Chrisman

Miller, John Vol. 15   4th Cpl. Pa. Mil.

Miller, John b. Mass. 1795 d. Wisc. 1885 m. Statira Booth   Pvt. Vt. Mil.
    son John C. m. Adelia Waite

Miller, John b. Md. 1778 d. Ind. 1866 m. Nancy   Col. U.S. Inf.
    daughter Katherine m. John Fox

Miller, John A. b. N.J. 1760 d. Mo. 1850 m. Isabel Little   Pvt. Conn. Mil.
    daughter Mary m. William Allen Webster

Miller, John Henry b. S.C. 1777 d. Miss. 1852   Surgeon & Maj. S.C.
    m. Jane (Or Jean) Pickens   Vol. 18
    son John Henry Jr. m. Eliza Dicia Giohan

Miller, Joseph b. Pa. 1790 d. Pa. 1850 m. Susanna Rice   Ens. Pa. Mil.
    daughter Sara Jane m. Samuel Blair Hood

Miller, Matthew b. Tenn. d. Tenn. 1813   Cpl. Tenn. Mil.
    m. Margaret John — daughter Rebecca m. Eli Epps

Miller, Michael b. Pa. 1783 d. Pa. 1860   Pvt. Pa. Mil. 1812
    m. Susannah Eisman — son John M. m. Sarah Fox

Miller, Michael b. S.C. 1784 d. S.C. 1874   Lt. S.C. Mil.
    m. (1) Frances Welsh — daughter Harriett M. m. John Rushing Welsh
    son Stephen D. m. Matilda Griffith

Miller, Peter b. N.Y. 1770 d. N.Y. 1834   Capt. U.S. Vol.
    m. Katherine Ann O'Sullivan — son Elias G. m. Sarah T. McCord

Miller, Peter Vol. 8   Ens. Ky. Mil.

Mliler, Peter b. Pa. 1786 d. Pa. 1851 m. Elizabeth Kline   Pvt. Pa. Mil.
    daughter Susan m. Benjamin Shollenberger

Miller, Peter b. Tenn. 1792 d. Tenn. 1863 m. Mary Hunt   Lt. Tenn. Mil.
    son James Sevier m. Mary Evans
    son Samuel H. m. Eliza Range

Miller, Reuben b. Mass. 1731 d. Conn. 1809 m. Sarah   Pat. Conn. 1784-1800
    son Ebenezer m. Dianthe Hutchinson

Miller, Robert b. Pa. 1775 d. Pa. 1829 m.—   Lt. Col. Pa. Mil.
    daughter Isabella m. James Bryan

Miller, Simon b. Va. 1791 d. Tenn. 1866 m. Elizabeth North Pvt. Va. Mil.
    son Simon m. Martha G. Rivers

Miller, Squire b. R.I. 1775 d. R.I. 1825 m. Amy Bishop   Capt. R.I. Mil.
    son Aurin m. Ruth Ann Hunt

Miller, Thomas b. Md. 1788 d. Pa. 1819   Capt. Ohio Mil.
    m. Elizabeth Simpson — son John m. Elizabeth Ellen Hamlin

Miller, Thomas Craig b. Pa. 1789 d. Pa. 1860   Capt. Pa. Mil.
    m. Margaret Maginly — son Mathew A. m. Matilde Ann Fechtig

Miller, Thomas D. b. Pa. 1796 d. Wisc. 1883   Pvt. Pa. Rifleman
    m. Phoebe Mershon — son Alfred m. Frances J. Rust

Miller, William b. Ire. 1768 d. Pa. 1830   Pvt. Pa. 1792
    m. Kezia Miller   Repaired Drum 1812
    daughter Margaret P. m. Sturley Cuthbert

Miller, William b. Pa. 1791 d. Pa. 1866 m. Mary Lemmon   Pvt. Pa. Mil.
    son John C. m. Elizabeth Schaffer

Millholland, Robert D. b. Pa. d. Md.   2nd Lt. & Pay Mst. Md. Mil.
    m. Nancy Day — daughter Lydia E. m. William Davy Maxwell

Milligan (Millikan), Elihu b. N.C. 1785 d. Tenn. 1864   Capt. Tenn. Mil.
  m. Nancy Hurst — son Pleasant m. Jemima Day

Millikin, William Sr. b. Md. 1780/89 d. Ky. 1836   Lt. Md. Mil.
  m. Elizabeth Giles — son Leonard m. Dorcas Wheatley

Milliman, George Vol. 16   Sgt. Md. Mil.

Mills, Daniel b. Conn. 1785 d. Conn. 1836 m. Ruth Higley   Pvt. Conn. Mil.
  daughter Fidelia m. Horace Norton

Mills, Edward b. Conn. 1781 d. Ill. 1869 m. Locina Stewart   Pvt. Pa. Mil.
  daughter Mary L. m. Nathan Wright

Mills, Ezekiel b. Md. 1757 d. Md. 1847   Pvt. Md. Art. Mil.
  m. Mary Jane Sands — son Ezekiel Jr. m. Jerusha Kilbourn

Mills, Lewis b. Conn. 1736 d. Conn. 1817   Pat. Conn.
  m. Hannah Hall   Memb. Council
  daughter Lydia m. Daniel Thompson

Mills, Robert Vol. 6   Pvt. N.Y. Mil.

Mills, Timothy b. Ger. 1789 d. N.Y. m. Katherine Taylor   Pvt. N.Y. Mil.
  son Deloss m. Pamelia Lansing

Mills, William A. Vol 9   Pat.

Mills, William b. Mass. (Me.) d. Me.   Sgt. Mass. (Me.) Mil.
  son James m. Dorcas Webber

Milner, Simeon b. Ga. 1786 d. Ga. 1828 m. Elizabeth Nall   Sgt. Ga. Mil.
  son Jonathan P. m. Eliza English

Milner, William b. Va. 1794 d. Ohio 1860   Sgt. Ohio Mil.
  m. Julia Maria Hart — daughter Philena m. James Crumbley

Milroy, Henry Vol. 14   Pvt. U.S. Inf.

Miltenberger, George b. Va. 1785 d. Ohio 1842 m. Mary Null   Pvt. Va. Mil.
  son Henry m. Mary Jane Warrick

Milton, Homer Virgil b. Ga. 1781 d. Ga. 1822   Col. U.S. Inf.
  m. Elizabeth Robinson — son John m. Susan Amanda Cobb

Mimmo, William b. Va. d. Va. m. Fanny Taylor   Maj. Va. Mil.
  daughter Fanny m. William Taylor

Mims, Samuel b.— d. Miss. Terr. 1813 m. Raine Vol. 19   Lt. Miss. Mil.
  daughter Harriet m. Benjamin S. Smoot

Minard, James S. b. Conn. 1787 d. Pa. 1875 m. (1) Roxy Lee   Cpl. N.Y. Mil.
  son James m. Lucy Foss

Minear, David b. (W.)Va. 1755 d. (W.)Va. 1834   Pvt. (W.)Va. Mil.
  m. Catherine Saylor — daughter Sarah Nancy m. Rodham Bonnifield

Minear, Nathan b. Va. d. W.Va. 1848   Pvt. Va. Mil.
  m. Mrs. Elizabeth Ferguson Bonnifield
  daughter Elizabeth m. Samuel Wesley Bowman

Minear, Phillip b. Ohio 1795 d. Ohio 1849   Pvt. Ohio
  m. Elizabeth McCollister — daughter Mary m. John Dunlap

Miner, Anderson b. Vt. 1795 d. Mich. 1878   Pvt. U.S. Art.
  m. Delilah Armstrong
  daughter Winfield S. m. Mary Elizabeth Willsey

Miner, Andrew b. N.Y. 1793 d. Ia. 1880   Pvt. & Corp. N.Y. Inf.
    m. Fanny Dart — son Luman A. m. Mary Haynes

Miner, Cyrus b. Conn. 1797 d. Conn. 1848   Pvt. Conn. Mil.
    m. Lucy Tracy Huntington — daughter Mary Louise m. Lyman W. Lee

Miner, Elisha b. Conn. 1758 d. Conn. 1816 m. Amey Way   Ens. N.Y. Mil.
    son Alvin G. m. Betsy Latham

Miner, Erastus b. N.Y. 1796 d. N.Y. 1876   Pvt. U.S. Inf.
    m. Margaret Sivers — daughter Marinda m. Charles Colmas

Miner, Seth b. 1777 d. 1860 m. Eleanor Smith   Lt. N.Y. Mil.
    son Elon Galushe m. Margaret Begley

Mingos (Minges—Menges), Conrad b.— d. Pa. 1873   Pvt. Pa. Mil.
    m. Sarah — son Charles m. Mary Teter (Teater)

Minicare, James Monroe Vol. 8   Pvt. Va. Mil.

Minkler, John b. N.H. 1780 d. Vt. 1866 m. Irene Call   Pvt. N.Y. Mil.
    son Harvey m. Elizabeth Ransom

Minnick, Charles G. b. Md. 1798 d. Ka. 1889   Pvt. Md. Mil.
    m. Franciscus Jamieson — son Cornelius R. m. Mary E. Minnick?

Minnis, Thomas Vol. 13   Pvt. Tenn. Vol.

Minor, Benjamin b. N.Y. 1780 d. N.Y. 1861 m.—   Capt. N.Y. Mil.
    daughter Julia m. Daniel Mason

Minor James b. Va. 1745 d. Va. 1791 m. Mary Carr   Coroner Va. 1788
    son James m. Christianna Tompkins

Minor, John b. Va. 1747 d. Pa. 1833   Maj. Pa. Mil.
    m. (2) Cassandra Williams   Memb. Pa. Leg. 1792/6
    son Eli W. m. Dorcas Brice
    son Otho W. m. Rebecca South

Minor, John Pierson b. Pa. 1791 d. Pa. 1874   Cpl. Pa. Mil.
    m. Isabelle McClelland — son Francis M. m. Mary Jane Gwynn

Minten, John b. N.J. 1763 d. Pa. 1830 m. Rebecca Hansbury   Adj. Pa. Mil.
    daughter Rebecca m. George Key

Minton, Nathan b. N.J. 1767/69 k. 1813 in serv.   Pvt. N.J. Mil.
    m. Nancy Johnson — son Jacob m. Philette Willison

Mioton, Francis Nicholas b. La. 1791 d. La. 1824   Brigadier Foot Dragoons
    m. Marie Emilie D'Aram   La. 1815
    son Eugene F. m. Odile Malochee

Mitchell, David b. Pa. 1792 d. Ohio 1886 m. Nancy Hunter   Soldier Ohio
    daughter Belinda m. George W. Cushman

Mitchell, David b. Pa. 1742 d. Pa. 1818   Pa. Leg. 1786/1805
    m. Martha Brown   Pres. Elector 1813
    daughter Margaret m. John English
    daughter Mary m. Robert McCartney

Mitchell, Eliphalet Vol. 5   Pvt. Mass. Mil.

Mitchell, Fleming b. Tenn. 1791 d. Mo. 1865   Pvt. Tenn. Vol.
    m. Mary Dillard — daughter Julia Ann m. W. S. Hughes

Mitchell, Greenberry b. S.C. 1786 d. Tenn. 1860 m.—   Sgt. Tenn. Mil.
    son John m. Sarah D. Churchman

Mitchell, Hendrick b. Md. 1798 d. Md. 1859   Pvt. Md. Mil.
    m. Mary Ann Duvall — son Hendrick G. m. Susan Artridge Owens

Mitchell, Henry Vol. 9   Pvt. Va. Mil.

Mitchell, Isaac b. N.H. 1760 d. N.Y. 1848 m. Jane Moore   Pvt. N.Y. Mil.
    son David m. Elizabeth Dezelle

Mitchell, John b. Eng. 1763 d. W.Va. 1840   Pvt. W.Va. Mil.
    m. Catherine Margaret Teter — son George m. Mary McCann

Mitchell, John b. Pa. 1792 d. Mo. 1874   Pvt. Pa. Mil.
    m. (2) Hannah Atkinson
    daughter Elizabeth m. George Bradshaw REAL DAUGHTER

Mitchell, John b. N.C. 1787 d. Ohio 1847   Pvt. Ohio Mil.
    m. Elizabeth Bilby — son Peter m. Harriet Maria Hawley

Mitchell, John Francis b. 1792 d. Ga. 1861 m. Sarah Stubbs   Sgt. Ga. Mil.
    daughter Sarah Elizabeth m. Alexander Compton Maddox

Mitchell, Joseph b. N.H. 1792/3 d. Me. 1880   Sgt. U.S. Art.
    m. Mercy Buzzell — son John H. m. Mary Ann Carpenter

Mitchell, Joseph b. 1787 d. 1814   Ens. Mil. 1813 (Md.?)
    m. Mary Jane Lynch — son Joseph m. Henrietta Davis

Mitchell, Minott b. Conn. 1784 d. N.Y. 1862   Pat. Town Clerk N.Y. 1812
    m. Elizabeth Leeds Silliman — son Josiah S. m. Elizabeth Anderson

Mitchell, Reuben b. N.C. 1775 d. N.C. 1844 m. Susan Brown   Pvt. N.C. Mil.
    daughter Elizabeth m. Eliah Wyatt

Mitchell, Robert Vol. 11   Sgt. Va. Mil.

Mitchell, Seth b.— d. Me. m. Ruth Merrill Vol. 30   Maj. Mass. Mil.
    daughter Julia m. Cadwallader Curry

Mitchell, Stephen b. Ga. 1784 d. Ga. 1848 m. Margaret Vann   Pvt. Ga. Mil.
    son John V. m. Janet Atkins
    son Richard D. m. Louisa Gordon Phelps
    son Thomas C. m. Martha Ann Adams

Mitchell, William b. Va. 1743 d. Tenn. 1823   Pvt. Ky. Mil.
    m. Mildred Brown — son Martin m. Margaret Gibbs

Mitchell, William b. Va. 1748 d. Ga. 1819   Ens. Ga. Mil.
    m. Harriet Randolph — son James m. Mary Moulder

Mitchell, William b. S.C. 1777 d. Ga. 1859   Pvt. U.S. Inf.
    m. Eleanor Thomasson — son Alexander W. m. Mary Ann McDaniel
    son Isaac m. Mary Dudley

Mix, Ebenezer Vol. 12   Capt. N.Y. Mil.

Mix, Elijah b. Conn. 1780 d. La. 1845   Master U.S. Navy 1813
    m. Maria Cooper — son Edwin m. Louise Kendig

Mixon, Obed b. S.C. 1777 d. Miss. 1847   Sgt. Miss. Terr. Mil.
    m. Levisia Sanders — son Obed Jr. m. Mary F. Barksdale

Mock, John b. N.C. 1780 d. Ohio 1862 m. Mary Horney   Pvt. Ohio Mil.
    daughter Phebe m. Abram Blessing

Mock, Jacob b. N.C. 1778 d. N.C. 1844 m. Julia Tise   Pvt. N.C. Mil.
    daughter Sarah m. Andrews Lindsay

Modena, Henry b. Va. 1792 d. Tenn. 1847   Pvt. Va. Mil.
    m. Lucy A. E. Duncan — daughter Virginia E. m. Merral D. Embry Jr.

Moffett, Gabriel A. b. S.C. 1782 d. Ala. 1837 m. Ann E.   Pvt. Ga. Mil.
son G. Hunter Poinsett m. Pauline Wasson

Moffett, George b. Va. 1735 d. Va. 1811   Pat. 1789 Va. Justice Ct. 1790
m. Sarah McDowell — daughter Margaretta m. Joseph McDowell Jr.

Moffett, Josiah b. Va. 1751 d. Va. 1841 m. Hanna Gass   Lt. Va. Mil.
daughter Hanna m. William Thrift

Moffit, Samuel b. N.J. 1775 d. Pa. 1842 m. Mary Lewis   Pvt. N.J. Mil.
son John J. m. Charlotte Eppley

Moffitt, Peter James b. Ire. 1781 d. Ohio 1849   Pvt. Ohio Mil.
m. Mary Snee — daughter Ann Eliza m. John Fletcher

Mohler, John b. Pa. 1757 d. Pa. 1821 m. Ann Bollinger   Pvt. Pa. Mil.
daughter Rebecca m. John Studebaker

Mohr (More), Herman b. Pa. 1754 d. Pa. 1840   Pvt. Pa. Mil.
m. Anna Margaret Deibert — son Herman Jr. m. Anna Maria Stettly

Mohr, Jacob b. Pa. 1784 d. Pa. 1844   Pvt. Pa. Light Inf.
m. Catherine Uberroth — son Charles m. Caroline Brunner

Mohr, Jacob b. Pa. 1788 d. Pa. 1855 m. Sarah Bachman   Pvt. Pa. Mil.
son Moses m. Caroline Straub

Moisson, Philip b. Fra. 1789 d. N.Y. 1831   Pvt. N.Y. Mil.
m. Sarah A. Waldron — son John W. m. Carolina Blauvelt

Moler, Henry b. (W.) Va. 1797 d. W.Va. 1875   Pvt. Inf. Va. Mil.
m. Harriet — son Benjamin F. m. Mary Robbins Allstadt
son Isaac N. m. Margaret Frances Backus

Monbreun, Jacques Timothe Boucher de   Lt. Ill. 1783-6
b. Canada 1747 d. Tenn. 1826 m. Marguerite Therese Archange Gibaut
daughter Therese Archange Boucher de Wid Jac. Chenier m. Alexis
Doza

Monroe, James b. Va. 1758 d. N.Y. 1831   Pat. D.C. Secy' State in
m. Elizabeth Kortwright   Pres. Madison's Cabinet
daughter Maria Hester m. Samuel L. Gouverneur

Monroe, Lemuel b. Mass. 1759 d. Mich. 1854   Pvt. N.Y. Mil.
m. Martha Rollins — daughter Nancy m. Jonathan Totman

Montague, John b. Mass. 1752 d. Mass. 1832   Town Clerk Mass.
m. Abigail Hubbard   Selectman 1782-1815
son Caleb m. Martha Warner

Montague, Julius Vol. 9   Pvt. N.Y. Mil.

Montan, Anthony b. La. 1793 d. La. m. Eliza McKee   Privateersman La.
daughter Leila m. William P. Harper REAL DAUGHTER

Montayne, Thomas B. b. N.Y. 1769 d. Pa. 1829   Chaplain Pa. Mil.
m. Anna Edmond — daughter Cornelia N. m. George Fetter

Montgomery, Andrew H. Jr. b. S.C. 1794 d. Tenn. 1864   Pvt. Tenn. Vol.
m. Elizabeth Norris — son David J. m. Louise Crabb

Montgomery, Henry b. Vt. 1792 d. Wisc. 1846 m. Maria Tracy Lt. N.Y. Mil.
son Tracy m. Persis Pauline Chadwick

Montgomery, Hugh Vol. 15   Pvt. Va. Mil.

Montgomery, Isaac b. Va. 1776 d. Ind. 1864   Lt. Ind. Mil. 1811
m. Martha McClure — daughter Jane R. m. John I. Neely

Montgomery, James Vol. 17   Capt. N.Y. Mil.

Montgomery, James b. N.C. 1791 d. Tenn. 1881   Pvt. U.S. Inf.
m. Dorcas Miller Russell — son Pulaski m. Sophia Louisa Guinn

Montgomery, James b. Mass. 1777 d. N.Y. 1824   Capt. N.Y. Mil.
m. Sarah Hills — daughter Jane m. Simeon Rising

Montgomery, James Vol. 6   Pvt. Md. Cavalry

Montgomery, John b. Md. 1793 d. Md. 1879   Capt. N.Y. Mil.
m. Mary Ann Ijams — daughter Johnna m. Charles Thomas Dixon

Montgomery, John Vol. 7   Capt. Va. Mil.

Montgomery, John b. Md. c. 1780 d. Md. 1848   Pvt. Md. Mil.
m. (2) Juliana Langley — son James H. m. Jane E. Berry

Montgomery, John b. Pa. d. S.C. 1847/8 m. Margaret Miller Capt. S.C. Mil.
daughter Elizabet m. Samuel Spigner

Montgomery, John b. Pa. 1787 d. Ia. 1858   Pvt. Ky. Mil.
m. Margaret Thompson — son Joseph T. m. Hadassah Dryden Glasgow

Montgomery, John Berrier b. N.J. 1794 d. Pa. 1873 Midshipman U.S. Navy
m. Mary Henry — daughter Delia H. m. James Foster

Montgomery, Robert b. N.C. 1758 d. N.C. 1808   Pat. Rep. & Senator N.C.
m. Mary Jones   1785-1807
daughter Anne C. m. Bensbury Walton

Montgomery, William b. Pa. 1736 d. Pa. 1816   Maj. Gen. Pa. Mil.
m. Margaret Nevin — son John m. Elizabeth Bell

Montgomery, William b. Scot. 1751 d. Pa. 1825   Pvt. Pa. Mil. 1785
m. Nancy Nichols —daughter Elizabeth m. John Miller

Montgomery, William b. Pa. 1791 d. Ohio 1851   Pvt. Ohio Mil.
m. Elizabeth Gregg — son Dr. John m. Harriet Newell Willard

Monty, John Vol. 9   Pvt. N.Y. Mil.

Montz, William b. Pa. 1787 d. Ky. 1869 m. Elizabeth Durst   Pvt. Pa. Mil.
son Andrew J. m. Sarah Rush
son Jeremiah m. Ailsa Eleanor Cain

Moody, Jameson b. Va. 1785 d. Va. 1842   Pvt. Va. Mil.
m. Mary Susan Lankford
son William L. m. Pherabe Elizabeth Bradley

Moody, Joseph b. Me. 1792 d. Me. 1856 m. Happy Hunnewell Pvt. Me. Mil.
daughter Sarah Frances m. Sampson Plummer

Moody, Nathan b. 1779 d. 1861 m. Lydia Weeks   Pvt. Ohio Mil.
daughter Affadilla m. Reuben Deaver

Moody, Nathaniel b. Me. 1793 d. Me. 1886 m. Mary Kimball   Pvt. Me. Mil.
son Leonard m. Marianna Quantin

Mooers, Benjamin b. Mass. 1758 d. N.Y. 1838   Maj. Gen. N.Y. Mil.
m. Hannah Platt — son Benjamin H. m. Margaret Platt Miller
son Charles S. m. Jane A. Palmer
daughter Charlotte E. m. Amasa Corbin Moore
daughter Hannah M. m. Theodore Platt Cady
son William P. m. Marion C.

Moon, Abraham b. N.Y. 1790 d. Ohio 1831   Pvt. N.Y. Mil.
m. Terissa Durand — daughter Cordelia Q. m. Ezra Star Jackson

---

Moon, John Anderson b. Ky. ca. 1785 d. Mo. 1858   Pvt. Ky. Mil.
    m. Jane M. Richards — daughter Ann Anderson m. William C. Jones

Moon, John Diggs b. Va. 1794 d. Va. 1862   Pvt. Va. Mil.
    m. Mary Elizabeth Barclay — son James N. m. Cary Ann Coleman

Mooney, Hercules b. Ire. d. N.H. 1800 m. Mary Jones   Pat. Legis. N.H. 1787
    son Obadiah m. Sarah Blanchard

Moor, Sylvanus b. N.Y. 1796 d. Ore. 1880   Pvt. Pa. Mil.
    m. Nancy Pettibone — son Henry P. m. Eliza Burton

Moore, Alexander b. Pa. 1756 d. S.C. 1813   Pat. Legis. S.C. 1799
    m. Dorcas Erwin — son James m. Sophia Springs

Moore, Cleon b. Va. 1789 d. Tenn. 1852   3rd Lt. Tenn. Mil.
    m. Margaret Creed — daughter Margaret m. Alexander Keith

Moore, Cato III b. Va. 1783 d. W.Va. 1864   Pvt. Va. Mil.
    m. Margaret Strother
    daughter Mary Catherine m. Robert William Baylor

Moore, Charles C. Vol. 10   Pvt. Ky. Mil.

Moore, David Vol. 15   Pvt. Va. Mil.

Moore, Elam Vol. 12   Pvt. Vt. Mil.

Moore, Firmin b. Ky. 1792 d. Ill. 1882 m. Anna Worley   Pvt. Ohio Mil.
    daughter Rebecca F. m. Leroy F. Smith

Moore, Francis C. b. N.Y. 1796 d. Neb. 1874 m. Mary Grant   Pvt. N.Y. Mil.
    daughter Lydia G. m. Ferdinand Chandler Sherman
    REAL DAUGHTER

Moore, Garret b. Pa. 1779 d. Pa. 1861 m. Sarah Grubbs   Pvt. Pa. Mil.
    daughter Mary m. James Anderson

Moore, Hugh b. Ire. 1765 d. N.H. 1854   Pvt. N.Y. Mil.
    m. Margaret Nesmith — daughter Jane m. D. James Cockran

Moore, Isaac b. N.Y. 1794 d. Ohio m.—   Pvt. Ohio Mil.
    son Clifton H. m. Elizabeth Richmond

Moore, James Vol. 8   Pvt. Pa. Mil.

Moore, James b. Mass. (Me.) 1783 d. Me. 1859   Capt. Mass. (Me.) Mil.
    m. Mary Dyer — son Robert m. Eliza Ann

Moore, John b. N.C. 1789 d. Ill. 1839 m. Elizabeth Kizer   Pvt. N.C. Mil.
    son James A. m. Nancy Ann King

Moore, John Vol. 17   Lt. Va. Mil.

Moore, John b. Pa. 1780 d. Ohio m. Jane Porter   Pat. Ohio
    son Samuel m. Leah McKay Phillipp

Moore, John b. Pa. 1765 d. Pa. 1842 m. Nancy Morrow   Pvt. Pa. Mil.
    daughter Sarah m. Joseph Pyle

Moore, John b. Va. 1780 d. Tenn. 1837   Pvt. Tenn. Mil.
    m. Nancy Ann Rogers — daughter Martha R. m. James Haley

Moore, John Wheeler Dr. b. S.C. 1793 d. Ark. 1868   Lt. S.C. Troops
    m. Laura Rebecca Moore (cousin)
    son Dr. Thomas P. m. Augusta G. Ellis

Moore, Joseph b. N.C. 1791 d. Mo. 1873 m. Sophia Root   Sgt. U.S. Inf.
    daughter Martha K. m. William L. Cornett REAL DAUGHTER
    daughter Leeco m. Henry C. Taggart REAL DAUGHTER

Moore, Joseph Appleton b. Mass. 1795 d. Mass. 1878 Pvt. Mass. Mil.
 m. Abigail Mead — daughter Rachel M. m. Edward Keyes

Moore, Michael b. N.Y. 1800 d. N.Y. 1897 Pvt. N.Y. Mil.
 m. Clarissa Merrick Collins
 daughter Irene m.— REAL DAUGHTER
 daughter Josephine REAL DAUGHTER

Moore, Michael Vol. 17 Drum 2nd Lt. U.S. Inf.
 daughter Laura m. J. Middleton Evans REAL DAUGHTER

Moore, Moses b. Pa. 1788 d. Ohio 1863 Ens. Ohio Mil.
 m. Margery Blackburn — son David A. B. m. Elizabeth Cross

Moore, Nicholas Buxton b.—d. Md. 1816 m. Sarah Kelso Lt. Col. Md. Mil.
 daughter Camilla m. William Swan McKean

Moore, Orson b. Conn. 1769 d. N.Y. m.— Capt. N.Y. Mil.
 daughter Mianda m Jonathan Richardson

Moore, Patrick b Ire. 1766 d. Pa. 1847 m. Alice Carskaddon Seaman N.Y.
 son James m. Jane Macklean
 daughter Mary m. John F. Stouck

Moore, Philip b. Va. 1767 d. Ohio 1831 Pvt. Ohio Mil.
 m. Catherine Hornbeck — son Anthony m. Mary Thompson

Moore, Reuben b. Va. 1791 d. Va. 1859 Cpl. Va. Mil.
 m. Martha Jane McWilliams — son Madison m. Lydia Harrison

Moore, Samuel b. Pa. d. Ind. 1828 m.— Pvt. Ind. Mil.
 daughter Magaret m. William C. Moore

Moore, Samuel b. Conn. 1780 d. Conn. 1857 Pvt. Conn. Mil.
 daughter Elizabeth m. Theodore E. Bancroft

Moore, Samuel Perry b. Canada 1800 d. N.Y. 1880 Pvt. Drum N.Y. Mil.
 m. Maria Irish — daughter Fannie A. m. Clarence Herbert Smith

Moore, Theron Sr. b. Mass. 1786 d. Wisc. Cpl. N.Y. Mil.
 m. Keziah Aldrich — son Theron Jr. m. Delia Ann Care

Moore, Thomas b. S.C. 1759 d. S.C. 1822 Brig. Gen. S.C. Mil.
 m. Patsy Price — son Charles H. m. Matilda C. Graham

Moore, Spencer b. Del. 1780 d. Ala. 1869 Pvt. Ga. Regt.
 m. Susannah Graham — daughter Elizabeth m. Willis Cox

Moore, Thomas Vol. 6 Brig. Gen. S.C. Mil.

Moore, Thomas b. Pa. 1781 d. Pa. 1849 m. Esther Heckman Capt. Pa. Mil.
 daughter Elizabeth m. David E. Evans

Moore, Thomas Preston b. Va. 1789 d. Va. 1830 Capt. U.S Inf.
 m. Rachel Pindall — daughter Emily W. m. Waldo P. Johnson
 daughter Harriet m. Waldo Porter Goff

Moore, Washington b. Mass. 1776 d. N.Y. 1856 Pvt. N.Y. Mil.
 m. Susannah Rice — son Loren m. Phelina Amsden

Moore, William b. Va. 1757 d. Mo. 1843 Cpl. Ky. Mil.
 m. Druscilla Weatherford — son Travis G. m. Edith Doss

Moore, William b. Ky. 1786 d. Tenn. 1871 m. Olivia Free Capt. Tenn. Mil.
 son William Jr. m. Elizabeth Lawson

Moore, William b. Ky. 1792 d. Ky. 1833 Pvt. Ky. Mil.
 m. Margaret Sanford Braun
 son Thomas Edwin m. Sarah Jane Shawhan

Moore, William b. N.C. 1789 d. Tenn. 1853 m. Frances   Pvt. N.C. Mil.
    son Alfred m. Elizabeth Frances Phillip

Moore, William Henshaw b. Va. 1795 d. La. 1840   Maj. U.S. Inf.
    m. Heloise Delphine Verritt — daughter Pamela H. m. Felix Dejiern

Moore, William b. N.H. 1798 d. Ill. 1869   Seaman U.S. Navy 1809-12
    m. Eunice Melinda — son Frank W. m. Villa Sprague

Moore, William Washington b. S.C. 1789 d. Ala. 1859   Pvt. S.C. Mil.
    m. Sally Smith — son Peyton J. m. Maria Ann Americus Crowder

Moorehead, Samuel b. Pa. 1749 d. Pa. 1814   Pvt. Pa. Mil.
    m. Elizabeth Sproul — son David m. Margaret Henderson

Mooreman, James Clark b. Va. 1779 d. Va. aft. 1830   Pat. Sheriff Va.
    m. Janet Robinson — daughter Jane R. m. James Calloway Anderson

Moran, Charles Jr. Vol. 12   Cpl. Mich. Mil.

Moreau, Joseph b. Mo. 1791 d. Mo. 1857   Pvt. Mo. Mil.
    m. Louise Eloise Detchemendy
    daughter Marie L. m. Samuel Stanton REAL DAUGHTER

Morehead, Charles b. Va. 1762 d. Ky. 1828   Maj. Ky. Mil. 1797
    m. Margaret Slaughter — daughter Elvira S. m. William Coombs Sr.

Morehead, Turner b. Va. 1757 d. Ky. 1820 m. Ann Ransdale   Pvt. Md. Vol.
    son Turner Jr. m. Martha G. Worthington

Morehouse, Gould b. Conn. 1781 d. N.Y. 1866   Lt. N.Y. Mil.
    m. Betsey Meeker — daughter Eleanor G. m. Seaman Lawrence

Morel, Pierre Louis b. Fra. 1778 d. La. 1828   Pvt. La.
    m. Victoria Marie D'Armas
    son Christoval m. Eulalie Correlie d'Nebecourt
    son Octave Pierre Louis m. Septima Street

Morey, Reuben b. Vt. 1779 d. Vt. 1870 m. Martha Frizzell   Pvt. Vt. Mil.
    son Andrew J. m. Laura Pamela Paine

Morgan, Abraham b. N.J. 1794 d. N.Y. 1872   Sgt. N.Y. Mil.
    m. Elizabeth Kettle — daughter Almira m. Enoch De Long

Morgan, Daniel Jr. b. Conn. 1778 d. Conn. 1820   Maj. Conn.
    m. Susanna Lester — son Edwin m. Harriet Tyler

Morgan, David Bannister b. Mass. d. La. 1846   Brig. Gen. U.S. Army
    m. Marie Constance Baham — daughter Josephine m. William Blair
    daughter Adeline m. Moses Eastman

Morgan, George b. Conn. 1785 d. Pa. 1846 m.— Vol. 6   Pvt. Conn. Mil.

Morgan, Gideon b. N.Y. 1776 d. Tenn. 1851 m. Margaret Sevier   Col.
    daughter Cherokee A. m. Andrew L. Rogers REAL DAUGHTER

Morgan, Israel b. Conn. 1757 d. Conn. 1816   Cpl. Conn. Mil.
    daughter Hannah m. Jonathan Stoddard

Morgan, James b. Va. 1779 d. W.Va. 1860 m. Rachel Bunner   Capt. Va. Mil.
    son David m. Pleasant Harris
    son James m. Pleasant Harris
    son John m. Mary Wilson
    son Stephen m. Salome Van Gilder

Morgan, James Vol. 4   Col. Pa. Mil.

Morgan, John Griffith b. W.Va. 1792 d. W.Va. 1878   Pvt. W.Va. Mil.
m. Susannah Martin — son Benjamin S. m. Eliza Kyle
daughter Jane M. m. Perry Flesher

Morgan, Joseph b. N.J. 1794 d. Pa. 1869   Pvt. N.J. Mil.
m. Anna Maria Deringer
daughter Catherine Jane m. Frederick Lafayette Foster

Morgan, Morgan II b. Va. 1750 d. W.Va. 1828   Pvt. Va. Mil.
m. Elizabeth Blades — daughter Sarah m. Elisha Ayres Jr.

Morgan, Morris b. Wales 1785 d. Pa. aft. 1850   Pvt. Pa. Dragoons
m. Susanna Stantz — daughter Susan m. John Ball

Morgan, Randal b. N.J. 1793 d. Ind. 1871   Pvt. N.J. 1814
m. Susannah Johnson
daughter Diadema ? Donna m. William S. Barekman

Morgan, Samuel b. Conn. 1789 d. Pa. 1861 m. Mary Holmes Pvt. Conn. Mil.
son Samuel Jr. m. Rebecca Stratton

Morgan, Selden b. N.Y. 1784 d. N.Y. 1837   Capt. N.Y. Mil.
m. Lucena Palmer — son Amos A. m. Mary J. Hitchcock

Morgan, William Vol. 15   Pat. Legis. Conn.

Morgan, William Avery Vol. 15   Capt. Conn. Mil.

Morgan, Zackell b. Va. 1735 d. Va. 1795   Col. Va.
m. Nancy Paxton and Drucilla Springer
daughter Catherine m. Jacob Scott

Morgrage, Lemuel Vol. 3   Pvt. Mass. (Me.) Mil.

Moross, Ignace b. 1776 d. Mich. 1850 m. Frances Chauvain Capt. Mich. Mil.
son Medard A. m. Cecilia Troubley

Morrall, George Washington Sr. b. S.C. 1786 d. S.C. 1836   Pat. Legis. S.C.
m. Phebe Fripp   1814
son George W. Jr. m. Sarah A. Dunbar

Morrell, Daniel Jr. b. Mass. 1788 d. Me. 1871   Pvt. Mass. Mil.
m. Hannah Currier — son William H. m. Angeline Graves

Morrell, Stephen Vol. 3   Lt. Mass. Mil.

Morrill, Abraham b. N.H. 1756 d. N.Y. 1845   Pat. Town Clerk Vt.
m. Sarah Hoyt   Selectman Legis. 1792-1812
daughter Sarah H. m. Samuel Hilton

Morrill, Paul b. N.H. 1789 d. N.H. 1865   Sgt. N.H. Mil.
son David m. Mary

Morris, Amos b. Va. 1788 d. Ks. 1878 m. Joanna Lantz   Pvt. Pa. Mil.
son Isaac m. Hannah Hollingsworth

Morris, Ezekiel b. Pa. 1744 d. Ohio 1822 m. Mary   Pat. Juror Ohio 1810
son John m. Elizabeth Wells

Morris, Garret b. 1790 d. 1875 m. Mary Ann Jones   Pvt. S.C. Mil.
son Andrew Jackson m. Martha Herring

Morris Garret b. Va. 1792 d. Ala. 1875 m. Lavonia Earp   Pvt. S.C. Mil.
daughter Mary L. m. John Alexander Thomas REAL DAUGHTER

Morris, Isaac b. Va. 1779 d. Ohio 1849   Pvt. Ohio Mil.
m. Elizabeth Enochs — daughter Rebecca m. Eldridge McKee

Morris, Jacob b. N.J. 1778 d. N.J. 1858 m. Anna L. Wolcott   Pvt. N.J. Mil.
son Jacob W. m. Elizabeth Louise Pearce

Morris, Jacob b. N.Y. 1755 d. N.Y. 1844   Brig. Gen. N.Y. Mil.
m. Sophia Pringle — son William A. P. m. Harriet Persis Grannis

Morris, James Ludlum b. N.Y. 1796 d. N.Y. 1878   Midshipman U.S. Navy
m. Lucretia Aremia Crary — daughter Francis m. Charles Bill Waring

Morris, Jesse b. Pa. 1785 d. Ind. 1850 m. Elizabeth Stingley   Pvt. Pa. Mil.
daughter Martha m. James Orr Cook

Morris, Jesse b. Pa. 1770 d. Ohio 1816 m. Sarah Blackman   Pvt. Pa. Mil.
daughter Cynthia H. m. Benjamin Franklin Vernon

Morris, John b. N.C. 1790 d. Tenn. 1885   Capt. Ky. Mil.
m. Sarah Stephenson — son Robert C. m. Rebecca Cannon Henderson

Morris, Joseph b. Mass. 1782 d. Conn. 1848   Pat. Civil Officer
m. Lydia Russell   1807-15
son Sylvester m. Frances King Carpenter

Morris, Joseph b. Pa. 1760 d. aft. 1801 m. Betsey   Pvt. Pa. Mil.
daughter Jane m. Cornelius Howard

Morris, Joshua b. Va. 1752 d. Va. 1824   Pat. Justice Va. 1814-15
m. Frances Sims — son William m. Sarah Hansford
daughter Elizabeth m. Edmund Price

Morris, Leonard b. Va. 1746 d. W.Va. 1838   Pat. Judge Va. 1798
m. Margaret Lykens — son Dickinson m. Susan S. Morris
daughter Parthenia m. John B. Crockett

Morris, Leonard b. Va. 1748 d. W.Va. 1838   Pat. Justice W.Va.
m. Margaret Price — daughter Sarah m. Fleming Cobb

Morris, Levi b. Pa. 1783 d. Pa. 1842 m. Lucretia Stevens   Pvt. Pa. Mil.
daughter Margaret m. Patrick Donley

Morris, Lewis Vol. 13   Brig. Gen. N.Y. Mil.

Morris, Morris b. 1774 d. Pa. 1825 m. Anna Springer   Sgt. Pa. Vol.
son William m. Elizabeth Marchand

Morris, Nicholas I. b. N.Y. 1792 d. Neb. 1877   Pvt. N.Y. Mil.
m Emma Van Tuyl
daughter Mary E. m. Nelson Morris REAL DAUGHTER
daughter Melvina C. m. Ebenezer Hards REAL DAUGHTER

Morris, Stephen b. Md. d. Del. 1852 m. Jane Collins   Pvt. Del. Mil.
son James m. Sarah Mitchell

Morris, William b. Pa. 1756 d. N.J. 1841 m. Mary Anna Reed   Pvt. N.J. Mil.
son Charles m. Patience Garrison

Morris, William Burton Vol. 15   Pvt. Del. Mil.

Morris, William V. Vol. 8   Qtr. Mst. Ky. Mil.

Morrison, Alexander b. Va. 1773 d. W.Va. 1825   Cpl. Va. Mil.
m. Elizabeth Heagle — son Archibald m. Selina Joseph

Morrison, Archibald b. Va. 1771 d. Ky. 1829 m. Lucy Sullivan   Capt. Ky.
son Sydney m. Elisha Sebree
m. Lucy Fox — daughter Sydney Louise m. Elijah Garth Sebree

Morrison, Alexander b. Va. 1760/70 d. Ga. 1839   Justice Ga. 1797
m. Mary Gathright — son Thomas m. Zemaly Storey

Morrison, Edward b. 1789 d. 1865 m. Lucy Brady   **Fifer Tenn. Mil.**
son Merida m. Lydia Catherine Hardin

Morrison, Ephraim b. Pa. 1784 d. Ia. 1845 m. Phoebe Owen   **Pvt. Pa. Mil.**
son Hiram Eugene m. Joanna Hadley

Morrison, George Leslie Vol. 12   **Pvt. Pa. Mil.**

Morrison, James b. Pa. 1761 d. Mo. 1848   **Maj. Mo. Mil.**
m. Emilie Lefavre — daughter Adele m. Francis Yosti

Morrison, James D. b. Pa. 1793 d. Mo. 1870   **Pvt. Franklin Co., Ind. 1813**
m. Lydia Lee — daughter Nancy Ann m. John Jay Turnbaugh
son Hugh Holmes m. Cynthia Chapman

Morrison, James M. b. Pa. 1796 d. Ohio 1874   **Pvt. Ohio Mil.**
m. Albina Meredith — son Benjamin M. m. Eliza Schrack

Morrison, Joseph b. Ire. 1796 d. Ohio 1852 m. Eliza McClure   **Pvt. Ohio Mil.**
son James m. Ruth Dunham

Morrison, Josiah b. N.C. 1788 d. Tenn. 1868 m. Nancy Wells   **Pvt. Tenn. Inf.**
son Wesley W. m. Mary Jane Hamlett

Morrison, Nathaniel Sr. b. bef. 1734 d. Va.(W.) 1806   **Pvt. Va.(W.) Mil.**
m. Thankful — son James m. Elizabeth Callison

Morrison, Neill b. N.C. 1796 d. Miss. 1869 m. Jane McCants   **Pvt. N.C. Mil.**
daughter Mary Jane m. Samuel M. Rosamond

Morrison, Robert b. 1780 d. Ohio 1848   **Maj. Ohio Mil.**
m. Catherine Carlisle — son Freeman m. Catherine Stump

Morrison, Robert Carson b. N.C. 1787 d. Ala. 1856   **Pvt. N.C. Mil.**
m. Prudence Alexander
daughter Prudence S. m. Nathan Gono Phillips

Morrison, Samuel Vol. 10   **Sgt. Pa. Mil.**

Morrison, Samuel b. Ire. 1779 d. W.Va. 1876   **Sgt. Va. Mil.**
m. (2) Eliza McCall
daughter Dollie C. REAL DAUGHTER
daughter Prudence m. John M. Swecker REAL DAUGHTER

Morrison, William b. Va. d. Ohio m. Nancy Carpenter   **Lt. Ohio Mil.**
son Samuel m. Sidney Allison (or Brown)

Morrison, William b. Md. 1781 d. Pa. 1867   **Capt. Pa. Mil.**
m. Sarah Slemmons — daughter Maria m. John Boston

Morrow, Alexander Jr. b. Pa. c. 1785 d. Ohio 1823   **Lt. Ohio Mil.**
m. Elizabeth Douglass — daughter Jane m. George Robinson Jr.

Morrow, Benjamin b. S.C. 1790 d. N.C. 1875   **Lt. S.C. Mil.**
m. Catherine Malinda White
daughter Martha M. m. Louis Henry Russell

Morrow,, Charles b. Ire. 1779 d. Ohio 1867   **3rd Lt. Pa. Mil.**
m. Heath Babcock — son Gusham m. Nancy Huffman

Morrow, Daniel b. S.C. 1800 d. Tenn. aft. 1860   **Pvt. Tenn. Mil.**
m. Eleanor Morrow (cousin)
daughter Elizabeth E. m. John Riley Thurman

Morrow, Wm., b. 1767 d. 1843 m. Mary Boyd   **Col. Pa. Mil. 1812**
son John Boyd m. Rebecca Stouffer

Morse, Caleb Vol. 16   **Pvt. Vt. Mil.**

Morse, Daniel Vol. 9   **Pvt. Mass. Mil.**

Morse, Ebenezer Vol. 13   Pvt. Mass. Mil.

Morse, Ephraim b. Mass. (Me.) 1764 d. Me. 1843   Pvt. Mass. (Me.) Mil.
   m. Rachel Noyes — daughter Jane M. m. John Barbour

Morse, Joseph b. Mass. 1731 d. Mass. 1802 m. Sarah Ellis   Pvt. Mass. Mil.
   daughter Charlotte m. Benjamin Johnson

Morse, Miner b. Conn. 1780 d. Mich. 1851   Cpl. N.Y. Mil.
   m. Minerva Everetts — daughter Evaline m. Abraham Quick
   son John L. m. Susan Cowles

Morse, Nathan Vol. 9   Lt. Mass. Mil.

Morse, Richard b. N.H. 1795 d. Vt. 1883 m. Sarah Jenkins   Pvt. N.H. Mil.
   son Charles Sr. m. Sarah Heath Blood

Morse, Russell, Sr. b. Mass. 1786 d. Mass. 1869   Pvt. Mass. Mil.
   m. Betsey Waite — son Russell Jr. m. Mary Ann Stebbins

Morse, Samuel Sr. b. Mass. 1718 d. Mass. 1787   Pat. Assessor Mass. 1787
   m. Catherine Clark — son Samuel Jr. m. Esther Woodward

Morse, Samuel Jr. b. Mass. 1759 d. Mass. 1853   Pat. Selectman Mass.
   m. Esther Woodward — son Russell Sr. m. Betsey Waite   1806/13

Morse, Samuel Vol. 7   Pvt. N.Y. Mil.

Morse, Simeon Vol. 17   Ens. N.Y. Mil.

Morse, Timothy b. Conn. 1754 d. N.Y. 1821 m. Miriam Lee   Capt. N.Y. Mil.
   daughter Eliza Anna m. Lt. Col. Matthew Rogers

Morseman, Martin T. b. Vt. 1785 d. N.Y. 1879   Pvt. N.Y. Mil.
   m. Abigail Phelps — son Ephraim P. m. Betsy

Morss, John Jr. b. N.Y. 1775 d. N.Y. 1846   Pat. Alderman N.Y. 1811-14
   m. Isabella Brevoort — daughter Ann Eliza m. Augustus Post Woodruff

Morton, Elijah b. Mass. 1718 d. Mass 1798   Pat. Selectman Mass.
   m. Eunice Morton (cousin) — son Elihu m. Lucy Wells   1784-94

Morton, George b. Mass. 1775 d. Mass. 1842   Gunner Mass. Mil.
   m. Hanna Hobbs — son Allen m. Olive Sawyer

Morton, James b. Va. 1782 d. Ky. 1853   Pvt. Dragoons Mil.
   m. Ruth Summers Riggs — daughter Martha m. Joseph Kannady

Morton, Quin Vol. 11   Capt. Tenn. Mil.

Morton, Thomas b. Mass. (Me.) 1780 d. Me. 1850   Pvt. Mass. Mil.
   m. Hannah Wescott — daughter Lucinda m. Rev. Israel Hills

Morton, Thomas M. b. Ky. 1789 d. Mo. 1859 m. Anna B.   Sgt. Va. Mil.
   daughter Anna Maria m. John Price Hubbell

Mosby, Hezekiah b. Va. 1760 d. Va. 1830 m. Mary Massie   Pat. Va.
   son Edward C. m. Elizabeth Barret

Mosby, John b. Tenn. 1791 d. Tenn. 1837 m. Nancy Smith   Pvt. Tenn. Mil.
   son Samuel Luke m. Eliza Letitia Lancanshire

Moseley, Elijah b. 1767 d. 1822 m. Susannah Hubbard   Sgt. Ga. Mil.
   daughter Anna m. Robert Parnell

Murphy, Robertson b. 1780 d. 1827   Pvt. Tenn. Mil.
   m. Mary (Polly) Lawrence — son Elias Georgo m. Nancy G. Williams

Moseley, John b. Va. 1766 d. Ky. 1847 m. Elizabeth Maxey   Maj. Ky. Mil.
   son Robert M. m. Polly Smith

Moseley, John Finney b. Va. 1790 d. Miss. 1862   Sgt. Va. Mil.
   m. Mary Elizabeth Cooper — son Hillery m. (2) Judith Ann Moseley

Moseley, Thomas Vol. 17   Cpl. Va. Mil.

Moser, Burkhart Jr. b. Pa. 1763 d. Pa. 1849   Capt. Pa. Mil.
   m. Catherine Hornberger — daughter Barbara m. John Whetstone

Mosher, William Vol. 10   Pvt. N.Y. Vol.

Moses, John F. b. N.H. 1792 d. N.H. 1877 m. Abigail C. Boyd   Sgt. N.H. Mil.
   daughter Katharine W. m.— REAL DAUGHTER

Mosher, William Vol. 10   Pvt. N.Y. Vol.

Moss, Joseph b. N.Y. 1782 d. N.Y. 1828 m. Betsey Collins   Pvt. N.Y. Mil.
   daughter Jenette m. Abel Bennett

Moss, Matthew b.— d. Tex. m. Sarah Hogan Vol. 69   Pvt. Tenn. Mil.
   daughter Rebecca m. James Campbell Ragsdale

Moss, Moses, b. Va. 1758 d. Ky. 1838   Ind. Fighter Ky.
   m. Lucretia Williams — son William H. H. m. Mary Crisman

Mossman, William H. b. 1765 d. 1851 m. Sarah Gillis   Capt. Pa. Mil.
   son Thomas m. Rebecca Gillespie

Motter, George b. Pa. 1771 d. Pa. 1855   Pvt. Pa. Mil.
   m. Catrina Rumberger — son Michael m. Sarah Crum

Moulthrop, Josiah b. Conn. 1794 d. Wisc. 1853   Pvt. Conn. Mil.
   m. Sophia Lanckton — son M. Nelson m. Clarissa Louise Parker

Moulton, Abel b. N.Y. 1792 d. N.Y. 1869 m. Hannah Noble   Pvt. N.Y.
   daughter Mary m. Frederick Hunt

Moulton, Jonathan Jr. b. Mass. 1766 d. Mass. 1845   Pvt. Mass. Mil.
   m. Rebecca — daughter Mary m. Ephraim Berry

Mounger, Edwin b. N.C. 1762 d. Ga. 1814   Pat. Justice Ga. 1794
   m. Fanny Clark — son Henry m. Celia Millsaps

Mounger, Henry b. Va. d. Ga. 1795 m. Mary   Pvt. Ga. Mil. 1790
   son Edwin m. Fanny Clarke

Mount, Ezekiel S. b. N.J. 1785 d. W.Va. 1878 m.—   Pvt. Va. Mil.
   son Ezekiel S. Jr. m. Catherine Bell Weaver

Mountjoy, John b. Va. 1741 d. Ky. 1826   Pat. Ky. Repr. 1796
   m. Mary Anne Gerrard — daughter Sally m. Robert Elliston

Moutan, Anthony b. La. 1793 d.— m. Eliza McKee   Seaman La. Navy
   daughter Lelia m. William P. Harper

Mowrey, Amasa b. R.I. 1778 d. R.I. m. Anne Hamilton   Sgt. R.I. 1810
   daughter Phila m. Barney Mowrey

Mowrey, Philip b. Pa. 1778 d. Pa. 1846   Brig. Qtr. Mst. Pa. Vol.
   m. Susan Boyle — daughter Mathilda M. m. James Gormly
   son Peter m. Mary Ann Mowry
   son Robert B. m. Catharine Richardson

Moyer, Daniel Jr. b. Pa. 1797 d. Pa. 1880   Pvt. Pa. Mil.
   m. (2) Margaret Gettle
   daughter Clara m. John D. Books REAL DAUGHTER

Moyer, Jonathan b. Pa. d. Pa. 1817 m. Gertrude Stamm   Sgt. Pa. Regt.
   son Amos m. Maria Petri

Mozena, Dennis b. Conn. 1786 d. Ohio 1873   Pvt. 1st Va. Mil. 1812/13
    m. Rachel McLarin — son Francis m. Hettie Ruskirk

Mudge, Joseph Vol. 3   Cornet Mass. Mil.

Muir, Robert E. b. Scot. 780 d. N.Y. 1860 m. Betsey Haynes   Cpl. N.Y. Mil.
    son George m. Delia L. Taft

Mulford, Ezekial b. 1788 d. Ohio 1871   Pvt. Ohio Mil.
    m. Sarah (Sallie) Cook — daughter Polly m. Thomas Fowler

Mulford, Jacob b. N.J. 1776 d. N.J. 1822 m.—   Pvt. N.J. Rifleman 1814
    daughter Clarissa m. Rev. Edward Stout
    daughter Elizabeth m. William Stuart Van Dyke

Mullen, William b. N.C. abt. 1775 d. Miss. 1833   Capt. Tenn. Mil.
    m. Eleanor Becton — daughter Mary B. m. Joseph Stephenson

Muller, Ferdinand Vol. 10   2nd Lt. La. Mil.

Muller, Louis Vol. 5   3rd Sgt. Md. Mil.

Mullikin, Benjamin b. Md. 1769 d. Md. 1848   Capt. Md. Mil.
    m. Sarah Harwood — son Mortimer H. m. Talitha W. Duvall

Mullikin, William b. Md. 1780-90 d. Ky. 1836   Lt. Md. Mil.
    m. Elizabeth Giles — son Leonard m. Dorcas Wheatley

Mullin, William Vol. 10   Pvt. Va. Mil.

Mullins, Hosea Vol 16   Pvt. S.C. Mil.

Mullins, William b. Va. d. Va. m. Nancy Proctor   Pvt. Lt. Inf. Va. Mil.
    daughter Serena m. Theodore Baker

Mundy, Burruss b. Va. d. Va. c. 1877   Pvt. Va. Mil.
    m. Elizabeth Crossthwaite — son James William m. Lucy Gilbert

Mundy, Edward Nelson b. N.J. 1789 d. N.Y. 1854   Sgt. N.Y. Art.
    m. Margaret (Fran) Sisco — son William N. m. Margaret Jane Harris

Munger, John b. Mass. 1744 d. Mass. 1810   Pat. Selectman Rep.
    m. Sybil Parsons — son Elijah m. Delilah Hinds   Mass. 1794-1810

Munger, Joseph b. Mass. 1792 d. Mass. 1860   Pat. Chief Justice
    m. Candace Jerome — son Joseph Jr. m. Phoebe Risley   Mass.

Munger, Simeon b. Conn. 1787 d. N.Y. 1849   Pvt. N.Y. Mil.
    m. Damaris Evarts — son William P. m. Phebe Bissell

Munn, David b. N.J. 1760 d. N.J. 1843 m. Abigail Baldwin   Sgt. U.S. Inf.
    son Benjamin m. Mary Stalsman

Munn, Rufus Vol. 8   Pvt. N.Y. Mil.

Munro, Daniel b. Va. 1782 d. Santa Fe Trail 1828   Pvt. Mo. Mil.
    m. Elizabeth Copeland — son John T. m. Rebecca Isadore Shepard

Munro, Joseph Jr. b. Mass. 1784 d. Mass. 1863   Sgt. Mass. Mil.
    m. Olive Brown — son Warren C. m. Emma Pearson

Munro, Squire b. Mass. 1758 d. N.Y. 1835   Pat. Rep., Judge N.Y.
    m. Mary Daggett — son Philip m. Sibyl Roberts

Munroe, Daniel b. Conn. 1774 d. N.Y. 1854   Lt. Mass. Mil.
    m. Deborah Sexton — daughter Fidelia m. Obadiah Tower

Munsell, John Vol. 3 & 4   Pvt. Conn. 1781

Munson, Amri R. Vol. 13   Pvt. Vt. Mil.

Munson, Elias Young Vol. 8   Cpl. N.J. Mil.

Munson, John b. Conn. 1769 d. Vt. 1864 m. Betsey Taylor   Capt. Vt. Mil.
daughter Angeline m. Elisha Miller Jr.

Munson, Reuben Vol. 10   Capt. N.Y. Rifles

Munson, William b. 1766 d. Vt. 1830 m. Anna   Pa. Rep., Town Clerk Vt.
daughter Frances m. James S. Platt

Murch, Ebenezer b. Mass. (Me.) 1875 d. Me. 1867   Pvt. Mass. Mil.
m. Anna Grant — daughter Eliza Jane m. Silas Dunham

Murdoch, Alexander b. Pa. 1771 d. Pa. 1837   Pat. Justice Pa.
m. Elizabeth Henderson — daughter Sarah B. m. Joseph Brennaman

Murfree, William Hardy Vol. 7   Pat. Mem. House Commons
daughter Elizabeth m. Henry S. Frazer   N.C. 1813-15

Murphin, William Vol. 6   Pvt. Ohio Mil.

Murphy, John b. Va. 1752 d. Ky. 1818   Pvt. Ky. Lt. Dragoons
m. Rachael Cook — son William m. Nancy Ferguson

Murphy, Pleasant, b. Va. 1776 d. Va. 1863/8   Pvt. Va. Mil.
m. Ann Robeson Shelton
daughter Virginia L. m. Peter E. Hedrick REAL DAUGHTER

Murphy, Simon b. S.C. 1790 d. Ga. 1850 m. Rebecca Harris   Pvt. S.C. Mil.
son Joseph H. m. Sarah McIntosh

Murphy, William b. Va. 1776 d. Va. 1845   Cpl. Ky. Mil.
m. Nancy Ferguson — daughter Margaret m. Thomas C. Wallace

Murray, David b. (Me.) 1775 d. N.H. 1851   Pvt. N.H. Mil.
m. Margaret Forsythe — son Orlando D. m. Mary Jane Wetherbee

Murray, David b. Va. 1760 d. Ala. 1840 m. Mary Walton   Pvt. Ga. Mil.
daughter Anna Eliza m. James M. Collins

Murray, Ebenezer b. Scot. d. Va. 1825 m. Elizabeth Saunders   Pvt. Va. Mil.
son William S. m. Mary Elizabeth Athey

Murray, James b. Pa. 1776 d. Ohio 1834 m. Mary Mitchell   Pvt. Ohio Mil.
daughter Eleanor m. William Collier

Murray, Seymour b. Conn. 1792 d. N.Y. 1852   Pvt. Conn. Mil.
m. Ann Elizabeth Ellsworth Sickles
daughter Emma L. m. Benjamin R. Boone

Murray, Thomas Walton b. Va. 1797 d. Ga. 1830   Pvt. Ga. Mil.
m. Elizabeth Harper
daughter Peninah A. m. William Alexander Noel

Murrell, John Vol. 14   Pvt. Tenn. Mil.

Murrell, Samuel M. b. Ky. 1792 d. Ky. 1890   Pvt. Ky. Mil.
m. Elizabeth Sterrett — son George M. m. Mary Melvina Skiles

Muse, Asa b. N.C. 1795 d. N.C. 1893 m. Isabella McPherson   Pvt. N.C. Mil.
son John M. m. Emelie Jane Timberman

Muse, Fauntleroy Jr. b. Pa. 1791 d. Ky. 1864   Cpl. Pa. Lt. Dragoons
m. Susan Graham — son Eben m. Clara Anderson

Muse, Fauntleroy b. Va. 1757 d. Pa. 1840 m. Mary Jones   Lt. Pa. Mil.
daughter Elizabeth m. John Harrison
son Fauntley Roy Jr. m. Susan Graham
son James m. Hannah Condit
son John J. m. Mrs. Ella Zan Craig Wilson

Muse, Henry Lawson b. Va. 1788 d. Pa. 1845   Pvt. Va. Mil.
    m. Elizabeth Swanson
    daughter Julia Ann m. Dr. William L. T. Hopkins

Muse, John Jones b. Pa. 1796 d. Pa. 1879   Sgt. Pa. Mil.
    m. (1) Rebecca Edmundson — son Joseph m. Cynthia Ann Campbell
    m. (2) Ella Zan Craig Wilson
    daughter Minnie Elia m. Thomas Calvin Jones REAL DAUGHTER

Musgrave, Job b. Va. 1784 d. 1814 m. Isabelle Watts   Pvt. Va. Mil.
    son Zebulon m. Elizabeth McGinty

Musick, Jesse b. Va. 1780 d. Ind. 1811   Rifleman Ind. Mil. 1811
    m. Hannah Gudgel — son Abraham m. Anna Allen

Musick, Uel b. N.C. 1793 d. Mo. 1877 m. Sarah Cason   Pvt. Mo.
    son Francis M. m. Martha Ann Twitty

Musick, Uri Vol. 11   Pvt. U.S. Vol.

Musselman, Daniel Neff b. Pa. 1781 d. Ill. 1852   Capt. Ohio Mil.
    m. Christine Widener — son David W. m. Anna
    daughter Elizabeth m. Dorsey Sands

Musser, Peter Jr. b. Pa. 1792 d. Ohio 1852   Maj. Ohio Mil.
    m. Nancy Anna Newcomer — son John C. m. Margaret Loffer

Mussey, John Vol. 9   Pvt. N.H. Mil.

Mustard, David Vol. 15   Capt. Del. Mil.

Mustard, William b. Md. 1789 d. Ind. 1881 m. Jane DeLoy   Pvt. Ohio Mil.
    son Jacob m. Nancy
    son William m. Elizabeth Bennett

Mustain, John b. Va. 1783 d. Va. 1869 m.—   Pvt. Va. Mil.
    son John Jr. m. Emily LeGrand

Myers (Moyers) Chrisley b. Pa. 1777 d. Va. 1845   Pvt. Pa. Mil.
    m. Barbara Hunt — daughter Elizabeth m. David Henton

Myers, David b. S.C. 1758 d. S.C. 1835 m. Phalby Mills   Pvt. S.C. Mil.
    son Dr. John J. m. Sarah English Peay

Myers, Jacob b. Pa. 1753 d. Pa. 1826 m. Mary Van Wander   Sgt. Pa. Mil.
    son Jacob W. m. Elizabeth Rittenhouse
    daughter Mary M. m. Joseph Malcolmson

Meyers, John b. N.Y. d. N.Y. 1827 m. Susannah Lambert   Pvt. N.Y. Mil.
    son Peter m. Keziah Groot

Myers, John b.— d. Ohio 1834 m. Rachel Rosebrook   Capt. Va. Mil.
    Vol. 40

Myers, John b. Pa. 1783 d. Ohio 1842 m. Rachael Wolfcale   Pvt. Pa. Mil.
    daughter Elizabeth m. Levi Miller Sinclair

Myers (Meyers) Michael b. Pa. 1762 d. Pa. 1836   Pvt. Pa. Mil.
    m. Marie Beeghly (Beekly) — son Michael Jr. m. Elizabeth Lichty

Myers, Michael b. Va. 1745 d. Ohio 1852   Capt. Ohio Mil.
    m. Katherine Stickler — son John m. Jane Cochran

Myers, Peter Jr. b. Pa. 1773 d. Ohio 1854   Pvt. Pa. Mil.
    m. Catherine Leymeister — son Henry m. Sarah Salome Klair

Myers, Peter b. Pa. 1778 d. Pa. 1824 m. Mary Grove   Pvt. Pa. Mil.
    son Peter Jr. m. Lucinda Guist

Myers, Samuel b. Pa. 1776 d. Ohio 1849   Capt. Ohio Mil.
    m. Elizabeth Smith — son John L. m. Catherine Vance

Myles, James b. Ky. 1784 d. Ky. 1872 m. Ann Thomas   Pvt. Ky. Mil.
    daughter Mary Hannah m. Albert A. Boswell

Mynderse, Barent b. N.Y. 1747 d. N.Y. 1815   2nd Maj. N.Y. Mil.
    m. Yanetta Van Vrarken — daughter Nancy m. John C. Toll

Myrick, Barnabas Vol. 13   Lt. Vt. Vol.

Mytinger, Jacob b. Ger. 1750 d. Pa. 1793   Lt. Pa. Mil.
    m. Elizabeth Matthews — daughter Mary m. Zachariah Gemmill

N

Nagel, Augustus Gotlieb b. Ger. 1786 d. Ga. 1866   Pvt. Ga.
    m. Martha Gray — daughter Augusta m. Henry Mims

Nagle, Frederick b. Pa. 1776 d. Pa. 1853   Pat. Town Council Pa. 1814
    m. Rachel Singer — son Christopher E. m. Susanna Shields

Nagle, George b. Pa. 1785 d. Pa. 1825 m. Barbara Huber   Pvt. Pa. Mil.
    son George Jr. m. Mary Yost

Nagle, Joseph b. Pa. 1755 d. Pa. 1808   Capt. Pa. Mil. 1798
    m. Maura Magdelena Lane — son George m. Barbara Huber

Nagle, Peter b. Ger. 1750 d. Pa. 1834 m. Sarah High   Pvt. Pa. Mil.
    son Peter Jr. m. Susan E. Filbert

Nagle, Peter Jr. b. Pa. 1782 d. Pa. 1846 m. Susan Filbert   Pvt. Pa. Mil.
    son Henry m. Mary A. Homan

Nagle, Philip Vol. 17   Pvt. Pa. Mil.

Nall, James b. Ky. 1787 d. Ky. 1842   Pat. Inspector Ky. 1796
    m. Amanda Boone — daughter Elizabeth m. Mahlon Hatfield

Napier, John Wills Vol. 4   Qtr. Mst. Tenn. Mil.

Napier, Thomas b. Va. 1758 d. Ga. 1838   Maj. Ga. Mil. 1807
    m. Tabetha Easter — son Shelton m. Jane Gago
    daughter Tabitha m. Nathan C. Moore

Naragong, Jacob b. Pa. 1773 d. Ohio 1846   Pvt. Ohio Mil.
    m. Barbara Gotschall — son William m. Nancy Ann Watters

Nash, Reuben b. Va. 1771 d. S.C. 1822 m. Nancy   Lt. Col. S.C. Vol.
    daughter Nancy A. O. m. John Nash (relative)

Nason, Edward b. (Me.) Mass. 1794 d. Me. 1872   Pvt. (Me.) Mass. Mil.
    m. Ann Elwell — daughter Phoebe m. Elbridge Gerry Warren

Nation, Sampson b. N.C. d. Ind. 1824   Pvt. Ky. Mil.
    m. Susannah Johnson — son Seth m. Charlotte Nash

Navarre, Francois b. Mich. 1767 d. Mich. 1826   Lt. Col. Mich. Mil.
    m. Marie Suzor (Suzore) — daughter Rosalie m. Louis Berthelot
    son Samuel m. Mary Gaffney

Navarre, James b. Mich. 1766 d. Mich. m. Basile LaPointe   Pvt. Ohio Mil.
    son Joseph m. Lucille Nadeau

Nave, Henry b. Tenn. 1788 d. Mo. 1884 m. Amanda Church   Pvt. Tenn. Mil.
    daughter Mahala m. Daniel M. Embrey REAL DAUGHTER

Nayler, Isaac Vol. 14   Sgt. Ind. Mil.

Naylor, Samuel b. Ky. 1794 d. Ohio 1853 m. Sarah Tucker   Cpl. Ohio Mil.
son R. T. m. Sarah Wade

Neal, Henry b. Del. 1791 d. Ohio 1868 m. Jane Owens   Pvt. Md. Mil.
daughter Mary m. Stephen Barr

Neal, James b. Ga. 1793 d. Ark. 1868   Capt. Ga. Mil.
m. Eliza Rawling Davenport — daughter Louisa m. S. F. Cooper

Neal, James b. Va. 1789 d. Ind. 1874 m. Mary Ann Martin   Pvt. Ky. Mil.
son Moses M. m. Luticia Adeline King

Neal, John b. Pa. 1792 d. Pa. 1870 m. Elizabeth Hartman   Pvt. Pa. Mil.
son William m. Elizabeth Harer

Neal (Neil or Neel), Jonathan b. Ga. 1783 d. Ga. 1844   Pat. Preacher Ga.
m. Charity Morris — daughter Matilda m. Samuel McArthur

Neal, Stephen b. Va. 1766 d. Ala. 1832 m.—   Pvt. Ala. Mil., Sheriff
son George W. m. Annie Malone   Miss. Terr.

Neal (Neill), Thomas b. Va. 1765 d. Ky. 1836   Pvt. Ky. Mil.
m. Phebe LaRue — daughter Nancy m. William Houston Hays

Neale, Benjamin b. Ky. 1779 d. Ky. 1854 m. Mary Hayden   Pvt. Ky. Mil.
daughter Elizabeth L. m. Elijah Gorham Schochoh

Neblett, Sterling Vol. 15   Surgeon's Mate Va.

Neblett, Robert C. b. Va. 1795 d. Tex. 1871 m. Mariah Powe   Pvt. Va. Mil.
daughter Hattie m. William Joseph Terrell

Needham, William Vol. 5   Pvt. Mass. Mil.

Neel, Benjamin b. Va. 1792 d. Ky. 1854 m. Polly Hoden   Pvt. Ky. Mil.
daughter Sarah m. Henson Barker

Neel, Thomas b. 1790 d. Ga. 1857 m. Nancy Veazey   Pvt. S.C. Mil.
daughter Mary E. m. Judge Dickerson H. Walker

Neeley, James b.— d. 1826 m. Elizabeth   Pvt. Ohio Mil.
daughter Margaret N. m. Alexander McClure

Neely (Neelly), Charles Lynch b. Va. 1795 d. Tenn. 1853   Pvt. Tenn. Vol.
m. Sarah Elizabeth Wells
daughter Mary Virginia m. John Wesley Jones

Neely, David b. Ire. 1772 d. Wisc. 1858 m. Jane Feathers   Pvt. Pa. Mil.
son Robert m. Helen Maria Chase

Neely, George b. S.C. 1761 d. Tenn. 1833 m. Rebecca Green   Pvt. Tenn. Mil.
son James m. Elizabeth Lee

Neely, Henry b. Pa. 1779 d. Pa. 1864 m. Barbara Fry   Capt. Pa. Mil.
daughter Frances m. John H. Sigworth

Neely, John I. b. Ky. 1790 d. Ill. 1867   Qtr. Mst. Ind. Mil.
m. Jane Robertson Montgomery
daughter Caroline m. William A. Thomas
daughter Elizabeth Jane m. Mr. Bryant REAL DAUGHTER

Neely, Natthew b. W.Va. 1793 d. W.Va. 1857 m. Mary Newlon   Pvt. Va. Mil.
son Alfred m. Mary Morris

Neff, Jacob b. Pa. 1763 d. 1834 m. Barbara Kaufmann   Pvt. Pa. Mil.
daughter Mary m. Christian Stoner

Neff, Jacob b. Va. 1791 d. Ill. 1873 m. Sarah Painter   Pvt. Va. Mil.
son George William m. Elizabeth Marshall

Neil, Joseph b. 1774 d. Tenn. aft. 1814 m. Mary Wallace   Pvt. Tenn. Mil.
daughter Margaret S. m. Samuel Hughes Card

Neill, Stephen Thompson Vol. 13   Pvt. Va. Mil.

Neilson, David b. N.Y. 1786 d. N.Y. 1830   Surgeon's Mate N.Y.
son Edwin m. Adeline Mendora Cory   Mil.

Neilson, Joseph Hale b. Tenn. 1792 d. Tenn. 1845   Pvt. Tenn. Mil.
m. Mary Smith — daughter Sarah H. W. m. George W. Day

Neilson, Hall Vol. 7   Pvt. Va. Mil.

Neilson, Robert b. Ire. 1791 d. Md. 1845   Pvt. Md. Mil.
m. Catherine Ellender — daughter Mary E. m. Charles P. Stevens

Neilson, Thomas Nelson b. Ire. 1780 d. Md. 1859   Sgt. Md. Mil.
m. Caroline Dawson
daughter Ella m. Mr. Gaillard REAL DAUGHTER

Neiswander, Christian b. Pa. d. Ohio 1830   Pvt. Pa. Mil.
m. Catherine Kachner — son Thomas m. Rebecca Ridenour

Nell, George b. Ky. 1794 d. Ky. 1855 m. Martha Thurman   Pvt. Ky. Mil.
son Edward M. m. Amanda Winston Kinniard
son Timothy F. m. Mollie (Polly Catherine) Hindman

Nellis, George H. b. N.Y. 1767 d. N.Y. m. Catherine   Lt. Col. N.Y. Mil.
daughter Anna m. George Ehlie

Nelson, David Vol. 17   Surgeon Tenn. Mil.

Nelson, David b. Va. 1780 d. Tenn. 1850 m. Phoebe White Pvt. Tenn. Mil.
son James W. m. Elizabeth Carriger

Nelson, George b. Va. 1784 d. Va. 1860   Pvt. Va. Mil.
m. Elizabeth Porter
daughter Mary Katherine m. John Taylor Stark REAL DAUGHTER

Nelson, Gilbert b. N.Y. 1783 d. N.Y. 1871   Pvt. N.Y. Mil.
m. Sarah Delemater — daughter Susan m. Gilbert I. Fitchett

Nelson, Hugh b. abt. 1750 d. 1800 m. Judith Page   Senator Pa. 1791
son Dr. Nathan m. Lucy Mann Page   Town Trustee 1784

Nelson, John b. N.Y. 1752 d. N.Y. 1832 m. Nancy Garter   Pvt. N.Y. Mil.
son Henry C. m. Gertrude Wemple

Nelson, Roger b. Md. 1760 d. Md. 1815   Pat. Civil Offices Md.
m. Elizabeth Harrison — son Madison m. Josephine Morrell Marcilley

Nelson, Samuel b. Mass. 1760 d. Mass. 1823 m.—   Lt. Col. Mass. Mil.
son Joseph m. Lydia Hayward

Nelson, Samuel b. Va. 1780 d. Va. 1845 m. Polly Adams   Pvt. Va. Mil.
son Thomas W. m. Catherine Ann Hale

Nesbit, James Sr. b. N.J. 1718 d. Pa. 1792   Pat. Justice Pa. 1781-8
m. Phebe Harrison — —son Abram m. Bethiah Wheeler

Nesbitt, William b.—d. S.C. 1831 m. Jemima Baker   Pvt. S.C. Mil.
daughter Anges m. Robert Fee Jr.

Nesmith, Alexander b. S.C. 1779 d. Tenn. abt. 1857   Pvt. Tenn. Mil.
m. Jane (Jennie) Martin — son Thomas m. Elizabeth Roberts

Nesmith, Robert b. N.H. 1769 d. N.H.   Pat. Selectman N.H.
m. Jane Anderson — son James m. Mary Corning   1798/1801

Nesmith, Sarah Ann b. N.H. 1787 d. Ohio 1873　　Pat. N.H. Nurse 1814
m. Samuel Wilson — son Joseph m. Elizabeth Miller

Nesmith, Thomas b. D.C. 1795 d. 1886 m. Nancy Dorsey　　Pvt. Md. Mil.
daughter Mary D. m. William S. Bosley REAL DAUGHTER

Nesom, Abraham b. S.C. 1771 d. La. 1857　　Pvt. La. Mil. 1812-15
m. Louanza Kirby — son James m. Emily Holden
son Nelson, m. Drucilla Holden

Nestlerode, Israel b. Pa. 1764 d. Pa. 1832 m. Christina Kline　Pvt. Pa. Mil.
daughter Anna m. Daniel Kendig

Netherland, George S. Vol. 17　　　　　　　　　　Sgt. Va. Mil.

Nevin, David b. Pa. 1782 d. Pa. 1848 m. Mary Peirce　　Lt. Pa. Mil.
daughter Caroline O. m. William Rankin
son William W. m. Sarah Herron Shields

Newberry, (Newbury), Chauncey, Jr.　　　　　　Pvt. Ohio Mil.
b. Conn. 1786 d. Ohio 1885 m. Frances Coe
son Frederick H. m. Aurelia Kent

Newbert, Christopher b. Mass. (Me.) 1796 d. Me. 1884　　Pvt. Mass. Mil.
m. — daughter Ellen m. Orrin Benner

Newbold, Thomas b. N.J. 1760 d. N.J. 1823　　Congressman 1809-13
m. Mary Taylor — daughter Ann m. William Black

Newcomb, Elisha b. Mass. 1770 d. Va. 1820　　　　Sgt. Va. Mil.
m. Mary Ann Bilups — son William m. Huldah Cummings

Newcomb, George Washington b. N.Y. 1796 d. N.Y. 1875　　Pvt. N.Y. Mil.
m. Eliza Ann Lawton
daughter Ellen E. m. David I. Rogers REAL DAUGHTER

Newcomb, William b. Mass. 1790 d. Me. 1850　　Pvt. Seaman Mass. Navy
m. Elizabeth Sidensparker
daughter Amira B. m. James Marion Gladson

Newel, James b. Ire. 1756 d. N.J. 1838 m. Amy Anderson　　Capt. N.J. Mil.
son W. I. m. Edith S. Stetzer

Newell, Jesse b. Conn. 1790 d. N.Y. 1880　　　　Capt. N.Y. Mil.
m. Amaryllis Cowles — son Thomas J. m. Emily Francis

Newell, John Montgomery b. Ky. 1790 d. Ky. 1871　　Pvt. Ky. Mil.
m. Margaret Beaty — daughter Hettie m. Robert Franklin Beatty

Newell, Josiah b. Mass. 1709 d. Mass. 1792　　Pat. Justice Mass. 1781/9
m. Sarah MacIntyre — daughter Elizabeth m. Jonathan Whiting

Newell, Rezin Bryant b. Pa. 1784 d. Ohio 1855　　Pvt. U.S. Rifleman
m. Sarah Newell Roll — daughter Irene m. Henry S. Stewart
daughter Mary m. John Irwin REAL DAUGHTER

Newell, Rezen Bryant m. Susanna Huddleston (2) ? ? ?
daughter Sarah Jane m. Peter George Roll

Newhall, Ezra b. Mass. 1733 d. Mass. 1798　　Coll. Internal Rev. 1798
m. Sarah Fuller — son Thomas m. Mehitable Cheever

Newkirk, Garret Cornelius b. N.Y. 1760 d. N.Y. 1839　　Capt. N.Y. Mil.
m. Rachel Gardenier — daughter Eleanor Maria m. Peter Enders

Newkirk, Matthew Vol. 75

Newland, John A. b. 1784 d. 1864 m. Celia Key   Pvt. Ky. Mil.
son Jacob m. Julian Cann

Newman, Francis b. Md. 1787 d. La. 1854   Lt. Art. U.S. Army
m. (2) Manuella Solis — son Francis Jr. m. Ezilda Daubert

Newman, Francis b. Md. d. Md. 1818 m.—   Lt. Col. Md. Mil.
son Francis m. Barbara Ronquille

Newman, Francis b. Md. 1787 d. La. 1851   Capt. La. Mil.
m. Barbara Ronquille — son Octavie B. m. Jean F. Legier

Newman, George b. Va. 1792 d. Ky. 1848   Pvt. Ky. Mil.
m. Patsy Williams — son Isaac m. Catherine Bryant

Newman, George b. Md. 1788 d. Ohio aft. 1871   Pvt. Ohio Mil.
m. Susannah Powell — son George Jr. m. Nancy Tanner

Newman, Isaac b. Va. 1775 d. Ky. 1862 m. Rachel Rhodes   Pvt. Ky.
son Jonathan m. (2) Eleanor O'Hare

Newman, Jacob b. S.C. 1793 d. Tex. 1856   Pvt. Ky. Mil.
m. Priscilla Thomas
daughter Sarah Ellen m. Moses Poindexter Payne
son Simon Bolivar m. Mary Susan Streetman White

Newman, John b. Va. 1781 d. Va. 1839   Pat. Surveyer Va.
m. Mary Moore — daughter Sarah Ann m. Richard Stafford Rice

Newman, Thomas b. Md. 1778 d. La. 1815   Pvt. Miss. Mil.
m. Philema Smith — son George R. m. Terese Travis

Newman, William Bonner b. N.C. 1775 d. N.C. 1827   Pvt. N.C. Mil.
m. Esther Little — son Richard G. m. Elizabeth Gilbert

Newsome, Robert b. Va. 1783 d. Ga. 1868 m. Nancy Asbury   Cpl. Va. Mil.
daughter Ruth m. Howard Fluellen Bunkley

Newsum, Joab b. N.C. 1779 d. Va. 1850   Pat. Mem. Gen. Assy. N.C. 1812
m. Elizabeth Simmes — daughter Elizabeth m. John Ledford

Newton, Benjamin Vol. 11   Sgt. U.S. Inf.

Newton, Clark E. b. N.Y. 1793 d. N.Y. 1884   Pvt. N.Y. Mil.
m. Abigail Healey — son Laurens C. m. Irene Scott

Newton, Josiah Vol. 17   Pvt. Vt. Mil.

Newton, Reuben b. Vt. 1779 d. N.Y. 1833 m. Eunice Manley   Ens. N.Y. Mil.
son Jesse m. Louise Puddy

Newton, Seth b. Mass. 1732 d. Mass. 1807   Pat. Mem. Conv. Const. Mass.
m. Miss Belknap — son Luther m. Miriam

Newton, Stephen b. Conn. 1761 d. Mass. 1831   Capt. Conn. Mil.
m Esther Witter — daughter Hannah m. Moses Culver

Newton, Younger Jr. b. 1792 d. 1867 m. Nancy Smith   Pvt. S. C. Mil.
son Giles m. Harriet Adams

Niblett, Robert Vol. 16   Pvt. Va. Mil.

Nicholas, David b. R.I. 1767 d. R.I. 1822   Capt. R.I. Blues
m. Lydia Burlingame — son Nelson m. Lovina G. Fairbanks

Nichols, George b. Va. 1754 d. Ky. 1799 Pat. Del. to Const. Conv. 1788 Va.
m. Mary Smith — daughter Elizabeth R. m. James Gabriel Trotter

Nichols, Ira b. Conn. 1794 d. Conn. 1874   Pvt. Conn. Mil.
  m. Bethiah Goodyear
  daughter Harriet Sophia m. William Harrison Fletcher

Nichols, John b. Va. 1783 d. Ohio 1856 m. Hannah   Lt. Ohio Mil.
  daughter Sarah m. Caldwell Dunn

Nichols, John b. Va. 1788 d. Tenn. 1879   Pvt. U.S. Inf.
  m. Elizabeth Shelton — daughter Chaney S. m. Irby H. Orr

Nichols, John b. Conn. 1775 d. Conn. 1862   Capt. Conn. Mil.
  m. Charity Burton — son John L. m. Emily Mallett

Nichols, John b. R.I. 1739 d. N.Y. 1828   Pat. Mem. Gen. Ct. Mass. 1785
  m. Susannah Clark — daughter Susannah m. Jesse Smith

Nichols, Luke b. Vt. 1780 d. N.Y. 1869 m. Polly Bump   Music N.Y. Mil.
  son Samuel G. m. Harriett Aylesworth

Nichols, Nathan b. Va. 1789 d. Va. 1827 m. Sarah Thomas   Pvt. Va. Mil.
  son George m. Julia Ann Bradfield

Nichols, Robert Humphreys b. N.Y. 1791 d. N.J. 1874   Midshipman
  m. Hannah Demuth   U.S. Navy
  daughter Virginia m. Jonathan Halsey

Nichols, Walter b. R.I. 1748 d. R.I. 1823   Naval Officer R.I.
  m. Rachel Stoddard — son Joshua m. Hannah Coggeshall

Nicholson, Benjamin b. Md. 1745 d. Md. 1792   Pat. Chief Judge Md. 1792
  m. Mary Ridgely — daughter Elizabeth m. Henry Darington Darden Sr.

Nicholson, James b. Md. 1737 d. N.Y. 1804   Commander Navy
  m. Frances Witter — son James W. m. Ann Griffin

Nicholson, Josiah b. N.C. 1750 d. Ala. 1830   Pat. Justice N.C.
  m. Rhoda Whitehead — son Isaac W. m. Martha Jefferson Goode

Nicholson, William P. b. Md. 1793 d. Mo. 1859   Pvt. Md. Mil.
  m. Mary Todd Webb
  daughter Lucy C. m. D. Herndon Lindsay REAL DAUGHTER
  daughter Elizabeth unm.— REAL DAUGHTER

Nickerson, Edward b. N.Y. 1766 d. N.Y. 1840   Pvt. N.Y. Mil.
  m. Mary Marshall — son Edward Jr. m. Sarah Dan

Nickerson, Joseph b. N.Y. 1793 d. Ohio 1881   Drum N.Y. Mil.
  m. Nancy A. Christ — son Ebenezer B. m. Mary Hand

Nickey, Samuel b. Ger. 1766 d. Va. 1832   Surgeon Va. Mil.
  m. Anna Catherine Balsley — daughter Rebecca m. Jesse Briggs
  son Samuel Jr. m. Elizabeth Gradeless

Nicks, John Quinton Vol. 11   Maj. U.S. Army
  daughter Elizabeth Perkins m. Samuel Lewis Griffith REAL DAU.

Nidiffer, Solomon b. Tenn. 1793 d. Ark. 1855 m.—   Lt. Tenn. Mil.
  son Isaac m. Lucy Arthur

Nields, Thomas b. Pa. 1772 d. Pa. 1816 m. Hannah Graham   Pvt. Pa. Mil.
  son Daniel m. Eliza Ann Smedley

Nighman, George b Pa. 1790 d. Ohio 1832 m. Lydia Killen   Pvt. Ohio Mil.
  son Thaddeus C. m. Emeline

Niles, George W. b. N.Y. 1795 d. N.Y. 1867   Cpl. N.Y. Mil.
  m. Lucy Frances Randall
  daughter Jennie Caroline m. Louis Edwin Granger REAL DAUGHTER
  daughter Mary Louise m. Dr. Pierson Crane Curtis REAL DAUGHTER

Niles, John b. 1786 d. 1868 m. Elizabeth Hawkins   Pvt. U.S. Inf. N.H.
son John Langdon m. Louisa Elizabeth Geggus

Nisbet, James Sr. b. Scot. 1765 d. Ky. 1845 m. Jane Bratton   Pat. Ky. 1807
son James R. m. Mary Ann B. Pritchett

Nisbet, Robert b. 1793 d. Ga. aft. 1871 m. Eliza Graves   Pvt. S. C. Mil.
daughter Martha Jane m. Samuel Lawson McNair

Nixon, George b. Eng. 1788 d. Ind. 1815   Maj. Pa. Mil.
m. Mary Ann Lewis — son Daniel K. m. Lizzie Ann Exline

Nixon, George Henry b. Va. 1778 d. Miss. 1824   Lt. Col. Miss. Mil.
m. Rebecca Bracey — son Theodore m. Frances Louisa Hill

Nixon, Jacob b. N.J. d. Ill. 1865 m.— Vol. 11   Pvt. N.J. Mil.
daughter Harriet Jane m. Aaron Hadden REAL DAUGHTER

Nixon, Jeremiah Smith Vol. 8   Pvt. N.. Mil.

Nixon, Moses b. Pa. 1774 d. Va. 1854 m. Jane Wynne   Capt. Pa. Mil.
son Moses J. m. Nancy Ann Latimer

Nixon, William H. b. Va. 1773 d. Ga. 1840   Pvt. U.S. Inf.
m. Priscilla Parker Pickett (2)
son Calvin W. m. Mary Elizabeth Orr
daughter Eliza Ann m. Murdock McCaskill

Noble, Alva b. Mass. 1791 d. Pa. 1873   Pvt. Mass. Mil.
m. Maria Amelia Buel — son Sexton m. Lavinia Fish

Noble, Daniel b. Mass. (Me.) 1793 d. Wisc. 1862   Pvt. Mass. Mil.
m. Asenath Knight — Abbie A. m. Clarendon E. Adams

Noble, Daniel b. Mass. 1768 d. Mich. 1837   Pat. Justice Peace N.Y.
m. Lucinda Drake — son Sylvester D. m. Pamela A. Wood

Noble, Eli b. N.H. 1739 d. Va. 1827   Pat. Justice Peace Vt.
m. Ruth Campbell — daughter Eunice m. Joel White

Noble, Ransom b. Conn. 1778 d. N.Y. 1863   Maj. N.Y. Mil.
m. Anne MacNeill — son Harmon m. Laura Ann Welch

Noble, Roger b. Mass. 1742 d. Vt. 1810 m. Olive Hunt   Pat. Shay's Reb.
son William m. Betsy Sherman

Noble, Thomas b. Del. 1794 d. Del. 1849   Pvt. Md. Mil.
m. Elizabeth Morriston — daughter Sara m. Isaac Jacobs

Noble, William Vol. 8   Pvt. Ohio Mil.

Noble, William b. Mass. 1782 d. N.Y. 1848   Pvt. N.Y. Mil.
m. Betsey Sherman — daughter Alice m. John Wesley Moon

Noe, John b. N.J. d. N.J. 1848 m. Mary Kelly   Pvt. N.J. Mil.
daughter Ann m. Jonas Schuyler Lasher

Noel, John Jr. b. Ohio 1793 d. Ind 1885   Pvt. Ohio Mil.
m. Margaret Lowry — daughter Ann m. George W. Thomas

Nolen, Littleberry b. Va. 1777 d. Ala. 1850 m. Rachel   Capt. Tenn. Mil.
daughter Michael m. Stephen Nolen

Nolen, William b. Va. c. 1760 d. Tenn. 1850 m. Sara   Pvt. Tenn. Gunmen
Cantrell—son William Jr. m. Margaret McCarroll

Nolin, Thomas b. Va. 1796 d. Ky. 1858   Pvt. Va. Mil.
m. Susannah Dora Terhune — daughter Martha C. m. Jacob K. Hardin

Noll, Henry b. Pa. 1792 d. Pa. 1847 m. Mary   Ens. Pa. Mil.
son Henry Robert m. Lucy Ann Spitler

Nones, Benjamin b. Fra. 1757 d. Pa. 1826   2nd Lt. Pa. Mil.
m. Miriam Marks — son Jefferson B. m. Mary Louise Marshall

Nooe, Zephaniah b. Va. d.— m. Sarah Susanna Kirtley   Pvt. U.S. Inf.
son Albert K. m. Eliza Jane Garnet

Norcross, John b. N.J. 1783 d. Ill. 1845   Pvt. Pa. Mil.
m. (1) Margaret McCann — son Hiram m. Elizabeth McClellan

Norman, Bailey b. Va. 1775 d. Ohio 1851 m. Tacy Tyson   Pvt. Va. Mil.
daughter Ezella m. Curtis Hayes

Norman, John b. Md. d. Md. 1816 m. Hannah Randall   Pvt. Md. Mil.
son Richard C. m. Zelda Groves

Norman, Thomas R. Vol. 15   Pvt. Del. Mil.

Norris, Henry b. N.Y. c. 1785 d. N.Y. aft. 1813   Pvt .N.Y. Mil.
m. Rhoda Scholfield (1) — son Abram m. Cynthia E. Horton

Norris, Jacob b. Md. d. Md. 1807 m. Avarilla Gallion   Capt. U.S. Inf.
son John C. m. Caroline Caldwell

Norris, John b. Vt. 1785 d. Vt. 1847 m. Lydia George   Pvt. Vt. Mil.
son William G. m. Mary Card

Norris, John Jr. b. N.C. 1750 d. N.C. 1822   Pvt. N.C. Mil.
m. Patience Pearson — daughter Charlotte m. Young Utley

Norris, Patrick b. N.C. 1798 d. Ala. 1871   Fifer N.C. Mil.
m. Charlotte Bullard
daughter Maria Josephine m. William Edwin Wood

Norris, Richard b. Va. 1795 d. Va. 1818 m. Sarah Stott   Pvt. Va. Mil.
son William O. m. Sarah Spillman

Norris, Samuel Pearson b. N.C. 1787 d. N.C. 1856   Ens. N.C. Mil.
m. Martha Worthington—son Jesse A. m. Amy Ann Adams

Norris, Thomas b. Md. 1756 d. Ga. 1818   Pat. Repr. Ga. 1789
m. Sarah Ann Billengsley
daughter Emily Frances m. Nathaniel Allen

Norris, Thomas b. Pa. 1791 d. Pa. a. 1862 m. Rebecca Tiller   Pvt. Pa. Mil.
son Robert m. Maria Shuttleworth

Norris, Thomas Hathaway b. N.Y. 1795 d. N.Y. 1883   Pvt. Md. Mil.
m. Electa Raplee — son Thomas R. m. Sarah Elizabeth Shearman

North, Anthony b. Ga. ca. 1795 d. Ga. 1868   Pvt. Ga. Mil.
m. Mary Hubbard — daughter Mary m. James Bridges

North, John b. Ire. 1771 d. Pa. 1843 m. Elizabeth Pogue   Cpl. Del. Mil.
son John Jr. m. Elizabeth Simpson

Northcraft, Hezekiah b. Md. 1784 d. Va. 1871   Lt. Va. Cavalry
m. Susannah Woodward — son Richard m. Rhuama Starcher

Northcutt, Alexander b. Va. 1780 d. Ga. 1844   Lt. Ga. Mil. 1808
m. Lucy Robinson — son Elijah m. Elizabeth Ann Harris
son Luke S. m. Frances Dorsett Marlow (2)

Northcutt, William b. Va. 1773 d. Ky. 1852 m. Annie Moore   Pvt. Va. Mil.
son Ely m. Elleanor Ellis

Northen, Peter b. N.C. 1794 d. Ga. 1863　　　　　　　Pvt. Ga. Inf.
　m. Louise Maria Davis
　daughter Louise Abigail m. Josiah Anthony Carter

Northway, Francis b. Vt. 1780 d. Ill. 1868 m. Lucy Case　　Lt. Vt. Mil.
　son Francis H. m. Minerva Stuart
　daughter Mary Ann m. Edwin Perry

Norton, Elijah Vol. 6　　　　　　　　　　　　　　　　Lt. N.Y. Mil.

Norton, Ephraim b. Mass. 1752 d. Me. 1839　　　Pvt. Mass. (Me.) Mil.
　m. Deborah Instance — daughter Mehitabel m. Freeman Butler

Norton, George b. N.J. 1790 d. N.J. 1851　　　　　　Capt. N.J. Mil.
　m. Sarah Bancroft — son Somers m. Dias Creek

Norton, Russell b. Conn. d. Conn. 1840 m. Dinah Buell　Pvt. Conn. Mil.
　daughter Thankful m. Charles Francis

Norton, William b. N.C. 1765 d. Ga. 1843　　　Lt. aft. Rev. War Ga.
　m. Polly Landrum
　daughter Emily Ann Morton m. Marion H. Watson

Norton, William b. Mass. 1776 d. Me. 1822　　　Ens. Mass. (Me.) Mil.
　m. Sarah Bradstreet — son Edward S. m. Caroline Hatch

Norton, William Christopher b. N.Y. 1787 d. N.Y. 1870　Sgt. N.Y. Mil.
　m. Catharine Ostrander — son William W. m. Catherine Hendricks

Nottingham, Jonathan b.—d. Zibiah Eldridge　　　Ens. & Lt. N.J.
　son Jonathan m. (2) Hannah Smith

Norvall, John Park b. Va. 1776 d. Ala. 1830　　　　Pvt. Tenn. Mil.
　m. Catherine Griffith — son James T. m. Martha Elder Carter

Norvell, John b. Md. 1789 d. Mich. 1850　　　　　　Pvt. Md. Art.
　m. Isabella Hodgkiss — daughter Emily V. m. Henry N. Walker

Norwood, Charles Wesley b. Tenn. 1794 d. Tenn. 1889　Pvt. Tenn. Mil.
　m. Melinda George — daughter Martha R. m. Samuel Anderson Patton

Norwood, Henry b. Tenn. abt. 1790 d. Ala. 1840　　　Lt. Tenn. Mil.
　m. Alethea Avis Caperton
　daughter Mary m. Macklin Morris McCutchen

Nourse, James b. Eng. 1731 d. Md. 1784　　　　　　Pat. Md. 1784
　m. Sarah Burton Fouace — daughter Catherine B. m. John Cooke
　son James Jr. m. Sarah Benoist

Nourse, (Nurse) John Vol. 8　　　　　　　　　　Pvt. U.S. Inf.

Nourse, Michael b. Va. 1778 d. D.C. 1860　　　　Lt. Col. D.C. Mil.
　m. Mary Rittenhouse — son James m. Sarah North Harvey
　son William m. Isabella Bond

Nourse, John b. Mass. 1780 d. Vt. 1850 m. Sabrey Lovell　Pvt. Vt. Mil.
　son John R. m. Hannah Rebecca Bisbee

Noyes, Henry b. N.H. 1789 d. N.H. 1875 m. Eliza Peabody　Pvt. N.H. Mil.
　daughter Lois Ann m. Joshua Flint Noyes (relative)

Noyes, John b. Mass. (Me.) 1782 d. Me. 1857　　Pvt. Mass. (Me.) Mil.
　m. Amy J. Norton — daughter Mary Elizabeth m. Elisha Burton Foster

Noyes, Joseph b. R.I. 1727 d. R.I. 1802　　　Pat. Gen. Assy. 1782-9 R.I.
　m. Barbara Wells — son Sanford m. Martha Babcock

Noyes, Joseph Vol. 1　　　　　　　　　　　　　　Sgt. Conn. Mil.

Noyes, Nathan b. N.Y. 1793 d. N.Y. 1873   Pvt. N.Y. Mil.
   m. Mariah Woodward
   daughter Malvina Maria m. Perkins Wilson Forsaith

Noyes, Thomas b. R.I. 1754 d. R.I. 1819   Pat. Gen. Assy. R.I. 1792
   m. Lydia Rogers — son Thomas Jr. m. Hannah Phelps

Nute, Samuel b. N.H. 1792 d. Me. 1855 m. Betsey Fockett   Pvt. Mass. Mil.
   son Orasmus m. Lovina Dunn Davis

Nutter, Thomas Christopher b. (W.) Va. 1786 d. W.Va. 1869   Lt. Ohio Mil.
   m. Mary Parks — daughter Mary m. William Douglas

Nye, Charles Vol. 3   Pvt. Mass. Mil.

Nye, George b. Md. 1779 d. Ohio 1854 m. Susanna Knode   Sgt. Ohio Mil.
   son Amos m. Lavinia Emory

Nye, Iram b. Mass. 1785 d. Vt. 1864 m. Orris Willie   Pvt. Vt. Mil.
   son Alfred m. Sarah Ribble Silverthorn

Nye, John Vol. 10   Capt. U.S. Inf.

Nye, Nyel (Neil) b. Conn. 1787 d. Ky. 1841   Sgt. Ohio Mil.
   m. Elizabeth Hall — son Lewis S. m. Sarah Huse Plumer

Nye, Solomon b. Vt. 1763 d. Vt. 1857 m. Lois Fuller   Pvt. Mass. Mil.
   daughter Lois m. Philip Covell

O

Oakes, (Oak) Joel b. Mass. 1767 d. Ohio 1822   Pvt. Scout Ohio Rangers
   m. Susanna Bent — son Daniel m. Julia Clough

Oaks, Abijah b. New Engl. 1789 d. Wisc. 1878   Pvt. N.Y. Mil.
   m. Dempsey Ann Frisbie — son John A. m. Sarah Mossman

Oaks, George b. Mass. 1790 d. N.Y. 1857   Pvt. N.Y. Mil.
   m. Martha Green Choate
   daughter Martha m. Everett A. Dexter REAL DAUGHTER

Oarebaugh, Jacob b. Va. 1794 d. Ohio 1852 m. Rachel Fry   Pvt. Va. Mil.
   son Henry m. Hannah Sprinkle

Oatman, Elijah Vol. 15   Pvt. N.Y. Mil.

Oats, William b. S.C. 1778 d. S.C. 1845 m. Sarah Espey   Pvt. S.C. Mil.
   son Franklin m. Sinia Abernathy

O'Brannon, John b. Va. 1771 d. Va. 1828 m. Elizabeth Allen   Pvt. Va. Mil.
   son Benjamin A. m. Mary Ann Byrd

O'Barr, Robert b. S.C. 1790 d. Ark. 1853-60   Pvt. Ga. Mil.
   m. Celia (Lilly) Bearden — son Roland m. Jemima Hayes

Obenshain, John b. Va. 1789 d. Ind. 1864 m. Elizabeth Stair   Lt. Va. Mil.
   son John Jr. m. Elmira Stevenson

Ober, Benjamin Vol. 5   Pvt. Pa. Mil.

Oberbaugh, Abraham b. N.Y. 1795 d. N.Y. 1852   Cpl. N.Y. Mil.
   m. Deborah Voorhees — son James E. m. Elizabeth Adams

Obold, Sebastian Vol. 14   Pvt. Pa. Mil.

O'Brant, James b.— d. Ohio 1844 m. Sarah Powelson   Pvt. Ohio Mil.
   son Johnson m. Catherine Rock

O'Bryan, Jordan b. N.C. 1794 d. Mo. 1858 m. Elinor Taylor   Cpl. Ky. Mil.
daughter Laura m. Henry Elliott

Odell, Abraham b. N.Y. d. N.Y. 1875   Pvt. Vt. Mil.
m. Rhoda Hervey (Harvey) — son John H. m. Caroline Higbie

Odell, Jacob Vol. 17   Brig. Gen. N.Y. Mil.

Oden, Joshua b. S.C. 1783 d. Ala. 1876   Ens. Ga. Mil.
m. Charlotte Funderberg
daughter Nettie Irene m. Lewis Henry Crumpler

Odenwelder, Philip b. Pa. 1748 d. Pa. 1848   Pvt. Pa. Mil.
m. Anna Marie Yeager — son Philip Jr. m. Elizabeth Koch

O'Donovan, James Hayes b. Va. 1797 d. Pa. 1871   Pvt. Va. Mil.
m. Mary Bryte — daughter Katherine m. William Wilson

O'Ferrall, John b. Va. c. 1784 d. (W.) Va. c. 1856   Pvt. U.S. Inf. Va.
m. Eliza Humrickhouse — son John Jr. m. Helen Walton

Offield, William b. Tenn. 1793 d. Ore. 1880   3rd Cpl. Ky. Mil.
m. Dorrie Jane Laughlin — son John L. m. Amanda Jane E. Vance

Offutt, Rezin Beall b. Md. 1778 d. D.C. 1837   Sgt. Md. Mil.
m. Catherine Knott — son Zachariah M. m. Eliza Ann Remington

Ogier, Lewis b. Eng. 1760 d. Mass. (Me.)   Pvt. Mass. (Me.) Mil.
m. Lucy Thorndike — son William E. m. Sarah Sawyer

Ogle, Hercules, Sr. b. Pa. 1731 d. Va. 1804   Pat. Va. Surveyor
m. Mary Carson — daughter Lucretia m. Mathew Scott

Ogle, Joseph b. Del. 1741 d. Ill. 1821   Pvt. Ill. 1785
m. Druscilla Biggs — daughter Catherine m. James Lemen Sr.

Ogilby, Peter Farrar b. Va. 1792 d. Ky. 1853   Pvt. Va. Mil.
m. Harriett Ball — daughter Harriet m. John Partain

O'Kelly, William b. 1763 d. N.C. 1820   Legis. N.C. 1812-15
m. Mary E. Merritt — son William Jeff m. Nancy Moring

Olcott, Abel b. Conn. 1769 d. N.Y. 1813 m. Mary Rounds   Sgt. N.Y. Vol.
son Abel Jr. m. Betsey Clark

Olcott, Timothy b. Conn. 1739 d. Vt. 1832   Pat. Vt. 1788-9
m. Elizabeth Chandler — son Thomas C. m. Betsey Mann

Oldenberg, Daniel Augustus Vol. 11   Capt. Pa. Mil.

Oldham, Caleb, b. N.C. 1789 d. Ky. m. Milly Covington   Pvt. Ky. Mil.
daughter Martha B. m. John Mills Park

Oldham, John b. Tenn. 1747 d. Ind. 1865 m. Nancy Keeney Pvt. U.S. Inf.
daughter Leah m. James C. Ross

Oldham, Samuel b. Va. 1749 d. Ky. 1823   Pat. Justice Ky. 1794
m. Ann Lipscomb — son Conway m. Fanny Ross

Olin, Gideon b. R.I. 17786 d. Ky. 1830 m. Polly Cole   Cpl. N.Y. Vol.
son Benjamin F. m. Rachel A. Herin
daughter Sarah m. Daniel K. Hall

Olin, Gideon b. Vt. 1743 d. Vt. 1823 m. (1) Patience Dwinell   Pat. Vt. Judge
daughter Susannah m. Daniel Dyer

Oliphant, William b. Pa. 1768 d. Ohio 1850   Maj. Pa. Mil.
m. Ellen (Eleanor) Ewing — daughter Mary m. Samuel Long

Olive, Isham Vol. 12 — Pvt S.C. Mil.

Oliver, Benjamin Sr. b. Va. 1755 d. Ga. 1809 m. Sarah — Cornet Ga. Mil.
son Terry m. Miss Tate (Tait)

Oliver, Charles b. Mass. 1789 d. N.Y. 1866 m. Phebe Wilson — Pvt. Vt. Mil.
daughter Seraph m. James L. Acomb

Oliver, Francis b. N.C. 1791 d. N.C. 1849 — Sgt. N.C. Mil.
m. (2) Mary Ann Pettus Love
daughter Mary Adaline REAL DAUGHTER
son William H. H. m. Eunice Walters

Oliver, James b. (Me.) Mass. d. Me. — Pvt. (Me.) Mass. Mil.
m. Anna Trafton — daughter Lydia A. m. Charles Lyman Shaw

Oliver, James DeGray b. N.Y. 1792 d. N.Y. 1871 — Pvt. N.Y. Mil.
m. Sarah Wright — daughter Emily A. m. James Oliver West

Oliver, William b. Va. 1754 d. Mo. 1851 — Pvt. Va. Mil.
m. Hester Groves (Graves) — son C. M. m. Mary Elizabeth Wells
son John L. m. Ann Virginia Marshall

Olivier, Pierre Du Closel b. La. 1783 d. La. 1840 — Cpl. La. Mil.
m. Marie Joseph Latiolais — son Charles Maurice m. Aminthe Berard

Olmsted, Ashbel b. Conn. 1750 d. N.Y. 1832 m. Ruth Cone — Ens. N.Y. Mil.
son Samuel m. Huldah Marvin

Olmsted, Ichabod b. Conn. 1725 d. Conn. 1799 — Pat. 1786-93 Conn.
m. Dorothy Bates — son Ashel m. Ruth Cone

Olmstead, Jared b. Conn. 1793 d. Conn. 1882 — Pvt. Conn. Mil.
m. Hannah Betts — son Jared, Jr. m. Polly Abbott

Olney, Sylvanus b. Nova Scotia 1773 d. Ohio 1866 — 2nd Lt. Ohio Mil.
m. (1) Annie Stack — son Henry m. Joanna White

Oman, Peter b. Pa. 1774 d. Mich. 1864 m. Sunnah Hilburn — Pvt. Pa. Mil.
daughter Elizabeth m. William Brittain

Omohundro, Richard b. Va. c. 1733 d. Va. 1811 — Pat. Va. 1798
m. Elizabeth Muse — son Richard Jr. m. Edith Seay

Onderdonk, George b. N.Y. 1772 d. N.Y. m. Margaret Smith — Pvt. N.Y. Mil.
daughter Anna M. m. Williams S. Wait

O'Neal, Barney b, N.Y. 1795 d. Mich. 1876 — Pvt. U.S. Art.
m. Casina Pettengel — son James F. m. Jenet McNish

O'Neal, William Jr. b. Md. 1767 d. Md. aft. 1838 — Pvt. Md. Mil.
m. Elizabeth Lodge — daughter Ann m. Samuel Spates

Oram, John b. N.J. 1780 d. Va. 1813 m. Mary Fields — Sgt. Va. Regt.
son John m. Louise Farr

Oram, Samuel Jr. b. N.J. 1791 d. N.J. 1857 — Pvt. N.J. Inf.
m. Martha Godfrey — daughter Caroline m. Samuel Young

Orcutt, John b. Mass. 1758 d. Conn. 1830 m. Irene Wales — Pvt. Conn. Mil.
son John Jr. m. Lurana Griggs

Ord, James b. 1786 d. Neb. 1872 m. Rebecca Ruth Cresap — Lt. U.S. Inf.
son Placidus m. Julia Clark Andre

Ordarondaux, John Vol. 4 — Capt. U.S. Navy

Orendorf, Frederick Vol. 9 — Pvt. N.Y. Mil.

Ormond, William Jr. Vol. 75   Pat. Justice N.C.

Orms, Jonathan b. Conn. 1764 d. Vt. 1812   Brig. Gen. Vt. Mil.
    m. Eunice Hines — son Dan m. Amelia Gaines

Orndorff, Frederick Jr. b. N.Y. 1758 d. N.Y. 1830   Pvt. N.Y. Mil.
    m. Laicy Fulmer — daughter Lany m. Jacob Phillipse

Orput, Richard b. Md. 1786 d. Ohio 1843 m. Selephe Hatch   Pvt. Ohio Mil.
    daughter Elizabeth J. m. William H. Scofield

Orr, David b. Ire. 1770 d. Ind. 1852   Asst. Wagon Mst. Va. Mil.
    m. Rebecca Stephens — son Joseph m. Harriet Foster

Orr, Greshom b. Mass. 1787 d. Me. 1831   Pvt. Mass. Mil.
    m. Elizabeth Cole Polly
    daughter Hannah Polly m. Stephen Bayley Sewell

Orr, James b. Va. or S.C. 1779 d. Miss. 1816   Pvt. Miss. Mil.
    m. Elibabeth DeLoach — daughter Evalina m. John McNulty

Orr, James b. Ky. d. Ky. m. Vol. 34   Pvt. Ky. Mil.
    son John m. Sarah Armstrong

Orr, John b. 1765 d. Ind. 1848 m. Susannah Luke   Sgt. Ky. Vol.
    son Joshua m. Anna Morley

Orr, William b. N.C. 1771 d. Ala. 1861 m. Sarah Anderson   Pvt. Ga.
    son William m. Cynthia Montgomery

Orr, William b. 1793 d. Ohio 1880 m. Hannah Meekal   Pvt. Ohio Mil.
    son Calvin T. m. Julia Ann Mills

Orth, Baltzer, b. Pa. 1736 d. Pa. 1794   Pat. Judge 1786-9 Pa.
    m. Rosina Kucher — son Godlove m. Sarah Steiner   Lt. Col. Pa.

Osborn, John b. N.Y. 1788 d. N.Y. 1872   Pvt. N.Y. Vol.
    m. Catharine Bell — daughter Amelia m. James S. Dawson

Osborn, John b. Va. 1770 d. Ga. 1849 m. Jane Claypole   Sgt. N.C. Mil.
    son Jonathan m. Harriet Grady

Osborn, Richard b. Pa. 1785 d. Pa. 1853   3rd Sgt. Pa. Mil.
    m. Eliza Gilbert — son James G. m. Catherine Mimi

Osborn, Shadrach b. Conn. 1747 d. Conn. 1838   Pat. Legis Conn. 1795
    m. Mary Hinman — daughter Mary Elizabeth m. Leman Dunning

Osborn, Thomas Vol. 11   Maj. N.Y. Mil.

Osborne, John Squire, b. N.J. 1790 d. N.J. 1863   Pvt. N.J. Mil.
    m. Sally Baldwin — son Horace B. m. Frances Buckner

Osborne, Thomas b. Mass. 1786 d. Mich. 1854   Ens. & Qtr.Mst. N.Y. Mil.
    m. Mary Hogarth — daughter Jane m. Thomas Blackwood

Osbun, Samuel b. N.J. 1742 d. Ohio 1832 m. Sarah Holmes   Pvt. Pa. Mil.
    son Isaac m. Amelia

Osburn, Enoch b. N.C. 1750 d. Va. 1818 m. Jane Hash   Capt. Va. Mil.
    daughter Jane m. George Reeves, Jr.

Osburn, Enos b. Va. 1796 d. Ill. 1868 m. Sarah Castleman   Pvt. Va. Mil.
    son George W. m. Martha Eubank
    daughter Laura m. Albert G. Nance REAL DAUGHTER

Osgood, Jesse b. 1793 d. 1873 m. Betsey Butler   Pvt. Vt. Mil.
    daughter Margaret Jane m. Wm. H. Comstock

Osgood, Luther b. Mass. 1780 d. N.Y. 1850 m. Lucy   Pvt. Mass. Mil.
son Luther P. m. Catharine M. Tole

Oster, William I. b. Pa. 1787 d. Pa. 1855   Pvt. Pa. Mil.
m. Margaret Schmidt — son William II m. Elizabeth Major

Otey, Walter b. Va. 1771 d. Ala. 1823 m. Mary Walton   Capt. Va. Cavalry
daughter Frances m. Janes B. Robinson

Otis, Ezekiel b. Vt. 1790 d. Ohio 1858   Pvt. Ohio Mil.
m. Mrs. Mary Miller Stansberry — son Merrill m. Tamer Meyers

Otis, John Vol. 12   Ens. N.Y. Troops

Otis, Solomon b. N.H. 1792 d. N.J. 1867 m. Sarah Booream   Pvt. U.S. Inf.
son Charles R. m. Mary Catherine Bennett

Ouilmette, Antoine b. c. 1770 d. Ill. 1830   Pat. At Ft. Dearborn
m. Elizabeth — daughter Elizabeth m. John Michael Welch

Overall, Isaac b. 1776 d. Va. 1844 m. Mary Ann Carson   Maj. Va. Mil.
son William C. m. Selma Joliffe

Overall, Wilson Lee b. Tenn. 1792 d. Mo. 1850   Pvt. U.S. Rangers
m. Mary Griffith — son Asa N. m. Mary T. Anderson

Overall, Wiilliam b. Va. 1754 d. Ky. 1793   Capt. N.C. Troops
m. Susannah Thomas — son Wilson Lee m. Mary Griffith

Overbagh, Frederick b. N.Y. 1784 d. N.Y. 1866 m. Hannah   Pvt. N.Y. Mil.
daughter Jane m. Francis Story

Overbagh, Jeremiah b. N.Y. 1759 d. N.Y. 1813   Pvt. U.S. Inf.
m. Sarah Van Orden — son Elias m. Angelica Van Orden

Overbaugh, Abraham b. N.Y. 1795 d. N.Y. 1852   Cpl. N.Y. Mil.
m. Deborah Voorhees — daughter Rachel C. m. George L. Van Emburg
son James Edwin m. Elizabeth Adams

Overstreet, James Jr. b. S.C. 1773 d. N.C. 1822   Pat. Legis. 1808-11
m. Eliza Bowen   Senate 1812-17
daughter Eliza C. m. Janes C. Owens

Overstreet, John b. Va. 1758 d. Ill. 1843 m. Nancy Dabney   Pvt. Va. Mil.
daughter Jane m. Abner Hall

Overstreet, Robert b. Va. 1789 d. Ky. 1855   4th Sgt. Ky. Mil.
m. Jane Lowry — son Milton m. Katherine Martin

Overton, David b. N.Y. 1739 d. N.Y. 1826 m. Mary Davis   Capt. N.Y.
son Davis m. Deborah Wells

Overton, Moses b. Va. 1772 d. Va. 1849   Capt. Va. Mil.
m. Mary Clements Booker
son Dr. Thomas C. m. Martha William White

Owen, Abraham b. Va. 1769 d. 1811 m. Martha DuPuy   Col. Ky. Mil.
son Clark L. m. Laura Wells   K/A—Battle of Tippocanoe
daughter Nancy m. Hugh Woolfork

Owen, Benjamin b. Pa. 1765 d. Pa. 1824 m. Lydia Evans   Pvt. Pa. Mil.
son William m. Louisa Smith

Owen, David Vol. 12   Pvt. S.C. Mil.

Owen, Horton Vol. 5   Pvt. N.Y. Mil.

Owen, Ira b. N.H. 1787 d. Vt. 1836 m. Harriet Mariah Doane   Cpl. Vt. Mil.
son Henry B. m. Mary Elizabeth Hodges

Owen, Jesse b. Va. 1774 d. Ark. 1839 m. Susannah Burks   3rd Sgt. Va. Mil.
son Jack m. Sallie Marshall
daughter Mary m. Joel Kelly

Owen, Jonathan Burden b. N.Y. 1773 d. N.Y. 1855   Capt. N.Y. Mil.
m. Martha Rackett — daughter Hannah m. Alexander Moore

Owen, Philip Vol. 15   Pat. Legis. Mass. 1812-14

Owen, William b. Ga. 1778 d. Ga. 1814 m. Nancy Dye   Capt. Ga. Mil.
daughter Nancy m. Thomas R. Davis

Owens, Beacham b. S.C. 1787 d. S.C. 1868   Pvt. S.C. Mil.
m. Nancy Ann Taylor
daughter Emily A. m. Thomas Hayden REAL DAUGHTER
son Lawrence D. m. Mary H. Yarborough
daughter Mary Elizabeth m. John Pinckney Hair

Owens, Edmund b. S.C. 1795 d. Ill. 1864 m. Anna Phelps   Pvt. Tenn. Mil.
son Payton m. Mary

Owens, James b. Md. 1776 d. Md. 1864 m. Anna Franklin   Pvt. Md. Mil.
daughter Mary Ann m. Henry Childs Drury

Owens, John b. S.C. 1775 d. Ga. 1858   Ens. Ga. Mil.
m. Elizabeth Attaway — daughter Emily m. William Owens

Owens, Joseph Vol. 15   Pvt. Md. Mil.

Owens, Philip Vol. 17   Sgt. Ky. Mil.

Owens, William b. S.C. c. 1761 d. S.C. 1836   Pvt. S.C. Cavalry
m. Sarah E. Overstreet — son Edmond T. m. Frances Ellis

Owens, William b. Ky. 1754 d. Ky. 1837 m. Margaret Newell   Pvt. Ky. Mil.
son William N. m. Docta Hobbs

Owings, Samuel b. N.C. 1793 d. Tenn. 1868   Pvt. Tenn. Vol.
m. Sarah Randolph — daughter Martha Susan m. John Kendrick

Owsley, Henry Hawkins b. Md. 1786 d. Ill. 1867   Cpl. Ky. Mil.
m. Mary Finley — daughter Elvira m. Alfred Hennen Davison

Oyshterbanks, Walter b. N.Y. 1792 d. N.Y. 1862   Pvt. N.Y. Mil.
m. Polly Dunbar — daughter Mary m. Ira Tiestsort

P

Packard, Cyrus b. Mass. (Me.) 1796 d. Ka. 1860   Pvt. Mass. Mil.
m. Sarah Barrows — daughter Georgianna m. George Packard (Cousin)

Packer, George b. Conn. 1794 d. Conn. 1872   Cpl. Conn. Mil.
m. Delight Eldridge — son Thomas E. m. Emma J. Burrous

Packer, John b. Vt. 1788 d. Ia. 1857 m. Sarah Welder   Cpl. U.S. Navy
son Henry H. m. Jane Robson

Packette, John b. (W.)Va. 1792 d. N.Y. 1819   Lt. Comm. U.S. Navy
m. Frances Ranken Hammond
son John W. B. m. Lucy Elizabeth Washington

Paddock, Joseph b. Ind. 1779 d. Ill. 1865 m. Mary   Lt. Col. Ind. Mil.
daughter Susanna m. William Graham

Paden (Pedan, Peadon), John b. Ire. 1791 d. Ohio 1866   Lt. Pa. Mil.
m. Amy Margaret — son Sidney m. William Thomas

Page, James Brown Vol. 1 or 2   Pvt. Mass. Mil.

Page, Josiah (Henry Elliott) b. Vt. 1793 d. Ont. 1881   **Pvt. Vt. Mil.**
  m. Catharine Rice Spencer
  daughter Lydia Frances m. Charles Houston Whitmore

Paine, Lemuel Corell b. Vt. 1787 d. N.Y. 1873   **Surgeon N.Y. Mil.**
  m. Hannah Buell — son Cyrus Fay m. Harriet Adelia Sage

Paine, Seth Jr. Vol. 16   **Pat. Mem. Const. Conv. Conn.**

Paintor (Payntor), William b. Va. d. Mo. 1861/5   **Pvt. Va. Mil.**
  m. Edith Southwood
  daughter Rebecca m. John Clay Lee REAL DAUGHTER

Palfrey, William b. Mass. 1741 d.—on way to France   **Diplomat to France**
  m. Abigail Briscoe — son Thomas m. Hannah Capper

Palmateer, Peter b. N.Y. 1742 d. N.Y. 1814   **Pvt. N.Y. Mil.**
  m. Catheryna Hegeman — daughter Elizabeth m. Thomas Esmay

Palmer, Daniel b. Conn. 1763 d. Pa. 1851   **Ens. NY. Mil.**
  m. Joanna Youngs —son Daniel Jr. m. Beulah Warner

Palmer, Elias Sanford b. Conn. 1742 d. Conn. 1827   **Pat. Conn.**
  m. Phoebe Palmer (Cousin) — son Luther m. Sarah Kenyon

Palmer, Elisha Vol. 13   **Pvt. N.Y. Mil.**

Palmer, John Hampton b. Vt. 1780 d. Vt. 1813   **Pvt. Vt. Mil.**
  m. Lydia Loomis — daughter Sophia Martesia m. Samuel Newton

Palmer, Jonathan b. Conn. 1724 d. N.Y. 1813   **Pat. Justice N.Y. 1806-7**
  m. Hannah Randle — son Gideon m. Hannah Thirza Collins

Palmer, Lewis D. b. Va. 1781 d. Ill. 1869   **Pvt. Ky. Rifles**
  m. Ann Hansford Tutt — son Elihu J. m. Eliza Gordon
  son John McAuley m. Malinda Ann Neeley

Palmer, Luther b. Conn. 1774 d. Conn. 1860   **Pvt. Conn. Mil**
  m. Sarah Kenyon — daughter Sarah m. Paul Greene

Palmer, Moses b. Conn. 1789 d. Conn. 1848   **Pvt. Conn. Mil.**
  m. Nancy Main — son Noyes W. m. Emily Avery

Palmer, Peter b. 1766 d. N.Y. m. Polly Osborn   **Pvt. N.Y. Mil.**
  son Ephraim m. Hannah Phelps

Palmer, Thomas Vol. 5   **Pvt. Vt. Mil.**

Palmer, William b. Conn. 1782 d. Vt. 1857   **Pvt. Vt. Mil.**
  m. Cynthia Branch — daughter Bolina m. Augustus McEnoch

Palmer, William b. 1777 d. Tenn. 1859   **Pvt. Tenn. Mil.**
  m. Sarah Ann Rankin — daughter Nancy m. Joab Goodall

Palmer, William Vol. 14   **Cpl. Va. Mil.**

Palmer, Zacharia Vol. 7   **Cpl. N.Y. Mil.**

Palmer, Zebulon Vol. 16   **Pvt. N.Y. Mil.**

Pancake, Isaac b. W.Va. 1786 d. Ohio 1872   **Capt. Ohio Mil.**
  m. Susanna Daily — son William S. m. Sarah Manlove

Pancake, John b. Va. 1789 d. Ohio 1853 m. Jane Wilson   **Pvt. Ohio Mil.**
  daughter Susanna Jane m. David Elder Johnson

Pancake, Joseph b. Va. 1789 d. Ohio 1853 m. Susan Linton **Pvt. Ohio Mil.**
  son Isaac m. Elizabeth Ann Steele

Pancoast, Shreve b. Pa. 1788 d. Ohio 1866 m. Polly Myers   Cpl. Ohio Mil.
    daughter Lettie m. Henry Fulton

Pannebecker, Daniel b. Pa. 1761 d. Pa. 1825   Ens. Pa. Mil.
    m. Anna Maria Mosser — daughter Elizabeth m. John Swartz

Parent, Thomas Vol. 15   Pvt. U.S. Inf.

Parham, Johnson b. N.C. 1794 d. Tenn. 1846   Pvt. Tenn. Mil.
    m. Druscilla Selby — son John m. Elizabeth Brown

Parish, David b. N.Y. 1783 d. Ill. 1856   Capt. N.Y. Troops
    m. Charlotte Braymer (Brimmer)
    daughter Phebe Ann m. Martin Munson

Parish, Jacob Kimball b. Vt. 1793 d. Vt. 1881   Ord. Sgt. Vt. Mil.
    m. Mehitabel Flint — son Jacob m. Mary Ann Converse

Park, Alexander Vol. 8   Pvt. Pa. Mil.

Park, Andrew b. N.H. 1749 d. N.H. 1820   Pat. N.H. 1806-14
    m. Mary Cochran — son Alexander m. Elizabeth Nesmith

Park, Avery b. Conn. 1781 d. N.Y. 1876   Capt. N.Y. Troops
    m. Betsey Meech — daughter Eliza m. Norton S. Collin

Park, John Jr. b. N.J. 1791 d. N.J. 1835 m. Susanna Green   Pvt. N.J. Mil.
    son Morris m. Elizabeth Ann Runyan

Parke, Solomon b. N.Y. 1765 d. N.Y. 1843   Sgt. N.Y. Mil.
    m. Susannah Burnham — son Barzilla m. Susan Maria Budd Burghardt

Parker, Aaron b. N.Y. 1786 d. Ill. 1849   Pvt. N.Y. Mil.
    m. Phebe Russell Frye
    daughter Matilda m. David Gillespie REAL DAUGHTER

Parker, Archibald Vol. 16   Pvt. N.Y. Mil.

Parker, Copeland b. Va. 1788 d. Va.   Pat. Va. Surveyor of Customs
    m. Elizabeth Sinclair
    daughter Elisabeth S. m. J. Coates Jones REAL DAUGHTER

Parker, Daniel b. Mass. 1782 d. D.C. 1846   Brig. Gen. Mass. Mil.
    m. Ann Collins — daughter Sarah Ann m. Clement Hill

Parker, Enos Sr. b. Conn. 1744 d. N.Y. 1814 m. Demaris   Pat. 1797
    son Enos Jr. m. Mehitabel Lovell

Parker, Ezra b. Conn. 1745 d. Mich. 1842 m. Elizabeth Perry   Cpl. U.S. Inf.
    son William M. m. Lydia Gilbert Bull

Parker, Ezra b. 1791 d. 1863 m. Hannah Burleigh   Cpl. U.S. Inf.
    daughter Hannah Burleigh m. Richard Wales Peabody

Parker, Foxhall Alexander b. Va. 1789 d. Va. 1857   Lt. U.S. Navy
    m. Sarah Jay Bogardus — son Foxhall A. Jr. m. Lydia Mallory

Parker, Gouldman b. Va. 1775 d. Tex. 1826   Cpl. Va. Mil.
    m. Frances Gresham — son Samuel m. Mary B. Dunn

Parker, Isaac b. Ga. 1793 d. Tex. 1883   Pvt. Tenn. Mil.
    m. Lucy W. Cheatham — daughter Lucy Ann m. Samuel C. Haile

Parker, Isaac Jr. b. Vt. 1791 d. N.Y. 1866   Pvt. N.Y. Mil.
    m. Sarah Emerson Culver
    daughter Lucy Adelaide m. Gardner Addison Child

Parker, James Vol. 5   Sgt. Del. Mil.

Parker, John Vol. 16   Pvt. Conn. Mil.

Parker, Jonas Vol. 11   Pat. Mass.

Parker, Kendall b.—d. Me. 1877 m. Abigail Mace   Pvt. Mass. Mil.
daughter Abbie U. m. Charles H. Forbes

Parker, Levi b. Conn. 1757 d. Conn. 1833   Capt. Conn. Mil. 1793
m. Lydia Bradley — daughter Polly m. Luther Buell

Parker, Mathew b. Va. 1783 d. Va. m. Lucy Bailey (cousins)   Sgt. Va. Mil.
son James T. m. Rebecca C. Moore

Parker, Milton b. N.Y. 1795 d. N.Y. 1871   Pvt. N.Y. Mil.
m. Frances J. Frothingham — daughter Anna B. m. Edmund Burke

Parker, Moody Vol. 5   Pvt. N.H. Mil.

Parker, Nathan Sr. b. Mass. 1753 d. Mass. 1830 m. Ann   Pvt. Mass. Mil.
son Andrew m. Rachel Smith

Parker, Peter Vol. 17   Lt. Qtr. Mst. Del. Mil.

Parker, Richard b. Tenn. 1795 d. Miss. 1839   Pvt. Tenn. Mil.
m. Priscilla Eppes — daughter Martha m. James Hitt

Parker, Samuel b. Va. d. Ark. 1861 m. Maria White   Pvt. Ky. Mil.
son Isaac M. m. Sarah Mary Bigham

Parker, Samuel b. Ire. 1770 d. Ky. 1843 m. Eliza Doyle   Lt. Col. Ky. Mil.
daughter Anne Virginia m. Benjamin F. Jameson

Parker, William b. Ky. 1796 d. Ohio 1864 m. Esther Gibson   Pvt. Ohio Mil.
daughter Louisa m. Joseph M. Evans

Parker, William b. Mass. (Me.) 1783 d. Me. 1856   Sgt. Mass. (Me.) Mil.
m. Hannah Larrabee — son Ammi m. Elizabeth Grover

Parker, William Brooks b. N.H. 1793/8 d. Ill. 1858   Pvt. Vt. Mil.
m. Eliza Clark
daughter Florence A. m. Rufus M. Cunningham REAL DAUGHTER
daughter Medora L. V. m. William Almour REAL DAUGHTER

Parkhill, Samuel b. Ire. 1793 d. 1865 m. Mary Ann Bott   Pvt. Lt. Inf.
son Samuel Miles m. Amanda William Hall

Parkhurst, Abel b. Conn. 1761 d. N.Y. 1824   Lt. N.Y. Cavalry Mil.
m. Polly Burroughs — daughter Phoebe m. Stephen Platt Chamberlin

Parkhurst, Alexander b. Mass. 1779 d. Mass. 1819   Pvt. Mass. Mil.
m. Mary Thayer — son Lebbeus G. m. Adeline Knight

Parkhurst, Isaac (Otis) b. Mass. 1781 d. Ind. 1869   Pvt. Ohio Mil.
m. Sarah Jones — son Lemuel m. Amelia Leavens

Parkhurst, Leonard b. Mass. 1763 d. Mass. 1821   Pat. Mass. 1786-1797
m. Hannah Hills — son John m. Anne Elizabeth Chapline

Parkhurst, Nathan b. Mass. 1778 d. N.Y. 1861   Pvt. Mass. Mil.
m. Mary Neely — son Jarvis m. Saloma Billings

Parkinson, Robert b. Scot. d. Pa. m. Maria Hatton   Pvt. N.Y. Mil.
son Robert Jr. m. Harriett Uhl

Parks, David b. Pa. d. Pa. 1820 m. Martha Jane   Pvt. Pa. Mil.
son David L. m. Mary Ann Heilman

Parks, Elisha b. Md. 1799 d. Md. 1871   Drum Md. Mil.
m. Mary Ann Worrell — son Elisha Jr. m. Jennie Millender

Parks, Henry b. Va. 1758 d. Ga. 1845 m. Martha Justice   Pat. Justice Ga.
son Henry Jr. m. Nancy Dorsey
daughter Mary m. Joshua Baker

Parks, James b. Conn. 1792 d. Mich. 1854 m. Lucretia   Cpl. Mass. Mil.
daughter Caroline m. Owen Kelley

Parks, John b. Ga. 1784 d. Miss. 1852 m. Nancy Cooksey   Pvt. Ga. Mil.
daughter Faythe Katherine m. Marshall Marion Trammell REAL DAU.

Parks, Robert Vol. 9   Capt. N.Y. Mil.

Parks, William Woodfin b. N.C. 1793 d. Tenn. 1875   Sgt. U.S. Inf.
m. Anna W. Ladle
daughter Marsha m. William C. Handly REAL DAUGHTER

Parlin, Abel b. Mass. (Me.) 1784 d Me.   Fifer Mass. Mil.
m. Lydia Phelps Goodrich
daughter Elizabeth m. Moses Gilman Libbey

Parlin, Jonas b. Mass. (Me.) 1780 d. Me. 1870   Capt. Mass. (Me.) Cavalry
m. Nancy Page Bodfish — son Andrew J. m. Stella Barton Picton

Parmelee, Jeremiah Vol. 3   Pvt. Mass. Mil.

Parnell, Daniel b. 1776 d. 1837 m. Eleanore Moseley   Pvt. Ga. Mil.
son Robert m. Anna Moseley

Parrett, Frederick b. Va. 1764 d. Ohio 1842   Ens. Va. Mil.
m. Elizabeth Kellar — daughter Sarah m. John McArthur
son Joseph m. Sarah Haas

Parish, Stephen b. Conn. 1755 d. Mich.—   Cpl. N.Y. Troops
m. Lena Houghtaling — son Jasper m. Joanna Wolcott

Parrott, Joseph b. Va. 1791 d. Ohio 1869 m. Sarah Haas   Lt. Va. Mil.
son Henry C. m. Emily Welsheimer
daughter Mary P. m. William Thomas Jr.

Parrott, Joseph b. Tenn. 1789 d. Ohio 1859   Adj. Ohio Mil.
m. Rebecca Fancher (Fanshir) — son Benjamin H. m. Nancy Allen
son Isaac m. Mary Ann Keplinger

Parson, James b. Mass. 1791 d. Pa. 1854 m. Anna Briggs   Pvt. Mass. Mil.
son Horatio B. m. Fannie L. Locke

Parsons, David b. Md. 1791 d. Ohio 1880   Pvt. Va. Lt. Inf. Mil.
m. Jane Pettigrew — daughter Nancy Jane m. John Wolfe

Parsons, Festus b. Mass. 1784 d. N.Y. 1853   Ens. N.Y. Mil.
m. Betsey Towne — daughter Emeline m. Thurlow Weed Carr

Parsons, Isaac b. (W.) Va. 1789 d. Ia. 1852   Pvt. Va. Mil.
m. Mary Elizabeth Green — son Thompson M. m. Mary Hale

Parsons, Isaac b. Va. 1752 d. Va. 1796 m. Mary Gregg   Capt. Va. Mil.
son James m. Catherine Casey

Parsons, Job Sr. b. Va. 1793 d. W.Va. 1883   Cpl. Va. Mil.
m. Sarah Losh — daughter Emma m. Solomon J. Parsons REAL DAU.

Parsons, Joseph b. Conn. 1763 d. Ohio 1851   Pvt. Conn. Mil.
m. Elizabeth Westcott — son Aaron m. Betsy Case

Parsons, Luther Vol. 5   Lt. Conn. Mil.

Parsons, Samuel b. S.C. 1765 d. S.C. 1840   Capt. S.C. Mil.
     m. Tabitha Goodwin — son Hampton G. m. Sarah Martin

Parson, Thomas b. Md. 1786 d. Md. 1849   Pvt. Md. Mil.
     m. Elizabeth Waltham — daughter Susanna m. Hugh Kelly

Parsons, William b. Va. 1760 d. W.Va. 1829   Capt. (W.) Va. Mil.
     m. Catherine Stoker — daughter Nancy R. m. Jacob Daniels

Parsons, William b. Md. 1769 d. (W.) Va. 1839   Capt. (W.) Va. Mil.
     m. Nancy Walker — son George W. m. Mary E. Asbury
     son Travis m. Mary Hess

Partridge, Calvin b. Mass. 1739 d. Mass. 1815   Pat. Rep. Selectman
     m. Mary Wakefield Alden   Mass. 1785
     daughter Hannah m. Samuel Soule

Patridge, Isaac Jr. Vol. 8   Pvt. Vt. Mil.
     daughter Minna m. Irvin B. Wright REAL DAUGHTER

Passwaters, Jesse b. Del. 1780 d. Del. 1836 m. Rebecca   Pvt. Del. Mil.
     son John m. Elizabeth Smith

Patch, Samuel b. Mass. 1774 d. Vt. 1843 m. Mary Corey   Pvt. Vt. Mil.
     daughter Laura m. Rev. Thomas Dodgson

Patchin, Freegift b. Conn. 1758 d. N.Y. 1830   Brig. Gen. N.Y. Mil.
     m. Molly Morehouse — daughter Pamela m. Frederic Hager

Paterson, John b. Conn. 1744 d. N.Y. 1808   Maj. Gen. Mass. Troops
     m. Elizabeth Lee — daughter Ruth m. Ira Seymour

Patrick, Daniel b. Mass. 1772 d. Vt. 1842   Sgt. Vt. Troops
     m. Susannah McClave — son Daniel Jr. m. Melinda Rollins
     son Rufus m. Arabelle Knox

Patrick, John Peetors Vol. 17   Lt. Ohio Mil.

Patrick, Martin b. N.Y. 1791 d. Ind. 1871 m. Ruth Parent   Cpl. N.Y. Mil.
     son Thomas m. Thamar Elizabeth Stewart

Patrick, Ralph b. Conn. d. N.Y. 1846 m. Mary   Lt. N.Y. Mil.
     son Martin m. Ruth Parent

Patrick, William J. b. N.Y. 1762 d. N.Y. 1837   Surgeon N.Y. Mil.
     m. Sally Ensign — son Reuben W. m. Emmeline Draughhan

Patten, George Ferguson b. (Me.) Mass. 1787 d. Me. 1869   Capt. Mass. Mil.
     m. Hannah Thomas — daughter Hannah T. m. Jarius Slade

Patten, Mighill b. Mass. 1795 d. Me. 1882   Pvt. U.S. Inf.
     m. Catherine Condon — son Samuel D. m. Lucy Ann Leach

Patterson, James b. 1779 d. N.Y. 1863   2nd Lt. N.Y. Art.
     m. Deborah Morhouse — daughter Rosannah m. Jeremiah O'Connell
     son William M. m. Matilda Artman

Patterson, Nathaniel b. Pa. 1794 d. Pa. 1874 m.—   Cpl. Pa. Mil.
     daughter Nancy m. Robert C. Duncan

Patterson, Nathaniel b. Ky. 1795 d. Pa. 1874   Cpl. Pa. Mil.
     m. Agnes S. Williams — son Isaac W. m. Sarah Evans

Patterson, Nathaniel b. Pa. 1794 d. Pa. 1874 m.—   Cpl. Pa.
     daughter Mary m. Meloney Joseph Ramsay REAL DAUGHTER

Patterson, Robert b. Pa. 1753 d. Ohio 1827   Pat. Ky. Legis. 1790
     m. Elizabeth Lindsay — daughter Jane m. John Steele

Patterson, Robert b. Ire. 1792 d. Pa. 1881   Capt. Pa. Mil.
   m. Sarah Ann Engle — son William H. m. Cornelia Graham

Patterson, Robert Vol. 7   Maj. Gen. U.S. Inf.

Patterson, Robert Vol. 6   Col. Pa. Mil.

Patteson, John Colridge b. Va. 1790 d. Va. 1867   Sgt. Va. Mil.
   m. Jane Scruggs — son Nelson A. m. Ann Bell Lowry

Pattie, Sylvester b. Ky. 1782 d. Ky. 1829   Lt. Mo. Rangers 1812-13
   m. Nancy Hubbard — daughter Jennie Maria m. Edwin Collins
   son Thomas m. Sarah McKnight

Pattison, Richard b. Md. 1759 d. Md. 1823 m. Mary McKeel   Pvt. Md. Mil.
   daughter Susan P. m. Nathaniel Greene Eccleston

Patton, Henry b. Va. c 1751 d. Va. 1849   Maj. Va. Mil. 1793
   m. Martha Jane Randolph — daughter Matilda m. Joseph Davidson

Patton, Isaac b. 1777 d. Tenn. m. Ann Henley   Capt. W. Tenn. Mil.
   son John W. m. Malinda Pickens

Patton, Robert b. Va. 1779 d. Ohio 1865 m. Phebe Sprague   Sgt. Va. Mil.
   daughter Esther A. m. Eden Moore REAL DAUGHTER
   son John m. Phoebe Leeper

Paul, Hosea b. Mass. (Me.) 1793 d. Ohio m. Nancy Carter   Pvt. N.Y. Mil.
   son James M. m. Louisa Payne

Paul, Jacob b. Pa. 1776 d. W.Va. 1859 m. Elizabeth Miller   Lt. Va. Mil.
   son Washington M. m. Jane Snider

Paul, William b. N.Y. 1777 d. Pa. 1840   Pvt. Pa. Mil.
   m. Hannah Slack (Slaught) — son Andrew S. m. Ann Walton
   son Nathan m. Henrietta Bell
   daughter Rosa m. Christopher Vannum

Paul, William W. b. N.J. 1782 d. N.J. 1864 m. Elizabeth   Pvt. Pa. Mil.
   daughter Caroline A. m. Janes M. Cassady

Paulin, Philip b. Fra. 1776 d. Pa. 1864   Pvt. Pa. Mil. 1814-15
   m. Hanna Bacon — daughter Anna E. m. Samuel Rusk

Paull, Lemuel b. Mass. 1761 d. N.Y. 1815 m. Ruth Jones   Capt. Mass. Mil.
   son Silvanus m. Jane Bibbens

Pawley, John b. Eng. 1784 d. Md. 1857 m.—   Pvt. Md. Mil.
   son James m. Mary Ann Vawter

Pawling, John b. N.Y. 1786 d. N.Y. 1862 m. Harriet Connor   Sgt. N.Y. Mil.
   daughter Maria m. Dennison Rathbun

Pawling, Joseph b. Pa. 1777 d. Ind. 1855 m. Sarah Riffert   Capt. Pa. Mil.
   son Albert m. Eliza McLees

Paxton, Joseph Vol. 12   Sgt. Va. Mil.

Paxton, Joseph b. Va. 1779 d. Va. 1839 m. Sarah Edmondson   Pvt. Va. Mil.
   son Rev. James T. m. Amanda J. Venable

Paxton, Richard Vol. 13   Pvt. N.J. Mil.

Paxton, Thompson b. Va. 1783 d. Ill. 1839   Pvt. Tenn. Vol.
   m. Cynthia Potts — son Jonathan m. Olive Fowler

Paxton, William b. Va. 1776 d. Ky. 1827 m. Nancy Logan   Capt. Va. Mil.
   son Archibald m. Mary Davidson

Payne, Daniel b. 1795 d. 1860   Pvt. Lt. Dragoons Ga. Mil.
    m. Elizabeth Dupree — son William J. m. Sybella Farmer

Payne, Ebenezer Leach Jr. b. N.Y. d. Conn.   Pvt. Conn. Mil.
    m. Keziah Kinney — son Stephen m. Ruth A. Smith

Payne, Isaac b. N.Y. 1783 d. N.Y. 1858   Pvt. N.Y. Mil.
    m. Lucretia Barnes — son Albert m. Helen M.

Payne, Jacob b. Va. 1778 d. Tenn. 1847   Sgt. Tenn. Mil.
    m. Susan Browder — son Sterling m. Minerva Saunders

Payne, John b. Va. 1764 d. Ky. 1827 Vol. 96 Qtr. Mst. Gen. Ky. Dragoons
    m. Betsy Johnson

Payne, John b. Va. 1785 d. Ky. 1854 m. Letitia Whiteman   Pvt. Ky. Inf.
    daughter Matilda M. m. Dr. Adolphus Pinckard

Payne, John b. Va. 1784 d. Tex. 1848   2nd Sgt. Ga. Mil.
    m. Margaret Williams — son John M. m. Mahala Oliphant

Payne, John Calvin b. Conn. 1778 d. N.Y. 1846   Capt. N.Y. Inf.
    m. Philena Pierce — daughter Maria Philena m. Seth F. Smalley

Payne, Lewis b. Va. 1761 d. Va. m. Nancy Davis   Pvt. Va. Mil.
    son George H. m. Sarah Ann Womack

Payne, (Paine) Pardon b. 1789 d. 1867 m. Betsy Boutwell   Capt. Co. at N.Y.
    son Albert Howard m. Mary Ann Bromley

Payne, Tavers (Travis) b. Va. 1788 d. Va. 1878   Pvt. Va. Inf.
    m. Mary Wise — son Charles H. m. Anne Eliza Anderson

Payne, Zacheus b. N.Y. c. 1775 d. N.Y. aft. 1820   Pvt. N.Y. Vol.
    m. Experience Soper — son William m. Lucy Eldridge

Payton, William b. Ky. 1790 d. Ind. 1878   Pvt. Ohio Mil.
    m. Mary Hoover — daughter Matilda m. Daniel Henry Rose

Payton, Yelverton Jr. b. Ky. 1793 d. Ky. 1859   Pvt. Ky. Vol.
    m. Mildred White — son Yelverton W. m. Sally Ann Geery

Payton, Yelverton b. Va. 1755 d. Ky. 1832   Pvt. Ky. Mil. 1786
    m. Anna Guffee — Yelverton Jr. m. Mildred White

Peabody, Asa b. Conn. 1784 d. N.Y. 1826   Seaman N.Y.
    m. Mary Van Ness — son Simon V. m. Eleanor Norton

Peabody, Eliphalet b. N.Y. 1773 d. N.Y. 1818   Pvt. U.S. Art.
    m. Orinda Bennett — son William m. Sabrina Strong

Peacock, Jesse b. N.C. 1792 d. Ark. 1780   Pvt. Ga. Cav. 1813-14
    m. Eliza Ann Hendy — daughter Eliza Ann m. James H. Bush

Peadon, (Peadan) Edward b. 1784-5 d. Pa. 1850   Commissary Pa. Mil.
    m. Mary Martha Simpson — daughter Mary Martha m. James Boyd

Peale, Charles Willson b. Md. 1741 d. Pa. 1827   Pat. Pa.
    m. Rachel Brewer — son Raphaelle m. Martha McGlathery

Pearce, Arthur Davis b. N.C. 1790 d. Ill. 1872   Pvt. Tenn. Mil.
    m. Miss E. Bissell — son Isaac Newton m. Clara E. Jones
    son McKinnie m. Mary Davis

Pearce, Samuel b. Va. 1780 d. Va. 1860 m. Mary Page   Pvt. Va. Mil.
    daughter Mary m. Joseph Potts Crockett

Pearce, Thomas b. 1778 d. Ill. 1853   Pvt. Ohio Mil.
    m. Mrs. Phoebe Little George — daughter Mary M. m. Ivory Quinby

Pearce (Pierce), William b. N.J. 1767 d. Ind. 1829   Pvt. N.Y. Mil.
m. Mary Shephard — son Eli K. m. Adelia Murray

Pearre, (Perry) James b. Md. 1760 d. Md. 1825   Pvt. Md. Mil.
m. Sarah Warfield — James Jr. m. Eliza Dudderer

Pearre, (Perry) Joshua W. b. Md. 1777 d. Tenn. 1839   Pvt. Tenn. Mil.
m. Elizabeth Hulme — daughter Margaret E. m. Elisha Dotson

Pearson, William b. N.C. 1788 d. N.C. 1869   Pvt. N.C. Mil.
m. Nancy Trice — daughter Mary J. m. Malbourne A. Angier

Peay, Austin Ford b. S.C. 1787 d. S.C. 1841   Pat. Legis. S.C.
m. Mary English — son Nicholas A. m. Martha Cary Lamar

Peay, Nicholas b. Ky. d. Ark. 1835   Pvt. Ky. Lt. Dragoons
m. Judith Elizabeth Neil — son Gordon N. m. Sue Crease

Pearsall, Peter R. b. N.Y. 1790 d. Ind. 1878 m. Hannah Frost Pvt. N.Y. Mil.
daughter Julia m. Edward H. Evans REAL DAUGHTER

Pearson, Chesterfield Vol. 15   Fifer N.Y. Mil.

Pearson, Harvey b. 1776 d. 1830 m. Lydia Holden   Pvt. La. Mil.
son Joel m. Sarah Fornea

Pease, Calvin b. Conn. 1776 d. Ohio 1839   Pat. Senator & Judge Ohio
m. Laura Want Risley — daughter Nancy m. John Erwin

Pease, Lemuel b. Conn. 1763 d. Conn. 1836   Pat. Conn. 1799
m. Mary Parsons — daughter Achsah m. Daniel G. Baker

Pease, Noah b. Conn. 1739 d. Conn. 1818 m. Mary Ward   Cpl. Conn. Mil.
son Giles m. Jerusha Pitkin

Pease, William Jr. b. N.Y. 1781 d. N.Y. 1868   Pvt. N.Y. Mil.
m. Obediance Stone — son William G. m. Electa Coburn

Pease, Ebenezer Martin b. N.Y. 1786 d. N.Y.   Ens. N.Y. Inf.
m. Pamelia Wandell — son Calvin m. Mary Frances

Pebbles, James b. (Me.) Mass. 1792 d. Me. 1878   Pvt. Mass. (Me.) Mil.
m. (3) Margaret Larrabee — son James W. m. (1) Caroline M. Penley

Peck, Andrew b. Conn. 1768 d. Conn. 1839 m. Betsy   Pvt. Conn. Mil.
son William P. m. Mary Caton

Peck, Enos Vol. 13   Pvt. N.Y. Mil.

Peck, Jacob B. b. Va. 1786 d. Va. 1860 m. Sarah Bates   Cpl. Va. Mil.
daughter Sallie m. George Inghram

Peck, Jacob Franklin b. Va. ca. 1794 d. Tenn. 1871   Pvt. Ens. Va. Mil.
m. Jane Waggoner — son William T. m. Nancy Cooper

Peck, Joel Vol. 5   Pvt. Artificer

Peck, John Jr. b. Vt. 1782 d. Vt. 1826   Pat. Sheriff Vt. 1810
m. Anna Benedict — son Lucius m. Martha Day

Peck, Josiah b. Conn. 1793 d. Ohio 1849   Pvt. Ohio Mil.
m. Elizabeth C. Bogue — son Josiah m. Minerva Charlotte Phillips

Peck, Nathaniel b. Conn. 1782 d. N.Y. 1871 m. Abigail Starr Pvt. N.Y. Mil.
daughter Louisa m. Cyrus Allen

Peck, Patrick b. Tenn. d. ca. 1815 m. Elizabeth Gale   Pvt. Miss. Mil.
daughter Elizabeth S. m. Henry H. Fry

Peck, Ransford Vol. 16   Drum Mass. Mil.

Peck, Richard Vol. 7   Capt. N.Y. Mil.

Peck, Thomas b. Conn. 1762 d. Vt. 1826 m. Priscilla Howard   Ens. Vt. Mil.
son Rueben m. Hannah Edson

Pecker, Jeremiah Sr. b. N.H. 1772 d. N.H. 1843   Pvt. N.H. Vol.
m. Mary Eastman Lang — daughter Ruth Maria m. Joseph A. Merriam

Peckham, Peleg b. R.I. 1759 d. R.I. 1858   Pvt. Conn. Mil.
m. Elizabeth Stetson — son Isaiah m. Nancy Darrow

Peckinpaugh, Jacob Frederick b. Pa. 1769 d. Pa. 1814   Pvt. Pa. Mil.
m. Elizabeth Varner — daughter Mary m. John Bell

Pedin, Edmund b. 1775 d. 1828 m. Priscilla Wills   3rd Cpl. Va. Mil.
son Edmund Mrewer m. Caroline Matilda Driver

Peeler, Jacob b. Ga. 1796 d. Fla. 1846 m. Sarah Martin   Pvt. Ga. Mil.
son Anderson J. m. Mary Amanda Lawless
son James m. Mary Lawless

Peeling (Pheeling), James b. Pa. 1790 d. Pa. 1870   Pvt. Pa. Mil.
m. Elimor Harper — daughter Eliza m. Jonathan Neff
son John m. Anna Funk
son Josiah m. Fannie Craley
daughter Lucinda m. Levi S. Flinchbaugh REAL DAUGHTER
daughter Rebecca m. John F. Gessey REAL DAUGHTER

Peery, William b. Va. 1755 d. Va. 1830 m. Sarah Evans   Pvt. Va. Mil.
daughter Cosby m. John J. Buren

Peery, William Vol. 17   Pvt. Tenn. Gunman

Peirce, Benajah b. Mass. 1771 d. Mass. 1841   Pvt. Mass. Mil.
m. Charity Leonard — son John N. m. Mary Miller Alden

Peirce, George b. Del. 1769 d. Del. 1826   Capt. Del. Mil.
m. Margaret Springer — son George Wales m. Mary Adler

Peirce, Moses b. N.C. 1781 d. Va. 1857 m. Elizabeth Poole   Pvt. Va. Mil.
son John B. m. Mary Malinda Bell

Peirce, Samuel b. N.H. 1775 d. Mass. 1817 m. Ann Hoover   Pvt. Pa. Mil.
daughter Elizabeth P. m. Daniel Clifton Baker

Pell, David Jones b. N.Y. 1760 d. N.Y. 1823   Lt. Col. N.Y. Mil.
m. Hester Sneden — son Stephen S. m. Adeline M. Turnbull

Pelter, Sampson b. Va. 1790 d. Va. 1865 m. Rebecca Long   Pvt. Va. Mil.
son George m. Estaline Branaman

Pelton, Enoch b. Conn. 1770 d. Va. 1829   Pvt. D.C. Mil.
m. Matilda Backman — son Lorenzo m. Mary Ashcome

Pelton, Jesse b. Conn. 1778 d. Pa. 1862 m. Ruhama Wolf   Pvt. Ohio Mil.
son Sidney R. m. Sarah Ann Breckinridge

Pemberton, William b. Va. 1752 d. Ohio 1832 m. Rhoda Luck   Pvt. Ohio Mil.
daughter Joyce m. Isaac East

Pence, Peter b. Va. 1777 d. Ohio 1845 m.—   Sgt. Ohio Mil.
son Aaron m. Elizabeth Moore

Pendleton, David b. R.I. 1779 d. Ohio 1858/9 m. Ann Richar   Pvt. N.Y. Mil.
daughter Rosell Fidelia m. Dr. John Wesley Moore

Pendleton, James b. N.Y. 1798 d. W.Va. 1876   Pvt. N.Y. Mil.
m. Sarah Reynolds — son Daniel m. Elizabeth McMinn

Pendleton, Nathanael Green Vol. 9   3rd Lt. U.S. Art.

Pendleton, Otis b. R.I. 1780 d. Conn. 1828 m. Betsey Kenyon   Pvt. Conn. Mil.
daughter Eliza Ann m. Ethan Allen Cheseborough

Pendleton, Nathan b. 1754 d. 1816 m. Amelia Babcock   Capt. R.I.
daughter Sara m. John Longworthy

Pendleton, William b. Va. 1748 d. Va. 1817   Pat. Justice Va. 1810
m. Elizabeth Ferguson
daughter Lucy C. m. John Benjamin Ferguson

Penfield, David b. Conn. 1779 d. N.Y. 1843   Capt. N.Y. Mil.
m. Voadicia Scoville — son Orrin S. m. Margaret Stewart Redzie

Penfield, Fowler b. N.Y. 1790 d. N.Y. 1857 m. Jane DeMilt   Pvt. N.Y. Mil.
son George Jesse m. Susan Anne Dishbrow

Penick, Nathan(iel) b. Va. 1769 d. Va. 1853   Capt. Va. Mil.
m. Tabitha Rudd — daughter Ellen Judith m. Joel Hawkins

Penn, Thomas b. Va. 1781 d. Va. 1842 m. Martha Leath   Pvt. Va. Mil.
son Columbus F. m. Frances Matilda Rives

Pennebaker, Samuel b. 1796 d. 1835 m. Sarah Finley   Pvt. Md. Mil.
daughter Cassandra m. Preston Hawks

Penny, Benjamin b. Mass. (Me.) 1782 d. Me. 1818   Pvt. Mass. Mil.
m. Miriam Tuttle — son Thomas m. Pamelia Lee

Penny, Benjamin b. (Me.) Mass. 1784 d. Me. 1876   Pvt. U.S. Inf.
m. Meribah Chick — daughter Abigail C. m. Thomas Graves

Penniman, Peter b. Mass. 1728 d. Mass. 1806   Pat. Del. Prov. Conv. Mass.
m. Huldah Wheelock — son Andrew m. Cynthia

Pennington, Dennis b. 1776 d. Ind. 1854   Rep. Ind. 1807-16
m. Elizabeth English — daughter Anna Mitchell m. Henry Wm. Sieg
daughter Jane m. Robert Davis

Pennington, Nathan b. N.J. 1758 d. N.J. 1810   Sgt. N.J. Troops
m. Margaret Brazure Westcott — son John m. Elizabeth Taylor

Pennington, William b. N.C. 1777 d. Tenn. 1838   Pvt. Tenn. Mil.
m. Elizabeth Eller — daughter Catherine m. Louis Johnson

Penoyer (Piner, Penier), Reuben b. N.Y. 1785 d. Mich. 1868   Pvt. N.Y. Mil.
m. Margria — daughter Sarah m. Alonzo Hathaway

Pentz, Daniel b. Pa. 1794 d. Md. 1871 m. Martha Hare   Pvt. Md. Art.
daughter Martha Ann m. Daniel Lambdin Holden Sr.

Pepper, Daniel B. b. Mass. 1788 d. Me. 1828   Capt. Mass. Mil.
m. Louisa Ward — daughter Sarah Ann m. David Hill

Percy, Ellis b. Mass. (Me.) 1787 d. Me. 1852   Capt. Mass. (Me.) Mil.
m. Elizabeth Couillard Whitmore
daughter Sophia m. Andrew Lennan Powers

Perez, Manuel Antonio Vol. 6   Gen. La. Troops

Perine, Peter b. N.J. 1792 d. N.J. 1874 m. Rachel Van Winkle   Pvt. N.J. Mil.
son Jacob m. Sarah Ann Scull

Perkins, Stephen b. Conn. 1790 d. Wisc. 1878   Prisoner of War 1813-14
m. Eliza Smith — daughter Eliza Ann m. William Douglas Hempstead

Perkins, Asa b. Conn. 1782 d. Conn. 1861 m. Phoebe Garde   Pvt. Conn. Mil.
daughter Sarah Ann m. Henry Charles Brown

Perkins, David b. Pa. 1769 d. Pa. 1854   Pat. Justice Pa. 1808-15
m. Sarah Ferrier — son John m. Eunice Miller

Perkins, Isaiah b. Mass. (Me.) 1791 d. Me.   Pvt. Mass. (Me.) Mil.
m. Matilda Peterson — son George F. m. Julia Houghton

Perkins, John Vol. 16   Pvt. Md. Vol.

Perkins, John b. Vt. 1773 d. Vt. 1813   Cpl. & Music Vt. Troops
m. Amelia Eastman — son Daniel m. Samantha Chamberlain

Perkins, John b. Md. 1781 d. Md. 1840 m. Harriet Corsuch   Pvt. Md. Vol.
daughter Sarah G. m. John Ryland
daughter Susanna m. Richard Duckett Hall
son William H. m. Laura Ann Pochon

Perkins, Philo Sr. b. Conn. 1767 d. Vt. 1836   Pat. Surveyor Vt.
m. Chloe Cook — daughter Almira m. Simeon Webster Payn

Perkins, Robert b. Va. 1794 d. Miss. 1874   Pvt. Va. Mil.
m. Elizabeth Hooper — son Elisha m. Editha Murphree
daughter Julia F. m. William D. York

Perkins, William b. 1788 d. Ky. 1850 m. Elizabeth Dougherty   Sgt. Ky. Mil.
daughter Martha Jane m. Vene P. Armstrong

Perkins, William b. Eng. 1757 d. Md. 1816 m. Susanna Clarke   Pvt. Md. Mil.
daughter Elizabeth m. Richard Duckett Hall

Perlee, Edmund b. N.Y. 1750 d. N.Y. 1822   Pat. Mem. Constit. Conv.
m. Zayde Winans   1801 N.Y.
daughter Samantha m. Peter Van Allen Pugsley

Perrett, Charles Pierre b. La. d. La.   Maj. La. Mil.
m. Constance Elizabeth DeVogine
son Pierre C. m. Anaise Alexandrine Boudousque

Perrin, Calvin b. Conn. 1793 d. Pa. 1824 m. Polly Lawton   Pvt. Conn. Mil.
daughter Betsey m. John Long

Perrin, Josephus Jr. b. Va. 1771 d. Ky. 1843   Pat. Mem. Ky. Legis.
m. Elizabeth Clopton   Lt. 1791 Ky. Mil.
daughter Edna m. Sol. C. Perrin
daughter Margaret m. James M. Berry

Perrin, Samuel Sr. b. 1770 d. S.C. 1828 m. Eunice Chiles   Capt. S.C. Mil.
son Samuel Jr. m. Emma Catherine Blocker

Perrine, John b. N.J. 1760 d. N.Y. 1831 m. Mary Ely   2nd Lt. N.J. Mil.
daughter Phoebe m. Daniel Barclay

Perrine, Joseph b. N.J. 1766 d. N.Y. 1824 m. Mary   Pvt. N.J. Cavalry
son Joseph m. Sarah Parks

Perrine, Peter b. Mass. 1777 d. N.Y. m. Ann Duncan   Capt. N.Y. Mil.
daughter Lydia m. Daniel Failing

Perrine, Robert b. N.J. 1763 d. N.J. 1824   Capt. N.J. Mil.
m. Catherine Anderson — daughter Elizabeth m. John Dill

Perritt, David b. S.C. 1781 d. S.C. 1871 m. Sally Bryant   Pvt. S.C. Mil.
son John Ervin m. Nancy Ann Campbell

Perry, Amos b. N.H. 1783 d. Ill. 1854 m. Hannah   Pvt. N.Y. Cav. Mil.
son Edwin m. Mary Ann Northway

Perry, Benjamin b. Mass. 1761 d. S.C. 1842 m. Anna Foster   Pvt. S.C. Mil.
son Nathaniel J. F. m. Elizabeth Davis

Perry, Calvin P. Vol. 7   Pvt. U.S. Inf.

Perry, Charles G. b. Md. 1738 d. Md. 1818   Pvt. Md. Art.
m. Priscilla Johnson — daughter Lydia R. m. John Henderson

Perry, Christopher Raymond b. R.I. 1760 d. R.I. 1818   Capt. U.S. Army
m. Sarah Alexander — daughter Jane T. m. William Butter

Perry, Demas b. Vt. 1794 d. N.Y. 1880 m. Lucy Allen   Pvt. N.Y. Mil.
son Hermon H. m. Nancy Jane Perry

Perry, Edward b. R.I. 1731 d. R.I. 1798   Justice R.I. 1784-5
m. Dorcas Gardner — son George m. Anna Perry

Perry, Erasmus Vol. 15   Pvt. Md. Mil.

Perry, Ezekiel Jr. b. S.C. 1770 d. S.C. 1840 m. Mary Watson   Lt. S.C.
son Ezekiel m. Mary Bates

Perry, Israel Bratain Vol. 17   Pvt. Vt. Vol.

Perry, James b. Ky. 1786 d. Ky. 1831 m. Jane Shirley   Pvt. Ky. Mil.
son Milton m. Isabella Morrow

Perry, James Jr. b. R.I. 1795 d. Tex. 1860   3rd Lt. U.S. Inf.
m. Sarah Barker Moulton — son Elton m. Lucy Smith

Perry, James Vol. 6   Capt. R.I. Vol.

Perry, Jonas b. N.Y. 1788 d. N.Y. 1859 m. Nancy Jones   Lt. N.Y. Mil.
son Seth m. Abigail Wilcox

Perry, Nathan Vol. 6   Pat. Mass.

Perry, Rowland b. 1781 d. N.Y. 1870 m. Orra Pierson   Pvt. N.Y. Mil.
daughter Charlotte m. Albert Tiffany Banning

Perry, Samuel Augustus b. N.Y. 1792 d. N.Y. 1880   Sgt. N.Y. Mil.
m. Ann Hoy — daughter Nancy Jane m. Hermon Healy Perry

Perry, Solomon b. N.C. 1765 d. N.C. c. 1820 m. Mary Crudup   Pvt. N.C. Mil.
daughter Elizabeth B. m. William Harris

Perry, Timothy Peckham b. Conn. 1792 d. Conn 1839   Pvt. Conn. Mil.
m. Mary Clarke — son Oliver H. m. Abby Williams

Petefish, George b. Va. 1790 d. Ill. 1867 m. Margaret Ream   Pvt. Va. Mil.
son Aaron W. m. Laurena Liter

Peters, George b. Pa. 1795 d. Pa. 1881 m. Nancy A. Culver   Pvt. Pa. Mil.
daughter Lydia A. m. William Moore

Peters, Joshua b. N.C. 1781 d. Tex. 1870 m. Mary Smith   Pvt. Tenn. Mil.
daughter Nancy m. Richard Vincent Eddins

Peters, Samuel b. N.C. c. 1797 d. Mo. 1859 m.— Byler   Pvt. Tenn. Mil.
daughter Sallie m. Charles H. Gallagher

Peters, Samuel Andrew b. Conn. 1770 d. Conn. 1854   Pat. Mem. Gen. Assy.
son John T. m. Sophie Chester   Conn. 1807-10

Peterson, John b. Mass. (Me.) 1792 d. Tenn. 1876   Music Mass. (Me.) Mil.
m. Elizabeth Laidley
daughter Emeline L. m. George William Stocking

Peterson, Martin (Michael) b. Va. 1795 d. Ohio 1868   Sgt. Ohio Mil.
  m. Elizabeth Coyner (Kiner)
  daughter Mary Jane m. William Franklin Hains

Pettibone, Silas Vol. 11   Pat. Conn.

Pettijohn, Abraham b. Va. 1788 d. Ill. 1852 m. Jane Sloan Pvt. Ohio Mil.
  daughter Hannah m. Henry Allpin

Pettit, Daniel b. N.Y. 1790 d. N.Y. 1876 m. Lorico Rugg Pvt. N.Y. Mil.
  daughter Eliza M. m. Walter Sargent
  daughter Hester R. m. Jacob Seeber

Pettit, James Jacob b. N.Y. 1777 d. N.Y. 1849 Surgeon N.Y. Mil.
  m. Lucy Felts — son James Jacob Jr. m. Sarah Hill

Pettit, John II b. N.Y. 1789 d. N.J. 1855 Pvt. N.Y. Mil.
  m. Sarah Parmelle Mitchell
  daughter Sarah Frances m. Amzi Brown Miller

Pettit, John William Addison b. Ga. 1797 d. Tenn. 1863 Pvt. Ga. Mil.
  m. Marie Louise James
  daughter Elizabeth m. John D. Ware REAL DAUGHTER

Pettit, William b. N.Y. 1777 d. N.Y. 1857 m. Elizabeth Soldier N.Y.
  son George Wm. m. Caron Perkins

Pettitt, John (Larimore) b. Va. 1782 d. Ark. 1850 Pvt. Ky. Mil.
  m. Sarah Summers Williams
  son William McA. m. Enna Adalphin Lenhart

Peyson, John H. b. Va. 1778 d. Va. 1847 Aid to Gen. Porterfield
  m. Ann Montgomery Lewis Va. Mil.
  daughter Cornelia m. Charles P. Winston
  daughter Mary m. Robert Asher Gray
  daughter Margaret m. George M. Cochran

Peyton, Rowzee b. Va. 1789 d. N.J. 1867 m. Eliza Murray Pvt. Va. Mil.
  daughter Olivia m. Henry Lawrence de Zeng

Phelps, Asahel b. Mass. 1775 d. Mass. 1826 m. Polly Sears Pvt. Mass. Mil.
  daughter Mary m. Lewis Bliss

Phelps, Benajah b. Conn. 1770 d. Vt. 1862 Pvt. Vt. Mil.
  m. Catharine Stark — son George m. Lucretia Winslow

Phelps, Elisha b. Conn. 1779 d. Conn. 1847 Pat. House Rep.
  m. Lucy Smith Conn. 1807-14
  son John S. m. Mary Jones Whitney

Phelps, Epaphrus Lord b. Conn. 1779 d. Ind. 1823 Capt. N.Y. Troops
  m. Esther Hill — daughter Lydia m. Franklin Warren

Phelps, John b. Conn. 1729 d. Conn. 1804 Pat. Del. to Legis.
  m. Mary Richardson Conn. 1786
  daughter Mary m. Nathan Beers

Phelps, Josiah b. Conn. 1789 d. Conn. 1861 m. Emily Allyn Pvt. Conn. Mil.
  daughter Emily Harriet m. Edwin Hubbel Hollister

Phelps, Richard b. N.C. 1777 d. Ill. 1843 m. Elizabeth Anderson Lt. Md. Mil.
  son John H. m. Phoebe Horton Kemp

Phifer, Caleb b. N.C. 1749 d. N.C. 1811 Mem. Legis. N.C. 1787-9
  m. Barbara Freelander — daughter Sarah m. William Houston (Dr.)

Philabar, Samuel b. Pa. 1776 d. Ia. 1855 m.— 2nd Cpl. Pa. Mil.
  daughter Sarah Caroline m. Rev. Isaac P. Sadler

Philbrick, David b. Mass. 1780 d. Mass. (Me.) aft. 1815 Pvt. Mass. Cav. Mil.
m. Ann Nancy Lyford — son George W. m. Julia Ann Flye

Philibert, Arnaudt b. La. 1755 d. La. 1830 m. Marie Doussan   Pvt. La. Mil.
daughter Eusebia m. Joseph Hymel

Phillippe, Abraham b. Pa. 1763 d. Pa. 1812   Pvt. Pa. Mil.
m. Susanna Kraemer — son Jacob m. Elizabeth Rightmyer

Phillippi, Jacob b. Pa. 1788 d. Pa. 1828   Pvt. Pa. Mil.
m. Elizabeth Rightmyer — daughter Mary E. m. George Foos

Philips, Isaac Jr. Vol. 8   Pvt. Md. Mil.

Philips, Josiah b. Pa. 1751 d. Pa. 1817 m. Sarah Thomas   Pvt. Pa. Mil.
daughter Martha m. Robert Frame
son Owen m. Rachel Evans

Phillips, Aaron Vol. 16   Pvt. Pa. Mil.

Phillips, Abraham (Abram) b. N.C. 1756 d. N.C. 1818   Mem. N.C. House
m. Sarah Caroline Ridings (Rydings)   1788/90
daughter Frances m. Jonathan William Shore

Phillips, Benjamin b. Pa. 1766 d. Tenn. 1846 m. Lucy   Pvt. Tenn. Vol. Mil.
son John m. (2) Elizabeth Scott

Phillips, Benjamin b. R.I. 1785 d. Mass. 1867   Pvt. Mass. Mil.
m. Peggy McFarland — son William S. m. Sarah Richardson

Phillips, Francis b. N.Y. d. N.Y. m. Hannah Story Vol. 20   Pvt. N.Y. Mil.
daughter Jane m. Eli Gior

Phillips, Gilbert Drake b. N.Y. 1791 d. N.Y. 1872   Cpl. N.Y. Mil.
m. Betsey Miller — daughter Maria Louisa m. Frederick Leroy Martin

Phillips, Hiram b. Va. 1790 d. Mo. 1869 m. Elizabeth Cave   Sgt. Ky. Mil.
son Hiram C. m. Frances Pemberton
daughter Martha m. Robert W. McClelland REAL DAUGHTER

Phillips, John b. Va. 1774 d. Pa. 1845   Pay Mst. Pa. Mil. 1812-14
m. Mary Waite — son Moses m. Elizabeth Winebiddle

Phillips, Joseph b. 1790 d. 1859 m. Sara Elizabeth Pressley   Pvt. S.C. Mil.
daughter Sara Ann m. Wm. Odell (2) John C. Cooper (1)

Phillips, Joseph b. Vt. 1804 d. Pa. 1849 m. Lydia Davis (2)   Pvt. Vt. Mil.
daughter Mary Louise m. Joseph Hennon McConahy
REAL DAUGHTER

Phillips, Matthew b. Ga. d. Ga. m. Nancy Harper   Capt. Ga. Mil.
son Mathew A. m. Nancy Dickson

Phillips, Nicholas H. Vol. 10   Pvt. N.Y. Mil.

Phillips, Peter B. Vol. 17   Lt. R.I. Mil.

Phillips, Pettus b. Va. 1794 d. Tenn. 1867 m. Dorcas Pettus   Pvt. Va. Mil.
son David Alex m. Harriett Rimes

Phillips, Samuel Vol. 17   Lt. R.I. Mil.

Phillips, William b. N.J. 1779 d. Ky. 1864   Capt. Ky. Mil.
m. Margaret Graham — daughter Rebecca m. Austin Piety Cox

Phinney, James H. Vol. 9   Sgt. U.S. Inf.
daughter Ellen P. m. Samuel C. Means REAL DAUGHTER

Pickkenpaugh, George b. Ger. 1764 d. W.Va. 1838   Capt. Va. Mil.
    m. Charlotte Barrickman — son Nichaolas m. Abigail Chadwick
    son Reason m. Mary Penn Harrison
    son Sanford m. Ann Elizabeth Ramsey

Pickens, Andrew b. S.C. 1739 d. S.C. 1817   Lt. Col. Mil. S.C. 1795
    m. Rebecca Calhoun — son Ezekiel m. (2) Elizabeth Barksdale
    daughter Jean m. John Henry Miller

Pickens, Leonard b. Mass. d. Me. 1863 m. Vashti   Pvt. Me. (Mass.) Mil.
    daughter Vashti m. Ephraim C. Gates

Pickett, James K. b. N.Y. 1786 d. 1857 m. Elizabeth Haven
    son Daniel S. m. Eliza Jane Graves

Pickett, John b. Va. d. Tenn. m. Rebecca Collier   Pvt. Tenn. Vol.
    son Edward M. m. Paralee Adams

Pickett, Martin b. Va. 1740 d. Va. 1804   Pat. Va. 1787-1803
    m. Ann Blackwell — son Steptoe m. Sarah Orrick Chilton

Pickett, Reuben b. Va. 1754 d. N. or S. Carolina   Pat. Va.
    m. Elizabeth Day — son John m. Rebecca Collier

Pickle, Jacob b. Va. 1772 d. Va. 1837 m. Susannah Loucks   Pvt. Va. Mil.
    son David m. Mrs. Polly Porter Gose

Pidgeon, William W. Vol. 17   Sgt. Pa. Mil.

Pierce, Aretas Vol. 14   Pvt. Vt. Mil.

Pierce, Dyer, Vol. 11   Sgt. N.Y. Mil.

Pierce, Jason b.— d.— m. Sallie Stickney   Pvt. N.Y. Mil.
    son Charles P. m. Louise Stevens

Pierce, John b. Mass. 1756 d. Mass. 1829 m. Mary Gilmore   Lt. Mass. Mil.
    daughter Nancy m. Spooner Alden

Pierce, Jonathan Vol. 9   Col. N.H. Mil.

Pierce, Joseph Vol. 6   Commander of "Ida"

Pierce, Phineas Vol. 11   Pvt. N.Y. Mil.

Pierce, Reuben b. Vt. 1787 d. N.Y. 1857 m. Florilla Swetland   Pvt. N.Y. Mil.
    daughter Flora L. m. Eli H. Babcock REAL DAUGHTER

Pierce, Samuel Vol. 7   Pvt. Pa. Mil.

Pierce, William b. Va. bef. 1795 d. Ind. 1849   Pvt. Ohio Mil.
    m. Sarah Thompson — son William C. m. Mary Miller

Pierce, William Henry b. N.Y. 1795 d. Md. 1879   Pvt. Drum N.Y. Mil.
    m. Ann Flemming — daughter Virginia m. David Keener Zollicoffer

Pierpont, Francis Vol. 4   Ens. Va. Mil.

Pierson, James b. 1750 d. N.J. m. Martha Pearson   Matross N.J.
    son Sylvanus m. Elizabeth Hinkle

Pierson, John b. Conn. 1783 d. N.Y. 1814   Pvt. N.Y. Mil.
    m. Cynthia Franklin — daughter Louise C. m. Asa A. Flint

Piggott, Edward b. (W.)Va. 1790 d. W.Va. 1879   Pvt. Va. Mil.
    m. Melissa A. Davis
    daughter Lottie m. Edward Harris REAL DAUGHTER

Piggott, Newton b. Ill. 1793 d. Mo. 1874 m. Sarah Massey   Sgt. Mo. Mil.
    daughter Asenath m. Howard G. Lame

Pigman, John b. Pa. 1798 d. Ky. 1884   Pvt. U.S. Inf. 1814-15
    m. Rosannah Amburgy
    daughter Queentena m. Andrew Jackson Smith

Pike, Artemus b. Mass. 1775 d. N.Y. 1814 m. Marion Parker   Pvt. N.Y. Mil.
    daughter Eunice B. m. Henry Dopp, Jr.

Pike, Ezra b. Vt. 1761 d. Vt. 1840 m. Mary Garlick   Pvt. Vt. Mil.
    daughter Mercy m. Calvin Hill

Pike, Joseph Vol. 14   Pvt. U.S. Inf.

Pilcher, Lewis b. 1788 d. 1854 m. Susan C. Moon   Pvt. Ky. Mil.
    daughter Zerlida m. Wm. Jackson Cornett

Pillow, Gideon Sr. b. Va. 1770 d. Tenn. 1843 m. Annie Payne   Pvt. Tenn. Mil.
    daughter Amanda M. m. West Humphreys
    son Gideon Jr. m. Mary Martin
    son Jerome B. m. Elvira Dale

Pillsbury, Ithamar b. Mass. 1794 d. Ill. 1862   Cpl. N.H. Mil.
    m. Caroline E. Miller — son Francis I. m. Millie I. Blockwedel

Pillsbury, Joshua b. Mass. 1743 d. N.H. 1825   Pvt. Mass. Mil.
    m. Elizabeth Sawyer — son Caleb m. Anna Underhill

Pillsbury, Micajah b. Mass. 1761 d. N.H. 1801   Pat. Selectman N.H. 1797
    m. Sarah Sargent — son Stephen m. Lavinia Hobart

Pillsbury, Tobias Vol. 7   Pvt. U.S. Inf.

Pinckney, William b. N.Y. d. N.Y. m.—   Maj. N.Y. Mil.
    daughter Sabrina m. Elijah Ward

Pine, Daniel Vol. 10   Pvt. N.Y. Mil.

Pine, William Sr. b. N.J. 1780 d. Ill. 1872   Pvt. Ohio Mil.
    m. Hannah Peacock — son William Jr. m. Mary McCleery

Pinkerton, William b. Pa. 1780 d. Ky. 1850   Capt. Md. Mil.
    m. Elizabeth Littig — son Collin M. m. Louisa T. Davis

Pinkham, Nathaniel b. Mass. (Me.) 1784 d. Me. 1866   Pvt. Mass. (Me.) Mil.
    m. Phoebe Bailey — daughter Sarah m. Solon Turner

Pinkney, William b. Md. 1764 d. D.C. 1822   Maj. Md. Mil.
    m. Ann Maria Rodgers
    daughter Elizabeth m. Cumberland D. Williams
    son Frederick m. Sophia Rodgers

Piper, James b. Mass. 1781 d. Mass. 1850 m. Sarah Edwards   Seaman Mass.
    son Joseph L. m. Sarah A. Fowle

Piper, John b. Pa. 1766 d. Pa. 1847   2nd Maj. Pa. Mil.
    m. Rachel Braily (Brickly) — daughter Maria m. William Spielman

Pipes, David Winsor b. Miss. 1791 d. La. 1873   Lt. Miss. Mil.
    m. Martha Withington — daughter Mary H. m. James Taylor

Pipkin, Philip b. N.C. 1770 d. Mo. 1841   Col. W. Tenn. Mil.
    m. Margaret Brown — son Enos m. Jane Sale
    daughter Martha m. Jonah Sappington Sr.

Pipkin, Phillip b. N.C. 1770 d. Mo.   Capt. W. Tenn. Vol.
    m. Sarah Morris — daughter Fannie E. m. John Fenton Long

Pitchlynn, John b. Scot. d. Miss. 1835   Lt., Adj. Miss. Mil. 1814
    m. Sophia Fulsom — daughter Eliza m. William Harris
    daughter Elizabeth m. Lorenza Harris

Pitkin, Joseph Vol. 4   Cpl. Conn. Mil.

Pitkin, William b. Conn. 1724 d. Conn. aft. 1788   Pat. Conn. Const. Conv.
    m. Elizabeth Stanley   1788
    son William Jr. m. Mary Woodbridge

Pittard, William b. Ga. 1784 d. Ga. 1870   Pvt. Ga. Mil.
    m. (2) Curicy (Meadows) McKelvey
    daughter Elizabeth m. Henry M. Lumpkin

Pittman, Dempsey b. N.C. 1760 d. N.C. 1824   Pvt. N.C. Mil.
    m. Abigail Jones — daughter Adeline Frances m. Jacob Higgs

Pittman, James b. Va. 1756 d. Ga. 1850 m. Martha Taylor   Pat. Judge Ga.
    daughter America T. m. Benjamin Woods Cash
    son Martin H. m. Nancy Smith

Pittman, John Green b. Ga. 1782 d. Ga. 1873   Lt. Col. Ga. Mil.
    m. Polly Moore — son George T. m. Irene Croxton

Pitts, Joseph b. S.C. 1795 d. Ga. 1873   Pvt. S.C. Mil.
    m. Ann Anderson Lemon
    daughter Rebecca M. m. James Harwell Wilson

Pitts, Obadiah Vol. 12   Pvt. S.C. Vol.

Pitzer, John b. Va. 1771 d. Va. 1823 m. Charlotte Davidson   Capt. Va. Mil.
    son John Jr. m. Elizabeth Atherton

Plants, Edward b. N.J. 1792 d. Mich. 1863   Cpl. N.Y. Mil.
    m. Elizabeth Beach — son Leonard m. Nancy Wilson

Platt, Asa b. Conn. 1767 d. Conn. 1842   Lt. Conn. Cavalry
    m. Martha Woodruff — daughter Martha m. Raymond Baldwin

Platt, Joseph b. Conn. 1754 d. Conn. 1833 m. Mabel Clark   Capt. Conn. Mil.
    son Nathan m. Sally Fowler

Platt, Zephaniah Jr. b. N.Y. 1735 d. N.Y. 1807   Pat. Const. Conv. N.Y. 1788
    m. Mary Van Wyck — son William P. m. Hannah Kent

Platts, John b. Mass. 1726 d. N.H. 1817 m. Deborah Page   Pat. N.H. 1796-7
    son Joseph Jr. m. Abigail Sawtelle

Plauche, Jacques Urbain b. La. 1787 d. La. 1856   Lt. La. Mil.
    m. Mary Brown — daughter Mary m. Henry Dart

Plauche, Jean Baptiste b. La. 1785 d. La. 1860   Maj. La.
    m. Mathilde Daspit de St. Amant
    daughter Mathilde m. Louis Edouard Forstall

Plecher, Jacob Vol. 13   Pvt. Va. Mil.

Plowman, Jonathan b. Md. 1792 d. Md. 1844   Pvt. Md. Mil.
    m. Hannah Herbert — son John m. Sarah Jane Stabler

Plummer, Michajah Sawyer b. Mass. 1796 d. Mass. 1888   Pvt. Mass. Mil.
    m. Betsey Haskell
    daughter Martha A. m. George Draper Everett REAL DAUGHTER
    son Osgood m. Dianah Houghton

Plummer, Moses b. Mass. 1765 d. Vt. Aft. 1803 m.—   Pat. Vt. 1803
    son Samuel m. Nancy Morrison   Town Clerk

Plummer, Nathaniel b. N.H. 1785 d. Me. 1868   Sgt. Mass. (Me.) Mil.
    m. Agnes Pennell — son Isaac m. Frances Augusts Merrow

Plummer, Samuel b. Me. (Mass.) 1791 d. Vt. 1881   Pvt. Vt. Mil.
    m. Nancy Morrison — son Ebenezer m. Anna Whitehill

Plymton, Joseph b. Mass. 1787 d. N.Y. 1860   Lt. U.S. Inf.
 m. Eliza Matilda Livingston
 daughter Cornelia DeP. m. Henry M. Black

Poage, Allen b. Va. 1774 d. Ill. 1853 m.— Vol. 10   Pvt. Ky. Mil.

Poage, James b. Va. 1760 d. Ohio 1820 m. Mary Woods Pvt. Va. Mil.
 daughter Ann m. Alexander Mooney

Poage, Thomas Hoge b. Va. 1792 d. Tex. 1841   Ens. Ky. Mil.
 m. Nancy Allen Frame — son Hugh C. m. Sarah E. Davenport

Pockett, John Balbridge Vol. 7   Lt. U.S. Navy

Poe, Andrew b. Pa. 1780 d. Ohio 1857 m. Nancy Hoy Teamster Ohio Mil.
 daughter Sarah m. John Montgomery

Poe, Isaiah b. N.C. 1792 d. Mo. 1875 m. Sarah Burrows Cpl. Mo. Mil.
 daughter Amanda m. Benjamin Miller

Poe, John b. 1785 d. 1864 m. Rebecca Hinkle   Pvt. Tenn. Mil.
 daughter Rebecca Jane m. Samuel H. Boyd

Poe, William Romulus b. Va. 1794 d. Ill. 1866   Cpl. Va. Mil.
 m. Mary Jane Dale
 daughter Lucy Jane m. Herbert William Blandy REAL DAUGHTER

Poffenberger, William b. Pa. 1782 d. Pa. 1842   Pvt. Pa. Mil.
 m. Catherine Noll — son Daniel m. Margaretta Heckerk

Pogue, Robert b. Va. 1766 d. Ky. 1831-2 m. Jane Hopkins Lt. Col. Ky. Mil.
 son John H. m. Sarah A. Moore
 son William L. m. Anne McCormack & Caroline Ann Roach

Poindexter, John b. Va. 1793 d. Ky. 1877   Lt. Va. Mil.
 m. Elizabeth Graves — daughter Ella m. James Lyle Glenn

Poindexter, William b. Va. 1766 d. N.C. 1844   Pvt. N.C. Mil.
 m. Elizabeth A. Ashburn — son Denson A. m. Sarah Jones

Pointer, Samuel Vol. 11   Pvt. Va. Mil.

Points, Joseph b. Pa. 1763 d. Va. m.— Vol. 2   Capt. Va. Mil.
 son George W. m. Delphine Stuart

Polhemus, Daniel Vol. 14   Pvt. N.Y. Mil.

Polhemus, Theodorus b. N.Y. 1791 d. N.Y. 1872   Cpl. N.J. Mil.
 m. Hetty Mandeville — daughter Mary m. Edward D. Bailey

Polhill, Thomas b. Ga. 1760 d. Ga. 1814 Pat. Ga. State Senator
 m. Mary Anderson — son James m. Martha Jones
 son Joseph m. Julia J. Guion

Polk, Charles b. Pa. 1732 d. Pa. 1821   Pat. N.C. 1794-5; 1800
 m. Philipina Helms   Repr. Gen. Assy.
 son George W. m. Margaret Garmon
 son Michael m. Susannah Pyron

Polk, Evan Shelby b. Tenn. 1791 d. Ark. 1875   Cpl. Tenn. Mil.
 m. Martha Jane Miller — son John S. m. Dorcas Armstrong

Polk, Ezekiel b. Pa. 1747 d. Tenn. 1824 m. Mary Wilson Pat. Justice Tenn.
 son Thomas m. Abigail Irwin

Polk, Whittington Vol. 15   Capt. Md. Mil.

Polkinhorn, Richard Wallace b. Va. 1795 d. D.C. 1871 Pvt. Md. Mil.
 m. Jane Stephenson — son Richard O. m. Hannah M. Thompson

Pollard, John b. Pa. 1777 d. Pa. 1830 m. Mary Smallman   Pvt. Pa. Blues
   daughter Valeria m. William Cowen

Pollard, John W. b. Conn. 1792 d. Conn. 1884   Pvt. Conn. Mil.
   m. Lucy Wade — daughter Jane M. m. George H. Deming

Pollard, Joseph b. Va. d. Ky. 1800 m. Elizabeth Thornton   Lt. Va. Mil.
   son William m. Electra Ann Catt

Pollard, Nicholas b. Pa. 1774 d. Pa. 1851 m. Julia Anne   Pvt. Pa. Mil.
   daughter Sarah m. John Mohney

Pollard, William b. Va. 1761 d. Va. 1841 m. Frances Hampton   Pvt. Va. Mil.
   son Elijah G. m. Elizabeth Y. Hiter

Polle, Stephen P. Vol. 12   Pvt. Va. Mil.

Pollerin, Louis Barthelony b. 1762 d. 1845   Pvt. La.
   m. Mary Ann Isabel Labat
   son Louis Armand m. Kulie Marie Malvina Kerr

Polley, Andrew b. Pa. c. 1760 d. Pa. 1826 m.—   Pvt. Pa. Mil.
   daughter Anna Maria m. William Woodburn Bell

Pollock, John b. Pa. 1791 d. Pa. 1871 m. Eliza Gormley   Pvt. Pa. Mil.
   son William m. Samantha McMains

Pomeroy, Daniel b. Conn. 1789 d. N.Y. 1867   Sgt. N.Y. Mil.
   m. Roanna Sexton — son Hiram m. Jane Elizabeth Morris

Pomeroy, Enos b. Mass. 1761 d. Mass. 1826   Pat. Selectman Mass. 1813-14
   m. Lucy Smith — son Stephen m. Dorothy Carter

Pond, Charles b. Conn. 1744 d. Conn. 1832/3   Capt. Conn. Mil.
   m. Martha Miles — daughter Sally m. William Harpin Fowler

Pond, Lewis b. Mass. ca. 1764 d. Vt. 1831   Pvt. Mass. Mil.
   m. Elizabeth Pond — son Lewis Jr. m. Elivra Smith

Pond, Luther b. Conn. 1790 d. Mich. 1843 m. Sarah White   Pvt. N.Y. Mil.
   daughter Mary Ann m. Alanson Sprague

Pontius, John Vol. 12   Pvt. Ohio Mil.

Pool(e), Adam b. N.C. 1794 d. N.C. aft. 1820   Cpl. Miss. Mil.
   m. Betsey Pennington — daughter Rebecca L. m. Henry Box McCain

Pool, Garrett J. b. N.Y. ca. 1774 d. 1813 in service   Capt. U.S. Inf.
   m. Catherine Cross — son Peter m. Mary Ann Empie

Pool, John P. (Petty) b. S.C. 1785 d. S.C. 1848   Pvt. U.S. Mil.
   m. Martha Boswell — daughter Ann m. Albert Alsey Neves

Pool, Thomas b. Mass. 1787 d. Me. 1883   Cpl. Mass. (Me.) Mil.
   m. Lydia Cobb — daughter Lucy P. m. Daniel Jackson

Poole, Caderick P. b. Va. 1789 d. Va. 1855   Pvt. Va. Mil.
   m. Elizabeth Varden — daughter Sarah F. m. Joseph R. Seward

Poole, Galen b. Mass. 1789 d. Mass. aft. 1871   Pvt. U.S. Art. Mass.
   m. Harriett Andrews — daughter Augusta m. William H. Pride

Poole, Samuel b. Mass. (Me.) 1736 d. Me. 1830   Sgt. Me. (Mass.) Mil.
   m. Ruth Fullerton — daughter Alethea m. James Hersey

Poole, Stephen P. Vol. 12   Pvt. Va. Mil.

Pooler, George b. Mass. (Me.) 1784 d. Me. 1866   Lt. Mass. (Me.) Mil.
   m. Cynthia Weston — daughter Almeda m. Nathan Weston

Poor, Christopher b. Mass. (Me.) 1780 d. N.Y. 1854   Pvt. N.Y. Mil.
   m. Mary Parkinson — son Aaron m. Lucena Clark

Pope, Burwell b. N.C. 1751 d. Ga. 1800   Pat. Ga. Const. Conv. 1798
   m. Priscilla Wootten — daughter Martha m. Wylie Hill

Pope, Burwell b. Ga. 1790 d. Ga. 1840 m. Sarah Key Strong   Ens. Ga. Mil.
   son John Hardeman m. Mary Francis Caldwell

Pope, John Whitaker b. N.C. 1793 d. Tenn. 1839   Pvt. W. Tenn. Mil.
   m. Elizabeth Campbell — son John O. m. Frances Anne Thompson

Pope, Leroy b. 1765 d. 1844 m. Judith Sale   Judge Mem. Legis. Ala. 1808
   son William m. Sarah Clark Hatfield

Pope, Nathaniel William b. Ky. d. La. 1836   Pvt. Ky. Mil.
   m. Martha Johnson — son Charles W. m. Leonora Holmes

Pope, Samuel b. 1781 d. Ia. 1877 m. Mary E. Bentley   Lt. Ohio Mil.
   son John A. m. Eliza Johnson

Pope, Doctor Samuel b. Mass. 1781 d. N.Y. 1834   Pat. Dr. Conn. 1787
   m. Freelove Waterman — son Anson W. m. Wealthy Sophronia Brown

Pope, Thomas b. Mass. 1789 d. Mass. 1872   Brig. Maj. Mass. Mil.
   m. Emily Brown — son John F. m. Malvina Lillibridge Yeomans

Poppleton, Samuel b. Vt. 1793 d. Ohio 1865   Pvt. N.Y. Mil.
   m. Julia Smith — daughter Zada C. m. Thomas H. Linnell

Porter, David b. Mass. 1754 d. Md. 1808 Vol. 8   Capt. Mass. Navy

Porter, Elias Vol. 9   Cpl. Ohio Mil.

Porter, Ezekiel b. Mass. 1762 d. N.Y. m. Betsey Wyman   Lt. Col. Mass. Mil.
   daughter Mary m. Joseph Holley

Porter, Francis b. N.H. 1787 d. N.Y. 1866 m. Phila Fuller   Pvt. N.Y. Mil.
   son James H. m. Mary Gardner

Porter, Hugh b. Pa. 1778 d. Ohio 1838 m. Susannah Porter   Pvt. Ohio Mil.
   daughter Rebecca m. Seth Baker

Porter, James Vol. 3   Pvt. Ohio Mil.

Porter, James b. Md. 1789 d. Ohio 1850   Sgt. Ohio Mil.
   m. Elizabeth Kinbourne — son James G. m. Gertrude Judy

Porter, John b. 1778 d. 1837 m. Margaret Culton   Capt. Tenn. Mil.
   daughter Mary m. Moses Cox III

Porter, John b. S.C. 1756 d. La.; Battle New Orleans   Pvt. La. Mil.
   m. Mary Cox — daughter Susan C. m. Dr. James Haynesworth

Porter, John b. 1782 d. S.C. 1826 m. Jane Graham   Cpl. S.C. Inf.
   son William G. m. Agnes M. Montgomery

Porter, John b. Pa. 1783 d. Md. 1863 m. Catherine Glissan   Sgt. Md. Mil.
   daughter Eleanor P. m. Douglas Percy

Porter, Lewis b. Conn. 1786 d. N.Y. 1862   Qtr. Mst. Inf. 1812
   m. Samantha King — son Asaph King m. Rachel Glazier

Porter, Nehemiah b. Mass. 1758 d. Me. 1848   Pvt. Me. Mil.
   m. Joanna Barbour — daughter Joanna m. William Stearns Jr.

Porter, Oliver b. Va. 1766 d. Ga. 1838 Maj. Ga. Mil. & Justice Ct. 1796/1815
   m. Margaret Watson — daughter Mary A. m. James Fears

Porter, Peter b. N.C. 1792 d. Mo. 1876   Pvt. U.S. Inf.
   m. Matilda Armstrong — son James S. m. Ruth Bigham
   daughter Sarah E. m. Robert Ralston

Porter, Robert b. Pa. 1773 d. Pa. 1859   Pvt. Pa. Mil.
   m. Elizabeth Penrose Alcock — son John A. m. Grazella Holmes

Porter, Shadrach b. S.C. 1780 d. La. 1827   Capt. La. Mil.
   m. Elizabeth Campbell — daughter Cyrena N. m. Alfred P. Moss

Porter, William b. N.C. 1746 d. S.C. 1817   Col. N.C. Mil.
   m. Margaret Steele — son David m. Jane Swaine
   son James m. Nancy Neely

Porter, Wrixam Lewis b. Md. 1771 d. Md. 1816   Pvt. Md. Mil.
   m. Priscilla Riggin — son William m. Sally Miles

Portman, James b. Pa. 1789 d. Mich. 1853 m. Lucy Gilson   Pvt. Pa. Mil.
   son James G. m. Caroline Miner

Posey, Thomas b. Va. 1750 d. Ill. 1818   Capt. Ky. Vol. Mil.
   m. Mary Alexander (Thornton)
   daughter Eliza Maria m. Joseph Montfort Street

Post, Abraham A. b. N.Y. 1785 d. N.Y. 1871   Lt. N.Y. Mil.
   m. Mary Leah Wynkoop — son Abram A. m. Elizabeth F. Blosson

Post, Augustus b. Conn. 1793 d. Conn. 1879   Pvt. Conn. Mil.
   m. Betsey Strong — son Charles A. m. Lucy Ann Bill

Post, Isaac Burns b.— d. N.Y. m. Mania   Cpl. N.Y. Mil.
   son John D. m. Luana Pierpont

Post, John b. N.Y. 1789 d. N.Y. 1872 m. Elizabeth Cruser   Pvt. N.Y. Mil.
   daughter Ann m. John Lake

Post, Myndert b. N.Y. 1785 d. N.Y. 1842 m. Maria Brink   Ens. N.Y. Mil.
   daughter Emeline m. Diah Turner

Postal, William Cunningham b. N.Y. 1789 d. Tenn. 1876   Pvt. N.Y. Mil.
   m. Luna Carter — daughter Mary m. Abram Hiner

Postlewaite, William b. Pa. 1760 d. Pa. 1831   Capt. Pa. Mil.
   m. Elizabeth Irwin — daughter Elizabeth m. Jonathan Doyle

Potter, Benjamin b. R.I. 1785 d. R.I. 1867   Lt. R.I. Mil.
   m. Elizabeth Greene — son John E. m. Margart Nemis Wilty

Potter, David Vol. 5   Col. N.J. Troops

Potter, George b. R.I. 1732 d. R.I. 1794   Pat. R.I. Gen. Assy. 1790
   m. Content Maxson — son George m. Mary Stillman

Potter, Horace b. Conn. 1781 d. Ohio 1841   Surgeon Ohio Mil.
   m. Abrilla Quinby — son Ephraim m. Adaline Miller

Potter, John b. N.C. 1761 d. Tenn. 1865 m. Mary Stout   Pvt. Tenn. Mil.
   daughter Hannah m. Samuel Dugger
   son John III m. Sarah McIntosh

Potter, John Vol. 10   Seaman Pa.

Potter, Joseph Ayer b. N.Y. 1794 d. Wisc. 1863   Pvt. N.Y. Mil.
   m. Rachel West
   daughter Seraphina m. Charles Rollin Head REAL DAUGHTER

Potter, Pardon b. R.I. 1772 d. N.Y. 1859 m. Rhoda Carver   Lt. R.I. Troops
   son George C. m. Harriett Robinson

Potter, William b. Conn. 1794 d. Conn. 1858   Capt. Conn. Mil.
   m. Mary Elizabeth Maxon — son Charles O. m. Sallie Marie Bennett

Potter, Loving Vol. 8   Pvt. U.S. Art.

Potts, John b. Va. c. 1790 d. Ohio 1862   Pvt. Ohio Mil.
   m. Margaret Kinder — daughter Rosannah m. David De Vore

Potts, Jonathan b. Va. 1744-54 d. Ohio 1831   Pvt. Pa. Mil. 1789
   m. Elizabeth English — son Jonas m. Elizabeth Johnson

Powell, Allen Beverly b. Ga. 1783 d. Ga. 1844   Pat. Justice/Senator Ga.
   m. Mary Calder — daughter Matilda m. Daniel McDonald

Powell, Hardy b. N.C. 1776 d. Ga. 1824 m. Sara Horn   Pvt. Ga. Mil.
   son James Lafayette m. Lucinda Johnson

Powell, Honourias b. Va. 1770 d. Ky. 1850-60 m. Milly   Pvt. Va. Mil.
   daughter Elizabeth m. Thornton C. Gorham   Surveyor Ky. 1815

Powell, John b. Pa. 1797 d. Pa. 1845 m. Elizabeth Thomas   Pvt. Pa. Mil.
   daughter Arabella Louise m. John Trenton

Powell, Levin b. Va. 1737 d. Pa. 1810   Const. Conv. Va. 1788
   m. Sarah Harrison   Congressman 1799
   son William H. m. Sarah Green

Powell, Lewis R. b. Va. 1792 d. Ga. bef. 1860 m.—   Pvt. Ga. Mil.
   son Newton m. Lucinda Mahan

Powell, Matthew Vol. 12   Sgt. Maj. Va. Mil.

Powell, Nathaniel b. Va. 1781 d. Va. 1830   Pvt. Va. Mil.
   m. Sally A. Turnall — son James H. m. Martha Eliza Oast

Powell, Norborne Berkeley b. Va. 1791 d. Ala. 1862   4th Sgt. Va. Art.
   m. Eliza Anne R. Holmes
   daughter Lucy J. m. Joseph Milton Cary REAL DAUGHTER

Powell, Richard Vol. 12   Pvt. N.Y. Mil.

Powell, Robert b. Ky. 1794 d. Mo. 1877 m. Celia Murphy   Pvt. Ky. Mil.
   son Thomas J. m. Fannie Hartt

Powell, Stephen b. N.Y. 1782 d. Ohio 1870   Pvt. N.Y. Mil.
   m. Margaret Norton — son Stephen W. m. Rhoda Woodard Sanger

Power, Robert b. Ky. 1782 d. Ky. aft. 1812 m. Frances Grisum   Pvt. Ky.
   son David G. m. Martha Tharp   Mil.

Powers, David b. N.J. 1770 d. N.J. 1840 m. Mary Hubbard   Pvt. N.J. Mil.
   son Jacob b. Mary Fairchild

Powers, Gideon b. N.H. 1794 d. N.H. 1873 m. Affia Russell   Sgt. Me. Mil.
   daughter Sarah R. m. Austin Partridge

Powers, Isaac b. Mass. 1789 d. Mass. 1860   Cpl. Mass. Mil.
   m. Betsey Hanson
   daughter Emeline Janette m. William Burrows Farmer

Powers, James W. b. Va. 1793 d. W.Va. 1880   Pvt. W.Va. Mil.
   m. Margaret Moore — son John R. m. Savanah Luvina Earthenhouse

Powers, John b. Conn. 1762 d. N.Y. 1837 m. Anna Napier   Lt. N.Y. Lt. Inf.
   son Sidney m. Adeline Doyle

Powers, Jonathan b. 1792 d. Ind. 1855 m. Lovia Fields   Pvt. Ohio Mil.
   son William m. Priscilla Garrigues

Powers, Major b. Vt. 1791 d. N.Y. 1879 m. Harriet Payson   Pvt. N.Y. Mil.
    daughter Harriet E. m. Thomas B. Watson

Powers, Thomas Vol. 10   Pvt. Tenn. Mil.

Poynter, Gilbert B. Vol. 15   Pvt. Pa. Mil.

Prather, Josiah Turner Sr. b. Md. 1777 d. D.C. 1849   Pvt. Md. Mil.
    m. Elizabeth Cadle Drummond — son Joseph m. Martha Jane Belt

Pratt, Ebenezer b. Mass. 1777 d. Ill. 1861 m. Sallie Aldrich   Pvt. Mass. Mil.
    son John m. Lydia M. Webster

Pratt, Jedidiah Vol. 8   Pvt. Mass. (Me.) Mil.

Pratt, John Jr. b. Mass. 1783 d. Vt. 1820   Qtr. Mst. Vt. Mil.
    m. Lavinia Burnap
    daughter Catherine D. m. Bowman Bishop Martin

Pratt, Jonathan b. Mass. 1773 d. Mass. 1846   Pvt. Mass. Mil.
    m. Abigail Phillips — son Luke m. Eliza Sage

Pratt, Josiah b.— d.— m. Althea Hull   Pvt. N.Y. Mil.
    son Delos m. Laura Waller

Pratt, Samson Vol. 17   Pvt. U.S. Inf.

Pratt, Samuel b. Ala. 1788 d. Tenn. ca. 1853   Sgt. Tenn. Mil.
    m. Polly Boyd — daughter Eliza m. Robert Harrison

Pratt, Samuel Vol. 6   Pvt. N.Y. Mil.

Pratt, Thomas b. Mass. 1798 d. Mass. 1870   Music Mass. Mil.
    m. Phoebe Waite — daughter Caroline H. m. Kimball Bowes

Pratt, Thomas b. Pa. 1764 d. Pa. 1820 m. Hannah Massey   Pvt. Pa. Mil.
    daughter Susanna m. William Potts

Pratt, William b. Mass. (Me.) 1779 d. Mass. (Me.) 1818   Pvt. Mass. (Me.)
    m. Martha Gurney — William Jr. m. Zilpha Bryant   Mil.

Pratte, Bernard b. Fra. 1772 d. Mo. 1836 m. Emilie Labbadie   Gen. Mo. Mil.
    daughter Emilie m. Ramsay Crooks

Pray, John b. R.I. 1783 d. Ohio 1872 m. Lucy Durham   Pvt. N.Y. Mil.
    son John L. m. Lucina Cross

Pray, Joseph b. Mass. (Me.) 1766 d. Me. 1840   Pvt. Mass. (Me.) Mil.
    m. Dorcas Yeaton — son Phineas m. Sarah Wood

Prentice, Daniel Vol. 13   Pvt. Conn. Troops

Prentice Henry b. Mass. 1776 d. Vt. 1850 m. Molly Pratt   Lt. Mass. Mil.
    daughter Susan P. m. Daniel Wheelock

Prentis, Eben b. Va. 1788 d. Mich. 1868   Color Sgt. Conn.
    m. Rebecca Cager — son George m. Lovina Griffin

Prentiss, Jessee Vol. 3   Pvt. Mass. (Me.) Mil.

Prentiss, Jonathan b. 1796 d. 1844 m. Eliza Hamer   Capt. Vt. Mil.
    son Samuel m. Lois J. Brown

Prentiss, Jonathan b. Vt. 1777 d. Vt. 1860   Capt. Vt. Mil.
    m. Hannah Sparhawk — son Joseph m. Catherine Fisher

Prentiss, Manasseh b. Conn. 1778 d. N.Y. 1814   Capt. N.Y. Mil.
    m. Susan Lothrop — son Nelson m. Electa Ingersoll

Prescott, Daniel b. Mass. (Me.) 1802 d. Me. 1888   Drum Mass. Mil.
    m. Betsy Meservey — son Cyrus S. m. Harriett Elizabeth Bisbee

Prescott, Imley b. N.Y. 1794 d. N.Y. 1850   Qtr. Mst. N.Y. Mil.
   m. Maria Cross — son James B. m. Juliette Durfree

Presher, John Richard b. 1792 d. 1870   Seaman 1813-14
   m. Hannah Garner & (2) Millison Turner
   daughter Ann m. George S. Hill

Preston, Francis b. Va. 1765 d. S.C. 1836   Col. Va. Mil.
   m. Sally Buchanan — daughter Maria T. C. m. John M. Preston

Preston, George Vol. 17   Pvt. Pa. Mil.

Preston, James b. Va. 1770 d. Tenn. 1840   Capt. Tenn. Vol.
   m. Charlotte Rector — daughter Jane m. John Jackson

Preston, John b. Va. 1781 d. Va. 1864   Col. Va. Mil.
   m. Margaret Brown — son Francis m. Virginia Moffett

Preston, John b. Mass. 1746 d. Mass. 1815   Pat. Selectman Mass.
   m. Rachel Clark — son John Jr. m. Eunice Moody

Preston, Nathan b. Conn. 1786 d. Conn. 1873   Ens. Conn. Mil.
   m. Polly Crawford — son Selden C. m. Marietta Spofford

Prewett, John Welch b. Ala. 1793 d. Ala. 1873   Pvt. Tenn. Mil.
   m. Elizabeth Cooper
   daughter Margaret Jane m. Edward Isaac Hagler

Prewitt, Robert Hurt b. Ky. 1791 d. Ind. 1845   Pvt. U.S. Inf. Ky.
   m. Elizabeth Clark — son James P. C. m. Sarah Burns

Price, Charles b. Md. d.— m. Hannah J. Swartz   Pvt. Md. Mil.
   daughter Hannah Jane m. Kent Mitchell Chesney

Price, Charles b. Va. 1755 d. Va. 1833   Pat. Va. 1793
   m. Elizabeth Anderson — son Nathaniel H. m. Nancy Lee

Price, David b. Va. 1770 d. Ill. 1845   Capt. Tenn. Mil. 1814/15
   m. Nancy Milly Parker — daughter Mary m. James F. Johnston
   daughter Nancy m. Willis Willeford

Price, David b. Va. 1789 d. Md. 1861 m. Margaret Crook   Pvt. D.C. Mil.
   daughter Priscilla m. Charles F. Munder

Price, Edmund b. (W.) Va. 1793 d. Va. 1862   Pvt. Va. Mil.
   m. Rebecca Murphy — daughter Merida m. Almeda Arnold

Price, Icabod Benton b. N.J. 1781 d. N.Y. 1862   Pvt. N.Y. Art.
   m. Susan Moore — son Joseph N. m. Anne Amelia Hiscox

Price, Jacob b. Va. 1785 d. Va. 1848   Sgt. Va. Mil.
   m. Sophia Montgomery — daughter Sophia M. m. Dr. Hugh M. Grant

Price, Joseph b. Ala. 1780 d. Ark. 1866   Pvt. Tenn. Mil.
   m. Rebecca Haywood — daughter Nancy m. Jacob Kennamur Jr.

Price, Josiah C. Vol. 14   Pvt. Md. Mil.

Price, Richard b.— d. Ohio 1813 m. Mary Waller   2nd Lt. Ky. Mil.
   daughter Sallie m. Lyddall Bacon Bowles

Price, William b. (W.) Va. 1792 d. Mo. 1839   Pvt. W.Va. Mil.
   m. Sarah Walkup — son Joseph m. Elizabeth Renfro

Prichard, William b. N.C. 1786 d. Miss. 1845   Lt. Miss. Mil.
   m. Frances Smith — son James S. m. Elizabeth H. Foster

Priest, Hankey b. Va. 1783 d. Ohio 1862 m. Delia Meeker   Pvt. Ohio Mil.
   daughter Eliza m. Jonas Wiltrour

Prigg, William b. Md. 1790 d. Ind. 1876   Cpl. Md. Mil.
m. Mary Campbell — son Edward C. m. Harriet Curry

Prigmore, Thomas b. Pa. 1787 d. Tenn. 1872   Capt. Tenn. Vol.
m. Mary Lane — daughter Kizziah m. Jacob Peak
daughter Lucinda m. Bryant W. Smith

Prime, Grant b. Conn. 1766 d. Vt. 1861 m. Electa Doud   Vol. N.Y. Mil.
son Henry m. Weltha Hasseltine

Prince, Abel b. Conn. 1764 d. Conn. 1819 m. Lucy Cady   Sgt. Conn. Mil.
son William m. Betsey Fargo

Prince, Lyman b. Conn. 1793 d. Mass. 1867 m. Polly Corbin   Pvt. Conn. Mil.
daughter Emily m. Anson Barrett

Prince, William b. N.Y. 1795 d. N.Y. 1869   Pvt. N.Y. Mil.
m. Charlotte Goodwin Collins
daughter Charlotte P. m. Edwin Henry

Prindle, Jesse H. b. 1797 d. N.Y. 1856 m. Mahalia Rawson   Pvt. N.Y. Mil.
daughter Olive S. m. Jesse H. Rising REAL DAUGHTER

Prindle, John b. Conn. 1756 d. Mass. 1838   Pvt. Mass. Mil.
m. Penelope Johnson — son Marshall E. m. Caroline Lamphier

Prior, Asa b. Va. 1783 d. Tex. 1854 m. Sarah Witcher   Pvt. Ga. Mil.
son Haden M. m. Nancy Ann S. Montfort

Prior, William b. Mass. 1783 d. Ohio 1872 m. Sarah Horton Pvt. Ohio Mil.
daughter Susannah m. Horatio N. Poole

Pritchard, John b. N.H. 1771 d. Me. 1823   Commander of Schooner
m. Margaret Hammond   Mary; Mass.
daughter Ann Marie m. Stephen Little Sawyer

Pritchard, William b. Va. 1777 d. W.Va. 1866   Pvt. Va. Mil.
m. Nancy Meridith — daughter Mary Anne m. John Conley Parrish

Probasco, Garret b. N.J. 1745 d. N.J. 1834 m. Mayke   Pat. N.J.
daughter Rebecca m. Tunis Van Middlesworth

Proctor, Francis Jr. b. Nova Scotia 1756 d. Pa. 1814   Gunner 1784 Pa. Mil.
m. Ann Henderson — son Thomas m. Mary Musser

Proctor, James Buchannon b. Ky. d. Ind. 1873   Pvt. Ky. Mil.
m. Eliza Tudor — daughter Annie m. James Duncan

Proctor, Jeremiah b. Va. 1777 d. Ala. 1839 m. Jane Davis   Pvt. Tenn. Mil.
son Micahjah m. Margaret Minerva

Proctor, Stephen Royal b. S.C. 1784 d. N.Y. 1841   Capt. U.S. Inf. in
m. Mary Bedon Sawan   Fla. War
son Joseph B. m. Elina Nogan

Proctor, William b. N.H. 1767 d. N.H. 1848   Maj. N.H. Mil.
m. Abigail Whitmore — son William m. Rhoda Bagley

Proper, Petre von Stronder b. N.Y.| 1792 d. N.Y. aft. 1850 Pvt. N.Y. Troops
m. Mary Stillwell — daughter Charlotte m. Minor Easling

Protsman, John b. Pa. 1793 d. Ind. 1871   Pvt. Ohio Mil.
m. Elizabeth Mitchell — daughter Sarah Ann m. John Scott

Provance, Benjamin b. Pa. 1786 d. Pa. 1814 m. Jane Hartley   Pvt. Pa. Vol.
son James S. m. Susan Swearingen

Pruet, Jacob b. 1761 d. Ala. 1845   Capt. Tenn. Mil. 1800
m. Nancy Agnes Richey   Capt. Ala. Mil. 1814
daughter Margaret m. John Hellums

Pruitt, James b. Va. 1788 d. Ill. 1857 m. Mary Costley   Maj. Va. Mil.
son Amos m. Mary Stout Halleford

Pryor, Green b. N.C. 1789 d. Tenn. 1862   Pvt. Tenn. Mil.
m. Obediance Holloway — son William m. Amanda Prigmore

Pryor, Luke Sr. b. Va. 1770 d. Ala. 1851   Qtr. Mst. Sgt. Va. Mil.
m. Anne Batte Lane — son Luke, Jr. m. Isabelle Virginia Harris

Puckett, Aaron B. b. Va. bet. 1775-90 d. Ga. aft. 1820   Ens. Ga. Mil.
m. Sarah — son Robert m. Mary C. Brown

Puff, Philip b. Pa. 1752 d. Pa. 1817 m. Mary   Pvt. Pa. Mil.
daughter Mary m. Casper Arnold Jr.

Puffer, Phineas b. Mass. 1741 d. Mass. 1817   Pat. Mass. 1792
m. Mary Stratton — son Deacon Samuel m. Joanna Eames

Puffer, Samuel b. Mass. 1765 d. Mass. 1842   Capt. Mass. Mil.
m. Joanna Eames — Samuel Jr. m. Sophronia Miles Brown

Pugh, David b. Wales 1771 d. Pa. 1852 m. Mary Shaver   Pvt. Pa. Mil.
son David m. Jame Higgins

Pugh, Elijah b. N.C. 1760 d. Ala. 1824   Justice Ga. 1811/12
m. Ruth de St. Julien — daughter Aehsah m. Amos Robinson

Pugh, James Augustine Vol. 12   Capt. N.C. Mil.

Pugh, John B. b. Va. 1787 d. N.C. m. Ann Smith   Pvt. N.C. Mil.
daughter Nannie m. John B. Richardson REAL DAUGHTER

Pulver, Marvin b. N.Y. 1763 d. N.Y. 1832   Capt. N.Y. Mil.
m. Margaret Poplar (Pepler) — son Jacob M. m. Abigail Lockwood

Pummel, John b. Va. 1792 d. Va. 1869 m. Margaret Frantz   Pvt. Va. Mil.
daughter Rebecca m. John Kellough

Pumpelly, Charles b. Conn. 1779 d. N.Y. 1855   Pay Mst. N.Y. Mil.
m. Frances Avery — daughter Frances Eliza m. Joseph Bosworth

Pumphrey, Zachariah b. (W.) Va. 1788 d. Ohio 1875   Pvt. Ohio Mil.
m. Mary Margaret Snider — daughter Eliza m. Lewis Hull

Purcell, Edward b. Eng. d. Minn. 1825   Maj. Surgeon Inf.
m. Elizabeth Shirk — son John m. Susannah Postlethwaite

Purcell, Hardy b. N.C. 1777/8 d. Tenn. 1830   Pvt. W. Tenn. Mil.
m. Elizabeth Manning — son Edward m. Nancy Browning

Purcell, John b. Va. 1756/7 d. Va. 1836   Pvt. Va. Mil.
m. Elizabeth Carter
daughter Julia m. John R. Gray REAL DAUGHTER

Purdy, Isaac Shaw b. N.Y. 1793 d. N.Y. 1876 m. Ann Owens Pvt. N.Y. Mil.
son Joseph m. Margaret Elizabeth Bennett

Purdy, Jonathan Vol. 8   Pvt. N.Y. Mil.

Purington, Isaac b. (Me.) Mass. d. Me. aft. 1833   Pvt. (Me.) Mass. Mil.
m. Mary Foster — daughter Beulah m. Robert Patten

Puviance, James b. Md. 1772 d. Md. 1836 m. Eliza Young   Pvt. Md. Mil.
son James m. Eliza

Putnam, Andrew Vol. 14   Capt. N.Y. Mil.

Putman, Daniel b. Mass. 1755 d. Vt. 1819   Capt. Mass. Mil.
    m. Kezia Pollard — daughter Mary E. m. Shepard Marvin

Putnam, Elisha b. N.H. 1768 d. N.Y. at Sackett's Harbor 1814   Pvt. N.H.
    m. Mrs. Lydia Durant Parker — son Nathan m. Nancy Grinnell   Mil.

Putnam, John b. N.Y. 1795 d. N.Y. 1816   Sgt. N.Y. Art.
    m. Catherine Van Horne
    daughter Anna Maria m. James Gay McCreery

Putnam, Nathan b. N.H. 1793 d. N.H. 1867   Capt. N.H. Mil.
    m. Nancy Grinell — daughter Charlotte m. Harry Hackett
    son Franklin W. m. Mary Rosette Putnam

Putz, (Butz) Jeremiah b. Pa. 1795 d. Pa. 1859   Pvt. Pa. Mil.
    m. Rebecca Ludwig — son Samuel L. m. Teressa Scott

Pye, James Booth Vol. 10   Midshipman U.S. Navy

Pyfer, Henry Vol. 17   Matross & Cpl. D.C. Art.

Pyron, James b. Ga. 1776 d. Ga. 1820 m. Lucy Johnson   Pvt. Ga. Mil.
    son James Jr. m. Elizabeth Ann Cox

Q

Quackenbush, Nicholas b. N.Y. 1750 d. N.Y. 1830   Pvt. N.Y. Mil.
    m. Helen Magdelene Collier — son Jacob m. Margaret Hugrain
    son Peter N. m. Volley Quackenbush

Quarles, Tunstil b. Va. 1770 d. Ky. 1856   Commander Ky. Mil.
    m. Permalia Stringer — son John m. Ellen Huling

Quattlebaum, John b. S.C. d. S.C. 1853 m. Matee Burkeet   Capt. S.C. Mil.
    son Joseph m. Lucy Ann Merritt
    son Wilks m. Tennie Cowan

Quay, Andrew Vol. 11   Pvt. U.S. Rifles

Queen, Charles Jerningham b. Md. d. Md. 1837   Lt. Md. & Va. Mil.
    m. Maria Purcell — son Henry Peter m. Mary Elizabeth Wildman

Quick, Tunis b. N.J. 1763 d. N.J. 1839 m. Rhoda Prall   Pvt. N.J. Mil. 1792
    daughter Mary m. Thomas A. Holcombe

Quigley, Robert b. Pa. 1744 d. Pa. 1815 m. Mary Jacob   Capt. Pa. Mil.
    son Joseph m. Mary Sterrett Sharp

Quin, Robert Arnet b. N.Y. 1793 d. N.Y. 1863   Pvt. N.Y.
    m. Mary Elizabeth Hartenburgh — daughter Agnes m. John DeGroff

Quinn, John b. N.C. 1753 d. N.C. 1816 m. Celie Moore   Ens. N.C. Mil.
    daughter Crissie m. Seaborn Hall

Quisenberry, James H. b. Ky. 1786 d. Ky. 1822 m. Lucy Thomas   Pvt.
    son James J. m. Frances Thomas

R

Raborg, Christopher II b. Md. 1779 d. Md. 1862   Sgt. Md. Mil.
    m. Ann Goddard — son Goddard m. Ann Hynson Livesey

Rabun, Matthew b. N.C. 1744 d. Ga. 1819   Capt. Ga. Mil. 1793/4
    m. Sarah Warren — daughter Jane m. John Veazy

Radcliffe, Daniel b. Va. 1784 d. Ill. 1873   Sgt. Ky. Mil.
    m. Rachel McMannus — daughter Juliet m. Roland P. Moseley

Radebaugh, John b. Pa. 1752 d. Ohio 1850   Pvt. Pa. Mil.
  m. Catherine Barbara Werner — daughter Susannah m. Adam Klaur

Rader, John b. Va. 1791 d. Va. 1875   Pvt. Va. Mil.
  m. Pamela Ann Gannaway
  daughter Wyrinda Pamela m. George Washington Deskins

Rader, Michael b. Va. 1787 d. W.Va. 1867   Pvt. Music Va. Mil.
  m. Catherine Roush — daughter Elvira m. Alexander Keeney

Ragan, Jacob b. Ky. d. Mo. 1878 m. Anna C. Carter   Pvt. Ky. Mil.
  son Stephen m. Josephine Childs

Ragland, Fendall   Vol. 15   Pvt. Va. Mil.

Ragland, John b. Va. d. Ky. 1832 m. Ann Dubley   Qtr. Mst. Sgt. Va. Mil.
  daughter Anne m. Henry Hopson Jr.

Ragsdale, Elijah b. Va. 1758 d. Ga. 1837 m. Mary Kennedy   Pvt. Ga. Mil.
  son John C. m. Nancy Lucas

Ragsdale, William b. Va. d. Ark. 1819   Pvt. U.S. Ranger
  m. Sarah Campbell — son James C. m. Rebecca Moss
  son Charles Campbell m. Sarah Scallorn

Rahn, John Michael b. Pa. 1755 d. Pa. 1795   2nd Lt. Pa. Mil.
  m. Mrs. Sophia Ross — son Melchoir m. Sarah Kapp

Rahn, Melchoir b. Pa. 1781 d. Pa. 1849 m. Sarah Kapp   Qtr. Mst. Pa. Mil.
  son David m. Hannah Pugh Davis

Raiford, Alexander Gray b. Ga. 1784 d. Ga. 1854   Ens. Ga. Mil.
  m. Eliza Battey — daughter Eliza R. m. Louis Numa Falligant

Raiford, John b. N.C. c. 1730 d. Ga. 1812   Pat. Justice Ga. 1787
  m. Lucy Spell — son Maurice m. (2) Asenath

Railey, Thomas b. Va. 1754 d. Ky. 1822 m. Martha Woodson Capt. Va. Mil.
  daughter Jane m. John Henry Berryman

Railsback, Thomas Fisher b. Va. 1795 d. Ill. 1864   Pvt. Va. Regt.
  m. Louisa — son James E. m. Susan
  daughter Mary Ellen m. Rodney J. Mitchell

Raines, William   Vol. 13   Pvt. Va. Mil.

Rainey, William b.—d. N.C. 1816 m. Mary Vol. 68   Pat. N.C.

Rainey (Raney) Zebulon b. 1779 d. Tenn. 1864   Pvt. Miss. Mil.
  m.— Henderson — son Isaac m. Parthena Rainey (cousin)

Rains, William Green b. S.C. 1797 d. Ga. 1860   Pvt. Ga. Mil.
  m. Catherine Elizabeth Boulware
  daughter Nancy Elizabeth m. Jeptha Boulware Pickett

Rall, Jacob b. S.C. d. S.C. m.—   Pat. Deputy Sheriff S.C.
  son Thomas m.—

Ralls, Charles b. Va. 1781 d. m. Anne Browne   Pvt. Va. Mil.
  son Nathaniel B. m. Anne Smither

Ralls, Robert b. N.C. 1795 d. Ill. 1856 m. Martha Edwards Pvt. Ky. Mil.
  daughter Susannah m. Thomas Williams
  son William m. Susan Dinnell

Ralston, James b. Scot. 1761 d. Ohio 1833   Pvt. Ohio Mil.
  m. Isabelle Ellison — daughter Margaret m. Wesley Satterfield

Ralston, William b.—d. Pa. 1862 m.— Vol. 19   Col. Pa. Mil.
son John A. m. Elizabeth A. Ladd

Ramey, Daniel b. Va. 1787 d. Ga. 1852 m. Mary Morton   4th Sgt. Ga. Vol.
daughter Sarah Ann m. John Evans Robinson

Ramey, John b. Va. 1785 d. Va. 1872 m. Mary Henry   Pvt. Va. Mil.
daughter Malinda m. Elison Brown

Ramey, William b. Ky. 1790 d. Ky. 1823 m. Jane Sanders   Pvt. Ky. Mil.
son James M. m. Nancy Reddick

Ramsay, William Vol. 5   Pvt. Ohio Mil.

Ramsdell, Aquila b. Mass. 1756 d. N.H. 1844   Pat. N.H. 1801
m. Esther Brown — daughter Italy m. Zadoc L. Taft

Ramsdell, Horace b. Mass. 1797 d. Ohio 1872 m. Sarah Bullard   Pat. Ohio
son Horace V. m. Alma Louise Bardwell

Ramsey, Albert Vol. 12   Pvt. Va. Mil.

Ramsey, John b. Pa. 1781 d. Ohio 1812   Capt. Ohio Mil.
m. Nancy McLaughlin — son George m. Margaret Kyle

Ramsey, Jonathan b. Va. 1775 d. Mo. 1860   Brig. Gen. Ky. Mil. 1812
m. Hannah Lamkin — daughter Jane m. Robert A. Ewing

Ramsey, Joseph b. Pa. 1798 d. Pa. 1866   Pvt. U.S. Inf.
m. Margaret Jane O'Conner
son Thomas m. Martha Van Sickles

Ramsey, Thomas Vol. 4   Capt. Rifle Regt.

Ramsey, William b. Va. 1776 d. Ohio 1861   Capt. Ohio Mil.
m. Rebecca Miller — daughter Jane m. William Huston

Ramsey, William b. S.C. 1795 d. S.C. aft. 1830 m. Nancy Giles Cpl. S.C. Mil.
daughter Susan Nancy m. Christopher Hilary Plant

Rancier, George Sr. b. N.Y. 1756 d. N.Y. 1840   2nd Sgt. N.Y. Mil. 1813
m. Anna Barbara — son Peter m. Althea Bordman

Rand, Barzilla b. Mass. (Me.) 1791 d. Me. 1861   Pvt. Mass. (Me.) Mil.
m. Thankful Garcelon — daughter Joan m. Albert Pierce

Randy, Nehemiah Vol. 9   Pvt. N.Y. Mil.

Randall, Abraham b. N.H. 1731 d. N.H. 1804 m. Sarah Lyon Pat. N.H. 1786
son Abraham Jr. m. Elizhaba Talbot

Randall, Elias b. N.Y. 1790 d. Ill. 1867 m. Mindwell Corning Pvt. Vt. Mil.
daughter Louise m. Elias Hinzie

Randall, George b. (W.)Va. 1794 d. Kansas 1878   Pvt. Va. Mil.
m. Mary Wynkoop — daughter Mary m. Joseph A. Weller
son William M. m. Rebecca E.

Randall, John b. Md. 1774 d. Md. 1851 m. Caroline Killen   Pat. Md.
daughter Mary m. Thomas Bond

Randell, Peter, b. N.Y. 1793 d. N.Y. 1867   Cpl. N.Y. Mil.
m. Catherine Hammond
daughter Rachel Amelia m. Cornelius Suydam Vanderhoof

Randolph, John b. Va. 1773 d. Ga. 1856   Lt. Ga. Mil.
m. Nancy Ann Hinton — son Joshua H. m. Nancy Oliver

Randolph, Thomas Beverly b. Va. 1792 d. Ia. 1867   Capt. U.S. Army
   m. Maria Barbara Mayer
   daughter Martha Elizabeth m. John High Keim

Randon, Robert b. Md. 1786 d. Md. 1819 m. Margery Ray   Pvt. Md. Mil.
   son James M. m. Hannah Cooper

Rankin, George b. Pa. 1779 d. Pa. 1868 m. Nancy Cowan   Pvt. Pa. Mil.
   son Alexander m. (1) Sarah J. Paden

Rankin, James b. Pa. 1770 d. Ill. 1839   Pvt. Tenn. Mil.
   m. Margaret Massey — daughter Isabel m. William W. Bryant

Rankin, James b. Va. 1762 d. Va. 1822 m. Mary   Lt. Va. Mil.
   daughter Mary m. William Sillings, Jr.

Rankin, John b. Ire. 1775 d. Pa. 1871 m. Mary Robb   Pvt. Pa. Mil.
   daughter Teresa m. Joseph LaFayette Budd

Rankin, John Kieth b. Ky. 1791 d. Tex. 1884   Sgt. Miss. Mil.
   m. Elizabeth Butler — daughter Malinda C. m. Valentine Cook

Ranney, Willett b. Conn. 1731 d. N.Y. 1818 m. Mary Butler Vol. N.Y. Mil.
   daughter Sybil m. Richard Willis
   son Willett m. Betsey Robbins

Ranson, Barzillia b. N.Y. 1795 d. N.Y. 1851 m. Mary Conley Cpl. N.Y. Mil.
   son Barzillia Jr. m. Harriet Jane Spelman

Ranson, George Palmer b. Conn. 1762 d. Pa. 1850   Lt. Col. Pa. Mil.
   m. Olive Utley — daughter Esther m. Abijah Smith
   daughter Lyvia m. Oliver Davenport
   son William m. Clarissa Davenport

Ranson, Hubbel b. Mass. 1787 d. Mich. 1862   Pvt. N.Y. Mil.
   m. Charlotte Elizabeth Graves
   daughter Helen m. William Hobson

Rasmussen, Andrew Sr. b. Denmark 1755 d. K/A Lake Ontario 1813
   m. Catherine Schryder   Gunner 1813 Navy
   son Andrew Jr. m. Sarah Irwin

Ratcliff, John Vol. 8   Pvt. Miss. Mil.

Rathbone, John Vol. 12   Pat. Legis. N.Y.

Rathbone, William Palmer b. N.J. 1782 d. W.Va. 1862 Paymst. U.S. Army
   daughter Mary B. m. John Atkinson

Rathbun, Valentine Whitman b. Vt. 1792 d. Ind. 1876 Pvt. N.Y. Mil.
   m. Mary Isabelle Hamilton
   daughter Nettie m. William F. Lindley REAL DAUGHTER
   daughter Minnie R. L. m. Ulyses McElroy REAL DAUGHTER

Rathburn, Joel b. N.Y. 1779 d. N.Y. 1820   Surgeon N.Y. Mil.
   m. Philomela Alden — daughter Dorlisha m. Luther Pratt

Rattan (Rottan) Thomas b. S.C. 1789 d. Tex. 1854 Pvt. Ill. Rangers
   m. Mary Green — son Thomas m. Gillian Hill

Rauch, Philip b. Pa. 1784 d. Ohio 1841   Pvt. Ohio Mil.
   m. Susannah Alspaugh — son John m. Naomi Wisley

Rawlings, Benjamin b. Va. 1791 d. Va. 1848   Pvt. Va. Mil.
   m. Clarissa Morris Lawrence
   daughter Elizabeth m. Lewis A. Boggs

Rawlins, Joseph b. Ky. 1796 d. Ind. 1885 m. Sallie McManus Pvt. Ind. Mil.
   daughter Susan E. m. David Thomas Mitchell
   daughter Mary m. Benjamin A. Hickman REAL DAUGHTER

Rawlins, Levi b. Va. 1788 d. Va. 1824 m. Eliza Hansborough   Pvt. Va. Mil.
daughter Frances V. m. Charles Hume

Rawlins, Thomas b. Va. 1784 d. Mo. 1851 m. Esther   4th Cpl. Ky. Mil.
son Commodore Perry m. Pauline Adams

Rawson, Samuel b. R.I. 1760 d. N.Y. 1814 m. Lydia Thurston   Pvt. N.Y. Mil.
son James m. Mary Franklin

Rawson, Samuel b. Mass. 1771 d. Me. 1829 m. Polla Freeland   Lt. Mass. Mil.
daughter Mary Ann m. Simeon Fuller

Ray, David b. N.C. 1794 d. N.C. aft. 1840 m. Annie Hatch   Pvt. N.C. Mil.
daughter Rhoda E. m. Isaiah Cates

Ray, Enos b. Md. 1792 d. D.C. 1881 m. Elizabeth Osborn   Pvt. Md. Mil.
daughter Martha m. Charles M. Keys

Ray, Simeon b. N.Y. 1781 d. N.Y. 1831   Ens. & Lt. N.Y. Mil.
m. Cornelia Simmons — son William H. m. Mabel Tolles

Ray, William b. Md. 1788 d. Md.1827 m. Eliza Ann Blake   Capt. Md. Mil.
son John B. m. Susanna Botfield

Raymond, Jonathan b. Mass. 1768 d. Mass. 1823 m.—   Pvt. Vt. Mil.
son Jonathan Jr. m. Catherine Holt

Raymond, Joshua b. Conn. 1723 d. Conn. 1790   Pat. Conn.
m. Lucy Jewett — daughter Charlotte m. Benajah Cardiner

Raymond, William b. Conn. 1747 d. N.Y. 1832   Sgt. Conn. Mil.
m. Ruth Hoyt — son Nathan H. m. Marcia Kellogg

Raynolds, William   Vol. 1 or 2   Pvt. Mich. Mil.

Raynolds, William   Vol. 8   Major Ohio Mil.

Rea, John b. Pa. 1755 d. Pa. 1829   Maj. Gen. Pa. Mil.
m. Elizabeth Culbertson — son Charles m. Elizabeth Cochrane
son William m. Matilda Robinson

Read, Elisha   Vol. 11   N.Y. Vol.

Read, Gideon b. Mass. 1779 d. N.Y. 1853   Lt. N.Y. Art.
m. Martha Read (cousin) — daughter Martha J. m. George Smith

Read, Joel b. N.J. 1787 d. N.J. 1846   Pvt. N.J. Blues
m. Margaret Mason — son John S. m. Margaret

Read, Thomas b. Mass. 1746 d. Vt. 1814 m. Ruth Carriel   Pvt. Vt. Mil.
daughter Ruth m. Salmon Wright

Read, William   Vol. 11   Pvt. Tenn. Mil.

Read, William b. Va. 1766 d. Tenn. 1854   Gunman Tenn. Vol.
m. Mary Bledsoe — daughter Martha m. Francis Rogan

Reading, Thomas b. N.J. 1734 d. N.J. 1814   Justice N.J. 1788-9
m. Rebecca Ellis — daughter Deborah m. David Bartron   1793-99

Ready, Charles b. 1770 d. 1859 m. Mary Palmer   Pat. Tenn.
daughter Jane m. Maj. Peter Coleman Talley

Reams, Bartlet b. Va. 1775 d. La. 1815 m. Sarah Driskill   Pvt. U.S. Inf.
daughter Nancy m. Joel Davis
daughter Jane m. Alfred Jefferson Moyers Sr.

Reagan, Philip b. Va. 1756 d. Pa. 1848 m. Esther Campbell   Pat. Pa. 1794
son Alexander m. Catherine

Reavis, Charles   Vol. 16   Pvt. Ill. Mil.

Reavis, Isham   Vol. 12   Pvt. U.S. Rangers

Rector, Stephen b. Va. 1762 d. Mo. 1828   Lt. U.S. Rangers
   m. Lydia Mary Ann Lee — son Jesse H. m. Cynthia Simpson Strother

Redden, Reuben b. Va. 1795 d. Ohio 1870 m. Nancy Lingo   Pvt. Ohio Mil.
   daughter Elvira m. Mark Crawford
   daughter Susannah Gertrude m. William Colbert Hatfield
   REAL DAUGHTER

Reddick, Jacob b. Pa. d. Pa. 1825 m. Maria Stough   Pvt. Pa. Vol.
   son John m. Lydia Pechart

Reddig, Henry b. Pa. 1779 d. Pa. 1855 m. Julia Reinoehl   Pvt. N.Y. Mil.
   son Jeremiah B. m. Barbara Ann Heck

Reddish, Joseph b. Va. 1783 d. Ky. 1873   Capt. Va. Mil.
   m. Lucy Lee Templeman
   daughter Frances m. Crawford Hart Barkley

Redfield, Heman J.   Vol. 1 or 2   Pvt. N.Y. Mil.

Redfield, James G.   Vol. 13   Sgt. N.Y. Mil.

Redfield, James Wilcox b. N.J. 1787 d. N.Y. 1854   Fifer N.Y. Mil.
   m. Olive De Camp
   daughter Augusta L. m. Benjamin F. Simpson REAL DAUGHTER

Redfield, Luther b. Mass. 1780 d. Mich. 1867 m. Mary Dryer   Capt. N.Y. Mil.
   son Berliah S. m. Cornelia Nancy Parkinson

Redfield, Sylvester b. Conn. 1776 d. Conn. 1841   Cpl. Conn. Mil.
   m. Clarissa Bronson — son Robert m. Betsey Stone

Redgrave, Samuel   Vol. 7   Pvt. Md. Mil.

Redin, George b. Va. 1780 d. La. 1864   Pvt. La. Mil.
   m. (2) Elizabeth DeArmand
   daughter Elizabeth m. Joseph R. Hackney REAL DAUGHTER

Redin, John b. Va. bef. 1760 d.— m. Sidney Sevier   Pvt. S.C. Mil.
   son George m. Elizabeth DeArmand

Redman, Jacob b. Pa. 1771 d. Ohio 1849   Pvt. Ohio Mil.
   m. Catharine Hemerling — son Henry m. Maria Irey

Reece, Daniel b. N.C. 1773 d. N.C. 1818 m. Rachel Hadley   Pvt. N.C. Mil.
   son John m. Elizabeth Crutchfield

Reece, John b. N.Y. 1786 d. N.Y. 1850   Pvt. N.Y. Mil.
   m. Catherine Johnson — daughter Harriett m. Michael Reece

Reed, Allen b. Pa. 1782 d. Ohio 1864   Lt. Ohio Mil.
   m. Margaret McGriff — son James Collins m. Rhoda Ward

Reed, David b. Pa. 1792 d. 1865 m. Elizabeth Mitchell   Pvt. Pa. Mil.
   daughter Esther m. Thomas McCleary

Reed, George b. Me. 1794 d. at sea 1830 m. Hannah Allen   Pvt. Mass. Mil.
   son Elijah W. m. Rebecca Herrick

Reed, Hamilton b. Va. 1792 d. Ind. 1843 m. Rebecca Pound   Pvt. Ind. Mil.
   daughter Eunice m. John E. Hunt

Reed, Henry Lucoricus b. Mass. 1790 d. Pa. 1886   Pvt. Va. Mil.
   m. Charlotte Stickney — daughter Charlotte m. William Smiley Everett

Reed, James   Vol. 9   Pvt. Pa. Mil.
daughter Jane m. John O'Donel REAL DAUGHTER

Reed, Jesse Emerson b. Ire. d. Tenn. m. Mary Andrews   Pvt. Tenn. Mil.
son John S. m. Nancy Elvira Martin

Reed, John b. Ky. 1784 d. Ill. 1858 m. Katherine Weight   Pvt. Ky. Mil.
daughter Ann Jane m. Samuel Reynolds

Reed, John (Denny) b. N.C. 1784 d. Mo. 1870   Pvt. N.C. Mil.
m. Elizabeth Jenkins — son Thomas B. m. Rachel E. Denny

Reed, John H. b. Mass. d. Mo. m.—   Lt. Mass. Art.
son John H. Jr. m. Amelia Heldt

Reed, John Savage b. 1784 d. N.Y. 1878 m. Submit Joiner   Sgt. N.Y. Mil.
son Samuel G. m. Abigail Anna Miller

Reed, Joseph b. Mass. 1793 d. Mass. 1866   Sgt. Mass. Mil.
m. Wealthy Williams — son Freedman W. m. Ruth Lucina Cole

Reed, Joseph H. b. N.J. 1793 d. Ill. 1847 m. Eliza Bell   Pvt. N.J. Mil.
daughter Eliza Ann m. Aaron Bunn
daughter Fanny Amelia m. Simmons Gunn REAL DAUGHTER

Reed, Josiah b. Mass. (Me.) 1760 d. Me. 1849   Maj. Mass. Vol.
m. Sarah Davis — son Charles A. m. Sarah Grant

Reed, Michael b. Pa. 1777 d. Texas 1859   Pvt. Pa. Mil. 1814
m. Martha Burnett — daughter Sarah m. William C. Sparks

Reed, Paul Jr. b.— d.— m. Mary Reed   Pvt. Me. Mil.
son Francis m. Martha Frances Kennedy

Reed, Robert   Vol. 6   Pvt. Pa. Mil.

Reed, Samuel b. Conn. 1794 d. Ohio 1865 m. Hannah Brown   Pvt. Conn. Mil.
son Samuel Jr. m. Georgiana

Reed, Thomas b. Pa. 1791 d. Mex. 1825 m. Stella McKnight   Cpl. Pa. Mil.
son Thomas Jr. m. Mary Patterson

Reed, Thomas Jr.   Vol. 16   Pvt. Vt. Mil.

Reed, Thomas b. Pa. 1759 d. Pa. 1813 m. Mary   Pat. Justice Pa.
daughter Elizabeth m. Samuel Rean Boyer

Reed, William b. Mass. 1783 d. N.Y. 1850   Pat. Aid to U.S. Army
m. Rebecca Nelson — son Thomas J. m. Eliza Chase

Reed, William b. 1794 d. Ohio 1866 m. Elizabeth McFarlin   Pvt. Ohio Mil.
daughter Catherine m. James Porter

Reed, William b. Pa. 1752 d. Pa. 1813   Adj. Gen. Pa. Mil.
m. Nancy Miller — son Samuel M. m. Mary Agnew
daughter Isabelle Mariah m. Richard Wilson Porter

Reed, William b. Mass. 1783 d. N.Y. 1850 m. Rebecca Nelson   Pat. N.Y. 1814
son Reuben R. m. Emily M. Hale

Reeder, Amos b. N.J. 1770 d. N.J. 1855 m. Mary Stillwell   Sgt. Pa. Mil.
daughter Mary S. m. Jasper Smith Scudder

Reeder, Richard H. Jr. b. Md. 1776 d. W.Va. 1878   Lt. W.Va. Mil.
m. Urah Butcher — daughter Jane Ellen m. Harman Ruble
daughter Priscilla m. Wm. L. Carder

Reel, Henry b. Ind. 1793 d. Ind. 1871 m. Katherine Neely   Pvt. Ind. Mil.
daughter Martha m. George Beloat

Rees (Reese) David b. Va. 1787 d. Ohio 1840   Sgt. Ohio Mil.
  m. Sarah Weyer — daughter Margaret m. Henry Foraker
  daughter Harriet m. William Elliott

Rees, James b. Pa. 1764 d. N.Y. 1851   Capt. N.Y. 1814
  m. Elizabeth Reynolds — son Charles m. Catherine Hallett

Reese, Cuthert b. Va. 1781 d. Ga. 1855 m. Tabitha Clark   Pvt. Ga. Mil.
  daughter Ann Eliza F. m. Dr. Benjamin F. Keene

Reese, George b. (W.)Va. 1774 d. W.Va. 1851   Cpl. Va. Mil.
  m. Nancy Jones — daughter Anzy m. Samuel Linn

Reeves, Manasseh b. N.Y. 1796 d. Ia. 1868 m. Ester Perry   Pvt. N.Y. Mil.
  son William P. m. Katherine Case

Regal, Abraham b. Pa. 1776 d. Pa. 1875 m. Elizabeth Sippy   Pvt. Pa. Mil.
  daughter Christina Jane m. William Samuel Fisher
  daughter Lucretia m. Joseph Drinkwine

Regan, Ralph b. N.C. 1776 d. Miss. 1833 m. Phoebe White   Capt. Miss. Inf.
  daughter Ann Matilda m. Thomas W. Brown

Regar, Henry b. Pa. 1788 d. Pa. 1856 m. Eve Keplinger   Pvt. Pa. Mil.
  son Cyrus K. m. Eliza Grant Hornberger

Reger, Abram b. Va. 1795 d. W.Va. 1886 m. Leah Brake   Lt. Va. Mil.
  son Albert G. m. Mary Rebecca Seay

Rehrer, Godfrey b. Pa. 1769 d. Pa. 1823   Capt. Ky. Mil.
  m. Eva Elizabeth Seisz — daughter Anna Maria m. John Kurr

Reid, Alexander b. N.C. 1768 d. Ga. 1832   Capt. Ga. Mil. 1790
  m. Elizabeth Brewer — son David Henry m. Sarah Adams
  son William m. Martha Wingfield

Reid, James b. Ga. 1795 d. Ala. 1853 m. Elizabeth Goodwin   Pvt. Ga. Inf.
  son James M. m. Susan W. Odem
  daughter Elizabeth m. T. J. S. Sanford

Reid, James b. Va. 1778 d. Ga. 1855 m. Rebecca Duke   Pvt. Ga. Mil.
  daughter Elizabeth m. William Wilfrey Peek
  daughter Martha S. m. Robert Simms Burch

Reid, Jesse b. Va. 1791 d. Ga. 1861 m. Susan Maclin   Lt. Va. Mil.
  daughter Anne Eliza m. Ebenezer Davies McKinley

Reid, John b. S.C. 1765 d. S.C. 1818 m. Mary Harden   Pvt. S.C. Mil.
  daughter Phoebe m. Henry White Inzer

Reid, John b. Va. 1784 d. Va. 1816   Maj. Tenn. Mil.
  m. Elizabeth Branch Maury
  son John Jr. m. Margaret Louisa Trimble

Reid, John S. b. N.J. 1780 d. Ohio 1831   Indian Fighter Ohio
  m. Ann Schuyler — son Conrad m. Abigail Murdock
  daughter Elizabeth m. Quartus Gillmore and Harry Brooks

Reid, Robert b. Ga. d. Ga. 1814 m. Susannah Stallings   Capt. Ga. Mil.
  son Archibald M. m. Elizabeth Ann Herbert

Reid, Samuel b. 1728 d. Ga. 1810 m. Agnes Kay   Pat. Justice Sheriff
  daughter Margaret m. John Bailey   Ga. 1808

Reiff, David b. Pa. 1798 d. Md. 1890 m. Anna (Nancy) Horst   Pvt. Pa. Mil.
  daughter Susan m. Abraham Lesher

Reiff, Jacob b. Pa. 1734 d. Pa. 1816   Pat. Legis. Pa. 1786/9
m. Rachel Pauling — daughter Cathoonie m. Jacob Groff

Renick, Henry b. Va. 1766 d. Mo. 1843 m. Prudence Hall   Col. Ky. Vol.
daughter Elizabeth m. Young Ewing
daughter Keziah m. John W. Warder

Reph, Henrich (Henry) b. 1771 d. 1833 m. Barbara Heiny   Pvt. Pa. 1814
son Peter m. Susanna Mersch

Rettew, Aaron Jr. b. Pa. 1753 d. Pa. 1811   Lt. Pa. Mil.
m. Rebecca Aston and Elizabeth McCloud
son William m. Ann Packingham by 1st wife
son Charles m. Sarah Bull by 2nd wife

Rex, William b. Pa. 1790 d. Pa. 1863 m. Mary Minnich   Pvt. Pa. Vol.
son Michael M. m. Elizabeth C. Bloom

Reynnells, Benjamin b. Vt. 1786 d. Mich. 1855   Sgt. Maj. Ohio Mil.
m. Mary Mitchell — daughter Experience m. Anson H. Hathaway

Reynolds, Amos b. N.Y. 1759 d. N.Y. 1830   Pvt. N.Y. Mil.
m. Elizabeth Mosher — daughter Sarah m. James Pendleton

Reynolds, Elisha b. 1782 d. 1852 m. Rachel Von Hossen   2nd Lt. N.Y. Mil.
daughter Pauline Catherine m. Caleb Joshua Carpenter

Reynolds, Ichabod b. Mass. 1773 d. Me. 1855   Capt. Mass. Mil.
m. Polly Brett — daughter Betsey m. J. Leonard Farrington

Reynolds, Jacob b. N.Y. 1788 d, N.Y. 1872 m. Sarah Wood   Pvt. N.Y. Mil.
son John m. Margaret Hislop

Reynolds, Jonathan b. Engl. d. R.I. 1814   Capt. R.I. on Privateer
m. Hester Hannah Owen — daughter Harriet Ann m. Caleb Baldwin

Reynolds, Joseph b. N.C. 1780 d. Ky. 1868   Pvt. N.C. Inf.
m. Mary Reynolds (cousin) — son Richard m. Mary Boyd

Reynolds, Nathaniel Gardner b. Mass. 1794 d. Ill. 1865   Sgt. N.Y. Mil.
m. Phoebe B. Brace — son Linius C. m. Sarah M. Conner

Reynolds, Nathaniel Sr. b. Va. 1770 d. Ill. bet. 1850-60   Pvt. Ky. Mil.
m. Elizabeth Ann Bowyer
son Nathaniel Jr. m. Mary Aurelia Clopton

Reynolds, Nathanial   Vol. 15   Drummer & Sgt. Mass. Mil.

Reynolds, Oliver b. Ohio 1794 d. Ohio 1866   Pvt. Ohio Mil.
m. Zilphia Middlewart — son Stephen m. Maria Moore

Reynolds, Richard b. Va. 1790 d. Tenn. 1835 m. Mary Stone   Pvt. Va. Mil.
son George Alfred m. Mary Elizabeth Cook

Reynolds, Robert b. Pa. ca. 1781 d. Ohio 1848   Pvt. Pa. Mil.
m. Elizabeth Shall — daughter Maria m. Asa Ellis

Reynolds, Thomas b. Va. 1776 d. Ga. 1828 m. Margaret   Capt. Ga. Mil.
son Thomas Jr. m. Mary Ann Baker

Reynolds, Williams b. S.C. 1783 d. Tenn. 1841   Ens. S.C. Mil.
m. Candance Matthews — son William Jr. m. Jasmor Matthews

Rhea, Robert b. Ire. 1784 d. Tenn. 1841 m. Elizabeth   Maj. Tenn. Mil.
son John W. m. Adaline Dodson
daughter Margaret m. Samuel Woods
daughter Sarah m. George W. Gaines

Rhea (Ray), James b. Va. 1780 d. Ill. 1843 m. Rachel Joliff   Pvt. Ky. Mil.
son John m. Julia A. Stark

Rhoades, Jonthan b. Pa. 1772 d. Pa. 1829   Capt. Pa. Mil.
   m. Barbara Wolgemuth — son Samuel m. Mary Ankeney

Rhodes, David b. N.Y. 1799 d. Ill. 1874   Pvt. N.Y. Mil.
   m. (2) Caroline Christine Carter
   daughter Elizabeth E. m. Edward Hill Lyman REAL DAUGHTER

Rhodes, David Addison b. Vt. 1797 d. Mich. 1857   Pvt. N.Y. Mil.
   m. Mary Parmenter — daughter Sally Aurilla m. Levi Merchant

Rhodes, John b. N.H. 1795/6 d. N.H. 1875 m. Sarah Streeter   Pvt. N.H. Mil.
   son John m. Rosina Taylor

Riblet, Solomon b. Md. 1782 d. Pa. 1853 m. Mary Riper   Capt. Pa. Mil.
   son Samuel m. Deborah Woods

Riblet, Michael b. Pa. 1779 d. Pa. 1851   2nd Sgt. Pa. Mil.
   m. Hannah Walker(2) — son Thomas C. m. Caroline Blair

Rice, Abel b. Mass. 1789 d. N.Y. 1871 m. Diana Doty   Pvt. N.Y. Mil.
   son Charles m. Elizabeth Louch

Rice, Edward b. Va. 1785 d. Ky. 1878 m. Annie Utz   Pvt. Va. Mil.
   daughter Emily m. John Stephens

Rice, Gardner b. Mass. 1767 d. Vt. aft. 1812 m. Lydia   Pat. Vt.
   daughter Patty m. Abel Colburn

Rice, Hercules b. Mass. 1765 d. N.Y. 1831   Lt. Col. N.Y. Mil.
   m. Mary Dewey — daughter Mary m. John King

Rice, Joel P.   Vol. 16   Lt. N.Y. Mil.

Rice, John F.   Vol. 5   Midshipman Pa.

Rice, John b. 1776 d. 1843 m. Jane McNight   Soldier Ind. & Ohio
   son Samuel J. m. Serepta Marshall

Rice, John Walter b. 1793 d. Va. 1862   Surgeon 1812 Va.
   m. Anna Maria Gilliam — son Jacob Walter m. Anna Maria Henkel
   son Richard Stafford m. Sarah Ann Newman

Rice, Roswell b. N.Y. 1783 d. Ohio 1861 m. Nancy Keyes   Pvt. N.Y. Mil.
   son Harvey m. (2) Martha Hoxter

Rice, Simon Stevens b. N.Y. 1794 d. Wisc. 1888   Pvt. N.Y. Mil.
   m. Elizabeth Harrington — son Samuel T. m. Matilda Judd

Rice, Theodorick Bland b. Va. 1781 d. Tenn. 1839   Lt. Tenn. Mil.
   m. Mary Crockett Harbert
   daughter Sarah Angeline m. William Bennett

Rice, William b. N.C. 1780 d. Tenn. 1859 m. Sarah Harper   Pvt. Tenn. Mil.
   son Henry A. C. m. Elizabeth Hester

Rice, William b. N.Y. 1789 d. N.Y. 1864 m. Rachel Waldo   Lt. N.Y. Mil.
   son William S. m. Sarah K. Davis

Rice, William b. S.C. 1791 d. S.C. 1871 m. Martha Tindal   Sgt. S.C. Mil.
   son Henry B. m. Narcissa Wright
   daughter Matilda Ann m. John Griggsby Smith

Rice, William Sr. b. Mass. 1737 d. Mass. 1819   Pat. Mass. 1783-90
   m. Sarah Noyes — son William Jr. Charlotte Whitman

Rice, William Jr. b. Mass. 1782 d. Mass. 1860   Capt. Mass. Mil.
    m. Charlotte Whitman — son John W. m. Martha Almarine Gerry

Rich, Calmi   Vol. 9   Vice Commander N.Y. Mil.

Rich, Charles b. Mass. 1771 d. Vt. 1824   Pat. Vt. Legis. 1813-15
    m. Molly Watts — son David m. Affia Wright

Rich, John Jr. b. N.Y. 1761 d. N.Y. 1849   Pvt. N.Y. Mil.
    m. Susanna Putney — son Ebenezer m. Mira Chappel Smith
    son Joel Sr. m. Jennette Higgins

Rich, Joel Sr. b. N.Y. 1787 d. N.Y. 1871   Pvt. N.Y. Mil.
    m. Jeannette Higgins
    son Gussie m. Edward Long III REAL DAUGHTER

Rich, Jonathan b. Mass. d. N.Y. m. Anna Sanders   Pvt. N.Y. Mil.
    son George W. m. Nina May Proctor

Rich, Thomas b. N.C. 1783 d. Ill. 1868 m. Catherine Noah   Pvt. Tenn. Mil.
    son George m. Sarah Owen
    son John M. m. Anne Uffendale
    son William C. m. Millicent Guthrie

Rich, Thomas b. N.C. 1783 d. Ill. 1866 m. Polly Ann   Pvt. Tenn. Mil.
    son Jacob Sr. m. Susan Dallas

Richards, Augustus b. Va. 1780 d. Ia. 1851   Surgeon's Mate Ohio Mil.
    m. Frances Lee Doggett — daughter Frances A. m. Alex Liles

Richards, Cyrus G. b. N.J. 1794 d. N.J. 1857   Pvt. N.J. Mil.
    m. Hannah Smith Force — son George W. m. Lydia Amelia Deland

Richards, David b. Conn. 1760 d. Pa. 1837   Pat. Pa. 1790-7
    m. Susannah Dilley — son William m. Mary Pruner

Richards, Matthias b. Pa. 1758 d. Pa. 1830   Justice Judge Pa. 1791/7
    m. (2) Maria Salome Muhlenberg — son John W. m. Andora Garber

Richards, Richard Sr. b. Va. 1780 d. Va. 1855   Pvt. Va. Rifleman
    m. Mary Adams — son Richard m. Nancy Overton

Richards, Street b. Conn. 1750 d. Vt. 1835   Capt. Conn. Mil. 1794
    m. Eunice Culver — son Luther Abijah m. Polly Page

Richards, William b. Va. 1782 d. Ala. 1850 m. Nancy Warren   Pvt. Va. Rgt.
    son Thomas W. m. Temperance Smith

Richardson, Abel b. c. 1773 d. Ill. 1838 m. Nancy Hayes   Pvt. Tenn. Mil.
    son Isaac m. Nancy Denton

Richardson, Abijah b. Mass. 1752 d. Mass. 1822   Surgeon Mass. Mil.
    m. Mercy Daniels — daughter Mercy m. John Steadman

Richardson, Abiathar b. Mass. 1749 d. Mass. 1832   Capt. Mass. Mil.
    m. Martha Faulkner — daughter Polly m. Thomas Williams

Richardson, Amstead b. Va. 1788 d. Ga. 1866   2nd Lt. Ga. Mil.
    m. Elizabeth Griggs — son Dr. E. H. Sr. m. Mary F. Janes

Richardson, Benjamin b. Mass. 1732 d. Mass. 1821   Pat. Legis. Justice Mass.
    m. Abigail French — son William m. Prudence Burpee

Richardson, Freeman b. N.Y. 1791 d. N.Y. 1875   Cpl. N.Y. Mil.
    m. Lavinia Fullmore — son Amaziah F. m. Betsey Taylor

Richardson, Ebenezer b. Mass. 1766 d. N.H. 1850   Pat. Selectman N.H.
    m. Rhoda Coolidge   1811-15
    daughter Sarah m. Solomon Van R. Allen

Richardson, Isaac   Vol. 7   Pat. Mich.

Richardson, Israel Putnam   Vol. 10   Pat. Vt. 1807

Richardson, John b. Ky. 1792 d. Ky. 1875 m. Barbara Park   Pvt. Ky. Mil.
  son Dudley m. Mary Jane Adams

Richardson, John   Vol. 2   Capt.
  son Samuel O. m. Sarah Bainbridge

Richardson, John b. Ga. 1776 d. Tenn. 1879 m. Mary Horner   Pvt. Tenn. Mil.
  daughter Jemima m. John McNairy Tinin

Richardson, John Smythe Sr. b. S.C. 1777 d. S.C. 1850   Pat. S.C. 1810
  m. Mrs. Elizabeth L. Buford Couterier
  son John S. Jr. m. Sophia Hyatt

Richardson, John Thomas   Vol. 5   Pvt. Md. Mil.

Richardson, Jonathan Jr. b. N.J. 1762 d. N.Y. 1850   Prisoner of War 1813
  m. Rhoda Thompson — son Jonathan III m. Miranda Moore

Richardson, Philip b. 1793 d. 1853 m. Nancy (Ann) Owens   Pvt. La. Mil.
  daughter Magaret Ann m. Geo. W. Brannon

Richardson, Richard Jr. b. Md. 1742 d. Md. 1802/3   Pat. 1787
  m. Mary Pierpont — daughter Sarah m. Baylis Coombs

Richardson, Roswell b. Conn. 1793 d. N.H. 1886   Pvt. Conn. Mil.
  m. Mara Huntington — daughter Rachel Rebecca m. George S. Ellis

Richardson, Rufus   Vol. 7   Pvt. Conn. Troops

Richardson, Stephen b. Mass. 1737 d. Mass. 1808   Pat. Mass. Legis. 1785
  m. Mary Fuller — son Moses m. Eliza Andrews

Richardson, William b. Va. abt. 1765 d. Ky. 1825   Pvt. Ky. Mil.
  m. Susannah Stewart — son Thomas S. m. Mrs. Martha Downing Bell

Richardson, William   Vol. 4   Pat. Mem. Const. Conv.

Richardson, William b. Pa. 1741 d. Md. 1818   Wagon Mst. Pa. 1794
  m. Mary Salome Schneider   Whiskey Rebellion
  daughter Emily Elizabeth m. John Young

Richardson, William b.— d. 1810   Vol. 2   Col. Md.
  son John m. Sarah Bainbridge

Richardson, William b. Mass. 1776 d. Ill. 1855   Lt. N.Y. Mil.
  m. Sarah Norton — daughter Lurancie m. Nathan Pendleton Wilcox

Richert, Ludwig b. N.Y. 1756/7 d. N.Y. 1819   Lt. N.Y.
  m. Catharine Getman — daughter Naomi m. Johannes Vrooman

Richey, Andrew b. 1795 d. Ohio 1870 m. Sarah Rogers   Pvt. Ohio Mil.
  daughter Elizabeth m. Jeremiah Dunham

Richey, William b. Pa. 1768 d. Pa. 1862 m. Mary Pinkerton   Pvt. Pa. Mil.
  daughter Susan m. Charles Ross Thornberg

Richart, Jacob b. Pa. 1778 d. Ohio 1868   Capt. Ohio Mil.
  m. Elizabeth Griffith — daughter Penelope m. Anthony L. Davenport

Richmon (Richmond), Joseph b. 1786/7 d. Ill. 1831   Pvt. Ohio Mil.
  m. Nancy Iler — daughter Sarah Ann m. Hiram Heavenhill

Richmond, David   Vol. 8   Pvt. N.Y. Vol.

Richmond, George b. Mass. 1780 d. N.Y. 1843   Pvt. N.Y. Vol.
  m. Esther Thomas — daughter Elizabeth m. Solomon Pierce

Richstein, George Sr.   Vol. 4   Pvt. Md. Mil.

Rickabaugh, Adam b. Va. 1761 d. Ohio 1836 m. Mary Koontz Pvt. Ohio Mil.
daughter Ann m. Senet Allen
son Joseph m. Ritta Troth
daughter Mahala m. William Barker

Rickart, George Jr. b. N.Y. 1756 d. N.Y. m. Elizabeth Hawes Pvt. N.Y. Mil.
son David George m. Margaret Nashold

Rickert, Ludwig (Lodewick) b. N.Y. 1756/7 d. N.Y. 1817/9   Lt. N.Y. Mil.
m. Catherine Getman — daughter Naomi m. John L. Vrooman

Ricker, Amos b. Mass. 1795 d. Wisc. 1858   Pvt. U.S. Inf.
m. Charlotte Parkhurst — daughter Sarah m. Elisha Pierce

Riddick, Joseph   Vol. 12   Pat. Senator N.C. 1781-1811

Riddick, Thomas Fiveash b. Va. 1781 d. Mo. 1830   Pat. La. 1805-12
m. Eliza Minor Carr — daughter Virginia C. B. m. Edward Brooks

Riddle, Hugh b. N.Y. 1787 d. N.Y. 1865 m. Eleanor Reese   Sgt. U.S. Inf.
son John m. Anna Cauley

Riddle, James Akin   Vol. 8   Pvt. Mass. Mil.

Riddle (Riddell) Thomas b. Mass. 1781 d. Ohio 1823   Sgt. Mass. Mil.
m. Minerva Merrick — Jose M. m. Caroline Hayden

Ridenour John b. Pa. 1778 d. Ohio 1848 m. Susannah   Pvt. Ohio Mil.
daughter Eleanor m. Dimmit Mackrill

Ridenhour, John b. Md. 1782 d. Ohio 1847   Pvt. Ohio Mil.
m. Hannah Spohn — son Jacob Jr. m. Catherine Oats

Ridenhour, Martin b. Md. 1762 d. Ohio m. Betsy   Cpl. Ohio Mil.
daughter Elizabeth m. Ephraim Bull

Ridenour, Samuel b. Md. 1793 d. Ohio 1850   Pvt. Ohio Mil.
m. Barbara Miller — son Charles P m. Catharine Near

Rider, Benjamin b. Mass. 1775 d. Mass. 1838   Pvt. Mass. Mil.
m. Azubah Morse — son Elisha M. m. Susan Carey Maxim

Rider, Joseph b. Conn. 1780 d. N.Y. 1877 m. Mary Hill   Pvt. N.Y. Mil.
son Joseph Jr. m. Lucy Edwards

Rider, Joseph Sr. b. N.Y. 1779 d. Mich. 1862 m. Sarah Peck   Pvt. N.Y. Mil.
son Joseph Jr. m. Isabel Maria Fishbeck

Ridgely, Henry Moore b. Del. 1779 d. Del. 1847   Lt. Col. Del. Mil.
m. Sarah Banning — daughter Ann m. Charles I. du Pont
son Eugene m. May Ann Mifflin
son Nicholas m. May H. Tilden

Ridgely, Richard b. Md. 1774 d. Ill. 1863 m. Mary Humes   Pvt. Md. Mil.
son Daniel m. Sarah Jane Ingmand
daughter Elizabeth m. William Kidd

Ridley, Daniel b. Mass. (Me.) 1773 d. Me. 1852   Pvt. Mass. (Me.) Mil.
m. Paulina Williams — daughter Paulina m. Charles Graves

Ridley, George b. Tenn. 1797 d. Tenn. 1873   1st Cpl. Tenn. Mil.
m. May Vaughn — son Thomas J. m. Martha Burke

Ridley, Henry Bromfield b. Va. 1745 d. N.C. 1796 Commissioner N.C. 1786
m. Frances Keeling Henderson — son James m. Elizabeth T. Lewis

Ridley, John b. N.Y. 1795 d. N.Y. 1865 m. Maria Robinson   Cpl. N.Y. Mil.
daughter Anna Maria m. Rufus Erastus Crane

Ridgway, Thomas b. N.J. 1779 d. Pa. 1857 m. Mary Joy   Pvt. Pa. Cavalry
daughter Sarah Ann m. John Bannan

Riegel, John George b. Pa. 1776 d. Ohio 1848   Pvt. Ohio Mil.
m. Eve Rose Ann — son Benjamin m. Mary

Riffe, Christopher b. Md. 1764 d. Ky. 1850   Pvt. Ky. Mil.
m. (2) Elizabeth Coffee — son Peter B. m. Juliana Watkins
m. Mary Spears — son George m. Elizabeth Anderson

Riffe, John b. Va. d. Ky. 1883 m. Elizabeth Clay   Pvt. Va. Mil.
son William M. m. Elizabeth Short

Riggs, Gideon b. N.C. 1790 d. Tenn. 1871   Pvt. Tenn. Vol.
m. Sophia Campbell — daughter Mary C. m. William Wyatt Haley

Riggs, Henry b. N.J. 1790 d. Ind. 1859 m. Jane Mather   Cpl. Ohio Mil.
daughter Martha Ann m. Rufus Mellett Johnson

Riggs, Joseph Jr. b. Conn. 1746 d. Conn. 1822   Pat. Conn. Legis. 1796-1805
m. Elizabeth Johnson — son Ranford m. Deborah Baldwin

Riggs, Joseph Sr. b. Conn. d. Conn. m. Mabel Johnson Pat. Selectman Conn.
son Joseph J. m. Elizabeth Johnson

Riggs, Ranford b. Conn. 1783 d. Conn. 1832   Cpl. Conn. Mil.
m. Deborah Baldwin — son John S. m. Marie Padee

Riley Charles b. Va. 1793 d. Tenn. 1861   Pvt. Va. Mil.
m. Margaret Orr — daughter Elizabeth m. James F. Grant

Riley, George b. S.C. 1748 d. S.C. 1840   Pvt. S.C. Mil.
m. Catherine Gramline — daughter Catherine m. Conrad Kemmerlin

Riley, James b. N.Y. 1789/95 d. Ohio 1875/80   Pvt. Ohio Mil.
m. Mary Williams — son William m. Ann Burney

Riley, Richard b. Va. 1777 d. Ohio 1863 m. Elizabeth Day   Soldier
son Israel m. Massa Myers

Riley, William b. S.C. 1769 d. Ga. 1850 m. Margaret Powell   Pvt. Ga. Mil.
son David F. m. Mary Neal

Rilleux, Vincent b. La. 1736 d. La. 1800   Lt. La. Mil. 1784
m. Marie Antonia Tronquet
daughter Marie Eugenia m. James Freret

Rimel, John b. Pa. 1760 d. Tenn. 1828   Pat. Juror Tenn. 1812-14
m. Rebecca Lincoln — daughter Polly m. John Bird Jr.

Rinehart, Arthur Inghram b. Pa. 1793 d. Pa. 1872   Pvt. Pa. 1812
m. Rebecca Roberts — daughter Elizabeth m. Joheil Rinehart
son Wesley m. Sarah Hays

Ring, Samuel   Vol. 10   Pvt. Mass. Mil.

Ringgold, Samuel b. Md. 1772 d. Md. 1850 m. Rachael   Sgt. Md. Mil.
son Samuel Jr. m. Mary Smith

Ringgold, Samuel Jr. b. Md. 1800 d. Md. 1874 m. Mary Smith Pvt. Md. Mil.
son William S. m. Hester Livingston Thomas

Ringle, Mathias b. Ger. 1742 d. Pa. 1811 m. Margaret   Pvt. Pa. Mil.
daughter Margaret m. David King

Ringler, Reuben b. Pa. 1788 d. Pa. 1870 m. Sarah Wilson Pvt. Pa. Mil.
 son Anthony W. m. Mary Ann Major

Ringo, John R. b. Ky. 1790 d. Ky. 1857 2nd Sgt. Ky. Mil.
 m. Nancy Preston Lewis — son John L. m. Catherine Leer

Ringo, Robert b. Ky. 1789 d. Mo. 1841 m. Sarah Hodge Pvt. Ky. Mil.
 daughter Emily m. Daniel Smith

Rinker, Abraham b. Pa. 1756 d. Pa. 1820 m. Gertrude Stacey Col. Ky. Mil.
 daughter Elizabeth m. John Miller
 son John m. Sarah Reeser

Riordan, George b. Va. 1794 d. Ohio 1864 m. Sarah Downs Pvt. Va. Mil.
 daughter Sarah L. m. John Uncles

Ripley, Jotham b. (Me.) Mass. 1797 d. Wisc. 1860 Pvt. Mass. Mil.
 son Jotham J. m. Hannah Maria Holbrook

Rise, Isaac Jr. b. Pa. 1787 d. Pa. 1854 Pvt. Pa. Rifleman
 m. Elizabeth McMillen — son Isaac P. m. Margaret Gibson

Rising, Allen Vol. 17 Pvt. U.S. Inf.

Risley, Eli b. N.J. 1792 d. N.J. 1852 m. Aura Maria Ireland Pvt. N.J. Mil.
 son David F. m. Lucretia Barrett

Rison, Peter, b. Va. 1786 d. Ky. 1834 Sgt. Va. Mil.
 m. Sallie Bibb Booker — son John William m. Harriet Clifton Jones

Ritchey, James b. Md. 1757 d. Ohio 1838 m. Elizabeth Wilson Lt. Pa. Mil.
 daughter Jane m. Thomas Spencer
 daughter Rebecca W. m. Martin Berkey

Ritchey, William b. Va. d. S.C. m.— Pvt. Va. Mil.
 son John C. m. Jane Campbell

Ritchhart, Jacob Vol. 9 Capt. Ohio Mil.

Ritchie, James b. 1791 d. Pa. 1863 m. Esther Moore Pvt. Pa. Mil.
 son James m. Mary E. Wiltbank
 son Robert M. m. Alice Walker

Ritchie, Samuel b. Pa. 1788 d. Ohio 1815 Pvt. Ohio Mil.
 m. Elizabeth Humbert — son Newton S. m. Anne Gwynne

Ritchie, William b. Va. 1768 d. Pa. 1862 Pvt. Ky. Vol.
 m. Mary Pinkerton — daughter Susan m. Charles Thornburg

Ritscher, John Adam b. Pa. 1767 d. Pa. 1842 Col. Pa. Mil.
 m. Elizabeth Kurtz — son Israel Adam m. Catherine Shindel

Rittenhouse, Freeman Vol. 14 Cpl. Ohio Mil.

Rittenour (Ridenour), Jacob b. Va. 1787 d. Ohio 1883 Pvt. Ohio Mil.
 m. Ann Claypool — son Isaac N. m. Sarah Orr

Ritter, Henry b. Ky. 1788 d. Ohio 1859 m. Elizabeth Harbor Pvt. Ohio Vol.
 son Richard m. Sarah Kiser

Ritz (Ritts), Elias b. Pa. 1760 d. Pa. 1830 Pvt. Pa. Mil.
 m. Catherine Snyder — son John m. Sophia Schell

Rivers, Richard b. Va. 1751 d. N.C. aft. 1801 Pat. Mem. House N.C.
 m. Nancy — daughter Mary m. Hardy Avery 1794-1801

Roach, John W. b. Ky. 1789 d. Ind. 1870 m. Elizabeth Morgan   Pvt. Ind.
son Henry m. Frances Allen

Roane, Samuel Calhoun   Vol. 16   Sgt. Maj. Tenn. Mil.

Roane, Andrew b. 1792 d. 1874 m. Sarah Jane Clark   Pvt. Tenn. Cavalry
son Wm. Arthur m. Minnie Martin

Roark, Asa b. N.C. d. Ky. 1862 m. Susan Tuder   Ord. Sgt. Tenn. Mil.
son Hiram m. Barbara Wade

Roark, John b. N.C. 1780 d. Ky. 1860   Pvt. Tenn. Spies
m. Elizabeth (Linville) Gibbs — son Henry m. Elizabeth Smith

Robb, John   Vol. 5   Sgt. Pa. Mil.

Robb, Robert b. Pa. 1727 d. Pa. 1814   Pat. Justice Pa. 1791-1814
m. Susanna Flemming — daughter Ann m. Abraham Webster

Robbe, Alexander b. Ire. 1726 d. N.H. 1806   Pat. Selectman N.H.
m. Elizabeth Cunningham — son Samuel m. Betsy Scott

Robbins, Benjamin b. Mass. (Me.) 1789 d. Me. 1869 Pvt. (Me.) Mass. Mil.
m. Sibyl Fose — son Cyrus S. m. Mary Rockwood

Robbins, (Robins) Brintnel b. Conn. 1756 d. Pa. 1836   Pat. Ohio 1813
m. Mary Boardman — son William m. Agnes Sloan

Robbins, Jonathan Newman b. N.Y. d. Ia. 1864   Pvt. N.Y. Mil.
m. Permelia Sutliff — daughter Alzina m. Truman Almonson Squier

Robbins, Stephens   Vol. 3   Qtr. Mst. Mass. Mil. 1787

Robbins, Willard b. Vt. 1792 d. Ia. 1880 m. Mary Johnston   Pvt. U.S. Inf.
son Francis K. m. Christena Peters

Robe, William David Sr. b. Va. 1760 d. Ohio 1818   Pvt. Ohio Mil.
m. Elizabeth Baldwin — son David Jr. m. Martha Miller

Robers, William b. Tenn. 1779 d. Tenn. 1851 m. Anne Brown Pvt. N.C. Mil.
son Cullen m. Elizabeth Jarnigan

Roberson, James b. Tenn. 1784 d. Tenn. 1852   2nd Maj. Tenn. Mil.
m. Margaret Worthington — son James M. m. Selina Elizabeth Kendall

Roberts, Alexander b. Va. 1772 d. Va. 1851   Cornet Va. Mil.
m. Sarah Shepherd — daughter Elizabeth m. William Clinton Nalley

Roberts, Amos b. Conn. 1786 d. Mich. 1873 m. Sally Hurd Adj. N.Y. Mil.
daughter Sarah L. H. m. John W. Peirce

Roberts, Archibald b. Va. 1784 d. Ill. 1860   Lt. Ill. 5th Regt.
m. Sarah Pennington — son Nathan m. Mary Bovee

Roberts, Benjamin b. Va. d. W.Va. 1885   Pvt. Va. Mil.
m. Permelia Rockhold
daughter Nancy Ann m. William Drake Richards

Roberts, David b. Pa. 1792 d. Ohio 1875   Pvt. Pa. Rangers
m. Emeline Munyan — son Charles W. m. Rebecca Walton

Roberts, Elisha b. Tenn. (N.C.) 1775 d. Tex. 1844   Lt. La. Mil.
m. Martha Gill — son Noel G. m. Maria Thomas

Roberts, James W. b. Mass. (Me.) d. Mass. (Me.)   Lt. Mass. (Me.) Mil.
m. Roxana   Vol. 24 — son Shadrack m. Harriet Cross

Roberts, John b. Pa. 1795 d. 1880 m. Margaret Mead   Pvt. Pa. Mil.
daughter Martha Belle m. Samuel Bainard Moore

Roberts, John b. N.Y. 1759 d. N.Y. 1842   Pvt. & Maj. N.Y. Mil.
    m. Ednah Hillyard — daughter Betsy m. Joseph W. Edwards

Roberts, John Jr. b. N.J. 1767 d. Ohio 1850   Pvt. Ohio Mil.
    m. Esther Somers — son John S. m. Martha Hooper Rhoads

Roberts, John b. Md. 1762 d. Md. 1824   Sgt. Md. Mil.
    m. Martha Roberts (cousin) — daughter Nellie m. Samuel Ford

Roberts, Jozedic b. Tenn. d. Tenn. 1838   Pvt. Tenn. Mil.
    m. Mary Luttrell — daughter Eliza m. Wyatte A. Leinster
    son George W. m. Mary Anne Harkey

Roberts, Henry b. Pa. 1794 d. Pa. 1886 m. Nancy Wilson   Lt. Pa. Mil.
    son David M. m. Lydia Adams

Roberts, Philip Benjamin b. N.Y. 1783 d. N.Y. 1884   Pvt. N.Y. Mil.
    m. Mary Tennant — son Owen T. m. Louise Kinsley

Roberts, William b. Tenn. 1787 d. Ill. aft. 1868 m. Eve Ruble, Pvt. La. Mil.
    son James A. m. Sarah Seymour
    son William H. m. Jane Seymour

Roberts, William b. Va. 1773/5 d. Tex. aft. 1836 m. Sarah   Pvt. La. Mil.
    daughter Urza Ann m. Benjamin William Payne

Robertson, Alexander b. Va. 1748 d. Ky. 1802   Pat. Const. Conv. Ky. 1788
    m. Margaret Robinson   Sheriff 1792
    son George m. Eleanor James Bainbridge

Robertson, Andrew b. 1793 d. 1879   Pvt. Va. Mil.
    m. Elizabeth Hamilton — son Jonathan R. m. Susan Harrell

Robertson, Charles b. Va. 1771 d. Ind. 1821/2 m. Nancy Ford   Pvt. U.S. Inf.
    daughter Frances m. Micah Burns
    daughter Margaret m. John Milton Wood
    son Reuben m. Elvira Littell

Robertson, Cornelius b. Md. 1790 d. Ky. 1819   Pvt. Ky. Mil.
    m. Clarissa Hill (Keech)
    son Jerome B. m. Mary Elizabeth Cummins

Robertson, Duncan Forbes b. Va. 1784 d. Ky.   Sgt. N.Y. Mil.
    m. Mary Downing
    daughter Ann Elizabeth G. m. Dr. William Dodd

Robertson, Ephraim b. Conn. 1746 d. Conn. 1826   Vol. 7   Cpl. Conn. Mil.

Robertson, Henry b. Va. 1786 d. Va. 1844   Cpl. Tenn. Cavalry
    m. Elizabeth Todd Shires — daughter Ann F. m. Mires Horton Bonner

Robertson, James b. Va. 1742 d. Tenn. 1814   Pat. Tenn.
    m. Charlotte Reeves — son Jonathan F. m. Ciddy Davis
    daughter Leodocia Erwin m. C. W. Harris REAL DAUGHTER

Robertson, James b.— d.— m. Jane Gay   Vol. 1   Pat. Gov. La.

Robertson, James   Vol. 13   Brig. Gen. Ohio Ky. Mil.

Robertson, James Ross   Vol. 9   Sgt. Maj. Va. Mil.

Robertson, John b. N.C. 1781 d. Tenn. 1858   Pvt. Tenn. Mil.
    m. Margaret Register — son James R. m. Mary Ann Hunt

Robertson, John Alexander b. Va. d.—   Pvt. Va. Mil.
    m. Frances Holmes Broadnax
    daughter Margaret H. m. John Haskins Winfree

Robertson, Matthew b. Va. c. 1740 d. Va. 1797/8   Pat. Va. 1795-7
     m. Mary Robertson (cousin)   Justice
     son John S. M. m. Polly Motley

Robertson, Sterling C. b. Tenn. 1772 d. Tenn. 1842 m.—   Deputy Qtr. Mst.
     son E. Sterling C. m. Mary Elizabeth Dickey   Gen. Tenn.
     daughter Luella m. Z. T. Fulmoe

Robey, William b. Md. 1777 d. Tex. 1875 m. May Collins   2nd Lt. Ohio Mil.
     son William W. m. Sarah Eleanor Young

Robins, John b. N.J. 1760 d. Pa. 1842 m. Sarah Dailey   Lt. & Maj. Pa. Mil.
     son Philip m. Nancy Boyd

Robinson (Robison) Andrew b. Ire. d. W.Va.   Capt. Pa. Mil.
     m. Elizabeth Harrison — daughter Eleanor m. Samuel Frazier

Robinson, Charles b. Mass. (Me.) 1790 d. Me. 1872   Sgt. Mass. Mil.
     m. Elsie Meservey — daughter Nancy m. John Campbell Mountfort

Robinson, Darius b. Va. 1785 d. Va. 1838 m. Elizabeth Powell   Ens. Va. Mil.
     son Jabez J. m. Juliette Bowen
     son James J. m. Ada Kirkland

Robinson, David b. Mass. 1789 d. Me. 1867   Pvt. Md. Mil.
     m. Elizabeth Payne (Paine) — son Richard L. m. Cornelia Shindler

Robinson, David b. N.Y. 1765 d. N.Y. 1835   Pat. N.Y.
     m. Althea Elizabeth Hunt — son Gideon m. Mary Hammond

Robinson, David b. Va. 1785 d. Ill. 1836 m. Mary Moore   Lt. Ill. Mil.
     daughter Caroline m. A. B. Hardy

Robinson, David   Vol. 7   Pvt. Md. Mil.

Robinson, Elias b. 1785 d. 1820 m. Anna Sloat   Pvt. N.Y. Mil.
     daughter Sarah m. Michael Barker

Robinson, George b. Ky. 1780 d. in SVC 1813   Pvt. Ky. Mil.
     m. Elizabeth Robinson — daughter Margaret m. Lewis Arnold

Robinson (Robison), George Sr. b. Pa. 1789 d. Ohio 1861   Pvt. Ohio Mil.
     m. Margaret Hunter — son George Jr. m. Jane Morrow

Robinson, Gordon Jr. b. Ire. 1797 d. Mo. 1877   Music N.Y. Mil.
     m. Deborah Annet — daughter Jane m. George Hardey

Robinson, Gordon Sr. b. Ire. 1773 d. N.Y. 1827   Pvt. U.S. Inf.
     m. Jane Young — son Gordon Jr. m. Deborah Annet

Robinson, Jabez   Vol. 12   Ens. N.Y. Mil.

Robinson, James b. (W.)Va. 1787 d. Ohio 1856   Lt. Col. Va. Mil.
     m. Amelia Wood — son Henry M. m. Nancy Allison

Robinson, James b. Me. 1782 d. Me. 1874   Lt. & Capt. Mass.
     m. Martha Stetson — son Edward m. Emily Farnsworth

Robinson, Jesse b. S.C. 1789 d. Fla. 1854   Capt. Art. 1812-13 Ga.
     m. Mary Ann Bostick — son Francis A. m. Lorena A. M. Bush

Robinson, John b. Va. 1774 d. Ohio 1853   Pvt. Ohio Mil.
     m. Gretchen Zane — son William H. m. Druscilla Worley

Robinson, John b. Va. 1792 d. S.C. 1841   Ens. Ky. Mil.
     m. Eliza Blassingame — daughter Esther B. m. James Earle Hagood

Robinson, John b. N.Y. 1789 d. N.Y. 1863 m. Nancy Spear   Pvt. N.Y. Mil.
     son John S. m. Jane Utter

Robinson, John Nathan b. Pa. 1798 d. Pa. 1870   Pvt. Pa. Mil.
m. Mary Yocum — daughter Isabella m. Mahlon Hall

Robinson, Joseph b. Engl. 1787 d. Md. 1863   2nd Maj. Md. Mil.
m. Catherine Miller — daughter Louise m. William Claggett Miller

Robinson, Joshua b. Va. 1779 d. Ohio 1865 m. Ann Bentley   Pvt. Va. Mil.
daughter Sally Maria m. Asa Walker

Robinson (Robison), Lyman b. Conn. 1794 d. Pa. 1871   Pvt. Pa. Mil.
m. (2) Lucina Scott
daughter Alice May m. Horace G. Cottrell REAL DAUGHTER

Robinson, Michael (Mitchell) b. Va. 1796 d. Mich. 1850   Pvt. Ky. Mil.
m. Maria Caldwell — daughter Mary m. John Jenkins

Robinson, Robert b. S.C. 1793 d. S.C. 1851   Pvt. S.C. Mil.
m. Jeannette Elliott — daughter Melinda m. Henry Reid Jennings

Robinson, Robert b. Pa. 1774 d. Pa.   Lt. Pa. Mil.
m. Prudence McElroy — daughter Prudence m. William Hart

Robinson, Ruel b. Pa. d. Pa. m. Abigail Miles Vol. 21   Pvt. Pa. Mil.
daughter Polly m. Myron Stevens

Robinson, Sampson Avent Vol. 16   Sgt. Va. Mil.

Robinson, Seaborn Jones b. Ga. 1799 d. Tex. 1864   Pvt. La. Mil.
m. Elizabeth Barclay — daughter Amanda B. m. Joseph D. Henderson

Robinson, Thomas b. Ire. 1754 d. Ohio 1852   Capt. Ohio
m. Nancy McMillan — son George m. Margaret Hunter

Robinson, William Jr. b. N.C. 1783 d. Ohio 1875   Pvt. Ohio Mil.
m. Hannah Horney — daughter Mahala m. Joshua Creamer

Robinson, William Vol. 7   Pvt. N.J. Mil.

Robuck, Aaron b. Ohio 1784 d. Ohio 1860   Pvt. Ohio Mil.
m. Betsy McGovney — son Johnson m. Jane Mahaffey
daughter Mary m. William McColm
son Thomas m. Margaret Haines

Roby, Townley b. Md. 1780 d. Ind. 1815 m. Rebecca Ellis   Pvt. Ind. Mil.
son Tillman m. Mary Ann Mauck

Roche, Charles b. Fra. d. La. 1819 m. Eulalie Lalanne   2nd Lt. La. Mil.
daughter Caroline m. Joseph Lallande de Ferriere

Rockefeller, Walter b. N.Y. 1796 d. N.Y. 1867   Pvt. N.Y. Mil.
m. Elizabeth Ellis — son DeWitt m. Mary J. Craig

Rockhold, Joseph b. Md. 1774 d. Ohio 1860   Capt. Ohio Mil.
m. Mary Rickets — son Elijah m. Juliana D. Carson

Rockwell, Caleb b. Conn. 1779 d. Ohio 1859   Lt. Ohio Mil.
m. Sarah Watrous — son John W. m. Hannah Benham Tyler

Rockwell, Joseph W. Vol. 17   Capt. Mass. Mil.

Rockwell, Merrett b. Vt. 1790 d. Vt. 1864 m. Nancy Grant   Cpl. N.Y. Mil.
son Ell B. m. Lucy McElroy
son Jabez m. Mary Louise Ewen

Rockwood, Cephas Leland b. Mass. 1786 d. Wisc. 1844   Capt. Vt. Mil.
m. Louisa Foote
daughter Eunice S. m. Daniel F. Melindy REAL DAUGHTER
daughter Louise m. Horace Wardner REAL DAUGHTER

Rockwood, Timothy Jr. Vol. 7   Pat. Rep. Mass. 1813-14

Roddy (Roddye), James b. Engl. 1750 d. Tenn. 1823   Pat. Const. Conv.
m. Lidda Russell   Tenn. 1796
daughter Margaret m. David Haston

Rodenbaugh, Jacob b. Pa. 1785 d. Pa. 1861   Ens. Pa. Mil.
m. Mary Magdaline Brown — son John m. Christena Beighley

Rodenheffer, George b. Pa. 1784 d. Va. 1852   Sgt. Va. Mil.
m. Elizabeth Black — daughter Elizabeth m. Henry Thomas Shearer

Roderfield, William b. Pa. 1788 d. Del. 1868   Lt. Pa. Mil.
m. Mary Custis Hamill — daughter Emma m. Luther Martin

Rodes, William b. Ky. 1792 d. Ky. 1856   Lt. Ky. Mil.
m. Sarah Waller Burch — son Joseph W. m. Sarah Evans Marshall

Rodgers, Henry b. N.C. 1787 d. N.C. 1835 m. Alleleljah   Pvt. N.C. Mil.
son William D. m. Virginia Rieves

Rodgers, James m. Rhoda Alexander   Vol. 6   Pvt. Tenn. Mil.

Rodgers, Matthew b. Pa. 1770 d. Pa. 1837 m. Mary Kennedy   Col. Pa. Mil.
son Alexander m. Susannah Thompson

Rodgers, McNease b. S.C. 1780 d. S.C. 1854   Cpl. S.C. Mil.
m. Mary Burnsides — son Matthews m. Elizabeth Thomason

Rodgers, Nathaniel Kerr b. Va. 1797 d. Mo. 1862   Pvt. Va. Mil.
m. Elizabeth Champ
son Robert W. m. Mariam Stark & Frances Montgomery

Rodgers, William b. Va. 1784 d. Ohio 1815 m. Rebecca Lewis   Pvt. Ohio Mil.
son Aniel m. (1) Cynthia Popence

Rodgers, William b. Tenn. 1794 d. Tenn. 1864   Lt. Tenn. Mil.
m. Mahala Lowe — daughter Samira Ann m. Samuel Love Russell

Rodney, John   Vol. 15   Capt. Del. Mil.

Roff, Frederick b. N.Y. 1795 d. N.Y. 1890 m. Mary Runkle   Pvt. N.Y. Mil.
daughter Helena m. James Henry Godfrey REAL DAUGHTER
son William m. Alida Ann Clute

Rogers, Benjamin b. Va. 1772 d. Ohio 1849   Cpl. Ohio Mil.
m. Elizabeth Jackson — son Jackson m. Nancy Jones

Rogers, Brittain b. N.C. 1761 d. Ga. 1835   Lt. Ga. Mil.
m. Elizabeth Lockett — son Osborn m. Mary Thorn

Rogers, David b. Va. 1779 d. Tenn. 1871   Maj. Tenn. Mil.
m. Mary Elizabeth Lewis — son Jesse L. m. Margaret Wilson

Rogers, Elisha b. Va. 1787 d. Tenn. 1858 m. Sarah Thurman   Lt. Tenn. Mil.
son Alfred K. m. Mary Ann Cobbs

Rogers, Ezra b. N.Y. 1797 d. Ind. 1869 m. Elizabeth Smith   Pvt. N.Y. Mil.
daughter Arkansas m. John W. Graves REAL DAUGHTER

Rogers, Harris b. Conn. 1787 d. Conn. 1835   Lt. Conn. Mil.
m. Joanna Strickland — son James S. m. Rebecca S. West

Rogers, Henry b. Conn. 1784 d. Conn. 1857   Music N.Y. Inf.
m. Eunice Wilcox —— daughter Arietta May m. Samuel Daskam

Rogers, Henry b. Pa. 1796 d. N.Y. 1840 m. Nancy Tucker   Music N.Y. Mil.
daughter Chloe m. Edward M. Watkins

Rogers, Isaiah b. N.Y. 1787 d. N.Y. 1873 m. Mary Colby   Pvt. U.S. Inf.
daughter Lucy Amelia m. Seth Charles Pond REAL DAUGHTER

Rogers, James b. N.H. 1798 d. Me. 1878   Pvt. N.H. Mil.
m. Clarissa Harlow Wiggins
daughter Caroline M. m. Oscar Horace Shepley REAL DAUGHTER

Rogers, James b. Va. 1742 d. Ky. 1823 m. Martha Blackburn   Pat. Ky.
son Jonathan m. Elizabeth Ray

Rogers, James b. N. Y. 1787 d. Ia. 1873 m. Eleanor Mage   Pvt. Pa. Mil.
son Thomas E. m. Susan Maria Curtis

Rogers, Joel   Vol. 14   Sgt. U.S. Inf.

Rogers, Dr. John b. Ire. 1794 d. Tenn. 1832   Midshipman Navy 1811
m. Margaret Lucia Shepperd
son Dr. James Webb m. Cornelia Anna Eliza Harris

Rogers, John   Vol. 4   Capt. Va. Mil.

Rogers, John b. N.Y. 1793 d. N.Y. 1870   Pvt. N.Y. Mil.
m. Mary Eggleston — son Allen P. m. Diana Hall

Rogers, John b. Va. 1796 d. Ill. 1853 m. Phoebe Beam   Pvt. Va. Mil.
daughter Phoebe m. John W. Low

Rogers, John b. Conn. 1790 d. Conn. 1867   Pvt. Conn. Mil.
m. Sarah Harris — daughter Sophia m. Jason L. Ryon

Rogers, John b. Pa. 1780 d. Ark. 1860 m.—   Pat. Mich.
daughter Emma Cecelia m. James Alonzo Johnston

Rogers, John b. 1796 d. Ark. 1875 m. Amy G. Adams   Pvt. Ga. Mil.
daughter Mary C. m. Randolph B. Creekmore

Rogers, John A. b. Tenn. 1789 d. Texas 1856   Capt. U.S. Inf.
m. Ann L. Coates — daughter Virginia S. m. Henry Clay Swan

Rogers, Jonathan b. Mass. 1795 d. Ill. 1882   Pvt. N.Y. Mil. 1814
m. Elizabeth Herring — son Nelson C. m. Sarah Pruden

Rogers, Joseph b. N.Y. 1789 d. Ohio 1881 m. Lydia Lowry   Pvt. Ohio Mil.
son Loren B. m. Betsy Chamberlain

Rogers, Joseph b. Va. 1765 d. Ky. 1828   Pvt. Md. Sea Fencibles
m. Martha Wilson — daughter Julia A. m. Sydnor George

Rogers, Luke   Vol. 3   Pvt. Mass. Mil.

Rogers, Matthew b. Conn. 1770 d. Ill. 1847   1st Maj. N.Y. Mil.
m. Eliza Anna Morse — daughter Anna M. m. Martin Higgins

Rogers, Micajah b. Tenn. 1795 d. Tex. 1873   Ens. Tenn. Mil.
m. Cynthia Cannon — son George m. Lucinda Gibbs

Rogers, Nathaniel b. Va. 1755 d. Ky. 1790   Pat. Ky. Const. Conv.
m. Frances Cobb — daughter Nancy m. William Roseberry

Rogers, Nathaniel   Vol. 3   Pvt. Conn. Mil.

Rogers, Peter   Vol. 7   Pvt. Tenn. Mil.

Rogers, Robert b. N.H. 1796 d. N.H. 1878 m. Sarah Lane   Pvt. N.H. Mil.
son James m. Abbie Hall

Rogers, Samuel J. b. Va. 1790 d. Mo. 1877   Maj. Tenn. Mil.
    m. Sarah Conner
    son Samuel St. G. m. Mary Drury & Josephine Boyard

Rogers, Thomas b. Va. 1782 d. Ohio 1873   Ens. Ohio Mil.
    m. Nancy Watts — daughter Mary m. James Peyton Leake

Rogers, Thomas   Vol. 11   Gen. N.Y. Mil.

Rogers, William   Vol. 15   Pvt. N.J. Mil.

Rogers, William b. N.Y. 1754 d. N.Y. 1803 m. Ester Hawley   Ens. N.Y. Mil.
    son William Jr. m. Charlotte van Velsor

Rogers, William Henry b. Va. 1787 d. Va. 1859   Lt. Va. Regt.
    m. Mary Page Carter — son Lewis Carter m. Martha Vernon

Rolfe, Ephraim C. b. N.Y. d. N.Y. m. Lydia Osborne   Pvt. N.Y. Inf.
    daughter Mercy m. George W. Moore

Roll, John b. Pa. 1755 d. Pa. 1816 m. Mary Frampton   Capt. Pa. Mil.
    daughter Mary m. William Bloom Jr.

Roney, William b. Ire. 1782 d. Md. 1844   Capt. Md. Mil.
    m. Alice McBlair — daughter Margaret Ann m. James Warden

Ronde, Pierre Dennis de La. II b. 1762 d. 1824   Commander Mil. La. 1812
    m. Eulalie Guerbois
    daughter Emilie Elizabeth m. Pierre de Hos Cacho

Rooks, John b. Va. 1794 d. Va. 1834 m. Harriet Bull   Pvt. Va. Mil.
    son Oliver P. m. Elizabeth Ann Nottingham

Roosevelt, Thomas Wilton b. N.Y. 1781 d. at Ft. Erie 1814   Lt. N.Y. Mil.
    m. Elizabeth Cook — son Nelson m. Sarah Armitage

Root, Abel b. N.H. 1765 d. Pa. 1839 m. Princess Lyman   Pvt. N.Y. Mil.
    daughter Polly m. Xury Williams

Root, Dr. Anson b. N.Y. 1786 d. Ill. 1866   Surgeon's Mate Inf.
    m. Lucinda Wilson — daughter Orpha m. Samuel Parker Burdick

Root, Asahel   Vol. 7   Lt. N.Y. Mil.

Root, Eli b. Conn. 1769 d. N.Y. 1840 m. Betsey Lord   Pat. N.Y.
    daughter Almira m. Amaziah Shattuck

Root, Spofford b. Vt. 1796 d. Ill. 1880   Pvt. Vt. Mil.
    m. Kezia Ann De Ford
    daughter Martha E. m. Albert L. Pitney REAL DAUGHTER

Roper, John b. Va. 1782 d. Tenn. 1858   Capt. Tenn. Mil.
    m. Margaret Franklin — daughter Mary Ann m. George Branner

Roquemore, Peter b. Ga. 1778 d. Tex. 1852 m. Katy Murphy   Pvt. Ga. Mil.
    daughter Mary Ann m. (2) William B. Garrard

Rorapaugh, Benjamin b. N.Y. 1795 d. Pa. 1883   Pvt. N.Y. Mil.
    m. Apama Blakeslee — son Charles m. Electa Blatchley
    daughter Hannah m. Cornish Gilbert Taylor

Rose, Cephus b. Mass. 1781 d. N.Y. 1857 m. Eunice   Pvt. N.Y. Mil.
    son Edwin m. Rosannah Clark

Rose, Dennison Robinson b. Vt. 1790 d. Mich. 1877   Pvt. Dragoons Art.
    m. Hannah Eldridge — son Dennison F. m. Mary Ann Foster

Rose, Henry b. Pa. 1785 d. Pa. 1867 m. Catherine Ault   Pvt. Pa. Mil.
    daughter Susan m. William Reading

Rose, Isaac Jr. b. Pa. 1787 d. Pa. 1854   Pvt. Pa. Mil.
     m. Elizabeth McMillen — son Isaac P. m. Margaret Gibson
     son William m. Anne McDaniel

Rose, James b. Conn. 1744 d. R.I. 1830 m. Elizabeth Elred   Pvt. R.I. Reds
     son James Jr. m. Thankful Miner

Rose, James b. Pa. 1785 d. Pa. 1865 m. Martha McKiney   Pvt. Pa. Mil.
     son William m. Martha Parmalee

Rose, John b. Pa. d. 1813 at Battle of Lake Erie   Gunner U.S. Navy
     m. Martha Taylor   on U.S.S. Lawrence
     daughter Matilda B. m. Elias Root Stevens or Stearns

Rose, Lewis   Vol. 17   Capt. Ky. Mil.

Rose, William P.   Vol. 17   Pvt. N.C. Mil.

Rose, William Pickney b. N.C. 1787 d. Tex. 1851   Pvt. or Capt. Tenn. Mil.
     m. Mary Vardeman — son Preston R. m. Mary Ann Scott

Rose, William Pickney b. N.C. d. Ga. m. Anne Langston   Pvt. La. Mil.
     son John m. Mary Washington

Roseberry, John W. b. N.J. 1791 d. Pa. 1825   2nd Cpl. Pa. Inf.
     m. Margaret Good — daughter Mary M. m. Jacob Oliver Roads

Roseberry, Michael b. Va. 1787 d. Ohio 1859   Pvt. Ohio Mil.
     m. Elizabeth Downing — son Ebenezer m. Mary Carter

Roseboom, Garret b. N.Y. 1778 d. N.Y. 1861   Lt. N.Y. Mil.
     m. Josena Halenback — daughter Esther m. George W. J. Bronson

Roseborough, John b. S.C. 1775 d. S.C. 1854   Pat. Clerk Ct. S.C.
     m. Elimor Key (Kee)
     son William Daniel m. Elizabeth Ann Williamson

Rosenkraus, Benjamin b. 1770 d. 1848   Maj. N.J. Inf.
     m. Margaret Schoonover — daughter Maria m. James C. Bevans
     daughter Rachel m. John W. Van Auken

Rosensteel, Henry b. Md. 1792 d. Pa. 1834   Pvt. Md. Mil.
     m. Margaret Ann Ryland
     son William Henry m. Elizabeth Anne Robinette

Ross, Arthur Brown b. N.C. 1746 d. Miss. 1806   Pat. Justice S.C.
     m. Hannah Conger — daughter Elizabeth m. Thomas Sims

Ross, David b. Ky. 1785 d. Ky. 1852 m. Betsy Smith   Pvt. Ky. Mil.
     son David Jr. m. Dulcena Paxton

Ross, George b. Pa. 1752 d. Pa. 1832   Pat. Pa. Congressman 1790
     m. Mary Bird — daughter Ann m. James Hopkins

Ross, John E.   Vol. 6   Pvt. N.Y. Mil.

Ross, John G. b. Tenn. 1787 d. Okla. 1858 m. Elizabeth   Sgt. Tenn. Mil.
     son John A. m. Elizabeth Wilkerson

Ross, Reuben   Vol. 17   2nd Lt. Md. Mil.

Ross, Reuben b. N.C. 1776 d. Ky. 1860 m. Mildred Yarrell   Pat. Tenn.
     son James m. Mary Walton Barker

Ross, Robert   Vol. 11   Pvt. N.J. Mil.

Ross, St. Clair b. Ire. 1782 d. Ohio 1872   Pvt. Ohio Mil.
     m. Rebecca S. Eakins — daughter A. Eliza m. John Allen Glaze

Ross, Stephen b. Va. 1764 d. Mo. 1837 m. Savanah   Sgt. Mo. Mil.
son John T. m. Nancy Lee

Ross, Theodorus b. N.Y. 1780 d. N.Y. 1844   Capt. N.Y. Cavalry
m. Elizabeth Richards — son Leonard G. m. Martha Gillispie Fain

Ross, Walter (Raleigh) b. Va. 1793 d. Ala. 1850   Pvt. La. Mil.
m. (3) Anne David Sorsby
daughter Annie m. Dr. J. T. Searcy REAL DAUGHTER

Ross, William b. Mass. 1792 d. Ill. 1873 m. Edna Adams   Col. U.S. Inf.
daughter Anna Edna m. Asa C. Matthews

Rossell, Zachariah Vol. 8   Maj. Pa. U.S. Army

Rosser, David b. Ga. 1780 d. Ga. 1828 m. Sarah Harris   Capt. Ga. Mil.
daughter Mary Ann m. Henry Chamber Kimbrough

Rothbaust, John b. Pa. 1762 d. Pa. 1841   Pat. Pa. 1809-11
m. Barbara Weaver — daughter Anna M. m. Godfrey Greenawalt

Rough, John (also Rauch) b. Md. 1776 d. Pa. 1849   Sgt. Pa. Mil.
m. Anna Maria Young — son John Jr. m. Catherine Bowman

Roulston, James b. Va. 1772 d. Tenn. 1844   Col. W. Tenn. Mil.
m. Jane Simmons — daughter Martha m. Owen Russel Beene

Round, Alfred b. R.I. 1786 d. N.Y. 1829 m. Martha Lynde   Fifer N.Y. Mil.
son Nelson m. Mary Comfort

Roundtree, William Jr. b. S.C. 1790 d. S.C. 1860 m. Jane   Pvt. S.C. Mil.
son James W. m. Providence Bruton

Roundy, Asahel b. Vt. 1784 d. N.Y. 1857   Capt. N.Y. Mil.
m. Hannah Weston — daughter Mary Ann m. Dr. John Collins

Roundy, John Sr. b. Mass. 1726 d. Me. Terr. 1799   Pat. Me. 1789
m. Elizabeth Rea — son John Jr. m. (2) Polly Trussell

Roup, Jacob Vol. 4   Chief Wagon Mst. U.S. Inf.

Roup, John b. Pa. 1782 d. Pa. 1867 m. Kitty Winebiddle   Pvt. Pa. Mil.
daughter Rebecca m. William Penn Baum

Rouse, Rudolphus John Farandes b. 1793 d. Ill. 1873   Surgeon's Mate
m. Margaret Banta   N.Y. Mil.
daughter Margaret m. Hugh James Sweeny

Roush, Abraham b. Va. 1794 d. W. Va. 1877   Pvt. Fifer Va. Mil.
m. Susanna Rickard — son Enos m. Barbara
son Marcus m. Mary Van Meter

Roush (Rouse), Henry b. Va. 1780 d. Ohio 1861   Pvt. Ohio Mil.
m. Barbara Pfantzler — daughter Susannah m. John Runyon

Rowe, Benjamin b. Mass. 1786 d. Me. 1849 m. Judith   Pvt. Mass. Mil.
daughter Betsy m. William Jones

Rowe, Isaiah Vol. 3   Ens. N.H. Mil.

Rowe, John b. Va. 1780 d. Ohio 1863 m. 2) Lydia Weaver   Cpl. Ohio Mil.
son James H. m. Eliza Jane Jenkins
son Willis m. Harriet Limes (thru wife Frances Anderson)

Rowe, John b. Mass. 1796 d. Mass. 1883 m. Angeline Kelly   Pvt. Mass. Mil.
son John Lewis m. Louise Butler

Rowe, Moses b. Mass. 1781 d. Me. 1858   Lt. Mass. Mil.
m. Joanna Atwood Swett
daughter Cordelia Snow m. Benj. F. S. Patten

Rowe, Robert b. N.C. 1793 d. Tex. 1869 m. Mary Hooper   Pvt. N.C. Mil.
daughter Nancy G. m. Stephen Ralph Cummings

Rowe, Zebulon b Mass. (Me.) 1787 d. Me. 1865   Pvt. Mass. (Me.) Mil.
m. Judith Eveleth — daughter Sarah E. m. Jonathan Hutchins

Rowell, Dustin b. N.H. 1782 d. N.H. 1866   Pvt. N.H. Mil. 1813
m. Jennie Gordon — daughter Nancy D. m. Harvey Adams

Rowland, Alfred b. N.C. 1777 d. N.C. 1829   Lt. Col. N.C. Mil.
m. Mary Eliza Clinton — son John A. m. Flora McKay

Rowland, George b. 1736 d. N.J. 1793 m. Rachel   Pat. Constable N.J. 1788
son George Jr. m.—

Rowland, John S. b. N.C. 1795 d. Ga. 1863   Pvt. S.C. Mil.
m. Francis M. Lewis — son William L. m. Serena Jane Dillard

Rowland, Jonathan b. Pa. 1782 d. Pa. 1854 m. Mary   Pvt. Penn.
son Maxwell m. Matilda Horner

Rowland, Samuel b. Del. 1792 d. Ohio 1865   Pvt. Ohio Mil.
m. Rebecca Dyer — son Elza m. Maria Jane Thomas

Rowlett, Thomas b. N.C. 1787 d. Va. 1841 m. Lucy Bruce   Lt. Va. Mil.
daughter Beluma (Belerma, Belekma) m. Turner Dennis Patterson

Rowley, Erastus b. Mass. 1775 d. Mass. 1834   Col. Mass. Mil.
m. Eunice Cone — son Erastus Jr. m. Martha Morris

Rowley, Roger b. Conn. 1782 d. N.Y. 1844   Pvt. N.Y. Mil.
m. Rebecca Latimer — son Roger E. m. (1) Hannah Sargent Osgood

Rowntree, Henry b. Va. 1780 d. Ky. 1845   Pvt. Ky. Mil. 1814-15
m. (3) Lucy Watkins — son John m. Nancy Ellen Cannon

Rowsey, Thomas b. Va. 1770 d. Ohio 1846 m. Mary Rose   Pvt. Va. Mil.
son Charles Allen m. Mary Traynor

Rowzee, John b. Va. 1760 d. Va. aft. 1814   Pvt. Va. Mil.
m. Elizabeth or Isabella Miller
daughter Frances m. John H. Harris

Roy, Joseph b. Mo. 1792 d. Mo. 1856   Pvt. Mo. Terr. 1815
m. Mary Louise Shalifaux (Chalifou)
daughter Victoria m. John Silvers

Royall, John Bedford   Vol. 12   Capt. Va. Cav. Mil.

Royall, William b. Eng. 1776 d. Va.   Capt. Va. Mil.
m. Ann H. Underwood — son Richard m. Elizabeth Bibb Harding

Royce, Jeremiah b.— d. N.Y. 1862 m. Hulda Tibbals   Pvt. N.Y. Mil.
daughter Hulda m. Silas Jones

Royce, Jonathan b. Conn. 1745 d. N.H. 1826   Pat.-Selectman &
m. Sarah Marvin — son Jonathan Jr. m. Mary Emery   Moderator N.H.

Royer, Daniel b. Penn. 1800 d. Ill. 1850   Pat. Frontier Defender Penn.
m. Mary Cockburn — son Jacob D. m. Mary Elizabeth McCullah

Royer, John b. Penn. 1774 d. Pa. 1846   Pat. Commissioner Penn. 1806
m. Susan Stover — daughter Catherine m. John A. Shank

Royer, John H. b. Penn. 1793 d. Penn. 1873   Pvt. Penn. Mil.
m. Rachel Lesher — daughter Susan L. m. Malcolm Palmer Cary

Royster, David   Vol. 11   Pvt. Va. Mil.

Royston, John b. Md. 1777 d. Ohio 1840   Pvt. Ohio Mil.
m. Elizabeth Coons — son Daniel m. Marie Joanne de Bobo

Ruch, Lawrence   Vol. 11   Sgt. Penn. Mil.

Ruch, Peter b. Penn. 1779 d. Penn. 1838   Capt. Penn. Mil.
m. Susannah Schreiber — son Charles m. Salome Burkhalter

Rucker, Isaac b. Va. c. 1740 d. Va. 1799   Capt. Va. Mil. 1785-6
m. Mildred Hawkins (Plunkett) — son John m. Nancy Shelton

Rucker, (Rev.) James b. Va. 1758 d. Tenn. 1819   Pvt. Tenn. Vol.
m. Nancy Ann Reade Tate
son Benjamin m. (3) Eliza Wharton Welch
son Jos. Burrus m. Susan Edmondson

Rucker, Jarvis b. Va. 1784 d. Va. 1851 m. Milly Grayson   Pvt. Va. Mil.
son John m. Mary Jane Smith

Rudd, Hezekiah b. Va. c. 1775 d. Va. 1833 m. Elizabeth   Pvt. Va. Mil.
son James m. Harriet Allen Worsham

Rudd, Thomas b. Va. 1790 d. Va. 1885 m. Winny Anderson   Pvt. Va. Mil.
son Benjamin F. m. Susan F. Parsons

Ruddach, John b. Penn. 1793 d. Penn. 1819   Pvt. Jr. Artil. 1814
m. Margaret Forebaugh   Phila., Pa.
son William A. m. Elizabeth Fizone

Rudisill, Henry b. N.C. 1760 d. N.C. 1834   Capt. N.C. Mil.
m. Salome or Susanna Sides (Seitz)
daughter Susan m. David Summerow

Rudolph, Michael b. Md. 1758 d. at Sea 1795   Maj. Lt. Drag. Inf. Ga.
m. Sarah Baker
daughter Amelia Rebecca m. John F. W. Courvoisier Jr.

Ruffner, David b. Va. 1767 d. W.Va. 1843 m. Ann Brombach   Pvt. Va. Mil.
daughter Anna m. Dr. R. E. Putney

Ruffner, Jacob b. Va. 1781 d. Ohio 1839   Pvt. Ohio Mil.
m. Magdalene Bibler — son Jacob Jr. m. Eliza Coplin

Ruger, John b. N.Y. 1782 d. N.Y. 1865 m.—   Pat. N.Y.
daughter Sarah Ann m. Robert Wood Meador REAL DAUGHTER

Rugg, Levi b. New Engl. 1794 d. 1875   Pvt. N.Y. Mil.
m. Eugenia Scoyen
daughter Eva E. m. Bishop Simpson Garrison REAL DAUGHTER

Ruggles, Gardner b. Mass. 1782 d. Mass. 1853   Lt. Mass. Mil.
m. Lydia Phinney — son Zenas P. m. Margaret I. Donaldson

Ruhe, Charles b. Penn. 1794 d. Penn. 1879   Pvt. Penn. Mil.
m. Susanna Scheirer — son Frederick A. m. Julia A. Koder

Rumbarger, John Sr. b. Penn. 1775 d. Penn. 1847   Pat. Road Supervisor
m. Elizabeth Ellenbarger   Penn. 1813
son John Jr. m. Eliza Earhart

Rumbaugh, David b. prob. Penn. 1761 d. Penn. 1847   Pvt. Pa. Mil. 1785
m. Maria — son Adam m. Elizabeth Lauffer

Rumph, Jacob b. S.C. 1752 d. S.C. 1812   Brig. Gen. S.C. Mil. 1810
m. Anne Mary Harrisperger — son David m. Elizabeth Carmichael
son John m. Mary Gholson (Golson)

Rundell, Jacob   Vol. 8   Capt. N.Y. Inf.

Rundell, John   Vol. 12   Pvt. N.Y. Mil.

Runkle, William b. Va. 1784 d. Ill. 1867 m. Mary Pence   Lt. Ohio Mil.
daughter Dicy m. Stephen Dunlap

Runnells, Benjamin b. Mass. 1748 d. Mass. (Me.) 1802   Pat. Rep. to Gen.
m.— son David m. Sarah McDonald   Ct. Me. (Mass.)

Runyan, Abraham b. Va. 1783 d. Ind. 1836 m. Sophia Lynch   Pvt. Ohio Mil.
son Peter L. m. Mary Ervin (Irwin)

Runyon, John b. N.J. 1743 d. N.J. 1792   Pat. Mem. Legis. N.J. 1790-2
m. Sarah Wheaton — daughter Mercy m. Charles Toms

Runyon, Vincent b. N.J. 1794 d. N.J. 1872   Pvt. N.J. Mil.
m. Asenah Burlew (Buckalew) — daughter Mary m. Isaac Suydam

Rury, William b. N.Y. 1790 d. N.Y. 1880 m. Lorina Cook   Pvt. N.Y. Mil.
daughter Mary M. m. Charles C. Chadwick

Rush, John b. Penn. 1785-6 d. Ill. 1857 m. Margaret Hanna   Pvt. Penn.
son James m. Sabina Mitchell

Rush (Rast), John William b. S.C. 1793 d. S.C. 1885   Pvt. S.C.
m. Elizabeth Jane Daniels — daughter Rebecca Jane m. James Kelly

Rush, Leonard b. Penn. 1769 d. Ind. 1840   Ens. Penn. Mil. 1796
m. Jemima Hormell — son John m. Rachel Heaton

Rushing, John b. S.C. 1764 d. Ga. 1843 m. Rachel Renfroe   Pvt. Ga. Mil.
son William m. Mary Cox

Rusler, John Lewis b. Va. 1799 d. Va. 1877   Pvt. Va. Mil.
m. Elizabeth Hout — daughter Eliza J. m. Abraham Correll

Russel, Albert b. Penn. 1755 d. Ala. 1818   Pat. Justice Va. 1790
m. Anne Frances Hooe   Lt. Col. Va. Mil. 1793
daughter Susan Catherine m. Dr. Alexander Erskine   Mem. House
Del. 1789-93

Russell, Augustus b. Conn. 1775 d. Conn. 1829   Capt. Lt. Inf. Mil. Conn.
m. Lydia Rose — son Alfred m. Caroline Russell

Russell, George b. Tenn. c. 1794 d. Ala. 1820   Pvt. Tenn. Mil.
m. Leah Jackson Hudson — son George D. m. Emily Menville Stovall

Russell, Gideon Granger b. N.H. 1791 d. Vt. 1838   Pvt. Vt. Mil.
m. Sarah Plant — daughter Lucy F. m. Charles Tyler

Russell, Gilbert Christian   Vol. 1 or 2   Pat. Protector of Settlers
daughter Virginia m. John Duncan Fowler   against Indians
REAL DAUGHTER

Russell, Hamlin b. Conn. 1781 Penn. 1852   1st Sgt. Qtr. Mast. Penn. Mil.
m. Sarah Norcross — son George J. m. Arminda J. Hayes

Russell, Henry b. N.Y. (Mass.) 1774 d. N.Y. in prison 1814   Pvt. N.Y. Mil.
m. Sophia Winship Barney — son Daniel m. Sally Hicks

Russell, Ira b. Vt. 1788 d. Ohio 1850 m. Elizabeth Parker   Pvt. N.Y. Mil.
son Benjamin F. m. Ellen Rawlings

Russell, James L.   Vol. 12   Cpl. Ky. Mil.

Russell, John b. Va. 1793 d. W.Va. 1847   Qtr. Mst. Sgt. Va. Mil.
m. Rebekah Buffington — daughter Sarah m. Joseph W. Morris

Russell, Joseph b. Va. 1793 d. Ohio 1864   Pvt. Va.-Ky. Mil.
m. Celia Talbot Philips — son Henry S. m. Sarah Ellen Lance

Russell, Leverett   Vol. 17 — Pvt. N.Y. Mil.

Russell, Robert   Vol. 7 — Pvt. Del. Mil.

Russell, Thomas b. Va. 1789 d. Ill. 1862 — Pvt. Va. Mil.
m. Cecelia Hixson
daughter Mary Virginia m. James Henry Wickersham

Russell, William b. Va. 1735 d. Va. 1793 — Pat. Mem. of Assembly
m. Tabitha Adams — Va. 1781-1793
daughter Mary H. m. Capt. William Bowen

Russell, William   Vol. 15 — Pvt. Vt. Mil.

Russell, William   Vol. 17 — Pvt. Conn. Mil.

Russey, James Sr. b. Fra. 1755 d. Tenn. 1835 m. Sarah — Ens. Tenn.
son James Jr. m. Mary Elizabeth Cloud

Rust, George b. 1788 d. 1857 m. Maria Clagett Marlow — Vol. Md. 1812
son George T. m. Rebecca Coleman Yellott

Rust, Samuel b. Md. 1781 d. Md. 1864 m. Martha Dean — Pvt. Md. Art.
daughter Lydia m. William Ogle

Ruth, John b. Penn. 1771 d. Penn. m.— — Pvt. Penn. Mil.
son John Jr. m. Mary Magdalene Weisel

Rutherford, Griffith b. Ire. 1730 d. Tenn. 1799 — Pat. Governor 1795
m. Elizabeth Graham — son John m. Margaret — State Senator Tenn.

Rutherford, Samuel b. Penn. 1769 d. Penn. 1833 — Pvt. Penn. Mil.
m. Elizabeth Brisbane — daughter Eliza m. John Parke Rutherford

Rutherford, Samuel Morton b. Va. 1797 d. Ark. 1867 — Sgt. W. Tenn. Mil.
m. Eloise Marie Beall
daughter Mary Eloise m. William Murphy Cravens REAL DAUGHTER
son Robert B. m. Sally Wallace Butler

Rutledge, Jesse b. 1774 d. Ga. 1857 m. Jennie McDavid — Pvt. U.S. Rifles
daughter Rosanna m. (2) Ezekiel Tribble

Rutledge, Michael b. Md. 1777 d. Ohio 1867 — Cpl. Ohio Mil.
m. Mrs. Lydia Emmons Ackley — son William m. Mary Coe

Rutledge, William b. Ohio 1783 d. Ohio 1866 — Pvt. Ohio Mil.
m. Mary Scarlot — son Thomas m. Eleanor Birney

Ryan, John   Vol. 11 — Pvt. Mass. Mil.

Ryan, John b. Va. 1779 d. Ark. 1839 m. Mary Holt — Pvt. E. Tenn. Mil.
daughter Irene m. George Rex Lewis

Ryan, Robert b. Penn. 1790 d. Ky. 1862 m. Mary Rowe — Pvt. Ky. Lt. Drag.
son Richard J. m. Elizabeth Hieronymus

Ryland, Sylvester b. Penn. 1763 d. Penn. 1824 — Pvt. Penn. Mil.
m. Eleanor Hagan — son Andrew m. Margaret Fearer

Ryland, William   Vol. 17 — Cpl. Penn. Mil.

Ryley, James Van Slyck b. N.Y. 1761 d. N.Y. 1848 — Pat. Assoc.
m. Jarnetze Smith — Justice N.Y.
daughter Jane Helen m. Jared Elliott Warner

S

Sabin, Beekman Sr. b. N.Y. d. N.Y. 1830 — Pvt. N.Y. Mil.
m. Elizabeth Baker — son Beekman Jr. m.—

Sabin, Beekman Jr.   Vol. 1 — Pvt. N.Y. Mil.

Sackett, Daniel b. Mass. 1792 d. Mich. 1879   Cpl. Mass. Mil.
   m. Nancy Fulton — son William Francis m. Lois Avis Huggett

Sackett, Elijah b. Mass. 1768 d. N.Y. 1813   Pat. Nurse N.Y.
   m. Dorothy Hitchcock — daughter Elizabeth m. John Parker

Sackett, Ezekiel b. N.Y. 1786 d. Mich. 1857   Sgt. N.Y. Mil.
   m. Elizabeth Woodward — son David m. Emeline Prindle

Sadler, Philip Benjamin b. Ger. 1771 d. Md. 1860   Capt. Md. Mil.
   m. Catherine Sauervein (?) — son George T. m. Ann Sophy Plitt

Safell, Samuel b. 1777 d. 1850   Jury Service Tenn. 1804-7
   m. Elizabeth Cox — son Clement Hale m. Mary Ann Duncan

Safford, Adam G.   Vol. 13   Capt. Ga. Mil.

Safford, Hiram Vol. 7   Capt. N.Y. Lt. Drag.

Sage, Giles b. Conn. 1780 d. N.Y. 1842 m. Lydia Herendeen   Pvt. N.Y.
   son Orson G. m. Eliza Ann Eckler

Sage, Ransom b. Conn. 1780 d. N.Y. 1852 m. Mary West   Pvt. N.Y. Art.
   daughter Freelove m. Carlton Holland Wood

Sager, Christian b. Penn. 1769 d. Ohio 1866   Pvt. Ohio Mil.
   m. Elizabeth Shover — son Abraham m. Emaline Smith

Sailly, Peter, b. Fra. 1754 d. N.Y. 1826   Pat.
   m. Marianne Adelaide Guellier   Memb. N.Y. Assy.
   son Frederick L. C. m. Elizabeth Sheldon Platt

St. Amand, Pierre Daspit b. 1775 d. La. 1837   Civil Officer & Justice La.
   m. Marie Maysaur — son Marcel Daspit m. Elise Baudoin

St. Clair, Alexander b. Ire. 1715 d. Va. 1800   Pat. Senate 1791-3
   m. Jane McClanahan   Pres. Elector 1800 Va.
   daughter Anna m. John Boys

St. Clair, Arthur b. Scot. 1734 d. Penn. 1818   Maj. Gen. U.S. Army
   m. Phoebe Bayard — daughter Louisa m. Samuel Robb

St. Clair, James Jr. b. Penn. 1775 d. Penn. 1855   Pvt. Penn. Mil.
   m. Jennie Slemmons — son William Sr. m. Jane Lewis

St. George, Peter b. Ontario 1774 d. Mich. 1875   Pvt. Mich. Terr. Vol.
   m.— Grifford — daughter Elizabeth m. Edmond Tibble
   daughter Mary m. Jerome Priest

St. John, Daniel b. N.Y. 1777 d. Ind. 1863 m. Mary Oakley   Capt. N.Y. Mil.
   daughter Mary m. Daniel Pursel

Sale, Joseph b. Va. 1792 d. Mo. 1870 m. Peggy Grey   Sgt. Va. Mil.
   son Joseph E. m. Syrena Wells

Sale, William b. Va. 1782 d. Ky. 1861 m. Lavina Duncan   Capt. Va. Cav.
   daughter Elizabeth Ann m. John Camden Staples

Salisbury, Atwell b. N.Y. 1797 d. Minn. 1875   Pvt. N.Y. Mil.
   m. Martha Beckwith — daughter Elizabeth m. Howard Hiram Stilwell

Salisbury, D'Estaing b. R.I. 1778 d. N.Y. 1813   Capt. N.Y. Mil. 1807-11
   m. Elizabeth Adams — daughter Lucinda m. Henry Smith

Salisbury, Milburn b. Mass. 1792 d. N.Y. 1865   Musician N.Y. Mil.
   m. Anne Wales Keith
   daughter Emma Louise m. Richard Knight REAL DAUGHTER

Salisbury, Reuben   Vol. 18   Lt. U.S. Inf.

Sallada, Jacob Philip b. Penn. 1788 d. Pa. 1863   Lt. Capt. Penn. Mil.
    m. Cartherine Showers — son Abner m. Joanna Dieffenbacher
    daughter Lydia m. Michael Fenstermaker

Sally (Sallee), William b. Va. 1771 d. Ky. 1831   Ens. Ky. Mil.
    m. Elizabeth Smith — son George S. m. Lucy Henderson

Salmon, Charles Vol. 5   Pvt. N.Y. Mil.

Salmon, Ranson b. N.Y. 1791 d. N.Y. 1880 m. Hannah Searl   Pvt. N.Y. Mil.
    daughter Sallie m. George Rogers

Salter, Isaac Harrington b. Mass. 1785 d. N.Y. 1872   Pvt. N.Y. Mil.
    m. Sally Worthen — son Lyman m. Lucy Hall

Saltsman, William b. Penn. 1777 d. Penn. 1829   Pvt. Penn. Mil.
    m. Jane Stevenson — son George W. m. Harriet A. Robbins

Sample, James b. Penn. 1756 d. Penn. 1830   Capt., Maj. Penn. Mil.
    m. Christina Taggart — son Robert A. m. Mary Simpson

Sams, Edmond Vol. 9   Pvt. E. Tenn. Mil.

Sanborn, Daniel b. N.H. 1796 d. N.J. 1858   Pvt. N.H. Mil.
    m. Charlotte Frances — daughter Charlotte F. m. Charles S. Batchelder

Sanborn, Josiah b. 1747 d. N.H. 1817   Pvt. N.H. Lt. Inf.
    m. Lucy Swain — son William m. Lois Woodman

Sanders, James b. Scot. 1790 d. Ill. 1847 m. Mary Ann Orrell   Pvt. Va. Mil.
    son John William m. Nancy Harper

Sanders, Jeremiah b. Ga. 1782 d. Miss. 1840 m. Mary Barnes   Capt. Ga. Mil.
    son James B. m. Cornelia Marion Janes

Sanders, John b. 1764 d. S.C. 1868 m.—   Capt. S.C. Mil.
    daughter Lucinda m. Martin Still

Sanders, Malachi Madison b. 1785 d. Ga. 1873   Pvt. Ga. Mil.
    m. Margaret Watson — son King m. Bethany Leslie

Sanders, Peter b. Penn. 1765 d. Ohio 1834   Capt. Penn. Mil.
    m. Elizabeth Stuckey — daughter Elizabeth m. John Iles (Oiles)

Sanders, William b. Va. 1765 d. S.C. 1826 m. Rebecca Williams   S.C. Mil.
    son William Seaborn m. Piety Peacock
    son Stephen m. Sina Cooper

Sanderson, James b. Penn. 1790 d. Ohio 1867   Sgt. Ohio Mil.
    m. Sarah Newman — daughter Barbara m. Henry Willis

Sanderson, John b. Mass. 1789 d. Ill. 1851 m. Lydia Harris   Pvt. Mass. Mil.
    daughter Caroline C. m. Arabut Ludlow

Sanford, Daniel b. Vt. 1786 d. Vt. 1876 m. Dortha Peck   Ord. Sgt. Vt. Mil.
    son Horatio m. Sarah Ann Dana

Sanford, David B. Vol. 10   Capt. U.S. Inf.

Sanford, John b. Vt. 1795 d. Vt. 1869 m. Anne Beck   Pvt. Vt. Mil.
    son Edgar m. Minerva Tilden

Sanford, Reuben b. Conn. 1780 d. Ohio 1855 m. Polly Lewis   Pvt. N.Y. Mil.
    daughter Phebe B. m. Elisha A. Adams

Sanford, Sala b. Conn. 1784 d. Ill. 1866   Sgt. N.Y. Mil.
    m. Margaret B. Smith — son James B. m. Maria Yeomans

Sands, Comfort b. 1748 d. N.Y. m. Ann   Pat. Material Aid
    son Joseph m. Teresa de Kamphlin

Sands, Ray b. R.I. 1737 d. R.I. 1808 m. Ann Niles   Pat. Del. to Gen. Assem.
    son Robert G. m. Anna Maynard Case   R.I.

Sands, Robert Guthrie b. R.I. 1764 d. R.I. 1824   Capt. R.I. Mil.
    m. Ann Maynard Case — son William C. m. Abigail Wickes

Sankey, Richard b. Ire. 1712 d. Va. 1789 m. Thomson   Pat. Civil Va.
    daughter Sarah m. William Hamersley

Santee, Valentine b. Penn. 1748 d. Penn. 1808   Pat. Constable 1797
    m. Margaret Funston — son James m. Rachel McNeel
    son John m. Janes Moore

Sappington, Hartley b. Ky. 1791 d. Mo. 1849   Pvt. U.S. Vol.
    m. Mary Richardson — daughter Nancy m. John Baxter

Sappington, John b. Ky. 1790 d. Mo. 1864   Cpl. Mo. Terr. Mil.
    m. Sarah Wells — daughter Jemima m. Henry Fenton Steinhauer
    son Thomas Jefferson m. Julia Ann Leffingwell

Sarber, John b. Penn. 1781 d. Penn. 1858   Lt. Penn. Mil.
    m. Hannah Haven — daughter Mary D. m. Samuel Sheridan

Sargent, John b. N.H. 1794 d. Ill. 1867 m. Irene Sweet   Pvt. N.H. Mil.
    daughter Louise C. m. Robert Nelson Murray
    daughter Maria m. Welling Marvin REAL DAUGHTER
    son Marquis D. m. Lois Ingalls
    son William S. m. Relinda McKillips

Sargent, Reuben b. N.H. 1768 d. N.Y. 1852   Pat. Selectman N.H. 1812
    m. Mary Tarbox — daughter Sophia m. Abel Plummer

Sargent, Samuel b. Mass. 1756 d. Mass. 1827   Pvt. Mass. Mil.
    m. Mary Darling — daughter Hannah m. Moses Osgood

Sarven (Serven), Abraham A. b. N.Y. 1791 d. N.Y. 1849   Cpl. N.Y. Mil.
    m. Martha Van Houten — son John A. m. Sarah Polhemus

Satterlee, James b. Mass. 1777 d. N.Y. 1856   Pvt. N.Y. Mil.
    m. Theodosia Wells — daughter Helen m. Albert J. Hovey

Satterlee, Joseph b. N.Y. 1789 d. N.Y. 1863   Pvt. N.Y. Mil.
    m. Dorcas Babcock — daughter Betsey m. Alonza Wood

Sauerwein, Peter Jr. b. Md. 1797 d. Md. 1858 m. Mary Rich   Pvt. Md. Mil.
    son Edwin A. m. Annie Proctor Taylor

Saugrain, Antoine Francois b. Fra. 1763 d. Mo. 1820   Surgeon's Mate
    m. Rosalie Mishaut   U.S. Army
    son Frederick m. Marie Elise Prevenchere

Saunders (Sanders), Benjamin b. N.Y. 1791 d. Mich. 1858   Pvt. N.Y. Mil.
    m. Keziah Bunn — daughter Melvina m. George Raymond

Saunders, David b. Va. 1760 d. Va. 1842 m. Lockey Leftwich   Col. Va. Mil.
    son James m. Ann Maria Rives

Saunders, Edward   Vol. 13   Fife Maj. Penn. Mil.

Saunders, Elisha Smith b. N.Y. 1776 d. in Battle 1812   Capt. N.Y. Mil.
    m. Lucy Wyburn — daughter Juliette m. John Tuckey

Saunders, John   Vol. 17   Pvt. Penn. Mil.

Saunders, Oliver b. Ky. 1798 d. Ky. 1868 m. Maria Burns   Pvt. Ky. Mil.
   daughter Ellen m. Abner Hord REAL DAUGHTER

Saunders, Peleg b. 1785 d. Ill. aft. 1858 m.—   Pvt. N.Y. Mil.
   son Isaac m.—

Saunders, William b. 1776 d. 1846 m. Mary   Pvt. W. Tenn. Mil.
   son Ferdinand P. m. Artemisia Wyly

Saurman, Sarah C. Voorhees b. N.J. 1803 d. Penn. 1899   Pat. 1812
   m. Jacob Saurman (Mrs. Jacob Saurman)   Fed. Soldiers
   daughter Maria R. m. Lucius C. Pierson

Savage, George b. Va. 1786 d. Tenn. 1873   Cpl. Tenn. Mil.
   m. Elizabeth Kenner
   daughter Josephine m. William Davidson Smartt

Savery, Ashel   Vol. 7   Pvt. N.Y. Mil.

Savitz (Sevitz, Sevits), George b. Penn. 1753 d. Penn. 1826   Capt. Penn. Mil.
   m. Mary Catherine — daughter Jane m. Dr. Jacob Martin

Savitz (Sevitz, Savits), Joseph b. Penn. 1734 d. Penn. 1794   Capt. Penn.
   m. Gloria Catharine Dieter   Mil. 1794
   son George m. Mary Catherine

Sawyer, Benjamin b. Penn. 1735 d. Penn. 1792   Pvt. Penn. Mil.
   m. Margaret Haynes — son Thomas m. Elizabeth Day

Sawyer, Daniel b. Conn. 1773 d. N.C. 1819   Pat. Mem. House Commons
   m. Theodosia Penoyer Bouton   N.C. 1812-15
   son John S. m. Elmira Harrison

Sawyer, Dempsey b. Tenn. d. Tenn. 1861   Pvt. W. Tenn. Mil.
   m. Courtney Vick (Kennedy) — son Brown S. m. Martha Forehand
   son Elisha D. m. Mrs. Margaret E. Pate Pearre

Sawyer, Horace B.   Vol. 9   Capt. U.S. Navy

Sawyer, Isaac b. (Me.) Mass. 1793 d. Me. 1880   Pvt. Mass. Mil.
   m. Eleanor Wescott — son Marshall m. Arazine Wilkins

Sawyer, James b. Mass. 1737 d. Vt. 1801   Pat. Moderator Selectman
   m. Lydia Flint — son Dudley m. Olive Field   Vt. 1791
   son Stephen L. m. Ann Marie Pritchard

Sawyer, Prescot b. Mass. 1794 d. Wisc. 1876   Pvt. N.Y. Mil.
   m. Zeruiah Lamb — daughter Cornelia S. m. James B. Wood

Sawyers, James b. Va. 1794 d. Ill. 1879   Pvt. Tenn. Mil.
   m. (2) Rachel Sherwood
   daughter Lucy m. Albert Henry Schnell REAL DAUGHTER

Saxton, Alanson   Vol. 17   Pvt. N.Y. Mil.
   daughter Sarah J. m. Lewis Beardsley REAL DAUGHTER

Saxton, Jehiel   Vol. 9   Capt. Vt. Mil.
   daughter Mary unmarried REAL DAUGHTER

Sayre, John b. N.Y. 1767 d. N.Y. 1848   Town Clerk 1797/1801
   m. Sally Brewster   Ct. Judge N.Y. 1811/13
   daughter Eliza m. Stephen R. Miller

Sayre, Pierson (Pearson) b. N.J. 1761 d. N.J. 1852   Maj. Penn. Mil. 1800
   m. Catherine Lewis — daughter Elizabeth m. John Gibson

Sayre, Seely b. N.Y. 1769 d. Va. 1815   Pvt. U.S. Inf.
   m. Mrs. Thompson Davis — son John m. Sarah R. Freeman

Scales, Nathaniel b. N.C. 1758 d. N.C. 1824   Pat. Mem. Gen. Assem. as
    m. Nancy Allen   Senator N.C. 1806-11
    daughter Mary m. Joseph McCain

Scales, Thomas b. Va. c. 1760 d. Ga. 1797   Pat. Justice of Peace
    m. Ann — son Thomas Jr. m. Elizabeth Glover   Ga. 1793-6

Scales, William b. N.C. 1785 d. Ind. 1848 m. Mary Skelton   Sgt. Ind. Mil.
    son Thomas m. Sarah Bogan

Scarborough, Allen b. N.C. 1768 d. Ga. 1819   4th Sgt. Ga. Mil. 1812
    m. Nancy Stringer — son Daniel M. m. Damaris Ann Alford

Scatterday, Aaron b. Va. 1795 d. Va. 1872   Pvt. Va. Mil.
    m. Anna Matilda Beatty
    daughter Frances m. John Hough REAL DAUGHTER
    daughter Laura m. Jonathan Bean REAL DAUGHTER
    daughter Permalia m. William Sappington REAL DAUGHTER

Schaeffer, Henry b. Penn. 1749 d. Penn. 1803 m.—   Pat. Judge Penn. 1803
    daughter Maria m. J. Frederick Oberly

Schall, George b. Penn. 1768 d. Penn. 1831   Pat. Mem. Legis. Penn. 1810
    m. Catharine Eister (Oyster) — son William m. Caroline Traxter

Schall, Michael b. Penn. 1770 d. Penn. 1855   Pvt. Penn. Mil.
    m. Catherine Hines (Hein) — daughter Leah m. Samuel Woodward

Schall, Michael b. Ger. 1739 d. Penn. 1830   Lt. Penn. Mil. 1784
    m. Anna Maria — son Andrew m. Mary Schaeffer

Schall (Shall), Tobias b. Penn. 1771 d. Penn. 1849   Pvt. Penn. Mil.
    m. Elizabeth Eyster — daughter Elizabeth m. Isaac Yoder

Schappell, Jeremiah b. Penn. 1774 d. Penn. 1845   Lt. Col. Penn. Mil.
    m. Wille — son John m. Susanna Unger

Schaeffner, Henry J. Vol. 6   Sgt. Penn. Mil.

Schell, Henry b. Penn. 1782 d. N.Y. 1839 m. Delia Harned   Capt. U.S. Inf.
    son Henry L. m. Hester Visscher

Schellinger, Aaron b. N.J. 1780-5 d. N.J. 1872   Matross N.J. Art.
    m. Sophia Bennett — daughter Elizabeth m. William Smith

Schermerhorn, Uriah J. b. N.Y. d. N.Y. m. Olive Cahoon   Pvt. N.Y. Mil.
    daughter Mary M. m. David Henry Hull

Schmyser, Michael b. Penn. 1740 d. Penn. 1810   Mem. Legis. House &
    m. Anna Maria   Senate Penn. 1784-8
    son Jacob m. Ann Margaret Yessler

Schneider, George b. Penn. 1771 d. Penn. 1844   Pvt. Penn. Mil.
    m. Katherine Kobel — son Peter m. Eva Reith

Schneider (Snider, Snyder), John b. 1749 d. Penn. 1827 m.—   Pvt. Penn.
    daughter Anna Katherine m. Samuel Bowser   Mil. 1786-9

Schneider (Snyder), John b. Penn. 1783 d. Penn. 1853   Maj. Penn. Mil.
    m. Anna Mary Rummel — son Samuel M. m. Matilda Edson

Schoch (Shock), Henry b. Penn. 1792 d. Penn. 1843   Pvt. Penn. Mil.
    m. Elizabeth Roberts — son Henry L. m. Rebecca Conover

Schock, Jonathan b.— d.— m. Mary Ann Kerper   Pvt. Penn. Mil.
    son Jonathan Jr. m. Maria Loisa Shermer

Schoff, Philip b. Penn. 1770 d. Ohio 1855   Pvt. Ohio Mil.
    m. Elizabeth Ramsay — daughter Fanny m. Josiah Walker

Scholl, Joseph b. Va. 1755-6 d. Ky. 1829-30　　　　Lt. Ky. Mil. 1792-3
　　m. Levina Boone — son Septimus m. Sarah, Sallie) Millar

Schooler, Benjamin　Vol. 10　　　　　　　　　　Capt. Ohio Mil.

Schreiner, George Michael b. Penn. 1773 d. Penn. 1815　　Pvt. Penn. Mil.
　　m. Anna Maria Zehmer — son Henry m. Christiana Bomberger

Schrock, Christopher b. Ger. 1781 d. Ohio 1846　　　　Pvt. Va. Mil.
　　m. Sarah Cade (Cate) — son David m. Mary Welte
　　son John L. m. Charlotta McArthur

Schryver, Peter Isaac b. N.Y. 1771 d. N.Y. 1830　　　　Capt. N.Y. Inf.
　　m. Susan Storms — son John E. m. Abigail Bartlett

Schureman, James b. N.J. 1756 d. N.J. 1824　　Mem. U.S. Congress 1789-91
　　m. Eleanor Williamson　　　　　　　　　　Senate 1799-1801 N.J.
　　daughter Catherine m. Rev. Richard Wyncoop

Schutt, John b. N.Y. 1787 d. N.Y. 1869　　　　　　Sgt. N.Y. Mil.
　　m. Hannah Kinn or Krum
　　son Francis G. m. Elizabeth T. Wallis or Thomas

Schutt, Richard b. N.Y. 1795 d. N.Y. 1854　　　　　　Pvt. N.Y. Mil.
　　m. Elizabeth Winfield
　　daughter Sarah m. M. B. Reed REAL DAUGHTER

Schutz, Henry　Vol. 4　　　　　　　　　　Maj. Gen. Penn. Mil.

Schuyler, Barent　Vol. 12　　　　　　　　　　Adj. N.Y. Mil.

Schuyler, Harmanus b. N.Y. 1727 d. N.Y. 1796　Assist. Deputy Commission
　　m. Christina Ten Broeck　　　　　　　　　　Gen. N.Y. Troops
　　son John H. m. Hendrika Fort

Schuyler, Peter b. N.Y. 1780 d. N.Y. 1826　　Lt. N.Y. Privateer 1812
　　m. Elizabeth White — daughter Eliza m. Charles Plater Turner

Schuyler, Philip S. b. N.Y. 1775 d. N.Y. 1846　　　　Lt. U.S. Inf.
　　m. Cynthia Carpenter
　　daughter Abigail Maria m. Ira Samuel Hitchcock

Schwenk, Jacob b. Penn. 1789 d. Penn 1852　　　　Pvt. Penn. Mil.
　　m. Magdalena Zeigler — daughter Elizabeth m. R. Y. Strassburger

Schweppenheiser, John　Vol. 8　　　　　　　　Capt. U.S. Inf.

Scobee, Robert b. Scot. 1775 d. Ky. 1835　　　　Capt. Ky. Mil.
　　m. Elizabeth Brohard — daughter Kitty m. Thomas Jefferson Grimes
　　son Robert m. (2) Lucy Pendleton

Scofield, Jacob Smith b. N.Y. 1791 d. Ohio 1848　　　Cpl. N.Y. Mil.
　　m. Cynthia Phillips — daughter Louisia S. m. John McKelvey

Schofield (Scofield), Joseph　Vol. 15　　　　　　Pvt. N.Y. Mil.

Scofield, Thomas E.　Vol. 16　　　　　　　　　Pvt. N.Y. Mil.

Scott, Abel S.　Vol. 16　　　　　　　　　　　Pvt. N.Y. Mil.

Scott, Alexander b. Penn. 1793 d. Ill. 1866　　　　Pvt. Penn. Mil.
　　m. Elizabeth Boyd — son Abram B. m. Margaret McMasters

Scott, Andrew b. Va. 1789 d. Ark. 1851　　　　Cornet Mo. Mil.
　　m. Elizabeth Rice Jones
　　son John Rice Homer m. Nancy Evans Jamison

Scott, Benjamin Rush b. Conn. 1791 d. S.C. 1843　　　Pvt. S.C. Mil.
　　m. Eliza M. Roper — son Ira S. m. Margaret Peay

Scott, Daniel b. Conn. 1780 d. N.Y. 1867   Lt. Qtr. Mst. N.Y. Mil.
m. Sarah Dunlap — son Gideon m. Delia Denton

Scott, Daniel b. Va. 1762 d. Ky. 1846   Cpl. Ky. Mil. 1814-15
m. Nancy Crosby Floyd — son Charles Lewis m. Martha Greenwell

Scott, Daniel L. b. Eng. 1760 d. Penn. 1828   Lt. Qtr. Mst. U.S. Vol.
m. Charlotte Chalmers — son Daniel m. Mary Jones
daughter Sarah W. m. Henry Miller

Scott, David b. Va. 1768 d. Va. 1846 m. Rachel   Maj. Va. Mil.
daughter Judith m. David Bouslog

Scott, Francis Jr. b. Va. 1782 d. Va. 1821 m. Nancy Wyatt   Lt. Va. Mil.
daughter Susan Ann m. Alexander C. Owen

Scott, Harry b. N.Y. 1790 d. Vt. 1837 m. Cornelia Wicker   Fifer Vt. Mil.
daughter Cornelia L. m. Henry Clay Hill
daughter Elvira M. m. Horace Dawson

Scott, Henry Vol. 7   Pvt. Ga. Mil.
daughter Sarah J. m. William T. Holderness REAL DAUGHTER

Scott, Henry b. Vt. 1763 d. Vt. 1834   Financial Aid Vt.
m. Christiana Rowley — son Harry m. Cornelia Wicker

Scott, Jacob b. N.Y. 1784 d. N.Y. 1863 m. Lany   Pvt. N.Y. Mil.
daughter Eliza m. DeWitt C. Jackson

Scott, James b. 1765 d. 1849 m. Amelia Daugherty   Lt. Col. Va. Mil.
daughter Matilda m. Thomas Hess

Scott, James b. S.C. 1778 d. Miss. m. Nancy Montague   Sgt. Miss. Terr. Vol.
daughter Beverly D. m. Hester Williams

Scott, James b. S.C. 1793 d. Tex. 1862   Pvt. S.C. Mil.
m. Martha Corless (Carlos) — son Francis M. m. Lucy Duncan

Scott, John b. Va. 1772 d. Ga. 1839   Brig. Gen. Ga. Mil. 1807/17
m. Eliza Coleman — daughter Mary Lucretia m. Elisha Coleman

Scott, John b. Penn. 1784 d. Penn. 1850 m. Agnes Irvine   Maj. Penn. Mil.
son George W. m. Rebekah Bucher

Scott, John b. N.Y. 1784 d. Ia. 1861   Pvt. Vt. Mil.
m. Martha Puilla Wicker — daughter Christiana m. Peter Fleury

Scott, John Vol. 7   Ens. U.S. Inf.

Scott, John Baytop b. Va. 1761 d. Va. 1814   Org. co. Rev. Vets. for War
m. Martha Thompson   of 1812
son Christopher m. Elizabeth Strother Smith

Scott, John Jay b. N.Y. 1788 d. N.Y. 1846 m. Pamelia Lambert   Capt.
daughter Dora K. m. Charles Peck Crittenden REAL DAUGHTER

Scott, Johnny b. Va. 1718 d. Va. aft. 1801   Justice Va. 1784
m. Mary Hackett — son John m. Sarah Terrell

Scott, Joseph b. Ky. 1792 d. Kan. 1872 m. Sarah Sutton   Pvt. Ky. Mil.
daughter Hester Ann m. Joseph M. Dill Alexander

Scott, Richard b. Md. 1792 d. Md. 1869 m. Elizabeth Brown   Pvt. Md. Mil.
daughter Elizabeth m. Daniel Joseph Pender

Scott, Samuel b. Penn. 1785 d. Penn. 1819   Capt. Penn. Mil.
m. Mary Ann Wylie — son Josiah N. m. Rachel Vance

Scott, Samuel b. 1771 d. Tenn. 1851   Pvt. Tenn. Gunman
m. Catherine Morrison — son David M. m. Frances Hogler

Scott, Samuel b. N.C. 1777 d. Ky. 1841 m. Lydia Long   Sgt. Ky. Mil.
son Samuel Jr. m. Abigail Victoria Smith

Scott, Samuel b. Md. c. 1790 d. Ohio aft. 1840 m. Mary   Pvt. Penn. Mil.
son William H. m. Virginia C. Ivory

Scott, Samuel b. Va. 1786 d. Ind. 1855 m. Milly Foster   Pvt. Ky. Mil.
son John T. M. m. Mary Gaines Abrell

Scott, Thomas b. N.Y. 1784 d. N.Y. 1867   Lt. Col. N.Y. Mil.
m. Elizabeth Cooper — son Thomas Jr. m. Charlotte Ann Towsley

Scott, Thomas b. Va. 1775 d. Va. 1837 m. Jane Haskins   Pvt. Va. Mil.
daughter Mary Jane m. Branch O.
daughter Betsy Anne m. John Turner Ligon

Scott, Toliver b. Va. 1782 d. S.C. 1862 m. Nancy Wright   2nd Lt. S.C. Mil.
son William B. m. Emily Mason

Scott, William   Vol. 12   Pvt. U.S. Inf.

Scott, William b. Va. 1754 d. Ga. 1806 m. Jane Thomas   Drag. Ga. Mil.
son Daniel m. Jemima Walker

Scott, William Coleman   Vol. 6   Capt. Va. Mil.

Scout, Lewis b. Penn. 1797 d. Ill. 1883 m. Priscilla Dean   Pvt. Penn. Mil.
daughter Alice Frances m. William James Crawford REAL DAU.

Scouten, Jacob b. N.Y. 1755 d. Penn. 1842   Pvt. N.Y. Mil.
m. Charity Roberts — daughter Lucy m. Peter Thompson

Scovil, Moses b. Conn. 1762 d. Ohio 1836 m. Rachel Baker   Lt. Penn. Mil.
son David m. Clara Harding

Scoville, Daniel b. Conn. 1767 d. Conn. 1846   Sgt. Conn. Mil.
m. Lucina Cook — son Riley m. Nancy Baldwin

Scoville, Levi b. Conn. 1762 d. N.Y. 1828 m. Content Dunbar   Maj. N.Y.
son James m. Abigail

Scribner, Enoch b. Conn. 1750 d. Conn. 1816   Sgt. Conn. Mil.
m. Betty Benedict — son Joseph m. Sarah Kellogg

Scibner, John b. N.Y. 1783 d. Mich. 1862   Pvt. N.Y. Mil.
m. Johannah Hartsough — daughter Angeline m. Solomon Armstrong

Scroggs, John b. Penn. 1771 d. Penn. 1844   Capt. Penn. Mil.
m. Isabella Walker — daughter Rachel m. John McNickle

Scruggs, Edward b. Va. 1794 d. Tenn. 1846-7   Pvt. W. Tenn. Mil.
m. Althea Hassell — son William m. Sarah Gooch Kimbrough
son Young m. Ida Bennett

Scudder, Elias b. N.J. 1769 d. N.J. 1811 m. Sarah Smith   Pvt. N.J. Mil.
son Jasper S. m. Mary Stillwell

Scudder, Ezekiel b. Conn. 1765 d. N.Y. 1854   Commission of Highways
m. Cynthia Gould   N.Y. 1812
daughter Clarissa m. Elisha Spaulding

Scull, Andrew b. N.J. 1793 d. N.J. 1888 m. Mary Gifford   Pvt. N.J. Mil.
daughter Ann H. m. Nicholas H. Hickman REAL DAUGHTER
daughter Elizabeth G. m. John H. Willets REAL DAUGHTER

Scull, John R.   Vol. 16   Capt. N.J. Mil.

Scull, Richard b. N.J. 1792 d. N.J. 1854   Pvt. N.J. Mil.
   m. Elizabeth Hickman — son Richard Jr. m. Eunice English

Seaborn, James   Vol. 13   Capt. Va.

Seagrave, Edward b. Eng. 1722 d. Mass. 1793   Pvt. Mass. Mil.
   m. Lois White   Shay's Rebellion
   son Bazaleel m. Jemima Aldrich

Seagraves, Bennett b. Ga. 1791 d. Ill. 1868   Pvt. Drum W. Tenn. Mil.
   m. Margaret Lockhart — daughter Margaret S. m. Sterling Smith
   daughter Sarah J. E. m. Jacky Sawrey

Seagraves, James b. N.J. 1774 d. Penn. 1861   Ens. Penn. Mil.
   m. Elizabeth Shades — daughter Euphemia m. James Adam Gangwer

Seagraves, Samuel b. N.J. 1782 d. N.J. 1847   Maj. N.J. Inf.
   m. Barbara Hepner — son William m. Rebecca Gardiner

Seahorn, Jacob b. Penn. 1773 d. Tenn. 1871 m. Polly Inman   Pvt. Tenn. Vol.
   daughter Jane m. Robert C. Lowe

Seale, Bluford b. S.C. 1791 d. Ala. 1871   Pvt. Ga. Mil.
   m. Elizabeth Lyon (2) — son Benjamin B. m. Malinda McMillin

Seaman, John b. Penn. 1753 d. Penn. 1820   Judge Penn. 1805
   m. Elizabeth Schlabbig(?) — son John Jr. m. Catherine E. Alwein

Seamonds, Manson b. Ky. 1786 d. Ky. 1850   Capt. Ky. Mil.
   m. Elizabeth Newton — daughter Elizabeth m. Kinzea Stone

Searle, John b. Mass. 1767 d. Ohio 1820 m. Abigail Safford   Pvt. Ohio Mil.
   son John m. Agnes Owens

Searles, Covington b. S.C. 1785 d. Ga. 1847 m.—   Pvt. S.C. Mil.
   son Thomas m. Caroline Louise Wynn

Sears, Benjamin b. Conn. 1771 d. Ohio 1822   Maj. N. Y. Mil.
   m. Anne Bigelow — —son Elkanah m. Desire Phelps

Sears, David b. 1791 d. 1879 m. Levicy Nobles   Pvt. Ga. Inf.
   daughter Mary Sears m. Fred Jackson Mills Jr.

Seaton, George Clark b. Penn. 1783 d. Penn. 1849   Pvt. Penn. Mil.
   m. Isabella McClelland — daughter Isabella m. William Flenniken

Seaver, Seth b. Mass. 1784 d. Ill. 1871 m. Clarissa Phelps   Sgt. N.Y. Mil.
   daughter Clarissa D. m. Ezra Wilcox

Seavey, Eli b. (Me.) 1788 d. Me. 1857 m.—   Vol. 9   Lt. Mass. Mil.

Seavey, Jonathan b. N.H. 1774 d. Me. 1866 m. Mary E. Prescott   Pvt. N.H.
   son Ira m. Sarah Brown

Seawell, Benjamin b. Va. 1741 d. Tenn. 1821   Justice N.C. 1786-7
   m. Mary Booker — son William m. Nancy Evans Mabry

Seawell, William b. Va. 1771 d. Tenn. 1846   Public Surveyor Tenn.
   m. Nancy Evans Mabry
   daughter Adelaide m. Jasper Rogers Ashworth Jr.

Seay, Abraham B. b. Va. 1780 d. La. 1845   Pvt. U.S. Inf.
   m. Rosey Perman Loving — son John B. m. Eliza Thompson

Seay, Jesse b. S.C. c. 1775 d. S.C. aft. 1820 m. Mary   Cpl. S.C.
   son John W. m. Barbara Lephart

Sebring, Cornelius C. b. N.Y. 1797 d. N.Y. 1863   Pvt. N.Y. Mil.
m. Agnes Copeland — daughter Margaret C. m. George Oscar Smith

Secor, Caleb b. N.Y. 1795 d. N.Y. 1840 m. Eliza Sloan   Pvt. N.Y. Mil.
daughter Anna Eliza m. James Seaman

Secord (Secor), Jacob I. b. N.Y. 1784 d. N.Y. 1863   Sgt. N.Y. Mil.
m. Catherine Jones — son John J. m. Catherine Van Pelt

Sedwick, John b. Md. 1775 d. Ind. 1849   Qtr. Mst. Md. Mil.
m. Elizabeth Rawlings — daughter Sophia m. Wm. Booth Munson

See, Garred b. Va. 1788 d. Ky. 1856 m. Florence   Pvt. Va. Mil.
daughter Emily m. William Short

See, John b. N.Y. 1787 d. N.Y. aft. 1814 m. Eunice Minor   Capt. N.Y. Mil.
son Benjamin m. Lavina Jennings

See, John b. N.Y. 1752 d. N.Y. 1813 m. Rachel Martling   Pvt. N.Y. Mil.
son Peter m. Eliza Ann Davids

See, Peter b. N.Y. 1788 d. N.Y. 1864 m. Eliza Ann Davids   Pvt. N.Y. Mil.
daughter Rosannah m. Willet Field

Seeley, Michael b. Conn. 1750 d. Penn. 1823   Cpl. Penn. Mil.
m. Elsche Van Campen — son John m. Mary Wels (Weltz)

Seeley, Samuel C. b. N.J. 1756 d. Penn. 1819   Brig. Gen. Penn. Mil.
m. Patience Morrell — daughter Harret m. Isaac Rurell

Seeley, Samuel Odel b. Conn. 1779 d. Conn. 1863   Pvt. Conn. Mil.
m. Sally Morehouse — son Henry m. Clarissa Bulkley

Seeleye, Abner b. Conn. 1776 d. Conn. 1819   Pvt. Conn. Mil.
m. Lucy Osboren — daughter Sabra m. Samuel Wheeler

Seifert (Johan), Michael b. Penn. 1753 d. Ohio 1818   Pvt. Penn. Mil. 1785-8
m. Maria Magdalene Wild (Wilt)
son George M. m. Anna Maria Leinbaugh

Seip, Jacob b. Ger. 1741 d. Penn. 1831   Ens. Penn. Mil.
m. Anna Rosina Mertz — son John m. Rachel Levitz

Seip, Jacob b. Penn. 1778 d. Penn. 1863   Pvt. Penn. Mil.
m. Elizabeth Doll— son Reuben m. Mary Ann Fenstermacher

Seip (Sipe), Peter b. Ger. 1735 d. Penn. 1809   Pvt. Penn. Mil.
m. Anna Maria Erb — daughter Christina m. Conrad Ihrie, Jr.

Selby, Eli b. Md. 1761 d. Ohio 1857 m. Ruth Shipey   Pvt. Md. Mil.
daughter Julia Ann m. Isaac Gardner

Selby, Jesse b. Md. 1781 d. Md. 1845 m. Martha Sasscer   Pvt. Md. Mil.
son James m. Alverda McKnew

Selby, Joseph b. Penn. d. Ga. c. 1814 m. Alcey Wotten   Pvt. Ga. Mil.
daughter Christiana m. James G. Smith

Selden, Samuel b. Conn. 1748 d. N.H. 1814   Adj. N.H. Mil.
m. Prudence Cook — daughter Eleanor m. Walter Watsworth

Seldon, Joseph   Vol. 6   Pvt. Conn. Mil.

Selin, Anthony Charles b. Penn. 1789 d. Penn. 1825   2nd Lt. Penn. Mil.
m. Mary Catherine Yome — daughter Elizabeth m. John Clayton

Selingham, Daniel b. N.H. 1794 d. N.H. 1882   Music N.H. Mil.
m. Matilda Clement — daughter Matilda Jane m. Henry W. Benton

Sellars (Sollars), Samuel b. Penn. 1784 d. Ohio 1842   Pvt. Ohio Mil.
   m. Elizabeth Train — son Allen m. Sarah J. Ballard

Seller(s), John Finley b. Ky. 1791 d. Ind. 1875   Pvt. Ky. Inf.
   m. Rebecca — son Western Wood m. Margaret Hammond Drew

Sellers, Abraham b. S.C. 1782 d. Miss. abt. 1855   Pvt. S.C. Mil.
   m. Mary Norwood — son Philip m. Nancy McCraney (McRaney)

Sellick, James b. Conn. d. Ohio 1879 m. Polly Hoye   Pvt. Conn. Mil.
   daughter Mary m. Barnett Woodbury

Sells, William H. b. Ohio 1790 d. Ohio 1872   Pvt. Ohio Mil.
   m. Elizabeth Ebey — son Elijah m. Harriet J. Wetmore

Semple, Samuel   Vol. 12   Sgt. Del. Mil.

Sensenderfer, Lewis b. Penn. 1776 d. W.Va. 1867   Capt. Va. Mil.
   m. Catherine Imboden — son Jacob m. Elizabeth Ann Boltz
   son Martin m. Margaret Stump

Senseny, Jeremiah b. 1761 d. 1844 m. Catherine Hoover   1st Lt. Penn. Mil.
   son Hiram C. m. Maria Hoover

Serrill, George   Vol. 4   Ens. Del. Fencibles

Seerin, William b. Md. 1791 d. D.C. 1852   Pvt. Md. (D.C.) Mil.
   m. Christianna Durr — son William D. m. Sarah Ann Cumberland

Serviss, George b. N.Y. 1753 d. N.Y. 1812   Lt. N.Y. Mil.
   m. Mary Overbaugh — son George Jr. m. Sally Vander Veer

Serviss, William G. b. N.Y. 1785 d. Ohio 1855   3rd Lt. U.S. Vol.
   m. Margaret M. Warwick — son Osceola K. m. Maria V. Forgy

Seth, James b. Md. 1780 d. Md. 1829 m. Sarah Lambdin   Pvt. Md. Mil.
   son Alexander m. Martha Haddaway
   son James M. m. Louisa Farland

Seth, William Clayland b. Md. d. Md. 1815   Pvt. Md. Mil.
   m. Martha Chamberlain — daughter Martha m. James DuHamel

Settle, Edward b. Va. 1764 d. Tenn. 1839   Capt. Tenn.
   m. Elizabeth Hubbard — daughter Esther m. Calvert Porter

Sevier, George Washington b. 1782 d. Miss. 1849   Col. Tenn. Mil.
   m. Catherine Chambers — son George W. Jr. m. Sarah Knox
   son Henry C. m. Nancy Nash

Sevier, John b. Va. 1745 d. Ala. 1815   Governor & Mem. Cong. Tenn.
   m. (1) Sarah Hawkins   1790-1815
   m. (2) Catherine Sherrill
   son George W. m. Catherine Chambers
   son Samuel m. Jane Rhea
   daughter Elizabeth m. Major William Clark
   son James m. Nancy Conway
   son John Jr. m. Elizabeth Lowrey (Betty)
   daughter Nancy m. Walter King

Sewall (Sewell), Jason b. (Me.) Mass. 1791 d. Me. 1881   Music Pvt.
   m. Hannah Joyce   Mass. Mil.
   son Stephen B. m. Hannah Polly Orr

Seward, Carey b. Va. 1778 d. Va. 1827   Pvt. Va. Mil.
   m. Mary J. Anson Thorpe — son Joseph R. m. Sarah Frances P. Poole

Seward, David b. N.Y. or Mass. 1778 d. Mich. 1853   Pvt. N.Y. Mil.
   m. Susannah Smith — daughter Paulina m. Thomas Lee

Seward, Isaac b. 1778 d. Ind. 1847   Pvt. Ohio Mil.
m. (1) Mary Van Dyne — son Byrum P. m. Nancy Carter

Seward, Nathan b. Conn. 1758 d. N.Y. 1815   Lt. Col. N.Y. 1792
m. Martha Gridley — son Timothy G. m. Elizabeth Dudley

Seward, Nathaniel   Vol. 1 or 2   Pvt. N.Y. Mil.
daughter Mary Alward m. William J. Taylor REAL DAUGHTER

Seward, Samuel b. Ohio 1793 d. Tex. 1870   Pvt. Ohio Mil.
m. Ann Stewart — daughter Elizabeth m. Tacitus Thomas Clay
son George R. m. Louise Robertson
son John H. m. Laura Roberts

Seward, Stephen   Vol. 10   Capt. N.Y. Mil.

Sewell, Nicholas b. Md. 1760 d. Ga. aft. 1840   Pvt. Ga. Mil. 1793
m. Sarah Lafferty — son Henry m. Mrs. Mary Cornelia Dorsey Smith
daughter Ritha m. Darius Redferen Weems

Sewell, Joshua b. Md. 1755 d. Ga. 1834-37   Pvt. Ga. Mil.
m. Jennie Willis — son John m. Elizabeth Christian

Seymour, Chauncey b. Conn. 1762 d. Conn. 1839   Ens. Conn. Mil.
m. Isabel Sedgwick — son Lovica m. Priscilla Moore
daughter Sally m. Royal Isaac Watson

Seymour, Horace b. Conn. 1791 d. Conn. 1868   Pvt. Conn. Mil.
m. Sophia Spencer
daughter Cornelia B. m. Dr. Daniel Dustin Hanson

Seymour, Leverett b. Conn. 1775 d. N.Y. 1848   Pvt. N.Y. Mil.
m. Sarah Woodworth
daughter Hannah m. John Wesley Remington

Shackleford, Edmond b. Va. 1755 d. Ga. 1821   2nd Lt. Ga. Mil.
m. Judith Easton — daughter Mary J. m. John Harris

Shackleford, Edmund b. Ga. 1786 d. Fla. 1857   Brig. Gen. Ala. Mil.
m. Rebecca Broadnax — daughter Elizabeth R. m. E. G. Carew
son John m. Clarissa Motley

Shackleford, James b. Va. 1728 d. Ky. 1810   Capt. Ky. Mil.
m. Mrs. Mary Stamps Allen — daughter Amelia m. John Metcalfe

Shackleford, Lyne Jr. b. Va. 1762 d. Va. 1806   Oath of Allegiance Va.
m. Elizabeth Price Dabney — son George C. m. Ann P. Bassett

Shacklett, Benjamin b. Penn. 1774 d. Ky. 1838   Maj. Ky. Mil.
m. Elizabeth Ashcraft — son Elijah m. Polly Saunders

Shadel, Michael Jr. b. Penn. 1773 d. Penn. 1850   Pvt. Penn. Mil.
m. Anna Mary Weise — son Jacob (Sheadle) m. Mary L. Treat

Shafer, John b. Penn. 1789 d. Penn. 1872   2nd Sgt. Penn. Mil.
m. Elizabeth Hess — son John H. m. Rosanna Beegle

Shaffer, John b. Penn. 1764 d. Penn. 1835   Capt. Penn. Mil.
m. Phoebe Hawk — son Elijah m. Susanna Lozier

Shaffner, Philip b. Penn. 1787 d. Penn. 1836   Pvt. Penn. Mil.
m. Charlotte Haines — son Henry m. Elizabeth Shimp

Shallcross, Joseph b. Penn. 1797 d. Ohio 1873   Cpl. Pa. Vol.
m. Emily Henderson
daughter Hannah Maria (Minnie) m. Charles D. Kerr REAL DAU.

Shallcross, William b. Penn. 1767 d. Penn. 1828   Cpl. Penn. Mil.
m. Mary Knight — son Thomas m. Rebecca Walton

Shallenberger (Shellenberger), Christian   Pvt. Penn. Mil.
    b. Penn. 1784 d. Penn. 1844
    m. Margaretta Zimmerman — son Levi m. Elizabeth Hassler

Shallus, Francis b. Penn. 1774 d. Penn. 1821   Lt. Penn. Mil.
    m. Anne Peters — daughter Elizabeth m. Henry Horter Paul

Shamblin, John b. Va. 1771 d. Va. 1864 m. Martha Howell   Pvt. Va. Mil.
    daughter Priscilla m. John Wesley Tomlinson

Shane, Casper b. Penn. 1780 d. Penn. 1872   Pvt. Penn. Mil.
    m. Sarah Williams — daughter Ann m. Jacob Ganzhorn

Shane, William   Vol. 3   Pvt. Va. Mil.

Shaner (Shoener), Henry b. Penn. 1757 d. Penn. 1832   Drum Penn. Mil.
    m. Mary Magadelene Starnes — son Charles Sr. m. Mary Ann Biery

Shannon, James   Vol. 30   Capt. W. Tenn. Mil.
    son Samual m.—

Shannon, Samuel b. 1770 d. 1857 m. Elizabeth Sproul   Lt. Penn. Mil. 1793
    daughter Margaret Ann m. Jesse Dodds

Shannon, Thomas   Vol. 6   Pvt. Ky. Vol.

Shapleigh, Richard b. Me. 1794 d. N.H. m. Olive Tobey   Sgt. Me.
    daughter Olive m. Sylvester Brooks

Sharp, Andrew b. Penn. 1750 d. Penn. 1794 m. Ann Woods   Capt. Penn. Mil.
    daughter Margaret m. Alexander McCullough
    daughter Nancy Agnes m. James Mitchell

Sharp, Andrew b. 1777 d. 1858 m. Elizabeth Watts   Pvt. Ohio Mil.
    son Edward J. m. Elizabeth Leaman

Sharp, Eli   Vol. 5   Pvt. N.J. Mil.

Sharp, Henry b. N.J. 1773 d. Ill. 1824 m. Hannah   Cpl. Ill. Terr. Mil.
    daughter Elizabeth m. Simeon Walker
    son Samuel m. Sally Bledsoe

Sharp, Hiram b. Del. 1789 d. Ga. 1875 m. Sarah Ann Owen   Pvt. Ga. Mil.
    daughter Eliza A. m. Landon Carter McCalman

Sharp, John b. 1752 d. Penn. 1843   Capt. Penn. Mil. 1786-8
    m. Elizabeth Crowell   Justice of Peace 1792
    daughter Eve m. John Stine

Sharp, John Sr. b. Ire. 1720 d. Tenn. 1796   Constable Overseer 1784
    m. Jane Hamilton — son Thomas m. Jean Maxwell

Sharp, Jonathan Sr. b. Penn. 1797 d. Ill. 1844   Pvt. Ill. Terr. Mil.
    m. Mary St. Clair — daughter Elizabeth W. m. Posey Maddux
    son Henry m. Margaret Jane Mills
    son Jonathan Jr. m. Mary McNeill

Sharp, Turner b. Va. 1773 d. Va. 1858   Pvt. Va. Mil.
    m. Eliza Phillips Jones
    daughter Asenath B. m. Joseph Andrews Seay
    daughter Matilda H. m. Andrew T. Harrison

Sharp, William W. b. Va. 1765 d. Va. 1838   3rd Sgt. Va. Mil.
    m. Frances Sebree — daughter Maria S. m. Montgomery Meglone

Sharretts, Frederic b. Penn. 1781 d. Penn. 1845   3rd Lt. Penn. Mil.
    m. Catharne Gougler — daughter Isabella P. m. William Schwartz
    daughter Susan m. John Shyrock

Shattuck, Parker b. N.H. 1777 d. Vt. 1869   Civil Offices Vt. 1803-8
    m. Sarah Spofford — son Parker Jr. m. Nancy Jewett

Shaull, David b. Va. 1796 d. Ohio 1878 m. Mary Hess   Pvt. Va. Mil.
    daughter Martha m. Willis A. Harris

Shaver, Henry b. N.Y. 1786 d. N.Y. 1853 m. Caroline Polley Pvt. N.Y. Mil.
    daughter Philena M. m. Hiram Walrath

Shaw, Abraham Vol. 3   Pvt. N.H. Mil.

Shaw, George b. Va. 1796 d. Ga. 1855 m. Louisa Trout   Pvt. Ga. Mil.
    son Augustus m. Flora Trout

Shaw, Isaiah LaFayette b. Md. 1786 d. Md. 1879   Pvt. Md. Mil.
    m. Eleanor Grimes — son Isaiah L. Jr. m. Rachel Colt

Shaw, Jacob Vol. 15   Capt. N.Y. Mil.

Shaw, James b. S.C. 1794 d. Miss. m. Nancy Jane Crawford   Pvt. S.C. Mil.
    son Benjamin F. m. Arminta Jane Chaney

Shaw, John C. b. N.C. 1789 d. La. 1867   Pvt. La. Lt. Art.
    m. Margaret R. Merriman Lyons
    daughter Mary Josephine m. Hugh Ochiltree

Shaw, Nathaniel b. Mass. 1763 d. Me. 1846 m. Betsey House   Pvt. Mass. Mil.
    daughter Hannah m. Nathan Sturtevant

Shaw, Philip Jr. b. Mass. 1777 d. N.Y. 1854 m. Lucy Woods   Pvt. N.Y. Mil.
    daughter Elizabeth A. m. Albert Gallatin Leonard
    son Stephen C. m. Frances Edelin

Shaw, Russel b. N.Y. 1781 d. Ohio 1864   Pvt. Ohio Mil. Cav.
    m. Johannah Reynolds — son Calvin C. m. Elizabeth Hiatt
    daughter Philena m. Robinson McManis

Shaw, Sargent Jr. Vol. 12   Pvt. Mass. (Me.) Mil.

Shaw, Simon b. N.J. 1792 d. N.J. 1872 m. Mary Fox   Pvt. N.J. Inf.
    son Charles m. Isabel York
    daughter Emma B. m. DeMott Shaw REAL DAUGHTER

Shaw, Thomas b. Eng. 1779 d. N.Y. 1829   Capt. N.Y. Art.
    m. Rebecah Johnstone — son James m. Katherine Fosler

Shaw, Thomas b. Penn. 1755 d. Penn. 1814 m. Eleanor Evans Lt. Penn. Mil.
    son Thomas Jr. m. Susan Dunica

Shaw, Thomas b. 1775 d. Ky. m. Katherine Ripperdan   Sgt. Ky. Vol.
    son John R. m. Charlotte William

Shawhan, Joseph b. Md. 1781 d. Ky. 1871 m. Sarah Ewalt   Pvt. Ky. Mil.
    son John m. Tabitha Rush

Shay, Thomas Vol. 17   Lt. Penn. Mil.

Sheakley, George Vol. 7   Lt. Penn. Mil.

Shear, John Peter b. N.Y. 1777 d. N.Y. 1862 m. Joanna Craft Lt. N.Y. Mil.
    daughter Margaret m. William McCord

Shearer, Michael b. Md. 1799 d. Penn. m. Catherine McCord   Pvt. Penn. Mil.
    son Silas m. Elizabeth Shenkle

Shearman, Samuel Martin b. Va. 1776 d. Va. 1815   Capt. Va. Mil.
    m. (1) Nancy Martin — daughter Hannah Mariah m. James Lewis Bell

Sheckels, William Amon Vol. 14   Capt. Md. Mil.

Sheer, Jacob b. Penn. 1776 d. Ohio 1844 m. Margaret Porter   Pvt. Ohio Mil.
son William m. Norilla Swetland

Sheetz, Henry b. Penn. 1761 d. Penn. 1848   Maj. Gen. Penn. Mil.
m. Elizabeth Hooker — daughter Margaret m. Jonathan Wentz

Sheetz, Mathias b. Hungary 1736 d. Penn. 1807   Pvt. Penn. Mil.
m. Maria Catherine Pheifer
daughter Ann Catherine m. George Trepperd

Sheftall, Levi b.. 1784 d. Ga. 1809   U.S. Agent Ga. 1789-1808
m. Sarah de La Motta — son Soloman m. Clara de la Motta

Sheibley, Sebastian b.—d. N.Y. 1855   Vol. 34   Drum N.Y. Mil.
daughter Evaline m. Thomas Beadle

Sheidl, James   Vol. 17   Sgt. Va. Mil.

Shelden, Roger b. 1743-4 d. 1816   Rept. to Gen. Assem. 1793
m. Huldah Streeter — son David m. Vienna Wilkinson

Shelby, Isaac b. Md. 1750 d. Ky. 1826 m. Susanna Hart   Governor Ky.
son Evan m. Nancy Wilcox Warren
son Isaac Jr. m. Maria Boswell Warren
daughter Letitia m. Charles S. Todd
daughter Sarah m. Ephraim McDowell

Sheldon, Gad b. N.Y. 1793 d. Ohio 1875 m. Eunice Hosford   Pvt. N.Y. Mil.
son Alexander m. Leanora Granger

Shell, Byren (Byron) b. Ga. 1779 d. Ala. 1856 m. Sallie S. (1)   Pvt. Ga. Mil.
son Bolen m. Nancy Avera

Shell, John b. Ohio 1788 d. Ohio 1851 m. Sarah Estep   Cpl. Ohio Mil.
son Joseph m. Anna Mary Fryfogle
son Peter P. m. Nancy Ann Oyster

Shelley, Jacob D. b. N.C. 1798 d. Ala. 1871   Pvt. N.C. Mil.
m. Mary Cravens — son James T. m. Martha Jane McElwee

Shellman, Jacob b. Md. 1793 d. Ohio 1883   Pvt. Md. Mil.
m. Charlotte Whipp — daughter Catherine m. Solomon Zimmerman

Shelton, James b. Va. 1770 d. Va. 1817 m. Fannie S. Allen   Capt. Va. Mil.
son Pines H. m. Rebecca Carter

Shelton, Samuel Jr. b. Conn. 1780 d. Conn. 1862   Pvt. Conn. Mil.
m. Anna Beardsley — son Joel m. Louisa Mallett

Shelton, Spencer b. Va. 1757 d. Va. 1832 m. Clary   Dep. Sheriff Capt. Maj.
daughter Milly m. John Lewis Jr.   Va. 1784, 7, & 90

Shelton, Thomas b. Ky. 1798 d. Ky. 1868 m. Pauline Noel   Pvt. Ky. Mil.
son Thomas m. Lucinda Frances Yeager

Shelton, Thomas L.   Vol. 11   Lt. Va. Mil.

Shepard, Calvin b. Mass. 1784 d. Ohio 1856   Capt. Ohio Mil.
m. Mahala Oliver — son Alexander O. m. Charlotte Maxon

Shepard, Obed b. Mass. 1786 d. N.Y. 1858   Pvt. N.Y. Mil.
m. Mary Yeomans — son Issac m. Sarah Lacore

Shepard, Peletiah b. Conn. 1779 d. Ohio 1870 m. Mary Sweet   Pvt.
son Richard m. Rowena Charity Stratton   Ohio Mil.

Shepard (Shepherd), William b. Conn. 1785 d. N.Y. 1816   Pvt. N.Y. Mil.
m. Tamar Halstead —daughter Persis Ann m. Abram Van Marter

Shepherd, Ayars b. N.J. 1789 d. Penn. 1857   Pvt. Penn. Mil.
  m. Mary Murray — daughter Sarah m. John S. Mullin

Shepherd, Charles b. Penn. 1748 d. N.Y. 1820   Matross Penn. Mil.
  m. Elizabeth Dyer — son Charles Jr. m. Mary Winters

Shepherd, Daniel   Vol. 8   Pvt. Vt. Mil.
  daughter Emma A. m. Oscar D. Scribner REAL DAUGHTER

Shepherd, John b. Va. 1776 d. Md. 1825 m. Mary Owens   Pvt. Md. Mil.
  son Joseph m. Priscilla Drury (?)

Shepherd, Luther b. Conn. 1783 d. Conn. 1879   Cpl. Conn. Mil.
  m. Eliza Nichols — daughter Eliza m. Zopher Tuttle

Shepherd, William b. (W.) Va. 1767 d. W.Va. 1830   Pvt. Ky. Mil.
  m. Mary Clark — daughter Sarah m. Benjamin Mills

Sheplar, Philip b. Penn. 1788 d. Penn. 1865 m. Mary Hill   Pvt. Penn. Vol.
  son James m. Sarah Teeters

Sheppard, Benjamin b. Va. 1778 d. Va. 1855   Capt. Va. Cav.
  m. Sarah Garland Young — daughter Sarah G. m. John Austin Hicks

Sheppard, Furman b. N.J. 1756 d. N.J. 1832   Maj. N.J. Cav.
  m. Hannah Haskell — son Thomas C. m. Sarah Mulford

Sheppard, John b. Penn. d. Penn. m. Susanna Douglas   Pvt. Penn. Mil.
  daughter Ella m. Benjamin Whiteman

Sheppard, Robert b. N.J. 1788 d. Penn. 1875   Cpl. N.J. Mil.
  m. Maria Stratton — son Jeremiah B. m. (2) Elizabeth Lukens

Sheppard, William b. N.C. 1746 d. N.C. 1822   Pvt. N.C. Mil.
  m. Elizabeth Haywood — son John m. Mary Turner

Sherburn, Hezekiah   Vol. 13   Pvt. N.Y. Mil.

Sherman, Abner b. N.Y. 1786 d. N.Y. 1862   Pvt. N.Y. Mil.
  m. Betsey Orton (1) Phoebe Ray (2)
  daughter Elizabeth m. Ephraim Mattison by 1st wife

Sherman, Alpheus b. N.Y. 1780 d. N.Y. 1866   Capt. U.S. Army
  m. Hester Utt — daughter Laura m. Jeremiah B.

Sherman, Asaph b. Mass. 1775 d. Vt. 1835   Sgt. Vt. Mil.
  m. Sophia Norton — son Benjamin F. m. Charlotte Chipman

Sherman, Daniel b. Conn. 1721 d. Conn. 1799   Legis. Conn. 1785-91
  m. Mindwell Taylor — daughter Hannah m. Daniel Manville

Sherman, Humphrey b. N.Y. or Vt. 1780 d. N.Y. 1861   Pvt. N.Y. Mil.
  m. Anne Reynolds — son Titus G. m. Parthena Sheldon

Sherman, James b. Mass. 1781 d. N.Y. 1872   Pvt. N.Y. Mil.
  m. Lucina Johnson — daughter Emaline Augusta m. Daniel Garfield

Sherman, Joseph   Vol. 9   Pvt. Conn. Mil.

Sherman, Joseph b. Mass. 1779 d. N.Y. 1834   Seaman U.S. Navy
  m. Sarah Gardner — son Josiah m. Maria Gedney

Sherman, Nathan   Vol. 9 or 10   Pvt. or Ord. Sgt. Conn. Mil. or Vt.

Sherman, Roger b. Mass. 1721 d. Conn. 1793   Signer of Constit.
  m. Elizabeth Hartwell   U.S. Senator
  son John m. Nancy Tucker

Sherman, Shadrack b. N.Y. 1769 d. N.Y. 1812   Mem. Assem. N.Y. 1811
m. Diadania N. Howland — daughter Amy m. Joseph Tabor

Sherman, Silas b. R.I. 1778 d. R.I. 1814 m. Mary Sweet   Capt. R.I. Mil.
daughter Eliza m. Elisha Gardiner

Sherriff, Levi b. Md. 1777 d. D.C. 1853 m. Matilda Wilson   Pvt. Md. Mil.
daughter Mary Cornelia m. John T. W. Deane

Sherrill, Jeremiah Jr. b. N.Y. 1775 d. N.Y. 1814   2nd Lt. N.Y. Mil.
m. Elizabeth Hand — son Darius m. Mary Day

Sherrod, Benjamin b. N.C. 1777 d. Ala. 1857   Material Aid Ga.
m. Tabitha Goode — son Crawford m. Amanda Morgan

Sherwood, Charles b. Conn. 1791 d. Conn. 1846   Pvt. Conn. Mil.
m. Lois Jennings Burr — daughter Harriet S. m. Charles S. Banks

Shew, Jacob   Vol. 17   Lt. N.Y. Mil.

Shiars, Samuel Martin   Vol. 14   Capt. Merchantman

Shields, Robert   Vol. 13   Pvt. Ohio Mil.

Shields, William   Vol. 6   Pvt. Penn. Mil.

Shillingford, James b. Penn. 1787 d. Penn. 1853   3rd Sgt. Penn. Art. Mil.
m. Mary Hoofstitler
daughter Mary Ann m. Charles Afflick Litzenberg

Shine, William   Vol. 11   Cpl. U.S. Inf.

Shipe (Schieb), Jacob b. Penn. 1789 d. Penn. 1852   Sgt. Penn. Mil.
m. Maria Florn — son Jacob S. m. Mary Ann Frey

Shipp, William b. Tenn. ca. 1796 d. Tenn. aft. 1870   Soldier La.
m. Parthenia Griner — son Josiah Horton m. Harriett Foster

Shippe, Zabin b. N.Y. 1790 d. N.Y. 1858 m. Harriett   Pvt. N.Y. Mil.
daughter Laura m. John Nims (Hadley)

Shippen, Henry b. Penn. 1788 d. Penn. 1839   Aid de Camp Penn. Mil.
m. Elizabeth Wallis Evans — son Joseph m. Elizabeth Winslow

Shirk, John b. Penn. 1787 d. Penn. 1867   Pvt. Penn. Mil.
m. Martha Ann Means — son Joseph m. Alvira Clark
son Morgan M. m. Nancy McGraw

Shirly, Richard b. Ga. 1781 d. Ga. 1833 m. Sarah Brooks   Pvt. Ga. Mil.
daughter Elizabeth m. John Gills Brown
daughter Kiziah m. (2) George Compton

Shive, Jacob b. Penn. 1791 d. Penn. 1863   Sgt. Penn. Mil.
m. Elizabeth Schamel — son Conrad S. m. Amanda Wertsner

Shobe, Jacob Jr. b. Va. 1770 d. Ohio 1824 m. Mary Bush   Pvt. Ohio Mil.
daughter Lucinda m. Joseph McLean

Shoe, Phillip b.— d. Ohio aft. 1819   Vol. 71   4th Sgt. Ohio Mil.
daughter Amelia m. John T. Bryan

Shoemaker, Charles Jr. b. Penn. 1779 d. Penn. 1822   Brig. Qtr. Mst.
m. Elizabeth Kershner   Penn. Mil.
daughter Rebecca m. Solomon B. Seidel

Shoemaker, Robert b. N.Y. 1782 d. Ill. 1838   Maj. U.S. Army
m. Catherine Myers — son Robert M. m. Mary Colegate Steiner

Shook, David b. Penn. 1789 d. Ohio 1868 m. Sarah Marks   Pvt. Ohio Mil.
daughter Mary S. m. Hugh Bowers
daughter Rebecca m. John Young

Sholes, Stanton b. Conn. 1772 d. Ohio 1865   Capt. U.S. Art.
m. Abigail Avery — son Stanton Jr. m. Elizabeth Munden

Shore, Thomas b. Va. 1791 d. Mo. 1848   Postmst. Va. 1811
m. Mary Harriett Bolling — son Dr. John m. Theodosia Harriett Powell

Shore, William b. Va. 1798 d. Va. 1835   Cpl. Va. Mil.
m. Frances Anderson Taylor — daughter Julianna m. James W. Manees

Shores, Levin b. Md. 1792 d. Md. aft. 1815   Cpl. Md. Mil.
m. Mary Somers — daughter Rebecca m. Jonathan Moore

Shotwell, Jabez b. Ky. 1791 d. Mo. 1871   Pvt. Ky. Mil.
m. Elizabeth Elliott Warder
daughter Fannie E. m. Milton F. Royle REAL DAUGHTER

Shouts (Shotts, Stouts), Jacob b. 1797 d. Ohio 1835   Pvt. Ohio Mil.
m. Sarah Toops — son David m. Catherine Long

Showalter, Jacob b. Europe 1740 d. Penn. 1809 m. Barbara   Pvt. Penn.
daughter Lydia m. Jacob Longanecker

Shower, Adam b. Md. 1774 d. Md. 1833   Capt. Md. Mil.
m. Anna Elizabeth Troxel — daughter Catharine m. George Everhart

Shredley, Andrew b. Penn. 1775 d. Penn. 1836   Pvt. Penn. Mil.
m. Susanna Lauber — daughter Helena m. John Demmy

Shreffler, George Miller   Vol. 6   Wagon Mst. Penn. Mil.

Shreve, Caleb b. Penn. 1781 d. Ill. 1835 m. Anna Slack   Pvt. Ohio Mil.
daughter Delilah m. John Alexander
son James m. Hester Ann Argo

Shreve, William C. b. Va. 1788 d. Ind. 1843 m. Susan Bluice   Pvt. Va. Mil.
daughter Elizabeth N. m. Henry Eller

Shrewsbury, Nathaniel b. Va. 1768 d. Ky. 1823   Capt. Va. Mil. 1800-2
m. Nancy Board — daughter Nancy m. Burell Horsley

Shrock, Christopher b. Ger. 1781 d. Ohio 1846 m. Sarah Cate   Pvt. Va. Mil.
son John m. Charlotte McArthur

Shrom, Joseph b. Penn. 1792 d. Penn. 1865   Pvt. Penn. Mil.
m. Mrs. Anne Fleming Randolph
daughter Margaret m. Joseph Weibly

Shryock, George b. Md. 1783 d. Md. 1872   Capt. Md. Mil.
m. Elizabeth Lewis — son John K. m. Susan Sharretts

Shubrick, John Templer b. S.C. 1788 d. S.C. 1815 at sea   Lt. U.S. Navy
m. Elizabeth Matilda Ludlow
son Edmund T. m. Elizabeth Carolina Ball

Shue, Jacob b. Penn. 1776 d. Ohio m. Fulk   Pvt. Md. Mil.
daughter Sarah m. Thomas Bachtel

Shuey, Martin b. Penn. 1785 d. Calif. 1876   Capt. Ohio Mil.
m. Margaret Shupert — son Robert Martin m. Nancy Margaret

Shufelt, John b. ca. 1792 d. N.Y. aft. 1830 m. Mary Sears   Sgt. N.Y. Mil.
daughter Adelia Augusta m. Daniel Webster Mead

Shugart, Michael b. Penn. 1771 d. Va. 1834   Cpl. Va. Mil.
m. Rebecca Craig — son Earl B. C. m. Elizabeth Woodward
son John m. Mary Jane Russell

Shull, Reuben C. b. N.J. 1792 d. N.J. m. Mary   Pvt. Fifer N.J. Mil.
    daughter Lydia G. m. Charles Pedrick

Shults, Henry H.   Vol. 10   Pvt. N.Y. Mil.

Shuman, John b. Penn. 1761 d. Penn. 1807   Pvt. Penn. Mil.
    m. Catherine Wilt — daughter Catherine m. Rev. George Weisz

Shumate, Lewis b. Va. 1770 d. Va. 1861   Pvt. Va. Mil.
    m. Mary Chadwell — daughter Augusta m. Robert Davis

Shupp, George b. Penn. 1786 d. Penn. 1862   Sgt. Penn. Mil.
    m. Susannah Hawk — son Charles m. Elizabeth Driesbach

Shur, Jacob b. Penn. 1776 d. Ohio 1844 m. Margaret Porter   Pvt. Ohio Mil.
    son William m. Marilla Swetland (see Sheer)

Shuttlesworth, Phillip   Vol. 12   Drum Tenn. Mil.

Shy, John b. 1789 d. Mo. 1869 m. Sarah C. Cummings   Pvt. Ky. Mil.
    daughter Sarah C. m. Reamus Morris

Shryock, Henry b. bef. 1744 d.   Del. to Conv. Md. 1788
    m. Catherine Soleday — son Jacob m. Amelia Heiskell

Sibbet, David b. Penn. 1792 d. N.J. 1869   Pvt. Penn. Mil.
    m. Elizabeth Ann Swift — son Henry m. Jessie M. Miller

Sibley, Jacob b. Penn. 1782 d. Penn. 1856   Pvt. Lt. Inf. Penn. Mil.
    m. Catherine Goodman — daughter Elizabeth m. Thomas M'Clintock

Sibley, John b. N.Y. 1783 d. N.Y. 1827 m. Sarah Carriel   Pvt. N.Y. Mil.
    daughter Sarah m. Judge J. T. Everest

Sibley, Jonathan b. Conn. 1750 d. Conn. 1828   Mem. Gen. Assy. Conn.
    m. Patty Brooks — son Abijah m. Lucy Marcy   1790-1801

Sibley, Sylvester b. Vt. 1795 d. Ind. 1879   Pvt. N.Y. Mil.
    m. Catherine Rockwell — daughter Jane Emily m. Thomas Long

Sickles, Cornelius b. N.Y. 1786 d. N.Y. 1868   Capt. N.Y. Mil.
    m. Leah Blanch — daughter Martha m. John R. Van Houten

Sidman, Samuel b. N.Y. 1788 d. N.Y. 1864   Capt. N.Y. Mil. 1814
    m. Sarah Conklin — son Henry L. m. Sarah Ann Henion

Siegfried, Joseph b. Penn. 1779 d. Penn. 1832   Pvt. Penn. Mil.
    m. Susannah Seem — son Joseph Jr. m. Hannah Schoenberger

Sifritt, Andrew b. Va. 1750 d. Ohio 1847 m. Hannah Marrel   Elec. of Pres.
    m. Susan Schrock — son John m. Harriet Chapman   Washington

Sigerson, Robert b. Penn. 1777 d. Mo. 1850 m. Polly Wallace   Cpl. Ohio Mil.
    daughter Margaret m. William Reed
    son Wallace m. Anna Maria Magaw

Siggins, Alexander b. on Ocean 1793 d. Penn. 1858   Sgt. Penn. Mil.
    m. Margaret Kinnear — son Benjamin B. m. Elizabeth Erma Walker

Siglin, Jesse   Vol. 9   Pvt. Penn. Mil.

Siling, John Andrew b. Va. 1797 d. Ind. 1878   Pvt. Md. Inf. Mil.
    m. Mary Ann Yost — son Francis Marion m. Rachel Helen Wilkinson
    daughter Melinda m. Francis Whitaker Peppard

Silliman, Gershom b. Conn. 1783 d. Ill. 1856 m. Mary Colman   Ens. Lt. N.Y.
    son Marshall m. Clarissa Hyde

Silsbe, Enos b. N.Y. 1797 d. Mich. 1845   Pvt. N.Y. Mil.
    m. Abigail Chichester — daughter Mary Esther m. Alfred W. Reynolds

Silvers, William b. Penn. 1800 d. 1888 m. Mary Jarvis   Pvt. Ohio Mil.
  daughter Harriett m. John Paul

Silvey, William b. Ire. 1795 d. N.J. 1871 m. Eliza Davis   Capt. N.J. Mil.
  daughter Margaret D. m. Nelson Pugsley

Silvius, Mark b. Penn. c. 1790 d. Penn. bef. 1850   Pvt. Penn. Mil.
  m. Elizabeth McKae — daughter Sarah m. Jacob Haberstick

Simcock (Simcox), William b. Penn. 1791 d. Ohio 1855   Pvt. Penn. Mil.
  m. (1) Esther Robinson
  son Tolbert (Talbot) m. Hannah Baughman (Bachman)

Simms (Simons), Absalom b. N.C. 1792 d. La. m. Jane Keefe   Sgt. U.S. Inf.
  daughter Margaret L. m. Francis A. Nephler

Simmons, James Jr. b. Md. 1780 d. Ind. 1844   Lt. Md. Mil.
  m. Rebecca Ford — son John F. m. Haretta Murdoch

Simmons, Joab b. Va. 1787 d. Ind. 1872   Pvt. Va. Mil.
  m. Sarah Ellen Miller — son Augustus m. Margaret Thompson

Simmons, John b. S.C. 1790 d. Mo. 1868 m. Naomi Jared   Pvt. La. Mil.
  daughter Elizabeth J. m. John Bascom Lee

Simmons, Peter b. R.I. 1735 d. N.Y. 1811   Capt. N.Y. Mil.
  m. Rebecca Rouse — son Rouse m. Mary Potter

Simmons, Richard b. S.C. 1770 d. Ala. 1814   Pvt. Miss. Terr. Mil.
  m. Ann Tyler — son Thomas m. Barcener Hope
  son William m. Nancy Hope

Simms, Isaac Davis b. Va. 1788 d. Va. 1836   Lt. Col. Va. Mil.
  m. Nancy Catterton — daughter Permele m. Samuel D. Crawford

Simonds, Jonathan b. 1789 d.— m. Priscilla Sandborn   Pvt. Ohio Mil.
  daughter Helen Almira m. Andrew Jackson Conklin

Simonson, John b. Penn. 1782 d. Md. 1862   Sgt. Md. Lt. Inf.
  m. (1) Margaret Christina Keener
  son Joseph K. m. Margaret Ann Christopher

Simonson, John Smith b. Penn. 1796 d. Ind. 1881   Pvt. Ind. Mil.
  m. Elizabeth Edmondson Watson
  daughter Jane m. George Vail Howk

Simonton, Abraham   Vol. 6   Pvt. Mass. Mil.

Simonton, Theophilus b. 1769 d. 1856 m. Mary Sale   Capt. Ohio
  son Adam m. Elizabeth Ford

Simpson, Ebenezer   Vol. 16   Pvt. Mass. Mil.

Simpson, Gilbert b. Tenn. d. Tenn. 1813   Pvt. Tenn. Mil.
  m. Susannah Zimmerman — son Gilbert m. Christia Atkins

Simpson, Hugh b. Va. 1761 d. Ky. bef. 1836 m.   Lt. S.C. Mil. 1787
  son Elias m. Nancy Briggs

Simpson, Jeremiah b. Mass. (Me). 1776 d. Me. 1857   Lt. Mass. Mil.
  m. Joanna Brooks — daughter Elsie P. m. Edward S. Pinney

Simpson, John White b. N.C. 1789 d. Tenn. 1862   Maj. W. Tenn. Mil.
  m. Jane Montgomery — daughter Jane M. m. Lewis Goodall

Simpson, Paul Rolfe b. N.H. 1791 d. Me. 1881   Cpl. U.S. Inf.
  m. Hannah M. Thomas — son Willard E. m. Hannah Mower

Simpson, Rezin Burgess b. Md. 1795 d. Md. 1842   Pvt. Md. Mil.
  m. Sarah Ann Ricaud — daughter Mary O. m. Robert Henry Yeatman

Simpson, Robert b. Md. 1785 d. Mo. 1873   Surgeon Mate Md. Mil. (D.C.)
    m. Brica Smith — son George S. m. Jennie Swasco

Simpson, Thomas b. (Me.) Mass. 1784 d. Me. 1875   Pvt. Gunner Mass.
    m. Eliza Whitehouse   (Me.) Art.
    daughter Mary m. Austin Sperry REAL DAUGHTER

Simpson, William b. Ire. 1778 d. Del. 1851   Sailor U.S. Navy
    m. Elizabeth Mathews — daughter Mary m. Joseph K. Whildin

Simpson, William b. Va. d. Va. 1815 m. Phoebe Butler   Cpl. Va. Mil.
    son George m. Helen McGee

Simpson, William b. Ire. d. Ala. 1816 m. Mary   Surgeon Ala. Terr. Mil.
    son John m. Margaret Ann Dickson

Simrall, James b. 1779 d. Ill. 1823 m. Rebecca Graham   Col. Ky. Drag.
    daughter Cornelia S. m. Thomas Pollard Smith
    son W. A. m. Clara Grisella Newell

Sims, Bernard b. Va. ca. 1770 d. Va. m. Nancy Walton   Ens. Va. Lt. Inf.
    son Edward Walton m. Polly L. Hobson

Sims, John b. S.C. 1790 d. Tex. 1867 m. Mahala Mackay   Col. S.C. Mil.
    daughter Jane Minerva m. John C. Abercrombie
    daughter Mahala C. m. (2) Joseph Benson Cottrell

Sims, John b. Va. 1761 d. Va. 1833 m. Frances Taylor   Pvt. Va. Mil.
    son John Jr. m. Catherine Branch

Sims, William b. S.C. 1795 d. Ga. 1866 m. Sarah Hull   Pvt. S.C. Mil.
    son Thomas W. m. Nancy America Clark

Sinclair, David b. Md. 1780 d. Ohio 1859 m. Lucy Bruton   Sgt. Penn. Mil.
    son Levi M. m. Elizabeth Myers

Sinclair, James Sr. b. Penn. 1741 d. Penn. 1806   Pvt. Penn. Mil.
    m. Miss Miller — son James Jr. m. Jennie Slemons

Sinclair, John   Vol. 1   Capt.

Sinclair, Samuel Conner b. Vt. 1795 d. N.Y. 1838   Cpl. Vt. Mil.
    m Samantha Barney — son Lucius A. m. Clara M. Heath

Singletary, Amos b. Mass. 1721 d. Mass. 1806   Mem. Prov. Congress
    m. Mary Curtis   Mass. 1787
    daughter Thankful m. Ebenezer Burnap

Singletary, Uriah Johnson b. Mass. 1791 d. Mich. 1840   Pvt. Ohio Mil.
    m. Elizabeth Bishop — son Anson R. m. Martha Matilda Chapman

Singleton, James b. Va. 1762 d. Va. 1815   Brig. Gen. Va. Mil.
    m. Judith Throckmorton Ball — son James W. m. Parthenia McDanold

Singleton, Jechonias b. Va. 1766 d. Ky. 1836   Capt. Ky. 1812
    m. Jane Taylor — son John m. Polly Phillips

Singleton, John F. b. Va. 1789 d. W.Va. 1859   Ens. Va. Mil.
    m. Lucinda Byrne — son John S. m. Louisa Thomas Bragg

Singleton, Robert b. S.C. 1763 d. S.C. 1820   Lt. S.C. Mil.
    m. Margaret Van Nuyse — son James m. Hester Medlock

Sites, George b. Va. 1784 d. Va. bef. 1869   Pvt. Va. Mil.
    m. Rebecca Matthews — daughter Melvina m. Benjamin Hoover

Sithen, William b. 1788 d. abt. 1850 m.—   Pvt. N.J. Inf.
    daughter Ruth Ann m. Virgil McCraken Updike

Sitler, Abraham b. Md. 1790 d. Penn. 1850 m. Annie Bear   Pvt. Penn. Mil.
    son Joseph m. Rachel Ann Morrow

Sitton, Jesse   Vol. 16   Sgt. W. Tenn. Mil.

Sizer, John G. b. Va. 1780 d. Va. 1845   Capt. Va. Mil.
    m. Elizabeth Gatewood — son Lucian m. Mary E. Radle

Skaggs, Abraham Moredock b. 1793 d. 1855   Pvt. Ky. Mil.
    m. Rhoda Boone Smith — daughter Eliza Jane m. John Jacob Myers

Skerrett, Joseph b. Eng. 1752 d. Penn. 1804   Capt. Penn. Mil.
    m. Mary Eve Humbert
    son William Henry m. Margaret Ferguson Gregg

Skerrett, William Henry b. Penn. 1792 d. Ohio 1864   Pvt. Penn. Vol.
    m. Margaret Ferguson Gregg
    son Joseph S. m. Margaret Love Taylor

Skiddy, William (Taylor) b. N.Y. 1794 d. Conn. 1870   Midshipman U.S.
    m. Mary Ann Anderson   Navy
    daughter Mary m. Edward Augustus Quintard

Skidmore, John b. Penn. 1783 d. Ind. 1863 m. Jane Hopper   Lt. Ohio Mil.
    son Alexander m. Sarah Jane Leighton

Skidmore, Joseph b. Va. 1761 d. Mo. 1852   Pvt. Ky. Inf. Mil.
    m. Mary Barker — son James m. Mary Abbott

Skiles, George b. 1778 d. 1868 m. Mary Justus   2nd Lt. Tenn.
    daughter Mary Ann m. (1) Reno (2) Hiram Alexander Scott

Skillman, Jacob b. N.J. 1764 d. N.J. 1854   Pvt. Penn. Mil. 1794
    m. Ellen Ten Broeck — son Abraham m. Susan Emma Palmer

Skinner, Henry b.— d. Ill. 1827   Vol. 17   Surgeon Ohio Mil. 1807

Skinner, Jedediah J. b. Conn. 1765 d. N.H. 1842   Pvt. N.H. Mil.
    m. Sarah Hurlburt — daughter Hannah m. William Fullington Folsom

Skinner, John b. Mass. 1792 d. Ohio 1859 m. Rachel Clapp   Pvt. Mass. Mil.
    daughter Sovia A. m. William Chauncey Niece

Skinner, Peter   Vol. 12   Pvt. Va. Mil.

Skinner, Thomas   Vol. 75   Pvt. Del. Mil.

Skinner, Zalmon b. 1777 d. N.Y. 1859 m. Eunice Patterson   Capt. N.Y. Mil.
    daughter Esther C. m. Charles D. Haight

Skrine, Benjamin b. Spain 1762 d. Ga. bef. 1827   Solic. Gen. of Circ. Ct. Ga.
    m. Martha — son Benjamin Jr. m. Virginia Davis   1801

Slack, John b. Penn. ca. 1776 d. Va. 1825-6   Pvt. Va. Mil.
    m. Nancy Huddleston — daughter Catherine m. Mills W. Calvert
    daughter Elizabeth Anne m John Lewis Calvert

Slack, (Slaught) Phillip b. Penn. 1751 d. Penn. 1837   Capt. Penn. Mil.
    m. Rosanna — daughter Hannah m. William Paul

Slade, Jeremiah b. N.C. 1775 d. N.C. 1824   Brig. Gen. N.C. Mil.
    m. Janet Bog — son William m. Penelope Williams

Slade, Lloyd b. Mass. 1787 d. Mass. 1857   Ens. Mass. Mil.
    m. Eliza Hudson Lewin — son Obadiah m. Hannah Thompson Munro

Slater, Joseph b. Vt. 1772 d. N.Y. 1861   Capt. N.Y. Mil.
    m. Hannah Spaulding — son A. Jackson m. Mary Dudley

Slater, Nathan b. R.I. 1784 d. Penn. 1870   Music N.Y.
    m. Freelove Crossman — daughter Calista F. m. Robert Luse

Slaughter, Pleasant b. Va. 1792 d. Va. 1834   Pvt. Va. Mil.
    m. Susanna Jarrett Jolly — son Rev. D. J. C. m. Mary Frances Pettitt

Slaughter, Robert Coleman b. Va. 1776 d. Ky. 1855   Sgt. Ky. Mil.
    m. Nancy Hynes — son Gilly C. m. Green Dye

Slaydon, William Everett   Vol. 13   Pvt. Va. Mil.

Sleeper, Jonathan b. N.J. 1794 d. Ind. 1864   Pvt. N.J. Mil.
    m. Elizabeth Hollingsworth — daughter Ann m. Job Osborn

Sleeper, Rufus b. Vt. 1792 d. N.Y. 1869 m. Sally Bumpus   Pvt. N.H. Mil.
    son Frank A. m. Isadora D. Follett

Slemmons, William b. Penn. 1760 d. Penn. 1820   Justice of Peace Penn. 1799
    m. — Boggs — daughter Jennie m. James St. Clair II

Slicer, Andrew   Vol. 4   Capt. Md. Mil.

Slingluff, John b. Penn. 1762 d. Penn. 1843   Pvt. Penn. Mil.
    m. Mary Hallman — son William m. Mary Knoer

Sloan, Alexander b. Ire. 1760 d. Mo. 1844 m. Agnes Dobson   Pvt. Ky. Mil.
    daughter Jane m. James Cunningham Burney

Sloan, David b. c. 1790 d. Vt. m. Mary Warwick   Pvt. Vt.
    son David W. m. Sophronia (Parker) Prentiss

Sloan, John Alfred b. N.H. d. N.Y. 1848 m. Lima Moody   Cpl. U.S. Inf.
    daughter Emily m. William Henry Loomis

Sloan, Walter b. Penn. 1788 d. Penn. 1867 m. Jane Mateer   Lt. Penn. Inf.
    son James m. Margaret Kelley

Sloan, William b. N.C. 1753 d. Mo. 1827   Judge Mo. 1812
    m. Jane Stevenson — son James m. Sarah Black

Sloat, John b. N.Y. 1779 d. N.Y. 1862 m. Hester Raymond   Pvt. N.Y. Mil.
    daughter Tammy m. James Hart

Slocum, George b. R.I. 1804 d. R.I. 1863 m. Susan Gould   Drum R.I. Mil.
    son William S. m. Sarah Ann Bradley

Slocum, Giles b. R.I. 1750 d. R.I. aft. 1790   Deputy R.I. Assem. Del.
    m. Susannah Brownell   to Constit. Conv.
    son Stephen m. Mary Fish

Slocum, Samuel b. R.I. 1785 d. Neb. 1865 m. Mary Sherman   Soldier Vt.
    son George m. Rhoda Mantor

Slusor (Schlosser, Slusser), Philip   Pvt. Penn. Mil.
    b. Penn. 1760 d. Ohio 1829 m. Sarah Ann Heller
    daughter Anna m. Jacob Danner

Small, George D. b. N.Y. 1790 d. N.J. 1852   Prisoner Dartmoor Eng.
    m. Sarah Sumners   U.S. Navy
    daughter Sarah Ann m. David Sidney Shields

Small, John   Vol. 14   Lt. Penn.

Smalley, Francis b. Vt. 1785 d. Vt. 1858 m. Martha Post Hyde   Pvt. Vt. Mil.
    daughter Diadema m. Lucius H. Noyes

Smallwood, Samuel b. Md. 1771 d. N.J. 1834   Pvt. N.J. Mil.
    m. (2) Elizabeth Perry Perkins
    son Samuel P. m. Mary Jane Allen and Rachel Peterson

Smallwood, Walter b. 1782 d. 1869 m. Amelia Martin   Mil. Officer Ohio 1812
son Col. Walter M. K. m. Emaline Reinhart

Smallwood, William b. Md. 1786 d. Ind. 1850   Artificer N.C. Mil.
m. Eleoner Noland — son Alexander m. Cascinda Zike

Smart, Joseph b. N.C. 1793 d. Me. 1874 m. Annah   Maj. (Me.) Mass. Mil.
son Reuben S. m. Almira Curtis

Smartt, William Cheek b. N.C. 1785 d. Tenn. 1863   Lt. Commander Tenn.
m. Margaret Colvile   Mil.
son Francis B. m. Margaret McDavidson

Smaw, Daniel b. Va. 1791 d. 1834 m. Anne Warren   Pvt. Va. Mil.
daughter Frances Ellen m. Jerome B. Hall

Smead, Charles E. b. Mass. 1792 d. N.Y. 1875   Cpl. N.Y. Mil.
m. Maliza Howe — daughter Emily m. Edwin M. Snow

Smilie, John b. 1742 d. 1812   Mem. Congress Penn. 1793-1813
m. Janet Porter — son Robert Porter m. Mary Ann Beattie

Smilie, Robert Porter b. Penn. 1767 d. Penn. 1851   in Whiskey Rebell.
m. Mary Ann Beattie   Penn. 1793
daughter Mary m. George L. Shellenbarger

Smilie, Stanton b. N.H. or Eng. d. N.H. 1814   Pvt. U.S. Inf.
m. Elizabeth J. Adams — daughter Elizabeth A. m. Loren H. Gordon

Smith, Abner b. Mass. 1780 d. Mass. m. Jemima Fisk   Pvt. Mass. Mil.
daughter Lavina m. Abner Fisher

Smith, Abraham b. Penn. 1794 d. Penn. 1878   Pvt. Penn. Mil.
m. Sarah Elizabeth Christman
son John C. m. Rebecca M. Pennypacker

Smith (Schmidt), Abraham b. N.C. 1792 d. Ia. 1867   Pvt. Tenn. Mil.
m. Eleanor Van Doran — daughter Mary Ann m. John Morgan Lee

Smith, Abigale   Vol. 9   Lt. N.Y. Mil.

Smith, Alexander b. Va. 1752 d. Va. 1819   Va. 1798-1802 Town Office
m. Margaret Douglass — son James D. m. Margaret F. Moore

Smith, Ambrose Edward b. N.Y. 1794 d. N.Y. 1879   Pvt. N.Y. Mil.
m. Mary Mead — son Ambrose E. Jr. m. Hannah Philena Knapp

Smith, Amos   Vol. 9   Ens. N.Y. Mil.

Smith, Archimedes b. Ky. 1792 d. Ill. 1866   Surgeon's Mate Penn. Mil.
m. Olive Selden — daughter Jane m. Gideon C. Clarke

Smith, Asa   Vol. 17   Pvt. Ky. Mil.

Smith, Ashford b. Va. 1790 d. Ill. 1877 m. Mary Wright   Pvt. Ky. Mil.
son Larkin B. m. Nancy Jane Nash

Smith, Augustine Charles b. Va. 1789 d. Va. 1843   Lt. Col. Va. Mil.
m. Elizabeth Dangerfield
daughter Anna J. m. William Augustine Morgan
son Augustine J. m. Elizabeth Bedinger Morgan

Smith, Benjamin b. Ky. 1793 d. Ky. 1876 m. Malinda Mills   Pvt. Ky. Mil.
son S. F. m. Julia Rebecca Cox

Smith, Benjamin b. Va. 1786 d. Ohio 1831   Cpl. Ill. Terr. Mil.
m. Mary Horton — daughter Phoebe Elizabeth m. Robert Dunlap

Smith, Benjamin b. 1761 d. Ind. 1850 m. Rebecca   Capt. Ind. Terr. Mil.
son Edwin D. m. Elizabeth Stephens

Smith, Benjamin Hayes b. Penn. 1765 d. Penn. 1806   Mem. Gen. Assy.
m. Margaret Dunn   Penn. 1801-2-3
daughter Elizabeth H. m. Dr. Isaaac Anderson

Smith, Bird (Byrd) b. Va. 1761 d. La. 1815   Brig. Gen. W. Tenn. Mil.
m. Rhoda Ingles —daughter Juliet L. m. William Beavers McClellan

Smith, Caleb b. 1782 d. 1872 m. Lucy Peck   Pvt. N.Y.
son Homer m. Mary Brickley

Smith, Charles b. Penn. 1765 d. Penn. 1836   Legis. Del. Const. Conv.
m. Mary Yeates   House of Rep. 1806-8 Pa.
daughter Whihelmina E. m. Thomas B. McElwee

Smith, Charles b. 1777 d. Me. 1829   Surgeon's Mate Mass. (Me.) Mil.
m. Susannah Taylor — son Gustavus A. m. Julia A. McKenney

Smith, Comstock O. S. b. Conn. 1793 d. Conn. 1825   Pvt. Conn. Mil.
m. Phebe J. Crocker — son Comstock C. Jr. m. Naomi King

Smith, Constant b. N.J. 1772 d. N.J. 1861 m. Eunice Somers   Pvt. N.J. Mil.
daughter Margaret m. Abel Lee

Smith, Daniel b. N.J. 1755 d. Penn. 1836   Col. Penn. 1788-1815
m. Elizabeth Shute — son Francis G. m. Eliza Mackie

Smith, Daniel b. Tenn. 1788 d. Tenn. 1871   Pvt. E. Tenn. Mil.
m. Mary Simerly — daughter Celia m. Johnson Simerly
son E. Jones m. Mary Smithpeter
daughter Mary E. m. James Davidson Smith

Smith, Daniel b. Va. d. Va. 1850   Mem. House Del. 1803-6
m. Frances Strother Duff   State Att'y. 1804-11 Judge Sup.
daughter Elizabeth m. Christopher C. Scott   Ct. 1811-50 Va.

Smith, Daniel b. Penn. 1790 d. Penn. 1874   Pvt. Penn. Mil.
m. May Anne Lusher — son Abraham m. Sarah Smith

Smith, David b. N.H. 1769 d. N.H. 1858   Ord. Sgt. N.H. Mil.
m. Eleanor Giddings — son Jerry m. Susanna Currier

Smith, David b. N.C. 1753 d. Miss. 1832   Capt. Ky. Cav. Mil.
m. Sarah Terry — daughter Mary m. Alfred Dillingham

Smith, David b. N.C. 1753 d. Miss. 1835   Capt. W. Tenn. Mil.
m. Margaret Terry — daughter Mary m. Alfred David Smith

Smith, David b. Va. 1786 d. Ind. 1851   Pvt. Ohio Mil. 1812
m. Elizabeth Hurd — son William m. Kathrine M. Wood

Smith, Diodate b. Conn. 1772 d. Penn. 1834   Pat. U.S. Mail Carrier
m. Rachel Alworth — son Benjamin m. Lydia Gardiner

Smith, Dow b. Conn. 1737 d. N.Y. 1841   Mem. Commissary N.Y. Mil.
m. Clarissa Cook — son Augustus m. Martha Howe

Smith, Ebenezer b. N.H. 1765 d. N.H. 1831   Lt. N.H. Mil.
m. Eleanor Hilton — son Hezekiah m. Eliza Jane Jewett

Smith, Ebenezer b. N.Y. 1796 d. Mich. 1886   Pvt. N.Y. Mil.
m. Dorothy Davenport — daughter Phebe L. m. (3) Jacob J. Rhead

Smith, Edward b. Penn. 1775 d. Ohio 1817   Pvt. Ohio Mil.
m. Margaret Casselman — daughter Mary m. Edward Taylor

Smith, Elijah b. Va. d. Ky. 1838 m. Lucy   Pvt. U.S. Inf. 1814
 son Fleetwood m. Harriett Keegan

Smith, Enoch b. Va. 1750 d. Ky. 1825   Capt. Ky. Mil.
 m. Nancy Belfield Lane — daughter Sarah m. Thomas Jameson

Smith, Ezekiel b. Tenn. 1790 d. Tenn. 1863   Pvt. E. Tenn. Mil.
 m. Nancy Gordon Doran — son Daniel m. Rachel Edmondson

Smith, Floyd b. N.Y. 1791 d. N.Y. 1874 m.—   Sgt. N.Y. Mil.
 daughter Matilda m. Francis W. Brooks

Smith, Francis Gurney b. Penn. 1784 d. Penn. 1873 Pvt. Penn. Cav. 1808-15
 m. Eliza Mackie — daughter Joanna m. Alexis Irenee de Pont

Smith, George A. b. Ky. 1788 d. Ky. 1854   Pvt. Ky. Mil.
 m. Elizabeth Monroe Edwards
 daughter Sally Ann m. Joseph Austin Hildreth

Smith, George M. b. 1789 d. Ind. 1845 m. Catherine Beeks Pvt. Ky.
 son James m. Mary Flesher

Smith, Henry Sr b. Penn. 1787 d. Penn. 1873 Pvt. Penn. Cav. Mil.
 m. Magdalena Reichard — son Henry Jr. m. Lovina Fiscus

Smith, Hewlett b. Conn. 1793 d. Penn. 1879   Pvt. Conn. Mil.
 m. Eunice Wheeler — son Elijah m. Mary J. Clover

Smith, Hugh Dunham b. N.J. 1793 d. N.J. 1853 Pvt. N.J. Mil.
 m. Clarissa Richmond — daughter Ruth Ann m. Jonathan Taylor

Smith, Humphrey b. N.Y. d. Mo. 1858   Pvt. N.Y. Mil.
 m. Nancy Atwater Walker — son Erastus m. Maria L. McArdel

Smith, Isaac b. Penn. 1773 d. Penn. 1834 m. Susan Baker Capt. Penn. Mil.
 daughter Eliza m. Oliver Baskin
 daughter Elspy m. George W. Finney

Smith, Isaac b. Conn. 1790-1 d. N.Y. 1883   Pvt. N.Y. Mil.
 m. Elizabeth Edwards — daughter Melissa E. m. Albert W. Roberts

Smith, Irwin b. Md. 1789 d. Ind. 1860 m. Lydia Manon Cpl. Va. Mil.
 son Irwin M. m. Meranda Collier

Smith, Isaac b. N.C. 1779 d. Ill. 1855   Cpl. Tenn. Mil. 1814
 m. Millie Hassell — son Jesse Hassell m. Eliza Jane Bliss

Smith, Isaac Vol. 12   Capt. Penn. Mil.

Smith, Jacob b. Tenn. 1784 d. Tenn. 1866 Pvt. Tenn. Mtd. Guman Mil.
 m. Lucy Williams — daughter Elizabeth m. Joseph Shelton

Smith, James b. Md. 1787 d. Md. 1840 m. Elizabeth Lynch Pvt. Md. Mil.
 daughter Susannah M. m. Daniel Henry Thomas

Smith, James b. 1761 d. 1835 m. Marianna Gough Sgt. S.C.
 daughter Emma m. William Robinson Taber

Smith, Jared Vol. 10   Pvt. N.Y. Mil.

Smith, Jedediah b. Mass. 1752 d. Mass. 1819 Rep. Gen. Ct. Mass. 1795-6
 m. Rhoda — son George m. Clarissa Parker

Smith, Jeremiah b. Va. (W.Va.) 1785 d. Ohio 1886 Pvt. Drum Ohio Mil.
 m. Rachel Parrett (Parrott) — son Samuel m. Christina Life

Smith, Job b. Md. 1794 d. Md. 1871 m. Rachel   Pvt. Md. Mil.
 daughter Louise m. Louis A. Brig

Smith, John   Vol. 2   Capt. Conn. Mil. Seaman
  daughter Susannah m. Elijah Mott

Smith, John b. N.C. 1772 d. N.C. 1851   Senator N.C. 1812-14
  m. Isabella Campbell—daughter Elizabeth m. Jonathan Evans
  son James C. m. Philadelphia Mathews

Smith, John b. Ire. 1722 d. Md. 1794   Senator Legis. Md. 1786-91
  m. Mary Buchanan — son John m. Elizabeth Smith
  daughter Mary m. George Nicholas

Smith, John b. Va. 1750 d. Va. 1836 m.—   Mem. Congress 1808
  daughter E. Jacqueline m. George William Murdock

Smith, John b. Penn. ca. 1782 d. Penn. 1851   Pvt. Penn. Mil.
  m. Margarett Butler — son Abia m. Sarah Summerwell

Smith, John b. Va. 1750 d. Va. m. Anna Bull   Brig. Gen. Va. Mil.
  daughter Eliza m. Robert Mills

Smith, John b. N.C. 1795 d. N.C. 1880 m. Sarah Daugety   Pvt. N.C. Mil.
  son John G. m. Martha Byrd

Smith, John Campbell b. Del. c. 1780 d. Ohio 1848   Pvt. Ohio Mil.
  m. Sophia Bond — daughter Eleanor m. James Wilson

Smith, John Keyzar b. N.Y. 1785 d. Mich. 1855   Pvt. N.Y. Mil.
  m. Catherine McDonald — daughter Sarah C. m. Samuel Russell

Smith, John Thomas   Vol. 14   Pvt. Ga. Mil.

Smith, Jonas b. N.J. 1773 d. N.J. 1848   Pvt. Penn. Mil.
  m. Elizabeth Clark Tucker—son Marshall Ney m. Jane Wilson Halsted

Smith, Jonathan b. Mass. 1760 d. Canada 1814   Pvt. U.S. Army
  m. Lucy Hobart — son Jonathan Jr. m. Elizabeth Davison

Smith, Joseph Jr.   Vol. 6   Pvt. Md. Mil.

Smith, Joseph b. Va. 1794 d. Ill. 1862 m. Sally Taylor   Pvt. Ky. Mil.
  son DeWitt m. Mercy Adelia McConnell

Smith, Joseph Harvey b. N.Y. 1795 d. N.Y. 1865   Pvt. N.Y. Mil.
  m. Achsah Richmond — daughter Christina A. m. Lewis Smith Davis

Smith, Joseph Lee b. Conn. 1779 d. Fla. 1846   Maj. U.S. Inf.
  m. Frances Marvin Kirby—son Frances M. m. Lucien B. Webster

Smith, Joseph Sim b. Md. 1758 d. Ind. 1822 m. Eliza Price   Maj. Md. Mil.
  daughter Susan Matilda m. Henry Naylor

Smith, Joshua   Vol. 11   Legis. N.Y.

Smith, Josiah m. Rachel Cook Early Vol.   Pvteersman

Smith, Josiah b. N.Y. 1789 d. N.Y. 1863 m. Polly Armstrong   Sgt. N.Y. Mil.
  daughter Sarah Jane m. John M. Webster

Smith, Josiah R. b. Tenn. 1797 d. Tenn. 1882   Pvt. Tenn. Mil.
  m. Barthena Cloud—daughter Emily m. Wade Paschal

Smith, Lemuel b. Va. 1756 d. N.C. 1821   Mem. Gen. Assy. N.C. 1784
  m. Bethenia Pekins — daughter Agnes W. m. John Silver

Smith, Lemuel b. Conn. 1774 d. Conn. 1852 m. Nancy Jones   Pvt. Conn. Mil.
  son William L. m. Mary Ann Bigler

Smith, Levi b. Del. c. 1780 d. Del. 1834 m. Lurania Robinson   Pvt. Del. Mil.
  daughter Elizabeth m. John Passwater

Smith, Levi b. N.J. 1752 d. N.J. 1831 m. Rachel   Commis. Officer N.J. Mil.
daughter Hannah m. Reuben Ludlam

Smith, Lewis b. N.H. 1773 d. Mass. 1837 m. Abigail Parker   Pvt. N.H. Mil.
son Hervey m. Clarissa Felt

Smith, Lewis b. Conn. 1788 d. Ohio 1831   Matross Conn. Mil.
m. Mrs. Marilla Curtis Stillman
daughter Marilla M. m. John Liberty Bean

Smith, Melancton b. N.Y. 1744 d. N.Y. 1790   Mem. Assy. N.Y.
m. Margaret Mott — son Sidney m. Phebe Alta Bailey

Smith, Meriweather b. Va. 1769 d. Va. 1823   Maj. E. Tenn. Mil.
m. Judith Woodson Chiles
daughter Huldah S. m. William Henry Tisdale

Smith, Michael b. Penn. 1767 d. Ohio 1843   Pvt. Penn. Mil.
m. Mary Eva Shuster — daughter Elizabeth m. Jeremiah Shaffer

Smith, Mitchell b. Va. 1781 d. Va. 1816 m. Olive Butt   Capt. Va. Mil.
son Edwin m. Margaret Phillips
daughter Elizabeth m. (2) Edward Cannon Land
son William D. m. Anne Butt

Smith, Mordecai b. Va. 1791 d. Ohio 1844   Sgt. Md. Mil.
m. Lydia Jane Handlin — daughter Rebecca F. m. Charles A. Taylor

Smith, Moses Jr. b. Conn. 1783 d. Ohio 1866   Pvt. Conn. Mil.
m. Sarah Niles Haley — daughter Lucy Ann m. Dennis A. Hine

Smith, Moses Rogers b. N.Y. 1768 d. N.Y. 1847   Gunboat
m. Mary Reid   Mst. N.Y. 1812-15
son Francis Shubael m. Mary Jellett Duff

Smith, Nathan b. Mass. 1731 d. Mass. 1801 m. Eunice   Treasurer Selectman
daughter Sarah m. Levi Taylor   Mass. 1784-1801

Smith, Nathan b. N.Y. 1746 d. N.Y. 1798   Legis. Judge N.Y.
m. Susan Mackintosh— daughter Susan m. William W. Sackett

Smith, Nathaniel b. Va. or Tenn. d. Tex. 1841   Lt. Tenn. Mil.
m Martha F. Smith — daughter May M. m. Dr. James Hunter

Smith, Nathaniel b. Mass. (Me.) 1792 d. Minn. 1876   Pvt. U.S. Inf.
m. Ann Harris — son Harris N. m. Mary Jane Flanders
daughter Mary m. J. Harrison

Smith, Oliver b. Conn. 1761 d. Penn. 1838   Assist. to Commodore Perry
m. Betsy Lothrop   Battleship on Lake Erie
son Charles F. m. Emily Leach

Smith, Peter Jr. b. Pa. 1774 d. Pa. 1843   Pvt. Penn. Vol.
m. Phoebe Loafman — son John Edward m. Martha Ann Yount

Smith, Peter b. N.J. 1780 d. N.J. or Penn. 1815 m. Elizabeth   Pvt. N.J. Inf.
daughter Elizabeth m. Daniel Dysart

Smith, Ransford b. Vt. 1793 d. Ky. 1868   Pvt. Vt. Mil.
m. (2) Catherine Graves Howard Parker
son Firman R. m. Alva Ella Jackson
daughter Frances E. m. James Madison Early REAL DAUGHTER

Smith, Reuben b. Va. 1782 d. Va. 1831   Pvt. Va. Mil.
m. Elizabeth — son Charles R. m. Elizabeth Dangerfield

Smith, Reuben b. Conn. 1770 d. N.Y. 1856   Lt. Conn. Mil.
m. Elizabeth Moss — daughter Lucy m. Lyman Robinson

Smith, Richard b. Conn. 1779 d. Conn. or N.Y.   Pvt. N.Y. Mil.
  m. Elizabeth Allen — son Avery m. Lament Wagener

Smith, Robert b. at Sea 1720 d. Penn. 1804   Rep. Penn. Legis. 1785
  m. Margaret Vaughan — daughter Susanna m. Nathan Grier

Smith, Robert b. Ire. 1760 d. Ga. 1853 m. Ferguson Wilson Pvt. S.C. Mil.
  son Hugh m. Elizabeth Yarborough

Smith, Robert b. Eng. 1735 d. N.Y. 1830   Civic Offices N.Y. 1798-1804
  m. Grace Braithwaite — son Abram m. Rachel Gray

Smith, Samuel b. Mass. 1714 d. Mass. 1785   Justice Mem. Comm. of
  m. Priscilla Gould   Safety 1784-5 Mass.
  son Asael m. Mary Duty

Smith, Samuel Vol. 7   Brig. Gen. Penn. Mil.

Smith, Samuel b. N.H. 1788 d. Vt. 1866 m. Elizabeth Rood Pvt. Vt. Mil.
  daughter Lucy H. m. Augustus Rudolphus Bailey

Smith, Samuel b. Miss. 1785 d. Tex. 1868   Pvt. Miss. Terr. Mil.
  m. Polly Henderson — daughter Rhoda m. Claiborne Harris

Smith, Samuel Vol. 9   Pvt. E. Tenn. Mil.

Smith, Samuel Sr. b. 1753 d. 1843 m. Mollie Rice   Pvt. (Sgt.) S.C.
  son Samuel Jr. m. Sallie Hays

Smith, Samuel Davenport b. N.Y. 1793 d. N.Y. 1862   Pvt. N.Y. Mil.
  m. Mary Morrell — son Mott D. m. Elizabeth Brown

Smith, Samuel S. b. Penn. 1793 d. Ind. 1865   Pvt. Penn. Mil.
  m. Martha McCool — son Samuel Jr. m. Flora Rogers

Smith, Seth b. 1777 d. 1854   Selectman 1799 & 1814 Vt.
  m. Sarah (Sally) Jones — son Charles m. Rachel Amy Bryant

Smith, Sheldon b. Conn. 1791 d. Conn. 1863   Fife Maj. Conn. Mil.
  m. Polly Summers — son Clifford m. Ann McCready

Smith, Sherman b. Conn. 1761 d. Ohio   Pvt. Ohio Mil.
  m. Amarilla Hotchkiss — daughter Sabrah m. Elliott Driggs

Smith, Simon b. S.C. 1760 d. S.C. 1857 m. Isabella McRae Pvt. S.C. Mil.
  daughter Jane m. Henry Bridges Covington

Smith, Stafford Vol. 14   Capt. Vt. Mil.

Smith, Sylvanus b. Conn. 1783 d. Ohio 1872   Pvt. Vt. Mil.
  m. Thankful Kelsey — son Axro m. Mary Inskeep

Smith, Terrance b. 1770 d. River Raisin 1813   Pvt. U.S. Inf.
  m. Christine Leiter — son Jacob m. Nancy Dennis

Smith, Thomas b. N.Y. 1793 d. N.Y. 1868   Pvt. N.Y. Mil.
  m. (2) Phoebe Raynor — son Samuel R. m. Phoebe Smith

Smith, Thomas b. Conn. 1784 d. Ind. 1870   Pvt. Conn. Mil.
  m. Phoebe Lush Johnson — son Joseph B. m. Amelia Pabody

Smith, Thomas Adams b. Va. 1781 d. Mo. 1844 Brig. Gen. U.S. Army
  m. Cynthia White — son Crawford E. m. Virginia Penn

Smith, Thomas Gibson b. Scot. 1756 d. N.Y. 1837   Chaplain N.Y. Mil.
  m. Jemima Allen — daughter Eliza m. Isaac Dilks

Smith, Thomas O. b. N.C. 1776 d. La. 1815   Pvt. W. Tenn. Mil.
  m. Sally Griffin — son Thomas O. J. m. Annie Elizabeth Kinzer

Smith, Thomas R. b. N.Y. 1789 d. Md. 1853 m. Eleanor Houser   Boatswain
daughter Eliza Janes m. W. C. Lewis

Smith, Timothy b. Mass. 1752 d. Mass. 1818   Pvt. Mass. 1814
m. Mehitabel Newell — daughter Lucy m. Timothy Broad Jr.

Smith, Wells, b. Conn. 1792 d. Conn. 1867   Pvt. Conn. Mil.
m. Catherine Towner — son Wilson M. m. Eliza Jane Bay

Smith, Whitaker b. S.C. 1787 d. S.C. 1850 m. Mary Moorhead   Cpl. S.C. Mil.
daughter Rebecca m. Lewis Moorehead

Smith, William b. Va. 1746 d. Ga. 1824 m. Mary Richards   Capt. Ga. Mil.
son Needham m. Tabitha Tillman

Smith, William   Vol. 12   Sgt. Mo. Terr. Mil.

Smith, William b. Ky. 1790 d. Ky. 1862   Maj. Ky. Mil.
m. Hariett Herndon — son Nicholas m. Eliza Peter Foree

Smith, William b. Md. 1789 d. Ga. 1853 m. Selah Mathews   Pvt. Ga. Mil.
son Elijah M. m. Elizabeth Scofil

Smith, William Hooker b. Penn. 1724 d. Penn. 1815   Lt. Penn. Mil.
m. Widow Smith — daughter Elizabeth m. Benjamin Bailey

Smith, William Sly b. Va. 1779 d. Ala. 1853   Pvt. Va. Art.
m. Mrs. Martha Knighton Stewart
daughter America A. T. m. Richard Evans Jones
daughter Laurice m. — Armstrong

Smither, John b. Va. 1779 d. Texas 1860   Pvt. Va. Mil.
m. Mary P. Greenway—son John R. m. Rebecca Ann Spivey

Smock, Aaron b. N.J. 1873 d. N.J. 1835   Lt. N. J. Mil.
m. Sarah Conover Schenck — daughter Elizabeth m. T. G. V. DuBois

Smock, Samuel b. Va. 1776 d. Ind. 1833   Ind. Judge Terr.
m. Rachel Robins Ryker—son John R. m. Elizabeth Tilford

Smoot, Benjamin Stoddert b. Md. 1781 d. Ala. 1844   Col. Md.
m. Hariet Mims — daughter Susan m. Lt. McLean

Smoot, Daniel Jenifer b. 1792 d. 1865 m. Harriet Medley   Pvt. Va. Mil.
daughter Frances Burton m. Jacob Howard Plecker

Smoot, John   Vol. 13   Pay. Mst. Md. Mil.

Smull, Jacob b. Md. 1776 d. Md. 1819   Surgeon Md. Coast Guard
m. Elizabeth Luce—son David B. m. Elizabeth Arnold Edes

Smurr, George b. Va. 1795 d. Ind. 1887 m. Anna Wise   Pvt. Va. Mil.
son Harvey m. Rachel Jennings
son Nelson G. m. Rebecca Kinsey

Smyley, John b. S.C. 1783 d. Ala. 1849 m. Rebecca DeWalt   Capt. S.C. Mil.
daughter Nancy Caroline m. John Thomas Bender

Smyser (Schmeisser), Henry b. Penn. 1770-2 d. Penn. 1860   Capt. Penn. Mil.
m. Jane Fibble — son George M. m. Martha Noel

Snapp, John b. Va. 1800 d. Tenn. 1882   Pvt. Bugler Va. Mil.
m. Katherine Newland — daughter Margaret m. James Hopkins

Snead, Jacob b—d. m. Mary Franklin   Pvt. Va. Mil.
daughter Rosina m. Fleming Phillips

Snead, Jesse b. Va. 1794 d. Va. 1855 m. Jane Jude Johnson   Pvt. Va. Mil.
daughter Ella m. Joseph Bozeman
daughter Jeannie m. William A. Watson REAL DAUGHTER

Snead, Tully   Vol. 11   Pvt. Va. Mil.

Snedaker, Ganett (Garrett) b. Penn. 1792 d. Ohio 1863   Pvt. Ohio Mil.
   m. Margaret Ashenhurst — son W. H. m. Anna Belle Urton

Snedeker, Abraham Bower b. N.Y. 1793 d. N.Y. 1884   Sgt. N.Y. Mil.
   m. Mary Anne Bell — daughter Antoinette m. William Magonigle

Sneed, Archibald H.   Vol. 4   Lt. Ga. Drag.

Sneed, Constantine P. b. Va. 1790 d. Tenn. 1864   Sgt. Tenn. Vol.
   m. Susannah Perkins Hardeman
   daughter Mary m. Robert Owen REAL DAUGHTER
   daughter Agatha A. m. William G. Bush
   son James Hardeman m. Margaret Caldwell Wilderson

Sneeringer, John b. Penn. d. Penn. 1848 m. Lydia House   Pvt. Penn. Mil.
   son William J. m. Mary Frances Umack

Snell, Appleton b. Me. 1796 d. Minn. 1864   Pvt. Mass. (Me.) Mil.
   m. Elizabeth Hubbell — daughter Mary m. William E. Henry

Snell, James b. N.C. c. 1760 d. Tenn. c. 1833   Juror Tenn. 1813
   m. Jannie Bell—son Willie Bell m. Elizabeth Cross

Snelling, Joshiah b. Mass. 1782 d. D.C. 1828   Col. U.S. Army
   m. Abigail Hunt — daughter Marion I. m. William S. Hazard

Snider, Solomon—b.— d. Ark. 1860 m. Jane Davidson   Pvt. Va. Mil.
   daughter Susannah m. William Sinnard

Sniffen, Joseph   Vol. 9   Pvt. N.Y. Mil.

Snoddy, Joseph Walker b. Ky. 1793 d. Mo. 1853   Ens. Ky. Mil.
   m. Narcissa Foster
   daughter Margaret Eliza m. Humphrey Denny REAL DAUGHTER
   daughter Mary Ann m. Alexander Denny REAL DAUGHTER
   daughter Narcissa m. Georgia Given Harvey REAL DAUGHTER
   son Samuel W. m. Susan Frances Harvey

Snook, John b. N.Y. 1768 d. N.Y. 1832 m. Agnes McGraw   Ens. N.Y. Mil.
   son William m. Nancy Hill

Snook, William b. N.Y. 1730 d. N.Y. 1814   Capt. N.Y. Mil.
   m Catarina Kleyn — daughter Christina m. Jacob Pettingill

Snow, Asher b. Mass. 1790 d. Ind. 1816 m. Maudana Matthew   Drum N.Y.
   daughter Polly Maria m. Asher Kellogg

Snow, David b. N.Y. 1793 d. N.Y. 1881 m. Laura Stoddard   Pvt. N.Y. Mil.
   son Edwin M. m. Emily Thomas Smead

Snow, Ephraim   Vol. 3   Pvt. Mass. Mil.

Snow, Isaiah Parker b. Vt. 1786 d. N.Y. 1855   Lt. N.Y. Inf.
   m. Sarah Forbes — son James C. m. Emily Carr

Snowden, Isaac Wayne   Vol. 17   Surgeon's Mate Penn. Mil.

Snowden, Nathaniel Randolph   Vol. 5   Chaplain Penn. Mil.

Snyder, Adam   Vol. 16   Pvt. Penn. Mil.

Snyder, Adam Vrooman b. N.Y. 1784 d. Penn. 1856   Sgt. N.Y. Mil.
   m. Catherine Van Wicklen — son Adam Jr. m. Freeborn S. Hoag

Snyder, Andrew b. N.Y. 1762 d. N.Y. 1832   Lt. N.Y. Mil. 1812
   m. Lydia Schoonmaker—son Jacob A. m. Sarah Schoonmaker

Snyder, Daniel b. Penn. 1777 d. Penn. 1847   Pvt. Penn. Mil.
m. Christina Kratzer — son Simon A. m. Elizabeth Couldron

Snyder, David b. Penn. 1789 d. Penn. 1872   Pvt. N.Y. Mil.
m. Hannah Haner — daughter Melinda m. Heman Morse

Snyder (Schneider), George b. Penn. 1771 d. Penn. 1844   Cpl. Md. Mil.
m. Katherine Kobel — son George Jr. m. Rebecca Gabe
son Peter m. Eva

Snyder, George Crosby   Vol. 6   2nd Lt. Penn. Mil.

Snyder, Jacob b. Penn. 1784 d. Penn. 1844   Capt. Penn. Mil.
m. Elizabeth Kahler — son Jacob J. m. Margaret Erisman

Snyder, Jacob b. N.Y. 1744 d. N.Y. 1785 m. Sarah Vrooman   Capt. N.Y. Mil.
son Adam V. m. Catherine Dockstader

Snyder, James b. Va. 1790 d. Mo. 1851 m. Sarah Ann Ayler   Pvt. Va. Mil.
son Benjamin F. m. Mary F. Warford
son Michael H. m. Minerva McCully

Snyder, John b. Penn. 1791 d. Penn. 1850 m.—   Capt. Penn. Vol.
son John m. Mary Huy
daughter Vanicia Irene m. George W. Walls

Snyder, John H. b. N.Y. 1788 d. N.Y. 1825   Lt. N.Y. Mil.
m. Gertrude Shultz — son Nelson m. Catherine Boucher

Snyder, Nicholas b. 1773 d. Pa. 1839   Pvt. Pa. Mil. 1792
m. Catherine Howard — son John N. m. Barbara Diehl

Snyder, Peter b. Penn. 1796 d. Penn. 1873   Pvt. Penn. State Guards 1814-15
m. Margaret McBride—daughter Maria m. William Wilson Beck

Snyder, Peter b. Penn. 1777 d. Penn. 1859   Capt. Penn. Mil.
m. Magdalena Wagener — son Daniel m. Kesia Miller

Snyder, Simon b. Penn. 1759 d. Penn. 1819   Governor Penn. 1808
m. Catherine Antes — son George A. m. Ann Ellen Duncan

Snyder, William b. N.Y. 1781 d. N.Y. 1865 m. Marie Yerdon   Pvt. N.Y. Mil.
daughter Marie m. George Pickard

Sober, Samuel b. N.Y. 1793 d. Mich. 1884 m. Clarisa Allen   Pvt. N.Y. Mil.
son Sylvester C. m. Lydia Dennis

Soliday (Soledy), Frederick b. Swit. 1791 d. Ohio 1875   Pvt. Ohio Mil.
m. May Rader — daughter Anna m. Jacob Auer

Solt (Sold), Paul b. Penn. 1758 d. Penn. 1849   Lt. Penn. Mil.
m. Eva Schaffer — daughter Maria m. Thomas Weiss

Somers, James b. N.C. d.—   Vol. 6   Pvt. U.S. Inf. Tenn.

Somers, Jesse b. N.J. 1763 d. N.J. 1859   Postmst. N.J. 1799-1804
m. Deborah Ludlam — son Richard L. m. Anna Braddock

Somers, Nicholas b. 1780 d. 1833 m. Phebe Scull   Pvt. N.J. Mil.
son Charles m. Sarah Stites

Somers, Samuel   Vol. 16   Pvt. N.J. Mil.

Sommers, Jacob Jr. b. Penn. 1775 d. Penn. 1842   Pvt. Penn. Mil.
m. Elizabeth Bright — son Gideon B. m. Mary Loper

Sorrell, George Washington b. N.C. 1785 d. Ark. 1855   Sgt. Miss. Mil.
m. Mary B. Chambers — daughter Cynthia m. Dodson Beverly Hine
daughter Anna Maria m. Russell Estes

Souder, Jacob b. Penn. 1781 d. Penn. 1854 m. Sarah Felton Cpl. Penn. Mil.
son Jacob Jr. m. Catherine Janus

Soule, Howard Vol. 11 Pvt. N.Y. Mil.

Soule, Howland b. N.Y. 1793 d. N.Y. 1826 m. Sally Downing Pvt. N.Y. Mil.
son Daniel E. m. Eliza Phelph Nooney

Soule, James b. Mass. 1761 d. Mass. 1821 Ens. Mass. Mil.
m. Patience Macomber — son James Jr. m. Nancy Wellman

Soule, Josiah b. Va. d. Tenn. m. Sally Young Pvt. Tenn. Mil.
son Edward M. m. Paralee Adams

Souter, George b. 1783 d. S.C. 1821 Cpl. Md. Mil.
m. Catherine Barbara Smith — daughter Charlotte m. Jacob Leitner

South, Samuel b. Md. 1770 d. Ky. 1833 m. Martha Glover Col. Ky. Vol.
daughter Eliza m. Richard Holtzclaw

Southall, Turner b. Va. 1736 d. Va. 1791 State Senator 1784-91 Va.
m. Martha Vanderwall — son James B. m. Mary Whitfield

Southerland, Robert b. Va. 1747 d. N.C. 1835 Justice N.C. 1793
m. Patience Twilly — son David m. Sarah Brown

Southern, Isaiah b. Va. 1777 d. Tenn. 1861 Pvt. Tenn. Mil. 1814
m. Caroline M. Smith — son Asa m. Temperance Williams

Sowders, Emanuel b. Tenn. 1795 d. Ky. 1872 Pvt. Tenn. Mil.
m. Milly Ferrell — son Henry m. Rachel Ausmus

Sower, Henry b. Penn. d. Ohio m. Catherine Ann Swigert Pvt. Penn. Mil.
son Philip m. Mary Swigert

Sowers, Moses Vol. 14 Sgt. Ohio Mil.

Spafford (Spofford), Eldad Constable N.H. 1784
b. Mass. 1745 d. N.H. 1806 m. Lucy Spaulding
daughter Milly m. Joel Patten

Spafford, Nathan b. Vt. 1791 d. Ohio 1858 Pvt. N.Y. Mil.
m. Mary Morrison — son Seth A. m. Irene Tannant

Spahr, James McFee b. Penn. 1793 d. Penn. 1870 Pvt. Ohio Mil.
m. Esther Parkison — son John P. m. Jane Yanaway
m. (3) Catherine Steffey
daughter Martha Esther m. George W. Hawk REAL DAUGHTER

Spain, Thomas Peterson b. Va. 1786 d. Tenn. 1836 Pvt. Va. Mil.
m. Catherine Mays — daughter Fannie m. Olyntheus D. Oliver

Spalding, Gilbert Richmond b. Conn. 1784 d. N.Y. 1870 Lt. Vt. Mil.
m. Orinda McClure — daughter Sophronia A. m. Roswell Lilley

Spalding, Jedediah b. Vt. 1797 d. Mich. 1864 Pvt. Vt. Mil.
m. Sally Tolman — daughter Elizabeth E. m. Henry Howard

Spalding, John b. Penn. 1765 d. Penn. 1828 Lt. Col. Penn. Mil.
m. Welthy Anne Gore — son Obediah m. Clotilda Hoyt

Spalding, Jonathan b. N.H. 1772 d. Penn. 1855 Pvt. Penn. Mil.
m. Margaret Stutz — daughter Lucinda m. William Freeman

Spalding, Jonathan b. Mass. 1770 d. Vt. 1823 Capt. N.H. Mil.
m. Milly Bennett — son Alva m. Lydia Taylor

Spalding, Simon b. Conn. 1742 d. Penn. 1814 Gen. Penn. Mil.
m. Ruth Shepard—son John m. Welthy Ann Gore

Spalding, Thomas b. Ga. 1774 d. Ga. 1851 m. Sarah Leake   U.S. Rep.
daughter Katherine Ann m. Michael J. Kenan

Spangler, George b. Penn. 1779 d. Ohio 1859 m.—   Sgt. Penn. Mil. & Ohio
daughter Mary m. — Cummings

Spangler, Jacob b. Penn. 1767 d. Penn. 1843   Lt. Penn. Mil. 1790 Postmst.
m. (1) Susannah Hay   1793 Penn. Deputy Survey
daughter Anna Maria m. Charles Weiser

Spangler, Jonas b. Penn. 1780 d. Penn. 1855   Pvt. Penn. Mil.
m. Sarah Sharp — son John m. Catherine Eyster

Spangler, Michael b. Penn. 1758 d. Penn. 1834   Pvt. Penn. Mil.
m. Catherine Schweisgood — daughter Elizabeth m. Wilhelm Eister
son Zacharia m. Anna Maria Menges

Spangler, Michael b. Penn. 1791 d. Penn. 1834   Capt. Penn. Mil.
m. Matilda Shriver — daughter Margaret M. m. William D. Elliot

Spangler, Solomon b. Penn. 1771 d. Va. 1830 m. Miss Taylor   Pvt. Va. Mil.
son Solomon P. m. Lucinda Tanquery

Sparkman, William b. N.C. 1764 d. Tenn. 1832   Cpl. Tenn. Mil.
m. Rosanna Williams — son Thomas W. m. Nellie Ann White

Sparks, Aaron Early Vol.   Pvt. N.J. Mil.

Sparks, Richard b. N.C. 1770-80 d. Tenn.   Pvt. N.C. Mil. 1814
m. Anna Smith—son Seneth m. Pearce Wade Bradshaw

Sparrow, Josiah b. Mass. 1775 d. Mass. 1851   Pvt. Mass. Mil.
m. Minerva Miller — son Josiah m. Priscilla Ellis

Spaulding, Benjamin b. Mass. 1739 d. Me. 1811   Civil Officer Me.
m. Patty Barrett — son Leonard m. Margaret Warren

Spaulding, Levi b. N.H. 1737 d. N.Y. 1825   Mod. of Town Meeting
m. Ann Burns   Mem. Gen. Ct. N.H. 1784
daughter Martha m. Joseph Knight

Speakman, Stephen b. Penn. 1767 d. Pa. 1849   Pvt. Penn. Mil.
m. Elizabeth Burkholder — son Miller Stephen m. Mary Jane Copeland

Spear, Isaac b. Mass. 1770 d. Mass. 1821 m. Constance   Pvt. Mass. Mil.
son Isaac J. m. Sally Thayer

Spear, Stephen Vol. 15

Spear, Thomas b. (Me.) Mass. 1794 d. Me. 1880   Pvt. (Me.) Mass. Mil.
m. Susan Randall (Andros) — son William m. Pauline Campbell

Spears, Nathaniel b. S C. 1790 d. Miss. 1855-69 m.—   Pvt. S.C. Mil. 1814
son David m. Reana

Specht, Peter b. Penn. 1782 d. Ohio 1852   Pvt. Penn. Mil.
m. Margaret Jones — daughter Judith m. Jacob Leist

Speed, John b. Va. 1772 d. Ky. 1840 m. Lucy Gilmer   Material Aid Ky.
son William P. m. Sarah Adell Hutchinson

Speer (Spear), Thomas b. Va. 1779 d. Ky. 1839   Cpl. Ky. Mil.
m. Sarah Bell — son Samuel m. Ripley Grant

Spencer, Calvin b. Vt. 1774 d. Iowa 1839   Pvt. Vt. Mil.
m. Ruth Hopkins Winchell — son Daniel R. m. Lavina Wheeler

Spencer, James Vol. 14 or 16   Capt. Ohio or Ky. Mil.

Spencer, John b. Va. 1786 d. Va. 1845 m. Betsey Price   Pvt. N.J. Mil.
daughter Ann L. m. Edward Bernard Sims

Spencer, John b. Conn. 1793 d. N.Y. 1883 m. Nancy Carr   Pvt. N.Y. Mil.
    son Richard m. Polly Smith

Spencer, John b. Conn. 1774 d. Ohio 1825   Pvt. Conn. Mil. & Naval
    m. Alma Harrison — daughter Mary E. m. Albert Miller

Spencer, Joseph b. Conn. 1714 d. Conn. 1789   Mem. Congress Conn. 1789
    m. Hannah Brown Southmayd — son Nehemiah m. Betsy Swan

Spencer, Thomas b. Va. 1778 d. Ill. 1853 m. Sarah Preston   Pvt. Va. Mil.
    daughter Deborah m. William Canada REAL DAUGHTER

Spencer, William b. Penn. 1757 d. Ill. 1841   Col. Ill. Mil. & Judge
    m. Susannah Allen — daughter Jane m. (1) William Lowre

Sperry, Gilead b. Vt. 1787 d. N.Y. 1825   Capt. N.Y. Cav.
    m. Catherine Kilburn Marsh — son George M. m. Emily C. Ripley

Spicer, Miner b. Conn. 1776 d. Ohio 1855 m. Cyntha Allyn   Maj. Ohio Mil.
    daughter Lucinda m. Stephen Ayres

Spicer, Thomas D. (raper)) b. N.Y. 1776 d. N.Y. 1870   Sgt. N.Y. Mil.
    m. Abigail Button — daughter Hannah F. m. Peter Corbet Potter

Spigner, Samuel b. S.C. 1791 d. S.C. 1827   Pvt. S.C. Mil.
    m. Eliza Belle Montgomery — son Benjamin F. m. Sarah Elizabeth Rose

Spinks, John b. N.C. 1786 d. Tenn. aft. 1861   Capt. Tenn. Mil.
    m. Sarah Crawford — son John C. m. Sarah Fogleman
    daughter Nancy S. m. William Smith

Spivey, Littleton b. Ga. 1780 d. Ga. 1836 m. Celia Cowart   Cpl. Ga. Mil.
    daughter Sophia E. m. John Madison Chastain

Spofford, Amos b. (Me.) Mass. 1788 d. Me. 1848   Lt. Col. Mass. Mil.
    m. Dorcas Harmon — son Josiah H. m. Frances Rogers

Spofford, Ira b. N.H. 1797 d. N.H. 1869   Pvt. Surgeon's Asst. N.H. Mil.
    m. Miriam — son George W. m. Hannah Morrison

Spohn, John b. Penn. 1754 d. Penn. 1822 m. Maria Beidler   2nd Maj.
    son Solomon m. Mary Jerger   Penn. Mil.

Spong, Barnard   Vol. 11   Lt. N.Y. Mil.

Spooner, Micah Sr. b. Mass. 1754 d. Mass. 1822   Pvt. Mass. Mil.
    m. Patience Crapo—son Micah Jr. m. Hannah Parker

Spotts, Samuel b. Penn. 1788 d. La. 1833   Maj. U.S. Army
    m. Mary Harris Hanna — son Harry Innes m. Jane Pearce Tunstall

Sprague, Anthony   Vol. 15   Lt. Col. N.Y. Mil.

Sprague, Ephraim   Vol. 13   Pvt. U.S. Inf.

Sprague, Eseck b. Mass. 1782 d. N.Y. 1863   Capt. Vt. Mil.
    m. Sophronia Huntington — son Edwin m. Orra Stickney Dickinson

Sprague, John b. N.Y. 1779 d. N.Y. 1861 m. Aurilla Sweet   Capt. N.Y. Mil.
    daughter Belinda m. Henry Weed

Sprague, Parmenas b. Conn. 1780 d. N.Y. 1871   Pvt. N.Y. Mil.
    m. Rebecca Nobles — daughter Rebecca m. Samuel Preston
    m. Mary Ann Fellows
    daughter Emma m. John Strange

Sprague, William b. Mass. 1759 d. Me. 1828   Lt. Col. Mass. Mil.
    m. Anna Morrow Winthrop — son Washington m. Abigail Pettengill

Spratt (Sprott), Blythe   Pvt. Tenn. Mtd. Rifleman
    b. N.C. 1792 d. Tenn. 1868 m. Rachel E. Blythe
    daughter Zorilda m. John Grigsby
    daughter Minerva m. Joseph Denton

Sprawls, Samuel b. S.C. 1780 d. S.C. 1837 m. Jane   Pvt. S.C. State Troops
    son Perry m. Susannah

Spring, Alpheus b. Mass. (Me.) 1791 d. Me. 1859   Capt. Mass. Mil.
    m. Sally Goodenow — daughter Caroline E. D. m. James Steele Bean

Spring, Amasa b. N.Y. 1795 d. N.Y. 1860   Pvt. N.Y. Mil.
    m. Juliette A. De La Mater
    daughter Josephine M. m. Daniel Reed REAL DAUGHTER

Springer, John b. Del. 1780 d. Ohio 1843   Pvt. Ohio Mil.
    m. Rebecca Stockwell — daughter Mary m. Thomas Florence

Sproat, David b. 1786 d. Ill. 1855 m. Margaret Mitchell   Pvt. Ohio Mil.
    daughter Lucinda m. Edward Barrett

Sprong, Bernard, Jr. b. N.Y. 1781 d. N.Y. 1832   Lt. N.Y. Mil.
    m. Mrs. Sarah Moore Peck — daughter Jane M. m. Henry Lewis Davis

Sprout, Ezra b. Mass. 1793 d. Mass. 1856   Pvt. Mass. Mil.
    m. Densy Newland—son Brigham D. m. Sarah Adaline Pope

Spry, George b. Md. c. 1771 d. Md. 1840   Capt. Md. Mil.
    m. Araminta Turner — daughter Araminta m. George W. Medders

Spurrier, Rezin b. Md. 1751 d. Md. 1828 m. Helen Ann Hall   Sgt. Md. Mil.
    daughter Rosetta m. W. H. Davison

Squier, Gurdon b. N.Y. 1790 d. N.Y. 1841   Pvt. N.Y. Mil.
    m. Sally Foster (Dolly) — daughter Lois Moss m. John Ladd Lewis

Squier, John b. N.Y. 1792 d. Mich. 1868 m. Mary Williams   Pvt. N.Y. Mil.
    daughter Myraette m. Seymour S. Burling

Squire (Squires), Nathaniel b. N.J. 1785 d. Penn. 1849   Pvt. Penn. Mil.
    m. Mary — daughter Mary m. Christian F. Reinholdt

Squires, Sturges b. Conn. 1791 d. Penn. 1879   Pvt. Conn. Mil.
    m. Almira Wood — son Frank D. m. Jennie Ann Preston
    daughter Minnie Jane m. Ernest F. Carter REAL DAUGHTER

Staats, Peter b. N.J. 1783 d. N.J. 1871   Capt. N.J. Mil.
    m. Catherine Voorhees — son James V. m. Mary Ann Wyatt

Stacy (Stacey), William b. Mass. 1733-4 d. Ohio 1804   Took Oath Alleg. as
    m. Sarah Day   Mem. of Order of Cincinnati
    son Nymphas m. Sarah Gibbs   Mass. 1784 Lt. Col.

Stackhouse, Jacob b. Ohio d. Ohio 1850 m. Nancy Cantwell   Pvt. Ohio Mil.
    son John m. America Ann Davidson

Stackhouse, Samuel b. Penn. 1794 d. Penn. 1873   Pvt. Penn. Mil.
    m. Ann Hamilton
    daughter Emma m. James M. Vandergrift REAL DAUGHTER

Stafford, Nicholas b. N.Y. 1792 d. N.Y. 1826   Pvt. N.Y. Mil.
    m. Sarah Havens — son Harris m. Sabre Royce

Stahl (Stall), Henry b. Penn. 1752 d. Penn. 1816   Col. Penn. Mil.
    m. Rosina Stemple — son Daniel m. Nancy Fox
    son Jacob m. Jane Meloy
    son John m. Barbari Harmon
    daughter Sarah m. James Benford

Stair, Daniel b. Penn. 1787 d. Penn. 1864 m. Ann Eve   Pvt. Md. Mil.
    son Daniel F. m. Henrietta H. Stromen

Stair, John b. Va. 1791 d. Mich. 1885   Pvt. Va. Mil.
    m. (2) Catherine Butler
    daughter Melinda m. (1) John H. Bowers REAL DAUGHTER
    (2) William L. Green
    daughter Rebecca Jane m. (1) — Wilson
    (2) John Lynn REAL DAUGHTER

Stake, George b. Penn. 1760 d. Penn. 1816   Pvt. Penn. Mil.
    m. Elizabeth Monninger — son David m. Ann Catherine Newkirk

Stalford, John Pawling b. Penn. 1788 d. Penn. 1863   Pvt. Penn. Mil.
    m. Lydia Horton — son John B. m. Emma Martin

Stallard, Joseph Bullett b. Va. 1787 d. Mo. 1875   Sgt. Va. Mil.
    m. Hannah Johnson
    daughter Adelia m. Thomas Monroe REAL DAUGHTER

Stallard, Walter b. Va. 1750 d. Ky. 1827   Pioneer Minister of
    m. Elizabeth Basey — son Pitt m. Sarah W. Stone   Gospel Ky. 1802

Stambaugh,
    (Stumbaugh), Philip b. Penn. 1774 d. Penn. 1852   Sgt. Penn. Mil.
    m. Mary Ann Simonton — daughter Sarah m. John McKee

Stamps, Moses b. 1772 d. Ga. 1829 m. Ann Eason   Capt. Ga. Mil.
    son Moses W. m. Sarah Freeman

Stanard, Asa b. Conn. 1776 d. N.Y. 1837 m. Sarah Bidwell   Capt. N.Y. Mil.
    son Walter W. m. Lavanche W. Sharp

Stanford, James Harvey b. 1791 d. N.Y. 1874   Pvt. N.Y. Mil.
    m. Lydia French — son Ezra W. m. Electa Clark

Stanford, John   Vol. 17   Pvt. Va. Mil.

Stanley, Abijah   Vol. 12   Pvt. Vt. Mil.

Stanley, James b. Penn. 1778 d. Ohio 1827   Pvt. Ohio Mil.
    m. Mary McClintock — daughter Martha m. Isaac Kennard

Stanley, Nash b. N.C. d. N.C. m. Patsey Allen   Pvt. N.C. Mil.
    son James B. m. Catherine Cole

Stanley, Nathaniel b. N.H. 1767 d. N.Y. 1814   Pvt. U.S. Lt. Drag.
    m. Anna Blodget—son Moses J. m. Mary Ames

Stanley, Nathaniel b Conn. 1768 d. Ohio 1848   Pvt. Ohio Mil.
    m. Mary Moore — son Marshall m. Sarah Wasson

Stanley, William b. Conn. 1774 d. Ohio 1835   Pvt. Ohio Mil.
    m. Margaret Bratton — son John B. m. Sarah Peterson

Stannard, Asa   Vol. 13   Capt. N.Y. Mil.

Stansbury, Edmund b. Md. 1746 d. Md. 1801   Justice Md. 1785-6
    m. Belinda Duany Talbot — daughter Elizabeth m. Aquila Miles

Stansbury, Tobias E. b. Md. 1758 d. Md. 1849   Brig. Gen. Md. Mil. 1809
    m. Ann Dew — son John L. m. Mary Osborne Smith

Stansell, Nicholas b. N.Y. 1784 d. Mich. 1847   Pvt. N.Y. Lt. Inf.
    m. Elizabeth Newcomb — daughter Julia Ann m. James Aldrich

Stansell, William b. N.Y. 1782 d. N.Y. 1857   Pvt. N.Y. Mil.
    m. Susanna Otto — son George m. Zada Prindle Bristol

Stanton, Charles Thompson   Vol. 17   Pvt. & Guard Conn. Mil.

Stanton, John b. Conn. 1753 d. Conn. 1851   Pvt. Music Conn. Mil.
    m. Elizabeth Fisher — daughter Hannah m. Lodowick B. Stanton

Stanton, Joseph b. R.I. 1780 d. N.Y. 1828   Capt. Conn. Mil.
    m. Susan M. Brewster — daughter Frances M. m. George Anson Avery

Stanwood, William b. Mass. 1752 d. Me. 1829   Capt. Me. Mil. Selectman
    m. Hannah Thompson — daughter Elizabeth m. Stephen Lee   Legis.

Stark, James b. Ky. 1792 d. Mo. 1874 m. Jane Watts   2nd Sgt. Ky. Mil.
    son Washington m. Martha Whitledge

Stark, Jeremiah b 1771 d. 1851 m. Sally   Juror Tenn. 1808-11
    daughter Sarah m. Obediah Stone

Stark, Sanford b. Conn. 1793 d. Conn. 1866   Pvt. Conn. Mil.
    m. Hannah Park — son Albert G. m. Hannah Wolf

Starkweather, John b. Conn. 1790 d. Conn. 1868   Pvt. N.Y. Mil.
    m. Lydia Button — son John Leonard m. Sarah Palmer Greene

Starkweather, Samuel b. Conn. 1719 d. Mass. 1786   Civil Officer Mass.
    m. Sarah Purple — son John m. Hannah Simpson

Starling, (Sterling) Harvey b. Md. 1763 d. Wisc. 1855   Pvt. Ky. Mil. Inf.
    m. Elizabeth Harper — son Levi m. Nancy Parish

Starn, Samuel b. N.J. 1785 d. N.J. 1827   Capt N.J. Mil.
    m. Rebecca Browning — son Conrad George m. Nancy Rains

Starr, Comfort b. Conn. 1731 d. Vt. 1812 m.—   Civil Service Vt.
    son Parley m. Jemima Coon

Starr, David b. Conn. 1781 d. Conn. 1854   Pvt. Conn. Mil.
    m. Eunice Lee — son Benjamin A. m. Hannah Maria Lockwood

Staton, Frederick b. N.C. 1772 d. N.C. 1864 m. Sallie   Capt. NC. Mil.
    son Uriah m. Elizabeth Lee

Stauffer, Abraham b. 1747 d. Pa. 1809   Pvt. Pa. Mil. 1784
    m. Barbara Hershey — daughter Magdeline m. John Metz

Stearns, Samuel b. 1794 d. Mich. 1857 m. Deborah Corwin   Pvt. Vt. Mil.
    daughter Annie m. Feliz Lemkie REAL DAUGHTER

Stearns, William Jr. b. Mass. 1790 d. Me. 1877   Lt. Me. Terr. Mil.
    m. Joanna Porter — son Sylvanus P. m. Isabel Partridge

Stearns, William Sr. b. Mass. 1765 d. Me. 1850 m. Mary   Selectman School
    son William Jr. m. Johanna Porter   Commissioner Me. (Mass.) 1796

Stebbins, Ezra b. Mass. 1731 d. Mass. 1796   Tax Collector Mass.
    m. Margaret Chapin — son William m. Margaret Newell

Stebbins, Josiah   Vol. 13   Pvt. N.Y. Mil.

Stebbins, Phineas b. Mass. 1739 d. Mass. 1837   Capt. Mass. Mil.
    m. Ann Chaffee — son Phineas Jr. m. Phoebe Dunham

Stedman, Abel b. Vt. 1785 d. Ohio 1859 m. Sallie Foster   Sgt. Ohio Mil.
    son William m. Rhoda Glass

Stedman, Lyman b. Conn. 1785 d. N.Y. 1847   Sgt. N.Y. Mil.
    m. Elizabeth Wilson — daughter Martha E. m. Samuel B. Babcock

Steed, Nathaniel b. Va. 1740 d. N.C. 1810   Justice N.C.
    m. Rachael Mordecai Clayton — son Charles m. Hannah Raines

Steel, Job b.—d. N.Y. 1813 m. Olive Stoddard   Pvt. N.Y. Mil.
    son Elisha m. Mary Hadden

Steel, Alexander b. 1790 d. Ohio 1857   Pvt. 1812-13 Ohio
    m. Nancy Galloway
    daughter Margaret Crawford m. Isaac Steel Jr.

Steele, Adam b. Penn. 1778 d. Penn. 1848 m. Mary Ross   Pvt. Penn. Mil.
    daughter Sarah m. John Hoffman

Steele, David b. Penn. 1782 d. Ind. 1855   Ens. Ohio Mil.
    m. Mrs. Bathsheba Lindley Reed
    daughter Samantha M. m. Henry B. Pershing

Steele, George b. Va. 1796 d. Ala. 1854   Pvt. Tenn. Mil.
    m. Elizabeth Weaver — son Matthew W. m. Catherine Erskine

Steele, John Jr.   Vol. 7   Capt. U.S. Inf.

Steele, John b. 1794 d. Ky. 1856 m. Anne   Pvt. Ky. Vol.
    son William J. m. Mary Dandridge Winston

Steele, John Jr. b. Penn. 1788 d. Penn. 1853   Capt. U.S. Inf.
    m. Jane Porter — son William P. m. Elizabeth W. Harris

Steele, John b. Va. 1790 d. Va. 1854 m. Eliza H. Moon   Ens. Va. Mil.
    son Peter m. Eliza Burks Meek

Steele, Levi b. Conn. 1776 d. N.Y. 1837   Ens. N.Y. Mil.
    m. Sarah Van Benthuysen — son Levi Jr. m. Marie Antoinette Wells

Steele, Samuel b. Va. d. Va. 1795 m. Margaret Campbell   Capt. Va. Mil.
    son Robert m. Jennie McClung

Steele, Samuel   Vol. 17   Pvt. Ky. Mil.

Steele, Samuel b. Va. 1782 d. Tenn. 1864   Capt. Va. Mil.
    m. Patience Shane — daughter Martha B. m. Joseph S. Binkley

Steele, Solomon b. Va. 1779 d. Ky. 1855 m. Nancy Lee   Pvt. Ky. Mil.
    daughter Sarah m. William Glass

Steele, William b. S.C. 1796 d. S.C. 1871   Midshipman S.C. Navy
    m. Esther Love—son William Jr. m. Margaret Watson Greyton

Steele, William Anson b. Penn. 1797 d. Penn. 1867   Pvt. Rifle Vol. Penn.
    m. Hannah Houghton—daughter Berthinda W. m. Justus Shawkey

Steelman, Daniel b. N.J. 1750 d. N.J. 1823   Justice N.J. 1806
    m. Eleanor Edwards — daughter Lydia m. Nicholas Reape (Rape)

Steelman, Frederick   Vol. 17   Pvt. N.J. Mil.

Steen, John b. Penn. 1778 d. Penn. 1859   Ord. Sgt. Art. Penn. Mil.
    m. Anna Cummins McDole — son Matthew m. Elizabeth Galbraith

Steen, Matthew b. Ire. 1755 d. Penn. 1835   Constable Supervisor
    m. Jane Taylor — son John m. Ann Cummins McDole   Penn. 1806

Stein, Jacob   Vol. 15   3rd Lt. Penn. Mil.

Steinbeck, Jacob Jr. b. Penn. 1792 d. Penn. 1827   Pvt. Penn. Mil.
    m. Ann Davies — daughter Elizabeth m. Henry Ambrose Allen

Steinbach, Jacob Sr. b. Penn. 1755 d. Penn. 1847   Pvt. Penn.
    m. Maria Steinmetz — son Jacob Jr. m. Anne Davies

Steiner, Henry b. Md. 1775 d. 1825   Capt. Md. Mil.
    m. Rachel Rebecca Murray
    daughter Mary C. m. Robert Myers Shoemaker

Stell (Still), George Washington b. 1780 d. Tex. 1870   Capt. W. Tenn. Mil.
  m. Mary Lewis Wynne — daughter Martha J. m. John Harmon Cook

Stemple, Jacob Sr. b. W.Va. 1792 d. Ohio 1859   Pvt. Va. Mil.
  m. Eve Easterday — son Jacob Jr. m. Mary Margaret Ernst
  daughter Katherine m. Jacob Helfrick
  son Levi m. Mary Gearhart

Stephen, Adam Jr. b. Penn. 1762 d. Penn. 1826 m. Margaret Pvt. Penn. Mil.
  daughter Elizabeth m. George R. Shaffer

Stephens, Eliphalet b. Conn. 1731 d. Penn. 1814 Signed Pledge of Allegiance
  m. Elsa Halloway — daughter Sarah m. Asa Cobb   Quaker

Stephens, Ira b. Conn. 1778 d. N.Y. 1852 m. Hannah Arthur   Pvt. N.Y. Mil.
  son George W. m. Cynthia Ann Brown

Stephens, Joseph b. Va. 1759 d. Ga. 1843 m. Nanah Cox   Pvt. S.C. Troops
  son Samuel m. Martha Tabitha Baker

Stephens, Levi b. Penn. 1744 d. Penn. 1808   Deputy Surveyor Penn.
  m. Elizabeth Brown — son Thomas m. Jane Gisbert

Stephens, Thomas b. Va. ca. 1790 d. Ky. 1870   Pvt. Ky. Mil.
  m. Charlotte Briggs — son Abraham m. Josephine Lucas

Stephenson, Benjamin b. Penn. 1769 d. Ill. 1822   Col. Ill. Terr. Mil.
  m. Lucy Van Swearingen — daughter Julia E. m. Palemon Howard

Stephenson, Elijah b. 1787 d. Ohio 1830   Pvt. Ohio Mil.
  m. Catherine Kilgore — son Thomas R. m. Sarah Rock

Stephenson, John Garner b. Va. 1787 d. Va. 1857   Ens. Va. Mil.
  m. Charity LeMaster — son Franklin m. Julia Ann

Sterett, Joseph   Vol. 5   Lt. Col. Md. Mil.

Sterling, Abijah b. Conn. d. Conn.   Vol. 9   Capt. Conn. Mil.
  m. Eunice Sherwood

Sterling, William b. Conn. 1768 d. Conn. 1827   Col. Conn. Mil.
  m. Jerusha Ely — son Thomas Sill m. Mary Falconer

Sterrett, Joseph   Vol. 3   Lt. Col. Md. Inf.

Sterrett, Thomas b. Va. 1771 d. Ky. 1846   Capt. Ky. Mil.
  m. Mary Ann Brooks — daughter Elizabeth m. Samuel M. Murell

Stetson, Oliver b. N.Y. 1756 d. N.Y. 1839   Pvt. N.Y. Mil.
  m. Jeanette Anderson — son Oliver Jr. m. Rhoda Alice Adams

Stevens, Benjamin Frothingham b. Mass. 1792 d. Mass. 1841   Pvt. Mass.
  m. Mary Esty — son John D. m. Louisa Kimball   Mil. 1814

Stevens, Elihu b. Conn. 1731 d. N.H. 1814   Mem. Congress N.H. 1792
  m. Rachel Meigs — son Ziba m. Lydia Kirtland

Stevens, James b. Md. 1776 d. Penn. 1859   Lt. Md. Navy
  m. Barbara Mercer — son Samuel R. m. Eliza M. Pinnell

Stevens, Jared b. Mass. 1782 d. N.Y. 1865 m. Polly Brown   Pvt. N.Y. Mil.
  daughter Philomelia m. Edwin Marsh

Stevens (Stephens), Jesse b. N.C. 1788 d. Ind. 1864   Pvt. Ohio Mil.
  m. Anna Tribble — son Walter G. m. Martha A. Jefferies

Stevens, John b. N.Y. 1708 d. N.J. 1792   Vice Pres. Council N.J.
  m. Elizabeth Alexander   Cont. Congress 1783-7
  daughter Mary m. Robert Livingston

Stevens, Jonathan b. Mass. (Me.) 1774 d. Me. 1851   Pvt. Mass. (Me.) Mil.
m. Tabitha Toby — son Daniel m. Sally S. Kimball

Stevens, Joseph b. Mass. (Me.) 1779 d. Me. 1853   Pvt. Mass. (Me.) Mil.
m. (2) Jane Jones — son Charles m. Miss Randilla

Stevens, Joseph Jr. b. N.Y. 1771 d. N.Y. 1843   Capt. N.Y. Mil.
m. Abigail Knowlton
daughter Haddassah m. Daniel Horton Campbell

Stevens, Paul Harris b. Mass. 1776 d. Me. 1870   Ens. Mass. Mil.
m. Christina Ulmer — daughter Mary M. m. Abel Bennett

Stevens, Silas b. Mass. 1755 d. N.Y. 1848   Ens. N.Y. Mil.
m. Lucy Simonds — son Jared m. Polly Brown

Stevens, William b. Va. 1773 d. Va. aft. 1812   Capt. Mtd. Rifleman Va.
m. Margaret Mills — daughter Margaret m. Isaac Finks Graves

Stevens, William b. Eng. 1787 d. N.J. 1850   Matross N.J. Art.
m. Elizabeth Baldwin — daughter Henrietta C. m. Monroe Howell

Stevenson, Alexander Vol. 17   Pvt. Md. Mil.

Stevenson, Hugh b. 1784 d. 1874 m. Susan Pillow   1st Sgt. Penn. Mil.
daughter Sarah Anne m. Thos. Harrison White

Stevenson, James b. Penn. 1754 d. Ind. 1845   Capt. E. Tenn. Cav. Mil.
m. Mary Gess — daughter Narcissa m. Robert Boyd

Stevenson, James b. Penn. 1755   State Senator Penn. aft. 1787
d. Penn. 1815 m. Catherine Bonar
daughter Ann m. David Brownlee

Stevenson, James b. Va. 1772 d. Ohio 1864 m Ann Galloway   Pvt. Ohio Mil.
daughter Jane Gay m. Vincent King

Stevenson, Josiah Espy b. Penn. 1790 d. Penn. 1864   Surgeon Penn. Mil.
m. Anne E. — daughter Narcissa Y. m. Rev. Edward Burns Griffin

Stevenson, Levi Lamb Vol. 11   Sgt. Maj. Va. Mil.

Stevesonn, Solomon b. Vt. 1786 d. Ohio 1851   Pvt. Mass.
m. Abigail Ring — son George m. Marinda Bennett

Stewart, Archibald b. Scot. d. N.Y. m. Jane Clark   Cpl. N.Y. Mil.
daughter Eliza m. John Guthrie

Stewart, Charles b. Va. 1776 d. Va. 1856   Pvt. Va. Mil.
m. Elenor B. McIntosh (MacIntosh) — son John B. m. Martha J.

Stewart, Charles Vol. 1   Admiral U.S. Navy
daughter Delia m. Charles Parnell REAL DAUGHTER

Stewart, Daniel b. Penn. 1769 d. Va. 1829 m. Ann Kelso   Capt. Va.
daughter Elizabeth m. David Miller

Stewart, Daniel b. Conn. 1762 d. Ohio 1853   Pvt. Ohio Mil.
m. Ruth Fulford — son Daniel m. Sarah Carter

Stewart, Daniel b. Ga. 1761 d. Ga. 1829   Brig. Gen. Ga. Mil.
m. Susannah Oswald — daughter Mary m. Josiah Thomas Wilson

Stewart, David b. Md. 1751 d. Md. 1810   Civil officer Md. 1785
m. Ann Ridgely — daughter Anne m. James T. Robinson

Stewart, James b. S.C. 1796 d. S.C. 1854   Pvt. S.C. Mil.
m. Mary Knott Harper — son John Pinkney m. Elizabeth Howard

Stewart, (Steward) James b. N.J. 1772 d. Penn. 1834   Pvt. N.J. Mil. 1813
m. Elizabeth Culver — son Dr. Thomas P. m. Susan Sherrod Beavers

Stewart (Stuart), James b. Penn. 1758 d. Penn. 1805   Lt. Penn. Mil.
   m. Margaret Armstrong — son James m. Rosanna McMullen

Stewart, John I. b. Md. 1785 d. Md. 1842   Pvt. Md. Mil.
   m. Mary E. Frazier
   daughter Elizabeth Ann m. Nicholas B. Pritchard

Stewart, Joseph b. Penn. 1789 d. Ohio 1867   Pvt. Ohio Mil.
   m. Catharine Long — son Amos m. Catharine Shelton

Stewart, Samuel b. Ohio 1793 d. Ohio 1872   Pvt. Ohio Mil.
   m. Elizabeth Long — son Jonas m. Anne Marie Herrold
   son John W. m. Susan DeHoff

Stewart, Thomas b. Penn. 1784 d. Penn. 1865   Capt. Penn. Mil.
   m. Tabitha Wallace — son James m. Mary Irwin Hodgson

Stiarwalt, William b. Penn. 1783 d. Ohio 1844   Cpl. Ohio Mil.
   m. Susannah Hickman — son Mervin R. m. Hester

Stice, Charles b. N.C. 1795 d. Ill. 1869   Pvt. Ill. Terr. Mil.
   m. Martha Whitley — daughter Sarah m. John Calvin Jamison

Stickney, Benjamin Raymond b. Mass. 1796 d. Mass. 1854   Pvt. Mass. Mil.
   m. Sarah Webber — daughter Helen m. Joseph B. Reed

Stiles, Ephraim b. Vt. 1794 d. Vt. 1841 m. Jerusha French   Pvt. Vt.
   son George m. Olive Field

Stiles, Isaac b. Conn. 1761 d. Conn. 1830   Material Aid Conn.
   m. Lavina Leavenworth — son Truman m. Ada Rowan

Stiles, Reuben b. N.H. 1780 d. N.Y. 1832 m. Phebe Dutton   Lt. N.Y. Mil.
   son David m. Henrietta Strait

Stiles, Samuel b. Conn. 1758 d. N.Y. 1814 m. Sarah Rose   Pvt. N.Y. Mil.
   son Epaphroditus m. Roxana Lincoln

Stiles, Truman b. Conn. 1761 d. Conn. 1839   Material Aid Conn.
   m. Ada Rowan — son Sherman m. Adele Brown

Stillman, Amos b. Conn. 1785 d. N.Y. 1813   Work in Munitions Factory
   m. Susannah French   Conn. 1808-13
   son Edwin A. m. Jane Craig Cochrane

Stillman, George IV b. R.I. 1739 d. R.I. 1817 m. Esther   Maj. R.I. Mil.
   son Maxson m. Esther Crandall

Stillman, Maxson b. 1775 d. 1857 m. Esther Crandall   Ens. R.I. 1799
   daughter Susan Rogers m. Wm. Pendleton Longworthy

Stillwagon, Jacob b. Holl. 1753 d. Penn. 1840   Pvt. Penn. Mil.
   m Elizabeth Zearfoss — son John m. Sarah Fitzrandolph

Stilwell, James Vol. 7   Pvt. Penn. Mil.

Stine, Jacob R. b. Penn. 1789 d. Mo. 1846 m. Emily Miller   Lt. Penn.
   daughter Ariadne m. Wm. Shannon Harper
   daughter Letitia Marie m. John Martin Taylor

Stiness, Samuel Jr. b. Mass. 1789 d. R.I. 1816   Capt. R.I. Navy
   m. Ruthy Bessom — daughter Elizabeth H. m. Noah Shumway

Stinsman (Stinceman), Casper b. 1774 d. 1848   Pvt. Pa. Mil.
   m. Rachel Robinett — daughter Margaret m. Joseph S. Myers

Stites, Benjamin Jr. b. Penn. 1772 d. Ohio 1846   Capt. Ohio Mil.
   m. Ann Ferris — Benjamin III m. Susan Eunice Stewart

Stivers, Robert b. Penn. 1789 d. Ohio 1855 m. Jane Meharry   Ens. Ohio Mil.
   daughter Sarah m. John Y. Bird

Stockard, John b. N.C. 1781 d. N.C. 1861   Capt. N.C. Mil.
   m Catherine Albright — daughter Jane S. m. Jacob Long

Stocker, Adam b. Penn. 1736 d. Penn. 1811   Pvt. Penn. Mil. 1784
   m. Maria Magdalena Beissel — son John m. Catherine Deily

Stockham, Aaron b. Penn. 1787 d. Ohio 1849   Col. Ohio Mil.
   m. Ruhama Sikes — son William m. Abigail Adams

Stocking, Herod Vol. 19   Pvt. Mass. Mil.

Stocks, Isaac b. N.C. 1740 d. Ga. 1796   Pvt. Ga. Drag. Inf.
   m. Catherine Heard — son John m. Carolyn Matilda Hunter

Stockton, Abraham b. N.J. 1749 d. N.J. 1827   N.J. Overseer of Poor
   m. Susanna Kemble   1783-5 Common Council
   son Charles m. Martha Huff

Stockton, George b. Penn. 1787 d. Ohio 1865   Pvt. Ohio Mil.
   m. Barbara Platter — son Joseph P. m. Emily Brown

Stockton, John Cox b. N.J. 1786 d. Ohio 1869   Qtr. Mst. Ohio Mil.
   m. Ann Stillwell — son John S. m. Mary Elizabeth Batcheller

Stockton, Samuel b. N.C. 1765 d. Ill. aft. 1831   Pvt. Tenn. Mil.
   m. Sarah Ellen Aikman — daughter Mary D. m. William Oglesby

Stoddard, Jonathan b. Conn. 1783 d. Conn. 1859   Pvt. Conn. Mil.
   m. Hannah Morgan — son James G. m. Margaret Barr

Stoddard, Mark b. Conn. 1743 d. Conn. 1829 Capt. Conn. Train 1786-1800
   m. Lucy Allyn — son Jonathan m. Hannah Morgan

Stoddard, Russell b. Conn. 1789 d. N.Y. 1873   Sgt. N.Y. Mil.
   m. Clarissa Elliot — son Russell F. m. Julia E. Powers

Stoddard, Stephen b. Conn. 1788 d. Conn. 1868   Sgt. Conn. Mil.
   m. Sarah Morgan — son Stephen m. Henrietta Allyn

Stoddard, Wait, S. T. b. Conn. 1781 d. N.Y. 1866   Pvt. N.Y. Mil.
   m. Rosamond Bates — son Addison m. Catherine E. Allen

Stone, Ebenezer b. Mass. 1771 d. Ill. 1843 m. Clarissa Lobdell Lt. N.Y. Mil.
   daughter Thankful Ann E. m. (2) William Dillon

Stone, Hiel b. Conn. 1766 d. N.Y. 1839 m. Ruth Norton 2nd Maj. N.Y. Mil.
   son Philo m. Jane Blain

Stone, Ira b. Conn. 1777 d. Ill. 1852 m. Rhoda Chapman   Lt. N.Y. Mil.
   son Oliver Perry m. Martha Taggart

Stone, James II b. Vt. 1796 d. Wisc. 1857   Pvt. Vt. Mil.
   m. Lucinda Danforth — daughter Eliza Elmina m. Sherman Comings

Stone, Jeremiah b. R.I. 1745 d. R.I. 1823   Lt. R.I. Mil. 1788 Justice
   m Dinah Knight — son Henry m. Lydia Blackmar of Peace R.I. 1795-7

Stone, John b. Va. 1779 d. Ky. m. Sallie   Pvt. Ky. Mil.
   daughter Elizabeth m. Cyrus Carroll Tevis

Stone, John b. Va. 1792 d. Miss. 1851 m. Mrs. Thomas Lewis Pvt. Va. Mil.
   daughter Clara — Unm. REAL DAUGHTER

Stone, Jonas A. b. N.H. 1780 d. Wisc. 1853   Carpenter U.S. Navy
   m. Elizabeth Gallagher
   daughter Maria Theresa m. Parmenas Camp REAL DAUGHTER

Stone, Nicholas C. b.— d. Tenn. 1835 m. Celia Evans   Pvt. Tenn. Mil.
daughter Ferraby m. James Franklin Fowler

Stone, Oliver b. N.Y. 1789 d. N.Y. 1878 m. Rhoda Brown   Pvt. N.Y. Mil.
daughter Meretta m. John Patterson REAL DAUGHTER

Stone, Philo b. N.Y. 1797 d. N.Y. 1880 m. Jane Blain   Pvt. N.Y. Mil.
daughter Martha m. Lester Wright
daughter Lucy B. m. Comfort Elwell REAL DAUGHTER

Stone, Phineas Vol. 3   Col. N.H. Mil.

Stone, Reuben b. Mass. 1790 d. N.Y. 1869   Ord. Sgt. N.Y. Mil.
m. Julia Porter Dunham — son Edwin m. Emily Crawford

Stone, Samuel b. Va. 1792 d. Tenn. 1857 m. Mary Ann Chunn   Pvt. Va. Mil.
daughter Martha A. R. m. John Hogue
daughter Mary Orphelia m. William Boyce REAL DAUGHTER
son Samuel T. m. Sarah N. Sawyer

Stone, Samuel Vol. 9   Pvt. N.Y. Mil.

Stone, Valentine b. Va. 1751 d. Ky. 1822   Pvt. Ky. Mil.
m. Keziah Franch Madden — son Samuel m. Sally Lane

Stone, William b. Va. 1775 d. Tenn. 1854   Capt. Va. Mil.
m. Nancy Allien Daniel
daughter Mary Jane D. m. Washington R. Dickerson REAL DAU.

Stone, David b. Penn. d. Penn. 1835 m.—   Pvt. Md. Mil.
daughter Mary Ann m. Daniel Trubey

Stone, Ira Vol. 5   Lt. Art. N.Y. Mil.

Stoneberger, Peter b. Penn. 1789 d. Ohio 1850   Lt. Penn. Mil.
m. Elizabeth Blosser — daughter Anne m. B. N. Beaver

Stoner, Michael b. Penn. 1748 d. Ky. 1813   Pvt. Ky. Mil.
m. Frances Tribble — daughter Frances m. Thomas Chilton

Stoothoff, William b. N.Y. d. N.Y. m. Sarah Whycoff   Pvt. N.Y. Mil.
son Cornelius m. Ellen Gorsline

Storms, Abraham b. N.Y. 1778 d. N.Y. 1824   Lt. N.Y. Mil.
m. Catherine Johnson — son William J. m. Sarah MacFerren

Story, Benjamin b. N.J. 1783 d. La. 1847   Pvt. La. Mil.
m. Ann Eliza Clement — son Henry C. m. Marie Amelia De Lesseps

Story, Edward Vol. 12   Pvt. Ga. Mil.

Story, Elijah b. Vt. 1778 d. Vt. 1830 m. Rhoda Crissey   Pvt. Vt. Mil.
son Ozias m. Charlotte Safford

Story, John Vol. 10   Pvt. Ga. Mil.

Story, John Vol. 11   Pvt. N.Y. Mil.

Stouffer, Abraham b. Penn. 1747 d. Penn. 1809   Pvt. Penn. Mil.
m. (1) Barbara Hershey — son Jacob m. (1) Catherine Whitmore
daughter Magdalena m. John Metz

Stough, Jacob b. Penn. 1753 d. Penn. 1823   Pvt. Penn. Mil.
m. Margaret McClelland — daughter Katharine m. Samuel Kelson

Stoughton, Augustus b. Conn. 1786 d. Penn. 1830   Cpl. Conn. Mil.
m. Hannah Perry — son Augustus III m. Rebecca Pettit

Stout, Abraham b. Penn. 1740 d. Penn. 1812 m.—   Del. to Const. Conv.
son Henry m. Elizabeth Kern   1790 Penn.

Stout, Daniel b. N.J. 1758 d. N.J. 1843 m. Anna Chadwick   Justice N.J.
    daughter Rachel m. John Williams

Stout, David b. Tenn. 1790 d. Tenn. 1888   Pvt. Tenn. Mil.
    m. Elizabeth Howard Johnson — daughter Dicey m. Valentine Garland
    son Godfrey D. m. Elizabeth Crosswhite

Stout, John b. 1785 d. Ohio 1841   Pvt. Ohio Mil. 1812
    m. Sarah Bradrick — daughter Mariba m. Boston Harmon

Stout, Joseph Hutchinson b. Va. 1787 d. Ky. 1860   Pvt. Ky. Mil.
    m. Martha Veech — daughter Martha Elizabeth m. James D. Allen
    daughter Mary Eleanor m. Adam Porter Carruthers

Stout, Peter Lott b. N.Y. 1788 d. N.J. 1860 m. Waite Luther   Sgt. N.Y. Mil.
    daughter Electa m. Benjamin Luther

Stout, Richard Montgomery b. N.J. 1782 d. Penn. 1872   Pvt. N.J. Mil.
    m. Ann Irwin — son James Montgomery m. Elizabeth Christy

Stover, Christopher b. 1772 d. Ohio 18— m. Sarah Whitefall Pvt. Ohio Mil.
    son Henry J. m. Margaret Rose Bogard

Stover, Daniel b. Tenn. 1775 d. Tenn. 1849   Sgt. E. Tenn. Vol.
    m. Phebe Ward — son Solomon m. Mary Ann Tredway

Stow, Stephen b. N.Y. 1786 d. N.Y. 1870 m. Anna De Long   Capt. N.Y. Mil.
    son Cyrus m. Sarah Ann Rider
    son George W. m. Lydia Ann Smith

Stow, Thomas b. Del. 1787 d. Md. 1848 m. Mary Thayer   Sgt. Md. Mil.
    son Charles W. m. Margaret Jane Collins

Stow, William b. Conn. 1773 d. Conn. 1858 m.—   Capt. Mass. Mil.
    son Frank m.—

Stow, William Vol. 12   Teamster Ohio Troops

Stowell, Lewis Barnard b Mass. 1793 d. Wisc. 1886   Cpl. Mass. Mil.
    m. Mary Barnard — son Lewis Jr. m. Laura Tuell

Stowell, Moses b. N.H. 1789 d. Mass. 1870   Seaman Mass. 1813
    m. Mary Chessmore — daughter Emily N. m. Stephen C. Hastings

Stowell, Samuel b. 1791 d. N.Y. 1885 m.—   Pvt. N.Y. Mil.
    daughter Mary m. Sydney Crocker

Stoy, Daniel b. Eng. 1742 d. Penn. 1835   Legis. Justice Penn.
    m. Sarah Hickens   1783-1813 Penn.
    daughter Margaret m. Abraham Spangler

Strang, William Vol. 13   Pvt. U.S. Inf.

Strange, Amos Bradford b. N.C. 1759 d. S.C. 1842   Capt. S.C. Mil.
    m. Frances Bailey — son William m. Mary L. Fowler

Strange, William Vol. 16   Pvt. U.S. Inf.

Stratton, Samuel Vol. 15   Cpl. Conn. Mil.

Stratton, Stephen b. Mass. 1743 d. Mass. 1814   Lt. Col. Mass. Mil.
    m. Martha Graves — daughter Hannah m. Benjamin Fairbanks

Street, Dudley b. Va. 1730 d. Va. 1816 m. Patty Miller   Pat. Va. 1791
    daughter Nancy m. Johnson Hudgins

Street, John b. Md. 1762 d. Md. 1837 m. Martha St. Clair Lt. Col. Md. Cav.
    son Shadrach m. Elizabeth Watkins

Street, Rodgers b. Md. c. 1793 d. Md. m. Catherine Glenn   Maj. Md. Mil.
daughter Belinda m. Otho Lease

Street, Thomas b. Md. 1765 d. Md. m. Jemimah McClure   2nd Lt. Md. Mil.
son John m. Hannah Jones

Street, Waddy b. Va. 1768 d. Va. 1819 m. Elizabeth Smith   Lt. Col. Va. Mil.
daughter Mary Anne m. Edward Montfort Jones

Streeter, David b. N.H. 1777 d. N.H. 1855   Pvt. U.S. Mil.
m. Elizabeth Spooner — daughter Hannah m. Jonathan Quimby

Streeper, Peter b. Penn. 1794 d. Penn. 1878 m Mary Hinkle   Pvt. Penn. Mil.
son Samuel m. Susanna Dager

Strickland, Henry b. S.C. 1789 d. Ala. 1844   Pvt. S.C. Mil.
m. Asenith Alexander — daughter Nancy m. Dr. John S. Hayes

Strickland, James Belcher b. Va. d. Va. 1860   Pvt. Va. Mil.
m. Lucreita Tanner — daughter Eliza B. m. Garrett Davis

Strickler, Henry b. 1750 d. 1816 m. Anna Rhode   Pvt. Pa. 1787
daughter Susannah m. Geo. Washington Shade

Stricklin, (Strickland) Samuel b.—d. Tenn. 1867   Ord. Sgt. W. Tenn. Mil.
m. Mary Chambers — daughter Martha Jane m. Thomas Ferguson

Strieby, Christopher Harper Vol. 8   Lt. Penn. Mil.

Stringer, John b. Penn. 1776 d. Ohio 1845   Ens. Penn. Mil.
m. Jane McCormick — daughter Sarah m. James Boots

Strode, James b. Va. 1765 d. Ky. 1828   Pvt. Ky. Mil.
m. Margaret Forman — daughter Susanna m. George Thomas

Strong, Daniel b. Conn. 1776 d. N.Y. 1859   Seaman U.S. Navy
m. Hannah Richmond — son Abner m. Henrietta Handy

Strong, Daniel b. Conn. 1771 d. Ohio 1816   Pvt. Ohio Mil.
m. Hannah Scribner — son Lucius C. m. Mahala Andrus

Strong, Elisha b. N.Y. 1777 d. N.Y. 1812 m.—   Capt. N.Y. Mil.
son John V. m. Sally Neal

Strong, Elisha b. Va. 1792 d. Miss. 1879 m. Ann Scott Hill   Lt. Ga. Mil.
daughter Georgia m. Richard L. Sykes

Strong, George b. Ala. 1773 d. Ala. 1834 m. Polly East   Pvt. Tenn. Mil.
son Robert m. Lucy James Douglass

Strong, Isaac b. Conn. 1765 d. N.Y. 1829 m. Mariam Bacon   Pvt. N.Y. Mil.
daughter Electa m. Amasa Lee

Strong, Joseph Churchill b. 1775 d. 1844   Asst. Surg. U.S. Navy 1797-1800
m. Catherine Neilson — daughter Martha m. Chas. Ready Jr.   Conn.

Strong, Levi Vol. 5   Pvt. N.Y. Mil.

Strong, Nathan Vol. 16   Capt. N.Y. Mil.

Strong, Return Vol. 9   Cpl. Vt. Mil.

Strother, George James b. S.C. 1791 d. S.C. 1817   Teamster S.C.
m. Charlotte Richardson — son David R. m. Mary Caroline Blocker

Stroud, Jacob b. N.J. 1735   Member 6th Gen. Assy. Pa. 1784/5
d. Penn. 1806 m. Elizabeth McDowell
daughter Elizabeth m. William Colbert

Stroud, Jonathan b. Penn. d. Penn. m. Catherine Eisenheiss   Pvt. Penn. Mil.
son Edward m. Susan Hetrick

Stroud, Orion b. Ga. 1795 d. Ga. 1875 m. Milcah Trammell   Pvt. Ga. Mil.
son Orion L. m. Sarah Henderson

Stryker, John Vol. 16   Ens. N.J. Mil.

Stuart (Stewart), Charles b. Penn. 1780 d. Penn.   Pvt. Penn. Mil.
m. Katherine — daughter Mary m. Thomas Grey Norris

Stuart (Stewart), Jacob b.— d. Penn. 1834-5   Ens. Penn. Mil.
m. Eunice Eliza Dunn — son Silas m. Mary Hendricks

Stuart (Stewart), John Vol. 13   Pvt. Penn. Mil.

Stuart, Philip b. Va. 1760 d. D.C. 1830   Congressman Md. 1811-19
m. Mary Fell Baynes — son John Philip m. Mary Eleanor Dent

Stubblefield, George b. Va. c. 1738 d. Va. 1801   High Sheriff 1784-6 Va.
m. Sarah — son Peter m. Sallie Harris

Stubbles, James b. Md. 1795 d. Md. 1873   Pvt. Md. Mil.
m. Mary Jane Pritchard — daughter Lydia m. Charles Husfelt

Stubbs, Charles b. Me. (Mass.) 1787 d. Me. 1858   Pvt. Me. (Mass.) Mil.
m. Nancy Ramsdell — son Charles R. m. Almira Sanborn

Stubbs, Eldad b. Mass. (Me.) 1787 d. Me. 1873 m. Huldah   Pvt. Mass. Mil.
daughter Mary m. William Wyman Rogers

Stubbs, James b. S.C. 1787 d. at Sea 1814   Capt. Privateer
m. Hachel Gove — daughter Amelia J. m. John Nicholas Pritchard

Stuckey, Abraham b. 1766 d. Ohio 1832   Capt. Ohio Mil.
m. Margaret Peterson — daughter Elizabeth m. James McCoy

Stuckey (Stukey), John b. Penn. 1742 d. Ohio 1818   Pvt. Penn. Mil. 1793-4
m. Salome Zimmerman — daughter Elizabeth m. Peter Sanders

Stuckey, John J. b. Penn. 1794 d. Ind. 1875   Pvt. Penn. Mil.
m. Martha Mary Miller — son William R. m. Helen Diana Beeson

Stull, John b. Md. 1733 d. Md. 1791   Pres. County Ct. 1791 Md.
m. Mercy Williams — daughter Susannah m. Mark Hardin

Stults (Stultz), Peter b. N.J. 1775 d. Ohio 1841   Pvt. Ohio Mil.
m. Jemima Meeks — son Jacob m. Nancy Smith

Stump, Michael b. Va. 1744 d. W.Va. 1799 m. Sarah   Justice Va. 1786
son Michael m. Magdalena Richards

Sturgeon, Reuben b. Penn. 1783 d. Ohio 1832   Pvt. Ohio Mil.
m. Elizabeth Atkinson — daughter Margaret m. Jeremiah Walton

Sturgeon, Robert II b. Penn. 1759 d. Penn. 1832   Capt. Penn. Lt. Inf.
m. Jennie Patrick — son Robert III m. Eliza Rogers

Sturgeon, William b. Penn. 1756 d. Penn. 1841   Capt. Penn. Mil.
m. Mary Crosscross — son William Jr. m. Jane Riddle

Sturtevant, Alexander S. b. Holl. 1773 d. N.Y. 1853 m.—   Pvt. N.Y. Mil.
son Nye G. m. Mahala Hadley

Sturtevant, Allender Stewart b. Va. 1787 d. N.Y. 1863   Pvt. N.Y. Mil.
m. Roby Nichols — son Allender S. Jr. m. Hannah Jackson

Sturtevant, Nathan b. Me. 1793 d. Me. aft. 1863   Music Me. 1814
m. Hannah Shaw — daughter May M. m. John Roundy Harding

Sublett, James b. Va. 1785 d. Ky. 1860 m. Susan Edzard   Pvt. Ky. Mtd. Mil.
daughter Mary Frances m. Israel Rowley Dodge

Sublett, William Allen b. Va. 1772 d. Tenn. 1839   Capt. Tenn. Mil.
   m. Sally Akin — daughter Mary Ann m. Robert Lawing

Suddarth, James Jr. b. Va. 1792 d. Tenn. 1848   Pvt. Va.
   m. Elizabeth Turner — son Jerome m. Lucinda

Suddeth, John b. d. Va m.—   Pvt. Va. Mil.
   daughter Mary m. Rev. Elijah C. Stone

Suggett, James b. Va. 1775 d. Mo. 1851 m. Sarah Redding   Maj. Ky. Mil.
   daughter Susan m. Washington Lynes

Suits, Adam P. b. N.Y. 1788 d. N.Y. 1865   Pvt. N.Y. Mil.
   m. Catherine Laning
   daughter Elizabeth m. Harry Dillin REAL DAUGHTER

Sullard, Stephen D. b. Penn. 1781 d. Penn. 1852   Pvt. Penn. Mil.
   m. Polly Spencer — son Oliver m. Elizabeth Watts

Sullivan, Jeremiah b. Va. 1794 d. Ind. abt. 1877   Sgt. Va. Rifleman
   m. Charlotte Rudesel Cutler — son Jeremiah C. m. Mary Jane Kelly

Sullivan, Samuel Wells b. Penn. 1777 d. Mo. 1860   Pvt. Va. Mil.
   m. Mary A. Mayfield — son Henry m. Mary Kenny

Sullivan, Wilson Vol. 16   Pvt. U.S. Inf.

Sullivant, Lucas b. Va. 1765 d. Ohio 1823   Pvt. Ohio Mil.
   m. Sarah Starling — son Joseph m. (3) Elizabeth Underhill
   son Michael m. Fanny Willis

Summerfield, Ephraim b. Va. 1789 d. Mich. 1867   Cpl. U.S. Inf.
   m. Adelaide Marsac — son William m. Mary Ann Chortie

Summers, John b. Tenn. 1794 d. Ill. 1869   Pvt. Ill. Terr. Mil.
   m. Louise Langford
   daughter Lucinda Belle m. — Landes REAL DAUGHTER

Summers, Paul b. Va. 1745 d. W.Va. 1831   Ens.Va. Mil.
   m. Elizabeth Hull — daughter Susannah E. m. Michael John Huffman

Summers, Thomas b. N.C. 1775 d. Ala. 1870   Pvt. Tenn. Mil.
   m. Elexia Pearson
   daughter Susan V. m. David C. Smith REAL DAUGHTER

Summers, William b. Ky. 1789 d. Mo. 1875   Pvt. Ky. Mil.
   m. Fannie Poindexter — son Harvey C. m. Martha Thornton
   son William T. m. Sallie Ann Hulen

Sumner Benjamin b. Conn. 1757 d. N.H. 1815   Rep. Legis. N.H. 1784-5
   m. Prudence Hubbard — daughter Prudence m. Stephen Dexter

Sumner, Joseph b. Mass. 1783 d. Me. 1861   Lt. Mass. (Me.) Mil.
   m. Sarah Wiggins — son Chauncey W. m. Catherine Stimpson

Sumner, Seth b. Mass. 1735 d. Mass. 1814   Repr. Mass.
   m. Elizabeth Davis — son Davis m. Dorothy Vose

Sumpter, William b. Va. c. 1741 d. N.C. 1828   Capt. N.C. Mil. Justice 1787
   m. Judith Randall — daughter Elizabeth m. Edward Owens

Sumwalt, John T. b. Md. 1791 d. Md. 1868   4th Cpl. Md. Mil.
   m. Rachel Sparks — daughter Mary Ann m. Charles Alexander Hough

Sunderland, Noah Vol. 9   Pvt. Vt. Mil.

Supplee, John b. Penn. 1779 d. Penn. 1844   Ens. Penn. Lt. Inf.
   m. Katharine Webb — son William B. m. Elizabeth Jarrett

Sutherland, Fendel T. Vol. 17   Pvt. Va. Mil.

Sutherland, Hannah b. Vt. 1795 d. Wisc. 1882   Teacher Vt.
    m. Sylvester Hills — daughter Chloe P. Hills m. Judson M. Purinton

Sutley, Christian b. 1783 d. Penn. 1858   Pvt. Penn. Mil.
    m. Elizabeth Schumacher — son Simon m. Mary Ann Schumacher

Sutter, Daniel Sr. b. Ger. 1743 d. Penn. 1828   Pvt. Penn. Mil.
    m. Anna Chatarine Gardner — daughter Catharine m. Samuel Brusstar

Suttle, Austin b. Va. c. 1778 d. Va. bef. 1833   Pvt. 1813; Corp. & Sgt.
    m. Sarah Bryan   25th Regt. Va. Mil.
    daughter Maria Elizabeth m. John W. de Rodier

Sutton, Aaron b. Penn. 1782 d. Penn. 1817   Cpl. Penn. Mil.
    m. Abigail Chips — daughter Lydia m. Benjamin Watson

Sutton, Daniel b. Penn. 1780 d. Penn. 1846   Pvt. Penn. Mil.
    m. Susannah Case — daughter Margaret m. Laertes White

Sutton, Edmund b. abt. 1780 d. Tenn. 1824   Pvt. Tenn. Mil.
    m. Mary Pierce — daughter Roxannah P. m. John Howard Wood

Sutton, Joseph b. N.J. 1772 d. N.J. 1858   Pvt. Penn. Vol.
    m. Henrietta Tomlin — daughter Eliza m. Reuben Tomlin
    daughter Henrietta S. m. William Cheston

Sutton, Joseph b. N.J. 1780 d. N.J. 1861 m. Sarah Lewis   Pvt. N.J.
    son John m. Lydia Hoffman

Sutton, Levi b. 1789 d. Ohio 1852 m. Katherine Crist   Cpl. Ohio
    son Alfred m. Sallie Ann Clark

Swagger (Swagert, Sweigert), Felix b. Penn. 1765 d. Penn. 1826   Pvt. Penn.
    m. Christiana — son Felix Jr. m. Catherine Bostick   Mil.

Swain, Isaac b. Eng. 1759 d. N.Y. 1838 m. Patience Dunn   Pvt. N.Y. Mil.
    son Issac m.—
    son William m. Sabrina Barrett

Swain, Isaac Vol. 11   Material Aid N.Y.

Swan, Nathan Jr. b. Mass. 1780 d. Me. 1835   Capt. Mass. Mil.
    m. Annabella Boynton Poor — daughter Lydia T. m. Ezra Bickford

Swan, Adin b. Conn. 1764 d. N.Y. m. Hannah Gardner   Maj. N.Y. Mil.
    daughter Lois m. Elijah Utley

Swan, Charles b. Va. 1749 d. Pa. 1832   Lt. Col. Penn. 1792-8
    m. Sarah Van Meter — daughter Elizabeth m. James C. Seaton
    son Richard m. Susan Gregg

Swan, Francis b. Mass. 1710 d. Mass. 1797   Town Clerk Mass. 1781-6
    m. Lydia Frye — daughter Dorcas m. Jonathan Gage

Swan, Stephen Vol. 3   Pvt. Mass. Lt. Inf.

Swan, William b. Md. 1787 d. Md. 1867 m. Martha Knox   Pvt. Md. Vol.
    daughter Eliza Jane m. Ross Campbell

Swaney, Thomas b. Penn. 1774 d. Penn. 1835   Pvt. Penn. Mil.
    m. Jane Patton — daughter Mary m. David Kerr

Swann, Thomas Thompson b. Va. d. Va. m. Sallie Woodson   Pvt. Va. Mil.
    son James S. m. Mattie Graves

Swanson, Richard b. Tenn. 1790 d. Tenn. 1873   3rd Lt. Tenn. Mil.
    m. Alvina Deborah Tarkington
    daughter Alvina D. m. Rufus Ezeel REAL DAUGHTER
    daughter Amanda m. William Harrison
    daughter Amelia Ann m. Marcus Cook
    daughter Margaret Jane m. Samuel Morton

Swartz, Daniel b. Penn. 1746 d. Penn. 1815   Pvt. Penn. Mil.
  m. Elizabeth Ruth — son Daniel Jr. m. Magdalena Webber

Swearingen, Samuel Vol. 13   Pvt. Ky. Mtd. Mil.

Swearingen, Van b. N.C. 1743 d. S.C. 1820 m. Miss Cloud   Sgt. S.C. Mil.
  son Moses m. Martha Mims

Swearingen, William Van b. 1766 d.— m. Elizabeth Dawson   Lt. 1799
  son George m. Elizabeth

Sweat, Gideon Allen b. S.C. 1789 d. S.C. 1871 m. Ellen Newman   Sgt. S.C.
  son James m. Ellen Futch

Sweeney, (Sweeny) James b. Penn. 1787 d. Penn. 1849   Pvt. Penn. Mil.
  m. Mary Margaret Todhunter — son Barnabas m. Elizabeth Robinson

Sweeny, Doyle Edward b. Penn. 1789 d. Mexico 1846   Sgt. Penn. Vol.
  m. Catherine O'Hanlon — daughter Roxanna m. Thomas H. Walsh

Sweesy, Mathias b.—d. Penn. 1859 m. Elizabeth Pounds   Sgt. Penn. Mil.
  son Thomas m. Alice Forbes

Sweet, Darius b. Canada 1782 d. N.Y. 1864   Pvt. N.Y. Vol.
  m. Susan Tiffany — daughter Mary m. Elmanson Chesebro

Sweet, James b. 1767 d. 1850 m. Eleanor Barbour   Lt. Col. N.Y. 1812
  son William m. Clara Catlin

Sweet, Sylvester b. Mass. 1792 d. Mass. 1849   Pvt. Mass. Mil.
  m. Mary Heath — daughter Orra Angeline m. James W. Horton

Sweet, Thomas Jr. b. N.H. 1791 d. N.H. 1874   Pvt. N.H. Mil.
  m. Sarah S. Prescott — son David K. m. Elizabeth Ann Lane

Sweet, Wilbur b. Vt. 1760 d. Mich. 1857 m. Ann Leech   Pvt. Vt. Mil.
  daughter Irene m. John Sargent Jr.

Sweetland, Eleazer b. Conn. 1782 d. Va. 1838   Ens. N.Y. Lt. Inf.
  m. Sallie Hawkins (Van Meter)
  daughter Elizabeth Ann m. Thomas J. Obenchain

Sweigart, Felix b. Ger. 1765 d. Penn. 1826   Pvt. Penn. Mil.
  m. Christiana Schwenk — son John m. Susanna Duke

Swett, Benjamin Jr. b. N.H. 1736 d. N.H. 1800   Selectman N.H. 1785-6
  m. Mary Eliot — daughter Mary m. Benjamin Rolfe

Swett, John b. Mass. 1781 d. Me. 1832 m. Mary Wood   Lt. Mass. Mil.
  son Nathaniel m. Catherine Wright

Swift, Edmund b. Va. 1787 d. Va. 1878 m. Dorothy Smith   Pvt. Va. Cav.
  son William Z. m. Eliza Margaret Thomas

Swift, Daniel Vol. 8   Pvt. La. Mil.

Swift, Joseph Vol. 5   Pvt. N.Y. Mil.

Swift, Joseph Jr. b. Mass. 1787 d. Me.   Pvt. Mass. Mil.
  m. Sarah Lovel Faunce — daughter Lucy Ann m. Moses Houghton Jr.

Swigert (Sweigert), Philip b. Penn. 1754 d. Penn. 1814   Pvt. Penn. Mil.
  m. Christina Shaurman — daughter Rachel m. Amenius Allen

Swinney (Sweeney), William b. Va. 1773 d. Va. 1841   Ens. Va. Mil.
  m. Sarah Wells — daughter Lucy Ann G. m. Joshua Flagg

Swisher, John b. N.H. 1782 d. Ohio 1861   Pvt. Ohio Mil.
  m. Mary Peterson — son Jacob m. Anah Needles

Swope, Samuel b. Penn. 1779 d. Penn. 1853   Pvt. Penn. Mil.
    m. Hannah Hanes — son George E. m. Mary (Moreley) Harley

Swoyer, Jacob b. Penn. 1789 d. Penn. 1864   2nd Lt. U.S. Inf.
    m. Mrs. Sarah Wild Newill — daughter Sara m. John Kistler

Sylvester, Nathaniel Vol. 17   Pvt. N.Y. Mil.

Sylvester, William b. Mass. 1792-3 d. Wisc. 1875   Pvt. Mass. Mil.
    m. 2nd Harriett Norton
    daughter Lilliam m. Ethan Bradish REAL DAUGHTER
    by wife Mary Jane (Nancy) Allen
    daughter Mary M. m. (2) Silas Spees REAL DAUGHTER
    daughter Susan Delia m. John Rider Kingsbury

Symonds, Joseph b. Mass. 1746 d. N.H. 1820   Selectman Town Clerk
    m. Mattie Cummings — son Charles m. Sally Dennis   N.H. 1788

Sympson, William b. Va. 1766 d. Ky. 1843   Pvt. Va. Mil. 1813-14
    m. Rebekah Clendenning — son George m. Mary Bogan

Sypert, Lawrence b. N.C. 1786 d. Tenn. 1877   Pvt. Tenn.
    m. Mary Lambeth — daughter Mary D. m. J. M. Anderson

Sypert, William L. b. N.C. 1789 d. Tenn. 1871   Pvt. Tenn. Mil.
    m. Elizabeth Dew — daughter Elizabeth m. Nathaniel Cooke

Sypert, Lawrence b. Va. 1778 d. Tenn. 1869   Pvt. Tenn. Mil.
    m. Mary Lambeth — daughter Mary D. m. Joseph Motley Anderson

T

Tabor, Hudson b. (La.) 1789 d. La. 1827   2nd Lieu. 10th La. Regt. Mil.
    m. Parine Mills — son Hudson W. m. Emilie Bernard

Tackitt, John Wesley b. Va. 1795 d. Mo. 1873   Pvt. Va. Mil.
    m. Mary Alderson — daughter Virginia m. John M. Rice

Taffe, George b. Ky. 1794 d. Ind. 1844   Pvt. Ind. Terr. Vols.
    m. Katharine Harrodd
    daughter Katharine unm. REAL DAUGHTER
    daughter Sarah m. Spencer W. Huntington

Taft, Jesse b. Mass. 1731 d. Mass. 1800   Civil Offices Worcester 1783-89
    m. Hannah Taft (cousin) — son Sibley m. Katharine Weiss

Taggart, John Vol. 14   Drummer Va. Mil.

Taggart, William b. Pa. 1773 d. Pa. 1853   Major Pa. Mil.
    m. (3) Elizabeth Steele — son James S. m. Eleanora —

Tainter, Loren b. Conn. 1799 d. Minn. 1864   Pvt. N.Y. Mil.
    m. Ruth C. Graves — son Benjamin Darwin m. Nancy B. Hillard

Tainter, Newhall b. Conn. 1782 d. Conn. 1858   Capt. Conn. Mil.
    m. Ruth Smith — son Solomon m. Harriet Bacheldor

Tainter, Samuel b. Vt. 1787 d. Me. —— m. Sarah Davis   Capt. Conn. Mil.
    daughter Nancy D. m. Josiah Bartlett

Tait, Bacon Vol. 5   Pvt. Va. Mil.

Tait, Charles b. Va. 1768 d. Ala. 1885   Judge 1803; U.S. Sen. 1809 Ga.
    m. Ann Lucas Simson — son James A. m. Caroline Goode

Tait, James Ashbury b. Md. 1791 d. Ala. 1855   Capt. Ga. Mil.
    m. Caroline Goode — son Charles William m. Louise Williams

Talbee, Stephen b. R.I. 1766 d. R.I. 1846 m. Mary Smith   Lieut. R.I. Mil.
son Stephen m. Eliza Denham

Talbot, Charles Moyle b. Va. 1771 d. Va. 1834   Pvt. Va. Mil.
m. Martha T. Prewitt
daughter Martha Ann m. Francis Epps Williams

Talbot, John b. Va. 1790 d. Texas 1854 m. Susannah Gholston   Pvt. Va. Mil.
son John F. m. Elinor Ann Derrick

Talbot, John N. b. Ky. 1790 d. Ala. 1868   Surgeon Tenn. Mil.
m. Mrs. Sarah Patton Basyne
daughter Laura m. John Oldham Ross REAL DAUGHTER
daughter Cordelia m. Madison Pyles REAL DAUGHTER

Talbot, John Williston b. Va. 1735 d. Ga. 1795   Memb. Ga. Leg. 1789
m. Phoebe Moseley — daughter Phoebe m. David Gresswell

Talbott, Richard b. Md. 1788 d. Mo. 1823 m. Martha Cave   Pvt. Ky. Mil.
daughter Sarah m. Joel Harris Haden

Talbott, Richard Vol. 17   Ensign Md. Mil.

Talbot, Williston b. Va. 1751 d. Va. 1827   Sheriff Campbell Co. Va.
m. Elizabeth Cook — son Charles M. m. Martha T. Prewitt
daughter Sarah m. Archibald McWilliams

Talcott, George Vol. 4   Capt. N.Y. Mil.

Taliaferro, Francis b. Va. 1750 d. Ky. 1826   Dep. Sheriff 1796/7
m. Letitia Hughes   Albemarle Co. Va.
son Samuel W. m. Sallie McClung Moore

Taliaferro, Zachariah Vol. 11   Pvt. Tenn. Mil.

Tallmadge, Benjamin Vol. 14   Conn. Congressman 1801/15

Tallmadge, William S. b. N.Y. 1784 d. N.Y. 1866   Major U.S. Arty.
m. Phoebe Golding — son Lewis m. Elizabeth McKinstry

Talmage, Joseph b. N.J. 1781 d. Ohio 1837   Pvt. Ohio Mil.
m. Catherine Beerse — daughter Nancy Cornelia m. Henry Snider

Talman, John b. Va. 1794 d. Va. 1872 m. Sarah Grant   Pvt. Va. Mil.
daughter Mary Frances m. William Ettenger

Talman, Peter D. Vol. 6   Pvt. N.Y. Mil.

Tamblin, Timothy Vol. 12   Capt. N.Y. Mil.

Tandy, Willis b. Ky. 1788 d. Ill. c. 1849 m. Martha H. Reid Pvt. Ky. Mil.
son Andrew Jackson m. Sarah Jane Clough

Tankersley, George G. b. Ga. 1791 d. Ala. 1862   2nd. Lieut. Ga. Mil.
m. Sarah F. Haley Jones — son Robert m. Evelyn L. Cunningham

Tanner, Abel b. R.I. 1740 d. R.I. ——   Dep. Gen. Assembly-
m. Phoebe Bent — son William m. Elizabeth Palmer   Justice R.I.

Tanner, Isaac Jr. b. R.I. 1771 d. N.Y. 1855   Corp. N.Y. Mil.
m. Tabitha D. Bentley — daughter Sarah m. John Richards

Tanner, Isaac Jr. b. N.Y. 1794 d. N.Y. 1880   Corp. N.Y. Mil.
m. Phoebe J. Percy
daughter Mary m. George Babcock REAL DAUGHTER

Tanner, Lemuel b. c. 1793 d. La. 1854 m. Celeste Ballenger Lieut. La. Mil.
daughter Bridget m. Henry B. Holcombe Jr.

Tanner, Zera b. Conn. 1770 d. N.Y. 1837   Ensign N.Y. Mil.
  m. Janett McWhorter — daughter Polly m. Lewis Wood

Tanquary, Abraham b. Va. 1773 d. Ohio 1858   Pvt. Ohio Mil.
  m. Judith Wilson — son Benjamin F. m. Carrie Olivia Tanquary

Tansil, William Vol. 13   Pvt. Va. Mil.

Tappan, Benjamin b. Mass. 1773 d. Ohio 1857   Major Ohio Mil.
  m. Nancy Wright — son Benjamin m. Nancy Lowther

Tarbell, Amos Vol. 15   Pvt. N.Y. Mil.

Tarbell, Joseph b. 1773 d. D.C. 1815 m. Ann Cassin   Capt. U.S. Navy
  daughter Ann Eliza m. Dr. William Laurie

Tate, Caleb b. Va. 1783 d. Ala. 1841   Pvt. Campbell Co. Va. Mil.
  m. Mary Middleton — son Netherland m. Carolyn Porter Childers

Tate, Isaac b. Va. 1777 d. Ky. 1852 m. Mary Steel   Brig. Inspector Ky.
  daughter Nancy Jane m. Thomas Weller Lisle

Tate, Samuel Bracken b. Va. 1775 d. Ky. 1845   Capt. Ky. Mtd. Vol. Mil.
  m. Nancy Owens — son John m. Lucy Hale (Hail, Hall)

Tatum, Howell b. N.C. 1753 d. Tenn. 1823   Major Tenn. Vols.
  m. Henrica Organ — son Howell m. Rebecca Pearce
  son Joshua P. m. Sarah Vardeman
  son Organ m. Ailsey Vardeman
  son Peter E. m. Martha Gause

Taul, Micah b. Md. 1785 d. Ala. 1850 m. Mary Hayter   Col. Ky. Vols.
  daughter Darthula m. Charles Bradford Roach
  daughter Florida m. Dr. Joseph J. Marsh
  son Micah m. Louisiana Roach

Tayloe, John b. Va. 1721 d. Va. 1829   Major U.S. Army 1799—built
  m. Rebecca Plater   Octagon House where Treaty of
  son John m. Ann Ogle   Ghent was signed (in D.C.)

Taylor, Andrew Sr. b. Va. 1735 d. N.C. 1787   Justice Wash. Co. N.C. 1787
  m. Elizabeth Wilson — son Andrew m. Isabella Cooper
  daughter Rhoda m. Archibald Williams

Taylor, David Preston b. Va. 1791 d. 1890   Pvt. 43rd. Regt. Va. Mil.
  m. Anna Moore — son Peter m. Martha Shipley

Taylor, Dudley b. Va. 1784 d. Ind. 1855   Pack Horse Driver, Ky. Mil.
  m. Nancy — son Chesley m. Mary G. Long

Taylor, Ezekiel b. Ga. 1780 d. Ga. 1825 m. Nancy Kellum   Pvt. Ga. Mil.
  daughter Louisa m. Robert N. Taylor

Taylor, George b. Dela. 1760 d. Wash, D.C. 1851   Justice Peace D.C.
  m. (3) Love Hooker — son Algernon S. m. Lasan M. Meecham

Taylor, George W. Vol. 8   Seaman, Mass. Navy on the "Hornet"

Taylor, Gilbert b. Conn. 1776 d. N.Y. 1840   Pvt. N.Y. State Mil.
  m. Clarissa Gibbs — son Clinton C. m. Eliza Marie Barnes

Taylor, Giles b. N.Y. 1791 d. N.Y. 1879   Pvt. N.Y. Mil.
  m. Asenath Devereux — son Giles m. Hesebeth Whitney

Taylor, Henry Pendleton b. S.C. 1784 d. S.C. 1832   Capt. U.S. Inf.
  m. Ann T. Trezvant
  daughter Elizabeth W. m. Dr. Alexander L. Moore

Taylor, Jacob b. Pa. 1760 d. Pa. —— m.— Pvt. Pa. Mil.
son Jacob m. Elizabeth Andrews

Taylor, James Vol. 1 and 17 Pvt. Md. Mil.

Taylor, James b. Va. 1769 d. Ky. 1848 Quartermaster Gen. U.S. Inf.
m. Mrs. Keurah Moss Leitch — daughter Keturah m. Horatio Harris

Taylor, John b. Mass. 1773 d. Mass. 1842 Capt. Mass. Mil.
m. Martha Thompson — son James m. Sarah Briley

Taylor, John b. N.J. 1782 d. Ohio 1863 m. Mary Peirce Pvt. Ohio Mil.
daughter Sarah m. John Tudor

Taylor, John b. Va. 1784 d. Va. 1855 Pvt. Va. Mil.
m. Elizabeth Smiley — son Joshua m. Patsy Higgins

Taylor, John b. Va. —— d. 1814 in hosp. Norfolk, Va. Pvt. Va. Mil.
m. Mary Ann Varney — son William Anderson m. Sarah Maynard

Taylor, Jonathan b. Va. 1774 d. Ind. 1833 Capt. Ind. Terr. Exp. against
m. Mary Ann Ashby — son John Henley m. Susanna Cupp Indians

Taylor, Jonathan b. Ky. 1791 d. Ky. 1838 Ensign Ky. Vol. Mil.
m. Nancy Baker — son Fielding C. m. Mary Jane Caseldine

Taylor, Joseph b. N.J. 1770 d. Ohio 1830 m. Jane Irwin Pvt. Ohio Mil.
son Jared m. Nancy Pepple

Taylor, Lemuel b. Md. 1791 d. Md. 1859 Pvt. Md. Cav. Mil.
m. Diademia Davis — daughter Sarah A. m. William H. Watson

Taylor, Leonard b. Vt. 1783 d. Vt. 1832 m. Mary Steele Pvt. N.Y. Mil.
daughter Maria m. George Veazie

Taylor, Leroy b. Va. 1758 d. Tenn. 1834 Memb. Leg. for Wash. Co. Tenn.
m. Mary Bradford made 1st seal of Tenn.
daughter Sarah m. John Campbell

Taylor, Mark b. Va. 1787 d. Va. 1824 Pvt. Rockbridge Co. Va. Mil.
m. Margaret Amys — daughter Adeline m. John Gish

Taylor, Matthew b. Mass. 1788 d. Me. 1851 Ensign Mass. (Me.) Mil.
m. Maria Thompson — son Horace W. m. Susan E. Branch

Taylor, Matthew b. Scotland d. Ohio 1834 Col. Ohio Mil.
m. Anna McNight — son Matthew A. m. Mary Kellem

Taylor, Matthew b. Pa. 1775 d. Pa. 1852 Pvt. Wash. Co. Pa. Mil.
m. Nancy Hutcheson — son Matthew m. Jane Forrest

Taylor, Nathan Vol. 3 Ch. Citizen's Mtg. 1814 Sanbornton, N.H.

Taylor, Nathaniel b. Va. 1771/2 d. Tenn. 1816 Brig. Gen. Tenn. Mil.
m. Mary Patton — daughter Ann m. Thomas Dillard Love
daughter Mary m. Dr. William R. Dulaney
son Nathaniel m. Mary Carter

Taylor, Parmenas b. Va. 1753 d. Tenn. 1827 Col. Tenn. Mil.
m. Betty White — son Willis m. Ann Harrison

Taylor, Richard b. Va. 1749 d. Ky. 1825 Commodore Va. Navy 1787
m. Catherine Davis — son Richard m. Mary Taylor
son Thompson m. Nancy Oldham

Taylor, Richard b. Md. 1792 d. Pa. 1873 Corp. U.S. Army
m. Martha Blackburn — daughter Martha m. Thomas Forrester Scott

Taylor, Robert b. Ky. 1772 d. Ky. 1852 m. Ossa Drake   Capt. Ky. Mil.
   son Robert m. Elizabeth Forman

Taylor, Robert Vol. 17   Pvt. Baltimore, Md. Ind. Arts.

Taylor, Robert Jr. b. Pa. 1793 d. Ohio 1849   Pvt. Ohio Mil.
   m. Margaret Stewart — son Hugh S. m. Catharine Shaffer

Taylor, Samuel b. S.C. 1777 d. Ala. 1833 m. Leah Reece   Lieut. S.C. Mil.
   son Samuel m. Narcissa Watkins

Taylor, Septimus b. Ga. 1790 d. Ga. aft. 1840   Pvt. Ga. Mil.
   m. Fanny Pruitt — son William B. m. Lavisia Pruitt

Taylor, Thompson b. Va. 1775 d. Ky. 1827   Dept. QM. Gen. Ky. Mil.
   m. Nancy Oldham — son William R. m. Mrs. Mary A. O. Kellar

Taylor, Timothy b. 1729 d. Pa. 1790   Justice Peace Bucks Co. Pa. 1784
   m. Letitia Kirkbride — son Joseph m. Mercy Knowles

Taylor, Timothy b. Pa. 1761 d. Va. —— m. Achsah Johnson   Col. Va. Mil.
   daughter Mary m. James Roane

Taylor, Titus b. Pa. 1755 d. Pa. 1825   Capt. Chester Co. Pa. Mil. 1814
   m. Rebecca Hunt — daughter Martha m. Jesse Buffington

Taylor, William Vannah b. Va. 1790 d. Tenn. 1873   Surgeon "Constitution"
   m. Frances McCoy   U.S. Navy
   son Archibald m. Lucy Turnage
   son Henry S. m. Jane E. Mayor
   son William m. Mary Cornelia Jarrad

Taylor, William M. Vol. 6   Memb. War. Comm. Md.

Teachout, John b. N.Y. 1771 d. N.Y. 1814   Pvt. N.Y. Mil.
   m. Hannah Swartout — daughter Sarah m. Peter S. Woodin

Teagarden, Abraham Vol. 12   Pvt. Pa. Mil.

Teagarden, William b. Pa. 1746 d. Pa. ——   Ranger Wash. Co. Pa. Mil.
   m. Bethia Craig — son John B. m. Rosa McGuire

Teas, Joseph Bartlett Vols. 16 and 17   Pvt. Ill. Terr. Mil.

Teasdale, Thomas b. Eng. or N.J. 1779 d. N.J. 1847   Capt. Sussex Co. N.J.
   m. Hannah Cox — daughter Emma m. Isaac Struble   Mil.
   son John m. Susan B. Losey

Tebbs, Warren, b. Va. 1791 d. Ind. 1868   Corp. Ind. Terr. Mil.
   m. Elizabeth Ashby — son Alvin G. m. Maria Snyder

Teel (Teal), Micajah b. Eng c. 1785 d. N.C. 1868   Pvt. N.C. Mil.
   m. Gatsy Llewellyn Cherry — daughter Ann M. m. Little Berry Bryan
   daughter Ethalynde M. m. Robert L. Grammer
   daughter Susan G. m. Stanley Moore

Teese, Daniel Vol. 17   Corp. Pa. Art.

Teeters, John b. Pa. 1781 d. Ohio 1866 m. Mary Cook   Col. Ohio Mil.
   son Elisha m. Eliza Webb

Teft, William D. b. N.Y. 1790 d. N.Y. 1852   Sgt. N.Y. Inf.
   m. Mary Kenyon — daughter Delinda m. Sidney S. Smith

Temple, Jesse b. S.C. 1790 d. Tenn. 1873   Pvt. Ky. Mil.
   m. Tabitha Tinsley — son John L. m. Susan Harriet Clark

Temple, John b. Mass. 1774 d. Mass. 1869   Capt. Mass. Mil.
   m. Abigail Johnson — son Josiah H. m. Mary Belden

Temple, Robert b. N.Y. 1796 d. Pa. 1888 m. Eliza Allen   Pvt. Pa. Mil.
    daughter Mary m. Hiram Greeley Butler

Temple, Robert Vol. 12   Drummer N.Y. Mil.

Templeton, James b. N.Y. 1794 d. Mich. 1859   Teamster N.Y. Mil.
m. Sarah Marvin — daughter Mary m. Ezekiel Henry Brown

Templeton, John W. b. Md. 1784 d. Pa. 1843   Pvt. Chester Co. Pa. Mil.
    m. Margaret Fullweiner — daughter Mary m. Cornelius Sutton

Templeton, Mijamin b. S.C. 1801 d. Mo.   Gave material aid 1815
    m. Mary Mackey — daughter Mollie unm. REAL DAUGHTER

Ten Broeck, Cornelius b. N.Y. 1719 d. N.J. 1790   Memb. Town Comm. 1786
    m. Margaret Louw — daughter Helena m. Samuel Beekman   N.J.

Ten Broeck, John Henry b. N.Y. 1782 d. N.Y. ——   Ensign N.Y. Mil.
    m. Frances Mary Bennett
    daughter Margaret Ann m. William Cook Ball

Ten Broeck, John I. Vol. 12   Pvt. N.Y. Mil.

Tennant, Peter b. Va. 1773 d. W.Va. 1847   Sgt. Va. Mil.
    m. Elizabeth Brown — daughter Rebecca m. Richard B. Tennant

Tenney, Silas Vol. 13   Pvt. N.H. Det. Mil.

Terrell, Alfred b. Va. 1794 d. Va. 1871 m. Frances C. Micou   Pvt. Va. Mil.
    daughter Annis E. m. James S. Reamy

Terrell, Simon b. N.C. 1755 d. Ga. 1836 m. Sarah Thompson   Pvt. Ga. Mil.
    son William m. Sarah Kendrick

Terrell, Timothy b. N.C. 1777 d. Ga. 1860   Justice Peace Franklin Co.
    m. Mary Davis — son Thomas F. m. Esther Camp   Ga. 1813

Terrell, Zachariah b. Va. 1779 d. Ky. 1861   Lieut. Ky. Vol. Mi.1
    m. Polly Floyd — son Henry C. m. Mrs. Eliza McDonald Sullivan

Terrill, Edmund b. Va. 1768 d. Ky. 1816   Pvt. Ky. Mtd. Mil.
    m. Mary Jane Maxwell — daughter Elizabeth m. George Banton

Terrill, Jeremiah b. Conn. 1770 d. Ohio 1831   Pvt. Conn. Mil.
    m. Millicent Hine — son Willard m. Elizabeth Matteson

Terry, Joshua b. Pa. 1764 d. N.Y. 1827   Capt. Ontario Co. N.Y. Mil.
    m. Elizabeth — son Jesse m. Lydia Marsh

Terry, Willet b. N.Y. 1781 d. Ill. 1863   Pvt. Putnam Co. Pa. Mil.
    m. Azubah Dykeman — daughter Charlotte m. Benjamin Knight

Terwillger, Jacob b. N.Y. 1784 d. Ohio 1828   Corp. N.Y. Mil.
    m. Elizabeth Sexton — daughter Amy m. John W. Wiggins

Teter, Jacob b. Va. 1769/70 d. W.Va. 1850   Pvt. Pendleton Co. Mil.
    m. Elizabeth Friend ——son Jacob m. Mary Coberly

Tewksbury, Bill b. Mass. 1780 d. Mass. 1855   Sgt. Mass. Mil.
    m. Martha A. Belcher — son Herman B. m. Charlotte M. Henderson

Tewksbury, Moses M. Vol. 4   Lieut. Mass. Mil.

Thacher, Allen b. Va. 1783 d. Ill. 1875 m. Harriet Vaughn   Pvt. Ky. Mil.
    son Tobias m. Sarah Rebecca McCaslin

Thacher, Amasa Jr. b. Conn. 1768 d. Ohio 1844   Pvt. Vt. Mil.
    m. Phoebe Green — son Horace m. Susannah Ewers

Thacher, Timothy b. Mass. 1774 d. Mass. 1833   Surveyor Highways Lee
   m. Dorothy Phelps   Mass. 1800
   son Crocker m. Lucy Howland Bassett

Thacker, Hiram b. N.C. 1793 d. La. or Calif. 1871   Pvt. La. Mil.
   m. Hannah Morgan — son Albin G. m. Nancy Winnifred Quarles

Thacker, James b. Va. 1776 d. Va. drowned 1815   Pvt. Va. Mil.
   m. Sarah McPherson — daughter Elizabeth m. Samuel Shaw Fearson

Thames, William b. N.C. 1796 d. Ga. 1892 m. twice   Pvt. 3d. Regt. Ga. Mil.
   by 1st wife Rachel Taylor — daughter Mary Ann m. Joshua Dodson
   by 2nd wife Susan Weaver
   daughter Susan m. Durward Seymour REAL DAUGHTER

Thatcher, Daniel b. Conn. 1789 d. Conn. 1867   Corp. Conn. Mil.
   m. Julia Ann Hubbell — son George W. m. Anne Biddle Chambers

Thatcher, Evan b. N.J. d. Va. 1877 m. Rachel Brannon   Pvt. Va. Mil.
   son Evan R. m. Mary Jane Anderson

Thayler, Ebenezer b. 1788 d. c. 1880   1st. Sgt. N.Y.C. disch. 1814
   m. Martha McNeal Edgar
   son George Washington m. Ruth Elvira Huntington

Thayer, Joseph b. Mass. 1786 d. Ill. 1877   Pvt. Mass. Mil.
   m. Susannah Cannon — son Erastus W. m. Angeline Alexander

Thayer, Reuben b. Mass. 1796 d. Mass. 1876   Pvt. Mass. Mil.
   m. Achsa Merick — son Savannah A. m. Mary Chapman

Theais, Samuel Martin b. Conn.—d. Lost at sea bef. 1817   Capt. Conn. Navy
   m. Sarah Feem Peck
   daughter Julia Ann m. William Henry De Forest

Thebaut, Jean Pierre b. France d. Cuba 1812 m. Mary   Lieut. La. Mil.
   son J. M. m. Elizabeth Ann

Theobald, Thomas Smith Vol. 6   Lieut. U.S. Mtd. Rangers

Thomas, Alanson b. N.Y. 1789 d. Mich. 1878   Pvt. N.Y. Mil.
   m. Sarah Saunders — son Lyman m. Angelina Barker

Thomas, Daniel b. Scot. 1794 d. Ohio 1845   Pvt. Pa. Mil.
   m. Elizabeth McDowell — son John P. m. Mary Ann France

Thomas, David b. Mass. 1779 d. 1865 m. Mary Kinney   Pvt. N.Y. Mil.
   daughter Nancy B. m. Isaac Clements

Thomas, Henry b. Tenn. 1797 d. Tenn. 1880   Pvt. 2nd. Regt. Tenn. Mtd. Vol.
   m. Sarah Mungle — daughter Louisa H. m. William J. P. Wise
   son John m. Elizabeth Freer

Thomas, Isaac b. Va. 1735 d. Tenn. 1818   Pres. Elector Tenn. 1799
   m. Elizabeth Massengale — daughter Lucretia m. Robert Wear

Thomas, Jacob b. 1777 d. Ohio 1837 m. Stacia Bruce   Pvt. Ohio Mil.
   son Jesse m. Catherine Turner

Thomas, James II b. N.C. c. 1760 d. Ky. 1832   Pvt. Christian Co. Ky. Mil.
   m. Mollie Stanley — son Starkie m. Mary Bridges

Thomas, James b. Md. 1785 d. Md. 1845   Major Calvert Co. Md. Mil.
   m. Eliza Courts — son James R. m. Jeannette Eleanor Briscoe

Thomas, Jehu b. Pa. 1783 d. Pa. 1850   3rd Sgt. Pa. Mil.
   m. Agnes Maria Engelman — daughter Frances m. James Henry Potts

Thomas, Jeremiah b. Va. d. Ohio 1828 m. Ellen Norris   Pvt. Ohio Mil.
    son John m. Abigail Van Buskirk

Thomas, John b. Tenn. 1794 d. Texas 1875   Pvt. Tenn. Mil.
    m. Hannah Andes — daughter Cynthia A. m. William Jenkins

Thomas, John b. Va. 1760 d. Ky. aft. 1808   Surveyor Mercer Co. Ky.
    m. Elizabeth Poague — daughter Ann m. John W. Davis   1786-1808

Thomas, John b. Va. 1725 d. Ky. 1789   Collector Levies; Sheriff
    m. Jemima Miller   Augusta Co. Va. 1784/5
    son Silas m. Mary Morrow

Thomas, Linza b. Va. 1786 d. Va. 1870 m. Nancy Hammet   Sgt. Va. Mil.
    son Peyton L. m. Mary Eliza Weatherall

Thomas, Michael b. Md. or Pa. 1774 d. Pa. 1852   Pvt. Pa. Mil.
    m. Magdalena Maust — daughter Anna m. Andrew Umbel
    son Christian m. Susannah Fike

Thomas, Joseph Sr. b. Va. 1779 d. W.Va. 1870   Pvt. Loudoun Co. Va. Mil.
    m. Nancy Riggs — son George m. Mary Clark

Thomas, Nathaniel b. Mass. 1775 d. Mass. 1850   Pvt. Mass. (Me.) Mil.
    m. Mehitabel — daughter Mehitabel m. Ephraim Ford

Thomas, Samuel b. S.C. 1794 d. Ill. 1873   Pvt. Ill. Terr. Mil.
    m. Elizabeth Ann Isley—daughter Matilda m. Dr. Coston P. Clemmons
    son William D. m. Mary Rainey

Thomas, Samuel J. b. Pa. 1795 d. Ohio 1880/1   Pvt. Ohio Mil.
    m. Sarah Talbot — daughter Mary Ruth m. Job Haynes Martin

Thomas, Silas b. Mass. 1780 d. Mich. 1850   Pvt. Va. Mil.
    m. Bertha Crooker — son William m. Phebe D. Wilder

Thomas, Silas b. Ohio 1789 d. Ill. 1849 m. Mary Morrow   Sgt. Ohio Mil.
    son John H. m. Mary McNeil

Thomas, Sterling b. Md. 1790 d. Md. 1865   Corp. Md. Mil.
    m. Elizabeth Pentz — daughter Mary Ann m. James Hooker

Thomas, Turbey F. Vol. 4   Lieut. Ga. Inf.

Thomas, William b. Va. 1772 d. Tenn. 1840   Surveyor Williamson Co.
    m. Eliza Bass — daughter Mary m. Opie Pope   Tenn. 1800/12

Thomason, Robert b. Ky. 1791 d. Mo. 1864   Pvt. Ky. Mtd. Vols.
    m. Bethany Jean — son Marcellus m. Isabelle B. Estes

Thompson, Alexander   Early Number   Pvt. N.Y. Mil.

Thompson, Aquilla b. Md.—d. Pa. aft. 1814   Lieut. Md. Mil.
    m. Mary Patterson — son James P. m. Sarah Loughhead

Thompson, Asa b. Va. 1764 d. Ky. 1842 m. Ann Quarles   Pvt. Ky.
    son John m. Ann Ellis

Thompson, David b. N.C. 1787 d. Ga. 1857   Pvt. Ga. Mil.
    m. Patience D. Camp
    daughter Mary C. m. 1st —— Thomas, 2nd. Alexander S. Buchanan

Thompson, David Vol. 15   General Ky. Troops

Thompson, David Vol. 8   Pvt. & Sgt. Mass. Mil.

Thompson, David b. Pa. 1787 d. Pa. 1828   Ensign Pa. Mil.
    m. Elizabeth Cooper — son Hugh G. m. Martha Nevins

Thompson, Festus L. b.—— 1788 d. R.I. 1851　　　2nd Lieut. U.S. Inf.
m. Eliza Greene — daughter Jane M. m. Richard S. Lathrop

Thompson, Henry b. Eng. 1774 d. Md. 1837　　Capt. Md. Light. Dragoons
m. Ann Lux Bowley — son Henry A. m. Julie Z. de Macklet

Thompson, Hugh b. Pa. 1768 d. Ohio 1846　　　　　　Capt. Pa. Cav.
m. Elizabeth Scroggs — son Alexander S. m. Jane Stringer Boots

Thompson, Isaac b. Mass. 1746 d. Mass. 1819　　Leg. Plymouth Co. Mass.
m. Lucia Sturtevant — son Ezra m. Cynthia Gifford

Thompson, Isaac b. Pa. 1751 d. Ohio 1823　　Justice Peace Geagua Co.,
m. Martha Larimore — son William m. Lucinda Walden　　Ohio 1807

Thompson, Isaac b. N.H. 1775 d. Vt.— m. Susan S. Parcher　　Pvt. Vt. Mil.
son Lewis O. m. Margaret Brown

Thompson, James b. Va. 1763 d. Ky. 1825　　　Memb. Ky. Senate from
m. Ruth Peyton　　　　　　　　　　　　　　　Garrad Co. 1803/6
daughter Jemima m. Rev. Burdette Kemper

Thompson, James b. 1773 d. Ohio 1815　　　　　　　　Pvt. Ohio Mil.
m. Eleanor Thompson — daughter Margaret m. Joseph Harvey

Thompson, James b. Md. 1790 d. Ohio 1878　　　　　　Pvt. Ohio Mil.
m. Micha Kelly — daughter Sarah Jane m. William Brown Bowdle

Thompson, James b. Pa. 1780 d. Ohio 1877 m. Sarah Wells　Capt. Ohio Mil.
son Isaac N. m Jedidah Ann Foot

Thompson, James b. Va.—d. Va. m. Sarah Dibrell　　　Capt. Va. Mil.
son Charles W. m. Martha V. Turpin
daughter Elizabeth Anne m. Richard D. Mitchell

Thompson, James H. b. Va. 1790 d. Va. 1860　　　　　Sgt. Va. Mil.
m. Isabella D. Miller — son Blair H. m. Hester Ann Hensel

Thompson, Jesse b. Ga. 1777 d. Miss. 1833　　　　　Sgt. Miss. Regt.
m. Margaret Harvey Watson — son John H. m. Margaret Ann Watson

Thompson, Joel b. N.Y. 1760 d. N.Y. 1833　　Judge Chenango Co. N.Y. 1808
m. Cynthia Root　　　　　　　　　　　　　Memb. Congress 1813
daughter Cynthia m. Charles Warren Lynde

Thompson, John b. Eng. d. Ky. c. 1823　　　　Memb. Ky. Leg. 1803/7
m. Margaret Gilbert — son Gilbert m. Jennie Shannon

Thompson, John b. N.Y. 1760 d. N.Y. 1813　　Capt. Dutchess Co. N.Y.
m. Mary Knapp — daughter Eunice m. Jacob S. Browne　　Mil. 1798

Thompson, John b. Ohio 1788 d. Ohio 1841 m. Polly Hyre　Pvt. Ohio Mil.
daughter Rachel m. Jacob Swisher

Thompson, John B. Vol. 4　　　　　　　　　　　　　Pvt. Pa. Mil.

Thompson, John T. b. 1788 d. Ohio 1836 m. Mary Nelson　Pvt. Va. Mil.
son James m. Catharine Gamble

Thompson, Lamuel b. Va. 1767 d. N.C. 1820　　　　　Pvt. N.C. Mil.
m. Patience Bridgers Kitchen
son Nathan T. m. Mary Thompson (cousin)

Thompson, Levi b. N.H. 1781 d. N.H. 1871　　　　　　Pvt. N.H. Mil.
m. Comfort Ellison — son Levi m. Climena B. Rundlett

Thompson, Moses Jr. b. Conn. 1792 d. Conn. 1854　　　Sgt. Conn. Mil.
m. Sallie A. Remyon — son George M. m. Ann Elizabeth Tipton

Thompson, Nathan b. N.Y. 1785 d. Ind. 1865   Lieut. Genesse Co. N.Y. Mil.
m. Nancy Vaughn — daughter Belsora m. Joseph L. Washburn

Thompson, Peter b. Pa. 1746 d. N.C. 1823 m. Mary Potts   Census Taker
son John m. Lucy Cox

Thompson, Reubin b. N.C. 1765 d. Ga. 1856   Pvt. Ga. Mil. 1798/1800
m. Rachel Chambers — son Henry m. Mary C. Webb

Thompson, Samuel b. N.Y. 1794 d. Ohio 1890 m. Delia Smith Pvt. U.S. Inf.
daughter Delia Ann m. Putnam J. Norton

Thompson, Smallwood b. Va. 1791 d. Ohio 1875   Pvt. Ohio Mil.
m. Margaret Kevit — daughter Mary m. Morgan Blue

Thompson, Timothy b. Mass. 1750 d. Mass. 1834   Memb. Mass. Leg. from
m. Mary Frothingham   Charlestown 1809
daughter Susannah m. William Sawyer

Thompson, Waddy b. Va. 1769 d. S.C. 1845   Chancellor S.C.
m. Eliza Blackborn Williams
daughter Eliza W. m. Dr. Robinson Earle

Thompson, William b. Ky. 1790 d. Ky. 1817   Pvt. Ky. Mil.
m. Martha B. Berryman — daughter Sarah A. m. Beverly W. Todd

Thompson, William b. Mass. 1748 d. Mass. 1816   Justice Peace Mass.
m. Deborah Sturtevant — son Ira m. Sophia Drew

Thompson, William b. Va. 1788 d. Va. 1846 m. Elizabeth   Pvt. Va. Mil.
daughter Sallie m. Dr. Thomas Martin Dunn

Thompson, William b. Va. 1785 d. Mo. 1845 m. Rebecca Ellis Pvt. Va. Mil.
daughter Ellen m. William F. Graves REAL DAUGHTER

Thomson, Alexander b. Pa. 1771 d. Pa. 1840   Capt. Pa. Mil.
m. Rebecca Smith — son Robert m. Mary E. Carnahan

Thomson, Archibald b. N.J. 1759 d. N.J. 1856   Pvt. Monmouth Co. N.J. Mil.
m. Maria Bodine — daughter Elizabeth S. m. Enoch Coddington

Thomson, Benjamin Vol. 17   Pvt. S.C. Mil.

Thomson, David b. Va. 1775 d. Mo. 1861   2nd Major Ky. Mil.
m. Betsey Sugget — son Manlius V. m. Mary Ann
daughter Mildred E. m. Lewis Redd Major
daughter Marian W. m. Thomas A. Gunnell
son Milton T. m. Amelia Ann Scroggin
son Mentor m. Cora Virginia Wooldridge
son Morton m. Sarah Powell

Thomson, John b. Mass. 1768 d. Me. 1844 m.—   Musician Conn. Mil.
daughter Elinor m. Nathan Pease

Thomson, Warren b. N.J. 1778 d. N.J. 1853 m.—   Pvt. N.J. Mil.
daughter Mehitabel m. David Kane

Thorn, Michael Jr. b. Va. 1764 d. Ind. aft. 1844   Pvt. Vincennes Ind. Mil.
m. Cassandra Harbin — son James m. Polly Garrett   1790

Thorn, Michael Sr. b. Va. bef. 1737 d. bef. 1802   Pvt. Vincennes Inds. Mil.
m. Catherine — son Michael m. Cassandra Harbin   1790

Thorn, William Vol. 7   Pilot Mich. Navy

Thorn, William Vol. 7   Pvt. N.Y. Arty—Pilot with American Fleet

Thornley, Robert b. Va. or Car. c. 1745 d. S.C. 1805   Memb. S.C. Senate
son John m. Elizabeth

Thornley, William b. Va. 1775 d. West Indies 1837   Major Va. Mil.
m. Jane Riding — son John m. Julia H. Payne

Thornton, Ethan Vol. 13   Lieut. R.I. Mil.

Thornton, Henry Presley b. N.C. 1778 d. Ky. 1865   Capt. Ky. Rangers
m. Martha Ward — daughter Harriet m. (2nd) Daniel W. Norris

Thornton, Presley b. Va. 1750 d. Va. 1807 m. Elizabeth   Capt. U.S. Inf. 1798
daughter Charlotte m. J. T. Lomax

Thornton, William Vol. 11   Pvt. Ga. Mil.

Thornton, William Vol. 7   Lieut. Tenn. Mil.

Thornton, Zachariah b. Va. 1763 d. Va. 1830   Patriot Pittsylvania Co. 1813
m. Mary Elizabeth Oakes — son George W. m. Mary Elizabeth Moore

Thorp, James b. N.Y. 1792 d. Mich. 1866 m. Elizabeth   Pvt. N.Y. Mil.
daughter Phoebe m. Psalter Blanchard

Thorp, Joel Vol. 17   Pvt. Conn. Mil.

Thrailkill, Benjamin F. b. Va. 1792 d. Ohio 1836   Pvt. Culpepper Co. Va. Mil.
m. Nancy A. Fitting — son Joseph C. m. Eliza Holland

Thrasher, Charles b. Conn. 1795 d. Ill. 1863   Corp. N.Y. State Mil.
m. Malinda Hicks — son George m. Hester Ann Hubbard

Threlkeld, Jesse b. Va. 1771 d. aft. 1840 prob. Ky.   Patriot Ky.
son James m. Mary Campbell

Thrift, Charles b. Va. 1753 d. Ky. 1826   Overseer of Poor Fairfax Co. Va.
m. Elizabeth Magruder — son Samuel m. Sarah Fleming Cowan

Thurman, John b. Va. 1793 d. Mo. 1870 m. Rebecca Crooke   Pvt. Va. Mil.
son John J. m. Cynthia Antoinette Moore

Thurman, William b. Va. 1769 d. Va. 1829   Pvt. Pr. Wm. Co. Va. Mil.
m. Sarah — son John m. Rebecca Crooke

Tibbitts, John b. Mass. 1783 d. Mich. 1860   Pvt. N.Y. Mil. 1814
m. Phoebe Smith — son George m. Therina Ward Hyde

Tibbitts, Jonathan b. R.I. 1776 d. N.Y. 1860   Capt. Oneida Co. N.Y. Mil.
m. Juda Niles — son Aylmer m. Polly Ann Grinnell

Tibuat, John Peter Vol. 14   1st Lieut. La. Vols.

Tichenor, Jacob b. N.J. 1765 d. Ill. 1835   Pvt. Ky. Lt. Dragoons
m. Elizabeth Ramy — son Isaac m. Susan Messertz

Tiel, Jacob b. Pa. 1794 d. Pa. 1870   Pvt. Pa. Artillery
m. Eleanor (Williams or Warner)
son George m. Martha P. Williams
son William M. m. Mary Hastings Mason

Tierman, Charles Vol. 1   Maine Marine Svc.

Tiffany, David b. N.Y. 1796 d. N.Y. 1875   Pvt. Onandaga Co. N.Y. Mil.
m. Charlotte Dwinnell
daughter Diana Adele m. John P. Blumer REAL DAUGHTER

Tiffany, Jacob b. 1796 d. N.Y. 1871 m. Lovina Andrews   Pvt. N.Y. Mil.
daughter Eliza Jane m. Luther S. Lyon

Tift, Joseph Burrows b. Conn. 1782 d. Fla.   Gunner's Mate on
m. Rebecca A. Braman   "Old Ironsides"
daughter Elizabeth R. m. Henry Loomis

Tiller, James Vol. 14   Deputy Sheriff Va.

Tiller, William James Vol. 6   Adj. N.Y. Mil.

Tillman, James b. N.C. 1776 d. Ga. 1855   Justice Inf. Ct. Bulloch Co.
   m. Martha Marlow — daughter Mary m. Jacob Moody Sr.   1815

Tillotson, David Vol. 9   Pvt. N.Y. Mil.

Tillotson, Jehu John b. 1790 d. 1876   Pvt. 2nd U.S. Arty. Vol. Reg.
   m. Phebe Ackerly, 2nd Jane
   daughter Eliza Tillotson m. Samuel Bassett

Tillotson, John b. Conn. 1756 d. N.Y. 1826   Brig. Gen. N.Y. Mil.
   m. Elizabeth Brookway — son Ira m. Harriet Southworth

Tilton, Daniel Jr. Vol. 16   Pvt. N.J. Mil.

Tilton, John b. N.J. 1760 d. Ohio 1849   Pvt. Pa. Troops while liv. Ohio 1812
   m. Mary Sutphen — son Ira S. m. Jane McLain

Tilton, Peter Vol. 13   Pvt. N.J. Mil.

Timberlake, Nathan b. Va. 1794 d. Va. 1837   Pvt. Va. Mil.
   m. Mary Hughes — daughter Mary m. Thomas B. Anthony

Timmerman, John S. Vol. 16   Pvt. N.Y. Mil.

Tiindall, John b. N.J. 1754 d. 1837 m. Hannah   Lieut. N.J. Det. Mil.
   son Noah m. Ann Blackwell

Tinker, Chauncy b. Mass. 1770 d. Mich. 1873   Pvt. Ohio Mil.
   m. Lydia Andrews
   daughter Luella A. m. Sidney T. Beam REAL DAUGHTER

Tinsley, Anderson b. Va. 1790 d. Ky. 1830   Pvt. Va. Mil.
   m. Cynthia Holliday — daughter Eliza Ann m. Samuel Russ Thrift

Tinsley, William b. Va. 1793 d. Ga. 1852 m.Mary Speer Pvt. Va. Riflemen
   daughter Mary S. m. Portlock Fowler

Tipton, Daniel b. Ky. 1793 d. Ill. 1869 m.— Vol. 8   Pvt. Ky. Mil.

Tipton, Edmund b. Pa. 1780 d. Ohio 1864   Capt. Pa. Det. Mil.
   m. Mary McCabe — daughter Mary Jane m. John Ross

Tipton, John b. Md. 1732/5 d. Tenn. 1813   Justice Ct. Wash. Co. N.C.
   m. Mary Butler   State Senator 1787/9/93
   son Jonathan m. Lavinia Williams
   son Samuel m. 2nd Susanna Reneau

Tipton, Thomas M. b. Ky. 1792 d. Mo. 1870   Pvt. Ky. Vol.
   m. 1st Casey Smith — son Thomas J. m. Sarah Ann Philpot

Tirrell, John b. Mass. 1752 d. drowned 1807 Pvt. Mass. Mil. at Shay's Reb.
   m. Lydia — son Samuel m. Deborah Richards

Tisdale, Reuben b. Mass. 1757 d. Canada 1798   Capt. Mass. Mil. 1789
   m. Rachel Crane — daughter Fannie m. 2nd Abner Sibley Jr.

Tisdale, Sherwood b. S.C. 1779 d. Ala. 1836   Pvt. S.C. Vols.
   m. Rebecca B. West — daughter Amanda P. m. Simon H. Williams

Tisdale, William b.— d. N.C. 1818 m. Adelia Whitfield   Capt. N.C. Mil.
   daughter Sophia B. m. Joab Martin Key

Titcomb, John Vol. 5 and 9   Sgt. Maine Mil.

Tittle, Jonathan b. Pa. 1784 d. Ohio 1856   Pvt. Pa. Mil.
   m. Susanna Beatty — son William R. m. Emma E. Johnston

Tittle, Peter Jr. b. Md. 1746 d. Pa. 1834   Capt. Westmoreland Co. Pa. Mil.
m. Sarah Whitesides — son James m. Ann Fraeme
son Jonathan m. Susanna Beatty

Titus, Anson b. Mass. 1787/8 d. Ohio 1869   Lieut. N.Y. Mil.
m. Hannah Moore — daughter Mary m. Leonard Cahoon
son Treat m. Dorothy Digg

Titus, Archibald b. Dela. 1770 d. Pa. 1834   Sgt. Pa. Mil.
m. Nancy Ann Hartford — daughter Elizabeth m. Elijah Baker

Titus, Samuel b. Mass. 1763 d. Mass. 1846 m. Chloe Tingley   Pvt. Mass. Mil.
daughter Julia m. John Field Jr.

Titus, Stiles b. Conn. 1794 d. Conn. 1845   Pvt. Conn. Troops
m. Loretta Arnold — daughter Hulda A. m. Benajah P. Beach

Tobey, Nathaniel b. Mass. 1796 d. Me. 1879   Corp. Mass. (Me.) Mil.
m. 2nd. Mrs. Besey A. Mills Waldoben
daughter Rebecca C. m. Alton J. Hall REAL DAUGHTER

Tobin, Joseph Hardin b. Pa. 1788 d. Ky. 1863   Ensign, Mass. Mil.
m. Sarah Rion — son Robert H. m. Martha Cartherine Daniels

Todd, Benjamin Vol. 9   Pvt. Ohio Mil.

Todd, Bernard b. Md. 1766 d. Md. 1816 m. Mary Green   Pvt. Md. Cav.
daughter Elizabeth F. m. James Porter
son Nathan G. m. Patience Paine

Todd, Charles Stewart b. Ky. 1791 d. La. 1871   Ensign Ky. Mil.
m. Letitia Shelby — son Thomas m. Bettie Bonney

Todd, James b. N.J. 1763 d. N.J. 1840 m. Katrina Mellick   Pvt. N.J. Inf.
son John I. m. Anne Castner

Todd, James b. Va. 1784 d. Va. 1816 m. Susanna Loving   Pvt. Va. Mil.
son Royal m. Elizabeth Todd (cousin)

Todd, John b. Ireland 1739 d. N.J. 1823   Capt. Somerset Co. N.J. Mil.
m. Sarah Ismay — daughter Sarah m. John Regar

Todd, Levi b. Pa. 1756 d. Ky. 1807 m. Jean Briggs   Col. Ky. Mil.
daughter Hannah m. Rev. Robert Stuart

Todd, Robert Smith b. Ky. 1791 d. Ky. 1849   Lieut. Ky. Vols.
m. Elizabeth L. Humphreys
daughter Margaret m. Charles H. Kellogg

Todd, Thomas b. N.C. 1771 d. Mo. 1857   Lieut. Ky. Mil.
m. Mary Chenault — daughter Hulda Ann m. Jeptha Todd Sr.

Toland, Aquila b. Md. 1793 d. Ohio 1866   Corp. Md. Mil.
m. Elizabeth Lewis — daughter Jane m. Charles Butler

Toll, John C. b. N.Y. 1780 d. N.Y. 1849   Chaplain N.Y. Mil.
m. Nancy Mynderse — son Philip R. m. Maria de Graff

Toll, Philip Ryley   Early Vol.   Pvt. recd. Bounty Land

Tolles, Amos Vol. 16   Pvt. N.Y. Mil.

Tombling, Abijah b. Mass. 1788 d. N.Y.   Surgeon N.Y. Mil.
m. Ann Maria Porter
daughter Mary Louise m. Joshiah Abijah Noonan

Tomlinson, Benjamin Vol. 13   Mem. Legis. Md. 1791

Tomlinson, Isaac b. 1778 d. Penn. 1852   3rd Sgt. Penn.
m. Ann Buffington — son John m. Sara Ring

Tomlinson, Solomon b. Va. 1789 d. Ia. 1877   Pvt. Penn. Mil.
m. Sarah Silcott — son John W. m. Priscilla Shamblin

Tomlinson, Stephen b. Conn. 1791 d. Conn. 1872   Sgt. Conn. Cav.
m. Caroline Hawley — daughter Elizabeth m. Rev. Ralph Perry

Tomlinson, Thomas b. N.C. 1795 d. N.C. 1847   Pvt. N.C. Mil.
m. Sarah Penny — daughter Altona Jane m. David Shepherd Maultsby
son William H. m. Sarah Jane Wooten Crossland

Tompkins, William b. Va. 1787 d. Va. 1858   Pvt. Va. Mil.
m. Elizabeth Goodwin — son Reuben R. m. Susan Hamilton

Toops, Daniel b. Penn. 1775 d. Ohio 1858 m. Mary Streve   Pvt. Ohio Mil.
daughter Sarah m. Jacob Shotts

Toole, William Sr. b. Tenn. 1791 d. Tenn. 1860   Pvt. E. Tenn. Mil.
m. Elizabeth Wallace — son William Jr. m. Hessie Gillespie

Torbert, John Vol. 7   Pvt. Penn. Mil.

Torr, Andrew b. N.H. 1774 d. N.H. 1817   Rcpr. N.II. Legis. 1789-95
m. Mary Jones — son Joseph J. m. Lois Hill

Torrey, Joshua Vol. 3   Prisoner Engl.

Torrey, Stephen b. N.Y. 1799 d. N.Y. 1883   Pvt. N.Y. Mil.
m. Eleanor Sharp — daughter Caroline m. Luther Washburn

Touchstone, Sampson b. Va. 1792 d. Va. 1876   Pvt. Va. Mil.
m. Margaret Bowles — son Jacob m. Henrietta McDonald

Toulmin, Henry b. Eng. 1766 d. Ala. 1823 m. Ann Tremlett   Judge Ala.
daughter Emma S. m. Thomas Hord Herndon Erie

Tourtellotte, Stephen b. Me. 1788 d. N.H. 1876   Music Mass. Mil.
m. Betsey Ring — son Franklin m. Mary Bryant

Tousley, Aaron b. Vt. 1800 d. N.Y. 1863 m. Electa Cook   Pvt. N.Y. Mil.
daughter Sarah m. Alexander C. King

Towell, John b. Va. d. Ohio 1821 m. Sarah Ewing   Pvt. Ohio Mil.
daughter Elizabeth Ewing m. John Winans Baker

Towles, Oliver b. Va. 1771 d. Mo. 1823 m. Agatha Lewis   Maj. Va. Mil.
son Alfred L. m. Jane Pleasants Vaughan
daughter Elizabeth L. m. Rev. John Blair Dabney

Towles, Therit b. Va. 1788 d. Va. 1836   Capt. Va. Mil.
m. Ann Walker Smith — son Thomas T. m. Elizabeth Sydney Coleman

Town, Joseph b. Mass. d. Ohio 1815 m. Mary Slocum   Pvt. Ohio Mil.
son William C. m. Esther Evans

Towne, Allen b. Vt. 1792 d. N.Y. 1872   Sgt. N.Y. Mil.
m. Zerniah Stowell — daughter Pauline m. Dr. Frederick F. Hoyer

Towne, Gardner Vol. 16   Pvt. N.Y. Mil.

Towner, Ephraim b. Conn. 1775 d. Mich. 1850   Capt. N.Y. Cav.
m. Anna Kellog — son Benjamin F. m. Eliza Moore

Townes, John Leigh b. Va. 1784 d. Ala. 1846   Capt. Va. Mil.
m. Polly Segar Eggleston
son Eggleston D. m. Martha Cousins Betts
daughter Frances Harriet m. William Gregg

Townley, Richard b. N.J. 1764 d. N.Y. 1840   Legis 1808 N.Y.
  m. Polly Lewis — son Effingham m. Fanny Bower (Bauer)

Townsend, Alanson b. N.Y. 1788 d. N.Y. 1882   Pvt. N.Y. Mil.
  m. Mary Parker — son William R. m. Lucy Resseguie

Townsend, Elijah b. N.Y. 1751 d. N.Y. 1824   Lt. Col. N.Y .Mil.
  m. Nancy Tredwell — daughter Sybil m. Gidley

Townsend, George Washington Sr. b. Mass. 1794 d. Ill. 1872 Pvt. N.Y. Mil.
  m. Sarah Day — daughter Lois Minerva m. John Gardener Smith

Townsend, Horace b. N.Y. 1782 d. N.Y. 1831   Sgt. N.Y. Mil.
  m. Rebecca Cornell
daughter Lavinia Maria m. William Edward Barnes

Townsend, John Dean b. 1795 d. N.Y. 1890   Pvt. N.Y. Mil.
  m. Amanda Pardee — John P. m. Cynthia Perkins

Townsend, Joseph b. N.J. 1795 d. Ill. 1875   Capt. N.J. Mil.
  m. Christia Ann Wheaton — daughter Hannah m. Able Scoles

Townsend, Stephen Vol. 15   Drum. Mass. Mil.

Towsend, William b N.Y. 1788 d. N.Y. 1863   Pvt. N.Y. Mil.
  m. Charlotte Tobias — son Isaac T. m. Eliza Ann Many

Townsley, Abijah b. N.Y. 1783 d. N.Y. 1865 m. Chloe Bigelow Pvt. Vt. Mil.
daughter Roba Delight m. Stephen Augustus Day

Tozzer, (Tozer, Towzer) William b. Mass. d. Mass. 1853 Pvt. Mass. Inf.
  m. Mary Lane — son William Jr. m. Catherine Stevens

Trabue, Aaron b. Ky. 1793 d. Ill. 1877   Sgt. Ky. Lt. Drag.
  m. Martha Cheatham
daughter Ella Frances m. John H. Simmons REAL DAUGHTER
daughter Martha G. m. Andrew T. Linbarger

Tracy, Ezekiel b. Conn. 1754 d. N.Y. 1820   Capt. N.Y. Mil.
  m. Patience Kimball — daughter Sarah m. Elias Foote

Tracy, Gardner b. Conn. 1792 d. Vt. 1868 m. Phoebe Mott Pvt. Vt. Vol.
daughter Clara REAL DAUGHTER

Tracy, Gilbert b. Conn. 1761 d. N.Y. 1841   Ens. N.Y. Mil.
  m. Deborah Woodworth — daughter Clarinda m. Lyman Murdock

Tracy, Joshua Vol. 13   Pvt. Md. Mil.

Tracy, Wornel b. Md. 1770 d. Ohio 1851   Pvt. Ohio Mil.
  m. (2) Mary Babb — son Jasper m. Jane Painter

Trafton, Benjamin b. Mass. 1739 d. Mass. 1825   Pat. 1812-14
  m. Eunice Fisher — daughter Nancy m. John Codding

Trafton, Thomas b. Me. c. 1793 d. Me. 1864   Pvt. Me. Mil. 1812
  m. Jerusha Oliver — Clark m. Almira Fisher

Traphagen, Henry b. N.J. 1768 d. N.J. 1857   PayMst. N.J. Mil.
  m. Eleanor Van Vorst — Henry M. m. Sarah Conselyea

Traquair, Thomas b. Penn. 1790 d. Penn. 1824   2nd Lt. Penn. Mil.
  m. Eliza Henderson — daughter Annie m. George S. Lang

Trask, Samuel b. Mass. 1721 d. Mass. 1790   Selectman Mass. 1785
  m. Bethiah Sibley — daughter Sarah m. Simon Tenney

Travis, Abraham b. Ky. 1792 d. Wisc. 1851 m. Sarah Cramer Pvt. Ohio Mil.
daughter Mahala F. m. David C. Phillips REAL DAUGHTER
daughter Margaret m. Samuel Griffith REAL DAUGHTER

Travis, Jeremiah b.—d.—m. Mercy Agor   Pvt. N.Y. Mil.
son Jeremiah Jr. m. Esther Jemima Baxter

Traxler, Eamunel b. Penn. 1760 d. Ohio m.—   Civil Officer Ohio 1800
son Jonathan m. Rachel Martin

Trayler, Archer b. Va. d. Va. m. Elizabeth Gill   Sgt. Va. Mil.
Son Edwin m. Mary Whitehead

Traylor, Jesse b. Va. 1790 d. Ill. 1859   Pvt. Ky. Mil.
m. Obedience Blankenship
daughter Mary Jane m. Robert Chambers Blunt

Treadwell, Thomas b. N.Y. d. N.Y. 1832 m. Anne Hazard   Lt. N.Y. Mil.
daughter Anne H. m. Isaac C. Platt

Treakle, Christopher b. Md. 1767 d. Ohio 1813   Constable Md. 1804
m. Mary Wilson — daughter Elizabeth m. Joseph Wright

Treat, John b. Conn. 1795 d. Ohio 1887   Pvt. Conn. Mil.
m. Marietta Humason — daughter Elizabeth Ann m. Lewis Bushnel

Treat, Oren b. Vt. 1787 d. N.Y. 1882 m. Maria Weeks   Pvt. N.Y. Mil.
daughter Frances Marie m. Delevan Calkins REAL DAUGHTER

Treat, Samuel b. Conn. 1749 d. Conn. 1795   Mem. Legis. Conn. 1793-4
m. Martha Wolcott — daughter Patty W. m. David McKinney

Treber, Jacob b. Penn. 1779 d. Ohio 1875   Pvt. Ohio Mil.
m. Jane Thoroman — son William m. Malissa Thoroman

Trefry, James Vol. 3   Seaman Mass.

Trent, Thomas Jr. b. Va. 1786 d. Va. 1861   Lt. Va. Mil.
m. Martha Dick Holland
daughter Emeline S. m. Benjamin T. Tinsley

Trexler, John b. Penn. 1729 d. Penn. 1795 m. Elizabeth   Maj. Penn. Mil.
son Emanuel

Trexler, Jonathan b. Penn. 1762 d. Penn. 1846   Pvt. Penn. Mil.
m. Elizabeth Harlacher — daughter Anna m. Benjamin Fogel

Trexler, Jonathan b. Pa. 1791 d. Ill. 1880   Pvt. Ohio Mil.
m. Rachel Martin — son John m. Polly Ann Dobbins

Trexler, Peter b. Penn. 1748 d. Penn. 1828   Memb. Legis. Penn. 1785-88
m. Catherine Gum (Grim) — son Reuben m. Anna Lesher

Tribby, John b. R.I. 1758 d. Ohio 1819   Lt. R.I. Mil. 1801-2
m. Abigail Hazard — son John Jr. m. Fanney Patton

Trickey, William C. b. Va. 1795 d. Ohio 1867   Pvt. Va. Mil.
m. Sarah Osborne — daughter Sarah m. Amos Memeley

Trigg, Daniel b. Va. 1749 d. Va. 1819 m. Anne Smith   Lt. Col. Va. Mil.
son Abram B. m. Mary Mitchel

Trigg, Daniel Sr. b. Va. 1776 d. Tenn. 1830 m. Nancy Hodge   Pvt. Ky. Mil.
son Haden S. m. Elizabeth Jane Wilson

Trigg, John b. Va. 1746 d. Va. 1804 m. Dinah Ayers   Memb. House Del. Va.
son Stephen m. Elizabeth Clark

Trigg, Stephen b. Va. 1771 d. Mo. 1834 m. Elizabeth Clark   Pvt. Ky. Mil.
daughter Dina A. m. Shubael Allen
daughter Elizabeth m. John Thornton
daughter Malinda m. Robert P. Clark

Trigler, John b. N.Y. 1777 d. N.Y. 1855 m. Mary Irving   Cornet N.Y. Art
daughter Henrietta m. Cornelius Orrok

Trimmier, William b. S.C. 1756 d. S.C. 1850   Sgt. Maj. S.C. Mil.
m. Arsino Cleveland — daughter Arsino m. James Blair Jr.

Triplett, Robert b. Va. 1772 d. W.Va. 1843   Sgt. Va. Mil.
m. Nancy Day (Davy) — son Burr m Effie Butcher

Tripp, Isaac b. Penn. 1767 d. Penn. 1830   Pvt. Penn. Lt. Drag
m. Hannah Lee — son Daniel m. Lydia Freeman

Tripp, John b. N.C. 1775 d. Ga. 1870 m. Elizabeth Hunt   Pvt. Ga. Troops
son Turner H. m. Mary Ann Gatewood

Trotter, James vol. 13   2nd. Lt. Va. Troops

Trotter, James b. Va. 1753 d. Ky. 1827 m. Margaret Downey   Pvt. Ky. Mil.
daughter Mary m. Andrew Gibbs Mills
son James G. m. Elizabeth R. Nicholas

Trotter, James b. Ire. 1774 d. Canada 1813   2nd. Lt. Ky. Mil.
m. Mary Beard — son James m. Cynthia Cory
daughter Nancy m. Thomas Goodson

Trotter, James b. Va. 1779 d. Va. 1862 m. Nancy Pritchett   Pvt. Va. Mil.
daughter Julia m. Jarrett Walthall Cook Swanson

Trotter, Joseph b. 1745 d. 1809 m. Nancy Allison   Capt. Ky. Mil. 1796
daughter Mary m. Andrew G. Mills

Trott, Laurence b. S.C. 1771 d. S.C. 1819   Legis. S.C. 1800-04
m. Nancy Ann McTeer — son Gasper J. m. Caroline Adams

Trousdale, John b. N.C. 1762 d. Tenn. 1837   Pvt. Tenn. Inf.
m. Elizabeth S. — daughter Elizabeth G. m. William McClain

Trout, George b. Va. 1782 d. Va. 1850 m. Mary Miller   Pvt. Va. Mil.
son John m. Eliza J. Shaver

Trovillo, Elijah b. Penn. 1783 d. Penn. 1856   Sgt. Penn. Mil.
m. Margaret Harris
daughter Emily m. George Hood and William Doak

Trovinger, Samuel b. 1780 d. Ohio 1852   2nd. Cpl. Ohio Mil.
m. Rebecca Gordon — son Christopher m. Jane Lyle

Trow, Israel Sr. b. Mass. 1737 d. Mass. 1825   Selectman Rep. Mass.
m. Mary Clapp — son Israel Jr. m. Hannah Makepeace   1784-93
son Orin m. Hannah Robinson

Trowbridge, Abner b. N.J. 1779 d. Mich. 1858   Pvt. N.Y. Mil.
m. Sally Casterline — son Benjamin L. m. Hulda Ward

Trowbridge, Jacob b. Vt. 1790 d. Ohio 1867   Capt. Ohio Mil.
m. Sarah Shephard — son Zeublon m. Ruth Crawford

Trowbridge, Willard b. Conn. 1796 d. Ohio 1885   Pvt. N.Y. 1812-14
m. Amy Sprague — son Cornelius m. Celina Minerva Bradley

Trowbridge, William b. Conn. 1748 d. Conn. 1834   Lt. Conn. Cav.
m. Susannah Sessions — daughter Selina m. Jacob Pratt

Trower, John b. Va. 1782 d. Va. 1840 m. Delitha Belote   Lt. Va. Mil.
    son John Jr. m. Elizabeth S. Fitchett

Truax, Abram Caleb Early Vol.   Pvt. 1800

Truby, Christopher, Sr. b. 1736 d. Penn. 1802   Col. Pa. Mil. 1789
    m. Isbelle Bowman   Justice Pa. 1786
    son Jacob m. Mary Ann Lauffer
    son John m. Mary Reamer

True, James b. Va. 1788 d. Tenn. 1841   Pvt. Va. Mil.
    m. (2) Nancy Ann Newton
    son Francis M. m. Harriet Ellen Bigbee
    daughter Susan m. Meredith McCurry

True, John b. Ky. 1778 d. Ill. 1860 m. Mary White   Pvt. Ky. Mil.
    daughter Elvira m. Basil Magee

True, Josiah b. N.H. 1776 d. Ohio 1855 m. Almira Tuttle   Pvt. Ohio Mil.
    son Austin m. Jane Fuller

Truesdell, John Kimball Vol. 15   Sgt. Vt. Mil.

Truett (Truitt), Purnal (Purnell) b. Del. or Md. 1767 or 57
    d. Ga. 1841 m. Polly Godfrey or Godley   Pvt. Ga. Mil.
    son Riley m. Bonetta Smith
    son Thomas m. Polly Foster
    daughter Nancy m. Ell Collins

Truitt, James b. 1792 d. Ind. 1873   Pvt. Ky. Mil.
    m. Loudica (Adkinson) Dumont
    daughter America Elizabeth m. Hugh McMullan Reid

Trull, Joel Vol. 5   Pvt. Conn. Mil.

Truly, James Vol. 8   Pvt. Miss. Mil.

Truman, William b. 1783 d. 1863 m. Emma Grant Ship   Pvt. Ky. Mil.
    son Edmund Armisted m. Amelia M. Nevill

Trumbo, Mathias b. Va. 1787 d. Ill. 1875 m. Rebecca Grove   Pvt. Va. Mil.
    daughter Barbara m. Joseph Jackson REAL DAUGHTER

Truxtun, Thomas b. N.Y. 1755 d. Pa. 1822   Capt. U.S. Navy
    m. Mary Von Drieull — daughter Sally m. Henry Benbridge, Jr.

Tubbs, Joel, Jr. b. Mass. 1774 d. N.Y. 1846 m. Jedida   Qtmtr. N.Y. Cav.
    son Joel B. m. Jane Anne Demelt

Tuck, William b. Mass. 1740 d. Mass. 1826   Selectman, Collector Justice,
    m. Sarah Hager   Rep. Mass. 1786-1806
    daughter Maria R. m. Stephen Story, Jr.

Tucker, Henry St. George b. Va. 1780 d. Va. 1848   Capt. Va. Mil.
    m. Evelina Hunter — daughter Virginia m. Henry Lawrence Brooks

Tucker, James (Haw) b. Va. 1788 d. Ky. 1870   Pvt. Ky. Mil.
    m. Nancy Kennett — daughter Elizabeth m. John Avritt

Tucker, Jesse b. Va. d. Va. 1817 m. Nancy Lane   Pvt. Va.
    daughter Martha m. Wm. Hudson

Tucker, John b. Va. 1750 d. Ky. 1790 killed by Indian   Patriot 1790 Ky.
    son James H. m. Nancy Kennett

Tucker, John b. Pa. 1790 d. Ohio 1856 m. Mary Ann McBride   Lt. Pa. Mil.
    daughter Susanna m. John Shanstrom REAL DAUGHTER

Tucker, John b. N.H. 1792 d. Ohio 1879 m. Mary Ward   Pvt. N.H. Mil.
daughter Serena m. Francis Harvey Wagar

Tucker, John b. Mass. 1748 d. Mass. 1826   Capt. Mass. Mil.
m. Rachel Thompson — son Robert T. m. Hannah Billings

Tucker, Joseph Pascal Vol. 12   Citizens Protector N.Y.

Tucker, Levi b. (W.) Va. 1786 d. W.Va. 1851   Pvt. U.S. Inf.
m. Mary Glisson — son John W. m. Mary Anne Thomas

Tucker, Samuel b. N.J. 1784 d. Iowa 1852   Pvt. N.Y. Mil.
m. Mary Tucker (cousin) — daughter Harriet m. John Burk

Tucker, Samuel b. Md. 1795 d. D.C. 1880 m. Belina Hodgkin   Pvt. Md. Mil.
son Samuel W. m. Martha Collins

Tucker, William b. Va. 1800 d. Miss. 1882   Ens. Tenn. Mil. Pensioner
m. Elizabeth Crebalt Taylor
daughter Mary Virginia m. John Muse Hart REAL DAUGHTER

Tufford, Philip b. N.J. 1795 d. N.Y. 1870 m. Harriet Childs   Sgt. U.S. Vol.
daughter Mary Ann m. David Ortt

Tuggle, Benjamin b. Va. 1792 d. Ky. 1876   Corp. Ky. Mil.
m. Maacha Tarrant — daughter Charity B. m. John Tye

Tull, John Vol. 13   Pvt. Md. Mil.

Tull, John b. Del. 1783 d. Mo. 1862 m. Eliza Victor   Pvt. Ky. Mil.
daughter Hannah m. Lewis N. Ress
son James F. m. Sallie Willie Cosby
daughter Nancy m. Isaac Smith

Tuller, Flavel b. Conn. 1795 d. Ohio 1881   Pvt. Ohio Mil.
m. Lucinda Holcomb — daughter Henrietta S. m. Horace W. Wright

Tunison, John b. N.J. 1786 d. Penn. 1854 m. Hannah Miller   Pvt. Pa. Mil.
daughter Samantha m. John Sherbondy REAL DAUGHTER

Tunstall, William b. Va. 1736 d. Va. 1795   Clerk of Court Pa. 1767-1791
m. Elizabeth Barker — son Peyton R. m. Rebecca B. Barnes

Tupper, Charles Vol. 12   Pvt. U.S. Inf.
Julia Tuper Mund REAL DAUGHTER

Tupper, Elam b. Vt. 1792 d. Vt. 1880 m. Maria Smith   Pvt. Vt. Mil.
daughter Emeline m. Elliott N. Stearns

Tupper, Norman Vol. 9   Pvt. Vt. Mil.

Turbett (Torbett), Thomas b. Ky. 1767 d. Pa. 1830   Pvt. Pa. Mil.
m. Mrs. Lucy Elliott — Thomas m. Elizabeth Wallace

Turbett (Torbett), Thomas b. Ky. 1792 d. Pa. 1839   Pvt. Pa. Mil.
m. Elizabeth Wallace — son James m. Armilda V. Rucker

Turbyfill, John b. Va. 1742 d. N.C. 1838 m. Nancy   Justice N.C. 1802-17
daughter Martha m. James Mays

Turley, Alexander b. Va. 1787 d. Va. 1853 m. Susan   Pvt. Va. Mil.
son Charles W. m. Ella Meredith Jones

Turner, Abel b. Vt. 1791 d. N.Y. 1865   Pvt. N.Y. Mil.
m. Mary Turner prob. Relative
son Chauncey m. Ellen Agnes Barnard
daughter Mary E. REAL DAUGHTER

Turner, Alexander J. b. N.Y. 1763 d. N.Y. 1806   2nd Maj. N.Y. Mil.
m. Sarah — daughter Mary m. Aretus Man Hitchcock

Turner, Benejah Wolcott Vol. 10   Ens. N.Y. Mil.

Turner, Carolinus Vol. 1   Pvt. Va. Mil.

Turner, Ezra b. Mass. 1763 d. N.Y. 1851   Maj. N.Y. Mil.
m. Amy Beaman — daughter Mary m. Abel Turner

Turner, Ferdinand b. Va. 1791 d. Ind. 1865   Pvt. Ind. Terr. Mil
m. Hannah Harris   Pvt. Ohio Mil.
daughter Elizabeth m. Jacob Augusta Cox

Turner, Francis b. Ire. 1750 d. Va. 1803   Justice Va. 1791
m. Elizabeth — son John m. Judith Robertson

Turner, George b. Ire. 1731 d. N.H. 1821   Capt. N.H. Art.
m. (2) Elizabeth Cutty — daughter Elizabeth m. Joseph Willard, Jr.

Turner, Henry b. Va. 1786 d. Va. 1863 m. Isabella Hopkins   Pvt. Va. Mil.
daughter Ann Margaret m. William Walton Blaine

Turner, Henry Vol. 7   Pvt. Mass. Mil.

Turner, Henry b. Ohio Ter. 1789 d. Ohio   Pvt. Green Co. Ohio Mil.
m. Anna Thomas — son Thomas K. m. Mary Moore

Turner, Isaac b. France 1788 d. Pa. 1867   Pvt. N.Y. Mil.
m. (2) Mrs. Nancy Kelley Van Gilder
daughter Rosella C. m. (1)Houser (2) A. Lockard REAL DAUGHTER
daughter Mathilda REAL DAUGHTER
daughter Mary E. REAL DAUGHTER

Turner, Jacob b. N.Y. 1789 d. Mich. 1866   Pvt. N.Y. Mil. 1813
m. Gertrude Decker — son Edward m. Lucretia Carney
son William m. Sophrenia Tuttle

Turner, James b. Va. 1786 d. Va. 1846 m. Winnefred   Pvt. Va. Mil.
son James M. m. Jane Elizabeth Moore

Turner, James Vol. 16   Pvt. N.Y. Inf.

Turner, John Vol. 13   Surveyor, Sheriff Va.

Turner, John b. N.J. d. N.J. m. Elizabeth Carter   Pvt. N.J. Mil.
daughter Joanna m. John Hurff

Turner, John b. Va. 1772 d. Tenn. 1856   Ens. 1794 Va. Justice Va. 1803
m. Judith Robertson — son Francis m. Mary Nance Garner

Turner, John b. N.Y. 1796 d. Ohio 1861   Pvt. N.Y. Mil.
m. Eliza Ann Bennet — daughter Sarah m. Warren J. Phillips

Turner, John Bryant Vol. 3   Pvt. Mass. Mil.

Turner, John Leeds b. N.J. 1796 d. N.J. 1869   Pvt. N.J. Mil.
m. Elizabeth Sooy — daughter Elizabeth Ann m. Joseph A. Barstow

Turner, Joseph b. Va. 1793 d. Ky. 1879 m. Ellen Wallace   Cpl. Va. Mil.
daughter Cynthia Belle m. George H. Pursley REAL DAUGHTER

Turner, Joseph Vol. 12   Pvt. N.Y. Mil.

Turner, Thomas Jr. b. S.C. c. 1792 d. Ga. 1873   Pvt. S.C. Mil.
m. Gincy Parrish — son George W. m. Fannie Eliza Smith

Turner, Wiley b. N.C. 1796 d. Tenn. 1860   3rd Cpl. E. Tenn. Inf.
m. Maria Thompson — son Charles New m. Hettie B. Sullivan

Turner, William S. b. Va. 1792 d. Va. 1852   Pvt. Va. Mil.
   m. Frances Cheatwood — daughter Annie m. Fayette R. Rosser

Turney, Andrew Vol. 9   Sgt. Conn. Mil.

Turpin, Francis b. Md. 1759 d. Md. 1829   Maj. Md. Mil.
   m. Mrs. Nancy Smith Reed — son Francis B. C. m. Mary Adeline Smoot

Turpin, William b. Md. 1776 d. Md. 1824   Pvt. Md. Mil.
   m. Elizabeth R. — son John m. Susan Bell

Turrentine, Samuel b. N.C. 1763 d. Tenn. 1824 m. Sarah Wilson   Maj. N.C.
son Archelaus m. Margaret Smith

Tuthill, Job Vol. 85   Cpl. N.Y. Mil.

Tuthill, Samuel b. N.Y. 1766 d. N.Y. 1851   Capt. N.Y. Mil.
   m. Parnall Cantine — daughter Cynthia m. Elijah Jones

Tuthill, William b. N.Y. 1782 d. N.Y. 1827 m. Grizel Culver   Capt. N.Y. Inf.
daughter Eveline m. Nelson Ketcham

Tuttle, David Vol. 12   Pvt. N.Y. Mil.

Tuttle, Eli b. Mass. (Me.) 1780 d. Maine 1860   Cpl. Mass. Mil.
   m. Ruth Scott — daughter Phoebe H. m. John D. Groesbeeck

Tuttle, Gersham Jr. b. Conn. 1767 d. Ind. 1823   Lt. Col. N.Y. Mil.
   m. Permelia Strong Clark
daughter Mary m. (2) Sylvanius Doolittle Manville

Tuttle, Harvey Vol. 10   Pvt. U.S. Inf.

Tuttle, Jared b. Conn. 1760 d. N.Y. 1837 m. Roxanna Ward   Lt. N.Y. Mil.
daughter Lovina m. Walter Pitt Walker

Tuttle, John b. Mass. 1797 d. N.Y. 1881 m. Rachel Phelps   Pvt. N.Y. Mil.
daughter Mary Ann m. Carter

Tuttle, Solomon b. Conn. 1794 d. Ind. 1848   Pvt. N.Y. Mil.
   m. Nancy Holdridge — daughter Emily Candace m. William H. Meloy

Twiggs, Levi Vol. 5   2nd Lt. U.S. Marines

Twitchell, Joshua b. Mass. 1784 d. Ill. 1828   Pvt. Tenn. Mil. 1815
   m. Margaret Wheeler — son Elanson m. Betsey Newell

Twitchell, Nathan F. b. (Me.) Mass. 1794 d. Me. 1878   Musician Mass.
   m. Sarah F. Burbank   (Me.) Mil.
daughter Nancy m. Asa Page Knight

Twogood, William b. N.Y. 1794 d. Ill. 1874 m.   Pvt. N.Y. Mil.
daughter Emily m. Merritt Lawrence Satterlee REAL DAUGHTER
daughter Sarah m. Alfred Rose Chapin REAL DAUGHTER

Tye, George b. N.C. 1782 d. Ky. 1845   Sgt. Ky. Mtd. Vol.
   m. Margaret Leah Pearce — son John P. m. Charity B. Tuggle
son Robert W. m. Catherine Ann Hayden

Tylee, Samuel b. Conn. 1766 d. Ohio 1845   Capt. Ohio Mil.
   m. Anna Sandford — daughter Anna m. David Augustus Adams
son William m. Juliette Hurlburt

Tyler, Austin b. N.H. 1790 d. N.H. 1844   Sgt. N.H. Mil.
   m. Almira Kingsbury — daughter Ellen Almira m. J. L. Lovering

Tyler, Daniel b. Mass. 17— d. Mass. 1857   Pvt. Mass. Mil.
   m. (3) Sarah Jones — son David m. Emeline Reed

Tyler, Dwight Ripley b. Conn. 1796 d. Conn. 1879   Cpl. Conn. Mil.
m. Mary Kinne Johnson
daughter Mary E. m. Thruston Browning Barber REAL DAUGHTER

Tyler, Elijah Vol. 9   Pvt. Mass. Mil.

Tyler, Elnathan Bissell b. Conn. 1755 d. Conn. 1817   Cpl. Qtmr. Conn. Mil.
m. Phoebe Atwater — son John B. m. Minerva Mallery

Tyler, Job b. Mass. 1770 d. N.Y. 1863   Pvt. N.Y. Mil.
m. Phoebe Phillis McDonald
son William G. m. Mary Lindsay Connally

Tyler, John b. Va. 1747 d. Va. 1813   Mem. Gen. Assbly. Speaker
m. Mary Marat Armistead   Gov. Va. 1811-1813
son Nat Henry m. Elizabeth Warren Walker

Tyler, Samuel b. Mass. 1754 d. Mass. 1832   Lt. Col. Mass. Mil.
m. Lewis Isham — daughter Clarissa m. Cowes Danforth

Tynes, Robert b. Va. d. Va. 1819 m. Martha Jordan   Capt. Va. Mil.
son Henry L. m. Anne Caroline Powell
son James J. m. Angenetta Harriet Corbell

Tyree, Thomas I. b. Va. d. Tenn. 1858 m. Charlotte Ellison   Pvt. Va. Mil.
daughter Nancy m. Samuel H. McWhirter

Tyson, Cornelius b. N.C. 1720 d. N.C. 1789   Justice of Peace N.C. 1784
m. (2) Mary Sherrod — son Moses m. Elizabeth Joyner

Tyson, William Vol. 8   Pvt. N.Y. Art.

U

Uhler, Jacob b. Penn. 1748 d. Penn. 1807   Pvt. Penn. Mil.
m. Margaret Messer — son Valentine J. m. Elizabeth Breidinger

Ulrey, Jacob Sr. b. Md. 1768 d. Ohio 1838   Pvt. Ky. Rangers
m. Hannah West — son Jacob Jr. m. Sarah

Unbenhauer, John Philip b. Penn. 1763 d. Ohio 1854   Pvt. Penn. Mil.
m. Elizabeth — son Francis Henry m. Mary Ann Sullivan

Umberger, Michael b. Penn. 1757 d. Penn. 1815   Cpl. Penn. Mil.
m. Mary Verner — daughter Margaret m. Henry Shaffer

Umberger, Michael b. Penn. 1778 d. Penn. 1850   Cpl. Penn. Mil.
m. Sarah Montgomery — son John m. Eleanor (Ellen) Garman

Umstead, Jacob b. Penn. 1777 d. Ohio 1865 m. Hannah Hallman   Penn. Vol.
daughter Lydia m. Frederick Brunner

Underhill, John Bonnett b. N.Y. 1791 d. N.Y. 1868   Pound Mst. N.Y. 1814
m. Alchea — son George W. L. m. Julia Ann Barker

Underwood, John b. Ire. 1739 d. Penn. 1827   Capt. Penn. Mil.
m. Sarah Morrison — daughter Ann m. Ephraim Steel

Underwood, Samuel b. R.I. 1756 d. R.I. 1830   2nd Lt. R.I. Mil.
m. Susannah Tripp — son William m. Elizabeth Sherman

Updegraff, Abner b. Penn. 1770 d. Penn. 1845   Sgt. Maj. Penn. Mil.
m. Jane Devine — daughter Lydia m. William Jordan Howard

Upson, Charles b. Conn. 1752 d. Conn. 1809   Rep. 1797-8 Treasurer
m. Mrs. Mary Hotchkiss Moulthrop   Selectman Conn. 1789-96
son Thomas m. Jerusha Upson

Upson, Isaac b. Conn. 1763 d. Conn. aft. 1811   Selectman Conn. 1809
     m. Sylvia Lewis — daughter Jerusha m. Thomas Upson (Cousin)

Upson, Samuel b. Conn. 1737 d. Conn. 1816   Town Moderator Conn. 1780-90
     m. Ruth Cowles — son Isaac m. Sylvia Lewis

Upton, Jeduthan Jr. b. Mass. 1785 d. Cuba. 1821   Capt. Mass. Navy
     m. Sarah Smith — daughter Mary E. m. George B. Ricker

Upton, Nathaniel Vol. 3   Pvt. Seaman on Sloop of War

Urwiler, George b. Penn 1774 d. Penn. 1856 m. Sarah Davis   Lt. Penn. Mil.
     son John m. Owinia Stout MacGill

Usher, James b. R.I. 1760 d. R.I. 1832   2nd Lt. 1812 on Brig
     m. Susannah Dimon — son Allen T. m. Mary I. Wardwell

Utley, Elijah b. Conn. 1765-6 d. Mass. 1820-30   Pvt. N.Y. Mil.
     m. Lois Swan — daughter Elizabeth m. Timothy Henry Gidley

V

Vail, Daniel b. N.Y. 1795 d. N.Y. 1882 m. Susan   Ens. N.Y. Inf.
     daughter Catherine m. Nathaniel Tuthill

Valentine, Stephen b. N.Y. 1776 d. N.Y. 1818   Capt. N.Y. Mil.
     m. Prudence Cady — son Sidney m. Elizabeth Bargy

Valentine, Robert b. Penn. 1790 d. Penn. 1876   Pvt. Penn. Mil.
     m. Betsy Ann Owen — son Elial T. F. m. Helen Parmlee

Valentine, Thomas b. N.Y. 1794 d. N.Y. 1872   Pvt. N.Y. Mil.
     m. Sarah Brooks — son Thomas Jr. m. Cornelia Esther Cornell

Valle, Francois b. Mo. 1779 d. Mo. 1849   Ens. Mo. Terr. Mil.
     m. Mary Ann Deguerre — son Francis Jr. m. Columbia E. Holden

Van Alen, Evert b. N.Y. 1772 d. N.Y. 1854   Capt. N.Y. Mil. Justice
     m. Derica Knickerbocker
     daughter Christiana m. Cornelius Van Reypen

Vanaman, Daniel b. N.J. 1790 d. N.J. 1833 m. Ulena Shaw   Sgt. N.J. Mil.
     daughter Hannah m. Charles H. Snyder

Van Amburgh, Abraham G. 1792 d. Ohio 1841   Pvt. Ohio Mil.
     m. Nancy Kilburn — daughter Sarah E. m. Henry S. Butts

Van Artsdalen, Christopher b. Penn. 1776 d. Penn. 1850   Capt. Penn. Lt.
     m. Jane Cornell — son John C. m. Maria   Inf. Mil.

Van Auken, John b. Penn. 1768 d. N.Y. 1854   Capt. N.Y. Mil.
     m. Margaret Westfall — son Dudley L. m. Betsey Barker

Van Auken, Solomon Vol. 12   Pvt. N.Y. Mil.
     daughter E. m. Elijah Madan REAL DAUGHTER

Van Bibber, John b. Md. 1734 d. Va. 1821   Commissioner Va. 1789
     m. Chloe Standiford — daughter Chloe m. Jesse Bryan Boone

Van Bokelen, Adrien Hubertus b. Holland 1784 d. N.Y.   Qtr. Mst. N.Y. Mil.
     m. Deborah Morris — daughter Elizabeth M. m. Alfred Roe

Van Brocklin, Nicholas b. N.Y. 1794 d. N.Y. 1883   Pvt. N.Y. Mil.
     m. Nancy Shell — son John m. (1) Nancy

Van Brunt, Daniel b. N.J. 1789 d. N.J. 1871   Pvt. N.J. Mil.
     m. Sarah Lane Branch — daughter Margaret m. Jordan Woolley

Van Buren, Lawrence b. N.Y. 1786 d. N.Y. 1868   Qtr.Mst. Capt. N.Y. Mil.
m. Harriet Vosburg — daughter Mary m. Elijah Wright

Van Camp, Cornelius b. N.Y. 1761 d. N.Y. 1839   Capt. N.Y. Mil.
m. (1) Barbara Diefendorf — son Cornelius Jr. m. Catherine Diefendorf

Vance, David b. Va. 1745 d. N.C. 1813   Legis. N.C. 1785-91
m. Priscilla Brank — son David M. Jr. m. Margaret Baird

Vance, Joseph b. Penn. 1786 d. Ohio 1852   Capt. Ohio Mil. & Legis.
m. Mary Leman — son Alexander F. m. Mary Rebecca Ward

Vance, Samuel b. Tenn. 1786 d. Tenn. 1836   Pvt. W. Tenn. Inf.
m. Elizabeth Rockett — daughter Eliza m. Samuel Caffee

Vance, Samuel b. S.C. 1789 d. S.C. 1869   Sgt. S.C. Troops
m. Elizabeth Kincaid — son James K. m. Laurens Watson

Van Cleef, Hendrick b. N.Y. 1782 d. N.Y. 1820   Pvt. N.Y. Mil.
m. Martha Van Dyke — son John H. m. Sara Ann Lake

Van Cleef, Peter b. N.J. 1774 d. N.J. 1842   Pvt. N.J. Mil.
m. Jane Perlee — son Peter Jr. m. Maria Schenck Cox

Vandemark, John S. b. N.Y. 1771 d. N.Y. 1837   Pvt. N.Y. Mil.
m. Cornelia Vandenberg — son Evert m Fanny Wontworth

Vandenbemden, Joseph b. Holland 1787 d. Ohio 1881   Sgt. Ohio Mil.
m. Mary Randall — daughter Susan m. John Kent Buck

Vanderbilt, John K. Vol. 14   Sgt. N.Y. Mil.

Vanderbilt, Oliver b. N.Y. 1794 d. N.Y. 1868   Pvt. N.Y.
m. Catherine Morris — son Edward m. Keziah Wellings

Van Der Cook, Michael S. b. N.Y. 1774 d. N.Y. 1852   Maj. N.Y. Mil.
m. Mehitabel Haskins — son Michael S. Jr. m. Matilda Brown

Vanderhoef, Samuel Carhart b. N.J. 1796 d. N.J. 1847   Lt. N.J. Inf.
m. Idah Van Brackle Holmes
son Nathaniel S. W. m. Mary Elizabeth Blauvelt

Vandervort, Paul b. (W.) Va. 1790 d. W.Va. 1833   Pvt. Va. Mil.
m. Mary Jenkins — daughter Margarey m. Alfred Fleming

Van Deursen, William b. N.J. 1791 d. N.J. 1873   Surgeon U.S. Inf.
m. Eleanor Hendrickson — son John m. Ann Dickson McClelland

Van Deusen, Cornelius Vol. 15   Sgt. N.Y. Mil.

Van Devanter, John b. Tenn. 1796 d. Mo. 1856   2 Sgt. Tenn. Mil.
m. Mary Downing — daughter Sarah m. Frank Joseph Schatz

Vandever, Ashbury b. Ky. 1777 d. Ky. 1839   Pvt. Ky. Vol.
m. Rachel Mason — son George m. Mary Pigg

Van Dolffen, John T. Vol. 7   Lt. Col. N.Y. Mil.

Van Dorn, Jacob b. N.J. 1763 d. N.J. 1836   Pvt. N.J. Mil.
m. Margaret Hunt — daughter Ann m. John Jerolamon Peapack

Van Dusen, John b. N.Y. 1783 d. Vt. 1858 m. Mrs. Brot   Pvt. N.Y. Mil.
daughter Frances m. John Buckbee

Van Dyke, Thomas J. b. Del. 1777 d. Ala. 1814   Surgeon Tenn. Vol.
m. Penelope Smith Campbell — son Thomas Nixon m. Eliza Deaderick

Vander Zee, Cornelius A. b. 1785 d. 1846   Lt. Cav. N.Y. Mil.
m. Maria Van Bergen — son Henry C. m. Caty Eliza Bradt

Van Etten, Peter b. N.J. 1784 d. N.Y. 1863   Sgt. N.Y. Rifleman 1813
m. Polly Pitcher — daughter Catherine m. Francis Reed

Van Fleet, Levi b. N.Y. 1793 d. Ohio   Pvt. N.Y. Mil.
m. Mary Ann Smith — son Henry H. m. Mary Strong

Van Gilder, Michael b. 1786 d. Ohio 1882 m. Hannah Young   Pvt. N.J. Mil.
daughter Mary m. Nathaniel Foster Walker

Van Gorder, Elias b. N.J. 1773 d. 1814 m. Mary Hays   Pvt. Penn. Mil.
son John m. Susanna Eckles

Van Heins, Henry Andrew Vol. 12   Capt. La. Mil.

Van Hohne, Christopher b. Md. 1760 d. Md. 1833   Lt. Md. Troops
m. Mary Holland — daughter Mary Ann m. Martin Fannen Revell

Van Horn, Isaac b. Va. 1788 d. Ohio 1830 m. Sarah Smythe   Capt. Va. Mil.
daughter Mary Ann m. Noah Harris Coole

Van Horne, Abraham b. N.J. 1738 d. N.Y. 1810   Mem. Assem. Sheriff N.Y.
m. Hannah Hoff — son Richard m. Cornelia Ten Eyck   1784

Van Horne, Abram b. N.J. 1763 d. N.Y. 1840   Pvt. N.Y. Mil.
m. Annie Couvenhoven — daughter Catherine m. John Putnam

Van Horne, Cornelius b. N.J. 1750 d. Penn. 1847   Capt. Penn. Mil.
m. Sarah Elizabeth Dunn — daughter Elizabeth Jane m. Samuel Sloan

Van Horne, Isaac Sr. b. Penn. 1789 d. Mich. 1814   Lt. Ohio Mil.
m. Mrs. Jane Horne Waglorn
son Isaac Jr. m. Rebecca Ann Springer

Van Houten, Abraham b. N.J. 1791 d. N.J. 1819   Fifer N.J. Mil.
m. Margaret Speer — son Abraham m. Eleanor Benson

Van Inger (Van Winger), Joseph b. N.Y. 1762 d. N.Y. 1842   Lt. 1784-
m. Neeltje Van Alstyne   1820 N.Y.
daughter Margaret m. Henry Plank

Van Keuren, Garret b. N.Y. 1785 d. 1868   Ens. Qtr. Mst. N.Y. Mil.
m. Sarah Hagadorn — daughter Julia A. m. Thomas Reed

Vanlandingham, George b. Va. d. Canada 1814   Pvt. Ky. Mil.
m. Jane Bromley — daughter Elizabeth m. Edmund Perkins

Van Meter, Jacob b. N.J. 1762 d. Ky. 1850 m. Letitia Strode   Col. W.Va. Mil.
son Jacob Jr. m. Elizabeth Rhodes

Van Meter, John b. Va. 1764 d. Ky. ca. 1819   Sgt. Ky. Mil.
m. Dinah Holtzclaw — son Cyrus m. Polly Jewell

Vann, Absalom b. S.C. 1784 d. Ind. 1845   Pvt. Ky. Mil.
m. Rebecca Rollison — son Joseph m. Elizabeth Rhodes
son William R. m. Ellen (Middleswart) Carney

Van Name, Michael b. N.Y. 1795 d. N.Y. 1883   Pvt. N.Y. Mil.
m. Gertrude Cortelyou — daughter Eliza m. Henry Miller

Van Name, Moses b. N.Y. 1788 d. N.Y. 1871   Pvt. N.Y. Mil.
m. Mary Pierson — daughter Deborah m. Cornelius B. Mersereau

Van Ness, Nehemiah b. N.Y. 1790 d. Kan. 1876   Pvt. N.Y. Mil.
m. Martha Jackson — daughter Pamelia m. Thomas S. Graves

Van Nest, John b. N.J. 1774 d. Ohio 1862   Pvt. N.J. Mil.
m. Abigail Warne — son Furman m. Harriet Elliott

Van Norman, Aaron b. Penn. 1778 d. Miss. 1861   Pvt. N.Y. Mil.
m. Lucretia Bailey — son Stephen R. m. Mary Seal

Van Nuys, Isaac b. N.Y. 1745 d. N.J. 1815 m. Nelly Quick   Lt. N.J. Mil.
son John m. Lucy Brokaw

Van Nuys, Isaac b. N.J. 1787 d. N.J. 1850 m. Sarah Staats   3rd Lt. N.J. Mil.
daughter Catherine Jane m. Isaac Hoagland

Van Nuys, John b. N.J. 1768 d. N.J. 1849 m. Lucy Brokaw   Pvt. N.J. Mil.
daughter Mary m. Abraham Brokaw Covert

Van Nuys, Peter b. N.J. 1785 d. N.J. 1874   Pvt. N.J. Mil.
m. Catherine Quick — son Peter Q. m. Rachel Ann Curser

Van Orden, Peter b. N.Y. 1761 d. N.Y. 1841   Capt. N.Y. Mil.
m. Mary Crooker — son David Peter m. Polly M. Turner

Vanosdol, James b. Penn. 1784 d. Ohio 1837   Pvt. Ohio Mil.
m. Lydia Meeker — daughter Amanda M. m. Henry J. Willis

Van Patten, Philip b. 1743 d. N.Y. 1812 m. Debora Vaile   Pvt. N.Y. Mil.
son Simon P. m. Hannah Toll

Van Pelt, John b. Va. 1789 d. Ohio 1857 m. Mary Brady   Pvt. Ohio Mil.
son Isaac m. Mary Jane Beattie

Van Saun, Lucas b. N.J. 1746 d. N.J. 1812   Patriot N.J.
m. Magdalena Berdan — son John L. m. Ellen Van Voorhis

Van Schaick, Egbert b. N.Y. 1764 d. 1816   2nd Lt. N.Y. Mil.
m. Maria Winne — daughter Maria A. m. Hiram Fanning

Van Sciver, Isaac b. N.J. 1794 d. N.J. 1880 m. Lucy   Sgt. N.J. Inf.
daughter Emily m.—

Van Sicklen, Abraham b. N.Y. 1761 d. N.Y. 1830   Capt. N.Y. Cav. Mil.
m. Cornelia Cornell — daughter Maria m. Charles Boerum Vanderveer

Van Slyck (Slyck), John b. N.Y. 1781 d. N.Y. 1867   Pvt. N.Y. Art.
m. Jane Schouten — daughter Jane Ann m. Henry Sylvester Baxter

Van Slyck, Peter b. N.Y. 1744 d. N.Y. 1821   Brig. Gen. N.Y. 1811
m. Engeltje Zeillie — daughter Sara E. m. Jost Borst

Van Swearingen, John b. Md. 1764 d. Ohio 1852   Cpl. Ohio Mil.
m. Amelia Daly — son John D. m. Julia Ann Crane

Van Swearingen, Thomas b. Va. 1779 d. Ill. 1863   Pvt. Va.
m. Theodocia Goodale — daughter Martha m. Chester Fitch

Van Tassell, William J. b. N.Y. 1796 d. N.Y. 1884   Pvt. N.Y. Mil.
m. Abigail See — daughter Adelia m. Matthew Church

Vanuxem, Louis Clark b. Penn. 1788 d. 1832 at sea   Pvt. Penn. Cav. Mil.
m. Esther Musgrave Shoemaker
son Frederick W. m. Elizabeth Kennedy

Van Valkenburgh, Henry Vol. 13   Pvt. N.Y. Inf.

Van Valkenburgh, Jacob b. N.Y. 1795 d. N.Y.   Pvt. N.Y. Lt. Inf.
m. Mary Bathia Higgins — son Gerrit S. m. Mary Tisdale

Van Velsor, Cornelius b. N.Y. 1756 d. N.Y. 1837   Maj. N.Y. Mil. 1791
m. Eliza Houston — daughter Phoebe m. James S. Holmes

Van Vranken, Cornelius b. N.Y. 1791 d. N.Y. aft. 1870   Cpl. N.Y. Mil.
m. Rachel Yates — son Jacob E. m. Eveline E. Gates

Van Vranken, Gerrit b. N.Y. c. 1730 d. N.Y. aft. 1803   Ens. N.Y. Mil.
   m. Susanna Egbertse (Ebbers) — daughter Maritie m. Michael Basset

Van Wagoner, Aurt P. b. N.Y. 1779 d. 1849   Pvt. N.Y. Mil.
   m. Mary Schoonmaker — daughter Rachel m. Daniel Aldrich

Van Winkle, Daniel b. Ohio 1791 d. Ohio 1862   Messenger Ohio
   m. Eve Gideon — son William R. m. Elizabeth Hockett

Varn, George b. S.C. 1789 d. S.C. 1835 m. Elizabeth Hires   Pvt. S.C.
   son Daniel R. m. Margaret Copeland

Varnado, Samuel b.—d. Miss. 1874 m. Keziah Newsom   Pvt. La. Mil. 1814-5
   son Archibald m. Penelope Sibley

Varner, Thomas b. Ga. 1760 d. Ga. 1828 m. Emeline   Pvt. Ga. Mil.
   son Alexander m. Elizabeth Head

Varnum, Joseps Bradley b. Mass. 1749-50   V. Pres. U.S. 1814
   d. Mass. 1821 m. Molly Butler   Maj. Gen. 1805 Mass.
   son Jacob B. m. Catherine Dodemead

Varnum, Phineas b. Mass. 1778 d. Me. 1858   Capt. Mass. Mil.
   m. Prudence Fox — son Phineas m. Elizabeth Thomas

Vary, William Thomas Vol. 1   Lt. Col. N.Y. Mil.

Vaughan, Daniel Bowen b. Vt. 1781 d. N.Y. 1826   Capt. N.Y. Art.
   m. Content Boorn — daughter Mercy C. m. Henry Parsons

Vaughan, John b. Wales 1765 d. Ohio 1848 m. Mary Jones   Cpl. Ohio Mil.
   son William m. Mary Bebb

Vaughan, John b. N.C. 1760 d. N.C. 1845 m. Sarah Rogers   Pvt. N.C. Mil.
   son William m. Elizabeth Lawrence

Vaughan, John D. b. Mass. 1763 d. Fla. 1860   Lt. Ga. Mil. 1796
   m. Rhoda Effingham — son Daniel m. Eliza C. Pilot Harrison

Vaughan, Thomas b. N.C. 1750 d. Va. 1840   Collector Va. 1778-94
   m. Martha Lewis — son Edmund H. m. Sarah H. Walker

Vaughan, William b. Penn. 1775 d. N.Y. 1821   Sailing Mst. N.Y.
   m. Abby McMullen — daughter Keziah m. Jerome Shepard Nickles
   daughter Maria C. m. Norman Gurney

Vaughn, Johnson b. Conn. 1783 d. Ohio 1845   Pvt. Ohio Mil.
   m. Jemima Allen — son George R. m. Mary Ann Achre
   son Russell m. Susan Carson

Vaulx (Vaux), James b. Tenn. 1783 d. Tenn. 1862   Pvt. Tenn. Vol.
   m. Eliza Fenner — son James J. m. Margaret Garside

Vawter, Beverly b. Va. 1789 d. Ind. 1872   Pvt. Ind. Terr. Mil.
   m. Elizabeth Crawford — son Richard B. m. Maria Lam or Lain

Veazey, Elisha b. Penn. ca. 1777 d. Ky. 1851   Pvt. Penn. Mil.
   m. Sarah Warnock — son Joseph W. m. Eliz. Campbell

Veazey, Thomas b. N.H. 1787 d. Mass. 1839   3rd. Lt. N.H. Mil.
   m. Margaret Wiggin — son William m. Mary Annette Hatch

Veeder, Abraham b. N.Y. 1745 d. N.Y. 1814   Maj Gen. N.Y. Mil.
   m. Annetie Fonda — daughter Anna m. Matthew Putman

Veeder, Robert Vol. 17   Ens. N.Y. Mil.

Veeter (Feeter), William b. N.Y. 1756 d. N.Y. 1844   Lt. Col. U.S. Mil.
   m. Maria Elizabeth Bellinger — daughter Mary m. John C. Bellinger

Veitch, John b. Eng. 1773 d. N.Y. 1820 m. Martha   Pvt. U.S. Inf.
    son Henry F. m. Selene Whistenhunt

Venable, Charles b. 1730-2 d. 1815 m. Elizabeth Smith   Judge Va. 1792
    daughter Mary m. Robert Martin

Venable, Joseph Morton b. Va. 1791 d. Ind. 1838   Surgeon Tenn. Mil.
    m. Mary Fleming Cowan
    daughter Judith Joyce m. Thomas King Hanna REAL DAUGHTER

Verity, William b. N.Y. 1777 d. N.Y. 1858 m. Jane Wilson   Pvt. N.Y. Mil.
    daughter Mary A. R. m. Daniel Van Nostrand

Vernon, Richard b. 1797 d. 1863 m. Frances Bledsoe   Pvt. N.Y. Mil.
    daughter Susan m. Artir Miller

Vernon, Richard b. Va. 1746 d. Ky. 1834   Pvt. Ky. Mil.
    m. Martha Lindsley — son Anthony m. Fanny Quinn

Vernon, William Washington b. Va. d. Mo. 1826   Pvt. Va. Mil.
    m. Maria Charlotte Maul
    daughter Lucinda A. m. James Thomas McIntosh

Verrill, Ezekial b. Mass. (Me.) 1790 d. Me. 1870   Cpl. Mass. (Me.) Mil.
    m. Rebecca Cushman Fuller — daughter Nancy W. B. m. William Perry

Vesey, William Vol. 12   Capt. Va. Mil.

Viall, Nathaniel Sr. b. Mass. 1762 d. Vt. 1846   Pvt. Vt. Mil.
    m. Betsey Clark — son Sullivan m. Mary Ann Freeby

Vibbert, Jesse b. Conn. 1759 d. Conn. 1830   Pvt. Conn. Mil.
    m. Martha Abbey — daughter Triphena m. Selah Wilson

Vickers, Samuel Vol. 9   Pvt. Md. Mil.

Viele, Charles H. Vol. 10   Pvt. N.Y. Mil.

Viele, Jacob b. N.Y. 1761 d. N.Y. 1843   Ens. N.Y. Mil.
    m. Catherine Palmentier — daughter Harriet m. Frederick Van Wormer

Viley, Willa b. Md. 1788 d.—m. Lydia Smith   Pvt. Ky. Mil.
    son Warren m. Catherine Jane Martin

Villere, Jacques Philippe b. La. 1761 d. La. 1830   Maj. Gen. La.
    m. Jeanne Fazenda — son Caliste m. Marie Duverje

Villere, Rene Gabriel b. La. 1785 d. La. 1852   Pvt. La. Mil.
    m. Madeleine Eulalie de la Ronde — son Edmond m. Odile Cruzat
    son Denis m. Malvina Cruzat

Vincent, John b. 1790 d. Ala. 1871   Indian Fighter Ga. 1813
    m. Eunice Hawes — daughter Louise C. m. Francis Marion Bledsoe

Vincent, Joseph b. Del. 1770 d. Del. 1840 m. Mary Elliott   Ens. Del. Mil.
    daughter Elizabeth m. Isaac Knowles

Vincent, Orren b. N.C. 1788 d. Tenn. 1861   Pvt. N.C. Mil.
    m. Mary S. Ezell — daughter Elizabeth C. m. John P. Andrew Hays

Vincent, Pleasant Hart b. N.J. 1781 d. Ga. aft. 1827   Ord. Sgt. Ga. Mil.
    m. Susan Edwards — son Aulsey Ayres m. Martha Upshur

Vincent, William b. N.Y. 1780 d. N.Y. 1859 m. Anna Wooden   Pvt. N.Y. Mil.
    daughter Phebe Anna m. Daniel Stiles

Vinson, Thomas Melvill Vol. 3   Col. U.S. Inf.

Virden, William Vol. 10   Seaman Del. Navy

Virgil, Elon b. N.Y. 1799 d. Ill. 1867 m. Polly Dimon   Pvt. N.Y. Mil.
daughter Sally Mariah m. Charles Bartlett

Vliet, William b. 1776 d. 1857 m.—   Capt. N.J.
daughter Ida Ann m. Daniel Castner Gaston

Vogler, Christopher b. N.C. 1765 d. N.C. 1827   Gun Maker N.C. 1798
m. Anna J. Stauber — son Nathaniel m. Anna Mary Fishel

Vollintime, William b. N.C. 1791 d. Ill. 1868   Pvt. Tenn. Mtd. Gunmen
m. Sophia Sugg
daughter Lettie Ann m. James S. Ridgway REAL DAUGHTER

Von Steuben, Peter Martin b. Denmark 1748   Surgeon Penn. Mil.
d. Penn. 1814 m. Susannah Shimer
son August Ludwig m. Hannah Dreisbach

Voorhees, Elizabeth E. Williams b. Penn. d. Penn   Furnished Food Md.
m. Hendrick Vorhees   to Troops
daughter Sarah C. m. Jacob Saurman

Voorhees, Hendrick b. Holland 1760 d. N.Y.   Pvt. N.J. Mil.
m. Elizabeth E. Williams — daughter Sarah C. m. Jacob Saurman

Voorhees, Jeremiah b. N.J. 1794 d. N.J. 1874   Pvt. N.J. Mil.
m. Aletta Wyckoff — son Jacob W. m. Maria Louisa Shelton

Vose, Jeremiah b. Mass. 1778 d. Mass. 1855   Sgt. Mass. Mil.
m. Hannah Holmes — son Jeremiah Jr. m. Elizabeth Morse

Vought, Achitius b. N.Y. 1773 d. Penn. 1845 m. Jane Oakley   Pvt. Penn. Mil.
daughter Phoebe m. Asa Stevens

Vreeland, John b. N.J. 1756 d. N.J. 1832   Pvt. N.J. Mil.
m. Annatje Spier — son John m. Margaret Kingsland

Vroman, John b. N.Y. 1794 d. N.Y. 1877 m. Maria Ehle   Pvt. N.Y. Mil.
son Charles Ehle m. Celia Pierce

Vroman, Simon b. N.Y. 1786-7 d. N.Y. 1863 m. Laney Sitts   Pvt. N.Y. Mil.
daughter Catharine m. Henry G. Gercher

Vroome (Vrome), Henry b. N.Y. 1773 d. N.Y. 1855   Pvt. N.Y. Mil.
m. Ann Burbank — son Abraham B. m. Anna Barbara Clapp

W

Waddell, William b. Va. 1758 d. Ky. 1831 m. Nancy White   Pvt. Va. Mil.
daughter Elizabeth m. James F. Sisson

Wade, Edward b. Conn. 1754 d. N.Y. 1845   Pvt. U.S. Inf.
m. Susan Florence — son Edward Jr. m. Polly Eddy

Wade, George b. N.C. 1747 d. S.C. 1823-4   Commissioner S.C. 1797
m. Mary McDonald — son Daniel m. Jane Brown Ross
daughter Rebecca m. Swanson Lunsford

Wade, Isaac Jr. b. Va. 1788 d. Va. 1882   Pvt. Va. Mil.
m. Mary Stephens — son John m. Eliza Oney
son Thomas Louis m. Mildred Burton

Wade, Jeremiah b. Va. 1780 d. Ky. 1815   Pvt. Ky. Mil.
m. Margaret Weeks — daughter Martha m. Joseph Thompson

Wagner, John Vol. 4   Pvt. Penn. Mil.

Wade, Lewis b. Mass. 1791 d. N.Y. 1862   Music Mass. Mil.
m. Harriet Bowen — son Benjamin C. m. Lovicea F. Gaskill
son Lewis W. m. Nancy Ann Brink

Wadhams, Luman b. Conn. 1781 d. N.Y. 1832 Brig. Gen. N.Y. Mil.
 m. Lucy Bostwick Prindle — daughter Jane Ann m. Benjamin Wells
 son William L. m. Emeline Loretta Cole

Wadlington, Spencer C. b. S.C. 1790 d. Tex. 1859 Pvt. S.C. Mil.
 m. Elizabeth Chambers — son William S. m. Ellen Cellum

Wadsworth, Alexander Scammel b. Mass. (Me.) 1790 2nd Lt. U.S. Navy
 d. D.C. 1852 m. Louisa Jerusha Dension
 daughter Annie L. m. John Doane Wells REAL DAUGHTER

Wadsworth, Joseph Vol. 11 Music N.Y. Art.

Wadsworth, Peleg b. Mass. 1748 d. Me. 1829 Mass. Legis. 1792
 m. Elizabeth Bartlett — son Alexander S. m. Louisa Denison

Waffle, William Vol. 16 Ord. Sgt. N.Y. Mil.

Wagg, James b. Mass. 1754 d. Mass. 1845 Pvt. Mass. Vol. Mil.
 m. (1) Lorcas Strought — son Samuel m. Mary Dingley

Waggoner, Abraham J. b. N.Y. 1796 d. Penn. 1875 Teamster 1814 N.Y. Mil.
 m. Catherine Wormwoth — son Grattan Hugh m. Helen Jane Hoard

Waggoner, David b. Penn. 1791 d. Penn. 1845 Pvt. Penn. Mil.
 m. Catherine Gessner — daughter Catherine W. m. Martin M. Angle
 daughter Sarah m. Henry Hollar
 son John C. m. Emma Morrow

Waggoner, George b. 1795 d. Ohio 1891 Pvt. Ohio Mil.
 m. Margaret Klingler — daughter Margaret m. Aaron Shreffler

Waggoner, Joseph Jr. b. N.Y. 1791 d. N.Y. 1855 Pvt. N.Y. Mil.
 m. Minerva Riggs — son Alfred Joseph m. Mary C. Crouse

Wagoner, John Vol. 4 Pvt. Penn. Mil.

Wagner, William b. Penn. 1779 d. Penn. 1865 Pvt. Penn. Mil.
 m. Maria Mechlin — son Paul M. m. Rebecca R. R. Phipps

Waid, Robert b. Va. 1785 d. Va. 1834 m. Anna Stanifor Capt. Va. Mil.
 son William O. m. Elizabeth Ferguson

Wailes, William b. Md. d. Md. 1856 Pvt. Del. Mil.
 m. Eleanor Townsend Dashiell
 daughter Mary Ann m. John Jay Dashiell

Wainwright, Freeman b. Va. d. Va. m.— Vol. 2 Pvt. Va. Mil.
 daughter Martha C. m. C. C. Pugh

Wait, Henry b. Vt. 1793 d. Ill. 1882 m. Sophia Wells Pvt. Vt. Mil.
 son Jacob m. Cordelia Powell

Wait, Reuben b. R.I. 1768 d. N.Y. 1827 m. Mary Swain Sgt. N.Y. Mil.
 daughter Adeline m. James McNutt

Waite, Aruna b. 1775 d. Wisc. 1857 m. Elizabeth Aldrich Ens. N.Y. Mil.
 son Russell m. (1) Elizabeth Small
 son Willis m. Sarah Rider

Waite, John b. N.Y. 1793 d. N.Y. 1884 Pvt. N.Y. Mil.
 m. Mary Ann Sherman — son William m. Louisia Breece
 daughter Elizabeth m. Benj. Gifford Hall
 m. Ruth Lawton
 daughter Mary Ann m. Edward B. Becker REAL DAUGHTER

Waite, Silas Ward b. N.Y. 1794 d. N.Y. 1869 Pvt. N.Y. Mil.
 m. Martha Odell — daughter Jane Annette m. Janes C. Allen

Wakefield, Matthew b. Ky. 1788 d. Ky. 1871   Pvt. Ky. Mil.
m. Rebecca Heady — son Stillwell H. m. Ann Miller Taggart

Wakefield, William b. Ky. 1773 d. Ky 1828   Lt. Col. Ky. Mil.
m. Abigail Huston — son Dr. Matthew F. m. Hannah Ann Roberts

Wakeley, Abijah b. Conn. 1785 d. Conn. 1856 m. Sally Peet   Pvt. Conn. Mil.
son David A. m. Hannah Melinda Mallett

Wakeman, Abijah b. Conn. 1772 d. Mo. 1838   Pvt. Conn. Mil.
m. Mary Buckley — son Charles m. Lydia Mitchell

Walbach, John de Barth Vol. 5   Aid de Camp

Walbridge, Henry Vol. 15   Sgt. Maj. Vt. Mil.

Walden, Ebenezer Vol. 9   Mem. Assem. N.Y.

Waldo, Jonathan b. Conn. 1738 d. N.Y. 1821   Capt. N.Y. Mil.
m. Ann Palmer — son Abiather m. Hannah Homan

Waldo, Joseph W. b. Conn. 1776 d. Conn. 1837   Pvt. S.C. Mil.
m. Elizabeth Lamar — son Benjamin m. Sarah Lipscomb

Waldron, Oliver b. Ga. 1787 d. Fla. 1867 m. Ann Sylvester   Pvt. Ga. Mil.
son George W. S. m. Rebecca Lane

Wales, Ebenezer Vol. 5   Del. Gen. Ct. Mass. 1788

Wales, Roger, b. Conn. 1768 d. N.J. 1835   Surgeon N.J. Inf.
m. Harriet Bentley — son Eli B. m. Sarah Hughes

Wales, Royal b. Mass. 1773 d. Mass. 1857   Mem. Legis. Mass. 1810-13
m. Ruby Porter Bliss — son Horatio m. Mary Eliza Williams

Walker, Aaron b. Mass. 1773 d. Wisc. 1861   Cornet 2nd. Lt. Vt. Mil. 1806-
m. Judith Sanborn   1810
daughter Carolina Louisa m. William Douglass

Walker, Benjamin b. Va. 1775 d. Va. 1824   Sgt. Va. Mil.
m. Matilda Wyche — son William H. m. Nannie Roe Wyche

Walker, Christopher Vol. 9   Lt. Ohio Mil.

Walker, Daniel b. Va. 1792 d. Va. 1878 m. Unity Bell   Pvt. Va. Mil.
son James m. Hannah Cleghorn
m. Elizabeth Gilpin
daughter Fannie L. m. William A. Taylor REAL DAUGHTER
daughter Susie m. A. J. Hicks REAL DAUGHTER
son Joseph m. Trenton E. Allen

Walker, Daniel b. Tenn. 1761 d. Tenn. 1834   Lt. Tenn. Mil.
m. Martha Kilgore — son John m. Sarah Jones

Walker, David b. N.Y. d. Ohio m. Elizabeth Mumford   Pvt. N.Y. Mil.
son Welcome B. m. Abigail E. Mitchell

Walker, Edward b. Tenn. 1795 d. Tenn. 1860   Pvt. Tenn. Mil.
m. Mahalah Tussey — son Henry m. Lucinda Overton
son Isaac m. Mary Haynes

Walker, Enos b. Vt. 1781 d. Vt. 1865 m. Hannah Nichols   Capt. Vt. Mil.
son Lemuel F. m. Mary Delory

Walker, George Jr. b. Ga. 1763 d. Ga. 1830 m. Betsy Walker   Pvt. Ga. Cav.
son David m. Ann Kisiah Dawson

Walker, George b. Penn. 1777 d. Penn. 1847   Pvt. Penn. Mil.
m. Catherine Coleman — son John m. Elizabeth Boger

Walker, George b. Va. 1765 d. Ky. 1819   Pat. Ky. 1814-15
  m. Rachel Caffery — son John C. m. Eliza P. Carter

Walker, Gideon b. Vt. 1772 d. Penn. 1859 m. Martha Knott   Maj. N.Y. Mil.
  daughter Elizabeth P. m. Isaac Pruden

Walker, Henry b. Va. 1742 d. Va. 1792   Sheriff 1785 Col. Va. Mil.
  m. Martha Bolling Eppes
  daughter Sarah H. m. Edmund Hall Vaughan

Walker, Horatio b.—d. Tenn. 1815 m. Martha   Sgt. U.S. Inf.
  daughter Harriet m. Jason Meadows

Walker, Isaac b. Md. 1786 d. N.Y. 1868   Pvt. Md. Mil.
  m. Guluena Foster — daughter Anne E. m. William M. Gawtry

Walker, Isaac b. Penn. 1780 d. Penn. 1850 m. Ann Ewing   Pvt. Penn. Mil.
  son Ewing m. Carolyn Young

Walker, James b. Penn. 1760 d. Tenn 1825 m. Rachel White   Pvt. N.C. Mil.
  son Samuel m. Nancy Dryden

Walker, Jeremiah b. N.C. 1747 d. Ga. 1792 m.—   Pat. 1786-90
  daughter Polly m. John Coleman Jr.

Walker, Joel b. Va. 1764 d. Tenn. 1834 m. Mary B.   Pvt. E. Tenn. Mtd.
  son Joseph Alfred m. Adeline Nelson   Gunman Mil.

Walker, Joel b. N.C. 1789 d. Tenn. 1844   Pvt. E. Tenn. Mil.
  m. Mary Botheral
  daughter Katharine Anne m. William Joseph Bynum

Walker, John b. S.C. 1777 d. S.C. 1866   Capt. S.C. Mil.
  m. Elizabeth Ross Douglas
  daughter Eliza Peninah m. Robert Bones Caldwell

Walker, John b. Va. 1787 d. Ohio 1844   Pvt. Va. Mil.
  m. Letitia Humphrey — daughter Winnie S. m. Joseph Dixon

Walker, John b. Va. 1785 d. Miss. 1849 m. Sarah Gates   Pvt. Miss. Terr. Vol.
  son David C. m. Ann Leggett

Walker, John Vol. 10   Pvt. Ga. Mil.

Walker, John b.—d. m. Sarah Peeples   S.C. House 1811
  daughter Elizabeth Ann m. Rev. Allen A. Hart

Walker, Josiah (Joseph) b. N.Y. 1773 d. N.Y. 1855   Pvt. N.Y. Mil.
  m. Joanna Tanner — son Ephraim S. m. Amanda Roots

Walker, Lewis Vol. 6   Capt. Vt. Mil.

Walker, Nelson b. Va. 1784 d. Ky. 1856 m.—   Pvt. Va. Mil.
  daughter Sarah m. John Terry

Walker, Robert b. Penn. 1774 d. Penn. 1861   Lt. Col. Penn. Mil.
  m. (2) Sarah Wilt
  daughter Sarah J. m. (1) Hugh Ray Heffelfinger REAL DAUGHTER

Walker, Sater Thomas b. Md. 1788 d. Md. 1849   Pvt. Art. Cav. Md.
  m. Catherine Ann Kelly
  daughter Ann Rebecca m. Charles George Ridgely
  daughter Caroline C. m. James Adams
  daughter Catherine C. m. William Thomas Bishop
  daughter Mary Jane m. Benj. Jefferson Clark

Walker, Thomas b. Mass. 1763 d. N.Y. 1836 m. Pamela   Pvt. N.Y. Mil.
  son Lewis m. Sally Ann Robbins

Walker, William b. S.C. 1777 d. S.C. 1837   Lt. S.C. (Servant not Soldier)
m. Lydia Ratliff — daughter Annie m. John J. Ray
son William P. m. (2) Mary Hankinson

Walker, William b. N.C. 1791 d. Tenn. 1863   Pvt. E. Tenn. Mil.
m. Rachel Eaden — son James m. Rebecca Billingsly

Walker, William b. Ky. bef. 1797 d. Ky 1818 m. Miss Petts   Pvt. Ky. Mil.
son Joseph m. Mary M. McClure Ross

Walker, William b. S.C. 1782 d. S.C. 1862 m. Annis Lee   Pvt. S.C. Mil.
daughter Lucinda m. Robert Wylie

Walker, William b. Ga. 1762 d. Ga. 1818 m. Elizabeth Bostick   Sgt. Ga. Mil.
son Charles H. m. Caroline E. Jones

Walker, William Vol. 105   **Pvt. Art. Md.**
daughter Rachel Walker m. Will Bowdle

Walker, William Sr. b. Va. 1755 d. Va. 1840   **Lt. Col. Va. Mil.**
m. Mary Ann Smith — daughter Rebecca B. m. Lindsay Blanton

Walker, William Sr. b. Va. 1770 d. Ohio 1824   Special Ind. Agent Ohio
m. Catherine Rankin — son Matthew R. m. Lydia Brown Ladd
daughter Nancy m. George Garrett

Walkley, Jonathan b. Conn. 1783 d. Ohio 1828   Pvt. Ohio Mil.
m. Nancy Niles — son Aaron G. m. Mary Frances Smith

Walkup, Christopher b. Va. (W.) 1778 d. W.Va. 1818   Capt. Va. Mil.
m. Margaret Rusk (Risk) — daughter Margaret m. Samuel Beard

Wall, Garret Vol. 13   **Qtr.Mst. Penn. Mil.**

Wall, Walter b. Penn. 1794 d. Penn. 1856   Pvt. Penn. Mil.
m. Susannah Scott
daughter Emma D. m. John B. Scott REAL DAUGHTER

Wallace, Andrew b. 1778 d. 1838 m. Eleanor Jones   **Pvt. Ind. Mil. 1813**
son David m. (2) Zerelda Gray

Wallace, Andrew Vol. 8   **Pvt. Ky. Vol.**

Wallace, Henry Vol. 17   **Pvt. Ky. Cav.**

Wallace, Henry b. Ky 1792 d. Mo. 1875   Pvt. U.S. Army
m. Elizabeth Carlyle — daughter Rose Ann m. George W. Carter

Wallace, Jesse b. N.C. 1767 d. Tenn. 1854   **Cornet Tenn. Mil.**
m. Martha George — daughter Rebecca m. William Thompson

Wallace, John b. N.C. d. N.C. 1846   Pvt. N.C. Mil.
m. Mary Ann Tutton — son William m. Mary Rogers

Wallace John Andrew b. Ire. 1790 d. Va. 1830   Pvt. Penn. Ohio Mil.
m. Elizabeth Errisman — daughter Eliza Ellen m. Hugh Nelson Hall

Wallace, John Culbertson b. 1771 d. Penn. 1827   Surgeon Lt. Col. Penn. Mil.
m. Margaret Heron — daughter Jane m. Otis Wheeler

Wallace, Joseph B. b. Tenn. 1795 d. Tenn 1849   Pvt. Tenn.
m. Melissa Wilson — son Zacheus m. Mary McCall

Wallace, Matthew b. Ire. d. N.C. 1824 m. Jane Alexander   Pvt. N.C. Mil.
daughter Mary Jane m. Robert Wallace

Wallace, Robert b. Penn. 1782 d. Penn. 1847   **Maj. Penn. Mil.**
m. Elizabeth Reeder — son William R. m. Isabella McCracken

Wallace, Robert b. Va. d. Ky. bef. 1828 m. Jemima Allingham   Pvt. Ky. Mil.
son Thomas C. m. Margaret Murphy

Wallace, Samuel b.— d. Tenn. bef. 1827 m. Martha Johns   Pvt. Tenn.
son Samuel m. M. W. Muse

Wallace, William Jr. b. Conn. 1748 d. Conn. 1832   Selectman Conn. 1796
m. Eleanor Drake — daughter Martha m. Pierpont Hollister

Wallace, William b. N.C. 1737 d. Tenn. 1799   Deputy Justice Tenn.
m. Mary Wallis — daughter Mary m. John McClellan

Wallace, William b. Tenn. 1794 d. Tenn. 1840   Pvt. E. Tenn. Mil.
m. Margaret Chamberlain
son Jesse G. m. (2) Margarey W. A. Hershall

Wallace, William b. Ky. 1787 d. Ohio 1816   Pvt. Ky. Ohio Mil.
m. Sallie Shannon — son William Jr. m. Lucy Wallace

Waller, George b. Va. 1777 d. Ky. 1860   Chaplain Ky. Vol. Mil.
m. Mary Ware — daughter Mariah W. m. Douglas Cowherd
daughter Nancy m. Wm. Warner McCubbin

Waller, Isaac Rhodes b. N.C. 1793 d. Ga. 1875   Surgeon's Mate Ga. Mil.
m. Frances Perry Dismukes
daughter Eliza H. W. m. William T. Garrard

Waller, James b. Va. 1768 d. Ga. 1817 m. Elizabeth Ellis   Capt. Ga. Mil.
daughter Mary Elizabeth m. Jonathan Davis & 2nd Robert C. Humber
daughter Elizabeth H. m. Wiley Traylor

Waller, John b. Va. 1772 d. N.C. aft. 1815   Pvt. Va. Troops
m. Frances Baker — son Benjamin R. m. Lucy Harris

Waller, Jonathan b. Del. 1783 d. Del. 1842   Capt. Del. Troops
m. Rachel Wilson — daughter Eleanore Ann m. James Ellis

Waller, Nathan b. Conn. 1753 d. Penn. 1831   Capt. Penn. Mil.
m. Elizabeth Weeks — daughter Elizabeth m. Nathan Miller Horton

Waller, William b. Va. 1797 d. D.C. 1856 m. Ann Lucas vol. 6   Lt. Va. Mil.

Walling, Joseph b. N.J. d. N.J. 1860   Pvt. N.J. Mil.
m. Margaret Lequier — son John L. m. Eleanor Cox Pettie

Walsworth, William Jr. b. Vt. 1786 d. Ia. 1878   Pvt. N.Y. Mil.
m. Elizabeth Tracy — son Stephen m. Wealthy Baldwin

Walsh, William b. Ire. 1773 d. N.Y. 1832   Capt. N.Y. Vol. Mil.
m. Margaret McMurry — daughter Mary Ann m. Patrick Doherty

Walters, Aaron b. N.Y. 1775 d. N.Y. 1846   Pvt. N.Y. Mil.
m. Susannah Roberts — son Peter m. Susan Norcross

Walters, Ephraim Sr. b. Mass. 1744 d. Penn. 1835   Pvt. Penn. Mil.
m. Mary Debolt — daughter Elizabeth m. John Kendall

Walter(s), John b. Penn 1792 d. Ind. 1873 m. Rachel Clever   Pvt. Penn. Mil.
son George m. Susana Zeigler

Walters, Robert Jr. b. Ga. 1752 d. Ga. 1827 m. Mary   Pvt. Ga. Mil.
daughter Mary m. Benjamin Pruitt

Walthall, Samuel White Vol. 8   Pvt. Va. Mil.

Waltman, Michael b. Va. d. Penn. 1811   Pvt. Penn. Mil.
m. Ann Eve Esling
daughter Catherine Ann m. James Montgomery Greene

Waltman, Peter b. Penn. 1779 d. Penn. 1836   Pvt. Penn. Mil.
     m. Elizabeth Fatzinger — daughter Rebecca m. Jeremiah Hinkle

Walton, George Washington Vol. 16   Pvt. N.H. Mil.

Walton, Isaac b. N.C. 1763 d. Tenn. 1840   Const. Conv. 1796 Tenn.
     m. Katharine Perry — daughter Sarah m. Bright Berry Harris
     daughter Carolin m. King Luton

Walton, John b. Vt. 1777 d. Mich. 1869   Sgt. Maj. N.Y. Art.
     m. Eleanor Nelson — son Philander J. m. Elmira S. Torrey

Walton, Peter Wyche b.—d. m. Mary F. Perkins   Pvt. Va. Mil.
     daughter Virginia m. David Edward Butler

Walton, Reuben b. (Me.) Mass. 1793 d. Mass. 1867   Pvt. N.H. Mil.
     m. Miranda Piper — daughter Caroline A. m. Charles Wentworth

Walton, Robert b. Va. 1754 d. Ga. 1800   Justice of Peace & Inf.
     m. Blanche Glasscock   Ct. Ga. 1785-99
     son Augustus George m. Martha Sally Williams

Walton, Thomas Hobson b. Va. 1774 d. Ark. 1872   Pvt. Va. Mil.
     m. Susanna Woodson Bates
     son Robert Alfred m. Emily Caroline Bates

Walworth, Hiram Vol. 11   Pvt. Miss. Mil.

Walworth, Reuben Hyde Vol. 7   Aide to Maj. Mooers N.Y. Mil.

Wamsher, David b. Penn. 1794 d. Penn. 1867   Pvt. Penn. Mil.
     m. Mary Boyles — daughter Mary Ann m. William Holloway

Wandle, Casperus b. N.J. 1777 d. N.J. m. Cornelia Blanch   Pvt. Pa. Mil.
     son Jasper m. Sarah A. Van Winkle

Warburton, Benjamin b. Va. 1773 d. Va. 1850   Pvt. Va. Mil.
     m. Catherine Paul — daughter Adelaide V. REAL DAUGHTER

Ward, Aaron Vol. 6   1st U.S. Inf.

Ward, Adonijah b. Va. 1785 d. Ga. 1834 m. Hannah Hull   Constable 1810
     son Levi m. Martha Wood

Ward, Artemas Vol. 10   Cpl. N.Y. Mil.

Ward, Artemas b. Mass. 1727 d. Mass. 1800   Rep. & Chief Justice
     m. Sarah Trowbridge   Councillor to Gov. Mass. 1785-91
     son Thomas W. m. Elizabeth Denny

Ward, David b. Va. 1784 d. Ohio 1879   Teamster U.S. Army Ohio
     m. Elizabeth Taylor — daughter Rhoda m. James C. Reed

Ward, Jacob b. (W.) Va. d. W.Va. 1834   Constable (W.)Va. 1794
     m. Elizabeth Scott — son Levi m. Catherine Whitman

Ward, Jasper b. N.Y. 1773 d. N.Y. 1834 m. Anne Egbert   Lt. Col. N.Y. Mil.
     daughter Caroline Matilda m. William Darby Cook

Ward, John b. 1789 d. 1872-4 m. Julia Kellogg   Sgt. N.Y. Mil.
     daughter Clara Almira m. Martin J. White

Ward, John b. Ohio 1738 d. Ohio 1819 m. Mary Putnam   Lt. Col. Mil.
     son Joseph m. Rebecca

Ward, Joshua b. N.Y. 1758 d. N.Y. 1833 m. Mary Forman   Cpl. N.Y. Mil.
     daughter Elizabeth m. James I. Ostrom

Ward, Josiah Vol. 3   Pvt. U.S. Army

Ward, Levi b. (W.)Va. d. W.Va. m. Catherine Whitman   Ens. Va. Mil.
son George m. Maria Earle

Ward, Moses b. Penn. 1792 d. Ohio 1861 m. Mary Martin   Pvt. Ohio
daughter Elizabeth m. Cyrus Higgs

Ward, Nehemiah b. Mass. (Me.) 1794 d. Me. 1865   Pvt. Mass. (Me.) Mil.
m. Mary Gould — son Nehemia m. Betsey Brewster

Ward, Stephen b. N.Y. 1730 d. N.Y. 1797   Member Senate & Pres. Elector
m. Ruth Gedney — son Jasper m. Ann Egbert   N.Y. 1792

Ward, Sylvester b. (W.)Va. d. (W.)Va. 1796   Pat. (W.)Va. 1790
m. Mary Cunningham — son Jacob m. Elizabeth Scott

Ward, Victor b. Conn. d. Conn. 1827 m. Ann Sherwood Mills Pvt. Conn. Mil.
daughter Elizabeth m. Daniel Moser

Warden, Gabriel b. Vt. 1777 d. Ohio 1838   Pvt. Ohio Mil.
m. Mary Seely — son Homer m. Susan Woodard

Warder, Walter Fairfax b. Md. 1774 d. Ky. 1851   Pvt. Va. Mil.
m. Celia Moss — son Hiram K. m. Mary Wallingford

Wardlaw, Hugh b. Va. 1791 d. Ohio 1864 m. Rebecca Irons   Pvt. Ohio
daughter Martha Jane m. Jonathan Sroufe

Wardwell, Jacob b. Conn. 1744 d. Conn. 1820   Cpl. Conn. Mil.
m. Hannah Whitney — son Joseph m. Elizabeth Scudder

Ware, Arial Vol. 7   Pvt. Vt. Mil.

Ware, Henry Sr. b. Va. 1730 d. Ga. 1802   Justice Ga. 1798
m. Martha Garrett — son Nicholas m. Mary Matthews

Ware, Robert E. b. Va. 1785 d. Ky. 1853   Sgt. Va. Mil.
m. (2) Frances Daniel — son Samuel m. Elizabeth Bigger Landrum

Warfield, Lindsey b. Md. 1784 d. N.Y. 1864   Sgt. N.Y. Mil.
m. Elizabeth Lamoreux — daughter Hester Jane m. Alvin Chamberlin
son Myron m. Frances Greene
son Richard N. m. Rachel Elona Hill

Waring, C. R. Early Vol.   Lt. Md. Art.

Waring, Francis b. Md. 1792 d. Md. 1837 m. Elizabeth Turner   Sgt. Md. Mil.
daughter Elizabeth Elenor m. Joseph Fry Jones

Waring, Thomas b. Md. 1752 d. Ky. 1818   Memb. Senate Ky.
m. Lydia Walton — son Bazel m. Tabitha Mackoy
daughter Lydia W. m. James Haddock

Waring, Thomas Trueman Greenfield b. Md. 1782   Lt. Ky. Mtd. Vol.
d. Ky. 1864 m. Nancy Mefford
daughter Francis m. Harriet W. Williams

Warne, Margaret Vliet b. N.J. 1751 d. N.J. 1836   Nurse N.J.
m. Elijah Warne — son Abraham m. Amy Inscho

Warner, Alexander b. Conn. 1778 d. N.Y. 1862   Pvt. N.Y. Mil.
m. Loretta Conklin
daughter Mary Ann m. Stillman Andrus REAL DAUGHTER

Warner, Asher b. Conn. 1777 d. N.Y. 1813   Pvt. N.Y. Mil. 1813
m. Susan Courtright — daughter Hannah m. David Seager

Warner, Elias Vol. 3   Pvt. Mass. Mil.

Warner, Elijah b. Mass. 1770 d. N.Y. 1841   Cpl. N.Y. Mil.
   m. Relief Marble — son Houghton m. Mary Frary

Warner, George b. Ger. 1765 d. N.Y. 1840   Pvt. N.Y. Mil.
   m. Margaret Buckhorn — son George Jr. m. Amelia Hockenberger

Warner, Henry b. Ohio 1797 d. Ohio 1871   Cpl. Ohio Mil.
   m. Caroline Turrell — son Anson m. Catherine Zeller

Warner, Jacob b. Penn. 1775 d. Ohio 1835   Pvt. Ohio Mil.
   m. (1) Roseanna Lingenfelter — son Jacob L. m. Sarah Eller

Warner, Jesse III b. Mass. 1786 d. Mich. 1861   Lt. N.Y. Mil.
   m. Margaret Hutchinson — daughter Sarah A. m. Curtis Harman

Warner, Jonathan b. Mass. 1744 d. Vt. 1803   Maj. Gen. 1787
   m. Hannah Mandell — daughter Harriet m. Alexander Holton

Warner, Jonathan b. Mass. 1743 d. Mass. 1828   Shay's Rebellion Mass.
   m. Eglah Shelton — son Nathan m. Rebecca Paine Washburn   1786-7

Warner, Michael b. Md. 1744 d. Md. 1848   Qtr. Mst. Md. Mil.
   m. Ann Marie Beckley
   daughter Ann Eliza m. John Hammond Inglehart

Warner, Nathan b. N.Y. 1765 d. Ohio 1844   Material Aid Ohio
   m. Ann Adelia Davis — son Nathan Jr. m. Mary Rathbun

Warner, Peter Vol. 17   Pvt. Ohio Mil.

Warner, Richard b. Tenn. 1794 d. Tenn. 1875 m. Lucy   Pvt. Tenn. Mil.
   son John H. m. Nancy

Warner, Thomas B. b. Md. 1775 d. Ohio 1848   Sgt. Ohio Mil.
   m. Elizabeth Bibler — son Benjamin F. m. Susan Kraner

Warner, Thomas Cargill b. S.C. 1772 d. La. 1830   Pvt. La. Mil.
   m. Tabitha Cargill — son William D. J. m. Mary Margaret Edwards

Warner, Walter W. b. Ky. 1798 d. Wisc. 1862   Pvt. N.Y. Mil.
   m. Clara Lord Potter
   daughter Martha J. m. Charles J. Warner REAL DAUGHTER

Warner, Wyncoop b. Ohio 1795 d. W.Va. 1836   Lt. Ohio Inf.
   m. Minerva S. Boone — daughter Russella E. m. James Albert Price

Warner, Zebulon b. Penn. 1773 d. Ohio 1821   Lt. Penn. Mil. 1798
   m. Mary Fulton — son Wynkoop m. Minerva Boone

Warrance, William b. Penn. 1785 d. Mo. 1870   Pvt. Penn. Vol.
   m. Hannah Louise How
   daughter Belle m. Herman Runde REAL DAUGHTER

Warren, Ashbel b. Conn. 1762 d. Conn. 1843   Pvt. Conn. Mil.
   m. Penelope Pratt — daughter Margaret m. James Colvin

Warner, Asher b. Conn. 1777 d. N.Y. 1813 m. Susan Courtright   Pvt. N.Y.
   daughter Hannah m. David Seager

Warren, Calvin Vol. 13   Cpl. Vt. Vol.

Warren, Charles Wesley b. Va. 1770 d. Ky. 1841   Cpl. Ky. Mil.
   m. Miss Earnest — son Charles W. Jr. m. Susan Armstrong

Warren, Daniel R. b. N.C. 1793 d. Miss. 1841 m. Martha Seal   Lt. Miss. Mil.
   son William C. m. Anne Wilmuth Smith

Warren, David Jr. b. Vt. 1781 d. Mich. 1840   Sgt. Vt. Mil.
   m. Susanna Spaulding — son Samuel N. m. Anna Keller West

Warren, Gideon b. Mass. 1730 d. N.Y. 1803   Town Supervisor & Justice
m. Eunice Chipman   Peace N.Y.
daughter Sarah m. Abijah Webster

Warren, Isaac b. Mass. 1787 d. Conn. 1857   Pvt. Conn. Mil.
m. Leonora Perkins — son Harris F. m. Marion Margery Griffin

Warren, Isaac A. b. Conn. 1790 d. Ontario 1862   Pvt. N.Y. Mil.
m. Abigail Hadley — daughter Anna m. Washington Walker

Warren, John Hubbard Vol. 14   Music Conn. Mil.

Warren, Josiah b. Mass. 1745 d. N.H. 1826   Selectman & Del. Const. Conv.
m. Jane Livingston   N.H. 1791
son Robert m. Prudence Butterfield

Warren, Josiah b. Ga. c. 1790 d. Ga. 1831   Pvt. Ga. Mil.
m. Mary Ann Lewis — son Josiah Jr. m. Leasyann E. Frier

Warren, Joshua Raymond b. Conn. 1789 d. Conn. 1854   3 Lt. U.S. Inf.
m. Harriet Way — daughter Eunice H. m. Eleazer Clark Peck

Warren, Oliver b. N.H. 1776 d. N.Y. 1842   Capt. N.H. Troops
m. Abiah Stanley — daughter Abiah S. m. William Hiller

Warren, William Barton b. Md. 1738 d. Ky. 1818   Justice Peace Ky. 1792
m. Mary Jane Yates
son William M. m. Maria Watkins Fauntleroy

Warrington, Lewis Vol. 14   Commodore U.S. Navy

Warth, George b. Va. 1775 d. Ohio 1838   Mail Carrier on Ohio
m. Ruth Fleehar   Frontier Rte
son Robert m. Mary Johnson

Warthen, Elijah b. Va. 1771 d. Ga. 1826 m. Nancy Holiday   Pvt. Ga. Mil.
son William m. Mrs. Clara Arnau Godolfuss

Warthen, James b. Va. 1756 d. Va. 1841 m. Martha   Pvt. Va. Mil.
son John m. Alice Durfey

Warwick, Nelson Reed b. Va. 1784 d. Ohio 1843   Pvt. Va. Mil.
m. Sarah Lewis Small — son Beverly Green m. Mary Fisher
son Nelson R. m. Eliza J. Smith

Washburn, Abraham b. Ohio 1789 d. Ohio 1876   Pvt. Ohio Mil.
m. Rebecca Marlott — son Ellis m. Elizabeth Hannah
daughter Sallie Ann m. John Plummer

Washburn, Amasa Asa b. Vt. 1768 d. Vt. 1857   Cpl. Vt. Mil.
m. Zermiah Stoddard — son Amasa C. m. Ann Parkard

Washburn, Cyrus Mellen b. Mass. (Me.) 1796 d. Me. 1880   Pvt. Mass. Mil.
m. Lois French — son William H. m. Osca Briggs

Washburn, Ephraim b. Mass. (Me.) 1798 d. At Sea 1815   Pvteer 1812
m. Sally Perkins — daughter Charlotte T. m. Samuel H. Chadbourne

Washburn, Israel b. Mass. 1784 d. Me. 1876   Town Officer (Mass.) Me.
m. Martha Benjamin — son Charles A. m. Sally C. Cleaveland

Washburn, Jonah b. Mass. 1733 d. Vt. 1810   Surveyor of Highways Vt.
m. Huldah Sears — son Abner m. Olive Standish

Washburn, Nahum b. Mass. 1791 d. Mass. 1865   Pvt. Mass. Mil.
m. Ann Mitchell — daughter Susan L. m. Noah Cushman

Washburn, Philip b. Conn. 1772 d. N.Y. 1828   Sgt. U.S. Inf.
m. Elizabeth Davenport — daughter Maranda m. Henry S. Baxter

Washburn, Roger b. Conn. 1792 d. N.Y. 1866   Cpl. N.Y. Mil.
m. Elizabeth Ross — son John R. m. Lucia Ann Lewis

Washburn, Rufus b. Conn. 1766 d. N.Y. 1817   Capt. N.Y. Mil.
m. Patience Washburn — son Nehemiah m. Katharine Thayer

Washburn, William b. Mass. 1765 d. Mich. 1839   Pvt. N.Y. Mil.
m. Lodema Durkee
daughter Mary J. m. William Jerome Wallace REAL DAUGHTER

Washington, Stark b. Va. d. Ark. 1850 m.—   Pvt. Va. Mil.
daughter Mary F. K. m. (2) Solon Boone Jones

Washington, Woodson b. N.C. 1791 d. N.C. 1874   Pvt. N.C. Mil.
m. Sarah Blalock — daughter Martha Ann m. William David Jones

Wason, Robert b. Vt. 1793 d. Mich. 1868   Pvt. Vt. Mil.
m. Betsey Jonson — son Jonson m. Amorette Sleeper

Wassom, Jonathan b. Tenn. d. Ia. m. Elizabeth Booker   2nd Lt. Tenn. Mil.
son Jesse m. Margaret Jackson

Waterbury, David b. Conn. 1722 d. Conn. 1801   Memb. Conn. 1794-5
m. Mary Maltbie — son William m. Sally Lockwood

Waterbury, William b. Conn. 1766 d. Conn. 1842   Rep. Leg. Conn. 1801-8
m. Sally Lodswood — son David m. Sarah Mead Selleck

Waterman, Elijah b. Mass. 1788 d. Ind. 1864   Fifer N.Y. Mil.
m. Sarah Lindsay — son Miles m. Susan Beard

Waters, Charles Alexander b. Md. 1793 d. Md. 1883   Pvt. Md. Mil.
m. Theresa Murphy — son Charles A. m. Ann Killian

Waters, Moses b. Mass. 1771 d. N.Y. 1852   Capt. N.Y. Mil.
m. Rebecca Wilcox — son Nathan m. Eliza Noble Weller

Waters, Philemon b. Va. 1734 d. S.C. 1796   Col. S.C. Mil.
m. Sarah Bandroyne — son Philemon Jr. m. Mary Berry

Waters, Philemon b. Va. d. S.C. m. Mary Berry   Judge Rep. 1783-94 S.C.
son Philemon B. m. Sarah Gilliam
daughter Rhoda m. William Farrow

Waters, Richard Rawlings b. Md. 1795 d. Md. 1885   Pvt. Md. Mil.
m. Jerusha Anne Shaw
daughter Margaret B. m. Jessie Thomas Higgins

Waters, Wilson Turner b. Md. 1793 d. Tenn. 1879   Pvt. Tenn. Vol.
m. Polly Lawrence   Mtd. Gunman
daughter Minerva Jane m. Nelson Jamison Byran
son Wilson m. Minerva Bryan

Watkins, Francis b. Va. c. 1763 d. Va. 1829   Ens. Ind. Wars 1788
m. Nancy Donnally or Nancy Henderson
daughter Mary m. John Kouns

Watkins, Gassaway b. Md. 1752 d. Md. 1840   Lt. Col. Md. Mil.
m. Eleanor Bowie Claggett
daughter Margaret G. m. Albert Gallatin Warfield
daughter Priscilla Agnes m. George Tyson Kenly
son William W. m. Laura Watkins

Watkins, George b. Va. 1770 d. Ga. 1825   Judge Justice Ga. 1799-1806 Lt.
m. Mary Early — daughter Catherune A. m. Ulric Bender Clarke
daughter Jane S. E. m. (2) Junius Hillyer

Watkins, Isaac b. Va. 1777 d. Ark. 1827   Maj. Ky. Mtd. Mil.
   daughter Mary Eliza m. John Joseph Clendenin

Watkins, Richard b. Md. 1777 d. Ohio 1868   Pvt. Va. Mil.
   m. Catherine Hedges — daughter Harriet m. John D. State

Watkins, Thomas b. Md. d.— m. Lucy Belt Vol. 2   Capt. Md. Art.
   son Tobias m. Mary Simpson

Watkins, Thomas W. b. Va. 1794 d. Tenn. 1877   Pvt. W. Tenn. Cav.
   m. Nancy Sims — son Vincent Lee m. Sarah Lloyd

Watkins, William Stearin b. Eng. 1776 d. La. 1830   Maj. La. Mil.
   m. Betsy Baker — daughter Sophia M. m. Nathaniel Dunn Fuqua

Watkins, William Winn b. 1787 d. N.Y. 1864   Pvt. N.Y. Cav. Mil.
   m. Phebe Sheldon — daughter Rachel m. Thomas Higgins

Watrous, Jonathan B. b. Conn. 1795 d. Penn. 1860   Pvt. Conn. Mil.
   m. Matilda Moore — daughter Winfield Scott m. Annie Maria Edwards

Watrous, Pomeroy Vol. 17   Sgt. Conn. Mil.

Watrous, Winthrop b. Penn. 1791 d. Ohio 1816   Pvt. Ohio Mil.
   m. Pamelia Castle
   daughter Mary m. Aaron Bishop Robbins REAL DAUGHTER

Watson, Alexander b. Mass. (Me.) 1795 d. Me. 1847   Pvt. Mass. Mil.
   m. Lydia Rumery — son George W. m. Lucy E. Foss

Watson, Benjamin Naylor b. Va. 1792 d. Mo. 1847   Pvt. Va. Mil.
   m. Wealthy Rundell — daughter Julina m. Thos. Warren Westlake

Watson, David Vol. 10   Pvt. N.Y. Vol.

Watson, Ebenezer b. Conn. 1777 d. N.Y.   Pvt. Conn. Mil.
   m. Hannah Sedgwick — son Ebenezer H. m. Elizabeth Jane Knapp

Watson, Elijah b. S.C. 1775 d. S.C. 1841   Pvt. S.C. Mil.
   m. (1) Chloe Winberley — son Elijah Jr. m. Jame Elizabeth Briggs
   daughter Sophia m. Burrell T. Boatwright

Watson, James Vol. 8   Pvt. Penn. Mil.

Watson, James Clelland b. Ohio Terr. 1786 d. Ohio 1856   Pvt. Ohio Mil.
   m. Rebecca Cunningham — son William H. m. Frances Almeda Brandon

Watson, John b. Va. d. Va. 1805 m.—   Justice Va. 1793
   son Samuel m. Mary Ann Allen

Watson, Thomas b. Penn. 1783 d. Tex.   Capt. Md. Mil.
   m. Rebecca Howard Freeman — son William H. m. Sarah A. Taylor

Watson, William b. S.C. 1789 d. S.C. 1854   Pvt. S.C. Mil.
   m. Margaret Parks — son Samuel D. m. Antonetta E. Breedlove

Watson, William b. N.J. 1794 d. Ill. 1874   Pvt. Ky. Mtd. Vol.
   m. Mrs. Marie Cape Humerickhouse
   daughter Ann Maria m. Thomas Spencer Little

Watson, William b. Va. d. Va. 1853 m. Elizabeth Barksdale   Pvt. Va. Mil.
   son James A. m. Mary Jane Brown

Watt, James b. Ohio 1767 d. Ohio 1851 m. Sarah Kerr   Pvt. Ohio Mil.
   son Alexander m. Martha Morrow

Watts, James D. b. Va. 1762 d. Va. 1821   Pvt. Va. Mil.
   m. Elizabeth Durrett — son James D. Jr. m. Eliza J. Hamilton

Watts, Julius b. Va. d. Ky. 1849 m. Mary Eve   Pvt. Ky. Mil.
daughter Frances m. Henry Lawrence Jr.

Watts, Nathaniel b. Md. 1795 d. Md. 1888   Pvt. Md. Mil.
m. Catherine Lauchlin — son Benjamin m. Henrietta Wise

Watts, Peter b. Va. 1756 d. Ky. 1833   Capt. Mil. Ky. 1798
m. Margaret Fisher — daughter Mary m. John Gill

Waugh, Moses b. Conn. 1788 d. Conn. 1839   Pvt. Conn. Mil.
m. Susan Raymond — son Henry H. m. Susannah Gunn

Way, Daniel Shaw b. Conn. 1772 d. Conn. 1823   Pvt. Conn. Mil.
m. Clarissa Latimer — son John M. m. Elizabeth Jerusha Welles

Way, Henry H. b. S.C. 1793 d. Ind. 1873   Teamster Md. Mil.
m. Rachel Manlove — daughter Sarah m. Daniel Townsend

Way, Seth b. N.C. 1788 d. Ind. 1861 m. Sarah Cranor   Pvt. Ind. Mil.
daughter Betsey m. Lorenzo D. King

Wayland, Henry W. b. Va. 1790 d. Mo. 1870   Pvt. Tenn. Gunman Vol.
m. Ara Malone — daughter Sidney m. Hiram Robertson

Wayland, Joel b. Va. 1781 d. Mo. 1870 m. Sarah Snyder   Pvt. Va. Mil.
son James S. m. Eliza Arnold

Wead, Samuel b. Mass. 1774 d. Vt. 1833   Capt. Vt. Vol.
m. Fanny Morse (2) — son DeLazon DeF. m. Elizabeth Miner

Wear (Weir), Samuel b. Va. 1753 d. Tenn. 1817   Commissioner Tenn. 1786
m. Mary Lisle Thompson — son James H. m. Elizabeth Gaunt
son Samuel Jr. m. Mary Bowman Stephens
daughter Elizabeth m. Robert Armstrong
son Pleasant M. m. Tryphena Whitson
son Robert m. Lucretia Thomas

Weatherby, Henry Chester b. Mass. 1796 d. Ia. 1880   Pvt. Mass. Mil.
m. Elizabeth Brooks — son Charles M. m. Charlotte Edsell de Lorimer

Weatherby, Septimus b. Ga. 1796 d. Miss. 1861   Pvt. Ga.
m. Harriett Young — son Norman m. Katherine Sims

Weatherred, Francis Marcus b. Va. 1781 d. Tex. 1854   Lt. Tenn. Mil.
m. Agnes Sudderth — son Francis M. Jr. m. Nancy Ann Dowell

Weatherwax, David b. N.Y. 1786 d. Mich. 1870   Pvt. N.Y. Mil.
m. Susan Hammond — son Issachar H. m. Mary Rosetta Goold

Weaver, Isaac Jr. Vol. 14   Senator Penn.

Weaver, Isham b. Ga. 1791 d. Ga. 1878 m. Mary Ardis   2nd Lt. Ga. Mil.
son Nicholas M. m. Ann Elizabeth Davidson

Weaver, Jacob b. abt. 1793 d. La. 1815   Pvt. Tenn. Vol. Mil.
m. Elizabeth Shell — daughter Thursey m Isaac Phipps Johnston

Weaver, John b. N.Y. 1777 d.— m. Hannah Wintermute   Pvt. Conn. Mil.
son Peter m. Mary Barton

Weaver, John b. Va. 1787 d. Va. 1867 m. 2d Nancy Doss   Pvt. Va. Mil.
son John H. m. Nancy V. Doss
daughter Sallie m. John Lee Robertson—REAL DAUGHTER

Weaver, Jonas b. Penn. 1762 d. Penn. 1838   Lt. Penn. Mil.
m. Elizabeth Miller — son Joseph m. Mary McKendry Savage

Weaver, Joseph Morey b. 1794 d. 1879   Pvt. N.Y.
m. Elizabeth Livermore — daughter Mary A. m. Robt. S. Moscrip

Weaver, Joseph b. Penn. 1786 d. Penn. 1833 m. Jane Girt   Music Penn.
daughter Harriet m. Henry Stokes

Weaver, Nicholas N. Vol. 13   Lt. N.Y. Mil.

Weaver, Peter b. Penn. 1768 d. Penn. 1845   Pvt. Penn. Mil.
m. Margaret Ellen Heffelfinger — daughter Mary m. Samuel Hamilton

Webb, Abram b. Va. d. N.C. m. Sarah Walton   Pvt. Va. Mil.
son Silas m. Eliza Ann Creech

Webb, Benjamin b. Va. 1789 d. W.Va. 1879 m. Martha Stuart   Pvt. Va. Mil.
daughter Elizabeth m. Samuel Hyman
daughter Louisa m. John R. Hostetter

Webb, Curtis b. Conn. 1793 d. N.Y. 1876   Music Conn. Troops
m. Margaret Hitchock — son Elisha m. Nancy Stebbins

Webb, David b. Conn. 1786 d. Ohio 1848   Pvt. U.S. Inf.
daughter Mary Jane m. Mathew Hampton Winton

Webb, Isaiah b. 1796 d. Ark. 1881 m. Frances May   Pvt. Tenn. Mil.
son Stephen B. m. Eliza Prudence Murphree

Webb, James b. Conn. 1788 d. N.Y. 1877 m. Abigail White   Sgt. Conn. Mil.
son George William m. Mary Esther Wood

Webb, James Jr. b. Mass. (Me.) 1795 d. 1833   Music Mass. (Me.) Mil.
m. Sophia Bell — son James B. m. Margaret Ann Laughinghouse

Webb, Jonathan b. Conn. 1785 d. N.Y. 1867 m. Rebecca Cole   Pvt. N.Y. Mil.
son Daniel S. m. Lucinda C. Coon
daughter Harriet m. Delano D. Calvin

Webb, Oliver b. N.Y. 1782 d. N.Y. 1849 m. Sally Nichols   Cpl. N.Y. Mil.
son Nichols m. Fanny D. Clark

Webb, Thomas b. Conn. 1784 d. Ill. 1840 m. Rebecca Clark   Cpl. N.Y. Mil.
son Thomas C. m. Elvira Coats

Webb, William R. b. Mass. (Me.) 1775 d. Me. 1824   Sgt. Mass. (Me.) Mil.
m. Sarah Crockett — daughter Olive Jane m. John Pickering

Webb, Samuel B. Vol. 5   Brig. Gen. U.S. Army

Webber, John b. N.Y. 1789 d. N.Y. 1875   Pvt. N.Y. Mil.
m. Elizabeth Washburn — daughter Mary Melvina m. Jesse L. Ryder

Weber, Christian II b. Penn. 1743 d. Penn. 1815   Justice & Commissioner
m. Elizabet Weidner   Penn.
son Christian III m. Charlotte Ann Casselberry

Webster, Chester b. N.Y. 1791 d. N.Y. 1860   Pvt. N.Y. Mil. Art.
m. Margaret Buchanan — daughter Helen A. REAL DAUGHTER
daughter Permelia M. m. George H. Failing REAL DAUGHTER

Webster, Eli Vol. 13   Pvt. N.Y. Mil.

Webster, Milo J. b. N.Y. 1798 d. N.Y. 1879 m. Julia Adams   Pvt. N.Y. Mil.
son Martin S. m. Marilla S. Dowd

Webster, Miner b. Conn. 1776 d. N.Y. 1820   Fife Maj. N.Y. Mil.
m. Lydia Savage — son Abel m. Carolina Doolittle

Webster, Stephen b. Mass. 1758 d. Mass. 1845   Pvt. Mass. Mil.
m. Chloe Wheeler — daughter Susannah m. Nathan Call

Webster, Thomas b. Va. 1788 d. Ohio aft. 1850 m. Eliza   Pvt. Ohio Mil.
daughter Lydia J. m. Jas. W. Shoemaker

Weddell, Daniel b. Penn. 1759 d. Penn. 1824   Lt. Penn. Mil. 1792
     m. Ellen McAteer — son George m. Nancy Nelson

Wenderstrandt, Philemon Charles Vol. 9   Commandant U.S. Navy

Weed, John b. N.H. 1770 d. Me. 1843   Sgt. Mass. (Me.) Mil.
     m. Polly Merrow — son Alvah m. Louise Libby

Weed, John b. N.Y. 1785 d. Vt. 1845 m. Mary Townsend   Capt. U.S. Inf.
     son Townsend m. Almira Maltby

Weedon, William b. Md. 1786 d. Ala.   Col. Ala. Mil.
     m. (2) Jane Eliza Urquhart — daughter Jane m. William Read

Weeks, David b. Mass. 1769 d. N.Y. 1852 m. Polly Willson   Pvt. N.Y. Mil.
     daughter Esther m. Western Wesley Wager

Weeks, Joseph b. N.H. 1780 d. N.H. 1834 m. Charity Hurd   Pvt. N.H. Mil.
     daughter Hannah m. Benjamin Welch

Weems, George Vol. 17   Capt. Md. Art.

Weibling, William G. b. Holl. 1781 d. Ohio 1851   Cpl. U.S. Art.
     m. Susannah Prudence O'Neil — son Harmon G. m. Anna McFall

Weigle (Weikel) John b. Penn. 1788 d. Ill. 1855   Pvt. Penn. Vol.
     m. Mary Ann Snyder
     daughter Cornelia Jane m. Charles Hinman REAL DAUGHTER
     daughter Mary Catherine m. Dr. Charles Henry Burroughs

Weir, Andrew b. 1755 d. 1821 m. Mary Grigsby   Lt. 1795-97
     daughter Hannah Malvino m. James Carter

Weir, Samuel b. Va. 1753 d. Tenn. 1817   Memb. Const. Conv. Tenn. 1798
     m. Mary Thompson — daughter Mary Analiza m. John Moore Rankin

Weirich, Jacob b. Penn. 1754 d. Penn. 1822   Sheriff, Legis. 1790-1806
     m. Margaret   Penn.
     daughter Catharine m. George Snaverly (Schnably)

Weitzel (Winsell), Adam b. Penn. 1749 d. Tenn. 1827   Capt. Tenn. Mil.
     m. Mary Davis — daughter Pegg m. David Wagner
     daughter Susan m. Peter Wills

Welborn, Levi b. Ga. 1790 d. Ala. 1841   3rd Lt. Ga. Mil.
     m. Rozanna Bethune — daughter Julia R. m. Batte Peterson

Welborn, Moses b. S.C. 1785 d. Ala. 1834 m. Sarah Halbert   Cpl. S.C. Mil.
     son Joel m. Martha Bowen

Welch, John Vol. 8   Pvt. N.Y. Inf.

Welch, John b. Conn. 1745 d. Ohio 1831   Commissioner, Ohio 1808
     m. Deborah Monroe — son Bildad m. Lucy Aspinwall

Welch, Joseph Vol. 11   Md. Mil.

Weld, Robert Farrell b. Vt. 1784 d. Penn. 1870   Pvt. Penn. Mil.
     m. Clarissa Howe
     daughter Sarah M. m. Washington Parker Cummings

Welden, James D. b. N.Y. 1796 d. N.Y. 1878   Pvt. N.Y. Mil.
     m. Margaret Cramer — son Moses m. Caty Roof

Welker, William b. 1780 d. Ohio 1814 m.—   Pvt. Ohio Mil.
     son Frederic m. Phoebe Travis

Wellborn, James b. N.C. 1767 d. N.C. 1854   Col. N.C. Mil.
     m. Rebecca Montgomery — daughter Nancy M. m. S. S. Starnes

Welles, Jared b. Conn. 1791 d. Conn. 1871 m. Milla Smith   Pvt. Conn.
    son Elijah m. Nancie Bancroft Root

Wellford, Robert b. Eng. 1753 d. Va. 1823   Med. Director 1790-5
    m. Catherine (Yates) Thornton
    son Beverly R. m. Elizabeth Burwell Page

Wellman, John b. Md. 1779 d. W.Va. 1865 m. Nancy Webb   Pvt. W.Va. Mil.
    son David m. Rebecca Wilson

Wellman, Samuel S. Vol. 12   Cpl. N.Y. Mil.

Wells, Alexander b. Penn. 1782 d. Ill. 1877 m. Mary Chance   Pvt. Ill. Mil.
    daughter Mary Jane m. Thomas Denby

Wells, Appleton b. 1781 d. N.Y. 1813 m. Rhoda Baldwin   Pvt. N.Y. Mil.
    son Leonidas m. Olive Batchelor

Wells, Asa b. N.Y. d. N.Y. m. Marcy Taylor   Pvt. N.Y. Mil.
    son Sidney D. m. Mary Appleyard

Wells, Augustine b. Va. 1760 d. W.Va. 1839   Pvt. Va. Mil.
    m. Lucy Doolittle — daughter Lucy Ann m. John Stevens Dorsey

Wells, Charles b. Md. 1745 d. W.Va. 1820   Justice, Rep. Va. 1778-1810
    daughter Mary m. Asa Owings

Wells, Charles b. Penn. 1773 d. Ga. 1830 m. Sarah Lewis   Pvt. Ga. Mil.
    son Samuel m. Mariah Scoles

Wells, Charles b. Md. 1745 d. W.Va. 1815   Mem. Assem. Va. 1792-98
    m. Elizabeth Prather — daughter Sarah m. John McCoy Jr.

Wells, Daniel b. Md. 1767 d. Md. 1818 m. Mary Trigger   Capt. Md. Mil.
    son John m. Elizabeth Haslup

Wells, Edward b. S.C. 1770 d. S.C. 1842   Sgt. S.C. Mil.
    m. Esther Perdriau — son Richard m. Sarah Beatson

Wells, Elisha b. Conn. 1793 d. N.Y. 1872 m. Anna Gardner   Pvt. U.S. Inf.
    son Elisha Jr. m. Mary Collins

Wells, George B. b. Conn. 1793 d. Conn. 1842   Pvt. R.I. Mil.
    m. Sophia Stillman — daughter Eliza m. Edward D. Spicer

Wells, James b. N.H. 1792 d. Ohio 1870 m. Persis Earll   Capt. U.S. Inf.
    son William W. m. Elizabeth Streeter

Wells, James b. Md. 1769 d. 1844 m. Eleanor Hall   Pvt. Md. Cav.
    son James Jr. m. Sarah Brogan

Wells, Joel b. Conn. 1791 d. Ohio 1831 m. Mila Ingham   Pvt. Ohio Vol.
    daughter Harriet m. Joseph Bell

Wells, Joshua b. N.Y. 1763 d. N.Y. 1855 m. Hannah Finch   Pvt. N.Y. Mil.
    son Asa m. Marcy Taylor

Well, Lewis Vol. 9   Pvt. Conn. Mil.

Wells, Marmaduke b. N.Y. 1779 d. N.Y. 1826   Sgt. N.Y. Vol.
    m. Martha Holmes — daughter Rebecca K. m. Thomas Long

Wells, Nathaniel b. S.C. 1781 d. Miss. 1848   Maj. Miss. Mil.
    m. Elizabeth Simmons — son Thomas m. Cynthia Thompson

Wells, Rice b. Ga. 1782 d. Tex. m. Christine Chaney Berry   Sgt. La. Mil.
    daughter Maria Louisa m. Thomas Rowan Swann

Wells, Richard b. Ky. 1793 d. Mo. 1854   Cpl. Ill. & Mo. Mil.
    m. Mary Sappington — daughter Drusilla m. Edward Coons

Wells, Samuel b. Va. 1754 d. Mo. 1830 m. Mary Pope   Col. Ky. Mil.
    son George m. Elizabeth Macke
    daughter Rebecca m. Nathan Heald

Wells, Samuel Vol. 15   Pvt. Penn. Mil.

Wells, Sheriff b. S.C. d. Ala. 1841 m. Rosanah Titshaw   Pvt. S.C. Mil.
    daughter Zana m. William Bryant

Wells, Walter b. N.Y. 1797 d. Ill. 1884   Cpl. N.Y. Mil.
    m. Abigail Lockwood — daughter Evelyn P. m. William H. Hubbard

Wells, William b.— d. 1812 m. Sweet Breeze (Indian Girl)   Capt. Mil.
    daughter Jane T. m. John H. Griggs   Ind. Terr.

Wells, William b. Del. 1760 d. Ky. aft. 1832   Cpl. S.C. Mil.
    m. Mattha Barnett — son Jehu m. Jane Daniel

Wells, William b. Vt. 1784 d. N.Y. 1872-3   Pvt. N.Y. Mil.
    m. Lucinda Streator — son Lester m. Fanny B. Welch

Welsh, Robert b. Md. 1779 d. Md. 1866 m. Patty Sellman   Pvt. Md.
    daughter Isabella m. Robert Hart

Welton, Arad W. Vol. 17   Pvt. Conn. Mil.

Welton, Job b. (W.)Va. 1784 d. W.Va. 1852   Ens. Va. Mil.
    m. Margaret Seymour — daughter Ann Elizabeth m. Joseph Harness

Welton, Philo b. Conn. 1782 d. Ohio 1852 m. Sina Blakeslee   Lt. N.Y. Mil.
    son Dr. S. H. m. Caroline Crocker

Wendover, Peter Hercules b. N.Y. 1768 d. N.Y. 1834   Del. Legis. N.Y. 1801
    m. Rachel Van Voorhees — daughter Harriet W. m. Augustus Bedford

Wentworth, Daniel b. N.H. 1777 d. N.Y. 1815   Pvt. (Me.) Mass. Mil.
    m. Eunice Lumber (Lombard) — son Daniel Jr. m. Peace Fly

Wentworth, James Vol. 14   Pvt. Mass. Mil.

Werley, Nicholas b. Penn. 1752 d. Penn. 1831   Ens. Penn. Mil.
    m. Margaret Hautz — son Sebastian m. Lydia Bittner
    son Valentine m. Sarah Messinger

Wertz, Adam Vol. 14   Pvt. Penn. Mil.

West, Amos b. Va. 1766 d. Ky. 1819   Surveyor, Overseer Ky.
    m. Frances Herndon   1796-98
    daughter Isabella m. Hiram Halcomb

West, Ezekial Vol. 9   Pvt. U.S. Inf.

West, Francis b. Penn. 1761 d. Penn. 1843   Pvt. Penn. Cav.
    m. Mary Dawson Nixon — son James m. Anne Bell Welsh

West, Jacob b. N.C. 1776 d. Ill. 1868   Pvt. W. Tenn. Vol.
    m. Barsheba Cooper — daughter Nancy m. Jonathan Latimer

West, Joseph b. Penn. 1783 d. Penn. 1849   Capt. Penn. Mil.
    m. Christiana Engarg
    daughter Elizabeth R. m. William Ferdinand Meyer

West, Keen b.— d. (Me.) m. Lavina George   Pvt. U.S. Inf.
    daughter Persis m. Sanford C. Swan

West, Leonard b. N.C. 1760 d. Ky. 1842   Pvt. Ky. Mtd. Mil.
  m. Phoeby Morgan — son Amos S. m. Elizabeth Washburn

West, Lynn b. Va. 1775 d. Ky. 1836   Capt. Ky. Vol. Mil.
  m. Susan Jackson — son Lewis m. Sallie Mahoney

West, Robert b. Va. 1775 d. Ohio 1848   Capt. Ohio Mil.
  m. Henrietta Fairfax — daughter Catherine m. Christopher McVey

West, Samuel b. Conn. 1776 d. Conn. 1863   Capt. Conn. Mil.
  m. Rebecca Little — son Samuel F. m. Charlotte Porter

West, Thomas b. Tenn. 1792 d. Tenn. 1870   Pvt. Tenn. Mil.
  m. Rachel Oliphant — son Thomas Jr. m. Amanda Thomas

Westbrook, Joseph b. N.Y. 1775 d. Ohio 1846   Ord. Sgt. Ohio Mil.
  m. Elizabeth Wright — daughter Harriet A. m. Joseph Oursler

Westbrook, Wessel Brodhead b. N.Y. 1785 d. N.Y. 1864   Lt. N.Y. Mil.
  m. Rachael Hoornbeck — daughter Maria m. Augustus Krom

Westbrooke, Andrew Early Vol.   U.S. Army

Westcott, David b. Vt. 1797 d. N.Y. 1862 m. Betsey Avery   Cpl. N.Y. Mil.
  daughter Andeline m. Daniel Harwood

Westcott, John b. N.Y. 1776 d. N.Y. 1847 m. Hannah Tibbitts   Col. N.Y. Mil.
  son John G. m. Elizabeth Edick

Wester, Daniel b. N.C. 1786 d. Tenn. 1857   Pvt. Tenn. Mil.
  m. Elizabeth Lloyd — son John W. m. Catherine Allsion

Westervelt, Abraham m. Marion McKenzie Vol. 1
  daughter Julia R. m. Richard George Berford

Westervelt, Peter Vol. 15   Pvt. N.Y. Mil.

Westervelt, Ralph b. N.Y. 1786 d. N.Y. 1848 m. Maria   Pvt. N.Y. Art.
  daughter Sarah m. Abram J.

Westfall, Henry (Harvey) Vol. 12   Pvt. Ohio Mil.

Westfall, Jacob b. Penn. d. W.Va. or Ky. m. Judith Booth   Sheriff Lt. Va.
  son Zachariah m. Hannah Wolfe   1784-90

Westmoreland, Reuben b. Va. 1770 d. Ga. 1845   Pvt. Ga. Mil.
  m. Keziah Simmons — daughter Angelina m. William De G. Tidwell

Westmoreland, Robert b. Va. 1783 d. Ga. 1851   Pvt. Miss. Mil.
  m. Ann Louise Forman — daughter Miranda m. Thomas Matthews

Weston, Eli Jr. b. Mass. (Me.) 1781 d. Me. 1860   QtrMst. Sgt. Mass. Mil.
  m. Lois Stewart — daughter Caroline L. m. Charles Edwin Lord

Weston, Stephen b. Me. 1770 d. Me. 1847 m. Martha Grey   Pvt. Mass. Mil.
  daughter Martha m. Joseph B. Webb
  son Samuel m. Sarah Healy

Weston, William A. Vol. 9   Pvt. U.S. Inf.

Wetherbee, Asa b. Mass. 1783 d. N.Y. 1852   Pvt. N.Y. Mil.
  m. Nancy Herrick — son John m. Ruth Roberts

Wetherbee (Weatherby), Joshua b. N.H. 1789 d. Vt. 1861   Pvt. Vt. Mil.
  m. Anna Barnes — son Amos m. Mary Allen

Wetmore, Chester b. N.Y. 1794 d. Mich. 1871   Pvt. N.Y. Mil.
  m. Mary Dumont — son Albert D. m. Elizabeth Hudson

Wetmore, Samuel Vol. 15   Pvt. N.Y. Vol. Mil.

Wetmore, Seth b. Conn. 1761 d. N.Y. 1836 m. Lois Bronson   **Legis. N.Y.**
daughter Abigail m. Dan Beach.

Wetmore, William Chauncey b. N.J. 1798 d. N.J. 1848   Midshipman
m. Susan Oram — son Francis G. m. Julia E. Tommele   N.J. Navy

Wetzel (Winsell, Vinsell), Adam b. Penn. 1749 d. Tenn. 1827   Pvt. E. Tenn.
m. Mary Davis — daughter Susan m. Peter Wills

Wetzel, John b. Penn. 1776 d. Ill. 1854   Pvt. Penn. Lt. Inf.
m. Elizabeth Cornman — daughter Sarah m. John Pratz

Weymouth, John b. Me. 1771 d. Me. 1850 m. Charlotte Clark   Pvt. Me.
son Edmund m. Hannah Roberts

Whaley, David b. N.Y. 1794 d. N.Y. 1836 m. Polly Wickham   Pvt. N.Y. Mil.
son Kellar V. m. Louise Perdue

Whaley, Elijah b. Md. 1792 d. Mo. 1859   Pvt. Tenn. Mil.
m. Rebecca Dougherty — son Lemuel B. m. Martha Hash

Whaley, James b. Penn. 1789 d. Penn. 1869   Capt. Penn. Mil.
m. Jane Vance Moreland — daughter Jane V. m. John Foster Gray

Whaley, James Adolphus b. S.C. 1781 d. Ga. 1848   Pvt. S.C. Mil.
m. Nancy Lake — son John D. m. (2) Martha Alice Parrott

Whaling, Jacob b. Mass. 1791 d. Ohio 1860   Cpl. Mass. Mil.
m. Sarah Woods — daughter Sarah Ann m. Benjamin Rose Jr.

Wharton, Andrew b. Va. d. Ohio m. Anna Richey   Pvt. Ohio Mil.
daughter Helen W. m. John Neal Harrah
son John R. m. Sarah Cowen

Wheaton, William H. b. N.C. 1794 d. La. 1884   Sgt. N.C. Mil.
m. Anna Church — daughter Mary m. Joshua Johnson

Wheeler, Alvin b. Conn. 1790 d. Ind. 1886   Drum Maj. Ohio Mil.
m. Sara Willa — daughter Mary Ann m. Samuel Rice Smith

Wheeler, Amos b. Mass. 1775 d. Vt. bef. 1836   Pvt. Vt. Mil.
m. Lydia Adams — daughter Arvilla m. Horace Bancroft

Wheeler, Asahel b. Mass. 1741 d. Mass. 1812   Constable, Selectman
m. Jerusha Haynes   Mass. 1786-93
daughter Ruth m. Israel Hunt

Wheeler, Barzilla b. N.H. 1792 d. Mich. 1878   Sgt. U.S. Inf.
m. Clarina Williams — daughter Lucy Ann m. Caleb Way Bailey

Wheeler, Charles b. Penn. 1791 d. Ill. ca. 1865   Pvt. Penn.
m. Hester DeFord — son Jacob m. Anville Footer

Wheeler, Cornelius b. Conn. d. Canada 1814   Pvt. U.S. Inf.
m. Abigail Oliver — son Joseph m. Mary Stevens Ames

Wheeler, Ebenezer b. Mass. 1790 d. N.Y. 1862   Teamster Vt. Mil.
m. Hannah Hills
daughter Mary m. Joseph Swift Williams REAL DAUGHTER

Wheeler, Ebenezer b. Conn. 1770 d. N.Y. 1814   Maj. N.Y. Mil.
m. Harriett B. Foster — daughter Hannah m. George Samuel Young

Wheeler, Eli b. Conn. 1770 d. N.Y. 1847 m. Crisel Wheeler   Ens. N.Y. Mil.
daughter Eunice m. Benjamin Crabtree

Wheeler, George Arnold Vol. 13   Maj. N.Y. Mil.

Wheeler, James b. Vt. 1786 d. (Vt.) N.Y. 1867   Sgt. Vt. Mil.
   m. Betsey Reed — daughter Cynthia m. William Edward Bailey

Wheeler, James Vol. 16   Sgt. N.Y. Mil.

Wheeler, John Vol. 12   Pvt. Penn. Mil.

Wheeler, Nathaniel b. Va. 1769 d. W.Va.   Pvt. Va. Mil.
   m. Averilla Gorsuch — son Nimrod B. m. Kittie Wheeler

Wheeler, Nicholas b. Md. 1784 d. Ohio 1845   Pvt. Ohio Mil.
   m. Druscilla Johnston — son Ezekiel m. Nancy Roberts

Wheeler, Nimrod Bates b. Va. 1795 d. Ark. 1853   Pvt. E. Tenn. Vol. Mil.
   m. Catherine Wheeler — daughter Jane O. m. William Addison Camp

Wheeler, Perez Vol. 17   Sgt. Conn. Mil.

Wheeler, Reuben Vol. 16   Pvt. Conn. Mil.

Wheeler, Shepard III b. Conn. 1781 d. Mich. 1846   Pvt. Conn. Mil.
   m. Phoebe Jordan — son Shepard IV m. Charlotte Temple Barton

Wheeler, Silas b. Mass. 1752 d. N.Y. 1828 m. Sarah Gardner   Pvt. N.Y. Mil.
   daughter Sarah m. William Holmes

Wheeler, Simeon b. Mass. 1783 d. N.Y. 1859   Pvt. Mass. Mil.
   m. Orpha Pierce — daughter Emily W. m. Thomas Padden

Wheeler, Thomas b. Md. 1766 d. Md. 1827   Pvt. Md. Mil.
   m. Alice (Kingsley) Blackburn
   son Thomas Jr. m. Roseanne E. Harrison

Wheeler, William Vol. 16   Capt. Mass. (Me.) Mil.

Wheelock, Eleazer b. Mass. 1749-50 d. Mass. 1831   Capt. Mass. Mil.
   m. Huldah Woodward — son Humphrey m. Sophia Lesure

Wheelock, Eleazer Louis Ripley b. N.H. 1793 d. Ill. 1847   Ens. U.S. Inf.
   m. Mary Prickett — son George R. m. Mary Ann Slauter

Wheelock, Simeon b. Mass. 1741 d. Mass. 1786   Lt. Mass. Mil.
   m. Deborah Thayer — daughter Hannah m. Abner Plimpton Jr.

Wherritt, George b. Md. d. Md. 1844 m. Barbara Grush   Capt. Md. Mil.
   son George Jr. m. Margaret Fischer

Whetstone, Henry b. Penn. 1751 d. Penn. 1816   Lt. Penn. Mil.
   m. Hannah Roof — son Samuel m. Delilah Koontz

Whigham, Thomas b. Penn. 1779 d. Penn. 1858   Pvt. Penn. Mil.
   m. Sarah McKee — son William m. Mary Ann Shields

Whipple, John b. Mass. 1790 d. Ohio 1859   Pvt. Mass. Mil.
   m. Catherine Carroll — son Ambrose m. Elizabeth Freeman
   son George m. Elizabeth Eversole
   son James m. Jeanette Freeman
   daughter Maria C. m. Hiram King Dickey

Whipple, Nathaniel Vol. 17   Pvt. N.Y. Mil.

Whipple, Roswell b. N.Y. 1794 d. Ohio 1862   Pvt. N.Y. Mil.
   m. Hannah Weeks
   daughter Jennie m. Irven Travis REAL DAUGHTER

Whipple, Russell b. N.Y. 1782 d. Ill. 1859   Adj. N.Y. Mil.
   m. (1) Laura Kellogg — daughter Marie E. m. John Lush Wilson

Whips, Benjamin b. Md. 1759 d. Md. 1831 m. Susanna   Pvt. Md. Mil.
daughter Susanna m. John Berkey

Whistler, John b. Ire. 1756 d. Mo. 1829 m.— Bishop   Capt. U.S. Army
son William m. Julia Fearson   1797-1815

Whistler, William b. Md. 1780 d. Ohio 1863 m. Julia Fearson   Ohio Mil.
daughter Caroline F. m. William Bloodgood

Whitaker (Whitacre), James II b. Penn. 1790 d. Penn. 1868   Qtrmst.
m. Nancy Gilson   Penn. Cav.
son Aaron II m. Susanna Collins Andrews

Whitaker, John b. N.C. d. Tenn. m. Miss Wilcox   Pvt. W. Tenn. Mil.
son John J. m. Sallie Hammond

Whitaker, Oreen Datus b. Ga. 1791 d. Ga. 1824   Pvt. Ga. Mil.
m. Martha Rivers Harris
daughter Ann H. m. George Hendree Winston

Whitcomb, Asa b. N.H. 1793 d. N.H. 1869 m. Olive Vickery   Pvt. N.H. Mil.
daughter Julia Ann m. J. Harvey Huntley

Whitcomb, Jonathan Priest b. Mass. 1739 d. N.H. 1792   Town Treasurer
m. Dorothy Carter   N.H. 1784-7
son Ephraim m. Charlotte Chamberlain (2)

Whitcomb, Philemon b. Mass. 1748 d. N.H. 1824   Maj. Gen. N.H. Mil. 1810
m. Martha Sawyer — daughter Martha m. Joel Foster

White, Aaron Vol. 17   Capt. N.Y. Vol. Mil.

White, Asa b. Conn. 1791 d. Conn. 1855   Pvt. Penn. Mil.
m. Eunice Scoville — son Edward E. m. Charlotte Anne Wells

White, Benjamin b. N.C. 1736 d. N.C. bef. 1789   Memb. Commission 1784
m. Anna Rachel — daughter Nancy m. Josiah Allen

White, Benjamin Vol. 15   Sgt. Del. Mil.

White, Benjamin b. Va. 1756 d. Ala. 1830   Pvt. E. Tenn. Vol.
m. Martha Jobe — daughter Phoebe m. David Nelson

White, Caleb B. b. Md. 1788 d. Md. 1849   Pvt. 1813 Md.
m. Eliza A. W. Cruse — son George Francis m. Louisa Brewer

White, Calvin b. Mass. 1783 d. Vt. 1818 m. Laura Stanton   Lt. Vt. Mil.
son Calvin Jr. m. Charlotte Tarbell

White, David Vol. 12   Sgt. Penn. Mil.

White, David b. Ky. 1793 d. Ky. 1845 m. Mary Denny   Pvt. Ky. Mil.
son Granville m. Evelyn B. Smith

White, Drury (Drewry) b. Ky. 1799 d. Ark. 1883   Pvt. Miss. Terr. Mil.
m. Jane Rutherford
daughter Frances m. Randolph Brunson REAL DAUGHTER
son Sterling H. m. Mary Rice

White, Ebenezer b. N.Y. 1763 d. N.Y. 1814   Pvt. U.S. Inf.
m. Susanna Franklin — daughter Lucinda m. Job Barton

White, Elijah b. Mass. 1778 d. Mass. 1856 m. Lucy Pierce   Pvt. Conn.
son Josiah m. Hannah Cushing

White, Eppie b. Ga. 1791 d. Ga. 1854   Cpl. Ga. Mil.
m. Catherine Herndon — daughter Mildred E. m. James W. Jones

White, Hiram Montgomery b. Va. 1797 d. Ia. 1882   Pvt. Ohio Mil.
  m. (2) Mary A. Redford
  daughter Elizabeth J. m. Clarence A. Whitney REAL DAUGHTER

White, Hugh b. Penn. 1737 d. Penn. 1822   Col. Penn. Mil.
  m. Margaret Allison — daughter William m. Hannah Jackson

Whitcomb, Samuel Jr. b. Mass 1792 d. Vt.   Pvt. U.S. Inf.
  m. Mary Simonds Mullet — son William W. m. Mary Hyde

White, Ira Allen b. N.Y. 1796 d. Canada 1887   Pvt. U.S. Inf. N.Y.
  m. Elizabeth Reesor — daughter Harriett N. m. Hugh Powell Crosby

White, James b. 1790 d. Ga. 1870 m. Hannah Huey   Pvt. Ga. Mil.
  son Joseph m. Harriet Golson

White, James b. N.C. 1747 d. Tenn. 1821 m. Mary Lawson   Tenn. 1785
  son Hugh L. m. Elizabeth Carrick

White, James b. Md. 1788 d. Md. 1857   Pvt. Md. Mil.
  m. Elizabeth Adams Sefton — son James R. m. Mary Jane Thomas
  son John H. m. Mary C. Deale

White, James b. N.C. 1758 d. Tenn. 1840 m. Mary Garner   Brig. Gen.
  son Craig m. Sally Lane   E. Tenn. Mil.

White, John b. Penn. 1773 d. Penn. 1838   Pvt. Penn. Mil.
  m. Elizabeth Pomeroy — daughter Mary m. J. Harvey Allen

White, John b. N.Y. 1795 d. N.Y. 1876 m. Polly Ann Conn   Pvt. N.Y. Mil.
  daughter Lydia Ann m. Milton Hazelton

White, John b. Penn. 1759 d. Penn. 1832   Capt. Penn. Mil.
  m. Mary Patton — son Samuel m. Isabella Hanna

White, John b. Mass. (Me.) 1776 d. Me. 1862   Capt. Mass. Mil.
  m. Elizabeth Thorne — daughter Sarah T. m. Samuel Whitmore

White, John Robins b. Va. 1792 d. Va. 1820 m. Lydia Wilson   Sgt. Va. Mil.
  daughter Eliza Ann m. George Douglas Happer

White, Josiah Vol. 14   Pvt. U.S. Inf.

White, Maunsel Sr. b. Ire. 1783 d. La. 1863   Capt. 1812
  m. (2) Heloise de la Ronde   La. Blues
  son Maunsel Jr. m. Bettie Bradford

White, Pelatiah b. Mass. 1769 d. Ohio 1832   Lt. Ohio Mil.
  m. Susanna Wells — son Thomas H. m. Susanna Wood

White, Peter Sr. b. N.Y. 1766 d. Ohio 1859 m. Nancy Allen   Pvt. N.Y. Mil.
  son Peter Jr. m. Martilla Hart

White, Robert Irvine b. Ire. 1775 d. Va. 1851   Lt. Va. Mil.
  m. Margaret Johnston
  son Zachariah J. m. (2) Eliza Jane Williams

White, Samuel b. Mass. 1781 d. Mass. 1821 m. Mary Williams   Capt. Mass.
  son Charles m. Sarah French

White, Thomas b. Md. 1763 d. Ill. 1843 m. Sarah Small   Pat. Ohio
  son Thomas Jr. m. Mary Hicks   Commissioner

White, Walter b. R.I. d. 1832 m. Sophia Brown   Legis. R.I. 1784-1814
  daughter Mary m. Clark Hiscox Jr.

White, William Sr. b. Va. 1720 d. Va. 1820 m. Ann   Assem. Va. 1785-6
  son Moses m. Sarah Elizabeth Poindexter

White, William b. N.J. 1751 d. N.J. 1836 m. Ann Paul   Pvt. N.J. Mil. 1787
    daughter Ann m. William Haines

White, William b. Va. 1783 d. Tenn. 1833   Maj. Gen. Tenn. Mil.
    m. Eliza Carolina Wharton — son George W. m. Margaret Louise Word

White, Zachariah b. N.C. 1794 d. Ala. 1866   Pvt. Ga. Mil.
    m. Elizabeth Blackwood — daughter Sarah Jane m. William Thaxton

Whitefield, Needham b. N.C. 1758 d. N.C. 1812   Pat. Mem. House
    m. Lucy Hatch   Commons Senator 1783-1803 N.C.
    daughter Rachel m. John Thomas Bryan

Whitehead, John G. b. Va. 1780 d. Ky. 1862   Capt. Ky. Mil. 1806
    m. Elizabeth Macklin — daughter Polly m. George C. Butts

Whitehill, Robert b. Penn. 1738 d. Penn. 1813   Penn. Senate
    m. Eleanor Reed   Congress 1784-1813
    daughter Rachel m. Alexander McBeth

Whitehurst, John Sheridan b. 1783 d. 1878   Pvt. Ga. Mil.
    m. Mary Collins and Mary Griffin
    son George Willard m. Mary Etta Edwards

Whitehurst, Nehemiah b. Va. 1790 d. Va. 1848   Pvt. Va. Mil.
    m. Annis Williamson — son Nehemiah J. m. Nannie Davenport

Whitehurst, William b. Va. d. Va. 1857   Lt. Va. Mil.
    m. Ann (Nancy) Simmons — son William W. m. Annis J. Lambert

Whiteman, Wendell b. 1761 d. Penn. 1834 m. Susanna   Pvt. Penn. Mil.
    son Benjamin m. Ella Sheppard

Whiteside, Abraham b. Penn. d. Penn. 1797 m. Rebeckah   Justice Penn.
    son Thomas m. Mary Jenkins   1786-93

Whiteside, James A. b. 1782 d. Ill. 1848   Capt. Ill. Mil.
    m. Margaret Penny — son William m. Rachel Anderson

Whitewright, William b. Scot. 1783 d. N.Y. 1874   Pvt. N.Y. Mil.
    m. Susannah Jones — daughter Elizabeth m. James Stuart

Whiting, Elisha b. Conn. 1785 d. Ia. 1848 m. Sally Hulet   Cpl. Mass. Mil.
    son Chauncey m. Editha Ann Morley

Whiting, Henry b. D.C. 1788 d. Mo. 1851   Lt. U.S. Inf.
    m. Orpha Danforth — son William D. m. Eliza Macomb

Whiting, Horatio Vol. 10   Pvt. Mass. Mil.

Whiting, Kimball b. Mass. 1784 d. Mass. 1851   Pvt. Mass. Mil.
    m. Desire Jordan — son George W. B. m. Ann Eliza Smith

Whiting, Mason b. Mass. 1774 d. N.Y. 1849   Capt. N.Y. Mil.
    m. Mary Edwards — daughter Catherine S. m. Uriah Morris Stowers

Whiting, Samuel b. Conn. 1783 d. N.Y. 1851   Pvt. N.Y. Mil.
    m. Zilpha Mather — son Nelson T. m. Polly Bailey

Whiting, William b. Conn. 1730 d. Mass. 1792   Justice Mass. 1781-7
    m. Anna Mason — son Mason m. Mary Edwards

Whitledge, Lyna b Va. 1780 d. Mo. 1849   Pvt. Ky. Vol.
    m. Mehetabel Mabry — son Thomas B. m. Christiana Jacoby

Whitlock, John Burr b. Conn. 1786 d. N.Y. 1863   Lt. N.Y. Mil.
    m. Rachel Olmsted — son Warren m. Amanda Reynolds

Whitlock, William b. N.C. or S.C. d. Tex. 1835   Pvt. La. Mil.
  m. Mary White — son Bernard m. (2) Ida Heiser

Whitman, Matthew b. Va. 1761 d. W.Va. 1836   Capt. 1800 Sheriff
  m. Katherine Carleck   Rep. 1804 Va.
  daughter Cathleen m. Levi Ward

Whitman, Zachariah b. Mass. 1747 d. Mass. 1806   Surveyor of Highways
  m. Abigail Wood   Mass. 1787
  daughter Charlotte m. William Rice Jr.

Whitmer, Peter b. Penn. 1760 d. Ohio 1835   Ens. Penn. Mil.
  m. Mary Magdalene Overmeyer
  daughter Mary Magdalene m. Peter King

Whitmire, Moses b.—d. m. Elizabeth Evans   Pvt. S.C. Vol.
  daughter Charity Ann m. Thomas Lawson Cofer

Whitmore, George b.— d. 1850 m. Rachel Wright   Pvt. Va. Mil.
  son Samuel Paxton m. Phoebe Elizab. Beach

Whitmore, Nathaniel b. Vt. 1753 d. Penn. 1860 m.—   Pvt. N.Y. Mil.
  daughter Clarissie A. m. Charles F. Barnett

Whitney, Benjamin b. Vt. 1777 d. Vt. 1843   Pvt. Vt. Mil.
  m. Mary Emmons — son Silas P. m. Marry O. Warren (Filkins)

Whitney, Dailing b. Conn. 1758 d. N.Y. 1834   Maj. N.Y. Mil.
  m. Sarah Valentine — daughter Esther m. Israel Youngs

Whitney, Elisha b. Va. 1755 d. Va. 1822 m. Nancy   Pvt. Va. Mil.
  son Elisha Jr. m.—

Whitney Israel b. 1781 d. 1858 m. Lucy Mabon   Lt. Mass. Mil.
  daughter Sarah m. Daniel Goddard

Whitney, Job b. Vt. 1791 d. N.Y. 1850 m. Sylvia Delano   Pvt. N.Y. Mil.
  son Egbert D. m. Ann Safford

Whitney, Jonathan b. Norway 1774 d. Ohio 1846   Pvt. Ohio Mil.
  m. Mary Gates — daughter Sallie m. Franklin Carel

Whitney, Joshua b. Conn. 1773 d. Conn. 1845   Pvt. Conn. Mil.
  m. Rhoda Jewell — son Franklin m. Julia Spalding

Whitney, Lemuel b. 1779 d. aft. 1813   Cpl. Ohio Mil.
  m. Ellen (Kimball) Durant — son Elijah K. m. Julana F. Jones

Whitney, Moses b. Mass. 1772 d. Mass. 1816 m. Lydia Allen   Pat. N.Y.
  daughter Thirza A. m. Albert Elmore

Whitney, Noah Ashley b. Conn. 1770 d. Ohio 1834   Capt. Mass. Mil.
  m. (1) Olive Dorwin
  daughter Harriet m. Sanford Langworthy Collins

Whitney, Parkhurst Vol. 6   Capt. N.Y. Mil.

Whitney, Samuel Platte b. Conn. 1775 d. Ohio 1871   Pvt. Mass. Lt. Inf.
  m. Lois Buttles — son John V. m. Mrs. Mary Lansing Graves

Whiton, Joseph b. Conn. 1760 d. Mass. 1828   Maj. Gen. Mass. Mil.
  m. Amanda Garfield — daughter Eliza m. Hiram Guthery Daniel

Whiton (Whiting), Israel b. Mass. 1758 d. Mass. 1840   Pvt. Mass. Mil.
  m. Hannah Stowall — son Kimball m. Desire Jordan

Whitsell, William b. Penn. 1752 d. Penn. 1840   Ens. Paymst. Ky. Vol.
  m. Hadessa Crawford — son Ralph C. m. Rachel Estep

Whitsett, John b. Va. 1765 d. Ky. 1845   Pvt. Ind. Terr. Mil.
     m. Lucy Ramsey — son William m. Elizabeth Whitsett

Whitridge, Joshua Barker b. R.I. 1789 d. S.C. 1865   Surgeon's Mate
     m. Sarah Bailey McLeod   U.S. Army
     daughter Electra m. Osmond Bailey

Whitsett, Absalom Sr. b. N.C. d. Ala. 1814   Cpl. W. Tenn. Mil.
     m. Elizabeth Kidd — son Absalom Jr. m. Mary C. V. E. Johnson

Whittelsey, Roger Newton b. Conn. 1754 d. Conn. 1835   Justice Conn. 1784
     m. Ann Woodruff — son Jabez m. Nancy Parker

Whittemore, John Vol. 3   Pvt. Mass. Mil.

Whittemore, Nathan b. N.H. 1778 d. Me. 1858   Pvt. Mass. Mil.
     m. Sally Lewis — son James B. m. Hannah Littlefield

Whitten, William b. Ky. 1797 d. Ind. 1881   Pvt. Ky. Mil.
     m. Rebecca Woolen — daughter Mary m. William H. Larkin

Whittier, Edmund b. Mass. 1787 d. Vt. 1872   Pvt. N.H. Mil.
     m. Abigail Moody — son John James m. Maryann Fox

Whittier, Nathaniel b. Mass. (Me.) 1783 d. Me. 1869   Capt. Mass. (Me.) Mil.
     m. Nancy Merrill — son Sewall C. m. Hanah Beede

Whittington, Azariah b. Md. 1794 d. Ill. 1855   Pvt. W. Tenn. Mil.
     m. Elizabeth Lacey — son John Wesley m. Elizabeth Poiner
     daughter Sarah m. Zechariah Dillon
     son William C. m. Lucinda Moore

Whorton, Abraham b. S.C. 1789 d. Ala. 1868   Pvt. Ga. Mil.
     m. Lydia Bridges — daughter Minerva m. Mortimer Black

Wiatt, Solomon b. Del. 1779 d. N.J. 1865 m. Sarah Needles   Preacher Penn.
     son Stephen N. m. Mary Martin

Wickes, Bernard b. Fla. 1788 d. Fla. 1817   Pvt. Fla. Urban Mil.
     m. Mary Ann Kunen — daughter Eliza m. Phillip Weidman

Wickes, Oliver b. R.I. 1757 d. R.I. 1855   Ens. R.I. Mil.
     m. Abigail Greene — daughter Abigail m. William Case Sands

Wickham John b. Ohio 1787 d. Ohio 1863   Pvt. Ohio Mil.
     m. Clarinda Culver — son Warren m. Harriett A. James

Wickham, William b. R.I. 1778 d. N.Y. 1875   Capt. N.Y. Navy
     m. Catherine Christian
     daughter Elizabeth W. m. Aldan Sprague Baker

Wickliffe, Charles Anderson b. Ky. 1788 d. Md. 1869   Mil. Aide Ky. Mil.
     m. Margaret Crepps
     son Robert Charles m. Mrs. Annie Davis Anderson

Widener, Jacob b. N.J. 1780 d. N.Y. 1873   Pvt. N.Y. Mil.
     m. Margaret Griswold — daughter Mehitabel m. William Stottle

Wigg, William Hazzard b.—d. S.C. 1808 m.—   Commissioner S.C.
     daughter Mary H. m. Edward Barnwell

Wright, James Vol. 6   Pvt. Ky. Vol.

Wightman, John Thomas b. S.C. 1784 d. S.C. 1875   Sgt. S.C. Mil.
     m. Eliza Stoll — daughter Martha H. m. Francis Pelmoin

Wiglesworth Claiborne b. Va. d. Va.   Capt. Va. Mil.
   m. Lavinia Ward Farish
   daughter Mary C. m. William N. Thompson Jr.
   daughter Virginia W. m. William N. Thompson

Wigton, Christopher b. Penn. 1777 d. Penn. 1864   Capt. Penn. Mil.
   m. Margaret Hines — daughter Mary Ann m. Joseph Dysart
   son Richard B. m. Eleanor Hamill

Wikoff, James b. Ohio 1782 d. Ohio 1818   Sgt. Ohio Mil.
   m. Rachel Ellis — daughter Elizabeth E. m. John M. Melvin

Wikoff, Peter b. N.Y. 1745 d. Ohio 1819 m. Sarah Beekman   Capt. Ohio Mil.
   Vol. 25

Wilbraham, Thomas b. Penn. 1750 d. Penn. 1798   Pvt. Penn. Mil.
   m. Margaret Dismant — daughter Elizabeth m. Barnabas Baer

Wilbur, Jesse Jr. b. R.I. 1789 d. R.I. 1881   Lt. R.I. Troops
   m. Abigail Gardiner — son Jesse Jr. m. Thankful Barber

Wilbur, William b. Vt. 1780 d. N.Y. 1854   Pvt. N.Y. Mil.
   m. Roxsa Tupper — daughter Harriet m. Orin Hughitt

Wilcher, Jeremiah b. Va. 1760 d. Ga. 1829-30 m. Jane   Juror Ga. 1798
   son Jordan m. Elizabeth

Wilcher, Josiah b. Ky. 1795 d. Ill m. Sarah Medows   Pvt. Ky. Mil.
   daughter Rebecca A. m. William H. Lockwood REAL DAUGHTER

Wilcox, Borden b. N.Y. 1798 d. Ill. 1837 m. Almira Kellogg   Pvt. N.Y. Mil.
   son Seymour m. Julia F. Maclin

Wilcox, Daniel b. R.I. 1764 d. Vt. 1828 m. Eunice Barnes   Capt. Vt. Mil.
   son John F. m. Lucretia Gordon

Wilcox, Daniel b. Md. 1785 d. Md. aft. 1827   Pvt. Md. Mil.
   m. Sarah Hollingsworth
   daughter Rachel Emily m. Joseph James French

Wilcox, Enoch b. Conn. 1792 d. Conn. 1884 m.   Pvt. Conn. Mil.
   daughter Julia m. Isaac Hough

Wilcox, Ezra Erin b. Conn. 1789 d. N.Y. 1872   Corp. N.Y. Mil. 1812
   m. Sarah Davis — son Chas. Wm. m. Mary P. Wilcox

Wilcox, George b. N.C. 1764 d. Mo. 1818   Lt. Col. Ky. Mil.
   m. Elizabeth Pinchbeck — son Lazarus m. Lucy Helm

Wilcox, Harry b. Mass. 1798 d. N.Y. 1880   Drum. N.Y. Mil.
   m. Harriett Olcott
   daughter Harriet m. William Maynard REAL DAUGHTER
   son Homer m. Natilda Griswold Corbier
   son Marcus m. Esther Doolittle

Wilcox, Hazard b. Conn. 1787 d. Conn. 1874   Pvt. Conn. Mil.
   m. Mary Wright — son Asa m. Nancy Allen

Wilcox, John Vol. 7   Pvt. Vt. Mil.

Wilcox, John Flavel b. Conn. 1775 d. Ohio 1860   Pvt. Conn. Mil.
   m. Johannah — daughter Mary m. Henry G. Waters

Wilcox, Nelson b. N.Y. 1800 d. Ill. 1876   Pvt. Drum N.Y. Mil.
   m. (2) Emaline Wescott
   daughter Emma R. m. Henman A. Brede REAL DAUGHTER

Wilcoxson, William b. Ky. 1790 d. Ky. 1874 m. Catherine   Pvt. Ky. Mil.
   daughter Nancy m. John Walker Dearing

Wilder, Artemas b. Mass. 1796 d. Mich. 1866   Pvt. N.Y. Mil.
m. Fannie Cooley — daughter Deborah m. Stimpson G. Harvey

Wilder, Ephraim Vol. 17   Pvt. Mass. Mil.

Wilderman, Dorsey b. Md. 1792 d. Ill. 1857   Pvt. Ill. Terr. Rangers
m. Phoebe Carr — son Francis A. m. Martha Pitt

Wile, Conrad b. Penn. 1794 d. Penn. 1814   Pvt. Penn. Mil.
m. Elizabeth R. — son Conrad Jr. m. Henrietta May

Wiles, Christian b. 1760 d. Ohio 1837 m. Catherine Mere   Pvt. Ohio Mil.
son Peter M. m. Martha Henry

Wiley, Eli. b. Penn. 1773 d. Ky. 1858 m. Elizabeth Seal   Pvt. Ky. Mil.
son James m. Rebecca Parker
son Adin m. Jane Wiley

Wiley, Evan Shelby b. N.C. 1783 d. Ala. 1825   Capt. N.C. Mil.
m. Mary McCaleb — son James M. m. Elizabeth Duckworth

Wiley, James b. Vt. c. 1750 d. N.Y. Killed at Plattsburg   Col. Vt. Mil.
son Joseph m. Sarah Vanocker

Wiley, John b. Penn. 1732 d. Ky m. Vernon   Pvt. Ky. Vol. Mil.
son Eli m. Elizabeth Seal

Wiley, Samuel b. Ala. 1792 d. Ala. 1878   Pvt. Tenn. Mil.
m. Margaret Shields — daughter Lauretta m. John W. Williams

Wiley, William b. N.C. 1762 d. Ind. 1838   Sgt. N.C. Mil.
m. Ann Shannon — son Abner m. Sarah Jane Shannon

Wilford, Jeremiah b. Conn. 1782 d. Penn. 1860   Sgt. N.Y. Mil.
m. Clarissa Waldo — daughter Sophronia m. Alonza Drake

Wilhelm, Jacob b. Ger. 1739 d. Penn. 1795   Capt. Penn. Mil.
m. Mary Elizabeth Haverstick
daughter Ann Catherine m. Martin Foltz

Wilkerson, Nicholas b. Va. 1782 d. Va. 1813   Sgt. Va. Mil.
m. Linnette Dewitt — daughter Cynthia m. James F. Watson

Wilkerson, Owen b. Va. d. Ky. m. Katherine   Pvt. Va. Mil.
daughter Elizabeth A. m. Jesse G. Sweeney

Wilkes, George Vol. 3   Pvt. N.Y. Mil. 1813

Wilkes, Henry Shoonmaker b. N.Y. 1791 d. N.Y. 1864   Cpl. N.Y. Mil.
m. Eveline Hilman — daughter Charlotte Ann m. Henry Wiltsie
son Henry m. Lydia Callanan
daughter Martha E. m. Charles A. McCullouch REAL DAUGHTER
daughter Sarah Jane S. m. Andrew Jackson Pasenger REAL DAU.

Wilkie, George b. N.Y. 1799 d. N.Y. 1883 m. Sally Wilson   Pvt. N.Y. Mil.
son Hiram m. Charlotte M. Brognard

Wilkin, Abraham b. N.Y. 1790 d. N.Y. 1863   Lt. N.Y. Mil.
m. Hannah M. Mills — daughter Ella Louise m. Adelbert M. Phillips

Wilkins, John b. Va. 1794 d. Ind. 1868 m. Eleanor Brouse   Pvt. Ohio Mil.
daughter Elizabeth Jane m. William Leviston Heiskell REAL DAU.
son John A. m. Lavinia King

Wilkins, Richard Vol. 3   Pvt. Vt. Mil.

Wilkinson, James b. Penn. d. Md. 1842   Seaman U.S. Navy
m. Ann Haney Eskridge
daughter Fannie V. m. William M. Abbott REAL DAUGHTER

Wilkinson, Joseph Biddle b. 1785 d. 1865   Pvt. Miss. Mil. 1814
m. Catherine Andrews — daughter Julia m. Dr. Frederick Egan

Wilkinson, Samuel b. Md. 1794 d. Md. 1868   Pvt. Md. Mil.
m. Susannah Clark — son Thomas C. m. Emma Virginis Bonn

Wilkinson, William b. 1793 d. 1843 m. Temperance Jackson Pvt. Miss. Mil.
son Micajah m. Jane Stokes

Willard, Charles b. Conn. 1785 d. N.Y. 1862   Ens. N.Y. Mil.
m. Mehitabel Bullard — son Charles W. m. Teresa Ann Turtelot

Willauer, John b. Penn. 1792 d. Penn. 1880 m. Barbara   Pvt. Penn. Mil.
daughter Eleanore m. William Berrett

Willcox, Thomas b. N.C. 1781 d. Ga. 1840   2nd Sgt. Ga. Mil.
m. Winifred Talley — son John m. Elizabeth Simmons

Willcoxon, Rezin b. Va. 1751 d. Va. 1855   Capt. Va. Mil.
m. Elizabeth DeNeale — daughter Jane m. John Hooe Sweeny

Willett, Samuel b. N.H. 1763 d. N.J. 1830   Pat. N.J. 1811
m. Elizabeth Sperling — daughter Mary m. Samuel Martin

Willets, Elijah Vol. 15   Pvt. Mich. Mil.

Willey, Isaac Vol. 11   Pvt. U.S. Inf.

Willhoite, Joshua b. Ind. Terr. d. Ill. 1855   Pvt. Ky. Mil.
m. Mary Sparkes — son Alexander m. Sarah Gossett

Williams, Burwell b. N.C. 1735 d. N.C. 1816 m.—   Pvt. N.C. Mil.
daughter Sarah m. Frederick Williams Ragland

Williams, Charles b. Penn. 1791 d. Penn. 1873   Pvt. U.S. Inf.
m. Elizabeth Chipps — daughter Lydia m. Mahlon Fell

Williams, Colmore b. Md. 1787 d. Md. 1857   3rd Lt. & Qtrmst. Md. Mil.
m. Mariel Howard — daughter Rebecca m. Alexander E. Soper

Williams, Cornelius b. Conn. 1750 d. Mass. 1821   Pvt. Mass. Mil.
m. Sarah Kellogg — daughter Amanda P. m. Lorenzo Hatch Rice

Williams, Crawford b. Va. d. Ky. 1852 m. Nancy Wisdom   Soldier Va. Mil.
son James m. Nancy Poss

Williams, Daniel b.—d. Ia. 1846 m. Mary Kimberlin   Pvt. Ind. Terr. Mil.
daughter Ruth m. Elisha Salladay

Williams, Daniel b. Conn. 1771 d. Mich. 1860   Capt. N.Y. Mil.
m. Vina Hovey — son Xury m. Polly Root

Williams, David Rogerson b. S.C. 1776 d. S.C. 1830 Brig. Gen. S.C. 1814-16
m. Sarah Power — son John Nicholas m. Esther Serena Chesnut

Williams, David b. S.C. 1772 d. S.C. 1830 m. Elizabeth Reeves Pvt. S.C. Mil.
son Uriah m. Esther Hilson

Williams, Edmund b. Wales d. N.C. 1795 m. Lucretia Adams   Sheriff 1789
son Archibald m. Rhoda Taylor

Williams, Elisha b. Ky. 1786 d. Ky. 1876 m. Lucinda McGrath Pvt. Ky. Vol.
son Merrill M. m. Lucy Lightfoot

Williams, Elisha b. Mass. 1791 d. N.Y. 1860 m. Lucy Hatch   Pvt. N.Y. Art.
daughter Rebecca m. Richard Reynolds

Williams, Ethelred b. Va. 1792 c.   Pvt. Tenn. Mil.
  m. Frances Amelia Martin — son William T. m. Elizabeth T. Brown

Williams, George b. N.Y. 1793 d. N.Y. 1874   Aid de Camp N.Y. Troops
  m. Alma Devoe — daughter Julia G. m. Willis Hall Fuller

Williams, George W. b. Va. or Md. 1777 d. Ohio 1830   Capt. Ohio Mil.
  m. Rebecca Weatherington — son George W. Jr. m. Laura Ann Moore

Williams, Gideon Glenn b. Ala. 1787 d. Tex. 1860   Sgt. Maj. Tenn. Mil.
  m. Mary Lane — son Nathan L. m. Lucy M. Williamson

Williams, Hector Crawford b. Va. d. Ky. 1852 m. Nancy   Capt. Va. Mil.
  son James m. Nancy Paso

Williams, Henry b. N.C. 1769 d. N.C. 1853   Capt. N.C. Mil.
  m. Nancy Herring — son Herring m. Nancy Ashcraft

Williams, Henry Guston b. N.C. 1775 d. N.C. 1857   Material Aid N.C. 1814
  m. Lucy Tunstall — son John B. m. Temperance Hilliard

Williams, Hezekiah b. La. 1788 d. Tex. m. Nancy Reams   Pvt. La. Mil.
  son Hezekiah R. m. Lydia Stevenson

Williams, Humphrey b. Md. ca. 1770 d. Md. bef. 1820   Lt. Md. Mil.
  m. Sarah Beall — son Dennis m. Margaret Hall

Williams, James Jr. b. Penn. or Md. 1778 d Ohio 1873   Justice Ohio
  m. Sarah Brower (Brewer)   1809-1812
  son Henry B. m. Jane Anderson

Williams, James b. Va. 1772 d. Ill. 1831   Pvt. Ky. Mtd. Mil.
  m. Hannah Mappin — son John m. Lydia Porter

Williams, James b. Va. d. Ga. 1794 m. Elizabeth Blackburn   Legis. Ga.
  daughter Elizabeth B. m. Waddy Thompson

Williams, James b. Va. 1765 d. Va. 1818 m. Anne Uncle   Pvt. Va. Vol.
  daughter Martha m. Peter Brunet

Williams, John b. Md. 1776 d. Ohio 1854 m. Mary Duncan   Capt. Ohio
  daughter Andesire m. Michael Earley

Williams, John b. N.C. 1782 d. Ga. 1839 m. Nancy Ross   Lt. Ga. Drag.
  son Reuben S. m. Mary Deborah Hill

Williams, John b. 1759 d. Ky. 1835 m. Judith King   Capt. Ky. Mtd. Mil.
  son John W. m. Nancy Lane

Williams, John b. Conn. 1789 d. Ohio 1865   Pvt. Ohio Mil.
  m. Sarah Walker — daughter Rachel m. Dr. John Cannon

Williams, John b. 1778 d. 1837 m. Melinda White   Col. U.S. Inf. 1813
  son John Jr. m. Rhoda Campbell Morgan

Williams, John Morgan b. 1790 d. 1866   Pvt. Va.
  m. Elizabeth A. Robinson — son Henry Clay m. Sally J. Jones

Williams, Jordan b. S.C. 1794 d. Ala. 1862 m. Edna Atkins   Pvt. U.S. Army
  daughter Sarah m. Robert P. Henry

Williams, Joseph b. N.C. 1786 d. Tenn. 1850   Pvt. N.C. Mil.
  m. Margaret Phillips — son Joseph P. m. Sarah Ann Pennington

Williams, Joseph Jr. b. N.C. 1775 d. N.C. 1840   Clerk of Superior Ct.
  m. Susan Taylor   N.C. 1812-14
  daughter Rebecca L. m. John Franklin Deaderick

Williams, Lawrence 1790 d. Ia. 1847 m. Mary McGaffick   Pvt. Ky. Mil.
son Alexander Lee m. Mary Ann Gorsuch

Williams, Lemuel b. Mass. 1751 d. Me. 1820   Civil Officer Mass. (Me.)
m. Anna Hilton — son William m. Amy Gray   1798/1803

Williams, Levi b. Va. 1777 d. Ia. 1858 m. Hannah Lemon   Pvt. Tenn. Mil.
son Heslip m. Chalotte Miskimen

Williams, Lewis Sr. b. Va. 1755 d. Va. 1836 m. Sally Oslin   Capt. Va. Mil.
son John m. Mary Pettus

Williams, Lewis b. Conn. 1780 d. Conn. 1842-3   Pvt. Conn. Mil.
m. Betsey Fisk — daughter Emma m. Gideon Morgan Hubbard

Williams, Lewis b. 1789 d. Mo. 1814 m. Elizabeth Hyatt   Pvt. Ky. Mil. Vol.
daughter Mary m. Lewis A. Herndon

Williams, Marmaduke b. N.C. 1774 d. Ala. 1850   Legis. N.C.
m. Agnes Payne Harris — daughter Mary Elizabeth m. James Guild

Williams, Martin Vol. 16   Pvt. Penn. Mil.

Williams, Nathaniel b. Mass. 1782 d. Md. 1864   Pvt. Md. Mil.
m. Maria Dalrymple — daughter Marie D. REAL DAUGHTER

Williams, Osborn b. Md. ca. 1752 d. Md. 1819   Brig. Gen. Md.
m. Elizabeth Magruder — son Theodore m. Caroline Gover

Williams, Philo b. Mass. 1796 d. Mass. 1856   Pvt. Mass. Mil.
m. Amittai Hart Blake — son Philo M. m. Mary H. Gilman

Williams, Robert b. N.C. 1758 d. N.C. 1840 m. E. Ellis   Legis. N.C.
daughter Elizabeth E. m. William S. Foreman
m. Fannie Randolph
daughter Harriet m. James May

Williams, Robert O. b. N.C. 1773 d. La. 1851   Gen. N.C. Inf., Governor
m. Rebecca Jane Smith — son Lanier W. m. Caroline Bolton   N.C.

Williams, Samuel b. Md. 1770 d. Mo. 1821   Lt. Md. Mil.
m. Elizabeth Threlkeld — daughter Jane T. m. Rev. John Davis

Williams, Samuel b. Mass. (Me.) 1785 d. Mass. 1837   Pvt. Mass. (Me.) Mil.
m. Sarah Story — son John S. m. Ruth Toolhaker

Williams, Samuel H. b. Va. 1769 d. Tenn. 1835 m. Ruth   Lt. Col. Tenn.
daughter Sarah Quincy m. Matt Martin

Williams, Samuel L. b. Va. 1781 d. Ky. 1872   Gen. Va. Mil.
m. Frances Cluke (Clough) — son John S. m. Anne Patton Harrison

Williams, Sheppard b. N.C. 1780 d. Ga. 1850   Recruiting Officer Ga.
m. Mary Hudson — daughter Jane A. M. m. Matthew Casewell

Williams, Sherrod b. N.C. 1776 d. Ala. 1831   Pvt. Tenn.
m. Mary Looney — son James m. Katherine Tally

Williams, Stephen b. N.C. 1786 d. Tex. 1846 m. Jean Black   Pvt. Vol. Miss.
daughter Louisa M. m. Charles William Tait

Williams, Stephen b. N.C. 1791 d. N.C. 1849   Lt. N.C. Mil.
m. Anna Jane Newkirk — son David Henry m. Asha Colwell
daughter Elizabeth m. James H. Alderman
daughter Harriet A. m. James Wells
son Samuel m. Lucinda Wallace

Williams, Thomas b. N.C. 1775 d. en route to Calif. 1852   Pvt. Ky. Vol.
m. Hannah Hibbard — son Jebediah m. Mary Grant Lewis
daughter Miranda m. James Riley Booth

Williams, Thomas b. N.J. d. N.J. 1848 m. May Briant   Pvt. N.J. Mil.
son Hampton m. Lydia Ann Jenkins

Williams, Timothy b. N.Y. 1756 d. N.Y. 1861   Postmaster N.Y.
m. Jane Oakley — son George W. m. Mary Wakelam

Williams, Walter b. N.H. 1770 d. N.H. 1848   Pvt. N.H. Mil.
m. Abigail Marshall—son George F. m. Rebecca Maria Parker

Williams, William Jr. b. Ga. 1791 d. Ga. 1860   Pvt. Ga. Mil. 1814
m. Cassandra Shepherd (2nd)
daughter Caroline m. Jonathan Donalson

Williams, William b. R.I. 1758 d. N.H. 1841   Pvt. N.H. Mil.
m. Susannah Pond — daughter Julia m. Everett Robinson

Williams, William Vol. 17   Pvt. Md. Mil.

Williamson, Adam b. Va. 1788 d. Ga. 1862 m. Betsy Horton   Pvt. Ga. Mil.
daughter Amelia m. Jeremiah Trout

Williamson, Benjamin Vol. 9   Pvt. Ga. Mil.

Williamson, Charles Vol. 4   Sgt. Va. Mil.

Williamson, Cuthbert Vol. 12   Pvt. Va. Mil.

Williamson, Douwe Ditmars b. N.J. 1789 d. N.Y. 1869   Pvt. N.J. Mil.
m. Mary Ann Abeel — son Nicholas m. Mary Rebecca Burlock

Williamson, George b.—d. m. Hannah Mabry   Capt. Tenn. Mil.
son Thomas E. m. Frances E. Williamson

Williamson, Henry b. Va. 1794 d. Ohio 1881   Cpl. Ohio Mil.
m. Rachel Aughee — daughter Lydia J. m. Benjamin F. Field
son William J. m. Elizabeth Patterson

Williamson, John b. Va. 1764 d. Tenn. 1829   Capt. Tenn. Mil.
m. Margaret Scott Cloyd — son James m. Lucy Smith

Williamson, John Stark b. Ky. 1782 d. Tenn. 1825   Pvt. Tenn. Mil.
m. Eliza Phillips — son Benjamin F. m. Martha Jane Cross
daughter Rebecca W. m. Aylett Buchner Taylor

Williamson, Moses b. Penn. 1756 d. Penn. 1809   Col. Penn. Mil.
m. Barbara Walters
daughter Mary Ann m. William Daling or Devlin
daughter Margaret m. James Porter
son Robert C. m. Ann Elizabeth Herr

Williamson, Samuel b. Penn. 1782 d. La. 1823   Pvt. U.S. Inf.
m. Isabella Huston — daughter Caroline R. m. John Dunbar Creigh

Willig, George b. Penn. 1794 d. Md. 1874   Pvt. Penn. Mil.
m. Amy Broston — daughter Maria C. m. Dr. John Ker

Willis, Abel b. Va. 1776 d. Tenn. 1873   Capt. W. Tenn. Mil.
m. Sally Fleming — daughter Sarah m. (2) Hugh Armstrong Blevins

Williamson, William II b. Va. c. 1725 d. Ga. c. 1800   Juror Ga. 1792-3
m. Molly — son William m. — Newman

Willis, Francis b. Va. 1745 d. Tenn. 1829   Congress Ga. 1792
m. Elizabeth Edwards — son Carver m. Frances Madison

Willis, James b. Tenn. 1800 d. Tenn. 1858   Pvt. Tenn. Mtd. Vol. Gunman
m. Sallie Stapleton — daughter Mary m. Iredell Campbell Brown

Willis, James b. Penn. 1792 d. Ia. 1865 m. Eliza Skinner   Pvt. Ohio Mil.
son James M. m. Elizabeth Porter

Willis, James b. N.C. 1777 d La. 1852   Capt. Ga. Mil.
m. Elleighfair Humphries
daughter Mary m. Archibald Murphey Campbell

Willis, Joel b. Penn. 1764 d. Ohio 1842 m. Hannah Jessop   Pvt. Penn. Mil.
daughter Achsah m. Amer Hiatt

Willis, John b. N.C. 1759 d. Miss 1802 m. Asenath Barnes   Col. N.C. Mil.
son Thomas A. m. Margaret Holden

Willis, Joshua b. Va. 1790 d. Ala. 1830-40   Lt. Ga. Mil.
m. Louisa Haney Porter — son Joshua Paul m. Martha Ann Roland

Willis, Larkin b. 1777 d. Tenn. 1859 m. Mary   Pvt. Tenn. Mtd. Mil.
son James m. Sallie Stapleton

Willis, Malachi b.—d. Ill. 1832 m. Elizabeth Lane   Pvt. Tenn. Mil.
daughter Elizabeth C. m. John B. Bailey

Willis, Pierson b. Va. 1787 d. Ky. 1872   Sgt. Ky. Lt. Drag.
m. Elizabeth Standiford
daughter Mary Frances m. Adam Middleton III

Willis, Robert b. Ga. 1772 d. S.C. 1844 m. Kesiah Watsin   Lt. Ga. Mil.
daughter Matilda m. Samuel Reed
daughter Winnifred m. (2) Jesse Lott

Willis, Thomas C. b. N.J. 1791 d. N.J. 1864   Sgt. N.J. Mil.
m. Deborah Farrand — son Edwin E. m. Electa Caroline Cook
daughter Francis H. m. Benjamin F. Howell REAL DAUGHTER

Willis, W. Reading Jr. b. 1792 d. 1848 m. Maria Brawner Lt. Inf. 1814 N.J.
son Edw. Wm. m. Caroline Oldham

Willits, Thomas b. Penn. 1762 d. Mich. 1830   Lt. Penn. Mil. 1798
m. Mary Allison — daughter Elizabeth m. Matthew Dolsen

Willits, Elijah b. Penn. 1792 d. Mich. 1868   Pvt. Mich. Mil.
m. Catherine Welch — son Wellington m. Martha Jane Beardslee

Willoughby, Wallace Vol. 10   Pvt. Va. Mil

Wills, James b. Ohio 1788 d. Ind. 1840   Pvt. Ohio Mil.
m. Mary Jane Baldwin — son William P. m. Catherine Swaggerty

Wills, Miles Cary b. Va. 1797 d. Va. 1872   Pvt. Va. Mil.
m. Rebecca Bowles Strange (Allaway)
son Thomas C. m. Maria Louisa Craven

Wills, Thomas b. Ky. 1791 d. Ky. 1872 m. Mariah Swango   Pvt. U.S. Inf.
son Jordan m. Judah Cox

Willson, John Quintard Vol. 17   2nd Cpl. N.Y. Art.

Willson, Samuel Warner b. Vt. 1785 d. N.Y. 1875   Pvt. N.Y. Mil.
m. Nancy Willson — daughter Experience m. John Bennett

Wilmarth, Amos b. Vt. 1786 d. Vt. 1874 m. Anna Elmer   Sgt. Vt. Mil.
daughter Julia Maria m. George Smith

Willmott, Robert b. Md. 1757 d. Ky. 1839   Legis. Ky. 1799
m. Priscilla Ridgely Dorsey
son Charles R. m. Sarah Jane Parker & Matilda Chinn

Wilson, Alexander Vol. 8   Qtrmst. Sgt. Del. Vol.

Wilson, Augustus Nathaniel Coburn b. Ky. c. 1790   Pvt. Ky. Lt. Drag.
d. La. 1829 m. Caroline Randolph Woodson
daughter Ann W. m. Caleb Smith Stone

Wilson, Benjamin Sr. b. Va. 1747 d. Va. 1827   Col. 1810 W.Va. Mil.
m. Ann Ruddell   Legis. Justice Va. 1788-1814
son Benjamin Jr. m. Martha Louise Davisson
son William B. m. Elizabeth Davisson

Wilson, Charles b. Penn. 1751 d. Penn. 1826   Pvt. Penn. Mil.
m. Esther Smith — daughter Esther m. John Adair

Wilson, David b. Va. 1790 d. Ohio 1881 m. Abigail Porter   Pvt. Ohio
son William m. Chiffonette Treat

Wilson, David Carson b. Del. d. Del. 1865 m. Letitia Kirke   Capt. Del. Mil.
daughter Anna m. Leonard G. Van Kluck

Wilson, Ezekial Vol. 17   Pvt. Penn. Rifleman

Wilson, Fielder b. Md. 1772 d. Ky. 1833 m. Mary Suit   Ens. Md. Mil.
son Tyler m. Emily Cawford

Wilson, James b. Md. 1769 d. Ind. 1851 m. Susanna Wesley   Maj. Ohio Mil.
daughter Lovey m. William Hulit

Wilson, James b. Va. 1758 d. W.Va. 1810   Pvt. W.Va. 1794
m. (2) Elizabeth Haptonstall — son Samuel m. Ann Siron

Wilson, (Willson) James b. Va. 1788 d. Va. 1830   Surgeon's Mate Va. Mil.
m. Elizabeth Kenney — son Robert K. m. Elizabeth J. Hooke

Wilson, James Vol. 8   Capt. Ga. Mil.
son Elihu Wilson

Wilson, John b. N.Y. 1781 d. N.Y. 1848   Capt. N.Y. Mil.
m. (2) Susannah Elwood
daughter Eve m. Abram Diefendorf Van Camp

Wilson, John b. Ire. 1775 d. Penn. 1852   2nd Maj. Penn. Mil.
m. Catherine Sutley — daughter Margaret m. Dr. William Hamilton

Wilson, John Early Vol.   Pvt. Mass. Mil.

Wilson, John Vol. 16   Pvt. Md. Mil.

Wilson, John Vol. 10   Pvt. N.C. Mil.

Wilson, John b. Penn. 1775 d. Penn. 1839   Sgt. Maj. Penn. Mil.
m. Rebecca McCrea — daughter Eliza m. Samuel Hughes

Wilson, John b. Penn. 1742 d. N.C. 1799   Town Trustee N.C. 1792
m. Mary Wray — son John Jr. m. Hannah Baird

Wilson, John b. Penn. 1789 d. Penn. 1864   Pvt. Pa. Mil.
m. Catharine Rhoades — daughter Emily Margaret m. Tilghman Rupp

Wilson, John b. Va. 1781 d. N.C. 1843 m. Sally Strong   Pvt. N.C. Mil.
daughter Elizabeth Ann m. John Wilson May

Wilson, John b. Va. 1776 d. W.Va. 1832   Capt. Va. Vol.
m. Catherine Donnally — son Alexander H. m. Mary Eliza Chilton
daughter Jane m. Guy P. Matthews
son John Christian m. Elizabeth Jane Neal
daughter Mary C. m. James H. Couch Jr.
daughter Sallie m. Samuel Stephenson

Wilson, John M. b. Va. 1801 d. Mo. 1873 m. Sarah   Sgt. Va. Mil.
daughter Nancy J. m. David Russell

Wilson, John Q. Vol. 16   2nd Cpl. N.Y. Art.

Wilson, Jonas H. b. Conn. 1784 d. Conn. 1841   Music Conn. Mil.
m. Mary Starr — daughter Mary S. m. William Clapp

Wilson, Joseph b. Mass. 1759 d. N.Y. 1846   Pvt. N.Y. Mil.
m. Elizabeth Caldwell or Margaret Johnson
son Moses m. Sarah Halleck

Wilson, Joseph b. Md. d. Penn. 1830-6 m. Prudence Booth   Capt. Penn. Mil.
son Jeremiah m. Lydia Davidson

Wilson, Josiah b. N.J. 1758 d. N.Y. m. Jane Plum   Gunner N.Y. Art.
daughter Gertrude m. Stephen Swezey

Wilson, George LeGrand b. Va. 1789 d. Va. 1850   Pvt. N.C. Mil.
m. Catherine Robinson Pass — daughter America m. James Pierce

Wilson, Lazarus Brown b. Penn. 1795 d. Ind. 1875   Pvt. Md. Mil.
m. Mary Todd Barbee — daughter Alma W. REAL DAUGHTER
son Henry C. m. Louisa Grant

Wilson, Moses DeWitte b. N.Y. 1794 d. Ohio 1858   Pvt. N.Y. Mil.
m. Jane McCoy — daughter Martha D. REAL DAUGHTER
daughter Nancy E. m. John V. Marshall

Wilson, Noah b. Vt. 1761 d. Penn. 1844   Pat. Penn.
m. Mary (Welch) Rowley — daughter Samantha m. Buel Smith

Wilson, Richard b. Penn. 1769 d. Pa. 1820   Pvt. Pa. Mil.
m. Mary Steel — daughter Sarah Ann m. Andrew Buzby Godshall

Wilson, Robert b. Penn. 1782 d. Ohio 1875   Pvt. Ohio Mil.
m. Esther Anderson — son Ovid N. m. Margaret Christie

Wilson, Samuel Vol. 8   Cpl. Md. Mil.

Wilson, Samuel Vol. 5   Cpl. N.Y. Mil.

Wilson, Samuel b. Mass. 1772 d. N.Y. 1864   Maj. N.Y. Mil.
m. Anna Austin — son Ebenezer m. Charlotte N. Reed

Wilson, Samuel b. Penn. 1775 d. Ky. 1831   Pvt. Ky. Mil.
m. Elizabeth Hughlett — daughter Sarah C. m. James Goolder

Wilson, Samuel b. Penn. 1791 d. Penn. 1880   Pvt. Penn. Mil.
m. Catherine Jack — daughter Susan m. John Henry Hahn

Wilson, Samuel James b. S.C. 1790 d. Ala. 1844   Pvt. S.C. Mil.
m. Elizabeth Frierson
daughter Francis J. m. Thomas Wilkes Coleman REAL DAUGHTER
son Samuel G. m. Maria Louisa Herdon

Wilson, Sarah Ann Nesmith b. N.H. 1787 d. N.H. 1873   Pat. 1812 Nurse
m. Samuel Wilson — son Joseph G. m. Elizabeth Millar

Wilson, Stephen b. 1777 d. Penn. 1812 m. **Mary Culbertson**   Col. Penn. Mil.
son Alexander C. m. (2) **Mary Campbell McFarland**

Wilson, Thomas b. Penn. 1792 d. Penn. 1855   Pvt. Penn. Mil.
m. Mrs. Maria Kunsman — son Thomas Jr. m. Sarah E. Arndt

Wilson, Valentine b. Va. 1785 d. Ohio 1855   Pvt. Ohio Mil.
m. Eleanor Judy — son James m. Eleanor Smith
son John m. Julia Ann Prugh
m. Nancy Roberts — daughter Caroline m. Robert Boyd

Wilson, William b. 1791 d. N.J. 1886 m. Jane Bergen   Pvt. N.J. Mil.
son Minard W. m. Elizabeth White

Wilson, William b. N.C. 1784 d. Ala. 1835   Pvt. Tenn. Mil.
m. Martha Clements — son Benjamin F. m. Elizabeth Arminta Bostick
son Jason m. Mary Ann D. White

Wilson, William b. Va. 1794 d. Ill. 1857 m. Mary S. Davidson   Pvt. Va. Mil.
son Charles J. F. m. Harriet Lucy

Wilson, William b. Va. 1765 d. Va. 1824 m. Ann Reid   Pvt. W.Va. Mil.
daughter Mary Ann m. John Reid Jr.

Wilson, William b. Md. 1755 d. Ohio 1821   Ohio Mil., Justice Capt.
m. Esther Fickle — daughter Elizabeth m. James Ritchey

Wilson, William b. Ire. 1794 d. Md. 1824   Legis. Md. 1798
m. Jane Stansbury — son William Jr. m. Mary Knox

Wilson, Zaccheus b. Penn. 1740 d. Tenn. 1824   Const. Conv. N.C. 1788
m. Mrs. Lizzie Conger Ross — son Stephen m. Mary McElrath

Wilt, Peter b. Penn. 1774 d. Penn. 1840   Pvt. Penn. Mil.
m. Catherine Ernst — son William A. m. Lydia Forrey

Wiltsie, James b. N.Y. 1782 d. N.Y. 1872   Ens. N.Y. 1808
m. Catherine Vermilya — son Joseph m. Sophronia Wright

Wiman, Gardner b.—d. N.Y. 1812 m. Hannah Bacon   Pvt. N.Y. Mil.
son Alonzo m. Ellen Haskins

Wiman, John Vol. 5   Lt. Mass. Mil.

Wimberly, Ezekiel b. N.C. 1781 d. Ga. 1825   Maj. Ga. Mil.
m. Dorothy Brooks — son Henry S. m. Caroline Durham

Wimberly, Ezekiel b. N.C. 1783 d. Ga. 1843   Col. Ga. Mil.
m. Mary (Polly) Bryan — son Ezekiel A. m. Louisa A. Horne
m. Sarah Mims — daughter Sarah m. John Jones

Winch, William b. N.H. 1788 d. N.Y. 1828 m. Mary Fonar   Pvt. U.S. Inf.
daughter Typhena m. Charles Prew

Winchester, James b. Md. 1752 d. Tenn. 1826   Brig. Gen. U.S. Army
m. Susan Black — son George N. m. Malvina Henderson Gaines

Winchester Stephen b. Md. 1761 d. Tenn. 1815   Lt. Col. Md. 1794
m. Sarah Howard — daughter Mary Hall m. Samuel H. Lauderdale

Windowmaker, Jacob b. N.Y. 1781 d. Ind. 1855 m.—   Pvt. Penn. Mil.
Vol. 7

Windsor, Abraham b. R.I. 1778 d. N.Y. 1844   Lt. N.Y. Mil.
m. Sophia Bigelow — son Samuel m. Anna

Wines, William b. N.Y. 1765 d. N.Y. 1832 m. Bethia Howell   Patriot N.Y.
son Harris m. Helen Martin

Winebrener, David Vol. 5   Pvt. Penn. Mil.

Wing, Abraham b. Mass. 1721 d. N.Y. 1795   Pat. N.Y. 1770-95
   m. Anstis Wood — daughter Sarah m. Ichabod Merritt

Wing, Moses Jr. Vol. 12   Maj. Mass. (Me.) Mil.

Wingate, John b. N.Y. 1733 d. Ohio 1851 m. Mary Dillon   Sgt. Ohio Mil.
   daughter Cassandra m. William Herod

Wingfield, Joseph Vol. 6   Pvt. Tenn. Mil.

Wingler, Henry b. Penn. 1786 d. Penn. 1866   Pvt. Penn. Mil.
   m. Elizabeth Scett
   daughter Mary L. m. Frank DeGarmo REAL DAUGHTER
   daughter Sarah J S m. D. O'Donnell

Winkley, Joseph W. b. Ky. 1779 d. Ind. 1833 m.—   Sgt. Ohio Mil.
   daughter Mary Ann m. Martin Tresler

Winn, Richard b. Va. 1750 d. Tenn. 1818   Brig. Gen. S.C. 1796
   m. Priscilla McKinley — son William m. Susan Blanton

Winslow, Isaac b. Mass. 1763 d. Mass. 1806   Maj. U.S. Army
   m. Mary Russell — daughter Mary m. Charles Bradford

Winslow, Theron b. Vt. 1795 d. Vt. 1867 m. Dolly Ingalls   Drum Vt. Mil.
   daughter Lucretia m. George Phelps

Winslow, William b. Va. 1766 d. Ky. 1838 m. Peggy Mills   Pat. Ky. 1813
   daughter Mary m. Joseph Myrick

Winsor (Windsor), Abraham b. R.I. 1778 d. N.Y. 1844   Lt. N.Y. Inf.
   m. Sophia Bigelow — son Samuel B. m. Anna Sears

Winston, Anthony Jr. b. Va. 1750 d. Ala. 1828   Memb. House Va. Del. 1788
   m. Keziah Jones — son Edmund m. (1) Martha Cocke

Winston, Joseph W. Jr. b. 1788 d. N.C.   2nd Maj. N.C. Mil.
   m. Letitia Dalton Hughes — son John H. m. Elizabeth Tebbs

Winston, Samuel L. b. Va. 1782 d. Miss. 1831   Ens. Miss. Terr. Mil.
   m. Ann W. Hoggatt — daughter Anna m. David Stanton

Winston, William b. Va. 1780 d. Ky. 186—   Pvt. Va. Mil.
   m. Martha Eliza Mosby
   daughter Sally Ann m. Dr. Samuel Garber Menzies

Winter, Jacob b. Penn. 1760 d. Penn. 1827 m. Mary   Pvt. Penn. Mil.
   son Abraham m. Elizabeth Lines
   son James m. Rhoda Mitchell

Wirt, William Vol. 7   Capt. La. Art.

Wisdom, William Jr. b. Va. c. 1765 d. Mo. aft. 1838   2nd Lt. W. Tenn. Mil.
   m. Dorcas Cruse — son Francis Marion m. Elizabeth Benthall

Wise, (Weise) Adam b. Penn. 1751 d. Penn. 1833   Justice Penn. 1799
   m. Margaret Elizabeth Wingard — son John G. m. Charlotte Mone

Wise, Christopher b. Pa. 1799 d. Ohio 1880 m. Catherine   Pvt. Penn. Mil.
   son Samuel m. Isabel Ingram Patterson

Wise, John b. va. ca. 1770 d. Miss abt. 1840 m. Judith Lacy   Pvt. Va. Mil.
   son Joseph m. Lucy Eliza Hall

Wise, Patton b. Va. 1773 d. Ga. 1815   Justice Ga. 1799-1812
   m. Elizabeth Johnson — daughter Polly m. Parham Lindsey

Wishart, Daniel b. N.Y. d. N.Y. m. Amelia Foote   Lt. U.S. Army
daughter Frances Maria m. Daniel Holmes

Wisner (Wesner), Daniel b. N.Y. 1778 d. N.Y. 1861   Capt. N.Y. Mil.
m. Sarah Guy — son Horace m. Rachel Hudnut

Wisner, Henry b. N.Y. 1742 d. N.Y. 1812   Brig. Gen. N.Y. Mil.
m. Susannah Goldsmith — son John m. Elizabeth Butolph

Wisner, Henry Sr. b. N.Y. 1720 d. N.Y. 1790   Const. Conv. Congress N.Y.
m. Sarah Norton — son Henry Jr. m. Sarah Barnett

Wisner, James b. N.Y. 1765 d. Mich. aft. 1840   Capt. N.Y. Mil.
m. Elizabeth Carpenter — daughter Sarah m. Sheldon Pardee

Wisner. Thomas b. N.Y. 1779 d. N.Y. 1851 m. Sarah Weed   Sgt. N.Y. Mil.
son Ira m. Sarah H. Thomas

Wiswell, John b. Mass. 1753 d. N.Y. 1838 m. Esther Trowbridge   Pat. 1812
son Henry m. Elizabeth Salter

Witcher, Ephraim b. Va. 1792 d. Mo. 1845 m. Winifred B.   Pvt. Va. Mil.
son Nathaniel L. m. Ruth Hollingsworth

Witherell, Asaph Potter b. N.H. 1781 d. Ill. 1862   Artificer N.Y. Mil.
m. Joanna White — daughter Charlotte m. Critten H. Hutchinson

Witherell, Simeon Jr. b. Mass. 1748 d. Vt. 1832   Pvt. Vt. Mil.
m. Hannah Presho — daughter Hannah m. Peter Conery

Withers, Mathew Keene b. Va. 1755 d. Ind. 1830   Pvt. Ky. Vol.
m. Nancy Jennings — son William L. m. Christina Snapp

Witt, David b. Va. 1756 d. Ga. 1802 m. Ann Luttrell   Maj. Ga. Mil.
daughter Margaret m. Jesse Witt

Witten, Thomas Jr. b. Md. d. Va. m. Eleanor Cecil   Assem. Va. 1801-4
son James S. m. Levice Thompson

Wittenmyer, Michael b. Penn. 1772 d. Penn. 1859   Paymst. Penn. Mil.
m. Magdalena — son Samuel m. Catherine Glass (Gloss)

Witts, Daniel b. Va. 1787 d. Ill. 1855 m. Martha W.   Sgt. Va. Rifleman
daughter Martha B. m. James William Saighman

Wohlfart, George b. Swit, 1725 d. Pa. 1793/4   Pvt. Pa. Mil.
m. Elizabeth Zimmerman — son John m. Barbara

Wolcott, Frederick b. Conn. 1767 d. Conn. 1837   Judge of Probate Conn.
m. Elizabeth Huntington — daughter Elizabeth m. John P. Jackson

Wolcott, Joseph b. Conn. 1775 d. Ohio 1866 m. Lucy Hills   Pvt. Vt. Mil.
son Simon Peter m. Nancy Wilder Codding

Wolcott, Samuel b. Conn. 1772 d. N.Y. 1823   Sgt. Mass. Mil.
m. Hulah Herrick — daughter Ann Eliza m. John Fairfield Dewey

Wolf, Abram b. Pa. 1787 d. Pa. 1835 m. Agnes Gibbon   Pvt. Pa. Mil.
son John m. Mary Ann Newling
daughter Matilda m. Robert Cunningham

Wolf, Alvain   Early Vol.   Sgt. Pa. Mil.

Wolf. George b. Pa. 1758 d. Ohio 1813 m. Mary Catherine   Cpl. Ohio Mil.
son Jacob m. Catherine Miller

Wolfe, George b. Pa. 1771 d. Ohio 1850   Pvt. Pa. Mil.
    m. Jane Piser (Pisor) — son George P. m. Elizabeth Wilkins

Wolfe, John b. Ky. 1749 d. Ind. 1838 m. Ann Aurand   Pvt. Ohio Mil.
    son George W. m. Mary Margaret Conrad

Wolff, Elias b. Pa. 1747 d. Pa. 1827 m. Marbara (?)   Pvt. Pa. Mil.
    son Johannes m. Elizabeth Schaffer

Wolff, Jacob b. Pa. 1760 d. Pa. 1842 m. Catherine E. Finkle   Pvt. Pa. Mil.
    son Peter m. Catherine Battorf

Wolgamot, John Jr. b. Md. d. Md. 1833   Cpl. Md. Mil.
    m. Elizabeth Rentch — son Andrew m. Mary Dorothy Tice

Wollam, Henry b. Va. 1777 d. Ohio 1870 m. Mary Bough   Pvt. Ohio Mil.
    son Archibald m. Catherine Smith

Wolmer, George Vol. 12   Pvt. Pa. Mil.

Womack, Abraham Sr. b. N.C. 1782 d. La. 1860   Pvt. La. Mil.
    m. Elizabeth Burton
    daughter Elizabeth Jane m. William Henry Tillery

Womack, Byrd b. Va. 1776 d. Va. 18— m. Rebecca Haskins   Pvt. Va. Mil.
    daughter Elizabeth m. Willis Reeves Dortch

Womack, Jacob (Green) b. N.C. 1782 d. La. 1865   Pvt. La. Mil.
    m. Nancy Jane Waller — son Abraham B. m. Elizabeth G. Wood

Womack, Jesse Vol. 13   Lt. Ga. Mil.

Womack, John b. Ga. 1776 d. Ala. 1848 m. Frances Coleman   Pvt. La. Mil.
    daughter Aurelia m. Isaac Baker

Womack, Michael b. Va. 1794 d. Ark. 1861   Pvt. W. Tenn. Mil.
    m. Sarah Jones — son David D. m. Lydia Lokey

Wood, Aaron b. Mass. 1762 d. Mass. 1815   Civil Officer Mass.
    m. Bethia Beard — son Moses m. Mary Come

Wood, Abner b. N.Y. 1768 d. N.Y. 1869 m. Malinda Weed   Pvt. N.Y. Mil.
    daughter Caroline m. David Rogers

Wood, Benjamin b. N.Y. 1780 d. N.Y. 1875   Capt. N.Y. Mil.
    m. Catherine Cole — son Jacob B. m. Mary E. Lippencott

Wood, Benjamin b. N.Y. 1787 d. N.Y. 1828   Ens. N.Y. Inf.
    m. Judith Spaulding — son Harvey m. Esther Ann Wilkinson

Wood, Elias b. N.Y. 1793 d. N.Y. 1873 m. Hulda Allen   Pvt. N.Y. Mil.
    daughter Susan m. George D. Ruggles

Wood, Freeman b. Mass. 1791 d. Mich. 1867   Pvt. N.Y. Mil.
    m. Marilla Gates — daughter Lydia Estelle m. Alonzo Colgrave

Wood, Henry (Harry) b. Ky. d. Ky. m.— Vol. 31   Lt. Ky. Mil.
    daughter Eliza m. Alton

Wood, Henry (Harry) b. N.Y. 1794 d. N.Y. 1862   Pvt. N.Y. Mil.
    m. Celinda Garden — daughter Maria C. m. Anson Strong

Wood, Hugh b. N.J. 1796 d. Ill. 1838 m. Sarah   Sgt. Maj. Ohio Mil.
    daughter Isabelle m. Samuel Clark Spencer

Wood, Isaac b. Mass. 1746 d. Mass. 1835   Selectman Mass.
    m. Elizabeth Hartwell — daughter Eunice m. Joseph Hartwell

Wood, Jabin b. N.Y. 1794 d. N.Y. m.—   Pvt. N.Y. Mil.
    daughter Catherine M. m. M. H. Cutting REAL DAUGHTER

Wood, James b. N.Y. 1778 d. N.Y. 1863 m. Barbary　　　Pvt. N.Y. Mil.
　　son Horace m. Emily Delight Chrisman

Wood, James b. Va. 1774 d. Ill. 1849 m. Susanna Renfro　　Pvt. Ky. Mil.
　　son Samuel m. Keziah Daugherty

Wood, James Wilson b. Mass. 1779 d. N.Y. 1838　Collector of Customs N.Y.
　　m. Mary E. Danforth — son Benjamin F. m. Mary B. Hammond

Wood, Joel b. Md. 1790 d. Md. m. Mary Null　　　　　Cpl. Md. Mil.
　　daughter Anna Marie m. William Zimmerman
　　son John N. m. Melinda Jane Hill

Wood, John Vol. 8　　　　　　　　　　　Lt. Col. Miss. Mil.

Wood, John Sr. b. Mass. 1765 d. Mass. 1836　　School Trustee Mass. 1814
　　m. Zeviah Woodbury — son John Jr. m. Abigail Lord

Wood, John b. Va. 1786 d. Va. 1825 m. Janetta Hutchins　　Sgt. Va. Cal.
　　daughter Mary J. m. Lewis Lyman Stiff

Wood, John b. Mass. 1781 d. Vt. 1857 m. Lucy Whitney　Teamster Vt. Mil.
　　son Wyllys m. Eliza C. Gove

Wood, Jonathan b. Mass. 1760 d. Ohio 1838 m. Rachel White　Surveyor Vt.
　　daughter Matilda m. Slocum Hussey Bunker

Wood, Lemuel b. Mass. 1787 d. N.Y. 1850　　　　　Ens. N.Y. Mil.
　　m. Hannah Sprague — son Lemuel S. m. Mary Sophia Johnson

Wood, Richard b. Va. 1781 d. Ill. 1865 m. Celia Gregory　　Pvt. Ky. Mil.
　　son Samuel m. Mrs. Martha Moore Smith

Wood, Solomon Vol. 16　　　　　　　　　Lt. Mass. Mil.

Wood, Solomon Carpenter b. N.Y. 1794 d. Wisc. 1885　　Pvt. N.Y. Mil.
　　m. Susan McCoy — daughter Abigail M. m. John A. Wallace

Wood, Thomas b. N.Y. 1770 d. N.Y. 1844 m. Hester Hilliker　Pvt. N.Y. Mil.
　　daughter Deborah m. Andrew Weatherwax

Wood, William Sr. b. Md. d. Ohio 1838/1　　　　1st Sgt. Ohio Mil.
　　m. Margaret Chance or Prane — son Hugh m. Sarah Spicer

Wood, William b. Va. 1784 d. Ill. 1854 m. Mary Ann Wilson　Cpl. Ohio Mil.
　　son Daniel m. Mary Elizabeth Johnson

Wood, William b. Va. 1772 d. Ky. 1851　　　　Memb. Ky. Leg. 23 yrs.
　　m. Nellie Ryan — son Thomas J. m. Martha Ann Brame

Woodall, Edward b. Md. 1778 d. Md. 1816 m. Mary Cooper　Sgt. Md. Mil.
　　son John m. Sarah A. Roche

Woodard, Anthony Vol. 13　　　　　　　　　Sgt. Va. Mil.

Woodridge, William b. Conn. 1780 d. Mich. 1860　Acting Gov. Mich. Terr.
　　m. Julian Trumbull — son Dudley B. m. Martha Jane Lee

Woodbury, John b. Mass. 1752 d. Mass.　　　　Capt. Mass. Mil. 1786
　　m. Mary Ward — daughter Susan m. Abel Bancroft

Woodbury, John b. Mass. 1749 d. Mass. 1831　　　Capt. Mass. Mil.
　　m Mary Chase — son Benjamin m. Brooksey Cole

Woodbury, Jonathan b. Mass. 1767 d. Vt. 1842　　　Selectman, Clerk
　　m. Sally Davis　　　　　　　　Treasurer Vt. 1794-1814
　　daughter Esther m. Joel Ellis

Woodbury, Peter b. Mass. 1736 d. Mass. 1806   Town Clerk, Selectman
   m. (2) Zeviah Greenwood   1782, Rep. to Gen. Ct. Mass. 1784-1794
daughter Zeviah m. John Wood, Sr.

Woodford, Isaac, Jr. b. Conn. 1774 d. Ohio 1838   Pvt. Ohio Mil.
   m. Statira Cowles — daughter Emily m. Homer Mills Leet

Woodford, John Thornton b. Va. 1763 d. Ky. 1845   Col. Va. Cal. 1812
   m. Mary Turner Taliaferro   Mem. House of Del. 1802-6 Va.
son William m. Anna Maria Archer
daughter Mildred G. m. Edmund Hockaday Didlake

Woodgate, Jonathan m. Sarah   Pvt. Ky. Mil.
daughter Sarah m. James Arnett

Woodhull, William b. N.Y. 1785 d. N.Y. 1847   Capt. N.Y. Regt.
   m. Phoebe Carl — daughter Caroline Phoebe REAL DAUGHTER

Woodington, James b. Pa. 1775 d. Pa. 1828 m. Rachel Skees   Pvt. Pa. Mil.
son William m Rebecca Dyer

Woodman, Jeremiah Hall b. N.H. 1775 d. N.H. 1854   Pvt. Mass. Mil.
   m. Sarah Chase — daughter Sarah Jane T. m. Joseph Russell Bradford

Woodman, Joseph b. Vt. 1776 d. Vt. 1856 m. Hannah Kimball   Capt. Vt. Mil.
son Joseph K. m. Priscilla Godfrey

Woodring, Philip b. Pa. 1741 d. Pa. 1819   Pvt. Pa. Mil.
   m. Maria Elizabeth Wagner — son Nicholas m. Catherine Meixsell

Woodruff, Jesse b. Va. 1746 d. Tenn. 1826   Land Com. mem. of Tenn.
   m. Esther Buchanan — daughter Mary Ann m. Elijah Yeates Ct. 1810

Woodruff, Joseph b. 1789 d. 1861 m. Lovina Blanchard   Pvt. N.Y. Mil.
son Joseph m. Eliza A. Codding

Woodruff, Joseph b. Ga. 1787 d. S.C. 1828   Maj. U.S. Army
   m. Jane Harris — son Julian S. m. Maria Egleston

Woodruff, Micah b. Conn. 1745 d. Conn. 1810   Capt. Conn. Mil.
   m. Elizabeth Curtis — son Alvin m. Mary Cowles

Woodruff, Morris M. b. Conn. 1792 d. N.Y. 1875   2nd Lt. N.Y. Mil.
   m. Roxanna T. Bush
daughter Lois P. m. Henry Cooper REAL DAUGHTER

Woodruff, Samuel b. N.J. 1777 d. N.J. 1821   Lt. N.J. Mil.
   m. Abigail Acken — daughter Elizabeth m. Cyrus Carrigues

Woodruff, William E. b. N.Y. 1795 d. Ark. 1885   Pvt. N.Y. Mil.
   m. Jane Eliza Mills — daughter Mary Eliza m. Samuel Slade Bell
daughter Evie m. Craddock Robinson Vaughan REAL DAUGHTER

Woods, Henry b. Mass. 1733 d. Mass. 1804   Big. Gen. Mass. Mil.
   m. Deborah Parker — son Henry Jr. m. Alice Fitch

Woods, James b. Va. 1748 d. Ky. 1822   Pvt. Ky. Mil.
   m. Mary Garland — daughter Mary Rice m. Overton Harris

Wood, John b. Va. 1751 d. Tenn. 1815   2nd Lt. Tenn. Vol.
   m. Abigail Estill — son James m. Elizabeth Embrey

Woods, Jonathan Vol. 3   Pvt. Mass. Mil.

Woods, Micah b. Pa. 1782 d. Ohio 1874 m. Hester Bowman   Capt. Ohio Mil.
son Francis M. m. Hannah Copple

Woods, William b. N.C. 1783 d. S.C. 1860 m. Jane Babbs   Pvt. S.C. Mil.
daughter Martha m. James Foster Boyd

Woods, William b. Mass. 1789 d. Ill. 1866 m. Lima Congdon   Pvt. N.Y. Mil.
son Cyrenus Nelson m. Mary Armstrong Sheldon

Woodson, Charles F. b. Va. 1794 d. Mo. 1887 m. Anne Wilson   Pvt. Va. Mil.
son Richard m. Grace Lee

Woodson, John b. Va. 1788 d. Va. 1840   Pvt. Va. Mil.
m. Elizabeth Gooch — daughter Elizabeth G. m. John Hampton

Woodson, Robert b. Va. 1775 d. Va. 1822   Pvt. Va. Mil.
m. Elizabeth Pledge — son Joseph m. Julia Ann Edwards

Woodward, Abraham b. Md. 1776 d. Md. 1832   Pvt. Md. Mil.
m. Priscilla Owens — daughter Louisa m. Absalom Anderson

Woodward, Benjamin b N.Y. 1780 d. N.Y. aft. 1826   Lt. Col. N.Y. Mil.
m. Mary Van Auken — son Charles S. m. Sarah Swartout

Woodward, Caleb b. Pa. 1776 d. Pa. 1856   Lt. Pa. Mil. 1793
m. Phoebe McCarthy — son Davis m. Mary Boyd

Woodward, Daniel Vol. 9   Pvt. N.Y. Mil.

Woodward, Elkanah b. Mass. 1792 d. Mass. 1868   Pvt. Mass. Mil.
m. Hannah Snow — son Daniel S. m. Rhoda Canston Macker

Woodward, Francis Marion b. Tenn 1787 d. Tenn. 1818   Lt. Tenn. Mil.
m. Jane Brandon — son Lemuel S. m. Jane Waggoner

Woodward, George b. N.J. 1744 d. N.J. 1817   Civil Officer N.J. 1785-1811
m. Margaret Mount — son George m. Margaret Wynkoop

Woodward, Henry b. Md. 1770 d. Md. 1822   Capt. Md. Mil.
m. Eleanor Williams — daughter Mary Katherine m. James Rawlings

Woodward, Jesse S. b. N.Y. 1782 d. N.Y. m. Joanna Tiffany   Sgt. N.Y. Mil.
daughter Almeda m. Isaac Waggoner

Woodward, (Woodard) Joshua b. Conn. (?) 1786   Capt. Ohio Mil.
d. Ohio 1851 m. Rebecca Wooden
son James m. Maria Hopkins

Woodward, Samuel b. Pa. 1777 d. Ohio 1834 m. Sarah Carson   Pvt. Pa. Mil.
daughter Maria m. John Greine

Woodward, William b. N.J. 1782 d. Ill. 1839   War worker Pa.
m. Nancy Miller — son James M. m. Sarah Jane Thrasher

Woodward, William b. S.C. 1762 d. S.C. 1820   Col. S.C. Mil.
m. Nancy Barrette — daughter Charlotte m. William Turner
son Joseph A. m. Malinda Rebecca Bones

Woodward, William b. Va. 1796 d. Ga. 1865   Pvt. N.C. Mil.
m. Mary Ann Holland — daughter Elizabeth A. REAL DAUGHTER

Woodward, William H. b. N.H. 1774 d. N.H. 1818 m.—   Chief Justice
daughter Olivia m. Paul Chamberlin REAL DAUGHTER   N.H. 1813
daughter Ada H. m. Albert Glaspell REAL DAUGHTER

Woodworth, Dudley b. Conn. 1766 d. Mass. 1822 m.—   Drummer Conn. Art.
son Edward P. m. Hannah Hulbert

Woodworth, Hiram b. N.Y. 1793 d. N.Y. 1876   Pvt. N.Y. Art. Regt.
m. Phebe Winans — son George m. Ann Eliza Stevenson

Woodworth, James Vol. 17 — Pvt. Mass. Mil.

Woodworth, John b. Vt. 1792 d. N.Y. 1876 m. Cyrene Perry — Pvt. U.S. Inf.
son George m. Sarah Green

Woodworth, William b. Conn. 1752 d. Conn. 1814 — Pvt. N.Y. Mil.
m. Lydia Bacon — son Lathrop m. Mary Ball

Woodyard, Henley b. Va. 1791 d. Va. 1847 — Sgt. Maj. Va. Mil.
m. Sally Wiseman
daughter Eliza m. Perry Gawthrop REAL DAUGHTER

Wooford, James b. S.C. 1771 d. S.C. 1848 m. Celia Bennett — Cpl. S.C. Mil.
son William B. m. Maria Chumbly

Woolever, Jacob b. N.Y. 1761 d. N.Y. 1827 — Pvt. N.Y. Mil.
m. Susanna Flagg — daughter Elizabeth m. Joseph Casler

Wooster, Levi b. Conn. 1781 d. Conn. 1859 m. Esther Terrill — Lt. Conn. Mil.
son Albert m. Mittie Chatfield

Wooten (Wootan), John b. S.C. c. 1760 d. k/a 1812-15 — Maj. Ga. Mil.
m. Mary Sims — daughter Alsey m. Joseph Selby

Wooten (Wootten), Shadrach b. N.C. 1739 d. N.C. 1812 — Rep. N.C. 1785-
m. Elizabeth Allen (2) — 1812
son Richard m. Eliza Jane Williams
son Council m. Mary Burney

Wooten, William Vol. 11 — Pvt. N.C. Mil.

Wootten, Richard B. b. Ga. 1796 d. Ga. 1850 — Ens. Ga. Mil.
m. Martha Hinton — son Powhatan B. m. Catherine Lynch
daughter Susan m. James Boiling

Wootters, David b. Md. d. Md. m. Ann — Pvt. Md. Mil.
son Ezekiel m. Ann Downes

Worcester, Noah Vol. 3 — Capt. N.H. Mil.

Worden, Walter b. Conn. 1757 d. N.Y. 1814 — Capt. N.Y. Vol.
m. Lucretia Hicks — son Jesse m. Catherine Halsted

Work, Robert Vol. 10 — Pvt. Pa. Mil.

Work, William b. Pa. 1760 d. Pa. 1828 — Pvt. Pa. Mil. 1793
m. Miriam Scroggs — daughter Rachel m. Robert Hamilton
son William Jr. m. Nancy Brown

Worley, Ezekiel b. Md. 1747 d. Pa. 1836 — Pvt. Pa. Mil. 1787
m. Narcissa Wallen — son Joseph m. Susanna Amine

Worley, John b. 1747 d. Tenn. m. Nancy Henry — Pvt. E. Tenn. Mil.
daughter Elizabeth m. Michael Carriger

Worley, Joseph b. Md. 1769 d. Ohio 1871 m. Susanna Amrine — Cpl. Md. Mil.
daughter Druscilla m. William H. Robinson

Wormer (Van Wormer), Jeremiah b. Mass. 1783 — Matross N.Y. Art.
d. Mich. 1851 m. Eunice Wattles
son Aaron m. Mary Wallis

Wormley, Englehart b. Pa. 1755 d. Pa. 1827 — Lt. Pa. Mil.
m. Mary Elizabeth Rupley — son George E. m. Barbara Kiner
son John m. Mary C. Loy

Wornall, Thomas Vol. 13 — Capt. Ky. Mtd. Vol.

Worrell, Isaac Vol. 13   Maj. Gen. Pa. Mil.

Worsham, Daniel b. Va. 1780 d. Va. 1864 m. Fannie Jones   Pvt. Va. Mil.
    daughter Frances m. Frederick Rudd REAL DAUGHTER
    daughter Harriet m. James Rudd
    daughter Ida m. Arthur Wilton Dickeson

Worsley, William N.C. 1787 d. N.C. aft. 1830 m. Elizabeth   Pvt. N.C. Mil.
    son John m. Emerlizer Spicer

Worster, James b. Pa. 1782 d. Ind. 1849 m. Nancy Milner   Pvt. Ky. Mil.
    daughter Hannah R. m. William Henry Evens

Worthington, Lloyd Dorsey b. Md. 1785-95 d. Mo. 1877   Pvt. Md. Mil.
    m. Elizabeth Ball — son John A. m. Margaret Jane Clare

Worthington, William b. (W.) Va. 1761 d. Ky. 1848   Sen. Ky. 1814
    m. Mary Mason — son Thomas m. Rebecca Pace

Wright, Alexander b. Ire 1746 d. Pa. 1838   Asst. Judge Pa. 1800-27
    m. Esther Silcox — daughter Elizabeth m. Samuel Porter Stewart

Wright, Alpheus b. Vt. 1792 d. N.Y. 1848 m. Anna Loveland   Cpl. Vt. Mil.
    daughter Mary Jane m. Abraham X. Parker

Wright, Amzi b. Vt. 1781 d. N.Y. 1875   Cornet N.Y. Cal.
    m. Huldah A. Kellogg — son Enos K. m. Louise Newell

Wright, Benjamin b. N.C. 1796 d. Ill. 1866 m. Mary Hill   Pvt. N.C. Mil.
    son Simeon m. Sarilda Jane Swinford
    daughter Nancy m. Lewis Job
    son Perry A. m. Sarah E. Swinford
    daughter Lucinda m. James Richardson REAL DAUGHTER

Wright, Bildad b. Conn. 1768 d. N.Y. 1853   Pvt. Conn. Mil.
    m. Chloe Shipman — son Joel S. m. Jennet Templeton

Wright, Caleb b. Va. 1790 d. Ohio 1860   Pvt. Ohio Mil.
    m. Mary Ann Hacker — son Nathan m. Mary Lucina Mills

Wright, Daniel b. Vt. 1778 d. Ohio 1873 m. Ruth Todd   Sgt. Vt. Mil.
    daughter Mary m. Masury Woodward
    daughter Caroline m. William Whigam

Wright, Daniel b. Mass. 1780 d. Vt. 1866   Pvt. Vt. Mil.
    m. Bathsheba Frost — son William S. m. Lucy C. Phillips

Wright, Edward Vol. 7   Maj. Pa. Mil.

Wright, George b. Va. 1784 d. Miss. 1869   Pvt. La. Mil.
    m. Charity Hamilton — son Mark m. Martha Shepherd

Wright, Henry b. N.C. (Tenn.) 1789 d. Tex. 1853   Cornet W. Tenn. Vol.
    m. Sarah Endsley — daughter Adeline M. m. James Martin Henderson

Wright, Isaac H. b. Va. 1792 d. Miss. 1858   Sgt. Va. Mil.
    m. Catherine Meredith — daughter Martha Ann E. m. Reuben Lee
    daughter Mahala m. William Sims

Wright, Jacob II b. N.H. 1788 d. N.H. 1873   Pvt. N.H. Mil.
    m. Mary Underwood — daughter Lucy m. Moses D. Proctor

Wright, Jacob b. N.H. 1788 d. N.Y. 1865 m. Sally Sanders   Pvt. N.H. Mil.
    daughter Mary Rebecca m. Christopher Page Brown

Wright, James b. N.C. 1791 d. Tenn. 1860 m. Patsy Stigall   Pvt. N.C. Mil.
    son James M. m. Martha R. Vann

Wright, Joab b. Conn. 1759 d. Ohio 1844 m. Mary Olive   Pvt. N.Y. Mil.
   daughter Mary m. Henry Jeffrey

Wright, Job b. Mass. 1737 d. Mass. 1823   Mass. Clerk, Treasurer
   m. Miriam — son Nehemiah m. Anne Connable   Selectman 1785-90

Wright, John b. Tenn. 1790 d. Tenn. 1876   Pvt. Tenn. Mil.
   m. Barbara Range — son Thomas m. Margaret Haynes Swingle

Wright, John P. b. Vt. 1794 d. Vt. 1882   Pvt. Vt. Mil.
   m. Susannah Hewet — son William H. m. Sarah Hogan

Wright, John W. b. N.C. 1791 d. Ill. 1875   Pvt. Va. Mil.
   m. Matilda Randle — son John S. m. Mary I. Randle

Wright, Joseph b. 1794 d. Ohio 1853   Sgt. Ohio Mil.
   m. Elizabeth Trickle — son Joseph Jr. m. Susan D. Maxfield

Wright, Joseph b. Mass. 1746 d. Mass. 1803   Civil Officer Mass.
   m. Martha Eveleth — son Charles m. Betsey Clark

Wright, Reuben b. Va. 1794 d. Ill. 1868   Pvt. Ky. Mil.
   m. Kazuriah Jackson
   daughter Lucretia S. m. Edward Johnson Kendall

Wright, Robert Sr. b. Va. 1796 d. Mo. 1877   Pvt. Va. Mil.
   m. Mary Hamilton Alexander — daughter Mary S. m. Charles A. Martin

Wright, Thomas b. Va. 1785 d. Ohio 1845   Pvt. Ky. Vol.
   m. Frances E. Taylor — daughter Mary E. m. Samuel Saltzgaver

Wright, Thompson b. N.C. 1779 d. Tenn. 1834   Pvt. Tenn. Vol.
   m. Clementine Smith — daughter Amanda m. Col. Josh F. Johnson

Wright, William b. Ire. 1777 d. Washington. D.C, 1838   Seaman U.S.
   m. Elizabeth — son William Jr. m. Elizabeth Boyd   Frigate 1800

Wright, William b. Ire. 1750 d. Pa. 1820   Pvt. Pa. Mil.
   m. Sarah Ann Osborne — son Benjamin D. m. Josephine de la Rue

Wroth, Benjamin b. 1793 d. Iowa aft. 1855   Pvt. Vt. Mil.
   m. Aurilla Bonney — son Charles F. m. May A. Clark

Wunderlich (Wonderleigh), David b. Pa. 1775 d. Pa. 1840   Pvt. Pa. Mil.
   m. Mary Magdalene Heckendorn Titzel
   daughter Eliza m. William Culp

Wyborn, Bevil G. b. N.Y. 1783 d. N.Y. 1872   Pvt. N.Y. Mil.
   m. Keturah Van Velzer — son William H. m. Lavinia Bailey

Wyche, Henry Vol. 13   Com. of Revenue Va. 1812

Wyckoff, Peter b. N.J. 1757 d. N.J. 1840   Pvt. N.J. Inf.
   m. Catharine Van Etten (Van Etta)
   daughter Mary Magdalen m. Joseph Johnson

Wychoff, William b. Va. 1784 d. W.Va. 1868   Pvt. Va. Mil.
   m. Mary Shellingburgh — son Samuel m. Mary Ann St. Clair

Wyckoff, John b. N.Y. 1782 d. N.Y. 1867   Pvt. N.Y. Mil.
   m. Lucretia Dover — son Henry J. m. Johanna Stryker

Wyckoff, Nicholas b. Md. 1789 d. Kan. 1869   Pvt. Ohio Mil.
   m. Margaret Tweed — son John m. Maria Jane Merrill

Wyeth, Ebenezer b. Mass. 1727 d. Mass. 1788   Mass. Selectman, other
   m. Mary Winship   Civil Offices 1781-90
   son Gad m. Mary Kendall

Wylie, William Jr. Vol. 10   Pvt. Ky. Vol.

Wyly, James Rutherford b. 1783 d. 1835-64 m. Sarah H. Clark   Captain
    son Jas. R. Jr. m. Ann B. Harshaw   Creek War

Wyman, Adam b. Ky. 1775 d. Ky. 1813   Ens. Ky. Mtd. Vol.
    m. Elizabeth Smith — daughter Frances m. Levi Wooden

Wyman, Francis b. Mass. 1788 d. Mass. 1863   Pvt. Mass. Mil.
    m. Abigail Gammon — daughter Josephine A. m. John Orrin Mason

Wyman, John Vol. 6   Qtmtr. Mass. Mil.

Wyman, William Vol. 3   Pvt. Mass. Mil. 1777-80

Wyncoop, Gerardus b. Pa. 1732 d. Pa. 1812/13   Gen. Assem. Pa. 1786-99
    m. Elizabeth Bennett — son Matthew m. Thomasine Stockholm
    son William m. Mary Langstroth

Wynkoop, Everet H. b. N.Y. 1787 d. N.Y. 1874   Pvt. N.Y. Mil.
    m. Maria Post — son Everet H. Jr. m. Aldia Russell

Wynekoop, Matthew b. Pa. 1763 d. Pa.   Pvt. Pa. Light Drag.
    m. Thomasine Stockholm — son David m. Jane McCune

Wynn(e), Isaac b. Pa. 1741 d. Pa. 1807 m. Mary   Pvt. Pa. Mil.
    son Isaac, Jr. m. Dorcas Mixon Ayer

Wynne, John K. b. Va. 1765 d. Tenn. 1847   Lt. Col. Tenn. Mil.
    m. Lucy Mabry — son Alanson G. m. Martha Hunt
    son Thomas K. m. Elizabeth Johnson

Wynne, William Sr. b. Va. 1727/9 d. Va. 1808   Defender Va. 1793
    m. Cynthia Harman
    son Oliver Sr. m. Elizabeth Johnson
    m. Phillis Whitley
    son Robert Whitley m. Mary Crabtree

Wynne, Williamson b. S.C. 1760 d. Alabama 1829   Pvt. N.C. Mil.
    m. Eleanor Magruder — son Eramus m. Jane Sophronia Anderson

Wynsong, Jacob b Va. 1757 d. Va. 1823 m. Mary Byers   Pvt. Va. Mil.
    daughter Elizabeth m. Nicholas Starry
    son John m. Helen Henrietta Hebb

Yancey, Layton b. Va. 1754 d. Va. 1813   Sheriff Va. 1794
    m. Frances Lynn Lewis   Justice Va. 1783-1800
    daughter Louisa M. m. Thomas Garland Garth
    son William B. m. Mary Kyle Smith

Yancey, Robert b. Va. 1748 d. Va. 1818   Pvt. Va. Mil.
    m. Miss Holliday — daughter Delphia m. John Tillotson

Yancey, Thornton b. Va. 1740 d. N.C. 1799   Mem. Gen. Assem. N.C.
    m. Elizabeth Mitchell — son Tryon Sr. m. Martha Harris   1778-1792

Yantis, John b. Md. or Va. 1778 d. Ky. 1836   Capt. Ky. Mil.
    m. Priscilla A. Lapsley or Catherine
    son Enoch m. Eleanor Wolford
    son John L. m. Eliza A. Montgomery

Yard, Joseph b. N.J. 1788 d. N.J. 1872   Lt. N.J. Mil.
    m. Elizabeth Bimley (Brinley) — son Joseph B. m. Sarah A. E. Neal

Yates, George b. Va. 1779 d. Va. aft. 1813   Pvt. Va. Cav.
    m. Mary Browning — son John B. m. Elizabeth Coley Murray

Yates, James Gaines b. Va. 1781 d. Tenn. 1845   Maj. Ky. Mil.
    m. Mary Malinda Browning — son Willie B. m. Amanda Poor

Yates, John Christopher b. N.Y. 1799 d. Mich. 1855   Pvt. N.Y. Mil.
m. Mary Elizabeth Stephenson
son Oscar Edgar m. Gertrude Isabelle Giddings

Yates, John G. b. N.Y. 1793 d. N.Y. 1837 m. Lydia Hallett   Capt. N.Y. Mil.
daughter Cornelia m. John Vandenbaugh

Yates, Nicholas b. Va. 1790/1 d. Ark. 1873   Pvt. Tenn. Mil.
m. Elizabeth Hays — son Lewis Willis m. Elizabeth Archer Hagood

Yates, William b. Ky. 1793 d. Ky. 1867   Pvt. Ky. Mtd. Mil.
m. Elizabeth Ruby — daughter Frances P. m. Joseph H. Owsley

Yeager, John b. Pa. 1762 d. W.Va. 1833   Constable Surveyor
m. Phoebe Anastasia Hull (Anis Hohl)   W.Va. 1797
son Jacob m. Sarah Ann Hidy

Yeager, Nicholas b. Pa. 1774 d. W.Va. 1829 m. Mary Green   Lt. Va. Mil.
daughter Mary Ellen m. Asa Musgrave
daughter Sarah Catherine m. Alexander Long

Yeates (Yates), Jasper b. Pa. 1745 d. Pa. 1817 m. Sarah Burd   Pvt. Pa.
daughter Mary m. Charles Smith

Yeatman, Henry Lewis b. Va. 1773 d. Ky. 1859   Qtmsr. Va. Mil.
m. Elizabeth Thompson — son Arthur H. m. Sarah Elizabeth Suter

Yeaton, Joseph b. Mass. (Me.) 1775 d. Mass. (Me.) 1836   Pvt. Mass. Mil.
m. Rhoda Bailey — son Seth C. m. Elizabeth LeB. Pattie

Yoeman, Moses b. N.Y. 1746 d. N.Y. 1814   Trustee Sheriff N.Y.
m. Elizabeth Nottingham — daughter Lydia m. Jacob DuBois

Yeomans, Erastus b. Conn. 1791 d. Mich. 1863   Pvt. Fifer Conn. Mil.
m. Phoebe Arnold — daughter Maria m. James Bronson Sanford Sr.

York, Eli b. N.C. c. 1769 d. N.C. 1854   Manufactured Gun Powder
son Brantley m. Mary Wells Lineberry   1812-15

Yost, Benjamin Beringer b. Pa. 1787 d. Pa. 1858   Pvt. Pa. Mil.
m. Sarah Feather — son Isaac F. m. Rosina Miller

Youmans, Abijah b. N.Y. 1789 d. Ill. 1872 m. Esther Organ   Sgt. N.Y. Mil.
son Joseph B. m. Abigail Squire

Youmans, Freddrick b. N.Y. 1780 d. N.Y. 1829 m. Elizabeth   Pvt. N.Y. Mil.
daughter Catherine m. Henri Cochen

Young, Alexander b. Ky. 1792 d. Iowa 1869   Pvt. Ky. Mtd. Mil.
m. Mary Davis — son John D. m. Maria Louisa Eyestone

Young, Charles b. Ger. 1757 d. Va. 1848   Pvt. Va. Mil.
m. Catherine Elizabeth Kint — son Adam m. Sally Crum

Young, Conrad Vol. 10   Pvt. Md. Mil.

Young, Dan b. N.H. 1783 d. Ohio 1864   Leg. N.H.
m. Mary Mills Glidden
daughter Nancy Marie m. Dr. George Belden Crane

Young, Daniel b. Mass. (Me.) 1790 d. Me. aft. 1819   Lt. Mass. Mil.
m. Betsey Purves — daughter Sarah Jane m. Henry B. McLaughlin

Young, Daniel b. Va. 1790 d. Va. 1873   Pvt. Va. Mil.
m. Elizabeth Rhodes — son William W. m. Arianna Adeline Smith

Young, David b. Pa. c. 1792 d. Ohio 1874   Pvt. Ohio Mil.
m. Elizabeth Seaman — son Joseph m. Betty Miller

Young, David b. Va. 1774 d. Va. 1829 m. Mary A. Hart   Capt. Va. Mil.
son Samuel H. m. Catharine Weedon Small

Young, Foster Vol. 10
        Pat. N.Y.

Young, George b. Pa. 1797 d. Pa. 1866 m. Susanna Scholl   Pvt. Pa. Mil.
son John S. m. Mary Ann Weigle

Young, Guilford Dudley b. N.Y. d. Mex.   Maj. N.Y. Mil.
m. Betsey Huntington — son Guilford D. Jr. m. Laura Frances Graham

Young, Henry II b. N.C. 1793 d. Miss. 1878   Cpl. Tenn. Mil.
m. Sallie T. Humphreys — daughter Louisa M. m. James Smith Burns

Young, Jacob b. Va. 1773 d. Ohio 1862 m. Mary Mason   Pvt. Pa. Mil.
daughter Amy m. John Carlisle Kerr

Young, James b. Va. 1771 d. Ky. 1841   Ky. Legis. 1812-13
m. Anna Frances Booker — daughter Elizabeth Ann m. Lindsey George

Young, James G. b. Virginia 1790 d. Ala. 1857   Lt. Va. Mil.
m. (3) Elizabeth Clements Young (cousin)
son Hardaway m. Minerva Jones Vaughan

Young, John b. N.H. 1796 d. Vt. 1888 m. Nancy A. Herrick   Pvt. U.S. Army
son Franklin A. m. Priscilla Hathaway

Young, John b. Pa. 1760 d. W.Va. 1850   Lt. (W.)Va. Mil.
m. Mrs. Keziah Tackett Townsend
son Jacob m. Nancy Ann Stephenson
son John D. m. Elizabeth James

Young, John b. Scot 1746 d. Ala. 1840   Pvt. S.C. Mil.
m. Mary Sarah Beckett
daughter Martha Jane m. Andrew Jackson Alexander

Young, John Landis b. Ky. 1796 d. Iowa 1882   Cpl. Ky. Mil.
m. Juda Goldsmith — daughter Juda m. Alexander Burrell Hanner

Young, John Tully b. Md. 1776 d. W.Va. 1860   Pvt. Northwest
m. Euphama Jarvis   Indian War
daughter Eleanor m. John A. Williams

Young, Joseph b. N.J. 1783 d. Ohio 1861   Pvt. N.J. Mil.
m. Elizabeth Hickman — son Joseph Michael m. Margaret Jones

Young, Leavin (Leaving) b. Md. 1777 d. Ky. ca. 1841   Pvt. Ky. Mil.
m. Elizabeth Weibel (Weible)
daughter Eliza Ann m. Joseph Milward
son Leving m. Mary Ford

Young, Mathias b. prob. Va. d. W.Va. 1845   Pvt. Va. Mil.
m. Nancy Hickman — son Thompson m. Nancy Isabelle Reveal

Young, Nathaniel Vol. 9   2nd Lt. Del. Mil.

Young, William b. (Me.) Mass. 1771 d. Me. 1861   Pvt. (Me.) Mass. Mil.
m. Betsey Brown — daughter Lydia Margaret m. Nathaniel Hayes Cate

Young, William b. Va. 1760 d. Ohio 1845   Pvt. Ohio Mil.
m. Susan Lancaster — son Penelton m. Susan Solemberger

Young, William Broby b. N.C. 1794 d. Md. 1865   Sgt. Va. Mil.
m. Susan Bradford Grice
daughter Sue H. m. Andrew C. Bradley REAL DAUGHTER

Youngblood, William b.— d. S.C. 1815   Lt. Col. S.C. Mil.
     m. Elizabeth Singleton — daughter Margaret m. Jacob Q. Alison

Younglove, John b. Pa. 1743 d. N.Y. 1821   Judge N.Y. 1794
     m. Martha Perrine — daughter Catherine m. Jedidiah Pierce

Yount (Yundt), Andrew b. Pa. 1760 d. Pa. 1841   Pvt. Pa. Mil.
     m. Barbara Dietrich — son Henry m. Maria M. Kinzer

Yount, David b. N.C. 1795 d. Mo. 1881   Cpl. Mo. Mil. 1814-15
     m. Catherine Shell — son Azariah m. Elizabeth Ann Jarvis Franks
     son Azariah m. Elizabeth Ann Jarvis Franks

Z

Zane, Ebenezer b. Va. 1747 d. W.Va. 1812   Patriot Ohio
     m. Elizabeth McCullough — daughter Gretchen m. John Robinson

Zearing, John Vol. 16   Pvt. Pa. Mil.
     Rebecca m. Martin Carse REAL DAUGHTER

Zellner, Peter b. Pa. 1787 d. Pa. 1827   Pvt. Pa. Mil.
     m. Elizabeth Behinger — son Charles m. Elizabeth Mifflin Bank

Zener, David b. Va. 1797 d. Ind. 1877 m. Phoebe Baker   Pvt. Ky. Mil.
     daughter Harriet m. Joseph Ayers

Zenor, George b. Pa. d. Ind. 1848 m. Mary Danner   Pvt. Ind. Vol.
     son Joseph m. Mary A. Deal

Zerbe, John Adam b. Pa. 1794 d. Pa. 1873   Pvt. Pa. Mil.
     m. Christina Bretz — daughter Henrietta m. Anthony Berdnaier

Zieber, Samuel b. Pa. 1794 d. Pa. 1868 m. Matilda Schmeltzer   Pvt. Pa. Mil.
     daughter Catherine E. m.— REAL DAUGHTER
     daughter Emma Malilda m.— REAL DAUGHTER

Ziegler, Killian b. Pa. 1742 d. Pa. 1808   Justice of Peace
     m. Anna Maria Lischy — son John m. Elizabeth Sharp   Pa. 1796

Ziegler, Philip b. Pa. 1761 d. Pa. 1839 m. Mary Kramer   Capt. Pa. Mil.
     son Jesse m. Mary Ann Peffer

Zimmerman, David b. Pa. 1786 d. Pa. 1857 m. Mary Kelly   Pvt. Pa. Mil.
     son Mathias m. Sarah

Zimmerman, Rev. Ezra Benedict b. 1795 d. 1878   Sgt. Ohio
     m. Anna Thompson — daughter Eleanor Kellogg m. Dr. Wyllys Hull

Zimmerman, William b. Pa. 1781 d. Pa. 1862   Emergency Soldier Pa.
     son Franklin m. Martha Miller

Zink (Sink), John b. Pa. 1792 d. Ohio 1843   Cpl. Pa. Mil. 1814
     m. Martha Davis — son James Davis m. Clarissa Murphey

Zink, Samuel b. Pa. 1793 d. Pa. 1883 m. Dorothy Kesler   Sgt. Pa. Mil.
     son David R. m. Eliza Jane Sedwick

Zittrauer, Ernest b. Ga. c. 1754 d. Ga. 1817   2nd Lt. Ga. Mil.
     m. Johannah Reiter — son Gotlieb m. Margaret Gugel

Zollinger, George b. Md. 1791 d. Mo. 1871   Pvt. Md. Mil.
     m. Catherine Myers — son Augusta L. m. Mary Louise Mayfield

Zollinger, Jacob Vol. 3   Pvt. Pa. Mil.

Zumwalt, Adam b. Pa. 1756 d. Mo. 1834 m. Mary Roth   Pvt. Mo. Terr. Mil.
    daughter Mary Sue m. Joseph Journey

Zumwalt, Andrew b. Ky. 1789 d. Ore. 1867   Pvt. Mo. Terr. Mil.
    m. Elizabeth Fraser — son Adam F. m. Louisa M. Crow
    son Isaac m. Sarah Crow

Zumwalt, Christopher b. Pa. 1750 d. Mo. 1819 m. Marilus —   Pvt. Ky. Mil.
    son Christopher Jr. m. Elizabeth Keller

Zumwalt, Jacob b. Va. 1752 d. Mo. 1820   Defender Terr. Mo.
    m. (1) Quati M. Miller   1789
    son George m. Mary Elizabeth Killebrew

SUPPLEMENTAL LIST

Alexander, John Sr. b. Tenn. c. 1780 d. Tenn. Pvt. E. Tenn. Mil. 1814
1831 m. Martha Ferguson — son John m. Delilah Woods

Allen, William b. Mass. 1746 d. Mass. 1830 Lieut. Mass. Mil. 1797
m. Deborah Clark — daughter Anna m. Lemuel Allen

Althouse (Allshouse) Henry Jr. b. Pa. 1757 Member Pa. Assembly
d. Pa. 1836 m. 1st Catharina Truxel — son Isaac 1802-15
m. Margaret Minimum

Ambrose, Jacob b. prob. Pa. c. 1770 d. Pa. 1846 Militia Duty Bedford
m. Esther Shock Co. 1789
daughter Elizabeth m. Francis Spearman

Anderson, David b. Pa. 1771 d. Ohio 1843 Pvt. Ohio Mil. 1812
m. Esther Hollinshead — daughter Jane Duer m. Isaac Miover

Armstrong, William L. b. N.C. 1773 d. Tenn. 1862 Justice Peace 1812/5
m. Mary Cavitt — daughter Huldy m. James Glidewell Tenn.

Aspinwall, Elijah b. Mass. 1764 d. West Indies 1804 Navy War of 1812
m. Nancy Spurr — son Elijah m. Barbara Dickson British prisoner

Bailey, James b. N.Y. 1785 d. N.Y. 1830 Pvt. 2nd N.Y. Regt. 1812
m. Polly — son Horace D. m. Harriet Jackson

Bankston, John b. Pa. 1754 d. La. 1823 Pvt. La. Mil.
m. Henrietta Coates — daughter Cecelia m. William Dyson

Beaty, James b. S.C. 1784 d. Ala. 1837 Pvt. S.C. Mil. 1813/14
m. Margaret Milford — son George m. Mary E. Biggs

Benedict, John Thomas b. Conn. 1773 d. N. Y. 1845 Pvt. 50th N. Y.
m. Betsey Dart — daughter Betsey m. John R. Walker Regt. 1814

Bird, Williamson b. Va. c. 1726 d. Ga. 1806 Juror 1795 King &
m. Phoebe Price — son Philemon m. Mary Lee Queen Co. Va.

Blair, Thomas b. N. C. 1773 d. Tenn. 1846 Pvt. 4th W. Tenn. Regt 1812
m. Eleanor Doak — daughter Amanda Jane m. Joseph Poindexter

Bowell, Thomas b. Wales 1754 d. Pa. 1815 Pvt. Fayette Co. Pa. Mil.
m. Ann — daughter Ruth m. Charles Brownfield 1812/13

Bowman, Jonas b. Mass. 1739 d. N. H. 1807 Repr. N. H. State Leg
m. Susannah Gregory — son Baxter fr Henniker 1800/2
m. Abigail Kimball

Brown, Hugh b. Ga. 1788 d. Ga. 1851 Repr. Ga. State Leg. & Sheriff
m. Elizabeth Dean — daughter Jane Dean Camden Co. 1811/14
m. Jacob T. Goodbread

Brown, William b. N.J. 1794 d. N.J. 1861 Pvt. 3rd N.J. Regt. 1814
m. Jemima Newbury — daughter Sarah m. James L. Brand

Buck, Horace b. Mass. 1791 d. N. Y. 1863 Fifer N. Y. Mil.
m. Besey Burgess — son Wetmore m. Mary Joslin

Burckhartt, George F. b. Md. 1782 d. Mo. 1864 Sgt. Major Ky Mil.
m. Ruth Dorsey — son Dr. C. F. m. Elizabeth Ann Hill

Cabell, Joseph b. Va. 1780 d. Ky. 1836 Capt. 16th Green Co. Ky. Regt.
m. Rachel Mann — son Samuel m. Catherine M. Allen 1803

Cadmus, Abraham H. b. N. J. 1789 d. N. J. 1864 Corp. N. J. Mil.
m. Mariah Brown — son Moses m. Sophia Jane Weakley

Camp, Orsemus b. S. C. 1797 d. Ga. 1860   Soldier War of 1812
  m. Margaret Henley — son Hosea Milton   prob. Ga.
  m. Elizabeth Jane Goodwin

Carver, John C. b. Va. 1788 d. Ky. 1873   Pvt. Va. Mil. 1814/15
  m. Nancy Carver (cousin) — son James m. Jane Thomas

Catt, Sebastian b. c. 1775 d. Ill. 1822   Pvt. 4th Ind. Regt. 1812
  m. 2d Sebra Conger — daughter Electra Ann m. Dr. William Pollard

Chamberlain, Jason b. Mass. 1782 d. Mass. 1849   Pvt. Co. fr Westboro,
  m. Betsey Burnap — son Jason Dexter   Mass. svc. at Boston 1814
  m. Elsey G. Crooker

Chapman, John b. Va. 1740 d. Va. 1815   Lieut. Va. Mil. 1790
  m. Sallie Abbott — son George m. Patience Clay

Cleveland, John b. Conn. 1779 d. Ohio 1861   Pvt. N. Y. Mil.
  m. Silvia Phillips — son John P. m. Sarah Hatch

Cleveland, Joseph b. Mass. 1738 d. Maine 1816   Sgt. Mass. (Me.) Mil.
  m. Dorothy Cragain — son Timothy m. Jane McFadden

Cleveland, Moses b. Vt. 1799 d. Wisc. 1894   Pvt. N. Y. Mil.
  m. Tryphena Bates — son Charles m. Sophia King

Cook, David b. Pa. 1797 d. Ohio aft. 1870   Ensign Pa. 16th Div. 1813
  m. Lucy — daughter Eliza m. James Brownlee

Cook, Theophilus b. S. C. 1788 d. Ill. 1858   Pvt. Tenn. Vols. 1813/5
  m. Elizabeth Caldwell — daughter Fariba m. Willis B. Holder

Cooper, Osborn b. Va. 1780/90 d. Ohio 1847   Pvt. 2nd Ohio Regt. 1813/14
  m. Mary Ryon (Ryan) — daughter Elizabeth Jones m. Jesse Lee Day

Cosbey, Samuel b. Pa. 1790 d. Ohio 1869   Pvt. Ohio Mil. 1812
  m. Eleanor Lee — son Adam Lee m. Mary Jane Ferris

Cox, Robert b. S.C.— d. S.C. aft. 1835   Pvt. S.C. Mil.
  m. Basheba McCoy — daughter Louisa m. Wellborn Barton Jr.

Cozby, James b. Va. 1753 d. Tenn. 1831   Major and Surgeon
  m. Isabella Woods — son John m. Abigail McBee   Indian War 1813

Crawford, Joel b. Ga. 1783 d. Ga. 1858   Major Ga. Mil. 1814/15
  m. Sarah L. Rhodes — daughter Sarah Louisa m. William A. Maxwell

Crown, Hezekiah b. Md. 1798 d. D.C. 1865   Pvt. D.C. Mil. War 1812
  m. Jane Gingell — son Robert Amos m. Mary Ann McKnee

Culbertson, Andrew b. Pa. 1765 d. N.Y. 1812   Pvt. 4th Pa. Bn. 1784
  m. Elizabeth Craig — son Samuel m. Nancy Johnston

Davis, Henry b. 1794 d. Tenn. 1867   Pvt. Tenn. Mil. 1812/14
  m. Susannah West — son Stephen m. Katherine Fite

Dougherty, John b. S.C. 1788 d. Ga. 1870   Pvt. Ga. Mil.
  m. Nancy Gantt — son Eli G. m. Mary Elizabeth Fletcher Vol. 19

Dowling, John b. S.C. 1759 d. S.C. 1826   Pvt. S.C. State Troops 1812
  m. Nancy Boutwell — son Allen m. Polly Heath

Dungan, Jesse b. Pa. 1756 d. Pa. 1823   Lieut. 1786 Phila. Co. Pa. Mil.
  m. Esther Johnson — son James m. Joanna Holland

Edmiston, William b. Va. 1795 d. Ill. 1885   Pvt. Tenn. or Va. Mil.
  m. Sarah Askins — daughter Mary m. Thomas Paul

Edmonds, Samuel b. N.Y. 1760 d. N.Y. 1826   Paymaster Gen. N.Y. Mil.
m. Lydia Worth — daughter Mary Ann m. Henry L. Webb

Edson, Jonah b. Mass. 1792 d. Mass. 1874   Pvt. Bridgewater Co. 1814
m. Jennet Bryant — daughter Fanny m. Levi B. Parker   svc at Boston

Euans, Joseph b. N.J. 1784 d. Ohio 1851   Capt. 3rd Ohio Regt.
m. 1st Rhoda Heppard Richards   1813/14
son Samuel m. 1st Jemima Buckley

Fielder, John b. Va. 1780 d. S.C. 1889   Pvt. S.C. Mil. 1814/15
m. Mary Miller — daughter Jane Caroline m. Nathaniel Wofford

Fisher, George b. Md. 1782 d. Pa. bur Md. 1848   Major York Co. Pa.
m. Christina Hovis — son Benjamin m. Elizabeth Hildebrand   1812

Fisher, Samuel b. Pa. — d. La. aft. 1819   Sgt. 16th La. Regt. Mil.
m. Mary Ann Roule Roper (widow)
son Jeremiah C. m. Sarah Ann Barrow

Fritz, William b. Pa. 1774 d. Pa. 1864   Pvt. Bedford Co. Pa. Mil. 1789
m. Elizabeth Palm — son John m. Eva Maurer

Fuller, Stephen b. Conn. 1730 d. Pa. 1813   Civil Offices Bradford
m. Mary Abbot — son Reuben m. Mary Cash   Co. Pa. 1795/6

Fulton, Alexander b. Pa. 1764 d. La. bef. 1817   Coroner 1805; member
m. Henrietta Wells   La. Leg. 1807
daughter Courtney Ann m. Leonard Waller Groce

Galbraith, John b. Penn. 1739 d. Penn. 1802   Capt. Pa. Mil. 1792
m. Mary McCalley — daughter Nancy m. Robert Stockton

Gibbs, James L. b. Ky. 1786 d. Ky. 1872   Pvt. 1812 Ky. Vol. Cav.
m. Elizabeth Guthrie — son Jacob C. m. Mary Ann Munday

Gillham, Reyderius Clark b. S.C. 1783 d. Ill. 1846   Lieut. 2nd Ill. Regt.
m. Susannah C. Brown   1814
son Samuel Parker m. Louisa Gillham (cousin)

Glasscock, Thomas R. b. Ky. 1796 d. Ky. 1872   Drummer Ky. Mil.
m. Elizabeth Asbury — daughter Emily m. Henry V. Riggen   1814

Glentworth, Plunkett Fleeson b. Pa. 1768 d. N.J.   Pvt. Phila. Mil. 1794
1833 m. Harriet Straken Budden Bostwick
daughter Harriett m. Rev. William Miller Carmichael

Goodbread, Philip Jr., b. N.C. 1761 d. Fla. 1839   Ensign 3rd Co. Camden
m. Catherine Souder   Co. Ga. Mil. 1798
son Adam Souder G. m. Elizabeth Van Zant

Graham, James b. Va. 1741 d. W. Va. 1813   Colonel Mil. 1799
m. Florence Graham (cousin)   Monroe Co. Va.
daughter Jane m. David Jarrett Jr.

Grimsley, Joseph b. S.C. 1780 d. Ga. 1860   Pvt. Ga. Mil. 1814/15
m. Miss Hamilton — son Jeremiah W. m. Elizabeth Hays

Gwynne, David b. Md. 1786 d. Ky. 1849 m. Alice Ann Claypoole   Major
son Abraham E. m. Rachel Moore Flagg   Md. 1814

Hackney, Barton Philpot b. Md. by 1788 d. Md. aft 1830   Capt. Md. Mil.
m. Mary Deaver — son Charles Philpot m. Mary Large   1813/14

Hale, Enoch b. Mass. 1733 d. Vt. 1813 — Repr. to Vt. Leg. 1804/5
m. Abigail Gould Stanley
daughter Lucy m. Hezekiah Wetherbee

Hall, Street b. Conn. 1721 d. Conn. 1809 — Del. Conv. 1788 Conn.
m. Hannah Fowler — daughter Hannah m. Joel Moss

Hallock, Augustus Van Courtland b. N.Y. 1794 — Pvt. N.Y. Mil. 1812
d. Mich. 1874 m. 2d Catherine O'Neil
daughter Martha m. Robert Roof

Hart, Moses b. Va. 1791 d. Ohio 1881 m. Margaret Nicely — Pvt. Va. Mil. 1812
daughter Margaret m. John Weeks

Hayes (Haas) John b. N.J. 1785 d. N.J. 1845 — Pvt. N.J. Rifleman 1814
m. Alletta Wyckoff — daughter Lydia m. John Hoffman

Hayes, John b. — 1791 d. Ga. 1881 m. Lucy Jarrell — Pvt. Ga. Mil.
daughter Martha Ann m. Drury Jackson

Head, Benjamin b. Va. 1731 d. Va. 1803 — Grand Juror 1797 Orange Co. Va.
m. Martha Marshall or Sherman
son Henry m. Elizabeth Sanford

Hill, Henry John Alexander b. N.C. 1774 — Mem. Tenn. Assy. 1807/9 1813/15
d. Tenn. 1825 m. Mrs. Susanna Swales Savage
son Jesse m. Frances Rogers

Hodges, George W. b. S.C. by 1769 d. S.C. 1851 — Capt. War 1812 Marlboro Co. S.C.
m. Sarah Cherry
son Robert G. W. m. Elvira Hale

Hollinger, George b. Pa. 1757 d. Pa. 1833 — Pvt. 1783 Lancaster Co. Pa. Mil.
m. Margaretha Lehner — son David m. Susanna Grube

How, Samuel b. Conn. 1769 d. — 1854 — Capt. N.Y. Art. Mil.
m. Caroline Fitch — son John F. m. Sarah M. Clark

Hughes, Henry b. S.C. 1760 d. Miss. 1851/2 — Pvt. La. Mil. 1814/15
m. Widow Nancy Mary Bell
son Calvin m. 2d Mary M. Sanders

Jenkins, Philip b. Pa. 1789 d. Ark. 1871 — Pvt. Hardin Co. Ky. Mil.
m. Mary Shaver — son John Elliot m. 5th Sarah Hallock

Jones, John b. N.C. 1784 d. Tenn. 1832/3 — Pvt. Tenn. Mil. 1814
m. Jane James — son Thomas Jefferson m. Minerva Underhill

Jones, John b. Pa. 1781 d. Pa. 1858 — Pvt. Pa. Regt. 1812
m. Catherine Clover — son Samuel m. Elizabeth McGonagle

Jones, Mathew b. Pa. 1788 d. Ohio 1848 — Pvt. Ohio Mil. 1813
m. Sarah Thorougham—son Mathew Jackson m. Margaret L. Roderick

Joor (Ioor), John b. S.C. 1780 d. Miss. 1836 — Capt. Indian War Miss. General at Battle N/O La.
m. Emily Richardson
son Joseph m. Ann Finley

Ketchum "Captain" (Chief Delaware Indians 1848) — Guide for Gen. Cass from Ft. Wayne O 1814 to Can line
b. Ohio 1780 d. Kans. Terr. 1857 m._____
son Howard O. m. Maria

Kyle, Robert b. Ire. 1751 d. Tenn. 1814, exposure — Pvt. Tenn. Vols. 1814
m. Sarah Runnels (Reynolds)—son Robert m. 1st Rachel Gillenwater

Lacy, James b. N.C. 1771 d. Tenn. 1847 m. Nancy Edens   Pvt. E. Tenn. Mil.
son John W. m. Nancy Hyder

Lacy, Stephen b. Va. 1781 d. Miss. aft. 1850   Pvt. Ky. Mil. 1812
m. 2d Martha Morearty Moss
daughter Sara m. George Mathewes Hughes

Lastinger, Andrew b. Ga. 1778   Ensign Bulloch Co. Ga. Mil. 1802
d. Ga. 1837 m. Mary Parker — son William m. Louise English

LeBlanc, Silvestre b. La. bef. 1785 d. La. aft. 1820   Pvt. La. Mil.
m. Perosine Duhon — daughter Marie Aspasie m.   Battle N/O
Jean Treville Thibodeaux

Lenox, William b. Va. 1782 d. Mo. aft. 1855   Pvt. Ky. and Mo. Mil. 1812-15
m. _____ Kitchens — son David m. Elizabeth Brown

Lewis, Charles b. Va. 1775 d. Va. 1829   Pvt. Fairfax Co. Va. Mil.
m. Jane Davison — son George W. m. Sophia Allen

Lewis, Charles Augustine Lightfoot b. Va. 1782   Pvt. 1814 Va. Troops
d. Va. 1845 m. Mary Warner Lewis (cousin)
daughter Catherine B. m. Henry T. Goodloe

Lewis, Charles Crawford b. Va. 1761 d. N.C. 1833   Magis. & Mem. S.C.
m. Elizabeth Russell—son Pitman m. Iantha Dalton   Leg. 1798/1832

Lincoln, Jesse b. Pa. 1787 d. Pa. 1869   Sgt. Fayette Co. Pa. 1814
m. Hannah Hones
son Richard Stokes m. Hannah Anna Haymaker

Lindsay, John b. N.C. 1789 d. Texas 1853   2nd Sgt. Tenn. Mil. 1814-15
m. Martha Ledford
son William Ransome m. Elizabeth Ann Woosley

Little, Moses b. N.H. 1739 d. N.H. 1798   Justice Peace & Capt. Mil.
m. Mary Milk   Grafton Co. N.H.
son Ebenezer m. Jane Burbeck

Lynch, William Hugh b. Md. c. 1784 d. Md. aft. 1836   Sgt. 1st Md. Mil.
m. Valinda Spates   War 1812
son William Henry G. m. Elizabeth E. Lightfoot

McCallum, Angus Sellars b. N.C. 1774 d. N.C. 1849   Pvt. Robeson Co.
m. Rebecca Brown — son Dougald m. Flora Brown   N.C. Regt. 1812

McCorkle, Alexander b. Va. 1773 d. Va. 1851   Capt. War 1812
m. Mildred Welch   Rockbridge Co. Va.
son Thomas m. Susan Alexander

McGlathery, Isaac b. Pa. 1753 d. Pa. 1834   Pvt. Pa. Mil.
m. Rachel _____ — son Isaac m. Anne Lewis

Marshall, John b. N.H. 1785 d. N.H. 1869 m.   Pvt. N.H. Mil. 1814
Hannah March — daughter Rhoda Ann m. George Ball Kenney

Martin, Joseph b. France 1781 d. La. 1861   Lieut. La. Mil.
m. Marguerite Constance Verret
daughter Justine C. m. Jean Materre

Masters, Richard b. by 1763 d. Ohio 1843   Pvt. 3rd Ohio Regt. 1812-13
m. Mary _____ — son Benjamin m. Susan Jane Stage

Miller, Elisha Jr. b. Vt. 1792 d. Vt. 1871   Sgt. Vt. Mil.
m. Angeline Munson — son Jackson m. Hannah Ferre

Millikan, John b. N.C. 1775 d. Ohio 1814   Lieut. Ohio Cav.—died
  m. Mary Wyatte   while in command British
  son William m. 3rd Emma Cleveland   prisoners Chilicothe

Mingus, William b. Ohio 1796 d. Ohio 1836   Pvt. Zanesville Ohio Co.
  m. Hannah Lewis — son William m. Syntha Ann Vore   1812-13

Morgan, John b. Pa. 1790 d. Pa. 1880   Pvt. Fayette Co. Pa. 1812
  m. Elizabeth Lyons — son David m. Caroline Stewart

Morgan, Luke b. Mass. 1794 d. Mass. 1874   Pa. Mil. 1814-15
  m. 2d Anna Brown Elliott
  son Thomas Appleton m. 2d Henrietta Carroll

Morris, Samuel b. prob. Md. bef. 1760 d. Md. 1804-7   On Mil. list 1794
  m. Mary maybe Rebecca Roe   Baltimore Co.
  son Samuel m. Jemima Palmer

Morton, James b. Va. 1756 d. Tenn. 1808   Capt. 22nd Tenn. Regt. 1807
  m. Catherine Wells — daughter Tabitha m. John Lytle

Motter, John b. Pa. c. 1777 d. Md. 1819   Pvt. Pa. State Troops 1814-15
  m. Anna Marie Hanelin — son Jacob m. Jemima Troxel

Newcomer, Jacob b. Pa. 1765 d. Pa. 1820   Pvt. Pa. Vols. 1812
  m. Mary Neukommer — son Jacob m. Nency Leckrone

Nisbet, Robert b. S.C. 1793 d. Ga. 1876 m. Eliza Graves   Pvt. S.C. Mil.
  daughter Mary Anne m. William Alexander Weldon

Norton, James b. N.J. 1791 d. Pa. 1884 m. Harriet Bruchman Pvt. Pa. Inf.
  son James H. m. Adelaide A.

Ogletree, James Thomas b. Va. 1787 d. Ga. 1833   Pvt. Ga. Mil. 1814-15
  m. Elizabeth Goins (Goyens)—son Seaborn m. Rebecca Jane Taylor

Pancake, Joseph b. Va. 1789 d. Ohio 1853   Pvt. Ohio Mil.
  m. Martha Jane Wilson — daughter Jane m. David Johnson
  (This anc. listed earlier with different family)

Parker, Amos b. Conn. 1726 d. Vt. aft. 1789   Sgt. 1789 Windsor Co. Vt.
  m. Lois Ives — daughter Sally m. Edward Fairbanks

Pattee, Asa b. Mass. 1734 d. N.H. 1825   Juror Warner N.H. 1788
  m. 2nd Mehitable Jewett — daughter Ruth m. Jacob Currier

Patton, Thomas b. Pa. 1776 d. Ohio 1850   Pvt. & Corp. Ohio Terr. Mil. 1812
  m. Nancy Quiggle — daughter Fanney m. John Tribby Jr.

Pendleton, David b. R.I. 1770 d. R.I. 1857   Sailing Master R.I. Navy
  m. Sarah Pendleton (cousin) — son William C. m. Phebe Hall

Pendleton, Henry b. Va. 1762 d. Va. 1822   Delegate Gen. Assy. 1804-6
  m. Alcey Ann Winston   Militia Officer—Justice Ct.
  daughter Barbara Overton m. William Barrett Phillips

Post, Ephraim b. N.J. 1779 d. 1869   Sgt. Pa. 1st Regt. 1812-14
  m. Matilda Elliott — son Jacob m. Phoebe Jane Gray

Pratt, Sampson b. N.Y. 1795 d. Ill. 1872 Pvt. Fair Haven Vt. Regt. 1813-15
  m. Elizabeth Tryon — daughter Elizabeth m. William Dunn

Rankin, David b. Pa. 1777 d. Ky. 1815-20   Pvt. Ky. Vols. 1813
  m. Nancy Roberts — son Willis m. Nancy Asbury

Ray, John b. Va. 1741 d. Mo. 1820   Repr. & Sen. Ky. Leg. 1803-1
m. 1st Jane Randolph, 2d Virlanda
daughter Ruth Clary by 2d wife m. Birkett D. Bowmer

Richards, Isaac b. Va. 1791 d. Ind. 1888   Pvt. E. Tenn. Mil. 1814
m. Margaret Snapp — daughter Catherine m. David M. Tyler

Roberts, Dr. Joseph Gill b. Va. 1789 d. Ky. 1867   Doctor on USS "Essex"
m. Martha Ann Todd—son Joseph W. m. Ann Mary Bacon   1811-14

Rogers, Israel b. S.C. 1789 d. La. 1877   Pvt. La. Troops
m. 1st Mary Knighton
daughter Arzeala m. Robert Marshall Sample

Schley, Henry b. Md. d. Md. m. Sarah Worrell Vol. 2   Lieut. Md. Mil.
son Charles m. Harriet M. Johnson

Schmelzel, John B. b. N.Y.C. 1790 d. N.Y.C. 1864   2nd Sgt. N.Y. Art.
m. Jane Ostheim — son George J. m. C. Louisa Kidabock

Scott, Joseph b. Ky. 1792 d. Kans. 1871   Pvt. Jessamine Co. Ky. Mil.
m. Sarah Sutton — son James William m. Margaret Lucas

Seagraves, Bennett b. Ga. 1791 d. Tenn. 1868   Drummer W. Tenn. Mil.
m. Margaret Lockhart—daughter Sarah J. E. m. 2nd James D. Widger

Sears, Thomas b. Va. 1789 d. Ohio 1864   Pvt. Va. Mil. 1812
m. Mary Daniel — son William m. Phebe Walter

Seldon, Dr. Wilson Cary b. Va. 1761 d. Va. 1835   Member Va. Assy. 1793
m. Mary Bowles Armistead Alexander   Loudon Co.
daughter Eliza Aristead m. John Janney Lloyd

Sharp, Dr. Marcus La Fayette b. N.C. 1789 d. Texas   1862 Surgeon's Mate
m. 1st Phoebe Featherstone   1st Tenn. Regt. 1813
son Benjamin Franklin m. Mary Crocket

Shenefelt, John b. Pa. 1789 d. Mich. 1884   Sgt. Pa. Mil. 1812
m. Sarah Collier — son Henry Clay m. Anna Elizabeth Bacon

Shoemaker, Jacob b. Pa. 1769-70 d. Ohio 1846   Pvt. Ohio Mil. 1813
m. Catherine _____ — son Abraham m. Mary Dever

Shreve, Israel b. N.J. 1739 d. Pa. 1799   Judge Burlington N.J. 1784
m. Mary Cokely   Justice Peace 1786
daughter Esther m. William Briggs

Smith, David b. Va. 1786 d. Ind. 1851   Pvt. Ohio Mil. 1812
m. Elizabeth Hurd — son William m. Kathrine M. Wood

Spencer, Gideon b. Conn. 1741 d. Vt. 1819   Member Vt. Leg. 1788 & 95
m. Seviah Buck — son Jonathan B. m. Joanna Seeger

Stewart, Andrew b. N.C. 1790 d. Tenn. 1850   Pvt. & Corp. E. Tenn.
m. Sarah Drake   Inf. 1813-14
daughter Rebecca m. Rev. Hamilton Parks

Stockton, Charles b. N.J. 1777 d. N.J. m. Martha Huff   Corp. N.J. Mil.
daughter Sarah Cecilia m. George E. Rogers

Sutton, James b. Pa. 1769 d. Ind. 1853   Pvt. Butler Co. Ohio Mil.
m. Susanna Buckingham
daughter Anna m. Benjamin Raymond Whitcomb

waine, Joseph b. Mass. 1754 d. Vt. 1831   Artificer Mass. Navy
  m. Millicent Barrett — son William B. m. Tamar Brooks

Swan, Charles b. Md. 1749 d. Pa. 1839   Lieut. Col. Pa. Mil.
  m. Sarah Van Meter — daughter Mary m. William Collins

Swan, Nathan Jr. b. Mass. 1780 d. Maine 1835   Capt. Mass. Mil.
  m. Annabella Boynton Poor
  daughter Lydia T. m. Ezra Bickford

Swing, Abraham b. N.J. 1771 d. N.J. 1832   Lieut. Salem Co. N.J. Mil. 1814
  m. Hannah Lummis — daughter Ruth m. David deBois

Tate, James b. S.C. c. 1790 d. La. 1861   Pvt. La. Mil. 1814-15
  m. Abagail Holden—son Eastman R. m. Martha A. Wheat

Taylor, Dr. Gibson Berry b. Ky. 1793 d. Ky. 1861   Sgt. War of 1812
  m. 2nd Mary Rives — son George Peter m. Volinda Offutt   Ky. Mil.

Taylor, Henry b. Md. 1738 d. Pa. 1801   Brig. Gen. Wash. Co. Pa. Mil. 1793
  m. Jean White — son George m. Martha Bellinger

Tew, William b. R.I. 1745 d. R.I. 1808   Lt. Col. 1st Newport Co. R.I.
  m. Sarah Wilson   Regt. 1783-9
  daughter Ruth Nichols m. Abraham D. Tilley

Thomas, Arthur b. Va. by 1770 d. Ohio 1813 scalped by Indians
  m. Mary Haynes   Commander Fort Findlay
  daughter Mary m. Samuel Stewart   1812-13 Ohio

Thomas, Philomen b. Va. 1764 d. La. 1847   Major Gen. 1813 La. Mil.
  m. 1st Mary Craig
  daughter Elizabeth m. Benjamin P. Thomas (cousin)

Thompson, Andrew b. Va. by 1768 d. Va. aft. 1853   Sheriff Montgomery
  m. 2d Harriet Simpkins   Co. Va. 1798
  daughter Sarah m. John R. Francis

Thompson, James b. Md. 1782 d. Md. 1852   Pvt. & Sgt. Md. Mil. 1813
  m. Mary Fooks — son James Bailey m. Margaret Lord

Thompson, Robert b. at sea 1763 d. Tenn. 1822   Ensign—Justice Peace
  m. Sarah Robertson   Davidson Co. Tenn. 1799
  son James m. Sara Goodwin

Turner, James III b. N.Y. 1791 d. Vt. 1856 bur. N.Y.   Pvt. 50th N.Y.
  m. Matilda Safford — son William J. m. Jan Van der Pool   Regt. 1813

Van Huys, Isaac b. N.J. 1745 d. N.J. 1815   Lieut. N.J. Det. Mil.
  m. Nelly Iswick — son John m. Lucy Brokow

Watson, Douglas Jr. b. Va. 1776 d. Ga. 1825   Lieut. Greene Co. Ga.
  m. Sarah Hunter Greene — daughter Ruth Hunter m.   Mil. 1801
  John St. Clair Marlin and Elijah McHenry Marlin

Welborn, Aaron b. S.C. 1795 d. Ark. 1858   Sgt. S.C. Mil. 1815
  m. Lucy Stephenson — son James Lawrence m. Tobitha Welch

Wellford, Dr. Robert b. Eng. 1753 d. Va. 1823   Regional Surgeon
  m. Catherine Randolph Yates Thornton   Gen. dur. Whiskey Reb.
  son Robert Y. m. Louisa Gittings   1794

Wellman, John b. Md. 1779 d. W. Va. 1865   Pvt. Kanawha Co. Va. Mil.
  m. Nancy Webb — son David m. Rebecca Wilson

White, Anthony Jr. b. S.C. 1748 d. S.C. 1798   Sheriff Georgetown S.C.
   m. Hannah Barton — daughter Lydia m. John Dozier   1798

White, James Taylor b. La. c. 1785 d. Texas 1852   Sgt. La. Mil. 1812
   m. Sarah Cade — daughter Permelia m. Benjamin Barrow Sr.

Williams, Benajah b. R.I. 1778 d. N.Y. 1861   Ensign 1806-9 R.I. Mil. 1810
   m. Ruth Webster — daughter Sally m. Daniel R. Weeks

Williams, Jeremiah b. Md. 1759 d. Ohio 1842   Pvt. Bedford Co. Pa.
   m. Mary Gaither — daughter Susannah m. Uriah Egbert   Mil. 1789

Winfree, Philip b. c. 1755 d. La. bef. 1838 Pvt. Opelosas La. Vol. Co. 1815
   m. Sarah Hayes — daughter Elizabeth m. Solomon Barrow